ECONOMICS IN ACTION

FOR INQUIRING MINDS

microeconomics

CANADIAN EDITION

microeconomics

CANADIAN EDITION

Paul Krugman
Princeton University

Robin Wells
Princeton University

Anthony Myatt
University of New Brunswick

WORTH PUBLISHERS

Publisher: Catherine Woods
Sponsoring Editor: Charlie Van Wagner
Development Editor: Bruce Kaplan
Associate Managing Editor: Tracey Kuehn
Project Editor: Kerry O'Shaughnessy
Marketing Manager: Scott Guile
Production Manager: Barbara Anne Seixas
Art Director, Cover Designer: Babs Reingold
Interior Design: Babs Reingold
Layout Design: Lee Ann Mahler and TSI Graphics
Illustrations: Paul Lacy and TSI Graphics
Photo Manager: Patricia Marx
Photo Editors: Ted Szczepanski and Patricia Marx
Photo Researcher: Julie Tesser
Composition: TSI Graphics
Printing and Binding: R. R. Donnelley & Sons

ISBN: 0-7167-8689-3 (EAN: 9780716786894)

Library of Congress Control Number: 2005925498

Printed in the United States of America

First printing

Cover photo credits appear on page xix, which constitutes a continuation of the copyright page.

Worth Publishers
41 Madison Avenue
New York, NY 10010

www.worthpublishers.com

About the Authors

Paul Krugman is Professor of Economics at Princeton University, where he regularly teaches the principles course. He received his BA from Yale and his PhD from MIT. Prior to his current position, he taught at Yale, Stanford, and MIT. He also spent a year on the staff of the Council of Economic Advisors in 1982-83. His research is mainly in the area of international trade, where he is one of the founders of the "new trade theory", which focuses on increasing returns and imperfect competition. He also works in international finance, with a concentration in currency crises. In 1991, Krugman received the American Economic Association's John Bates Clark medal. In addition to his teaching and academic research, Krugman writes extensively for nontechnical audiences. Krugman is a regular op-ed columnist for *The New York Times.* His latest trade book is a best-selling collection of his *Times* articles entitled *The Great Unraveling: Losing Our Way in the New Century.* His earlier books, *Peddling Prosperity* and *The Age of Diminished Expectations,* have become modern classics.

Robin Wells is Researcher in Economics at Princeton University, where she regularly teaches undergraduate courses. She received her BA from the University of Chicago and her PhD from the University of California at Berkeley; she then did post-doctoral work at MIT. She has taught at the University of Michigan, the University of Southampton (U.K.), Stanford, and MIT. Her teaching and research focus on the theory of organizations and incentives. She writes regularly for academic journals.

Anthony Myatt received his PhD from McMaster University with a distinction in theory. He has taught at McMaster University, Western University, Nipissing University College, the University of Toronto, and the University of New Brunswick, where he has been Professor of Economics since 1992. His research interests have included the supply-side effects of interest rates, labour market discrimination against women, the causes of provincial unemployment disparities, and the methods and content of economic education. With Bill Scarth, he has written several articles exploring the effect on stabilization policy when interest rates are allowed to have cost effects. To date, Professor Myatt has authored 32 published papers. His interest in textbooks stems from re-evaluating what is typically taught at the introductory level. As a result, he has developed several different introductory courses as vehicles for teaching principles of economics, including Economics of Everyday Life, Economics in the Real World, and Economics Through Film. Professor Myatt has regularly been nominated for the distinguished teacher award at UNB.

Preface

"What is above all needed is to let the meaning choose the word, and not the other way about."

George Orwell,
"Politics and the English Language," 1946

FROM PAUL

Robin and I like to think that we wrote this book with a similar principle in mind. We wanted to write a different sort of book, one in which making sure the student understands how the models apply to the real world is given as much attention as the models themselves. We wanted to adapt Orwell's principle to the writing of an economics textbook: to let the purpose of economics—to achieve a deeper understanding of the world—rather than the mechanics of economics dictate the writing.

We believe that writing in this style reflects a commitment to the reader—a commitment to approach the material from a beginner's point of view, to make the material entertaining and accessible, to make discovery a joy. That's the fun part. But we also believe that there is another, equally compelling obligation on the part of an author of a principles of economics text. Economics is an extremely powerful tool. Many of us who are economists originally started in other disciplines (I started in history, Robin in chemistry). And we fell in love with economics because we believed it offers what most other disciplines don't—a coherent worldview that offers real guidelines to making the world a better place. (Yes, most economists are idealists at heart.) But like any powerful tool, economics should be treated with great care. For us, this obligation became a commitment that students would learn the appropriate use of the models—understand their assumptions and know their limitations as well as their positive uses. Why do we care about this? Because we don't live in a "one model of the economy fits all" world. To achieve deeper levels of understanding of the real world through economics, students must learn to appreciate the kinds of trade-offs and ambiguities that economists and policy makers face when applying their models to real-world problems. We hope this approach will make students more insightful and more effective participants in our common economic, social, and political lives.

To those familiar with my academic work, this perspective will probably look familiar. There I tried to make the problem to be solved the focus, and to avoid unnecessary technique. I tried to simplify. And I tried to choose topics that had important real-world implications. Writing for a large, nontechnical audience has only reinforced and expanded these tendencies. I had to begin with the working assumption that readers initially have no reason to care about what I am writing about—that it is my responsibility to show them why they should care. So the beginning of each chapter of this book is written according to the dictum: "If you haven't hooked them by the third sentence, then you've lost them". I've also learned that about all you can take for granted in writing for a lay audience is basic numeracy—addition and subtraction, but no more than that. Concepts must be fully explained; likely confusions must be anticipated and headed off. And most of all, you must be judicious in choosing the content and pacing of the writing—don't overwhelm your reader.

FROM ROBIN

Like Paul, I wanted to write a book that appeals to students without unduly sacrificing an instructor's obligation to teach economics well. I arrived at a similar perspective on how this book should be written, but by a different path. It came from my experiences teaching economics in a business school for a few years. Facing students who were typically impatient with abstraction and often altogether unhappy to be taking economics (and who would often exact bloody revenge in teaching evaluations), I learned how important it is to "hook" the students into the subject matter. Teaching with case studies, I found that concepts had been truly learned only when students could successfully apply them. And one of the most important lessons I learned was not to patronize. We—economists, that is—often assume that people who aren't familiar with conceptual thinking aren't smart and capable. Teaching in a business school showed me otherwise. The majority of my students were smart and capable, and many had shouldered a lot of responsibility in their working lives. Although adept at solving practical problems, they weren't trained to think conceptually. I had to learn to acknowledge the practical skills that they did have, but also show them the importance of the conceptual skills they didn't have. Although I eventually returned to an economics department, the lessons I learned about teaching economics in a business school stayed with me and, I believe, have been crucial ingredients in writing this textbook.

FROM TONY

My interest in writing a textbook stems from re-evaluating my own effectiveness as a teacher, which led me to question what I teach and how. During this period of questioning, one thing that struck me was the contrast between the dryness of the textbooks and the rich heritage of subject matter that economics embraces. Couldn't books be less dry? Couldn't they be more immediate and compelling, like a novel one can't put down?

So when I was approached to Canadianize a new text by Krugman and Wells, I was curious. Paul Krugman's academic work had earned him a reputation for originality and insight, for being able to bring new realism and simplicity to the theoretical treatment of many difficult topics. And his popular writing demonstrated a rare talent to transmit complicated ideas in crystal clear prose for the non-specialist.

I was not disappointed with the U.S. text. Here was no boring sleepy prose. And the text was full of real-world examples and applications, rather than the hypothetical examples used by some textbooks. But what most grabbed my attention was its story-driven approach set in an everyday context. I was intrigued to see how these stories could become chapter themes that would involve students and relate to their lives.

Frankly, the U.S. textbook was so good I felt a little intimidated at the prospect of trying to Canadianize it. Fortunately, however, many of the examples and themes already had a Canadian dimension. For example, in Chapter 3 Wayne Gretzky's last game is perfect for a Canadian audience. And since basic economic principles work just as well in Canada as in the United States (or any country), my task has generally been relatively simple—to provide Canadian data, institutional context, and legal framework, as well as Canadian applications, so the finished product will resonate even more with a Canadian reader.

However, deep surgery was required in several places. In particular, chapter 4, 17, and 21 had to be recast to fit the Canadian experience while still keeping the spirit of the original Krugman/Wells text. Chapter 4 rested too much on taxicab licensing to illustrate the effect of quotas, whereas agricultural quotas are much more important in Canada. Chapter 17 on international trade had to be re-focused to reveal Canada's greater reliance on trade than is the case with the United States. And Chapter 21 concerning taxing, income distribution, and poverty had to be overhauled to reflect Canada's unique experience.

The result is thoroughly Canadianized text that preserves the Krugman/Wells story-driven approach and their flair for writing, which is honed to be an effective teaching tool for Canadian teachers and an effective learning device for Canadian students.

Advantages of This Book

Why should any instructor use our text? We believe our book distinguishes itself in several ways that will make your introductory economics course an easier and more successful undertaking for the following reasons:

- **Chapters build intuition through realistic examples.** In every chapter, we use real-world examples, stories, applications, and case studies to teach the core concepts and motivate student learning. We believe that the best way to introduce concepts and reinforce them is through real-world examples; students simply relate more easily to them.

- **Pedagogical features reinforce learning.** We've worked hard to craft a set of features that will be genuinely helpful to students. We describe these features in the next section, "Tools for Learning".

- **Chapters have been written to be accessible and entertaining.** We have used a fluid and friendly writing style that makes the concepts accessible. And we have tried whenever possible to use examples that are familiar to students: for example, choosing which course to take, buying a used textbook, or deciding where to eat at the food court at the local shopping mall.

- **Although easy to understand, the book also prepares students for further coursework.** Too often, instructors find that selecting a textbook means choosing between two unappealing alternatives: a textbook that is "easy to teach" but leaves major gaps in students' understanding, or a textbook that is "hard to teach" but adequately prepares students for future coursework. We have worked very hard to create an easy-to-understand textbook that offers the best of both worlds.

- **The book permits flexible yet conceptually structured use of chapters.** We recognize that many instructors will prefer to teach the chapters in a sequence different from the one found in the book. Chapters were written with this in mind. Instructors can use the chapters in any order they wish. Our overarching goal was flexibility of organization for everyone. For a detailed look at the organization of chapters and ways to use them, see pages ix through xv of this preface.

Tools for Learning

We have structured each of the chapters around a common set of features. The following features are intended to help students learn better while also keeping them engaged.

"What You Will Learn in This Chapter"

To help readers get oriented, the first page of each chapter contains a preview of the chapter's contents, in an easy-to-review bulleted list format, that alerts students to the critical concepts and details the objectives of the chapter.

Opening Story

In contrast to other books in which each chapter begins with a recitation of some aspect of economics, we open each chapter with a compelling story that often extends through the entire chapter. Stories were chosen to accomplish two things: to illustrate important concepts in the chapter and then to encourage students to want to read on to learn more.

As we've mentioned, one of our main goals is to build intuition with realistic examples. Because each chapter is introduced with a real-world story, students will relate more easily to the material. For example, Chapter 3 teaches supply and demand in the context of a market for scalped tickets to a sports event (our opening story on page 58 is "Gretzky's Last Game"). A complete list of our opening stories appears on the inside front cover.

"Economics in Action" Case Studies

In addition to introducing chapters with vivid stories, we conclude virtually every major text section with still more examples: a real-world case study called "Economics in Action". This feature provides a short but compelling application of the major concept just covered in that section. Students will experience an immediate payoff from being able to apply the concepts they've just read about to real phenomena. For example in Chapter 7 we discuss urban sprawl and the loss of farmland, to communicate the concept of opportunity cost (see the "Economics in Action" entitled "Urban Sprawl and the Loss of Farmland in Canada" on pages 174–175). For a complete list of all the "Economics in Action" cases in the text, see the page facing the inside front cover and also our table of contents.

Unique End-of-Section Review: "Quick Review" and "Check Your Understanding" Questions

In contrast to most other textbooks, which offer a review of concepts only at the end of each chapter, we include review material at the end of each major section within a chapter.

Economics contains a lot of jargon and abstract concepts that can quickly overwhelm the principles student. So we provide **Quick Reviews,** short bulleted summaries of concepts at the end of each major section. This review helps ensure that students understand what they have just read.

The **Check Your Understanding** feature, which appears along with every "Quick Review," consists of a short set of review questions; solutions to these questions appear at the back of the book in the section set off with a burgundy tab at the edge of each page. These questions and solutions allow students to immediately test their understanding of the section just read. If they're not getting the questions right, it's a clear signal for them to go back and reread before moving on.

The "Economics in Action" cases, followed by the "Quick Reviews" and "Check Your Understanding" questions comprise our unique end-of-section pedagogical set that encourages students to apply what they've learned (via the "Economics in Action") and then review it (with the "Quick Reviews" and "Check Your Understanding" questions). Our hope is that students will be more successful in the course if they make use of this carefully constructed set of study aids.

"For Inquiring Minds" Boxes

To further our goal of helping students build intuition with real-world examples, each chapter contains one or more "For Inquiring Minds" boxes, in which concepts are applied to real-world events in unexpected and sometimes surprising ways, generating a sense of the power and breadth of economics. These boxes help impress on students that economics can be fun despite being labeled "the dismal science".

In a Chapter 10 box, for example, students learn how prices in a budget line serve the same function as the numbers of points assigned to different foods in a Weight Watchers' diet plan (see the "For Inquiring Minds" entitled "Food for Thought on Budget Constraints," on page 252.) For a list of all "For Inquiring Minds" boxes, see the page facing the inside front cover and our table of contents.

"Pitfalls" Boxes

Certain concepts are prone to be misunderstood when students are beginning their study of economics. We have tried to alert students to these mistakes in the "Pitfalls" boxes. Here common misunderstandings are spelled out and corrected—for example, the difference between increasing total cost and increasing marginal cost (see the "Pitfalls" box on this topic on page 177). For a list of all the "Pitfalls" boxes in chapters, see the table of contents.

Student-Friendly Graphs

Comprehending graphs is often one of the biggest hurdles for principles students. To help alleviate that problem, this book has been designed so that figures are large, clear, and easy for students to follow. Many contain helpful annotations—in an easy-to-see balloon label format—that link to concepts within the text. Figure captions have been written to complement the text discussion of figures and to help students more readily grasp what they're seeing.

We've worked hard to make these graphs student-friendly. For example, to help students navigate one of the stickier thickets—the distinction between a shifting curve and movement along a curve—we encourage students to see this difference by using two types of arrows: a shift arrow (⟶) and what we call a "movement-along" arrow (⟶). You can see these arrows at work in Figures 3-12 and 3-13 on pages 75 and 77.

In addition, several graphs in each chapter are accompanied by the icon >web..., which indicates that these graphs are available online as simulations (the graphs are animated in a Flash format and can be manipulated). Every interactive graph is accompanied by a quiz on key concepts to further help students in their work with graphs.

Helpful Graphing Appendix For students who would benefit from an explanation of how graphs are constructed, interpreted, and used in economics, we've included a detailed graphing appendix after Chapter 2 on page 42. This appendix is more comprehensive than most because we know that some students need this helpful background, and we didn't want to breeze through the material. Our hope is that this comprehensive graphing appendix will better prepare students to use and interpret the graphs in this textbook and then out in the real world (in newspapers, magazines, and elsewhere).

Definitions of Key Terms

Every key term, in addition to being defined in the text, is also placed and defined in the margin to make it easier for students to study and review.

A Look Ahead

The text of each chapter ends with an "A Look Ahead" section, a short overview of what lies ahead in upcoming chapters. This concluding section provides students with a sense of continuity among chapters.

End-of-Chapter Review

In addition to the "Quick Review" at the end of each major section, each chapter ends with a complete but brief **Summary** of the key terms and concepts. In addition, a list of the **Key Terms** is placed at the end of each chapter along with page references.

Finally, we have created for each chapter a comprehensive set of **End-of-Chapter Problems**—problems that test intuition as well as the ability to calculate important variables. Much care and attention have been devoted to the creation of these problems so that instructors can be assured that they provide a true test of students' learning.

Upcoming Variations of This Book

The text you are now holding is our introduction to microeconomics, intended for the one-semester principles course in microeconomics.

Here is an overview of other textbooks in this series:

- ***Economics:*** The complete version of this textbook, containing all microeconomics chapters plus the full complement of macroeconomics chapters, is intended for the two-semester principles course.
- ***Macroeconomics:*** The complete introduction to macroeconomics is intended for a one-semester principles course in macroeconomics.

The Organization of This Book and How to Use It

This book is organized as a series of building blocks in which conceptual material learned at one stage is clearly built upon and then integrated into the conceptual material covered in the next stage. These building blocks correspond to the ten parts into which the chapters are divided. It's equally important to remember that an instructor need not teach these parts in the same sequence as they are found in the book. We recognize that a number of chapters will be considered optional and that many instructors will prefer to teach the chapters using a different order. Chapters and sections have been written to incorporate a degree of flexibility in the sequence in which they are taught, without sacrificing conceptual continuity. So an instructor can achieve some course customization through the choice of which chapters to cover and in which order to cover them. We will give a brief overview of each part and chapter, followed by a discussion of the various ways in which an instructor can tailor this book to meet his or her needs.

Part 1: What Is Economics?

In the **Introduction, "The Ordinary Business of Life"**, students are initiated into the study of economics in the context of a shopping trip on any given Saturday in everyday Canada. It provides students with basic definitions of terms such as *economics,* the *invisible hand,* and *market structure.* In addition it serves as a "tour d'horizon" of economics, explaining the difference between microeconomics and macroeconomics.

In **Chapter 1, "First Principles"**, nine principles are presented and explained: four principles of individual choice, covering concepts such as opportunity cost, marginal analysis, and incentives; and five principles of interaction between individuals, covering concepts such as gains from trade, market efficiency, and market failure. In later chapters, we build intuition by frequently referring to these principles in the explanation of specific models. Students learn that these nine principles form a cohesive conceptual foundation for all of economics.

Chapter 2, "Economic Models: Trade-offs and Trade", shows students how to think like economists by using three models—the production possibility frontier, comparative advantage and trade, and the circular-flow diagram—to analyse the world around them. It gives students an early introduction to gains from trade and to international comparisons. The **Chapter 2 appendix** contains a comprehensive math and graphing review for those students and instructors who wish to cover this material.

Part 2: Supply and Demand

Chapter 3, "Supply and Demand", covers the standard material in a fresh and compelling way: supply and demand, market equilibrium, and surplus and shortage are all illustrated using an example of the market for scalped tickets to a sports event. Students learn how the demand and supply curves of scalped tickets shift in response to the announcements of a star player's impending retirement.

Chapter 4, "The Market Strikes Back", covers various types of market interventions and their consequences: price and quantity controls, inefficiency and deadweight loss, and excise taxes. Through tangible examples such as rent control regulations and agricultural quotas, the costs generated by attempts to control markets are made real to students.

In Chapter 5, "Elasticity", the actions of OPEC and their consequences for the world market for oil taken together are the real-world motivating example in our discussion of the price elasticity of demand. In this chapter, we introduce the various elasticity measures and show how elasticities are used to evaluate the incidence of an excise tax.

Part 3: Individuals and Markets

Through examples such as a market for used textbooks and eBay, students learn how markets increase welfare in **Chapter 6, "Consumer and Producer Surplus"**. Although the concepts of market efficiency and deadweight loss are strongly emphasized, we also preview the ways in which a market can fail.

Chapter 7, "Making Decisions", is a unique chapter. Microeconomics is fundamentally a science of how to make decisions. But that aspect is rarely highlighted in introductory microeconomics. Rather, other textbooks place much of the emphasis on comprehending the consequences of decision making instead of on developing an understanding of how decisions should be made in any context. For example, due to the almost exclusive emphasis that economics textbooks place on marginal analysis, we believe that students are often unable to distinguish between what is and what isn't a marginal decision. To remedy this, we have included an entire section on "either-or" versus "how much" decisions—a distinction that is particularly useful in later chapters where we compare a firm's output decision to its entry/exit decision. In addition, in Chapter 7 we reprise the concept of opportunity cost; present a thorough treatment of marginal analysis; explain the concept of sunk cost; and, for instructors who wish to teach it, cover present discounted value. Full coverage of sunk cost at this point will help students later in understanding the irrelevance of fixed cost in the firm's short-run output decision. We think this chapter will be an important teaching aid because it helps students develop a deeper intuition about the common conceptual foundations of microeconomic models.

What Comes Next: The Firm or the Consumer? You may have noticed that we have placed the chapters covering the producer before the chapters covering the consumer. Why have we done this? Because we believe that it is a more natural conceptual progression to cover the producer after Chapter 7, "Making Decisions", than it is to cover the consumer. Since students have just studied opportunity cost, economic profit versus accounting profit, marginal benefit and marginal cost, and sunk cost, we think examining the firm's cost curves, its output decision, and its entry/exit decision is an easier next step for them to undertake.

We are aware that some instructors are likely to be skeptical of this approach. We have often heard instructors say that the consumer should be studied before the producer because students can relate to being a consumer but not to being the owner of a firm. We hope, however, to change that viewpoint because what we really want students to do is not just relate to being a consumer but *think like a rational consumer—a consumer who maximizes utility subject to scarce resources.* And we believe that it is easier for students to understand utility maximization (utility being an inherently slippery concept) after they have come to understand profit maximization.

Nonetheless, we want to strongly emphasize that it is very easy for instructors who wish to follow a traditional chapter sequence—with the consumer before the firm—to do just that. We wrote the chapters so that there is no loss whatsoever if an instructor follows Chapter 7 with Chapter 10, "The Rational Consumer", and Chapter 11, "Consumer Preferences and Consumer Choice" (an optional chapter).

Part 4: The Producer

In Chapter 8, "Behind the Supply Curve: Inputs and Costs", we develop the production function and the various cost measures of the firm. There is an extensive discussion of the difference between average cost and marginal cost, illustrated by examples such as a student's grade point average. **Chapter 9, "Perfect Competition and the Supply Curve"**, explains the output decision of the perfectly competitive firm, its entry/exit decision, the industry supply curve, and the equilibrium of a perfectly competitive market. We draw on examples such as generic pharmaceuticals and the precarious nature of Canada's airline industry to illustrate the shut-down rule and highlight the pressures of competition.

Part 5: The Consumer

Chapter 10, "The Rational Consumer", provides a complete treatment of consumer behavior for instructors who don't cover indifference curves. There is a simple, intuitive exposition of the budget line, the optimal consumption choice, diminishing marginal utility, and income and substitution effects and their relationship to market demand. Students learn, for example, that a budget line constructed using prices is much like a Weight Watchers' diet plan constructed using a point system. **Chapter 11, "Consumer Preferences and Consumer Choice"**, offers a more detailed treatment for those who wish to cover indifference curves. It contains an analysis of the optimal consumption choice using the marginal rate of substitution as well as income and substitution effects.

What Comes Next: Markets and Efficiency or Market Structure? Many instructors are likely to consider the next two chapters—Chapter 12, "Factor Markets and the Distribution of Income", and Chapter 13 "Efficiency and Equity"—optional. For those who wish to skip them, the next topic area will be market structure beyond perfect competition: monopoly, oligopoly, and monopolistic competition. Chapters 12 and 13 are likely to be used by instructors who want more in-depth coverage of microeconomics, as well as those who wish to emphasize labour markets, welfare, and public policy issues.

Instructors who prefer a traditional sequence of topics may wish to go from Part 5 ("The Consumer") to Part 4 ("The Producer") to Part 7 ("Market Structure: Beyond Perfect Competition"), bypassing Part 6 ("Markets and Efficiency") altogether or covering it later. This is a good choice for those who wish to contrast the difference between the perfectly competitive firm's output decision and the monopolist's output decision. But, those who follow the existing chapter sequence—"The Producer" followed by "The Consumer" followed by "Market Structure: Beyond Perfect Competition"—will be able to draw a tighter connection among consumer behavior, monopoly pricing, price discrimination, product differentiation, and monopolistic competition. We have written the chapters so that either sequence works equally well.

Part 6: Markets and Efficiency

Chapter 12, "Factor Markets and the Distribution of Income", covers the competitive factor market model and the factor distribution of income. It also contains modifications and alternative interpretations of the labour market: the efficiency-wage model of the labour market is discussed, and the influences of education, discrimination, and market power are also addressed. It presents, we hope, a balanced and well-rounded view of the strengths and limitations of the competitive market model of labour markets and leads to a greater appreciation of the issues of efficiency and equity discussed in the next chapter. For instructors who covered indifference curves in Chapter 11, the **Chapter 12 appendix** offers a detailed examination of the labour-leisure trade-off and the backward-bending labour supply curve.

In **Chapter 13, "Efficiency and Equity"**, after recapping efficiency in a single market, we compare and contrast this to what it means to have efficiency in a market economy as a whole. Some may wonder why it is useful to draw the distinction between partial equilibrium and general equilibrium in a principles course. We believe that doing so gives students a deeper understanding of the often-conflicting objectives of efficiency and equity—something that really can't be fully explored in a partial equilibrium setting. As a real-world example, we discuss the reunification of Germany in terms of the trade-offs faced by German policy makers, who sacrificed some efficiency-enhancing measures in order to reduce the income differences between East and West Germans. Students should come away from this chapter with a fuller appreciation of the complexity of real-world economic policy making—that is, how democracies may sometimes choose to sacrifice some efficiency for equity purposes.

Part 7: Market Structure: Beyond Perfect Competition

Chapter 14, "Monopoly", is a full treatment of monopoly, including topics such as price discrimination and the welfare effects of monopoly. We provide an array of compelling examples, such as De Beers Diamonds, electricity pricing in Canada, and airline ticket-pricing. In **Chapter 15, "Oligopoly"**, we present basic game theory in both a one-shot and repeated-game context, as well as an integrated treatment of the kinked demand curve model. The models are applied to a wide set of actual examples, such as Archer Daniels Midland, a European vitamin cartel, OPEC, and airline ticket-pricing wars. In **Chapter 16, "Monopolistic Competition and Product Differentiation"**, students are brought face to face early on with an example of monopolistic competition that is a familiar feature of their lives: the food court at the local mall. We go on to cover entry and exit, efficiency considerations, and advertising in monopolistic competition.

What Comes Next: Extending Market Boundaries or Microeconomics and Public Policy? The next section of the book, "Extending Market Boundaries", is devoted to applications and extensions of the competitive market model: Chapter 17, "International Trade", and Chapter 18, "Uncertainty, Risk, and Private Information". Both of these chapters are optional. Instructors who prefer to skip one or both of these chapters can proceed to the following section, "Microeconomics and Public Policy".

Part 8: Extending Market Boundaries

In Chapter 2, we presented a full exposition of gains from trade and the difference between comparative and absolute advantage, illustrated with an international example (trade between high-wage and low-wage countries). **Chapter 17, "International Trade"**, builds on that material. It contains a recap of comparative advantage in a Canadian context, traces the sources of comparative advantage, considers tariffs and quotas, and explores the politics of trade protection. In response to current events, we give in-depth coverage to the controversy over imports from low-wage countries, trade protection in Canada, the role of the WTO, and the implications of globalization.

The inclusion in a principles text of **Chapter 18, "Uncertainty, Risk, and Private Information"**, may come as a surprise to some—a common reaction being "Isn't this material too hard for principles students?" We believe that, with our treatment, the answer is "no" for many more students than is typically expected. In this chapter we explain attitudes towards risk in a careful and methodical way, grounded in the basic concept of diminishing marginal utility. This allows us to analyse a simple competitive insurance market, and to examine the benefits and limits of diversification. Next comes an easily comprehensible and intuitive presentation of private information in the context of adverse selection and moral hazard, with illustrations drawn from the market for lemons (used cars) and franchising. We believe that instructors will be surprised by how easy it is to teach this material and how much it will enlighten students about the relevance of economics to their everyday lives.

Part 9: Microeconomics and Public Policy

Chapter 19, "Externalities", covers negative externalities and solutions such as Coasian private trades, emissions taxes, and a system of tradable permits. We also examine positive externalities, technological spillovers, and the resulting arguments for industrial policy. **Chapter 20, "Public Goods and Common Resources"**, makes an immediate impression by opening with the story of how "The Great Stink of 1858" compelled Londoners to build a public sewer system. Students learn how to classify goods into four categories (private goods, common resources, public goods, and artificially scarce goods) based on two dimensions: excludability and rivalry in consumption. With this system, they can develop an intuitive understanding of why some goods but not others can be efficiently managed by markets.

Chapter 21, "Taxes, Social Insurance, and Income Distribution", begins with a review of the burden of taxation and considerations of equity versus efficiency. Next, it examines the structure of taxes, current tax policy, and public spending in Canada. This is followed by an investigation into the sources of poverty and their implications for government tax and transfer policies. From this chapter, students can gain an appreciation of the difficult questions policy makers face in addressing issues of economic efficiency and welfare.

Part 10: New Directions for Markets

The final section of the book contains one chapter, **Chapter 22, "Technology, Information Goods, and Network Externalities"**.

We believe that Chapter 22, even though providing real economic models and relevant cases, will be enjoyable for both instructors and students. Starting with the example of sharing music files over the Internet, it introduces the concept of information goods and network externalities and analyses the problems they cause for efficient pricing. We discuss the implications for standard-setting and the ambiguities that network externalities present for regulatory policy. Students will see how these issues affect their daily lives through references to Kazaa, Apple Computers, and Microsoft.

What's Core, What's Optional?

As noted earlier, we realize that some of our chapters will be considered optional. On the following page is a listing of what we view as core chapters and those that could be considered optional. We've annotated the list of optional chapters to indicate what they cover should you wish to consider incorporating them into your course.

A Selection of Possible Outlines

To illustrate how instructors can use this book to meet their specific goals, we've constructed a selection of three possible outlines (see page xv). By no means exclusive, these outlines reflect a likely range of different ways in which this book could be used:

- **Traditional Outline** (consumer first, producer second)
- **Public Policy and Welfare Outline** (includes factor markets and efficiency)
- **Applied Microeconomics Outline** (includes international trade and uncertainty, risk, and private information)

Although we don't outline it here, we also offer a Decision-Based Outline. The choice between a Traditional Outline and the Decision-Based Outline is primarily a choice about the sequencing of Parts 4 and 5. An instructor who prefers to cover "The Consumer" before "The Producer" will choose the Traditional Outline. An instructor who wants to emphasize decision making should instead cover "The Producer" before "The Consumer", just covering Parts 4 and 5 as ordered.

At this point, instructors can skip immediately to Part 7, to cover monopoly, oligopoly, and monopolistic competition. However, instructors who wish to focus more intensely on international economics, tools of microeconomics, or public policy (the Applied Microeconomics Outline or the Public Policy and Welfare Outline) may choose to teach Part 6, which addresses factor markets and economy-wide efficiency, before moving on to Part 7. After Part 7, instructors who have adopted an applied microeconomics or public policy focus may wish to cover some or all of Part 8, which contains a chapter on international trade and a chapter on risk and private information. Others, however, will prefer to skip to Part 9, which covers externalities, public goods, common resources, and tax policy. Finally, Part 10, consisting solely of Chapter 22 on the network economy, is a suitable choice for any of these outlines. But it will be a particularly good chapter for those who wish to focus on public policy.

Supplements and Media

Worth Publishers is pleased to offer an exciting and useful supplements and media package to accompany this textbook. The package has been crafted to help instructors teach their principles course and to help students grasp concepts more readily.

Since accuracy is so critically important, all the supplements have been scrutinized and double-checked by members of the supplements team, reviewers, and a team of additional accuracy checkers. The time and care that have been put into the supplements and media ensure a seamless package.

Companion Website for Students and Instructors

econXchange

(www.worthpublishers.com/krugmanwellsmyatt)

The companion website for the Krugman/Wells/Myatt text offers valuable tools for both the instructor and students.

For instructors, this completely customized website offers many opportunities for quizzing and, most important, powerful grading tools. The site gives you the ability to track students' interaction with the Homework Advantage Center, the Practice Quizzing Center, and the Graphing Center by accessing separate online gradebooks for each category.

For students, the site offers many opportunities to practice, practice, practice. On the site, students can find online simulations, practice quizzes, video resources, graphing tutorials, and links to many other resources designed to help them master economic concepts. In

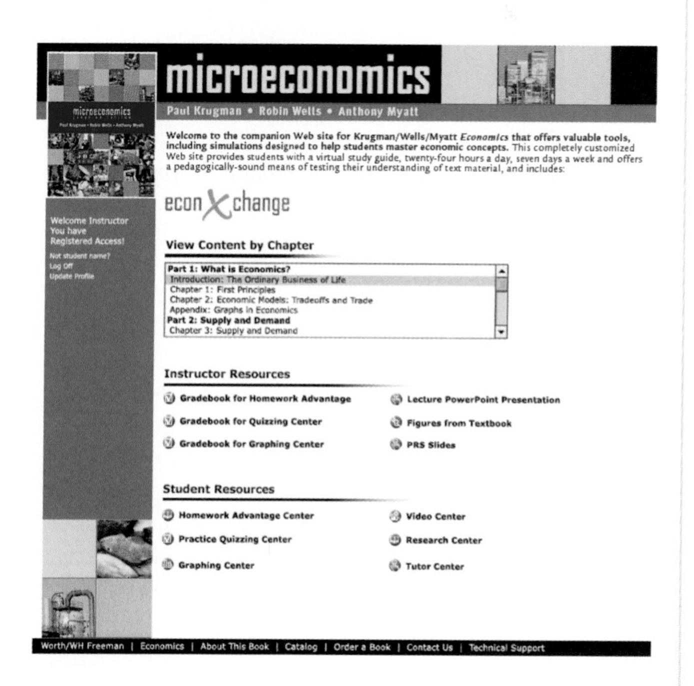

WHAT'S CORE, WHAT'S OPTIONAL: AN OVERVIEW

Core	Optional
	Introduction: The Ordinary Business of Life
1. First Principles	
2. Economic Models: Trade-offs and Trade	**Appendix: Graphs in Economics** A comprehensive review of graphing and math for students who would find such a refresher helpful.
3. Supply and Demand	
4. The Market Strikes Back	
5. Elasticity	
6. Consumer and Producer Surplus	
	7. Making Decisions A unique chapter aimed at helping students understand how decisions should be made in any context. Includes coverage of marginal analysis and cost-benefit analysis. Pairs well with Chapter 6. Prepares students for coverage of models in upcoming chapters.
8. Behind the Supply Curve: Inputs and Costs	
9. Perfect Competition and the Supply Curve	
10. The Rational Consumer	
	11. Consumer Preferences and Consumer Choice This chapter offers a more detailed treatment of consumer behavior for instructors who wish to cover indifference curves.
	12. Factor Markets and the Distribution of Income Plus Appendix: Indifference Curve Analysis of Labour Supply For instructors who want to go more in depth, this chapter covers the efficiency-wage model of the labour market as well as the influences of education, discrimination, and market power. The appendix examines the labour-leisure trade-off and the backward-bending labour supply curve.
	13. Efficiency and Equity A unique chapter that explores what it means to have efficiency in a market economy as a whole. Gives students a deeper understanding of the often-conflicting objectives of efficiency and equity. Intended for instructors who emphasize welfare and public policy issues.
14. Monopoly	
15. Oligopoly	
16. Monopolistic Competition and Product Differentiation	
	17. International Trade This chapter recaps comparative advantage, considers tariffs and quotas, and explores the politics of trade protection. Coverage here links back to the international coverage in Chapter 2.
	18. Uncertainty, Risk, and Private Information A unique, applied chapter that explains attitudes towards risk, examines the benefits and limits of diversification, and considers private information in the context of adverse selection and moral hazard.
19. Externalities	
20. Public Goods and Common Resources	
21. Taxes, Social Insurance, and Income Distribution	
	22. Technology, Information Goods, and Network Externalities A unique chapter that shows students how to use economic models to analyze information goods. A nice treat for students and instructors!

THREE POSSIBLE OUTLINES

Traditional

Part 1
1. First Principles
2. Economic Models: Trade-offs and Trade
   Appendix: Graphs in Economics

Part 2
3. Supply and Demand
4. The Market Strikes Back
5. Elasticity

Part 3
6. Consumer and Producer Surplus
7. Making Decisions

Part 5*
10. The Rational Consumer
11. Consumer Preferences and Consumer Choice

Part 4*
8. Behind the Supply Curve: Inputs and Costs
9. Perfect Competition and the Supply Curve

Part 7
14. Monopoly
15. Oligopoly
16. Monopolistic Competition and Product Differentiation

Part 9
19. Externalities
20. Public Goods and Common Resources
21. Taxes, Social Insurance, and Income Distribution

Public Policy and Welfare

Part 1
1. First Principles
2. Economic Models: Trade-offs and Trade
   Appendix: Graphs in Economics

Part 2
3. Supply and Demand
4. The Market Strikes Back
5. Elasticity

Part 3
6. Consumer and Producer Surplus
7. Making Decisions

Either **Part 4, then 5**
Or, **Part 5, then Part 4**

Part 6
12. Factor Markets and the Distribution of Income
   Appendix: Indifference Curve Analysis of Labour Supply
13. Efficiency and Equity

Part 7
14. Monopoly
15. Oligopoly
16. Monopolistic Competition and Product Differentiation

Part 8
17. International Trade
18. Uncertainty, Risk, and Private Information

Part 9
19. Externalities
20. Public Goods and Common Resources
21. Taxes, Social Insurance, and Income Distribution

Part 10
22. Technology, Information Goods, and Network Externalities

Applied Microeconomics

Part 1
1. First Principles
2. Economic Models: Trade-offs and Trade
   Appendix: Graphs in Economics

Part 2
3. Supply and Demand
4. The Market Strikes Back
5. Elasticity

Part 3
6. Consumer and Producer Surplus
7. Making Decisions

Either **Part 4, then 5**
Or, **Part 5, then Part 4**

Part 6
12. Factor Markets and the Distribution of Income
   Appendix: Indifference Curve Analysis of Labour Supply
13. Efficiency and Equity

Part 7
14. Monopoly
15. Oligopoly
16. Monopolistic Competition and Product Differentiation

Part 8
17. International Trade
18. Uncertainty, Risk, and Private Information

Part 9
19. Externalities
20. Public Goods and Common Resources
21. Taxes, Social Insurance, and Income Distribution

***Instructors who wish to follow a decision-based sequence should use the parts of this text as we've ordered them: Part 4, "The Producer", followed by Part 5, "The Consumer".**

essence, this site provides students with a virtual study guide, twenty-four hours a day, seven days a week by offering a pedagogically sound means of testing their understanding of text material.

This helpful, powerful site contains the following:

- Numerous reports can be customized and printed with an interactive print preview.
- Results can be merged from TheTestingCenter.com.
- Student rosters can be imported and exported.

Practice Quizzing Center This quizzing engine provides 20 multiple-choice questions per chapter with appropriate feedback and page references to the textbook. The questions as well as the answer choices are randomized to give students a different quiz with every refresh of the screen. All student answers are saved in an online database that can be accessed by instructors.

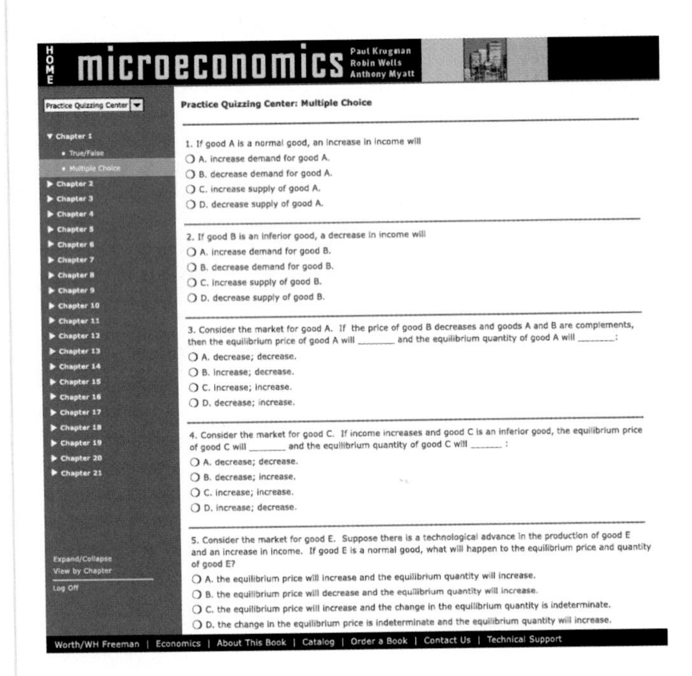

Graphing Center The Graphing Center includes selected graphs from the textbook that have been animated in a Flash format, allowing students to manipulate curves and plot data points when appropriate. Approximately five graphs from each chapter have been animated and are identified in the textbook by a web icon >*web*... within the appropriate figure. Having the ability to manipulate graphs and observe the results of the manipulation provides students with a keen understanding of the effects of the shifts and movements of the curves. Every interactive graph is accompanied by questions that quiz students on key concepts from the textbook and provide instructors with feedback on student progress. Student responses and interactions are tracked and stored in an online database that can be accessed by the instructor.

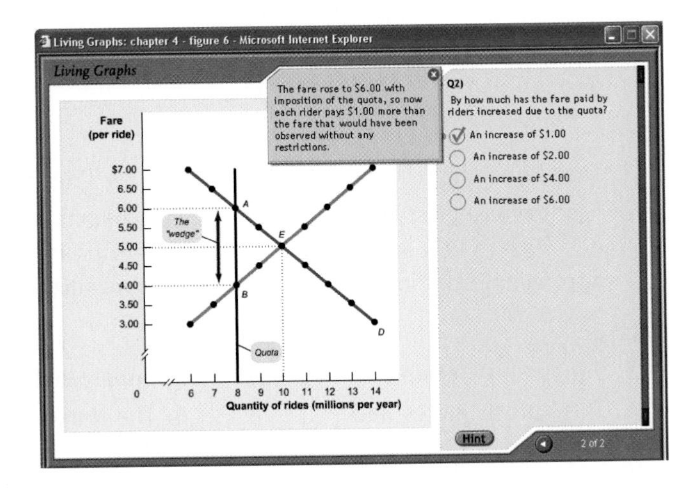

Research Center The Research Center allows students to easily and effectively locate outside resources and readings that relate to topics covered in the textbook. It lists web addresses that hotlink to relevant websites; each URL is accompanied by a detailed description of the site and its relevance to each chapter, allowing students to conduct research and explore related readings on specific topics with ease. Also hotlinked are relevant articles by Paul Krugman and other leading economists.

Video Center In video interviews, Paul Krugman and Robin Wells comment on specific aspects of each chapter and their relevance to students' lives. Each video is embedded in a Flash format with other pedagogical features and a running transcript of the authors' remarks. Videos can be presented in class to generate discussion or assigned as homework to give students a deeper understanding of key topics in the textbook.

Student PowerPoints Created by Gustaro Indart, University of Toronto, this PowerPoint presentation is ideal for students who need extra help in understanding the concepts in each chapter. The PowerPoint presentations for each chapter come complete with animations, notes, summaries, and graphics. This tool enables students to review and practice and helps them to more readily grasp economic concepts. The PowerPoints nicely complements the already extensive learning apparatus within the text itself.

Additional Student Supplement

Study Guide Prepared by Rashid Khan, McMaster University, the Study Guide reinforces the topics and key concepts covered in the text. For each chapter, the Study Guide provides an introduction, fill-in-the-blank chapter review, learning tips with graphical analysis, four or five comprehensive problems and exercises, 20 multiple-choice questions, and solutions to all fill-in-the-blank reviews, problems, exercises, and quizzes found within the Study Guide.

Additional Instructor Supplements

Instructor's Resource Manual The Instructor's Resource Manual, written by Rod Hill, University of New Brunswick, Saint John, is an ideal resource for instructors teaching principles of economics. The manual includes chapter-by-chapter learning objectives, chapter outlines, teaching tips and ideas, hints on how to create student interest, common misunderstandings that are typical among students, and activities that can be conducted in or out of the classroom. Detailed solutions to every end-of-chapter problem from the textbook have also been included.

Printed Test Bank The Test Bank, prepared by Oliver Franke, Athabasca University, provides a wide range of creative and versatile questions ranging in levels of difficulty. Selected questions are paired with original graphs and graphs from the textbook to reinforce comprehension. The Test Bank offers both multiple-choice and true/false questions assessing comprehension, interpretation, analysis, and synthesis. Each question is conveniently cross referenced to the page number in the text where the appropriate topic is discussed. Questions have been checked by the entire supplements team, reviewed extensively, and checked again for accuracy.

Diploma 6.3 Computerized Test Bank The Krugman/Wells/Myatt printed Test Bank is also available in CD-ROM format, powered by Brownstone, for both Windows and Macintosh users. With Diploma, you can easily create tests, write and edit questions, and create study sessions for students. You can add an unlimited number of questions, scramble questions, and include pictures, equations, and multimedia links. Tests can be printed in a wide range of formats or administered to students with Brownstone's network or Internet testing software. The software's unique synthesis of flexible word-processing and database features creates a program that is extremely intuitive and capable. With the new Diploma 6.3, you can:

BROWNSTONE

- Work with complete word processing functions (including creating tables).
- Work with myriad question formats, including multiple choice, true/false, short answer, matching, fill in the blank, and essay.
- Attach feedback (rationales) to questions (or answers).
- Create, install, and use an unlimited number of question banks.
- Incorporate references (including tables, figures, and case studies).
- Attach customized instructions.
- Use multiple graphic formats (BMP, DIB, RLE, DXF, EPS, FPX, GIF, IMG, JPG, PCD, PCX, DCX, PNG, TGA, TIF, WMF, and WPG).
- Take advantage of a powerful algorithm engine for complex, dynamic question types and dynamic equations.
- Export self-grading tests (in HTML formats) for use with web browsers.
- Export test files in Rich Text File format for use with any word-processing program.
- Export test files to EDU, WebCT, and Blackboard course management systems.
- Preview and re-format tests before printing them.
- Include custom splash screens that feature graphics or images.
- Post tests to Diploma's online testing site, TheTestingCenter.com.

This computerized Test Bank is accompanied by a gradebook that enables you to record students' grades throughout a course; it also includes the capacity to track student records and view detailed analyses of test items, curve tests, generate reports, add weights to grades, and allows you to:

- Organize grades into as many as 25 related categories.
- Adjust letter grade cutoffs and create customized grading.
- Enter/display assignment scores and category averages as percentages, points, letter grades, or according to your own customized grading scheme.
- Report final averages as points earned across all categories.
- Customize student properties (including ID number, password, e-mail address, and status).
- Drop grades either manually or automatically.
- Import and export student rosters.

Diploma Online Testing at www.brownstone.net is another useful tool within the Brownstone software that allows instructors to provide online exams for students using Test Bank questions. With Diploma, you can easily create and administer secure exams over a network and over the Internet, with questions that incorporate multimedia and interactive exercises. The program allows you to restrict tests to specific computers or time blocks, and it includes an impressive suite of gradebook and result-analysis features.

PowerPoint Slides The enhanced PowerPoint presentation slides are designed to assist you with lecture preparation and presentation by providing original animations, graphs from the textbook, data tables, and bulleted lists of key concepts suitable for large lecture presentation. You can customize these slides to suit your individual needs by adding your own data, questions, and lecture notes. You can access these files on the instructor's side of the website or on the Instructor's Resource CD-ROM.

Instructor's Resource CD-ROM Using the Instructor's Resource CD-ROM, you can easily build classroom presentations around a variety of still and moving images—from the Krugman/Wells/Myatt text, from your own sources, and even from the web. This customized presentation CD-ROM contains all text figures (in JPEG and GIF formats), animated graphs, and enhanced PowerPoint slides. All these resources are compatible with Microsoft PowerPoint software but can also be used independently to create a classroom presentation providing an unbeatable combination of convenience and power. This CD allows you to combine all the publisher-provided instructor materials with your own materials into a customized presentation suitable for all lecture needs.

EduCue Personal Response System (PRS)—"Clickers" Instructors can create a dynamic, interactive classroom environment with a personal response system, powered by EduCue. This wireless remote system allows you to ask your students questions, record their responses, and calculate grades instantly during lectures. Students use a hand-held wireless device (about the size of a television remote control) to transmit immediate feedback to a lecture hall receiver.

Acknowledgments

Writing a textbook is a team effort. Obviously, my greatest debt of gratitude goes to Paul Krugman and Robin Wells for providing such a splendid text to begin with. Next, I could never have reached this point without the insightful comments offered by many thoughtful reviewers. I am indebted to the following reviewers for their suggestions and advice on portions of the manuscript:

Jeremiah Allen, *University of Lethbridge*
Mike Fellows, *Mount Royal University*
Oliver Franke, *Athabasca University*
David Goodwin, *University of New Brunswick*
Shadhidul Islam, *Grant MacEwan College*
Michael Leonard, *Kwantlen University*
Shahram Manouchehri, *Grant MacEwan College*
David Murrell, *University of New Brunswick*
V. Nallainayagam, *Mount Royal College*
Donald Reddick, *Kwantlen University, Langley Campus*
David Sabiston, *Mount Royal College*
Angela Trimarchi, *University of Waterloo*
Peter Wylie, *University of British Columbia, Okanagan*
Yuri Yevdokimov, *University of New Brunswick*

I would also like to acknowledge those individuals who developed supplementary material for the Krugman/Wells text. The supplement authors of this text are indebted to their contributions:

Rosemary Cunningham, *Agnes Scott College*
Can Erbil, *Brandeis University*
Jack Chambless, *Valencia Community College*
Ardeshir Dalal, *Northern Illinois University*
Mark Funk, *University of Arkansas–Little Rock*
Lynn Gillette, *University of Kentucky*
Gus W. Herring, *Brookhaven College*
Jules Kaplan, *University of Colorado-Boulder*
Diane Keenan, *Cerritos Community College*
Elizabeth Sawyer Kelly, *University of Wisconsin-Madison*
Debbie Mullin, *University of Colorado-Colorado Springs*
Martha Olney, *University of California-Berkeley*
Ranita Wyatt, *Dallas Community College District*

Special thanks go to Rod Hill, who did a wonderful job checking the final manuscript for accuracy. I would also like to thank Bruce Kaplan, the development editor, for excellent suggestions, criticism, and encouragement, and the acquisitions editor Charles Van Wagner, who put together the team and nurtured the process through to its successful completion. Thanks go to Marie McHale for assembling the supplements authors and shepherding the supplements to completion. The numerous production people at Worth Publishers who took the manuscript and turned it into this attractive book are owed a special thanks: Kerry O'Shaughnessy, who as project editor guided the book throughout the production process; Lisa Story, who as copyeditor tightened the prose and smoothed the language; Patricia Marx, who as photo editor provided the dramatic visuals; and Babs Reingold for creating such a wonderful design and cover. Scott Guile, the marketing manager, provided energy and creativity in marketing this Canadian book to a Canadian audience.

Finally, I would like to thank my wife, Muriel, both for her help with the manuscript and her understanding and support.

Tony Myatt

Credits

Photo Credits

Grateful acknowledgment is given for permission to reprint the following cover photos:

Front Cover

Row 1 (left to right): Fresh vegetables, Photodisc/Getty Images; **Row 2 (left to right):** Vancouver Skyline Photodisc/Getty Images; Parliament, Toronto, Ontario, Digital Vision; **Row 3 (left to right):** Chemical plant, EyeWire; Refinery, EyeWire; **Row 4 (left to right):** Trishaw, Phnom Penh, Cambodia, Photodisc/Getty Images; New York Stock Exchange interior, Image Source/Veer; Businessman on cell phone in front of Petronas Towers, Kuala Lumpur, Malaysia, ©image100 Ltd./Veer; Meeting with laptop, Photodisc/Getty Images; British Columbia, Canada, Brand X Pictures/Getty Images; Buying shoes, Photodisc/Getty Images; **Row 5 (left to right):** Big Ben and Commonwealth of Flags, Photodisc/Getty Images; Bar-B-Q sign, Photodisc/Getty Images; Logging truck, Eye Wire; Postal worker dropping letter in mail slot, Photodisc/Getty Images; Seagulls and cooling tower, EyeWire; Electronic components assembly, Photodisc/Getty Images; **Row 6 (left to right):** Old building reflecting in windows of modern skyscraper, Toronto, Ontario, Digital Vision; Indian woman on cell phone and computer, Thinkstock/Getty Images; Satellite dish, Stockbyte; Couple crossing street with sales signs in background, Image Source/Picture Quest; Empty shopping cart, Photodisc/Getty Images; Chateau Frontenac and roofs in Quebec City, Photodisc/Getty Images; **Row 7 (left to right):** Making cappuccino, Photodisc/Getty Images; Hip kids sharing headphones, ©image100 Ltd./Veer; Man checking classified ads, Photodisc/Getty Images; Market fruit stand, Photodisc/Getty Images; Busy Hong Kong intersection, Photodisc/Getty Images; Office building under construction, EyeWire.

Back Cover

Row 1 (left to right): Wood frame building under construction, EyeWire; Fresh fish, Photodisc/Getty Images; Woman making bicycle on assembly line, EyeWire; Nuclear plant cooling tower with steam, EyeWire; **Row 2 (left to right):** East River tugboat, EyeWire; Man making pizza at a pizza stand, Photodisc/Getty Images; Shoe repair shop window, Photodisc/Getty Images; Antique store, Photodisc/Getty Images; **Row 3 (left to right):** Bunches of asparagus, Photodisc/Getty Images; Electrician working, Photodisc/Getty Images; Dark meeting with laptop and videoconference, Photodisc/Getty Images; **Row 4 (left to right):** European hotel, Photodisc/Getty Images; Manhattan, Photodisc/Getty Images; **Row 5 (left to right):** Window display in men's shop, Photodisc/Getty Images; **Row 6 (left to right):** Tractor hauling hay bales, Stockbyte.

Author Photos

Page v: Paul Krugman and Robin Wells, Ted Szczepanski; Anthony Myatt, Geoffrey Gammon.

brief contents

BRIEF CONTENTS

CONTENTS

microeconomics

CANADIAN EDITION

>>Introduction: The Ordinary Business of Life

ANY GIVEN SATURDAY

It's a typical Saturday afternoon in the winter of 2004, and the West Edmonton Mall is a busy place. Thousands of people crowd the stores, restaurants, and entertainment complexes that fill the equivalent of 48 city blocks. In this, the world's largest shopping centre, most of the shoppers are cheerful—and why not? The stores offer an extraordinary range of choices; you can buy everything from sophisticated electronic equipment to fashionable clothes to organic carrots. There are probably 100,000 distinct items available under one roof. And most of these items are not luxury goods that only the rich can afford; they are products that millions of Canadians can and do purchase every day.

The scene in the West Edmonton Mall that winter day was, of course, perfectly ordinary—very much like the scene in hundreds of other malls, all across Canada, that same afternoon. But the discipline of economics is mainly concerned with ordinary things. As the great nineteenth-century economist Alfred Marshall put it, economics is "a study of mankind in the ordinary business of life".

What can economics say about this "ordinary business"? Quite a lot, it turns out. What we'll see in this book is that even familiar scenes of economic life pose some very important questions—questions that economics can help answer. Among these questions are:

Charted Media

The market economy in action in the West Edmonton Mall.

- How does our economic system work? That is, how does it manage to deliver the goods?
- When and why does our economic system go astray, leading people into counterproductive behaviour?
- Why are there ups and downs in the economy? That is, why does the economy sometimes have a "bad year"?
- Finally, why is the long run mainly a story of "ups" rather than "downs"? That is, why has Canada, along with other advanced nations, become so much richer over time?

Let's take a look at these questions, and offer a brief preview of what you will learn in this book.

The Invisible Hand

That ordinary scene in your local shopping mall would not have looked at all ordinary to a Canadian from colonial times. Imagine that you could transport such a person forward in time to our own era and place him or her in your shopping mall. What would amaze this time-traveller? Surely the most amazing thing would be the sheer prosperity of modern Canada—the range of goods and services that ordinary families can afford. Looking at all that wealth, our transplanted colonial would wonder, "How can I get some of that?" Or perhaps he or she would ask, "How can my society get some of that?"

The answer is that to get this kind of prosperity you need a well-functioning system for coordinating productive activities—the activities that create the goods and services people want and get them to the people who want them. That kind of system is what we mean when we talk about the **economy**. And **economics** is the study of economies, at the level both of individuals and of society as a whole.

An **economy** is a system for coordinating society's productive activities.

Economics is the study of economies, at the level both of individuals and of society as a whole.

An economy succeeds to the extent that it, literally, delivers the goods. And a time-traveller from the eighteenth century—or even from 1950—would be amazed at how many goods and services the modern Canadian economy delivers, and at how many people can afford them. Compared with any past economy and compared with all but a few other countries, Canada has an incredibly high standard of living.

So our economy must be doing something right, and the time traveller might want to compliment the person in charge. But guess what? There isn't anyone in charge. Canada has a **market economy**, in which production and consumption are the result of decentralized decisions by many firms and individuals. There is no central authority telling people what to produce or where to ship it. Each individual producer makes what he or she thinks will be most profitable; each consumer buys what he or she chooses.

A **market economy** is an economy in which decisions about production and consumption are made by individual producers and consumers.

The alternative to a market economy is a *command economy*, in which there *is* a central authority making decisions about production and consumption. Command economies have been tried, most notably in the Soviet Union between 1917 and 1991. But they didn't work very well. Producers in the Soviet Union routinely found themselves unable to produce because they did not have crucial raw materials, or they succeeded in producing but then found that nobody wanted their products. Consumers were often unable to find necessary items—command economies are famous for long lines at shops.

Market economies, however, are able to coordinate even highly complex activities, and to reliably provide consumers with the goods and services they want. Indeed, people quite casually trust their lives to the market system: residents of any major city would starve in days if the unplanned yet somehow orderly actions of thousands of businesses did not deliver a steady supply of food. Surprisingly, the unplanned "chaos" of a market economy turns out to be far more orderly than the "planning" of a command economy.

In 1776, in a famous passage in his book *The Wealth of Nations,* the pioneering Scottish economist Adam Smith wrote about how individuals, in pursuing their own interests, often end up serving the interests of society as a whole. Of a businessman whose pursuit of profit makes the nation wealthier, Smith wrote: "[H]e intends only his own gain, and he is in this, as in many other cases, led by an invisible hand to promote an end which was no part of his intention." Ever since, economists have used the term **invisible hand** to refer to the way a market economy manages to harness the power of self-interest for the good of society.

The study of how individuals make decisions, and of how these decisions interact, is called **microeconomics**. One of the key themes in microeconomics is the validity of Adam Smith's insight: Individuals pursuing their own interests often do promote the interests of society as a whole.

So part of the answer to our time-traveller's question—"How can my society achieve the kind of prosperity you take for granted?"—is that his society should learn to appreciate the virtues of a market economy and the power of the invisible hand.

But the invisible hand isn't always our friend. It's also important to understand when and why the individual pursuit of self-interest can lead to counterproductive behaviour.

The **invisible hand** refers to the way in which the individual pursuit of self-interest can lead to good results for society as a whole.

Microeconomics is the branch of economics that studies how people make decisions and how these decisions interact.

My Benefit, Your Cost

One thing that our time-traveller would not admire about the Canadian shopping mall experience would be trying to get out of the parking lot. In fact, while most things have gotten better in Canada over time, traffic congestion has become a lot worse.

When traffic is congested, each driver is imposing a cost on all the other drivers on the road—he is literally getting in their way (and they are getting in his way). This cost can be substantial: in major metropolitan areas, each time someone drives to work, as opposed to taking public transportation or working at home, he can easily impose $15 or more in hidden costs on other drivers. Yet when deciding whether or not to drive, commuters have no incentive to take the costs they impose on others into account.

Traffic congestion is a familiar example of a much broader problem: sometimes the individual pursuit of one's own interest, instead of promoting the interests of society as a whole, can actually make society worse off. When this happens, it is known as **market failure**. Other important examples of market failure involve air and water pollution as well as the overexploitation of natural resources such as fish and forests.

When the individual pursuit of self-interest leads to bad results for society as a whole, there is **market failure.**

The good news, as you will learn as you use this book to study microeconomics, is that economic analysis can be used to diagnose cases of market failure. And often, economic analysis can also be used to devise solutions for the problem.

Good Times, Bad Times

We have imagined your local mall as bustling with shoppers eager to buy at the best price. These are the good times—the times when the economy is growing and most people who want jobs can get them. Unfortunately, things are not always like that. The fact is that the economy does not always run smoothly: it experiences "fluctuations", a series of ups and downs.

Troubled periods are a regular feature of modern economies. By the time he or she reaches middle age, a typical Canadian will have experienced three or four downs, known as **recessions**. (The Canadian economy experienced serious recessions beginning in 1982 and 1990.) During a severe recession, millions of workers may lose their jobs, and millions more may be afraid of losing theirs. In such times, your local mall may be short of shoppers.

A **recession** is a downturn in the economy.

Like market failure, recessions are a fact of life; but also like market failure, they are a problem to which economic analysis offers some solutions. Recessions are one of the main concerns of the branch of economics known as **macroeconomics**, which is concerned with the overall ups and downs of the economy. If you study macroeconomics, you will learn how economists explain recessions, and how government policies can be used to minimize the damage from economic fluctuations.

Macroeconomics is the branch of economics that is concerned with overall ups and downs in the economy.

Despite the occasional recession, however, over the long run the story of the Canadian economy contains many more ups than downs. And that long-run ascent is the subject of our last question.

Onward and Upward

At the beginning of the twentieth century, most Canadians lived under conditions that we would now consider extremely primitive. Less than 10% of homes had flush toilets, only 2% had electricity, and nobody had a car, let alone a washing machine or air conditioning.

Such comparisons are a stark reminder of how much our lives have been changed by **economic growth**, the growing ability of the economy to produce goods and services.

Economic growth is the growing ability of the economy to produce goods and services.

Why does the economy grow over time? And why does economic growth occur faster in some times and places than in others? These are key questions for economics because economic growth is a good thing, as those shoppers in your local mall can attest, and most of us want more of it.

An Engine for Discovery

We hope we have convinced you that the "ordinary business of life" is really quite extraordinary, if you stop and think about it, and that it can lead us to ask some very interesting and important questions.

In this book, we will describe the answers economists have given to these questions. But this book, like economics as a whole, isn't a list of answers: it's an introduction to a discipline, a way to address questions like those we have just asked. Or as Alfred Marshall, who described economics as a study of the "ordinary business of life", put it: "Economics . . . is not a body of concrete truth, but an engine for the discovery of concrete truth."

So let's turn the key in the ignition.

KEY TERMS

chapter 1

>>First Principles

COMMON GROUND

The annual meeting of the Canadian Economics Association draws hundreds of economists, young and old, famous and obscure. There are booksellers and business meetings, but mainly the economists gather to talk and listen. During the busiest times, 20 or more presentations may be taking place simultaneously on questions that range from the future of the stock market to who does the cooking in two-earner families.

What do these people have in common? An expert on the stock market probably knows very little about the economics of housework, and vice versa. Yet an economist who wanders into the wrong seminar and ends up listening to presentations on some unfamiliar topic is nonetheless likely to hear much that is familiar. The reason is that all economic analysis is based on a set of common principles that apply to many different issues.

One must choose.

Richard Hamilton Smith/Corbis

Some of these principles involve *individual choice*—for economics is, first of all, about the choices that individuals make. Do you choose to work over the summer or take a backpacking trip? Do you buy a new CD or go to a movie? These decisions involve *making a choice* among a limited number of alternatives—limited because no one can have everything that he or she wants. Every question in economics at its most basic level involves individuals making choices.

But to understand how an economy works, you need to understand more than how individuals make choices. None of us is Robinson Crusoe, alone on an island—we must make decisions in an environment that is shaped by the decisions of others. Indeed, in a modern economy even the simplest decisions you make—say, what to have for breakfast—are shaped by the decisions of thousands of other people, from the banana grower in Costa Rica who decided to grow the fruit you eat to the farmer in Saskatchewan who provided the wheat in your toast. And because each of us in a market economy depends on so many others—and they, in turn, depend on us—our

What you will learn in this chapter:

- A set of principles for understanding the economics of how individuals make choices
- A set of principles for understanding how individual choices interact

choices interact. So although all economics at a basic level is about individual choice, in order to understand how market economies behave, we must also understand economy-wide *interaction*—how my choices affect your choices, and vice versa.

In this chapter, we will look at nine principles of economics—four "basic principles" involving individual choice, and five "principles of interaction" involving the way individual choices interact.

Individual Choice: The Core of Economics

Individual choice is the decision by an individual of what to do, which necessarily involves a decision of what not to do.

Every economic issue involves, at its most basic level, **individual choice**—decisions by an individual about what to do and what *not* to do. In fact, you might say that it isn't economics if it isn't about choice.

Step into a big store like a Sears or Canadian Tire. There are thousands of different products available, and it is extremely unlikely that you—or anyone else—could afford to buy everything that you might want to have. And anyway, there's only so much space in your dorm room or apartment. So will you buy another bookcase or a mini-refrigerator? Given limitations on your budget and your living space, you must choose which products to buy and which to leave on the shelf.

The fact that those products are on the shelf in the first place involves choice—the store manager chose to put them there, and the manufacturers of the products chose to produce them. All economic activities involve individual choice.

Four basic economic principles underlie the economics of individual choice, as shown in Table 1-1. We'll now examine each of these principles in more detail.

TABLE 1-1

Principles That Underlie the Economics of Individual Choice

1. Resources are scarce.
2. The real cost of something is what you must give up to get it.
3. "How much?" is a decision at the margin.
4. People usually exploit opportunities to make themselves better off.

Basic Principle #1: Resources Are Scarce

You can't always get what you want. Everyone would like to have a beautiful house in a great location (and help with the housecleaning), two or three luxury cars, and frequent vacations in fancy hotels. But even in a rich country like Canada not many families can afford all of that. So, they must make choices—whether to go to Disney World this year or buy a better car, whether to make do with a small backyard or accept a longer commute in order to live where land is cheaper.

Limited income isn't the only thing that keeps people from having everything they want. Time is also in limited supply: there are only 24 hours in a day. And because the time we have is limited, choosing to spend time on one activity also means choosing not to spend time on a different activity—spending time studying for an exam means forgoing a night at the movies. Indeed, many people are so limited by the number of hours in the day that they are willing to trade money for time. For example, convenience stores normally charge higher prices than a regular supermarket. But they fulfill a valuable role by catering to time-pressured customers who would rather pay more than travel farther to the supermarket.

A **resource** is anything that can be used to produce something else.

Resources are **scarce**—the quantity available isn't large enough to satisfy all productive uses.

Why do individuals have to make choices? The ultimate reason is that *resources are scarce*. A **resource** is anything that can be used to produce something else. Lists of the economy's resources usually begin with land, labour (the available time of workers), capital (machinery, buildings, and other man-made productive assets), and human capital (the educational achievements and skills of workers). A resource is **scarce** when the quantity of the resource available isn't large enough to satisfy all productive uses. There are many scarce resources. These include natural resources—resources that come from the physical environment—such as minerals, lumber, and petroleum. There is also a limited quantity of human resources—labour, skill, and intelligence. And in a growing world economy with a rapidly increasing human population, even clean air and water have become scarce resources.

Just as individuals must make choices, the scarcity of resources available to an economy means that society as a whole must make choices. One way for a society to make choices is simply to allow them to emerge as the result of many individual choices, which is what usually happens in a market economy. For example, Canadians as a group have only so many hours in a week: how many of those hours will they spend going to supermarkets to get lower prices, rather than saving time by shopping at convenience stores? The answer is the sum of individual decisions: each of the millions of individuals in the economy makes his or her own choice about where to shop, and the overall choice is simply the sum of those individual decisions.

But for various reasons, there are some decisions that a society decides are best not left to individual choice. For example, recently there has been a house-building boom in Canada, with many new urban communities springing up in previously undeveloped areas. Most local residents feel that a community will be a more pleasant place to live if some of the land is left undeveloped and made available as public parks or play areas. But no individual has an incentive to keep his or her land as open space, rather than selling it to a developer. As a result, provincial governments legislate, in their community planning acts, that a certain minimum amount of space must be set aside (by the developers) for community parks and playgrounds. We'll see in later chapters why decisions about how to use scarce resources are often best left to individuals, but sometimes should be made at a higher, community-wide level.

Basic Principle #2: The Real Cost of Something Is What You Must Give Up to Get It

It is the last term before you graduate from university, and your class schedule allows you to take only one elective. There are two, however, that you would really like to take: History of Jazz and Introduction to Canadian Film.

Suppose that you decide to take the History of Jazz course. What's the cost of that decision? It is the fact that you can't take the film course. Economists call that kind of cost—what you must forgo in order to get something you want—the **opportunity cost** of that item. So the opportunity cost of the History of Jazz class is the enjoyment you would have derived from the film class.

The real cost of an item is its **opportunity cost:** what you must give up in order to get it.

The concept of opportunity cost is crucial to understanding individual choice because, in the end, all costs are opportunity costs. Sometimes critics claim that economists are concerned only with costs and benefits that can be measured in dollars and cents. But that is not true. Much economic analysis involves cases like our elective course example, where it costs no extra tuition to take one elective course—that is, there is no direct monetary cost. Nonetheless, the elective you choose has an opportunity cost—the other desirable elective course that you must forgo because your limited time permits taking only one.

You might think that opportunity cost is an add-on—that is, something *additional* to the monetary cost of an item. Suppose that an elective course costs additional tuition of $750; now there is a monetary cost to taking History of Jazz. Is the opportunity cost of taking that course something separate from that monetary cost?

Well, consider two cases. First, suppose that taking Introduction to Canadian Film also costs $750. In this case you would have to spend that $750 no matter which class you take. So what you give up to take the History of Jazz class is still the film class, period—you would have to spend that $750 either way. But suppose there isn't any fee for the film class. In that case, what you give up to take the jazz class is the film class *plus* whatever you would have bought with the $750.

Either way, the cost of taking your preferred class is what you give up to get it. *All* costs are ultimately opportunity costs.

Sometimes the money you have to pay for something is a good indication of its opportunity cost. But many times it is not. One very important example of how

FOR INQUIRING MINDS

GOT A PENNY?

At many cash registers—for example, the one in our university cafeteria—there is a little basket full of pennies. People are encouraged to use the basket to round their purchases up or down: if it costs $5.02, you give the cashier $5 and take two pennies from the basket; if it costs $4.99, you pay $5 and the cashier throws in a penny. It makes everyone's life a bit easier. Of course, it would be easier still if we just abolished the penny, a step that some economists have urged.

But then why do we have pennies in the first place? If it's too small a sum to worry about, why calculate prices that exactly?

The answer is that a penny wasn't always such a negligible sum: the purchasing power of a penny has been greatly reduced by inflation. Forty years ago, a penny had more purchasing power than a nickel does today.

Why does this matter? Well, remember the saying: "A penny saved is a penny earned." But there are other ways to earn money, so you must decide whether saving a penny is a productive use of your time. Could you earn more by devoting that time to other uses?

Forty years ago, the average wage was about $2 an hour. A penny was equivalent to 18 seconds' worth of work—it was worth saving a penny if doing so took less than 18 seconds. But wages have risen along with overall prices, so that the average (industrial) worker in Canada is now paid around $16 per hour. A penny is, therefore, equivalent to about 2 seconds of work—and so it's not worth the opportunity cost of the time it takes to worry about a penny more or less.

In short, the rising opportunity cost of time in terms of money has turned a penny from a useful coin into a nuisance.

AP/Wide World Photos

Tiger Woods understood the concept of opportunity cost. The rest is history.

poorly monetary cost can indicate opportunity cost is the cost of attending university. Tuition and housing are major monetary expenses for most students; but even if these things were free, attending university would still be an expensive proposition because most university students, if they were not in university, would have a job. That is, by going to university, students *forgo* the income they could have made if they had worked instead. This means that the opportunity cost of attending university is what you pay for tuition and housing *plus* the forgone income that you would have earned in a job.

It's easy to see that the opportunity cost of going to university is especially high for people who could be earning a lot during what would otherwise have been their university years. That is why star athletes often skip university or, like Tiger Woods, leave before graduating.

Basic Principle #3: "How Much?" Is a Decision at the Margin

Some important decisions involve an "either–or" choice–for example, you decide either to go to university or to begin working; you decide either to take economics or to take something else. But other important decisions involve "how much" choices–for example, if you are taking both economics and chemistry this semester, you must decide how much time to spend studying for each. When it comes to understanding "how much" decisions, economics has an important insight to offer: "how much" is a decision made at the *margin*.

Suppose you are taking both economics and chemistry. And suppose you are a pre-med student, so that your grade in chemistry matters more to you than your grade in economics. Does that therefore imply that you should spend *all* your study time on chemistry and wing it on the economics exam? Probably not; even if you think your chemistry grade is more important, you should put some effort into studying for economics.

You make a **trade-off** when you compare the costs with the benefits of doing something.

Spending more time studying for economics involves a benefit (a higher expected grade in that course) and a cost (you could have spent that time doing something else, such as studying to get a higher grade in chemistry). That is, your decision involves a **trade-off**–a comparison of costs and benefits.

How do you decide this kind of "how much" question? The typical answer is that you make the decision a bit at a time, by asking how you should spend the next hour. Say both exams are on the same day, and the night before the exams you spend time reviewing your notes for both courses. At 6 P.M., you decide that it's a good idea to spend at least an hour on each course. At 8 P.M., you decide you'd better spend another hour on each course. At 10 P.M., you are getting tired and figure you have one more hour to study before bed—chemistry or economics? If you are pre-med, it's likely to be chemistry; if you are pre-MBA, it's likely to be economics.

Note how you've made the decision to allocate your time: at each point the question is whether or not to spend *one more hour* on either course. And in deciding whether to spend another hour studying for chemistry, you weigh the costs (an hour forgone of studying for economics or an hour forgone of sleeping) versus the benefits (a likely increase in your chemistry grade). As long as the benefit of studying one more hour for chemistry outweighs the cost, you should choose to study for that additional hour.

Decisions of this type—what to do with your next hour, what to do with your next dollar, and so on—are **marginal decisions**. They involve making trade-offs *at the margin*: comparing the costs and benefits of doing a little bit more of an activity versus doing a little bit less. The study of such decisions is known as **marginal analysis**.

Decisions about whether to do a bit more or a bit less of an activity are **marginal decisions**. The study of such decisions is known as **marginal analysis**.

Many of the questions that we face in economics—as well as in real life—involve marginal analysis: How many workers should I hire in my shop? After how many kilometres should I change the oil in my car? What is an acceptable rate of negative side effects from a new medicine? Marginal analysis plays a central role in economics because it is the key to deciding "how much" of an activity to do.

Basic Principle #4: People Usually Exploit Opportunities to Make Themselves Better Off

Every weeknight, CBC Radio broadcasts a show called *As It Happens.* It directly follows *The World at Six,* and delves deeper into the news. It has a special fondness for stories that are weird or wacky. One evening it reported on a story that the best way to park your car in Manhattan is to go to Jiffy Lube for an oil change—they keep your car all day and it only costs US$19.95. In comparison, parking in a garage would run you at least US$30 a day. What was amusing was what happened when the host of the show tried to talk to the owner of the Jiffy Lube for his comment. They discovered that there is no Jiffy Lube in Manhattan. It's a great story, but unfortunately it turned out not to be true.

It's too bad there's no Jiffy Lube in Manhattan. But if there were, you can be sure there would be a lot of oil changes there. Why? Because when people are offered opportunities to make themselves better off, they normally take them—and if they could find a way to park their car all day for $19.95 rather than $30, they would.

When you try to predict how individuals will behave in an economic situation, it is a very good bet that they will exploit opportunities to make themselves better off. Furthermore, individuals will *continue* to exploit these opportunities until they have been fully exhausted—that is, people will exploit opportunities until those opportunities have been fully taken.

If there really were a Manhattan Jiffy Lube and an oil change really were a cheap way to park your car, we can safely predict that before long the waiting list for oil changes would be weeks, if not months.

In fact, the principle that people will exploit opportunities to make themselves better off is the basis of *all* predictions by economists about individual behaviour. If the earnings of those who get MBAs soar while the earnings of those who get law degrees decline, we can expect more students to go to business school and fewer to go to law school. If the price of gasoline rises and stays high for an extended period of time, we

FOR INQUIRING MINDS

PAYING FOR GRADES IN FLORIDA? PAYING FOR BABIES IN QUÉBEC?

Do people always respond to incentives? Would you work harder for an exam if you were given a cash bonus for doing well? Would you have a baby if the government gave you a cash bonus for doing so? You may answer 'no' to these questions. You may feel that there is already enough pressure to do well on exams. You may feel that you will start a family only when you are ready, and that a financial incentive would not affect you. Indeed, you may feel that having children because of a financial incentive is immoral. But statistically, incentives have been shown to work for both grades and babies.

For example, a few years ago, some Florida schools stirred widespread debate by offering actual cash bonuses—up to $50 in a savings bond—to students who scored high on the state's standardized exams. They did this because the state government had introduced a pay-for-performance scheme for schools: schools whose students earned high marks on the state exams received extra state funds. Interviews with students suggested that the cash bonuses did spur at least some students to try harder. And the schools themselves reported substantial improvements in student performance.

With regard to babies, Québec offered its residents baby bonuses between 1988 and 1997—starting at $500 for a first baby and rising to $8000 for a third. They did this to combat declining fertility rates. And it worked. Fertility in the province grew overall by 12 percent during the period.

The point is that these incentives are likely to affect people *at the margin*. Couples don't have babies for the baby bonus—it's too small an amount. But for a couple on the borderline between having another child and not, or between having a baby sooner rather than later, the baby bonus tips the scales.

can expect people to buy smaller cars with better fuel economy—making themselves better off in the presence of higher gas prices by driving more fuel-efficient cars.

An **incentive** is anything that offers rewards to people who change their behaviour.

When changes in the available opportunities offer rewards to those who change their behaviour, we say that people face new **incentives**. If the price of parking in Manhattan rises, those who can find alternative ways to get to their Wall Street jobs will save money by doing so—and so we can expect fewer people to drive to work.

One last point: economists tend to be sceptical of any attempt to change people's behaviour that *doesn't* change their incentives. For example, a plan that calls on manufacturers to reduce pollution voluntarily probably won't be effective; a plan that gives them a financial incentive to reduce pollution is a lot more likely to work.

Individual Choice: Summing It Up

We have just seen that there are four basic principles of individual choice:

- *Resources are scarce.* It is always necessary to make choices.
- *The real cost of something is what you must give up to get it.* All costs are opportunity costs.
- *"How much?" is a decision at the margin.* Usually the question is not "whether", but "how much". And that is a question whose answer hinges on the costs and benefits of doing a bit more.
- *People usually exploit opportunities to make themselves better off.* As a result, people will respond to incentives.

So are we ready to do economics? Not yet—because most of the interesting things that happen in the economy are not merely the result of individual choices, but of the way those individual choices *interact*.

economics in action

A Woman's Work

One of the great social transformations of the twentieth century was the change in the nature of women's work. In 1900, only 6 percent of married women worked for pay outside the home. By the early twenty-first century, the number was around 65 percent.

What caused this transformation? Changing attitudes towards work outside the home certainly played a role: in the first half of the twentieth century it was often considered improper for a married woman to work outside the home if she could afford not to, whereas today it is considered normal. But an important driving force was the invention and growing availability of home appliances, especially washing machines. Before these appliances became available, housework was an extremely laborious task—much more so than a full-time job. In 1945, government researchers clocked a farm wife as she did the weekly wash by hand; she spent 4 hours washing clothes and 4½ hours ironing, and she walked more than a mile. Then she was equipped with a washing machine; the same wash took 41 minutes, ironing was reduced to 1¾ hours, and the distance walked was reduced by 90 percent.

The point is that in pre-appliance days the opportunity cost of working outside the home was very high: it was something women typically did only in the face of dire financial necessity. With modern appliances, the opportunities available to women changed—and the rest is history.

>> QUICK REVIEW

- All economics involves *individual choice.*
- People must make choices because *resources* are *scarce.*
- The cost of anything is what you must give up to get it—all costs are *opportunity costs*. Monetary costs are sometimes a good indicator of opportunity costs, but not always.
- Many choices are not *whether* to do something, but *how much*. "How much" choices are made by making a trade-off at the margin. The study of marginal decisions is known as *marginal analysis*.
- Because people usually exploit opportunities to make themselves better off, *incentives* can change people's behaviour.

>> CHECK YOUR UNDERSTANDING 1-1

1. Explain how each of the following situations illustrates one of the four principles of individual choice.
   a. You are on your third trip to a restaurant's all-you-can-eat dessert buffet and are feeling very full. Although it would cost you no additional money, you forgo another slice of coconut cream pie but have a slice of chocolate cake.
   b. Even if there were more resources in the world, there would still be scarcity.
   c. Different teaching assistants teach several Economics 101 tutorials. Those taught by the teaching assistants with the best reputations fill quickly, with spaces left unfilled in the ones taught by assistants with poor reputations.
   d. To decide how many hours per week to exercise, you compare the health benefits of one more hour of exercise to the effect on your grades of one less hour spent studying.
2. You make $45,000 per year at your current job with Whiz Kids Consultants. You are considering a job offer from Brainiacs, Inc., which will pay you $50,000 per year. Which of the following are elements of the opportunity cost of accepting the new job at Brainiacs, Inc.?
   a. The increased time spent commuting to your new job.
   b. The $45,000 salary from your old job.
   c. The more spacious office at your new job.

Solutions appear at back of book.

Interaction: How Economies Work

As we learned in the Introduction, an economy is a system for coordinating the productive activities of many people. In a market economy, such as the one we live in, that coordination takes place without any coordinator: each individual makes his or her own choices. Yet those choices are by no means independent of each other: each individual's opportunities, and hence choices, depend to a large extent on the choices made by other people. So to understand how a market economy behaves, we have to examine this **interaction**, in which my choices affect your choices, and vice versa.

Interaction of choices—my choice affects your choices, and vice versa—is a feature of most economic situations. The results of this interaction are often quite different from what the individuals intend.

When studying economic interaction, we quickly learn that the end result of individual choices may be quite different from what any one individual intends.

For example, over the past century farmers in Canada have eagerly adopted new farming techniques and crop strains that have reduced their costs and increased their yields. Clearly, it's in the interest of each farmer to keep up with the latest farming techniques. But the end result of each farmer trying to increase his or her own income has actually been to drive many farmers out of business. Because Canadian

TABLE 1-2

Principles That Underlie the Interaction of Individual Choices

1. There are gains from trade.
2. Markets move toward equilibrium.
3. Resources should be used as efficiently as possible to achieve society's goals.
4. Markets usually lead to efficiency.
5. When markets don't achieve efficiency, government intervention can improve society's welfare.

farmers (and their counterparts in the U.S. and Europe) have been so successful at producing larger yields, agricultural prices have steadily fallen. These falling prices have reduced the incomes of many farmers, and as a result fewer and fewer people find farming worth doing. That is, an individual farmer who plants a better variety of wheat is better off; but when many farmers plant a better variety of wheat, the result may be to make farmers as a group worse off.

A farmer who plants a new, more productive wheat variety doesn't just grow more wheat. Such a farmer also affects the market for wheat through the increased yields attained, with consequences that will be felt by other farmers, consumers, and beyond.

Just as there are four economic principles that fall under the theme of choice, there are five principles that fall under the theme of interaction. These five principles are summarized in Table 1-2. We will now examine each of these principles more closely.

Principle of Interaction #1: There Are Gains from Trade

Why do the choices I make interact with the choices you make? A family could try to take care of all its own needs—growing its own food, sewing its own clothing, providing itself with entertainment, writing its own economics textbooks. But trying to live that way would be very hard. The key to a much better standard of living for everyone is **trade**, in which people divide tasks among themselves and each person provides a good or service that other people want in return for different goods and services that he or she wants.

In a market economy, individuals engage in **trade**: they provide goods and services to others and receive goods and services in return.

There are **gains from trade**: people can get more of what they want through trade than they could if they tried to be self-sufficient. This increase in output is due to **specialization**: each person specializes in the task that he or she is good at performing.

The reason we have an economy, not many self-sufficient individuals, is that there are **gains from trade**: by dividing tasks and trading, two people (or 6 billion people) can each get more of what they each want than they could get by being self-sufficient. Gains from trade arise, in particular, from this division of tasks which economists call **specialization**, a situation in which different people each engage in a different task.

The advantages of specialization, and the resulting gains from trade, were the starting point for Adam Smith's 1776 book *The Wealth of Nations,* which many regard as the beginning of economics as a discipline. Smith's book begins with a description of an eighteenth-century pin factory where, rather than each of the 10 workers making a pin from start to finish, each worker specialized in one of the many steps in pin-making:

> One man draws out the wire, another straightens it, a third cuts it, a fourth points it, a fifth grinds it at the top for receiving the head; to make the head requires two or three distinct operations; to put it on, is a particular business, to whiten the pins is another; it is even a trade by itself to put them into the paper; and the important business of making a pin is, in this manner, divided into about eighteen distinct operations. . . . Those ten persons, therefore, could make among them upwards of forty-eight thousand pins in a day. But if they had all wrought separately and independently, and without any of them having been educated to this particular business, they certainly could not each of them have made twenty, perhaps not one pin a day. . . .

"I hunt and she gathers—otherwise we couldn't make ends meet."

The same principle applies when we look at how people divide tasks among themselves and trade in an economy. *The economy, as a whole, can produce more when each person specializes in a task and trades with others.*

The benefits of specialization are the reason a person typically chooses only one career. It takes many years of study and experience to become a doctor; it also takes many years of study and experience to become a commercial airline pilot. Many doctors might well have had the potential to become excellent pilots, and vice versa; but it is very unlikely that anyone who decided to pursue both careers would be as good a pilot or as good a doctor as someone who decided at the beginning to specialize in that field. So it is to everyone's advantage that individuals specialize in their career choices.

Markets are what allow a doctor and a pilot to specialize in their own fields. Because markets for commercial flights and for doctors' services exist, a doctor is assured that she can find a flight, and a pilot is assured that he can find a doctor. As long as individuals know that they can find the goods and services that they want in the market, they are willing to forgo self-sufficiency and are willing to specialize. But what assures people that markets will deliver what they want? The answer to that question leads us to our second principle of economy-wide interaction.

Principle of Interaction #2: Markets Move towards Equilibrium

It's a busy afternoon at the supermarket; there are long lines at the checkout counters. Then one of the previously closed cash registers opens. What happens?

The first thing that happens, of course, is a rush to that register. After a couple of minutes, however, things will have settled down; shoppers will have rearranged themselves so that the line at the newly opened register is about the same length as the lines at all the other registers.

How do we know that? We know from our fourth principle of individual choice that people will exploit opportunities to make themselves better off. This means that people will rush to the newly opened register in order to save time standing in line. And things will settle down when shoppers can no longer improve their position by switching lines—that is, when the opportunities to make themselves better off have all been exploited.

Chuck Keeler/Stone/Getty Images

See equilibrium in action at the checkout lines in your neighbourhood supermarket.

A story about supermarket checkout lines may seem to have little to do with economy-wide interactions, but in fact it illustrates an important principle. A situation in which individuals cannot make themselves better off by doing something different—the situation in which all the checkout lines are the same length—is what economists call an **equilibrium**. An economic situation is in equilibrium when no individual would be better off doing something different.

An economic situation is in **equilibrium** when no individual would be better off doing something different.

Recall the story about the mythical Jiffy Lube, where it was supposedly cheaper to leave your car for an oil change than to pay for parking. If that opportunity had

FOR INQUIRING MINDS

CHOOSING SIDES

Why do people in North America drive on the right side of the road? Of course, it's the law. But long before it was the law, it was an equilibrium.

Before there were formal traffic laws, there were informal "rules of the road", practices that everyone expected everyone else to follow. These rules included an understanding that people would normally keep to one side of the road. In some places, such as England, the rule was to keep to the left; in others, such as France, it was to keep to the right.

Why would some places choose the right and others, the left? That's not completely clear, although it may have depended on the dominant form of traffic. Men riding horses and carrying swords on their left hip preferred to ride on the left (think about getting on or off the horse, and you'll see why). On the other hand, right-handed people walking but leading horses apparently preferred to walk on the right.

In any case, once a rule of the road was established, there were strong incentives for each individual to stay on the "usual" side of the road: those who didn't would keep colliding with oncoming traffic. So once established, the rule of the road would be self-enforcing—that is, it would be an equilibrium.

Nowadays, of course, which side you drive on is determined by law; some countries have even changed sides (Sweden went from left to right in 1967). But what about pedestrians? There are no laws—but there are informal rules. In Canada, urban pedestrians normally keep to the right. But if you should happen to visit Japan, watch out: the Japanese, who drive on the left, also typically walk on the left. So when in Japan, do as the Japanese do. You won't be arrested if you walk on the right, but you will be worse off than if you accept the equilibrium and walk on the left.

really existed, and people were still paying $30 to park in garages, the situation would *not* have been an equilibrium.

And that should have been a giveaway that the story couldn't be true.

In reality, people would have seized an opportunity to park cheaply, just as they seize opportunities to save time at the checkout line. And in so doing they would have eliminated the opportunity! Either it would have become very hard to get an appointment for an oil change, or the price of a lube job would have increased to the point that it was no longer an attractive option (unless you really needed a lube job).

As we will see, markets usually reach equilibrium via changes in prices, which rise or fall until no opportunities for individuals to make themselves better off remain.

The concept of equilibrium is extremely helpful in understanding economic interactions because it provides a way of cutting through the sometimes complex details of those interactions. To understand what happens when a new line is opened at a supermarket, you don't need to worry about exactly how shoppers rearrange themselves, who moves ahead of whom, which register just opened, and so on. What you need to know is that any time there is a change, the situation will move to an equilibrium.

The fact that markets move toward equilibrium is why we can depend on markets to work in a predictable way. In fact, we can trust markets to supply us with the essentials of life. For example, people who live in big cities can be sure that the supermarkets shelves will always be fully stocked. Why? Because if some merchants who distribute food *didn't* make deliveries, a big profit opportunity would be created for any merchant who did—and there would be a rush to supply food, just like the rush to a newly opened cash register. So the market ensures that food will always be available for city-dwellers. And, returning to our previous principle, this allows city-dwellers to be city-dwellers—to specialize in doing city jobs rather than living on farms and growing their own food.

A market economy also allows people to achieve gains from trade. But how do we know how well such an economy is doing? The next principle gives us a standard to use in evaluating an economy's performance.

Principle of Interaction #3: Resources Should Be Used as Efficiently as Possible to Achieve Society's Goals

Suppose you are taking a course in which the classroom is too small for the number of students—many people are forced to stand or sit on the floor—despite the fact that large, empty classrooms are available nearby. You would say, correctly, that this is no way to run a university. Economists would call this an *inefficient* use of resources.

But if an inefficient use of resources is undesirable, just what does it mean to use resources *efficiently*? You might imagine that the efficient use of resources has something to do with money, maybe that it is measured in dollars-and-cents terms. But in economics, as in life, money is only a means to other ends. The measure that economists really care about is not money but people's happiness or welfare. Economists say that *an economy's resources are used efficiently when they are used in a way that has fully exploited all opportunities to make everyone better off.* To put it another way, an economy is **efficient** if it takes all opportunities to make some people better off without making other people worse off.

An economy is **efficient** if it takes all opportunities to make some people better off without making other people worse off.

In our classroom example, there clearly was a way to make everyone better off—moving the class to a larger room would make people in the class better off without hurting anyone else in the university. Assigning the course to the smaller classroom was an inefficient use of the university's resources, while assigning the course to the larger classroom would have been an efficient use of the university's resources.

When an economy is efficient, it is producing the maximum gains from trade possible given the resources available. Why? Because there is no way to rearrange how resources are used in a way that can make everyone better off. When an economy is efficient, one person can be made better off by rearranging how resources are used *only* by making someone else worse off. In our classroom example, if all larger classrooms were already occupied, the university would have been run in an efficient way: your class could be made better off by moving to a larger classroom only by making people in the larger classroom worse off by making them move to a smaller classroom.

Should economic policy-makers always strive to achieve economic efficiency? Well, not quite, because efficiency is not the only criterion by which to evaluate an economy. People also care about issues of fairness or **equity.** And there is typically a trade-off between equity and efficiency: policies that promote equity often come at a cost of decreased efficiency in the economy, and vice versa.

Equity means that everyone gets his or her fair share. Since people can disagree about what's "fair", equity isn't as well-defined a concept as efficiency.

To see this, consider the case of disabled-designated parking spaces in public parking lots. Many people have great difficulty walking due to age or disability, so it seems only fair to assign closer parking spaces specifically for their use. You may have noticed, however, that a certain amount of inefficiency is involved. To make sure that there is always an appropriate space available should a disabled person want one, there are typically quite a number of disabled-designated spaces. So at any one time there are typically more such spaces available than there are disabled people who want one. As a result, desirable parking spaces are unused. (And the temptation for non-disabled people to use them is so large that we must be dissuaded by fear of getting a ticket.) So, short of hiring parking valets to allocate spaces, there is a conflict between *equity,* making life 'fairer' for disabled people, and *efficiency,* making sure that all opportunities to make people better off have been fully exploited by never letting close-in parking spaces go unused.

Exactly how far policy-makers should go in promoting equity over efficiency is a very difficult question that goes to the heart of the political process. As such, it is not a question that economists can answer. What is important for economists, however, is to always seek to use the economy's resources as efficiently as possible in the pursuit of society's goals, whatever those goals may be.

Principle of Interaction #4: Markets Usually Lead to Efficiency

No branch of the Canadian government is entrusted with ensuring the general economic efficiency of our market economy—we don't have agents who go around making sure that brain surgeons aren't ploughing fields, that Saskatchewan farmers aren't trying to grow oranges, that prime beachfront property isn't taken up by used-car dealerships, that universities aren't wasting valuable classroom space. The government doesn't need to enforce efficiency because in most cases the invisible hand does the job.

In other words, the incentives built into a market economy already ensure that resources are usually put to good use, that opportunities to make people better off are not wasted. If a university were known for its habit of crowding students into small classrooms while large classrooms went unused, it would soon find its enrolment dropping, putting the jobs of its administrators at risk. The "market" for university students would respond in a way that induces administrators to run the university efficiently.

A detailed explanation of why markets are usually very good at making sure that resources are used well will have to wait until we have studied how markets actually work. But the most basic reason is that in a market economy, in which individuals are free to choose what to consume and what to produce, opportunities for mutual gain are normally taken. If there is a way that some people can be made better off, people will usually be able to take advantage of that opportunity. And that is exactly what defines efficiency: all of the opportunities to make everyone better off have been exploited.

As we learned in the Introduction, however, there are exceptions to this principle that markets are generally efficient. In cases of *market failure,* the individual pursuit of self-interest found in markets makes society worse off—that is, the market outcome is inefficient. And, as we will see in examining the next principle, when markets fail, government intervention can help. But short of instances of market failure, the general rule is that markets are a remarkably good way of organizing an economy.

Principle of Interaction #5: When Markets Don't Achieve Efficiency, Government Intervention Can Improve Society's Welfare

Let's recall from the Introduction the nature of the market failure caused by traffic congestion—a commuter driving to work has no incentive to take into account the cost that his or her action inflicts on other drivers in the form of increased traffic congestion. There are several possible remedies to this situation; examples include charging road tolls, subsidizing the cost of public transportation, or taxing sales of gasoline to individual drivers. All of these remedies work by changing the incentives of would-be drivers—motivating them to drive less and use alternative transportation. But they also share another feature: each relies on government intervention in the market.

This brings us to our fifth and last principle of interaction: *when markets don't achieve efficiency, government intervention can improve society's welfare.* That is, when markets go wrong, an appropriately designed government policy can sometimes move society closer to an efficient outcome by changing how society's resources are used.

A very important branch of economics is devoted to studying why markets fail and what policies should be adopted to improve social welfare. We will study these problems and their remedies in depth in later chapters, but here we give a brief overview of why markets fail. They fail for three principal reasons:

- Individual actions have *side effects* that are not properly taken into account by the market.
- One party prevents mutually beneficial trades from occurring in the attempt to capture a greater share of resources for itself.
- Some goods, by their very nature, are unsuited for efficient management by markets.

An important part of your education in economics is to learn to identify not just when markets work, but also when they don't work—and to judge which government policies are appropriate in each situation.

economics in action

Restoring Equilibrium on the Freeways

In 1994 a powerful earthquake struck the Los Angeles area, causing several freeway bridges to collapse and thereby disrupting the normal commuting routes of hundreds of thousands of drivers. The events that followed offer a particularly clear example of interdependent decision making—in this case, the decisions of commuters about how to get to work.

In the immediate aftermath of the earthquake, there was great concern about the impact on traffic, since motorists would now have to crowd onto alternative routes or detour around the blockages by using city streets. Public officials and news programs warned commuters to expect massive delays and urged them to avoid unnecessary travel, reschedule their work to commute before or after the rush, or use mass transit. These warnings were unexpectedly effective. In fact, so many people heeded them that in the first few days following the quake, those who maintained their regular commuting routine actually found the drive to and from work faster than before.

Of course, this situation could not last. As word spread that traffic was actually not bad at all, people abandoned their less convenient new commuting methods and reverted to their cars—and traffic got steadily worse. Within a few weeks after the quake, serious traffic jams had appeared. After a few more weeks, however, the situation stabilized: the reality of worse-than-usual congestion discouraged enough drivers to prevent the nightmare of city-wide gridlock from materializing. Los Angeles traffic, in short, had settled into a new equilibrium, in which each commuter was making the best choice he or she could, given what everyone else was doing. ■

>> QUICK REVIEW

- A feature of most economic situations is the *interaction* of choices made by individuals, the end result of which may be quite different from what was intended. In a market economy, this takes the form of *trade* between individuals.
- Individuals interact because there are *gains from trade*. Gains from trade arise from *specialization*.
- Economic situations normally move toward *equilibrium*.
- As far as possible, there should be an *efficient* use of resources to achieve society's goals. But efficiency is not the only way to evaluate an economy; *equity* may also be desirable, and there is often a trade-off between equity and efficiency.
- Markets normally *are* efficient, except for certain well-defined exceptions.
- When markets fail to achieve efficiency, government intervention can improve society's welfare.

>>CHECK YOUR UNDERSTANDING 1-2

1. Explain how each of the following situations illustrates one of the five principles of interaction.
   a. Using the university's student website, any student who wants to sell a used textbook for at least $X is able to sell it to another who is willing to pay $X.
   b. At a university tutoring co-op, students can arrange to provide tutoring in subjects they are good in (like economics) in return for receiving tutoring in subjects they are poor in (like philosophy).
   c. The local municipality imposes a law that requires bars and nightclubs near residential areas to keep their noise levels below a certain threshold.
   d. To provide better care for low-income patients, the city of Toronto has decided to close some underutilized neighbourhood clinics and shift funds to the main hospital.
   e. On the university website, books of a given title with approximately the same level of wear and tear sell for about the same price.
2. Which of the following describes an equilibrium situation? Which does not? Explain your answer.
   a. The restaurants across the street from the university dining hall serve better-tasting and cheaper meals than those served at the university dining hall. The vast majority of students continue to eat at the dining hall.
   b. You currently take the subway to work. Although taking the bus is cheaper, the ride takes longer. So you are willing to pay the higher subway fare in order to save time.

Solutions appear at back of book.

• A LOOK AHEAD •

The nine basic principles we have described lie behind almost all economic analysis. Although they can be immediately helpful in understanding many situations, they are usually not enough. Applying the principles to real economic issues takes one more step.

That step is the creation of *models*—simplified representations of economic situations. Models must be realistic enough to provide real-world guidance but simple enough that they allow us to see clearly the implications of the principles described in this chapter. So our next step is to show how models are used to actually do economic analysis.

SUMMARY

1. All economic analysis is based on a short list of basic principles. These principles apply to two levels of economic understanding. First, we must understand how individuals make choices; second, we must understand how these choices interact.
2. Everyone has to make choices about what to do and what not to do. **Individual choice** is the basis of economics—if it doesn't involve choice, it isn't economics.
3. The reason choices must be made is that **resources**—anything that can be used to produce something else—are **scarce**. Individuals are limited in their choices by money and time; economies are limited by their supplies of human and natural resources.
4. Because you must choose among limited alternatives, the true cost of anything is what you must give up to get it—all costs are **opportunity costs**.

5. Many economic decisions involve questions not of "whether", but of "how much"—how much to spend on some good, how much to produce, and so on. Such decisions must be taken by performing a **trade-off** *at the margin*—by comparing the costs and benefits of doing a bit more or a bit less. Decisions of this type are called **marginal decisions**, and the study of them, **marginal analysis**, plays a central role in economics.
6. The study of how people *should* make decisions is also a good way to understand actual behaviour. Individuals usually exploit opportunities to make themselves better off. If opportunities change, so does behaviour: people respond to **incentives.**
7. **Interaction**—my choices depend on your choices, and vice versa—adds another level to economic understanding. When individuals interact, the end result may be different from what anyone intends.
4. The reason for interaction is that there are **gains from trade**: by engaging in the **trade** of goods and services with one another, the members of an economy can all be made better off. Underlying gains from trade are the advantages of **specialization**, of having individuals specialize in the tasks they are good at.
9. Economies normally move toward **equilibrium**—a situation in which no individual can make himself or herself better off without taking a different action.
10. An economy is **efficient** if all opportunities to make someone better off without making others worse off are taken. Resources should be used as efficiently as possible to achieve society's goal. But efficiency is not the sole way to evaluate an economy: **equity**, or fairness, is also desirable, and there is often a trade-off between equity and efficiency.
11. Markets usually lead to efficiency, with some well-defined exceptions.
12. When markets fail and do not achieve efficiency, government intervention can improve society's welfare.

KEY TERMS

Individual choice, p. 6
Resource, p. 6
Scarce, p. 6
Opportunity cost, p. 7
Trade-off, p. 8
Marginal decisions, p. 9
Marginal analysis, p. 9
Incentive, p. 10
Interaction, p. 11
Trade, p. 12
Gains from trade, p. 12
Specialization, p. 12
Equilibrium, p. 13
Efficient, p. 14
Equity, p. 15

PROBLEMS

1. In each of the following situations, identify which of the nine principles is at work:
   - **a.** You choose to shop at the local discount store rather than pay a higher price for the same merchandise at the local department store.
   - **b.** On your spring vacation trip, your budget is limited to $35 a day.
   - **c.** The student union provides a website on which departing students can sell items such as used books, appliances, and furniture rather than giving them away to their roommates as they formerly did.
   - **d.** You decide how many cups of coffee to have when studying the night before an exam by considering how much more work you can do by having another cup versus how jittery it will make you feel.
   - **e.** There is limited lab space available to do the project required in Chemistry 101. The lab supervisor assigns lab time to each student based on when that student is able to come.
   - **f.** You realize that you can graduate a semester early by forgoing a semester of study abroad.
   - **g.** At the student union there is a bulletin board on which people advertise used items for sale, such as bicycles. Once you have adjusted for differences in quality, all the bikes sell for about the same price.
   - **h.** You are better at performing lab experiments, and your lab partner is better at writing lab reports. So, the two of you agree that you will do all the experiments, and she will write up all the reports.
   - **i.** Provincial governments mandate that it is illegal to drive without passing a driving exam.
2. Describe some of the opportunity costs when you decide to do the following.
   - **a.** Attend university instead of taking a job
   - **b.** Watch a movie instead of studying for an exam
   - **c.** Ride the bus instead of driving your car
3. Liza needs to buy a textbook for the next economics class. The price at the university bookstore is $65. One online site offers it for $55 and another site for $57. All prices include sales tax. The accompanying table indicates the typical shipping and handling charges for the textbook ordered online.

Shipping method	Delivery time	Charge
Standard Shipping	3–7 days	$3.99
Second-day air	2 business days	$8.98
Next-day air	1 business day	$13.98

a. What is the opportunity cost of buying online?

b. Show the relevant choices for this student. What determines which of these options the student will choose?

4. Use the concept of opportunity cost to explain the following:

a. More people choose to get graduate degrees when the job market is poor.

b. More people choose to do their own home repairs when the economy is slow.

c. There are more parks in suburban areas than in urban areas.

d. Convenience stores, which have higher prices than supermarkets, cater to busy people.

e. Fewer students enrol in classes that meet before 10 A.M.

5. In the following examples, state how you would use the principle of marginal analysis to make a decision:

a. Deciding how many days to wait before doing your laundry

b. Deciding how much library research to do before writing your term paper

c. Deciding how many bags of chips to eat

d. Deciding how many lectures of a class to skip

6. This morning you made the following individual choices: you bought a bagel and coffee at the local café, you drove to school in your car during rush hour, and you typed your roommate's term paper because you are a fast typist—in return for which she will do your laundry for a month. In each of these actions, describe how your individual choices interacted with the individual choices made by others. Were other people left better off or worse off by your choices in each case?

7. On the east side of the Miramichi River lives the Hatfield family, while the McCoy family lives on the west side. Each family's diet consists of fried chicken and corn-on-the-cob, and each is self-sufficient, raising their own chickens and growing their own corn. Explain the conditions under which each of the following would be true:

a. The two families are made better off when the Hatfields specialize in raising chickens, the McCoys specialize in raising corn, and the two families trade.

b. The two families are made better off when the McCoys specialize in raising chickens, the Hatfields specialize in raising corn, and the two families trade.

8. Which of the following situations describes an equilibrium? Which does not? If the situation does not describe an equilibrium, what would an equilibrium look like?

a. Many people regularly commute from the suburbs to downtown Pleasantville. Due to traffic congestion, the trip takes 30 minutes when you travel by highway, but only 15 minutes when you go by the side streets.

b. At the intersection of Main and King are two gas stations. One station charges 90 cents a litre for regular gas and the other charges 85 cents a litre. Customers can get service immediately at the first station, but must wait in a long line at the second.

c. Every student enrolled in Economics 101 must also attend a weekly tutorial. This year there are two sections offered: Section A and Section B, which meet at the same time in adjoining classrooms and are taught by equally competent instructors. Section A is overcrowded, with people sitting on the floor and often unable to see the chalkboard. Section B has many empty seats.

9. In each of the following cases, explain whether you think the situation is efficient or not. If it is not efficient, why not? What actions would make the situation efficient?

a. Electricity is included in the rent at your dorm. Some residents in your dorm leave lights, computers, and appliances on when they are not in their rooms.

c. Although they cost the same amount to prepare, the cafeteria in your dorm consistently provides too many dishes that diners don't like, such as tofu casserole, and too few dishes that diners do like, such as roast turkey with dressing.

d. The enrolment for a particular course exceeds the spaces available. Some students who need to take this course to complete their major are unable to get a space, while others who are taking it as an elective do get a space.

10. Discuss the efficiency and equity implications of each of the following policies. How would you go about balancing the concerns of equity and efficiency in these areas?

a. The government pays the full tuition for every college student to study whatever subject he or she wishes.

b. When people lose their jobs, the government provides unemployment benefits until they find new ones.

11. Governments often adopt certain policies in order to promote desired behaviour among their citizens. For each of the following policies, determine what the incentive is and what behaviour the government wishes to promote. In each case, why do you think that the government might wish to change people's behaviour, rather than allow their actions to be solely determined by individual choice?

a. A tax of $5 per pack is imposed on cigarettes.

b. The government pays parents $100 when their child is vaccinated for measles.

c. The government pays for university students to tutor children from low-income families.

d. The government imposes a tax on the amount of air pollution that a company discharges.

12. In each of the following situations, explain how government intervention could improve society's welfare by changing people's incentives. In what sense is the market going wrong?

a. Pollution from auto emissions has reached unhealthy levels.

b. Everyone in Woodville would be better off if streetlights were installed in the town. But no individual resident is willing to pay for installation of a streetlight in front of his or her house because it is impossible to recoup the cost by charging other residents for the benefit they receive from it.

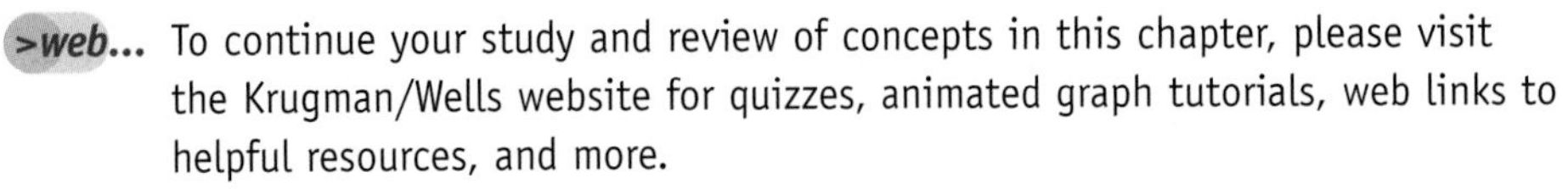

>web... To continue your study and review of concepts in this chapter, please visit the Krugman/Wells website for quizzes, animated graph tutorials, web links to helpful resources, and more.

www.worthpublishers.com/krugmanwellsmyatt

chapter 2

>>Economic Models: Trade-Offs and Trade

TUNNEL VISION

In 1901 Wilbur and Orville Wright built something that would change the world. No, not the airplane—their successful flight at Kitty Hawk would come two years later. What made the Wright brothers true visionaries was their wind tunnel, an apparatus that let them experiment with many different designs for wings and control surfaces. These experiments gave them the knowledge that would make heavier-than-air flight possible.

A miniature airplane sitting motionless in a wind tunnel isn't the same thing as an actual aircraft in flight. But it is a very useful model of a flying plane—a simplified representation of the real thing that can be used to answer crucial questions, such as how much lift a given wing shape will generate at a given airspeed.

Needless to say, testing an airplane design in a wind tunnel is cheaper and safer than building a full-scale version and hoping it will fly. More generally, models play a crucial role in almost all scientific research—economics very much included.

In fact, you could say that economic theory consists mainly of a collection of models, a series of simplified representations of economic reality that allow us to understand a variety of economic issues. In this chapter, we will look at three economic models that are crucially important in their own right and also illustrate why such models are so useful. We'll conclude with a look at how economists actually use models in their work.

Landov Photos

Clearly, the Wright brothers believed in their model.

What you will learn in this chapter:

- Why **models**—simplified representations of reality—play a crucial role in economics
- Three simple but important models: the **production possibility frontier**, the **comparative advantage**, and the **circular-flow diagram**
- The difference between **positive economics**, which tries to describe the economy and predict its behavior, and **normative economics**, which tries to prescribe economic policy
- When economists agree and why they sometimes disagree

Models in Economics: Some Important Examples

A **model** is a simplified representation of a real situation that is used to better understand real-life situations.

A **model** is any simplified representation of reality that is used to better understand real-life situations. But how do we create a simplified representation of an economic situation?

One possibility—an economist's equivalent of a wind tunnel—is to find or create a real but simplified economy. For example, economists interested in the economic role of money have studied the system of exchange that developed in World War II prison camps, in which cigarettes became a universally accepted form of payment even among prisoners who didn't smoke.

Another possibility is to simulate the workings of the economy on a computer. For example, when changes in tax law are proposed, government officials use tax models—large computer programs—to assess how the proposed changes would affect different types of people.

The **other things equal assumption** means that all other relevant factors remain unchanged.

The importance of models is that they allow economists to focus on the effects of only one change at a time. That is, they allow us to hold everything else constant and study how one change affects the overall economic outcome. So the **other things equal assumption,** which means that all other relevant factors remain unchanged, is an important assumption when building economic models.

FOR INQUIRING MINDS

MODELS FOR MONEY

What's an economic model worth, anyway? In some cases, quite a lot of money.

Although many economic models are developed for purely scientific purposes, others are developed to help governments make economic policies. And there is a growing business in developing economic models to help corporations make decisions.

Who models for money? All economic consultants—of which there are probably hundreds in Canada—use models and data in their analysis. But very few firms go so far as to build a complete model of the Canadian economy and then use that model to predict future trends, offer advice based on their models, or develop custom models for business and government clients. There are about five operations that do this in Canada—the biggest of which is a firm called "Informetrica", which employs around 20 full-time professionals.

One particularly lucrative branch of economics is finance theory, which helps investors figure out what assets, such as shares in a company, are worth. Finance theorists often become highly paid "rocket scientists" at big Bay Street firms because financial models demand a high level of technical expertise.

Unfortunately, the most famous business application of finance theory came spectacularly to grief in the United States. In 1994 a group of Wall Street traders teamed up with famous finance theorists—including two Nobel prize winners—to form Long-Term Capital Management (LTCM), a fund that used sophisticated financial models to invest the money of wealthy clients. At first, the fund did very well. But in 1998 bad news from all over the world—with countries as disparate as Russia, Japan, and Brazil in trouble at the same time—inflicted huge losses on LTCM's investments. For a few anxious days, many people feared not only that the fund would collapse but also that it would bring many other companies down with it. Thanks in part to a rescue operation organized by government officials, this did not happen; but LTCM was closed a few months later, with some of its investors losing most of the money they had put in.

What went wrong? Partly it was bad luck. But experienced hands also faulted the economists at LTCM for taking too many risks. Their models said that a run of bad news like the one that actually happened was extremely unlikely—but a sensible economist knows that sometimes even the best model misses important possibilities.

But you can't always find or create a small-scale version of the whole economy, and a computer program is only as good as the data it uses. (Programmers have a saying: garbage in, garbage out.) For many purposes the most effective form of economic modeling is the construction of "thought experiments": simplified, hypothetical versions of real-life situations.

In Chapter 1 we illustrated the concept of equilibrium with the example of how customers at a supermarket would rearrange themselves when a new cash register opens. Though we didn't say it, this was an example of a simple model—an imaginary supermarket, in which many details were ignored (what are the customers buying?—never mind)—that could be used to answer a "what if" question: what if another cash register were opened?

As the cash register story showed, it is often possible to describe and analyze a useful economic model in plain English. However, because much of economics involves changes in quantities—in the price of a product, the number of units produced, or the number of workers employed in its production—economists often find that using some mathematics helps clarify an issue. In particular, a numerical example, a simple equation, or—especially—a graph can be the key to understanding an economic concept.

Whatever the form it takes, a good economic model can be a tremendous aid to understanding. The best way to make this point is to consider some simple but important economic models and what they tell us. First, we will look at the *production possibility frontier,* a model that helps economists think about the trade-offs every economy faces. Then we will turn to *comparative advantage,* a model that clarifies the principle of gains from trade—trade both between individuals and between countries. Finally, we'll examine the *circular-flow model,* which helps economists analyze the monetary transactions taking place in the economy as a whole.

In discussing these models, we make considerable use of graphs to represent mathematical relationships. Such graphs will play an important role throughout this book. If you are already familiar with the use of graphs, the material that follows should not present any problem. If you are not, this would be a good time to turn to the appendix of this chapter, which provides a brief introduction to the use of graphs in economics.

The **production possibility frontier** illustrates the trade-offs facing an economy that produces only two goods. It shows the maximum quantity of one good that can be produced for any given quantity produced of the other.

Trade-offs: The Production Possibility Frontier

The hit movie *Cast Away,* starring Tom Hanks, was an update of the classic story of Robinson Crusoe, the hero of Daniel Defoe's eighteenth-century novel. Mr. Hanks played the sole survivor of a plane crash, stranded on a remote island. As in the original story of Robinson Crusoe, the character played by Mr. Hanks had limited resources: the natural resources of the island, a few items he managed to salvage from the plane, and, of course, his own time and effort. With only these resources, he had to make a life. In effect, he became a one-man economy.

The first principle of economics we introduced in Chapter 1 was that resources are scarce, and that as a result any economy—whether it contains one person or millions of people—faces trade-offs. For example, if a castaway devotes resources to catching fish, he cannot use those same resources to gather coconuts.

To think about the trade-offs that face any economy, economists often use the model known as the **production possibility frontier**. The idea behind this model is to improve our understanding of trade-offs by considering a simplified economy that produces only two goods. This simplification enables us to show the trade-off graphically.

What to do? Even a castaway faces trade-offs.

Figure 2-1 shows a hypothetical production possibility frontier for Tom, a castaway alone on an island, who must make a trade-off between production of fish and production of coconuts. The frontier—the curve in the diagram—shows the maximum number of fish Tom can catch during a week *given* the quantity of coconuts he gathers, and vice versa. That is, it answers questions of the form, "What is the maximum number of fish Tom can catch if he also gathers 20 (or 25, or 30) coconuts?" (We'll explain the bowed-out shape of the curve in Figure 2-1 shortly, after we've seen how to interpret the production possibility frontier.)

There is a crucial distinction between points *inside* or *on* the curve (the shaded area) and *outside* the curve. If a production point lies inside or on the frontier—like the point labelled *C*, at which Tom catches 20 fish and gathers 20 coconuts—it is feasible. After all, the frontier tells us that if Tom catches 20 fish, he could also gather a maximum of 25 coconuts, so he could certainly gather 20 coconuts. On the other hand, a production point that lies outside the frontier—such as the hypothetical production point shown in the figure as point *D*, where Tom catches 40 fish and gathers 30 coconuts—isn't feasible. (In this case, Tom could catch 40 fish and gather no coconuts, *or* he could gather 30 coconuts and catch no fish, but he can't do both.)

In Figure 2-1 the production possibility frontier intersects the horizontal axis at 40 fish. This means that if Tom devoted all his resources to catching fish, he would catch 40 fish per week but would have no resources left over to gather coconuts. The production possibility frontier intersects the vertical axis at 30 coconuts; this means that if Tom devoted all his resources to gathering coconuts, he could gather 30 coconuts per week but would have no resources left over to catch fish.

The figure also shows less extreme trade-offs. For example, if Tom decides to catch 20 fish, he is able to gather 25 coconuts; this production choice is illustrated by point *A* in Figure 2-1. If Tom decides to catch 30 fish, he can gather at most only 20 coconuts, as shown by point *B*.

Thinking in terms of a production possibility frontier simplifies the complexities of reality. The real-world economy produces millions of different goods. Even a castaway on an island would produce more than two different items (for example, he would need clothing and housing as well as food). But in this model we imagine an economy that produces only two goods.

If we simplify reality, however, the production possibility frontier helps us understand some aspects of the real economy better than we could without the model.

Figure 2-1

The Production Possibility Frontier

The production possibility frontier illustrates the trade-offs facing an economy that produces two goods. It shows the maximum quantity of one good that can be produced given the quantity of the other good produced. Here, the maximum number of coconuts that Tom can gather depends on the number of fish he catches, and vice versa. His feasible production is shown by the area *inside or on* the curve. Production at point *C* is feasible but not efficient. Points *A* and *B* are feasible and efficient, but point *D* is not feasible. **>web...**

>web... Throughout our book, this icon will be used to indicate which graphs are available in an interactive format on our text's website. You can work with these interactive graph tutorials and find additional learning resources if you go to www.worthpublishers.com/krugmanwells.

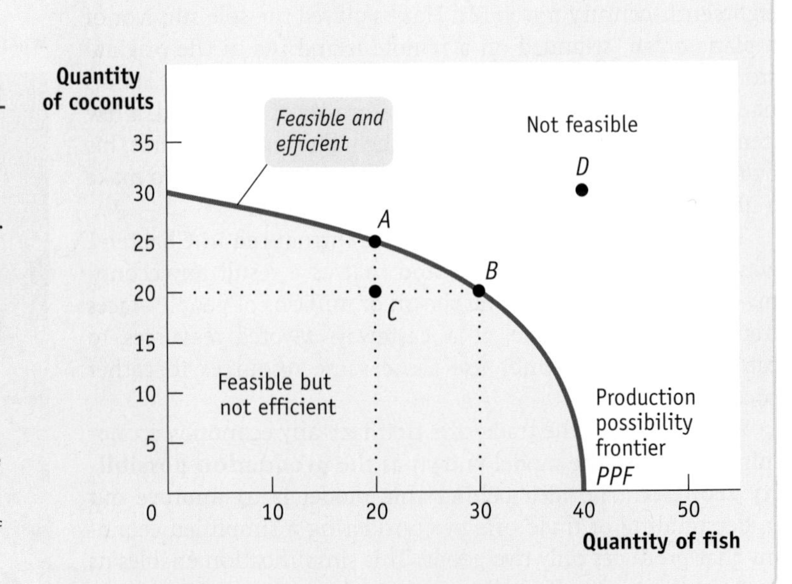

First of all, the production possibility frontier is a good way to illustrate the general economic concept of *efficiency*. Recall from Chapter 1 that an economy is *efficient* if there are no missed opportunities—if there is no way to make some people better off without making other people worse off. A key element of efficiency is that there are no missed opportunities in production—there is no way to produce more of one good without producing less of other goods.

As long as Tom is on the production possibility frontier, his production is efficient. At point *A*, the 25 coconuts he gathers are the maximum number he can get *given* that he has chosen to catch 20 fish; at point *B*, the 20 coconuts he gathers are the maximum he can get *given* his choice to catch 30 fish; and so on.

But suppose that for some reason Tom was at point *C*, producing 20 fish and 20 coconuts. Then this one-person economy would definitely be *inefficient*: it could be producing more of both goods.

The production possibility frontier is also useful as a reminder of the fundamental point that the true cost of any good is not just the amount of money it costs to buy, but everything else in addition to money that must be given up in order to get that good—the *opportunity cost*. If Tom were to catch 30 fish instead of 20, he would be able to gather only 20 coconuts instead of 25. So the opportunity cost of those 10 extra fish is the 5 coconuts not gathered. And if 10 extra fish have an opportunity cost of 5 coconuts, each one fish has an opportunity cost of $5/10 = 0.5$ coconuts.

We can now explain the bowed-out shape of the production possibility frontier we saw in Figure 2-1: it reflects an assumption about how opportunity costs change as the mix of output changes. Figure 2-2 shows the same production possibility frontier as Figure 2-1. The arrows in Figure 2-2 illustrate the fact that with this bowed-out production possibility frontier, Tom faces *increasing opportunity cost*: the more fish he catches the more coconuts he has to give up to catch an additional fish, and vice versa. For example, to go from producing zero fish to producing 20 fish, he has to give up 5 coconuts. That is, the opportunity cost of those 20 fish is 5 coconuts. But to increase his fish production to 40—that is, to produce an additional 20 fish—he must give up 25 more coconuts, a much higher opportunity cost.

Economists believe that opportunity costs are usually increasing. The reason is that when only a small amount of a good is produced, the economy can use resources that are especially well suited for that production. For example, if an

Figure 2-2

Increasing Opportunity Cost

The bowed-out shape of the production possibility frontier reflects increasing opportunity cost. In this example, to produce the first 20 fish, Tom must give up 5 coconuts. But to produce an additional 20 fish, he must give up 25 more coconuts. **>*web...***

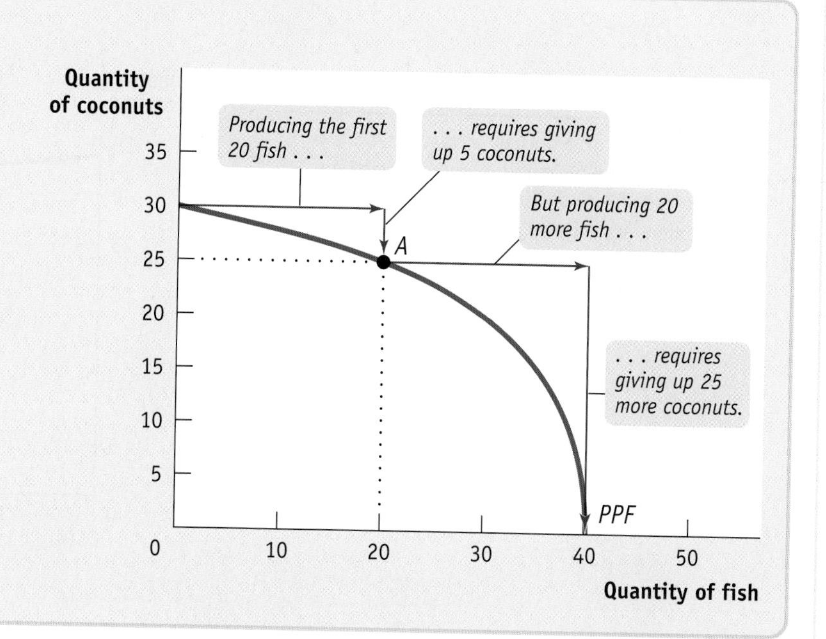

economy grows only a small amount of corn, that corn can be grown in places where the soil and climate are perfect for corn growing, but less suitable for growing anything else, like wheat. So growing that corn involves giving up only a small amount of potential wheat production. If the economy grows a lot of corn, however, land that isn't so great for corn and would have been well suited for wheat must be pressed into service, so the additional corn production will involve sacrificing considerably more wheat production.

Finally, the production possibility frontier helps us understand what it means to talk about *economic growth*. We introduced the concept of economic growth in the Introduction, defining it as *the growing ability of the economy to produce goods and services*. As we saw, economic growth is one of the fundamental features of the real economy. But are we really justified in saying that the economy has grown? After all, although the Canadian economy produces more of many things than it did a century ago, it produces less of other things—for example, horse-drawn carriages. Production of many goods, in other words, is actually down. So how can we say for sure that the economy as a whole has grown?

The answer, illustrated in Figure 2-3, is that economic growth means an *expansion of the economy's production possibilities*: the economy *can* produce more of everything. For example, if Tom's production is initially at point *A* (20 fish and 25 coconuts), economic growth means that he could move to point *E* (25 fish and 30 coconuts). *E* lies outside the original frontier; so in the production possibility frontier model, growth is shown as an outward shift of the frontier.

What the economy actually produces depends on the choices people make. After his production possibilities expand, Tom might not actually choose to produce both more fish and more coconuts—he might choose to increase production of only one good, or he might even choose to produce less of one good. But even if, for some reason, he chooses to produce either fewer coconuts or fewer fish than before, we would still say that his economy has grown—because he *could* have produced more of everything.

The production possibility frontier is a very simplified model of an economy. Yet it teaches us important lessons about real-life economies. It gives us our first clear sense of a key element of economy efficiency, it illustrates the concept of opportunity cost, and it makes it clear what economic growth is all about.

Figure 2-3

Economic Growth

Economic growth results in an *outward shift* of the production possibility frontier because production possibilities are expanded. The economy can now produce more of everything. For example, if production is initially at point *A* (20 fish and 25 coconuts), it could move to point *E* (25 fish and 30 coconuts).

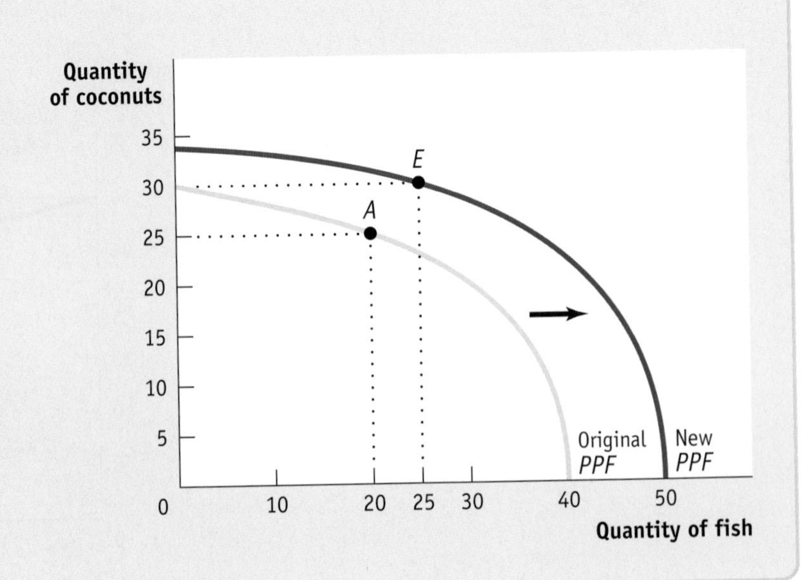

Comparative Advantage and Gains from Trade

Among the nine principles of economics described in Chapter 1 was that of *gains from trade*—the mutual gains that individuals can achieve by specializing in doing different things and trading with one another. Our second illustration of an economic model is one particularly useful model of gains from trade—trade based on *comparative advantage*.

Let's stick with Tom stranded on his island, but let's now suppose that a second castaway, *Dumb and Dumber*'s Lloyd, is washed ashore. Can they benefit from trading with each other?

It's obvious that there are potential gains from trade if the two castaways do different things particularly well. For example, if Tom is a skilled fisherman while Lloyd is very good at climbing trees, clearly it makes sense for Tom to catch fish and Lloyd to gather coconuts—and for the two men to trade the products of their efforts.

But one of the most important insights in all of economics is that there are gains from trade even if one of the trading parties isn't especially good at anything. Suppose, for example, that Lloyd is less well suited to primitive life than Tom; he's not nearly as good at catching fish, and compared to Tom even his coconut gathering leaves something to be desired. Nonetheless, what we'll see is that both Tom and Lloyd can live better by trading with each other than either could alone.

For the purposes of this example, let's slightly redraw Tom's production possibilities represented by the production possibility frontier in panel (a) of Figure 2-4. According to this diagram, Tom could catch at most 40 fish, but only if he gathered no coconuts, and could gather 30 coconuts, but only if he caught no fish, as before.

In Figure 2-4, we have replaced the curved production possibility frontier of Figure 2-1 with a straight line. Why do this, when we've already seen that economists regard a bowed-out production possibility frontier as normal? The answer is that it simplifies our discussion—and as we have explained, modeling is all about simplification. The principle of comparative advantage doesn't depend on the assumption of straight-line production possibility frontiers, but it is easier to explain with that assumption.

Figure 2-4 Production Possibilities for Two Castaways

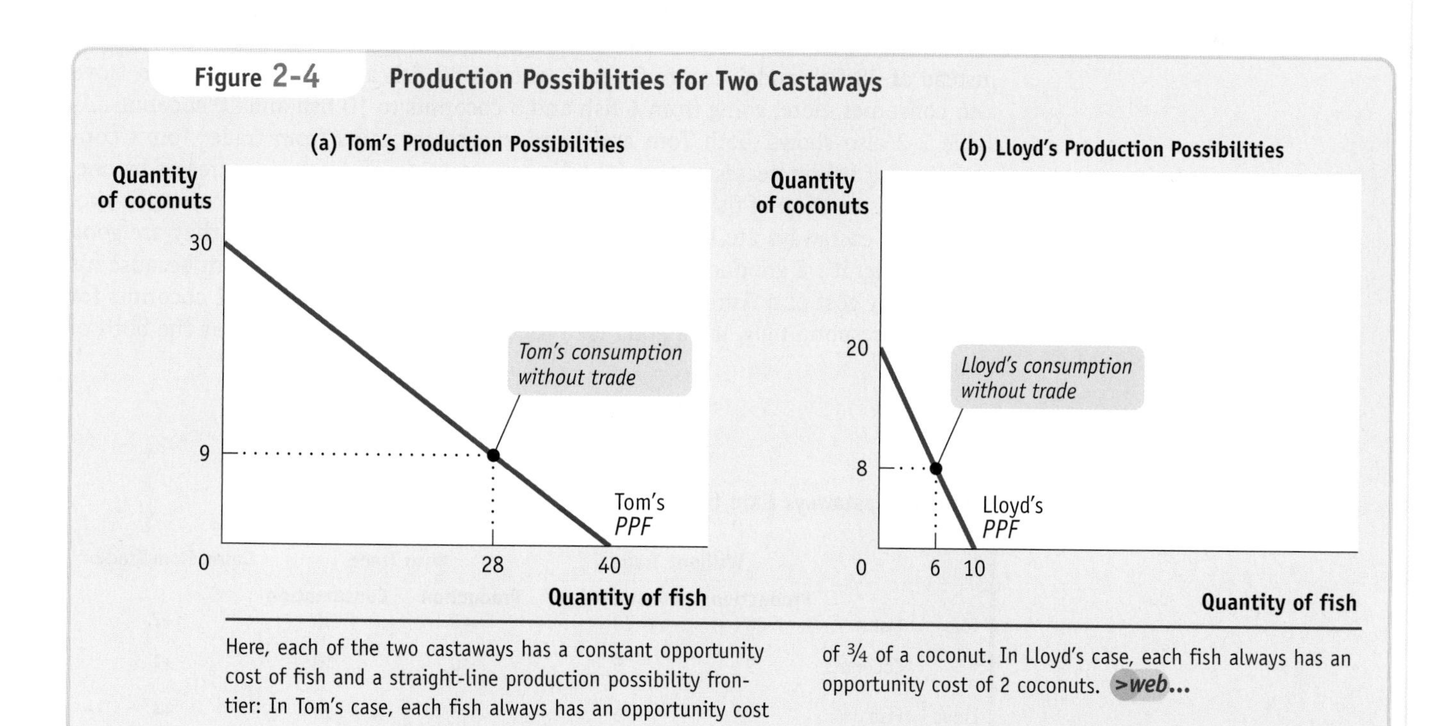

Here, each of the two castaways has a constant opportunity cost of fish and a straight-line production possibility frontier: In Tom's case, each fish always has an opportunity cost of ¾ of a coconut. In Lloyd's case, each fish always has an opportunity cost of 2 coconuts. >web...

The straight-line production possibility frontier in panel (a) of Figure 2-4 has a constant *slope* of −¾. (The appendix to this chapter explains how to calculate the slope of a line.) That is, for every 4 additional fish that Tom chooses to catch, he gathers 3 fewer coconuts. So Tom's opportunity cost of a fish is ¾ of a coconut regardless of how many or how few fish he catches. In contrast, a production possibility frontier is curved when the opportunity cost of a good changes according to how much of the good has already been produced.

For example, you can see from Figure 2-2 that if Tom starts at the point of having caught zero fish and gathers 30 coconuts, his opportunity cost of catching 20 fish is 5 coconuts. But once he has already caught 20 fish, the opportunity cost of an additional 20 fish increases to 25 coconuts.

Panel (b) of Figure 2-4 shows Lloyd's production possibilities. Like Tom's, Lloyd's production possibility frontier is a straight line, implying a constant opportunity cost of fish in terms of coconuts. His production possibility frontier has a constant slope of −2. Lloyd is less productive all around: at most he can produce 10 fish or 20 coconuts. But he is particularly bad at fishing; whereas Tom sacrifices ¾ of a coconut per fish caught, for Lloyd the opportunity cost of a fish is 2 whole coconuts. Table 2-1 summarizes the two castaways' opportunity costs for fish and coconuts.

TABLE 2-1

Tom's and Lloyd's Opportunity Costs of Fish and Coconuts

	Tom's Opportunity Cost	Lloyd's Opportunity Cost
One fish	¾ coconut	2 coconuts
One coconut	4/3 fish	½ fish

Now, Tom and Lloyd could go their separate ways, each living on his own side of the island, catching his own fish and gathering his own coconuts. Let's suppose that they start out that way and make the consumption choices shown in Figure 2-4: in the absence of trade, Tom consumes 28 fish and 9 coconuts per week, while Lloyd consumes 6 fish and 8 coconuts.

But is this the best they can do? No, it isn't. Given that the two castaways have different opportunity costs, they can make a deal that makes both of them better off.

Table 2-2 shows how such a deal works: Tom specializes in the production of fish, catching 40 per week, and gives 10 fish to Lloyd. Meanwhile, Lloyd specializes in the production of coconuts, gathering 20 per week, and gives 10 coconuts to Tom. The result is shown in Figure 2-5. Tom now consumes more of both goods than before: instead of 28 fish and 9 coconuts, he consumes 30 fish and 10 coconuts. And Lloyd also consumes more, going from 6 fish and 8 coconuts to 10 fish and 10 coconuts. As Table 2-2 also shows, both Tom and Lloyd experience gains from trade: Tom's consumption of fish increases by two, and his consumption of coconuts increases by one. Lloyd's consumption of fish increases by four, and his consumption of coconuts by two.

So both castaways are better off when they each specialize in what they are good at and trade. It's a good idea for Tom to catch the fish for both of them because his opportunity cost of a fish is only ¾ of a coconut not gathered, versus 2 coconuts for Lloyd. Correspondingly, it's a good idea for Lloyd to gather coconuts for the both of them.

TABLE 2-2

How the Castaways Gain from Trade

		Without Trade		With Trade		Gains from Trade
		Production	Consumption	Production	Consumption	
Tom	Fish	28	28	40	30	+2
	Coconuts	9	9	0	10	+1
Lloyd	Fish	6	6	0	10	+4
	Coconuts	8	8	20	10	+2

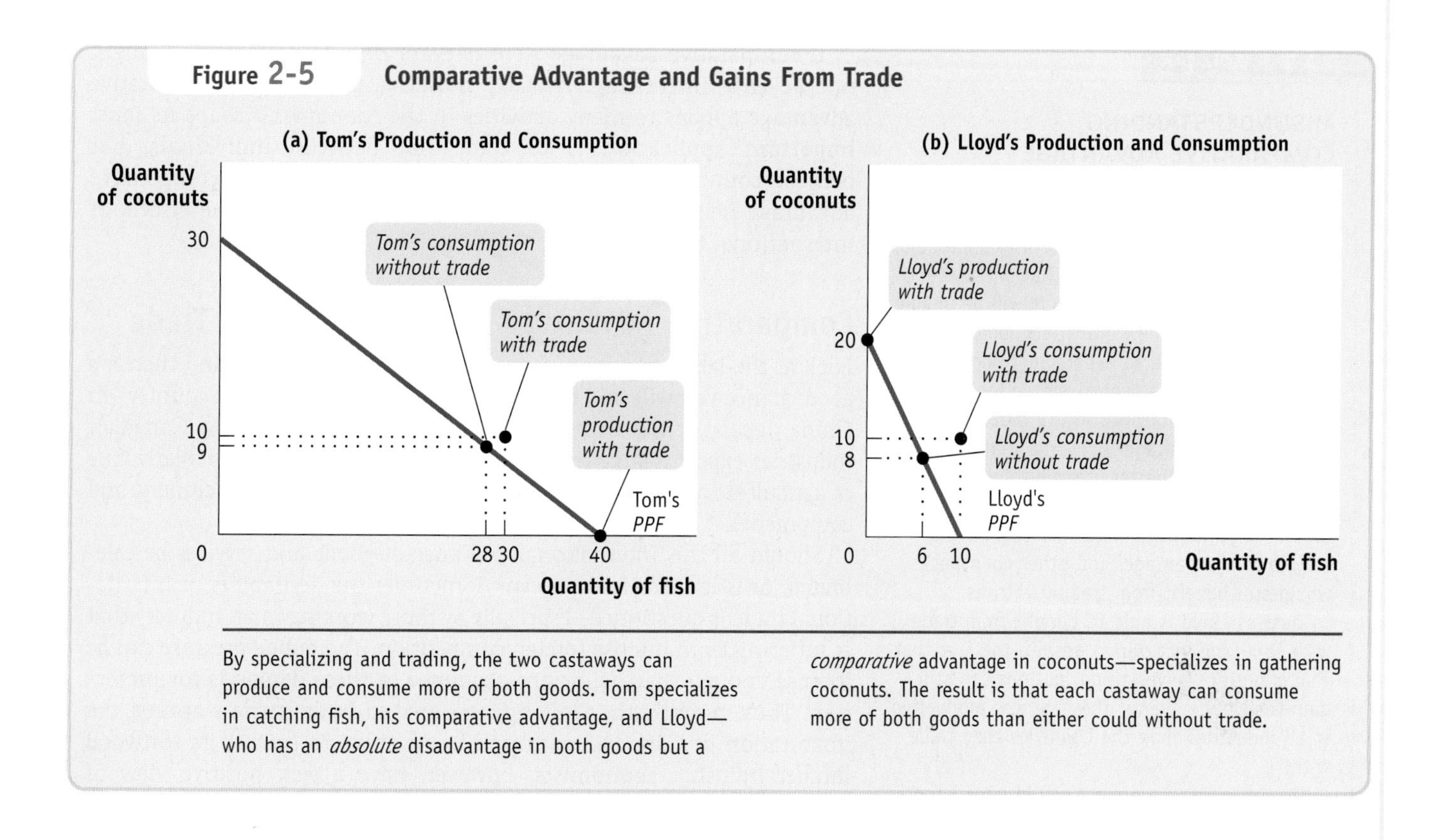

Figure 2-5 Comparative Advantage and Gains From Trade

By specializing and trading, the two castaways can produce and consume more of both goods. Tom specializes in catching fish, his comparative advantage, and Lloyd—who has an *absolute* disadvantage in both goods but a *comparative* advantage in coconuts—specializes in gathering coconuts. The result is that each castaway can consume more of both goods than either could without trade.

Or we could put it the other way around: Because Tom is so good at catching fish, his opportunity cost of gathering coconuts is high: $\frac{4}{3}$ fish not caught for every coconut gathered. Because Lloyd is a pretty poor fisherman, his opportunity cost of gathering coconuts is much less, only $\frac{1}{2}$ fish per coconut.

What we would say in this case is that Tom has a **comparative advantage** in catching fish and Lloyd has a comparative advantage in gathering coconuts. An individual has a comparative advantage in producing something if the opportunity cost of that production is lower for that individual than for other people. In other words, Lloyd has a comparative advantage over Tom in producing a particular good or service if Lloyd's opportunity cost of producing that good or service is less than Tom's.

An individual has a **comparative advantage** in producing a good or service if the opportunity cost of producing the good is lower for that individual than for other people.

The story of Tom and Lloyd clearly simplifies reality. Yet it teaches us some very important lessons that apply to the real economy too.

First, the model provides a clear illustration of the gains from trade: by agreeing to specialize and provide goods to each other, Tom and Lloyd can produce more, and therefore both are better off than if they tried to be self-sufficient.

Second, the model demonstrates a very important point that is often overlooked in real-world arguments: as long as people have different opportunity costs, *everyone has a comparative advantage in something, and everyone has a comparative disadvantage in something.*

Notice that in our example Tom is actually better than Lloyd at producing both goods: Tom can catch more fish in a week, and he can also gather more coconuts. That is, Tom has an **absolute advantage** in both activities: he can produce more output with a given amount of input (in this case, his time) than Lloyd. You might therefore be tempted to think that Tom has nothing to gain from trading with the less competent Lloyd.

An individual has an **absolute advantage** in an activity if he or she can do it better than other people. Having an absolute advantage is not the same thing as having a comparative advantage.

But we've just seen that Tom can indeed benefit from a deal with Lloyd, because *comparative*, not *absolute*, advantage is the basis for mutual gain. It doesn't matter that it takes Lloyd more time to gather a coconut; what matters is that for him the opportunity cost of that coconut in terms of fish is lower. So Lloyd, despite his absolute disadvantage, even in coconuts, has a comparative advantage in coconut gathering.

PITFALLS

MISUNDERSTANDING COMPARATIVE ADVANTAGE

Students do it, pundits do it, and politicians do it all the time: they confuse *comparative* advantage with *absolute* advantage. For example, one can often hear dire warnings that unless we improve our productivity, Canada will be unable to compete in the new global economy—as if we would be unable to export anything, and would lose all those export-related jobs.

Those commentators confuse *absolute* and *comparative* advantage. It is true that if our competitors were better at everything than we were, then we would have no *absolute* advantage in anything. But we would still have a *comparative* advantage, and other countries would still benefit from trading with us.

Just as Lloyd is able to benefit from trade with Tom (and vice versa) despite the fact that Tom is better at everything, nations can still gain from trade even if they are less productive in all industries than the countries they trade with.

Low productivity growth would have important ramifications for our ability to sustain high standards of living. But it would not affect our ability to trade with other countries.

If comparative advantage were relevant only to castaways, it might not be that interesting. In fact, however, the idea of comparative advantage applies to many activities in the economy. Perhaps its most important application is to trade—not between individuals, but between countries. So let's look briefly at how the model of comparative advantage helps in understanding both the causes and the effects of international trade.

Comparative Advantage and International Trade

Look at the label on a manufactured good sold in Canada, and there's a good chance you will find that it was produced in some other country—in China, Japan, or the United States. On the other side, many Canadian industries export a large fraction of their output (this is particularly true of agriculture and forestry products, automotive products, machinery, and equipment).

Should all this international exchange of goods and services be celebrated, or is it cause for concern? Sometimes the desirability of international trade is questioned—especially by those working in an industry that is suffering from intense foreign competition. The public pressure can be intense enough that politicians acquiesce to these demands for protection. Thus, recently the United States erected trade barriers against the importation of Canadian softwood in an effort to protect its softwood lumber industry. Economists, however, have a very positive view of international trade. Why? Because they view it in terms of comparative advantage.

Figure 2-6 shows, with a simple example, how international trade can be interpreted in terms of comparative advantage. Although the

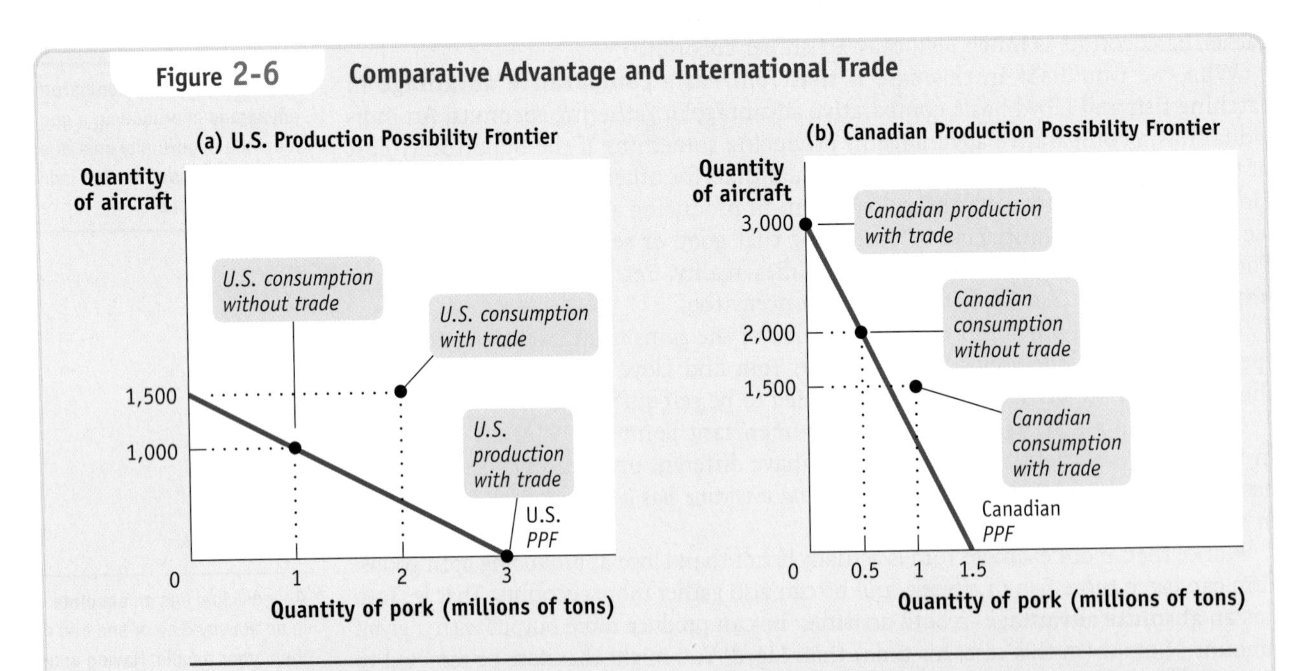

Figure 2-6 Comparative Advantage and International Trade

In this hypothetical example, Canada and the United States produce only two goods: pork and aircraft. Aircraft are measured on the vertical axis and pork on the horizontal axis. Panel (a) shows the U.S. production possibility frontier. It is relatively flat, implying that the United States has a comparative advantage in pork production. Panel (b) shows the Canadian production possibility frontier. It is relatively steep, implying that Canada has a comparative advantage in aircraft production. Just like two individuals, both countries gain from specialization and trade. >web...

example as constructed is hypothetical, it is based on an actual pattern of international trade: Canadian exports of aircraft to the United States and American exports of pork to Canada. Panels (a) and (b) of Figure 2-6 illustrate hypothetical production possibility frontiers for the United States and Canada, with pork measured on the horizontal axis and aircraft measured on the vertical axis. The U.S. production possibility frontier is flatter than the Canadian frontier, implying that the United States has a comparative advantage in pork, while Canada has a comparative advantage in aircraft.

Although the consumption points in Figure 2-6 are hypothetical, they illustrate a general principle: just like the example of Tom and Lloyd, the United States and Canada can both achieve mutual gains from trade. If the United States concentrates on producing pork and ships some of its output to Canada, while Canada concentrates on aircraft and ships some of its output to the United States, both countries can consume more than if they insisted on being self-sufficient.

Moreover, these mutual gains don't depend on each country being better at producing one kind of good. Even if one country has, say, higher output per person-hour in both industries—that is, even if one country has an absolute advantage in both industries—there are still mutual gains from trade.

But how does trade actually take place in market interactions? This brings us to our final model, the circular-flow diagram, which helps economists analyze the transactions that take place in a market economy.

Transactions: The Circular-Flow Diagram

The little economy created by Tom and Lloyd on their island lacks many features of the economy modern Canadians live in. For one thing, though millions of Canadians are self-employed, most workers are employed by someone else, usually in a company with hundreds of employees. Also, Tom and Lloyd engage in only the simplest of economic transactions, **barter**, in which an individual trades a good or service he or she has directly for a good or service he or she wants. In the modern economy, simple barter is rare: usually people trade goods or services for money—pieces of coloured paper with no inherent value—then trade those pieces of coloured paper for the goods or services they want. That is, they sell goods or services and buy other goods or services.

Trade takes the form of **barter** when people directly exchange goods or services that they have for goods or services that they want.

And they both sell and buy a lot of different things. The Canadian economy is a vastly complex entity, with more than 15 million workers employed by tens of thousands of companies, producing a vast array of different goods and services. Yet you can learn some very important things about the economy by considering the simple representation shown in Figure 2-7, the **circular-flow diagram.** This diagram represents the transactions that take place in an economy by two kinds of flows around a circle: flows of physical things like goods, services, labour, or raw materials in one direction, and flows of money that pay for these physical things in the opposite direction. In this case the physical flows are shown in yellow, the money flows in green.

The **circular-flow diagram** is a model that represents the transactions in an economy by flows around a circle.

The simplest circular-flow diagram models an economy that contains only two kinds of "inhabitants": **households** and **firms**. A household consists of either an individual or a group of people (usually, but not necessarily, a family) that share their income. A firm is an organization (usually, but not necessarily, a corporation) that produces goods and services for sale—and that employs members of households.

A **household** is a person or a group of people that share their income.

A **firm** is an organization that produces goods and services for sale.

As you can see in Figure 2-7, there are two kinds of markets in this model economy. On one side (here the left side) there are **markets for goods and services** in which households buy the goods and services they want from firms. This produces a flow of goods and services to households and a return flow of money to firms.

Firms sell goods and services that they produce to households in **markets for goods and services**.

On the other side, there are **factor markets**. A **factor of production** is a resource used to produce goods and services. Economists usually use the term *factor of production* to refer to a resource that is not used up in production. For example, workers use sewing machines to convert cloth into shirts; the workers and the

Firms buy the resources they need to produce—**factors of production**—in **factor markets**.

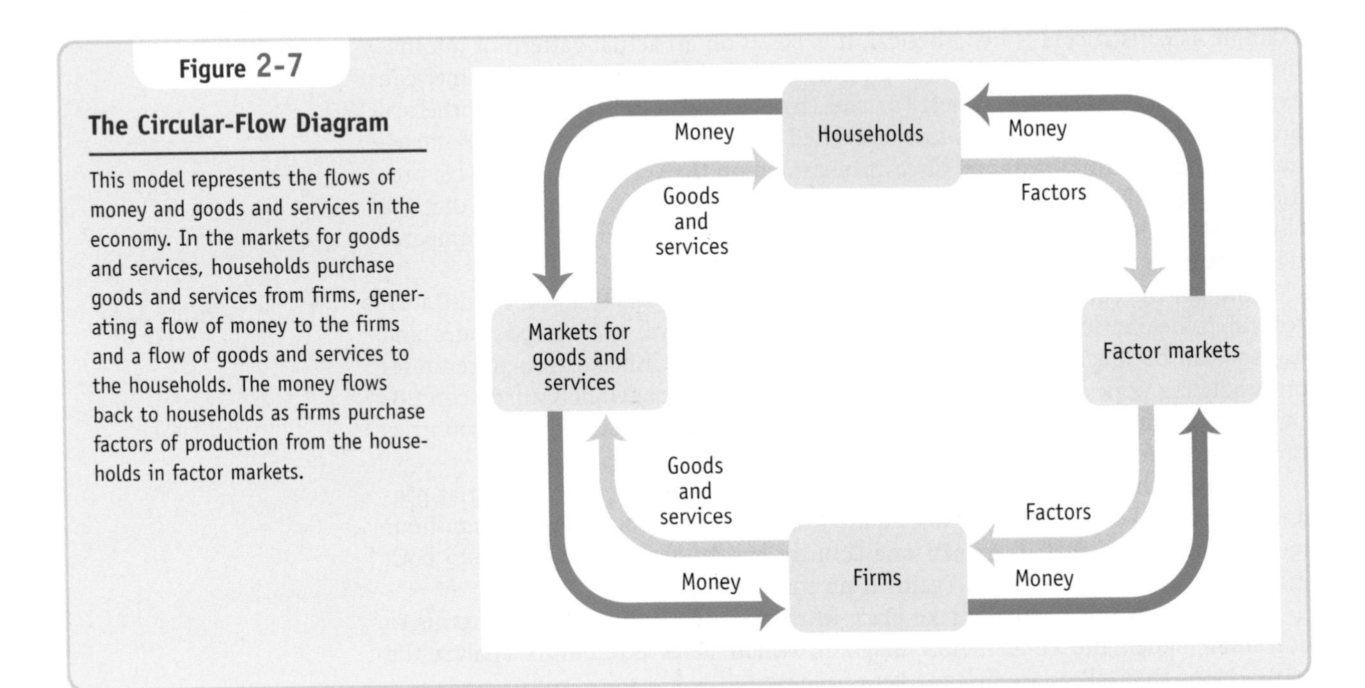

Figure 2-7

The Circular-Flow Diagram

This model represents the flows of money and goods and services in the economy. In the markets for goods and services, households purchase goods and services from firms, generating a flow of money to the firms and a flow of goods and services to the households. The money flows back to households as firms purchase factors of production from the households in factor markets.

sewing machines are factors of production, but the cloth is not. Broadly speaking, the main factors of production are land, labour, and capital. Land is a resource supplied by nature; labour is the work of human beings; and capital refers to "created" resources such as machines and buildings. Of course, each of these is really a category rather than a single factor: land in northern Quebec is quite different from land in southern Ontario. And just as it is possible to invest capital in improving the productivity of land, so it is possible to invest in improving the productivity of labour. Such investment—through education and skill acquisition—creates "human capital", and results in enhancing the productivity of the labour force.

The factor market most of us know best is the *labour market,* in which workers are paid for their time. Besides labour, we can think of households as owning and selling the other factors of production to firms. For example, when a corporation pays dividends to its stockholders, who are members of households, it is in effect paying them for the use of the machines and buildings that ultimately belong to those investors.

In what sense is Figure 2-7 a model? That is, in what sense is it a *simplified* representation of reality? The answer is that this picture ignores a number of real-world complications. A few examples:

- In the real world, the distinction between firms and households isn't always that clear-cut. Consider a small, family-run business—a farm, a shop, a small hotel. Is this a firm or a household? A more complete picture would include a separate box for family businesses.
- Many of the sales firms make are not to households but to other firms; for example, steel companies sell mainly to other companies such as auto manufacturers, not to households. A more complete picture would include these flows of goods and money within the business sector.
- The figure doesn't show the government, which in the real world diverts quite a lot of money out of the circular flow in the form of taxes but also injects a lot of money back into the flow in the form of spending.

Figure 2-7, in other words, is by no means a complete picture either of all the types of "inhabitants" of the real economy or of all the flows of money and physical items that take place among these inhabitants.

Despite its simplicity, the circular-flow diagram, like any good economic model, is a very useful aid to thinking about the economy.

For example, a circular-flow diagram can help us understand how the economy manages to provide jobs for a growing population. To illustrate, consider the huge expansion in the Canadian labour force—the number of people who want to work—between the early 1960s and the late 1980s. This increase was partly caused by the 15-year baby boom that followed World War II; the first "baby boomers" began looking for jobs in the early 1960s, and the last of them went to work in the late 1980s. In addition, social changes led a much higher percentage of women to seek paid work outside the home. As a result, between 1962 and 1988 the number of Canadians employed or seeking jobs increased by 110%.

That's a lot of new job seekers. But luckily, the number of jobs also expanded during the same period, by almost exactly the same percentage.

Or was it luck? The circular-flow diagram helps us understand why the number of jobs available grew along with the expansion of the labour force. Figure 2-8 compares the money flows around the circle for the Canadian economy in 1962 and 1988. Both the money paid to households and the money spent by households increased enormously over the period—and that was no accident. As more people went to work—that is, as more labour was sold in the factor markets—households had more income to spend. They used that increased income to buy more goods and services in the market for goods and services. And in order to produce these goods and services, firms had to hire more workers!

So, despite being an extremely simple model of the economy, the circular-flow diagram helps us to understand some important facts about the real Canadian economy. The number of jobs isn't fixed, the model tells us, because it depends on how much households spend; and the amount households spend depends on how many people are working. It is, in other words, no accident that the economy somehow creates enough jobs even when the working population grows rapidly.

Figure 2-8 Money Flows in the Canadian Economy in 1962 and in 1988

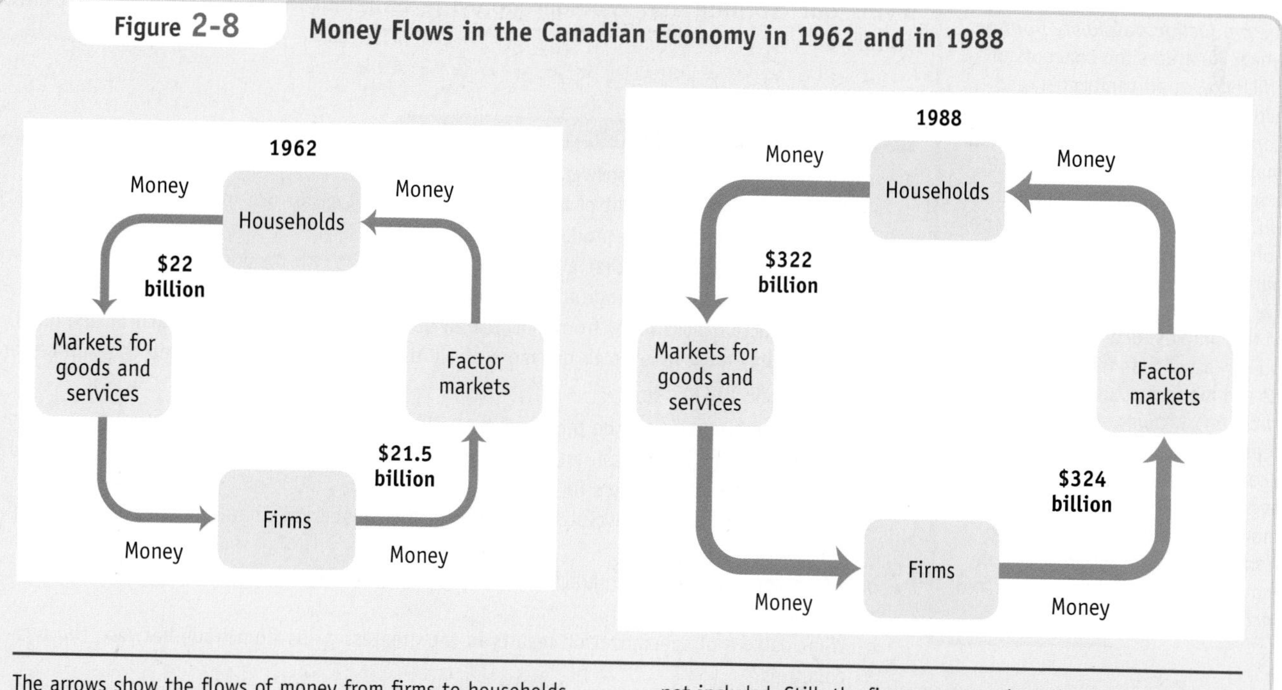

The arrows show the flows of money from firms to households and from households to firms in two years, 1962 and 1988. Notice that the numbers don't quite match—that's because there are other groups in the economy (government and foreigners) not included. Still, the figure suggests how the economy was able to find jobs for a rapidly growing labour force: the increased incomes of households made possible greater spending, which in turn was returned to households via the factor markets.

Robert Nickelsberg/Getty Images

Although less productive than Canadian workers, Bengali workers have a comparative advantage in clothing production.

economics in action

Rich Nation, Poor Nation

Try taking off your clothes—at a suitable time and in a suitable place, of course—and take a look at the labels inside that say where they were made. It's a very good bet that much, if not most, of your clothing was manufactured overseas, in a country that is much poorer than Canada—say, in El Salvador, Sri Lanka, or Bangladesh.

Why are these countries so much poorer than we are? The immediate reason is that their economies are much less *productive*—firms in these countries are just not able to produce as much from a given quantity of resources as comparable firms in Canada or other wealthy countries. Why countries differ so much in productivity is a deep question—indeed, one of the main questions that preoccupy economists. But in any case, the difference in productivity is a fact.

But if the economies of these countries are so much less productive than ours, how is it that they make so much of our clothing? Why don't we do it for ourselves?

The answer is "comparative advantage". Just about every industry in Bangladesh is much less productive than the corresponding industry in Canada. But the productivity difference between rich and poor countries varies across goods; it is very large in the production of sophisticated goods like aircraft but not that large in the production of simpler goods like clothing.

The point is that Bangladesh, though it is at an absolute disadvantage compared with Canada in almost everything, has a comparative advantage in clothing production. This means that both Canada and Bangladesh are able to consume more because they specialize in producing different things, with Bangladesh supplying our clothing and Canada supplying Bangladesh with more sophisticated goods. ■

>> QUICK REVIEW

- Most economic *models* are "thought experiments" or simplified representations of reality, which rely on the *other things equal assumption*.
- An important economic model is the *production possibility frontier*, which illustrates the concepts of efficiency, opportunity cost, and economic growth.
- *Comparative advantage* is a model that explains the source of gains from trade but is often confused with *absolute advantage*. Every person and every country has a comparative advantage in something, giving rise to gains from trade.
- In the simplest economies people *barter* rather than trade with money as in a modern economy. The *circular-flow diagram* is a model representing transactions within the economy as flows of goods and services, *factors of production*, and money between *households* and *firms*. These transactions occur in *markets for goods and services* and *factor markets*.

>> CHECK YOUR UNDERSTANDING 2-1

1. True or false? Explain your answer.
   a. An increase in the amount of resources available to Tom for use in producing coconuts and fish does not change his production possibility frontier.
   b. A technological change that allows Tom to catch more fish for any amount of coconuts gathered results in a change in his production possibility frontier.
   c. The production possibility frontier is useful because it illustrates how much of one good an economy must give up to get more of another good regardless of whether resources are being used efficiently.
2. In Italy, an automobile can be produced by 8 workers in one day and a washing machine by 3 workers in one day. In Canada, an automobile can be produced by 6 workers in one day and a washing machine by 2 workers in one day.
   a. Which country has an absolute advantage in the production of automobiles? In washing machines?
   b. Which country has a comparative advantage in the production of washing machines? In automobiles?
   c. What pattern of specialization results in the greatest gains from trade between the two countries?
3. Use the circular-flow diagram to explain how an increase in the amount of money spent by households results in an increase in the number of jobs in the economy. Describe in words what the circular-flow model predicts.

Solutions appear at back of book.

Using Models

Economics, we have now learned, is mainly a matter of creating models that draw on a set of basic principles but add some more specific assumptions that allow the modeller to apply those principles to a particular situation. But what do economists actually *do* with their models?

Positive versus Normative Economics

Imagine that you are an economic adviser to the Premier of your province. What kinds of questions might the Premier ask you to answer?

Well, here are three possible questions:

1. How much revenue will the provincial fuel tax yield next year?
2. How much would that revenue increase if the tax were raised 20 percent?
3. Should the government increase the tax, bearing in mind that the tax increase will raise much-needed revenue and reduce traffic and air pollution—but may impose some financial hardship on frequent commuters, will adversely affect the trucking industry, and may discourage tourism?

There is a big difference between the first two questions and the third one. The first two are questions about facts. Your forecast of next year's tax collection will be proved right or wrong when the numbers actually come in. Your estimate of the impact of a change in the tax is a little harder to check—revenue depends on other factors besides the tax rate, and it may be hard to disentangle the causes of any change in revenue. Still, in principle there is only one right answer.

But the question of whether the government should raise the fuel tax may not have a "right" answer—two people who agree on the effects of a higher fuel tax could still disagree about whether raising the tax is a good idea. For example, someone who walks to work probably won't care much about the increased commuting costs but may care about the reduced traffic and noise pollution. On the other hand, a regular commuter may have the opposite priorities.

This example highlights a key distinction between two roles of economic analysis. Analysis that tries to answer questions about the way the world works, which have definite right and wrong answers, is known as **positive economics**. In contrast, analysis that involves saying how the world *should* work is known as **normative economics**. To put it another way, positive economics is about description, normative economics is about prescription.

Positive economics is the branch of economic analysis that describes the way the economy actually works.

Normative economics makes prescriptions about the way the economy *should* work.

Positive economics occupies most of the time and effort of the economics profession. And models play a crucial role in almost all positive economics. The Canadian government uses computer models to assess proposed changes in national tax policy, and many provincial governments have similar models to assess the effects of their own tax policies.

It's worth noting that there is a subtle but important difference between the first and second questions we imagined the Premier asking. Question 1 asked for a simple prediction about next year's revenue—a **forecast**. Question 2 was a "what if" question, asking how revenue would change if the tax were to change. Economists are often called upon to answer both types of questions, but models are especially useful for answering "what if" questions.

A **forecast** is a simple prediction of the future.

The answers to such questions often serve as a guide to policy, but they are still predictions, not prescriptions. That is, they tell you what will happen if a policy is changed; they don't tell you whether that result is good or not. Suppose that your economic model tells you that the government's proposed increase in fuel taxes will raise inner city property values but will hurt those people who must use their cars to commute to work. Does that make this proposed tax increase a good idea or a bad one? It depends on whom you ask. As we've just seen, someone who is very concerned about the environmental pollution caused by automobiles may support the increase. But someone who is very concerned with the welfare of drivers will feel differently. That's a value judgement—it's not a question of economic analysis.

Still, economists often do end up giving policy advice. That is, they do engage in normative economics. How can they do this when there may be no "right" answer?

One answer is that economists are also citizens, and we all have our opinions. But economic analysis can often be used to show that some policies are clearly better than others, regardless of anyone's opinions.

Suppose that policy A makes everyone better off than policy B, or at least makes some people better off without making anyone else worse off. Then A is clearly more efficient than B. That's not a value judgement: we're talking about how best to achieve a goal, not about the goal itself.

For example, two different policies have been used to help low-income families obtain housing: rent control, which limits the rents landlords are allowed to charge, and rent subsidies, which provide low-income families with additional money to pay rents. Almost all economists agree that subsidies are the more efficient policy. (In Chapter 4 we'll see why this is so.) And so the great majority of economists, whatever their personal politics, favour subsidies over rent control.

When policies can be clearly ranked in this way, economists generally agree. But it is no secret that economists sometimes disagree. Why does this happen?

When and Why Economists Disagree

Economists have a reputation for arguing with each other. Where does this reputation come from?

One important answer is that media coverage tends to exaggerate the real differences in views among economists. If nearly all economists agree on an issue—for example, the proposition that rent controls lead to housing shortages—reporters and editors are likely to conclude that there is no story worth covering, and so the professional consensus tends to go unreported. But when there is some issue on which prominent economists take opposing sides—for example, whether cutting taxes right now would help the economy—that does make a good news story. So you hear much more about the areas of disagreement within economics than you do about the large areas of agreement.

It is also worth remembering that economics is, unavoidably, often tied up in politics. On a number of issues powerful interest groups know what opinions they want to hear; they therefore have an incentive to find and promote economists who profess those opinions, giving these economists a prominence and visibility out of proportion to their support among their colleagues.

But although the appearance of disagreement among economists exceeds the reality, it remains true that economists often *do* disagree about important things. For example, some very respected economists argue strongly that the Canadian government should replace the income tax with a "consumption tax". This is sometimes called an expenditure tax because it taxes only a person's expenditures (or income less all savings). Other equally respected economists disagree. Why this difference of opinion?

There are two main reasons. First, there may be a normative element to the disagreement. Replacing income taxes with consumption taxes would reduce taxes on savings and perhaps stimulate savings. Everyone would benefit from this. But since the rich save a larger proportion of their income than the poor, the rich would benefit the most. This redistribution of income to the rich *could* be offset using other government policies, such as sales tax rebates to the poor. But *would* it? Economists may disagree, on normative grounds, as to the desirability of the income redistribution; and they may further disagree on positive grounds as to the likelihood that the government would bring in other measures to offset the gains to the rich, such as sales tax rebates to the poor.

Suppose, however, that the government absolutely guaranteed that they would bring in offsetting policies, so that the shift from income taxes to consumption taxes would have no income redistribution effects. Why might economists still disagree over the desirability of such changes?

The answer is that because economists base their conclusions on models—which are simplified representations of reality—two economists can legitimately disagree about which simplifications are appropriate, and therefore arrive at different conclusions.

Economist *A* may rely on a model that focuses on the administrative costs of tax systems—that is, the costs of monitoring, processing papers, collecting the tax, and so on. He or she might then point to the well-known high costs of running a consumption tax, and argue against the change. But Economist *B* may think that the right way to approach the question is to ignore the administrative costs and focus on how the proposed law would change savings behaviour; he or she might point to studies that suggest that consumption taxes promote higher consumer saving, a desirable result.

Because the economists have used different models, that is, made different simplifying assumptions, they arrive at different conclusions. And so the two economists may find themselves on different sides.

Most such disputes are eventually resolved by the accumulation of evidence that shows which of the various models proposed by economists does a better job of fitting the facts. However, in economics as in any science it can take a long time before research settles important disputes—decades, in some cases. And since the economy is always changing, in ways that make old models invalid or raise new policy questions, there are always new issues on which economists disagree. The policy maker must then decide which economist to believe.

The important point is that economic analysis is a method, not a set of conclusions.

FOR INQUIRING MINDS

WHEN ECONOMISTS AGREE

"If all the economists in the world were laid end to end, they still couldn't reach a conclusion." So goes one popular economist joke. But do economists really disagree that much?

Not according to a classic survey of members of the American Economic Association, reported in the May 1992 issue of the *American Economic Review*. The authors asked respondents to agree or disagree with a number of statements about the economy; what they found was a high level of agreement among professional economists on many of the statements. At the top, with more than 90 percent of the economists agreeing, were "Tariffs and import quotas usually reduce general economic welfare" and "A ceiling on rents reduces the quantity and quality of housing available." What's striking about these two statements is that many non-economists disagree: tariffs and import quotas to keep out foreign-produced goods are favoured by many voters, and proposals to do away with rent control in cities like Toronto and Winnipeg have met fierce political opposition.

So is the stereotype of quarrelling economists a myth? Not entirely: economists do disagree quite a lot on some issues, especially in macroeconomics. But there is a large area of common ground.

economics in action

Economists in Government

Many economists are mainly engaged in teaching and research. But quite a few economists have a more direct hand in events.

As described in the For Inquiring Minds on page 22, economists play a significant role in the business world, especially in the financial industry. But the most striking involvement of economists in the "real" world is their extensive participation in government.

This shouldn't be surprising: One of the most important functions of government is to make economic policy, and almost every government policy decision must take economic effects into consideration. So governments around the world employ economists in a variety of roles.

Economists work in almost every branch of the Canadian government. Consider the mandates of the departments dealing with aboriginal affairs, agriculture, environment, immigration, interprovincial relations, natural resources, transportation, or science and technology! No matter what department comes to mind, there is a strong economic dimension involved. However, the strongest concentration of economists is likely to be found in the Department of Finance, which plans and prepares the federal government's budget, and analyzes and designs tax policies. This department also develops policies on international finance and helps design Canada's tariff policies.

It's also worth noting that economists play an especially important role in two international organizations headquartered in Washington, D.C.: the International Monetary Fund, which provides advice and loans to countries experiencing economic difficulties, and the World Bank, which provides advice and loans to promote long-term economic development.

Do all these economists in government disagree with each other all the time? Are their positions largely dictated by political affiliation? The answer to both questions is no. Although there are important disputes over economic issues in government, and politics inevitably plays some role, there is broad agreement among economists over many issues, and most economists in government try very hard to assess issues as objectively as possible. ■

>> QUICK REVIEW

- Economists do mostly *positive economics,* analysis of the way the world works, in which there are definite right and wrong answers and which involve making *forecasts.* But in *normative economics,* which makes prescriptions about how things ought to be, there are often no right answers and only value judgments.
- Economists do disagree—though not as much as legend has it—for two main reasons. One, they may disagree about which simplifications to make in a model. Two, economists may disagree—like everyone else—about values.

>> CHECK YOUR UNDERSTANDING 2-2

1. Which of the following statements is a positive statement? Which is a normative statement?
   a. Society should take measures to prevent people from engaging in dangerous personal behaviour.
   b. People who engage in dangerous personal behaviour impose higher costs on society through higher medical costs.
2. True or false? Explain your answer.
   a. Policy choice A and policy choice B attempt to achieve the same social goal. Policy choice A, however, results in a much less efficient use of resources than policy choice B. Therefore economists are more likely to agree on choosing policy choice B.
   b. When two economists disagree on the desirability of a policy, it's typically because one of them has made a mistake.
   c. Policymakers can always use economics to figure out which goals a society should try to achieve.

Solutions appear at back of book.

• A LOOK AHEAD •

This chapter has given you a first view of what it means to do economics, starting with the general idea of models as a way to make sense of a complicated world and then moving on to three simple introductory models.

To get a real sense of how economic analysis works, however, and to show just how useful such analysis can be, we need to move on to a more powerful model. In the next two chapters we will study the quintessential economic model, one that has an amazing ability to make sense of many policy issues, predict the effects of many forces, and change the way you look at the world. That model is known as "supply and demand".

SUMMARY

1. Almost all economics is based on **models,** "thought experiments" or simplified versions of reality, many of which use mathematical tools such as graphs. An important assumption in economic models is the **other things equal assumption,** which allows analysis of the effect of a change in one factor by holding all other relevant factors unchanged.
2. One important economic model is the **production possibility frontier.** It illustrates opportunity cost (showing how much less of one good can be produced if more of the other good is produced); efficiency (an economy is efficient if it produces on the production possibility frontier); and economic growth (an expansion of the production possibility frontier).
3. Another important model is **comparative advantage,** which explains the source of gains from trade between individuals and countries. Everyone has a comparative advantage in something—some good or service in which that person has a lower opportunity cost than everyone else. But it is often confused with **absolute advantage,** an ability to produce a particular good or service better than anyone else. This confusion leads some to erroneously conclude that there are no gains from trade between people or countries.
4. In the simplest economies people **barter**—trade goods and services for one another—rather than trade them for money, as in a modern economy. The **circular-flow diagram** is a model representing transactions within the economy as flows of goods, services, and income between **households** and **firms**. These transactions occur in **markets for goods and services** and **factor markets,** markets for **factors of production** such as labor. It is useful in understanding how spending, production, employment, income, and growth are related in the economy.
5. Economists use economic models for both **positive economics,** which describes how the economy works, and for **normative economics,** which prescribes how the economy should work. Positive economics often involves making **forecasts.** Economists can determine correct answers for positive questions, but typically not for normative questions, which involve value judgments. The exceptions are when policies designed to achieve a certain prescription can be clearly ranked in terms of efficiency.
6. There are two main reasons economists disagree. One, they may disagree about which simplifications to make in a model. Two, economists may disagree—like everyone else—about values.

KEY TERMS

PROBLEMS

1. Atlantis is a small, isolated island in the South Atlantic. The population grows potatoes and catches fresh fish. The accompanying table shows the maximum annual output combinations of potatoes and fish that can be produced. Obviously, given their limited resources and available technology, as they use more of their resources for potato production, there are fewer resources available for catching fish.

Maximum annual output options	Quantity of potatoes (pounds)	Quantity of fresh fish (pounds)
A	1,000	0
B	800	300
C	600	500
D	400	600
E	200	650
F	0	675

a. Draw a production possibility frontier illustrating these options, showing points A–F.

b. Can Atlantis produce 500 pounds of fish and 800 pounds of potatoes? Explain. Where would this point lie relative to the production possibility frontier?

c. What is the opportunity cost of expanding the annual output of potatoes from 600 to 800 pounds?

d. What is the opportunity cost of increasing the annual output of potatoes from 200 to 400 pounds?

e. Can you explain why the answers to c and d above are not the same? What does this imply about the slope of the production possibility frontier?

2. In the ancient country of Roma, only two goods, spaghetti and meatballs, are produced. There are two tribes in Roma, the Tivoli and the Frivoli. By themselves, the Tivoli tribe each month can produce either 30 pounds of spaghetti and no meatballs, or 50 pounds of meatballs and no spaghetti, or any combination in between. The Frivoli, by themselves, each month could produce 40 pounds of spaghetti and no meatballs, or 30 pounds of meatballs and no spaghetti, or any combination in between.

a. Assume that all production possibility frontiers are straight lines. Draw one diagram showing the monthly production possibility frontier for the Tivoli and another diagram showing the monthly production possibility frontier for the Frivoli. Show how you calculated them.

b. Which tribe has the comparative advantage in spaghetti production? In meatball production?

In 100 A.D. the Frivoli discover a new technique for making meatballs that doubles the quantity of meatballs they can produce monthly.

c. Draw the new monthly production possibility frontier for the Frivoli.

d. After the innovation, which tribe now has the absolute advantage in producing meatballs? In producing spaghetti? Which has the comparative advantage in meatball production? In spaghetti production?

3. Peter Pundit, an economics reporter, states that the European Union is increasing its productivity very rapidly in all the major industries. He claims that this productivity advance is so rapid that output from the EU in these industries will soon exceed that of Canada and, as a result, Canada will no longer benefit from trade with the EU.

a. Do you think Peter Pundit is correct or not? If not, what do you think is the source of his mistake?

b. If the EU and Canada continue to trade, what do you think characterizes the goods that the EU exports to Canada? What characterizes the goods that Canada exports to the EU?

4. You are in charge of allocating members of your dormitory to the dormitory baseball and basketball teams. You are down to the last four people, where two must be allocated to baseball and two to basketball. The following table gives each person's batting average and free-throw average. Explain how you would use the concept of comparative advantage to allocate the players. Begin by establishing each player's opportunity cost of free throws in terms of batting averages.

Name	Batting average	Free-throw average
Kelley	70%	60%
Jackie	50%	50%
Curt	10%	30%
Gerry	80%	70%

Why is it likely that the other basketball players will be unhappy about this arrangement, but the other baseball players will be satisfied? Nonetheless, why would an economist say that this is an efficient way to allocate players for your dormitory sports teams?

5. The economy of Atlantis has developed, and the inhabitants now use money in the form of cowry shells. Draw a circular-flow diagram showing households and firms. Firms produce potatoes and fish, and households buy potatoes and fish. Households also provide the land and labour to firms. Identify where in the flows of cowry shells or physical things (goods and services, or resources) each of the following impacts would occur. Describe how this impact spreads around the circle.

a. A devastating hurricane floods many of the potato fields.

b. There is a very productive fishing season with very large numbers of fish caught.

c. The residents of Atlantis discover the Macarena and spend several days a month at dancing festivals.

6. An economist might say that universities "produce" education, using faculty members and students as inputs. According to this line of reasoning, education is then "consumed" by households. Construct a circular-flow diagram like the one found in this chapter to represent the sector of the economy devoted to university education: universities represent firms, and households both consume education and provide faculty and students to universities. What are the relevant markets in this model? What is being bought and sold in each direction? What would happen in the model if the government decided to subsidize 50% of all university students' tuition?

7. Your dormitory roommate plays loud music most of the time, while you would prefer more peace and quiet. You suggest that she buy some earphones. She responds that although she would be happy to use earphones, she has many other things that she would prefer to spend her money on right now. You discuss this situation with a friend who is an economics major. The following exchange takes place:

She: How much would it cost to buy earphones?
You: $15.
She: How much do you value having some peace and quiet for the rest of the semester?
You: $30.

She: It is efficient for you to buy the earphones and give them to your roommate. You gain more than you lose; the benefit exceeds the cost. You should do that.

You: It just isn't fair that I have to pay for the earphones when I'm not the one making the noise.

a. Which parts of this conversation contain positive statements and which parts contain normative statements?

b. Compose an argument supporting your viewpoint that your roommate should be the one to change her behaviour. Similarly, compose an argument from the viewpoint of your roommate that you should be the one to buy the earphones. If your dormitory has a policy which gives residents unlimited rights to play music, whose argument is likely to win? If your dormitory has a rule in which a person must stop playing music whenever a roommate complains, whose argument is likely to win?

8. A representative of the Canadian clothing industry recently made the following statement: "Workers in Asia often work in sweatshop conditions earning only pennies an hour. Canadian workers are more productive and as a result earn higher wages. In order to preserve the dignity of the Canadian workplace, the government ought to enact legislation banning imports of low-wage Asian clothing."

a. Which parts of this quote are positive statements? Which parts are normative statements?

b. Is the policy that is being advocated consistent with the preceding statements about the wages and productivities of Canadian and Asian workers?

c. Would such a policy make some Canadians better off without making any other Canadians worse off? That is, would this policy be efficient from the viewpoint of all Canadians?

d. Would low-wage Asian workers benefit or be hurt by such a policy?

9. Are the following statements true or false? Explain your answer.

a. "When people must pay higher taxes on their wage earnings, it discourages their incentive to work" is a positive statement.

b. "We should lower taxes to encourage more work" is a positive statement.

c. Economics can never be used to completely decide upon what society ought to do.

d. "The system of public education in this country generates greater benefits to society than the cost of running the system" is a normative statement.

e. All disagreements among economists are generated by the media.

10. Evaluate the following statement: "It is easier to build an economic model that accurately reflects events that have already occurred than to build an economic model to forecast future events." Do you think that this is true or not? Why? What does this imply about the difficulties of building good economic models?

11. Economists who work for the government are often called upon to make policy recommendations. Why do you think it is important for the public to be able to differentiate normative statements from positive statements in these recommendations?

12. The mayor of Ottawa is worried about a potential epidemic of deadly influenza this winter. She asks her economic adviser the following series of questions. Categorize these questions according to whether they require the economic advisor to make a positive assessment or a normative assessment.

a. How much vaccine will be in stock in the city by the end of November?

b. If we offer to pay 10% more per dose to the pharmaceutical companies providing the vaccines, will they provide additional doses?

c. If there is a shortage of vaccine in the city, who should we vaccinate first—the elderly or the very young? (Assume that a person from one group has an equal likelihood of dying from influenza as a person from the other group.)

d. If the city charges $25 per shot, how many people will pay?

e. If the city charges $25 per shot, it will make a profit of $10 per shot, money that can go to pay for inoculating poor people. Should the city engage in such a scheme?

13. Assess the following statement: "If economists just had enough data, they could solve all policy questions in a way that maximizes the social good. There would be no need for divisive political debates, such as whether the government should provide free daycare."

>web... To continue your study and review of concepts in this chapter, please visit the Krugman/Wells website for quizzes, animated graph tutorials, web links to helpful resources, and more.

www.worthpublishers.com/krugmanwellsmyatt

>>Chapter 2 Appendix: Graphs in Economics

Getting the Picture

Whether you're reading about economics in the *Globe and Mail* or in your economics textbook, you will see many graphs. Visual images can make it much easier to understand verbal descriptions, numerical information, or ideas. In economics, graphs are the type of visual image used to facilitate understanding.

To fully understand the ideas and information being discussed, you need to be familiar with how to interpret these visual aids. This appendix explains how graphs are constructed and interpreted and how they are used in economics.

Graphs, Variables, and Economic Models

One reason to attend university is that a bachelor's degree provides access to higher-paying jobs. Additional degrees, such as MBAs or law degrees, increase earnings even more. If you were to read an article about the relationship between educational attainment and income, you would probably see a graph showing the income levels for workers with different amounts of education. And this graph would depict the idea that, in general, more education increases income. This graph, like most of those in economics, would depict the relationship between two economic variables. A **variable** is a quantity that can take on more than one value, such as the number of years of education a person has, the price of a can of pop, or a household's income.

A quantity that can take on more than one value is called a **variable**.

As you learned in this chapter, economic analysis relies heavily on *models*, simplified descriptions of real situations. Most economic models describe the relationship between two variables, simplified by holding constant other variables that may affect the relationship. For example, an economic model might describe the relationship between the price of a can of pop and the number of cans that consumers will buy, assuming that everything else that affects the number of cans stays constant. This type of model can be described mathematically or verbally, but illustrating the relationship in a graph makes it easier to understand. Next we show how graphs that depict economic models are constructed and interpreted.

How Graphs Work

Most graphs in economics are based on a grid built around two perpendicular lines that show the values of two variables, helping you visualize the relationship between them. So a first step in understanding the use of such graphs is to see how this system works.

Two-Variable Graphs

Figure 2A-1 shows a typical two-variable graph. It illustrates the data in the accompanying table on outside temperature and the cans of pop a typical vendor can expect to sell at a baseball stadium during one game. The first column shows the values of outside temperature (the first variable) and the second column shows the values of number of cans sold (the second variable). Five combinations or pairs of the two variables are shown, each denoted by *A* through *E* in the third column.

Now let's turn to graphing the data in this table. In any two-variable graph, one variable is called the *x*-variable and the other is called the *y*-variable. Here we have made outside temperature the *x*-variable and quantity of pop sold the *y*-variable.

Figure 2A-1 Plotting Points on a Two-Variable Graph

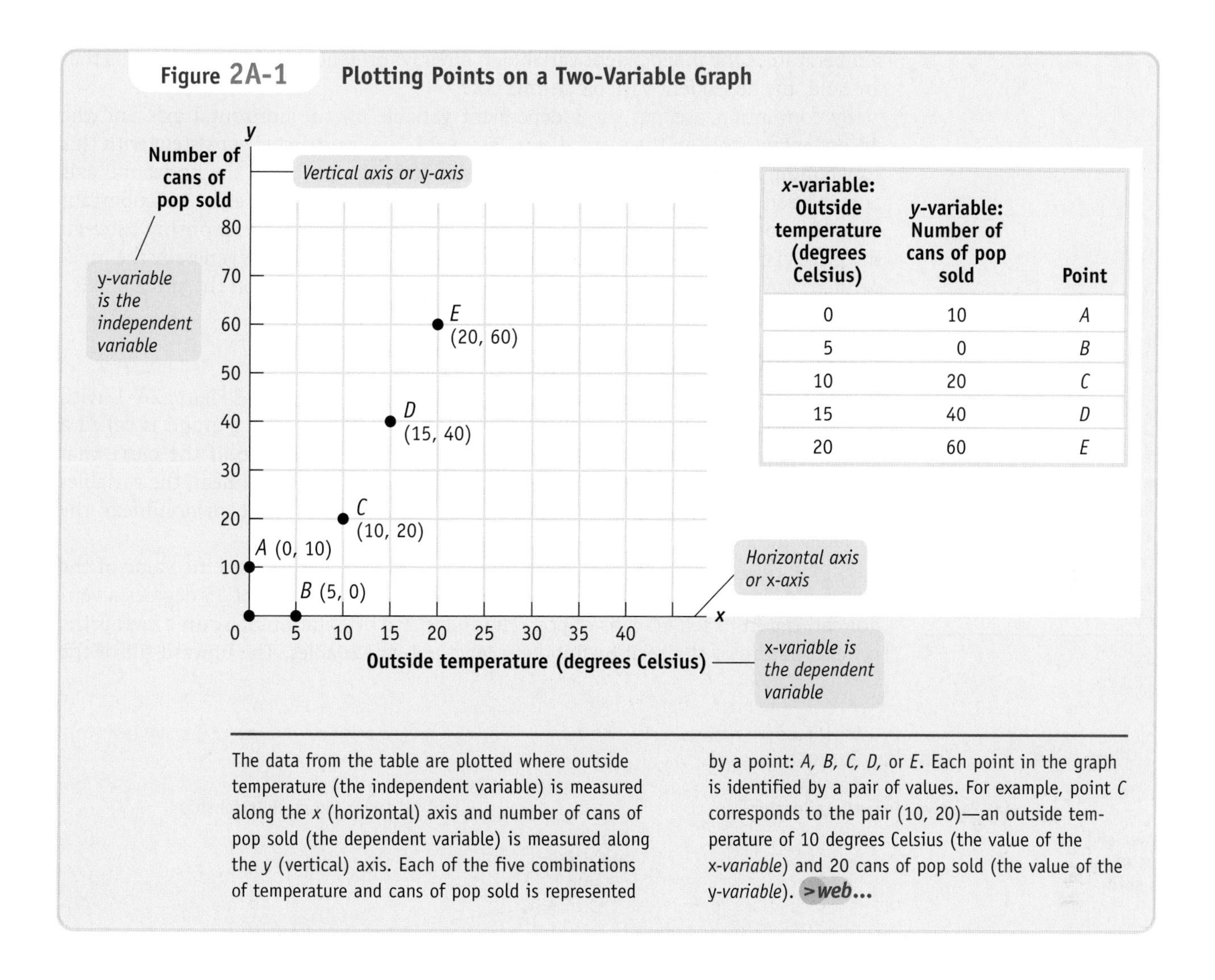

x-variable: Outside temperature (degrees Celsius)	*y*-variable: Number of cans of pop sold	Point
0	10	*A*
5	0	*B*
10	20	*C*
15	40	*D*
20	60	*E*

The data from the table are plotted where outside temperature (the independent variable) is measured along the *x* (horizontal) axis and number of cans of pop sold (the dependent variable) is measured along the *y* (vertical) axis. Each of the five combinations of temperature and cans of pop sold is represented by a point: *A, B, C, D,* or *E*. Each point in the graph is identified by a pair of values. For example, point *C* corresponds to the pair (10, 20)—an outside temperature of 10 degrees Celsius (the value of the *x-variable*) and 20 cans of pop sold (the value of the *y-variable*). **>web...**

The solid horizontal line in the graph is called the **horizontal axis** or ***x*-axis,** and values of the *x*-variable—outside temperature—are measured along it. Similarly, the solid vertical line in the graph is called the **vertical axis** or ***y*-axis,** and values of the *y*-variable—cans of pop sold—are measured along it. At the **origin,** the point where the two axes meet, each variable is equal to zero. As you move rightward from the origin along the *x*-axis, values of the *x*-variable are positive and increasing. And as you move up from the origin along the *y*-axis, values of the *y*-variable are positive and increasing.

You can plot each of the five points *A* through *E* on this graph by using a pair of numbers—the values that the *x*-variable and the *y*-variable take on for a given point. These values are called the ***x*-coordinate** and the ***y*-coordinate.** In Figure 2A-1, at point C, the *x*-variable takes on the value 10 and the *y*-variable takes on the value 20. You plot point C by drawing a line straight up from 10 on the *x*-axis and a horizontal line across from 20 on the *y*-axis. We write point C as (10, 20). We write the origin as (0, 0). Looking at point *A* and point *B* in Figure 2A-1, you can see that when one of the variables for a point has a value of zero, it will lie on one of the axes. If the value of *x* is zero, the point will lie on the vertical axis, like point *A*. If the value of *y* is zero, the point will lie on the horizontal axis, like point *B*.

Most graphs that depict relationships between two economic variables represent a **causal relationship,** a relationship in which the value taken by one variable directly influences or determines the value taken by the other variable. In a causal relationship, the determining variable is called the **independent variable;** the variable it determines is called the **dependent variable.** In our example of pop sales, the outside

The line along which values of the *x*-variable are measured is called the **horizontal axis** or ***x*-axis.**The line along which values of the *y*-variable are measured is called the **vertical axis** or ***y*-axis.** The point where the axes of a two-variable graph meet is the **origin.** The value that the *x*-variable takes on for a given point is called the ***x*-coordinate.** The value that the *y*-variable takes on for a given point is called the ***y*-coordinate.**

A **causal relationship** exists between two variables when the value taken by one variable directly influences or determines the value taken by the other variable. In a causal relationship, the determining variable is called the **independent variable;** the variable it determines is called the **dependent variable.**

temperature is the independent variable. It directly influences the number of cans that are sold, the dependent variable in this case.

By convention, we put the independent variable on the horizontal axis and the dependent variable on the vertical axis. Figure 2A-1 is constructed consistent with this convention; the independent variable (outside temperature) is on the horizontal axis and the dependent variable (cans of pop sold) is on the vertical axis. An important exception to this convention is in graphs showing the economic relationship between the price of a product and quantity of the product: although price is generally the independent variable that determines quantity, it is always measured on the vertical axis.

Curves on a graph

A **curve** is a line on a graph that depicts a relationship between two variables. It may be either a straight line or a curved line. If the curve is a straight line, the variables have a **linear relationship**. If the curve is not a straight line, the variables have a **nonlinear relationship**.

Panel (a) of Figure 2A-2 contains some of the same information as Figure 2A-1, with a line drawn through the points *B*, *C*, *D*, and *E*. Such a line on a graph is called a **curve**, regardless of whether it is a straight line or a curved line. If the curve that shows the relationship between two variables is a straight line, or linear, the variables have a **linear relationship.** When the curve is not a straight line, or nonlinear, the variables have a **nonlinear relationship.**

A point on a curve indicates the value of the *y*-variable for a specific value of the *x*-variable. For example, point *D* indicates that at a temperature of 15 degrees a vendor can expect to sell 40 cans of pop. The shape and orientation of a curve reveals the general nature of the relationship between the two variables. The upward tilt of the

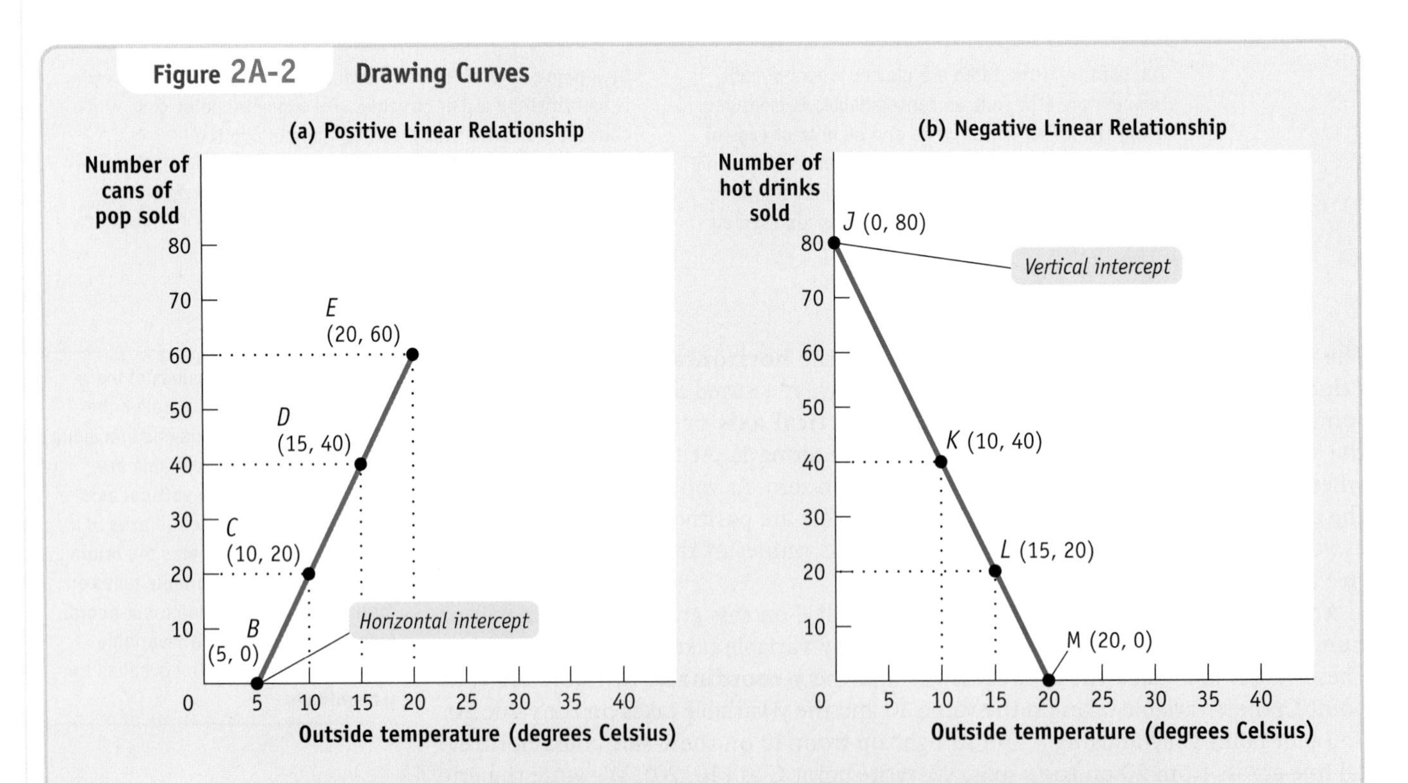

The curve in panel (a) illustrates the relationship between the two variables, outside temperature and number of pops sold. The two variables have a positive linear relationship: positive because the curve has an upward tilt, and linear because it is a straight line. It implies that an increase in *x* (outside temperature) leads to an increase in *y* (number of pops sold). The curve in panel (b) is also a straight line, but it tilts downwards. The two variables here, outside temperature and number of hot drinks sold, have a negative linear relationship: an increase in *x* (outside temperature) leads to a decrease in *y* (number of hot drinks sold). The curve in panel (a) has a horizontal intercept at point *B*, where it hits the horizontal axis. The curve in panel (b) has a vertical intercept at point *J*, where it hits the vertical axis, and a horizontal intercept at point *M*, where it hits the horizontal axis. **>web...**

curve in panel (a) of Figure 2A-2 suggests that vendors can expect to sell more cans of pop at higher outside temperatures.

When variables are related this way—that is, when an increase in one variable is associated with an increase in the other variable—the variables are said to have a **positive relationship.** It is illustrated by a curve that slopes upwards from left to right. Because this curve is also linear, the relationship between outside temperature and cans of pop sold, illustrated by the curve in panel (a) of Figure 2A-2, is a positive linear relationship.

When an increase in one variable is associated with a decrease in the other value, the two variables are said to have a **negative relationship.** It is illustrated by a curve that slopes downwards from left to right, like the curve in panel (b) of Figure 2A-2. Because this curve is also linear, the relationship it depicts is a negative linear relationship. Two variables that might have such a relationship are the outside temperature and the number of hot drinks that a vendor can expect to sell at a baseball stadium.

Return for a moment to the curve in panel (a) of Figure 2A-2 and you can see that it hits the horizontal axis at point *B*. This point, known as the **horizontal intercept,** shows the value of the *x*-variable when the value of the *y*-variable is zero. In panel (b) of Figure 2A-2, the curve hits the vertical axis at point *J*. This point, called the **vertical intercept,** indicates the value of the *y*-variable when the value of the *x*-variable is zero.

Two variables have a **positive relationship** when an increase in the value of one variable is associated with an increase in the value of the other variable. It is illustrated by a curve that slopes upwards from left to right.

Two variables have a **negative relationship** when an increase in the value of one variable is associated with a decrease in the value of the other variable. It is illustrated by a curve that slopes downwards from left to right.

The **horizontal intercept** of a curve is the point at which it hits the horizontal axis; it indicates the value of the *x*-variable when the value of the *y*-variable is zero.

The **vertical intercept** of a curve is the point at which it hits the vertical axis; it shows the value of the *y*-variable when the value of the *x*-variable is zero.

A Key Concept: The Slope of a Curve

The **slope** of a line or curve is a measure of how steep it is and indicates how sensitive the y-variable is to a change in the *x*-variable. In our example of outside temperature and the number of cans of pop a vendor can expect to sell, the slope of the curve would indicate how many more cans of pop the vendor could expect to sell with each one-degree increase in temperature. Interpreted this way, the slope gives meaningful information. Even without numbers for *x* and *y*, it is possible to arrive at important conclusions about the relationship between the two variables by examining the slope of a curve at various points.

The **slope** of a line or curve is a measure of how steep it is. The slope of a line is measured by "rise over run"—the change in the *y*-variable between two points on the line divided by the change in the *x*-variable between those same two points.

The Slope of a Linear Curve

Along a linear curve the slope, or steepness, is measured by dividing the "rise" between two points on the curve by the "run" between those same two points. The rise is the amount that *y* changes and the run is the amount that *x* changes. Here is the formula:

$$\frac{\text{Change in } y}{\text{Change in } x} = \frac{\Delta y}{\Delta x} = \text{Slope}$$

In the formula, the symbol Δ (the Greek uppercase delta) stands for "change in". When a variable increases, the change in that variable is positive; when a variable decreases, the change in that variable is negative.

The slope of a curve is positive when the rise (the change in the *y*) has the same sign as the run (the change in the *x*). That's because when two numbers have the same sign, the ratio of those two numbers is positive. The curve in panel (a) of Figure 2A-2 has a positive slope: along the curve, both the *y* variable and the *x* variable increase. The slope of a curve is negative when the rise and the run have different signs. That's because when two numbers have different signs, the ratio of those two numbers is negative. The curve in panel (b) of Figure 2A-2 has a negative slope: along the curve, an increase in the *x*-variable is associated with a decrease in the *y*-variable.

Figure 2A-3 illustrates how to calculate the slope of a linear curve. Let's focus first on panel (a). From point *A* to point *B* the value of *y* changes from 25 to 20 and the value of *x* changes from 10 to 20. So the slope of the line between these two points is:

$$\frac{\text{Change in } y}{\text{Change in } x} = \frac{\Delta y}{\Delta x} = \frac{-5}{10} = -\frac{1}{2} = -0.5$$

Figure 2A-3 Calculating the Slope

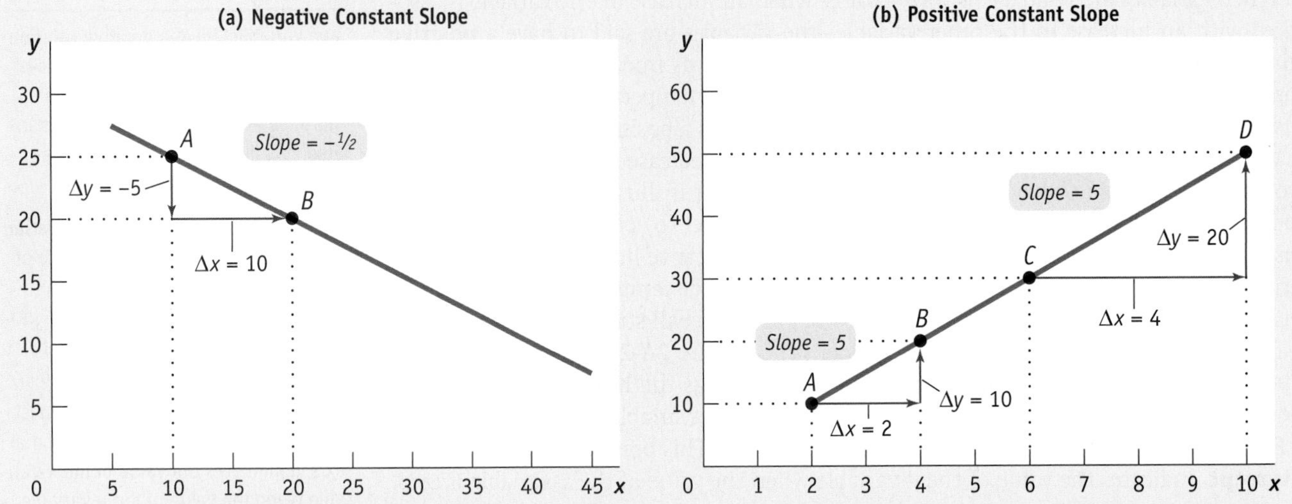

(a) Negative Constant Slope

(b) Positive Constant Slope

Panels (a) and (b) show two linear curves. Between points A and B on the curve in panel (a), the change in y (the rise) is −5, while the change in x (the run) is 10. Therefore, the slope from A to B is $\Delta y/\Delta x = -5/10 = -1/2 = -0.5$, where the negative sign indicates that the curve is downward sloping. In panel (b), the curve has a slope from A to B of $\Delta y/\Delta x = 10/2 = 5$. The slope from C to D is $\Delta y/\Delta x = 20/4 = 5$. The slope is positive, indicating that the curve is upward sloping. Furthermore, the slope between A and B is the same as the slope between C and D, making this a linear curve. The slope of a linear curve is constant: it is the same regardless of where it is calculated along the curve. **>web...**

Because a straight line is equally steep at all points, the slope of a straight line is the same at all points. In other words, a straight line has a constant slope. You can check this by calculating the slope of the linear curve between points A and B and between points C and D in panel (b) of Figure 2A-3.

Between A and B: $$\frac{\Delta y}{\Delta x} = \frac{10}{2} = 5$$

Between C and D: $$\frac{\Delta y}{\Delta x} = \frac{20}{4} = 5$$

Horizontal and Vertical Curves and Their Slopes

When a curve is horizontal, the value of y along that curve never changes—it is constant. Everywhere along the curve, the change in y is zero. Now, zero divided by any number is zero. So, regardless of the value of the change in x, the slope of a horizontal curve is always zero.

If a curve is vertical, the value of x along the curve never changes—it is constant. Everywhere along the curve, the change in x is zero. This means that the slope of a vertical line is a ratio with zero in the denominator. A ratio with zero in the denominator is equal to infinity—that is, an infinitely large number. So the slope of a vertical line is equal to infinity.

A vertical or a horizontal curve has a special implication: it means that the x-variable and the y-variable are unrelated. Two variables are unrelated when a change in one of the variables (the independent variable) has no effect on the other variable (the dependent variable). Or to put it a slightly different way, two variables are unrelated when the dependent variable is constant regardless of the value of the independent variable. If, as is usual, the y-variable is the dependent variable, the curve is horizontal. If the dependent variable is the x-variable, the curve is vertical.

The Slope of a Nonlinear Curve

A **nonlinear curve** is one in which the slope changes as you move along it. Panels (a), (b), (c), and (d) of Figure 2A-4 show various nonlinear curves. Panels (a) and (b) show nonlinear curves whose slopes change as you move along them, but the slopes always remain positive. Although both curves tilt upwards, the curve in panel (a) gets steeper as you move from left to right in contrast to the curve in panel (b), which gets flatter. A curve that is upward sloping and gets steeper, as in panel (a), is said to have *positive increasing* slope. A curve that is upward sloping but gets flatter, such as the curve in panel (b), is said to have *positive decreasing* slope.

A **nonlinear curve** is one in which the slope is not the same between every pair of points.

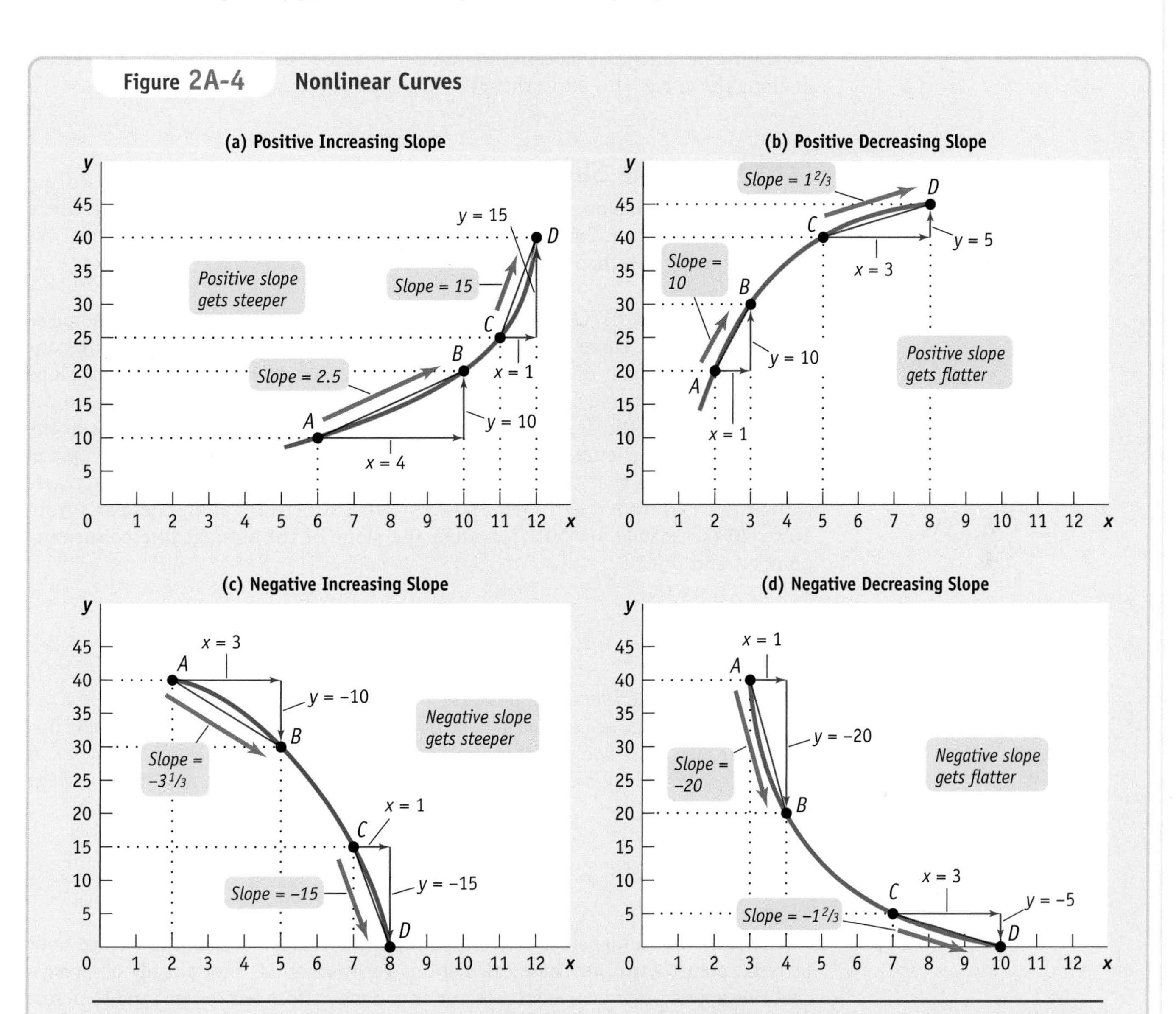

Figure 2A-4 Nonlinear Curves

In panel (a), the slope of the curve from *A* to *B* is $\Delta y/\Delta x = 10/4 = 2.5$, and from *C* to *D* it is $\Delta y/\Delta x = 15/1 = 15$. The slope is positive and increasing; it gets steeper as you move to the right. In panel (b), the slope of the curve slope from *A* to *B* is $\Delta y/\Delta x = 10/1 = 10$, and from *C* to *D* it is $\Delta y/\Delta x = 5/3 = 1\frac{2}{3}$. The slope is positive and decreasing; it gets flatter as you move to the right. In panel (c) the slope from *A* to *B* is $\Delta y/\Delta x = -10/3 = -3\frac{1}{3}$, and from *C* to *D* it is $\Delta y/\Delta x = -15/1 = -15$. The slope is negative and increasing; it gets steeper as you move to the right. And in panel (d) the slope from *A* to *B* is $\Delta y/\Delta x = -20/1 = -20$, and from *C* to *D* it is $\Delta y/\Delta x = -5/3 = -1\frac{2}{3}$. The slope is negative and decreasing; it gets flatter as you move to the right. The slope in each case has been calculated by using the arc method—that is, by drawing a straight line connecting two points along a curve. The average slope between those two points is equal to the slope of the straight line between those two points. >web...

When we calculate the slope along these nonlinear curves, we obtain different values for the slope at different points. How the slope changes along the curve determines the curve's shape. For example, in panel (a) of Figure 2A-4, the slope of the curve is a positive number that steadily increases as you move from left to right, whereas in panel (b), the slope is a positive number that steadily decreases.

The **absolute value** of a negative number is the value of the negative number without the minus sign.

The slopes of the curves in panels (c) and (d) are negative numbers. Economists often prefer to express a negative number as its **absolute value,** which is the value of the negative number without the minus sign. In general, we denote the absolute value of a number by two parallel bars around the number; for example, the absolute value of –4 is written as $|-4| = 4$. In panel (c), the absolute value of the slope steadily increases as you move from left to right. The curve therefore has *negative increasing* slope. And in panel (d), the absolute value of the slope of the curve steadily decreases along the curve. This curve therefore has *negative decreasing* slope.

Calculating the Slope Along a Nonlinear Curve

We've just seen that along a nonlinear curve, the value of the slope depends on where you are on that curve. So how do you calculate the slope of a nonlinear curve? We will focus on two methods: the *arc method* and the *point method.*

The Arc Method of Calculating the Slope An arc of a curve is some piece or segment of that curve. For example, panel (a) of Figure 2A-4 shows an arc consisting of the segment of the curve between points *A* and *B*. To calculate the slope along a nonlinear curve using the arc method, you draw a straight line between the two end-points of the arc. The slope of that straight line is then a measure of the average slope of the curve between those two end-points. You can see from panel (a) of Figure 2A-4 that the straight line drawn between points *A* and *B* increases along the *x*-axis from 6 to 10 (so that $\Delta x = 4$) as it increases along the *y*-axis from 10 to 20 (so that ($\Delta y = 10$). Therefore the slope of the straight line connecting points *A* and *B* is:

$$\frac{\Delta y}{\Delta x} = \frac{10}{4} = 2.5$$

This means that the average slope of the curve between points *A* and *B* is 2.5.

Now consider the arc on the same curve between points *C* and *D*. A straight line drawn through these two points increases along the *x*-axis from 11 to 12 ($\Delta x = 1$), as it increases along the *y*-axis from 25 to 40 ($\Delta y = 15$). Thus the average slope between points *C* and *D* is:

$$\frac{\Delta y}{\Delta x} = \frac{15}{1} = 15$$

Therefore the average slope between points *C* and *D* is larger than the average slope between points *A* and *B*. These calculations verify what we have already observed—that this upward-tilted curve gets steeper as you move from left to right and therefore has positive increasing slope.

A **tangent line** is a straight line that just touches, or is tangent to, a nonlinear curve at a particular point. The slope of the tangent line is equal to the slope of the nonlinear curve at that point.

The Point Method of Calculating the Slope The point method calculates the slope of a nonlinear curve at a specific point on that curve. Figure 2A-5 illustrates how to calculate the slope at point *B* on the curve. First, we draw a straight line that just touches the curve at point *B*. Such a line is called a **tangent line:** the fact that it just touches the curve at point *B* and does not touch the curve at any other point on the curve means that the straight line is *tangent* to the curve at point *B*. The slope of this tangent line is equal to the slope of the nonlinear curve at point *B*.

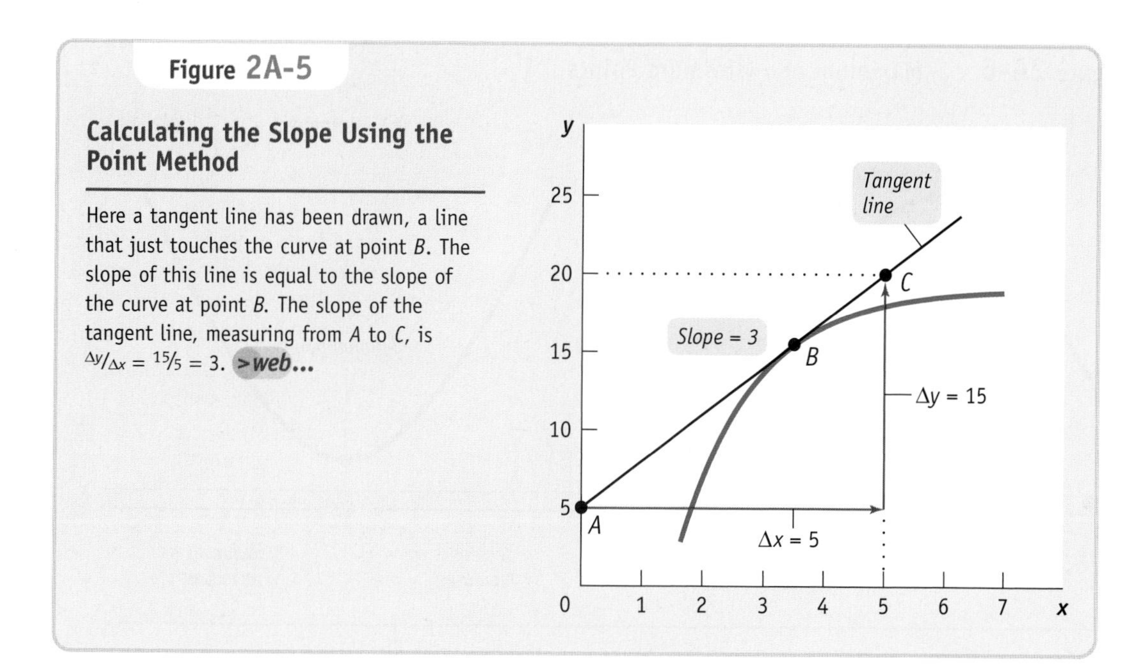

Figure 2A-5

Calculating the Slope Using the Point Method

Here a tangent line has been drawn, a line that just touches the curve at point *B*. The slope of this line is equal to the slope of the curve at point *B*. The slope of the tangent line, measuring from *A* to *C*, is $\Delta y/\Delta x = 15/5 = 3$. **>web...**

You can see from Figure 2A-5 how the slope of the tangent line is calculated: from point *A* to point *C*, the change in *y* is 15 units and the change in *x* is 5 units, generating a slope of:

$$\frac{\Delta y}{\Delta x} = \frac{15}{5} = 3$$

By the point method, the slope of the curve at point *B* is equal to 3.

A natural question to ask at this point is to determine which method to use—the arc method or the point method—in calculating the slope of a nonlinear curve. The answer depends on the curve itself and the data used to construct it. You use the arc method when you don't have enough information to be able to draw a smooth curve. For example, suppose that in panel (a) of Figure 2A-4 you had only the data represented by points *A*, *C*, and *D* and don't have the data represented by point *B* or any of the rest of the curve. Clearly, then, you couldn't use the point method to calculate the slope at point *B*; you would have to use the arc method to approximate the slope of the curve in this area by drawing a straight line between points *A* and *C*. But if you had sufficient data to draw the smooth curve shown in panel (a) of Figure 2A-4, then you could use the point method to calculate the slope at point *B*—and at every other point along the curve as well.

Maximum and Minimum Points

The slope of a nonlinear curve can change from positive to negative or vice versa. When the slope of a curve changes from positive to negative, it creates what is called a *maximum* point of the curve. When the slope of a curve changes from negative to positive, it creates a *minimum* point.

Panel (a) of Figure 2A-6 illustrates a curve in which the slope changes from positive to negative as you move from left to right. When *x* is between 0 and 50, the slope of the curve is positive. At *x* equal to 50, the curve attains its highest point—the largest value of *y* along the curve. This point is called the **maximum** of the curve. And as *x* exceeds 50, the slope becomes negative as the curve turns downwards. Many important curves in economics, such as the curve that represents how the profit of a firm changes as it produces more output, are hill-shaped like this.

A nonlinear curve may have a **maximum** point, the highest point along the curve. At the maximum, the slope of the curve changes from positive to negative.

In contrast, the curve shown in panel (b) of Figure 2A-6 is U-shaped: it has a slope that changes from negative to positive. At *x* equal to 50, the curve reaches its lowest

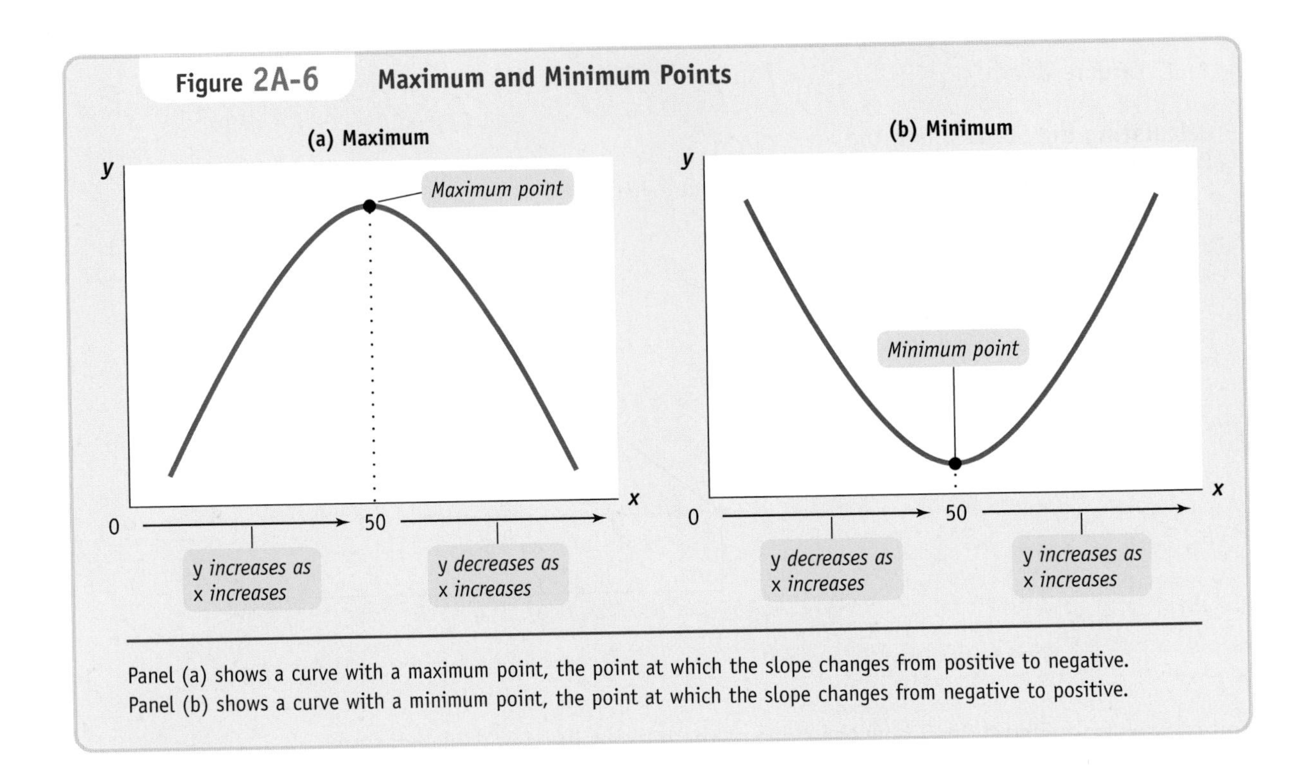

Panel (a) shows a curve with a maximum point, the point at which the slope changes from positive to negative. Panel (b) shows a curve with a minimum point, the point at which the slope changes from negative to positive.

A nonlinear curve may have a **minimum** point, the lowest point along the curve. At the minimum, the slope of the curve changes from negative to positive.

point—the smallest value of y along the curve. This point is called the **minimum** of the curve. Various important curves in economics, such as the curve that represents how the costs of some firms change as output increases, are U-shaped like this.

Graphs That Depict Numerical Information

Graphs can also be used as a convenient way to summarize and display data without assuming some underlying causal relationship. Graphs that simply display numerical information are called *numerical graphs*. Here we will consider four types of numerical graphs: *time-series graphs*, *scatter diagrams*, *pie charts*, and *bar graphs*. These are widely used to display real, empirical data about different economic variables because they often help economists and policy makers identify patterns or trends in the economy. But as we will also see, you must be careful not to misinterpret or draw unwarranted conclusions from numerical graphs. That is, you must be aware of both the usefulness and the limitations of numerical graphs.

Types of Numerical Graphs

A **time-series graph** has dates on the horizontal axis and values of a variable that occurred on those dates on the vertical axis.

You have probably seen graphs in newspapers that show what has happened over time to economic variables such as the unemployment rate, stock prices, or the exchange rate of the Canadian dollar. A **time-series graph** has successive dates on the horizontal axis and the values of a variable that occurred on those dates on the vertical axis. For example, Figure 2A-7 shows the unemployment rate in Canada from 1976 to 2003. A line connecting the points that correspond to the value of the unemployment rate for each year gives a clear idea of the overall trend in unemployment over these years.

Figure 2A-8 is an example of a different kind of numerical graph. It represents information from a sample of 158 countries on average life expectancy and gross national product (GNP) per capita—a rough measure of a country's standard of living. Each point here indicates an average resident's life expectancy and the log of

Figure 2A-7

Time-Series Graph

Time-series graphs show successive dates on the *x*-axis and values for a variable on the *y*-axis. This time-series graph shows the unemployment rate in Canada from 1976 to the end of 2003.

Source: Statistics Canada, Labour Force Survey. Cansim series: V206815.

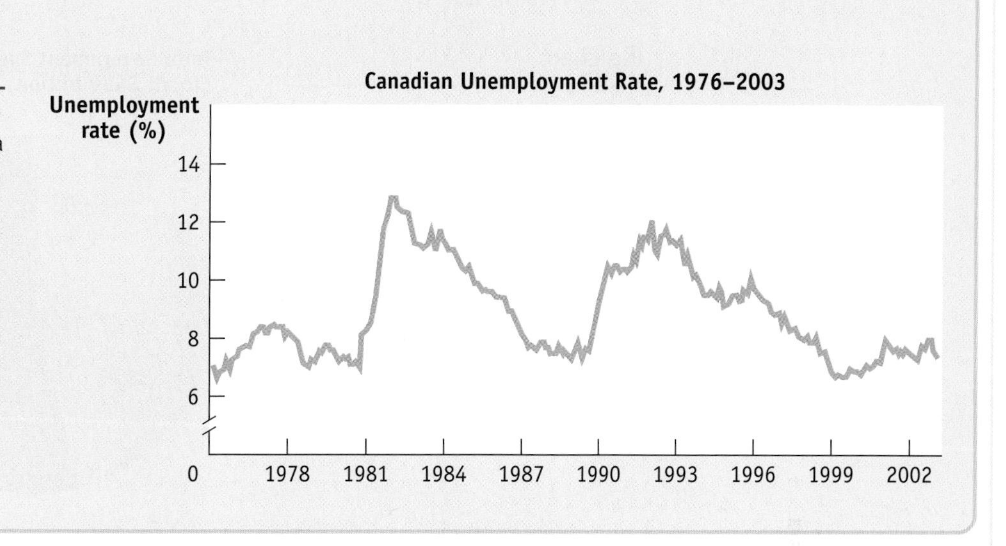

GNP per capita for a given country. (Economists have found that the log of GNP rather than the simple level of GNP is more closely tied to average life expectancy.) The points lying in the upper right of the graph, which show combinations of high life expectancy and high log GNP per capita, represent economically advanced countries such as Canada. Points lying in the bottom left of the graph, which show combinations of low life expectancy and low log GNP per capita, represent economically less advanced countries such as Afghanistan and Sierra Leone. The pattern of points indicates that there is a positive relationship between life expectancy and log GNP per capita: on the whole, people live longer in countries with a higher standard of living. This type of graph is called a **scatter diagram,** a diagram in which each point corresponds to an actual observation of the *x*-variable and the *y*-variable. In scatter diagrams, a curve is typically fitted to the scatter of points; that is, a curve is drawn that approximates as closely as possible the general relationship between the variables. As you can see, the fitted curve in Figure 2A-8 is upward sloping,

A **scatter diagram** shows points that correspond to actual observations of the *x*- and *y*-variables. A curve is usually fitted to the scatter of points.

Figure 2A-8

Scatter Diagram

In a scatter diagram, each point represents the corresponding values of the *x*- and *y*-variables for a given observation. Here, each point indicates the observed average life expectancy and the log of GNP per capita of a given country for a sample of 158 countries. The upward-sloping fitted line drawn here is the best approximation of the general relationship between the two variables.

Source: Eduard Bos et al., *Health, Nutrition, and Population Indicators: A Statistical Handbook* (Washington, DC: The World Bank, 1999).

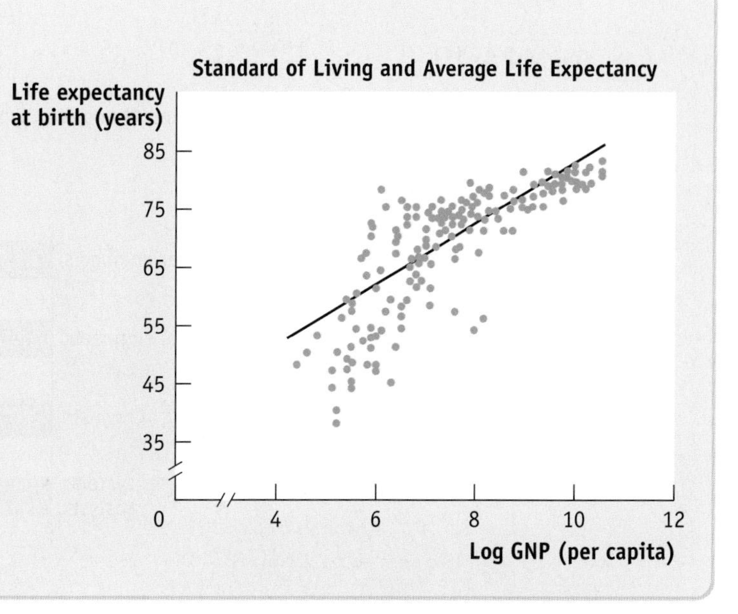

Figure 2A-9

Pie Chart

A pie chart shows the percentages of a total amount that can be attributed to various components. This pie chart shows the breakdown of total government spending into its major categories.

Source: Finances of the Nation, 2001, table A.4.

Total Government Spending, 2001 (Total: $439 billion)

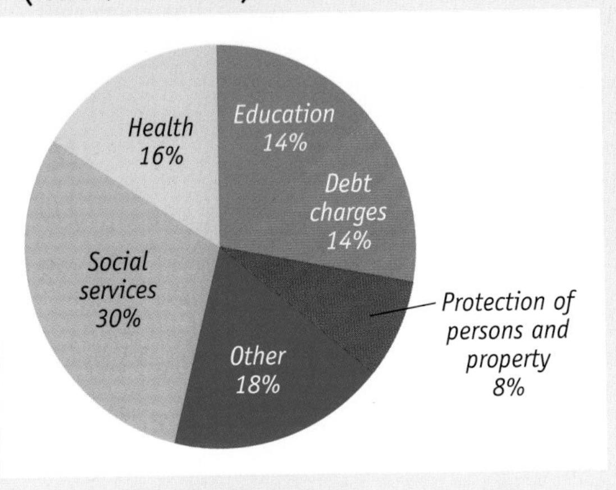

indicating the underlying positive relationship between the two variables. Scatter diagrams are often used to show how a general relationship can be inferred from a set of data.

A **pie chart** shows how some total is divided among its components, usually expressed in percentages.

A **pie chart** shows the share of a total amount that is accounted for by various components, usually expressed in percentages. For example, Figure 2A-9 is a pie chart that depicts the total spending by all levels of government in Canada for the year 2001. As you can see, social services were the largest single government expenditure item, absorbing 30 percent of total expenditures. This category includes employment insurance, the Canada Pension Plan, and social welfare payments.

A **bar graph** uses bars of varying height or length to show the comparative sizes of different observations of a variable.

Bar graphs use bars of various heights or lengths to indicate values of a variable. In the bar graph in Figure 2A-10, the bars show the projected percent change from 2002 to 2012 in the number of jobs in occupations that usually require at least a bachelor's degree. Exact values of the variable that is being measured may be written at the end of the bar, as in this figure. But even without the precise values, comparing the heights or lengths of the bars can give useful insight into the relative magnitudes of the different values of the variables.

Figure 2A-10

Bar Graph

A bar graph measures a variable by using bars of various heights or lengths. This bar graph shows the projected percentage change between 2002 and 2012 in the number of jobs in certain occupations that require a bachelor's degree or higher.

Source: Canadian Occupational Projection System, HRDC, Canada.

Projected Changes in Employment for Degree Holders, 2002–2012

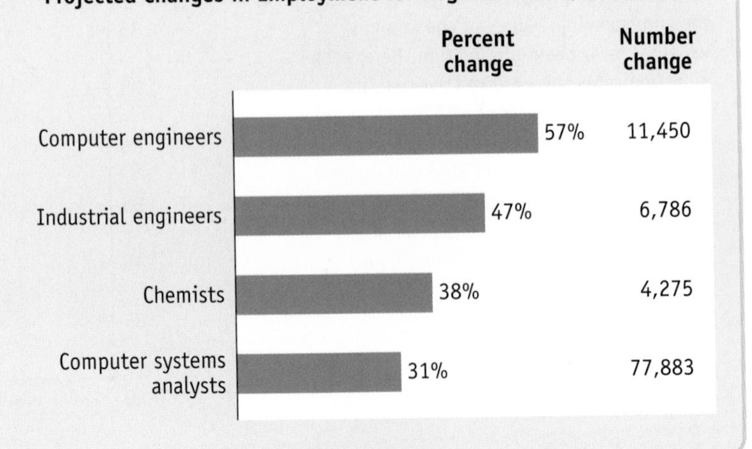

Problems in Interpreting Numerical Graphs

Although the beginning of this appendix emphasized that graphs are visual images that make ideas or information easier to understand, graphs can be constructed (intentionally or unintentionally) in ways that are misleading and can lead to inaccurate conclusions. This section raises some issues that you should be aware of when you interpret graphs.

Features of Construction Before drawing any conclusions about what a numerical graph implies, you should pay attention to the scale, or size of increments, shown on the axes. Small increments tend to visually exaggerate changes in the variables, whereas large increments tend to visually diminish them. So the scale in construction of a graph can influence your interpretation of the significance of the changes it illustrates—perhaps in an unwarranted way.

Take, for example, Figure 2A-11, which shows the unemployment rate in Canada during the year 2001. It is constructed using a 0.2% scale, and you can see from it that the unemployment rate rose from 6.8% at the beginning of 2001 to 8.0% by the end of 2001. Here, the 1.2% rise in the unemployment rate looks enormous and it could lead a policy-maker to conclude that the economy was in a nosedive. But if you go back and re-examine Figure 2A-7, which shows the unemployment rate in Canada from 1976 to 2003, you can see that this would be a misguided conclusion. Figure 2A-7 includes the same data shown in Figure 2A-11, but it is constructed with a 1% scale rather than a 0.2% scale. From it you can see that the 1.2% rise in the unemployment rate during 2001 was, in fact, relatively modest, at least compared to the rise in unemployment that occurred during 1982 or during 1990. This comparison shows that if you are not careful to factor in the choice of scale in interpreting a graph, you can arrive at very different, and possibly misguided, conclusions.

Related to the choice of scale is the use of *truncation* in constructing a graph. An axis is **truncated** when part of the range is omitted. This is indicated by two slashes (//) in the axis near the origin. You can see that the vertical axis of Figure 2A-7 has been truncated—the range of values from 0 to 6.0 has been omitted and a // appears in the axis. Truncation saves space in the presentation of a graph and allows larger increments to be used in constructing it. As a result, changes in the variable depicted on a graph that has been truncated appear larger compared to a graph that has not been truncated and that uses smaller increments.

An axis is **truncated** when some of the values on the axis are omitted, usually to save space.

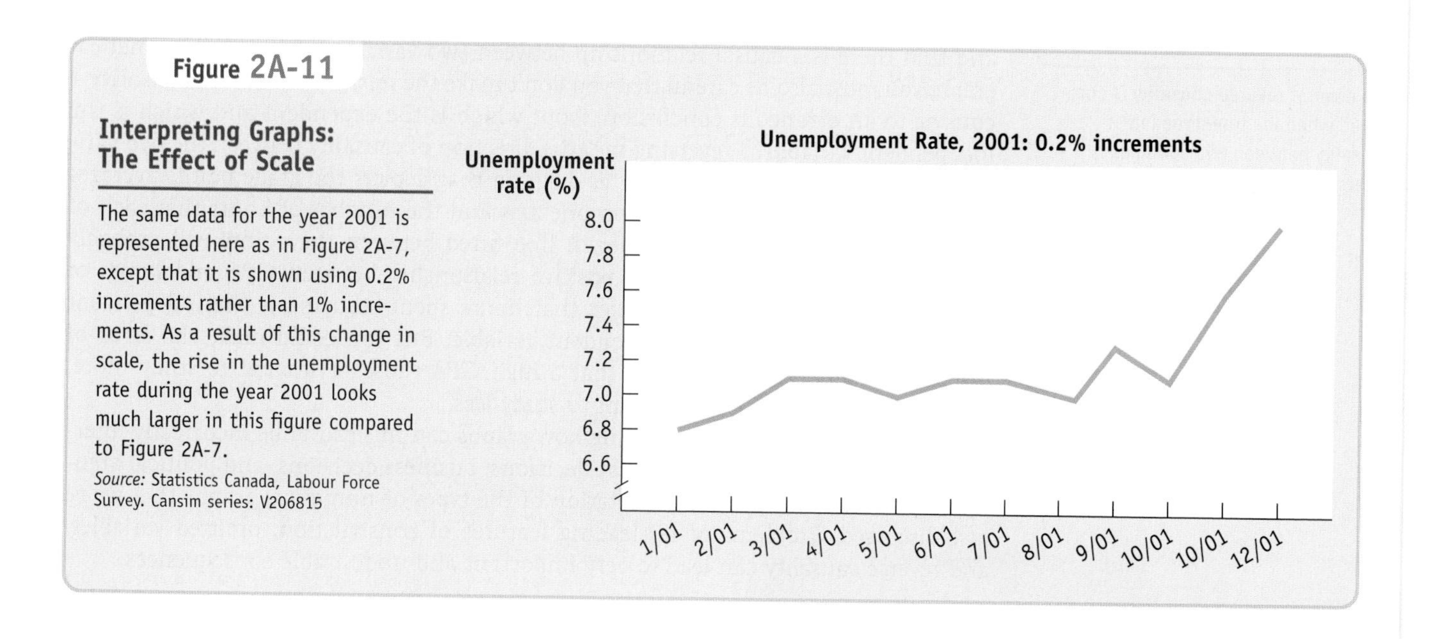

Figure 2A-11

Interpreting Graphs: The Effect of Scale

The same data for the year 2001 is represented here as in Figure 2A-7, except that it is shown using 0.2% increments rather than 1% increments. As a result of this change in scale, the rise in the unemployment rate during the year 2001 looks much larger in this figure compared to Figure 2A-7.

Source: Statistics Canada, Labour Force Survey. Cansim series: V206815

You must also pay close attention to exactly what a graph is illustrating. For example, in Figure 2A-10, you should recognize that what is being shown here are percentage changes, not numerical changes. The occupation with the longest bar represents computer engineers, showing a projected percentage increase in jobs of 57% from 2002 to 2012. If you confused numerical changes with percentage changes, you would erroneously conclude that the greatest number of new jobs created will be for computer engineers. But, in fact, a correct interpretation of Figure 2A-10 shows that the greatest number of new jobs will be for computer systems analysts. This is detailed in the right column of the figure—a projected increase in jobs of 77,883 for computer systems analysts is greater than the projected increase of 11,450 for computer engineers. Although engineers have a higher *percentage* increase in jobs than analysts, the current *number* of engineers is smaller than the number of analysts, leading to a smaller number of new jobs for engineers than for analysts.

Omitted Variables From a scatter diagram that shows two variables moving either positively or negatively in relation to one another, it is easy to conclude that there is a causal relationship. But relationships between two variables are not always due to direct cause and effect. Quite possibly, an observed relationship between two variables is due to the *unobserved* effect of a third variable on each of the other two variables. An unobserved variable that, through its influence on other variables, creates the erroneous appearance of a direct causal relationship among those variables is called an **omitted variable.** For example, in New Brunswick, a greater amount of snowfall during a given week will typically lead people to buy more snow shovels. It will also cause people to buy more de-icer fluid. But if you omitted the influence of the snowfall and simply plotted the number of snow shovels sold versus the number of bottles of de-icer fluid, you would produce a scatter diagram that showed an upward tilt in the pattern of points, indicating a positive relationship between snow shovels sold and de-icer fluid sold. To attribute a causal relationship between these two variables, however, is misguided; more snow shovels sold do not cause more de-icer fluid to be sold, or vice versa. They move together because they are both influenced by a third, determining, variable—the weekly snowfall—which is the omitted variable in this case. So before assuming that a pattern in a scatter diagram implies a cause-and-effect relationship, it is important to consider whether the pattern is instead the result of an omitted variable. Or to put it succinctly: Correlation is not causation.

An **omitted variable** is an unobserved variable that, through its influence on other variables, creates the erroneous appearance of a direct causal relationship among those variables.

Reverse Causality Even when you are confident that there is no omitted variable and that there is a causal relationship between two variables shown in a numerical graph, you must also be careful that you don't make the mistake of **reverse causality**—coming to an erroneous conclusion about which is the dependent and which is the independent variable by reversing the true direction of causality between the two variables. For example, imagine a scatter diagram that depicts the grade points averages (GPAs) of 20 of your classmates on one axis and the number of hours that each of them spends studying on the other. A line fitted between the points will probably have a positive slope, showing a positive relationship between GPA and hours of studying. We could reasonably infer that hours spent studying is the independent variable and that GPA is the dependent variable. But you could make the error of reverse causality: you could infer that a high GPA causes a student to study more, whereas a low GPA causes a student to study less.

The error of **reverse causality** is committed when the true direction of causality between two variables is reversed.

The significance of understanding how graphs can mislead or be incorrectly interpreted is not purely academic. Policy decisions, business decisions, and political arguments are often based on interpretation of the types of numerical graphs that we've just discussed. Problems of misleading features of construction, omitted variables, and reverse causality can lead to very important and undesirable consequences.

SUMMARY

1. Graphs are often used to illustrate conceptual or numerical information about economic variables. A 2-variable graph uses a *horizontal axis,* or *x-axis,* and a *vertical axis,* or *y-axis,* to generate a grid. Each point on this grid can be identified by the pair (*x, y*), where *x* denotes the *x-coordinate* and *y* denotes the *y-coordinate.* The two axes cross at the *origin,* where each variable is equal to zero.
2. In a *causal relationship,* the *independent variable* (usually plotted on the horizontal axis) determines the value of the *dependent variable* (usually plotted on the vertical axis). An important exception to this plotting convention is the case of price (independent variable plotted on the vertical axis) and quantity (dependent variable plotted on the horizontal axis).
3. A *curve* is a line depicting the relationship between two variables. If it is straight, the relationship is *linear;* if it is not, the relationship is *nonlinear.* If it slopes upwards from left to right, the relationship is *positive* (higher *x* leads to higher *y*); if it slopes downwards from left to right, the relationship is *negative* (higher *x* leads to lower *y*).
4. The *slope* of a linear curve is equal to the change in *y* divided by the change in *x.* The slope of a linear curve is constant along the entire curve. The slope of a nonlinear curve changes along the curve. Its slope can be measured two ways: the arc method or the point method. A nonlinear curve may have *positive increasing, positive decreasing, negative increasing,* or *negative decreasing* slope. It may also have a *maximum* or a *minimum.*
5. Numerical graphs are used to illustrate numerical information, but they can mislead unless interpreted carefully. The principal types are *time-series graphs, scatter diagrams, pie charts,* and *bar graphs.* The scale used in the graph can influence your estimation of the magnitude of changes illustrated. You must also be careful to avoid errors of *omitted variables* or *reverse causality.*

KEY TERMS

Variable, p. 42
Horizontal axis or *x*-axis, p. 43
Vertical axis or *y*-axis, p. 43
Origin, p. 43
X-coordinate, p. 43
Y-coordinate, p. 43
Causal relationship, p. 43
Independent variable, p. 43
Dependent variable, p. 43
Curve, p. 44
Linear relationship, p. 44
Nonlinear relationship, p. 44
Positive relationship, p. 45
Negative relationship, p. 45
Horizontal intercept, p. 45
Vertical intercept, p. 45
Slope, p. 45
Nonlinear curve, p. 47
Absolute value, p. 48
Tangent line, p. 48
Maximum, p. 49
Minimum, p. 50
Time-series graph, p. 50
Scatter diagram, p. 51
Pie chart, p. 52
Bar graph, p. 52
Truncation, p. 53
Omitted variable, p. 54
Reverse causality, p. 54

PROBLEMS

1. Study the four diagrams below. Consider the following statements and indicate which diagram matches each statement and which variable would appear on the horizontal and which on the vertical axis. In each of these statements, is the slope described as positive, negative, zero, or infinity?
   a. If the price of movies increases, fewer consumers go to see movies.
   b. More experienced workers typically have higher incomes than less experienced workers.
   c. Whatever the temperature outside, Canadians consume the same number of hot dogs per day.
   d. Consumers buy more frozen yogurt when the price of ice cream goes up.
   e. Research finds no relationship between how selective a college is and the average salaries earned by its graduates.
   f. Regardless of the price of salt, Canadians buy the same quantity of salt.

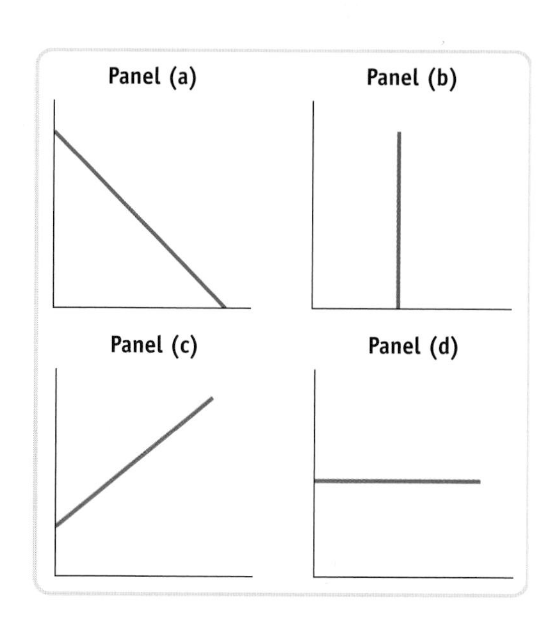

2. In the early 1980s, economist Arthur Laffer argued in favor of lowering income tax rates in order to increase tax revenues. He believed, like most economists, that at low income tax rates tax revenue increases as income tax rates increase. But he also claimed that if income tax rates increase beyond a certain level, tax revenue would fall because high taxes discourage people from working. This relationship between tax rates and tax revenue is graphically summarized in what is widely known as the "Laffer Curve". Plot the Laffer Curve relationship. The following questions help you construct the graph.
   a. Which is the independent variable? Which is the dependent variable? On which axis do you therefore measure the income tax rate? On which axis do you measure income tax revenue?
   b. The minimum possible income tax rate is 0%. What would tax revenue be at a 0% income tax rate?
   c. The maximum possible income tax rate is 100%. What would tax revenue be at a 100% income tax rate?
   d. Estimates now show that the maximum point on the Laffer curve is (approximately) at a tax rate of 80%. For tax rates less than 80%, how would you describe the relationship between the tax rate and tax revenue, and how is this relationship reflected in the slope? For tax rates higher than 80%, how would you describe the relationship between the tax rate and tax revenue, and how is this relationship reflected in the slope?
3. In the diagram below, the numbers on the axes have been lost. All you know is that the units shown on the vertical axis are the same as the units on the horizontal axis.
   a. In panel (a), what is the slope of the line? Show that the slope is constant along the line.
   b. In panel (b), what is the slope of the line? Show that the slope is constant along the line.

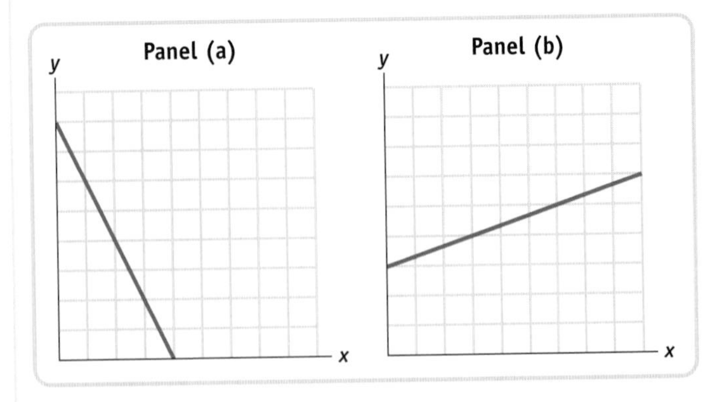

4. Answer each of the following questions by drawing a schematic diagram.
   a. Taking measurements of the slope of a curve at three points further and further to the right along the horizontal axis, the slope of the curve changes from −0.3, to −0.8, to −2.5, measured by the point method. Draw a schematic diagram of this curve. How would you describe the relationship illustrated in your diagram?
   b. Taking measurements of the slope of a curve at five points further and further to the right along the horizontal axis, the slope of the curve changes from 1.5, to 0.5, to 0, to −0.5, to −1.5, measured by the point method. Draw a schematic diagram of this curve. Does this figure have a maximum or a minimum?
5. The table below shows the relationship between workers' hours of work per week and their hourly wage. Apart from the fact that they receive a different hourly wage and work different hours, these five workers are otherwise identical.

Name	Hours worked per week	Hourly wage
Amy	30	$15
Bill	35	30
Charlie	37	45
Doug	36	60
Emily	32	75

   a. Which variable is the independent variable? Which is the dependent variable?
   b. Draw a scatter diagram illustrating this relationship. Draw a (nonlinear) curve which connects the points. Put the hourly wage on the vertical axis.
   c. As the wage increases from $15 to $30, how does the number of hours worked respond? What is the average slope of the curve between Amy's and Bill's data points?
   d. As the wage increases from $60 to $75, how does the number of hours worked respond? What is the average slope of the curve between Doug's and Emily's data points?
6. Studies have found a relationship between a country's yearly rate of economic growth and the yearly rate of increase in airborne pollutants. It is believed that a higher rate of economic growth allows a country's residents to have more cars and travel more, thereby releasing more airborne pollutants.
   a. Which variable is the independent variable? Which is the dependent variable?
   b. Suppose that in the country of Sudland, when the yearly rate of economic growth fell from 3.0% to 1.5%, the yearly rate of increase in airborne pollutants fell from 6% to 5%. What is the average slope of a nonlinear curve between these points?
   c. Now suppose that when the yearly rate of economic growth rose from 3.0% to 4.5%, the yearly rate of increase in airborne pollutants rose from 5.5% to 7.5%. What is the average slope of a nonlinear curve between these two points?
   d. How would you describe the relationship between the two variables here?
7. An insurance company has found that the severity of property damage in a fire is positively related to the number of firefighters arriving at the scene.
   a. Draw a graph that depicts this finding. What is the argument made by your graph?

b. In order to reduce its payouts to policy holders, should the insurance company therefore ask the city to send fewer firefighters to any fire?

8. The table below illustrates annual salaries and income tax owed by five individuals. Apart from the fact that they receive different salaries and owe different amounts of income tax, these five individuals are otherwise identical.

Name	Annual salary	Annual income tax owed
Susan	$22,000	$3,304
Bill	63,000	14,317
John	3,000	454
Mary	94,000	23,927
Peter	37,000	7,020

a. If you were to plot these points on a graph, what is the slope of the curve between the points for Bill's and Mary's salaries and taxes? How would you interpret this value for slope?

b. What is the slope of the curve between the points for John's and Susan's salaries and taxes? How would you interpret that value for slope?

c. What happens to the slope as salary increases? What does this relationship imply about how the level of income taxes a person must pay affects his or her incentive to earn a higher salary?

>web... To continue your study and review of concepts in this chapter, please visit the Krugman/Wells website for quizzes, animated graph tutorials, web links to helpful resources, and more.

www.worthpublishers.com/krugmanwellsmyatt

chapter 3

>>Supply and Demand

What you will learn in this chapter:

- What **a competitive market** is and how it is described by the **supply and demand model**
- What the **demand curve** is and what the **supply curve** is
- The difference between **movements along a curve** and **shifts of a curve**
- How the supply and demand curves determine a market's **equilibrium price** and **equilibrium quantity**
- In the case of a **shortage** or **surplus**, how price moves the market back to equilibrium

GRETZKY'S LAST GAME

THERE ARE SEVERAL WAYS YOU CAN get tickets for a sporting event. You might have a season pass that gives you a seat at every home game, you could buy a ticket for a single game from the box office, or you could buy a ticket from a *scalper*. Scalpers buy tickets in advance—either from the box office or from season ticket holders who decide to forgo the game—and then resell them shortly before the event.

Scalping is not always legal, but it is often profitable. A scalper might buy tickets at the box office and then, after the box office has sold out, resell them at a higher price to fans who have decided at the last minute to attend the event. Of course, the profits are not guaranteed. Sometimes an event is unexpectedly "hot" and scalped tickets can be sold for high prices, but sometimes an event is unexpectedly "cold" and scalpers end up selling at a loss. Over time, however, even with some unlucky nights, scalpers can make money from eager fans.

Ticket scalpers in the city of Ottawa had a good few days in April 1999. Why? Because Wayne Gretzky, the Canadian hockey star, unexpectedly announced that he would retire from the sport and that the April 15 match between the Ottawa Senators and his team, the New York Rangers, would be his last game on Canadian soil. Many Canadian fans wanted to see the great Gretzky play one last time—and would not give up just because the box office had long since sold out.

Clearly, scalpers who had already stocked up on tickets—or who could acquire more tickets—were in for a bonanza. After the announcement, scalped tickets began selling for four or five times their face value. It was just a matter of supply and demand.

Shelly/Castellanos/Zuma

AFB/Corbis

Ronal Siemoneit/Corbis

Fans paid hundreds, even thousands, of dollars to see Wayne Gretzky and Michael Jordan play their last games. How much would you pay to see a music star, such as Shania Twain, one last time? What about your favorite athlete?

But what do we mean by that? Many people use the phrase *supply and demand* as a sort of catchphrase to mean "the laws of the marketplace at work". To economists, however, the concept of supply and demand has a precise meaning: it is a *model of how a market behaves,* a model that is extremely useful for understanding many—but not all—markets.

In this chapter we lay out the pieces that make up the model known as the supply and demand model, put them together, and show how this model can be used to understand how many—but not all—markets behave.

Supply and Demand: A Model of a Competitive Market

Ticket scalpers and their customers constitute a market—a group of sellers and buyers. More than that, they constitute a particular type of market, known as a competitive market. Roughly, a **competitive market** is a market in which there are many buyers and sellers of the same good or service. More precisely, the key feature of a competitive market is that no individual's actions have a noticeable effect on the price at which the good or service is sold.

A **competitive market** is a market in which there are many buyers and sellers of the same good or service.

It's a little hard to explain why competitive markets are different from other markets until we've seen how a competitive market works. So let's take a rain check—we'll return to that issue at the end of this chapter. For now, let's just say that it's easier to model competitive markets than other markets. When taking an exam, it's always a good strategy to begin by answering the easier questions. In this book we're going to do the same thing. So we will start with competitive markets.

When a market is competitive, its behaviour is well described by a model known as the **supply and demand model.** And because many markets *are* competitive, the supply and demand model is a very useful one indeed.

The **supply and demand model** is a model of how a competitive market works.

There are five key elements in this model:

- The *demand curve*
- The *supply curve*
- The set of factors that cause the demand curve to shift, and the set of factors that cause the supply curve to shift
- The *equilibrium price*
- The way the equilibrium price changes when the supply and demand curves shift

To understand the supply and demand model, we will examine each of these elements.

The Demand Curve

How many people wanted to buy scalped tickets to see the New York Rangers and the Ottawa Senators play that April night? You might at first think the answer was: every hockey fan in Ontario who didn't already have a ticket. But although every hockey fan wanted to see Wayne Gretzky play one last time, most fans weren't willing to pay four or five times the normal ticket price. In general, the number of people who want to buy a hockey ticket, or any other good, depends on the price. The higher the price, the fewer people who want to buy the good; the lower the price, the more people who want to buy the good.

So the answer to the question "How many people will want to buy a ticket to Gretzky's last game?" depends on the price of a ticket. If you don't yet know what the price will be, you can start by making a table of how many people would want to buy at a number of different prices. Such a table is known as a *demand schedule*. This, in turn, can be used to draw a *demand curve*, which is one of the key elements of the supply and demand model.

The Demand Schedule and the Demand Curve

A **demand schedule** shows how much of a good or service consumers will want to buy at different prices.

A **demand schedule** is a table showing how much of a good or service consumers will want to buy at different prices. At the right of Figure 3-1, we show a hypothetical demand schedule for tickets to a hockey game.

According to the table, if scalped tickets are available at $100 each (roughly their face value), 20,000 people will be willing to buy them; at $150 some fans will decide that this price is too high, and only 15,000 will be willing to buy. At $200, even fewer people want tickets, and so on. So the higher the price, the fewer tickets people want to purchase. In other words, as the price rises, the quantity of tickets demanded falls.

A **demand curve** is a graphical representation of the demand schedule. It shows how much of a good or service consumers want to buy at any given price.

The **quantity demanded** is the actual amount consumers are willing to buy at some specific price.

The graph in Figure 3-1 is a visual representation of the information in the table. (You might want to review the discussion of graphs in economics in the appendix to Chapter 2.) The vertical axis shows the price of a ticket, and the horizontal axis shows the quantity of tickets. Each point on the graph corresponds to one of the entries in the table. The curve that connects these points is a **demand curve.** A demand curve is a graphical representation of the demand schedule, another way of showing how much of a good or service consumers want to buy at any given price.

Suppose that scalpers are charging $250 per ticket. We can see from Figure 3-1 that 8,000 fans are willing to pay that price; that is, 8,000 is the **quantity demanded** at a price of $250.

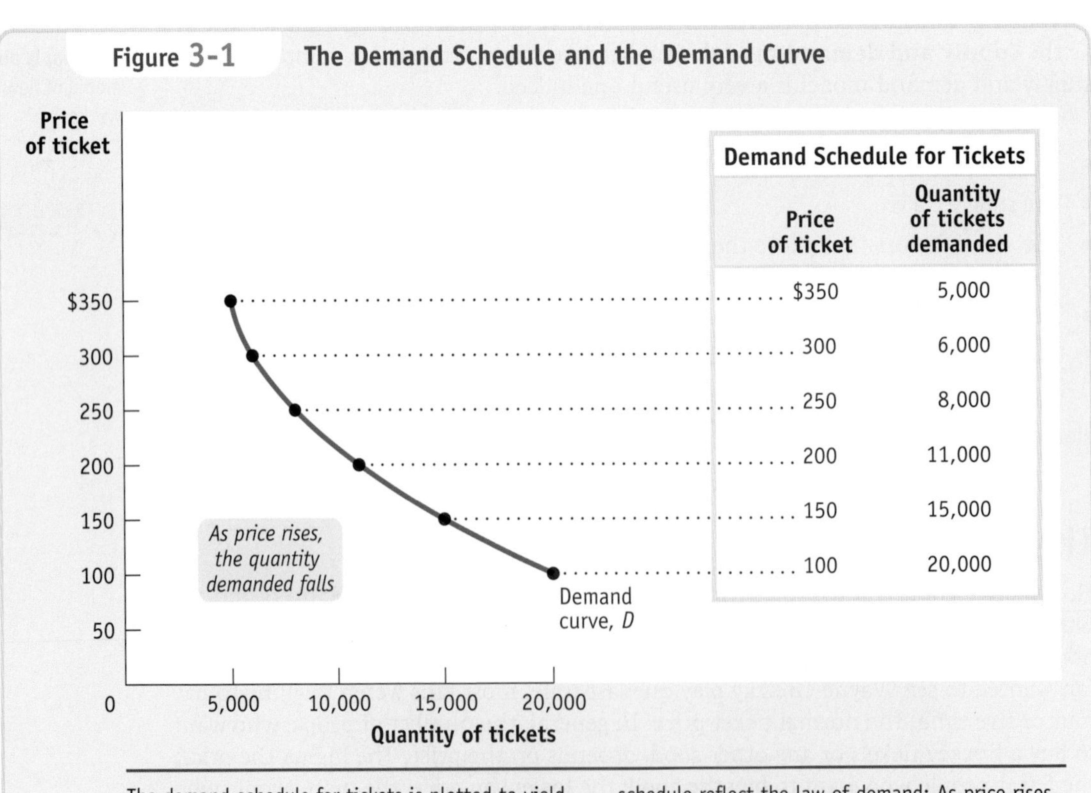

Price of ticket	Quantity of tickets demanded
$350	5,000
300	6,000
250	8,000
200	11,000
150	15,000
100	20,000

The demand schedule for tickets is plotted to yield the corresponding demand curve which shows how much of a good consumers want to buy at any given price. The demand curve and the demand schedule reflect the law of demand: As price rises, the quantity demanded falls. Similarly, a decrease in price raises the quantity demanded. As a result the demand curve is downward sloping.

Note that the demand curve shown in Figure 3-1 slopes downwards. This reflects the general proposition that a higher price reduces the number of people willing to buy a good. In this case, many people who would have laid out $100 to see the great Gretzky aren't willing to pay $350. In the real world, demand curves almost always, with some very specific exceptions, *do* slope downwards. The exceptions are goods called "Giffen goods", but economists think these are so rare that for practical purposes we can ignore them. Generally, the proposition that a higher price for a good, *other things equal,* leads people to demand a smaller quantity of that good is so reliable that economists are willing to call it a "law"—the **law of demand.**

The **law of demand** says that a higher price for a good, other things equal, leads people to demand a smaller quantity of the good.

Shifts of the Demand Curve

When Gretzky's retirement was announced, the immediate effect was that more people were willing to buy tickets for that April 15 game at any given price. That is, at every price the quantity demanded rose as a consequence of the announcement. Figure 3-2 illustrates this phenomenon in terms of the demand schedule and the demand curve for scalped tickets.

The table in Figure 3-2 shows two demand schedules. The second one shows the demand schedule after the announcement, the same one shown in Figure 3-1. But the first demand schedule shows the demand for scalped tickets *before* Gretzky announced his retirement. As you can see, after the announcement the number of people willing to pay $350 for a ticket increased, the number of people willing to pay $300 increased, and so on. So at each price, the second schedule—the schedule after the announcement—shows a larger quantity demanded. For example, at $200, the quantity of tickets fans were willing to buy increased from 5,500 to 11,000.

Figure 3-2 An Increase in Demand

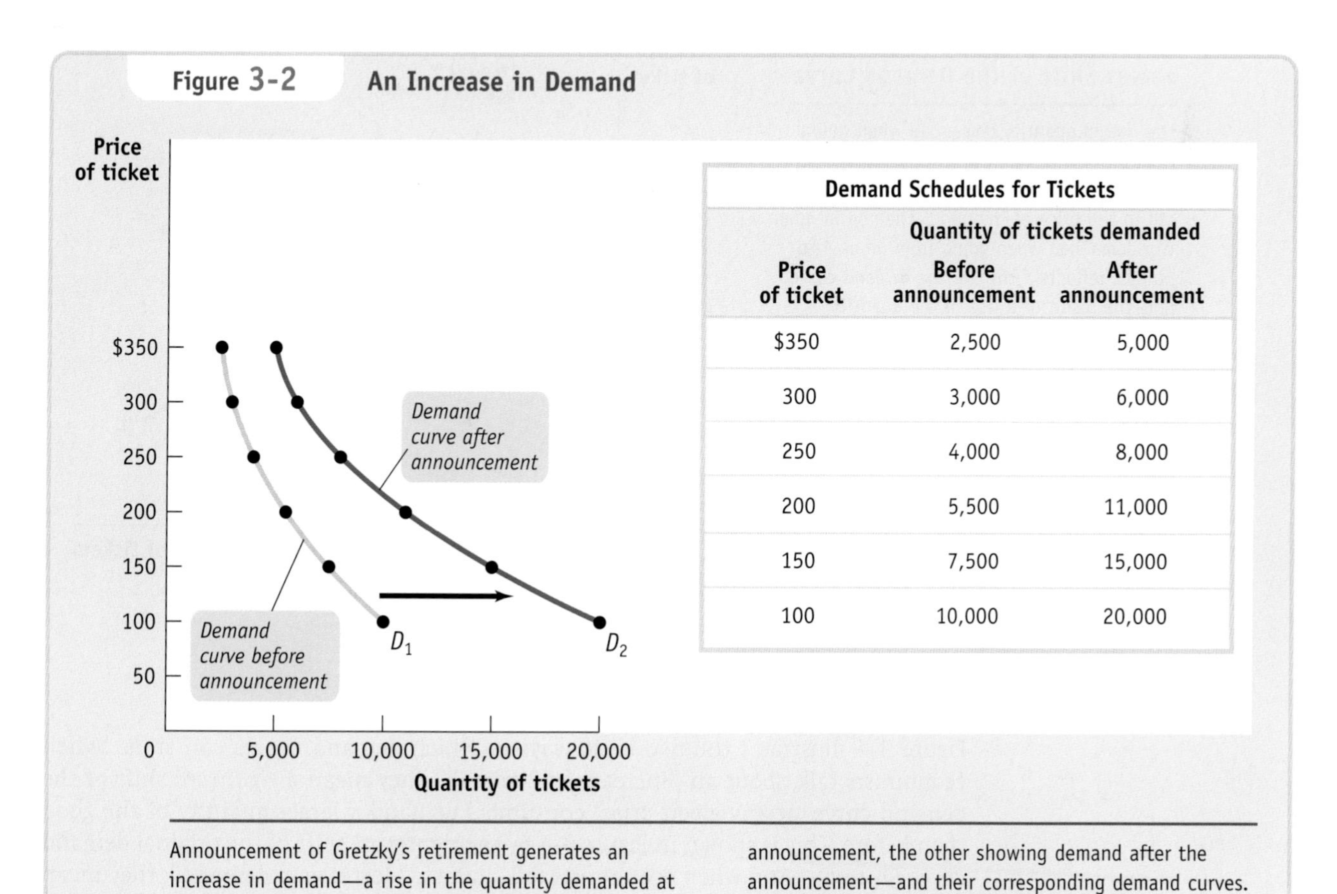

Price of ticket	Before announcement	After announcement
	Quantity of tickets demanded	
$350	2,500	5,000
300	3,000	6,000
250	4,000	8,000
200	5,500	11,000
150	7,500	15,000
100	10,000	20,000

Demand Schedules for Tickets

Announcement of Gretzky's retirement generates an increase in demand—a rise in the quantity demanded at any given price. This event is represented by the two demand schedules—one showing demand before the announcement, the other showing demand after the announcement—and their corresponding demand curves. The increase in demand shifts the demand curve to the right. >*web*...

The announcement of Gretzky's retirement generated a *new* demand schedule, one in which the quantity demanded is greater at any given price than in the original demand schedule. The two curves in Figure 3-2 show the same information graphically. As you can see, the new demand schedule after the announcement corresponds to a new demand curve, D_2, that is to the right of the demand curve before the announcement, D_1. This **shift of the demand curve** shows the change in the quantity demanded at any given price, represented by the change in position of the original demand curve D_1 to its new location at D_2.

A **shift of the demand curve** is a change in the quantity demanded at any given price, represented by the change of the original demand curve to a new position, denoted by a new demand curve.

A **movement along the demand curve** is a change in the quantity demanded of a good that is the result of a change in that good's price.

It's crucial to make the distinction between such shifts of the demand curve and **movements along the demand curve,** changes in the quantity demanded of a good that result from a change in that good's price. Figure 3-3 illustrates the difference.

The movement from point *A* to point *B* is a movement along the demand curve: the quantity demanded rises due to a fall in price as you move down D_1. Here, a fall in price from $350 to $215 generates a rise in the quantity demanded from 2,500 to 5,000 tickets. But the quantity demanded can also rise when the price is unchanged if there is an increase in demand—a rightward shift of the demand curve. This is illustrated in Figure 3-3 by the shift of the demand curve D_1 to D_2. Holding price constant at $350, the quantity demanded increases from 2,500 tickets at point *A* on D_1 to 5,000 tickets at point *C* on D_2.

When economists say "the demand for X increased" or "the demand for Y decreased", they mean that the demand curve for X or Y shifted—*not* that the quantity demanded rose or fell because of a change in the price.

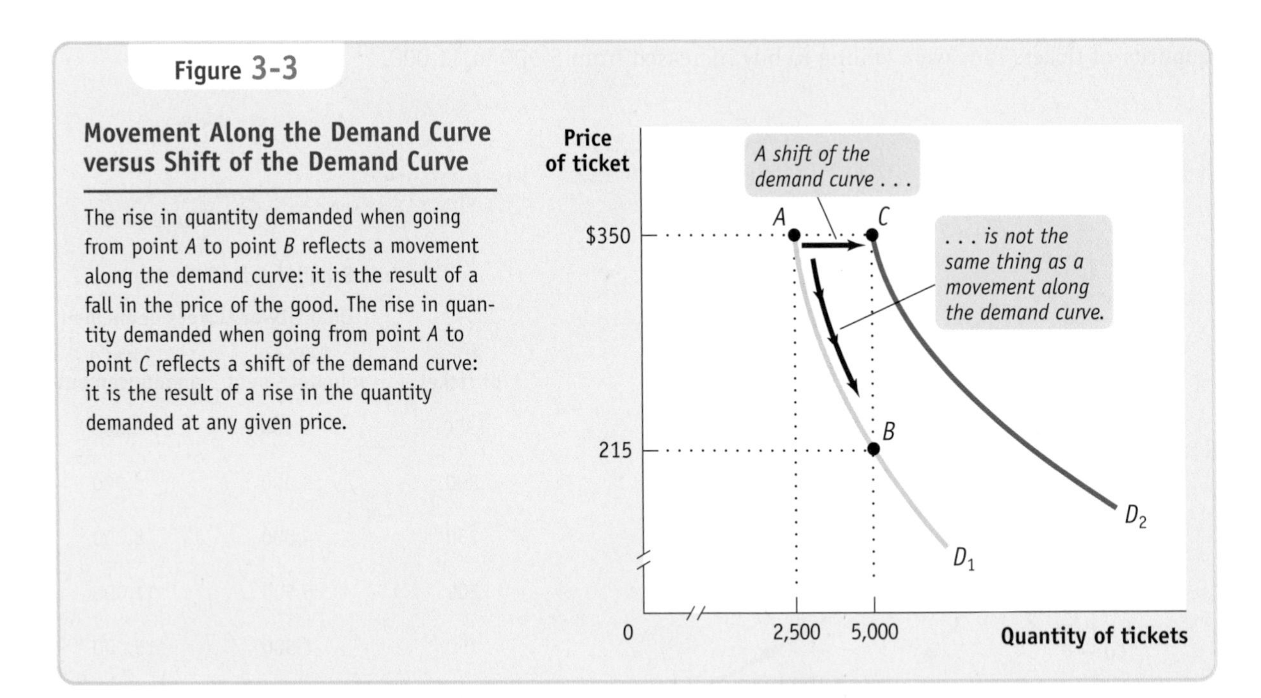

Figure 3-3

Movement Along the Demand Curve versus Shift of the Demand Curve

The rise in quantity demanded when going from point *A* to point *B* reflects a movement along the demand curve: it is the result of a fall in the price of the good. The rise in quantity demanded when going from point *A* to point *C* reflects a shift of the demand curve: it is the result of a rise in the quantity demanded at any given price.

Understanding Shifts of the Demand Curve

Figure 3-4 illustrates the two basic ways in which demand curves can shift. When economists talk about an "increase in demand", they mean a *rightward* shift of the demand curve: at any given price, consumers demand a larger quantity of the good than before. This is shown in Figure 3-4 by the rightward shift of the original demand curve D_1 to D_2. And when economists talk about a "decrease in demand", they mean a *leftward* shift of the demand curve: at any given price, consumers demand a smaller quantity of the good than before. This is shown in Figure 3-4 by the leftward shift of the original demand curve D_1 to D_3.

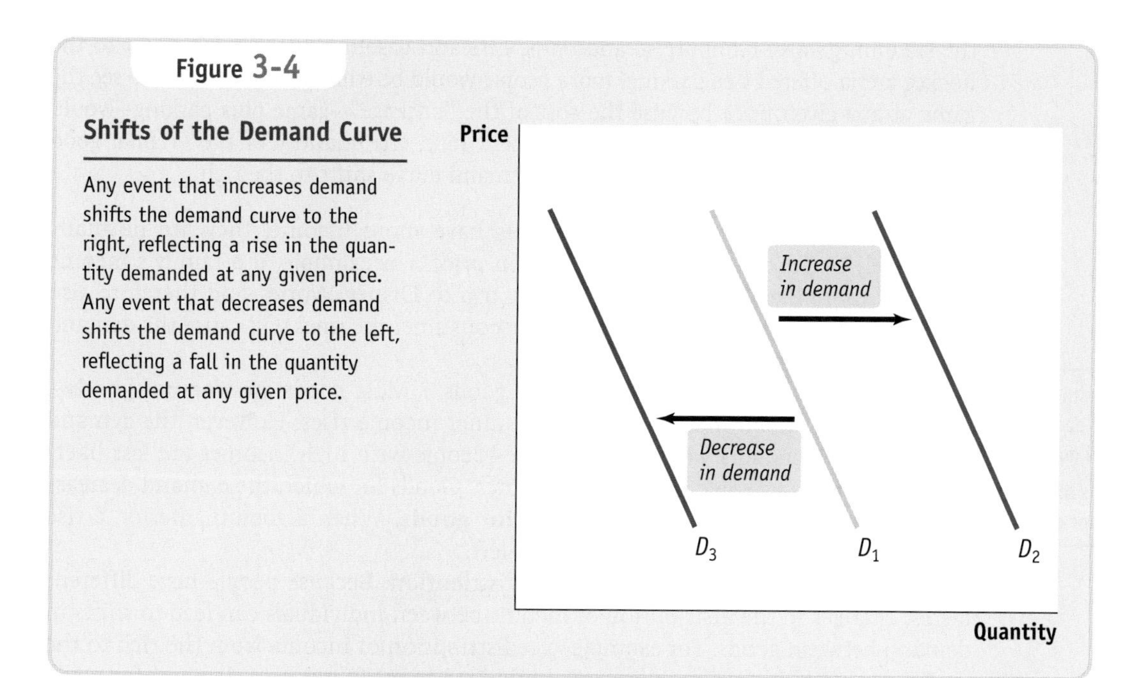

Figure 3-4

Shifts of the Demand Curve

Any event that increases demand shifts the demand curve to the right, reflecting a rise in the quantity demanded at any given price. Any event that decreases demand shifts the demand curve to the left, reflecting a fall in the quantity demanded at any given price.

But what causes a demand curve to shift? In our example, the event that shifted the demand curve for tickets is the announcement of Gretzky's imminent retirement. But if you think about it, you could come up with other things that are likely to shift the demand curve for those tickets. For example, suppose there is a music concert the same evening as the hockey game, and the band announces that it will sell tickets at half-price. This is likely to cause a decrease in demand for hockey tickets: hockey fans who also like music will prefer to purchase half-price concert tickets rather than hockey game tickets.

Economists believe that there are five principal factors that shift the demand curve for a good:

- Changes in the prices of related goods
- Changes in income
- Changes in tastes
- Changes in population
- Changes in expectations

Although this is not an exhaustive list, it contains the five most important factors that can shift demand curves. When we said before that the quantity of a good demanded falls as its price rises, *other things equal,* we were referring to the factors that shift demand as remaining unchanged.

Changes in the Prices of Related Goods If you want to have a good night out but are not too particular about what you do, a music concert is an alternative to the hockey game—it is what economists call a *substitute* for the hockey game. A pair of goods are **substitutes** if a fall in the price of one good (music concerts) makes consumers less willing to consume the other good (hockey games). Substitutes are usually goods that in some way serve a similar function: concerts and hockey games, muffins and donuts, trains and buses. A fall in the price of the alternative good induces some consumers to purchase it *instead of* the original good, shifting the demand for the original good to the left.

But sometimes a fall in the price of one good makes consumers *more* willing to consume another good. Such pairs of goods are known as **complements.** Complements are usually goods that in some sense are consumed together: sports tickets and parking at

Two goods are **substitutes** if a fall in the price of one of the goods makes consumers less willing to buy the other good.

Two goods are **complements** if a fall in the price of one good makes people more willing to buy the other good.

the stadium garage, hamburgers and buns, cars and gasoline. If the garage next to the hockey arena offered free parking, more people would be willing to buy tickets to see the game at any given price because the cost of the "package"—game plus parking—would have fallen. When the price of a complement falls, the quantity of the original good demanded at any given price rises; so the demand curve shifts to the right.

Changes in Income When individuals have more income, they are normally more likely to purchase a good at any given price. For example, if a family's income rises it is more likely to take that summer trip to Disney World—and therefore also more likely to buy plane tickets. So a rise in consumer incomes will cause the demand curves for most goods to shift to the right.

When a rise in income increases the demand for a good—the normal case—we say that the good is a **normal good**.

When a rise in income decreases the demand for a good, it is an **inferior good**.

Why do we say "most goods", not "all goods"? Most goods are **normal goods**—the demand for them increases when consumer income rises. However, the demand for some products falls when incomes rise—people with high incomes are less likely to take buses than people with lower incomes. Goods for which the demand decreases when income rises are known as **inferior goods.** When a good is inferior, a rise in income shifts the demand curve to the left.

An important aspect of income is its distribution. Because people have different tastes, changes in the distribution of income between individuals can lead to shifts in demand between goods. For example, a redistribution of income from the rich to the poor (with total income unchanged) could lead to an increase in demand for small or second-hand cars and a decrease in demand for new luxury automobiles.

Changes in Tastes Why do people want what they want? Fortunately, we don't need to answer that question—we just need to acknowledge that people have certain preferences, or tastes, that determine what they choose to consume and that these tastes can change. Economists usually lump together changes in demand due to fads, beliefs, cultural shifts, and so on under the heading of changes in *tastes* or *preferences*.

For example, once upon a time men routinely wore undershirts (or vests). But then came a dramatic moment—American actor Clark Gable removed his shirt in Frank Capra's classic film *It Happened One Night* (1934)—revealing bare skin rather than an undershirt! Reportedly, the sales of vests immediately plummeted. Fashion had changed overnight, and the demand for men's undershirts never recovered.

The main distinguishing feature of changes in tastes is that economists have little to say about them, and usually take them as given. When tastes change in favour of a good, more people want to buy the good at any given price, so the demand curve shifts to the right. When tastes change against a good, fewer people want to buy it at any given price, so the demand curve shifts to the left.

Changes in Population An increase in the population would not necessarily create new demand. Sure, it may create new needs, but for needs to be translated into demands those needs must be backed up with purchasing power. If we assume any additional population has the same average income as the existing population, we would expect the demand for all goods and services to increase.

An important aspect of population is its demographic breakdown, or age distribution. For example, as a result of the "baby boom", almost one-third of the Canadian population was in their teens or early 20s during the early 1970s. This created a boom for the products enjoyed by that age group—Volkswagen vans, guitars, and tie-dyed T-shirts. By 2020 this generation will be turning 70, and their sheer numbers will shift up the demand for nursing homes and health care services.

Changes in Expectations You could say that the increase in demand for tickets to the April 15 hockey game was the result of a change in expectations: fans no longer expected to have future opportunities to see Gretzky in action, so they became more eager to see him while they could.

Depending on the specifics of the case, changes in expectations can either decrease or increase the demand for a good. For example, savvy shoppers often wait for seasonal sales—say, buying holiday gifts during the post-holiday markdowns. In this case, expectations of a future drop in price lead to a decrease in demand today. Alternatively, expectations of a future rise in price are likely to cause an increase in demand today.

Expected changes in future income can also lead to changes in demand: If you expect your income to rise in the future, you will typically borrow today and increase your demand for certain goods; and if you expect your income to fall in the future, you are likely to save today and reduce your demand for some goods.

economics in action

Beating the Traffic

All big cities like Toronto, Montreal, and Vancouver have traffic problems, and many local authorities try to discourage driving in the crowded city centre. If we think of an auto trip to the city centre as a good that people consume, we can use the economics of demand to analyze anti-traffic policies.

One common strategy of municipal governments is to reduce the demand for auto trips by lowering the prices of substitutes. For example, most Canadian municipalities subsidize bus and rail service, hoping to lure commuters out of their cars.

An alternative strategy is raising the price of complements: several major U.S. cities impose high taxes on commercial parking garages, both to raise revenue and to discourage people from driving into the city. In Canadian cities, the dominant tactic seems to be short time limits on parking meters, combined with vigilant parking enforcement.

However, few cities have been willing to adopt the politically controversial direct approach: reducing congestion by raising the price of driving. So it was a shock when, in 2003, London, England, imposed a "congestion charge" of £5 (about $12) on all cars entering the city centre during business hours.

Compliance with the charge is monitored using automatic cameras that photograph license plates. People can either pay the charge in advance or pay it by midnight of the day they have driven. Those who don't pay and are caught are fined £80 (about $192) for each transgression. (A full description of the rules can be found at www.cclondon.com.)

Not surprisingly, the result of the new policy confirms the law of demand: according to an August 2003 news report, traffic into central London had fallen 32 percent and cars were traveling more than a third faster as a result of the congestion charge. ■

>>QUICK REVIEW

- The *demand schedule* shows how the *quantity demanded* changes as the price changes. The relationship is illustrated by a *demand curve*.
- The *law of demand* asserts that demand curves normally slope downwards—that is, a higher price reduces the quantity demanded.
- When economists talk about increases or decreases in demand, they mean *shifts of the demand curve*. An increase in demand is a rightward shift: the quantity demanded rises for any given price. A decrease in demand is a leftward shift: the quantity demanded falls for any given price.
- A change in price results in a *movement along the demand curve* and a change in the quantity demanded.
- The five main factors that can shift the demand curve are changes in (1) the price of a related good, such as a *substitute* or a *complement*, (2) income, (3) tastes, (4) population, and (5) expectations.

>>CHECK YOUR UNDERSTANDING 3-1

1. Explain whether each of the following events represents (i) a *shift* of the demand curve or (ii) a *movement along* the demand curve.
   a. A store owner finds that customers are willing to pay more for umbrellas on rainy days.
   b. When XYZ Telecom, a long-distance telephone service provider, offered reduced rates on weekends, the volume of weekend calling increased sharply.
   c. People buy more long-stem roses the week of Valentine's Day, even though the prices are higher than at other times of the year.
   d. The sharp rise in the price of gasoline leads many commuters to join carpools in order to reduce their gasoline purchase.

Solutions appear at back of book.

The Supply Curve

Ticket scalpers have to acquire the tickets they sell, and many of them do so from ticket-holders who decide to sell. The decision of whether to sell your own ticket to a scalper depends in part on the price offered: the higher the price offered, the more likely that you will be willing to sell.

The **quantity supplied** is the amount of a good or service people are willing to sell at some specific price.

So just as the quantity of tickets that people are willing to buy depends on the price they have to pay, the quantity that people are willing to sell—the **quantity supplied**—depends on the price they are offered. (Notice that this is the supply of tickets *to the market in scalped tickets*. The number of seats in the stadium is whatever it is, regardless of the price—but that's not the quantity we're concerned with here.)

The Supply Schedule and the Supply Curve

A **supply schedule** shows how much of a good or service would be supplied at different prices.

The table in Figure 3-5 shows how the quantity of tickets made available varies with the price—that is, it shows a hypothetical **supply schedule** for tickets to Gretzky's last game.

A supply schedule works the same way as the demand schedule shown in Figure 3-1: in this case, the table shows the quantity of tickets season subscribers are willing to sell at different prices. At a price of $100, only 2,000 people are willing to part with their tickets. At $150, some more people decide that it is worth passing up the game in order to have more money for something else, increasing the quantity of tickets available to 5,000. At $200 the quantity of tickets supplied rises to 7,000, and so on.

A **supply curve** shows graphically how much of a good or service people are willing to sell at any given price.

In the same way that a demand schedule can be represented graphically by a demand curve, a supply schedule can be represented by a **supply curve,** as shown in Figure 3-5. Each point on the curve represents an entry from the table.

Suppose that the price scalpers offer rises from $200 to $250; we can see from Figure 3-5 that the quantity of tickets sold to them rises from 7,000 to 8,000. This is the normal situation for a supply curve, reflecting the general proposition that a higher price leads to a higher quantity supplied. So just as demand curves normally slope downwards, supply curves normally slope upwards: the higher the price being offered, the more hockey tickets people will be willing to part with—the more of any good they will be willing to sell.

Figure 3-5 The Supply Schedule and the Supply Curve

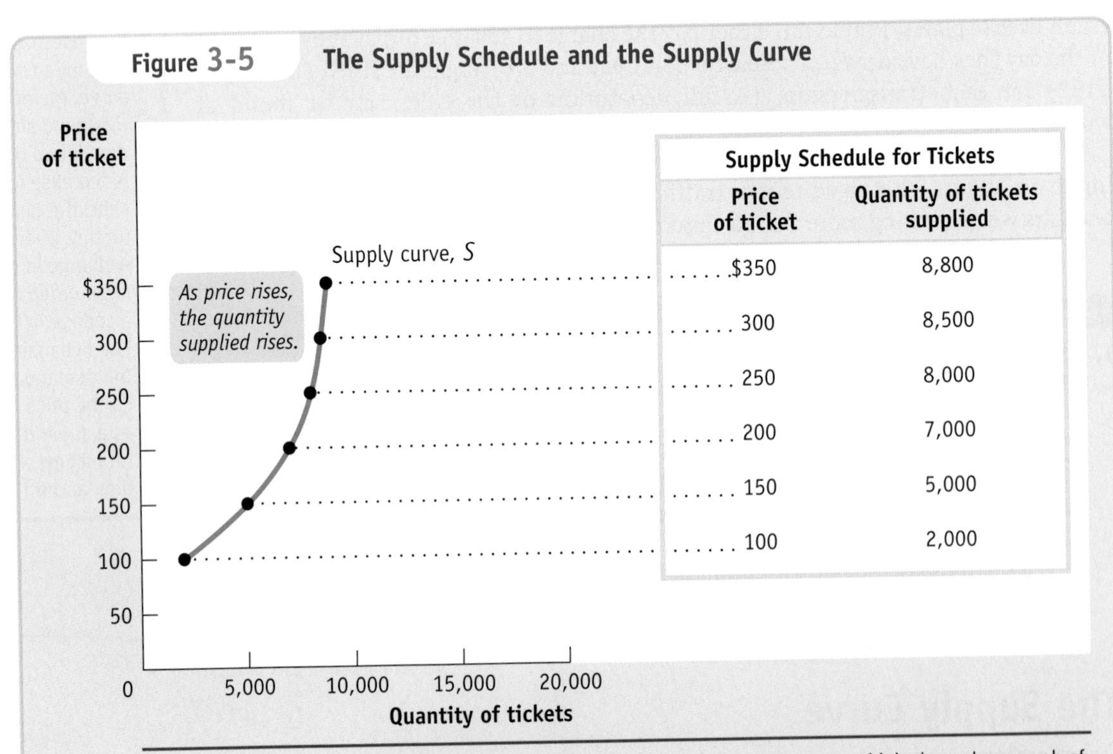

Supply Schedule for Tickets

Price of ticket	Quantity of tickets supplied
$350	8,800
300	8,500
250	8,000
200	7,000
150	5,000
100	2,000

The supply schedule for tickets is plotted to yield the corresponding supply curve which shows how much of a good people are willing to sell at any given price. The supply curve and the supply schedule reflect the fact that supply curves are usually upward sloping: the quantity supplied rises when the price rises.

Shifts of the Supply Curve

When Gretzky's retirement was announced, the immediate effect was that people who already had tickets for the April 15 game became less willing to sell those tickets to scalpers at any given price. So the quantity of tickets supplied at any given price fell: the number of tickets people were willing to sell at $350 per ticket fell, the number they were willing to sell at $300 fell, and so on. Figure 3-6 shows us how to illustrate this event in terms of the supply schedule and the supply curve for tickets.

The table in Figure 3-6 shows two supply schedules; the schedule after the announcement is the same one as in Figure 3-5. The first supply schedule shows the supply of scalped tickets *before* Gretzky announced his retirement. And just as a change in demand schedules leads to a shift of the demand curve, a change in supply schedules leads to a **shift of the supply curve**—a change in the quantity supplied at any given price. This is shown in Figure 3-6 by the shift of the supply curve before the announcement, S_1, to its new position after the announcement S_2. Notice that S_2 lies to the left of S_1, a reflection of the fact that quantity supplied decreased at any given price in the aftermath of Gretzky's announcement.

A **shift of the supply curve** is a change in the quantity supplied of a good or service at any given price. It is represented by the change of the original supply curve to a new position, denoted by a new supply curve.

As in the analysis of demand, it's crucial to draw a distinction between such shifts of the supply curve and **movements along the supply curve**—changes in the quantity supplied that result from a change in price. We can see this difference in Figure 3-7. The movement from point A to point B is a movement along the supply curve: the quantity supplied falls along S_1 due to a fall in price. Here, a fall in price from $250 to $200 leads to a fall in the quantity supplied from 9,000 to 8,000 tickets. But the quantity supplied can also fall when the price is unchanged if there is a decrease in supply—a leftward shift of the supply curve.

A **movement along the supply curve** is a change in the quantity supplied of a good that is the result of a change in that good's price.

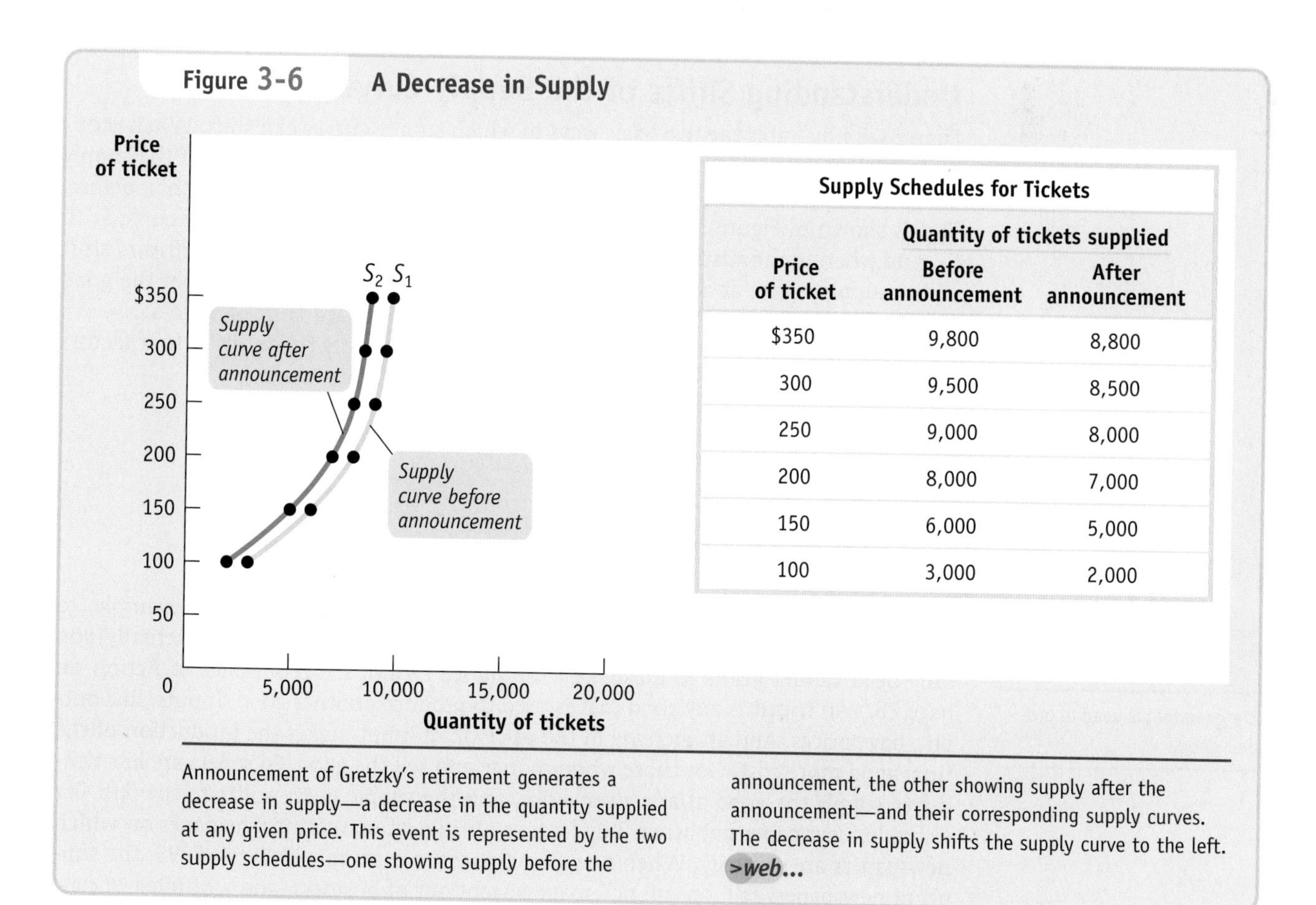

Supply Schedules for Tickets

Price of ticket	Quantity of tickets supplied: Before announcement	Quantity of tickets supplied: After announcement
$350	9,800	8,800
300	9,500	8,500
250	9,000	8,000
200	8,000	7,000
150	6,000	5,000
100	3,000	2,000

Announcement of Gretzky's retirement generates a decrease in supply—a decrease in the quantity supplied at any given price. This event is represented by the two supply schedules—one showing supply before the announcement, the other showing supply after the announcement—and their corresponding supply curves. The decrease in supply shifts the supply curve to the left. >web...

This is shown in Figure 3-7 by the leftward shift of the supply curve S_1 to S_2. Holding price constant at $250, the quantity supplied falls from 9,000 tickets at point *A* on S_1 to 8,000 at point *C* on S_2.

Figure 3-7

Movement Along the Supply Curve versus Shift of the Supply Curve

The fall in quantity supplied when going from point *A* to point *B* reflects a movement along the supply curve: it is the result of a fall in the price of the good. The fall in quantity supplied when going from point *A* to point *C* reflects a shift of the supply curve: it is the result of a fall in the quantity supplied at any given price.

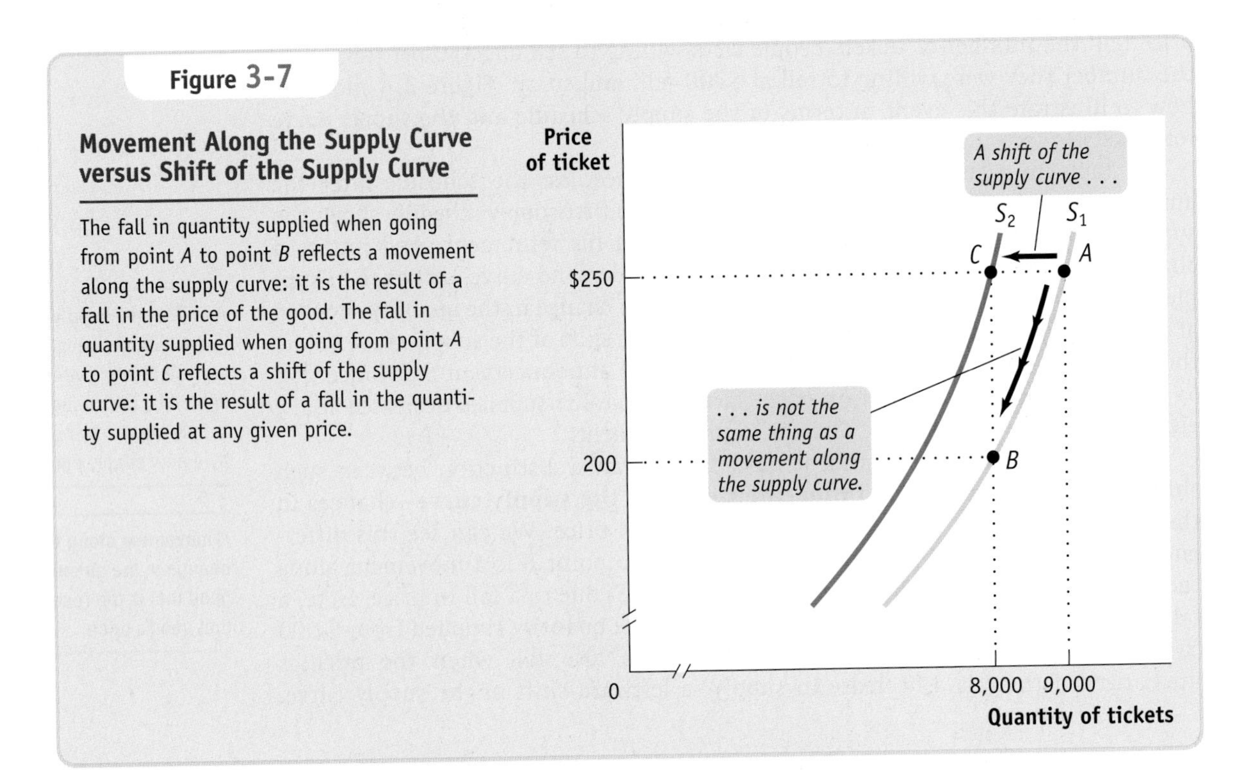

Understanding Shifts of the Supply Curve

Figure 3-8 illustrates the two basic ways in which supply curves can shift. When economists talk about an "increase in supply", they mean a *rightward* shift of the supply curve: at any given price, people will supply a larger quantity of the good than before. This is shown in Figure 3-8 by the shift to the right of the original supply curve S_1 to S_2. And when economists talk about a "decrease in supply", they mean a *leftward* shift of the supply curve: at any given price, people supply a smaller quantity of the good than before. This is represented in Figure 3-8 by the leftward shift of S_1 to S_3.

Economists believe that shifts of supply curves are mainly the result of four factors (though, as in the case of demand, there are other possible causes):

- Changes in input prices
- Changes in technology
- Changes in the number of suppliers
- Changes in expectations

An **input** is a good that is used to produce another good.

Changes in Input Prices To produce output, you need inputs—for example, to make vanilla ice cream you need vanilla beans, cream, sugar, and so on. (Actually, you only need vanilla beans to make *good* vanilla ice cream; see Economics in Action on page 78.) An **input** is any good that is used to produce another good. Inputs, like output, have prices. And an increase in the price of an input makes the production of the final good more costly for those who produce and sell the good. So sellers are less willing to supply the good at any given price, and the supply curve shifts to the left. For example, newspaper publishers buy large quantities of newsprint (the paper on which newspapers are printed). When newsprint prices rose sharply in 1994–1995, the supply of newspapers fell: several newspapers went out of business, and a number of new

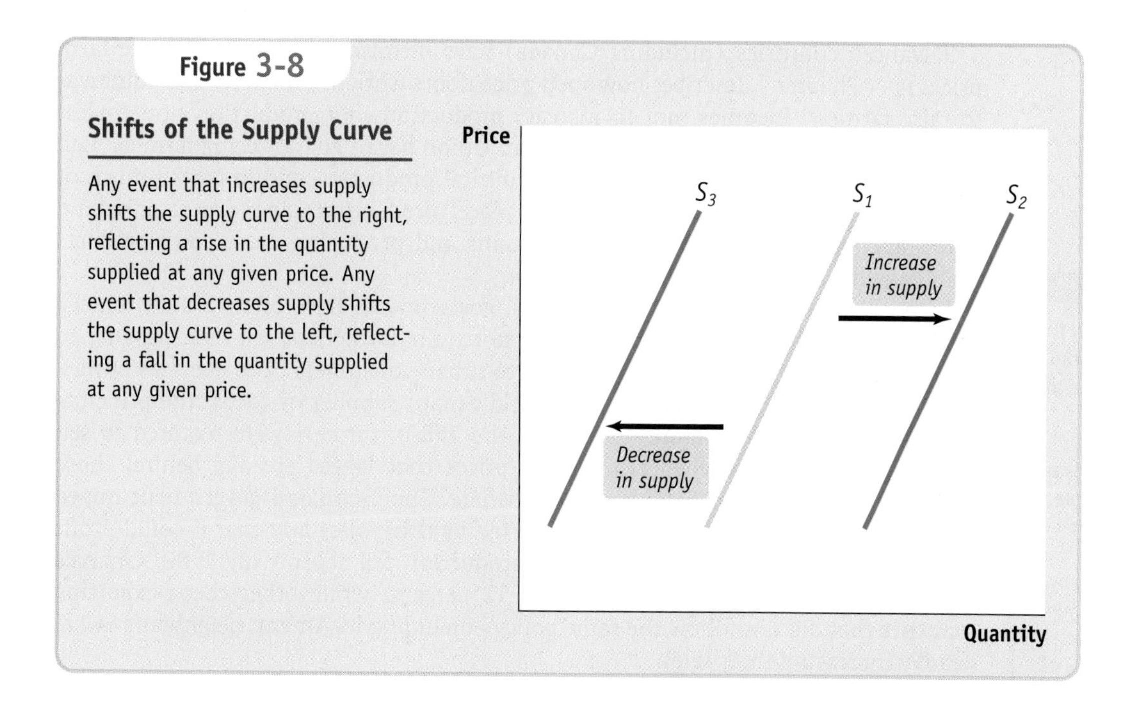

Figure 3-8

Shifts of the Supply Curve

Any event that increases supply shifts the supply curve to the right, reflecting a rise in the quantity supplied at any given price. Any event that decreases supply shifts the supply curve to the left, reflecting a fall in the quantity supplied at any given price.

publishing ventures were cancelled. Similarly, a fall in the price of an input makes the production of the final good less costly for sellers. They are more willing to supply the good at any given price, and the supply curve shifts to the right.

Changes in Technology When economists talk about "technology", they don't necessarily mean high technology—they mean all the ways that people can turn inputs into useful goods. The whole complex of activities that turns wheat from a Saskatchewan farm into toast on your breakfast table is technology in this sense. And when a better technology becomes available, reducing the cost of production—that is, letting a producer spend less on inputs, yet produce the same output—supply increases, and the supply curve shifts to the right. For example, an improved strain of corn that is more resistant to disease makes farmers willing to supply more corn at any given price.

Changes in the Number of Suppliers. Given input prices and technology, the more firms that produce a good, the greater is the supply of that good. As firms enter an industry, supply in that industry increases. As firms leave an industry, supply decreases. As we will see in Chapter 9, firms enter and leave an industry in response to profit signals. Profits encourage entry; losses encourage exit.

Changes in Expectations Imagine that you had a ticket for the April 15th game but couldn't go. You'd want to sell the ticket to a scalper. But if you heard a credible rumour about Gretzky's imminent retirement, you would know that the ticket would soon skyrocket in value. So you would hold off on selling the ticket until his decision to retire was made public. This illustrates how expectations can alter supply: an expectation that the price of a good will be higher in the future causes supply to decrease today, but an expectation that the price of a good will be lower in the future causes supply to increase today.

economics in action

Down (and Up) on the Farm

Many countries have designed farm policies based on the belief—or maybe the hope—that producers *won't* respond much to changes in the price of their product. But they have found out, to their dismay, that the price does indeed matter.

Advanced countries (including Canada) have historically tried to legislate farm prices *up*. (Chapter 4 describes how such price floors work in practice.) The point was to raise farmers' incomes, not to increase production—but production nonetheless did go up. Until the nations of the European Union began guaranteeing farmers high prices in the 1960s, they had limited agricultural production and imported much of their food. Once price supports were in place, production expanded rapidly, and European farmers began growing more grains and producing more dairy products than consumers wanted to buy.

In poorer countries, especially in Africa, governments have often sought to keep farm prices *down*. The typical strategy was to require farmers to sell their produce to a "marketing board", which then resold it to urban consumers or to overseas buyers. A famous example is Ghana, once the world's main supplier of cocoa, the principal ingredient in chocolate. From 1965 until the 1980s, farmers were required to sell their cocoa beans to the government at prices that lagged steadily behind those chocolate manufacturers were paying elsewhere. The Ghanaian government hoped that cocoa production would be little affected by this policy and that it could profit by buying low and selling high. In fact, production fell sharply. By 1980, Ghana's share of the world market was down to 12 percent, while other cocoa-exporting countries that did not follow the same policy—including its African neighbours—were steadily increasing their sales.

Today Europe is trying to reform its agricultural policy, and most developing countries have already abandoned their efforts to hold farm prices down. Governments seem finally to have learned that supply curves really do slope upwards, after all. ■

>>QUICK REVIEW

- The *supply schedule* shows how the *quantity supplied* depends on the price. The relationship between the two is illustrated by the *supply curve*.
- Supply curves are normally upward sloping: at a higher price, people are willing to supply more of the good.
- A change in price results in a *movement along the supply curve* and a change in the quantity supplied.
- As with demand, when economists talk of increases or decreases in supply, they mean *shifts of the supply curve*, not changes in the quantity supplied. An increase in supply is a rightward shift: the quantity supplied rises for any given price. A decrease in supply is a leftward shift: the quantity supplied falls for any given price.
- The four main factors that can shift the supply curve are changes in (1) input prices, (2) technology, (3) the number of suppliers, and (4) expectations.

>>CHECK YOUR UNDERSTANDING 3-2

1. Explain whether each of the following events represents (i) a *shift* of the supply curve or (ii) a *movement along* the supply curve.
   a. More homeowners put their houses up for sale during a real estate boom that causes house prices to rise.
   b. Many strawberry farmers open temporary roadside stands during harvest season, even though prices are usually low at that time.
   c. Immediately after the school year begins, fast-food chains must raise wages to attract workers.
   d. Many construction workers temporarily move to provinces that have suffered forest fire damage, lured by the hope of higher wages.
   e. Since new technologies have made it possible to build larger cruise ships (which are cheaper to run per passenger), Vancouver-to-Alaska cruise lines have offered more berths, at lower prices, than before.

Solutions appear at back of book.

Supply, Demand, and Equilibrium

We have now covered the first three key elements in the supply and demand model: the supply curve, the demand curve, and the set of factors that shift each curve. The next step is to put these elements together to show how they can be used to predict the actual price at which a good will be bought and sold.

What determines the price at which a good is bought and sold? In Chapter 1 we learned the general principle that *markets move toward equilibrium*, a situation in which no individual would be better off taking a different action. In the case of a competitive market, we can be more specific: a competitive market is in equilibrium when the price has moved to a level at which the quantity demanded of a good equals the quantity supplied of that good. At that price, no individual seller could make herself better off by offering to sell either more or less of the good and no individual buyer could make himself better off by offering to buy more or less of the good.

The price that matches the quantity supplied and the quantity demanded is the **equilibrium price;** the quantity bought and sold at that price is the **equilibrium quantity.** The equilibrium price is also known as the **market-clearing price:** it is the price that "clears the market" by ensuring that every buyer willing to pay that price finds a seller willing to sell at that price, and vice versa.

You may notice from this point on that we will no longer focus on middlemen such as scalpers but focus directly on the market price and quantity. Why? Because the function of a middleman is to bring buyers and sellers together to trade. But what makes buyers and sellers willing to trade is in reality not the middleman, but the price they agree upon—the equilibrium price. By going deeper and examining how price functions within a market, we can safely assume that the middlemen are doing their job and leave them in the background.

So, how do we find the equilibrium price and quantity?

A competitive market is in equilibrium when price has moved to a level at which the quantity demanded of a good equals the quantity supplied of that good. The price at which this takes place is the **equilibrium price,** also referred to as the **market-clearing price.** The quantity of the good bought and sold at that price is the **equilibrium quantity.**

Finding the Equilibrium Price and Quantity

The easiest way to determine the equilibrium price and quantity in a market is by putting the supply curve and the demand curve on the same diagram. Since the supply curve shows the quantity supplied at any given price and the demand curve shows the quantity demanded at any given price, the price at which the two curves cross is the equilibrium price: the price at which quantity supplied equals quantity demanded.

Figure 3-9 combines the demand curve from Figure 3-1 and the supply curve from Figure 3-5. They *intersect* at point *E*, which is the equilibrium of this market; that is, $250 is the equilibrium price and 8,000 tickets is the equilibrium quantity.

PITFALLS

BOUGHT *AND* SOLD?

We have been talking about the price at which a good is bought *and* sold, as if the two were the same. But shouldn't we make a distinction between the price received by sellers and that paid by buyers? In principle, yes; but it is helpful at this point to sacrifice a bit of realism in the interest of simplicity—by assuming away the difference between the prices received by sellers and those paid by buyers. In reality, people who sell hockey tickets to scalpers, although they sometimes receive high prices, generally receive less than those who eventually buy these tickets pay. No mystery there: that difference is how a scalper, or any "middleman"—someone who brings buyers and sellers together—makes a living. In many markets, however, the difference between the buying and selling price is quite small. It is therefore not a bad approximation to think of the price paid by buyers as being the *same* as the price received by sellers. And that is what we will assume in the remainder of this chapter.

Figure 3-9

Market Equilibrium

Market equilibrium occurs at point *E*, where the supply curve and the demand curve intersect. In equilibrium, the quantity demanded is equal to the quantity supplied. In this market, the equilibrium price is $250 and the equilibrium quantity is 8,000 tickets. >*web*...

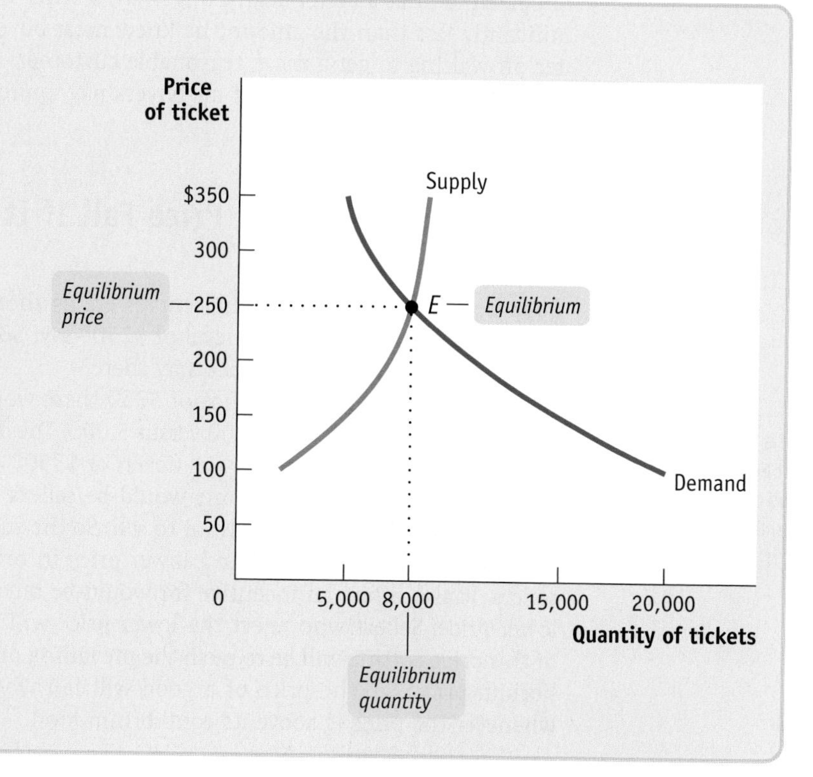

Let's confirm that point *E* fits our definition of equilibrium. At a price of $250 per ticket, 8,000 ticket-holders are willing to resell their tickets and 8,000 people who do not have tickets are willing to buy. So at the price of $250 the quantity of tickets supplied equals the quantity demanded. Notice that at any other price the market would not clear: every willing buyer would not be able to find a willing seller, or vice versa. In other words, if the price were more than $250, the quantity supplied would exceed the quantity demanded. If the price were less than $250, the quantity demanded would exceed the quantity supplied.

The model of supply and demand, then, predicts that given the demand and supply curves shown in Figure 3-9, 8,000 tickets would change hands at a price of $250 each.

But how can we be sure that the market will arrive at the equilibrium price? We begin by answering three simpler questions:

1. Why do all sales and purchases in a market take place at the same price?
2. Why does the market price fall if it is above the equilibrium price?
3. Why does the market price rise if it is below the equilibrium price?

Why Do All Sales and Purchases in a Market Take Place at the Same Price?

There are some markets where the same good can sell for many different prices, depending on who is selling or who is buying. For example, have you ever bought a souvenir in a "tourist trap" and then seen the same item on sale somewhere else (perhaps even in the next store) for a lower price? Because tourists don't know which shops offer the best deals and don't have time for comparison shopping, sellers in tourist areas can charge different prices for the same good.

But in any market where the buyers and sellers have both been around for some time, sales and purchases tend to converge at a generally uniform price, so that we can safely talk about *the* market price. It's easy to see why. Suppose a seller offered a potential buyer a price noticeably above what the buyer knew other people to be paying. The buyer would clearly be better off shopping elsewhere—unless the seller was prepared to offer a better deal. Conversely, a seller would not be willing to sell for significantly less than the amount he knew most buyers were paying; he would be better off waiting to get a more reasonable customer. So in any well-established, active market, all sellers receive and all buyers pay approximately the same price. This is what we call the *market price*.

Why Does the Market Price Fall If It Is Above the Equilibrium Price?

Suppose the supply and demand curves are as shown in Figure 3-9, but the market price is above the equilibrium level of $250—say, $350. This situation is illustrated in Figure 3-10. Why can't the price stay there?

There is a **surplus** of a good when the quantity supplied exceeds the quantity demanded. Surpluses occur when the price is above its equilibrium level.

As the figure shows, at a price of $350 there would be more tickets available than hockey fans wanted to buy: 8,800 versus 5,000. The difference of 3,800 is the **surplus**—also known as the *excess supply*—of tickets at $350.

This surplus means that some would-be sellers are being frustrated: they cannot find anyone to buy what they want to sell. So the surplus offers an incentive for those 3,800 would-be sellers to offer a lower price in order to poach business from other sellers. It also offers an incentive for would-be buyers to seek a bargain by offering a lower price. Sellers who reject the lower price will fail to find buyers, and the result of this price cutting will be to push the prevailing price down until it reaches the equilibrium price. So, the price of a good will fall whenever there is a surplus—that is, whenever the price is above its equilibrium level.

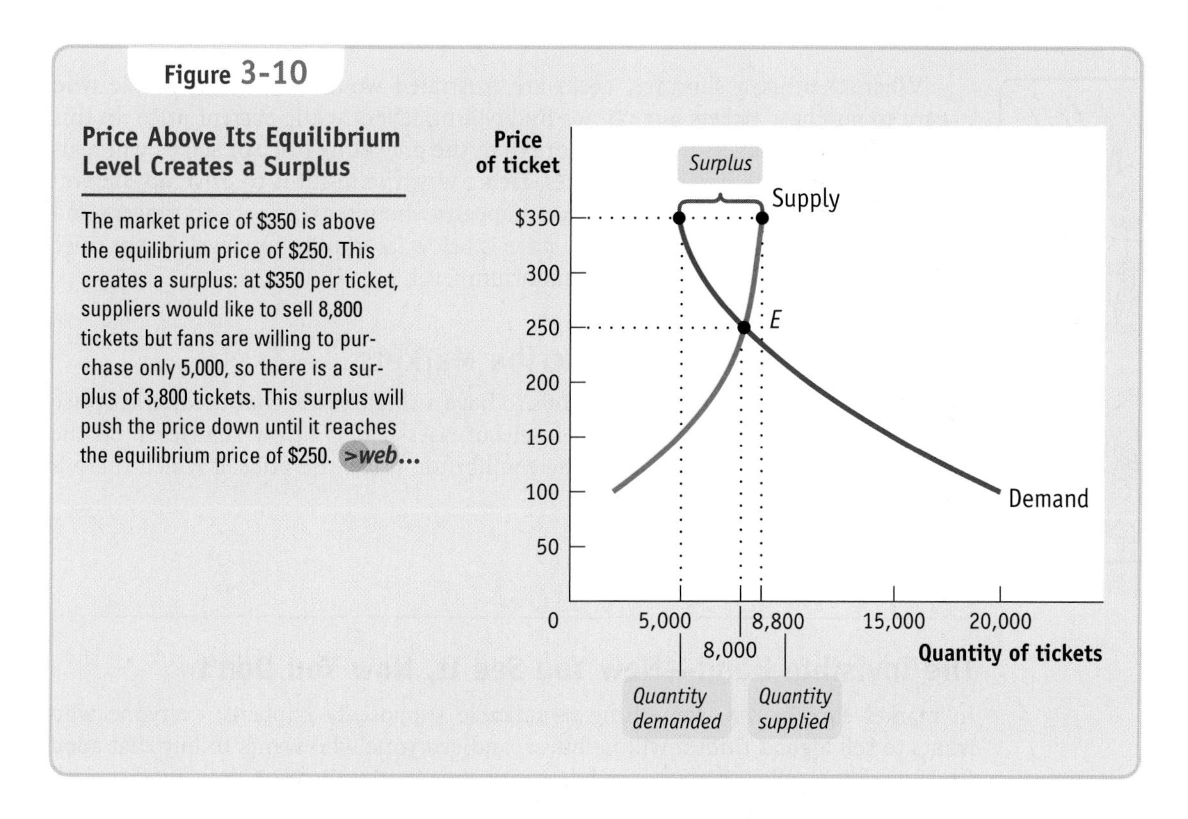

Figure 3-10

Price Above Its Equilibrium Level Creates a Surplus

The market price of $350 is above the equilibrium price of $250. This creates a surplus: at $350 per ticket, suppliers would like to sell 8,800 tickets but fans are willing to purchase only 5,000, so there is a surplus of 3,800 tickets. This surplus will push the price down until it reaches the equilibrium price of $250. >web...

Why Does the Market Price Rise If It Is Below the Equilibrium Price?

Now suppose the price is below its equilibrium level—say, at $150 per ticket, as shown in Figure 3-11. In this case, the quantity demanded (15,000 tickets) exceeds the quantity supplied (5,000 tickets), implying that there are 10,000 would-be buyers who cannot find tickets: there is a **shortage,** also known as an *excess demand,* of 10,000 tickets.

There is a **shortage** of a good when the quantity demanded exceeds the quantity supplied. Shortages occur when the price is below its equilibrium level.

Figure 3-11

Price Below Its Equilibrium Level Creates a Shortage

The market price of $150 is below the equilibrium price of $250. This creates a shortage: fans want to buy 15,000 tickets but only 5,000 are offered for sale, so there is a shortage of 10,000 tickets. This shortage will push the price up until it reaches the equilibrium price of $250. >web...

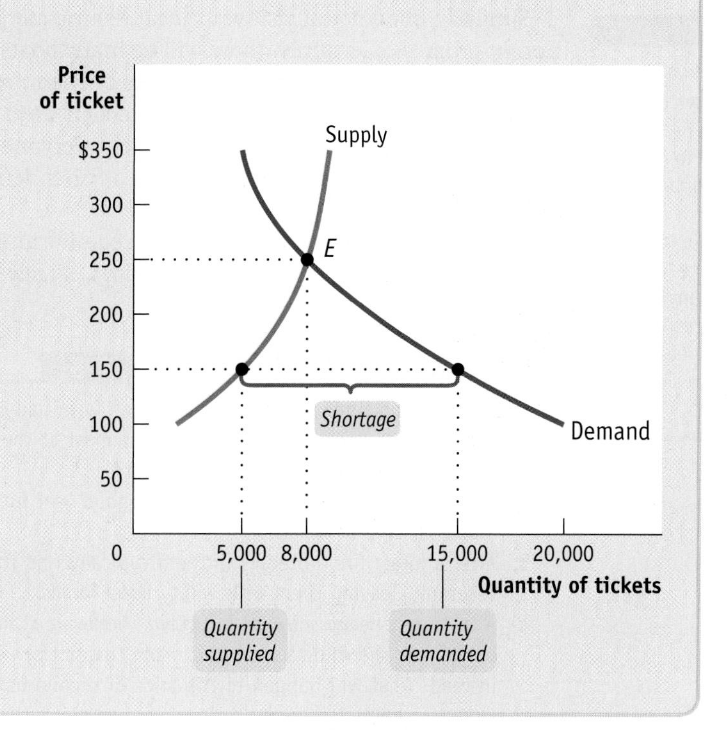

When there is a shortage, there are frustrated would-be buyers—people who want to purchase tickets but cannot find willing sellers at the current price. In this situation, either buyers will offer more than the prevailing price or sellers will realize that they can charge higher prices. Either way, the result is to drive up the prevailing price. This bidding up of prices happens whenever there are shortages—and there will be shortages whenever the price is below its equilibrium level. So the price will always rise if it is below the equilibrium level.

Using Equilibrium to Describe Markets

We have now seen that a market tends to have a single price; that the market price falls if it is above the equilibrium level but rises if it is below that level. So the market price always *moves toward* the equilibrium price, the price at which there is neither surplus nor shortage.

economics in action

The Invisible Hand—Now You See It, Now You Don't

In market equilibrium, something remarkable supposedly happens: everyone who wants to sell a good finds a willing buyer, and everyone who wants to buy that good finds a willing seller. It's a beautiful theory—but is it realistic? Can a market with nobody in charge really match up sellers and buyers?

As educators, we love graphic, visual examples. Prior to 1997, perhaps the best example would have been the trading floor of a stock exchange. Even better, had you lived close to one of Canada's five stock exchanges (Toronto, Montreal, Winnipeg, Calgary, and Vancouver) you could have visited and watched in amazement at how the traders—clutching bits of paper and screaming at each other from across the floor—accomplished their trades and established market-clearing prices. But alas, this is no more. Since 1997, all the traders sit in front of computer terminals. You can still visit, and the traders still succeed in establishing market-clearing prices, but now there is nothing much to see.

Similarly, should you visit your local fishing pier, you probably will not see an auction in progress. Certainly, there will be many boats unloading their catches; and certainly there will be many buyers—scores of them, mostly middlemen wanting to buy in large quantities. You won't see much (if any) haggling, since the market very quickly establishes the going price, which everyone knows. If a buyer offered a price below that, no one would sell to him; if a fisher demanded a price above that, no one would buy from him.

So, the tendency for markets to reach equilibrium isn't just theoretical speculation. Market forces are powerful—and nowadays, largely invisible. ■

>> QUICK REVIEW

- Price in a competitive market moves to the *equilibrium price*, or *market-clearing price*, where the quantity supplied is equal to the quantity demanded. This quantity is the *equilibrium quantity*.
- All sales and purchases in a market take place at the same price. If the price is above its equilibrium level, there is a *surplus* that drives the price down. If the price is below its equilibrium level, there is a *shortage* that drives the price up.

>> CHECK YOUR UNDERSTANDING 3-3

1. In the following three situations, the market is initially in equilibrium. After each event described below, does a surplus or shortage exist at the original equilibrium price? What will happen to the equilibrium price as a result?
   a. Due to good weather, 1997 was a very good year for Prairie wheat growers, who produced a bumper crop of wheat.
   b. After a forest fire, hoteliers in Banff typically find that many vacationers cancel their vacations, leaving them with empty hotel rooms.
   c. After a very heavy snowfall in Ottawa, hardware store owners find that they quickly sell out of new snowblowers, so that many customers want to buy second-hand snowblowers instead. What will happen to the price of second-hand snowblowers?

Solutions appear at back of book.

Changes in Supply and Demand

Wayne Gretzky's announcement that he was retiring may have come as a surprise, but the subsequent rise in the price of scalped tickets for his last Canadian game was no surprise at all. Suddenly the number of people who wanted to buy tickets at any given price increased—that is, there was an increase in demand. And at the same time, because those who already had tickets wanted to see Gretzky's last game, they became less willing to sell them—that is, there was a decrease in supply.

In this case, there was an event that shifted both the supply and the demand curves. However, in many cases something happens that shifts only one of the curves. For example, a freeze in Florida reduces the supply of oranges, but doesn't change the demand for oranges. A medical report suggesting that eggs are bad for your health reduces the demand for eggs, but does not affect the supply. That is, events often shift either the supply curve or the demand curve, but not both; it is therefore useful to ask what happens in each case.

We have seen that when a curve shifts, the equilibrium price and quantity change. We will now concentrate on exactly how the shift of a curve alters the equilibrium price and quantity.

What Happens When the Demand Curve Shifts

Coffee and tea are substitutes: if the price of tea rises, the demand for coffee will increase, and if the price of tea falls, the demand for coffee will decrease. But how does the price of tea affect the *market* for coffee?

Figure 3-12 shows the effect of a rise in the price of tea on the market for coffee. The rise in the price of tea increases the demand for coffee. Point E_1 shows the equilibrium corresponding to the original demand curve, with P_1 the equilibrium price and Q_1 the equilibrium quantity bought and sold.

An increase in demand is indicated by a *rightward* shift of the demand curve from D_1 to D_2. At the original market price P_1, this market is no longer in equilibrium: a shortage occurs because the quantity demanded exceeds the quantity supplied. So the

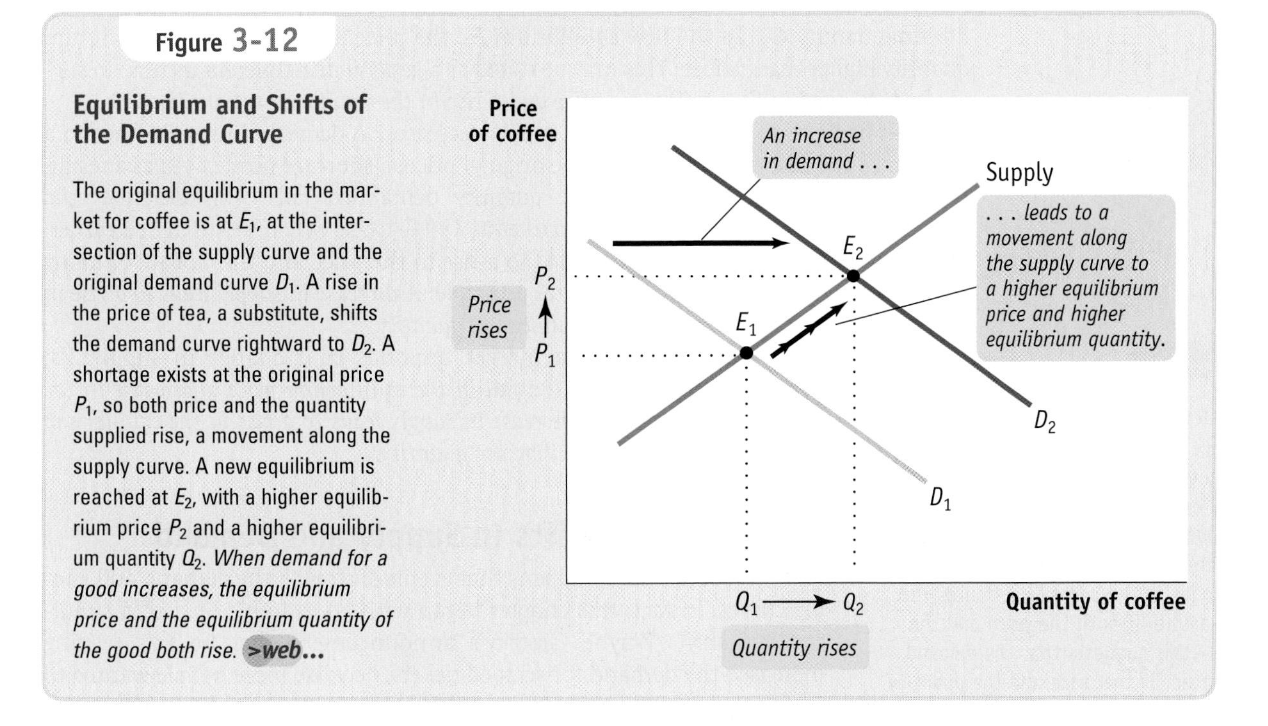

Figure 3-12

Equilibrium and Shifts of the Demand Curve

The original equilibrium in the market for coffee is at E_1, at the intersection of the supply curve and the original demand curve D_1. A rise in the price of tea, a substitute, shifts the demand curve rightward to D_2. A shortage exists at the original price P_1, so both price and the quantity supplied rise, a movement along the supply curve. A new equilibrium is reached at E_2, with a higher equilibrium price P_2 and a higher equilibrium quantity Q_2. *When demand for a good increases, the equilibrium price and the equilibrium quantity of the good both rise.* **>web...**

price of coffee rises and generates an increase in the quantity supplied, an upward *movement along the supply curve.* A new equilibrium is established at point E_2, with a higher equilibrium price P_2 and higher equilibrium quantity Q_2. This sequence of events reflects a general principle: *When demand for a good increases, the equilibrium price and the equilibrium quantity of the good both rise.*

And what would happen in the reverse case, a fall in the price of tea? A fall in the price of tea decreases the demand for coffee, shifting the demand curve to the *left*. At the original price, a surplus occurs as quantity supplied exceeds quantity demanded. The price falls and leads to a decrease in the quantity supplied, with a lower equilibrium price and a lower equilibrium quantity. This illustrates another general principle: *When demand for a good decreases, the equilibrium price of the good and the equilibrium quantity both fall.*

To summarize how a market responds to a change in demand: *An increase in demand leads to a rise in both the equilibrium price and the equilibrium quantity. A decrease in demand leads to a fall in both the equilibrium price and the equilibrium quantity.*

What Happens When the Supply Curve Shifts

In the real world, it is a bit easier to predict changes in supply than changes in demand. Physical factors that affect supply, like the availability of inputs, are easier to get a handle on than the fickle tastes that affect demand. Still, with supply as with demand, what we really know are the *effects* of shifts of the supply curve.

A spectacular example of a change in technology increasing supply occurred in the manufacture of semiconductors—the silicon chips that are the core of computers, video games, and many other devices. In the early 1970s, engineers learned how to use a process known as photolithography to put microscopic electronic components onto a silicon chip; subsequent progress in the technique has allowed ever more components to be put on each chip. Figure 3-13 shows the effect of such an innovation on the market for silicon chips. The demand curve does not change. The original equilibrium is at E_1, the point of intersection of the original supply curve S_1 and the demand curve, with equilibrium price P_1 and equilibrium quantity Q_1. As a result of the technological change, supply increases and S_1 shifts rightward to S_2. At the original price P_1, a surplus of chips now exists and the market is no longer in equilibrium. The surplus causes a fall in price and a rise in quantity demanded, a downward movement along the demand curve. The new equilibrium is at E_2, with an equilibrium price P_2 and an equilibrium quantity Q_2. In the new equilibrium E_2, the price is lower and the equilibrium quantity higher than before. This may be stated as a general principle: *An increase in supply leads to a fall in the equilibrium price and a rise in the equilibrium quantity.*

What happens to the market when supply decreases? A decrease in supply leads to a *leftward* shift of the supply curve. At the original price, a shortage now exists; as a result, the equilibrium price rises, and the quantity demanded falls. This describes the sequence of events in the newspaper market in 1994–1995, which we discussed earlier: a decrease in the supply of newsprint led to a rise in the price and the closure of many newspapers. We can formulate a general principle: *A decrease in supply leads to a rise in the equilibrium price and a fall in the equilibrium quantity.*

To summarize how a market responds to a change in supply: *An increase in supply leads to a fall in the equilibrium price and a rise in the equilibrium quantity. A decrease in supply leads to a rise in the equilibrium price and a fall in the equilibrium quantity.*

PITFALLS

WHICH CURVE IS IT, ANYWAY?

When the price of some good changes, in general we can say that this reflects a change in either supply or demand. But it is easy to get confused about which one. A helpful clue is the direction of change in the quantity. If the quantity sold changes in the *same* direction as the price—for example, if both the price and the quantity rise—this suggests that the demand curve has shifted. If the price and the quantity move in *opposite* directions, the likely cause is a shift in the supply curve.

Simultaneous Shifts in Supply and Demand

Finally, it sometimes happens that events shift *both* the demand and supply curves. In fact, this chapter began with an example of such a simultaneous shift. Wayne Gretzky's announcement that he was retiring increased the demand for scalped tickets, because more people wanted to see him play one last time; but it also decreased the supply because those who already had tickets became less willing to part with them.

Figure 3-13

Equilibrium and Shifts of the Supply Curve

The original equilibrium in the market for silicon chips is at E_1, at the intersection of the demand curve and the original supply curve S_1. After a technological change increases the supply of silicon chips, the supply curve shifts rightward to S_2. A surplus exists at the original price P_1, so price falls and the quantity demanded rises, a movement along the demand curve. A new equilibrium is reached at E_2, with a lower equilibrium price P_2 and a higher equilibrium quantity Q_2. *When supply of a good increases, the equilibrium price of the good falls and the equilibrium quantity rises.* **>web...**

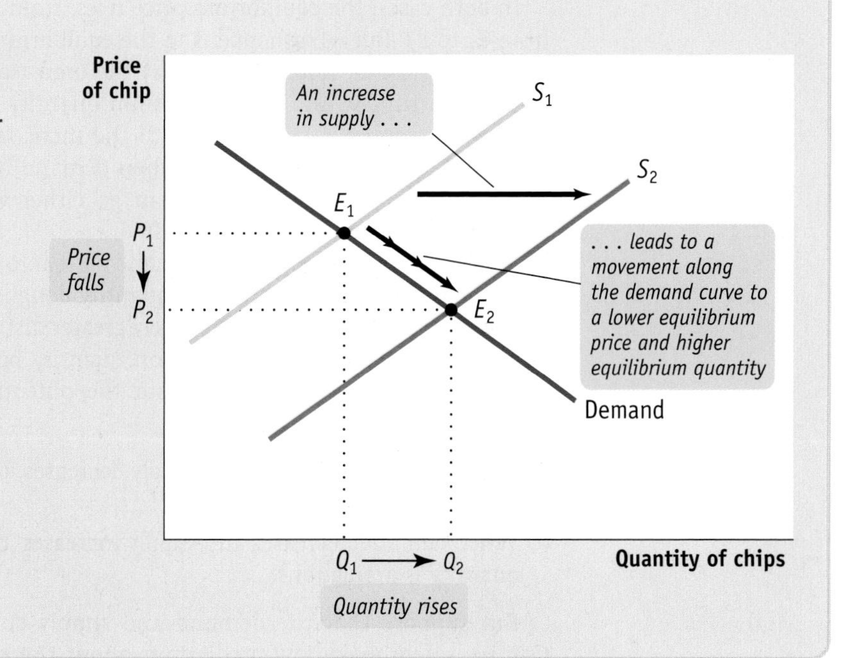

Figure 3-14 illustrates what happened. In both panels we show an increase in demand—that is, a rightward shift of the demand curve, from D_1 to D_2. Notice that the rightward shift in panel (a) is relatively larger than the one in panel (b). Both panels also show a decrease in supply—that is, a leftward shift of the supply curve, from S_1 to S_2. Notice that the leftward shift in panel (b) is relatively larger than the one in panel (a).

Figure 3-14 Simultaneous Shifts of the Demand and Supply Curves

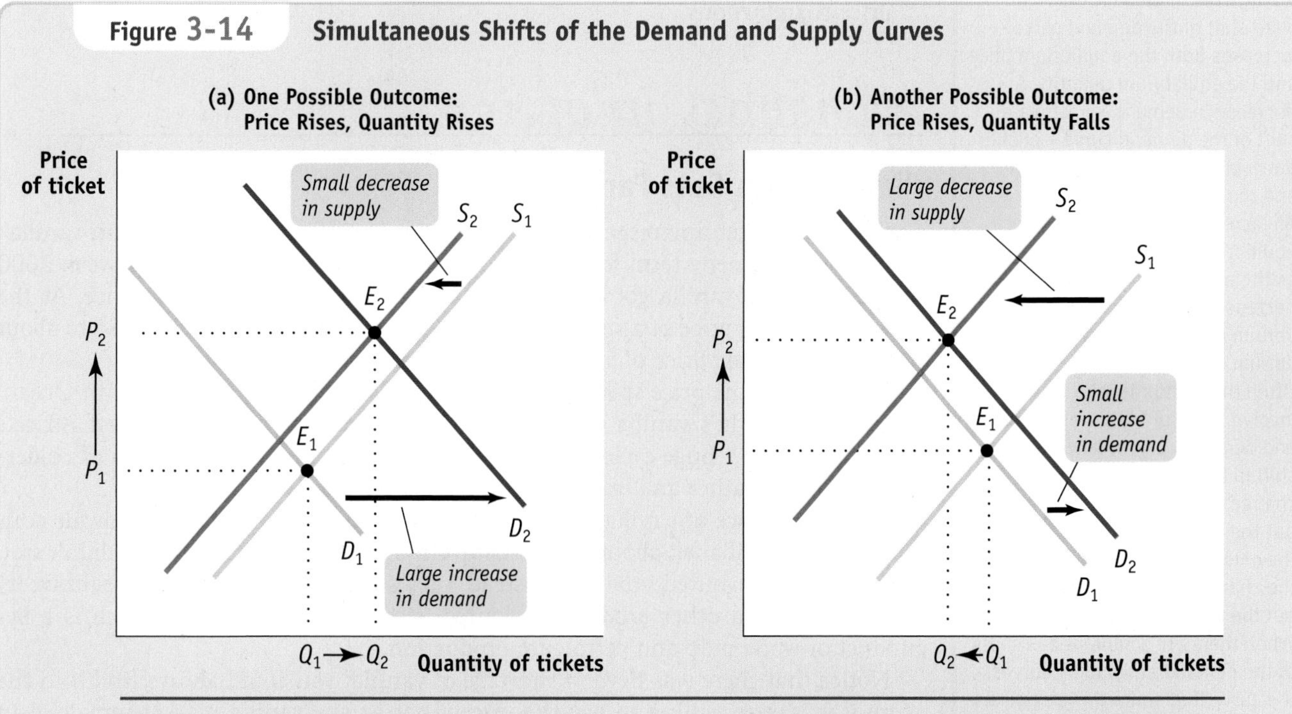

In panel (a) there is a simultaneous rightward shift of the demand curve and leftward shift of the supply curve. Here the increase in demand is relatively larger than the decrease in supply, so the equilibrium price and equilibrium quantity both rise.

In panel (b) there is also a simultaneous rightward shift of the demand curve and leftward shift of the supply curve. Here the decrease in supply is relatively larger than the increase in demand, so the equilibrium price rises and the equilibrium quantity falls.

In both cases, the equilibrium price rises, from P_1 to P_2, as the equilibrium moves from E_1 to E_2. But what happens to the equilibrium quantity, the quantity of scalped tickets bought and sold? In panel (a) the increase in demand is large relative to the decrease in supply, and the equilibrium quantity rises as a result. In panel (b) the decrease in supply is large relative to the increase in demand, and the equilibrium quantity falls as a result. That is, when demand increases and supply decreases, the actual quantity bought and sold can go either way, depending on *how much* the demand and supply curves have shifted.

In general, when supply and demand shift in opposite directions, we can't predict what the ultimate effect will be on quantity bought and sold. What we can say is that a curve that shifts a disproportionately greater distance than the other curve will have a disproportionately greater effect on quantity bought and sold. That said, we can make the following prediction about the outcome when the supply and demand curves shift in opposite directions:

- When demand increases and supply decreases, the price rises but the change in the quantity is ambiguous.
- When demand decreases and supply increases, the price falls but the change in the quantity is ambiguous.

But suppose that the demand and supply curves shift in the same direction. Can we safely make any predictions about the changes in price and quantity? In this situation, the change in quantity bought and sold can be predicted but the change in price is ambiguous. The two possible outcomes when the supply and demand curves shift in the same direction (which you should check for yourself) are as follows:

- When both demand and supply increase, the quantity increases but the change in price is ambiguous.
- When both demand and supply decrease, the quantity decreases but the change in price is ambiguous.

economics in action

Plain Vanilla Gets Fancy

Vanilla doesn't get any respect. It's such a common flavouring that "plain vanilla" has become a generic term for ordinary, unembellished products. But between 2000 and 2003, plain vanilla got quite fancy—at least if you looked at the price. At the supermarket, the price of a small bottle of vanilla extract rose from about $5 to about $15. The wholesale price of vanilla beans rose 400 percent.

The cause of the price spike was bad weather—not here, but in the Indian Ocean. Most of the world's vanilla comes from Madagascar, an island nation off Africa's southeast coast. A huge cyclone struck there in 2000, and a combination of colder-than-normal weather and excessive rain impeded recovery.

The higher price of vanilla led to a fall in the quantity demanded: worldwide consumption of vanilla fell about 35 percent from 2000 to 2003. Consumers didn't stop eating vanilla-flavoured products; instead, they switched (often without realizing it) to ice cream and other products flavoured with synthetic vanillin, which is a by-product of wood pulp and petroleum production.

Notice that there was never a shortage of vanilla: you could always find it in the store if you were willing to pay the price. That is, the vanilla market remained in equilibrium. ■

QUICK REVIEW

- Changes in the equilibrium price and quantity in a market are the result of shifts in the supply curve, in the demand curve, or both.
- An increase in demand—a rightward shift of the demand curve—increases both the equilibrium price and the equilibrium quantity. A decrease in demand—a leftward shift of the demand curve—pushes down both the equilibrium price and the equilibrium quantity.
- An increase in supply drives the equilibrium price down but increases the equilibrium quantity. A decrease in supply raises the equilibrium price but reduces the equilibrium quantity.
- Often the fluctuations in markets involve shifts of both the supply and demand curves. When they shift in the same direction, the change in quantity is predictable but the change in price is not. When they move in opposite directions, the change in price is predictable but the change in quantity is not. When there are simultaneous shifts of the demand and supply curves, the curve that shifts the greater distance has a greater effect on the change in price and quantity.

FOR INQUIRING MINDS

SUPPLY, DEMAND, AND CONTROLLED SUBSTANCES

The big "issue" movie of the year 2000 was *Traffic*, a panoramic treatment of the drug trade. The movie was loosely based on the 1989 British TV miniseries *Traffik*. Despite the lapse of 11 years, the basic outlines of the situation—in which the drug trade flourishes despite laws that are supposed to prevent it—had not changed. Not only has the so-called "war on drugs" by law enforcement officials not succeeded in eliminating the trade in illegal drugs; according to most assessments, it has not even done much to reduce consumption.

The failure of the war on drugs has a historical precedent: during the era known as Prohibition, the sale and consumption of alcohol was illegal. In the United States this period lasted from 1919 to 1933, but it was much shorter in Canada. Quebec and British Columbia were the first to reject it, as early as 1920, while most of the remaining provinces were "wet" by 1927. This early rejection of prohibition in Canada created quite an export opportunity for Canadian breweries and distilleries! Indeed, legend has it that at least one famous Canadian family fortune began with old-fashioned smuggling and rum running to the States. Canadian suppliers, as well as U.S. domestic "bootleggers", ensured that liquor remained widely available in the United States throughout the Prohibition era. In fact, by 1929 U.S. per capita consumption of alcohol was higher than it had been a decade earlier. As with illegal drugs today, the production and distribution of the banned substance became a large enterprise that flourished despite its illegality.

Why is it so hard to choke off markets in alcohol and drugs? Think of the war on drugs as a policy that shifts the supply curve but has not done much to shift the demand curve.

Although it is illegal to use drugs such as cocaine, just as it was once illegal to drink alcohol, in practice the war on drugs focuses mainly on the suppliers. As a result, the cost of supplying drugs includes the risk of being caught and sent to jail (and, in some countries, perhaps even of being executed). This undoubtedly reduces the quantity of drugs supplied *at any given price;* in effect shifting the supply curve for drugs to the left. In Figure 3-15, this is shown as a shift in the supply curve from S_1 to S_2. If the war on drugs had no effect on the price of drugs, and the price remained at P_1, this leftward shift would reflect a reduction in the quantity of drugs supplied equal in magnitude to the leftward shift of supply.

But as we have seen, when the supply curve for a good shifts to the left, the effect is to raise the market price of that good. In Figure 3-15 the effect of the war on drugs would be to move the equilibrium from E_1 to E_2, and to raise the price of drugs from P_1 to P_2, a movement along the demand curve. Because the market price rises, the actual decline in the quantity of drugs supplied is less than the decline in the quantity that would have been supplied at the original price.

The crucial reason Prohibition was so ineffective was that as the market price of alcohol rose, consumers trimmed back only slightly on their consumption—yet the higher prices were enough to induce many potential suppliers to take the risk of jail time. So while Prohibition raised the price of alcohol, it did not do much to reduce consumption. Unfortunately, the same seems to be true of current drug policy. The policy raises the price of drugs to those who use them, but this does not do much to discourage consumption. Meanwhile, the higher prices are enough to induce suppliers to provide drugs despite the penalties. (By the way, despite recent talk in Canada of decriminalizing use of small amounts of cannabis, penalties are expected to remain severe for dealing.)

What is the answer? Some argue that policy should be refocused on the demand side—more anti-drug education, more counselling, and so on. If these policies worked, they would shift demand to the left. Others argue that drugs, like alcohol, should be made legal but heavily taxed. While the debate goes on, so does the war on drugs.

Figure 3-15

Effects of the War on Drugs

The war on drugs shifts the supply curve to the left. However, we can see by comparing the original equilibrium E_1 with the new equilibrium E_2 that the actual reduction in the quantity of drugs supplied is much smaller than the shift of the supply curve. The equilibrium price rises from P_1 to P_2—a movement along the demand curve. This leads suppliers to provide drugs despite the risks.

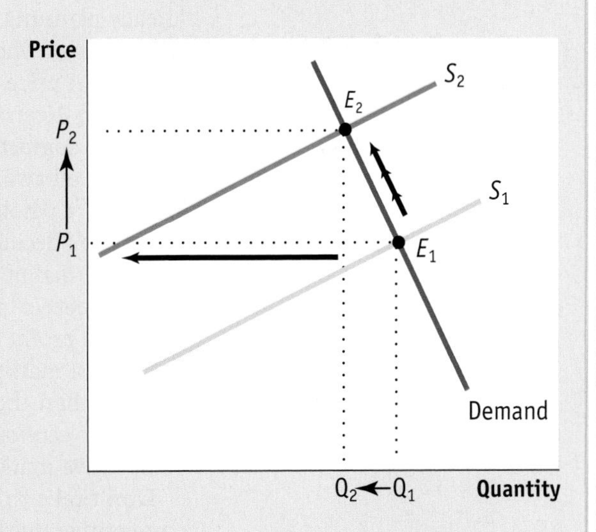

>>CHECK YOUR UNDERSTANDING 3-4

1. In each of the following examples, determine (i) the market in question; (ii) whether a shift in demand or supply occurred, the direction of the shift, and what induced the shift; and (iii) the effect of the shift on the equilibrium price and the equilibrium quantity.
   a. As the price of gasoline fell in Canada during the 1990s, auto dealers found that more auto buyers chose large cars.
   b. As technological innovation has lowered the cost of recycling used paper, fresh paper made from recycled stock is used more frequently.
   c. As a local cable company offers cheaper "pay-per-view" films, local movie theatres have more unfilled seats.
2. Periodically, a computer chip maker like Intel introduces a new chip that is faster than the previous one. In response, demand for computers using the earlier chip decreases as customers put off purchases in anticipation of machines containing the new chip. Simultaneously, computer makers increase their production of computers containing the earlier chip in order to clear out their stocks of those chips.

   Draw two diagrams of the market for computers containing the earlier chip: (a) one in which the equilibrium quantity falls in response to these events and (b) one in which the equilibrium quantity rises. What happens to the equilibrium price in each diagram?

Solutions appear at back of book.

Competitive Markets—and Others

Early in this chapter, we defined a competitive market and explained that the supply and demand framework is a model of competitive markets. But we took a rain check on the question of why it matters whether or not a market is competitive. Now that we've seen how the supply and demand model works, we can offer some explanation.

To understand why competitive markets are different from other markets, compare the problems facing two individuals: a wheat farmer who must decide whether to grow more wheat, and the president of a giant aluminium company—say, Alcan—who must decide whether to produce more aluminium.

For the wheat farmer, the question is simply whether the extra wheat can be sold at a price high enough to justify the extra production cost. The farmer need not worry about whether producing more wheat will affect the price of the wheat he or she was already planning to grow. That's because the wheat market is competitive. There are thousands of wheat farmers, and no one farmer's decision will have much impact on the market price.

For the Alcan executive, things are not that simple, because the aluminium market is *not* competitive. There are only a few big players, including Alcan, and each of them is well aware that its actions *do* have a noticeable impact on the market price. This adds a whole new level of complexity to the decisions producers have to make. Alcan can't decide whether or not to produce more aluminium just by asking whether the additional product will sell for more than it costs to make. The company also has to ask whether producing more aluminium will drive down the market price and reduce its profit.

When a market is competitive, individuals can base decisions on less complicated analyses than those used in a non-competitive market. This in turn means that it's easier for economists to build a model of a competitive market than of a non-competitive market.

Don't take this to mean that economic analysis has nothing to say about non-competitive markets. On the contrary, economists can offer some very important insights into how other kinds of markets work. But those insights require other models. In the next chapter, we will focus on what we can learn about competitive markets from the very useful model we have just developed: supply and demand.

• A LOOK AHEAD •

We've now developed a model that explains how markets arrive at prices, and why markets "work" in the sense that buyers can almost always find sellers, and vice versa. But this model could use a little more clarification.

Well, nothing demonstrates a principle quite as well as what happens when people try to defy it. And governments do, fairly often, try to defy the principles of supply and demand. In our next chapter, we consider what happens when they do—the revenge of the market.

SUMMARY

1. The **supply and demand model** illustrates how a **competitive market,** one with many buyers and sellers, works.
2. The **demand schedule** shows the **quantity demanded** at each price and is represented graphically by a **demand curve.** The **law of demand** says that demand curves slope downward.
3. A **movement along the demand curve** occurs when price changes and causes a change in quantity demanded. When economists talk of increasing or decreasing demand, they mean **shifts of the demand curve**—a change in the quantity demanded at any given price. An increase in demand causes a rightward shift of the demand curve. A decrease in demand causes a leftward shift.
4. There are five main factors that shift the demand curve:
   - A change in the prices of related goods, such as **substitutes** or **complements**
   - A change in income: when income rises, the demand for **normal goods** increases and the demand for **inferior goods** decreases
   - A change in tastes
   - A change in population
   - A change in expectations
5. The **supply schedule** shows the **quantity supplied** at each price and is represented graphically by a **supply curve.** Supply curves usually slope upward.
6. A **movement along the supply curve** occurs when price changes and causes a change in the quantity supplied. When economists talk of increasing or decreasing supply, they mean **shifts of the supply curve**—a change in the quantity supplied at any given price. An increase in supply causes a rightward shift of the supply curve. A decrease in supply causes a leftward shift.
7. There are four main factors that shift the supply curve:
   - A change in **input** prices
   - A change in technology
   - A change in the number of suppliers
   - A change in expectations
8. The supply and demand model is based on the principle that the price in a market moves to its **equilibrium price** or **market-clearing price,** the price at which the quantity demanded is equal to the quantity supplied. This quantity is called the **equilibrium quantity.** When the price is above its market-clearing level, there is a **surplus** that pushes the price down. When the price is below its market-clearing level, there is a **shortage** that pushes the price up.
9. An increase in demand increases both the equilibrium price and the equilibrium quantity; a decrease in demand has the opposite effect. An increase in supply reduces the equilibrium price and increases the equilibrium quantity; a decrease in supply has the opposite effect.
10. Shifts of the demand curve and the supply curve can happen simultaneously. When they shift in opposite directions, the change in price is predictable but the change in quantity is not. When they shift in the same direction, the change in quantity is predictable but the change in price is not. In general, the curve that shifts the greater distance has a greater effect on the changes in price and quantity.

KEY TERMS

Competitive market, p. 59
Supply and demand model, p. 59
Demand schedule, p. 60
Demand curve, p. 60
Quantity demanded, p. 60
Law of demand, p. 61
Shift of the demand curve, p. 62
Movement along the demand curve, p. 62
Substitutes, p. 63
Complements, p. 63
Normal good, p. 64
Inferior good, p. 64
Quantity supplied, p. 66
Supply schedule, p. 66
Supply curve, p. 66
Shift of the supply curve, p. 67
Movement along the supply curve, p. 67
Input, p. 68
Equilibrium price, p. 71
Equilibrium quantity, p. 71
Market-clearing price, p. 71
Surplus, p. 72
Shortage, p. 73

PROBLEMS

1. A survey indicated that chocolate ice cream is Canada's favourite ice-cream flavour. For each of the following, indicate the possible effects on demand and/or supply and the equilibrium price and quantity of chocolate ice cream.

a. A severe drought causes dairy farmers to reduce the number of milk-producing cattle in their stocks by a third. These dairy farmers supply cream that is used to make chocolate ice cream.

b. A new report by the Canadian Medical Association reveals that chocolate does, in fact, have significant health benefits.

c. The discovery of cheaper synthetic vanilla flavouring lowers the price of vanilla ice cream.

d. New technology for mixing and freezing ice cream lowers manufacturers' cost of producing chocolate ice cream.

2. In a supply and demand diagram, draw the shift in demand for hamburgers in your home town due to the following events. In each case, show the effect on equilibrium price and quantity:

a. The price of tacos increases.

b. All hamburger sellers raise the price of their french fries.

c. Income falls in town. Assume that hamburgers are a normal good for most people.

d. Income falls in town. Assume that hamburgers are an inferior good for most people.

e. Hot dog stands cut the price of hot dogs.

3. The market for many goods changes in predictable ways according to the time of year, in response to things such as holidays, vacation times, seasonal changes in production, and so on. Using supply and demand, explain the change in price in each of the following cases. Note that supply and demand may shift simultaneously in these examples.

a. Lobster prices usually fall during the summer peak harvest season, despite the fact that people like to consume lobster during the summer months more than during any other time of year.

b. The price of a Christmas tree is lower after Christmas than before, despite the fact that tree growers harvest and supply fewer trees for sale after Christmas than before.

c. The price of a round-trip air ticket to Paris on Air France falls by over $200 after the end of school vacation in September. This happens despite the fact that generally worsening weather increases the cost of operating flights to Paris, and Air France therefore reduces the number of flights to Paris at any given price.

4. Show in a graph the effect on the demand curve, the supply curve, the equilibrium price, and the equilibrium quantity for each of the following events.

a. The market for newspapers in your town.

Case 1: The salaries of journalists go up.
Case 2: There is a big news event in your town that is reported in the newspapers.

b. The market for Edmonton Eskimos' football cotton T-shirts.

Case 1: The Eskimos win the Grey Cup.
Case 2: The price of cotton increases.

c. The market for bagels.

Case 1: People realize how fattening bagels are.
Case 2: People have less time to make themselves a cooked breakfast.

d. The market for the Krugman, Wells, and Myatt *Microeconomics* textbook.

Case 1: Your professor makes it required reading for all of his or her students.
Case 2: Printing costs for textbooks are lowered by the use of synthetic paper.

5. In a recent study, the supply schedule of lobsters from the Atlantic provinces was determined to be:

Price of lobster (per pound)	Quantity of lobster supplied (pounds)
$25	800
20	700
15	600
10	500
5	400

Suppose these lobsters can only be sold in Canada. The Canadian demand schedule for Atlantic lobsters is:

Price of lobster ($ per pound)	Quantity of lobster demanded (pounds)
$25	200
20	400
15	600
10	800
5	1,000

a. Draw the demand curve and the supply curve of Atlantic lobsters. What is the equilibrium price and quantity of lobsters?

Suppose now Atlantic lobsters can be sold in France. The French demand schedule for Atlantic lobsters is given below:

Price of lobster ($ per pound)	Quantity of lobster demanded (pounds)
$25	100
20	300
15	500
10	700
5	900

b. What is the demand schedule for Atlantic lobsters now that French consumers can also buy them? Draw a supply and demand diagram that illustrates the new equilibrium price and quantity of lobsters. What will happen to the price at which Atlantic lobster fishermen can sell lobster? What will happen to the price paid by Canadian consumers of Atlantic lobster? What will happen to the quantity of Atlantic lobster consumed by Canadians?

6. Find the flaws in reasoning in the following statements, paying particular attention to the distinction between shifts of and movements along the supply and demand curves. Draw a diagram to illustrate what actually happens in each situation.

a. "A technological innovation that lowers the cost of producing a good might seem at first to result in a reduction in the price of the good to consumers. But a fall in price will increase demand for the good, and higher demand will send the price up again. It is not certain, therefore, that an innovation will really reduce price in the end."

b. "A study shows that eating a clove of garlic a day can help prevent heart disease, causing many consumers to demand more garlic. This increase in demand results in an increase in the price of garlic. Consumers, seeing that the price of garlic has increased, reduce their demand for garlic. This causes the demand for garlic to decrease and the price of garlic to fall. Therefore, the ultimate effect of the study on the price of garlic is uncertain."

7. Some points on a linear demand curve for a normal good are given below:

Price	Quantity demanded
$23	70
21	90
19	110
17	130

Do you think that the increase in quantity demanded (from 90 to 110 in the table) when price decreases (from 21 to 19) is due to a rise in consumers' income? Explain clearly (and briefly) why or why not.

8. Assume that Devon Spank is a star hitter for the Toronto Blue Jays baseball team. He is close to breaking the major league record for home runs hit during one season, and it is widely anticipated that in the next game he will break that record. As a result, tickets for the team's next game have been a hot commodity. But today it is announced that, due to a knee injury, he will not in fact play in the team's next game. Assume that season ticket-holders are able to resell their tickets if they wish. Use supply and demand diagrams to explain the following:

a. Show the case in which this announcement results in a lower equilibrium price and a lower equilibrium quantity than before the announcement.

b. Show the case in which this announcement results in a lower equilibrium price and a higher equilibrium quantity than before the announcement.

c. What accounts for whether case (a) or case (b) occurs?

d. Suppose that a ticket scalper had secretly learned before the announcement that Devon Spank would not play in the next game. What actions do you think he would take?

9. In *Rolling Stone* magazine, several rock stars, including Pearl Jam, and fans were bemoaning the high price of concert tickets. One superstar argued, "It just isn't worth $75 to see me play. No one should have to pay that much to go to a concert." Assume this star sold out arenas around the country at an average ticket price of $75.

a. How would you evaluate the arguments that ticket prices are too high?

b. Suppose that due to this star's protests, ticket prices were lowered to $50. In what sense is this price "too low"? Draw a diagram using supply and demand curves to support your argument.

c. Suppose Pearl Jam really wanted to bring down ticket prices. Since the band controls the supply of its services, what do you recommend they do? Explain using a supply and demand diagram.

d. Suppose the band's next CD was a total dud. Do you think they would still have to worry about ticket prices being "too high"? Why or why not? Draw a supply and demand diagram to support your argument.

e. Suppose the group announced this was going to be their last tour. What effect would this likely have on the demand and price of tickets? Illustrate with a supply and demand diagram.

10. The following table gives the quarterly Canadian demand and supply schedules for Ford trucks.

Price ($ per truck)	Quantity of trucks demanded (thousands)	Quantity of trucks supplied (thousands)
$20,000	20	14
25,000	18	15
30,000	16	16
35,000	14	17
40,000	12	18

a. Plot the demand and supply curves using the above schedules. Indicate on your graph the equilibrium price and quantity.

b. Supposing the tires used by Ford were found to be defective. What would you expect would happen in the market for Ford trucks? Show this on your graph.

c. Suppose further that the Canadian Department of Transportation imposes restrictions on Ford that cause the car manufacturer to reduce supply by one-third, or 33%, at any given price. Calculate and plot the new supply schedule and indicate the new equilibrium price and quantity on your graph.

11. After several years of decline, the market for handmade acoustic guitars is making a comeback. These guitars are usually made in small workshops employing relatively few highly skilled luthiers. Assess the impact on the equilibrium price and quantity of handmade acoustic guitars as a result of each of the following events. In your answers, indicate which curves. shifts. and in which direction.

a. Environmentalists succeed in having the use of Brazilian rosewood banned in Canada, forcing luthiers to seek out alternative, more costly woods.

b. A foreign producer re-engineers the guitar-making process and floods the market with similar guitars.

c. Music using handmade acoustic guitars makes a comeback as audiences tire of heavy metal and grunge music.

d. Canada goes into a deep recession in which the income of the average Canadian falls sharply.

12. *Demand Twisters*: Try to sketch and explain the demand relationship in each of the following situations.

a. I would never buy a Britney Spears CD! You couldn't even give me one for nothing.

b. I generally buy a bit more coffee as the price falls. But once the price falls to $4/kilo, I will buy out the entire stock of the supermarket.

c. I spend more on orange juice even as the price rises. (Does this mean that I must be violating the law of demand?)

d. Due to a tuition rise, most students find themselves with less disposable income. Almost all of them eat more frequently at the university cafeteria and less often at restaurants, even though prices at the cafeteria have risen too. (This one requires that you draw both demand and supply curves for dormitory cafeteria meals.)

13. Will Shakespeare is a struggling playwright in sixteenth-century London. As the price he receives for writing a play increases, he is willing to write more plays. In the following questions, use a diagram to illustrate how each event affects the equilibrium price and quantity in the market for Shakespeare's plays.

a. The playwright Christopher Marlowe, Shakespeare's chief rival, is killed in a bar brawl.

b. The bubonic plague, a deadly infectious disease, breaks out in London.

c. In order to celebrate the Royal Navy's victory over the Spanish Armada, Queen Elizabeth commissions several weeks of festivities, including new plays.

14. The small town of Middling experiences a sudden doubling of the birth rate. After three years, the birth rate returns to normal. Use a diagram to illustrate the effect of these events on the following:

a. The market for an hour of babysitting services in Middling today.

b. The market for an hour of babysitting services 14 years into the future after the birth rate has returned to normal, by which time children born today are old enough to work as babysitters.

c. The market for an hour of babysitting services in Middling 30 years into the future, when children born today are likely to be having children of their own.

15. In the following questions, use a diagram to illustrate how each event affects the market equilibrium price and quantity of pizza.

a. The price of mozzarella cheese rises.

b. The health hazards of hamburgers are demonstrated in a widely advertised campaign.

c. The price of tomato sauce falls.

d. The incomes of consumers rise and pizzas are inferior goods.

e. Consumers expect the price of pizzas to fall next week.

16. Draw the appropriate curve in each of the following cases. Is it like or unlike the curves you have seen so far? Explain.

a. The demand for cardiac bypass surgery, given that the government pays the full cost for any patient

b. The demand for elective cosmetic plastic surgery, where the patient pays the full cost of the surgery

c. The weekly supply of locally grown tomatoes during the month of August at your local market

>web... To continue your study and review of concepts in this chapter, please visit the Krugman/Wells website for quizzes, animated graph tutorials, web links to helpful resources, and more.

www.worthpublishers.com/krugmanwellsmyatt

chapter 4

>>The Market Strikes Back

BIG COUNTRY, SMALL IDEAS

"THINK BIG, THEN THINK EVEN bigger." This was Sir William Van Horne's motto, and he certainly lived by it. Sir William's vision, energy, and indomitable will were largely responsible for the successful completion, in five dramatic years, of the Canadian Pacific Railway. This railway played a fundamental role in the settlement and development of the Canadian West, and became the lifeline that united Canada's vast territory. Its completion in 1885 fulfilled a dream—the vision of a nation stretching from the Pacific coast to the Atlantic Ocean.

Of course, its completion also meant that Van Horne's pockets were bulging with money. And what better way to spend it than to build a luxury summer residence on his own 500-acre island and become a "gentleman farmer"?

So, the self-made millionaire equipped his summer residence with a gigantic livestock barn to house his prized herd of Dutch belted cattle, a creamery where the milk and butter were prepared for consumption, and a heated greenhouse where exotic plants, peach trees, and grape vines were grown. In this way, Sir William was able to provide himself and his guests (there were 17 bedrooms) with fresh milk, butter, fruits, and vegetables. And when he visited his Montreal residence, he had these provisions sent to him by overnight rail—Canadian Pacific, naturally.

But if you have similar thoughts of becoming a gentleman farmer after you've made your nest egg, perhaps you should think again—especially if you actually want to sell your product on the market. While there's nothing to stop you from making lots of money, government regulations might prevent you from becoming a producer of turkey, chicken, eggs, milk, butter, or cheese. All these products are protected by "marketing boards", the main purpose of which is not to "market" the product, but to set a price floor for the producer and to impose quotas to prevent surplus production. Without a quota—which is an actual piece of paper giving you the right to produce a certain amount of the product—you can't produce. And since they're not giving any more away, to obtain the necessary quota you might have to pay several

Buddy Mays/CORBIS

The Van Horne mansion, Minister's Island, New Brunswick: "Think big, then think even bigger".

What you will learn in this chapter:

- The meaning of **price controls** and **quantity controls**, two kinds of government intervention in markets
- How price and quantity controls create problems and make a market **inefficient**
- Why economists are often deeply sceptical of these attempts to control markets
- Who benefits and who loses from market interventions, and why they are used despite their well-known problems
- What an **excise tax** is and why its effect is similar to a quantity control
- Why the **deadweight loss** of a tax means that its true cost is more than the amount of tax revenue collected

hundred thousand dollars to an existing producer wanting out.

Agricultural quotas were imposed to help support and stabilize farm incomes, and to ensure quality control. Their result, however, has been to raise the price of some of the cheaper forms of protein, without actually benefiting many of the producers in those industries.

Quotas aren't that unusual. They are just one of many government policies that, in one way or another, try to prevail over the market forces of supply and demand. For example, to keep prices down, governments impose price ceilings; and to keep prices up, governments impose price floors.

In the previous chapter we learned the principle that a market moves towards equilibrium—that the market price rises or falls to the level at which the quantity of a good people are willing to supply is equal to the quantity that other people want to buy. When governments try to defy that principle, the market strikes back in predictable ways. And our ability to predict what will happen when governments try to defy supply and demand shows the power and usefulness of supply and demand analysis itself.

In this chapter, we begin by examining what happens when governments try to control market prices, keeping the price in a market either below its equilibrium level (a *price ceiling*) or above it (a *price floor*). We then turn to schemes such as agricultural quotas that attempt to dictate the quantity of a good bought or sold, and, finally, consider the effects of taxes on sales or purchases.

Why Governments Control Prices

You learned in Chapter 3 that a market moves to equilibrium—that is, the market price moves to the level at which the quantity supplied equals the quantity demanded. But this equilibrium price does not necessarily please either buyers or sellers.

After all, buyers would always like to pay less if they could; and sometimes they can make a strong moral or political case that they ought to pay lower prices. For example, what if the equilibrium between supply and demand for oil leads to prices so high that lower-income homeowners can't afford to heat their homes in the winter? This might well create pressure for governments to impose limits on the price of heating oil. Or what if the equilibrium between the supply and demand for apartments leads to rental rates that an average working person can't afford? Again, the government might well find itself pressured to impose limits on the rents landlords can charge.

On the other hand, sellers would always like to get more money for what they sell, and sometimes they can make a strong moral or political case that they should receive higher prices. This is especially easy to do if the price in question is the price of labour (wages). For example, what if the equilibrium between the supply and demand for less-skilled workers leads to wage rates that are below the poverty level? In that case, a government might well find itself pressured to require employers to pay wage rates no lower than a given minimum wage. Similarly, if farmers find that prices for their produce are too low for them to survive, governments might be pressured into measures that support farm prices.

In other words, there is often a strong political demand for governments to intervene in markets. When a government intervenes to regulate prices, we say that it imposes **price controls.** These controls typically take the form either of an upper limit, a **price ceiling;** or a lower limit, a **price floor.**

Unfortunately, it's not that easy to tell a market what to do. As we will now see, when a government tries to control prices—whether it legislates them *down* by imposing a price ceiling or *up* by imposing a price floor—there are certain predictable and unpleasant side effects.

Price controls are legal restrictions on how high or low a market price may go. They can take two forms: a **price ceiling,** a maximum price sellers are allowed to charge for a good, or a **price floor,** a minimum price buyers are allowed to pay for a good.

Using the Competitive Model

We should note an important caveat here: our analysis in this chapter considers only what happens when price controls are imposed on *competitive markets*—which, as you should recall from Chapter 3, are markets in which there are many buyers and sellers of the *same* good, and in which no buyer or seller can have a *noticeable* effect on the market price. When these conditions do not hold—for example, when a good is differentiated by brand or by quality, or when either buyers or sellers can have a noticeable effect on the price—price controls don't necessarily cause the same problems.

If we ended the discussion here, we would miss an important point: what constitutes a "noticeable" effect on price? And how similar do goods have to be to be called the "same" good? Even wheat has different strains of quality, and every landlord has some leeway with regard to the rent she charges.

To answer these questions, we should remember from Chapter 2 that a model is a simplification. All models abstract from some aspects of reality. As a result, economists sometimes disagree on which model is best applied to any given situation. But they try to resolve these disputes by appealing to the empirical evidence. All economists agree that the model that "best fits the facts" is the appropriate model to use.

This means that questions about what constitutes a noticeable effect, and how similar the goods have to be, are essentially empirical questions that depend upon what "facts" we are trying to explain. The questions we're asking, and the facts we're trying to explain, determine the appropriate model to use.

For example, the fact that landlords have some leeway over the rent they charge may be important for explaining differences in rents between apartments, but is probably unimportant for explaining average rents. Therefore, we can't use a competitive model to explain rental differences between apartments; but we should be able to use it to explain average rents and the effects of government-imposed rent ceilings. Whether we can or not depends on whether the model's predictions best fit the facts.

The key point is that we shouldn't judge the relevance of any model—and its associated predictions—by the "realism" of the assumptions it makes. Economists do not assume that the competitive model is relevant to a particular market simply because that market has a large number of buyers and sellers. We test the model's predictions against the facts we're trying to explain.

Price Ceilings

Price ceilings are typically imposed during crises—wars, harvest failures, natural disasters—because these events often lead to sudden price increases, which hurt many people but produce big gains for a lucky few. During World War II, for example, Canada imposed a general ceiling on prices, wages, and rents in an effort to control inflation and ensure a fair distribution of goods. These controls were dismantled in 1951.

Figure 4-1 **The Market for Apartments in the Absence of Government Controls**

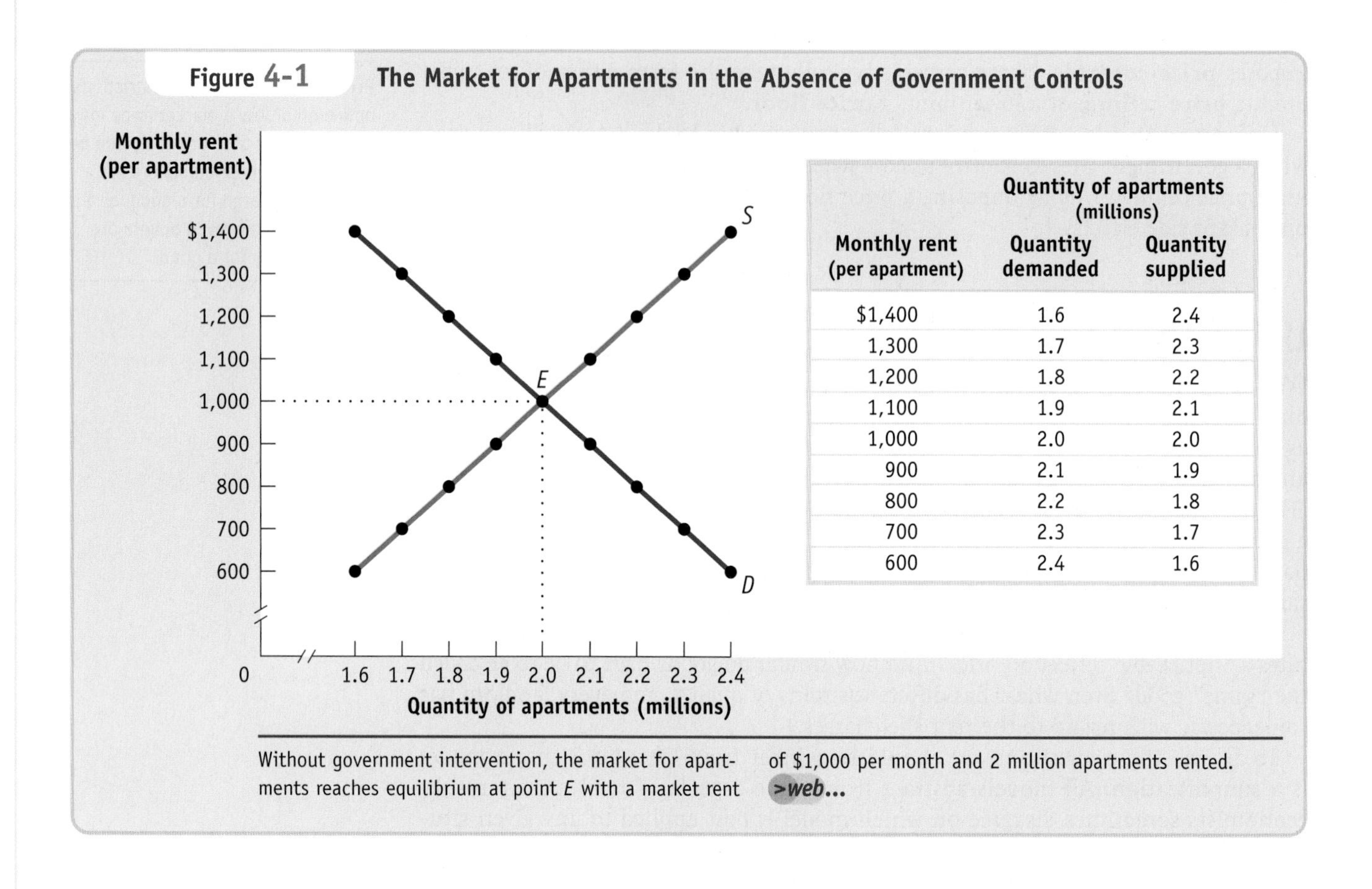

Monthly rent (per apartment)	Quantity of apartments (millions) Quantity demanded	Quantity supplied
$1,400	1.6	2.4
1,300	1.7	2.3
1,200	1.8	2.2
1,100	1.9	2.1
1,000	2.0	2.0
900	2.1	1.9
800	2.2	1.8
700	2.3	1.7
600	2.4	1.6

Without government intervention, the market for apartments reaches equilibrium at point *E* with a market rent of $1,000 per month and 2 million apartments rented. **>*web...***

To see what can go wrong when a government imposes a price ceiling on a competitive market, consider Figure 4-1, which shows a simplified model of the market for apartments. For the sake of simplicity, we imagine that all apartments are exactly the same, and that they would therefore rent for the same price in an uncontrolled market. In this context, we will develop five key predictions from the competitive model.

But before we start, we need to emphasize an important point: price ceilings will have no effect if they are set *above* the equilibrium price. For example, suppose that, as Figure 4-1 illustrates, the equilibrium rental rate on apartments is $1,000 per month, and that the local government now sets a rent ceiling of $1,200 per month. Who cares? In this case, the price ceiling won't be binding—it won't actually constrain market behaviour—and it will have no effect.

In what follows, we shall assume that the price ceiling is set below the equilibrium price. In other words, our predictions relate to cases in which the price ceiling is **binding.**

A price ceiling set below the equilibrium price is a **binding price constraint.**

Price Ceilings: Five Key Predictions

The table in the figure shows the demand and supply schedules; the implied supply and demand curves are shown on the left. On the horizontal axis of the figure, we show the number of apartments rented; on the vertical axis, the monthly rent per apartment. You can see that in an unregulated market the equilibrium would be at point *E*: 2 million apartments would be rented for $1,000 per month.

Now suppose that the government imposes a price ceiling, limiting rents to a price below the equilibrium price, say no more than $800.

Figure 4-2 shows the effect of the price ceiling, represented by the line drawn at $800. At the enforced rental rate of $800, at point A on the supply curve, only 1.8 million apartments are offered for rent, 200,000 less than in the free-market situation. At the same time, more people would want to rent apartments at a monthly rate of $800

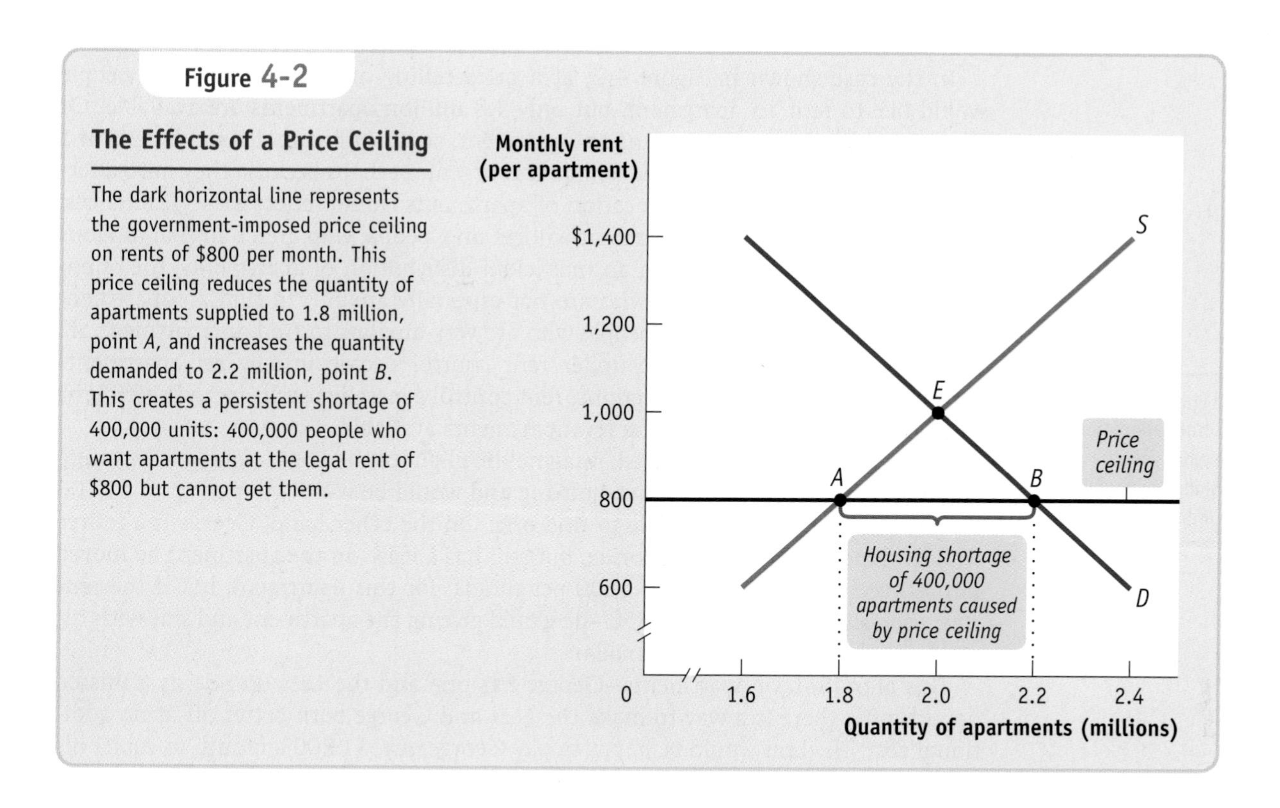

Figure 4-2

The Effects of a Price Ceiling The dark horizontal line represents the government-imposed price ceiling on rents of $800 per month. This price ceiling reduces the quantity of apartments supplied to 1.8 million, point *A*, and increases the quantity demanded to 2.2 million, point *B*. This creates a persistent shortage of 400,000 units: 400,000 people who want apartments at the legal rent of $800 but cannot get them.

than at the equilibrium rate of $1,000. More people will decide to live on their own rather than share accommodation, and more people will decide that renting is a better option than buying. As shown at point *B* on the demand curve, at a rent of $800 per month the number of apartments demanded rises to 2.2 million, 200,000 more than in the free-market situation, and 400,000 more than are actually available at the rate of $800. So there is now a rental housing shortage, a persistent excess demand: at that rate, 400,000 more people want to rent than are actually able to find apartments.

#1: Shortages That Get Worse over Time So, our first key prediction is that binding price controls imposed on competitive markets lead to shortages. We can expand this prediction by delving a little deeper into the reason why the quantity of apartments supplied decreases at the ceiling price of $800, and how long it takes for this decrease to occur.

The reduction in the quantity of apartments supplied most likely will not happen all at once. Given an existing number of apartment buildings, there may be *initially* only a small reduction in the number of apartments offered—caused, perhaps, by homeowners having less incentive to rent out a room or a basement. However, over time more reductions will occur. For example, given time, it is possible to convert apartment buildings to condominiums or to knock them down and build shopping malls. So, the full reduction in supply (of 200,000 units in our example) may take some time to occur. This means that the shortage of apartments generated by rent controls gets worse the longer the controlled price (the rent ceiling) stays below the equilibrium price.

#2: Inefficient Allocation to Consumers The housing shortage shown in Figure 4-2 is not merely annoying: like any shortage induced by price controls, it can be seriously harmful because it leads to *inefficiency*. In Chapter 1, we learned that an economy is efficient if there is no way to make some people better off without making others worse off. A market or an economy becomes **inefficient** when there are missed opportunities—ways that production or consumption could be rearranged that would make some people better off at no cost to anyone else.

A market or an economy is **inefficient** if there are missed opportunities: some people could be made better off without making other people worse off.

In the case shown in Figure 4-2, at a price ceiling of $800, 2.2 million people would like to rent an apartment, but only 1.8 million apartments are available. Of those 2.2 million who are seeking an apartment, some will be in desperate need of a place to live. For others the need will be less urgent, perhaps because they have alternative housing. An efficient allocation of apartments would reflect these differences: people who really want an apartment will get one, people who aren't all that anxious to have an apartment won't. In an inefficient distribution of apartments, the opposite will happen: some people who are not especially anxious to find an apartment will get one, even while some people who are very anxious to find an apartment are unable to do so. And because under rent control people usually get apartments through luck or personal connections, rent control generally results in an **inefficient allocation to consumers** of the few apartments available.

Price ceilings often lead to inefficiency in the form of **inefficient allocation to consumers:** people who want the good badly don't get it, while those who care relatively little about the good do get it.

To see the inefficiency involved, imagine the plight of the Lees, a family with young children, who have no alternative housing and would be willing to pay up to $1,500 for an apartment but are unable to find one. On the other hand, George is a retiree who lives most of the year in Florida, but still has a lease on the apartment he moved into 40 years ago. George pays $800 per month for this apartment, but if the rent were even slightly more—say, $850—he would give up the apartment and stay with his children when he returns to Canada.

This allocation of apartments—George has one and the Lees do not—is a missed opportunity: there is a way to make the Lees and George both better off at no additional cost. The Lees would be happy to pay George, say, $1,200 a month to sublet his apartment, which he would happily accept since the apartment is worth no more to him than $850 a month. George would be $350 a month better off. The Lees, too, are $300 a month better off since they would have been willing to pay up to $1,500 for an apartment. So both would be made better off by this transaction—and nobody else would be hurt.

More generally, if people who really want apartments could sublet them from people who are less eager to stay in them, both those who gain apartments and those who trade their leases for more money would be better off. However, subletting is illegal under rent control because it would take place at prices above the price ceiling. But just because subletting is illegal doesn't mean it never happens. This illegal subletting is a kind of *black market activity*, which we will discuss in full shortly.

#3: Wasted Resources A third reason a price ceiling causes inefficiency is that it leads to **wasted resources.** Under rent control, the Lees will spend all their spare time for several months searching for an apartment. This time has an *opportunity cost* measured in terms of the foregone leisure or income they could have had if they hadn't had to search for an apartment for so long. If the market for apartments worked freely, the Lees would quickly find an apartment at $1,000 and have spare time to enjoy themselves—an outcome that would make the Lees better off at no expense to anyone else. Again, rent control creates missed opportunities that are pure waste.

Price ceilings typically lead to inefficiency in the form of **wasted resources:** people spend money and expend effort in order to deal with the shortages caused by the price ceiling.

#4: Inefficiently Low Quality Our fourth prediction is that under a price ceiling, goods tend to be of **inefficiently low quality.** To see what we mean, consider the situation under rent control. Landlords facing rent control have no incentive to provide better conditions, since they cannot raise rents to cover their repair costs and are able to find tenants easily regardless of the conditions. In many cases, tenants would be willing to pay much more for improved conditions—for example, the repair and upgrade of an antiquated electrical system that cannot safely run air conditioners or computers—than it would cost for the landlord to provide them. But any additional payment for such improvements would be legally considered a rent increase, which is prohibited. This is a missed opportunity—some tenants would be happy to pay for better conditions, and landlords would be happy to provide them for payment. But this exchange could occur only if the market were allowed to operate freely.

Price ceilings often lead to inefficiency in that the goods being offered are of **inefficiently low quality:** sellers offer low-quality goods at a low price even though buyers would prefer a higher quality at a higher price.

#5: Black Markets And that leads us to our final prediction about the effects of price ceilings: they provide an incentive for *illegal activities*, specifically the emergence of **black markets.**

A **black market** is a market in which goods or services are bought and sold illegally—either because it is illegal to sell them at all or because the prices charged are prohibited by a price ceiling or a price floor.

We have already described one kind of black market activity—illegal subletting by tenants. But there are others. Clearly, a building owner may be tempted to say to a potential tenant, "Look, you can have the place if you slip me an extra few hundred in cash each month."And, if the tenant is one of those people who would be willing to pay much more than the legal maximum rent, he or she will be equally tempted to agree.

Figure 4-3 shows how to predict the likely size of these side-payments (or bribes). At the ceiling rent, 1.8 million apartments are supplied. But buyers are willing to pay up to $1,200 a month for an apartment when supply is this low—$400 more than the legal ceiling. So, we can expect side-payments as high as $400 a month.

Ironically, the emergence of a black market may ameliorate the inefficiencies we have enumerated. On the black market, those who really need (or want) the commodity have the opportunity to back up that need with cash and acquire it. For example, on the black market, that illegal sublet between the Lees and George can occur.

But before we sing the praises of the black market, we need to emphasize that the bigger a black market, the more people who are breaking the law. And when laws are routinely flouted for personal gain, we can have the worst of all possible worlds.

Moreover, illegal activity worsens the position of those who try to be honest. If the Lees were scrupulous about not breaking the rent control law, while other families—families that may need an apartment less than the Lees do—were willing to go ahead and bribe the landlords, the Lees may *never* find an apartment.

So, here is one way to think about our five predictions and to organize them in our minds: First, price ceilings lead to shortages (prediction 1). Next, the fundamental reason why shortages are bad is that they are inefficient, and this inefficiency manifests itself in three distinct ways (predictions 2, 3, and 4). Finally, whenever there are unsatisfied wants because of legal restrictions, crime will always arise to profit from them (prediction 5).

Figure 4-3

The Black Market Price

The price ceiling reduces the quantity of apartments supplied to 1.8 million, point *A*. From the demand curve, we see that the maximum willingness to pay for an apartment, at this quantity, is $1,200 per month, point *B*. This is $400 more than the legal ceiling rent. We predict bribes, or side-payments, of up to $400 a month.

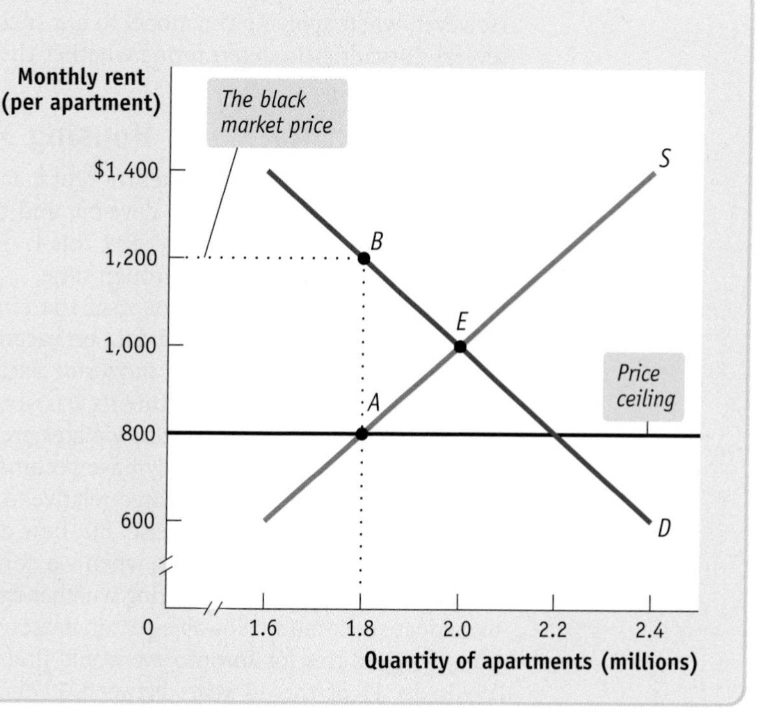

Comparing the Predictions to the Facts

How do our predictions compare to the facts? There is a rich array of data from which to choose. Price controls have been imposed on different commodities, in different countries, in different times.

During World War II, price ceilings were imposed on many commodities in both Britain and Canada—commodities such as meat, milk, eggs, sugar, and gasoline. In every case, shortages instantly developed, confirming prediction #1. In an attempt to avoid the costs associated with an inefficient distribution of these commodities amongst consumers (prediction #2) and the cost of the time wasted in searching for the good (prediction #3), families were issued ration coupons based on need. Despite the fact that the amount of ration coupons issued was approximately equal to the available supply, the rationing schemes did not succeed in avoiding these costs completely—they merely transferred the costs from private citizens to the government. Instead of individuals wasting time searching for the commodity, the government "wasted" time and labour issuing ration coupons.

Was it a pure waste, though? To the extent to which rationing succeeded in establishing a more equitable distribution of essential commodities, many would consider the cost of issuing ration coupons a worthwhile trade-off for the increased equity—at least in the short run during wartime. However, the fact that extensive black markets for rationed goods did exist in both countries (bearing out prediction #5) suggests that the aim of establishing a more equitable distribution was only partly achieved, and that not everyone bought into the "worthwhile trade-off" point of view. Finally, since the best cuts of meat were often sold on the black market, only lesser quality cuts were available to be sold legally, bearing out prediction #4.

As another example, when OPEC restricted oil supplies in 1979, leading to an approximate doubling of world prices, President Jimmy Carter responded to the public outcry in the U.S. by imposing price ceilings on gasoline. Again, the historical record bears out all the competitive model's predictions. In particular, the price ceiling produced gasoline shortages, and millions of Americans ended up spending hours each week waiting in lines at gas stations. This wasn't exactly what the public expected, despite the clear predictions from our model.

The above examples clearly vindicate the competitive model's predictions. However, when applying the model to our main example, rent control, we encounter several difficulties in determining whether the model fits the facts.

The Distinct Nature of Housing Markets

First, in the context of the market for rental accommodation, the model predicts that the shortages may take time to develop, and the longer the rent control is in effect, the worse the shortages become. But this is only true if the rent control is binding, and remains equally binding through time.

For example, suppose we looked at the effects of rent control in Toronto in the 1990s; and suppose we obtained data on vacancy rates (which are an inverse measure of shortages), and we observed *increasing* vacancy rates over this period. This would suggest that any scarcity of apartments was not getting worse, but was moderating over time. Should we conclude that this violates prediction #1? It would be a mistake to do so, because the price ceiling may have become less binding throughout the 1990s. If maximum allowable rents increased relative to equilibrium rents, we would expect the shortage to moderate, not increase. But how do we know what equilibrium rents are, or how they move through time, when we don't necessarily observe them?

One imperfect way of estimating whether the rent ceiling did become less binding is to compare maximum allowable rent increases with the province's average rate of inflation. If we did this for Toronto, we would find that rent controls were relaxed over the 1990s. In 11 of the 13 years between 1991 and 2003, the maximum allowed rent increase exceeded Ontario's rate of inflation. By contrast, in the 11 years prior to 1990, this occurred only 3 times. Hence, the observation of increasing vacancy rates in Toronto during the 1990s is perfectly consistent with the predictions of the competitive model.

The second main difficulty we encounter is that rent controls are one of the more complicated types of price ceiling. Rarely does rent control simply stipulate a ceiling price for rents. That type of rent control occurred during World War II, but disappeared in Canada in 1951 with the general dismantling of price controls. More complicated controls were reintroduced in the 1970s, but this more modern legislation (known as "second-generation" rent control) is much more flexible than the rigid wartime price ceilings. For example, it commonly allows automatic rent increases geared to increasing costs, excludes luxury high-rent buildings, and provides incentives for landlords to maintain or improve quality. Often it allows for decontrol once the unit is vacated. Clearly, this is very different from a rigid rent freeze.

Fortunately for us, there is one city where the rigid wartime controls were not abolished in the 1950s—New York City. Let's first see how the competitive model's predictions fare there, before trying to evaluate the effect of more complicated second-generation controls in Canada.

The Singular Case of New York City Of all the cities in North America that imposed rent controls during World War II, only New York City retained them. This is what makes New York's experience unique and valuable—it shows us the consequences of having a rigid form of rent control for a very long period of time. The effects in New York have been devastating—and have strongly borne out the competitive model's predictions concerning the effects of a rigid rent freeze.

In any market, the extent of a shortage can be gauged by the size of the black market, since there would be no need for a black market if there were no shortage. And New York is infamous for its bribes. In fact, they are so widespread that people felt the need to coin the term "key-money" as a euphemism for these bribes. Moreover, talking about key-money allows a pretence to be maintained that the money is actually paying for something—like the cutting of a new key. But "new keys" in New York can be very expensive—in fact, they can run into thousands of dollars.

Another easily observable fact about New York is the deteriorating quality of its rental housing stock. Apartments are notoriously badly maintained, rarely painted, subject to frequent electrical and water problems, and sometimes even hazardous to inhabit. But the problems go far beyond that. The quality of some buildings has deteriorated to the point where entire city blocks in the Harlem and Bronx districts have been abandoned by landlords as unprofitable. This abandonment has caused social havoc, since the buildings attract crime and drugs.

In sum, New York's experience prompted Swedish economist Assar Lindbeck to quip, "rent controls are the most effective means yet for destroying cities—in his opinion rent controls are even more effective than bombing."

FOR INQUIRING MINDS

WHY RENT CONTROL PERSISTS IN NEW YORK

Given the unpleasant consequences, why does rent control persist in New York?

One answer is that while price ceilings may have adverse effects, they do benefit some people. While the majority of New Yorkers have worse housing than they would in the absence of rent controls, a sizeable minority gets a better deal—slightly worse quality but a much lower price. And those who benefit from the controls are typically better organized and more vocal than those who lose.

Indeed, one of the ironies of New York's rent control system is that some of the biggest beneficiaries are not the working-class families the system was intended to help, but affluent and powerful tenants whose families have lived for many decades in choice apartments that would now command very high rents.

Rent Controls in Canada Because rent control is under provincial jurisdiction, Canada's experience with it has been quite diverse. All the provinces acceded to the federal government's request to reintroduce rent control in the mid-1970s as part of its general wage and price controls. But when that came to an end in 1978, some provinces moved quickly to decontrol, some moved to voluntary arbitration schemes, and some moved to "permanent" mandatory controls. By 1988, six of the ten provinces had abolished mandatory controls. The four that didn't were Manitoba, Ontario, PEI, and Nova Scotia.

This remaining rent control is all "second-generation"—meaning that it is relatively flexible and allows, for example, automatic rent increases geared to increasing costs. What effects has this legislation had?

In reviewing the empirical evidence, Richard Arnott[1] suggests that, in comparison with other factors affecting the housing market—like tax policy related to housing, local real estate cycles, changes in the national and regional economy, and major government housing programs—the effects of second-generation rent controls in Canada have been almost imperceptible.

The one exception to this is Ontario, and in particular the city of Toronto. Ontario suffered from poorly designed legislation, especially throughout the 1970s and 1980s. Generally speaking, the maximum allowed rent increase in Ontario did not keep up with costs in this early period. Moreover, Ontario was the only province that controlled the rent of luxury units and failed to exempt new construction from rent control. The situation got so bad that in the early 1980s Ontario found it necessary to pass legislation prohibiting the demolition of rental property or its conversion to condominiums. Moreover, vacancy rates were the lowest of any province across Canada. Some even compared Toronto's experience with rent control during this period to the situation in New York.

However, this comparison is no longer valid today. While rent control remains nominally in effect in Ontario, its influence has been moderated by two factors. First, the maximum allowed rent increase has generally exceeded the rate of inflation since 1990, lessening the extent to which rent control is binding. Second, the Progressive Conservative government of Mike Harris implemented significant reforms in June 1998. In particular, rental units built after 1998 will never be subject to rent control, and vacant apartments now become decontrolled. These changes have effectively begun the process of decontrol in Ontario.

So the message of this section is that second-generation rent controls are not the same as a rigid rent freeze, and we shouldn't judge their effects by the experience of New York. Apparently, their effects in Canada have been, on the whole, almost imperceptible.

Could Second-Generation Rent Control Be Beneficial? The traditional economics answer to this question is 'no'. If the controls are binding (and cause rents to fall below their equilibrium values), they cause efficiency losses. If the controls are not binding (so that the legal rent exceeds the equilibrium rent), then the controls are redundant—in which case a level of bureaucracy (the rent control board) is being maintained for no reason, and hence there is still an efficiency loss.

However, in recent years some housing economists have begun to challenge the orthodox view (see Arnott, 1995). Remember, our five predictions apply only when price controls are imposed on *competitive markets,* and the market for apartments has some *non-competitive* elements. Because apartments differ in location and other attributes, and tenants face high costs searching for an alternative apartment and moving to it, landlords have some ability to influence the price. In addition, there is a lack of information about who is a good landlord (and who is a good tenant). Because of these features, *moderate* and *well-designed* rent control *could* be beneficial. It can prevent, for example, uninformed tenants from being taken advantage of by an unscrupulous landlord.

---

[1]Richard Arnott, "Time for Revisionism in Rent Control?" *Journal of Economic Perspectives* 9 (1995): 99–120.

But it is one thing to say that it is *theoretically possible* to design legislation that improves over the unrestricted free market solution. It is altogether another to say that this legislation has actually been implemented in any given jurisdiction. If you come across any, do let us know!

economics in action

Alternatives to Rent Controls in Canada

In practice, there are better ways to provide affordable housing than to implement rent control. Even though most provinces have now abandoned rent control, all provinces in Canada try to provide affordable housing for low-income families. They do this through social assistance programs: public housing, cooperative housing, shelter allowances, or rental supplements.

However, the system has been under increasing stress since 1993 as a result of cuts in federal spending. For every public housing unit, there is usually a family on a waiting list needing to get in. As a result, the effort nowadays is to try to use existing units more effectively as a *temporary* stopgap, and to give the occupants of the units the skills necessary to move towards self-sufficiency. The aim is to avoid the often-encountered situation in which people born in public housing are now raising their own families there. ■

>> QUICK REVIEW

- *Price controls* take the form of either legal maximum prices—*price ceilings*—or legal minimum prices—*price floors*.
- A price ceiling below the equilibrium price benefits successful buyers, but causes predictable adverse effects such as persistent *shortages*, which lead to three types of *inefficiencies: inefficient allocation to consumers, wasted resources*, and *inefficiently low quality*.
- Price ceilings also produce *black markets*, as buyers and sellers attempt to evade the price restriction.

>> CHECK YOUR UNDERSTANDING 4-1

1. Homeowners near McGill University's stadium used to rent out spaces in their driveways at a going rate of $11 to fans who had no other place to park. A new town ordinance now sets a maximum parking fee of $7.

   Use the accompanying supply and demand diagram to show how each of the following corresponds to a price-ceiling concept.

   a. Some homeowners think that it's not worth the hassle to rent out spaces.
   b. Some fans who used to carpool to the game now drive there alone.
   c. Some fans can't find parking and leave without seeing the game.

   Explain how each of the following phenomena arises from the price ceiling:

   d. Determined fans arrive several hours early to find parking.
   e. Family or friends of homeowners near the stadium regularly attend games, even if they aren't big fans. But some serious fans have given up because of the parking situation.
   f. Some homeowners rent spaces for more than $7 but pretend that the buyers are friends or family.

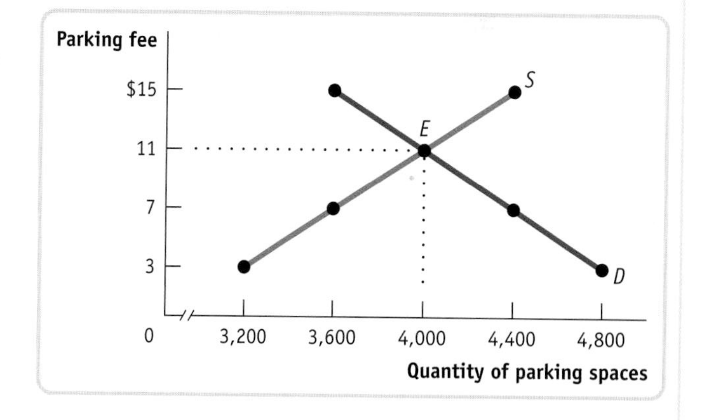

2. True or false? Explain your answer. Compared to a free market, price ceilings at a price below the equilibrium price do the following:

   a. Increase quantity supplied.
   b. Make some people who want to consume the good worse off.
   c. Make all producers worse off.

Price Floors

Sometimes governments intervene to push market prices up instead of down. Just as price ceilings are often imposed because they benefit some influential buyers of a good, price floors are often imposed because they benefit influential *sellers*.

For example, Europe's Common Agricultural Policy (CAP)—born out of the 1957 Treaty of Rome that created the European Economic Community—was an intensely political scheme designed to keep French farmers happy in exchange for Germany's winning a bigger market for its industrial goods. Price floors form the cornerstone of this agricultural policy, and are set at levels that support the incomes of farmers.

Historically, there have also been price floors on services such as air travel. These were phased out in Canada in the early 1980s.

Finally, if you have ever worked in a fast-food restaurant you are likely to have encountered a price floor: all provinces in Canada maintain a lower limit on the hourly wage—that is, a floor on the price of labour. This price floor on labour is called the **minimum wage.**

The **minimum wage** is a legal floor on the wage rate, which is the market price of labour.

Just like price ceilings, price floors are intended to help some people. The problem is that when they are imposed on competitive markets, our model predicts that there will be undesirable side effects. Let's consider in detail the predictions of our competitive model and then see if these predictions fit the facts.

Price Floors: Five Key Predictions

Figure 4-4 shows hypothetical supply and demand curves for blueberries. Left to itself, the market would move to equilibrium at *E*, with 10 million pint boxes of blueberries bought and sold at a price of $4 per pint box.

But now suppose that the government, in order to help blueberry growers, imposes a price floor on blueberries of $5 per pint box. Its effects are shown in Figure 4-5, where the line drawn at $5 represents the price floor.

Figure 4-4 The Market for Blueberries in the Absence of Government Controls

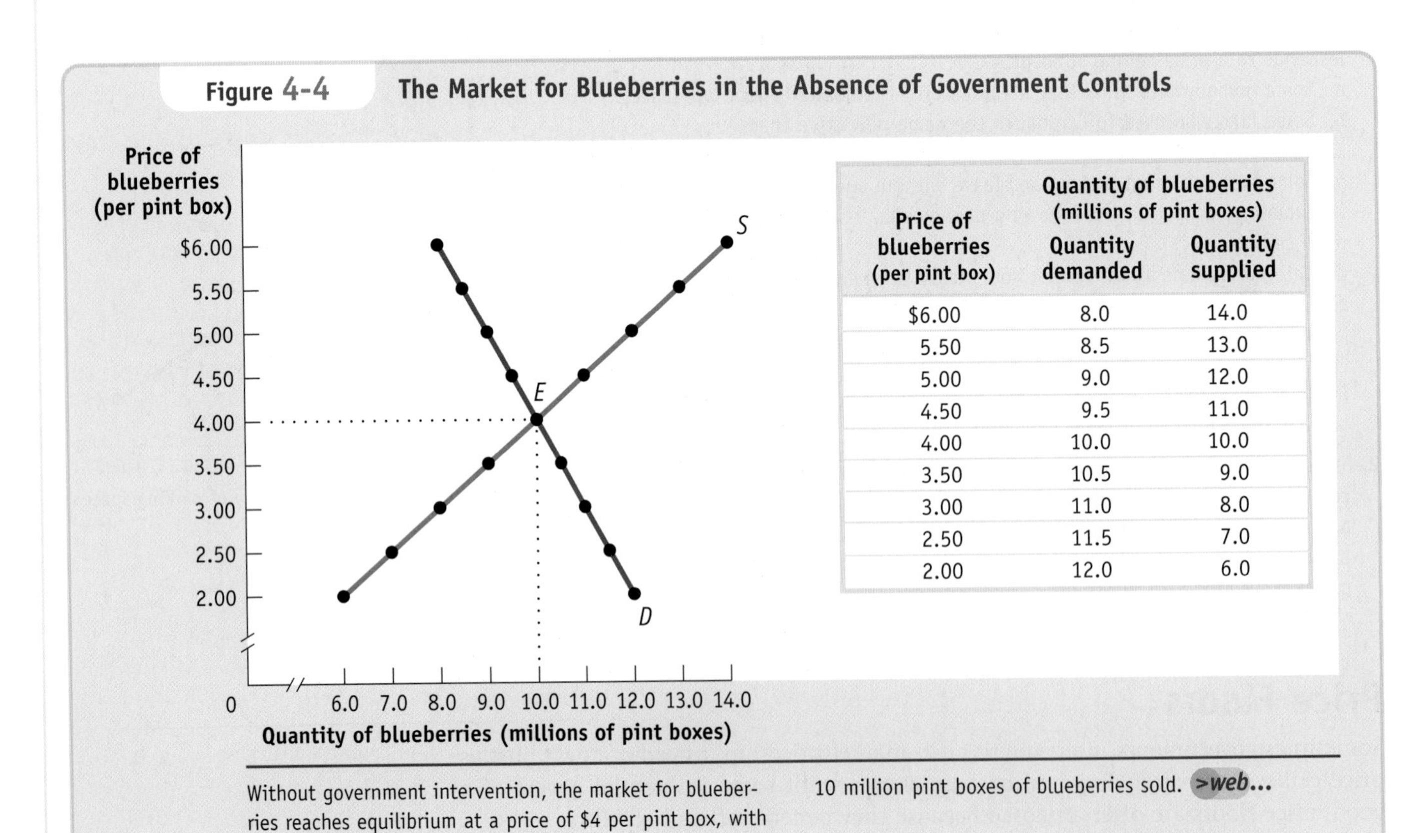

Price of blueberries (per pint box)	Quantity of blueberries (millions of pint boxes) Quantity demanded	Quantity supplied
$6.00	8.0	14.0
5.50	8.5	13.0
5.00	9.0	12.0
4.50	9.5	11.0
4.00	10.0	10.0
3.50	10.5	9.0
3.00	11.0	8.0
2.50	11.5	7.0
2.00	12.0	6.0

Without government intervention, the market for blueberries reaches equilibrium at a price of $4 per pint box, with 10 million pint boxes of blueberries sold. >web...

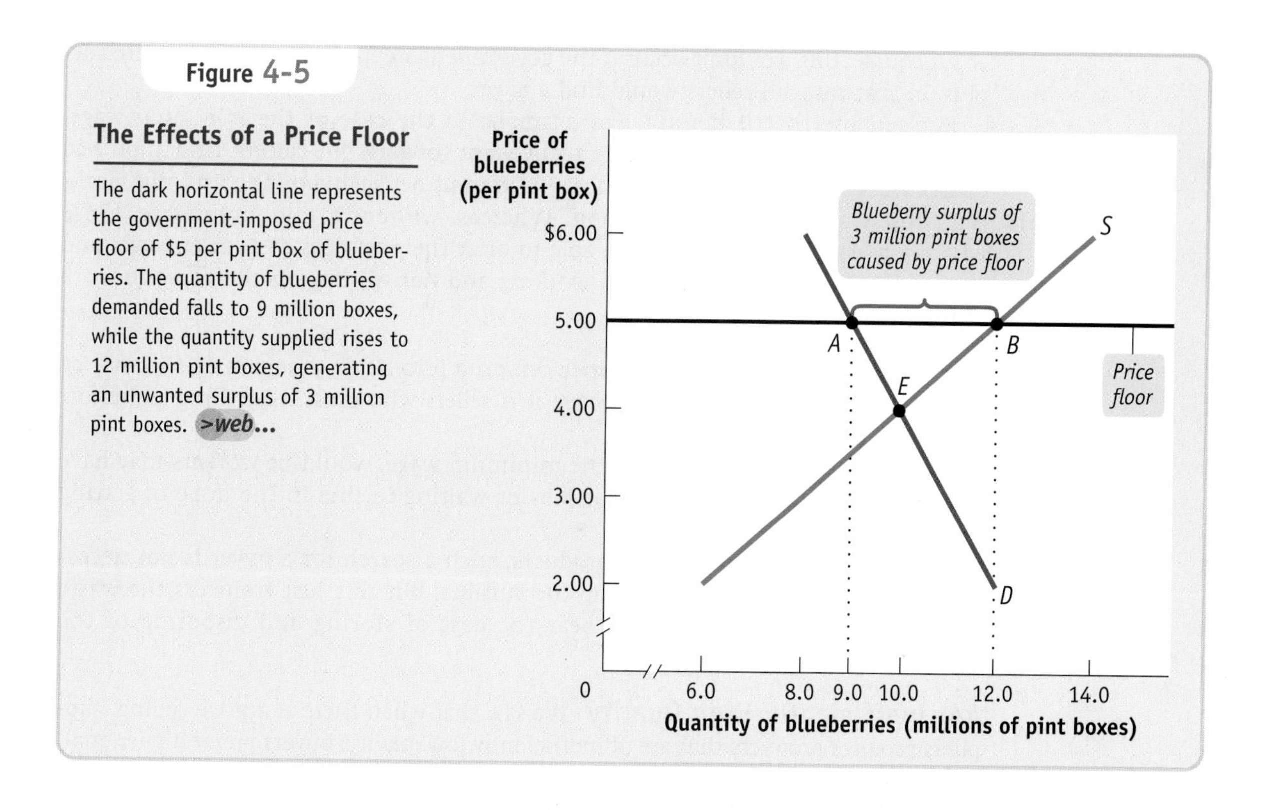

Figure 4-5

The Effects of a Price Floor

The dark horizontal line represents the government-imposed price floor of $5 per pint box of blueberries. The quantity of blueberries demanded falls to 9 million boxes, while the quantity supplied rises to 12 million pint boxes, generating an unwanted surplus of 3 million pint boxes. ***>web...***

#1: Surplus production At a price of $5 per pint box, growers would want to supply 12 million boxes (point *B* on the supply curve), while consumers would want to buy only 9 million boxes (point *A* on the demand curve). Thus, there would be a surplus—a persistent excess supply—of 3 million pint boxes of blueberries.

Does a price floor always lead to an unwanted surplus? No: just as in the case of a price ceiling, the floor may not be binding—that is, it may be irrelevant. If the equilibrium price of blueberries were $4 per pint, while the floor is set at only $3.50, the floor has no effect.

But suppose that a price floor is binding: what happens to the unwanted surplus? With agricultural products, governments invariably buy up the surplus production at the floor price. What happens to it next depends on government policy. But one thing is certain: this surplus must not be subsequently resold on the domestic market, or it will depress the price below the floor. So, the surplus may be stored, destroyed, given away as foreign aid, or sold abroad at a lower price.

When the government is not prepared to purchase the unwanted surplus, a price floor means that would-be sellers cannot find buyers. This is what happens in the case of the minimum wage. The competitive model predicts that when the *minimum wage* is above the equilibrium wage rate, some people who are willing to work will not be able to find employers willing to give them jobs. In other words, it leads to unemployed workers.

#2: Inefficient Allocation Of Sales Among Sellers The persistent unwanted surplus that results from a price floor creates missed opportunities—inefficiencies—that resemble those created by the shortage that results from a price ceiling.

Like a price ceiling, a price floor can lead to an *inefficient allocation*—but in this case an **inefficient allocation of sales among sellers** rather than an inefficient allocation to consumers.

Price floors lead to **inefficient allocation of sales among sellers:** those who would be willing to sell the good at the lowest price are not always those who manage to sell it.

Of course, this wouldn't occur if the government stepped in to buy the entire surplus. In that case, all sellers would find a buyer.

But suppose that it doesn't. For example, in the case of the minimum wage, there may be some job seekers who really want to work but cannot find a job and others who have a job but are almost indifferent between working and not working. This is an inefficient allocation. Whereas, without a minimum wage, those who really want to work would be able to offer their services at a lower wage, and those who are indifferent between working and not working would cease to work at the lower wage.

#3: Wasted Resources Like a price ceiling, a price floor generates inefficiency by *wasting resources*. In this case, however, it is sellers who must waste time and effort searching for a buyer.

For example, in the context of the minimum wage, would-be workers may have to spend many hours searching for jobs or waiting in line in the hope of getting jobs.

In the context of agricultural products, such a search for a buyer is not necessary when the government buys up the surplus. But this just transfers the waste to the government, which must bear the cost of storing and disposing of the surplus.

#4: Inefficiently High Quality We saw that when there is a price ceiling, suppliers produce products that are of inefficiently low quality: buyers prefer higher quality products and are willing to pay for them, but sellers refuse to raise the quality of their products because the price ceiling prevents them from being compensated for it. This same logic applies to price floors, but in reverse: suppliers offer **inefficiently high quality.**

Price floors often lead to inefficiency in that goods of **inefficiently high quality** are offered: sellers offer high-quality goods at a high price, even though buyers would prefer a lower quality at a lower price.

How can this be? Isn't high quality a good thing? Yes, but only if it is worth the cost. Suppose that suppliers spend a lot to make their goods of very high quality, but that this quality is not worth all that much to consumers, who would rather receive the money spent on that quality in the form of a lower price. Then this represents a missed opportunity: suppliers and buyers could make a mutually beneficial deal in which buyers got goods of somewhat lower quality for a much lower price.

#5: Illegal Activity Finally, like price floors, price ceilings can provide an incentive for *illegal activity*—only in this case it is sellers who will be bribing buyers.

Comparing the Predictions to the Facts

To sum up, a price floor creates various negative side-effects:

- An artificially-induced *surplus* of the good;
- Inefficiency that arises from the artificially-induced surplus, which can manifest itself in three ways—an inefficient allocation of sales among sellers, wasted resources, and an inefficiently high level of quality offered by suppliers;
- Temptation to engage in illegal activity, particularly bribery and corruption of government officials.

How well do these predictions fit the facts? Let's begin by considering price floors imposed on agricultural commodities, where the government buys up any unsold production at the floor price. This was the method employed by European Community in the 1970s for commodities such as butter, milk, and grains. The result? It soon found itself the proud owner of a so-called "butter mountain", which was followed in the 1980s with a "grain mountain", and then a "milk lake". Similarly, the United States government has at times found itself warehousing thousands of tons of butter, cheese, and other farm products. So, in the context of a variety of agricultural commodities, prediction #1 is supported by the facts.

What about the associated inefficiencies? As we have noted above, when the government commits itself to buying up the surplus production, all sellers will find a buyer; so it is difficult to argue that there will be an inefficient distribution of sales among sellers, or that sellers waste time and effort finding a buyer. Similarly, there is no need for sellers to produce an inappropriately high quality of the good in order to attract buyers. Instead, the inefficiency manifests itself in the tax dollars spent accumulating an unwanted surplus that may end up being either destroyed or thrown away because of spoilage—and this is pure waste. Moreover, this waste causes great political embarrassment, given the food shortages that exist in many parts of Africa. To avoid these occurrences, government officials have to spend time and effort disposing of the unwanted goods. Some governments, such as the European Union, end up paying exporters to sell products at a loss overseas. In the United States, the government has paid farmers to not produce the products at all.

Only when the surplus production is not sold will sellers waste time and effort finding buyers, and react by producing excessive quality. A good example comes from the days when trans-Atlantic airfares were set artificially high by international treaty. Surplus production manifested itself in empty seats. Forbidden to compete for customers by offering lower ticket prices, airlines tried to attract more customers by providing expensive services, like lavish in-flight meals—food that went largely uneaten. At one point, the regulators tried to restrict this practice by defining maximum service standards—for example, that a "snack service" should consist of no more than a sandwich. One airline then introduced what it called a "Scandinavian Sandwich", a towering affair, forcing the convening of another conference to define "sandwich". All of this was wasteful, especially considering that what passengers really wanted was less food and lower airfares.

Finally, if sellers are still unable to attract buyers they may resort to illegal behaviour. For example, workers desperate for jobs might agree to work off the books for employers who conceal their employment from the government—or who bribe the government inspectors. This practice is known in Europe as "black labour", and is especially common in Southern European countries, including Italy and Spain.

"Black Labour" in Southern Europe The best-known example of a price floor is the minimum wage rate. While there is some controversy over the effects of small increases in the minimum wage (as we will discuss in the next section), most economists believe that if the minimum wage is increased to a sufficiently high level, there will be adverse employment effects, especially on the least-skilled workers. This prediction is borne out in many European countries, where minimum wages, as a proportion of average weekly wages, have been set much higher than in Canada. The higher minimum wage in these countries is exacerbated by significantly higher payroll taxes than in Canada, which further increases the cost of hiring labour. (Payroll taxes make the actual cost of hiring a worker higher than the worker's pay cheque.)

The result is that in Europe the minimum wage is well above the wage rate that would make the quantity of labour supplied by workers equal to the quantity of labour demanded by employers. This results in high unemployment—an artificially induced surplus of millions of workers, especially young workers, who seek jobs but cannot find them.

In countries where the enforcement of labour laws is lax, however, there is a second, entirely predictable result: widespread evasion of the law. In both Italy and

Spain, officials believe that there are hundreds of thousands, if not millions, of workers who are employed by companies that pay them less than the legal minimum, fail to provide the required health or retirement benefits, or both. In many cases the jobs are simply unreported: Spanish economists estimate that about a third of the country's reported unemployed are actually working at unreported jobs in the black labour market. In fact, Spaniards waiting to collect cheques from the unemployment office have been known to complain about the long lines that keep them from getting back to work!

Employers in these countries have also found legal ways to evade the wage floor. For example, Italy's labour regulations apply only to companies with 15 or more workers. This gives a big cost advantage to small Italian firms, many of which remain small in order to avoid having to pay higher wages and benefits. And sure enough, in some Italian industries there is an astonishing proliferation of tiny companies. For example, one of Italy's most successful industries is the manufacture of fine woollen cloth, centred in the Prato region. The average textile firm in that region employs only four workers!

Some Controversy over the Effects of Minimum Wages We should not conclude without mentioning that there is currently a controversy in the economics profession about whether small increases in the minimum wage above the equilibrium do have negative employment effects. This controversy partly reflects the work of David Card and Alan Krueger,[2] which has set off a heated debate and eroded the consensus on the issue.

Looking at Figure 4-6, you may well think to yourself that adverse employment effects *must* occur as long as the minimum wage is binding (meaning that it is above the equilibrium wage of $6). This certainly is the prediction of the competitive model. But the question is whether the competitive model is the best framework to use when analysing minimum wage effects. Even though there may be large num-

[2]Much of this work is summarized in their book *Myth and Measurement: The New Economics of the Minimum Wage*, Princeton University Press, 1995.

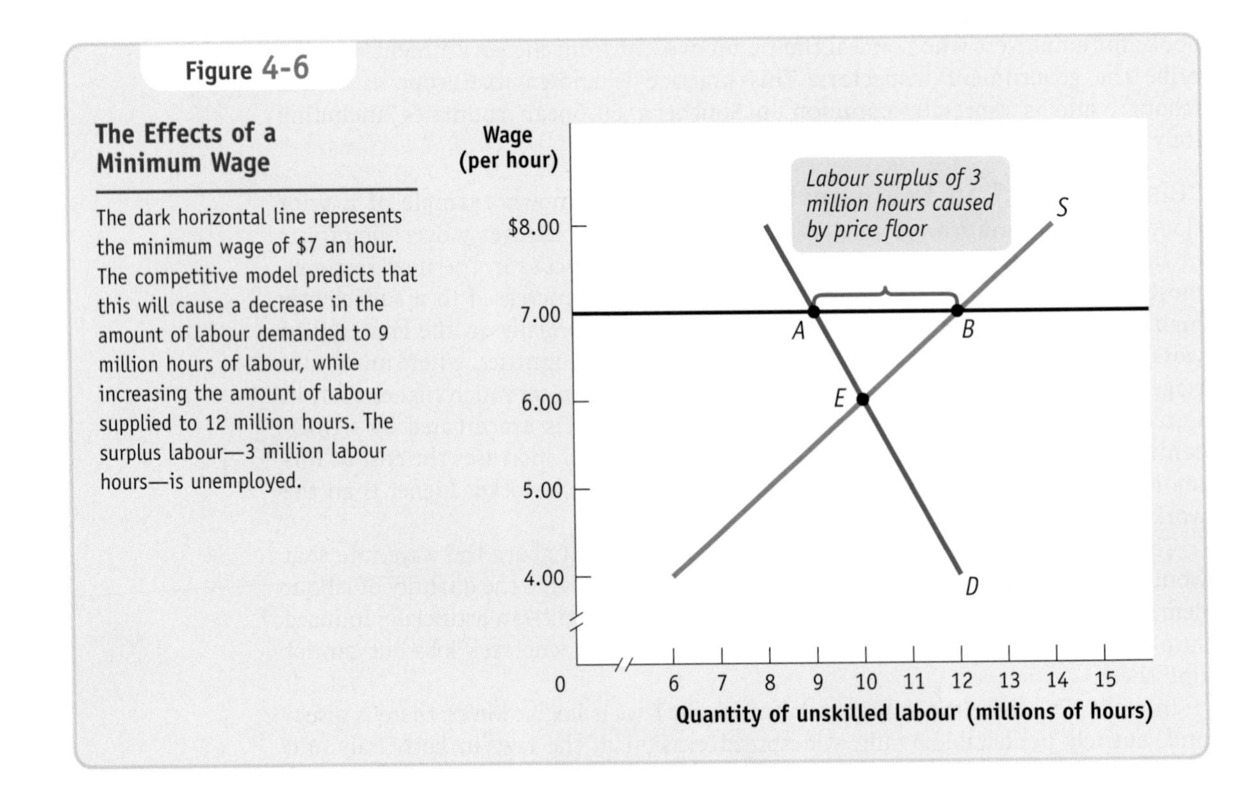

Figure 4-6

The Effects of a Minimum Wage

The dark horizontal line represents the minimum wage of $7 an hour. The competitive model predicts that this will cause a decrease in the amount of labour demanded to 9 million hours of labour, while increasing the amount of labour supplied to 12 million hours. The surplus labour—3 million labour hours—is unemployed.

bers of buyers and sellers of unskilled labour, the market may have some non-competitive elements. Like the housing market, the good in question is not identical. All jobs are slightly different—as are workers. Moreover, information is difficult to acquire, and finding the right job can involve a costly search process. This may give employers some ability to influence the market price. Of course, whether this matters or not is an empirical question.

There is another difference between labour markets and the markets for grain, butter, or blueberries: labour cares how much it sells for, whereas blueberries do not. This means that labour might work harder if it is paid better, and might be less inclined to shirk and less inclined to change jobs. These effects might stimulate demand for labour, but these are issues that Figure 4-6 does not incorporate. But again, whether they are important or not is an empirical matter.

Interestingly, at this point the empirical debate has not been resolved. Neumark and Wascher[3] observe that evidence is mixed for almost every country in the world, including the United States, France, the United Kingdom, New Zealand, and Portugal.

Only in Canada has the evidence been consistent—showing significant and increasingly important negative employment effects of minimum wages. But even here, new work by McDonald and Myatt,[4] suggests that whether minimum wages do have a negative employment effect in Canada depends crucially on the overall state of the economy. When the overall unemployment rate is low, only a very small effect is found.

To conclude, no one doubts that if the minimum wage were increased high enough, jobs would be lost and unemployment created. The debate is whether this conclusion holds true for small increases in the minimum wage above the equilibrium level. At stake is whether the competitive model is entirely appropriate to analyse all aspects of the labour market.

economics in action

If Minimum Wages Are Not a Good Way of Helping Labour, Then What Is?

Minimum wages in Canada are, on average, lower in terms of purchasing power than at any time in the last 30 years. They vary from a low of $5.90 an hour in Alberta to a high of $8.50 an hour in Nunavut (as of July 2004), and average around $7.00 an hour. Working 40 hours a week, 52 weeks a year at minimum wage pretty much guarantees an income below the poverty line. While many minimum-wage earners are young people from well-off families, more than 40 percent of minimum-wage earners come from poor households.[5] So, should minimum wages be increased?

One could certainly make a case for increasing the minimum wage. First, a small increase may not adversely affect the number of jobs available, especially in the context of low overall unemployment. Second, even if it did reduce the available jobs, it would still succeed in increasing the incomes of those who retain their jobs. This benefit may more than offset the cost of some young part-time workers being forced out of the labour market and some older full-time workers being forced onto welfare.

---

[3]David Neumark and William Wascher, "Minimum Wages, Labor Market Institutions, and Youth Employment: A Cross-National Analysis", *Industrial and Labour Relations Review* 57 (2004): 223–248.

[4]Ted McDonald and Tony Myatt, "The Minimum Wage Effect on Youth Employment in Canada: Testing the Robustness of Cross-Province Panel Studies", University of New Brunswick Working Paper 01-05 (2005).

[5]Nicole Fortin and Thomas Lemieux, "Income Redistribution in Canada: Minimum Wages Versus Other Policy Instruments", in *Public Policies in a Labour Market in Transition*, eds. W. C. Riddell and F. St-Hilaire (Montreal: Institute for Research on Public Policy, 2004).

Figure 4-7

The Effects of Job Training Schemes

If workers receive job training that makes them more productive, firms will be willing to hire more labour at all wage rates. In this way, the hourly wage can be increased to, say, $7 an hour, while avoiding lost jobs and unemployment. In this example, the number of jobs increases to 12 million labour hours. **>*web...***

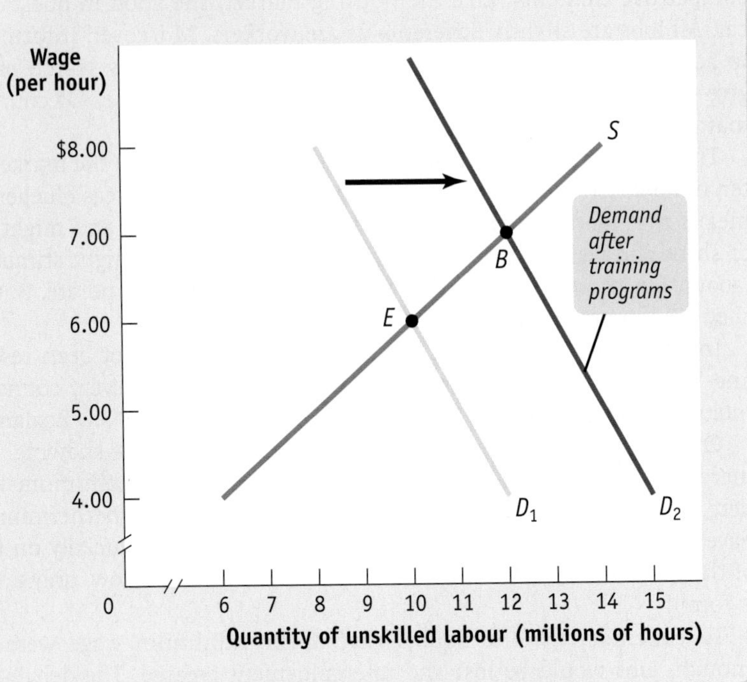

But can't we do better? Isn't it possible to help some workers without hurting others? The answer is 'yes', and the way to do that is through job training programs targeted specifically to low-income workers. If it is possible to make workers more productive, firms will be willing to hire more workers at any given wage. In other words, the demand for labour will shift out to the right, as shown in Figure 4-7. This figure shows that job training schemes can increase the equilibrium wage for less skilled workers and at the same time increase, rather than reduce, the number of jobs available. ■

>> QUICK REVIEW

- The most familiar price floor is the *minimum wage.* Price floors are also commonly imposed on agricultural goods.
- A price floor above the equilibrium price benefits successful sellers, but causes predictable adverse effects such as a persistent *surplus,* which leads to three kinds of inefficiencies: *inefficient allocation of sales among sellers, wasted resources,* and *inefficiently high quality.*
- Price floors encourage illegal activity such as workers who work "off the books", often leading to official corruption.

>> CHECK YOUR UNDERSTANDING 4-2

1. The provincial government mandates a price floor for gasoline of $1.30 per litre. Assess the following statements and illustrate your answer using the accompanying figure:
   a. Proponents of the law claim that it will increase the income of gas station owners. Opponents claim that it will hurt gas station owners as they lose customers.
   b. Proponents claim that consumers will be better off because gas stations will provide better service. Opponents claim that consumers will be generally worse off because they prefer to buy gas at cheaper prices.
   c. Proponents claim that they are helping gas station owners without hurting anyone else. Opponents claim that consumers are hurt and that they will end up doing things like driving across the provincial or international borders or buying gas on the black market.

Price ($ per litre of gas)
1.50
1.40
1.30
1.20
1.10
1.00
0.90
0.80
0
0.6 0.7 0.8 0.9 1.0 1.1 1.2 1.3 1.4 1.5
Quantity (millions of litres of gas)
B C S A D
Price floor

Controlling Quantities

We have seen that in an attempt to help farmers, the European Union established price floors for many agricultural commodities and bought up the resulting surpluses. We have also seen that this led to costly and embarrassing consequences—"mountains" of stored produce, much of which ended up being thrown away. The United States has tried to avoid this consequence of price floors by paying farmers not to produce. However, this has led to the comic (and very inefficient!) situation where farmers can make more money by *not* producing than they can by producing. Canada's approach has been to restrict the production of the supported commodity through quotas.

In general, governments try to regulate not only prices but also quantities. A **quota** is a form of **quantity control.** The total amount of the good that can be transacted under the quantity control is called the **quota limit.** Unlike price controls that can set upper or lower limits on prices, quantity controls always set an upper (not a lower) limit on quantities. Typically, the government limits quantity in a market by issuing **quota licenses**—which are actual pieces of paper giving you the right to produce a certain amount of the product.

A **quantity control** or **quota** is an upper limit on the quantity of some good that can be bought or sold. The total amount of the good that can be legally transacted is the **quota limit.**

A **quota license** gives its owner the right to supply a certain quantity of the good.

There are many examples of quantity controls, ranging from limits on the number of taxis that are allowed to operate in a metropolitan area, to limits on the quantity of salmon that West Coast fishers are allowed to catch. Some attempts to control quantities are undertaken for good economic reasons, some for bad ones; in many cases, as we will see, quantity controls introduced to address a temporary problem become politically hard to remove later because the beneficiaries don't want them to stop, even after the original reason for their existence is long gone. But whatever the reasons for such controls, they have certain predictable—and usually undesirable—economic consequences.

Canadian Agricultural Quotas

In Canada, the most important example of the use of quantity controls is in agriculture. In the early 1970s "marketing boards" were created for turkey, chicken, eggs, milk, butter, and cheese—the main purpose of which was not to "market" the product, but to set a price floor for the producer and to impose quotas to prevent surplus production. The idea was to help support and stabilize farm incomes, and ensure quality control.

Because poultry and dairy products are mobile across provincial and national borders, the schemes operate nationally under a set of federal/provincial agreements. The Canadian Dairy Commission sets national prices and determines provincial quotas for milk, butter, and cheese products; the National Farm Products Council does the same for eggs and poultry. Foreign imports are prevented with the use of high tariff barriers.

The marketing boards eliminate all competition. Competition among provinces is avoided since quotas are always stated in terms of market share (percentage of the total market), and these shares haven't been changed since the scheme was introduced in the 1970s. So, if the national body deemed that production must be lowered to maintain the floor price, all provinces would suffer the same percentage decrease in production. The provincial marketing boards would then pass on these percentage reductions to its own registered producers.

Competition between producers is also eliminated, since the producer is guaranteed the same price whether his output is sold to the public or to food processors, or ends up being destroyed. Competition with new producers is likewise eliminated, since new producers can only enter the market if they buy a quota from an existing producer.

So, high prices and the elimination of risk explain why farmers generally like the marketing boards. But consumers pay for these gains to farmers in the form of higher prices. We can estimate the extent of these higher prices in two ways: first, by the size of the tariffs required to keep out imports; and second, by the value of the quota itself. Since tariffs in some cases are as high as 300 percent, and since quota rights to become an average-size chicken producer (for example) can cost as much as half a million dollars, both methods suggest that Canadian consumers pay inflated prices for their cheapest sources of protein.

The Anatomy of Quotas

To understand why agricultural quotas are worth so much money, let's consider the market for milk, shown in Figure 4-8. The table in the figure shows hypothetical supply and demand schedules in terms of millions of litres of milk per week. The equilibrium, indicated by point *E* in the figure and by the shaded entries in the table, is a price of $1 per litre, with 13 million litres bought per week.

Until now, we have derived the demand curve by answering questions of the form: "How many litres of milk will customers want to buy if the price is $1 per litre?" But it is possible to reverse the question and ask instead: "At what price will consumers want to buy 13 million litres of milk?" The price consumers are willing to pay for a given quantity is known as the **demand price** of that quantity. You can see from the demand schedule in Figure 4-8 that the demand price of 13 million litres is $1.00 per litre, the demand price of 15 million litres is $0.60, and so on.

The **demand price** of a given quantity is the price at which consumers will demand that quantity.

Similarly, we have derived the supply curve by answering questions of the form: "How many litres of milk would dairy farmers supply at a price of $1 per litre?" But we can also reverse this question to ask: "At what price will suppliers be willing to supply 13 million litres?" The price at which suppliers will supply a given quantity is the **supply price** of the quantity. We can see from the supply schedule in Figure 4-8 that the supply price of 13 million litres is $1 per litre, the supply price of 15 million litres is $1.20, and so on.

The **supply price** of a given quantity is the price at which producers will supply that quantity.

Figure 4-8 The Market for Litres of Milk in the Absence of Government Controls

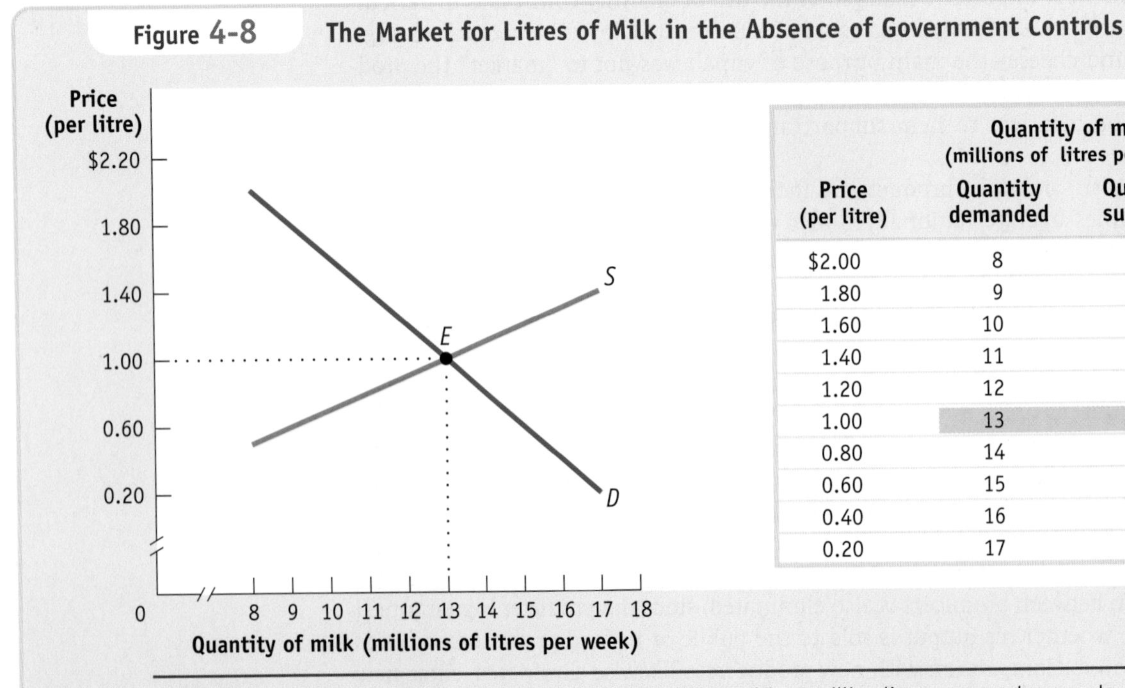

Price (per litre)	Quantity of milk (millions of litres per week) Quantity demanded	Quantity supplied
$2.00	8	23
1.80	9	21
1.60	10	19
1.40	11	17
1.20	12	15
1.00	13	13
0.80	14	11
0.60	15	9
0.40	16	7
0.20	17	5

Without government intervention, the market reaches equilibrium with 13 million litres consumed per week, at a price of $1 per litre.

Figure 4-9 Effect of a Quota on the Market for Milk

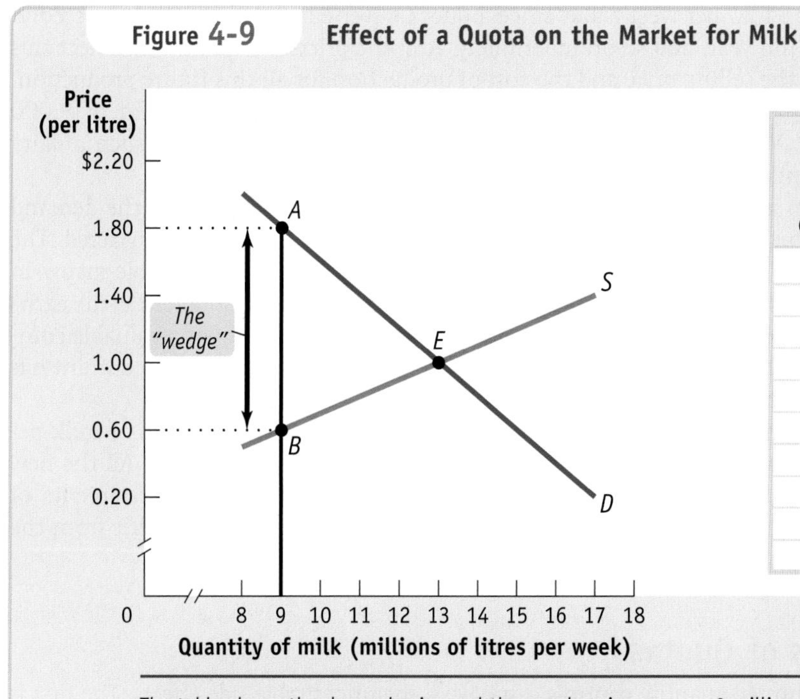

Price (per litre)	Quantity of milk (millions of litres per week) Quantity demanded	Quantity supplied
$2.00	8	23
1.80	9	21
1.60	10	19
1.40	11	17
1.20	12	15
1.00	13	13
0.80	14	11
0.60	15	9
0.40	16	7
0.20	17	5

The table shows the demand price and the supply price corresponding to each quantity: the price at which that quantity would be demanded and supplied, respectively. The government imposes a quota of 9 million litres, represented by the dark vertical line. The price paid by consumers rises to $1.80 per litre, the demand price of 9 million litres, shown by point *A*. The supply price of 9 million litres is only $0.60 per litre, shown by point *B*. The difference between these two prices is the quota rent per litre per week, the earnings that accrue to the owner of a quota. The quota rent drives a wedge between the demand price and the supply price. **>*web...***

Now, suppose the milk marketing board limits production to 9 million litres of milk per week. Figure 4-9 shows consumers must be at point *A* on the demand curve, corresponding to the shaded entry in the demand schedule: the demand price of 9 million litres of milk is $1.80 per litre. Meanwhile, milk producers must be at point *B* on the supply curve, corresponding to the shaded entry in the supply schedule: the supply price of 9 million litres of milk is $0.60 per litre.

But how can the price paid by consumers be $1.80 while the price received by milk producers is $0.60? The answer is that in addition to the market for milk, there will also be a market for milk quotas. Quota-holders may not always want to produce milk. In this event, they can sell their quotas to others for a fee. So we need to consider two sets of transactions here, and hence two prices: (1) transactions in milk, and the price at which these will occur; and (2) transactions in milk quotas, and the price at which these will occur. It will turn out that since we are looking at two markets, the prices $1.80 and $0.60 will both be right.

To see how this works, consider how much a prospective producer would be willing be pay for the right to produce a litre of milk. The supply price of a litre of milk is $0.60, yet that litre will sell for $1.80. So, the value of the right to produce that litre is the difference between these two prices. And the price of a quota will exactly equal this value. How can we be sure of that? Because competition among new entrants to acquire quotas will drive their price up until it exactly equals what they are worth.

In our example, the value of a quota allowing a producer to sell one litre of milk is $1.20 per week ($1.80 minus $0.60). Now we can see why quotas are worth so much money. Over the course of a year, this one-litre quota is worth $62.40

(52 weeks at $1.20 per week). But since a quota never expires, there is also a second year, and a third year, and so on indefinitely. And the price of a quota will reflect this difference in the selling price and the cost of production for all this future production.

Moreover, a moderately sized dairy operation would produce upward of 9,000 litres a week. We now see why, in real life, the quotas associated with such a dairy operation would cost about $1.5 million.

The reason a quota is valuable comes back to the difference between the demand price of the quantity transacted and the supply price of the quantity transacted. The quota drives a **wedge** between these two prices, illustrated by the double arrow in Figure 4-9. This wedge has a special name: the **quota rent.** The quota rent is the earnings that accrue to the holder of the quota license from ownership of a valuable commodity, the right to sell the good. This is precisely the amount that a new entrant has to pay for a quota on a per-litre, per-week basis.

A quantity control or quota drives a **wedge** between the demand price and the supply price of a good; that is, the price paid by buyers ends up being higher than that received by sellers. The difference between the demand and supply price at the quota limit is the **quota rent,** the earnings that accrue to the holder of the quota license from ownership of the right to sell the good. It is equal to the market price of the quota when quotas are traded.

So, a new entrant into the dairy business would make $1.80 per litre of milk per week. But $1.20 of this is going to pay for the cost of buying the quota. All the new entrant really makes is $0.60 per litre, per week. Only the original recipients of quotas—when they were given away back in the 1970s—receive any benefit from the quota system in terms of increased income.

The Costs of Quotas

Like price controls, quantity controls can have some undesirable side effects. The first is the by-now familiar problem of *inefficiency* due to missed opportunities: quantity controls prevent mutually beneficial transactions from occurring—transactions that would benefit both buyers and sellers. Looking back at the table in Figure 4-9, you can see that starting at the quota limit of 9 million litres, individuals would be willing to pay at least $1.60 per litre for an additional 1 million litres and that milk producers would be willing to produce that milk as long as they get at least $0.70 per litre. Thus, this is milk that would have been consumed if the quota limit were not in place. The same is true for the next 1 million litres: individuals are willing to pay at least $1.40 per litre when the number of litres is increased from 10 to 11 million, and milk producers are willing to produce that milk as long as they get at least $0.80 per litre. Again, this milk would have been consumed without the quota limitation, and again it represents missed opportunities.

Generally, *as long as the demand price of a given quantity exceeds the supply price, there is a missed opportunity.* A buyer would be willing to buy the good at a price that the seller would be willing to accept, but such a transaction does not occur because the quota forbids it.

And because there are transactions that people would like to make but are not supposed to, quantity controls generate an incentive to engage in manoeuvres to evade them or even to break the law. This means that the marketing boards must not only set the quotas but also enforce them. They must investigate cases in which farmers illegally supply milk to stores and supermarkets, or illegal egg producers package their eggs in the discarded boxes of a legal producer. In sum, quantity controls typically create the following undesirable side effects:

- Inefficiencies, or missed opportunities, in the form of mutually beneficial transactions that don't occur
- Incentives for illegal activities

The Future of Quotas

So agricultural quotas are inefficient, generate incentives for illegal activity, raise the prices of inexpensive sources of protein, and don't even benefit many of the producers in the industry. Why don't we just abolish them?

If only it were so simple. New farmers purchased their quotas, and the higher prices they derive for their output represents the return on their investment. If quotas were ever abolished, they would have a legal case for compensation. In addition, many farmers look to sell their quotas upon retirement, and depend upon this for their retirement income.

The main threat to agricultural quotas, and the main hope for Canadian consumers, comes from international trade agreements. Less developed countries are increasingly impatient with agricultural trade barriers in developed countries and are demanding their removal. But the farming lobby in the developed countries has, up to this point, succeeded in blocking these initiatives. As a result, the last round of World Trade Organization negotiations, in Cancun in 2003, ended in complete disarray.

Quotas, once created, are hard to eliminate. This problem doesn't arise only with agricultural quotas. In most major Canadian cities, taxicab regulation limits the number of taxis to only those who hold taxi licenses (or "plates" or "medallions"). For example, in 2001 only about 4,000 medallions existed for the entire city of Toronto. These traded for about $100,000 each. Abolishing these quotas without compensation would be hard on the 25 percent of medallion owners who are drivers and depend on selling them for their retirement income. It would also be hard on other owners—lawyers, dentists, and middlemen—who regard the medallion as an investment, just like a bond.

But abolishing these medallions and compensating the owners would cost $400 million (4,000 medallions worth $100,000 each). Is this the best way to spend scarce tax dollars? Certainly the municipality of Toronto could not afford so steep a bill. So quotas, once created, are hard to eliminate.

economics in action

The Atlantic Lobster Fishery

We have seen how quotas in agricultural produce have had pernicious effects on the prices consumers pay. We now want to look at an instance where quotas have helped.

Without quota limitations, there would almost certainly be overfishing. Indeed, overfishing undoubtedly contributed to the death of Newfoundland's cod fishery. Fortunately for the East coast, however, there remains a profitable and vibrant lobster fishery that provides direct employment for about 32,000 people and has a substantial impact on the Atlantic community. In an effort to protect this fishery, a quota system was established in 1967. Only people with lobster fishing licenses are allowed to catch lobster.

It is important to note that fishing licenses are an example of a quota that is justified by broader environmental considerations—unlike taxicab medallions or Canadian agricultural quotas. Nevertheless, Atlantic lobster licenses work the same way as any quota system. In particular, the main beneficiaries are the recipients of the original licenses. Today, the going price of a lobster license depends on the fishing area for which it is designated. A license for Grand Manan Island in the Bay of Fundy will change hands for around $250,000.[6] That expense is in addition to that of your boat, your traps, and all the rest of your gear. But the lobster fishers of Grand Manan are grateful for quotas despite their expense, for without them there would be no lobsters to catch. ■

>> QUICK REVIEW

- *Quantity controls* or *quotas* are government-imposed limits on how much of a good may be bought or sold. The quantity allowed for sale is the *quota limit.* The government then issues a quota license—the right to sell a given quantity of a good under the quota.
- Because the quota limit is smaller than the amount of the good transacted in an unregulated market, the *demand price* is higher than the *supply price,* at the quota limit. This difference is called a *wedge.*
- This wedge is the *quota rent,* the earnings that accrue to the owner of the quota-license from possessing the valuable right to sell the good.
- Like price controls, quantity controls create inefficiencies and encourage illegal activity.

[6]Fisheries Resource Conservation Council, "A Conservation Framework for Atlantic Lobster" (Ottawa, ON: FRCC, November 1995).

>>CHECK YOUR UNDERSTANDING 4-3

1. Suppose that Figure 4-8 gives the supply and demand for milk, but that the quota is set at 10 million litres per week instead of 9 million. Find the following and indicate them on Figure 4-8:
   a. The price of a litre of milk
   b. The quota rent
2. Illustrate the answer to the following using Figure 4-8.
   a. Suppose the quota limit is further increased to 12 million litres. What happens to the quota rent?
   b. Assume that the quota limit is 12 million litres. Suppose demand falls due to a health scare about hormones given to dairy cattle adversely affecting humans. What is the smallest decrease in demand that would result in the quota no longer having an effect on the market?

A Surprise Parallel: Taxes

To provide the services we want, from national defence to public parks, governments must collect taxes. But taxes impose costs on the economy. Among the most important roles of economics is tax analysis: figuring out the economic costs of taxation, determining who bears those costs, and suggesting ways to change the tax system that will reduce the costs it imposes. It turns out that the same analysis that we have just used to understand quotas can be used, with hardly any modification, to make a preliminary analysis of taxes too.

Why a Tax Is Like a Quota

Suppose that the supply and demand curves for milk were exactly as shown in Figure 4-8. Again, this means that in the absence of government action, the equilibrium price of a litre of milk will be $1, and 13 million litres will be bought and sold.

An **excise tax** is a tax on sales of a particular good or service.

Now suppose that instead of imposing a quota on the number of rides, the government imposes an **excise tax**—a tax on sales of a particular good or service. Specifically, it charges milk producers $1.20 for each litre they sell. What is the effect of the tax?

From the point of view of a milk producer, the tax means that he or she doesn't get to keep all of the price: if a customer pays a $2 a litre, $1.20 goes in tax, so the producer gets only $0.80. This increases the *supply price* corresponding to any given number of litres produced—for example, dairy farmers will now require a price of $2.20 to supply as many litres as they would have been willing to supply at a price of $1 in the absence of the $1.20 tax.

So, the tax on sales shifts the supply curve up by the amount of the tax. This is shown in Figure 4-10, where S_1 is the supply curve before the tax is imposed, and S_2 is the supply curve after the tax is imposed. The market equilibrium moves from *E*, where the price is $1 per litre and 13 million litres are bought and sold, to *A*, where the price is $1.80 per litre and 9 million litres are bought and sold. *A* is, of course, on both the demand curve *D* and the new supply curve S_2.

But how do we know that 9 million litres will be supplied at a price of $1.80? Because the price *net of the tax* is $0.60, and the pre-tax supply price of 9 million litres is $0.60, as shown by point *B* in Figure 4-10.

Does all this look familiar? It should. The equilibrium with a $1.20 tax on a litre of milk, which reduces the quantity bought and sold to 9 million litres, looks just like the equilibrium with a quota of 9 million litres, which leads to a quota rent of $1.20. Just like a quota, the tax *drives a wedge* between the demand price and the supply price.

The only difference is that instead of paying $1.20 towards the cost of a quota, producers pay a $1.20 tax to the government. In fact, there is a way to make an excise tax and a quota completely equivalent. Imagine that instead of issuing a limited number of quotas, the government simply rented them at $1.20 per litre per week. This $1.20 quota rent charged by the government would, for all practical purposes, be a $1.20 excise tax.

Figure 4-10

Effect of an Excise Tax Levied on the Sales of Milk

S_1 is the supply curve before the tax. After the government requires producers to pay a tax of $1.20 for every litre they produce, the supply curve shifts up by $1.20, to the new supply curve S_2. This means that the price producers receive net of tax is $0.60, represented by point *B* on the old supply curve S_1. And the price paid by consumers is $1.80, represented by point *A* on the new supply curve S_2. The tax drives a wedge between the demand price, $1.80, and the supply price, $0.60.

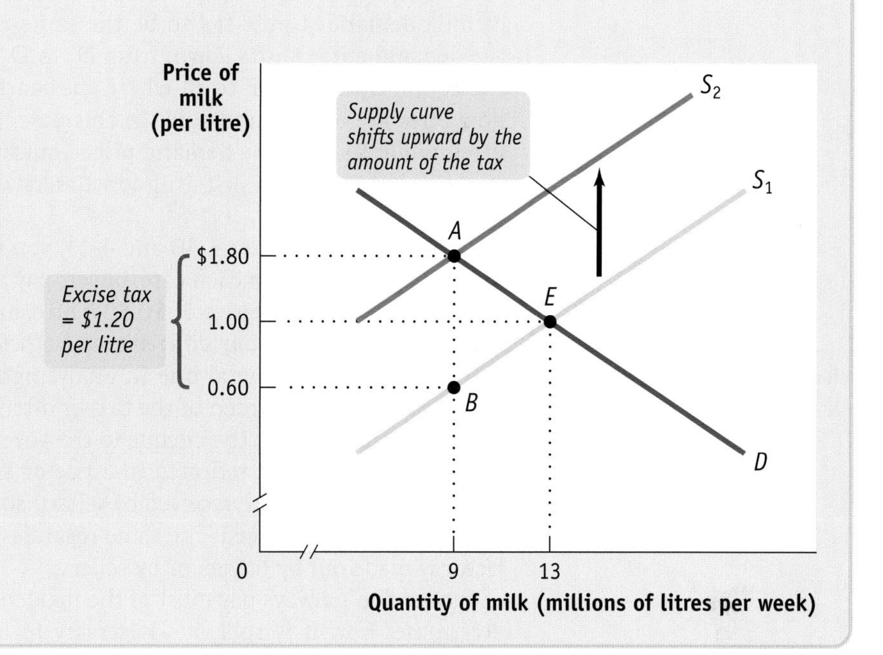

Who Pays an Excise Tax?

We have just imagined a tax that must be paid by the *sellers* of a good. But what would happen if the tax was instead paid by the *buyers*—if, say, to buy a litre of milk you had to pay a special $1.20 tax?

The answer is shown in Figure 4-11. If a milk consumer must pay a $1.20 tax on each litre, this means that a price of $0.60 a litre is in effect a price of $1.80 a litre.

Figure 4-11

Effect of an Excise Tax Levied on Purchases of Milk

D_1 is the demand curve before the tax. After the government requires consumers to pay the $1.20 tax per litre, the demand curve shifts down by $1.20 to the new demand curve D_2. Producers again receive, net of tax, $0.60, represented by point *B*, while consumers again pay a total price of $1.80, represented by point *A*. The *incidence* of the tax is exactly the same as in Figure 4-10; this shows that who officially pays a tax is irrelevant when answering the question of who bears the burden of the tax.

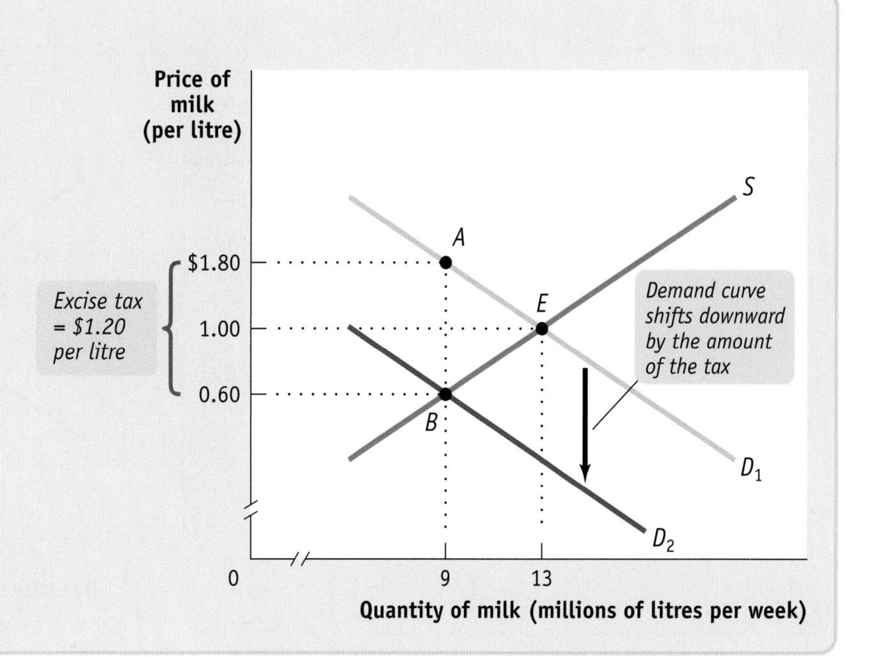

That is, the price buyers pay must be $1.20 lower in order for the number of litres of milk demanded post-tax to be the same number as that demanded pre-tax. So the demand curve shifts *down*, from D_1 to D_2, by the amount of the tax. This shifts the equilibrium from *E* to *B*, where the market price is $0.60 per litre and 9 million litres are bought and sold. In this case, $0.60 is the supply price of 9 million litres, while $1.80 is the demand price—but in effect, buyers do pay $1.80 when the tax is included. So it is just as if consumers were on their original demand curve at point *A*.

If you compare Figures 4-10 and 4-11, you will immediately notice that they show the same price effect. In each case, buyers pay an effective price of $1.80 per litre, sellers receive an effective price of $0.60 a litre, and 9 million litres are bought and sold. *It doesn't seem to make any difference who officially pays the tax.*

The **incidence** of a tax is a measure of who really pays it.

This insight is a general one in analyzing taxes: the **incidence** of a tax—that is, who *really* bears the burden of the tax—is often not a question you can answer by asking who actually writes the cheque to the government. In this particular case a $1.20 per litre tax on milk is reflected in a rise of $0.80 in the price paid by buyers and a fall of $0.40 in the price received by sellers; so the incidence of the tax is mostly paid by buyers. This incidence is the same regardless of whether the cheque to the tax collector is made out by buyers or by sellers.

Buyers don't always pay most of the incidence of an excise tax; to understand what determines how it *is* split, it's necessary to use information about the supply and demand curves.

The Revenue from an Excise Tax

While both buyers and sellers lose from an excise tax, the government does collect revenue—which is the whole point of the tax. How much revenue does the government collect? The answer is that the revenue is equal to the area of the shaded rectangle in Figure 4-12.

To see why this is the revenue collected by a $1.20 per litre tax on milk, notice that the *height* of the rectangle is $1.20. This is the amount of the tax per litre; it is also, as we have seen, the size of the wedge that the tax drives between the supply price and

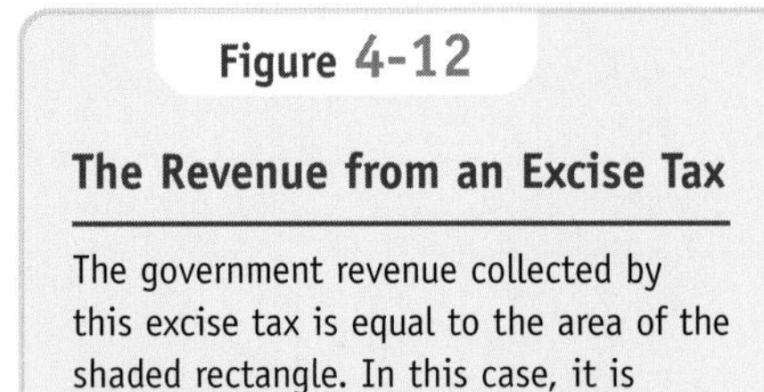

Figure 4-12

The Revenue from an Excise Tax

The government revenue collected by this excise tax is equal to the area of the shaded rectangle. In this case, it is $1.20 per litre x 9 million litres = $10.8 million.

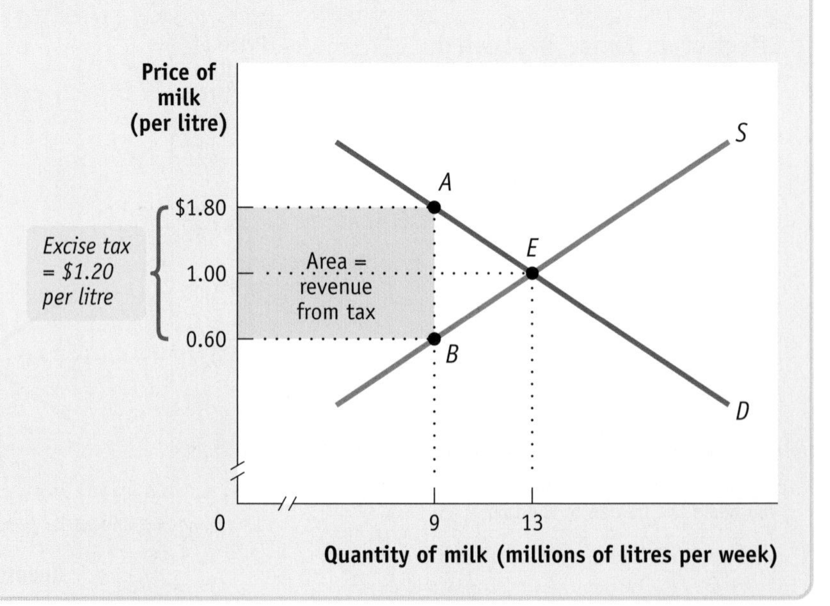

the demand price. Meanwhile, the *width* of the rectangle is 9 million litres, which is the equilibrium number of litres given that $1.20 tax.

The revenue collected by the tax is

$$\text{Revenue} = \$1.20 \text{ per litre} \times 9 \text{ million litres} = \$10.8 \text{ million}$$

But the area of the rectangle is

$$\text{Area} = \text{height} \times \text{width} = \$1.2 \times 9 \text{ million} = \$10.8 \text{ million}$$

This is a general principle: *the revenue collected by an excise tax is equal to the area of the rectangle whose height is the wedge that the tax drives between the supply and demand curves, and whose width is the quantity bought and sold under the tax.*

The Costs of Taxation

What is the cost of a tax? You might be inclined to answer that it is the money taxpayers pay to the government. But suppose that the government used that money to provide services everyone wants, or for that matter simply handed out the money to taxpayers. Would we then say that the tax didn't cost anything?

No—because a tax, like a quota, prevents mutually beneficial transactions from occurring. Consider Figure 4-12 once more. With a $1.20 per litre tax on milk, consumers pay $1.80 per litre, while producers receive only $0.60 per litre. There are therefore some potential consumers who would be willing to drink milk if the price were only, say, $1.40 per litre; and there are producers who would be willing to supply those litres for a price of, say, $0.80. If those producers and consumers could be brought together, this would be a mutually beneficial transaction. But such a deal would be illegal, because the $1.20 tax would not have been paid.

More broadly, we know that the tax reduces consumption by 4 million litres of milk each week. This milk would have been consumed in the absence of the tax, to the mutual benefit of the consumers and producers.

So an excise (or sales) tax imposes additional costs, in the form of inefficiency, over and above the money actually paid in taxes. This inefficiency occurs because the tax discourages mutually beneficial transactions. This is referred to as the **excess burden** or **deadweight loss** from a tax. And all real-world taxes do impose some excess burden, although badly designed taxes impose bigger excess burdens than well-thought-out taxes.

The **excess burden** or **deadweight loss** from a tax is the extra cost in the form of inefficiency that results because the tax discourages mutually beneficial transactions.

Economists sometimes say that the real cost of a tax is not the taxes that people pay but the taxes that they *don't* pay. What they mean is that people change their behaviour in order to avoid taxes—for example, by going hungry instead of drinking a glass of milk—and in so doing miss opportunities for mutual benefit.

One final point: like all of the other government policies analyzed in this chapter, taxes create incentives for illegal activity. The following Economics in Action explains how excise taxes on cigarettes have given rise to a substantial smuggling business. And, of course, even seemingly respectable people have been known to be a bit creative with their income taxes.

economics in action

When a Canadian Tax Became Too High

Cigarettes have long been subject to excise taxes. But from 1982 to 1993, as the anti-smoking movement gained political power, cigarette taxes in Canada rose from an average of $0.59 to $3.86 per pack. Governments saw this as a way of raising more revenue while discouraging a bad habit.

However, U.S. sales taxes (which are a state rather than a federal matter) remained relatively low. In particular, the states bordering Canada had much lower taxes than we did. For example, in early 1994 the state of Michigan had a tax rate of only $0.25 per pack. This divergence created an opportunity for those who didn't mind breaking the law. By 1994, organized crime was conducting massive smuggling operations into Canada. Violence increased, merchants suffered, and in one year alone the federal and provincial governments lost over $2 billion in tax revenues. Estimates suggested that nearly one in three cigarettes in Canada was contraband. This led to a fall in the average price paid for cigarettes, which undermined the government's health policy objectives of reducing tobacco consumption—particularly among youth.

By 1994, shaken by the crime explosion and lost tax revenues, Canadian Prime Minister Jean Chrétien said the cigarette tax threatened "the very fabric of Canadian society". Even the Federal Health Minister argued that a tax cut was needed to force children to rely on regular stores for their cigarettes where purchases could be better controlled. As a result, in July 1994 federal and provincial cigarette taxes were slashed (by around $1.40 a pack). This, combined with an increase in taxes in Michigan (from $0.25 to $0.75 a pack), essentially eliminated cigarette smuggling into Canada.

>>QUICK REVIEW

- Like a quota, an *excise tax* drives a wedge between the demand price and the supply price.
- The *incidence* of an excise tax does not depend on who officially pays the tax, the buyer or the seller.
- Like a quota, an excise tax creates inefficiency by preventing mutually beneficial transactions between buyers and sellers. This *excess burden* or *deadweight loss* from a tax means that its true cost is always larger than the amount paid in taxes.
- Also like quotas, taxes create an incentive for illegal activity.

>>CHECK YOUR UNDERSTANDING 4-4

Use Figure 4-4 to answer the following questions.

a. What amount of excise tax generates the same level of inefficiency as a quota of 9 million pint boxes of blueberries?

b. What quota level generates the same level of inefficiency as an excise tax of $3.00 per pint box of blueberries?

c. In a and b, find how the burden of an excise tax is split between buyers and sellers. That is, explain how much of the tax is paid by buyers and how much is paid by sellers in each case.

• A LOOK AHEAD •

In the last two chapters, we have gotten a first taste of how economic models help us understand the real world. As we've seen, supply and demand—a simple model of how markets work—can be used to understand and predict the effects of everything from bad weather to misconceived government policies.

In the chapters to come, we'll see how models—including supply and demand, but others as well—can shed light on a wide variety of economic phenomena and issues.

SUMMARY

1. Governments often intervene in markets in attempts to "defy" supply and demand. Interventions take the form of **price controls** or **quantity controls.** But they generate predictable and undesirable side effects, consisting of various forms of inefficiency and illegal activity.
2. A **price ceiling**—a maximum market price—below the equilibrium price benefits buyers but creates shortages: because price is maintained below the equilibrium price, it increases the quantity demanded and reduces the quantity supplied compared to the equilibrium quantity. This leads to predictable problems: **inefficiencies** in the form of **inefficient allocation to consumers, wasted resources,** and **inefficiently low quality.** It also encourages illegal activity as people turn to **black markets** to get the good. Because of these problems, price ceilings have generally lost favour as an economic policy tool. But some governments continue to impose them, either because they don't understand the effects or because the price ceilings benefit some influential group.
3. A **price floor**—a minimum market price—above the equilibrium price benefits sellers but creates persistent surplus: because price is maintained above the equilibrium price, it reduces the quantity demanded and increases the quantity supplied compared to the equilibrium quantity. This leads to predictable problems: inefficiencies in the form of **inefficient allocation of sales**

among sellers, wasted resources,** and **inefficiently high quality.** It also encourages illegal activity and black markets. The most well-known kind of price floor is the minimum wage law, but price floors are also commonly applied to agricultural products.

4. **Quantity controls,** or **quotas,** limit the quantity of a good that can be bought or sold. The amount allowed for sale is called the **quota limit.** The government issues **licenses** to individuals, the right to sell a given quantity of the good. The owner of a license earns a **quota rent,** earnings that accrue from the right to sell the good. It is equal to the **demand price** at the quota limit—what consumers are willing to pay for that amount—and to the **supply price** at the quota limit, what suppliers are willing to accept for that amount. Economists say that a quota drives a **wedge** between the demand price and the supply price, and this wedge is equal to the quota rent. Quantity controls generate inefficiency in the form of mutually beneficial transactions that don't occur, as well as encouraging illegal activity.
5. **Excise taxes**—taxes on the purchase or sale of a good—have effects similar to quotas. They raise the price paid by buyers and reduce the price received by sellers, driving a wedge between the two. The **incidence** of the tax—the division of higher prices to consumers and lower prices to sellers—does not depend upon who officially pays the tax. Excise taxes cause inefficiency because they prevent some mutually beneficial transactions. This inefficiency is the **excess burden** or **deadweight loss** caused by the tax. Excise taxes also encourage illegal activity in attempts to avoid the tax.

KEY TERMS

Price controls, p. 87
Price ceiling, p. 87
Price floor, p. 87
Binding, p. 88
Inefficient, p. 89
Inefficient allocation to consumers, p. 90
Wasted resources, p. 90
Inefficiently low quality, p. 90
Black market, p. 91
Minimum wage, p. 96
Inefficient allocation of sales among sellers, p. 97
Inefficiently high quality, p. 98
Quantity control, p. 103
Quota, p. 103
Quota limit, p. 103
Quota license, p. 103
Demand price, p. 104
Supply price, p. 104
Wedge, p. 106
Quota rent, p. 106
Excise tax, p. 108
Incidence, p. 110
Excess burden, p. 111
Deadweight loss, p. 111

PROBLEMS

1. Suppose it is decided that rent control in Toronto will be abolished and that market rents will now prevail. Assume that all rental units are identical and are therefore offered at the same rent. To address the plight of low-income residents who may be unable to pay the market rent, an income supplement will be paid to all low-income households equal to the difference between the old controlled rent and the new market rent.

    a. Use a diagram to show the effect on the rental market of the elimination of rent control. What will happen to the quality and quantity of rental housing supplied?

    b. Use a second diagram to then show the additional effect of the income supplement policy on the market. What effect does the income supplement policy have on the market rent and quantity of rental housing supplied in comparison to your answers to part a?

    c. Are tenants better or worse off as a result of these policies? Are landlords better or worse off as a result of these policies?

    d. From a political standpoint, why do you think cities have been more likely to resort to rent control rather than a policy of income supplements to help low-income people pay for housing?

2. In order to ingratiate himself with voters, the mayor of Gotham City decides to lower the price of taxi rides in the city. Assume, for simplicity, that all taxi rides are the same distance and therefore cost the same. The following table shows the demand and supply schedules for taxi rides.

Fare (per ride)	Quantity demanded (millions of rides per year)	Quantity supplied (millions of rides per year)
$7.00	10	12
6.50	11	11
6.00	12	10
5.50	13	9
5.00	14	8
4.50	15	7

    a. Assume that there are no restrictions on the number of taxi rides that can be supplied in the city (i.e., there is no medallion system). Find the market equilibrium price and quantity.

b. Suppose that the mayor sets a price ceiling of $5.50. How large is the shortage of rides? Illustrate with a diagram. Who loses and who benefits from this policy?

c. Suppose that the stock market crashes and, as a result, people in Gotham City are poorer. This reduces the quantity of taxi rides demanded by 6 million rides per year at any given price. What effect will the mayor's new policy have now? Illustrate with a diagram.

d. Suppose that the stock market rises and the demand for taxi rides returns to normal (that is, returns to the demand schedule given in the table). The mayor now decides to ingratiate himself with taxi drivers. He announces a policy in which operating licences are given to existing taxi drivers; the number of licences is restricted so that only 10 million rides per year can be given. Illustrate the effect of this policy on the market, and indicate the resulting price and quantity transacted. What is the quota rent per ride?

3. Suppose that Gotham City controls the price of bread, set at a predetermined price that is above the market price.

a. Draw a diagram that shows the effect of the policy. Will the policy act as a price ceiling or a price floor?

b. What kinds of inefficiencies are likely to arise when the controlled price of bread is above the market price?

Suppose that for a one-year period a poor wheat harvest causes a leftward shift in the supply of bread and therefore an increase in the market price of bread. Bakers now find that the controlled price of bread is below the market price.

c. Draw a diagram that shows the effect of the price control on the market for bread during this one-year period. Did the policy act as a price ceiling or a price floor?

d. What kinds of inefficiencies do you think occurred during this period? Explain in detail.

4. The accompanying table shows the demand and supply schedules for blueberries. Suppose the Canadian government decides that the incomes of blueberry farmers should be maintained at a level that allows the traditional family blueberry business to survive. The government therefore implements a price floor of $1 per quart. It does this by buying surplus blueberries until the price is $1 per quart.

Price (per quart)	Quantity demanded (millions of quarts per year)	Quantity supplied (millions of quarts per year)
$1.20	550	850
1.10	600	800
1.00	650	750
0.90	700	700
0.80	750	650

a. How many surplus blueberries will be produced as a result of this policy?

b. What will be the cost to the government of this policy?

c. Since blueberries are an important part of the Canadian diet, the government decides to provide the surplus blueberries it purchases to elementary schools at a price of only $0.60 per quart. Assume that schools will buy any amount of blueberries available at this low price. But parents now reduce their purchases of blueberries at any price by 50 million quarts per year because they know that their children are getting blueberries at school. How much will the blueberry program now cost the government?

d. Give two examples of inefficiencies arising from wasted resources that are likely to result from this policy. What is the missed opportunity in each case?

5. As noted in the text, European governments tend to make greater use of price controls than does the Canadian government. For example, the French government sets minimum starting yearly wages for new hires who have completed *le bac,* a diploma roughly equivalent to a high school diploma. The demand schedule for new hires with *le bac* and the supply schedule of new job seekers with *le bac* are given in the accompanying table. The price here—given in euros, the currency used in France—is the same as the yearly wage.

Wage (per year)	Quantity demanded (new hires per year)	Quantity supplied (new job seekers per year)
$45,000	200,000	325,000
40,000	220,000	320,000
35,000	250,000	310,000
30,000	290,000	290,000
25,000	370,000	200,000

a. In the absence of government interference, what is the equilibrium wage and number of graduates hired per year? Illustrate with a diagram. Will there be anyone who seeks a job at the equilibrium wage who is unable to find one—that is, will there be anyone who is involuntarily unemployed?

b. Suppose the French government sets a minimum yearly wage of 35,000 euros. Is there any involuntary unemployment at this wage? If so, how much? Illustrate with a diagram. What if the minimum wage is set at 40,000 euros? Also illustrate with a diagram.

c. Given your answer to part b and the information in the table, what do you think is the relationship between the level of involuntary unemployment and the level of the minimum wage set by the government? Who benefits from such a policy? Who loses? What is the missed opportunity here?

6. Until recently, the standard number of hours worked per week for a full-time job in France was 40 hours, just as in Canada. But in response to social unrest over high levels of involuntary unemployment, the French government instituted a 35-hour workweek—a worker could not work more than 35 hours per week even if both the worker and employer wanted it. The motivation behind this policy was that if current employees worked fewer hours, employers would be forced to hire more new workers. Assume that it is costly to employers to train new workers. French employers were greatly opposed to this policy and threatened to move their operations to neighbouring countries that did not have such employment restrictions. Can you explain their attitude? Give an example of both an inefficiency and an illegal activity that are likely to arise from this policy.

7. Suppose the Canadian government is considering the use of price supports to provide income assistance to Canadian wheat farmers. It has two schemes in mind. Scheme A uses price floors, which it will maintain by buying up the surplus wheat production. Scheme B uses target prices in combination with quotas. In Scheme B, the government limits overall production and gives the farmer an amount equal to the difference between the market price and the target price for each unit sold. Consider the market for wheat depicted in the accompanying diagram:

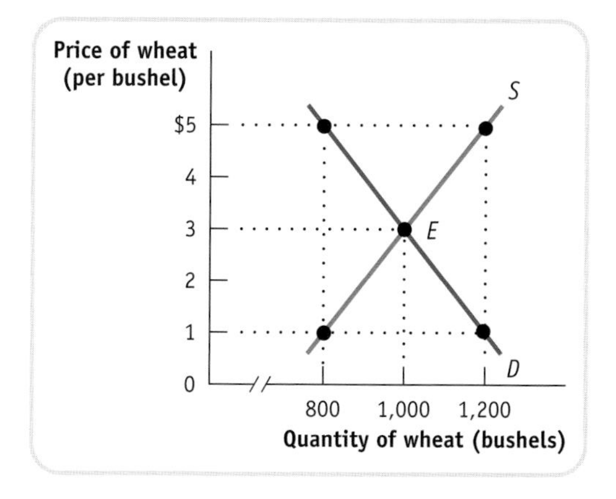

a. If the government sets a price floor of $5.00, how many bushels of wheat are produced? How many are purchased by consumers? By the government? How much income do wheat farmers earn? How much does the program cost the government?

b. Suppose the government sets a target price of $5.00 and a quota of 1,000 bushels. How many bushels of wheat are purchased by consumers and at what price? By the government? How much revenue do wheat farmers receive? How much does the program cost the government?

c. Which program costs wheat consumers more? Which program costs the government more? Explain.

d. What are the inefficiencies that arise in each case?

8. The waters off the Pacific coast were once teeming with salmon. Now, due in part to overfishing by the commercial fishing industry, the stocks of salmon are seriously depleted. Since 1985, under the Pacific Salmon Treaty, the United States and Canada have tried to agree on quotas to allow fish stocks to recover. Canada's quota limits the amount of salmon caught per year by all Canada-licensed fishing boats. As soon as the Canadian fishing fleet meets the quota limit, the salmon fishery is closed down for the rest of the year. The following table gives hypothetical demand and supply schedules for salmon caught in Canada. Suppose the quota is set at 7 million kilograms.

Price of salmon (per kilogram)	Quantity of salmon (millions of kilograms per year)	
	Quantity demanded	Quantity supplied
$20	6	15
18	7	13
16	8	11
14	9	9
12	10	7

a. Use a diagram to show the effect of this policy on the market for Canadian salmon in 1991.

b. How do you think fishermen will change how they fish in response to this policy?

c. Use your diagram from part a to show an excise tax that achieves the same reduction in the amount of salmon caught as the quota. What is the amount of the tax per kilogram?

d. What kinds of activities do you think an excise tax will tempt people to engage in?

e. The excise tax is collected from the fishermen, who protest that they alone are bearing the burden of this policy. Why might this protest be misguided?

9. Since the Auto Pact was abandoned in February 2001 as a result of a World Trade Organization ruling, Canada has had free trade in cars and trucks. Suppose, however, that the government decides it would like to help Canadian truck manufacturers compete against foreign imports. It could do this by imposing a quota on the number of foreign trucks imported into Canada, or it could impose an excise tax on each foreign truck sold in Canada. Hypothetical demand and supply schedules for imported trucks are given in the following table:

Price ($ per truck)	Quantity demanded (hundreds of trucks)	Quantity supplied (hundreds of trucks)
$32,000	100	400
31,000	200	350
30,000	300	300
29,000	400	250
28,000	500	200
27,000	600	150

a. In the absence of government interference, what is the price of an imported truck? How many are sold in Canada? Illustrate with a diagram.

b. Suppose the Canadian government adopts a quota, allowing no more than 20,000 foreign trucks to be imported. What is the effect on the market for these trucks? Illustrate using your diagram from part a and explain.

c. Now suppose that, instead of a quota, the government imposes an excise tax of $3,000 per truck. Illustrate the effect of this excise tax in your diagram from part a. How many trucks will now be purchased and at what price? What will the foreign automaker receive per truck?

d. Calculate the government revenue raised by the excise tax in part c. Then illustrate it on your diagram from that part. Do you think the government, from a revenue standpoint, prefers an excise tax or a quota?

e. Explain how the government policy, whether it be a quota or an excise tax, benefits Canadian truck manufacturers. Whom does it hurt? What is the missed opportunity here, and how does it reflect inefficiency?

10. To preserve the Atlantic lobster fisheries, quota restrictions limit harvests. To catch lobster, one must have a lobster fishing license. Today, about 12,000 licenses are active in the Atlantic community, and each license permits between 250 and 400 traps per season (depending on the exact lobster fishing area). Suppose that these restrictions limit the catch in Atlantic Canada to 80,000 pounds of lobster a year. The accompanying figure shows hypothetical demand and supply curves for pounds of Atlantic lobsters.

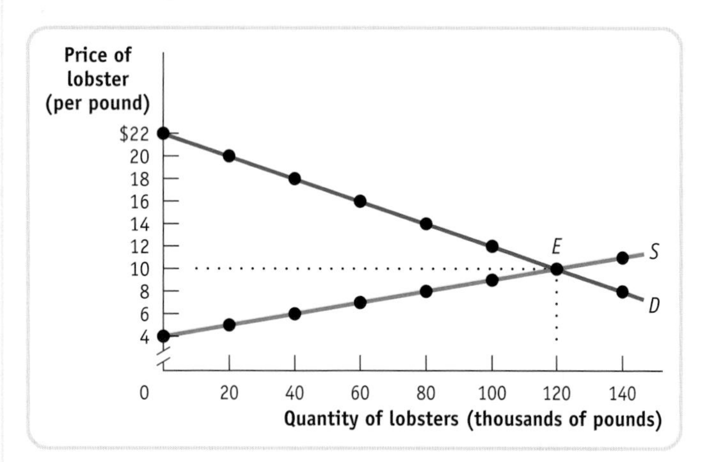

a. In the absence of quotas, what are the equilibrium price and quantity?

b. What is the *demand price* at which consumers wish to purchase 80,000 pounds of lobsters?

c. What is the *supply price* at which suppliers are willing to supply 80,000 pounds of lobsters?

d. What is the *quota rent* per pound of lobster when 80,000 pounds are sold?

e. Find an excise tax that achieves the same reduction in the harvest of lobsters as the quota system. Show it on the figure. What is the government revenue collected from this tax?

f. Explain a transaction that benefits both buyer and seller but is prevented by the quota restriction. Explain a transaction that benefits both buyer and seller but is prevented by the excise tax.

11. In each of the following cases involving taxes, explain: 1) whether the incidence of the tax falls more heavily on consumers or producers, 2) why government revenue raised from the tax is not a good indicator of the true cost of the tax, and 3) what missed opportunity, or inefficiency, arises.

a. The government imposes an excise tax on the sale of all college textbooks. Before the tax was imposed, 1 million textbooks were sold every year at a price of $50. After the tax is imposed, 600,000 books are sold yearly; students pay $55 per book, while publishers receive $30 per book.

b. The government imposes an excise tax on the sale of all airplane tickets. Before the tax was imposed, 3 million airline tickets were sold every year at a price of $500. After the tax is imposed, 1.5 million tickets are sold every year; travelers pay $550 per ticket, while airlines receive $450 per ticket.

c. The government imposes an excise tax on the sale of all toothbrushes. Before the tax, 2 million toothbrushes were sold yearly at a price of $2.00. After the tax is imposed, 800,000 toothbrushes are sold yearly; consumers pay $1.75 per toothbrush, while producers receive $1.25 per toothbrush.

>web... To continue your study and review of concepts in this chapter, please visit the Krugman/Wells website for quizzes, animated graph tutorials, web links to helpful resources, and more.

www.worthpublishers.com/krugmanwellsmyatt

chapter 5

>>Elasticity

DRIVE WE MUST

In early 1998, Luis Tellez held a secret meeting with his Saudi Arabian counterpart. Mr Tellez was Mexico's oil minister, the government official who decided how many barrels of oil Mexico would produce and sell to other countries. The purpose of the secret meeting? To increase their earnings, or revenues, from selling oil by raising the world price of oil, which had fallen 50 percent over the previous two years. This low world price was creating serious problems for both governments, which depended on revenue from oil sales. But a plan to raise oil prices would not succeed unless other oil-exporting countries were also willing to commit to reductions in oil production.

Why was it necessary to reduce production? Why not just raise prices? Because by the *law of demand,* a price increase leads to a fall in the quantity demanded. So if output didn't also fall, there would soon be a surplus of oil on the market, pushing the price right back down again. To make the plan work, Tellez had to persuade his fellow oil ministers to produce less. But how much less?

If consumers responded to the price increase by using a lot less oil, output would have to fall by a large amount. And if output fell by a large enough amount in response to the price increase, revenue would decline, not increase. The crucial question for Tellez, then, was how responsive the quantity of oil demanded was to changes in the price of oil.

But how do we define *responsiveness?* The answer, and what Tellez needed to know in this case is a particular number: the *price elasticity of demand.* In this chapter, we will show how the price elasticity of demand is measured and why it is the best measure of how the quantity demanded responds to changes in the price. We will then see that the price elasticity of demand is only one of a family of related concepts, including the *income elasticity of demand* and the *price elasticity of supply*. Finally, we will see how elasticities are used to determine who bears the greater share of the burden of a tax—producers or consumers.

Charted Media

Gassing up: A hard habit to break.

What you will learn in this chapter:

- The definition of **elasticity**, a measure of responsiveness to changes in prices or income
- The importance of the **price elasticity of demand**, which measures the responsiveness of the quantity demanded to price
- The meaning and importance of the **income elasticity of demand**, a measure of the responsiveness of demand to income
- The significance of the **price elasticity of supply**, which measures the responsiveness of the quantity supplied to price
- What factors influence the size of these various elasticities
- How elasticity affects the **incidence** of a tax, the measure of who bears its burden

Defining and Measuring Elasticity

Luis Tellez, who is a trained economist, knew that to calculate the cut in oil output needed to achieve his price target, he would have to know the *price elasticity of demand* for oil.

The Price Elasticity of Demand

Figure 5-1 shows a hypothetical world demand curve for oil. At a price of $20 per barrel, world consumers would demand 10 million barrels of oil per day (point *A*); at a price of $21 per barrel, the quantity demanded would fall to 9.9 million barrels (point *B*).

Figure 5-1, then, tells us the response of the quantity demanded to a particular change in the price. But how can we turn this into a measure of price responsiveness? The answer is to calculate the *price elasticity of demand.*

The price elasticity of demand compares the *percent change in quantity demanded* to the *percent change in price* as we move along the demand curve. As we'll see later in this chapter, the reason economists use percent changes is to get a measure that doesn't depend on the units in which a good is measured (say, litres versus barrels of oil). But before we get to that, let's look at how elasticity is calculated.

To calculate the price elasticity of demand, we first calculate the percent change in the quantity demanded and the corresponding percent change in the price as we move along the demand curve. These are defined as follows:

$$\textbf{(5-1)} \quad \text{\% change in quantity demanded} = \frac{\text{Change in quantity demanded}}{\text{Initial quantity demanded}} \times 100$$

and

$$\textbf{(5-2)} \quad \text{\% change in price} = \frac{\text{Change in price}}{\text{Initial price}} \times 100$$

In Figure 5-1, we see that when the price rises from $20 to $21, the quantity demanded falls from 10 million to 9.9 million barrels, yielding a change in the

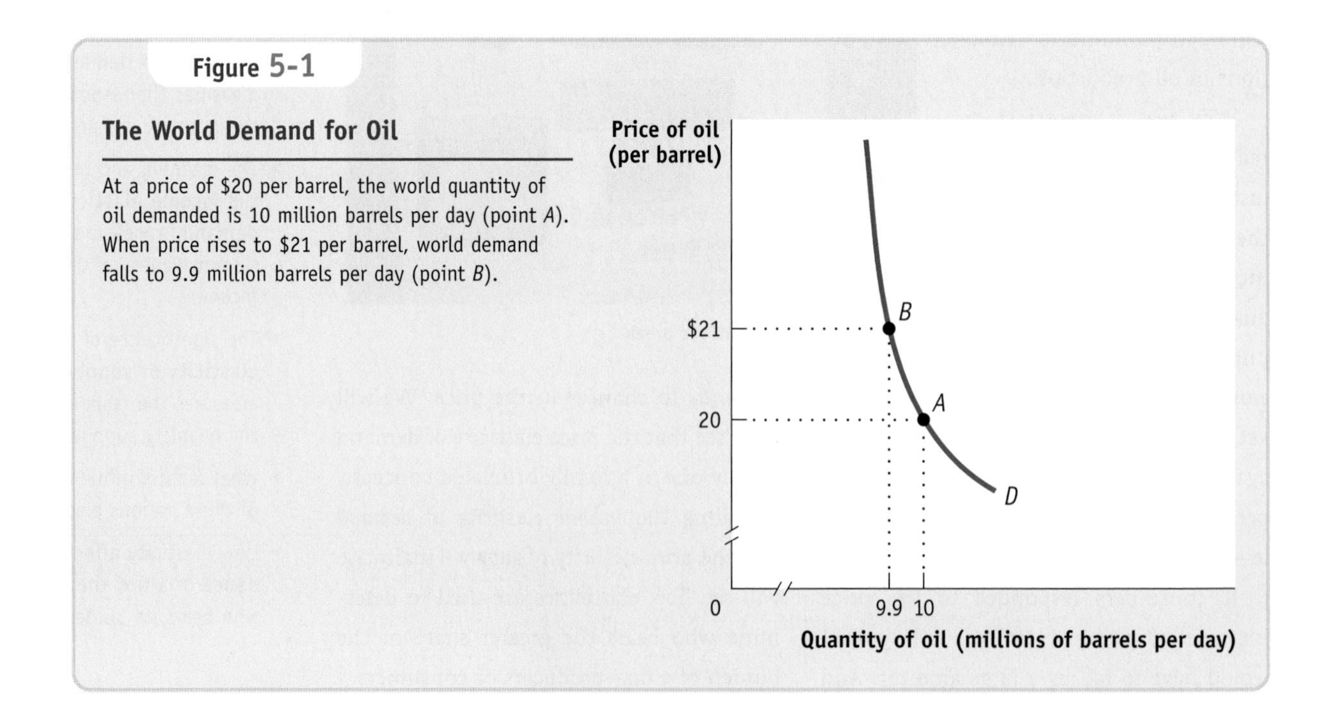

Figure 5-1

The World Demand for Oil

At a price of $20 per barrel, the world quantity of oil demanded is 10 million barrels per day (point *A*). When price rises to $21 per barrel, world demand falls to 9.9 million barrels per day (point *B*).

quantity demanded of 0.1 million barrels. So the percent change in the quantity demanded is

$$\text{\% change in quantity demanded} = \frac{0.1 \text{ million barrels}}{10 \text{ million barrels}} \times 100 = 1\%$$

The initial price is $20 and the change in the price is $1, so the percent change in price is

$$\text{\% change in price} = \frac{\$1}{\$20} \times 100 = 5\%$$

To calculate the price elasticity of demand, we find the ratio of the percent change in the quantity demanded to the percent change in the price:

$$\text{(5-3)} \quad \textbf{Price elasticity of demand} = \frac{\text{\% change in quantity demanded}}{\text{\% change in price}}$$

The **price elasticity of demand** is the ratio of the percent change in the quantity demanded to the percent change in the price as we move along the demand curve.

In Figure 5-1, the price elasticity of demand is therefore

$$\frac{1\%}{5\%} = 0.2$$

The *law of demand* says that demand curves slope downward. This means that the price elasticity of demand is, in strictly mathematical terms, a negative number (if the price rises, which is a positive percent change, the quantity demanded falls, which is strictly speaking a *negative* percent change). However, it is a nuisance to keep writing that minus sign. So when economists talk about the price elasticity of demand, they usually drop the minus sign and report the absolute value of the elasticity. In this case, for example, economists would usually say "the price elasticity of demand is 0.2", taking it for granted that you understand they mean *minus* 0.2. As we have just done, we follow this convention and drop the minus sign when referring to the price elasticity of demand.

The larger the price elasticity of demand, the more responsive the quantity demanded is to the price. When the price elasticity of demand is large—when consumers change their quantity demanded by a large percentage compared with the percent change in the price—economists say that demand is highly elastic.

As we'll see shortly, a price elasticity of 0.2 indicates a small response of quantity demanded to price. That is, the quantity demanded will fall by a relatively small amount when price rises. This is what economists call *inelastic* demand. And inelastic demand was exactly what Tellez needed for his strategy to increase revenue by raising oil prices.

Using the Midpoint Method to Calculate Elasticities

Price elasticity of demand compares the *percent change in quantity demanded* with the *percent change in price.* When we look at some other elasticities, which we will do shortly, we'll see why it is important to focus on percent changes. But at this point we need to discuss a technical issue that arises when you calculate percent changes in variables and how economists deal with it.

The best way to understand the issue is with a real example. Suppose you were trying to estimate the price elasticity of demand for gasoline by comparing gasoline prices and consumption in different countries. Because of high taxes, gasoline usually costs about twice as much per litre in Europe as it does in Canada. So what is the percent difference between Canadian and European gas prices?

Well, it depends on which way you measure it. The price of gasoline in Europe is two times higher than in Canada, so it is 100 percent higher. The price of gasoline in Canada is half as high as in Europe, so it is 50 percent lower.

This is a nuisance: we'd like to have a percent measure of the difference in prices that doesn't depend on which way you measure it. A good way to avoid computing different elasticities for rising and falling prices is to use the *midpoint method*.

The **midpoint method** is a technique for calculating the percent change. In this approach, we calculate changes in a variable compared with the average, or midpoint, of the starting and final values.

The **midpoint method** replaces the usual definition of the percent change in a variable, X, with a slightly different definition:

$$\textbf{(5-4)} \quad \% \text{ change in } X = \frac{\text{Change in } X}{\text{Average value of } X} \times 100$$

where the average value of X is defined as

$$\text{Average value of } X = \frac{\text{Starting value of } X + \text{final value of } X}{2}$$

When calculating the price elasticity of demand using the midpoint method, both the percent change in the price and the percent change in the quantity demanded are found using this method.

To see how this method works, suppose you have the following data for some good:

	Price	**Quantity demanded**
Situation A	$0.90	1,100
Situation B	$1.10	900

To calculate the percent change in quantity going from situation A to situation B, we compare the change in the quantity demanded—200 units—with the *average* of the quantity demanded in the two situations. So we calculate

$$\% \text{ change in quantity demanded} = \frac{200}{(1{,}100 + 900)/2} \times 100 = \frac{200}{1{,}000} \times 100$$

$$= 20\%$$

In the same way, we calculate

$$\% \text{ change in price} = \frac{\$0.20}{(\$0.90 + \$1.10)/2} \times 100 = \frac{\$0.20}{\$1.00} \times 100$$

So in this case we would calculate the price elasticity of demand to be

$$\text{Price elasticity of demand} = \frac{\% \text{ change in quantity demanded}}{\% \text{ change in price}} = \frac{20\%}{20\%} = 1$$

The important point is that we would get the same result, a price elasticity of demand of 1, whether we go up the demand curve from situation A to situation B, or down from situation B to situation A.

To arrive at a more general formula for price elasticity of demand, suppose that we have data for two points on a demand curve. At point 1, the quantity demanded and price are (Q_1, P_1); at point 2, they are (Q_2, P_2). Then the formula for calculating the price elasticity of demand is

$$\textbf{(5-5)}\ \text{Price elasticity of demand} = \frac{\dfrac{Q_2 - Q_1}{(Q_1 + Q_2)/2}}{\dfrac{P_2 - P_1}{(P_2 + P_1)/2}} = \frac{\dfrac{Q_2 - Q_1}{Q_2 + Q_1}}{\dfrac{P_2 - P_1}{P_2 + P_1}}$$

As before, when reporting a price elasticity of demand calculated by the midpoint method, we usually drop the negative sign and report the absolute value.

economics in action

Estimating Elasticities

You might think it's easy to estimate price elasticities of demand from real-world data: just compare percent changes in prices with percent changes in quantities demanded. Unfortunately, it's rarely that simple because changes in price aren't the only thing affecting changes in the quantity demanded: other factors—such as changes in income, changes in population, and changes in the prices of other goods—shift the demand curve, thereby changing the quantity demanded for any given price. To estimate price elasticities of demand, economists must use careful statistical analysis to separate the influence of these different factors, holding other things equal.

The most comprehensive effort to estimate price elasticities of demand was a mammoth study by the economists Hendrik S. Houthakker and Lester D. Taylor. Some of their results are summarized in Table 5-1. Although they used U.S. data, the thrust of their results easily carries over to Canada too. These estimates show a wide range of price elasticities. There are some goods, like eggs, for which demand hardly responds at all to changes in the price; there are other goods, most notably foreign travel, where the quantity demanded is very sensitive to the price.

Notice that Table 5-1 is divided into two parts: inelastic and elastic demand. We'll explain in the next section the significance of that division. ■

TABLE 5-1

Some Estimated Price Elasticities of Demand

Good	Price elasticity of demand
Inelastic demand	
Eggs[1]	0.1
Beef[1]	0.4
Stationery[2]	0.5
Gasoline[2]	0.5
Elastic demand	
Housing[3]	1.2
Restaurant meals[3]	2.3
Airline travel[2]	2.4
Foreign travel[2]	4.1

[1]Kuo S. Huang and Biing-Hwan Lin (2000). "Estimation of Food Demand and Nutrient Elasticities from Household Survey Data", *United States Department of Agriculture Economic Research Service Technical Bulletin 1887.*
[2]H. S. Houthakker and Lester D. Taylor (1966). *Consumer Demand in the United States, 1929–1970: Analyses and Projections.* Cambridge, Mass.: Harvard University Press.
[3]H. S. Houthakker and Lester D. Taylor (1970) *Consumer Demand in the United States: Analyses and Projections,* 2nd ed. Cambridge, Mass.: Harvard University Press.

>> QUICK REVIEW

- The *price elasticity of demand* is equal to the percent change in the quantity demanded divided by the percent change in the price as you move along the demand curve.
- Percent changes are best measured using the *midpoint method,* in which the percent change in each variable is calculated using the average of starting and final values.

>> CHECK YOUR UNDERSTANDING 5-1

1. The price of strawberries falls from $1.50 to $1.00 per carton, and the quantity demanded goes from 100,000 to 200,000 cartons. Use the midpoint method to find the price elasticity of demand.
2. At the present level of consumption, 4,000 movie tickets, and at the current price, $5 per ticket, the price elasticity of demand for movie tickets is 1. Using the midpoint method, calculate the percentage by which the owners of movie theatres must reduce price in order to sell 5,000 tickets.
3. The price elasticity of demand for ice-cream sandwiches is 1.2 at the current price of $0.50 per sandwich and the current consumption level of 100,000 sandwiches. Calculate the change in the quantity demanded when price rises by $0.05. Use Equations 5-1 and 5-2 to calculate percent changes, and Equation 5-3 to relate price elasticity of demand to the percent changes.

Solutions appear at back of book.

Interpreting the Price Elasticity of Demand

Mexico and other oil-producing countries believed they could succeed in driving up world oil prices with only a small decrease in the quantity sold because the price elasticity of oil demand was low. But what does that mean? How low does a price elasticity have to be for us to classify it as low? How high does it have to be for us to consider it high? And what determines whether the price elasticity of demand is high or low, anyway?

To answer these questions, we need to look more deeply at the price elasticity of demand.

How Elastic Is Elastic?

As a first step toward classifying price elasticities of demand, let's look at the extreme cases.

First, consider the demand for a good when people pay no attention to the price—say, shoelaces. Suppose that Canadian consumers will buy 100 million pairs of shoelaces per year regardless of the price. In this case, the demand curve for shoelaces would look like the curve shown in panel (a) of Figure 5-2: it would be a vertical line at 100 million pairs of shoelaces. Since the percent change in the quantity demanded is zero for *any* change in the price, the price elasticity of demand in this case is zero. The case of a zero price elasticity of demand is known as **perfectly inelastic demand.**

Demand is **perfectly inelastic** when the quantity demanded does not respond at all to changes in the price. When demand is perfectly inelastic, the demand curve is a vertical line.

The opposite extreme occurs when even a tiny rise in the price will cause the quantity demanded to drop to zero or even a tiny fall in the price will cause the quantity demanded to get extremely large. Panel (b) of Figure 5-2 shows the case of pink tennis balls; we suppose that tennis players really don't care what colour their tennis balls are and that other colours, such as neon green and vivid yellow, are available at $5 per dozen balls. In this case, consumers will buy no pink balls if they cost more than $5 per dozen but will buy only pink balls if they cost less than $5. The demand curve will therefore be a horizontal line at a price of $5 per dozen balls. As you move back and forth along this line, there is a change in the quantity demanded but no change in the price. Roughly speaking, when you divide a number by zero, you get infinity, so a horizontal demand curve implies an infinite price elasticity of demand. When the price elasticity of demand is infinite, economists say that demand is **perfectly elastic.**

Demand is **perfectly elastic** when any price increase will cause the quantity demanded to drop to zero. When demand is perfectly elastic, the demand curve is a horizontal line.

Figure 5-2 Two Extreme Cases of Price Elasticity of Demand

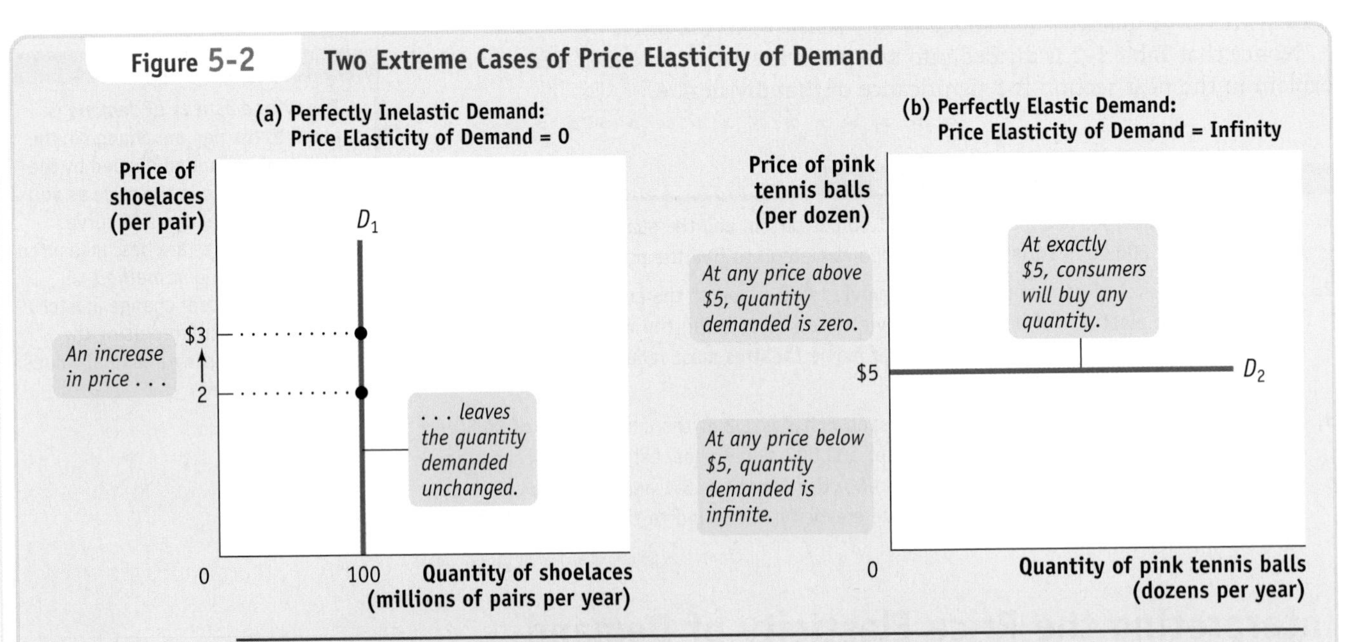

Panel (a) shows a perfectly inelastic demand curve, which is a vertical line. The quantity of shoelaces demanded is always 100 million pairs, regardless of price. As a result the price elasticity of demand is zero—the quantity demanded is unaffected by the price. Panel (b) shows a perfectly elastic demand curve, which is a horizontal line. At a price of $5, consumers will buy any quantity of pink tennis balls, but will buy none at a price above $5. If price falls below $5, they will buy an extremely large number of pink tennis balls and none of any other color.

The price elasticity of demand for the vast majority of goods is somewhere between these two extreme cases. Economists use one main criterion for classifying these intermediate cases: they ask whether the price elasticity of demand is higher or lower than 1. When the price elasticity of demand is greater than 1, economists say that demand is **elastic.** When the price elasticity of demand is less than 1, they say that demand is **inelastic.** The borderline case is **unit-elastic demand,** where the price elasticity of demand is—surprise—exactly 1.

Demand is **elastic** if the price elasticity of demand is greater than 1, **inelastic** if the price elasticity of demand is less than 1, and **unit-elastic** if the price elasticity of demand is exactly 1.

To see why a price elasticity of demand equal to 1 is a useful dividing line, let's consider a hypothetical example: a toll bridge operated by the department of transportation. Other things equal, the number of drivers who use the bridge depends on the toll, the price charged for crossing the bridge: the higher the toll, the fewer the drivers who use the bridge.

Figure 5-3 shows three hypothetical demand curves—one in which demand is unit-elastic, one in which it is inelastic, and one in which it is elastic. In each case,

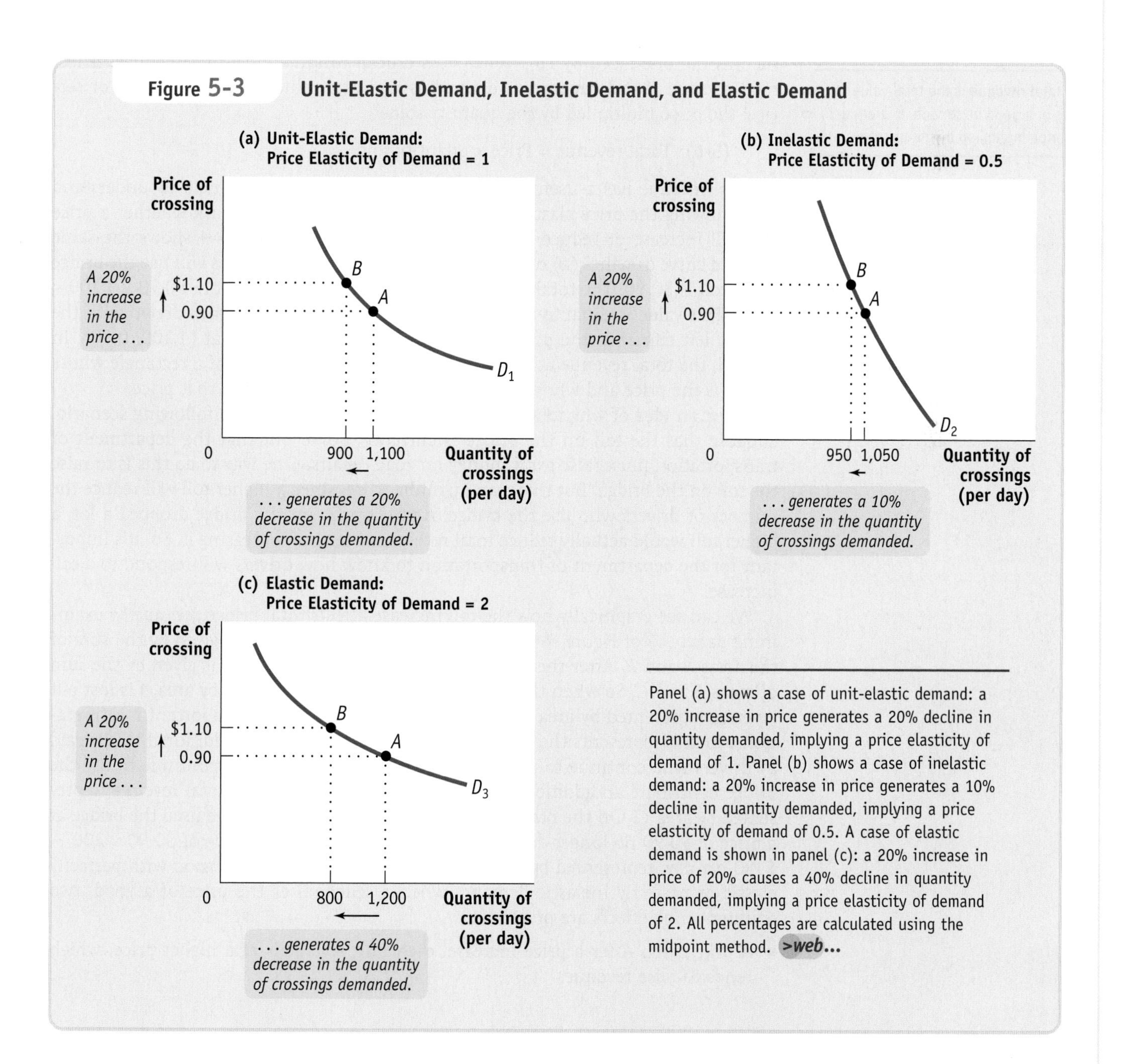

Panel (a) shows a case of unit-elastic demand: a 20% increase in price generates a 20% decline in quantity demanded, implying a price elasticity of demand of 1. Panel (b) shows a case of inelastic demand: a 20% increase in price generates a 10% decline in quantity demanded, implying a price elasticity of demand of 0.5. A case of elastic demand is shown in panel (c): a 20% increase in price of 20% causes a 40% decline in quantity demanded, implying a price elasticity of demand of 2. All percentages are calculated using the midpoint method. >web...

point *A* shows the quantity demanded if the toll is $0.90 and point *B* shows the quantity demanded if the toll is $1.10. An increase in the toll from $0.90 to $1.10 is an increase of 20% if we use the midpoint method to calculate percent changes.

Panel (a) shows what happens when the toll is raised from $0.90 to $1.10 and the demand curve is unit-elastic. Here the 20% price increase leads to a fall in the quantity of cars using the bridge each day from 1,100 to 900, which is a 20% decline (again using the midpoint method). So the price elasticity of demand is 20%/20% = 1.

Panel (b) shows a case of inelastic demand when the toll is raised from $0.90 to $1.10. The same 20% price increase reduces the quantity demanded from 1,050 to 950. That's only a 10% decline, so in this case the price elasticity of demand is 10%/20% = 0.5.

Panel (c) shows a case of elastic demand when the toll is raised from $0.90 to $1.10. The 20% price increase causes the quantity demanded to fall from 1,200 to 800—a 40% decline, so the price elasticity of demand is 40%/20% = 2.

Why does it matter whether demand is unit-elastic, inelastic, or elastic? Because this classification predicts how changes in the price of a good will affect the *total revenue* earned by producers from the sale of that good. And in many real-life situations, such as the one faced by Luis Tellez, it is crucial to know how price changes affect total revenue. **Total revenue** is defined as the total value of sales of a good or service: the price multiplied by the quantity sold.

The **total revenue** is the total value of sales of a good or service. It is equal to the price multiplied by the quantity sold.

(5-6) Total revenue = Price × quantity sold

Total revenue has a useful graphical representation that can help us understand why knowing the price elasticity of demand is crucial when we ask whether a price rise will increase or reduce total revenue. Panel (a) of Figure 5-4 shows the same demand curve as panel (a) of Figure 5-3. We see that 1,100 drivers will use the bridge if the toll is $0.90. The total revenue at a price of $0.90 is therefore $0.90 × 1,100 = $990. This value is equal to the area of the green rectangle, which is drawn with the bottom left corner at the point (0, 0) and the top right corner at (1,100, 0.90). In general, the total revenue at any given price is equal to the area of a rectangle whose height is the price and whose width is the quantity demanded at that price.

To get an idea of why total revenue is important, consider the following scenario. Suppose that the toll on the bridge is currently $0.90 but that the department of transportation must raise extra money for road repairs. One way to do this is to raise the toll on the bridge. But this plan might backfire, since a higher toll will reduce the number of drivers who use the bridge. And if traffic on the bridge dropped a lot, a higher toll would actually reduce total revenue instead of increasing it. So, it's important for the department of transportation to know how drivers will respond to a toll increase.

We can see graphically how the toll increase affects total bridge revenue by examining panel (b) of Figure 5-4. At a toll of $0.90, total revenue is given by the sum of the areas *A* and *B*. After the toll is raised to $1.10, total revenue is given by the sum of areas *B* and *C*. So when the toll is raised, revenue represented by area *A* is lost but revenue represented by area *C* is gained. These two areas have important interpretations. Area *C* represents the revenue gain that comes from the additional $0.20 paid by drivers who continue to use the bridge. That is, the 900 who continue to use the bridge contribute an additional $0.20 × 900 = $180 per day to total revenue, represented by area *C*. On the other hand, 200 drivers who would have used the bridge at a price of $0.90 no longer do so, generating a loss to total revenue of $0.90 × 200 = $180 per day, represented by area *A*. Except in the rare case of a good with perfectly elastic or perfectly inelastic demand, when a seller raises the price of a good, two countervailing effects are present:

- *A price effect.* After a price increase, each unit sold sells at a higher price, which tends to raise revenue.

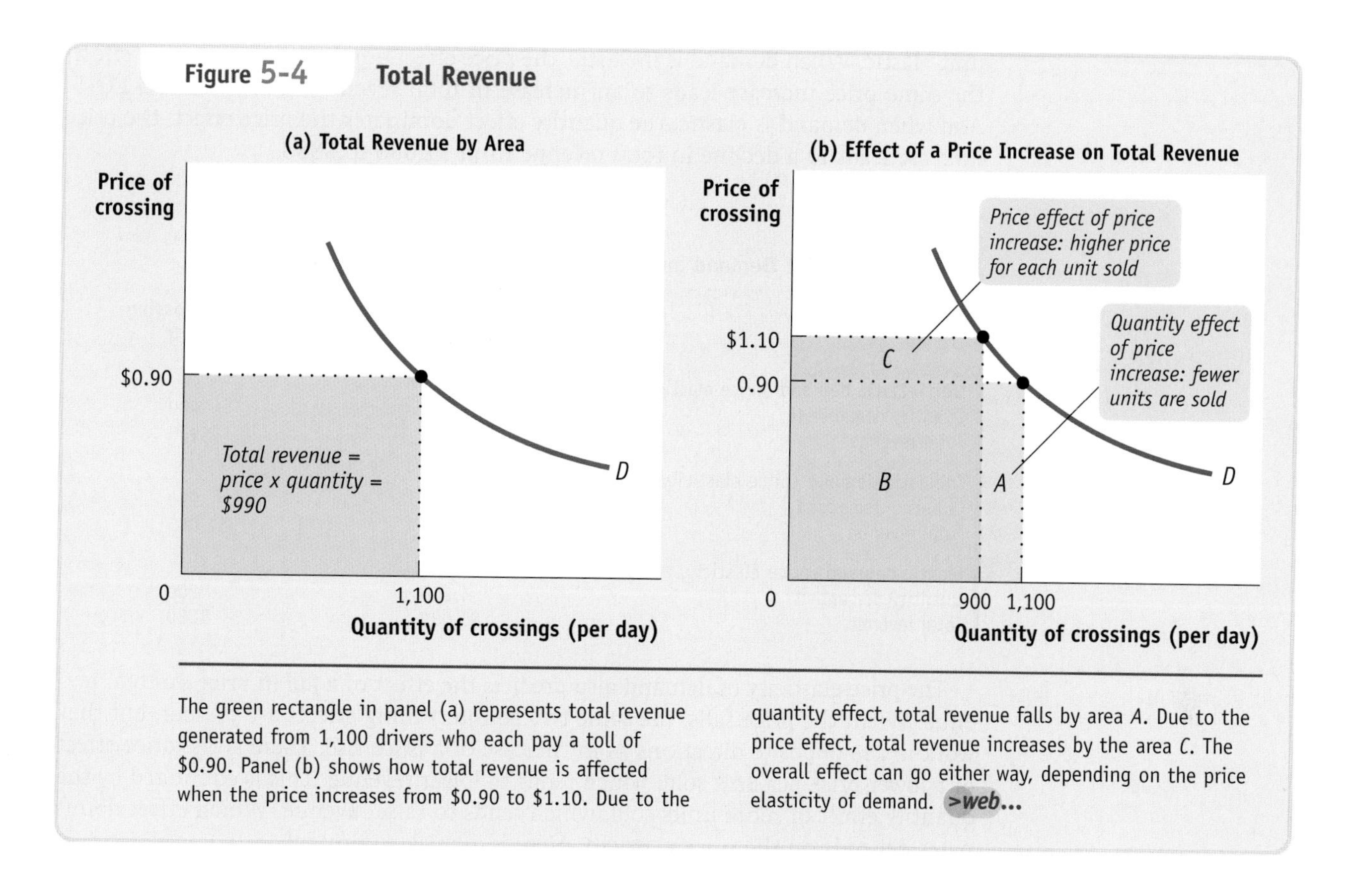

The green rectangle in panel (a) represents total revenue generated from 1,100 drivers who each pay a toll of $0.90. Panel (b) shows how total revenue is affected when the price increases from $0.90 to $1.10. Due to the quantity effect, total revenue falls by area *A*. Due to the price effect, total revenue increases by the area *C*. The overall effect can go either way, depending on the price elasticity of demand. >web...

- *A quantity effect.* After a price increase, fewer units are sold, which tends to lower revenue.

But then, you may ask, what is the ultimate effect on total revenue: does it go up or down? The answer is that, in general, the effect on total revenue can go either way—a price rise may increase total revenue or may lower it. If the price effect, which tends to raise total revenue, is the stronger of the two effects, then total revenue goes up. If the quantity effect, which tends to reduce total revenue, is the stronger, then total revenue goes down. And if the strengths of the two effects are exactly equal—as in our toll bridge example, where a $180 gain offsets a $180 loss—total revenue is unchanged by the price increase.

The price elasticity of demand tells us what happens to total revenue when price changes: its size determines which effect—the price effect or the quantity effect—is stronger. Specifically:

- If demand for a good is *elastic* (the price elasticity of demand is greater than 1), an increase in price reduces total revenue. In this case, the quantity effect is stronger than the price effect.
- If demand for a good is *inelastic* (the price elasticity of demand is less than 1), a higher price increases total revenue. In this case, the price effect is stronger than the quantity effect.
- If demand for a good is *unit-elastic* (the price elasticity of demand is 1), an increase in price does not change total revenue. In this case, the quantity effect and the price effect exactly offset each other.

Table 5-2 (page 126) shows how the effect of a price increase on total revenue depends on the price elasticity of demand, using the same data as in Figure 5-3. An increase in the price from $0.90 to $1.10 leaves total revenue unchanged at $990 when demand is unit-elastic. When demand is inelastic, the price effect dominates the quantity effect; the same price increase leads to an increase in total revenue from $945 to $1,045. And when demand is elastic, the quantity effect dominates the price effect; the price increase leads to a decline in total revenue from $1,080 to $880.

TABLE 5-2

Price Elasticity of Demand and Total Revenue

	Price of crossing = $0.90	Price of crossing = $1.10
Unit-elastic demand (price elasticity of demand = 1)		
Quantity demanded	1,100	900
Total revenue	$990	$990
Inelastic demand (price elasticity of demand = 0.5)		
Quantity demanded	1,050	950
Total revenue	$945	$1,045
Elastic demand (price elasticity of demand = 2)		
Quantity demanded	1,200	800
Total revenue	$1,080	$880

The price elasticity of demand also predicts the effect of a *fall* in price on total revenue. When the price falls, the same two countervailing effects are present, but they work in the opposite directions as in the case of a price rise. There is the price effect of a lower price per unit sold, which tends to lower revenue. This is countered by the quantity effect of more units sold, which tends to raise revenue. Which effect dominates depends on the price elasticity. Here is a quick summary:

- When demand is *elastic*, the quantity effect dominates the price effect; so a fall in price increases total revenue.
- When demand is *inelastic*, the price effect dominates the quantity effect; so a fall in price reduces total revenue.
- When demand is *unit-elastic*, the two effects exactly balance; so a fall in price has no effect on total revenue.

Price Elasticity Along the Demand Curve

Suppose that an economist says that "the price elasticity of demand for coffee is 0.25". What he or she means is that *at the current price* the elasticity is 0.25. In the previous discussion of the toll bridge, what we were really describing was the elasticity *at the price* of $0.90. Why this qualification? Because for the vast majority of demand curves, the price elasticity of demand at one point along the curve is different from the price elasticity at other points along the same curve.

To see this, consider the table in Figure 5-5, which shows a hypothetical demand schedule. It also shows in the last column the total revenue generated at each price and quantity combination in the demand schedule. The upper panel of Figure 5-5 shows the corresponding demand curve. The lower panel illustrates the same data on total revenue: the height of a bar at each quantity demanded—which corresponds to a particular price—measures the total revenue generated at that price.

In Figure 5-5, you can see that when the price is low, raising the price increases total revenue: starting at a price of $1, raising the price to $2 increases total revenue from $9 to $16. This means that when the price is low, demand is inelastic. Moreover, you can see that demand is inelastic on the entire section of the demand curve from a price of $0 to a price of $5.

When the price is high, however, raising it further reduces total revenue: starting at a price of $8, raising the price to $9 reduces total revenue, from $16 to $9. This

Figure 5-5 **The Price Elasticity of Demand Changes Along the Demand Curve**

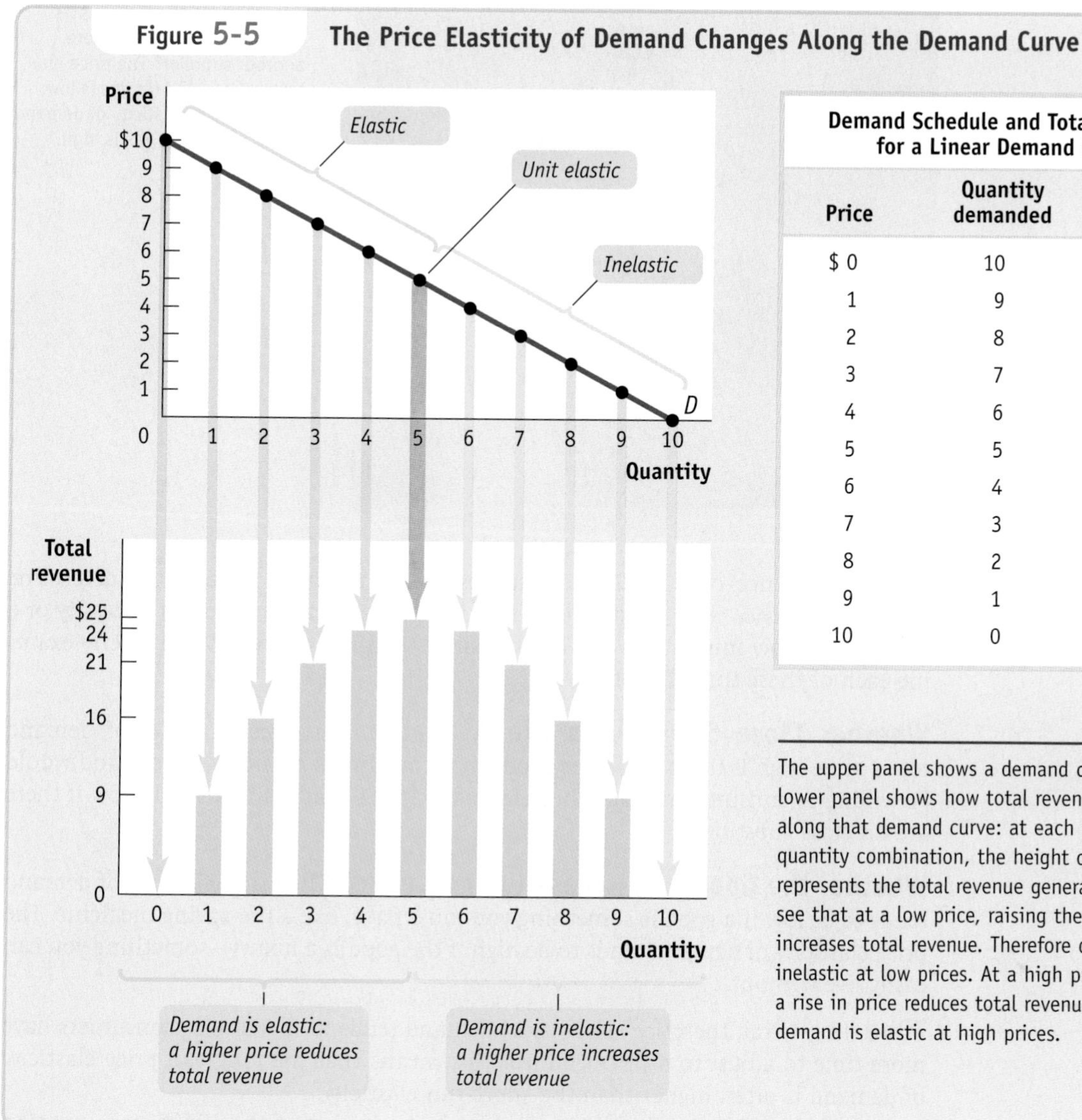

Demand Schedule and Total Revenue for a Linear Demand Curve

Price	Quantity demanded	Total revenue
$ 0	10	$ 0
1	9	9
2	8	16
3	7	21
4	6	24
5	5	25
6	4	24
7	3	21
8	2	16
9	1	9
10	0	0

The upper panel shows a demand curve. The lower panel shows how total revenue changes along that demand curve: at each price and quantity combination, the height of the bar represents the total revenue generated. You can see that at a low price, raising the price increases total revenue. Therefore demand is inelastic at low prices. At a high price, however, a rise in price reduces total revenue. Therefore demand is elastic at high prices.

means that when the price is high, demand is elastic. Furthermore, you can see that demand is elastic over the section of the demand curve from a price of $5 to $10.

For the vast majority of goods, the price elasticity of demand changes along the demand curve. So whenever you measure the elasticity, you are really measuring it at a particular point or section of the demand curve.

What Factors Determine the Price Elasticity of Demand?

1998 was not the first time that oil-exporting countries tried to raise oil prices. Oil exporters succeeded in quadrupling world oil prices between 1973 and 1974, and in raising prices another 150 percent in 1979. Canadian oil prices increased in response to these rising world prices. So, how did the quantity demanded respond to these price hikes? Consumers in North America initially reacted by changing their consumption of gasoline very little. Over time, however, North American drivers gradually adapted to the higher gasoline prices. After a few years, drivers had cut their consumption of gasoline in various ways: increased carpooling, greater use of public transportation, and, most important, replacement of large, gas-guzzling cars with smaller, more fuel-efficient models.

When Petro Canada raises its prices, do you buy gas from another supplier? The price elasticity of demand for gas is low, but the price elasticity of demand for Petro Canada gas is high.

The experience of the 1970s illustrates the three main factors that determine elasticity: whether close substitutes are available, whether the good is a necessity or a luxury, and how much time has elapsed since the price change. We'll briefly examine each of these three factors.

Whether Close Substitutes Are Available The price elasticity of demand tends to be high if there are other goods that consumers regard as similar and would be willing to consume instead. The price elasticity of demand tends to be low if there are no close substitutes.

Whether the Good Is a Necessity or a Luxury The price elasticity of demand tends to be low if a good is something you must have, like a life-saving medicine. The price elasticity of demand tends to be high if the good is a luxury—something you can easily live without.

Time In general, the price elasticity of demand tends to increase as consumers have more time to adjust to a price change. This means that the long-run price elasticity of demand is often higher than the short-run elasticity.

So when gasoline prices first jumped at the beginning of the 1970s, consumption fell very little because there were no close substitutes for gasoline and because driving their cars was necessary for people to carry out the ordinary tasks of life. Over time, however, North Americans changed their habits in ways that enabled them to gradually reduce their gasoline consumption. The result was a steady decline in gasoline consumption throughout the 1980s even though the price of gasoline did not continue to rise, confirming that the long-run price elasticity of demand for gasoline was indeed much larger than the short-run elasticity.

economics in action

Reversing Falls and Reversing Flows

In Saint John, New Brunswick, the Reversing Falls is a popular tourist attraction. This occurs where the flow of the mighty Saint John River enters the Bay of Fundy—a place where some of the highest tides in the world periodically reverse the flow of the river.

Tourists might be interested in another reversal of flows, one that was produced not by natural phenomena but by changes in the value of the Canadian dollar—reversing flows of tourists. In 1992, 18.6 million Canadians visited the United States, but only 11.8 million U.S. residents visited Canada. By 2002, however, roles had been reversed: more U.S. residents visited Canada than vice versa.

Why did the tourist traffic reverse direction? Canada didn't get any warmer from 1992 to 2002—but it did get cheaper for Americans. The reason was a large change in the exchange rate between the two nations' currencies: in 1992 a Canadian dollar was worth US$0.80, but by 2002 it had fallen in value by nearly 20 percent to about US$0.65. This meant that our goods and services—particularly hotel rooms and meals—were about 20 percent cheaper for Americans in 2002 compared to 1992. Thus, Canada had become a cheap vacation destination for Americans by 2002. Things were not so rosy, however, for the tourist industry in the United States: American vacations had become 20 percent more expensive for Canadians. Canadians responded by choosing to spend holidays in their own country or in other parts of the world besides the United States.

Foreign travel is an example of a good that has a high price elasticity of demand: as we saw in Table 5-1, it has been estimated at about 4.1. One reason is that foreign travel is a luxury good for most people—you may regret not going to Paris this year, but you can live without it. A second reason is that a good substitute for foreign travel typically exists—domestic travel. A Canadian who finds it too expensive to vacation in San Francisco this year is likely to find that Vancouver is a very good alternative.■

>> QUICK REVIEW

- Demand is *perfectly inelastic* if it is completely unresponsive to price. It is *perfectly elastic* if it is infinitely responsive to price.
- Demand is *elastic* if the price elasticity of demand is greater than 1; it is *inelastic* if the price elasticity of demand is less than 1; and it is *unit-elastic* if the price elasticity of demand is exactly 1.
- When demand is elastic, the quantity effect of a price increase dominates the price effect, and *total revenue* falls. When demand is inelastic, the price effect of a price increase dominates the quantity effect, and *total revenue* increases.
- Because the price elasticity of demand can change along the demand curve, economists mean a particular point on the demand curve when referring to "the" price elasticity of demand.
- The availability of close substitutes makes demand for a good more elastic, as does the length of time elapsed since the price change. Demand for a necessary good is less elastic; demand for a luxury good is more elastic.

>> CHECK YOUR UNDERSTANDING 5-2

1. For each case, choose the condition that characterizes demand: elastic demand, inelastic demand, or unit-elastic demand.
   a. Total revenue decreases when price increases.
   b. The additional revenue generated by an increase in quantity sold is exactly offset by revenue lost from the fall in price received per unit.
   c. Total revenue falls when output increases.
   d. Producers in an industry find they can increase their total revenues by working together to reduce industry output.
2. For the following goods, what is the elasticity of demand? Explain. What is the shape of the demand curve?
   a. Demand by a snake-bite victim for an antidote
   b. Demand by students for green erasers

Solutions appear at back of book.

Other Demand Elasticities

The quantity of a good demanded depends not only on the price of that good but on other variables. In particular, demand curves shift because of changes in the prices of related goods and changes in consumers' incomes. It is often important to have a measure of these other effects, and the best measures are—you guessed it—elasticities. Specifically, we can best measure how the demand for a good is affected by prices of other goods using a measure called the *cross-price elasticity of demand*, and we can best measure how demand is affected by changes in income using the *income elasticity of demand.*

The Cross-Price Elasticity of Demand

In Chapter 3 you learned that the demand for a good is often affected by the prices of other, related goods—goods that are substitutes or complements. There you saw that a change in the price of a related good shifts the demand curve of the original good, reflecting a change in the quantity demanded at any given price. The strength of such a "cross" effect on demand can be measured by the **cross-price elasticity of demand,** defined as the ratio of the percent change in the quantity demanded of one good to the percent change in the price of the other.

The **cross-price elasticity of demand** between two goods measures the effect of the change in one good's price on the quantity demanded of the other good. It is equal to the percent change in the quantity demanded of one good divided by the percent change in the other good's price.

(5-7) Cross-price elasticity of demand between goods A and B

$$= \frac{\text{\% change in quantity of A demanded}}{\text{\% change in price of B}}$$

When two goods are substitutes, like hot dogs and hamburgers, the cross-price elasticity of demand is positive: a rise in the price of hot dogs increases the demand for hamburgers—that is, it causes a rightward shift of the demand curve for hamburgers. If the goods are close substitutes, the cross-price elasticity will be positive and large; if they are not close substitutes, the cross-price elasticity will be positive and small. So when the cross-price elasticity of demand is positive, it is a measure of how closely substitutable for each other two goods are.

When two goods are complements, like hot dogs and hot dog buns, the cross-price elasticity is negative: a rise in the price of hot dogs decreases the demand for hot dog buns—that is, it causes a leftward shift of the demand curve for hot dog buns. As with substitutes, the size of the cross-price elasticity of demand between two complements tells us how strongly complementary they are: if the cross-price elasticity is only slightly below zero, they are weak complements; if it is very negative, they are strong complements.

Note that in the case of the cross-price elasticity of demand, the sign (plus or minus) is very important: it tells us whether the two goods are complements or substitutes. So we cannot drop the minus sign as we did for the price elasticity of demand.

Our discussion of the cross-price elasticity of demand is a useful place to return to a point we made earlier: elasticity is a *unit-free* measure—that is, it doesn't depend on the units in which goods are measured.

To see the potential problem, suppose that someone told you that "If the price of hot dog buns rises by $0.30, Canadians will buy 1 million fewer hot dogs this year." If you've ever bought hot dog buns, you'll immediately wonder: is that a $0.30 increase in the price *per bun*, or is it a $0.30 increase in the price *per package* (buns are usually sold by the dozen)? It makes a big difference what units we are talking about! However, if someone says that the cross-price elasticity of demand between buns and hot dogs is –0.3, it doesn't matter whether buns are sold individually or by the package. So elasticity is defined as a ratio of percent changes, as a way of making sure that confusion over units doesn't arise.

The Income Elasticity of Demand

The **income elasticity of demand** is the percent change in the quantity of a good demanded when a consumer's income changes divided by the percent change in the consumer's income.

The **income elasticity of demand** is a measure of how much the demand for a good is affected by changes in consumers' incomes. It allows us to determine whether a good is a normal or inferior good as well as measure how intensely the demand for the good responds to changes in income.

$$\text{(5-8)} \quad \text{Income elasticity of demand} = \frac{\text{\% change in quantity demanded}}{\text{\% change in income}}$$

Just as the cross-price elasticity of demand between two goods can be either positive or negative, depending on whether the goods are substitutes or complements, the income elasticity of demand for a good can also be either positive or negative. Recall from Chapter 3 that goods can be either *normal goods*, for which demand increases when income rises, or *inferior goods*, for which demand decreases when income rises. These definitions relate directly to the sign of the income elasticity of demand:

- When the income elasticity of demand is positive, the good is a normal good—that is, the quantity demanded at any given price increases as income increases.
- When the income elasticity of demand is negative, the good is an inferior good—that is, the quantity demanded at any given price decreases as income increases.

Economists often use estimates of the income elasticity of demand to predict which industries will grow most rapidly as the incomes of consumers grow over time. In doing this, they often find it useful to make a further distinction among normal goods, identifying which are *income-elastic* and which are *income-inelastic*.

FOR INQUIRING MINDS

CANADA—NO LONGER A NATION OF FARMERS

At one time, most Canadians lived and worked on farms; and as recently as the 1940s, one-quarter of Canadian workers were still in agriculture. But the importance of agriculture has been steadily declining, and it is no longer true that we are a nation of farmers. Though farmers still swing a lot of political weight, nowadays less than 2 percent of the Canadian labour force works in agriculture. What accounts for this decline?

The immediate answer is that consumers in Canada spend a much smaller share of their income on food and other agricultural products than they used to. And since farm products command a smaller share of spending, the producers must receive a smaller share of total income.

But why has the share of spending for food declined? It turns out that there are two answers, both having to do with elasticities. First, the income elasticity of demand for food is much less than one. So as an economy gets richer, other things being the same, it will spend only slightly more on food.

Second, throughout the twentieth century agriculture was a technologically progressive sector; as a result, the prices of farm products have steadily fallen compared with the prices of nonagricultural goods. This could either raise or lower total spending on agricultural products, other things being the same; it depends on whether demand is elastic or inelastic. But all the evidence is that the price elasticity of demand for agricultural products is less than one—an inelastic demand—so falling prices reduced the total revenue, and hence the income, of farmers.

In short, the Canadian farm sector is a victim of its own success; indeed, it has been so successful that it has almost disappeared.

The demand for a good is **income-elastic** if the income elasticity of demand for that good is greater than 1. When income rises, the demand for income-elastic goods rises *faster* than income. Luxury goods such as second homes and international travel tend to be income-elastic. The demand for a good is **income-inelastic** if the income elasticity of demand for that good is positive, but less than 1. When income rises, the demand for income-inelastic goods rises, but more slowly than income. Necessities such as food and clothing tend to be income-inelastic.

The demand for a good is **income-elastic** if the income elasticity of demand for that good is greater than 1.

The demand for a good is **income-inelastic** if the income elasticity of demand for that good is positive but less than 1.

economics in action

Spending It

Statistics Canada carries out extensive surveys of how families spend their incomes. This is not just a matter of intellectual curiosity. Quite a few government programs involve some adjustment for changes in the cost of living; to estimate those changes, the government must know how people spend their money. But an additional payoff to these surveys is evidence on the income elasticity of demand for various goods.

What stands out from these studies? The classic result is that the income elasticity of demand for "food eaten at home" is considerably less than 1: as a family's income rises, the share of its income spent on food consumed at home falls. Correspondingly, the lower a family's income, the higher the share of its income spent on food consumed at home. In poor countries, many families spend more than half their income on food consumed at home. Few people in Canada are that poor, but the income elasticity for "food eaten at home" is usually estimated at less than 0.5. "Food eaten away from home" has a much higher income elasticity, perhaps close to 1—families with higher incomes eat out more often and at fancier places. In fact, a sure sign of rising income levels in developing countries is the arrival of fast-food restaurants that cater to newly affluent customers. For example, McDonald's can now be found in Jakarta, Shanghai, and Bombay.

AP/Wide World Photos

Judging from the activity at this busy McDonald's, incomes are rising in Jakarta, Indonesia.

There is one clear example of an inferior good found in the surveys: rental housing. Families with higher income actually spend less on rent than families with lower income, because they are much more likely to own their own homes. And the category identified as "other housing"—which basically means second homes—is highly income-elastic: only higher-income families can afford a vacation home at all, so "other housing" has an income elasticity of demand greater than 1. ■

>> QUICK REVIEW

- Goods are substitutes when the *cross-price elasticity of demand* is positive. Goods are complements when the cross-price elasticity of demand is negative.
- Inferior goods have a negative *income elasticity of demand.* Most goods are normal goods, which have a positive income elasticity of demand.
- Normal goods may be either *income-elastic,* with an income elasticity of demand greater than 1, or *income-inelastic,* with an income elasticity of demand that is positive, but less than 1.

< < < < < < < < < < < < < < < < < <

>> CHECK YOUR UNDERSTANDING 5-3

1. After Kathy's income increased from $12,000 to $18,000 a year, her purchases of CDs increased from 10 to 40 CDs a year. Calculate Kathy's income elasticity of demand for CDs using the midpoint method.
2. Expensive restaurant meals are income-elastic goods for most people, including Sanjay. Suppose his income falls by 10% this year. What can you predict about the change in Sanjay's consumption of expensive restaurant meals?
3. As the price of margarine rises by 20%, a manufacturer of baked goods increases its quantity of butter demanded by 5%. Calculate the cross-price elasticity of demand between butter and margarine. Are butter and margarine substitutes or complements for this manufacturer?

Solutions appear at back of book.

The Price Elasticity of Supply

The Tellez plan to drive up the price of oil would have been much less effective if a higher price had induced large increases in output by countries that were not party to the agreement. For example, if Canadian oil producers had responded to the higher price by significantly increasing their production, they could have pushed the price of oil back down. But they didn't—in fact, producers of oil who were not members of OPEC (Organization of Petroleum Exporting Countries) did not respond much to the higher price. This was another critical element in the success of the Tellez plan: a low responsiveness in output to a higher price of oil from other oil producers. To measure the response of producers to price changes, we need a measure parallel to the price elasticity of demand—the *price elasticity of supply.*

Measuring the Price Elasticity of Supply

The **price elasticity of supply** is a measure of the responsiveness of the quantity of a good supplied to the price of that good. It is the ratio of the percent change in the quantity supplied to the percent change in the price as we move along the supply curve.

The **price elasticity of supply** is defined the same way as the price elasticity of demand:

$$\textbf{(5-9)}\quad \text{Price elasticity of supply} = \frac{\%\text{ change in quantity supplied}}{\%\text{ change in price}}$$

The only difference is that this time we consider movements along the supply curve rather than movements along the demand curve.

Suppose that the price of tomatoes rises by 10 percent. If the quantity of tomatoes supplied also increases by 10 percent in response, the price elasticity of supply of tomatoes is 1 (10%/10%), and supply is unit-elastic. If the quantity supplied increases by 5%, the price elasticity of supply is 0.5 and supply is inelastic; if the quantity increases by 20%, the price elasticity of supply is 2, and supply is elastic.

As in the case of demand, the extreme values of the price elasticity of supply have a simple graphical representation.

Panel (a) of Figure 5-6 shows the supply of cell phone frequencies, the portion of the radio spectrum that is suitable for sending and receiving cell phone signals. Governments own the right to sell the use of this part of the radio spectrum to cell phone operators inside their borders. In Chapter 7, we will discuss how many governments recently sold off their cell phone frequencies to the highest bidder in an auction. But governments can't increase or decrease the number of cell phone frequencies that they have to offer—for technical reasons, the quantity of frequencies suitable for cell phone operation is a fixed quantity. So the supply curve for cell phone frequencies

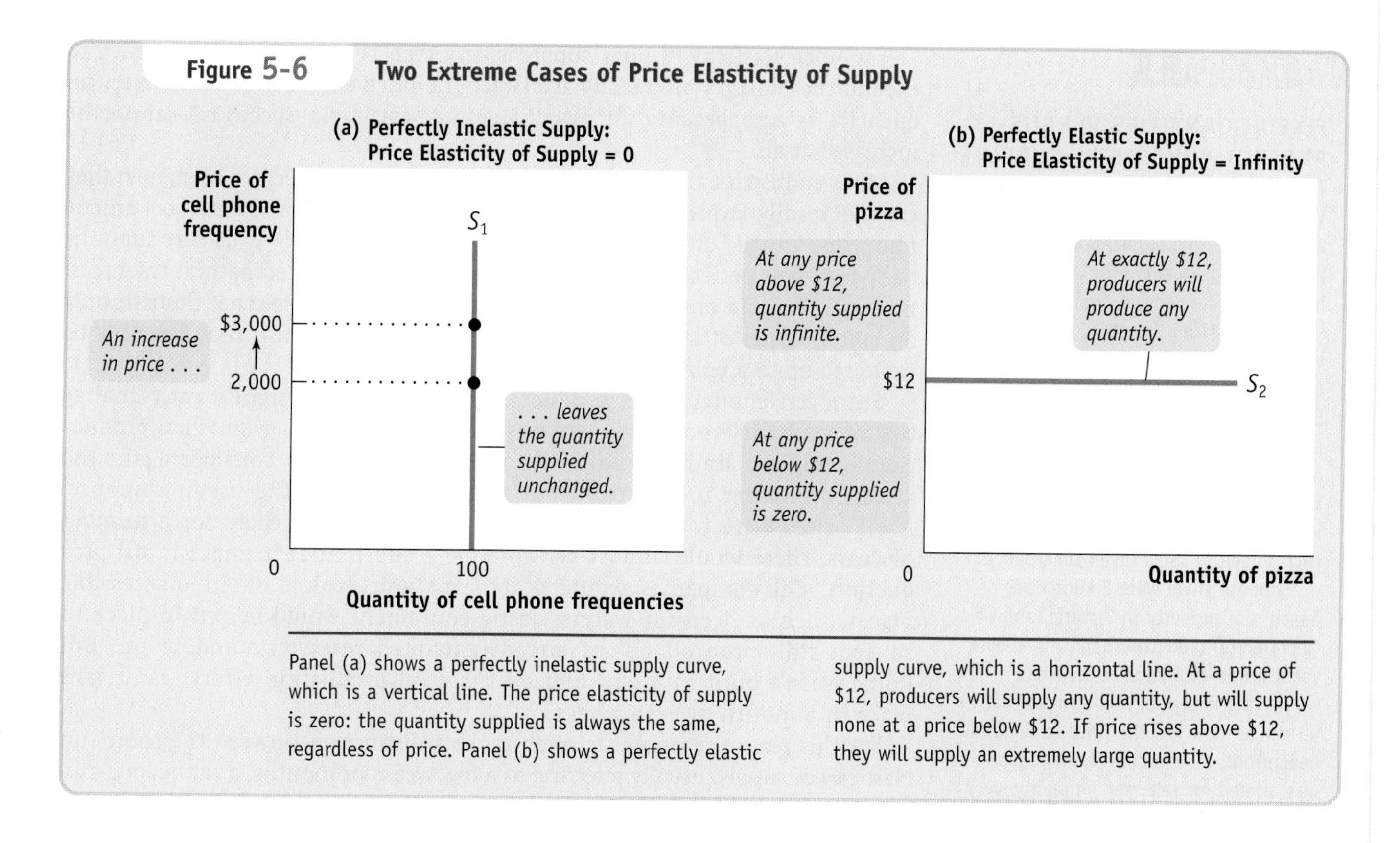

Panel (a) shows a perfectly inelastic supply curve, which is a vertical line. The price elasticity of supply is zero: the quantity supplied is always the same, regardless of price. Panel (b) shows a perfectly elastic supply curve, which is a horizontal line. At a price of $12, producers will supply any quantity, but will supply none at a price below $12. If price rises above $12, they will supply an extremely large quantity.

is a vertical line, which we have assumed is set at the quantity of 100 frequencies. As you move up and down that curve, the change in quantity supplied by the government is zero, whatever the change in price. So panel (a) illustrates a case in which the price elasticity of supply is zero. This is a case of **perfectly inelastic supply.**

Panel (b) shows the supply curve for pizza. We suppose that it costs $12 to produce a pizza, including all opportunity costs such as the implicit cost of capital invested in pizza parlours. At any price below $12, it would be unprofitable to produce pizza, and all the pizza parlours in Canada would go out of business. Alternatively, there are many producers who could operate pizza parlours if they were profitable. The ingredients—dough, tomatoes, cheese—are plentiful. And if necessary, more tomatoes could be grown, more milk could be produced to make mozzarella, and so on. So any price above $12 would elicit an extremely large quantity of pizzas supplied. The implied supply curve is therefore a horizontal line at $12. Since even a tiny increase in the price would lead to a huge increase in the quantity supplied, the price elasticity of supply would be more or less infinite. This is a case of **perfectly elastic supply.**

As our cell phone frequencies and pizza examples suggest, real-world instances of both perfectly inelastic and perfectly elastic supply are relatively easy to find—much easier than their counterparts in demand.

There is **perfectly inelastic supply** when the price elasticity of supply is zero, so that changes in the price of the good have no effect on the quantity supplied. A perfectly inelastic supply curve is a vertical line.

There is **perfectly elastic supply** when even a tiny increase or reduction in the price will lead to very large changes in the quantity supplied, so that the price elasticity of supply is infinite. A perfectly elastic supply curve is a horizontal line.

What Factors Determine the Price Elasticity of Supply?

Our examples tell us the main determinant of the price elasticity of supply: the availability of inputs. In addition, as with the price elasticity of demand, time may also play a role in the price elasticity of supply. Here we briefly summarize the two factors.

The Availability of Inputs The price elasticity of supply tends to be large when inputs are easily available. It tends to be small when inputs are difficult to obtain.

Time The price elasticity of supply tends to become larger as producers have more time to respond to a price change. This means that the long-run price elasticity of supply is often higher than the short-run elasticity.

PITFALLS

FIXED QUANTITIES VERSUS PERFECTLY INELASTIC SUPPLY

The quantity of beachfront property in Victoria is fixed—there is a certain amount, and that's that. Does this mean the supply curve for Victoria beachfront is a vertical line? Not necessarily. Recall from Chapter 3 that there was a fixed quantity of tickets to Gretzky's last hockey game in Canada. But the supply curve of tickets was upward sloping, because supply is not only what exists but what is offered for sale. Remember, the "quantity supplied" is defined as the amount that sellers wish to sell in some given time period.

Suppose there were 2 kilometres of beachfront property in Victoria, and we (incorrectly) drew the supply curve as a vertical line at 2 kilometres. What would this imply? It would imply that no matter how low the price for Victoria beachfront, all the beachfront property was offered for sale. Yet, in reality, very high prices would be required to tempt some existing owners to put their property on the market. At low prices, some property may be offered for sale, but probably very little. The same analysis suggests, for example, that even though there is fixed quantity of genuine Picasso paintings in existence, the supply curve is not necessarily a vertical line. Supply is the quantity offered for sale in any given period of time, not the quantity in existence.

The price elasticity of pizza supply is very high because the inputs needed to expand the industry are readily available. The price elasticity of cell phone frequencies is zero because an essential input—the radio spectrum—cannot be increased at all.

Many industries are like pizza and have high price elasticities of supply: they can be readily expanded because they don't require any special or unique resources. On the other hand, the price elasticity of supply is usually substantially less than perfectly elastic for goods that involve limited natural resources: minerals like gold or copper, agricultural products like coffee that flourish only on certain types of land, renewable resources like ocean fish that can only be exploited up to a point without destroying the resource.

But given enough time, producers are often able to significantly change the amount they produce in response to a price change, even when production involves a limited natural resource. For example, consider again the effects of a surge in oil prices, but this time focus on the supply response. If oil prices were to rise to US$55 per barrel and stay there for a number of years, there would almost certainly be a substantial increase in oil production. Oil companies would search for and exploit oil in inaccessible places, such as deep-sea waters; costly equipment would be put in place to squeeze still more oil out of already-exploited reservoirs; and so on. But Rome wasn't built in a day, and all these oil-production efforts can't take place in a month or even a year.

For this reason, economists often make a distinction between the short-run elasticity of supply, usually referring to a few weeks or months, and the long-run elasticity of supply, usually referring to several years. In most industries, the long-run elasticity of supply is higher than the short-run elasticity.

economics in action

European Farm Surpluses

One of the policies we analysed in Chapter 4 was the imposition of a *price floor*, a lower limit on the price of a good. We saw that price floors are often used by governments to support the incomes of farmers but create large unwanted surpluses of farm produce. The most dramatic example of this is found in the European Union, where price floors have created a "butter mountain", a "wine lake", and so on.

Were European politicians unaware that their price floors would create huge surpluses? They probably knew that surpluses would arise, but underestimated the price elasticity of agricultural supply. In fact, when the agricultural price supports were put in place, many analysts thought they were unlikely to lead to big increases in production. After all, European countries are densely populated, and there was little new land available for cultivation.

What the analysts failed to realize, however, was how much farm production could expand by adding other resources, especially fertilizer and pesticides. So although farm acreage didn't increase much, farm production did! ■

>>QUICK REVIEW

- The *price elasticity of supply* is the percent change in the quantity supplied divided by the percent change in the price.
- Under *perfectly inelastic supply*, the quantity supplied is completely unresponsive to price and the supply curve is a vertical line. Under *perfectly elastic supply*, the supply curve is horizontal at some specific price. If the price falls below that level, the quantity supplied is zero. If the price rises above that level, the quantity supplied is infinite.
- The price elasticity of supply depends on the availability of inputs and upon the period of time that has elapsed since the price change.

>>CHECK YOUR UNDERSTANDING 5-4

1. Using the midpoint method, calculate the price elasticity of supply for web-design services when the price per hour rises from $100 to $150 and the number of hours transacted increases from 300,000 hours to 500,000. Is supply elastic, inelastic, or unit-elastic?
2. True or false? If the demand for milk were to rise, in the long run milk-drinkers would be better off if supply were elastic rather than inelastic.

3. True or false? Long-run price elasticities of supply are generally larger than short-run price elasticities of supply. Therefore the short-run supply curves are generally flatter than the long-run supply curves.
4. True or false? When supply is perfectly elastic, changes in demand have no effect on price.

Solutions appear at back of book.

An Elasticity Menagerie

We've just run through quite a few different elasticities. Keeping them all straight can be a problem. So in Table 5-3 we provide a summary of all the elasticities we have discussed and their implications.

TABLE 5-3

An Elasticity Menagerie

Name	Possible Values	Significance
Price elasticity of demand = $\frac{\text{\% change in quantity demanded}}{\text{\% change in price}}$ (use absolute value)		
Perfectly inelastic demand	0	Price has no effect on quantity demanded (vertical demand curve).
Inelastic demand	Between 0 and 1	A rise in price increases total revenue.
Unit-elastic demand	Exactly 1	Changes in price have no effect on total revenue.
Elastic demand	Between 1 and ∞	A rise in price reduces total revenue.
Perfectly elastic demand	∞	A rise in price causes quantity demanded to fall to 0. A fall in price leads to an infinite quantity demanded (horizontal demand curve).
Cross-price elasticity of demand: = $\frac{\text{\% change in quantity } \textit{of one good} \text{ demanded}}{\text{\% change in price } \textit{of another good}}$		
Complements	Negative	Quantity demanded of one good falls when the price of another rises.
Substitutes	Positive	Quantity demanded of one good rises when the price of another rises.
Income elasticity of demand = $\frac{\text{\% change in quantity demanded}}{\text{\% change in income}}$		
Inferior good	Negative	Quantity demanded falls when income rises.
Normal good, income-inelastic	Positive, less than 1	Quantity demanded rises when income rises, but not as rapidly as income.
Normal good, income-elastic	Greater than 1	Quantity demanded rises when income rises, and more rapidly than income.
Price elasticity of supply = $\frac{\text{\% change in quantity supplied}}{\text{\% change in price}}$		
Perfectly inelastic supply	0	Price has no effect on quantity supplied (vertical supply curve).
	Greater than 0, less than ∞	Ordinary upward-sloping supply curve.
Perfectly elastic supply	∞	Any fall in price causes quantity supplied to fall to 0. Any rise in price elicits an infinite quantity supplied (horizontal supply curve).

Using Elasticity: The Incidence of an Excise Tax

In Chapter 4 we introduced the concept of the *incidence* of a tax—the measure of who really bears the burden of the tax. We saw in the case of an excise tax—a sales tax imposed on sales or purchases of a specific product—that the incidence does not depend on who literally pays the money to the government. It doesn't matter, in other words, whether the tax is a tax assessed on the sellers or the buyers. But we also noted that to determine who really pays the tax, we needed the concept of elasticity.

We are now ready to see how the price elasticity of demand and the price elasticity of supply determine the incidence of an excise tax.

When an Excise Tax Is Paid Mainly by Consumers

Figure 5-7 shows an excise tax that falls mainly on consumers: an excise tax on gasoline, which we set at $0.50 a litre. (There really is an excise tax on gasoline. Indeed, in Canada, taxes comprise over half the price of a litre of gasoline.) According to Figure 5-7, in the absence of the tax, gasoline would sell for $0.45 a litre.

Two key assumptions are reflected in the supply and demand curves. First, the price elasticity of demand for gasoline is very low, so the demand curve is relatively steep. Second, the price elasticity of supply is very high, so the supply curve is relatively flat.

We know from Chapter 4 that an excise tax drives a wedge, equal to the size of the tax, between the price paid by consumers and the price received by producers. This wedge drives the price paid by consumers up, the price received by producers down. But as we can see from the figure, in this case those two effects are very unequal in size. The price received by producers falls only slightly, from $0.45 to $0.40, while the price paid by consumers rises by a lot, from $0.45 to $0.90.

This example illustrates a general principle: When the price elasticity of demand is low and the price elasticity of supply is high, the burden of an excise tax falls mainly on consumers. This is probably a good description of the main excise taxes actually collected in Canada today, such as taxes on cigarettes and alcoholic beverages.

Figure 5-7

An Excise Tax Paid Mainly by Consumers

The relatively steep demand curve here reflects a low price elasticity of demand for gasoline. The relatively flat supply curve reflects a high price elasticity of supply. The pre-tax price of a litre of gas is $0.45, and a tax of $0.50 per litre is imposed. The cost to consumers doubles (it rises by $0.45), reflecting the fact that most of the burden of the tax falls on consumers. Only a small portion of the tax is borne by producers: the price they receive falls by only $0.05.

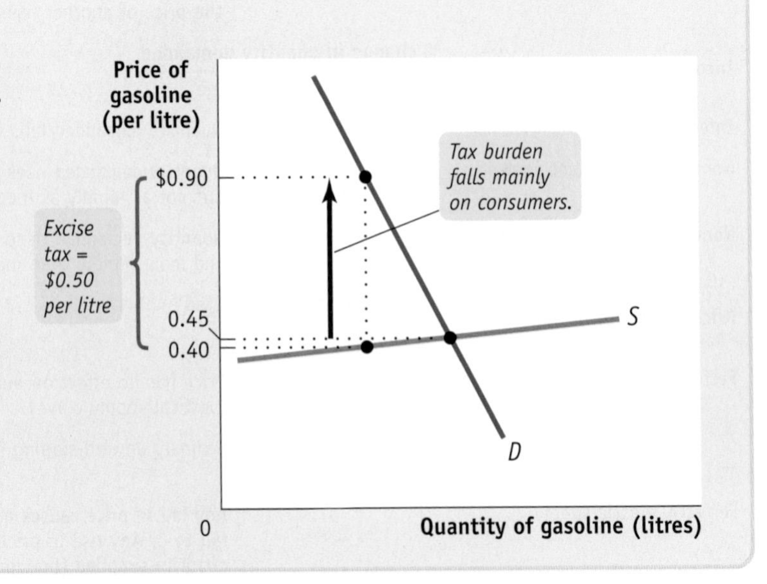

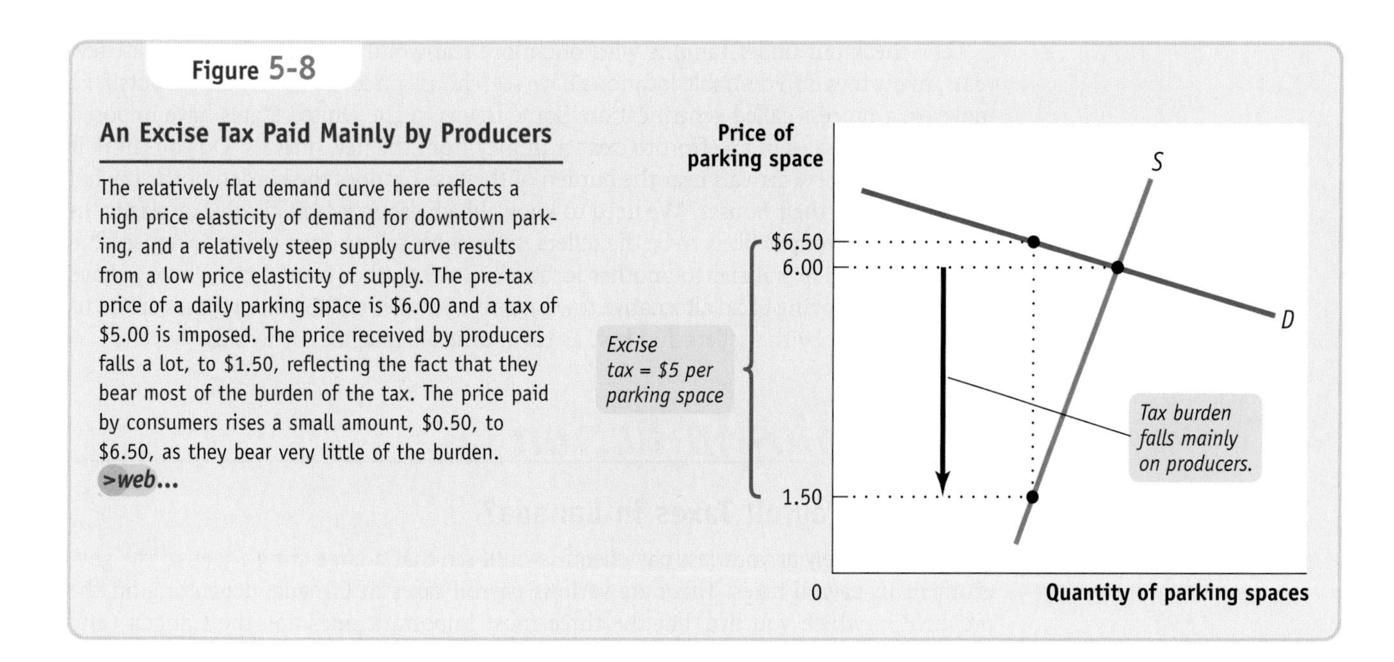

Figure 5-8

An Excise Tax Paid Mainly by Producers

The relatively flat demand curve here reflects a high price elasticity of demand for downtown parking, and a relatively steep supply curve results from a low price elasticity of supply. The pre-tax price of a daily parking space is $6.00 and a tax of $5.00 is imposed. The price received by producers falls a lot, to $1.50, reflecting the fact that they bear most of the burden of the tax. The price paid by consumers rises a small amount, $0.50, to $6.50, as they bear very little of the burden.
>web...

When an Excise Tax Is Paid Mainly by Producers

Figure 5-8 shows an excise tax paid mainly by producers. In this case we consider a $5.00-per-day tax on downtown parking in a small city. In the market equilibrium, parking would cost $6.00 per day in the absence of the tax.

The price elasticity of supply is assumed to be very low because the lots used for parking have very few alternative uses. So the supply curve is relatively steep. The price elasticity of demand, however, is high: consumers can easily switch to other parking spaces a few minutes' walk from downtown. So the demand curve is relatively flat.

The tax drives a wedge between the price paid by consumers and the price received by producers. This time, however, the price to consumers rises only slightly, from $6.00 to $6.50, but the price received by producers falls a lot, from $6.00 to $1.50. So a consumer bears only $0.50 of the $5 tax, with a producer bearing the remaining $4.50.

Again, this example illustrates a general principle: When the price elasticity of demand is high and the price elasticity of supply is low, the burden of an excise tax falls mainly on producers.

Putting It All Together

We've just seen that when the price elasticity of supply is high and the price elasticity of demand is low, an excise tax falls mainly on consumers; when the price elasticity of supply is low and the price elasticity of demand is high, an excise tax falls mainly on producers. This leads us to the general rule: when the price elasticity of demand is higher than the price elasticity of supply, an excise tax falls mainly on the producers. When the price elasticity of supply is higher than the price elasticity of demand, an excise tax falls mainly on consumers. So elasticity—not who literally pays the tax—determines the incidence of an excise tax.

One handy way to remember this is to think of an analogy—Tai Chi. Originally, Tai Chi was a martial art emphasizing flexibility and responsiveness. When two practitioners fight, the one to be hit will invariably be the one who is least flexible and least responsive. The same goes for the incidence of taxes. The hit of the tax will always fall on the group that is least responsive and least flexible—least elastic.

Let's check our understanding with one more real-world example. Over the past few years, many towns in desirable locations have seen house prices go up as well-off outsiders move in, a process called gentrification. Some towns in the United States have imposed taxes on house sales in an effort to extract money from the new arrivals. Do you think it works? Do the new arrivals bear the burden of the tax? Or does the burden of the tax fall on those selling their houses? We need to know which group is least flexible or elastic. In this case, that group is likely to be the sellers, since most sellers must sell their houses due to things like a job transfer to another location. On the other hand, buyers always have the option of moving to an alternative town nearby. So taxes on home purchases are actually paid mainly by the sellers and not, as town officials imagine, by wealthy buyers.

economics in action

Who Pays Payroll Taxes in Canada?

If you look closely at your last pay cheque, you'll see that a large chunk goes to the government in payroll taxes. There are various payroll taxes in Canada, depending on the province in which you live, but the three most important ones are: the Canada (and Québec) pension plan contributions, employment insurance (EI) premiums, and workers' compensation premiums. Payroll taxes have grown considerably since the early 1980s when they were only about 5% of total wages and salaries, but this growth has levelled off since 1992. In 2001, payroll taxes amounted to about 12% of total wages and salaries.

Payroll taxes in Canada are shared between workers and employers, and this sharing seems to favour the worker—at least superficially. Employers and workers pay equally into the Canada (and Quebéc) pension plan, but employer contributions towards EI (employment insurance) are 1.4 times the amount of worker contributions, while the employer pays the entire payroll tax that supports workers' compensation.

But we have learned that the incidence of a tax does not really depend on who actually makes out the cheque. So, who really bears the burden of payroll taxes in Canada? Almost all economists who have studied the issue agree that the incidence of payroll taxes falls almost entirely on workers, not on their employers. This is because wages are lower than they would be without payroll taxes. If payroll taxes paid by employers lead to offsetting reductions in wages, then workers will bear the entire burden—not only of the part they pay themselves, but also of the part paid by the employer.

The reason for this conclusion lies in a comparison of the price elasticities of supply and demand for labour. The evidence suggests that the price elasticity of demand for labour is quite high, at least 3. That is, an increase in average wages of 1% would lead to at least a 3% decline in the number of hours of work demanded. On the other hand, the price elasticity of supply of labour is generally believed to be very low. The reason is that although a rise in the wage rate increases the incentive to work, it also makes people richer and more able to afford leisure; so the number of hours people are willing to work increases very little, if at all, when the wage per hour goes up.

Our analysis already tells us that when the price elasticity of demand is much higher than the price elasticity of supply, the burden of an excise tax falls mainly on the suppliers. So payroll taxes fall mainly on the suppliers of labour, that is, workers—even though, on paper, employers pay more than half of these taxes.

< < < < < < < < < < < < < < < < < < <

>>QUICK REVIEW

- The price elasticity of demand and the price elasticity of supply determine the incidence of a tax.
- In general, the higher the price elasticity of supply and the lower the price elasticity of demand, the more heavily the burden of an excise tax falls on consumers. The lower the price elasticity of supply and the higher the price elasticity of demand, the more heavily the burden falls on producers.

>>CHECK YOUR UNDERSTANDING 5-5

1. The demand for economics textbooks is very inelastic, but the supply is somewhat elastic. What does this imply about the incidence of a tax? Illustrate with a diagram.
2. True or false? When a substitute for a good is readily available to consumers, but it is difficult for producers to adjust the quantity of the good produced, then the burden of a tax on the good falls more heavily on producers.

3. The supply of bottled spring water is very inelastic, but the demand for it is somewhat elastic. What does this imply about the incidence of a tax? Illustrate with a diagram.
4. True or false? Other things equal, consumers would prefer to face a less elastic supply curve when a tax is imposed.

Solutions appear at back of book.

• A LOOK AHEAD •

The concept of elasticity deepens our understanding of supply and demand, among other things helping us predict not only in which direction prices will move but also by how much. For example, we now know that supply and demand elasticities determine how the burden of a tax will be divided between producers and consumers. And, to come back to an example from very early on in this chapter, the concept of elasticity was just what Luis Tellez needed to be able to engineer a reduction in output by oil-exporting countries that led to an increase in oil prices and an increase in their total revenues.

But we don't yet have a way to translate the changes in prices that result from a tax, or from any other change in the situation, into a measure of gains or losses to individuals. In the next chapter, we show how to make that translation—how to use the supply and demand curves to calculate gains and losses to producers and consumers.

SUMMARY

1. Many economic questions depend on the size of consumer or producer response to changes in prices or other variables. *Elasticity* is a general measure of responsiveness that can be used to answer such questions.
2. The **price elasticity of demand**—the percent change in the quantity demanded divided by the percent change in the price (dropping the minus sign)—is a measure of the responsiveness of the quantity demanded to changes in the price. In practical calculations, it is usually best to use the **midpoint method,** which calculates percent changes in prices and quantities based on the average of starting and final values.
3. The responsiveness of the quantity demanded to price can range from **perfectly inelastic demand,** where the quantity demanded is unaffected by the price, to **perfectly elastic demand,** where there is a unique price at which consumers will buy as much or as little as they are offered. When demand is perfectly inelastic, the demand curve is a vertical line; when it is perfectly elastic, the demand curve is a horizontal line.
4. The price elasticity of demand is classified according to whether it is more or less than 1. If it is greater than 1, demand is **elastic;** if it is less than 1, demand is **inelastic;** if it is exactly 1, demand is **unit-elastic.** This classification determines how **total revenue,** the total value of sales, changes when the price changes. If demand is elastic, total revenue falls when the price increases, and rises when the price decreases. If demand is inelastic, total revenue rises when the price increases and falls when the price decreases.
5. The price elasticity of demand depends on whether there are close substitutes for the good in question, whether the good is a necessity or a luxury, and the length of time that has elapsed since the price change.
6. The **cross-price elasticity of demand** measures the effect of a change in one good's price on the quantity of another good demanded. The cross-price elasticity of demand can be positive, in which case the goods are substitutes, or negative, in which case they are complements.
7. The **income elasticity of demand** is the percent change in the quantity of a good demanded when a consumer's income changes divided by the percentage change in income. The income elasticity of demand indicates how intensely the demand for a good responds to changes in income. It can be negative; in that case, the good is an inferior good. Goods with positive income elasticities of demand are normal goods. If the income elasticity is greater than 1, a good is **income-elastic;** if it is positive and less than 1, the good is **income-inelastic.**
8. The **price elasticity of supply** is the percent change in the quantity of a good supplied divided by the percent change in the price. If the quantity supplied does not change at all, we have an instance of **perfectly inelastic supply;** the supply curve is a vertical line. If the quantity supplied is zero below some price but infinite above that price, we have an instance of **perfectly elastic supply;** the supply curve is a horizontal line.
9. The price elasticity of supply depends on the availability of resources to expand production and on time. It is

higher when inputs are easily available, and the longer the time elapsed since the price change.

10. The incidence of an excise tax depends on the price elasticities of supply and demand. If the price elasticity of demand is higher than the price elasticity of supply, the tax falls mainly on producers; if the price elasticity of supply is higher than the price elasticity of demand, the tax falls mainly on consumers.

KEY TERMS

Price elasticity of demand, p. 119
Midpoint method, p. 120
Perfectly inelastic demand, p. 122
Perfectly elastic demand, p. 122
Elastic demand, p. 123
Inelastic demand, p. 123
Unit-elastic demand, p. 123
Total revenue, p. 124
Cross-price elasticity of demand, p. 129
Income elasticity of demand, p. 130
Income-elastic demand, p. 131
Income-inelastic demand, p. 131
Price elasticity of supply, p. 132
Perfectly inelastic supply, p. 133
Perfectly elastic supply, p. 133

PROBLEMS

1. TheNile.com, an online bookseller, wants to increase its total revenue. Currently, every book they sell is priced at $10.50. One suggested strategy is to offer a discount that lowers the price of a book to $9.50, a 10% reduction in price using the midpoint method. TheNile.com knows that its customers can be divided into two distinct groups according to their likely responses to the discount. The following table shows how the two groups respond to the discount.

	Group A (Sales per week) (millions)	Group B (Sales per week) (millions)
Volume of sales before the 10% discount	1.55	1.50
Volume of sales after the 10% discount	1.65	1.70

   a. Using the midpoint method, calculate the price elasticities of demand for Group A and Group B.

   b. Explain how the discount will affect total revenue from each group.

   c. Suppose TheNile.com knows which group each customer belongs to when he or she logs on and can choose whether or not to offer the 10% discount. Should discounts be offered to Group A or to Group B, to neither group, or to both groups?

2. Do you think the price elasticity of demand for Ford sport-utility vehicles (SUVs) will increase, decrease, or remain the same when each of the following events occurs? Explain your answer.

   a. Other car manufacturers, such as General Motors, decide to make and sell SUVs.

   b. SUVs produced in foreign countries are banned from the Canadian market.

   c. Due to ad campaigns, Canadians believe that SUVs are much safer than ordinary passenger cars.

   d. The time period over which you measure the elasticity lengthens. During that longer time, new models such as four-wheel drive cargo vans appear.

3. Canadian wheat production increased dramatically in 1999 after a bumper harvest. The supply curve shifted rightward and, as a result, the price fell and the quantity demanded increased (a movement along the demand curve). The table below describes what happened to prices and the quantity of wheat demanded.

Demand Data for Canadian Wheat	1998	1999
Bushels produced	1.74 billion	1.9 billion
Average price per bushel	$3.70	$2.72

   a. Using the midpoint method, calculate the price elasticity of demand for wheat.

   b. What is the total revenue for Canadian wheat farmers in 1998 and 1999?

   c. How did the bumper harvest affect the incomes of Canadian wheat farmers? How could you have predicted this from your answer to part a?

4. The table below gives part of the supply schedule for personal computers in Canada.

Price of computer	Quantity of computers supplied (thousands)
$1,100	12,000
900	8,000

   a. Calculate the price elasticity of supply when the price rises from $900 to $1,100, using the midpoint method.

   b. Suppose firms produce 1,000 more computers at any given price due to improved technology. As price increases from $900 to $1,100, is the price elasticity of supply now greater than, less than, or the same as it was in part a?

c. Suppose a longer time period under consideration means that the quantity supplied at any given price is 20% higher than the figures given in the table. As price increases from $900 to $1,100, is the price elasticity of supply now greater than, less than, or the same as it was in part a?

5. The following table lists the cross-price elasticities of demand for several goods, where the percent price change is measured for the first good of the pair, and the percent quantity change is measured for the second good.

	Cross-price elasticities of demand
Air-conditioning units and kilowatts of electricity	−0.34
Coke and Pepsi	+0.63
High-fuel-consuming sport-utility vehicles (SUVs) and gasoline	−0.28
McDonald's burgers and Burger King burgers	+0.82
Butter and margarine	+1.54

a. Explain the sign of each of the cross-elasticities. What does it imply about the relationship between the two goods in question?

b. Compare the absolute values of the cross-price elasticities and explain their magnitudes. For example, why is the cross-price elasticity for McDonald's and Burger King less than the cross-elasticity of butter and margarine?

c. Use the information above to calculate how a 5% increase in the price of Pepsi affects the quantity of Coke demanded.

d. Use the information above to calculate how a 10% fall in the price of gasoline affects the quantity of SUVs demanded.

6. What can you conclude about the price elasticity of demand in each of the following statements?

a. "The pizza delivery business in this town is very competitive. I'd lose half my customers if I raised prices by as little as 10%."

b. "I owned both of the two Jerry Garcia autographed lithographs in existence. I sold one on eBay for a high price. But when I sold the second one, the price dropped a lot."

c. "My economics professor has chosen to use the Krugman, Wells, Myatt textbook for this class. I have no choice but to buy this book."

d. I always spend exactly $10 per week on coffee.

7. Take a linear demand curve like that drawn in Figure 5-5, where the range of prices for which demand is elastic and inelastic is labelled. In each of the following scenarios, the supply curve shifts. Show along which portion of the demand curve (that is, the elastic or the inelastic portion) the supply curve must have shifted in order to generate the event described. In each case, show on the diagram the quantity effect and the price effect.

a. Recent attempts to stop the flow of illegal drugs into Canada have actually benefited drug dealers.

b. New construction increased the number of seats in the football stadium and resulted in greater total revenue from ticket sales.

c. Increasing production of Porsches has led to a decline in total revenue for the Porsche Company.

8. The following table shows the price and yearly quantity sold of souvenir T-shirts in Charlottetown according to the average income of the tourists visiting.

Price of T-shirt	Quantity of T-shirts demanded when average tourist income is $20,000	Quantity of T-shirts demanded when average tourist income is $30,000
$4	3,000	5,000
5	2,400	4,200
6	1,600	3,000
7	800	1,800

a. Using the midpoint method, calculate the price elasticity of demand when the price of a T-shirt rises from $5 to $6 when the average tourist income is $20,000. Also calculate it when the average tourist income is $30,000.

b. Using the midpoint method, calculate the income elasticity of demand when the average tourist income increases form $20,000 to $30,000 when the price of a T-shirt is $4. Also calculate it when the price is $7.

9. A recent study determined the following elasticities for Volkswagen Beetles:

Price elasticity of demand = 2
Income elasticity of demand = 1.5

The supply of Beetles is elastic. Based on this information, are the following statements true or false? Explain your reasoning for each.

a. A 10% increase in the price of a Beetle will reduce the quantity demanded by 20%.

b. An increase in consumer income will increase the price and quantity of Beetles. Since price elasticity of demand is greater than 1, total revenue will go down.

10. In each of the following cases, do you think the price elasticity of supply is (i) perfectly elastic; (ii) perfectly inelastic; (iii) elastic, but not perfectly elastic; or (iv) inelastic, but not perfectly inelastic? Explain, using a diagram.

a. An increase in demand this summer for luxury cruises leads to a huge jump in the sales price of a cabin on the *Queen Mary 2.*

b. The price of a kilowatt of electricity is the same during periods of high electricity demand as during periods of low electricity demand.

c. Fewer people want to fly during February than during any other month. The airlines cancel about 10% of their flights as ticket prices fall about 20% during this month.

d. Owners of vacation homes in Nova Scotia rent them out during the summer. Due to the soft economy this year, a 30% decline in the rental rate leads more than half of homeowners to occupy their vacation homes themselves during the summer.

11. Use an elasticity concept to explain each of the following observations:

a. During economic boom times, the number of new personal care businesses, such as gyms and tanning salons, is proportionately greater than the number of other new businesses, such as grocery stores.

b. Cement is the primary building material in Mexico. After new technology makes cement cheaper to produce, the supply curve for the Mexican cement industry becomes relatively flatter.

c. Some goods that were once considered luxuries, such as telephones, are now considered virtual necessities. As a result, the demand curve for telephone services has become steeper over time.

d. People in a less developed country like Guatemala spend proportionately more of their income on equipment for producing things at home, like sewing machines, than people in a more developed country like Canada.

12. Taiwan is a major world supplier of semiconductor chips. A recent earthquake in Taiwan severely damaged the production facilities of Taiwanese chip-producing companies, sharply reducing the amount of chips they could produce.

a. Assume that the total revenue of a typical non-Taiwanese chip manufacturer rises due to these events. In terms of elasticity, what must be true for this to happen? Illustrate the change in total revenue with a diagram, indicating the "price effect" and the "sales effect" of the Taiwan earthquake on this company's total revenue.

b. Now assume that the total revenue of a typical non-Taiwanese chip manufacturer falls due to these events. In terms of elasticity, what must be true for this to happen? Illustrate the change in total revenue with a diagram, indicating the price effect and the quantity effect of the Taiwan earthquake on this company's total revenue.

13. There is a debate about whether sterile hypodermic needles should be passed out free of charge in cities with high drug use. Proponents argue that doing so will reduce the incidence of diseases, such as HIV/AIDS, that are often spread by needle sharing among drug users. Opponents believe that it will encourage more drug use by reducing the risks of this behaviour. As an economist asked to assess the policy, you must know the following: (i) how responsive the spread of diseases like AIDS/HIV is to the price of sterile needles; and (ii) how responsive drug use is to the price of sterile needles. Assuming that you know these two things, use the concepts of price elasticity of demand for sterile needles and cross-price elasticity between drug use and sterile needles to answer the following questions.

a. In what circumstances do you believe that this is a beneficial policy?

b. In what circumstances do you believe that this is a bad policy?

14. Suppose that the government imposes an excise tax of 25 cents for every litre of gas sold. Before the tax, the price of a litre of gas is 50 cents. Consider the following four after-tax scenarios. In each of the cases, (i) use a concept from elasticity to explain what must be true for this scenario to arise; (ii) determine who bears relatively more of the burden of the tax, producers or consumers; and (iii) illustrate your answer with a diagram.

a. The price of gasoline paid by consumers rises to 75 cents per litre. Assume that the demand curve is downward sloping.

b. The price paid by consumers remains at 50 cents a litre after the tax is imposed. Assume that the supply curve is upward sloping.

c. The price of gasoline paid by consumers rises to 70 cents.

d. The price of gasoline paid by consumers rises to 55 cents.

15. Describe how the following events will affect the incidence of taxation—that is, after the event, will the tax fall more heavily on consumers or producers in comparison to before the event? Use the concept of elasticity to explain your answer.

a. Sales of gasoline are taxed. Ethanol, a substitute for gasoline, becomes widely available.

b. Sales of electricity to Quebec residents are taxed. Regulations are introduced that make it much more difficult for Quebec utility companies to divert supplies of electricity from the Quebec market to markets in neighbouring states in the U.S.

c. Sales of electricity to Quebec residents are taxed. Regulations are introduced that make it much easier for Quebec utility companies to divert supplies of electricity from the Quebec market to markets in neighbouring states in the U.S.

d. The sale of municipally provided water is taxed. Legislation is introduced that forbids the use of private sources of water such as wells and the diversion of rivers.

16. In devising taxes, there is often a debate about (i) who bears the burden of the tax; and (ii) whether the tax achieves some desirable social goal, such as discouraging undesirable behaviour by making it more expensive. In the case of cigarettes, smokers tend to be highly addicted and have lower income than the average nonsmoker. Taxes on cigarettes have historically had the effect of raising the price to consumers almost one for one with the size of the tax.

a. Why might such a tax be undesirable when considering issues of tax equity—that is, whether or not more of the tax burden falls more heavily on lower-income people? How do the elasticities of supply and demand for cigarettes affect the equity of cigarette taxation?

b. How do the elasticities of supply and demand for cigarettes affect the effectiveness of the tax in discouraging smoking?

c. In light of your answers to parts a and b and the historical response of price to the tax, what trade-offs must policy makers make when considering a cigarette tax?

16. Worldwide, the average coffee grower has increased the amount of acreage under cultivation over the past few years. The result has been that the average coffee plantation produces significantly more coffee than it did 10 to 20 years ago. Unfortunately for the growers, however, this has also been a period in which their total revenues have plunged. In terms of elasticity, what must be true for these events to have occurred? Illustrate these events with a diagram, indicating the quantity effect and the price effect that gave rise to these events.

>web... To continue your study and review of concepts in this chapter, please visit the Krugman/Wells website for quizzes, animated graph tutorials, web links to helpful resources, and more.

www.worthpublishers.com/krugmanwellsmyatt

chapter 6

>>Consumer and Producer Surplus

MAKING GAINS BY THE BOOK

THERE IS A LIVELY MARKET IN SECOND-hand university textbooks. At the end of each term, some students who took a course decide that the money they can get by selling their used books is worth more to them than keeping the books. And some students who are taking the course next term prefer to buy a somewhat battered but inexpensive used textbook rather than pay the full price for a new one.

Textbook publishers and authors are not happy about these transactions, because they cut into sales of new books. But both the students who sell used books and those who buy them clearly benefit from the existence of the market. That is why many university bookstores facilitate their trade, buying used textbooks and selling them alongside the new books.

But can we put a number on what used textbook buyers and sellers gain from these transactions? Can we answer the question, "*How much* do the buyers and sellers of textbooks gain from the existence of the used-book market?"

Yes, we can. In this chapter, we will see how to measure benefits, such as those to buyers of used textbooks, from being able to purchase a good—known as *consumer surplus.* And we will see that there is a corresponding measure, *producer surplus,* of the benefits sellers receive from being able to sell a good.

The concepts of consumer surplus and producer surplus are extremely useful for analyzing a wide variety of economic issues. They let us calculate how much benefit producers and consumers receive from the existence of a market. They also allow us to calculate how the welfare of consumers and producers is affected by changes in market prices. Such calculations play a crucial role in evaluating many economic policies.

David Young-Wolff/PhotoEdit

How much am I willing to pay for that used textbook?

What information do we need to calculate consumer and producer surplus? The answer, surprisingly, is that all we need are the demand and supply curves for a good. That is, the supply and demand model isn't just a model of how a competitive market works—it's also a model of how much consumers and producers gain from participating in that market. So our first step will be to learn how consumer and producer surplus can be derived from the demand and supply curves. We will then see how these concepts can be applied to actual economic issues.

What you will learn in this chapter:

- The meaning of **consumer surplus** and its relationship to the demand curve
- The meaning of **producer surplus** and its relationship to the supply curve
- The meaning and importance of **total surplus** and how it can be used both to measure the gains from trade and to evaluate the efficiency of a market
- How to use changes in total surplus to measure the deadweight loss of taxes

Consumer Surplus and the Demand Curve

The market in used textbooks is not a big business in terms of dollars and cents. But it is a convenient starting point for developing the concepts of consumer and producer surplus.

So let's look at the market for used textbooks, starting with the buyers. The key point, as we'll see in a minute, is that the demand curve is derived from their tastes or preferences—and that those same preferences also determine how much they gain from the opportunity to buy used books.

Willingness to Pay and the Demand Curve

A used book is not as good as a new book—it will be battered and coffee-stained, may include someone else's highlighting, and may not be completely up to date. How much this bothers you depends on your own preferences. Some potential buyers would prefer to buy the used book if it is only slightly cheaper than a new book, while others would buy the used book only if it is considerably cheaper. Let's define a potential buyer's **willingness to pay** as the maximum price at which he or she would buy a good, in this case a used textbook. An individual won't buy the book if it costs more than this amount but is eager to do so if it costs less. If the price is just equal to an individual's willingness to pay, he or she is indifferent between buying and not buying.

A consumer's **willingness to pay** for a good is the maximum price at which he or she would buy that good.

The table in Figure 6-1 shows five potential buyers of a used book that costs $100 new, listed in order of their willingness to pay. At one extreme is Anne, who will buy a second-hand book even if the price is as high as $59. Brad is less willing to have a

Figure 6-1 The Demand Curve for Used Textbooks

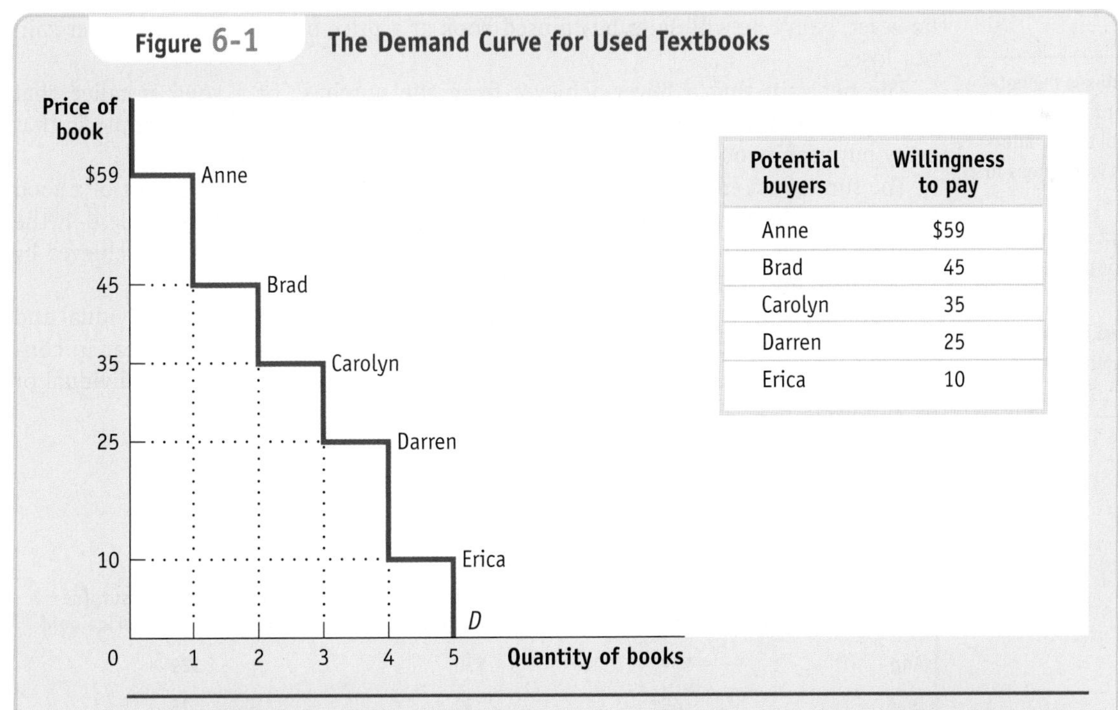

Potential buyers	Willingness to pay
Anne	$59
Brad	45
Carolyn	35
Darren	25
Erica	10

With only five potential consumers in this market, the demand curve is step-shaped. Each step represents one consumer, and its height indicates that consumer's willingness to pay, the maximum price at which each student will buy a used textbook, as indicated in the table. Anne has the highest willingness to pay at $59, Brad has the next highest at $45, and so on down to Erica with the lowest at $10. At a price of $59 the quantity demanded is one (Anne); at a price of $45 the quantity demanded is two (Anne and Brad), and so on until you reach a price of $10 at which all five students are willing to purchase a book.

used book, and will buy one only if the price is $45 or less. Carolyn is willing to pay only $35, Darren only $25. And Erica, who really doesn't like the idea of a used book, will buy one only if it costs no more than $10.

How many of these five students will actually buy a used book? It depends on the price. If the price of a used book is $55, only Anne buys one; if the price is $40, Anne and Brad both buy used books, and so on. So the information in the table on willingness to pay also defines the *demand schedule* for used textbooks.

As we saw in Chapter 3, we can use this demand schedule to derive the market demand curve shown in Figure 6-1. Because we are considering only a small number of consumers, this curve doesn't look like the smooth demand curves of earlier chapters, where markets contained hundreds or thousands of consumers. This demand curve is step-shaped, with alternating horizontal and vertical segments. Each horizontal segment—each step—corresponds to one potential buyer's willingness to pay. However, we'll see shortly that for the analysis of consumer surplus it doesn't matter whether the demand curve is stepped, as in this figure, or whether there are many consumers, making the curve smooth.

Willingness to Pay and Consumer Surplus

Suppose that the campus bookstore makes used textbooks available at a price of $30. In that case, Anne, Brad, and Carolyn will buy books. Do they gain from their purchases, and if so, how much?

The answer, shown in Table 6-1, is that each student who purchases a book does achieve a net gain but that the amount of the gain differs among students.

Anne would have been willing to pay $59, so her net gain is $59 - $30 = $29. Brad would have been willing to pay $45, so his net gain is $45 – $30 = $15. Carolyn would have been willing to pay $35, so her net gain is $35 – $30 = $5. Darren and Erica, however, won't be willing to buy a used book at a price of $30, so they neither gain nor lose.

Individual consumer surplus is the net gain to an individual buyer from the purchase of a good. It is equal to the difference between the buyer's willingness to pay and the price paid.

Total consumer surplus is the sum of the individual consumer surpluses of all the buyers of a good.

The term **consumer surplus** is often used to refer to both individual and to total consumer surplus.

The net gain that a buyer achieves from the purchase of a good is called that buyer's **individual consumer surplus.** What we learn from this example is that every buyer of a good achieves some individual consumer surplus.

The sum of the individual consumer surpluses achieved by all the buyers of a good is known as the **total consumer surplus** achieved in the market. In Table 6-1, the total consumer surplus is the sum of the individual consumer surpluses achieved by Anne, Brad, and Carolyn: $29 + $15 + $5 = $49.

Economists often use the term **consumer surplus** to refer to both individual and total consumer surplus. We will follow this practice; it will always be clear in context whether we are referring to the consumer surplus achieved by an individual or by all buyers.

TABLE 6-1

Consumer Surplus When the Price of a Used Textbook Is $30

Potential buyer	Willingness to pay	Price paid	Individual consumer surplus = willingness to pay – price paid
Ann	$59	$30	$29
Brad	45	30	15
Carolyn	35	30	5
Darren	25	—	—
Erica	10	—	—
			Total consumer surplus: $49

Figure 6-2

Consumer Surplus in the Used Textbook Market

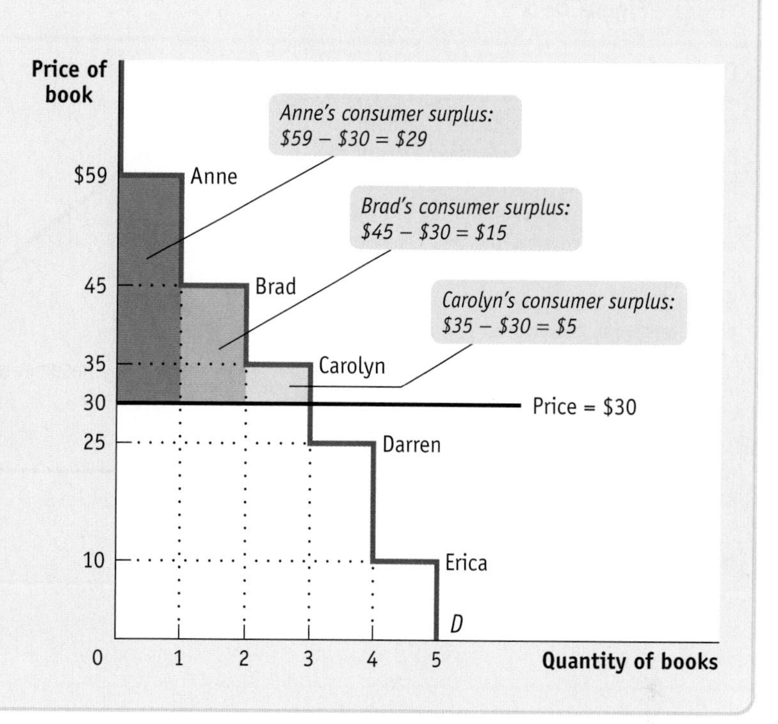

At a price of $30, Anne, Brad, and Carolyn each buy a book but Darren and Erica do not. Anne, Brad, and Carolyn get individual consumer surpluses equal to the difference between their willingness to pay and the price, illustrated by the areas of the shaded rectangles. Both Darren and Erica have a willingness to pay less than $30, so are unwilling to buy a book in this market; they receive zero consumer surplus. The total consumer surplus is given by the entire shaded area—the sum of the individual consumer surpluses of Anne, Brad, and Carolyn—equal to $29 + $15 + $5 = $49.

Total consumer surplus can be represented graphically. Figure 6-2 reproduces the demand curve from Figure 6-1. Each step in that demand curve is one book wide and represents one consumer. For example, the height of Anne's step is $59, her willingness to pay. This step forms the top of a rectangle, with $30—the price she actually pays for a book—forming the bottom. The area of Anne's rectangle, ($59 – $30) × 1 = $29, is her consumer surplus from purchasing a book at $30. So the individual consumer surplus Anne gains is the *area of the dark blue rectangle* shown in Figure 6-2.

In addition to Anne, Brad and Carolyn will also buy books when the price is $30. Like Anne, they benefit from their purchases, though not as much, because they each have a lower willingness to pay. Figure 6-2 also shows the consumer surplus gained by Brad and Carolyn; again, this can be measured by the areas of the appropriate rectangles. Darren and Erica, because they do not buy books at a price of $30, receive no consumer surplus.

The total consumer surplus achieved in this market is just the sum of the individual consumer surpluses received by Anne, Brad, and Carolyn. So total consumer surplus is equal to the combined area of the three rectangles—the entire shaded area in Figure 6-2. Another way to say this is that total consumer surplus is equal to the area that is under the demand curve but above the price.

This illustrates the following general principle: *The total consumer surplus generated by purchases of a good at a given price is equal to the area below the demand curve but above that price.* The same principle applies regardless of the number of consumers.

When we consider large markets, this graphical representation becomes extremely helpful. Consider, for example, the sales of personal computers to millions of potential buyers. Each potential buyer has a maximum price that he or she is willing to pay. With so many potential buyers, the demand curve will be smooth, like the one shown in Figure 6-3 (page 148).

Suppose that at a price of $800, a total of 1 million computers are purchased. How much do consumers gain from being able to buy those 1 million computers? We

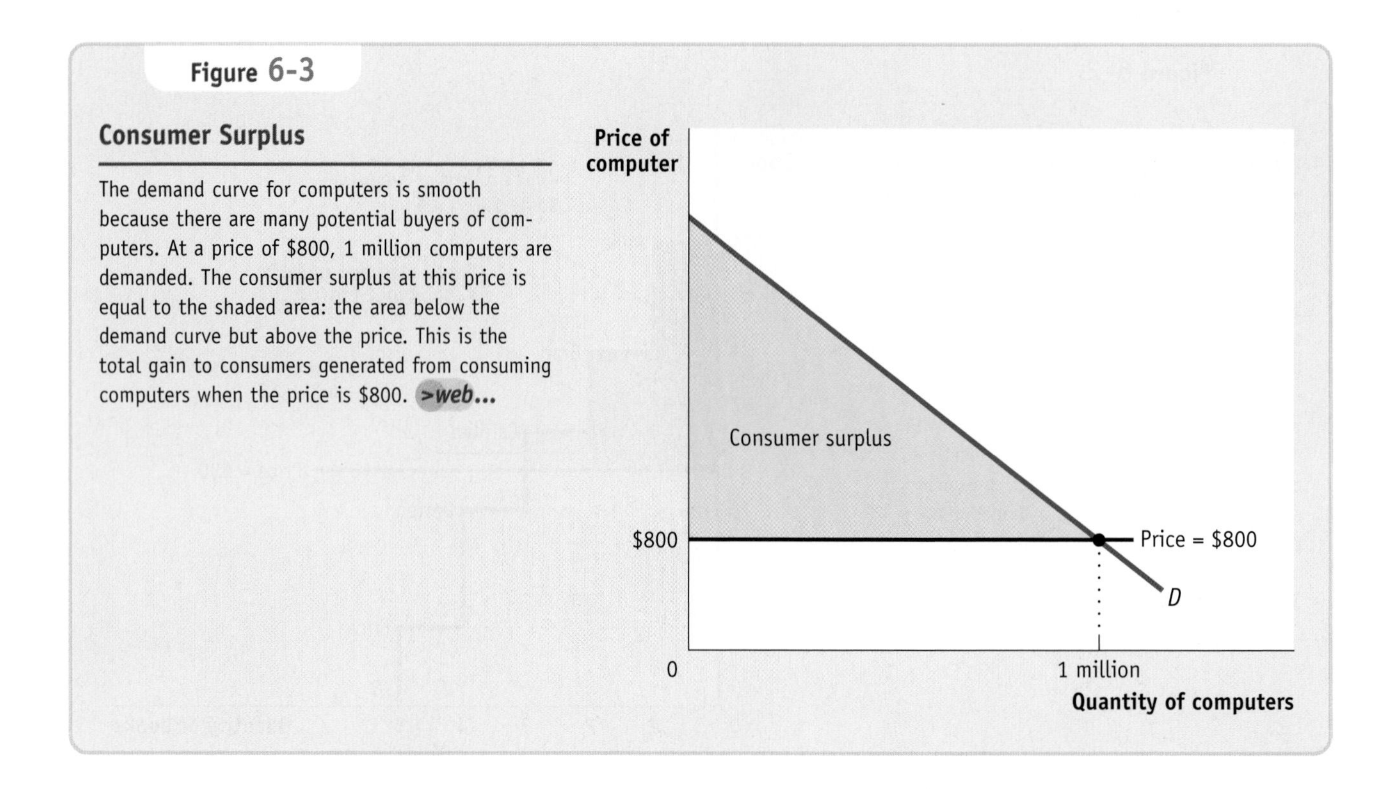

Figure 6-3

Consumer Surplus

The demand curve for computers is smooth because there are many potential buyers of computers. At a price of $800, 1 million computers are demanded. The consumer surplus at this price is equal to the shaded area: the area below the demand curve but above the price. This is the total gain to consumers generated from consuming computers when the price is $800. >*web*...

could answer that question by calculating the consumer surplus of each individual buyer and then adding these numbers up to arrive at a total. But it is much easier just to look at Figure 6-3 and use the fact that the total consumer surplus is equal to the shaded area. As in our original example, consumer surplus is equal to the area below the demand curve but above the price.

How Changing Prices Affect Consumer Surplus

It is often important to know how much consumer surplus *changes* when the price changes. For example, we may want to know how much consumers are hurt if a frost in Florida drives up orange prices, or how much consumers gain if an expansion of fish farming makes salmon less expensive. The same approach we have used to derive consumer surplus can be used to answer questions about how changes in prices affect consumers.

Let's return to the example of the market for used textbooks. Suppose that the bookstore decided to sell used textbooks for $20 instead of $30. How much would this increase consumer surplus?

The answer is illustrated in Figure 6-4. As shown in the figure, there are two parts to the increase in consumer surplus. The first part, shaded dark blue, is the gain of those who would have bought books even at the higher price. Each of the students who would have bought books at $30—Anne, Brad, and Carolyn—pays $10 less, and therefore each gains $10 in consumer surplus from the fall in price to $20. So the dark blue area represents the $30 increase in consumer surplus to those three buyers. The second part, shaded light blue, is the gain to those who would not have bought a book at $30 but are willing to pay more than $20. In this case that means Darren, who would not have bought a book at $30 but does buy one at $20. He gains $5—the difference between his willingness to pay $25 and the new price of $20. So the light blue area represents a further $5 gain in consumer surplus. The total increase in consumer surplus is the sum of the shaded areas, $35. Likewise, a rise in

Figure 6-4

Consumer Surplus and a Fall in the Price of Used Textbooks

There are two parts to the increase in consumer surplus generated by a fall in price from \$30 to \$20. The first is given by the dark blue rectangle: each person who would have bought at the original price of \$30—Anne, Brad, and Carolyn—receives an increase in consumer surplus equal to the total fall in price, \$10. So the area of the dark blue rectangle corresponds to an amount equal to $3 \times \$10 = \$30$. The second part is given by the light blue rectangle: the increase in consumer surplus for those who would *not* have bought at the original price of \$30 but who buy at the new price of \$20—namely, Darren. Darren's willingness to pay is \$25, so he now receives consumer surplus of \$5. The total increase in consumer surplus is $3 \times \$10 + \$5 = \$35$, represented by the sum of the shaded areas. Likewise, a rise in price from \$20 to \$30 would decrease consumer surplus by an amount equal to the sum of the shaded areas.

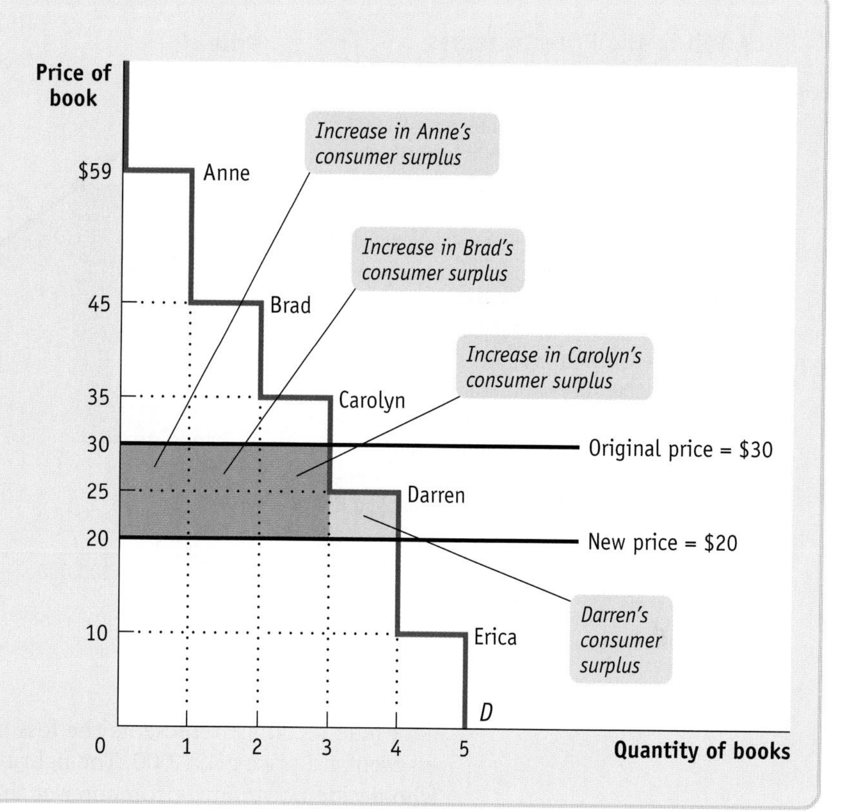

price from \$20 to \$30 would decrease consumer surplus by an amount equal to the sum of the shaded areas.

Figure 6-4 illustrates that when the price of a good falls, the area under the demand curve but above the price—which we have seen is equal to the total consumer surplus—increases. Figure 6-5 (page 150) shows the same result for the case of a smooth demand curve, the demand for personal computers. Here we assume that the price of computers falls from \$5,000 to \$800, leading to an increase in the quantity demanded from 200,000 to 1 million units. As in the used-textbook example, we divide the gain in consumer surplus into two parts. The dark blue rectangle in Figure 6-5 corresponds to the dark blue area in Figure 6-4: it is the gain to the 200,000 people who would have bought computers even at the higher price of \$5,000. As a result of the price fall, each receives additional surplus of \$4,200. The light blue triangle in Figure 6-5 corresponds to the light blue area in Figure 6-4: it is the gain to people who would not have bought the good at the higher price but are willing to do so at a price of \$800. For example, the light blue triangle includes the gain to someone who would have been willing to pay \$3,000 for a computer, and therefore gains \$2,200 in consumer surplus when he or she is able to buy a computer for only \$800. As before, the total gain in consumer surplus is the sum of the shaded areas, the increase in the area under the demand curve but above the price.

What would happen if the price of a good were to rise instead of fall? We would do the same analysis in reverse. Suppose, for example, that for some reason the price of computers increased from \$800 to \$5,000. This would lead to a fall in consumer surplus, equal to the shaded area in Figure 6-5. This loss consists of two parts. The

Figure 6-5

A Fall in the Price Increases Consumer Surplus

A fall in the price of a computer from $5,000 to $800 leads to an increase in the quantity demanded and an increase in consumer surplus. The change in total consumer surplus is given by the sum of the shaded area: the total area below the demand curve but between the old and new prices. Here, the dark blue area represents the increase in consumer surplus for the 200,000 consumers who would have bought a computer at the original price of $5,000; they each receive an increase in consumer surplus of $4,200. The light blue area represents the increase in consumer surplus for those willing to buy at a price equal to or greater than $800 but less than $5,000. Similarly, a rise in the price of a computer from $800 to $5,000 generates a decrease in consumer surplus equal to the sum of the two shaded areas. >web...

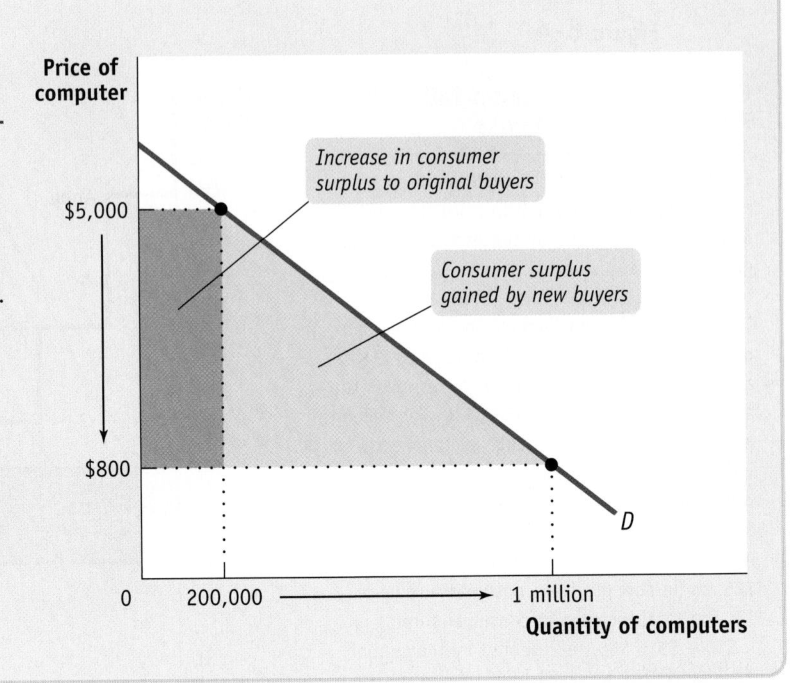

dark blue rectangle represents the loss to consumers who would still buy a computer, even at a price of $5,000. The light blue triangle represents the loss to consumers who decide not to buy a computer at the higher price.

FOR INQUIRING MINDS

I WANT A NEW DRUG . . .

The pharmaceutical industry is constantly introducing new prescription drugs. Some of these drugs do the same thing as other, existing drugs, but a bit better—for example, pretty good allergy medicines have been around for years, but newer versions that are somewhat more effective or have fewer side effects keep emerging. Other drugs do something that was previously considered impossible—a famous example from the late 1990s was Propecia, the pill that slows and in some cases reverses hair loss.

Such innovations raise a difficult question for the people who are supposed to measure economic growth: how do you calculate the contribution of a new product to the economy?

You might at first say that it's just a matter of dollars and cents. But that could be wrong, in either direction. A new painkiller that is just slightly better than aspirin might have huge sales, because it would take over the painkiller market—but it wouldn't really add much to consumer welfare. On the other hand, the benefits of a drug that cures the previously incurable might be much larger than the money actually spent on it—after all, people *would have been willing* to pay much more.

Consider, for example, the benefits of antibiotics. When penicillin was introduced in 1941, it transformed the treatment of infectious disease; illnesses that had previously crippled or killed millions of people were suddenly easy to treat. Presumably most people would be willing to pay a lot not to go back to the days before penicillin. Yet the average Canadian spends only a few dollars per year on antibiotics.

The right way to measure the gains from a new drug—or any new product—is therefore to try to figure out what people would have been willing to pay for the good, and subtract what they actually pay. In other words, the gains from a new drug should be measured by calculating consumer surplus!

economics in action

When Money Isn't Enough

The key insight we get from the concept of consumer surplus is that purchases yield a net benefit to the consumer, because the consumer pays a price that is less than the amount he or she would have been willing to pay for the good. Another way to say this is that the right to buy a good at the going price is a valuable thing in itself.

Most of the time we don't think about the value associated with the right to buy a good. In a market economy, we take it for granted that we can buy whatever we want, as long as we are willing to pay the price. But that hasn't always been true. For example, during World War II many goods in Canada were rationed in order to make resources available for the war effort. To buy sugar, eggs, butter, or gasoline and many other goods, you not only had to pay cash; you also had to present stamps or coupons from special books that were issued to each family by the government. These pieces of paper, which represented nothing but the right to buy goods at the market price, quickly became valuable commodities in themselves. As a result, black markets in sugar stamps and gasoline coupons sprang into existence. Moreover, criminals began stealing coupons, and even counterfeiting stamps.

The funny thing was that even if you had bought a gasoline coupon on the black market, you still had to pay the regular price of gasoline to fill your tank. So what you were buying on the black market was not the good but *the right to buy the good*—that is, people who bought ration coupons on the black market were paying for the right to get some consumer surplus. ■

>>QUICK REVIEW

- The demand curve for a good is determined by the *willingness to pay* of each potential consumer.
- *Individual consumer surplus* is the net gain an individual consumer gets from buying a good.
- The *total consumer surplus* in a given market is equal to the area under the demand curve but above the price.
- A fall in the price of a good increases consumer surplus through two channels: a gain to consumers who would have bought at the original price and a gain to consumers who are persuaded to buy by the lower price. A rise in the price of a good reduces consumer surplus in a similar fashion.

>>CHECK YOUR UNDERSTANDING 6-1

1. Consider the market for cheese-stuffed jalapeno peppers. There are two consumers, Casey and Josie, and their willingness to pay for each pepper is given in the accompanying table. Use the table (i) to construct the demand schedule for peppers for prices of $0.00, $0.10, and so on, up to $0.90; and (ii) to calculate the total consumer surplus when the price of a pepper is $0.40.

Quantity of peppers	Casey's willingness to pay	Josie's willingness to pay
1st pepper	$0.90	$0.80
2nd pepper	0.70	0.60
3rd pepper	0.50	0.40
4th pepper	0.30	0.30

Solutions appear at back of book.

Producer Surplus and the Supply Curve

Just as buyers of a good would have been willing to pay more for their purchase than the price they actually pay, sellers of a good would have been willing to sell it for less than the price they actually receive. We can therefore carry out an analysis of producer surplus and the supply curve that is almost exactly parallel to that of consumer surplus and the demand curve.

Cost and Producer Surplus

Consider a group of students who are potential sellers of used textbooks. Because they have different preferences, the various potential sellers differ in the price at which they are willing to sell their books. The table in Figure 6-6 (page 152) shows the prices at which several different students would be willing to sell. Andrew is willing to sell the book as long as he can get anything more than $5; Betty won't sell unless she can get at

Figure 6-6 The Supply Curve for Used Textbooks

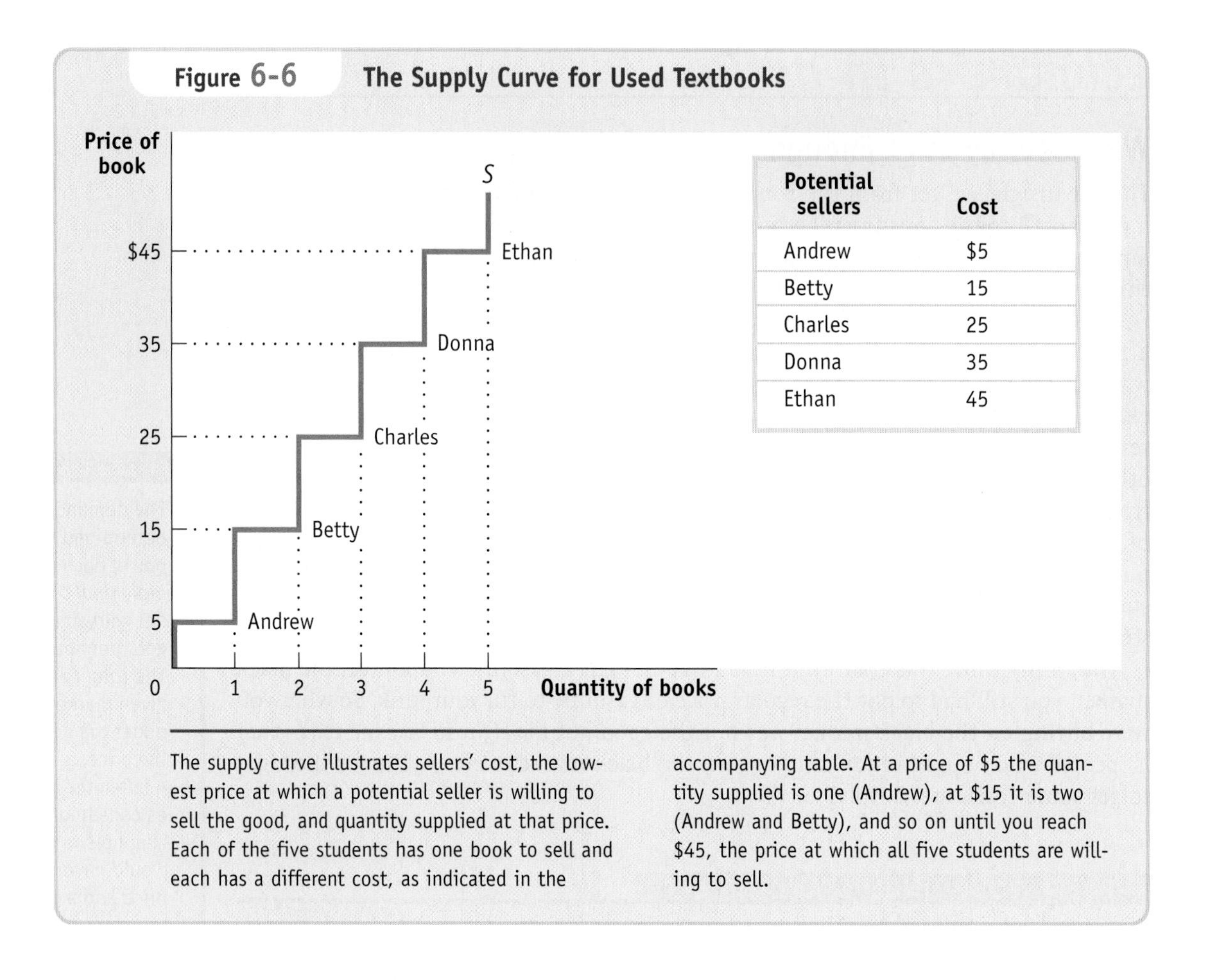

Potential sellers	Cost
Andrew	$5
Betty	15
Charles	25
Donna	35
Ethan	45

The supply curve illustrates sellers' cost, the lowest price at which a potential seller is willing to sell the good, and quantity supplied at that price. Each of the five students has one book to sell and each has a different cost, as indicated in the accompanying table. At a price of $5 the quantity supplied is one (Andrew), at $15 it is two (Andrew and Betty), and so on until you reach $45, the price at which all five students are willing to sell.

least $15; Charles, unless he can get $25; Donna, unless she can get $35; Ethan, unless he can get $45.

A potential seller's **cost** is the lowest price at which he or she is willing to sell a good.

The lowest price at which a potential seller is willing to sell has a special name in economics: it is called the seller's **cost.** So Andrew's cost is $5, Betty's is $15, and so on.

Using the term *cost*, which people normally associate with the monetary cost of producing a good, may sound a little strange when applied to sellers of used textbooks. The students don't have to manufacture the books, so it doesn't cost the student who sells a book anything to make that book available for sale, does it?

Yes, it does. A student who sells a book won't have it later, as part of a personal collection. So there is an *opportunity cost* to selling a textbook, even if the owner has completed the course for which it was required. And remember that one of the basic principles of economics is that the true measure of the cost of doing anything is always its opportunity cost—the real cost of something is what you must give up to get it.

So it is good economics to talk of the minimum price at which someone will sell a good as the "cost" of selling that good, even if he or she doesn't spend any money to make the good available for sale. Of course, in most real-world markets the sellers are also those who produce the good—and therefore *do* expend money to make the good available for sale. In this case the cost of making the good available for sale *includes* monetary costs—but it may also include other opportunity costs.

Individual producer surplus is the net gain to a seller from selling a good. It is equal to the difference between the price received and the seller's cost.

Getting back to the example, suppose that Andrew sells his book for $30. Clearly he has gained from the transaction: he would have been willing to sell for only $5, so he has gained $25. This gain, the difference between the price he actually gets and his cost—the minimum price at which he would have been willing to sell—is known as his **individual producer surplus.**

Just as we derived the demand curve from the willingness to pay of different consumers, we can derive the supply curve from the cost of different producers. The step-shaped curve in Figure 6-6 shows the supply curve implied by the costs shown in the accompanying table. At a price less than $5, none of the students are willing to sell; at a price between $5 and $15, only Andrew is willing to sell, and so on.

As in the case of consumer surplus, we can add the individual producer surpluses of sellers to calculate the **total producer surplus,** the total gains to sellers in the market. Economists use the term **producer surplus** to refer to either total or individual producer surplus. Table 6-2 shows the net gain to each of the students who would sell a used book at a price of $30: $25 for Andrew, $15 for Betty, and $5 for Charles. The total producer surplus is $25 + $15 + $5 = $45.

Total producer surplus in a market is the sum of the individual producer surpluses of all the sellers of a good. Economists use the term **producer surplus** to refer both to individual and to total producer surplus.

TABLE 6-2

Producer Surplus When the Price of a Used Textbook Is $30

Potential seller	Cost	Price received	Individual producer surplus = price received − cost
Andrew	$5	$30	$25
Betty	15	30	15
Charles	25	30	5
Donna	35	—	—
Ethan	45	—	—
			Total producer surplus: $45

As with consumer surplus, the producer surplus gained by those who sell books can be represented graphically. Figure 6-7 reproduces the supply curve from Figure 6-6. Each step in that supply curve is one book wide and represents one seller. The height of Andrew's step is $5, his cost. This forms the bottom of a rectangle, with $30, the price he actually receives for his book, forming the top. The area of this rectangle, ($30 − $5) × 1 = $25, is his producer surplus. So the producer surplus

Figure 6-7

Producer Surplus in the Used Textbook Market

At a price of $30, Andrew, Betty, and Charles each sell a book but Donna and Ethan do not. Andrew, Betty, and Charles get individual producer surpluses equal to the difference between the price and their cost, illustrated here by the shaded rectangles. Donna and Ethan each have a cost that is greater than the price of $30, so are unwilling to sell a book and therefore receive zero producer surplus. The total producer surplus is given by the entire shaded area, the sum of the individual producer surpluses of Andrew, Betty, and Charles, equal to $25 + $15 + $5 = $45.

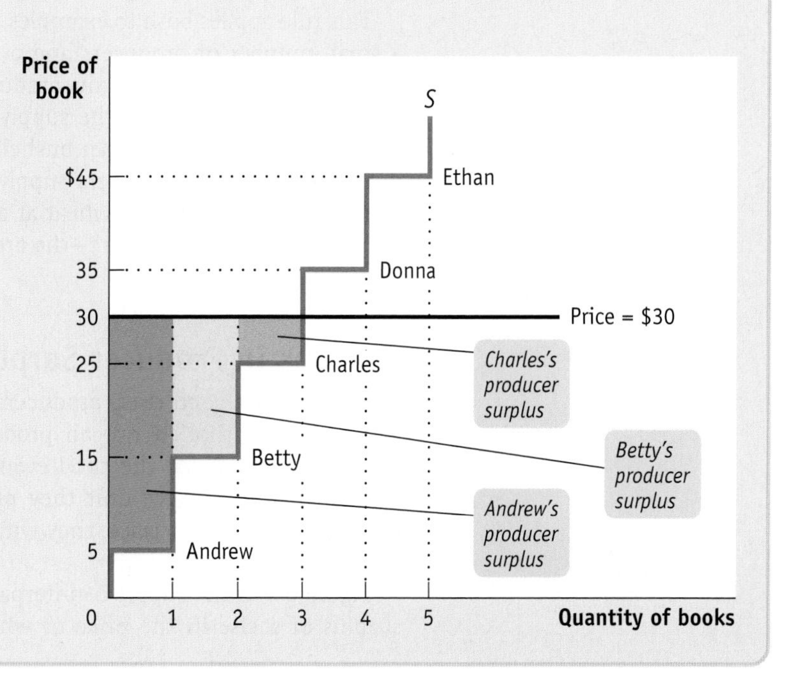

Figure 6-8

Producer Surplus

Here is the supply curve for wheat. At a market price of $5 per bushel, farmers supply 1 million bushels. The producer surplus at this price is equal to the shaded area: the area above the supply curve but below the price. This is the total gain to producers—farmers in this case—from supplying their product when the price is $5. ***>web...***

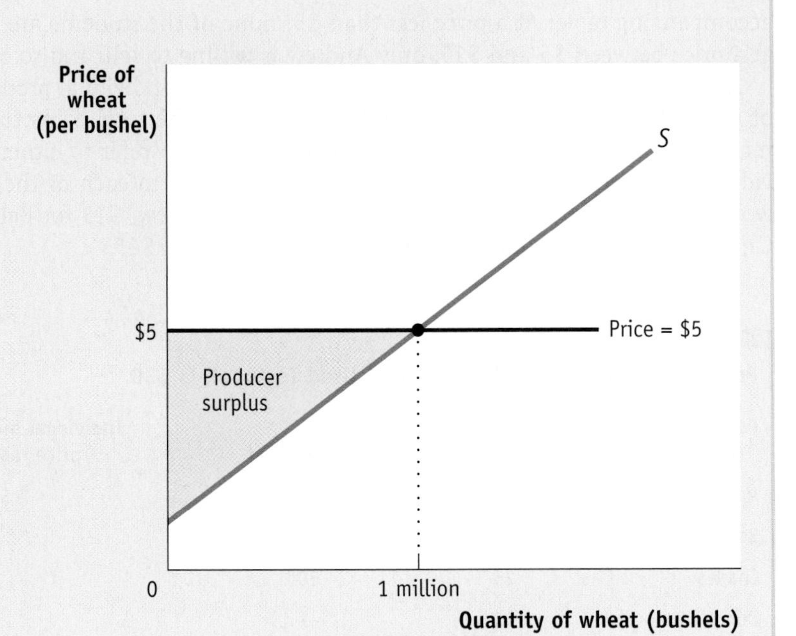

Andrew gains from selling his book is the *area of the dark red rectangle* shown in the figure.

Let's assume that the campus bookstore is willing to buy all the used copies of this book that students are willing to sell at a price of $30. Then, in addition to Andrew, Betty and Charles will also sell their books. They will also benefit from their sales, though not as much as Andrew, because they have higher costs. Andrew, as we have seen, gains $25. Betty gains a smaller amount: since her cost is $15, she gains only $15. Charles gains even less, only $5.

Again, as with consumer surplus, we have a general rule for determining the total producer surplus from sales of a good: *The total producer surplus from sales of a good at a given price is the area above the supply curve but below that price.*

This rule applies both to examples like the one shown in Figure 6-7, where there are a small number of producers and a step-shaped supply curve, and to more realistic examples where there are many producers and the supply curve is more or less smooth.

Consider, for example, the supply of wheat. Figure 6-8 shows how producer surplus depends on the price per bushel. Suppose that, as shown in the figure, the price is $5 per bushel and farmers supply 1 million bushels. What is the benefit to the farmers from selling their wheat at a price of $5? Their producer surplus is equal to the shaded area in the figure—the area above the supply curve but below the price of $5 per bushel.

Changes in Producer Surplus

If the price of a good rises, producers of the good will experience an increase in producer surplus, though not all producers gain the same amount. Some producers would have produced the good even at the original price; they will gain the entire price increase on every unit they produce. Other producers will enter the market because of the higher price; they will gain only the difference between the new price and their cost.

Figure 6-9 is the supply counterpart of Figure 6-5. It shows the effect on producer surplus of a rise in the price of wheat from $5 to $7 per bushel. The increase in

Figure 6-9

A Rise in the Price Increases Producer Surplus

A rise in the price of wheat from $5 to $7 leads to an increase in the quantity supplied and an increase in producer surplus. The change in total producer surplus is given by the sum of the shaded areas: the total area above the supply curve but between the old and new prices. The red area represents the gain to the farmers who would have supplied 1 million bushels at the original price of $5; they each receive an increase in producer surplus of $2 for each of those bushels. The triangular pink area represents the increase in producer surplus achieved by the farmers who supply the additional 500,000 bushels because of the higher price. Similarly, a fall in the price of wheat generates a decrease in producer surplus equal to the shaded areas. **>*web*...**

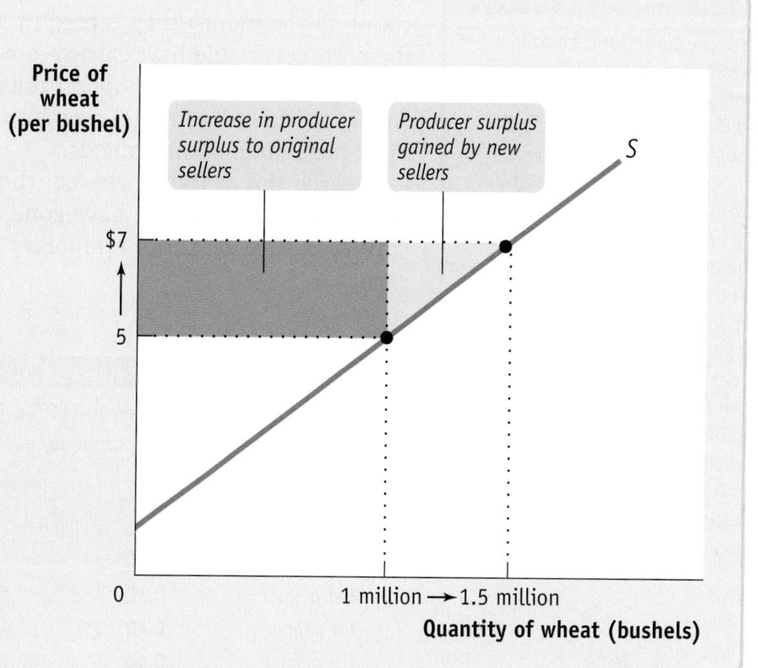

producer surplus is the entire shaded area, which consists of two parts. First, there is a red rectangle corresponding to the gains to those farmers who would have supplied wheat even at the original $5 price. Second, there is an additional pink triangle that corresponds to the gains to those farmers who would not have supplied wheat at the original price but are drawn into the market by the higher price.

If the price were to fall from $7 to $5 per bushel, the whole story would run in reverse. The whole shaded area would now be the decline in producer surplus, the fall in the area above the supply curve but below the price. The loss would consist of two parts, the loss to farmers who would still grow wheat at a price of $5 (the red rectangle) and the loss to farmers who decide not to grow wheat because of the lower price (the pink triangle).

economics in action

Gaining from Disaster

On September 28, 2003, Hurricane Juan hit Nova Scotia, destroying many homes and cutting electricity throughout the province. It was weeks before many Nova Scotians had power restored, and many businesses, especially agricultural businesses, were badly affected.

Hurricane Juan was one of the most powerful and damaging hurricanes to ever affect Canada. But as bad as it was, Juan was only a category 1 hurricane (with gusts measured at 129 kilometres per hour). Imagine, then, what it must have been like to be in Florida on August 21, 1992, when Hurricane Andrew hit. Andrew was a category 5 hurricane, with winds gusting at 284 kilometres per hour. It carved through Florida, causing as much as $26.5 billion in damage.

Florida quickly began rebuilding, with the help of thousands of construction workers who temporarily moved there. These construction workers were not motivated mainly by sympathy for Florida residents. They were lured by the high wages available there—and they took home billions of dollars.

>> QUICK REVIEW

- The supply curve for a good is determined by the *cost* to each potential seller.
- The difference between the price and cost is the seller's *individual producer surplus*.
- The *total producer surplus* is equal to the area above the supply curve but below the price.
- When the price of a good rises, producer surplus increases through two channels: the gains of those who would have supplied the good even at the original, lower price and the gains of those who are induced to supply the good by the higher price. A fall in the price of a good similarly leads to a fall in producer surplus.

But how much did the temporary workers actually gain? Certainly we should not count all the money they earned in Florida as a net benefit. For one thing, most of these workers would have earned something—though not as much—if they had stayed home. In addition to this opportunity cost, the temporary move to Florida had other costs: the expense of motel rooms and of transportation, the wear and tear of being away from families and friends.

Clearly the workers viewed the benefits as being larger than the costs—otherwise they wouldn't have gone to Florida in the first place. But the producer surplus earned by those temporary workers was much less than the money they earned. ■

< < < < < < < < < < < < < < < < < < <

>> CHECK YOUR UNDERSTANDING 6-2

1. Consider the market for cheese-stuffed jalapeno peppers. There are two producers, Cara and Jamie, and their costs of producing each pepper are given in the accompanying table. Use the table (i) to construct the supply schedule for pepper for prices of $0.00, $0.10, and so on, up to $0.90; and (ii) to calculate the total producer surplus when the price of a pepper is $0.70.

Quantity of peppers	Cara's cost	Jamie's cost
1st pepper	$0.10	$0.30
2nd pepper	0.10	0.50
3rd pepper	0.40	0.70
4th pepper	0.60	0.90

Solutions appear at back of book.

Consumer Surplus, Producer Surplus, and the Gains from Trade

One of the nine core principles of economics we introduced in Chapter 1 is that markets are a remarkably effective way to organize economic activity: they generally make society as well off as possible given the available resources. The concepts of consumer surplus and producer surplus can help us deepen our understanding of why this is so.

The Gains from Trade

Let's go back to the market in used textbooks but now consider a much bigger market—say, one at a university the size of the University of Toronto or the University of British Columbia—where there are many potential buyers and sellers. Let's line up incoming students—who are potential buyers of the book—in order of their willingness to pay, so that the entering student with the highest willingness to pay is potential buyer number 1, the student with the next highest willingness to pay is number 2, and so on. Then we can use their willingness to pay to derive a demand curve, like the one in Figure 6-10. Similarly, we can line up outgoing students, who are potential sellers of the book, in order of their cost, starting with the student with the lowest cost, then the student with the next lowest cost, and so on, to derive a supply curve like the one shown in the same figure.

Let's abstract from any markup charged by the bookstore. For simplicity, we'll suppose it is a non-profit store run by the student union, and offering its services for free. As we have drawn the curves, the market reaches equilibrium at a price of $30 per book, and 1,000 books are bought and sold at that price. The two shaded triangles show the consumer surplus (blue) and the producer surplus (red) generated by this market. The sum of consumer and producer surplus is known as the **total surplus** generated in a market.

The **total surplus** generated in a market is the total net gain to consumers and producers from trading in the market. It is the sum of the producer and the consumer surplus.

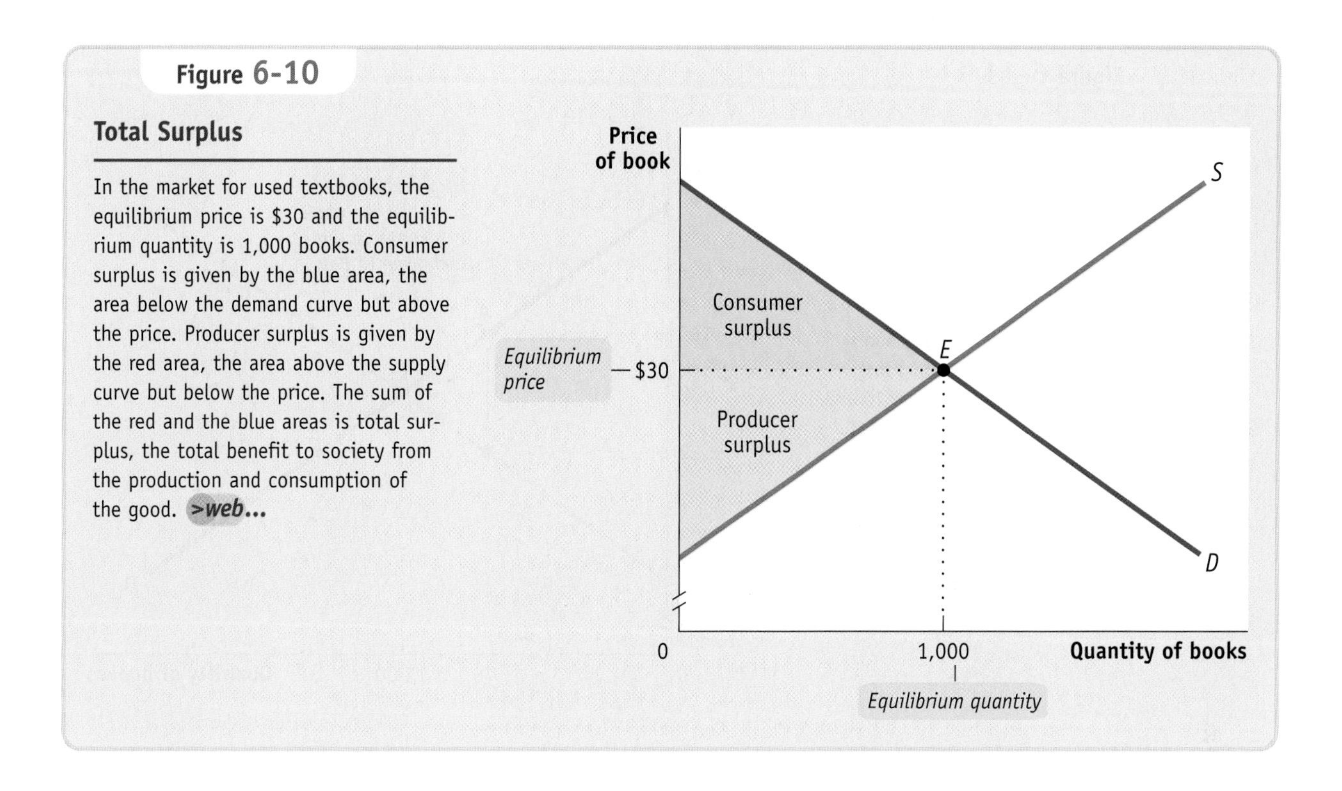

Figure 6-10

Total Surplus

In the market for used textbooks, the equilibrium price is $30 and the equilibrium quantity is 1,000 books. Consumer surplus is given by the blue area, the area below the demand curve but above the price. Producer surplus is given by the red area, the area above the supply curve but below the price. The sum of the red and the blue areas is total surplus, the total benefit to society from the production and consumption of the good. >*web*...

The striking thing about this picture is that both consumers and producers gain—that is, both consumers and producers are better off because there is a market in this good. But this should come as no surprise—it illustrates another core principle of economics: there are *gains from trade*. These gains from trade are the reason everyone is better off participating in a market economy than they would be if each individual tried to be self-sufficient.

But are we as well off as we could be? This brings us to the question of the efficiency of markets.

The Efficiency of Markets: A Preliminary View

Markets produce gains from trade, but in Chapter 1 we made a bigger claim: that markets are usually *efficient*. That is, we claimed that once the market has produced its gains from trade, there is usually no way to make some people better off without making others worse off (with some well-defined exceptions).

We're not yet ready to carry out a full discussion of the efficiency of markets—that will have to wait until we've looked in more detail at the behaviour of producers and consumers. However, we can get an intuitive sense of the efficiency of markets by noticing a key feature of the market equilibrium shown in Figure 6-10: the maximum possible total surplus is achieved at market equilibrium. That is, the market equilibrium allocates the consumption of the good among potential consumers and sales of the good among potential sellers in a way that achieves the highest possible gain to society.

How do we know this? By comparing the total surplus generated by the consumption and production choices in the market equilibrium to the surplus generated by a different set of consumption and production choices. We can show that any change from the market equilibrium reduces total surplus.

Let's consider three ways in which you might try to increase the total surplus:

1. *Reallocate consumption among consumers*—take the good away from buyers who would have purchased the good in the market equilibrium, and instead give it to potential consumers who would not have bought it in equilibrium.

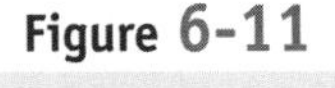

Figure 6-11

Reallocating Consumption Lowers Consumer Surplus

Ana (point *A*) has a willingness to pay of $35. Bob (point *B*) has a willingness to pay of only $25. At the market equilibrium price of $30, Ana purchases a book but Bob does not. If we rearrange consumption by taking a book from Ana and giving it to Bob, consumer surplus declines by $10 and, as a result, total surplus declines by $10. The market equilibrium generates the highest possible consumer surplus by ensuring that those who consume the good are those who value it the most. **>web...**

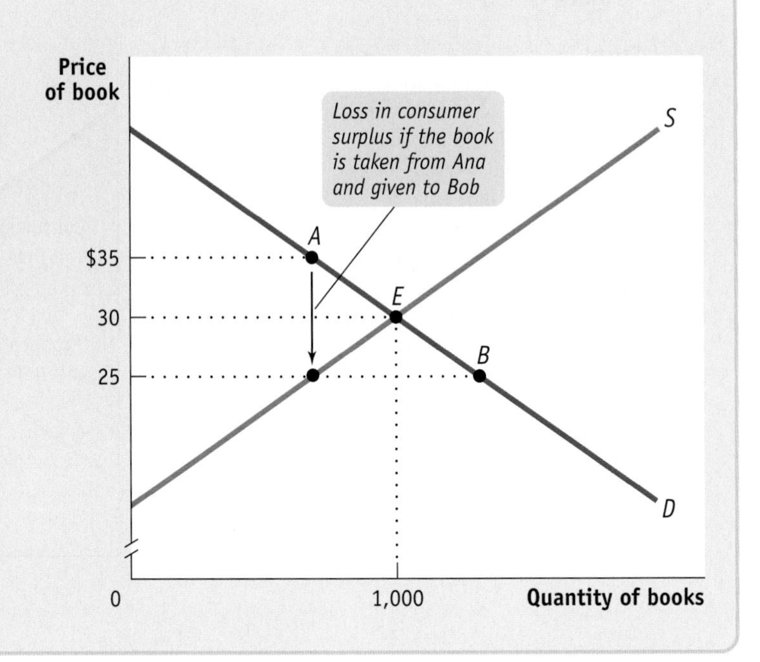

2. *Reallocate sales among sellers*—take sales away from sellers who would have sold the good in the market equilibrium, and instead compel potential sellers who would not have sold the good in equilibrium to sell it.
3. *Change the quantity traded*—compel consumers and producers to transact either more or less than the equilibrium quantity.

It turns out that each of these actions will not only fail to increase the total surplus; in fact, each will reduce the total surplus.

Figure 6-11 shows why reallocating consumption of the good among consumers will reduce the total surplus. Points *A* and *B* show the positions on the demand curve of two potential buyers of a used book, Ana and Bob. As we can see from the figure, Ana is willing to pay $35 for a book, but Bob is willing to pay only $25. Since the equilibrium price is $30, Ana buys a book and Bob does not.

Now suppose that we try to reallocate consumption. This would mean taking a book away from somebody who *would* have bought one at the equilibrium price of $30, like Ana, and giving that book to someone who would *not* have bought at that price, like Bob. But since the book is worth $35 to Ana, but only $25 to Bob, this would *reduce total consumer surplus* by $35 – $25 = $10.

This result doesn't depend on which two students we pick. Every student who buys a book in equilibrium has a willingness to pay that is *more* than $30, and every student who doesn't buy a book has a willingness to pay that is *less* than $30. So reallocating the good among consumers always means taking a book away from a student who values it more and giving it to a student who values it less, which necessarily reduces consumer surplus.

A similar argument, illustrated by Figure 6-12, holds for producer surplus. Here points *X* and *Y* show the positions on the supply curve of Xavier, who has a cost of $25, and Yvonne, who has a cost of $35. At the equilibrium price of $30, Xavier would sell his book but Yvonne would not. If we reallocated sales, forcing Xavier to keep his book and forcing Yvonne to give up hers, total producer surplus would be reduced by $35 – $25 = $10. Again, it doesn't matter which two students we choose. Any student who sells a book in equilibrium has a lower cost than any student who

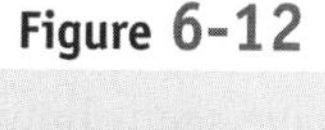
Figure 6-12

Reallocating Sales Lowers Producer Surplus

Yvonne (point *Y*) has a cost of $35, $10 more than Xavier (point *X*) who has a cost of $25. At the market equilibrium price of $30, Xavier sells a book, but Yvonne does not. If we rearrange sales by preventing Xavier from selling his book and compelling Yvonne to sell hers, producer surplus declines by $10 and, as a result, total surplus declines by $10. The market equilibrium generates the highest possible producer surplus by assuring those who sell the good are those who value the right to sell it the most. **>*web...***

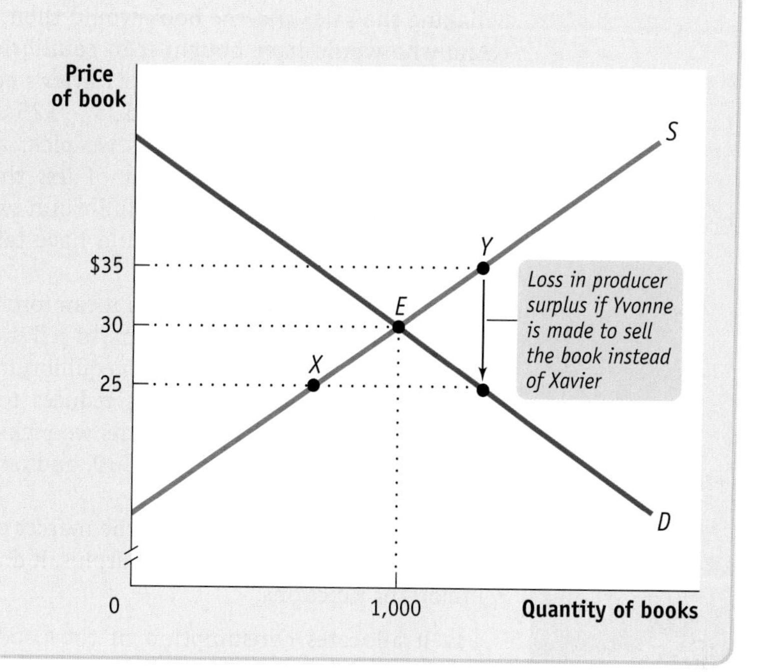

does not, so reallocating sales among sellers necessarily increases total cost and reduces producer surplus. In this way the market equilibrium generates the highest possible producer surplus: it ensures that those who sell their books are those who most value the right to sell them.

Finally, changing the quantity bought and sold reduces the sum of producer and consumer surplus. Figure 6-13 shows all four students: potential buyers Ana and Bob, and potential sellers Xavier and Yvonne. To reduce sales, we would have to

Figure 6-13

Changing the Quantity Lowers Total Surplus

If Xavier (point *X*) were prevented from selling his book to someone like Ana (point *A*), total surplus would fall by $10, the difference between Ana's willingness to pay ($35) and Xavier's cost ($25). This means that total surplus falls whenever fewer than 1,000 books—the equilibrium quantity—are transacted. Likewise, if Yvonne (point *Y*) were compelled to sell her book to someone like Bob (point *B*), total surplus would also fall by $10, the difference between Yvonne's cost ($35) and Bob's willingness to pay ($25). This means that total surplus falls whenever more than 1,000 books are transacted. These two examples show that at market equilibrium, all beneficial transactions—and only beneficial transactions—occur.

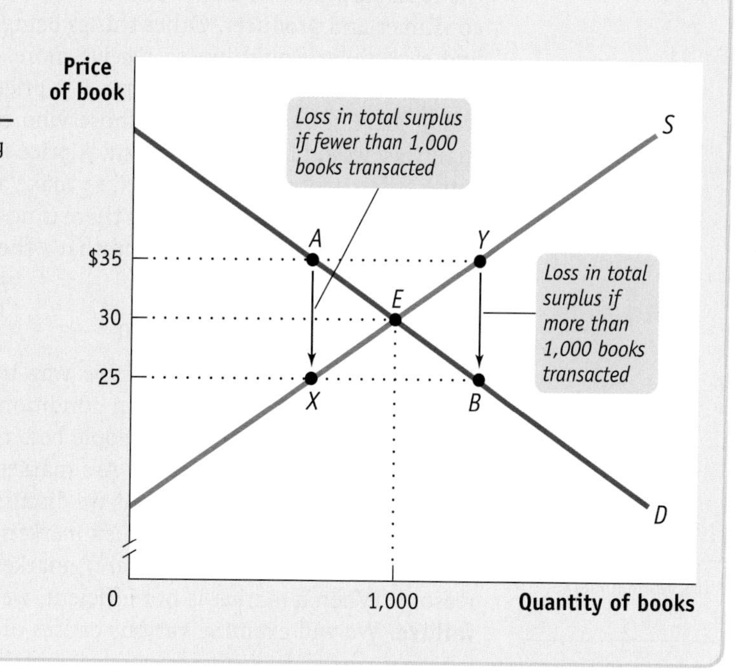

prevent someone like Xavier, who would have sold the book in equilibrium, from making the sale; and the book would then not be made available to someone like Ana who would have bought it in equilibrium. As we've have seen, however, Ana would be willing to pay $35, but Xavier's cost is only $25. So preventing this sale would reduce total surplus by $35 – $25 = $10. Once again, this result doesn't depend on which two students we pick: any student who would have sold the book in equilibrium has a cost of *less* than $30, and any student who would have purchased the book in equilibrium would be willing to pay *more* than $30, so preventing any sale that would have taken place in equilibrium reduces total surplus.

Finally, to increase sales would mean forcing someone like Yvonne, who would not have sold her book in equilibrium, to sell it, and giving it to someone like Bob, who would not have bought a book in equilibrium. Because Yvonne's cost is $35 but Bob is willing to pay only $25, this reduces total surplus by $10. And once again it doesn't matter which two students we pick—anyone who wouldn't have bought the book is willing to pay less than $30, and anyone who wouldn't have sold has a cost of more than $30.

Photodisc Red/Getty Images

Maximizing total surplus at your local hardware store.

What we have shown is that the market equilibrium maximizes total surplus—the sum of producer and consumer surplus. It does this because the market performs four important functions:

1. It allocates consumption of the good to the potential buyers who value it the most, as indicated by the fact that they have the highest willingness to pay.
2. It allocates sales to the potential sellers who most value the right to sell the good, as indicated by the fact that they have the lowest cost.
3. It ensures that every consumer who makes a purchase values the good more than every seller who makes a sale, so that all transactions are mutually beneficial.
4. It ensures that every potential buyer who doesn't make a purchase values the good less than every potential seller who doesn't make a sale, so that no mutually beneficial transactions are missed.

A caveat: it's important to realize that although the market equilibrium maximizes the total surplus, this does not mean that it is the best outcome for every individual consumer and producer. Other things being equal, each buyer would like to pay less, and each seller would like to receive more. So some people would benefit from the price controls discussed in Chapter 4. A price ceiling that held down the market price would leave some consumers—those who managed to make a purchase—better off than they would be at equilibrium. A price floor that kept the price up would benefit some sellers—those who managed to make a sale.

But in the market equilibrium there is no way to make some people better off without making others worse off—and that's the definition of efficiency.

A Few Words of Caution

Markets are an amazingly effective way to organize economic activity; we've just demonstrated that, under certain conditions, a market is actually efficient—there is literally no way to make some people better off without making others worse off.

But how secure is this result? Are markets really that good?

The answer is "not always". As we discussed briefly in Chapter 1 in our ninth and final principle of economics (*when markets don't achieve efficiency, government intervention can improve society's welfare*), markets can fail to be efficient for a number of reasons. When a market is not efficient, we have what is known as a case of **market failure.** We will examine various causes of *market failure* in depth in later chapters;

Market failure occurs when a market fails to be efficient.

for now, let's review the three main reasons why markets sometimes fall short of efficiency in reality.

First, markets can fail when, in an attempt to capture more resources, one party prevents mutually beneficial trades from occurring. This situation arises, for instance, when a market contains only a single seller of a good, known as a *monopolist.* In this case, the assumption we have relied on in supply and demand analysis—that no individual buyer and seller can have a noticeable effect on the market price—is no longer valid; the monopolist can determine the market price. As we'll see in Chapter 14, this gives rise to inefficiency as a monopolist manipulates the market price in order to increase profits, thereby preventing mutually beneficial trades from occurring.

For example, suppose a monopolist were to take over the student-run bookstore. The monopolist might decide that the best way to maximize its profits would be to charge a big markup—say, buying books for $5 and selling them for $40. This price manipulation would prevent many mutually beneficial trades from occurring.

Second, actions of individuals sometimes have *side effects* on the welfare of other individuals that markets don't take into account. The best-known example of such an *externality* is pollution. We'll see in Chapter 19 that pollution and other externalities also give rise to inefficiency.

Third, markets for some goods can fail because these goods, by their very nature, are unsuited for efficient management by markets. In Chapter 18, we will analyze goods that fall under this category because of problems of *private information*—information about a good that some people possess but others don't. In Chapter 20, we will encounter other types of goods that fall under this category—*public goods, common resources,* and *artificially scarce goods.* These are goods for which markets fail because of problems in limiting people's access to and consumption of the good. And in Chapter 22 we will learn about *information goods*: goods like a downloaded tune, which are costly to create but, once created, cost nothing to consume. But even with these caveats, it's remarkable how well markets work at maximizing the gains from trade.

economics in action

eBay and Efficiency

Garage sales are an old Canadian tradition: they are a way for families to sell items they don't want to other families that have some use for them, to the benefit of both parties. But many potentially beneficial trades were missed. For all Mr. Smith knew, there was someone 1,000 miles away who would have really loved that 1930s gramophone he had in the basement; for all Ms. Jones knew, there was someone 1,000 miles away who had that 1930s gramophone she had always wanted. But there was no way for Mr. Smith and Ms. Jones to find each other.

Enter eBay, the online auction service. eBay was founded in 1995 by Pierre Omidyar, a programmer whose fiancée was a collector of Pez candy dispensers and wanted a way to find potential sellers. The company, which says that its mission is "to help practically anyone trade practically anything on earth", provides a way for would-be buyers and would-be sellers of unique or used items to find each other, even if they don't live in the same neighbourhood or even the same city.

"I got it from eBay"

The potential gains from trade were evidently large: in 2003, 95 million people were registered by eBay, and in the same year almost $24 billion in goods were bought and sold using the service. The Omidyars now possess a large collection of Pez dispensers. They are also billionaires. ■

< < < < < < < < < < < < < < < < < < <

>>QUICK REVIEW

- *Total surplus* measures the gains from trade in a market.
- Markets are usually efficient. We can demonstrate this by considering what happens to total surplus if we start from the equilibrium and rearrange consumption, rearrange sales, or change the quantity traded. Any outcome other than the market equilibrium reduces total surplus, which means that the market equilibrium is efficient.
- Under certain conditions, *market failure* occurs and the market produces an inefficient outcome. The three principal sources are attempts to capture more resources that produce inefficiencies, side effects from certain transactions, and problems in the nature of the goods themselves.

>>CHECK YOUR UNDERSTANDING 6-3

1. Using the tables in Check Your Understanding 6-1 and 6-2, find the equilibrium price and quantity in the market for cheese-stuffed jalapeno peppers. What is the total surplus in the equilibrium in this market, and who receives it?
2. Show how each of the following three actions reduces total surplus:
   a. Having Josie consume one less pepper, and Casey one more pepper, than in the market equilibrium
   b. Having Cara produce one less pepper, and Jamie one more pepper, than in the market equilibrium
   c. Having Josie consume one less pepper, and Cara produce one less pepper, than in the market equilibrium

Solutions appear at back of book.

Applying Consumer and Producer Surplus: The Efficiency Costs of a Tax

The concepts of consumer and producer surplus are extremely useful in many economic applications. Among the most important of these is assessing the efficiency cost of taxation.

In Chapter 4 we introduced the concept of an *excise tax*, a tax on the purchase or sale of a good. We saw that such a tax drives a *wedge* between the price paid by consumers and that received by producers: the price paid by consumers rises, and the price received by producers falls, with the difference equal to the tax per unit. The *incidence* of the tax—how much of the burden falls on consumers, how much on producers—does not depend on who actually writes the cheque to the government. Instead, as we saw in Chapter 5, the burden of the tax depends on the price elasticity of supply and demand: the higher the price elasticity of demand, the greater the burden on producers; the higher the price elasticity of supply, the greater the burden on consumers.

We also learned that there is an additional cost of a tax, over and above the money actually paid to the government. A tax causes a *deadweight loss* to society, because less of the good is produced and consumed than in the absence of the tax. As a result, some mutually beneficial trades between producers and consumers do not take place.

Now we can complete the picture, because the concepts of consumer and producer surplus are what we need to pin down precisely the deadweight losses that an excise tax imposes.

Figure 6-14 shows the effects of an excise tax on consumer and producer surplus. In the absence of the tax, the equilibrium is at *E*, and the equilibrium price and quantity are P_E and Q_E, respectively. An excise tax drives a wedge equal to the amount of the tax between the price received by producers and the price paid by consumers, reducing the quantity bought and sold. In this case, where the tax is *T* dollars per unit, the quantity bought and sold falls to Q_T. The price paid by consumers rises to PC, the demand price of the reduced quantity, Q_T, and the price received by producers falls to P_P, the supply price of that quantity. The difference between these prices, $P_C - P_P$, is equal to the excise tax, *T*.

What we can now do, using the concepts of producer and consumer surplus, is show exactly how much surplus producers and consumers lose as a result of the tax.

We saw earlier, in Figure 6-5, that a fall in the price of a good generates a gain in consumer surplus that is equal to the sum of the areas of a rectangle and a triangle. A price increase causes a loss to consumers that looks exactly the same. In the case

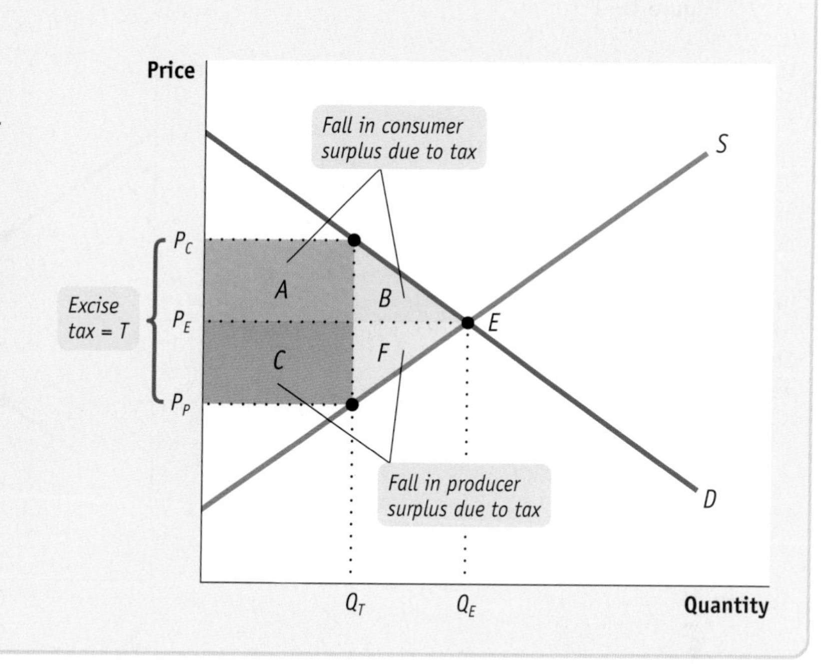

Figure 6-14

A Tax Reduces Consumer and Producer Surplus

Before the tax, the equilibrium price and quantity are P_E and Q_E respectively. After an excise tax of T per unit is imposed, the price to consumers rises to P_C and consumer surplus falls by the sum of the dark blue rectangle, labelled *A*, and the light blue triangle, labelled *B*. The tax also causes the price to producers to fall to P_P; producer surplus falls by the sum of the red rectangle, labelled *C*, and the pink triangle, labelled *F*. The government receives revenue from the tax, $Q_T \times T$, which is given by the sum of the areas *A* and *C*. Areas *B* and *F* represent the losses to consumer and producer surplus that are not collected by the government as revenue; they are the deadweight loss to society of the tax. **>web...**

of an excise tax, the rise in the price paid by consumers causes a loss equal to the sum of the area of the dark blue rectangle labelled *A* and the area of the light blue triangle labelled *B* in Figure 6-14.

Meanwhile, the fall in the price received by producers causes a fall in producer surplus. This, too, is the sum of the areas of a rectangle and a triangle. The loss in producer surplus is the sum of the areas of the red rectangle labelled *C* and the pink triangle labelled *F* in Figure 6-14.

Of course, although consumers and producers are hurt by the tax, the government gains revenue. The revenue the government collects is equal to the tax per unit sold, *T*, multiplied by the quantity sold, Q_T. This revenue is equal to the area of a rectangle Q_T wide and T high. And we already have that rectangle in the figure: it is the sum of the rectangles labelled *A* and *C*. So the government gains part of what consumers and producers lose from an excise tax.

But there is a part of the loss to producers and consumers from the tax that is not offset by a gain to the government—specifically, the two triangles labelled *B* and *F*. The deadweight loss caused by the tax is equal to the combined area of these triangles. It represents the total surplus that would have been generated by transactions that do not take place because of the tax.

Figure 6-15 (page 164) is a version of the same picture, leaving out the shaded rectangles—which represent money shifted from consumers and producers to the government—and showing only the deadweight loss, this time as a triangle shaded yellow. The base of that triangle is the tax wedge, *T*; the height of the triangle is the reduction the tax causes in the quantity sold, $Q_E - Q_T$. Notice that if the excise tax didn't reduce the quantity bought and sold in this market—if Q_T weren't less than Q_E—the deadweight loss represented by the yellow triangle would disappear. This observation ties in with the explanation given in Chapter 4 of why an excise tax generates a deadweight loss to society: the tax causes inefficiency because it discourages mutually beneficial transactions between buyers and sellers.

The idea that deadweight loss can be measured by the area of a triangle recurs in many economic applications. Deadweight-loss triangles are produced not only by excise taxes but also by other types of taxation. They are also produced by other kinds of distortions of markets, such as monopolies. If a monopolist took over the student bookstore and

Figure 6-15

The Deadweight Loss of a Tax

A tax leads to a deadweight loss because it creates inefficiency: some mutually beneficial transactions never take place because of the tax, namely the transactions $Q_E - Q_T$. The yellow area here represents the value of the deadweight loss: it is the total surplus that would have been gained from the $Q_E - Q_T$ transactions. If the tax had not discouraged transactions—had the number of transactions remained at Q_E—no deadweight loss would have been incurred.

>web...

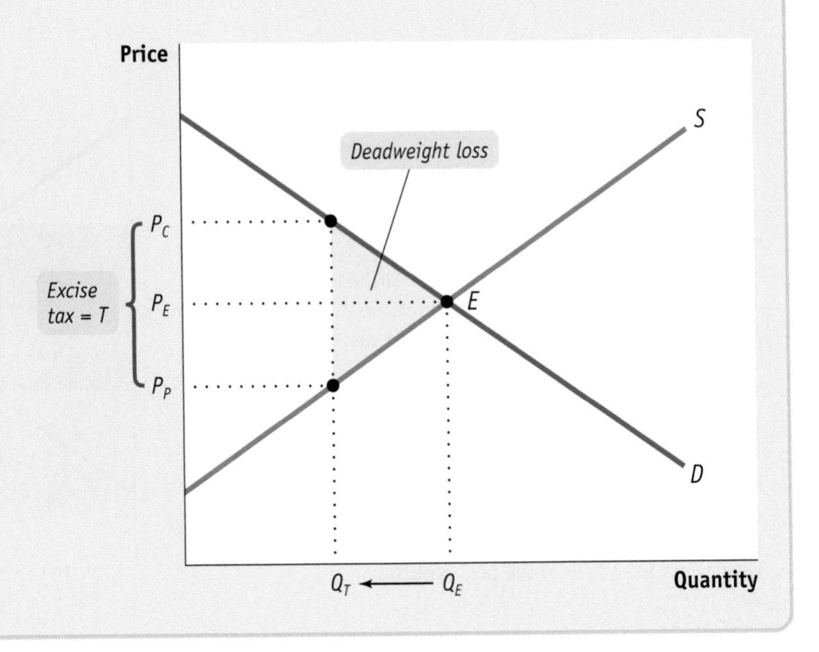

charged enormous markups on the sale of used books, the effect would very similar to that of the excise tax we've just analysed. And triangles are often used to evaluate other public policies besides taxation—for example, decisions about whether to build new highways.

The general rule for economic policy is that, other things equal, you want to choose the policy that produces the smallest deadweight loss. This principle gives valuable guidance on everything from the design of the tax system to environmental policy. But how can we predict the size of the deadweight loss associated with a given policy? For the answer to that question, we return to a familiar concept: elasticity.

Deadweight Loss and Elasticities

The deadweight loss from an excise tax arises because it prevents some mutually beneficial transactions from occurring. In particular, the producer and consumer surplus that is forgone from these missing transactions is equal to the size of the deadweight loss itself. This means that the larger the number of transactions that are impeded by the tax, the larger the deadweight loss.

This gives us an important clue in understanding the relationship between elasticity and the size of deadweight loss from a tax. Recall that when demand or supply is elastic, it means that the quantity demanded or the quantity supplied is relatively responsive to price. So a tax imposed on a good for which either demand or supply, or both, is elastic will cause a relatively large decrease in the quantity bought and sold and a large deadweight loss. And when we say that demand or supply is inelastic, we mean that the quantity demanded or the quantity supplied is relatively unresponsive to price. As a result, a tax imposed when demand or supply, or both, is inelastic will cause a relatively small decrease in the quantity bought and sold and a small deadweight loss.

The four panels of Figure 6-16 illustrate the positive relationship between price elasticity of either demand or supply and the deadweight loss of taxation. In each panel, the size of the deadweight loss is given by the area of the shaded triangle. In panel (a), the deadweight-loss triangle is large because demand is relatively elastic—a large number of transactions fail to occur because of the tax. In panel (b), the same supply curve is drawn as in panel (a), but demand is now relatively inelastic; as a result the triangle is small because only a small number of transactions are forgone. Likewise, panels (c) and (d) contain the same demand curve but different supply curves. In panel (c),

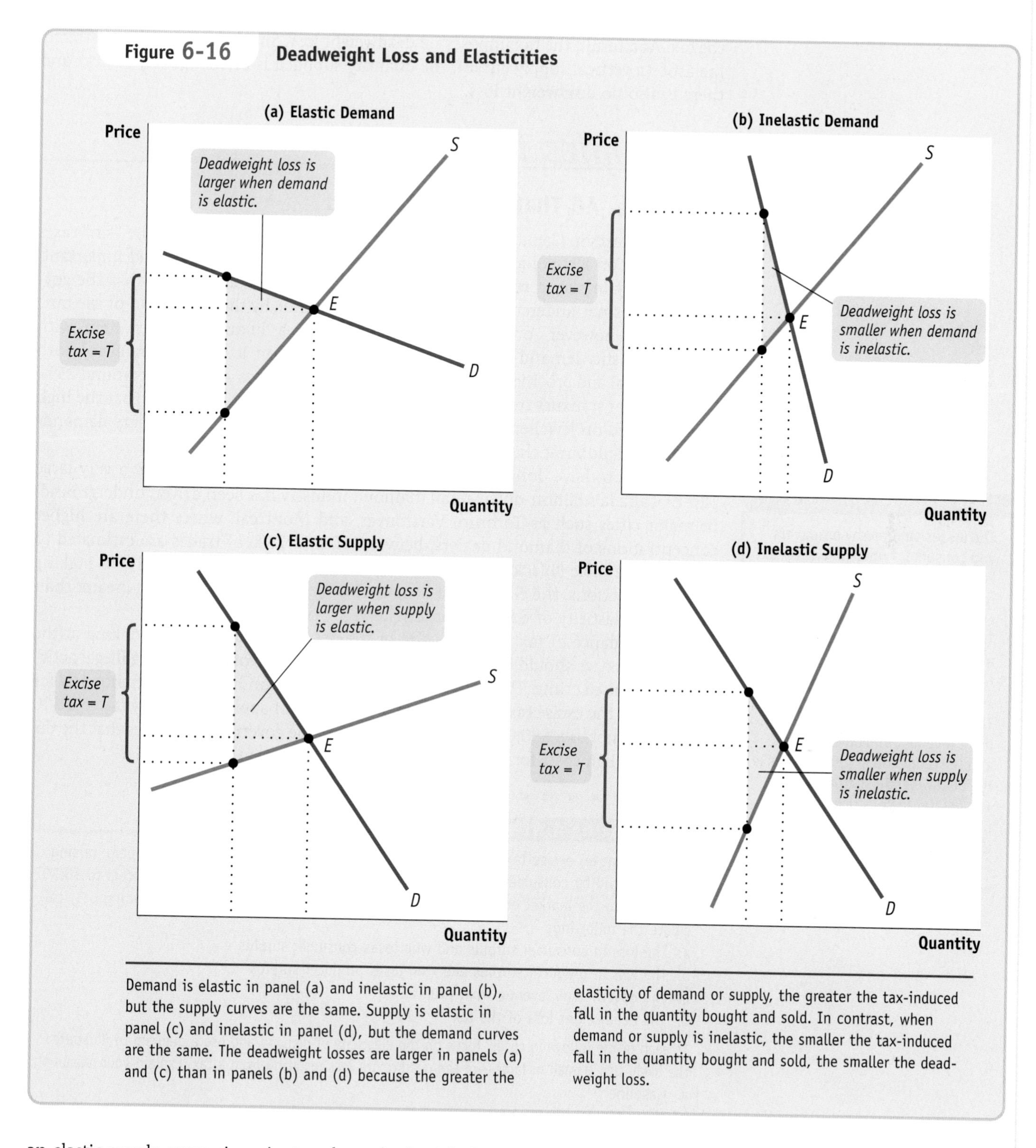

Figure 6-16 Deadweight Loss and Elasticities

Demand is elastic in panel (a) and inelastic in panel (b), but the supply curves are the same. Supply is elastic in panel (c) and inelastic in panel (d), but the demand curves are the same. The deadweight losses are larger in panels (a) and (c) than in panels (b) and (d) because the greater the elasticity of demand or supply, the greater the tax-induced fall in the quantity bought and sold. In contrast, when demand or supply is inelastic, the smaller the tax-induced fall in the quantity bought and sold, the smaller the deadweight loss.

an elastic supply curve gives rise to a large deadweight-loss triangle, but in panel (d) an inelastic supply curve gives rise to a small deadweight-loss triangle.

As the following story illustrates, the implication of this result is clear: if you want to lessen the efficiency costs of taxation, you should devise taxes to fall on goods for which either demand or supply, or both, is relatively inelastic. And this lesson carries a flip side: using a tax to purposely decrease the amount of a harmful activity, such as underage drinking, will have the most impact when that activity is elastically demanded or supplied. In the extreme case in which demand is perfectly inelastic (a vertical demand curve), the quantity demanded is unchanged by the imposition of the tax. As a result, the tax imposes no deadweight loss. Similarly, if supply is perfectly inelastic (a vertical supply curve), the quantity supplied is unchanged by the tax and there is also no deadweight loss.

economics in action

In Canada, All That Glitters Is Taxed

Most excise taxes in Canada are placed on goods with inelastic demand—the "sin" taxes (excise taxes on alcohol and cigarettes) being two of the most visible and important. This not only implies a relatively small deadweight loss but also means that the government does not undercut the source of its tax revenue by the imposition of the tax.

There is, however, one excise tax imposed on a luxury item—an item with relatively elastic demand—the 10% federal excise tax on jewellery. Combined with regular federal and provincial sales taxes, jewellery is subject to a tax rate of around 25%.

Because most luxury items have an elastic demand, one would expect that the high taxes imposed on jewellery would seriously reduce the amount of jewellery demanded, which would limit the tax revenue raised.

It appears to have done more than that. A recent report claimed that a very large part of Canada's billion-dollar retail diamond industry has been driven underground. In major cities such as Toronto, Vancouver, and Montreal, where there are higher concentrations of diamond dealers, between 50 and 75% of trades are estimated to be under-the-table "black market" transactions. Because of the possibility of making illegal transactions, the elasticity of demand for "legal jewellery" is much greater than the overall elasticity of demand for jewellery.

Such avoidance of tax limits the size of the deadweight loss. But in looking at the cost of the tax, we should include the broader societal costs of encouraging illegal activity and organised crime. The Canadian Jewellers Association has lobbied strenuously for the repeal of the excise tax. It notes the inconsistency of applying a luxury tax to a $10 gold pin but not to a $50,000 automobile. It hopes the government realises that the tax is imposing high costs for relatively little gain in equity or in tax revenue. ■

>>QUICK REVIEW

- The losses suffered by producers and consumers when an excise tax is imposed can be measured by the reduction in consumer and producer surplus.
- The government gains revenue from an excise tax, but this government revenue is less than the loss in total surplus.
- The difference between the government revenue from an excise tax and the reduction in total surplus is the deadweight loss from the tax.
- The greater the elasticities of supply or demand, or both, the larger the number of transactions prevented by a tax and the larger the deadweight loss.

>>CHECK YOUR UNDERSTANDING 6-4

1. Suppose that an excise tax of $0.40 is imposed on cheese-stuffed jalapeno peppers, raising the price paid by consumers to $0.70, and lowering the price received by producers to $0.30. Compared to the market equilibrium without the tax from Check Your Understanding 6-3, calculate the following:
   a. The loss in consumer surplus and who loses consumer surplus
   b. The loss in producer surplus and who loses producer surplus
   c. The government revenue from this tax
   d. The deadweight loss of the tax
2. In each of the following cases, focus on the elasticity of demand and use a diagram to illustrate the likely size—small or large—of the deadweight loss resulting from a tax. Explain your reasoning.
   a. Gasoline
   b. Milk chocolate bars

Solutions appear at back of book.

• A LOOK AHEAD •

We have now almost completed our tour of the supply and demand model. But there is one more topic we need to address: how do producers and consumers make decisions? Up to now we have looked at simple situations where it is immediately clear what an individual should do. For example, a consumer should buy if the price is less than his or her willingness to pay. But not all situations are that simple. In the next chapter, we take a deeper look at how producers and consumers make decisions.

SUMMARY

1. The **willingness to pay** of each individual consumer determines the demand curve. When price is less than or equal to the willingness to pay, the potential consumer purchases the good. The difference between price and willingness to pay is the net gain to the consumer, the **individual consumer surplus.**
2. The **total consumer surplus** in a market, the sum of all individual consumer surpluses in a market, is equal to the area below the demand curve but above the price. A rise in the price of a good reduces consumer surplus; a fall in the price increases consumer surplus. The term **consumer surplus** is often used to refer both to individual and to total consumer surplus.
3. The **cost** of each potential producer, the lowest price at which he or she is willing to supply a unit of that good, determines the supply curve. If the price of a good is above a producer's cost, a sale generates a net gain to the producer, known as the **individual producer surplus.**
4. The **total producer surplus,** the sum of the individual producer surpluses, is equal to the area above the supply curve but below the price. A rise in the price of a good increases producer surplus; a fall in the price reduces producer surplus. The term **producer surplus** is often used to refer both to the individual and to the total producer surplus.
5. **Total surplus,** the total gain to society from the production and consumption of a good, is the sum of consumer and producer surplus.
6. Usually, markets are efficient and achieve the maximum total surplus. Any possible rearrangement of consumption or sales, or change in the quantity bought and sold, reduces total surplus.
7. Under certain conditions, **market failure** occurs and markets fail to be efficient. This arises from three principal sources: attempts to capture more resources that create inefficiencies, side effects of some transactions, and problems in the nature of the good.
8. Economic policies can be evaluated by their effect on total surplus. For example, an excise tax generates revenue for the government but lowers total surplus. The loss in total surplus exceeds the tax revenue, resulting in a deadweight loss to society. The value of this deadweight loss is shown by the triangle that represents the value of the transactions discouraged by the tax. The greater the elasticity of demand or supply, or both, the larger the deadweight loss of a tax.

KEY TERMS

PROBLEMS

1. Determine the amount of consumer surplus generated in each of the following situations:
   - **a.** Paul goes to the clothing store to buy a new T-shirt, for which he is willing to pay up to \$10. He picks out one he likes with a price tag of exactly \$10. At the cash register, he is told that his T-shirt is on sale for half the posted price.
   - **b.** Robin goes to the CD store in town hoping to find a used copy of the *Eagles Greatest Hits* for up to \$10. The store has one copy selling for \$10.
   - **c.** After soccer practice, Phil is willing to pay \$2 for a bottle of mineral water. The 7-Eleven sells mineral water for \$2.25 per bottle.
2. Determine the amount of producer surplus generated in each of the following situations:
   - **a.** Bob lists his old Lionel electric trains on eBay. He sets a minimum acceptable price, known as his *reserve price,* of \$75. After five days of bidding, the final high bid is exactly \$75.
   - **b.** Jenny advertises her car for sale in the used car section of the student newspaper for \$2,000, but she is willing to sell the car for any price higher than \$1,500. The best offer she gets is \$1,200.
   - **c.** Sanjay likes his job so much that he would be willing to do it for free. However, his annual salary is \$80,000.
3. Hollywood writers have a new agreement with movie producers that the writers will receive 10% of the revenue from every video rental of a movie they worked on. They have no such agreement for movies shown on pay-per-view television.
   - **a.** When the new writers' agreement comes into effect, what happens in the market for video rentals—that is, will supply or demand shift, and how? As a result, how will consumer surplus in the market for video rentals change? Illustrate with a diagram. Do you think the writers' agreement will be popular with consumers who rent videos?
   - **b.** Consumers consider rental videos and pay-per-view movies substitutable to some extent. When the new

writer's agreement comes into effect, what will happen in the market for pay-per-view movies—that is, will supply or demand shift, and how? As a result, how will producer surplus in the market for pay-per-view movies change? Illustrate with a diagram. Do you think the writers' agreement will be popular with cable television companies that show pay-per-view movies?

4. There are 6 potential consumers of computer games. Consumer 1 is willing to pay $40 for a computer game, consumer 2 is willing to pay $35, consumer 3 is willing to pay $30, consumer 4 is willing pay $25, consumer 5 is willing to pay $20, and consumer 6 is willing to pay $15.

   a. Suppose the market price is $29. What is the total consumer surplus?

   b. The market price decreases to $19. What is the total consumer surplus now?

   c. When the price fell from $29 to $19, how much did each consumer's individual consumer surplus change?

5. In an effort to provide more affordable rental housing for low-income families, the city council of Belleville, Manitoba, decides to impose a rent ceiling well below the current market equilibrium rent.

   a. Illustrate the effect of this policy in a diagram. Indicate consumer and producer surplus before and after the introduction of the rent ceiling.

   b. Will this policy be popular with renters? With landlords?

   c. An economist explains to the city council that this policy is creating a deadweight loss. Illustrate the deadweight loss in your diagram.

6. On Thursday nights, a local restaurant has a pasta special. Ted likes the restaurant's pasta, and his willingness to pay for each serving is shown in the accompanying table.

Quantity of pasta (servings)	Willingness to pay for pasta (per serving)
1	$10
2	8
3	6
4	4
5	2
6	0

   a. If the price of a serving of pasta is $4, how many servings will Ted buy? How much consumer surplus does he receive?

   b. The following week, Ted is back at the restaurant again, but now the price of a serving of pasta is $6. By how much does his consumer surplus decrease compared to the previous week?

   c. One week later, he goes to the restaurant again. He discovers that the restaurant is offering an "all you can eat" special for $25. How much pasta will Ted eat, and how much consumer surplus does he receive now?

   d. Suppose you own the restaurant and Ted is a "typical" customer. What is the highest price you can charge for the "all you can eat" special, and still attract customers?

7. The accompanying diagram shows the market for cigarettes. The current equilibrium price per pack is $4, and every day 40 million packs of cigarettes are sold. In order to recover some of the health care costs associated with smoking, the government imposes a tax of $2 per pack. This will raise the equilibrium price to $5 per pack, and reduce the equilibrium quantity to 30 million packs.

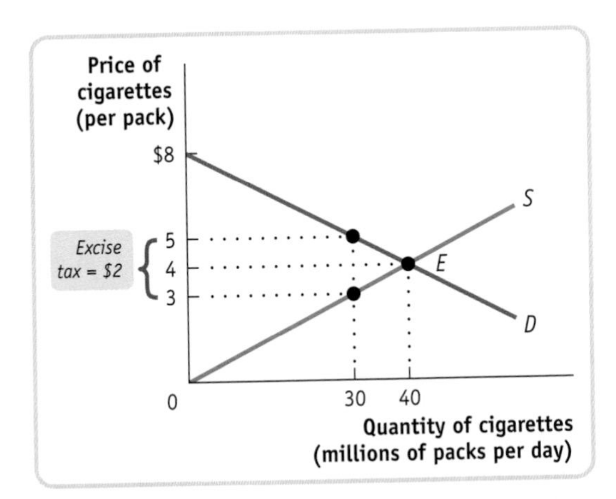

The economist working for the tobacco lobby claims that this tax will reduce the consumer surplus for smokers by $40 million per day, since 40 million packs now cost $1 more per pack. The economist working for the lobby for sufferers of second-hand smoke argues that this is an enormous overestimate, and that the reduction in consumer surplus is only $30 million per day, since after the imposition of the tax only $30 million packs of cigarettes will be bought and each of these packs now costs $1 more. They are both wrong. Why?

8. Consider the original market for pizza in Middleton, Ontario, illustrated in the accompanying table. Town officials decide to impose to impose an excise tax on pizza of $4 per pizza.

Price of pizza	Quantity of pizza demanded	Quantity of pizza supplied
$10	0	6
9	1	5
8	2	4
7	3	3
6	4	2
5	5	1
4	6	0
3	7	0
2	8	0
1	9	0

a. What is the quantity of pizza bought and sold after the imposition of the tax? What is the price paid by consumers? What is the price received by producers?

b. Calculate the consumer surplus and the producer surplus after the imposition of the tax. By how much has the imposition of the tax reduced consumer surplus? By how much has it reduced producer surplus?

c. How much tax revenue does Middleton earn from this tax?

d. Calculate the deadweight loss from this tax.

9. Consider once more the original market for pizza in Middleton, Ontario, illustrated in the table in Problem 8. Now Middleton officials impose a price floor on pizza of $8.

a. What is the quantity of pizza bought and sold after the imposition of the price floor?

b. Calculate the consumer surplus after the imposition of the price floor, and the producer surplus after the imposition of the price floor.

10. You are the manager of Fun World, a small amusement park in Beaver, British Columbia. The accompanying diagram shows the demand curve of a typical customer at Fun World.

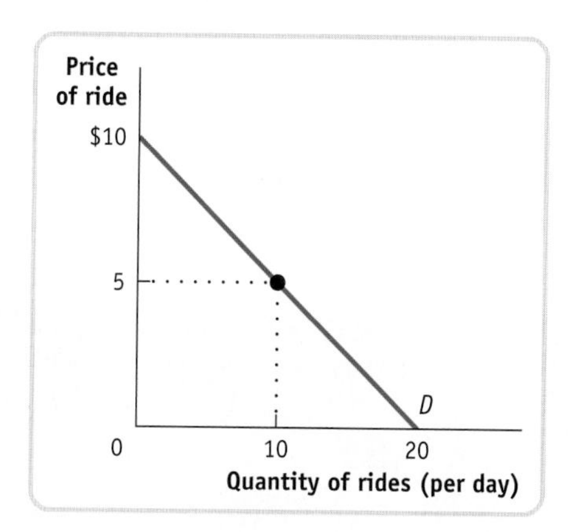

a. Suppose that the price of each ride is $5. At that price, how much consumer surplus does an individual consumer get? (Recall that the area of a triangle is $1/2 \times$ the base of the triangle $\times$ the height of the triangle.)

b. Suppose that Fun World considers charging an admission fee, while maintaining the price of each ride at $5. What is the maximum admission fee it could charge? (Assume that all potential customers have enough money to pay the fee.)

c. Suppose that Fun World lowered the price of each ride to zero. How much consumer surplus does an individual consumer get? What is the maximum admission fee Fun World could therefore charge?

11. The accompanying diagram illustrates a taxi driver's individual supply curve (assume that each taxi ride is the same distance).

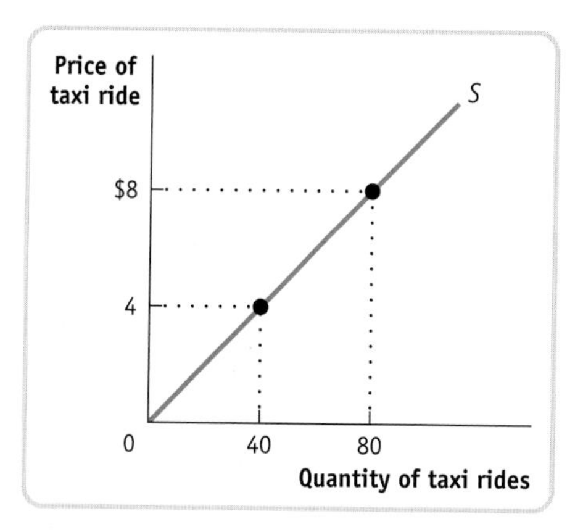

a. Suppose the city sets the price of taxi rides at $4 per ride. What is this taxi driver's producer surplus? (Recall that the area of a triangle is $1/2 \times$ the base of the triangle $\times$ the height of the triangle.)

b. Suppose now that the city keeps the price of a taxi ride set at $4, but it decides to charge taxi drivers a "licensing fee". What is the maximum licensing fee the city could extract from this taxi driver?

c. Suppose that the city allowed the price of taxi rides to increase to $8 per ride. How much producer surplus does an individual taxi driver now get? What is the maximum licensing fee the city could charge this taxi driver?

12. The province needs to raise money, and the premier has a choice of imposing an excise tax of the same amount on one of two previously untaxed goods: the province can either tax sales of restaurant meals or sales of gasoline. Both the demand for and the supply of restaurant meals are more elastic than the demand for and the supply of gasoline. If the premier wants to minimize the deadweight loss caused by the tax, which good should be taxed? For each good, draw a diagram that illustrates the deadweight loss from taxation.

>web... To continue your study and review of concepts in this chapter, please visit the Krugman/Wells website for quizzes, animated graph tutorials, web links to helpful resources, and more.

www.worthpublishers.com/krugmanwellsmyatt

chapter 7

>> Making Decisions

A TALE OF TWO INVASIONS

On June 6, 1944, Allied soldiers stormed the beaches of Normandy, beginning the liberation of France from German rule. Long before the assault, however, Allied generals had to make a crucial decision: *where* would the soldiers land?

They had to make what we call an "either–or" decision. *Either* the invasion force could cross the English Channel at its narrowest point, Calais—which was what the Germans expected—*or* it could try to surprise the Germans by landing farther west, in Normandy. Since men and landing craft were in limited supply, the Allies could not do both. In fact, they chose to rely on surprise. The German defences in Normandy were too weak to stop the landings, and the Allies went on to liberate France and win the war.

Thirty years earlier, at the beginning of World War I, German generals had to make a different kind of decision. They, too, planned to invade France, in this case via land, and had decided to mount that invasion through Belgium. The decision they had to make was not an "either–or" but a "how much" decision: *how much* of their army should be allocated to the invasion force, and how much should be used to defend Germany's border with France? The original plan, devised by General Alfred von Schlieffen, allocated most of the German army to the invasion force; on his deathbed, Schlieffen is supposed to have pleaded, "Keep the right wing [the invasion force] strong!" But his successor, General Helmuth von Moltke, weakened the plan: he reallocated some of the divisions that were supposed to race through Belgium to the defence. The weakened invasion force wasn't strong enough: the defending French army stopped it 30 miles from Paris. Most military historians believe that by allocating too few men to the attack, von Moltke cost Germany the war.

So Allied generals made the right decision in 1944; German generals made the

MGM/The Kobal Collection

Decision: Attack here? Or there?

What you will learn in this chapter:

- How economists model decision making by individuals and firms
- The importance of **implicit** as well as **explicit costs** in decision making
- The difference between **accounting profit** and **economic profit**, and why economic profit is the correct basis for decisions
- The difference between "either–or" and "how much" decisions
- The **principle of marginal analysis**
- What **sunk costs** are and why they should be ignored
- How to make decisions in cases where time is a factor

wrong decision in 1914. The important point for this chapter is that in both cases the generals had to apply the same logic that applies to economic decisions, like production decisions by businesses and consumption decisions by households.

In this chapter we will survey the principles involved in making economic decisions. These principles will help us understand how any individual—whether a consumer or a producer—makes an economic decision. We begin by taking a deeper look at the significance of opportunity cost for economic decisions and the role it plays in "either–or" decisions. Next we turn to the problem of making "how much" decisions and the usefulness of *marginal analysis*. We then examine what kind of costs should be ignored in making a decision—costs which economists call *sunk costs*. We end by considering the concept of *present value* and its importance for making decisions when costs and benefits arrive at different times.

Opportunity Cost and Decisions

In Chapter 1 we introduced some core principles underlying economic decisions. We've just seen two of those principles at work in our tale of two invasions. The first is that *resources are scarce*—the invading Allies had a limited number of landing craft, and the invading Germans had a limited number of divisions. Because resources are scarce, the true cost of anything is its *opportunity cost*—that is, the real cost of something is what you must give up to get it. When it comes to making decisions, it is crucial to think in terms of opportunity cost, because the opportunity cost of an action is often considerably more than the simple monetary cost.

Explicit versus Implicit Costs

Suppose that, upon graduation from university, you have two options: to go to school for an additional year to get an advanced degree or to take a job immediately. You would like to take the extra year in school but are concerned about the cost.

But what exactly is the cost of that additional year of school? Here is where it is important to remember the concept of opportunity cost: the cost of that year spent getting an advanced degree is what you forgo by not taking a job for that year.

This cost, like any cost, can be broken into two parts: the *explicit cost* of the year's schooling and the *implicit cost*.

An **explicit cost** is a cost that involves actually laying out money. An **implicit cost** does not require an outlay of money; it is measured by the value, in dollar terms, of the benefits that are forgone.

An **explicit cost** is a cost that requires an outlay of money. For example, the explicit cost of the additional year of schooling includes tuition. An **implicit cost,** on the other hand, does not involve an outlay of money; instead, it is measured by the value, in dollar terms, of all the benefits that are forgone. For example, the implicit cost of the year spent in school includes the income you would have earned if you had taken that job instead.

A common mistake, both in economic analysis and in real business situations, is to ignore implicit costs and focus exclusively on explicit costs. But often the implicit cost of an activity is quite substantial—indeed, sometimes it is much larger than the explicit cost.

Table 7-1 (page 172) gives a breakdown of hypothetical explicit and implicit costs associated with spending an additional year in school instead of taking a job. The explicit cost consists of tuition, books, supplies, and a home computer for doing assignments—all of which require you to spend money. The implicit cost is the salary you would have earned if you had taken a job instead. As you can see, the forgone salary is $35,000 and the explicit cost is $9,500, making the implicit cost more than three times as much as the explicit cost. So ignoring the implicit cost of an action can lead to a seriously misguided decision.

TABLE 7-1

Opportunity Cost of an Additional Year of School

Explicit cost		Implicit cost	
Tuition	$7,000	Forgone salary	$35,000
Books and supplies	1,000		
Home computer	1,500		
Total explicit cost	**9,500**	**Total implicit cost**	**35,000**
Total opportunity cost = Total explicit cost + Total implicit cost = $44,500			

There is another, slightly different way of looking at the implicit cost in this example that can deepen our understanding of opportunity cost. The forgone salary is the cost of using your own resources—your time—in going to school rather than working. The use of your *time* for more schooling, despite the fact that you don't have to spend any money, is nonetheless costly to you. This illustrates an important aspect of opportunity cost: in considering the cost of an activity, you should include the cost of using any of your own resources for that activity. You can calculate the cost of using your own resources by determining what they would have earned in their next best use.

FOR INQUIRING MINDS

FAMOUS UNIVERSITY DROPOUTS

What do Bill Gates, Tiger Woods, and Sarah Michelle Gellar (a.k.a. Buffy the Vampire Slayer) have in common? None of them has a university degree.

Nobody doubts that all three are easily smart enough to have gotten their diplomas. However, they all made the rational decision that the implicit cost of getting a degree would have been too high—by their late teens, each had a very promising career that would have had to be put on hold to get a university degree. Gellar would have had to postpone her acting career; Woods would have had to put off winning one major tournament after another and becoming the world's best golfer; Gates would have had to delay developing the most successful and most lucrative software ever sold, Microsoft's computer operating system.

In fact, extremely successful people—especially those in careers like acting or athletics, where starting early in life is especially crucial—are often university dropouts. It's a simple matter of economics: the opportunity cost of their time at that stage in their lives is just too high to postpone their careers for a university degree.

Accounting Profit versus Economic Profit

As the example of going to school suggests, taking account of implicit as well as explicit costs can be very important for individuals making decisions. The same is true of businesses.

Consider the case of Kathy's Copy Shop, a small business operating in a local shopping centre. Kathy makes copies for customers, who pay for her services. Out of that revenue, she has to pay her expenses: the cost of supplies and the rent for her store space. We suppose that Kathy owns the copy machines themselves. This year Kathy has $100,000 in revenues and $60,000 in expenses. Is her business profitable?

At first it might seem that the answer is obviously yes: she receives $100,000 from her customers and has expenses of only $60,000. Doesn't this mean that she has a profit of $40,000? Not according to her accountant, who reduces the number by $5,000 for the yearly *depreciation* (reduction in value) of the copy machines.

Depreciation occurs because machines wear out over time. The yearly depreciation amount reflects what an accountant estimates to be the reduction in the value of the machines due to wear and tear that year. This leaves $35,000, which is the business's **accounting profit.** Basically, the accounting profit of a company is its revenue minus its explicit costs and depreciation. The accounting profit is the number that Kathy has to report on her income tax forms and that she would be obliged to report to anyone thinking of investing in her business.

The **accounting profit** of a business is the business's revenue minus the explicit cost and depreciation.

Accounting profit is a very useful number, but suppose that Kathy wants to decide whether to keep her business going or to do something else. To make this decision, she will need to calculate her **economic profit**—the revenue she receives minus her opportunity cost, which may include implicit as well as explicit costs. In general, when economists use the simple term *profit*, they are referring to economic profit. (We will adopt this simplification in later chapters of this book.)

The **economic profit** of a business is the business's revenue minus the opportunity cost of its resources. It is usually less than the accounting profit.

Why does Kathy's economic profit differ from her accounting profit? Because she may have implicit costs over and above the explicit cost her accountant has calculated. Businesses can face implicit costs for two reasons. First, a business's **capital**—its equipment, buildings, tools, inventory, and financial assets—could have been put to use in some other way. If the business owns its capital, it does not pay any money for its use, but it pays an implicit cost because it does not use the capital in some other way. Second, the owner devotes time and energy to the business that could have been used elsewhere—a particularly important factor in small businesses, whose owners tend to put in many long hours.

The **capital** of a business is the value of its assets—equipment, buildings, tools, inventory, and financial assets.

If Kathy had rented her copy machines from the manufacturer, their rent would have been an explicit cost. But because Kathy owns her own machines, she does not pay rent on them and her accountant deducts an estimate of their depreciation in the profit statement. However, this does not account for the opportunity cost of the machines—what Kathy forgoes by owning them. Suppose that instead of using the machines for her own business, the best alternative Kathy has is to sell them for $50,000 and put the money into a bank account where it would earn yearly interest of $3,000. This $3,000 is an implicit cost of running the business.

It is generally known as the **implicit cost of capital,** the opportunity cost of the capital used by a business; it reflects the income that could have been realized if the capital had been used in its next best alternative way. It is just as much a true cost as if Kathy had rented the machines instead of owning them.

The **implicit cost of capital** is the opportunity cost of the capital used by a business—the income the owner could have realized from that capital if it had been used in its next best alternative way.

Finally, Kathy should take into account the opportunity cost of her own time. Suppose that instead of running her own shop, she could earn $34,000 as an office manager. That $34,000 is also an implicit cost of her business.

Table 7-2 summarizes the accounting for Kathy's Copy Shop, taking both explicit and implicit costs into account. It turns out, unfortunately, that although the business makes an accounting profit of $35,000, its economic profit is actually negative.

TABLE 7-2

Profits at Kathy's Copy Shop

Revenue	$100,000
Explicit cost	– 60,000
Depreciation	– 5,000
Accounting profit	**35,000**
Implicit cost of business	
Income Kathy could have earned on capital in the next best way	– 3,000
Income Kathy could have earned as manager	– 34,000
Economic profit	**–2,000**

"I've done the numbers, and I will marry you."

This means that Kathy would be better off financially if she closed the business and devoted her time and capital to something else.

In real life, discrepancies between accounting profits and economic profits are extremely common. As the following Economics in Action explains, this is a message that has found a receptive audience among real-world businesses.

economics in action

Urban Sprawl and the Loss of Farmland in Canada

It seems irrational that some of the most fertile agricultural land in Canada is buried under concrete and tarmac—a victim of urban sprawl. Why does this occur and what, if anything, can be done about it?

The root cause is simple enough. Historically, people congregated in fertile areas, and villages and cities grew up in the middle of the most productive land, especially if there were also water routes nearby that facilitated trading. Given these beginnings, city growth almost inevitably absorbs some of the best farmland.

The mechanics of urban growth work like this. As land prices increase on the edge of an urban area, so the implicit cost of farming increases. It doesn't matter whether the farmer owns the land or not. Because land is a form of capital used to run the business, keeping one's land as a farm instead of selling it to a developer constitutes an implicit cost of capital. Higher land prices increase the implicit cost of capital, which raises the cost of farming—even if the farmer owns the land. This puts intense pressure on farmers to generate incomes that are substantial enough to justify keeping the land in agriculture. Eventually, these pressures become too great and the land is sold for development.

How great are these pressures? Well, farmland in Canada can sell for anything from $100 to $100,000 an acre, depending on its quality and location. Around small urban centres, one would expect to pay about $7000 an acre for good farmland in 2004, depending on the province. But around large metropolitan areas, prices are much higher. For example, a farm within 30 miles of the greater Toronto area, where urban development is foreseeable within the next 5 to 10 years, would command prices of about $100,000 an acre. It's nearly impossible to operate a farm with such a high implicit cost of capital. That's why developers succeed in buying up land where development is foreseen many years before the development takes place. They buy it and hold it as an investment—a so-called "land bank".

Before we get too alarmed about urban sprawl, we should note that urban areas do need space to grow. We should be happy we've got it. Moreover, we should bear in mind that much of the decrease in the amount of land devoted to farming over the last 100 years has nothing to do with the growth of urban centres. Rather, it is due to the replacement of the horse with the tractor as the primary farm vehicle, which reduced the amount of land needed to produce hay and led to the abandonment of much pastureland.

Nevertheless, all provinces feel the need to control urban sprawl in various ways. Most attempt to do this through zoning regulations and urban plans created by the municipality or local service district. The big drawback with this approach is that farmers comprise only about 3% of the rural population, so rural zoning laws may not offer much effective protection against urban development. Partly as a result of this problem, British Columbia set up an Agricultural Land Reserve in the 1970s. In essence, this took zoning decisions out of local hands and put them under provincial jurisdiction, and it has been very effective in preventing urban sprawl around southwestern BC and the Okanagan Valley.

But there are other options for controlling urban sprawl. For example, New Brunswick has a farmland identification program under which provincial property taxes can be deferred indefinitely while the land remains farmland; but should the land be abandoned or developed, the last 15 years' worth of property taxes (plus accrued interest) becomes due immediately. Another method, more common in the U.S. than in Canada, is to sell the development rights to a trust. Any developer must then not only buy the land from the farmer but also must buy the development rights from the trust. This insulates the farmer against increases in the implicit cost of capital due to higher land prices caused by impending development. Moreover, farmers benefit from the money they receive from selling the development rights to the land trust, but can meanwhile continue to use the land for agriculture.

So, the main point is two-pronged: first, high implicit costs of capital put enormous pressure on farmers to sell their land to urban developers; and second, attempts to contain this pressure use zoning, farmland identification programs, and land trusts. ■

>> QUICK REVIEW

- All costs are opportunity costs. They can be divided into *explicit costs* and *implicit costs.*
- Companies report their *accounting profit,* which is not necessarily equal to their *economic profit.*
- Due to the *implicit cost of capital,* the opportunity cost of a company's *capital,* and the opportunity cost of the owner's time, economic profit is often substantially less than accounting profit.

>>CHECK YOUR UNDERSTANDING 7-1

Karma and Don run a furniture-refinishing business from their home. Which of the following represent an explicit cost of the business and which represent an implicit cost?

a. Supplies such as paint stripper, varnish, polish, sandpaper, and so on
b. Basement space that has been converted into a workroom
c. Wages paid to a part-time helper
d. A van that they inherited and use only for transporting furniture
e. The job at a larger furniture restorer that Karma gave up in order to run the business

Solutions appear at back of book.

Making "How Much" Decisions: The Role of Marginal Analysis

As the story of the two wars at the beginning of this chapter demonstrated, there are two types of decisions: "either–or" decisions and "how much" decisions. To help you get a better sense of that distinction, Table 7-3 offers some examples of each kind of decision.

TABLE 7-3

"How Much" versus "Either–Or" Decisions

"How much" decisions	"Either–or" decisions
How many days before you do your laundry?	Tide or Cheer?
How many miles do you go before an oil change in your car?	Buy a car or not?
How many jalapenos on your nachos?	An order of nachos or a sandwich?
How many workers should you hire in your company?	Run your own business or work for someone else?
How much should a patient take of a drug that generates side effects?	Prescribe drug A or drug B for your patients?
How many troops do you allocate to your invasion force?	Invade at Calais or in Normandy?

Although many decisions in economics are "either–or", many others are "how much". Not many people will stop driving if the price of gasoline goes up, but many people will drive less. How much less? A rise in wheat prices won't necessarily persuade a lot of people to take up farming for the first time, but it will persuade farmers who were already growing wheat to plant more. How much more?

To understand "how much" decisions, we use an approach known as *marginal analysis.* Marginal analysis involves comparing the benefit of doing a little bit more of some activity with the cost of doing a little bit more of that activity. The benefit of doing a little bit more of something is what economists call its *marginal benefit,* and the cost of doing a little bit more of something is what they call its *marginal cost.*

Why is this called "marginal" analysis? A margin is an edge; what you do in marginal analysis is push out the edge a bit, and see whether that is a good move.

We will begin our study of marginal analysis by focusing on marginal cost, and we'll do that by considering a hypothetical company called Felix's Lawn-mowing Service, operated by Felix himself with his tractor-mower.

Marginal Cost

Felix is a very hardworking individual; if he works continuously, he can mow 7 lawns in a day. It takes him an hour to mow each lawn. The opportunity cost of an hour of Felix's time is $10.00 because he could make that much in his next best job.

His one and only mower, however, presents a problem when Felix works this hard. Running his mower for longer and longer periods on a given day takes an increasing toll on the engine and ultimately necessitates more—and more costly—maintenance and repairs.

The second column of Table 7-4 shows how the total daily cost of Felix's business depends on the quantity of lawns he mows in a day. For simplicity, we assume that Felix's only costs are the opportunity cost of his time and the cost of upkeep for his mower.

TABLE 7-4

Felix's Marginal Cost of Mowing Lawns

Quantity of lawns mowed	Felix's total cost	Felix's marginal cost of lawns mowed
0	$0	
		$10.50
1	10.50	
		11.25
2	21.75	
		13.25
3	35.00	
		15.50
4	50.50	
		18.00
5	68.50	
		20.75
6	89.25	
		23.75
7	$113.00	

At only 1 lawn per day, Felix's daily cost is $10.50: $10.00 for an hour of his time plus $0.50 for some oil. At 2 lawns per day, his daily cost is $21.75: $20 for 2 hours of his time and $1.75 for mower repair and maintenance. At 3 lawns per day, the daily cost has risen to $35.00: $30.00 for 3 hours of his time and $5.00 for mower repair and maintenance.

The third column of Table 7-4 contains the cost incurred by Felix for each *additional* lawn he mows, calculated from information in the second column. The 1st lawn he mows costs him $10.50; this number appears in the third column between the lines representing 0 lawns and 1 lawn because $10.50 is Felix's cost of going from 0 to 1 lawn mowed. The next lawn, going from 1 to 2, costs him an additional $11.25. So $11.25 appears in the third column between the lines representing the 1st and 2nd lawns, and so on.

The **marginal cost** of an activity is the additional cost incurred by doing one more unit of that activity.

There is **increasing marginal cost** from an activity when each additional unit of the activity costs more than the previous unit.

The increase in Felix's cost when he mows one more lawn is his **marginal cost** of lawn-mowing. In general, the marginal cost of any activity is the additional cost incurred by doing one more unit of that activity.

The marginal costs shown in Table 7-4 have a clear pattern: Felix's marginal cost is greater the more lawns he has already mowed. That is, each time he mows a lawn, the additional cost of doing yet another lawn goes up. Felix's lawn-mowing business has what economists call **increasing marginal cost:** each additional lawn costs

Figure 7-1

The Marginal Cost Curve

The height of each bar is equal to the marginal cost of mowing the corresponding lawn. For example, the 1st lawn mowed has a marginal cost of $10.50, equal to the height of the bar extending from 0 to 1 lawn. The bars ascend in height, reflecting increasing marginal cost: each additional lawn is more costly to mow than the previous one. As a result, the marginal cost curve (drawn by plotting points in the top center of each bar) is upward sloping. >web...

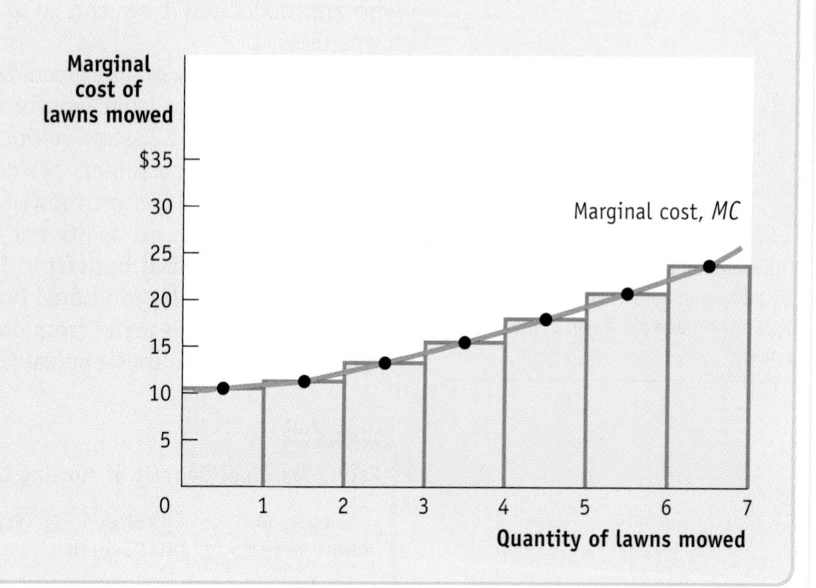

more to mow than the previous one. Or, to put it slightly differently, with increasing marginal cost, the marginal cost of an activity rises as the quantity already done rises.

Figure 7-1 is a graphical representation of the third column in Table 7-4. The horizontal axis measures the quantity of lawns mowed, and the vertical axis measures the marginal cost of a mowed lawn. The height of each shaded bar represents the marginal cost incurred by mowing a given lawn. For example, the bar stretching from 4 to 5 lawns is at a height of $18.00, equal to the cost of mowing the 5th lawn. Notice that the bars form a series of ascending steps, a reflection of the increasing marginal cost of lawn mowing. The **marginal cost curve,** the red curve in Figure 7-1, shows the relationship between marginal cost and the quantity of the activity already done. We draw it by plotting a point in the center at the top of each bar and connecting the points.

The **marginal cost curve** shows how the cost of undertaking one more unit of an activity depends on the quantity of that activity that has already been done.

The marginal cost curve is upward sloping, due to increasing marginal cost. Not all activities have increasing marginal cost; for example, it is possible for marginal cost to be the same regardless of the number of lawns already mowed. Economists call this case *constant* marginal cost. It is also possible for some activities to have a marginal cost that initially falls as we do more of the activity and then eventually rises. These sorts of activities involve gains from specialization: as more output is produced, more workers are hired, allowing each one to specialize in the task that he or she performs best. The gains from specialization yield a lower marginal cost of production.

Now that we have established the concept of marginal cost, we move to the parallel concept of marginal benefit.

PITFALLS

INCREASING TOTAL COST VERSUS INCREASING MARGINAL COST

The concept of *increasing marginal cost* plays an important role in economic analysis, but students sometimes get confused about what it means. That's because it is easy to wrongly conclude that whenever total cost is increasing, marginal cost must also be increasing. But the following example shows that this conclusion is misguided.

Suppose that we change the numbers of our example: the marginal cost of mowing the 6th lawn is now $20, and the marginal cost of mowing the 7th lawn is now $15. In both instances total cost increases as Felix does an additional lawn: it increases by $20 for the 6th lawn and by $15 for the 7th lawn. But in this example marginal cost is *decreasing:* the marginal cost of the 7th lawn is less than the marginal cost of the 6th lawn. So we have a case of increasing total cost and decreasing marginal cost. What this shows us is that, in fact, totals and marginals can sometimes move in opposite directions.

Marginal Benefit

Felix's business is in a town where some of the residents are very busy but others are not so busy. For people who are very busy, the opportunity cost of an hour of their time spent mowing the lawn is very high. So they are willing to pay Felix a fairly high sum to do it for them. People with lots of free time, however, have a lower opportunity cost of an hour of their time spent mowing the lawn. So they are willing to pay

Felix only a relatively small sum. And between these two extremes lie other residents who are moderately busy and so are willing to pay a moderate price to have their lawns mowed.

We'll assume that on any given day, Felix has one potential customer who will pay him $35 to mow her lawn, another who will pay $30, a third who will pay $26, a fourth who will pay $23, and so on. Table 7-5 lists what he can receive from each of his seven potential customers per day, in descending order according to price. So if Felix goes from 0 to 1 lawn mowed, he can earn $35; if he goes from 1 to 2 lawns mowed, he can earn an additional $30; and so on. The third column of Table 7-5 shows us the **marginal benefit** to Felix of each additional lawn mowed. In general, marginal benefit is the additional benefit derived from undertaking one more unit of an activity. Because it arises from doing one more lawn, each marginal benefit value appears between the lines associated with successive quantities of lawns.

The **marginal benefit** from an activity is the additional benefit derived from undertaking one more unit of that activity.

TABLE 7-5

Felix's Marginal Benefit of Mowing Lawns

Quantity of lawns mowed	Felix's total benefit	Felix's marginal benefit of lawns mowed
0	$0	
		$35.00
1	35.00	
		30.00
2	65.00	
		26.00
3	91.00	
		23.00
4	114.00	
		21.00
5	135.00	
		19.00
6	154.00	
		18.00
7	$172.00	

It's clear from Table 7-5 that the more lawns Felix has already mowed, the smaller his marginal benefit from mowing one more. So Felix's lawn-mowing business has what economists call **decreasing marginal benefit:** each additional lawn mowed produces less benefit than the previous lawn. Or, to put it slightly differently, with decreasing marginal benefit, the marginal benefit of an activity falls as the quantity already done rises.

There is **decreasing marginal benefit** from an activity when each additional unit of the activity produces less benefit than the previous unit.

The **marginal benefit curve** shows how the benefit from undertaking one more unit of an activity depends on the quantity of that activity that has already been done.

Just as marginal cost could be represented with a marginal cost curve, marginal benefit can be represented with a **marginal benefit curve,** shown in blue in Figure 7-2. The height of each bar shows the marginal benefit of each additional lawn mowed; the curve through the middle of each bar's top shows how the benefit of each additional unit of the activity depends on the number of units that have already been undertaken.

Felix's marginal benefit curve is downward sloping, because he faces decreasing marginal benefit from lawn-mowing. Not all activities have decreasing marginal benefit; in fact, there are many activities for which marginal benefit is constant—that is, it is the same regardless of the number of units already undertaken. In later chapters where we study firms, we will see that the shape of a firm's marginal benefit curve from producing output has important implications for how it behaves within its industry. We'll also see in Chapters 10 and 11 why economists assume that declining marginal benefit is the norm when considering choices made by consumers. Like increasing marginal cost, decreasing marginal benefit is so common that for now we can take it as the norm.

Now we are ready to see how the concepts of marginal benefit and marginal cost can be brought together to answer the question of "how much" of an activity an individual should undertake.

Figure 7-2

The Marginal Benefit Curve

The height of each bar is equal to the marginal benefit of mowing the corresponding lawn. For example, the 1st lawn mowed has a marginal benefit of $35, equal to the height of the bar extending from 0 to 1 lawn. The bars descend in height, reflecting decreasing marginal benefit: each additional lawn produces a smaller benefit than the previous one. As a result, the marginal benefit curve (drawn by plotting points in the top center of each bar) is downward sloping. >web...

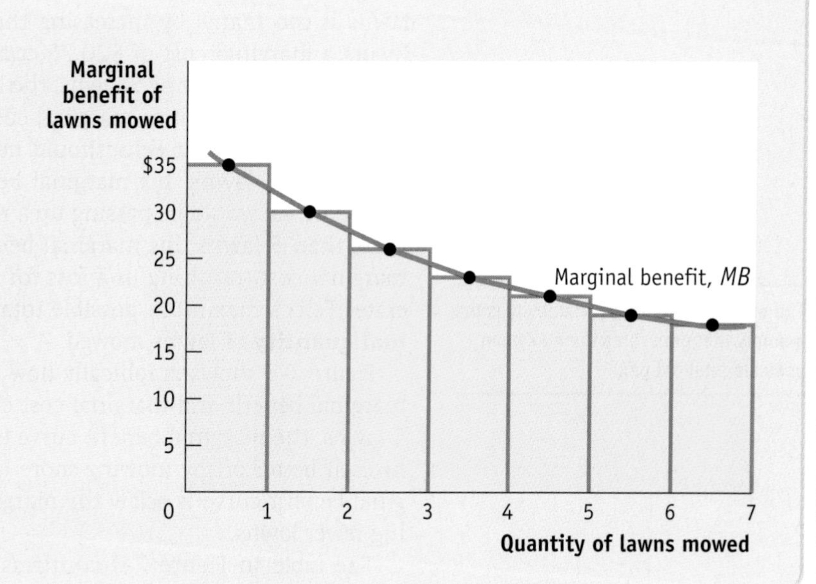

Marginal Analysis

Table 7-6 shows the marginal cost and marginal benefit numbers from Tables 7-4 and 7-5. It also adds an additional column: the net gain to Felix from one more lawn mowed, equal to the difference between the marginal benefit and the marginal cost.

We can use Table 7-6 to determine how many lawns Felix should mow. To see this, imagine for a moment that Felix planned to mow only 3 lawns today. We can immediately see that this is too small a quantity. If Felix mows an additional lawn, increasing the quantity of lawns mowed from 3 to 4, he realizes a marginal benefit of $23.00 and incurs a marginal cost of only $15.50—so his net gain would be $23 – $15.50 = $7.50. But even 4 lawns is still too few: if Felix increases the quantity from 4 to 5, his marginal benefit is $21.00 and his marginal cost is only $18.00, for a net gain of $21.00 – $18.00 = $3.00 (as indicated by the highlighting in the table).

But if Felix goes ahead and mows 7 lawns, that is too many. We can see this by looking at the net gain from mowing that 7th lawn: Felix's marginal benefit is $18.00, but his marginal cost is $23.75. So mowing that 7th lawn would produce a

TABLE 7-6

Felix's Net Gain from Mowing Lawns

Quantity of lawns mowed	Felix's marginal benefit of lawns mowed	Felix's marginal cost of lawns mowed	Felix's net gain of lawns mowed
0			
	$35.00	$10.50	$24.50
1			
	30.00	11.25	18.75
2			
	26.00	13.25	12.75
3			
	23.00	15.50	7.50
4			
	21.00	18.00	3.00
5			
	19.00	20.75	–1.75
6			
	18.00	23.75	–5.75
7			

net gain of \$18.00 – \$23.75 = –\$5.75; that is, a net *loss* for his business. And even 6 lawns is too many: by increasing the quantity of lawns mowed from 5 to 6, Felix incurs a marginal cost of \$20.75 compared with a marginal benefit of only \$19.00. He is best off at mowing 5 lawns, the largest quantity of lawns at which marginal benefit is at least as great as marginal cost.

The upshot is that Felix should mow 5 lawns—no more and no less. If he mows fewer than 5 lawns, his marginal benefit from one more is greater than his marginal cost; he would be passing up a net gain by not mowing more lawns. If he mows more than 5 lawns, his marginal benefit from the last lawn mowed is less than his marginal cost, resulting in a loss for that lawn. So 5 lawns is the quantity that generates Felix's maximum possible total net gain; it is what economists call the **optimal quantity** of lawns mowed.

The **optimal quantity** of an activity is the quantity that generates the maximum possible total net gain.

Figure 7-3 shows graphically how the optimal quantity can be determined. Felix's marginal benefit and marginal cost curves are both shown. If Felix mows fewer than 5 lawns, the marginal benefit curve is *above* the marginal cost curve, so he can make himself better off by mowing more lawns; if he mows more than 5 lawns, the marginal benefit curve is *below* the marginal cost curve, so he would be better off mowing fewer lawns.

The table in Figure 7-3 confirms our result. The second column repeats information from Table 7-6, showing marginal benefit minus marginal cost—or the net gain—for each lawn. The third column shows total net gain according to the quantity of lawns mowed. The total net gain after doing a given lawn is simply the sum of numbers in the second column up to and including that lawn. For example, the net

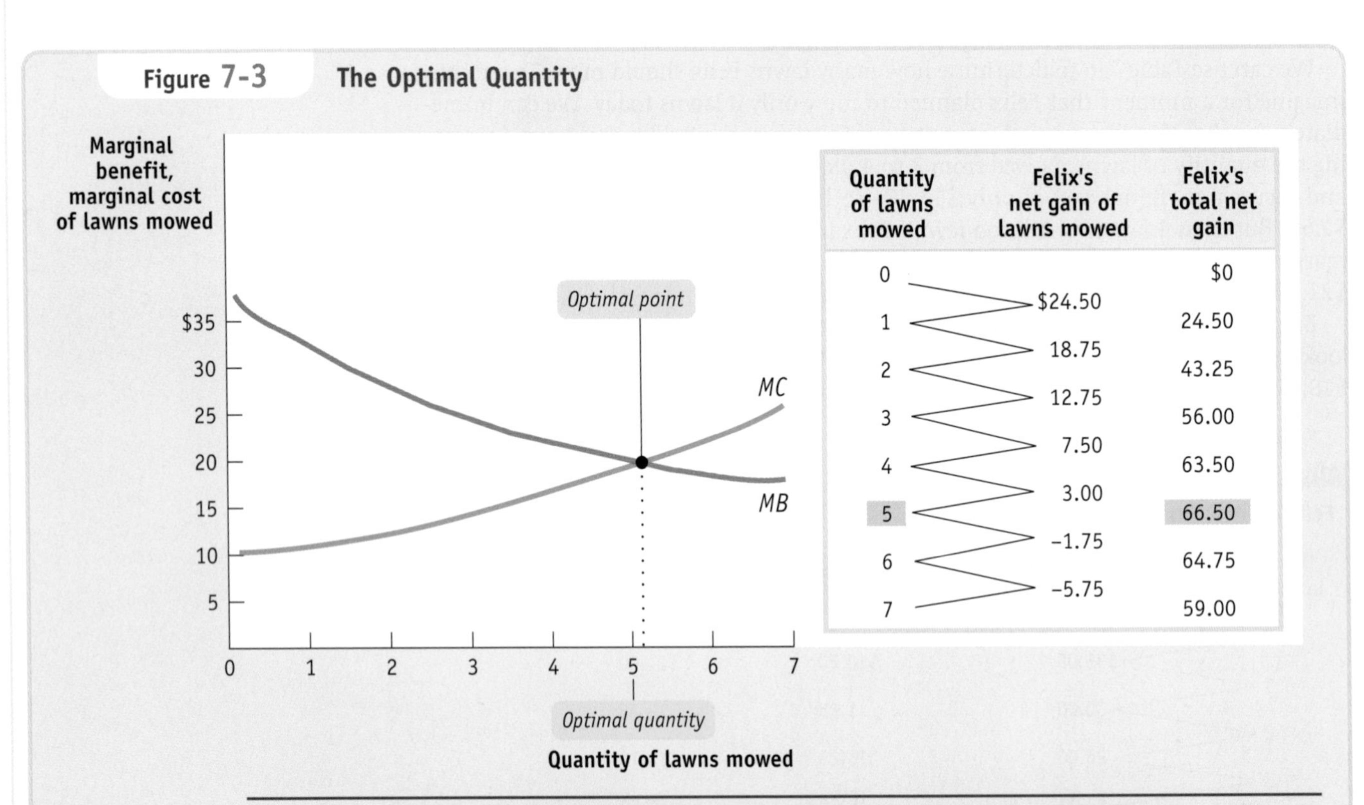

Quantity of lawns mowed	Felix's net gain of lawns mowed	Felix's total net gain
0		\$0
	\$24.50	
1		24.50
	18.75	
2		43.25
	12.75	
3		56.00
	7.50	
4		63.50
	3.00	
5		66.50
	–1.75	
6		64.75
	–5.75	
7		59.00

The optimal quantity of an activity is the quantity that generates the highest possible total net gain. It is the quantity at which marginal benefit is equal to marginal cost. Equivalently, it is the quantity at which the marginal benefit curve and the marginal cost curve intersect. Here they intersect at approximately 5 lawns. The table beside the graph confirms that 5 is indeed the optimal quantity: the total net gain is maximized at 5 lawns, generating \$66.50 in total net gain for Felix.

gain is $24.50 for the first lawn and $18.75 for the second. So the total net gain after doing the first lawn is $24.50, and the total net gain after doing the second lawn is $24.50 + $18.75 = $43.25. Our conclusion that 5 is the optimal quantity is confirmed by the fact that the greatest total net gain, $66.50, occurs when the 5th lawn is mowed.

The example of Felix's lawn-mowing business shows how you go about finding the optimal quantity: increase the quantity as long as the marginal benefit from one more unit is greater than the marginal cost, but stop before the marginal benefit becomes less than the marginal cost.

In many cases, however, it is possible to state this rule more simply. When a "how much" decision involves relatively large quantities, the rule simplifies to this: the optimal quantity is the quantity at which marginal benefit is equal to marginal cost.

To see why this is so, consider the example of a farmer who finds that her optimal quantity of wheat produced is 5,000 bushels. Typically, she will find that in going from 4,999 to 5,000 bushels, her marginal benefit is only very slightly greater than her marginal cost—that is, the difference between marginal benefit and marginal cost is close to zero. Similarly, in going from 5,000 to 5,001 bushels, her marginal cost is only very slightly greater than her marginal benefit—again, the difference between marginal cost and marginal benefit is very close to zero. So a simple rule for her in choosing the optimal quantity of wheat is to produce the quantity at which the difference between marginal benefit and marginal cost is approximately zero—that is, the quantity at which marginal benefit equals marginal cost.

PITFALLS

MUDDLED AT THE MARGIN

The idea of setting marginal benefit equal to marginal cost sometimes confuses people. Aren't we trying to maximize the *difference* between benefits and costs? And don't we wipe out our gains by setting benefits and costs equal to each other? But what we are doing is setting *marginal,* not *total,* benefit and cost equal to each other.

Once again, the point is to maximize the total net gain from an activity. If the marginal benefit from the activity is greater than the marginal cost, doing a bit more will increase that gain. If the marginal benefit is less than the marginal cost, doing a bit less will increase the total net gain. So only when the *marginal* benefit and cost are equal is the difference between *total* benefit and cost at a maximum.

Economists call this rule the **principle of marginal analysis.** It says that the optimal quantity of an activity is the quantity at which marginal benefit equals marginal cost. Graphically, the optimal quantity is the quantity of an activity at which the marginal benefit curve *intersects* the marginal cost curve. In fact, this graphical method works quite well even when the numbers involved aren't that large. For example, in Figure 7-3 the marginal benefit and marginal cost curves cross each other at about 5 lawns mowed—that is, marginal benefit equals marginal cost at about 5 lawns mowed, which we have already seen is Felix's optimal quantity.

The **principle of marginal analysis** says that the optimal quantity of an activity is the quantity at which marginal benefit is equal to marginal cost.

A Principle with Many Uses

The principle of marginal analysis can be applied to just about any "how much" decision—including those decisions where the benefits and costs are not necessarily expressed in dollars and cents. Here are a few examples:

- The number of traffic deaths can be reduced by spending more on highways, requiring better protection in cars, and so on. But these measures are expensive. So we can talk about the marginal cost to society of eliminating one more traffic fatality. And we can then ask whether the marginal benefit of that life saved is large enough to warrant doing this. (If you think no price is too high to save a life, see the following Economics in Action.)
- Many useful drugs have side effects that depend on the dosage. So we can talk about the marginal cost, in terms of these side effects, of increasing the dosage of a drug. The drug also has a marginal benefit in helping fight the disease. So the optimal quantity of the drug is the quantity that makes the best of this trade-off.
- Studying for an exam has costs because you could have done something else with the time, such as studying for another exam or sleeping. So we can talk about the marginal cost of devoting another hour to studying for your chemistry final. The optimal quantity of studying is the level at which the marginal benefit in terms of a higher grade is just equal to the marginal cost.

economics in action

The Cost of a Life

What's the marginal benefit to society of saving a human life? You might be tempted to answer that human life is infinitely precious. But in the real world, resources are scarce, so we must decide how much to spend on saving lives since we cannot spend infinite amounts. After all, we could surely reduce highway deaths by dropping the speed limit on major highways to 60 kilometres per hour, but the cost of such a lower speed limit—in time and money—is more than anyone is willing to pay.

Generally, people are reluctant to talk in a straightforward way about comparing the marginal cost of a life saved with the marginal benefit—it sounds too callous. Sometimes, however, the question becomes unavoidable.

For example, the cost of saving a life became an object of intense discussion in the United Kingdom in 1999, after a horrifying train crash near London's Paddington Station killed 31 people. There were accusations that the British government was spending too little on rail safety. However, the government estimated that improving rail safety would cost an additional $4.5 million per life saved. But if that amount was worth spending—that is, if the estimated marginal benefit of saving a life exceeded $4.5 million—then the implication was that the British government was spending way too little on *traffic safety.* The estimated marginal cost per life saved through highway improvements was only $1.5 million, making it a much better deal than saving lives through greater rail safety. ■

>> QUICK REVIEW

- A "how much" decision is made by using marginal analysis.
- The *marginal cost* of an activity is represented graphically by the *marginal cost curve.* An upward-sloping marginal cost curve reflects *increasing marginal cost.*
- The *marginal benefit* of an activity is represented by the *marginal benefit curve.* A downward-sloping marginal benefit curve reflects *decreasing marginal benefit.*
- The *optimal quantity* of an activity is found by applying the *principle of marginal analysis.* It says that the optimal quantity of an activity is the quantity at which marginal benefit is equal to marginal cost. Equivalently, it is the quantity at which the marginal cost curve intersects the marginal benefit curve.

>> CHECK YOUR UNDERSTANDING 7-2

1. In each of the "how much" decisions listed in Table 7-3, describe the nature of the marginal cost and of the marginal benefit.
2. Suppose that Felix's marginal cost, instead of increasing, is the same for every lawn he mows.
   a. Assume Felix's marginal cost is $18.50. Using Table 7-6, find the optimal quantity of mowed lawns. What is his total net gain?
   b. How high would marginal cost have to be such that Felix's optimal quantity of lawns mowed is 0? Can you specify a marginal cost for which the optimal quantity is 3?

Solutions appear at back of book.

Sunk Costs

When making decisions, knowing what to ignore is important. Although we have devoted much attention in this chapter to costs that are important to take into account when making a decision, some costs should be ignored when doing so. In this section we will focus on the kinds of costs that people should ignore—what economists call *sunk costs*—and why they should be ignored.

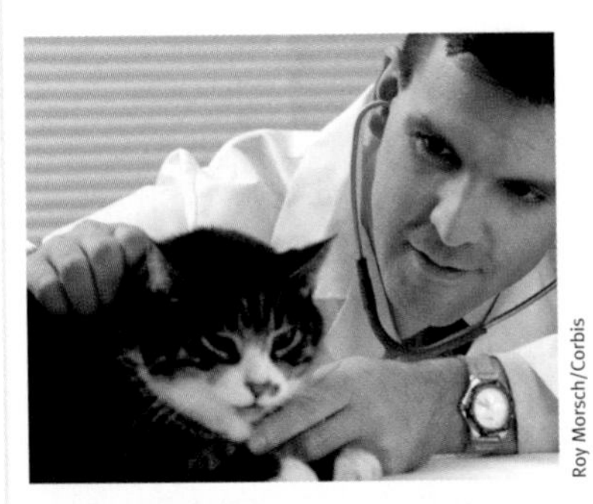

Roy Morsch/Corbis

This vet left law school to pursue his dream career. The cost for a year of law school was lost—a sunk cost. But he and his patients are now happy.

To gain some intuition, consider the following scenario. You own a car that is a few years old, and you have just replaced the brake pads at a cost of $250. But then you find out that the entire brake system is defective and must be replaced—including the newly installed brake pads. This will cost you an additional $1,500. Alternatively, you could sell the car and buy another of comparable quality, but with no brake defects, by spending an additional $1,600. What should you do: fix your old car, or sell it and buy another?

Some might say that you should take the latter option. After all, this line of reasoning goes, if you repair your car you will end up having spent $1,750: $1,500 for the brake system and $250 for the brake pads you replaced. If you were instead to sell your old car and buy another, you would spend only $1,600.

But this reasoning, although it sounds plausible, is wrong. It is wrong because it ignores the fact that you have *already* spent the amount of $250 on brake pads, and that $250 is *non-recoverable*. That is, having been spent already, the $250 cannot be recouped. Therefore, it should be ignored and should have no effect on your decision whether to repair your car and keep it or not. From an economist's viewpoint, the real cost at this time of repairing and keeping your car is $1,500 and not $1,750. Therefore, the correct decision is to repair your car and keep it rather than spend $1,600 on a new car.

In this example, the $250 that has already been spent and cannot be recovered is what economists call a **sunk cost.** Sunk costs should be ignored in making decisions about future actions because they have no influence on their costs and benefits. It's like the old saying, "There's no use crying over spilt milk": once something is gone and can't be recovered, it is irrelevant in making decisions about what to do in the future.

A **sunk cost** is a cost that has already been incurred and is non-recoverable. A sunk cost should be ignored in decisions about future actions.

It is often psychologically hard to ignore sunk costs. And if, in fact, the costs haven't yet been incurred, then they should be taken into consideration. That is, if you had known at the beginning that it would cost $1,750 to repair your car, then the right choice *at that time* would have been to buy a new car for $1,600. But once the $250 had already been paid for brake pads, it is no longer something that should be included in your decision making about your next actions. It may be hard to accept that "bygones are bygones", but it is the right thing to do.

economics in action

The Next Generation

In 2000 and early 2001, several European countries held "spectrum auctions", auctions in which telephone companies bid for portions of a country's airwave space. The telephone companies planned to use this airwave space to offer new mobile phone services to consumers. Companies believed they could earn large profits by providing these new services, so-called third-generation, or 3G, mobile phone services, which included features such as video calling and mobile Internet access. Eager to capture what they expected to be large future profits, telephone companies paid billions of dollars for portions of the European airwave space.

But some technology experts were worried. They believed that the companies had exaggerated expectations of future profits and, as a result, had paid too much for the airwave space. These experts feared that once the companies realized that the airwave space was worth much less than what they had paid, the companies would be unwilling to put up the additional money needed for physical infrastructure, such as the towers used to transmit the signals that are necessary to the 3G services.

It turned out that the technology experts were right about the exaggerated expectations: within a few months of the spectrum auctions, telephone companies realized that they had paid far more for the portions of airwave space than they were really worth.

But was the experts' second conjecture correct: would the overpayment for the airwaves really prevent the future investment needed to provide 3G services? The answer at this point is no. Several companies, including Vodaphone, the British company that owns a substantial part of the American company Verizon, have pushed ahead in building the required infrastructure. As of 2004, 3G was available in over 30 countries worldwide.

Technology experts were wrong about the effect of overpayment because they didn't understand the concept of sunk costs. That is, they didn't understand that once made, those payments for airwave space couldn't be recovered; therefore, they wouldn't affect the telephone companies' willingness to spend additional money to complete the project. After the companies came to the painful—and quite embarrassing—realization of their overpayment, it didn't change the fact that it was still profitable to build the infrastructure needed to provide the new services. In the end, they appear to have made the right economic calculation—and in the process admitted to themselves that there's no use crying over a lost billion or two. ■

< < < < < < < < < < < < < < < < < < <

>> QUICK REVIEW

- *Sunk costs*, costs that have already been incurred and that cannot be recovered, should be ignored in decisions regarding future actions. Because they have already been incurred and are unrecoverable, they have no influence on future costs and benefits.

>> CHECK YOUR UNDERSTANDING 7-3

1. You have decided to go into the ice-cream business and have bought a used ice-cream truck for $8,000. Now you are reconsidering. What is your sunk cost in the following scenarios?
   a. The truck cannot be resold.
   b. It can be resold, but only at a 50% discount.
2. You have gone through two years of medical school but are suddenly wondering whether you wouldn't be happier as a musician. Which of the following statements are potentially valid arguments and which are not?
   a. "I can't give up now, after all the time and money I've put in."
   b. "If I had thought about it from the beginning, I never would have gone to med school, so I should give it up now."
   c. "I wasted two years, but never mind—let's start from here."
   d. "My parents would kill me if I stopped now." (*Hint*: we're discussing *your* decision-making ability, not your parents'.)

Solutions appear at back of book.

The Concept of Present Value

In many cases, individuals must make decisions whose consequences extend some ways into the future. For example, when you decide to attend university, you are committing yourself to years of study, which you expect will pay off for the rest of your life. So the decision to attend university is the decision to embark on a long-term project.

As we have already seen, the basic rule in deciding whether or not to undertake a project is that you should compare the benefits of that project with its costs, implicit as well as explicit. But sometimes there can be a problem in making these comparisons: the benefits and costs of a project may not arrive at the same time.

Sometimes the costs of a project come at an earlier date than the benefits. For example, going to university involves large immediate costs: tuition, income forgone because you are in school, and so on. The benefits, such as a higher salary in your future career, come later, often much later.

In other cases, the benefits of a project come at an earlier date than the costs. If you take out a loan to pay for a vacation cruise, the satisfaction of the vacation will come immediately, but the burden of making payments will come later.

But why is time an issue?

Borrowing, Lending, and Interest

In general, having a dollar today is worth more than having a dollar a year from now. To see why, let's consider two examples.

First, suppose that you get a new job that comes with a $1,000 bonus, which will be paid at the end of the first year. But you would like to spend the extra money now—say, on new clothes for work. Can you do that?

The answer is yes—you can borrow money today, and use the bonus to repay the debt a year from now. But if that is your plan, you cannot borrow the full $1,000 today. You must borrow less than that, because a year from now you will have to repay the amount borrowed *plus interest*.

Now consider a different scenario. Suppose that you are paid a bonus of $1,000 today, and you decide that you don't want to spend the money right now. What do you do with it? You put it in the bank; in effect, you are lending the $1,000 to the bank, which in turn lends it out to its customers who wish to borrow. At the end of a year, you will get more than $1,000 back—you will have the $1,000 plus the interest earned.

What all of this means is that $1,000 today is worth more than $1,000 a year from now. The reason is that if you want to have the money today, you must borrow it and pay interest. That is, you must pay a price for using the money today. And, correspondingly, if you forgo using the money today and lend it to someone else, you earn interest on the money. That is, you earn something by letting someone else use your money. When someone borrows money for a year, the **interest rate** is the price, calculated as a percentage of the amount borrowed, charged by the lender.

When someone borrows money for a year, the **interest rate** is the price, calculated as a percentage of the amount borrowed, charged by the lender.

Because of the interest paid on borrowing, you can't evaluate a project just by adding up all the costs and benefits when those costs and benefits arrive at different times. You must take time into account when evaluating the project because a $1 benefit that comes today is worth more than a $1 benefit that comes a year from now; and a $1 cost that comes today is more burdensome to you than a $1 cost that comes next year. Fortunately, there is a simple way to adjust for these complications.

What we will now see is that the interest rate can be used to convert future benefits and costs into what economists call their *present values*. By using present values in evaluating a project, you can evaluate a project *as if* all its costs and benefits were occurring today rather than at different times. This allows people to "factor out" the complications created by time. We'll start by defining exactly what the concept of present value is.

Defining Present Value

The key to the concept of present value is to understand that you can use the interest rate to compare the value of a dollar realized today with the value of a dollar realized later. Why the interest rate? Because the interest rate correctly measures the cost of delaying a dollar of benefit and, correspondingly, the benefit of delaying a dollar of cost. Let's illustrate this with some examples.

Suppose, first, that you are evaluating whether or not to take a job in which your employer promises to pay you a bonus at the end of the first year. What is the value to you today of $1 of bonus money to be paid to you one year in the future? A slightly different way of asking the same question: what would you be willing to accept today in place of receiving $1 one year in the future?

The way to answer this question is to observe that you need *less* than $1 today in order to be assured of having $1 one year from now. Why? Because any money that you have today can be lent out at interest, turning it into a greater sum at the end of the year.

The symbol r is used to represent the rate of interest, expressed as a fraction—that is, if the interest rate is 10%, then $r = 0.10$. If you lend out $X, at the end of a year you will receive your $X back, plus the interest on your $X, which is $\$X \times r$. Thus, at the end of the year you will receive $\$X + \$X \times r$, which is $\$X \times (1 + r)$. What we want to know is how much you would have to lend out today to have $1 a year from now. If the amount you lend out is $X, it must be true that

(7-1) $$\$X \times (1 + r) = \$1$$

Rearranging, we can solve for $X, the amount you need today in order to generate $1 one year from now.

(7-2) $$\$X = \$1/(1 + r)$$

This means that you would be willing to accept $X today for every $1 to be paid one year from now. The reason is that by lending out $X today, you can be assured of having $1 one year from now. If we plug into the equation the value of the yearly interest rate—say it is 10%, which means that $r = 0.10$—then we can solve for $X: $X

The **present value** of \$1 realized one year from now is equal to \$1/(1 + *r*): the amount of money you must lend out today in order to have \$1 in one year. It is the value to you today of \$1 realized one year from now.

is equal to \$1/1.10, which is approximately \$0.91. So you would be willing to accept \$0.91 today in exchange for every \$1 to be paid to you one year from now. Economists have a special name for \$X—it's called the **present value** of \$1.

To see that this technique works for future costs as well as future benefits, consider the following example. Suppose you enter into an agreement that obliges you to pay \$1 one year from now—say to pay off your student loan when you graduate in a year. How much money would you need today to ensure that you have \$1 in a year? The answer is \$X, the present value of \$1, which in our example is \$0.91. The reason \$0.91 is the right answer is that if you lend it out for one year at an interest rate of 10%, you will receive \$1 in return at the end.

What these two examples show us is that the present value concept provides a way to calculate the value today of \$1 that is realized in the future—regardless of whether that \$1 is realized as a benefit (the bonus) or a cost (the student loan payback). This means that to evaluate a project today that has benefits and/or costs to be realized in the future, we just use the relevant interest rate to convert those future dollars into their present values. In that way, we have "factored out" the complication that time creates for decision making.

In the next section we will work out an example of using the present value concept to evaluate a project. But before we do that, it is worthwhile to note that the present value method can be used for projects in which the \$1 is realized more than a year later—say two, three, or even more years.

Suppose you are considering a project that will pay you \$1 *two* years from today. What is the value to you today of \$1 received two years into the future? We can find the answer to that question by expanding our formula for present value.

Let's call \$V the amount of money you need to lend today at an interest rate of r in order to have \$1 in two years. So if you lend \$V today, you will receive $\$V \times (1 + r)$ in one year. And if you *re-lend* that sum for yet another year, you will receive $\$V \times (1 + r) \times (1 + r) = \$V \times (1 + r)^2$ at the end of the second year. At the end of two years, \$V will be worth $\$V \times (1 + r)^2$; if $r = 0.10$, then this becomes $\$V \times (1.10)^2 = \$V \times (1.21)$.

Now we are ready to answer the question of what \$1 realized two years in the future is worth today. In order for the amount lent today, \$V, to be worth \$1 two years from now, it must satisfy this formula:

(7-3) $$\$V \times (1 + r)^2 = \$1$$

Rearranging, we can solve for \$V:

(7-4) $$\$V = \$1/(1 + r)^2$$

Given $r = 0.10$, this means that $\$V = \$1/1.21 = \$0.83$. So when the interest rate is 10%, \$1 realized two years from today is worth \$0.83 today because by lending out \$0.83 today you can be assured of having \$1 in two years. And that means that the present value of \$1 realized two years into the future is \$0.83.

From this example we can see how the present value concept can be expanded to a number of years even greater than two. If we ask what value of \$1 realized *N* number of years into the future is, the answer is given by a generalization of the present value formula: it is equal to $\$1/(1 + r)^N$.

Using Present Value

Suppose you have to choose one of three projects to undertake. Project A has an immediate payoff to you of \$100, while project B requires that you put up \$10 of your own money today in order to receive \$115 a year from now. Project C gives you an immediate payoff of $119 but requires that you pay $20 a year from now. We'll assume that the annual interest rate is 10%—that is, $r = 0.10$.

The problem in evaluating these three projects is that they have costs and benefits that are realized at different times. That is, of course, where the concept of present value becomes extremely helpful: by using present value to convert any dollars realized in the future into today's value, you factor out the issue of time. This allows you to calculate the **net present value** of a project—the present value of current and future benefits minus the present value of current and future costs. And the best project is the one with the highest net present value.

The **net present value** of a project is the present value of today's and future benefits minus the present value of today's and future costs.

Table 7-7 shows how this is done for each of the three projects. The second and third columns show how many dollars are realized and when they are realized; costs are indicated by a minus sign. The fourth column shows the equations used to convert the flows of dollars into their present value, and the fifth column shows the actual amounts of the total net present value for each of the three projects.

TABLE 7-7

The Net Present Value of Three Projects

Project	Dollars realized today	Dollars realized one year from today	Present value formula	Net present value given $r = 0.10$
A	$100	—	$100	$100.00
B	−$10	$115	$-\$10 + \$115/(1 + r)$	$94.55
C	$119	−$20	$\$119 - \$20/(1 + r)$	$100.82

For instance, to calculate the net present value of project B, we need to calculate the present value of $115 received in one year. The present value of $1 received in one year would be $\$1/(1 + r)$. So the present value of $115 is 115 times $\$1/(1 + r)$; that is, $\$115/(1 + r)$. The net present value of project B is the present value of today's and future benefits minus the present value of today's and future costs: $-\$10 + \$115/(1 + r)$.

From the fifth column, we can immediately see which is the preferred project—it is project C. That's because it has the highest net present value, $100.82, which is higher than the net present value of project A ($100) and much higher than the net present value of project B ($94.55).

This example shows how important the concept of present value is. If we had failed to use the present value calculations and instead had simply added up the dollars generated by each of the three projects, we could have easily been misled into believing that project B was the best project and project C was the worst one.

economics in action

Should You Take the "Set for Life" or the "Cash Out" Option?

Many lotteries in Canada are organised nationally through the Interprovincial Lotteries Corporation. Both Lotto 649 and Super 7 are national lotteries offering large one-time tax-free winnings. Other lotteries are run provincially and geared to specific regional tastes. However, one common game offers the winner a fixed sum over an extended period of time. For example, Loto-Québec has a game called "La Grande Vie" which pays the lucky winner $100,000 each year for life; in Ontario the game is called "Cash for Life" and pays out $2000 a week for life; and in Atlantic Canada and British Columbia, the game is called "Set for Life" and pays out $1000 a week for 25 years. This adds up to a cool $1.3 million ($\$1000 \times 52 \times 25$); hence the name "Set for Life." In all these cases, the lottery corporation in question offers a "cash-out" option.

For example, the Atlantic Lottery Corporation routinely offers a one-time upfront cash payment of $675,000 instead of the weekly payments. Even though this seems like a stingy amount for a quick payoff, most lucky winners have chosen this "cash-out" option instead of the weekly payments. Are they making good decisions? What would you do?

As economics students, we should calculate the present value of the "set for life" income stream. There are two stages to this. First, we suppose we invest each $1000 payment, and calculate the amount we would have after 25 years, including all the interest earned. In the second stage, we take this amount and discount it back to the present to find its present value. While stage one is quite laborious, these calculations are not that difficult with a calculator or computer. But the result depends crucially on the interest rate used.

It turns out that the present value of the "Set for Life" income stream of $1000 per week for 25 years equals the cash-out option of $675,000 at an interest rate of 6½ percent. At higher interest rates, the cash-out option is worth more; at lower interest rates, the income stream is worth more. In April 2004, the yield on long-term government of Canada bonds was only 4.8 percent; therefore, the best decision at that time was to take the income stream. So, why have most winners chosen the cash-out option?

The most likely explanation is they were just impatient to get all the money as quickly as possible. But in that case, they should have taken the income stream and borrowed the $675,000 at 4.8%. Their weekly payments on this loan would be less than their weekly lottery payments. That's called having your cake and eating it too. See how useful a bit of economics can be? ■

< < < < < < < < < < < < < < < < < <

>>QUICK REVIEW

- When costs or benefits arrive at different times, you must take the complication created by time into account. This is done by transforming any dollars realized in the future into their *present value.*
- $1 in benefit realized a year from now is worth $1/(1 + r) today, where *r* is the *interest rate.* Similarly, $1 in cost realized a year from now is valued at a cost of $1/(1 + r) today.
- When comparing several projects in which costs and benefits arrive at different times, you should choose the project that generates the highest *net present value.*

>>CHECK YOUR UNDERSTANDING 7-4

1. Consider the three alternative projects shown in Table 7-7. This time, however, suppose that the interest rate is only 2%.
   a. Calculate the net present values of the three projects. Which one is now preferred?
   b. Explain why the preferred choice is different with a 2% interest rate than with a 10% rate.

Solutions appear at back of book.

• A LOOK AHEAD •

This chapter laid out the basic concepts that we need to understand economic decisions. These concepts, as we will soon see, provide the necessary tools for understanding not only the behaviour behind the supply and demand curves, but also the implications of markets for consumer and producer welfare.

But to get there we need a bit more context—we need to know something more about the kinds of decisions that producers and consumers must make. We start with producers: in the next two chapters we will see how marginal analysis determines how much a profit-maximizing producer chooses to produce.

SUMMARY

1. All economic decisions involve the allocation of scarce resources. Some decisions are "either–or" decisions, in which the question is whether or not to do something. Other decisions are "how much" decisions, in which the question is how many resources to put into some use.
2. The cost of using a resource for a particular activity is the opportunity cost of that resource. Some opportunity costs are **explicit costs;** they involve a direct payment of cash. Other opportunity costs, however, are **implicit costs;** they involve no outlay of money but represent the inflows of cash that are forgone. Both explicit and implicit costs should be taken into account in making decisions. Companies use **capital** and their owners' time. So companies should base decisions on **economic profit,** which takes into account implicit costs such as the opportunity cost of the owners' time and the **implicit**

cost of capital. The **accounting profit,** which companies calculate for the purposes of taxes and public reporting, is often considerably larger than the economic profit because it includes only explicit costs and depreciation, not implicit costs.

3. A "how much" decision is made using marginal analysis, which involves comparing the benefit to the cost of doing an additional unit of an activity. The **marginal cost** of an activity is the additional cost incurred by doing one more unit of the activity, and the **marginal benefit** of an activity is the additional benefit gained by doing one more unit. The **marginal cost curve** is the graphical illustration of marginal cost, and the **marginal benefit curve** is the graphical illustration of marginal benefit.
4. Marginal cost and marginal benefit typically depend on how much of the activity has already been done. In the case of **increasing marginal cost,** each additional unit costs more than the unit before; this is represented by an upward-sloping marginal cost curve. In the case of **decreasing marginal benefit,** each additional unit produces a smaller benefit than the unit before; this is represented by a downward-sloping marginal benefit curve.
5. The **optimal quantity** of an activity is the quantity that generates the maximum possible total net gain. According to the **principle of marginal analysis,** the optimal quantity is the quantity at which marginal benefit is equal to marginal cost. It is the quantity at which the marginal cost curve and the marginal benefit curve intersect.
6. A cost that has already been incurred and that is nonrecoverable is a **sunk cost.** Sunk costs should be ignored in decisions about future actions because they have no effect on future benefits and costs.
7. In order to evaluate a project in which costs or benefits are realized in the future, you must first transform them into their **present values** using the **interest rate,** r. The present value of \$1 realized one year from now is $\$1/(1 + r)$, the amount of money you must lend out today to have \$1 one year from now. Once this transformation is done, you should choose the project with the highest **net present value.**

KEY TERMS

Explicit cost, p. 171
Implicit cost, p. 171
Accounting profit, p. 173
Economic profit, p. 173
Capital, p. 173
Implicit cost of capital, p. 173
Marginal cost, p. 176
Increasing marginal cost, p. 176
Marginal cost curve, p. 177
Marginal benefit, p. 178
Decreasing marginal benefit, p. 178
Marginal benefit curve, p. 178
Optimal quantity, p. 180
Principle of marginal analysis, p. 181
Sunk cost, p.183
Interest rate, p. 185
Present value, p. 186
Net present value, p. 187

PROBLEMS

1. Scott owns and operates a small business that provides economic consulting services. During the year he spends \$55,000 on travel to clients and other expenses, and the computer that he owns depreciates by \$2,000. If he didn't use the computer, he could sell it and earn yearly interest of \$100 on the money created through this sale. Scott's total revenue for the year is \$100,000. Instead of working as a consultant for the year, he could teach economics at a small local college and make a salary of \$50,000.
   a. What is Scott's accounting profit?
   b. What is Scott's economic profit?
   c. Should Scott continue working as a consultant, or should he teach economics instead?
2. Jackie owns and operates a web-design business. Her computing equipment depreciates by \$5,000 per year. She runs the business out of a room in her home. If she didn't use the room as her business office, she could rent it out for \$2,000 per year. Jackie knows that if she didn't run her own business, she could return to her previous job at a large software company that would pay her a salary of \$60,000 per year. Jackie has no other expenses.
   a. How much total revenue does Jackie need to make in order to break even in the eyes of her accountant? That is, how much total revenue would give Jackie just zero accounting profit?
   b. How much total revenue does Jackie need to make in order for her to want to remain self-employed? That is, how much total revenue would give Jackie just zero economic profit?
3. You own and operate a bike store. Each year, you receive revenue of \$200,000 from your bike sales, while it costs you \$100,000 to obtain the bikes. In addition, you pay \$20,000 for electricity, taxes, and other expenses per year. Instead of running the bike store, you could become an accountant and receive a yearly salary of \$40,000. A large clothing retail chain wants to expand and offers to rent the store from you for \$50,000 per year. How do you explain to your friends that despite making a profit, it is too costly for you to continue running your store?

4. Suppose you have just paid your non-refundable fees of $1,000 for your meal plan for this academic term. This allows you to eat dinner in the cafeteria every evening.

   a. You are offered a part-time job in a restaurant where you can eat for free each evening. Your parents say that you should eat dinner in the cafeteria anyway, since you have already paid for those meals. Are your parents right? Explain why or why not.

   b. Now suppose that you are offered a part-time job in a restaurant, but rather than being able to eat there for free, the restaurant only gives you a large discount on your meals there. Each meal at the restaurant will cost you $2, and if you eat there each evening this semester it will add up to $200. Your roommate says that you should eat in the restaurant since it costs less than the $1,000 that you paid for the meal plan. Is your roommate right? Explain why or why not.

5. You have already bought a $10 ticket for the university soccer game in advance. The ticket cannot be resold. You know that going to the soccer game will give you a benefit equal to $20. After you have bought the ticket to the soccer game, you hear that there will be a professional baseball post-season game at the same time. Tickets to the baseball game cost $20, and you know that going to the baseball game will give you a benefit equal to $35. You tell your friends the following: "If I had known about the baseball game before buying the ticket to the soccer game, I would have gone to the baseball game instead. But now that I have the ticket to the soccer game already, it's better for me to just go to the soccer game." Are you making the correct decision? Justify your answer by calculating the benefits and costs of your decision.

6. Amy, Bill, and Carla all mow lawns for money. Each of them operates a different lawnmower. The accompanying table shows the total cost to Amy, Bill, and Carla of mowing lawns.

Quantity of lawns mowed	Amy's total cost	Bill's total cost	Carla's total cost
0	$0	$0	$0
1	20	10	2
2	35	20	7
3	45	30	17
4	50	40	32
5	52	50	52
6	53	60	82

   a. Calculate Amy's, Bill's, and Carla's marginal costs, and draw each of their marginal cost curves.

   b. Who has increasing marginal cost, who has decreasing marginal cost, and who has constant marginal cost?

7. You are the manager of a gym, and you have to decide how many customers to admit each hour. Assume that each customer stays exactly one hour. Customers are costly to admit because they inflict wear and tear on the exercise equipment. Moreover, each additional customer generates more wear and tear than the customer before. As a result, the gym faces increasing marginal cost. The table below shows the marginal costs associated with each number of customers per hour.

Quantity of customers per hour	Marginal cost of customer
0	
	$14.00
1	
	14.50
2	
	15.00
3	
	15.50
4	
	16.00
5	
	16.50
6	
	17.00
7	

   a. Suppose that each customer pays $15.25 for a one-hour workout. Use the principle of marginal analysis to find the optimal number of customers that you should admit per hour.

   b. You increase the price of a one-hour workout to $16.25. What is the optimal number of customers per hour that you should admit now?

8. Georgia and Lauren are economics students who go to a karate class together. Both have to choose how many classes to go to per week. Each class costs $20. The table below shows Georgia's and Lauren's estimates of the marginal benefit that each of them gets from each class per week.

Quantity of classes	Lauren's marginal benefit of each class	Georgia's marginal benefit of each class
0		
	$23	$28
1		
	19	22
2		
	14	15
3		
	8	7
4		

   a. Use marginal analysis to find Lauren's optimal number of karate classes per week.

   b. Will Georgia be willing to go to the same number of classes per week that are optimal for Lauren?

9. Recently, the Atlanta-based Center for Disease Control and Prevention (CDC) recommended against vaccination of the whole population of the United States against the smallpox virus because the vaccination has undesirable, and sometimes

fatal, side effects. Suppose the accompanying table gives the available data about the effects of a smallpox vaccination program.

Percent of population vaccinated	Deaths due to smallpox	Deaths due to vaccination side effects
0	200	0
10	180	4
20	160	10
30	140	18
40	120	33
50	100	50
60	80	74

a. Calculate the marginal benefit (in terms of lives saved) and the marginal cost (in terms of lives lost) of each 10% increment of smallpox vaccination. Calculate the net gain of a 10% increment in population vaccinated.

b. Using marginal analysis, decide what percentage of the population should optimally be vaccinated.

10. Patty delivers pizza using her own car, and she is paid according to how many pizzas she delivers. The accompanying table shows Patty's total benefit and total cost when she works a specific number of hours.

Quantity of hours worked	Total benefit	Total cost
0	$0	$0
1	30	10
2	55	21
3	75	34
4	90	50
5	100	70

a. Use marginal analysis to decide how many hours Patty should work. In other words, what is the optimal number of hours Patty should work?

b. Calculate the total net gain to Patty from working 0 hours, 1 hour, 2 hours, and so on. Now suppose Patty chooses to work for 1 hour. Compare her total net gain from working for 1 hour with the total net gain from working the optimal number of hours. How much would she lose from working for only 1 hour?

11. Assume De Beers is the sole producer of diamonds. When it wants to sell more diamonds, it must lower its price in order to induce consumers to buy more. Furthermore, each additional diamond that is produced costs more than the previous one due to the difficulty of mining for diamonds. De Beers's total benefit schedule is given in the accompanying table, along with its total cost schedule.

Quantity of diamonds	Total benefit	Total cost
0	$0	$0
1	1,000	50
2	1,900	100
3	2,700	200
4	3,400	400
5	4,000	800
6	4,500	1,500
7	4,900	2,500
8	5,200	3,800

a. Draw the marginal cost curve and the marginal benefit curve and, from your diagram, graphically derive the optimal quantity of diamonds to produce.

b. Calculate the total net gain to De Beers from producing each quantity of diamonds. Which quantity gives De Beers the highest total net gain?

12. You have won the provincial lottery. There are two ways in which you can receive your prize: You can either have $1 million in cash now, or you can have $1.2 million that is paid out as follows: you get $300,000 now, $300,000 in one year's time, $300,000 in two years' time, and $300,000 in three years' time. The interest rate is 20%. How would you prefer to receive your prize?

13. The drug company Pfizer is considering whether to invest in the development of a new cancer drug. Development will require an initial investment of $10 million now; beginning one year from now, the new drug will generate annual profits of $4 million for three years.

a. If the interest rate is 12%, should Pfizer invest in the development of the new drug? Why or why not?

b. If the interest rate is 8%, should Pfizer invest in the development of the new drug? Why or why not?

>web... To continue your study and review of concepts in this chapter, please visit the Krugman/Wells website for quizzes, animated graph tutorials, web links to helpful resources, and more.

www.worthpublishers.com/krugmanwellsmyatt

chapter 8

Behind the Supply Curve: >> Inputs and Costs

THE FARMER'S MARGIN

THOUGH FARMERS ARE NOW ONLY A small minority of Canada's population, our agricultural industry is immensely productive and feeds much of the world. If you look at agricultural statistics, however, something may seem a bit surprising: when it comes to yield per hectare, Canadian farmers are often nowhere near the top. For example, farmers in western European countries grow about three times as much wheat per hectare as their Canadian counterparts. Are the Europeans better at growing wheat than we are?

No: European farmers are very skilful, but no more so than Canadians. They produce more wheat per hectare because they employ more inputs—more fertilizer and, especially, more labour—per hectare. Of course, this means that European farmers have higher costs than their Canadian counterparts. But because of government policies, European farmers receive a much higher price for their wheat than Canadian farmers. This gives them an incentive to use more inputs and to expend more effort at the margin to increase the crop yield per hectare.

Notice our use of the phrase "at the margin". Like most decisions that involve a comparison of benefits and costs, decisions about inputs and production involve a comparison of marginal quantities—the marginal cost versus the marginal benefit of producing a bit more from each hectare.

In Chapter 7 we used the example of Felix's Lawn-Mowing Service to illustrate the *principle of marginal analysis*, showing how Felix could use marginal analysis to determine the optimal number of lawns to mow daily—that is, the number that generates the maximum total net gain or profit.

What you will learn in this chapter:

- The importance of the firm's **production function**, the relationship between quantity of inputs and quantity of output
- Why production is often subject to **diminishing returns** to inputs
- What the various forms of a firm's costs are and how they generate the firm's **marginal** and **average cost curves**
- Why a firm's costs may differ in the **short run** versus the **long run**
- How the firm's technology of production can generate **economies of scale**

W. Wayne Lockwood, M. D./Corbis

Peter Dean/Agripicture/Grant Heilman Photography

Canadian farming practices (at left) or European farming practices (at right)? How intensively a hectare of land is worked—a decision at the margin—depends on the price of wheat a farmer faces.

In this chapter and in Chapter 9, we will show how marginal analysis can be used to understand the output decisions that lie behind the supply curve. The first step in this analysis is to show how the relationship between a firm's inputs and its output—its *production function*—determines its *cost curves,* the relationship between cost and quantity of output produced. That is what we do in this chapter. In Chapter 9, we will see how to go from the firm's cost curves to the supply curve.

The Production Function

A *firm* is an organization that produces goods or services for sale. To do this, it must transform inputs into output. The quantity of output a firm produces depends on the quantity of inputs; this relationship is known as the firm's **production function.** As we'll see, a firm's production function underlies its *cost curves*. But as a first step, let's look at the characteristics of a hypothetical production function.

A **production function** is the relationship between the quantity of inputs a firm uses and the quantity of output it produces.

Inputs and Output

To understand the concept of a production function, let's consider a farm that we assume, for the sake of simplicity, produces only one output, wheat, and uses only two inputs, land and labour. This particular farm is owned by a couple named George and Martha. They hire workers to do the actual physical labour on the farm. Moreover, we will assume that all potential workers are of the same quality—they are all equally knowledgeable and capable of performing farm work.

George and Martha's farm sits on 10 hectares of land; no more hectares are available to them, and they are currently unable to either increase or decrease the size of their farm by selling, buying, or leasing land. Land here is what economists call a **fixed input**—an input whose quantity is fixed and cannot be varied. On the other hand, George and Martha are free to decide how many workers to hire. The labour provided by these workers is called a **variable input**—an input whose quantity the firm can vary. (In Chapter 7, when we considered the example of Felix's Lawn-Mowing Service, Felix's fixed input was his lawn mower and his variable input was his own labour.)

A **fixed input** is an input whose quantity is fixed and cannot be varied.

A **variable input** is an input whose quantity the firm can vary.

In reality, whether or not the quantity of an input is really fixed depends on the time horizon. In the **long run**—that is, given that a long enough period of time has elapsed—firms can adjust the quantity of any input. So there are no fixed inputs in the long run, only in the **short run.** Later in this chapter we'll look more carefully at the distinction between the short run and the long run. But for now, we will restrict our attention to the short run and assume that at least one input is fixed.

The **long run** is the time period in which all inputs can be varied.

The **short run** is the time period in which at least one input is fixed.

George and Martha know that the quantity of wheat they produce depends on the number of workers they hire. Given modern farming techniques, one worker can cultivate the 10-hectare farm, albeit not very intensively. When an additional worker is added, the land is divided equally among all the workers: each worker has 5 hectares to cultivate when 2 workers are employed, each cultivates $3\frac{1}{3}$ hectares when 3 are employed, and so on. So as additional workers are employed, the 10 hectares of land are cultivated more intensively and more bushels of wheat are produced. The relationship between the quantity of labour and the quantity of output, for a given amount of the fixed input, constitutes the farm's production function. The production function for George and Martha's farm is given in the first two columns of the table in Figure 8-1 (page 194); the diagram there shows the same information graphically. The curve in Figure 8-1 shows how the quantity of output depends on the quantity of the variable input, for a given quantity of the fixed

Figure 8-1 **Production Function and Total Product Curve for George and Martha's Farm**

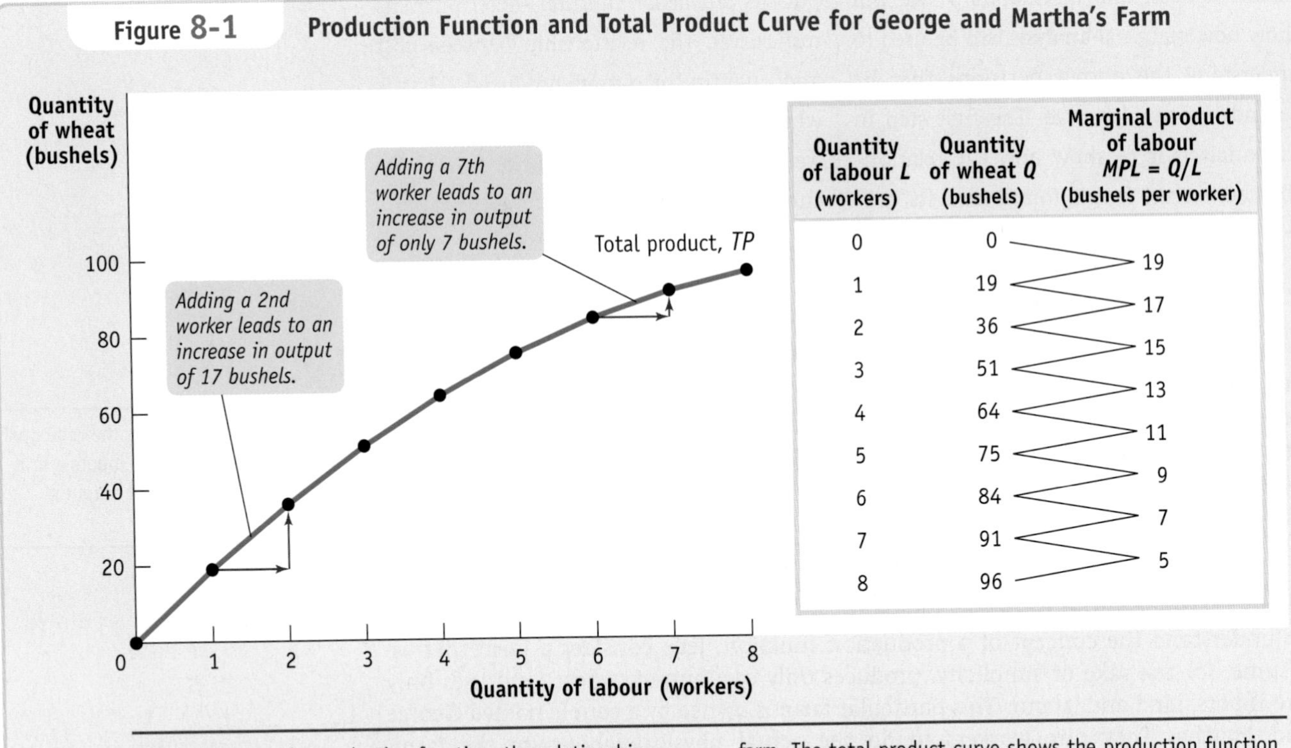

Quantity of labour L (workers)	Quantity of wheat Q (bushels)	Marginal product of labour $MPL = Q/L$ (bushels per worker)
0	0	
		19
1	19	
		17
2	36	
		15
3	51	
		13
4	64	
		11
5	75	
		9
6	84	
		7
7	91	
		5
8	96	

The table shows the production function, the relationship between the quantity of the variable input (labour, measured in number of workers) and the quantity of output (bushels of wheat) for a given quantity of the fixed input. It also calculates the marginal product of labour on George and Martha's farm. The total product curve shows the production function graphically. It slopes upward because more wheat is produced as more workers are employed. It also becomes flatter because the marginal product of labour declines as more and more workers are employed.

The **total product curve** shows how the quantity of output depends on the quantity of the variable input, for a given quantity of the fixed input.

The **marginal product** of an input is the additional quantity of output that is produced by using one more unit of that input.

input; it is called the farm's **total product curve.** The physical quantity of output, bushels of wheat, is measured on the vertical axis, while the quantity of the variable input, labour—that is, the number of workers employed—is measured on the horizontal axis. The total product curve here is upward sloping, reflecting the fact that more bushels of wheat are produced as more workers are employed.

Although the total product curve in Figure 8-1 slopes upward along its entire length, the slope isn't constant: as you move up the curve to the right, it flattens out. To understand this changing slope, look at the third column of the table in Figure 8-1, which shows the *change in the quantity of output* that is generated by adding one more worker. That is, it shows the **marginal product** of labour: the additional quantity of output from using one more unit of labour (that is, one more worker).

In this case, we have data at intervals of 1 worker—that is, we have information on the quantity of output when there are 3 workers, 4 workers, and so on. Sometimes data aren't available in increments of 1 unit—for example, you might have information only on the quantity of output when there are 40 workers and when there are 50 workers. In this case, you can use the following equation to figure out the marginal product of labour:

$$\text{(8-1)}\quad \text{Marginal product of labour} = \frac{\text{Change in quantity of output}}{\text{Change in quantity of labour}} = \text{Change in quantity of output generated by one additional unit of labour}$$

or

$$MPL = \Delta Q/\Delta L$$

In this equation, Δ, the Greek uppercase delta, represents the change in a variable.

Now we can explain the significance of the slope of the total product curve: it is equal to the marginal product of labour. Remember from the Chapter 2 Appendix that the slope of a line is equal to "rise" over "run" (see p. 45). This implies that the slope of the total product curve is the change in the quantity of output (the "rise") divided by the change in the quantity of labour (the "run"). And this, as we can see from Equation 8-1, is simply the marginal product of labour. So the fact that the marginal product of the first worker is 19 also means that the slope of the total product curve in going from 0 to 1 worker is 19. Similarly, the slope of the total product curve in going from 1 to 2 workers is the same as the marginal product of the second worker, 17, and so on.

In this example, the marginal product of labour steadily declines as more workers are hired—that is, each successive worker adds less to output than the previous worker. So as employment increases, the total product curve gets flatter.

Figure 8-2 shows how the marginal product of labour depends on the number of workers employed on the farm. The marginal product of labour, *MPL*, is measured on the vertical axis in units of physical output—bushels of wheat—produced per additional worker, and the number of workers employed is measured on the horizontal axis. You can see from the table in Figure 8-1 that if 5 workers are employed instead of 4, output rises from 64 to 75 bushels; so in this case the marginal product of labour is 11 bushels—the same number found in Figure 8-2. To indicate that 11 bushels is the marginal product when employment rises from 4 to 5, we place the point corresponding to that information halfway between 4 and 5 workers.

In this example the marginal product of labour falls as the number of workers increases. That is, there are *diminishing returns to labour* on George and Martha's farm. In general, there are **diminishing returns to an input** when an increase in the quantity of that input, holding the quantity of all other inputs fixed, reduces that input's marginal product.

To grasp why diminishing returns can occur, think about what happens as George and Martha add more and more workers, without increasing the number of hectares. As the number of workers increases, the land is farmed more intensively and the number of bushels increases. But each additional worker is working with a smaller share of the 10 hectares—the fixed input—than the previous

There are **diminishing returns to an input** when an increase in the quantity of that input, holding the levels of all other inputs fixed, leads to a decline in the marginal product of that input.

PITFALLS

WHAT'S A UNIT?

The marginal product of labour (or any other input) is defined as the increase in the quantity of output when you increase the quantity of that input by one unit. But what do we mean by a "unit" of labour? Is it an additional hour of labour, an additional week, or a person-year?

The answer is that it doesn't matter, *as long as you are consistent.* One common source of error in economics is getting units confused—say, comparing the output added by an additional *hour* of labour with the cost of employing a worker for a *week.* Whatever units you use, always be careful that you use the same units throughout your analysis of any problem.

Figure 8-2

Marginal Product of Labour Curve for George and Martha's Farm

The marginal product of labour curve plots each worker's marginal product, the increase in the quantity of output generated by each additional worker. The change in the quantity of output is measured on the vertical axis and the number of workers employed on the horizontal axis. The first worker employed generates an increase in output of 19 bushels, the second worker generates an increase of 17 bushels, and so on. The curve slopes downward due to diminishing returns. >web...

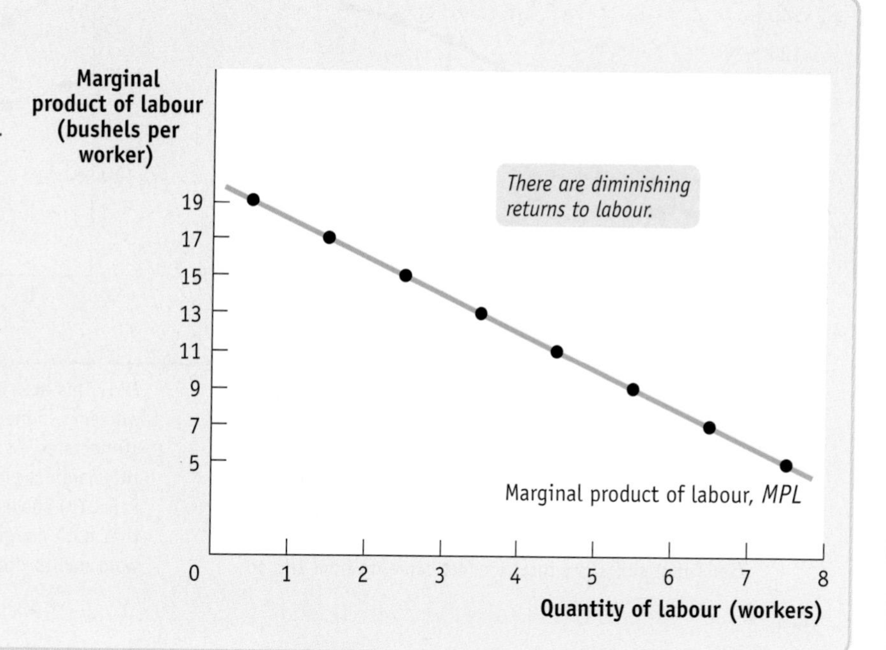

worker. As a result, the additional worker cannot produce as much output as the previous worker. So it's not surprising that the marginal product of the additional worker falls.

The crucial thing to emphasize about diminishing returns is that, like many propositions in economics, it is an "other things equal" proposition: each successive unit of an input will raise production by less than the last *if the quantity of all other inputs is held fixed.*

What would happen if the levels of other inputs were allowed to change? You can see the answer in Figure 8-3. Panel (a) shows two total product curves, TP_{10} and TP_{20}. TP_{10} is the farm's total product curve when its total area is 10 hectares (the same curve as in Figure 8-1). TP_{20} is the total product curve when the farm has increased to 20 hectares. Except when 0 workers are employed, TP_{20} lies everywhere above TP_{10} because with more hectares available, any given number of workers produces more output. Panel (b) shows the corresponding marginal product of labour curves. MPL_{10} is the marginal product of labour curve given 10 hectares to cultivate (the same curve as in Figure 8-2) and MPL_{20} is the marginal product of labour curve given 20 hectares. Both curves slope downward because, in each case, the amount of land is fixed, albeit at different levels. But MPL_{20} lies everywhere above MPL_{10}, reflecting the fact that the marginal product of the same worker is higher when he or she has more of the fixed input to work with.

Figure 8-3 demonstrates a general result: the position of the total product curve depends on the quantities of other inputs. If you change the quantity of the other inputs, both the total product curve and the marginal product curve of the remaining input will shift. The importance of the "other things equal" assumption in discussing diminishing returns is illustrated in the following For Inquiring Minds.

Figure 8-3 Total Product, Marginal Product, and the Fixed Input

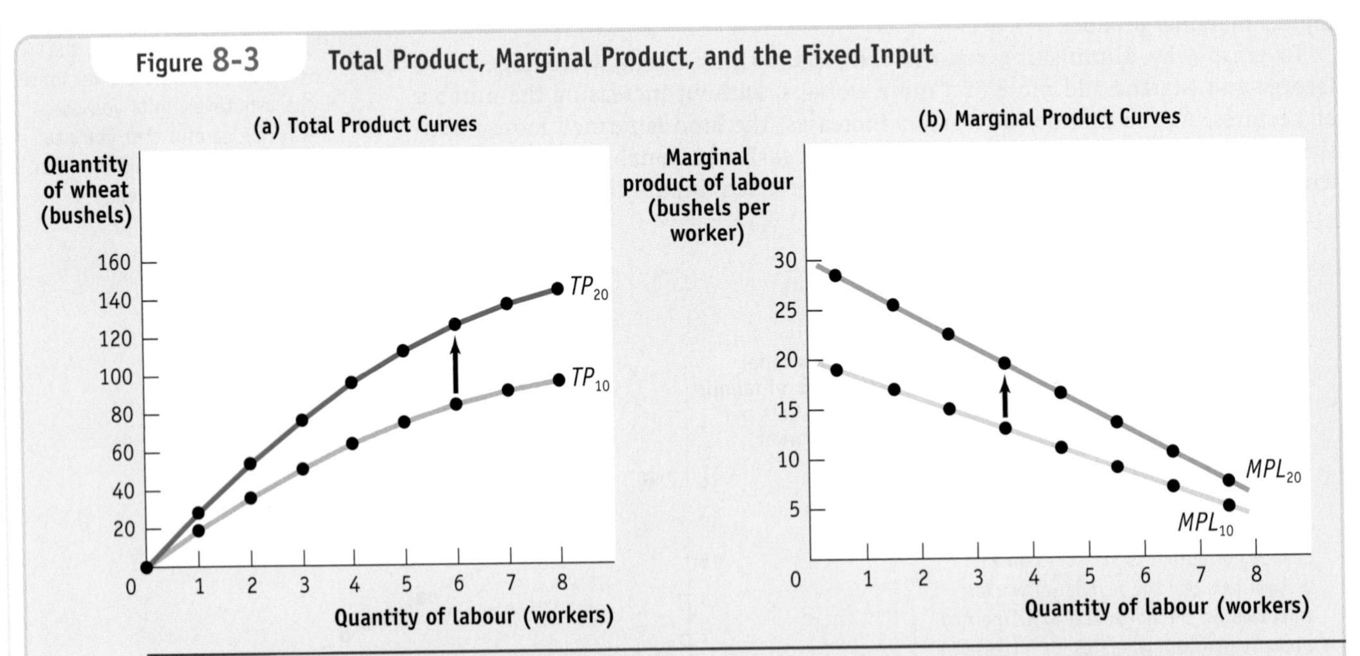

This figure shows how the quantity of output—illustrated by the total product curve—and marginal product depend on the level of the fixed input. Panel (a) shows two total product curves for George and Martha's farm, TP_{10} when their farm is 10 hectares and TP_{20} when it is 20 hectares. With more land, each worker can produce more wheat. So an increase in the fixed input shifts the total product curve up from TP_{10} to TP_{20}. This also implies that the marginal product of each worker is higher when the farm is 20 hectares than when it is 10 hectares. As a result, an increase in acreage also shifts the marginal product of labour curve up from MPL_{10} to MPL_{20}. Panel (b) shows the marginal product of labour curves. Note that both marginal product of labour curves still slope downward due to diminishing returns.

FOR INQUIRING MINDS

WAS MALTHUS RIGHT?

The idea of diminishing returns first became influential with the writings of Thomas Malthus, an English pastor whose 1798 book *An Essay on the Principle of Population* was deeply influential in its own time and continues to provoke heated argument to this day.

Malthus argued that as its population grew (while its land area remained fixed), a country would find it increasingly difficult to grow enough food. Though more intensive cultivation of the land could increase yields, each successive farmer would add less to the total than the last as the marginal product of labour declined. Eventually, food production per capita (the average output of an existing worker) would decline as the population exceeded some level.

He drew a powerful conclusion from this argument—namely, that misery was the normal condition of humankind. Imagine a country in which land was abundant and population low, so that everyone had plenty to eat. Then families would, he argued, be large (as they were at the time in Canada, where land was abundant), and the population would grow rapidly—until the pressure of population on the land had reduced the condition of most people to a level where starvation and disease held the population in check. (It was arguments like these that led the historian Thomas Carlyle to dub economics the "dismal science".)

Happily, Malthus's prediction has turned out to be quite wrong. The world's population has increased from about 1 billion people when Malthus wrote to more than 6 billion today, but in most of the world people eat better now than ever before. In England, in particular, a fivefold increase in population was accompanied by a dramatic rise in the standard of living.

So was Malthus completely wrong? And does the wrongness of his prediction refute the whole idea of diminishing returns? No, on both counts.

First of all, the Malthusian story actually works pretty well as a description of 57 out of the last 59 centuries: peasants in eighteenth-century France probably did not live much better than Egyptian peasants in the age of the pyramids. It just so happens that scientific and technological progress since the eighteenth century has been so rapid that it has far outpaced any problems caused by diminishing returns.

The concept of diminishing returns does not mean that using more labour to grow food, even on a given amount of land, will lead to a decline in the marginal product of labour—*if* there is also a radical improvement in farming technology. It does mean that the marginal product declines when *all* other things—land, farming technology, and a host of other factors—remain the same. And so the happy fact that Malthus's predictions were wrong does not invalidate the concept of diminishing returns.

From the Production Function to Cost Curves

Once George and Martha know their production function, they know the relationship between inputs of labour and land and output of wheat. But if they want to maximize their profits, they need to translate this knowledge into information about the relationship between the quantity of output and cost. Let's see how they can do this.

To translate information about a firm's production function into information about its cost, we need to know how much the firm must pay for its inputs. We will assume that George and Martha face either an explicit or an implicit cost of $400 for the use of the land. As we learned in Chapter 7, it is irrelevant whether George and Martha must rent the land for $400 from someone else, or they own the land themselves and forgo earning $400 by renting it to someone else. Either way, they pay an opportunity cost of $400 by using the land to grow wheat. Moreover, since the land is a fixed input, the $400 George and Martha pay for it is a **fixed cost,** denoted by *FC*—a cost that does not depend on the quantity of output produced. In business, fixed cost is often referred to as "overhead cost".

We also assume that George and Martha must pay each worker $200. Using their production function, George and Martha know that the number of workers they must hire depends on the amount of wheat they intend to produce. So the cost of labour, which is equal to the number of workers multiplied by $200, is a **variable cost,** denoted by *VC*—a cost that depends on the quantity of output produced. Adding the fixed cost and the variable cost of a given quantity of output gives the **total cost,** or *TC*, of that quantity of output. We can express the relationship among fixed cost, variable cost, and total cost as an equation:

A **fixed cost** is a cost that does not depend on the quantity of output produced. It is the cost of the fixed input.

A **variable cost** is a cost that depends on the quantity of output produced. It is the cost of the variable input.

The **total cost** of producing a given quantity of output is the sum of the fixed cost and the variable cost of producing that quantity of output.

(8-2) Total cost = Fixed cost + Variable cost

or

$$TC = FC + VC$$

The table in Figure 8-4 shows how total cost is calculated for George and Martha's farm. The second column shows the number of workers employed. The third column shows the corresponding level of output, taken from the table in Figure 8-1. The fourth column shows the variable cost, equal to the number of workers multiplied by \$200. The fifth column shows the fixed cost, which is \$400 regardless of how many workers are employed. The sixth column shows the total cost of output, which is the variable cost plus the fixed cost.

The **total cost curve** shows how total cost depends on the quantity of output.

The first column labels each row of the table with a letter, from *A* to *I*. These labels will be helpful in understanding our next step: drawing the **total cost curve,** a curve that shows how total cost depends on the quantity of output.

George and Martha's total cost curve is shown in the diagram in Figure 8-4, where the horizontal axis measures the quantity of output in bushels of wheat and the vertical

Figure 8-4

Total Cost Curve for George and Martha's Farm

The table shows the variable cost, fixed cost, and total cost for various output quantities on George and Martha's 10-hectare farm. The total cost curve shows how total cost (measured on the vertical axis) depends on the quantity of output (measured on the horizontal axis). The labelled points on the curve correspond to the rows of the table. The total cost curve slopes upward because the number of workers employed, and hence total cost, increases as the quantity of output increases. The curve gets steeper as output increases due to diminishing returns to labour.

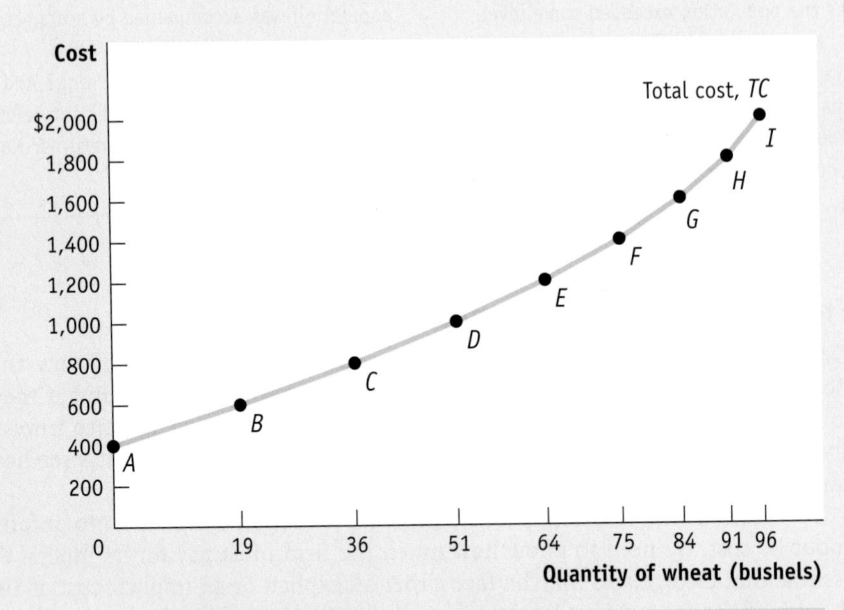

Point on graph	Quantity of labour *L* (workers)	Quantity of wheat *Q* (bushels)	Variable cost *VC*	Fixed cost *FC*	Total cost *TC = FC + VC*
A	0	0	\$0	\$400	\$400
B	1	19	200	400	600
C	2	36	400	400	800
D	3	51	600	400	1,000
E	4	64	800	400	1,200
F	5	75	1,000	400	1,400
G	6	84	1,200	400	1,600
H	7	91	1,400	400	1,800
I	8	96	1,600	400	2,000

axis measures total cost in dollars. Each point on the curve corresponds to one row of the table in Figure 8-4. For example, point *A* shows the situation when 0 workers are employed: output is zero, and total cost is equal to fixed cost, $400. Similarly, point *B* shows the situation when 1 worker is employed: output is 19 bushels, and total cost is $600, equal to the sum of $400 in fixed cost and $200 in variable cost.

Like the total product curve, the total cost curve is upward sloping: due to the variable cost, the more output produced, the higher the farm's total cost. But unlike the total product curve, which gets flatter as employment rises, the total cost curve gets *steeper*. That is, the slope of the total cost curve is greater as the amount of output produced increases. And as we will soon see, the steepening of the total cost curve is also due to diminishing returns to the variable input. Before we can understand this, we must first look at the relationship among several useful measures of cost.

economics in action

The Mythical Man-Month

The concept of diminishing returns to an input was first formulated by economists during the late eighteenth century. These economists, notably including Thomas Malthus, drew their inspiration from agricultural examples; they noticed, in particular, that as an individual tried to employ more workers in agriculture, he or she was forced to cultivate poorer quality land. Although still valid, such examples can seem somewhat musty and old-fashioned in our modern information economy.

However, the idea of diminishing returns to an input applies with equal force to the most modern of economic activities—such as, say, the design of software. In 1975 Frederick P. Brooks Jr., a project manager at IBM during the days when it dominated the computer business, published a book titled *The Mythical Man-Month* that soon became a classic—so much so that a special anniversary edition was published 20 years later.

The chapter that gave its title to the book is basically about diminishing returns in the writing of software. Dr. Brooks observed that multiplying the number of programmers assigned to a project did not produce a proportionate reduction in the time it took to get the program written. A project that could be done by 1 programmer in 12 months could *not* be done by 12 programmers in 1 month—hence the "mythical man-month", the false notion that the number of lines of programming code produced was proportional to the number of code writers employed. In fact, above a certain number, adding another programmer on a project actually *increased* the time to completion.

The argument of *The Mythical Man-Month* is summarized in Figure 8-5. The upper part of the figure shows how the quantity of the project's output, as measured by the number of lines of code produced per month, varies with the number of programmers. Each additional programmer accomplishes less than the previous one, and beyond a certain point an additional programmer is actually counterproductive. The lower part of the figure shows the marginal product of each successive programmer, which falls as more programmers are employed, and eventually becomes negative. In other words, programming is

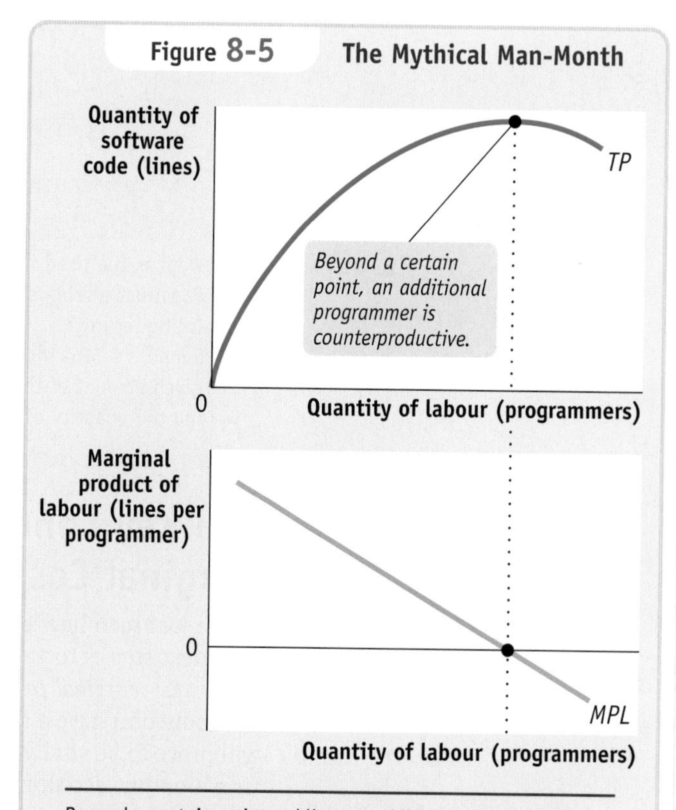

Beyond a certain point, adding an additional programmer is counterproductive—output falls and the slope of the total product curve becomes negative. At this point the marginal product of labour curve crosses the horizontal axis—and the marginal product of labour becomes negative.

subject to diminishing returns so severe that at some point more programmers actually have negative marginal product. The source of the diminishing returns lies in the nature of the production function for a programming project: each programmer must coordinate his or her work with that of all the other programmers on the project, leading to each person spending more and more time communicating with others as the number of programmers increases. In other words, other things equal, there are diminishing returns to labour. It is likely, however, that if fixed inputs devoted to programming projects are increased—say, installing a faster e-mail system—the problem of diminishing returns for additional programmers can be mitigated.

A reviewer of the reissued edition of *The Mythical Man-Month* summarized the reasons for these diminishing returns: "There is an inescapable overhead to yoking up programmers in parallel. The members of the team must 'waste time' attending meetings, drafting project plans, exchanging e-mail, negotiating interfaces, enduring performance reviews, and so on . . . At Microsoft, there will be at least one team member that just designs T-shirts for the rest of the team to wear." (from www.ercb.com, Dr. Dobb's Electronic Review of Computer Books) ■

>> QUICK REVIEW

- The firm's *production function* is the relationship between quantity of inputs and output. The *total product curve* shows how the quantity of output depends upon the quantity of the *variable input* for a given quantity of the *fixed input*, and its slope is equal to the *marginal product* of the variable input. In the *short run*, the fixed input cannot be varied; in the *long run* all inputs are variable.
- When the levels of all other inputs are fixed, *diminishing returns to an input* may arise, yielding a downward-sloping marginal product curve and a total product curve that becomes flatter as more output is produced.
- The *total cost* of a given quantity of output equals the *fixed cost* plus the *variable cost* of that output. The *total cost curve* becomes steeper as more output is produced due to diminishing returns.

>> CHECK YOUR UNDERSTANDING 8-1

1. Bernie's ice-making company produces ice cubes using a 10-ton machine and electricity. The quantity of output, measured in terms of kilograms of ice, is given in this table:

Quantity of electricity (kilowatts)	Quantity of ice (kilograms)
0	0
1	1,000
2	1,800
3	2,400
4	2,800

a. What is the fixed input? What is the variable input?

b. Construct a table showing the marginal product of the variable input. Does it show diminishing returns?

c. Suppose a 50% increase in the size of the fixed input increases output by 100% for any given amount of the variable input. What is the fixed input now? Construct a table showing the quantity of output and marginal product in this case.

Solutions appear at back of book.

Two Key Concepts: Marginal Cost and Average Cost

We've just seen how to derive a firm's total cost curve from its production function. Our next step is to take a deeper look at total cost by deriving two extremely useful measures: *marginal cost* and *average cost*. As we'll see, these two measures of the cost of production have a somewhat surprising relationship to each other. Moreover, they will prove to be vitally important in Chapter 9, where we will use them to analyze the firm's output decision and the market supply curve.

Marginal Cost

We defined marginal cost in Chapter 7: it is the change in total cost generated by producing one more unit of output. We've already seen that marginal product is easiest to calculate if data on total cost are available in increments of one unit of input. Similarly, marginal cost is easiest to calculate if data on total cost are available in increments of

TABLE 8-1

Costs at Ben's Boots

Quantity of boots Q (pairs)	Fixed cost FC	Variable cost VC	Total cost $TC = FC + VC$	Marginal cost of pair $MC = \Delta TC/\Delta Q$
0	$108	$0	$108	
				$12
1	108	12	120	
				36
2	108	48	156	
				60
3	108	108	216	
				84
4	108	192	300	
				108
5	108	300	408	
				132
6	108	432	540	
				156
7	108	588	696	
				180
8	108	768	876	
				204
9	108	972	1,080	
				228
10	108	1,200	1,308	

one unit of output. When the data come in less convenient increments, it's still possible to calculate marginal cost over each interval. But for the sake of simplicity, let's work with an example in which the data come in convenient increments.

Ben's Boots produces leather footwear; Table 8-1 shows how its costs per day depend on the number of boots it produces per day. The firm has fixed cost of $108 per day, shown in the second column, which represents the daily cost of its boot-making machine. The third column shows the variable cost, and the fourth column shows the total cost. Panel (a) of Figure 8-6 plots the total cost curve. Like the total

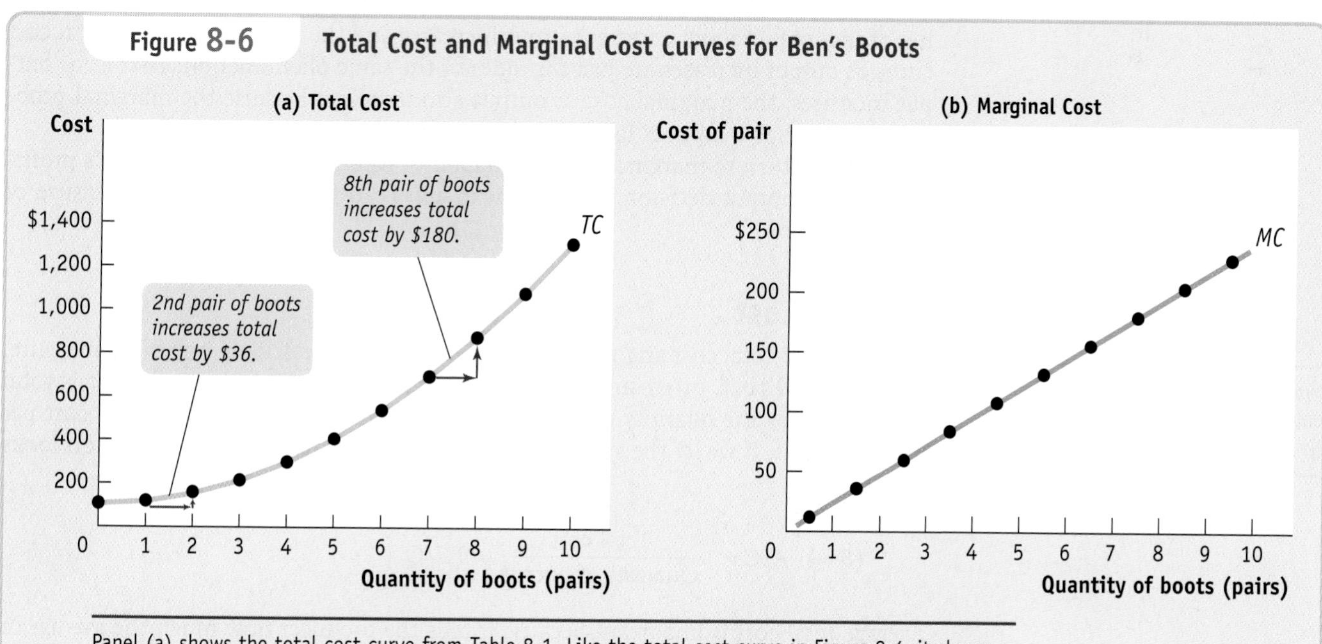

Panel (a) shows the total cost curve from Table 8-1. Like the total cost curve in Figure 8-4, it slopes upward and gets steeper as we move up it to the right. Panel (b) shows the marginal cost curve. It also slopes upward, reflecting diminishing returns to the variable input. >web...

cost curve for George and Martha's farm in Figure 8-4, this curve is upward sloping, getting steeper as you move up it to the right.

The significance of the slope of the total cost curve is shown by the fifth column of Table 8-1, which calculates *marginal cost*: the cost of each additional unit. The general formula for marginal cost is

$$\textbf{(8-3)}\quad \text{Marginal cost} = \frac{\text{Change in total cost}}{\text{Change in quantity of output}} = \begin{array}{c}\text{Change in total cost}\\ \text{generated by one}\\ \text{additional unit of}\\ \text{output}\end{array}$$

or

$$MC = \Delta TC/\Delta Q$$

As in the case of marginal product, marginal cost in this equation is equal to "rise"—(the increase in total cost) divided by "run"—(the increase in the quantity of output). So just as marginal product is equal to the slope of the total product curve, marginal cost is equal to the slope of the total cost curve.

Now we can understand why the total cost curve gets steeper as we move up it to the right: as you can see in Table 8-1, the marginal cost at Ben's Boots rises as output increases. Panel (b) of Figure 8-6 shows the *marginal cost curve* corresponding to the data in Table 8-1. Notice that, as in Figure 8-2, we plot the marginal cost for increasing output from 0 to 1 pair of boots halfway between 0 and 1, the marginal cost for increasing output from 1 to 2 pairs of boots halfway between 1 and 2, and so on.

Why is the marginal cost curve upward sloping? Because there are diminishing returns to inputs in this example. As output increases, the marginal product of the variable input declines. This implies that more and more of the variable input must be used to produce each additional unit of output as the amount of output already produced rises. And since each unit of the variable input must be paid for, the cost per additional unit of output also rises.

In addition, recall that the flattening of the total product curve is also due to diminishing returns to inputs in production: the marginal product of an input falls as more of that input is used if the quantities of other inputs are fixed. The flattening of the total product curve as output increases and the steepening of the total cost curve as output increases are just flip sides of the same phenomenon. That is, as output increases, the marginal cost of output also increases because the marginal product of the variable input is falling.

We will return to marginal cost in Chapter 9, when we consider the firm's profit-maximizing output decision. But our next step is to introduce another measure of cost: *average cost*.

Average Cost

Average total cost, often referred to simply as **average cost**, is total cost divided by quantity of output produced.

In addition to total cost and marginal cost, it's useful to calculate one more measure, **average total cost,** often simply called **average cost.** The average total cost is total cost divided by the quantity of output produced; that is, it is equal to total cost per unit of output. If we let the symbol *ATC* denote average total cost, the equation looks like this:

$$\textbf{(8-4)}\quad ATC = \frac{\text{Total cost}}{\text{Quantity of output}} = TC/Q$$

Average total cost is important because it tells the producer how much the *average* or *typical* unit of output costs to produce. Marginal cost, meanwhile, tells the producer how much *one more* unit of output costs to produce. Although they may look very similar, these two measures of cost typically differ. And confusion between them is a

TABLE 8-2

Average Costs for Ben's Boots

Quantity of boots *Q* (pairs)	Total cost *TC*	Average total cost of pair *ATC* = *TC*/*Q*	Average fixed cost of pair *AFC* = *FC*/*Q*	Average variable cost of pair *AVC* = *VC*/*Q*
1	$120	$120.00	$108.00	$12.00
2	156	78.00	54.00	24.00
3	216	72.00	36.00	36.00
4	300	75.00	27.00	48.00
5	408	81.60	21.60	60.00
6	540	90.00	18.00	72.00
7	696	99.43	15.43	84.00
8	876	109.50	13.50	96.00
9	1,080	120.00	12.00	108.00
10	1,308	130.80	10.80	120.00

major source of error in economics, both in the classroom and in real life, as illustrated by Economics in Action at the end of this section.

Table 8-2 uses the data from Ben's Boots to calculate average total cost. For example, the total cost of producing 4 pairs of boots is $300, consisting of $108 in fixed cost and $192 in variable cost (see Table 8-1). You can see from Table 8-2 that as quantity of output increases, average total cost first falls, then rises.

Figure 8-7 plots that data to yield the *average total cost curve,* which shows how average total cost depends on output. As before, cost in dollars is measured on the vertical axis and quantity of output is measured on the horizontal axis. The average total cost curve has a distinctive U shape that corresponds to how average total cost

Figure 8-7

Average Total Cost Curve for Ben's Boots

The average total cost curve at Ben's Boots is U-shaped. At low levels of output, average total cost falls because the "spreading effect" of falling average fixed cost dominates the "diminishing returns effect" of rising average variable cost. At higher levels of output, the opposite is true and average total cost rises. At point *M*, corresponding to an output of 3 pairs of boots per day, average total cost is at its minimum level, the minimum average total cost. **>*web...***

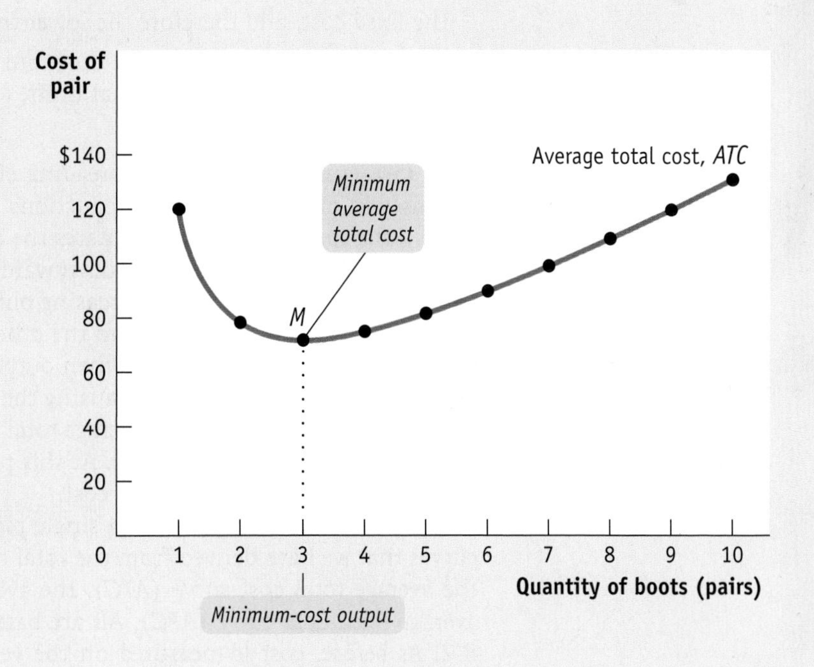

A **U-shaped average total cost curve** falls at low levels of output, then rises at higher levels.

Average fixed cost is the fixed cost per unit of output.

Average variable cost is the variable cost per unit of output.

first falls and then rises as output increases. Economists believe that such **U-shaped average total cost curves** are the norm for producers in many industries.

To help our understanding of why the average total cost curve is U-shaped, Table 8-2 breaks average total cost into its two underlying components, *average fixed cost* and *average variable cost*. **Average fixed cost,** or *AFC*, is fixed cost divided by the quantity of output, also known as the fixed cost per unit of output. For example, if Ben's Boots produces 4 pairs of boots, average fixed cost is $\$108/4 = \$27$ per pair of boots. **Average variable cost,** or *AVC*, is variable cost divided by the quantity of output, also known as variable cost per unit of output. At an output of 4 pairs of boots, average variable cost is $\$192/4 = \$48$ per pair. Writing these in the form of equations,

$$\textbf{(8-5)} \quad AFC = \frac{\text{Fixed cost}}{\text{Quantity of output}} = FC/Q$$

$$AVC = \frac{\text{Variable cost}}{\text{Quantity of output}} = VC/Q$$

Average total cost is the sum of average fixed cost and average variable cost; it has a U shape because these components move in opposite directions as output rises.

Average fixed cost falls as more output is produced because the numerator (the fixed cost) is a fixed number but the denominator (the quantity of output) increases as more is produced. Another way to think about this relationship is that, as more output is produced, the fixed cost is spread over more units of output; the end result is that the fixed cost *per unit of output*—the average fixed cost—falls. You can see this effect in the fourth column of Table 8-2: average fixed cost drops continuously as output increases.

Average variable cost, however, rises as output increases. As we've seen, this reflects diminishing returns to the variable input: each additional unit of output incurs more variable cost to produce than the previous unit. So variable cost rises at a faster rate than the quantity of output increases.

Increasing output, therefore, has two opposing effects on average total cost—the "spreading effect" and the "diminishing returns effect":

- The spreading effect: the larger the output, the more production that can "share" the fixed cost, and therefore the lower the average fixed cost.
- The diminishing returns effect: the more output produced, the more variable input it requires to produce additional units, and therefore the higher the average variable cost.

At low levels of output, the spreading effect is very powerful because even small increases in output cause large reductions in average fixed cost. So at low levels of output, the spreading effect dominates the diminishing returns effect and causes the average total cost curve to slope downward. But when output is large, average fixed cost is already quite small, so increasing output further has only a very small spreading effect. Diminishing returns, on the other hand, usually grow increasingly important as output rises. As a result, when output is large, the diminishing returns effect dominates the spreading effect, causing the average total cost curve to slope upward. At the bottom of the U-shaped average total cost curve, point *M* in Figure 8-7, the two effects exactly balance each other. At this point average total cost is at its minimum level, the minimum average total cost.

Figure 8-8 brings together in a single picture four members of the family of cost curves that we have derived from the total cost curve: the marginal cost curve (*MC*), the average total cost curve (*ATC*), the average variable cost curve (*AVC*), and the average fixed cost curve (*AFC*). All are based on the information in Tables 8-1 and 8-2. As before, cost is measured on the vertical axis and the quantity of output is measured on the horizontal axis.

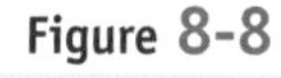

Marginal Cost and Average Cost Curves for Ben's Boots

Here we have the family of cost curves for Ben's Boots: the marginal cost curve (*MC*), the average total cost curve (*ATC*), the average variable cost curve (*AVC*), and the average fixed cost curve (*AFC*). Note that the average total cost curve is U-shaped and the marginal cost curve crosses the average total cost curve at the bottom of the U, point *M*, corresponding to the minimum average total cost from Table 8-2 and Figure 8-7. **>*web...***

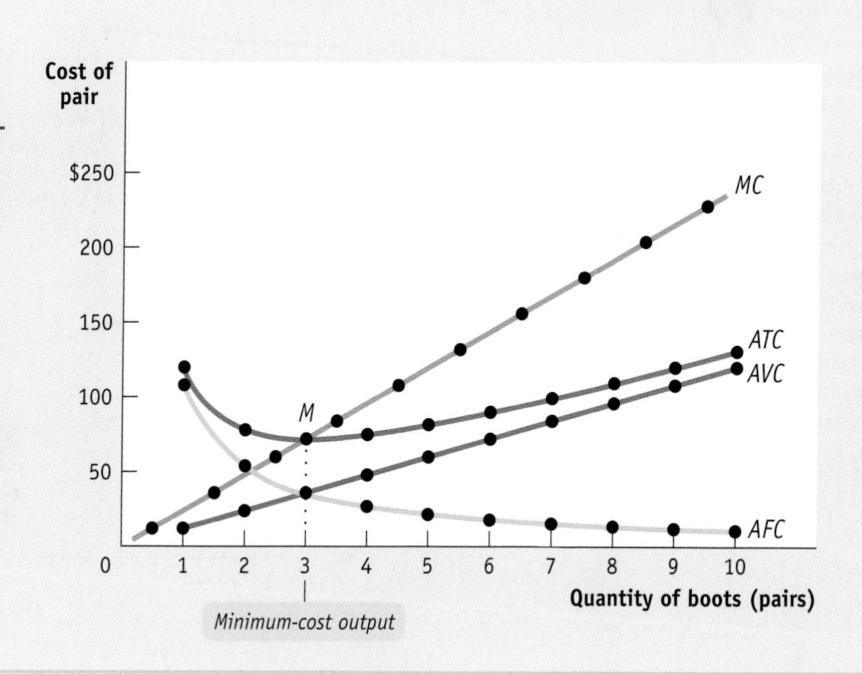

Let's take a moment to note some features of the various cost curves. First of all, marginal cost is upward sloping—the result of diminishing returns that makes an additional unit of output more costly to produce than the one before. Average variable cost also is upward sloping—again, due to diminishing returns—but is flatter than the marginal cost curve. That is because the higher cost of an additional unit of output is averaged across all units, not just the additional units, in the average variable cost measure. Meanwhile, average fixed cost is downward sloping because of the spreading effect.

Finally, notice that the marginal cost curve intersects the average total cost curve from below, crossing it at its lowest point, point *M* in Figure 8-8. This last feature is our next subject of study.

Minimum Average Total Cost

For a U-shaped average total cost curve, average total cost is at its minimum level at the bottom of the U. Economists call the quantity that corresponds to the minimum average total cost the **minimum-cost output.** In the case of Ben's Boots, the minimum-cost output is three pairs of boots per day.

The **minimum-cost output** is the quantity of output at which average total cost is lowest—the bottom of the U-shaped average total cost curve.

In Figure 8-8, the bottom of the U is at the level of output at which the marginal cost curve crosses the average total cost curve from below. Is this an accident? No—it reflects general principles that are always true about a firm's marginal cost and average total cost curves:

- At the minimum-cost output, average total cost *is equal to* marginal cost.
- At output less than the minimum-cost output, marginal cost *is less than* average total cost and average total cost is falling.
- And at output greater than the minimum-cost output, marginal cost is *greater than* average total cost and average total cost is rising.

To understand this principle, think about how your grade in one course—say, a 3.0 in physics—affects your overall grade point average. If your GPA before receiving that grade was more than 3.0, the new grade lowers your average.

Figure 8-9

The Relationship Between the Average Total Cost and the Marginal Cost Curves

To see why the marginal cost curve (*MC*) must cut through the average total cost curve at the minimum average total cost (point *M*), corresponding to the minimum-cost output, we look at what happens if marginal cost is different from average total cost. If marginal cost is *less* than average total cost, an increase in output must reduce average total cost, as in the movement from A_1 to A_2. If marginal cost is *greater* than average total cost, an increase in output must increase average total cost, as in the movement from B_1 to B_2.

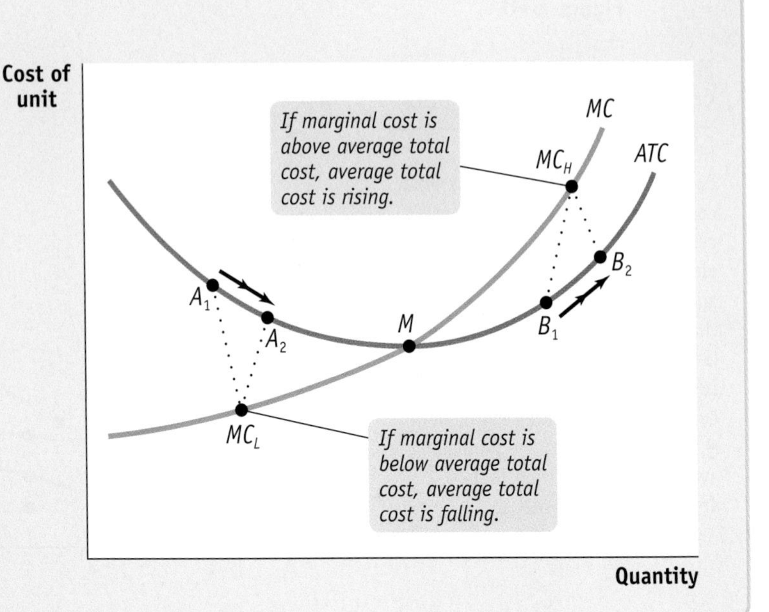

Similarly, if marginal cost—the cost of producing one more unit—is less than average total cost, producing that extra unit lowers average total cost. This is shown in Figure 8-9 by the movement from A_1 to A_2. In this case, the marginal cost of producing an additional unit of output is low, as indicated by the point MC_L on the marginal cost curve. And when the cost of producing the next unit of output is less than average total cost, increasing production reduces average total cost. So any quantity of output at which marginal cost is less than average total cost must be on the downward-sloping segment of the U.

But if your grade in physics is more than the average of your previous grades, this new grade raises your GPA. Similarly, if marginal cost is greater than average total cost, producing that extra unit raises average total cost. This is illustrated by the move from B_1 to B_2 in Figure 8-9, where the marginal cost, MC_H, is higher than average total cost. So any quantity of output at which marginal cost is greater than average total cost must be on the upward-sloping segment of the U.

Finally, if a new grade is exactly equal to your previous GPA, the additional grade neither raises nor lowers that average—it stays the same. This corresponds to point M in Figure 8-9: when marginal cost equals average total cost we must be at the bottom of the U, because only at that point is average total cost neither falling nor rising.

Does the Marginal Cost Curve Always Slope Upward?

Up to this point we have emphasized the importance of diminishing returns, which lead to a marginal product curve that is always downward sloping and a marginal cost curve that is always upward sloping. In practice, however, economists believe that marginal cost curves often slope *downward* as a firm increases its production from zero up to some low level, sloping upward only at higher levels of production: they look like the curve *MC* in Figure 8-10.

This initial downward slope occurs because a firm that employs only a few workers often cannot reap the benefits of specialization of labour. For example, one individual producing boots would have to perform all of the tasks involved: making soles, shaping the upper part, sewing the pieces together, and so on. As more workers are employed, they can divide the tasks, with each worker specializing in one or a few aspects of boot making. This specialization can lead to *increasing* returns at first, and so to a downward-sloping

More Realistic Cost Curves

In practice, the marginal cost curve often begins with a section that slopes downward. As output rises from a low level, a firm is capable of engaging in specialization and division of labour, which leads to increasing returns. At higher levels of output, however, diminishing returns lead to upward-sloping marginal cost. When marginal cost has a downward-sloping section, average variable cost is U-shaped. However, the basic results—U-shaped average total cost, and marginal cost that cuts through the minimum average total cost—remain the same. >web...

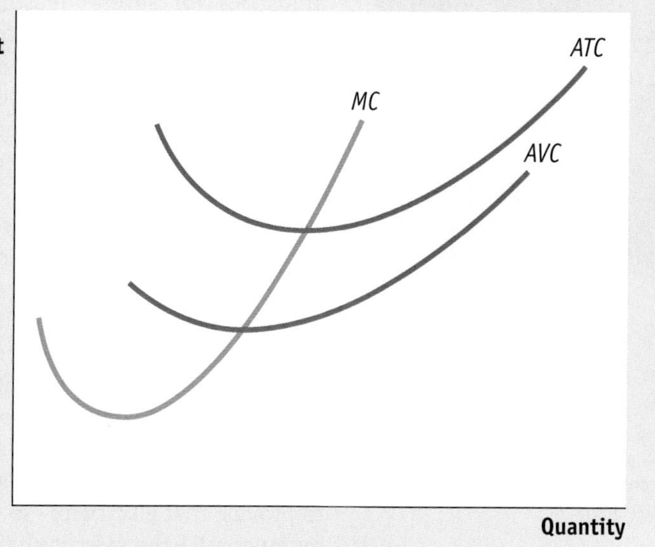

marginal cost curve. Once there are enough workers to permit specialization, however, diminishing returns set in. So, typical marginal cost curves actually have the "swoosh" shape shown by *MC* in Figure 8-10. For the same reason, average variable cost curves typically look like *AVC* in Figure 8-10: they are U-shaped rather than strictly upward sloping.

However, as Figure 8-10 also shows, the key features we saw from the example of Ben's Boots remain true: the average total cost curve is U-shaped, and the marginal cost curve passes through the point of minimum average total cost as well as through the point of minimum average variable cost.

economics in action

The Cost of Hydroelectricity in Canada

One of Canada's great resources is the availability of suitable sites for producing hydroelectric power. When conditions are right—basically, when a large river runs through a deep but narrow valley—hydropower can be much cheaper than electricity generated using fossil fuels, such as coal, or nuclear power. Indeed, the three cheapest producers of electricity in North America are all Canadian: Manitoba Hydro, Hydro-Québec, and BC Hydro. It is no coincidence that hydroelectricity accounts for more than 90% of the total power generation for all three of these provincially owned crown-corporations.

Because hydroelectricity is cheap, all three provinces not only export electricity but have also managed to attract industries (like metal smelting or pulp and paper) that are heavy users of electricity. A natural question is whether these provinces should do more to attract industries to move into their jurisdictions that would benefit from cheap power.

The answer to this question is far from simple. All three corporations charge a higher price for their exported electricity than they do for domestically consumed electricity. So, the corporations can make more profits by encouraging domestic conservation of power and increasing their exports. On the other hand, since provincial governments own these corporations, their ultimate objective is not maximization of their profits, but rather the general good of the province.

As a result, Manitoba Hydro, which exports as much as 40 percent of its electricity generation, has a division actively seeking to attract business into the

Royalty Free/Corbis

Confusing marginal cost and average total cost proved a very costly mistake for the company that built this dam and for its customers.

province. It wishes to attract "energy-reliant" industries, for which reliability of supply is the key issue. It does not particularly want to attract "energy-intensive" industries for several reasons. First, these industries are often highly capital-intensive, with few jobs created; second, such industries would gobble up Manitoba Hydro's energy surplus and eliminate its lucrative export business; and third, the company is aware that the cost of providing additional power capacity will always be higher than the cost of the existing capacity. This is because the best hydroelectric sites are already developed, and new capacity would require the development of less productive sites.

Another way of saying this is that while the current average total cost of producing electricity is low, the marginal cost of developing new capacity is much higher. Therefore, if too much energy-intensive industry were attracted into the province, the power company would find itself having to add high-cost new capacity that would increase average total costs of production. As a regulated industry (something we'll discuss in Chapter 14), the rates electricity companies charge consumers are generally set to reflect average total cost. So, we could have a seemingly paradoxical effect: if an energy-intensive industry moved into the province, it would pay less for the electricity it consumed than the extra, or marginal, cost incurred by the utility company to provide that electricity—so to cover its higher average total cost, the power company must raise the rates it charges all consumers.

This paradoxical situation occurred in the western United States—a region that also had a seemingly plentiful supply of hydroelectricity. Until the 1980s, politicians and business leaders encouraged energy-intensive industries to move into the region. But then, to the surprise and anger of consumers, Western power companies began demanding higher prices, saying that they were no longer able to cover their costs at the old electricity rates. The problem was that officials had confused the *average total cost* of producing electricity with the *marginal cost* of producing it. If public officials had understood the difference between average total cost and marginal cost, they might have avoided this trap—either by charging new electricity users higher rates, or by discouraging new electricity-using businesses from moving to their states.

Judging from the policy of Manitoba Hydro, it seems that Canada's power companies may have learned from the mistakes of our southern neighbours. ■

>> QUICK REVIEW

- *Marginal cost* is equal to the slope of the total cost curve. Diminishing returns cause the marginal cost curve to be upward sloping.
- *Average total cost* (or *average cost*) is equal to the sum of *average fixed cost* and *average variable cost*. When the *U-shaped average total cost curve* slopes downward, the spreading effect dominates: fixed cost is spread over more units of output. When it slopes upward, the diminishing returns effect dominates: an additional unit of output requires more variable inputs.
- Marginal cost is equal to average total cost at the *minimum-cost output*. At higher output levels, marginal cost is greater than average total cost and average total cost is rising. At lower output levels, marginal cost is lower than average total cost and average total cost is falling.
- At low levels of output there are often increasing returns to an input due to the benefits of specialization, making the marginal cost curve "swoosh"-shaped: initially sloping downward before sloping upward.

>>CHECK YOUR UNDERSTANDING 8-2

1. Alicia's Apple Pies is a roadside business. Alicia must pay $9.00 in rent each day. In addition, it costs her $1.00 to produce the first pie of the day, and each subsequent pie costs 50% more to produce than the one before. For example, the second pie costs $1.00 x 1.5 = $1.50 to produce, and so on.
   a. Calculate Alicia's marginal cost, variable cost, average total cost, average variable cost, and average fixed cost as her daily pie output rises from 0 to 6. (*Hint*: The variable cost of two pies is just the marginal cost of the first, plus the marginal cost of the second pie, and so on.)
   b. Indicate the range of pies for which the spreading effect dominates and the range for which the diminishing returns effect dominates.
   c. What is Alicia's minimum-cost output? Explain why making one more pie lowers Alicia's average total cost when output is lower than the minimum-cost output. Similarly, explain why making one more pie raises Alicia's average total cost when output is greater than the minimum-cost output.

Solutions appear at back of book.

Short-Run versus Long-Run Costs

Up to this point, we have treated fixed cost as completely outside the control of a firm because we have focused on the short run. But as we noted earlier, all inputs are variable in the long run: this means that in the long run, fixed cost may also be varied. In the long run, in other words, a firm's fixed cost becomes a variable it can choose. For example, given time, Ben's Boots can acquire additional boot-making machinery or dispose of some of its existing machinery. In this section, we will examine how a firm's costs behave in the short run and in the long run. We will also see that the firm will choose its fixed cost in the long run based on the level of output it expects to produce.

Let's begin by supposing that Ben's Boots is considering whether to acquire additional boot-making machines. Acquiring additional machinery will affect its total cost in two ways. First, the firm will have to either rent or buy the additional machinery; either way, that will mean higher fixed cost in the short run. Second, if the workers have more equipment they will be more productive: fewer workers will be needed to produce any given output, so variable cost for any given output level will be reduced.

The table in Figure 8-11 shows how acquiring an additional machine affects costs. In our original example, we assumed that Ben's Boots had a fixed cost of

Figure 8-11

Choosing the Level of Fixed Cost for Ben's Boots

There is a trade-off between higher fixed cost and lower variable cost for any given output level, and vice versa. ATC_1 is the average total cost curve corresponding to a fixed cost of $108; it leads to high variable cost. ATC_2 is the average total cost curve corresponding to a higher fixed cost of $216 but lower variable cost. At low output levels, fewer than 4 pairs of boots per day, ATC_1 lies below ATC_2: average total cost is lower with only $108 in fixed cost. But as output goes up, average total cost is lower with the higher amount of fixed cost, $216: at more than 4 pairs of boots per day, ATC_2 lies below ATC_1.

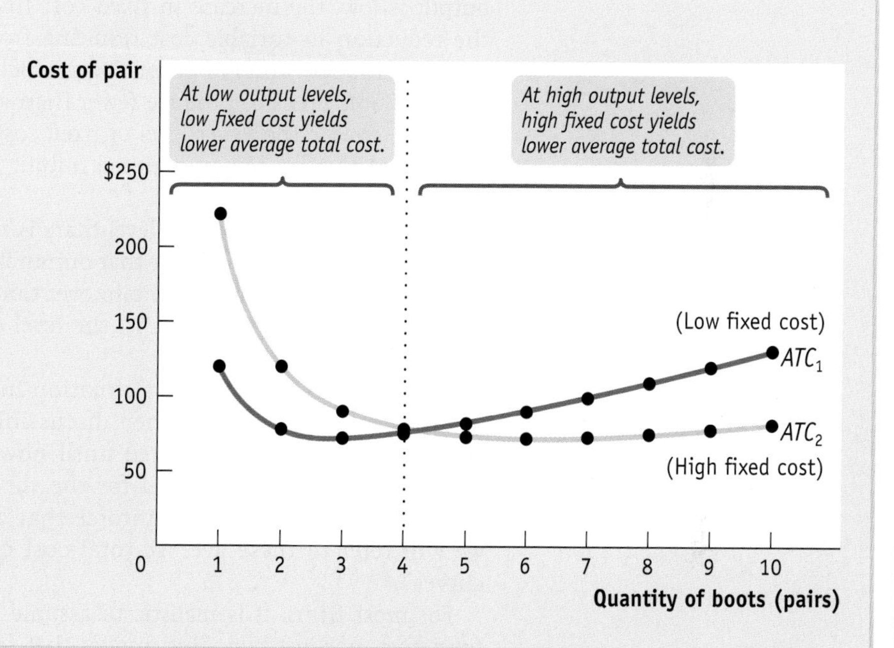

	Low fixed cost (FC = $108)			High fixed cost (FC = $216)		
Quantity of boots (pairs)	High variable cost	Total cost	Average total cost of pair ATC_1	Low variable cost	Total cost	Average total cost of pair ATC_2
1	$12	$120	$120.00	$6	$222	$222.00
2	48	156	78.00	24	240	120.00
3	108	216	72.00	54	270	90.00
4	192	300	75.00	96	312	78.00
5	300	408	81.60	150	366	73.20
6	432	540	90.00	216	432	72.00
7	588	696	99.40	294	510	72.90
8	768	876	109.50	384	600	75.00
9	972	1,080	120.00	486	702	78.00
10	1,200	1,308	130.80	600	816	81.60

\$108. The left half of the table shows variable cost as well as total cost and average total cost assuming a fixed cost of \$108. The average total cost curve for this level of fixed cost is given by ATC_1 in Figure 8-11. Let's compare that to a situation in which the firm buys an additional boot-making machine, doubling its fixed cost to \$216 but reducing its variable cost at any given level of output. The right half of the table shows the firm's variable cost, total cost, and average total cost with this higher level of fixed cost. The average total cost curve corresponding to \$216 in fixed cost is given by ATC_2 in Figure 8-11.

From the figure you can see that when output is small, 4 pairs of boots per day or fewer, average total cost is smaller when Ben's Boots forgoes the additional machinery and maintains the lower fixed cost of \$108: ATC_1 lies below ATC_2. For example, at 3 pairs of boots per day, average total cost is \$72 without the additional machinery and \$90 with the additional machinery. But as output increases beyond 4 pairs per day, the firm's average total cost is lower if it acquires the additional machinery, raising its fixed cost to \$216. For example, at 9 pairs of boots per day, average total cost is \$120 when fixed cost is \$108, and only \$78 when fixed cost is \$216.

Why does average total cost change like this when fixed cost increases? When output is low, the increase in fixed cost from the additional machinery outweighs the reduction in variable cost resulting from higher worker productivity—that is, there are too few units of output over which to spread the additional fixed cost. So if Ben's Boots plans to produce fewer than 4 pairs of boots per day, it would be better off to choose the lower level of fixed cost, \$108, to achieve a lower average total cost of production. When planned output is high, however, it should acquire the additional machinery.

In general, for each output level there is some choice of fixed cost that minimizes the firm's average total cost for that output level. So when the firm has a desired output level that it expects to maintain over time, it should choose the level of fixed cost appropriate to that level—that is, the level of fixed cost that minimizes its average total cost.

Now that we are studying a situation in which fixed cost can change, we need to take time into account when discussing average total cost. All of the average cost curves we have considered until now are defined for a given level of fixed cost—that is, they are defined for the short run, the period of time over which fixed cost doesn't vary. To reinforce that distinction, for the rest of this chapter we will refer to these average total cost curves as "short-run average total cost curves".

For most firms, it is realistic to assume that there are many possible choices of fixed cost, not just two. This implies that for such a firm, many possible short-run average total cost curves will exist, each corresponding to a different choice of fixed cost and so giving rise to what is called a firm's "family" of short-run average total cost curves.

At any given time, a firm will find itself on one of its short-run cost curves, the one corresponding to its current level of fixed cost; a change in output will cause it to move along that curve. If the firm expects that change in output level to be longstanding, then it is likely that the firm's current level of fixed cost is no longer appropriate. Given sufficient time, it will want to adjust its fixed cost to a new level that minimizes average total cost for its new output level. For example, if Ben's Boots had been producing 2 pairs of boots per day with a fixed cost of \$108 but found itself increasing its output to 8 pairs per day for the foreseeable future, then in the long run it should increase its fixed cost to a level that minimizes average total cost at the 8-pairs-per-day output level.

Suppose we do a thought experiment and calculate the lowest possible average total cost that can be achieved for each output level if the firm were to choose its

Figure 8-12

Short-Run and Long-Run Average Total Cost Curves

If Ben's Boots has chosen the level of fixed cost that minimizes short-run average total cost at an output of 6 pairs of boots per day and actually ends up producing 6 pairs per day, it will be on *LRATC* at point *C*. But if it produces more or less, in the short run it will be on the short-run average total cost curve ATC_6, and not on *LRATC*. So if it produces only 3 pairs per day, its average total cost is shown by point *B*, not point *A*. If it produces 9 pairs per day, its average total cost is shown by point *Y*, not point *X*. There are economies of scale when long-run average total cost declines as output increases, and there are diseconomies of scale when long-run average total cost increases as output increases.

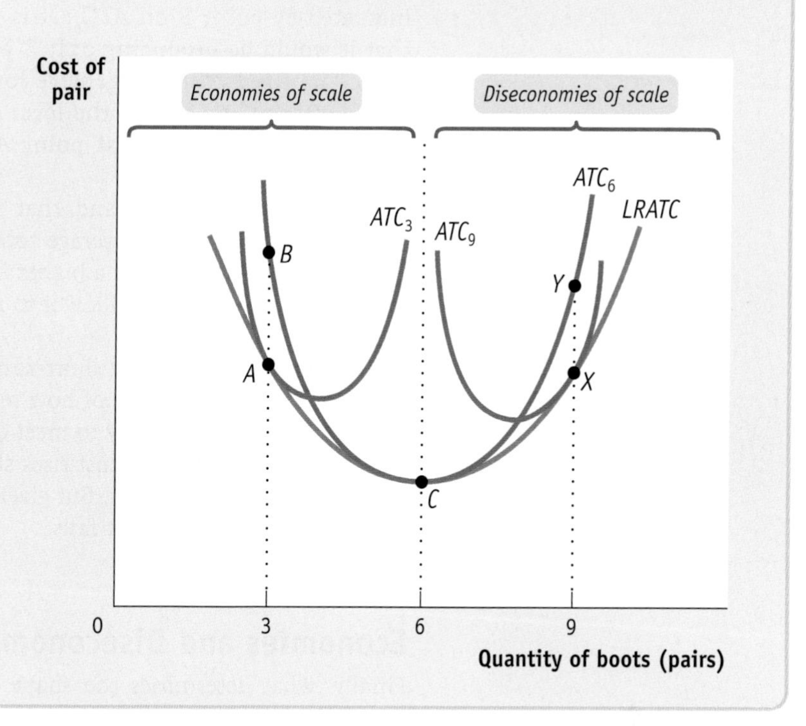

fixed cost for each output level. Economists have given this thought experiment a name: it is the *long-run average total cost curve.* Specifically, the **long-run average total cost curve,** or *LRATC,* is the relationship between output and average total cost when fixed cost has been chosen to minimize average total cost *for each level of output.* If there are many possible choices of fixed cost, the long-run average total cost curve will have the familiar, smooth U shape, as shown by *LRATC* in Figure 8-12.

The **long-run average total cost curve** shows the relationship between output and average total cost when fixed cost has been chosen to minimize average total cost for each level of output.

We can now draw the distinction between the short run and the long run more fully. In the long run, when a producer has had time to choose the fixed cost appropriate for its desired level of output, that producer will be on some point on the long-run average total cost curve. But if the output level is altered, the firm will no longer be on its long-run average total cost curve and will instead be moving along its current short-run average total cost curve. It will not be on its long-run average total cost curve again until it readjusts its fixed cost for its new output level.

Figure 8-12 illustrates this point. The curve ATC_3 shows short-run average total cost if a boot producer has chosen the level of fixed cost that minimizes average total cost at an output of 3 pairs of boots per day. This is confirmed by the fact that at 3 pairs per day, ATC_3 touches *LRATC*, the long-run average total cost curve. Similarly, ATC_6 shows short-run average total cost if a boot producer has chosen the level of fixed cost that would minimize average total cost if its output is 6 pairs of boots per day. It touches *LRATC* at 6 pairs per day. And ATC_9 shows short-run average total costs if a boot producer has chosen the level of fixed cost that would minimize average total cost if its output is 9 pairs of boots per day. It touches *LRATC* at 9 pairs per day.

Suppose that the firm has initially chosen to be on ATC_6. If the firm actually produces 6 pairs of boots per day, it will be at point C on both its short-run and long-run average total cost curves. Suppose, however, that the firm ends up producing only 3 pairs of boots per day. In the short run, its average total cost is indicated by point *B* on ATC_6; it is no longer on *LRATC*. If the firm had known that it would be producing only 3 pairs per day, it would have been better off to reduce its fixed cost and achieve lower average total cost. That is, it would have been better off to choose the level of fixed cost corresponding to ATC_3. Then it would have found itself at point *A*, on the long-run average total cost curve, which lies below point *B*.

Suppose, on the other hand, that the firm ends up producing 9 pairs of boots per day. In the short run its average total cost is indicated by point *Y* on ATC_6. But it would be better off to incur a higher fixed cost in order to reduce its variable cost and move to ATC_9. This would allow it to reach point *X* on the long-run average total cost curve, which lies below *Y*.

The distinction between short-run and long-run average total costs is extremely important in making sense of how real firms operate over time. A company that has to increase output suddenly to meet a surge in demand will typically find that in the short run its average total cost rises sharply because it is hard to get extra production out of the existing facilities. But given time to build new factories or add machinery, short-run average total cost falls.

Economies and Diseconomies of Scale

Finally, what determines the shape of the long-run average total cost curve? The answer is that *scale,* the size of a firm's operations, is often an important determinant of its long-run average total cost of production. Firms that experience scale effects in production find that their long-run average total cost changes substantially depending on the quantity of output they produce. There are **economies of scale** when long-run average total cost declines as output increases. As you can see in Figure 8-12, Ben's Boots experiences economies of scale over output levels ranging from 0 to 6 pairs of boots—the output levels over which the long-run average total cost curve is declining. There are **diseconomies of scale** when long-run average total cost increases as output increases. For Ben's Boots, diseconomies of scale occur at output levels of 6 pairs of boots or more, the output levels over which its long-run average total cost curve is rising.

There are **economies of scale** when long-run average total cost declines as output increases.

There are **diseconomies of scale** when long-run average total cost increases as output increases.

There are **constant returns to scale** when long-run average total cost is constant as output increases.

Although it is not shown in Figure 8-12, there is a third possible relationship between long-run average total cost and scale: firms experience **constant returns to scale** when long-run average total cost is constant as output increases. In this case, the firm's long-run average total cost curve is horizontal over the output levels for which there are constant returns to scale.

What explains these scale effects in production? The answer ultimately lies in the firm's technology of production. Economies of scale often arise from the increased *specialization* that larger output levels allow—a larger scale of operation means that individual workers can limit themselves to more specialized tasks, becoming more skilled and efficient at doing them. Another source of economies of scale is very large initial set-up cost; in some industries—such as auto manufacturing, electricity generating, or petroleum refining—a very large initial cost in the form of plant and equipment is necessary to produce any output. As we'll see in Chapter 14, where we study monopoly, economies of scale have very important implications for how firms and industries interact and behave.

Diseconomies of scale, on the other hand, typically arise in large firms due to problems of coordination and communication: as the firm grows in size, it becomes ever more difficult and therefore costly to communicate and organize its activity. While economies of scale induce firms to get larger, diseconomies of scale tend to limit their size. And when constant returns to scale exist, scale has no effect on a firm's long-run average total cost: it is the same regardless of whether the firm produces 1 unit or 100,000 units.

Summing Up Costs: The Short and Long of It

If a firm is to make the best decisions about how much to produce, it has to understand how its costs relate to the quantity of output it chooses to produce. Table 8-3 provides a quick summary of the concepts and measures of cost you have learned about.

TABLE 8-3

Concepts and Measures of Cost

	Measurement	Definition	Mathematical term
Short run	Fixed cost	Cost that does not depend on the quantity of output produced	*FC*
	Average fixed cost	Fixed cost per unit of output	$AFC = FC/Q$
Short run and long run	Variable cost	Cost that depends on the quantity of output produced	*VC*
	Average variable cost	Variable cost per unit of output	$AVC = VC/Q$
	Total cost	The sum of fixed cost (short-run) and variable cost	$TC = FC$ (short-run) $+ VC$
	Average total cost (average cost)	Total cost per unit of output	$ATC = TC/Q$
	Marginal cost	The change in total cost generated by producing one more unit of output	$MC = \Delta TC/\Delta Q$
Long run	Long-run average total cost	Average cost when fixed cost has been chosen to minimize total cost for each level of output	*LRATC*

economics in action

No Business Like Snow Business: Montreal versus Victoria

Anyone who has lived both in a snowy city, like Montreal, and in a city that only occasionally experiences significant snowfall, like Victoria, is aware of the differences in total cost that arise from making different choices about fixed cost.

In Victoria, even a minor snowfall—say, an inch or two overnight—is enough to create chaos for the next morning's commute. The same snowfall in Montreal has hardly any effect at all. The reason is not that Victorians are wimps and Montrealers are made of sterner stuff; it is that Victoria, where it rarely snows, has only a fraction as many snowploughs and other snow-clearing equipment as cities where heavy snow is a fact of life.

In this sense Victoria and Montreal are like two producers who expect to produce different levels of output, where the "output" is snow removal. Victoria, which rarely has significant snow, has chosen a low level of fixed cost in the form of snow-clearing equipment. This makes sense under normal circumstances, but leaves the

AP/Wide World Photos

A lesson in economies of scale: cities with higher average annual snowfall maintain larger snowplow fleets.

city unprepared when major snow does fall. Montreal, which knows that it will face lots of snow, chooses to accept the higher fixed cost that leaves it in a position to respond effectively. ■

< < < < < < < < < < < < < < < < < < <

>> QUICK REVIEW

- In the long run, firms choose fixed cost according to expected output. Higher fixed cost reduces average total cost when output is high. Lower fixed cost reduces average total cost when output is low.
- There are many possible short-run average total cost curves, each corresponding to a different level of fixed cost. The *long-run average total cost curve*, *LRATC*, shows average total cost over the long run, when the firm has chosen fixed cost to minimize average total cost for each level of output.
- A firm that has fully adjusted its fixed cost for its output level will operate at a point that lies on both its current short-run and long-run average total cost curves. A change in output moves the firm along its current short-run average total cost curve. Once it has readjusted its fixed cost, the firm will operate on a new short-run average total cost curve and on the long-run average total cost curve.
- Scale effects arise from the technology of production. *Economies of scale* tend to make firms larger. *Diseconomies of scale* tend to limit their size. With *constant returns to scale*, scale has no effect.

>> CHECK YOUR UNDERSTANDING 8-3

1. The accompanying table shows three possible combinations of fixed cost and average variable cost.
   a. For each of the three choices, calculate the average total cost of producing 12,000, 22,000, and 30,000 units. For each of these quantities, which choice results in the lowest average total cost?
   b. Suppose that the firm, which has historically produced 12,000 units, experiences a sharp, permanent increase in demand that leads it to produce 22,000 units. Explain how its average total cost will change in the short run and in the long run.
   c. Explain what the firm should do instead if it believes the change in demand is temporary.

Choice	Fixed cost	Average variable cost
1	$8,000	$1.00
2	12,000	0.75
3	24,000	0.25

2. In each of the following cases, explain what kind of scale effects you think the firm will experience and why.
   a. A telemarketing firm in which employees make sales calls using computers and telephones
   b. An interior design firm in which design projects are based on the expertise of the firm's owner
   c. A diamond-mining company

Solutions appear at back of book.

• A LOOK AHEAD •

We've now seen how to use information about how a firm produces to analyse that firm's costs. Our next step is to go from our analysis of costs to an analysis of the supply curve. To understand the supply curve for a particular good, we will need to look both at how a profit-maximizing firm chooses its quantity of output and at how it decides whether to enter or exit the industry producing that good.

SUMMARY

1. The relationship between inputs and output is a producer's **production function.** In the **short run,** the quantity of a **fixed input** cannot be varied but the quantity of a **variable input** can. In the **long run,** the quantities of all inputs can be varied. For a given amount of fixed input, the **total product curve** shows how the quantity of output changes as the quantity of the variable input changes. We may also calculate the **marginal product** of an input, the increase in output from using one more unit of that input.
2. There are **diminishing returns to an input** when its marginal product declines as more of the input is used, holding the quantity of all other inputs fixed.
3. **Total cost,** represented by the **total cost curve,** is equal to the sum of **fixed cost,** which does not depend on output, and **variable cost,** which does depend on output. Due to diminishing returns, marginal cost, the increase in total cost generated by producing one more unit of output, normally increases as output increases.
4. **Average total cost** (also known as **average cost**), total cost divided by quantity of output, is the cost of the average unit of output, while marginal cost is the cost of one more unit produced. Economists believe that **U-shaped average total cost curves** are typical, because average total cost consists of two parts: **average fixed cost,** which falls when output increases (the spreading effect) and **average variable cost,** which rises with output (the diminishing returns effect).
5. When average total cost is U-shaped, the bottom of the U is the level of output at which average total cost is minimized, the point of **minimum-cost output.** This is also the point at which the marginal cost curve crosses

the average total cost curve from below. Due to gains from specialization, the marginal cost curve may slope downward initially before sloping upward, giving it a "swoosh" shape.

6. In the long run, a producer can change its fixed input and its level of fixed cost. By accepting higher fixed cost, a firm can lower its variable cost for any given output level, and vice versa. The **long-run average total cost curve** shows the relationship between output and average total cost when fixed cost has been chosen to minimize average total cost at each level of output. A firm moves along its short-run average total cost curve as it increases output, and returns to a point on both its short-run and long-run average total cost curves once it has adjusted fixed cost to its new output level.
7. As output increases, there are **economies of scale** if long-run average total cost declines; **diseconomies of scale** if it increases; and **constant returns to scale** if it remains constant. Scale effects depend on the technology of production.

KEY TERMS

Production function, p. 193
Fixed input, p. 193
Variable input, p. 193
Long run, p. 193
Short run, p. 193
Total product curve, p. 194
Marginal product, p. 194
Diminishing returns to an input, p. 195
Fixed cost, p. 197
Variable cost, p. 197
Total cost, p. 197
Total cost curve, p. 198
Average total cost, p. 202
Average cost, p. 202
U-shaped average total cost curve, p. 204
Average fixed cost, p. 204
Average variable cost, p. 204
Minimum-cost output, p. 205
Long-run average total cost curve, p. 211
Economies of scale, p. 212
Diseconomies of scale, p. 212
Constant returns to scale, p. 212

PROBLEMS

1. Marty's Frozen Yogurt is a small shop that sells cups of frozen yogurt in a university town. Marty owns three frozen yogurt machines. His other inputs are refrigerators, frozen yogurt mix, cups, sprinkle toppings, and, of course, workers. He estimates that his daily production function when he varies the number of workers he employs (and at the same time, of course, yogurt mix, cups, and so on) is as shown in the accompanying table.

Quantity of labour (workers)	Quantity of frozen yogurt (cups)
0	0
1	110
2	200
3	270
4	300
5	320
6	330

a. What are the fixed inputs and variable inputs in the production of cups of frozen yogurt?

b. Draw the total product curve. Put the quantity of labour on the horizontal axis and the quantity of frozen yogurt on the vertical axis.

c. What is the marginal product of the first worker? The second worker? The third worker? Why does marginal product decline as the number of workers increases?

2. The production function for Marty's Frozen Yogurt is given in Problem 1. Marty pays each of his workers $80 per day. The cost of his other variable inputs is $0.50 per cup of yogurt. His fixed cost is $100 per day.

a. What are Marty's variable cost and total cost when he produces 110 cups of yogurt? 200 cups? Calculate variable and total cost for every level of output given in Problem 1.

b. Draw Marty's variable cost curve. On the same diagram, draw his total cost curve.

c. What is the marginal cost per cup of yogurt for the first 110 cups of yogurt? For the next 90 cups? Calculate the marginal cost for all remaining levels of output.

3. The production function for Marty's Frozen Yogurt is given in Problem 1. The costs are given in Problem 2.

a. For each of the given levels of output, calculate the average fixed cost (*AFC*), average variable cost (*AVC*), and average total cost (*ATC*), per cup of frozen yogurt.

b. On one graph, draw the *AFC* curve, the *AVC* curve, and the *ATC* curve.

c. What principle explains why the *AFC* declines as output increases? What principle explains why the *AVC* increases as output increases? Explain your answers.

d. How many cups of frozen yogurt are produced when average total cost is minimized?

4. The accompanying table shows a car manufacturer's total cost of producing cars.

Quantity of cars	*TC*
0	$500,000
1	540,000
2	560,000
3	570,000
4	590,000
5	620,000
6	660,000
7	720,000
8	800,000
9	920,000
10	1,100,000

a. What is this manufacturer's fixed cost?

b. For each level of output, calculate the variable cost (*VC*). For each level of output except zero output, calculate the average variable cost (*AVC*), the average total cost (*ATC*), and the average fixed cost (*AFC*). What is the minimum-cost output?

c. For each level of output, calculate this manufacturer's marginal cost (*MC*).

d. On one diagram, draw the manufacturer's *AVC*, *ATC*, and *MC* curves.

5. Magnificent Blooms is a florist specializing in floral arrangements for weddings, graduations, and other events. Magnificent Blooms has a fixed cost associated with space and equipment of $100 per day. Each worker is paid $50 per day. The daily production function for Magnificent Blooms is shown in the accompanying table.

Quantity of labour (workers)	Quantity of floral arrangements
0	0
1	5
2	9
3	12
4	14
5	15

a. What is the marginal product (*MPL*) of the first worker, second, third, fourth, and fifth workers? What principle explains why the marginal product per worker declines as the number of workers employed increases?

b. What is the marginal cost (*MC*) of producing each of the first five floral arrangements? The sixth through ninth floral arrangements? The remaining levels of output? What principle explains why the marginal cost per floral arrangement increases as the number of arrangements increases?

6. You have the information shown in the accompanying table about a firm's costs. Complete the missing data.

Quantity	*TC*	*MC*	*ATC*	*AVC*
0	$20			
		$20		
1	?		?	?
		10		
2	?		?	?
		16		
3	?		?	?
		20		
4	?		?	?
		24		
5	?		?	?

7. Evaluate each of the following statements: If a statement is true, explain why; if it is false, identify the falsity and try to correct it.

a. A decreasing marginal product tells us that marginal cost must be rising.

b. An increase in fixed cost increases the minimum-cost output.

c. An increase in fixed cost increases marginal cost.

d. When marginal cost is above average total cost, average total cost must be falling.

8. Mark and Jeff operate a small company that produces souvenir footballs. Their fixed cost is $2,000 per month. They can hire workers for $1,000 per worker per month. They estimate their monthly production function for footballs is as given in the accompanying table.

Quantity of labour (workers)	Quantity of footballs
0	0
1	300
2	800
3	1,200
4	1,400
5	1,500

a. For each quantity of labour, calculate average variable cost (*AVC*), average fixed cost (*AFC*), average total cost (*ATC*), and marginal cost (*MC*).

b. On one diagram, draw in the *AVC*, *ATC*, and *MC* curves.

c. At what level of output is Mark and Jeff's average total cost minimized?

9. You produce widgets. Currently you produce 4 widgets at a total cost of $40.

a. What is your average total cost?

b. Suppose you could produce one more (the fifth) widget at a marginal cost of $5. If you do produce that fifth widget, what will your average total cost be? Has your average total cost increased or decreased? Why?

c. Suppose instead that you could produce one more (the fifth) widget, but at a marginal cost of $20. If you do produce that fifth widget, what will your average total cost be? Has your average total cost increased or decreased? Why?

10. In your economics class, each homework problem set is graded on the basis of a maximum score of 100. You have completed 9 out of 10 of the problem sets for the term, and your current average grade is 88. What range of grades for your 10th problem set will raise your overall average? What range will lower your overall average? Explain.

11. Don owns a small concrete-mixing company. His fixed cost is the cost of the concrete-batching machinery and his mixer trucks. His variable cost is the cost of the sand, gravel, and other inputs for producing concrete; the gas and maintenance for the machinery and trucks; and his workers. He is trying to decide how many mixer trucks to purchase. He has estimated the costs shown in the accompanying table based on estimates of the number of orders his company will receive per week:

Quantity of trucks	*FC*	*VC* 20 orders	*VC* 40 orders	*VC* 60 orders
2	$6,000	$2,000	$5,000	$12,000
3	7,000	1,800	3,800	10,800
4	8,000	1,200	3,600	8,400

a. For each level of fixed cost, calculate Don's total cost for producing 20, 40, and 60 orders per week.

b. If Don is producing 20 orders per week, how many trucks should he purchase and what will his average total cost be? Answer the same questions for 40 and 60 orders per week.

12. Consider Don's concrete company described in Problem 11. Suppose Don purchased 3 trucks, expecting to produce 40 orders per week.

a. Suppose that, in the short run, business declines to 20 orders per week. What is Don's average total cost per order in the short run? What will Don's average total cost per order in the short run be if his business booms to 60 orders per week?

b. What is Don's long-run average total cost for 20 orders per week? Explain why his short-run average total cost of producing 20 orders per week when the number of trucks is fixed at 3 is greater than his long-run average total cost of producing 20 orders per week.

c. Sketch Don's long-run average total cost curve. Sketch his short-run average total cost curve if he owns 3 trucks.

13. True or False? Explain your reasoning.

a. The short-run average total cost can never be less than the long-run average total cost.

b. The short-run average variable cost can never be less than the long-run average total cost.

c. In the long run, choosing a higher level of fixed cost shifts the long-run average total cost curve upward.

14. Wolfsburg Wagon (WW) is a small carmaker. The accompanying table shows WW's long-run average total cost.

Quantity of cars	*LRATC* of car
1	$30,000
2	20,000
3	15,000
4	12,000
5	12,000
6	12,000
7	14,000
8	18,000

a. For which levels of output does WW experience economies of scale?

b. For which levels of output does WW experience diseconomies of scale?

c. For which levels of output does WW experience constant returns to scale?

>**web...** To continue your study and review of concepts in this chapter, please visit the Krugman/Wells website for quizzes, animated graph tutorials, web links to helpful resources, and more.

www.worthpublishers.com/krugmanwellsmyatt

chapter 9

>>Perfect Competition and the Supply Curve

DOING WHAT COMES NATURALLY

FOOD CONSUMERS IN CANADA ARE concerned about health issues. This concern really began to take off in 1993, and it has persisted over the past decade. Demand for "natural" foods and beverages, such as bottled water and organically grown fruits and vegetables, increased rapidly, and the small group of farmers who had pioneered organic farming techniques prospered thanks to higher prices.

But everyone knew that the high prices of organic produce were unlikely to persist even if the new, higher demand for naturally grown food continued: the supply of organic food, while not that price-elastic in the short run, was surely much more price-elastic in the long run. Over time, farms already producing organically would increase their capacity, and conventional farmers would enter the organic food business. So the increase in the quantity supplied in response to the increase in price would be much larger in the long run than in the short run.

Where does the supply curve come from? Why is there a difference between the short-run and the long-run supply curve? In this chapter we will use our understanding of costs, developed in Chapter 8, as the basis for an analysis of the supply curve. As we'll see, this will require that we understand the behaviour both of individual firms and of an entire industry, composed of these many individual firms.

Our analysis in this chapter assumes that the industry in question is characterized by *perfect competition*. We begin by explaining the concept of perfect competition, providing a brief introduction to the conditions that give rise to a perfectly competitive industry. We then show how a producer under perfect competition decides how much to produce. Finally, we use the cost curves of the individual producers to derive the *industry supply curve* under perfect competition. By analysing the way a competitive industry evolves over time, we will come to understand the distinction between the short-run and long-run effects of changes in demand on a competitive industry—such as, for example, the effect of Canada's new taste for organic food on the organic farming industry. We will conclude with a deeper discussion of the conditions necessary for perfect competition.

Peter Dean/Agriculture/Grant Heilman Photography

Whether it's organic strawberries or satellites, how a good is produced determines its cost of production.

What you will learn in this chapter:

- The meaning of **perfect competition** and the characteristics of a **perfectly competitive industry**
- How a **price-taking producer** determines its profit-maximizing quantity of output
- How to assess whether or not a producer is profitable and why an unprofitable producer may continue to operate in the short run
- Why industries behave differently in the short run and the long run
- What determines the **industry supply curve** in both the short run and the long run

Perfect Competition

Suppose that Yves and Zoe are neighbouring farmers, both of whom grow organic tomatoes. Both sell their output to the same grocery store chains that carry organic foods; so, in a real sense, Yves and Zoe compete with each other.

Does this mean that Yves should try to stop Zoe from growing tomatoes or that Yves and Zoe should form an agreement to grow less? Almost certainly not: there are hundreds or thousands of organic tomato farmers, and both Yves and Zoe are competing with all of those other growers as well as with each other. Because so many farmers sell organic tomatoes, if any one of them produced more or less, there would be no measurable effect on market prices.

When people talk about business competition, the image they often have in mind is a situation in which two or three rival firms are intensely struggling for advantage. But economists know that when a business focuses on a few main competitors, it's actually a sign that competition is fairly limited. As the example of organic tomatoes suggests, when there is enough competition it doesn't even make sense to identify your opponents: there are so many competitors that you cannot single out any one of them as a rival.

We can put it another way: Yves and Zoe are **price-taking producers.** A producer is a price-taker when its actions cannot affect the market price of the good it sells. As a result, a price-taking producer considers the market price as given. When there is enough competition—when competition is what economists call "perfect"—then every producer is a price-taker. And there is a similar definition for consumers: a **price-taking consumer** is a consumer who cannot influence the market price of the good by his or her actions. That is, the market price is unaffected by how much or how little of the good the consumer buys.

A **price-taking producer** is a producer whose actions have no effect on the market price of the good it sells.

A **price-taking consumer** is a consumer whose actions have no effect on the market price of the good he or she buys.

Defining Perfect Competition

In a **perfectly competitive market,** all market participants—both consumers and producers—are price-takers. That is, neither consumption decisions by individual consumers nor production decisions by individual producers affect the market price of the good.

A **perfectly competitive market** is a market in which all market participants are price-takers.

The supply and demand model, which we introduced in Chapter 3 and have used repeatedly since then, is a model of a perfectly competitive market. It depends fundamentally on the assumption that no individual buyer or seller of a good, such as scalped tickets to a hockey game or organic tomatoes, believes that he or she can affect the price at which he or she can sell or buy the good.

As a general rule, consumers are indeed price-takers. Instances in which consumers are able to affect the prices they pay are rare. It is, however, quite common for producers to have a significant ability to affect the prices they receive, a phenomenon we'll address in Chapter 14. So the model of perfect competition is appropriate for some but not all markets. An industry in which producers are price-takers is called a **perfectly competitive industry.** Clearly, some industries aren't perfectly competitive; in later chapters we'll see how to analyse industries that don't fit the perfectly competitive model.

A **perfectly competitive industry** is an industry in which producers are price-takers.

Under what circumstances will all producers be price-takers? In the next section we will see that there are three necessary conditions for a perfectly competitive industry.

Three Necessary Conditions for Perfect Competition

The markets for major grains, like wheat and corn, are perfectly competitive: individual wheat and corn farmers, as well as individual buyers of wheat and corn, take market prices as given. (The Canadian Wheat Board is merely a marketing agency unable to influence the world wheat price.) In contrast, the markets for some of the food items made from these grains—in particular, breakfast cereals—are by no means perfectly competitive. There is intense competition among cereal brands, but not *perfect* competition. To understand the difference between the market for wheat and the market for shredded wheat cereal is to understand the three necessary conditions for perfect competition.

A producer's **market share** is the fraction of the total industry output represented by that producer's output.

First, for an industry to be perfectly competitive, it must contain many producers, none of whom has a large **market share.** A producer's market share is the fraction of the total industry output represented by that producer's output. The distribution of market share constitutes a big difference between the grain industry and the breakfast cereal industry. There are thousands of wheat farmers, none of whom account for more than a small fraction of 1% of total wheat sales. The breakfast cereal industry, however, is dominated by four producers: Kellogg's, General Mills, Post, and Quaker Foods. Kellogg's alone accounts for about one-third of all cereal sales. Kellogg's executives know that if they try to sell more corn flakes, they are likely to drive down the market price of corn flakes. That is, they know that their actions influence market prices, simply because they are so large a part of the market that changes in their production will significantly affect the overall quantity supplied. It makes sense to assume that producers are price-takers only when an industry does *not* contain any large players like Kellogg's.

Second, an industry can be perfectly competitive only if consumers regard the products of all producers as equivalent. This clearly isn't true in the breakfast cereal market: consumers don't consider Cap'n Crunch to be a good substitute for Raisin Bran. As a result, the maker of Raisin Bran has some ability to raise its price without fear that it will lose all its customers to the maker of Cap'n Crunch. Contrast this with the case of a **standardized product,** sometimes known as a **commodity.** Consumers regard the output of one wheat producer as a perfect substitute for that of another producer. Consequently, one farmer cannot increase the price for his or her wheat without losing all his or her sales to other wheat farmers. So the second necessary condition for a competitive industry is that the industry output is a standardized product.

A good is a **standardized product,** also known as a **commodity,** when consumers regard the products of different producers as the same good.

Third, all perfectly competitive industries have one more feature: it is easy for new firms to enter the industry or for firms that are currently in the industry to leave. That is, no obstacles in the form of government regulations or limited access to key resources prevent new producers from entering the market. And no additional costs are associated with shutting down a company and leaving the industry. Economists refer to the arrival of new firms into an industry as *entry*; they refer to the departure of firms from an industry as *exit*. When there are no obstacles to entry into or exit from an industry, we say that the industry has **free entry and exit.**

There is **free entry and exit** into and from an industry when producers can easily enter into or leave that industry.

Free entry and exit is not strictly necessary for price-taking behaviour. In Chapter 4 we described the case of the Atlantic lobster fishery, where regulations have the effect of limiting the number of fishers. Despite this, there are enough fishers that they operate as price-takers. But free entry and exit is a key factor in *perfectly* competitive industries. It ensures that the number of producers in an industry can adjust to changing market conditions. And, in particular, this assumption ensures that producers in an industry cannot artificially keep other firms out of the industry. Finally, it ensures (as we will see later in this chapter) that in long-run equilibrium, perfectly competitive firms make zero economic profits.

To sum up, then, perfect competition depends on three necessary conditions. First, the industry must contain many producers, each having a small market share. Second, the industry must produce a standardized product. Third, there must be free entry and exit.

How does an industry that meets these three criteria behave? As a first step toward answering that question, let's look at how an individual producer in a perfectly competitive industry maximizes profit.

FOR INQUIRING MINDS

WHAT'S A STANDARDIZED PRODUCT?

A perfectly competitive industry must produce a standardized product. But is it enough for the products of different firms actually to be the same? No: people must also *think* that they are the same. And producers often go to great lengths to convince consumers that they have a distinctive, or *differentiated,* product, even when they don't.

Consider, for example, champagne—not the super-expensive premium champagnes but the more ordinary stuff. Most people cannot tell the difference between champagne actually produced in the Champagne region of France, where the product originated, and similar products from Spain or California. But the French government has sought and obtained legal protection for the firms of Champagne, ensuring that around the world only bubbly wine from that region can be called champagne. If it's from someplace else, all the seller can do is say that it was produced by the *méthode Champenoise*. This creates a differentiation in the minds of consumers and lets the champagne producers of Champagne charge higher prices.

AP/Wide World Photos

In the end, only *kimchi* eaters can tell you if there is truly a difference between Korean-produced *kimchi* and the Japanese-produced variety.

In a less Eurocentric example, Korean producers of *kimchi*, the spicy fermented cabbage that is the national side dish, are doing their best to convince consumers that the same product packaged by Japanese firms is just not the real thing. The purpose, of course, is to ensure higher prices for Korean *kimchi*.

So is an industry perfectly competitive if it sells products that are indistinguishable except in name but that consumers, for whatever reason, don't think are standardized? No. When it comes to defining the nature of competition, the consumer is always right.

economics in action

The Pain of Competition

Sometimes it is possible to see an industry become perfectly competitive. In fact, it happens on a regular basis in the case of pharmaceuticals: the conditions for perfect competition are often met as soon as the patent on a popular drug expires.

When a company develops a new drug, it is usually able to receive a patent—a legal monopoly that gives it the exclusive right to sell that drug. In Canada, pharmaceutical patents last for 20 years from the date of filing. When the patent expires, the field is open for other companies to sell their own versions of the drug—marketed as "generics" and sold under the medical name of the drug rather than the brand name used by the original producer. Generics are standardized products, much like aspirin, and are often sold by many producers.

A good example came in 1984, when Upjohn's patent on ibuprofen—a painkiller that the company still markets under the brand name Motrin—expired. Most people who use ibuprofen, like most people who use aspirin, now purchase a generic version made by one of many producers.

The shift to perfect competition, not coincidentally, is accompanied by a sharp fall in market price. When its patent expired, Upjohn immediately cut the price of Motrin by 35 percent, but as more companies started selling the generic drug, the price of ibuprofen eventually fell by another two-thirds.

Ten years later the patent on the painkiller naproxen—sold under the brand name Naprosyn—expired. The generic version of naproxen was soon selling at only one-tenth of the original price of Naprosyn.

> > > > > > > > > > > > > > > > > >

>> QUICK REVIEW

- Neither the actions of a *price-taking producer* nor those of a *price-taking consumer* can influence the market price of a good.
- In a *perfectly competitive market,* all producers and consumers are price-takers. Consumers are almost always price-takers, but this is often not true of producers. An industry in which producers are price-takers is a *competitive industry.*
- A *perfectly* competitive industry contains many producers, each of which produces a *standardized product* (also known as a *commodity*) but none of which has a large *market share.*
- Perfectly competitive industries are also characterized by *free entry and exit.*

>>CHECK YOUR UNDERSTANDING 9-1

1. In each of the following situations, do you think the industry described will be perfectly competitive or not? Explain your answer.
   a. There are two producers of aluminium in the world, a good sold in many places.
   b. Only a handful of companies produce natural gas from the North Sea. The price of natural gas is determined by global supply and demand, of which North Sea production represents a small share.
   c. Dozens of designers sell high-fashion clothes. Each designer has his or her own distinctive style and a loyal clientele.
   d. There are many hockey teams in Canada, one or two for each major city, and each selling tickets to its events.

Solutions appear at back of book.

Production and Profits

Consider Jennifer and Jason, who run an organic tomato farm. Suppose that the market price of organic tomatoes is $18 per bushel and that Jennifer and Jason are price-takers—they can sell as much as they like at that price. Then we can use the data in Table 9-1 to find their profit-maximizing level of output by direct calculation.

TABLE 9-1

Profit for Jennifer and Jason's Farm When Market Price Is $18

Quantity of tomatoes *Q* (bushels)	Total revenue *TR*	Total cost *TC*	Profit *TR* – *TC*
0	$0	$14	$–14
1	18	30	–12
2	36	36	0
3	54	44	10
4	72	56	16
5	90	72	18
6	108	92	16
7	126	116	10

The first column shows the quantity of output in bushels, and the second column shows Jennifer and Jason's total revenue from their output: the market value of their output. Total revenue, *TR*, is equal to the market price per unit multiplied by the quantity of output:

$$\textbf{(9-1)}\quad TR = P \times Q$$

In this example, total revenue is $18 per bushel times the quantity of output in bushels.

The third column of Table 9-1 shows Jennifer and Jason's total cost. The fourth column of Table 9-1 shows their profit, equal to total revenue minus total cost:

$$\textbf{(9-2)}\quad \text{Profit} = TR - TC$$

As indicated by the numbers in the table, profit is maximized at an output of 5 bushels, where profit is equal to $18. But we can gain more insight into the profit-maximizing choice of output by viewing it as a problem of marginal analysis, a task we'll do next.

Using Marginal Analysis to Choose the Profit-Maximizing Quantity of Output

Recall from Chapter 7 the *principle of marginal analysis:* the optimal amount of an activity is the level at which marginal benefit is equal to marginal cost. To apply this principle, consider the effect on a producer's profit of increasing output by 1 unit. The marginal benefit of that unit is the additional revenue generated by selling it; this measure has a name—it is called the **marginal revenue** of that output. The general formula for marginal revenue is:

Marginal revenue is the change in total revenue generated by an additional unit of output.

$$\textbf{(9-3)}\quad \text{Marginal revenue} = \frac{\text{Change in total revenue}}{\text{Change in output}} = \begin{array}{c}\text{Change in total revenue}\\ \text{generated by one}\\ \text{additional unit of output}\end{array}$$

or

$$MR = \Delta TR/\Delta Q$$

So Jennifer and Jason would maximize their profit by producing bushels up to the point at which the marginal revenue is equal to marginal cost. We can summarize this as the producer's **optimal output rule:** profit is maximized by producing the quantity at which the marginal revenue of the last unit produced is equal to its marginal cost. That is, $MR = MC$ at the optimal quantity of output.

The **optimal output rule** says that profit is maximized by producing the quantity of output at which the marginal revenue of the last unit produced is equal to its marginal cost.

We can learn how to apply the optimal output rule with the help of Table 9-2, which provides various short-run cost measures for Jennifer and Jason's farm. The second column contains the farm's variable cost, and the third column shows its total cost of output based on the assumption that the farm incurs a fixed cost of $14. The fourth column shows their marginal cost. Notice that, in this example, the marginal cost falls as output increases from a low level before rising, so that the marginal cost curve has the "swoosh" shape described in Chapter 8. (Shortly it will become clear that this shape has important implications for short-run production decisions.)

The fifth column contains the farm's marginal revenue, which has an important feature: Jennifer and Jason's marginal revenue is constant at $18 for every output level. The sixth and final column of Table 9-2 shows the calculation of the net gain per bushel of tomatoes, which is equal to marginal revenue minus marginal cost—or, equivalently, market price minus marginal cost. As you can see, it is positive for the 1st through 5th bushels; producing each of these bushels raises Jennifer and Jason's profit. For the 6th and 7th bushels, however, net gain is negative: producing them

PITFALLS

WHAT IF MARGINAL REVENUE AND MARGINAL COST AREN'T EXACTLY EQUAL?

The optimal output rule says that to maximize profit, you should produce the quantity at which marginal revenue is equal to marginal cost. But what do you do if there is no output level at which marginal revenue equals marginal cost? In that case, you produce the largest quantity for which marginal revenue exceeds marginal cost. This is the case in Table 9-2 at an output of 5 bushels. The simpler version of the optimal output rule applies when production involves large numbers, such as hundreds of thousands of units. In such cases marginal cost comes in small increments, and there is always a level of output at which marginal cost almost exactly equals marginal revenue.

TABLE 9-2

Short-Run Costs for Jennifer and Jason's Farm

Quantity of tomatoes Q (bushels)	Variable cost VC	Total cost TC	Marginal cost of bushel $MC = \Delta TC/\Delta Q$	Marginal revenue of bushel	Net gain of bushel = $MR - MC$
0	$0	$14			
			$16	$18	$2
1	16	30			
			6	18	12
2	22	36			
			8	18	10
3	30	44			
			12	18	6
4	42	56			
			16	18	2
5	58	72			
			20	18	−2
6	78	92			
			24	18	−6
7	102	116			

would decrease, not increase, profit. (You can verify this by examining Table 9-1.) So 5 bushels are Jennifer and Jason's profit-maximizing output; it is the level of output at which marginal cost is equal to the market price, $18.

The **price-taking firm's optimal output rule** says that a price-taking firm's profit is maximized by producing the quantity of output at which the market price is equal to the marginal cost of the last unit produced.

This example, in fact, illustrates another general rule derived from marginal analysis—the **price-taking firm's optimal output rule,** which says that a price-taking firm's profit is maximized by producing the quantity of output at which the market price is equal to the marginal cost of the last unit produced. That is, $P = MC$ at the *price-taking firm's* optimal quantity of output. In fact, the price-taking firm's optimal output rule is just an application of the optimal output rule to the particular case of a price-taking firm. Why? Because in the case of a price-taking firm, *marginal revenue is equal to price.* A price-taking firm cannot influence the market price by its actions. It always takes the market price as given because it cannot lower the market price by selling more or raise the market price by selling less. So, for a price-taking firm, the additional revenue generated by producing one more unit is always the market price. We will need to keep this fact in mind in future chapters, where we will learn that marginal revenue is not equal to the market price if the industry is not perfectly competitive and, as a result, firms are not price-takers.

The **marginal revenue curve** shows how marginal revenue varies as output varies.

For the remainder of this chapter, we will assume that the firms in question are, like Jennifer and Jason's farm, perfectly competitive. Figure 9-1 shows that Jennifer and Jason's profit-maximizing quantity of output is, indeed, the number of bushels at which the marginal cost of production is equal to price. The figure shows the marginal cost curve, *MC*, drawn from the data in the last column of Table 9-1. As in Chapter 8, we plot the marginal cost of increasing output from 1 to 2 bushels halfway between 1 and 2, and so on. The horizontal line at $18 is Jennifer and Jason's **marginal revenue curve, *MR*.** Note that whenever a firm is a price-taker, its marginal revenue curve is a horizontal line at the market price: it can sell as much as it likes at the market price. Regardless of whether it sells more or less, the market price is unaffected. In effect, the individual firm faces a horizontal, perfectly elastic demand curve for its output—an individual demand curve for its output that is equivalent to its marginal revenue curve. The marginal cost curve crosses the marginal revenue curve at point *E*. Sure enough, the quantity of output at *E* is 5 bushels.

Figure 9-1

The Price-Taking Firm's Profit-Maximizing Quantity of Output

At the profit-maximizing quantity of output, the market price is equal to marginal cost. It is located at the point where the marginal cost curve crosses the marginal revenue curve, which is a horizontal line at the market price. Here, the profit-maximizing point is at an output of 5 bushels of tomatoes, the output quantity at point *E*.

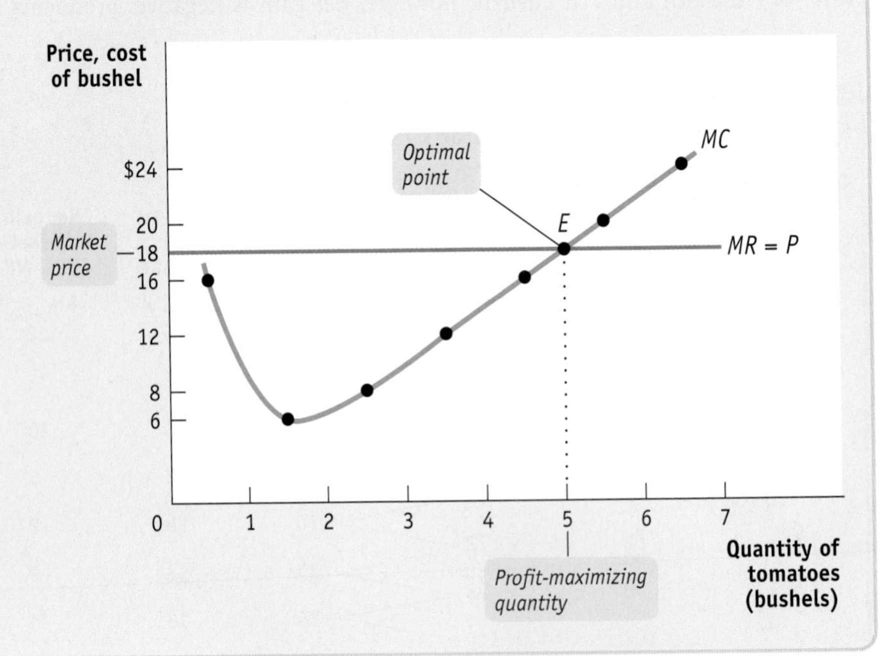

Does this mean that the firm's production decision can be entirely summed up as "produce up to the point where the marginal cost of production is equal to the price"? No, not quite. Before applying the principle of marginal analysis to determine how much to produce, a potential producer must as a first step answer an "either–or" question: should it produce at all? If the answer to that question is yes, it then proceeds to the second step—a "how much" decision: maximizing profit by choosing the quantity of output at which marginal cost is equal to price.

To understand why the first step in the production decision involves an "either–or" question, we need to ask how we determine whether it is profitable or unprofitable to produce at all.

When Is Production Profitable?

Recall from Chapter 7 that a firm's decision whether or not to stay in a given business depends on its *economic profit*—a measure based on the opportunity cost of resources used in the business. To put it a slightly different way: in the calculation of profit, a firm's total cost incorporates the implicit cost—the benefits forgone in the next-best use of the firm's resources—as well as the explicit cost in the form of actual cash outlays.

We will assume that all costs, implicit as well as explicit, are included in the cost numbers given in Table 9-1; as a result, the profit numbers in Table 9-2 are economic profit. So what determines whether Jennifer and Jason's farm earns a profit or generates a loss? The answer is that, given the farm's cost curves, whether or not it is profitable depends on the market price of tomatoes—specifically, *whether the market price is more or less than the farm's minimum average total cost.*

Table 9-3 calculates short-run average variable cost and short-run average total cost for Jennifer and Jason's farm. These are short-run values, because we take fixed cost as given. (We'll turn to the effects of changing fixed cost shortly.) The short-run average total cost curve, *ATC*, is shown in Figure 9-2 (page 226), along with the marginal cost curve, *MC*, from Figure 9-1. As you can see, average total cost is minimized at point *C*, corresponding to an output of 4 bushels—the *minimum-cost output*—and an average total cost of $14 per bushel.

To see how these curves can be used to decide whether production is profitable or unprofitable, recall that profit is equal to total revenue minus total cost, $TR - TC$. This means:

- If $TR > TC$, the firm is profitable.
- If $TR = TC$, the firm breaks even.
- If $TR < TC$, the firm incurs a loss.

TABLE 9-3

Average Costs for Jennifer and Jason's Farm

Quantity of tomatoes Q (bushels)	Variable cost VC	Total cost TC	Average variable cost of bushel $AVC = VC/Q$	Average total cost of bushel $ATC = TC/Q$
1	$16.00	$30.00	$16.00	$30.00
2	22.00	36.00	11.00	18.00
3	30.00	44.00	10.00	14.67
4	42.00	56.00	10.50	14.00
5	58.00	72.00	11.60	14.40
6	78.00	92.00	13.00	15.33
7	102.00	116.00	14.57	16.57

Figure 9-2

Costs and Production in the Short Run

This figure shows the marginal cost curve, *MC*, and the short-run average total cost curve, *ATC*. When the market price is $14, output will be 4 bushels of tomatoes (the minimum-cost output), represented by point *C*. The price of $14, equal to the firm's minimum average total cost, is the firm's *break-even price*. 

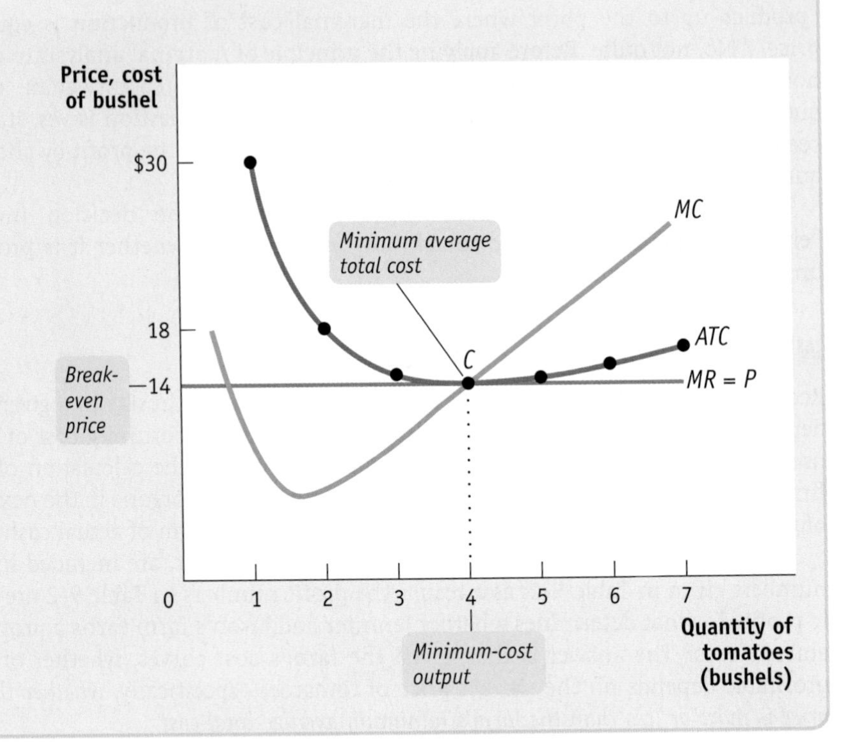

We can also express this idea in terms of revenue and cost per unit of output. If we divide profit by the number of units of output, Q, we obtain the following expression for profit per unit of output:

(9-4) $\text{Profit}/Q = TR/Q - TC/Q$

TR/Q is average revenue—that is, the market price. *TC/Q* is average total cost. So a firm is profitable if the market price for its product exceeds the average total cost of the quantity the firm produces; a firm loses money if the market price is less than the average total cost of the quantity the firm produces. This means:

- If $P > ATC$, the firm is profitable.
- If $P = ATC$, the firm breaks even.
- If $P < ATC$, the firm incurs a loss.

Figure 9-3 illustrates this result, showing how the market price determines whether a firm is profitable. It also shows how profits are depicted graphically. Each panel shows the marginal cost curve, *MC*, and the short-run average total cost curve, *ATC*. Average total cost is minimized at point *C*. Panel (a) shows the case we have already analyzed, in which the market price of tomatoes is $18 per bushel. Panel (b) shows the case in which the market price of tomatoes is lower, $10 per bushel.

In panel (a), we see that at a price of $18 per bushel the profit-maximizing quantity of output is 5 bushels, indicated by point *E* where the marginal cost curve, *MC*, intersects the marginal revenue curve—which for a price-taking firm is a horizontal line at the market price. At that quantity of output, average total cost is $14.40 per bushel, indicated by point *Z*. Since the price per bushel exceeds average total cost per bushel, Jennifer and Jason's farm is profitable.

Jennifer and Jason's total profits when the market price is $18 are represented by the area of the shaded rectangle in Panel (a). To see why, notice that total profit can be expressed in terms of profit per unit:

(9-5) Profit = $TR - TC = (TR/Q - TC/Q) \times Q$

or, equivalently,

$$\text{Profit} = (P - ATC) \times Q$$

since P is equal to TR/Q and ATC is equal to TC/Q. The height of the shaded rectangle in panel (a) corresponds to the vertical distance between points E and Z. It is equal to $P - ATC$ = \$18.00 – \$14.40 = \$3.60 per bushel. The shaded rectangle has a width equal to the output: Q = 5 bushels. So the area of that rectangle is equal to

Figure 9-3

Profitability and the Market Price

In panel (a) the market price is \$18. The farm is profitable because price exceeds minimum average total cost, the break-even price, \$14. The farm's optimal output choice is indicated by point *E*, corresponding to an output of 5 bushels. The average total cost of producing 5 bushels is indicated by point *Z* on the *ATC* curve, corresponding to an amount of \$14.40. The vertical distance between *E* and *Z* corresponds to the farm's per-unit profit, \$18.00 – \$14.40 = \$3.60. Total profit is given by the area of the shaded rectangle, 5 × \$3.60 = \$18.00.

In panel (b) the market price is \$10; the farm is unprofitable because the price falls below the minimum average total cost, \$14. The farm's optimal output choice when producing is indicated by point *A*, corresponding to an output of 3 bushels. The farm's per-unit loss, \$14.67 – \$10.00 = \$4.67, is represented by the vertical distance between *A* and *Y*. The farm's total loss is represented by the shaded rectangle, 3 × \$4.67 = \$14.00 (adjusted for rounding error). >web...

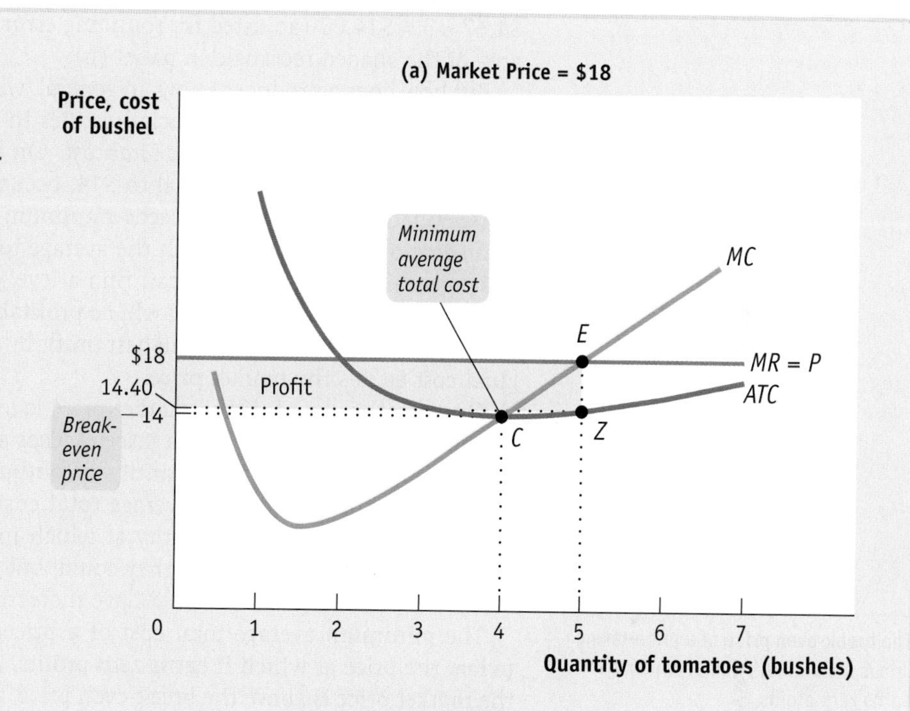

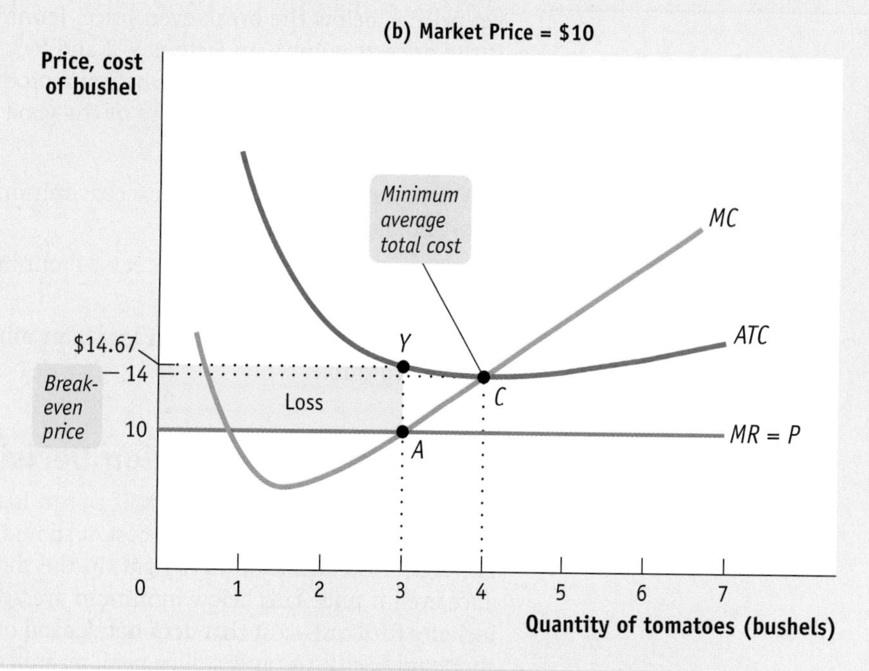

Jennifer and Jason's profit: 5 bushels × \$3.60 profit per bushel = \$18—the same number we calculated in Table 9-2.

What about the situation illustrated in panel (b)? Here the market price of tomatoes is \$10 per bushel. Setting price equal to marginal cost leads to a profit-maximizing output of 3 bushels, indicated by point *A*. At this output, Jennifer and Jason have an average total cost of \$14.67 per bushel, indicated by point Y. At their profit-maximizing output quantity—3 bushels—average total cost exceeds the market price. This means that Jennifer and Jason's farm generates losses, not profits.

How much do they lose by producing when the market price is \$10? On each bushel they lose $ATC - P$ = \$14.67 – \$10.00 = \$4.67, an amount corresponding to the vertical distance between points *A* and Y. And they would produce 3 bushels, which corresponds to the width of the shaded rectangle. So, the total value of the losses is \$4.67 × 3 = \$14.00 (adjusted for rounding error), an amount that corresponds to the area of the shaded rectangle in panel (b).

But how does a producer know, in general, whether or not its business will be profitable? It turns out that the crucial test lies in a comparison of the market price to the producer's *minimum average total cost.* On Jennifer and Jason's farm, minimum average total cost, which is equal to \$14, occurs at an output quantity of 4 bushels. Whenever the market price exceeds minimum average total cost, the producer can find some output level for which the average total cost is less than the market price. That means that the producer can find a level of output at which the firm makes a profit. Jennifer and Jason's farm will be profitable whenever the market price exceeds \$14. And they will achieve the highest profit by producing the quantity at which marginal cost equals the market price.

On the other hand, if the market price is less than minimum average total cost, there is no output level at which price exceeds average total cost. As a result, the firm will be unprofitable at any quantity of output. As we saw, at a price of \$10—an amount less than minimum average total cost—Jennifer and Jason did indeed lose money. By producing the quantity at which marginal cost equals the market price, Jennifer and Jason did the best they could, but the best that they could do was a loss of \$14. Any other quantity would have increased the size of their loss.

The **break-even price** of a price-taking firm is the market price at which it earns zero profits.

The minimum average total cost of a price-taking firm is called its **break-even price,** the price at which it earns zero profits. A firm will earn positive profits when the market price is above the break-even price, and it will suffer losses when the market price is below the break-even price. Jennifer and Jason's break-even price of \$14 is the price at point C in Figures 9-2 and 9-3.

So the rule for determining whether a producer of a good is profitable depends on a comparison of the market price of the good to the producer's break-even price—its minimum average total cost:

- Whenever the market price exceeds minimum average total cost, the producer is profitable.
- Whenever the market price equals minimum average total cost, the producer breaks even.
- Whenever the market price is less than minimum average total cost, the producer is unprofitable.

The Short-Run Production Decision

You might be tempted to say that if a firm is unprofitable because the market price is below its minimum average total cost, it shouldn't produce any output. In the short run, however, this conclusion isn't right. In the short run, sometimes the firm should produce even if price falls below minimum average total cost. The reason is that total cost includes *fixed cost*—cost that does not depend on the amount of output produced. In the short run fixed cost must still be paid, regardless of whether or not a firm produces. For example, if Jennifer and Jason have rented a tractor for the year, they have to pay that rent regardless of whether they produce any tomatoes. Since it cannot be changed in the short run, their fixed cost is irrelevant to their decision about whether to produce or shut down in the short run. Although fixed costs should play no role in the decision about whether to produce at all in the short run, other costs—variable costs—do matter. An example of variable costs is the wages of workers who must be hired to help with planting and harvesting. Variable costs can be saved by *not* producing, so they should play a role in determining whether or not to produce in the short run.

Let's turn to Figure 9-4: it shows both the short-run average total cost curve, *ATC*, and the short-run average *variable* cost curve, *AVC*, drawn from the information in Table 9-3. Recall that the difference between the two curves—the vertical distance between them—represents average fixed cost, the fixed cost per unit of output, *FC/Q*. Because the marginal cost curve has a "swoosh" shape—falling at first before rising—the short-run average variable cost curve is U-shaped: the initial fall in marginal cost causes average variable cost to fall as well, before rising marginal cost eventually pulls it up again. The short-run average variable cost curve reaches its minimum value of $10 at point *A*, at an output of 3 bushels.

We are now prepared to fully analyze the optimal production decision in the short run. We need to consider two cases:

- When the market price is below minimum average *variable* cost
- When the market price is greater than or equal to minimum average *variable* cost

When the market price is below minimum average variable cost, the price the firm receives is not covering its variable cost per unit. A firm in this situation should cease production immediately. Why? Because there is no level of output at which the firm's total revenue covers its variable costs—the costs it can avoid by not operating. In this case, the firm maximizes its profits by not producing at all—by, in effect, minimizing its losses. It will still incur fixed cost in the short run, but it will no longer incur any variable cost. This means that the minimum average variable cost is equal to the **shut-down price,** the price at which the firm ceases production in the short run.

A firm will cease production in the short run if the market price falls below the **shut-down price,** which is equal to minimum average variable cost.

Figure 9-4

The Short-Run Individual Supply Curve

When the market price exceeds Jennifer and Jason's *shut-down price* of $10, the minimum average variable cost indicated by point *A*, they will produce the output quantity at which marginal cost is equal to price. So at any price above minimum average *variable* cost, the short-run individual supply curve is the firm's marginal cost curve; this corresponds to the upward-sloping segment of the individual supply curve. When market price falls below minimum average variable cost, the firm ceases operation in the short run. This corresponds to the vertical segment of the individual supply curve along the vertical axis.

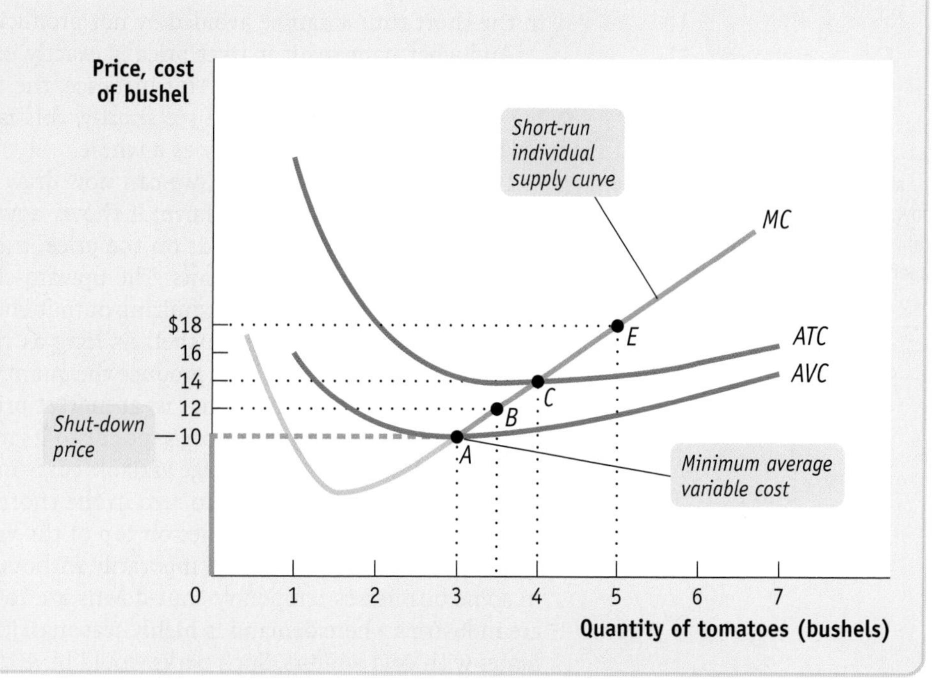

When price is greater than minimum average variable cost, however, the firm should produce in the short run. In this case, the firm maximizes profit—or minimizes losses—by choosing the output quantity at which its marginal cost is equal to the market price. For example, if the market price of tomatoes is $18 per bushel, Jennifer and Jason should produce at point *E* in Figure 9-4, corresponding to an output quantity of 5 bushels. Note that point *C* in Figure 9-4 corresponds to the farm's break-even price of $14 per bushel. Since *E* lies above *C*, Jennifer and Jason's farm will be profitable; they will generate a per-bushel profit of $18.00 – $14.40 = $3.60 when the market price is $18.

But what if the market price lies between the shut-down price and the break-even price—that is, between minimum average *variable* cost and minimum average *total* cost? In the case of Jennifer and Jason's farm, this corresponds to prices anywhere between $10 and $14—say, a market price of $12. At $12, Jennifer and Jason's farm is not profitable; since the market price is below minimum average total cost, the farm is losing the difference between price and average total cost per unit produced. Yet, even if it isn't covering its total cost per unit, it is covering its variable cost per unit and some—but not all—of the fixed cost per unit. If a firm in this situation shuts down, it would incur no variable cost but would incur the *full* fixed cost. As a result, shutting down generates an even greater loss than continuing to operate.

This means that whenever price falls between minimum average total cost and minimum average variable cost, the firm is better off producing some output in the short run. The reason is that by producing, it can cover its variable cost per unit and at least some of its fixed cost, even though it is incurring a loss. In this case, the firm maximizes profit—that is, minimizes its loss—by choosing the quantity of output at which its marginal cost is equal to the market price. So if Jennifer and Jason face a market price of $12 per bushel, their profit-maximizing output is given by point *B* in Figure 9-4, corresponding to an output of 3.5 bushels.

It's worth noting that the decision to produce when the firm is covering its variable costs but not all of its fixed cost is similar to the decision to ignore *sunk costs,* a concept we studied in Chapter 7. You may recall that a sunk cost is a cost that has already been incurred and cannot be recouped; and because it cannot be changed, it should have no effect on any current decision. In the short-run production decision, fixed cost is, in effect, like a sunk cost—it has been spent, and it can't be recovered in the short run. This comparison also illustrates why variable cost does indeed matter in the short run: it can be avoided by not producing.

And what happens if market price is exactly equal to the shut-down price, minimum average variable cost? In this instance, the firm is indifferent between producing 3 units or 0 units. As we'll see shortly, this is an important point when looking at the behaviour of an industry as a whole.

The **short-run individual supply curve** shows how an individual producer's profit-maximizing output quantity depends on the market price, taking fixed cost as given.

Putting everything together, we can now draw the **short-run individual supply curve** of Jennifer and Jason's farm; it shows how the profit-maximizing quantity of output in the short run depends on the price, the red line in Figure 9-4. As you can see, the curve is in two segments. The upward-sloping segment starting at point *A* shows the short-run profit-maximizing output choice when market price is above the shut-down price of $10 per bushel. As long as the market price is above the shut-down price, Jennifer and Jason produce the quantity of output at which marginal cost is equal to the market price. That is, at market prices above the shut-down price, the firm's short-run supply curve corresponds to its marginal cost curve. But at any market price below minimum average variable cost—in this case, $10 per bushel—the firm shuts down and output drops to zero in the short run. This corresponds to the vertical segment of the curve that lies on top of the vertical axis.

Do firms really shut down temporarily without going out of business? Yes. In fact, in some businesses temporary shut-downs are routine. The most common examples are industries where demand is highly seasonal, like outdoor amusement parks in climates with cold winters. Such parks would have to offer very low prices to entice customers during the colder months—prices so low that the owners would not cover their variable costs (principally wages and electricity). The wiser choice economically is to shut down until warm weather brings enough customers who are willing to pay a higher price.

Changing Fixed Cost

Although fixed cost cannot be altered in the short run, in the long run firms can acquire or get rid of machines, buildings, and so on. As we learned in Chapter 8, in the long run the level of fixed cost is a matter of choice. We saw that a firm will choose the level of fixed cost that minimizes the average total cost for its desired output quantity. Now we will focus on an even bigger question facing a firm when choosing its fixed cost: whether to incur *any* fixed cost at all by remaining in its current business.

In the long run, a producer can always eliminate fixed cost by selling off its plant and equipment. If it does so, of course, it can't ever produce—it has exited the industry. In contrast, a potential producer can take on some fixed cost by acquiring machines and other resources, which puts it in a position to produce—it can enter the industry. In most perfectly competitive industries the set of producers, although fixed in the short run, changes in the long run as firms enter or leave the industry.

Consider Jennifer and Jason's farm once again. In order to simplify our analysis, we will sidestep the problem of choosing among several possible levels of fixed cost. Instead, we will assume from now on that Jennifer and Jason have only one possible choice of fixed cost if they operate, the amount of $14 that was the basis for the calculations in Tables 9-1, 9-2, and 9-3. Alternatively, they can choose a fixed cost of zero if they exit the industry. (With this assumption, Jennifer and Jason's short-run average total cost curve and their long-run average total cost curve are one and the same.)

Suppose that the market price of organic tomatoes is consistently less than $14 over an extended period of time. In that case, Jennifer and Jason never fully cover their fixed cost: their business runs at a loss. In the long run, then, they can do better by closing their business and leaving the industry. In other words, *in the long run* firms will exit an industry if the market price is consistently less than their break-even price, their minimum average total cost.

On the other hand, suppose that the price of organic tomatoes is consistently above the break-even price, $14, for an extended period of time. Because their farm is profitable, Jennifer and Jason will remain in the industry and continue producing. But things won't stop there. The organic tomato industry meets the criterion of *free entry:* there are many potential organic tomato producers, because the necessary inputs are easy to obtain. And the cost curves of those potential producers are likely to be similar to those of Jennifer and Jason, since the technology used by other producers is likely to be very similar to that used by Jennifer and Jason. If the price is high enough to generate profits for existing producers, it will also attract some of these potential producers into the industry. So *in the long run* a price in excess of $14 should lead to entry: new producers will come into the organic tomato industry.

As we will see in the next section, exit and entry lead to an important distinction between the *short-run industry supply curve* and the *long-run industry supply curve.*

PITFALLS

ECONOMIC PROFITS, AGAIN

Some readers may wonder why firms would enter an industry when they will do little more than break even. Wouldn't people prefer to go into other businesses that yield a better profit?

The answer is that here, as always, when we calculate costs, we mean *opportunity costs*—that is, costs that include the return a business owner could get by using his or her resources elsewhere. And so the profit that we calculate is *economic profit;* if the market price is above the break-even level, potential business owners can earn more in this industry than they could elsewhere.

Summing Up: The Perfectly Competitive Firm's Profitability and Production Conditions

In this chapter, we've studied where the supply curve for a perfectly competitive firm comes from. Every perfectly competitive firm makes its production decisions by maximizing profit, and these decisions determine the supply curve. Table 9-4 (page 232) summarizes the competitive firm's profitability and production conditions. It also relates them to entry and exit from the industry.

TABLE 9-4

Summary of the Perfectly Competitive Firm's Profitability and Production Conditions

Profitability Condition (minimum *ATC* = break-even price)	Result
$P >$ minimum *ATC*	Firm profitable. Entry into industry in the long run.
$P =$ minimum *ATC*	Firm breaks even. No entry into or exit from industry in the long run.
$P <$ minimum *ATC*	Firm unprofitable. Exit from industry in the long run.
Production Condition (minimum *AVC* = shut-down price)	**Result**
$P >$ minimum *AVC*	Firm produces in the short run. If $P <$ minimum *ATC*, firm covers variable cost and some but not all of fixed cost. If $P >$ minimum *ATC*, firm covers all variable cost and fixed cost.
$P =$ minimum *AVC*	Firm indifferent between producing in the short run or not. Just covers variable cost.
$P <$ minimum *AVC*	Firm shuts down in the short run. Does not cover variable cost.

economics in action

The Shut-Down Rule and Air Canada

Post-9/11, airlines incurred significant additional costs of doing business—costs associated with tighter security procedures and mammoth increases in their insurance rates. On top of this, the price of crude oil has spiralled upwards. This has shifted the supply curve for air travel up and to the left. At the same time, fears of renewed terrorist attacks decreased the demand for air travel. This combination has drastically reduced the amount of air travel and caused havoc in the airline industry. Many airlines have gone bankrupt. Others, like Air Canada, are continuing to operate at a loss. The loss implies that Air Canada is not covering its average total costs. The fact that it's still operating implies that it is more than covering its average variable costs.

One would think that the gap between the break-even price and the shut-down price would be huge in the airline industry, since fixed costs constitute a significant proportion of total costs. One Boeing 747 costs about $270 million. Sure, variable costs like personnel and fuel are expensive. But imagine the interest on the capital expenditure and the depreciation, maintenance, and storage costs for a whole fleet of aircraft, not to mention other fixed costs like lease of airport gates and runway and office space. That's why we see so many airlines continuing to operate at a loss.

How long can an airline continue to operate at a loss? In part, this question involves asking how long the "short run" is. This depends in part on how quickly an airline can liberate itself of its fixed costs. Having a "fire sale" of Boeing 747s might involve substantial capital losses—especially in a depressed air-travel environment. Beyond that, it depends on whether there is any prospect of an improved business climate on the horizon, or possibly even government bailouts. Without them, let's say that in this case the short run is two or three years at the most. Keep your fingers crossed, Air Canada. ■

>>QUICK REVIEW

- A producer chooses output according to the *optimal output rule.* For a price-taking firm, *marginal revenue* is equal to price and it chooses output according to the *price-taking firm's optimal output rule.*
- A firm is profitable whenever market price exceeds its *break-even* price, equal to its minimum average total cost. A firm is unprofitable whenever price falls below its break-even price. And a firm breaks even when price is equal to its break-even price.
- Fixed cost is irrelevant to the firm's optimal short-run production decision. When price exceeds its *shut-down price*—minimum average variable cost—the price-taking firm produces the quantity of output at which marginal cost equals price. When price is lower than its shut-down price, it ceases production in the short run. This defines the firm's *short-run individual supply curve.*
- In the long run, fixed cost matters. If price falls below minimum average total cost for an extended period of time, a firm will exit the industry. If price exceeds minimum average total cost, the firm is profitable and will remain in the industry; in addition, other firms will enter the industry.

>>CHECK YOUR UNDERSTANDING 9-2

1. Draw a short-run diagram showing a U-shaped average total cost curve, a U-shaped average variable cost curve, and a "swoosh"-shaped marginal cost curve. On it, indicate the range of output and the range of price for which the following actions are optimal.
   a. The firm shuts down immediately.
   b. The firm operates in the short run despite sustaining a loss.
   c. The firm operates while making a profit.

2. The province of New Brunswick has a very active lobster industry, which harvests lobsters during the summer months. During the rest of the year, lobsters can be obtained from other parts of the world but at a much higher price. New Brunswick is also full of "lobster shacks", roadside restaurants serving lobster dishes that are open only during the summer. Explain why it is optimal for lobster shacks to operate only during the summer.

Solutions appear at back of book.

The Industry Supply Curve

Why will an increase in the demand for organic tomatoes lead to a large price increase at first but a much smaller increase in the long run? The answer lies in the behaviour of the **industry supply curve**—the relationship between the price and the total output of an industry as a whole. The industry supply curve is what we referred to in earlier chapters as *the* supply curve or the market supply curve. But here we take some extra care to distinguish between the *individual supply curve* of a single firm and the supply curve of the industry as a whole.

As you might guess from the previous section, the industry supply curve must be analyzed in somewhat different ways for the short run and the long run. Let's start with the short run.

The **industry supply curve** shows the relationship between the price of a good and the total output of the industry as a whole.

The Short-Run Industry Supply Curve

Recall that in the short run, the number of producers in an industry is fixed—there is no entry or exit. We can best understand how the industry supply curve emerges from individual producer supply curves by imagining that all the producers are alike. So let's assume that there are 100 organic tomato farms, each with the same costs as Jennifer and Jason's farm.

Each of these 100 farms will have an individual short-run supply curve like the one in Figure 9-4. At a price below $10, no farms will produce. At a price of more than $10, each farm will produce the quantity of output at which its marginal cost is equal to the market price. As you can see from Figure 9-4, this will lead them to produce 4 bushels if the price is $14 per bushel, 5 bushels if the price is $18, and so on. So if there are 100 organic tomato farmers, and the price of organic tomatoes is $18 per bushel, the industry as a whole will produce 500 bushels, corresponding to 100 farmers × 5 bushels per farmer, and so on. The result will be the **short-run industry supply curve,** shown as *S* in Figure 9-5. This curve shows

The **short-run industry supply curve** shows how the quantity supplied by an industry depends on the market price given a fixed number of producers.

Figure 9-5

The Short-Run Market Equilibrium

The short-run industry supply curve, *S*, is the industry supply curve taking the number of producers—here, 100—as given. It is generated by adding together the individual supply curves of the 100 producers. Below the shut-down price of $10, no producer wants to produce in the short run. Above $10, the short-run industry supply curve slopes upward, as each producer increases output as price increases. It intersects the demand curve, *D*, at point E_{MKT}, the point of short-run market equilibrium, corresponding to a market price of $18 and a quantity of 500 bushels. >web...

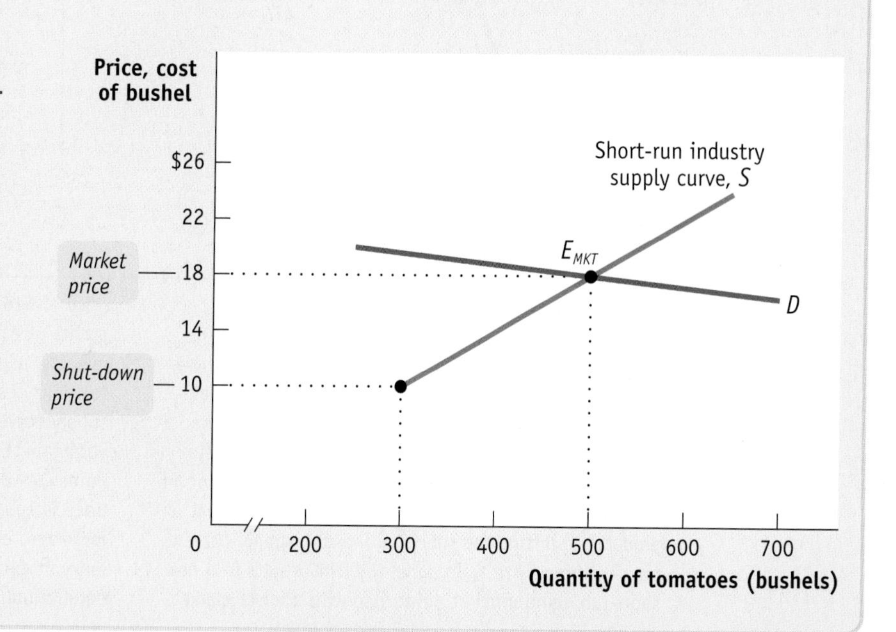

the quantity that producers will supply at each price, *taking the number of producers as given.*

The demand curve D in Figure 9-5 crosses the short-run industry supply curve at the point labelled E_{MKT}, corresponding to a price of $18 and a quantity of 500 bushels. Point E_{MKT} is a **short-run market equilibrium:** the quantity supplied equals the quantity demanded, taking the number of producers as given. But the long run may look quite different, because in the long run farms may enter or exit the industry.

There is a **short-run market equilibrium** when the quantity supplied equals the quantity demanded, taking the number of producers as given.

The Long-Run Industry Supply Curve

Suppose that in addition to the 100 farmers currently in the organic tomato business, there are many other potential producers. Suppose also that each of these potential producers would have the same cost curves as existing producers like Jennifer and Jason if it entered the industry.

When will additional producers enter the industry? Whenever existing producers are making a profit—that is, whenever the market price is above the break-even price of $14 per bushel, the minimum average total cost of production. For example, at a price of $18 per bushel, new firms will enter the industry.

What will happen as additional producers enter the industry? Clearly, the quantity supplied at any given price will increase. The short-run industry supply curve will shift to the right. This will, in turn, alter the market equilibrium and result in a lower market price. Existing firms will respond to the lower market price by reducing their output, but the total industry output will increase because of the larger number of firms in the industry.

Figure 9-6 illustrates the effects of this chain of events on an existing firm and on the market; panel (a) shows how an individual existing firm responds to entry,

Figure 9-6 The Long-Run Market Equilibrium

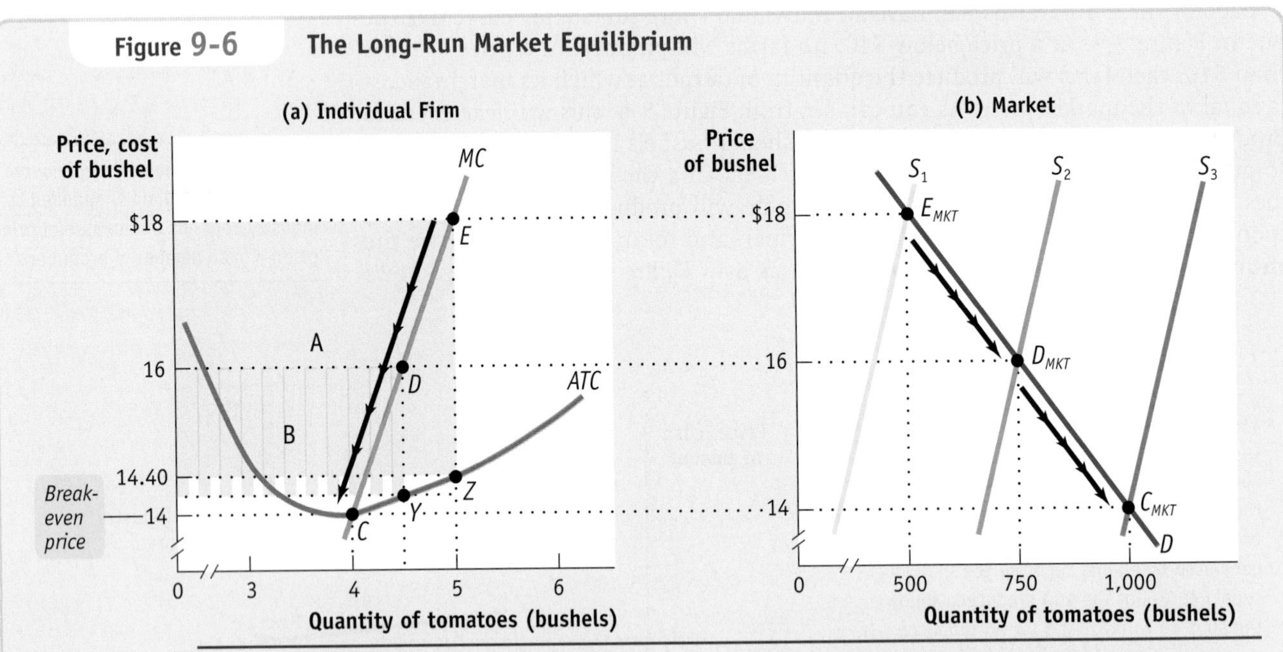

Point E_{MKT} of panel (b) shows the initial short-run market equilibrium, at the intersection of the demand curve, D, and the initial short-run industry supply curve, S_1. Because the market price ($18) is above the break-even price ($14), each of the 100 existing producers makes an economic profit; this is illustrated in panel (a), where the rectangle labeled A shows the profit of an existing firm. These profits induce entry by additional producers, shifting the short-run industry supply curve outward from S_1 to S_2 in panel (b). This results in a new short-run equilibrium at point D_{MKT} with a lower market price of $16 and higher industry output. The output and profits of existing firms are reduced; but some profit remains, as shown by the rectangle labeled B in panel (a). Entry continues shifting out the short-run industry supply curve, as price falls and industry output increases yet again. Entry finally ceases once an equilibrium, at point C_{MKT} on supply curve S_3, is reached. Here market price is equal to the break-even price; existing producers make zero economic profits and there is no incentive for entry or exit. Therefore C_{MKT} is also a long-run market equilibrium.

and panel (b) shows how the market responds to entry. (Note that these two graphs have been rescaled in comparison to Figure 9-4 to better illustrate how profit changes in response to price.) In panel (b), S_1 is the initial short-run industry supply curve, based on the existence of 100 producers. The initial short-run market equilibrium is at E_{MKT}, with an equilibrium market price of $18 and a quantity of 500 bushels. At this price existing producers are profitable, which is reflected in panel (a): an existing firm makes a total profit represented by the shaded rectangle *A* when market price is $18.

These profits will induce new producers to enter the industry, shifting the short-run industry supply curve to the right. For example, the short-run industry supply curve when the number of producers has increased to 167 is S_2. Corresponding to this supply curve is a new short-run market equilibrium labelled D_{MKT}, with a market price of $16 and a quantity of 750 bushels. At $16, each firm produces 4.5 bushels, so that industry output is $167 \times 4.5 = 750$ bushels (rounded). From panel (a) you can see the effect of the entry of 67 new producers on an existing firm: the fall in price causes it to reduce its output, and its profits to fall to the area represented by the striped rectangle labelled *B*.

Although diminished, the profit of existing firms at D_{MKT} means that entry will continue and the number of firms will continue to rise. If the number of producers rises to 250, the short-run industry supply curve shifts out again to S_3, and the market equilibrium is at C_{MKT}, with a quantity supplied and demanded of 1,000 bushels and a market price of $14 per bushel.

Like E_{MKT} and D_{MKT}, C_{MKT} is a short-run equilibrium. But it is also something more. Because the price of $14 is each firm's break-even price, an existing producer makes zero economic profits—neither a profit nor a loss—when producing its profit-maximizing output of 4 bushels. At this price there is no incentive either for potential producers to enter or for existing producers to exit the industry. So C_{MKT} corresponds to a **long-run market equilibrium**—a situation in which quantity supplied equals the quantity demanded given that sufficient time has elapsed for producers to either enter the industry or exit the industry. In a long-run market equilibrium, all existing and potential producers have fully adjusted to their optimal long-run choices; as a result, no producer has an incentive to either enter or exit the industry.

A market is in **long-run market equilibrium** when the quantity supplied equals the quantity demanded, given that sufficient time has elapsed for entry into and exit from the industry to occur.

To explore further the significance of the difference between short-run and long-run equilibrium, consider the effect of an increase in demand on an industry with free entry that is initially in long-run equilibrium. Panel (b) in Figure 9-7 (page 236) shows the market adjustment; panels (a) and (c) show how an existing individual firm behaves during the process.

In panel (b) of Figure 9-7, D_1 is the initial demand curve and S_1 is the initial short-run industry supply curve. Their intersection at point X_{MKT} is both a short-run and a long-run market equilibrium, because the equilibrium price of $14 leads to zero economic profits—and therefore neither entry nor exit. It corresponds to point *X* in panel (a), where an individual existing firm is operating at the minimum of its average total cost curve.

Now suppose that the demand curve shifts out for some reason, to D_2. As shown in panel (b), in the short run, industry output moves along the short-run industry supply curve S_1 to the new short-run market equilibrium at Y_{MKT}, the intersection of S_1 and D_2. The market price rises to $18 per bushel and industry output increases from Q_X to Q_Y. This corresponds to the movement from *X* to *Y* in panel (a), as an existing firm increases its output in response to the rise in the market price.

But we know that Y_{MKT} is not a long-run equilibrium, because $18 is higher than minimum average total cost, so existing producers are making economic profits. This will lead additional firms to enter the industry. Over time entry will cause the short-run industry supply curve to shift to the right. In the long run, the short-run industry supply curve will have shifted out to S_2, and the equilibrium will be at Z_{MKT}—with the price falling back to $14 per bushel and industry output increasing yet again, from Q_Y to Q_Z. Like X_{MKT} before the increase in demand, Z_{MKT} is both a short-run and a long-run market equilibrium.

Figure 9-7 The Effect of an Increase in Demand in the Short Run and the Long Run

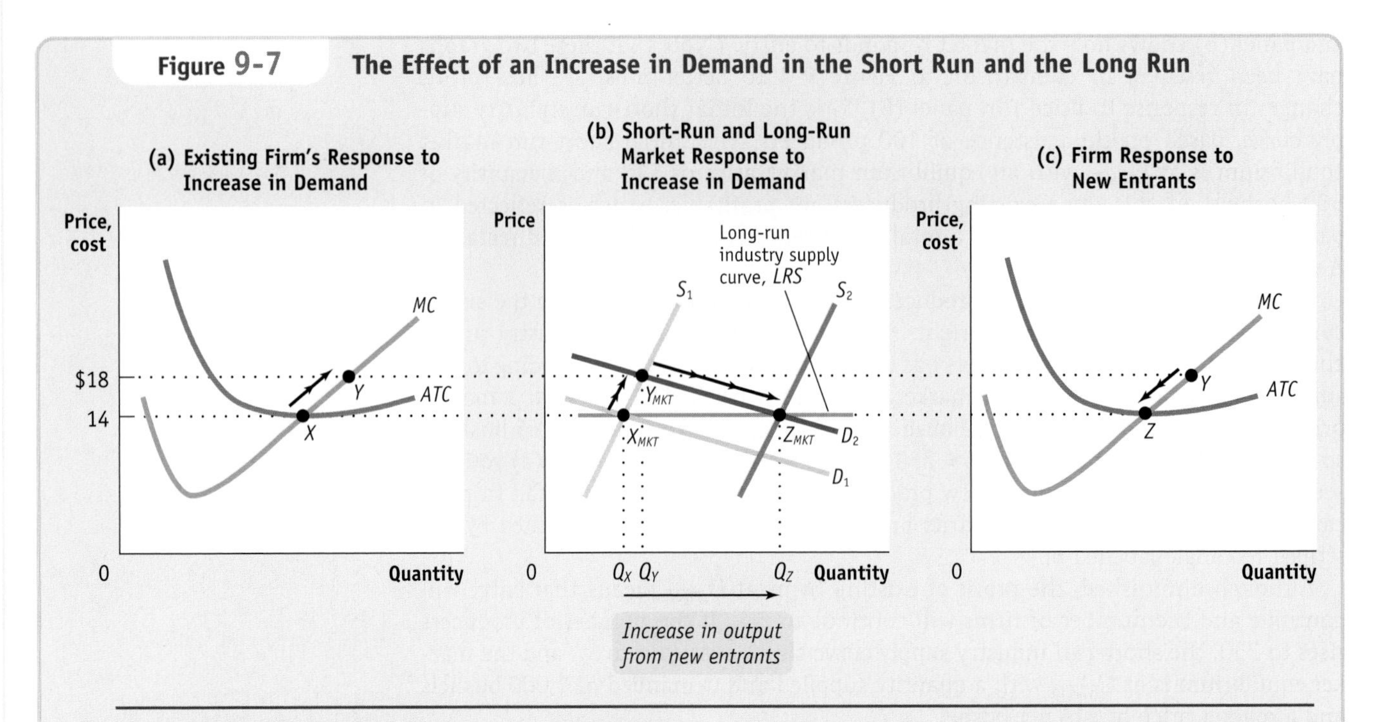

Panel (b) shows how an industry adjusts in the short and long run to an increase in demand; panels (a) and (c) show the corresponding adjustments by an existing firm. Initially the market is at point X_{MKT} in panel (b), a short-run and long-run equilibrium at a price of \$14 and industry output of Q_X. An existing firm makes zero profit, operating at point *X* in panel (a) at minimum average total cost. Demand increases as D_1 shifts rightward to D_2, and raises the market price to \$18. Existing firms increase their output and industry output moves along the short-run industry supply curve S_1 to a short-run equilibrium at Y_{MKT}. Correspondingly, the existing firm in panel (a) moves from point *X* to point *Y*. But at a price of \$18 existing firms are profitable. As shown in panel (b), in the long run new entrants arrive and the short-run industry supply curve shifts rightward, from S_1 to S_2. There is a new equilibrium at point Z_{MKT}, at a lower price of \$14 and higher industry output of Q_Z. An existing firm responds by moving from *Y* to *Z* in panel (c), returning to its initial output level and zero profit. Production by new entrants accounts for the total increase in industy output, $Q_X - Q_Z$. Like X_{MKT}, Z_{MKT} is also a short-run and long-run equilibrium: with existing firms earning zero economic profits, there is no incentive for any firms to enter or exit the industry. The horizontal line passing through X_{MKT} and Z_{MKT}, *LRS*, is the *long-run industry supply curve*: at the break-even price of \$14, producers will produce any amount that consumers demand in the long run.

The effect of entry on an existing firm is illustrated in panel (c), in the movement from *Y* to *Z* along the firm's individual supply curve. The firm reduces its output in response to the fall in price, ultimately arriving back at its original output quantity, corresponding to the minimum of its average total cost curve. In fact, every firm that is now in the industry—the initial set of firms and the new entrants—will operate at the minimum of its average total cost curves, at point *Z*. This means that the entire increase in industry output, from Q_X to Q_Z, comes from production by new entrants.

The line *LRS* that passes through X_{MKT} and Z_{MKT} in panel (b) is the **long-run industry supply curve.** It shows how the quantity supplied by an industry responds to the price given that producers have had time to enter or exit the industry.

The **long-run industry supply curve** shows how the quantity supplied responds to the price once producers have had time to enter or exit the industry.

In this particular case, the long-run industry supply curve is horizontal at \$14. In other words, in this industry supply is *perfectly elastic* in the long run—given time to enter or exit, producers will supply any quantity consumers demand at a price of \$14. Perfectly elastic long-run supply is actually a good assumption for many industries. However, in other industries, even the long-run industry supply curve is upward sloping. The usual reason even the long-run industry supply curve is upward sloping is

Comparing the Short-Run and Long-Run Industry Supply Curves

The long-run industry supply curve may slope upward, but it is always flatter—more elastic—than the short-run industry supply curve. This is because of entry and exit: a higher price attracts new entrants in the long run, resulting in a rise in industry output and a fall in price; a fall in price induces existing producers to exit in the long run, generating a fall in industry output and a rise in price. >web...

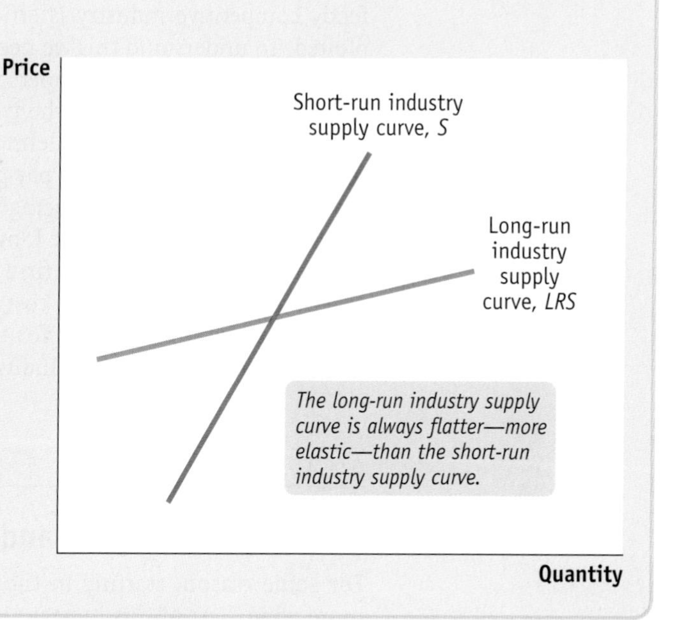

that the producers must use some input that is in limited supply and as the industry expands, the price of that input is driven up. For example, beach-resort hotels must compete for a limited quantity of prime oceanfront property.

Whether the long-run industry supply curve is horizontal or upward sloping, however, the long-run price elasticity of supply is *higher* than the short-run price elasticity whenever there is free entry and exit. As shown in Figure 9-8, the long-run industry supply curve is always flatter than the short-run industry supply curve. The reason is entry and exit: a high price attracts entry by new producers, resulting in a rise in industry output and a fall in price; a low price induces existing firms to exit, leading to a fall in industry output and an increase in price.

The distinction between the short-run industry supply curve and the long-run industry supply curve is very important in practice. We often see a sequence of events like that shown in Figure 9-7: an increase in demand initially leads to a large price increase, but prices return to normal once new firms have entered the industry. Or we see the sequence in reverse: a fall in demand reduces prices in the short run, but they return to normal as producers exit the industry.

The Cost of Production and Efficiency in Long-Run Equilibrium

Our analysis leads us to three conclusions about the cost of production and efficiency in the long-run equilibrium of a perfectly competitive industry. These results will be important in our discussion in Chapter 14 of how monopoly gives rise to inefficiency.

First, in a perfectly competitive industry in equilibrium, the value of marginal cost is the same for all firms. That's because all firms produce the quantity of output at which marginal cost equals the market price, and as price-takers they all face the same market price.

Second, in a perfectly competitive industry with free entry and exit, each firm will have zero economic profit in long-run equilibrium. Each firm produces the quantity of output that minimizes its average total cost—corresponding to point *Z* in panel (c) of Figure 9-7. So the total cost of production of the industry's output is minimized in a perfectly competitive industry.

The third and final conclusion is that the long-run market equilibrium of a perfectly competitive industry is efficient: no mutual beneficial transactions go unexploited. To understand this we need to recall a fundamental requirement for efficiency from Chapter 6: all consumers who have a willingness to pay greater than or equal to seller's costs actually get the good. And we also learned that a market is efficient (except under certain, well-defined conditions)—the market price matches all consumers with a willingness to pay greater than or equal to the market price to all sellers who have a cost of producing the good less than or equal to the market price.

How do we know that the long-run equilibrium of a perfectly competitive industry is efficient? Because each firm produces the output level at which price is equal to marginal cost. And marginal cost is in fact the same as seller's cost—the lowest price the firm is willing to accept for the good. So the long-run equilibrium of a market with a perfectly competitive industry is indeed efficient.

economics in action

The Grape in Canada and California

For some reason, starting in the mid-1990s, North Americans began drinking lots more wine. Part of this increase in demand may have reflected a booming economy, but the surge in wine consumption continued even after the economy stumbled in 2001. By 2002, North Americans were consuming about 36 percent more wine than they did in 1993.

At first, this increase in wine demand led to sharply higher prices; between 1993 and 2000, the price of red wine grapes rose 50%, and grape growers earned high profits. Now, according to our theory, these high profits should encourage entry, which would bid down prices. Did this occur?

Kate Kline/Foodpix/Getty Images

As production expanded and prices fell, profits in the California wine industry shriveled.

Yes, though not in Canada. The key wine regions in Canada—the Okanagan Valley in British Columbia, the Niagara Peninsula in Ontario, and the Annapolis Valley in Nova Scotia—are geographically limited either by mountains, lakes, or the sea, and this physically restricted the expansion of production by existing producers or new entrants.

But there were no such physical restrictions in California. As a result, there was a rapid expansion of the industry south of the border, both because existing grape growers expanded their capacity and because new growers entered the market. Between 1994 and 2002, American production of red wine grapes almost doubled.

The result was predictable: the price of grapes fell as the supply curve shifted out. As demand growth slowed in 2002, prices plunged by 17 percent. The effect was to end the California wine industry's expansion. In fact, some grape producers began to exit the industry.

As a footnote, just as Canada's wineries avoided the expansion, so continued improvements in quality, and a relatively secure niche market in icewine, allowed them to avoid the bust. Canada's wineries have enjoyed slow but continued growth in both the volume and the value of their sales.

But our main point is that when markets are competitive, as in the California grape market, profits induce new entrants and prices eventually fall. ■

>> QUICK REVIEW

- The *industry supply curve* corresponds to the supply curve of earlier chapters. In the short run, the time period over which the number of producers is fixed, the *short-run market equilibrium* is given by the intersection of the *short-run industry supply curve* and the demand curve. In the long run, the time period over which producers can enter or exit the industry, the *long-run market equilibrium* is given by the intersection of the *long-run industry supply curve* and the demand curve. In the long-run market equilibrium, no producer has an incentive to enter or exit the industry.
- The long-run industry supply curve is often horizontal, although it may be upward sloping when a necessary input is in limited supply; it is always more elastic than the short-run industry supply curve.
- In the long-run market equilibrium of a perfectly competitive industry, each firm produces at the same marginal cost, which is equal to the market price, and the total cost of production of the industry's output is minimized. It is also efficient.

>>CHECK YOUR UNDERSTANDING 9-3

1. Which of the following events will induce firms to enter an industry? Which will induce firms to exit? When will entry or exit cease? Explain your answer.
   a. A technological advance lowers the fixed cost of production of every firm in the industry.
   b. The wages paid to workers in the industry go up.
   c. A change in consumer tastes increases demand for the good.
   d. The price of a key input rises due to a shortage of that input.
2. Assume that the beef industry is perfectly competitive and is in long-run equilibrium with a perfectly elastic long-run industry supply curve. Health concerns about BSE ("mad cow" disease) then lead to a fall in demand. Construct a figure similar to Figure 9-7, showing the short-run behaviour of the industry and how long-run equilibrium is reestablished.

Solutions appear at back of book.

• A LOOK AHEAD •

In this chapter, we have seen how the rational decisions of producers in a perfectly competitive industry give rise to that industry's supply curve. But this is, of course, only half the story. To complete the picture we must turn next to the decisions made by rational consumers and how these decisions give rise to the demand curve.

SUMMARY

1. In a **perfectly competitive market,** all producers are **price-taking producers** and all consumers are **price-taking consumers**—no one's actions can influence the market price. Consumers are normally price-takers, but producers often are not. In a **perfectly competitive industry,** all producers are price-takers.
2. There are three necessary conditions for a perfectly competitive industry: there are many producers, none of whom have a large **market share;** the industry produces a **standardized product** or **commodity**—goods that consumers regard as equivalent; and there is **free entry and exit** into and from the industry.
3. A producer chooses output according to the **optimal output rule:** produce the quantity at which **marginal revenue** equals marginal cost. For a price-taking firm, marginal revenue is equal to price and its marginal revenue curve is a horizontal line at the market price. It chooses output according to the **price-taking firm's optimal output rule:** produce the quantity at which price equals marginal cost. However, a firm that produces the optimal quantity may not be profitable.
4. A firm is profitable if total revenue exceeds total cost or, equivalently, if the market price exceeds its **break-even price**—minimum average total cost. If market price exceeds the break-even price, the firm is profitable; if it is less, the firm is unprofitable; if it is equal, the firm breaks even. When profitable, the firm's per-unit profit is $P - ATC$; when unprofitable, its per-unit loss is $ATC - P$.
5. Fixed cost is irrelevant to the firm's optimal short-run production decision, which depends on its **shut-down price**—its minimum average variable cost—and the market price. When the market price exceeds the shut-down price, the firm produces the output quantity where marginal cost equals the market price. When the market price falls below the shut-down price, the firm ceases production in the short run. This generates the firm's **short-run individual supply curve.**
6. Fixed cost matters in the long run. If the market price is below minimum average total cost for an extended period of time, firms will exit the industry. If above, existing firms are profitable and new firms will enter the industry.
7. The **industry supply curve** depends on the time period. The **short-run industry supply curve** is the industry supply curve given that the number of firms is fixed. The **short-run market equilibrium** is given by the intersection of the short-run industry supply curve and the demand curve.
8. The **long-run industry supply curve** is the industry supply curve given sufficient time for entry into and exit from the industry. In the **long-run market equilibrium**—given by the intersection of the long-run industry supply curve and the demand curve—no producer has an incentive to enter or exit. The long-run industry supply curve is often horizontal. It may slope upward if there is limited supply of an input, but it is always flatter than the short-run industry supply curve.
9. In the long-run market equilibrium of a competitive industry, profit maximization leads each firm to produce at the same marginal cost, which is equal to market price. Free entry and exit means that each firm earns zero economic profit—producing the output corresponding to its minimum average total cost. So the total cost of production of an industry's output is minimized. The outcome is efficient because every consumer with a willingness to pay greater or equal to marginal cost gets the good.

KEY TERMS

Price-taking producer, p. 219
Price-taking consumer, p. 219
Perfectly competitive market, p. 219
Perfectly competitive industry, p. 219
Market share, p. 220
Standardized product, p. 220
Commodity, p. 220
Free entry and exit, p. 220
Marginal revenue, p. 223
Optimal output rule, p. 223
Price-taking firm's optimal output rule, p. 224
Marginal revenue curve, p. 224
Break-even price, p. 228
Shut-down price, p. 229
Short-run individual supply curve, p. 230
Industry supply curve, p. 233
Short-run industry supply curve, p. 233
Short-run market equilibrium, p. 234
Long-run market equilibrium, p. 235
Long-run industry supply curve, p. 236

PROBLEMS

1. For each of the following, is the business a price-taking producer? Explain your answers.

a. A cappuccino café in a university town where there are dozens of very similar cappuccino cafés

b. The makers of Pepsi-Cola

c. One of many sellers of zucchini at a local farmers' market

2. For each of the following, is the industry perfectly competitive? Referring to market share, standardization of the product, and/or free entry and exit, explain your answers.

a. Aspirin

b. Shania Twain concerts

c. SUVs

3. Kate's Catering provides catered meals, and the catered meals industry is perfectly competitive. Kate's machinery costs $100 per day and is the only fixed input. Her variable cost consists of the wages paid to the cooks and the food ingredients. The variable cost associated with each level of output is given in the accompanying table.

Quantity of meals	*VC*
0	$0
10	200
20	300
30	480
40	700
50	1,000

a. Calculate the total cost, the average variable cost, the average total cost, and the marginal cost for each quantity of output.

b. What is the break-even price? What is the shut-down price?

c. Suppose that the price at which Kate can sell catered meals is $21 per meal. In the short run, will Kate earn a profit? In the short run, should she produce or shut down?

d. Suppose that the price at which Kate can sell catered meals is $17 per meal. In the short run, will Kate earn a profit? In the short run, should she produce or shut down?

e. Suppose that the price at which Kate can sell catered meals is $13 per meal. In the short run, will Kate earn a profit? In the short run, should she produce or shut down?

4. Bob produces DVD movies for sale. Production of DVD movies requires just a building and a machine that copies the original movie onto a DVD. Bob rents a building for $30,000 per month and rents a machine for $20,000 a month. Those are his fixed costs. His variable cost is given in the accompanying table.

Quantity of DVDs	*VC*
0	$0
1,000	5,000
2,000	8,000
3,000	9,000
4,000	14,000
5,000	20,000
6,000	33,000
7,000	49,000
8,000	72,000
9,000	99,000
10,000	150,000

a. Calculate Bob's average variable cost, average total cost, and marginal cost for each quantity of output.

b. There is free entry into the industry: anyone who enters the industry will face the same costs as Bob. Suppose that currently the price of a DVD is $23. What will the price of DVD movies be in the long run? Explain your answer.

5. Consider Bob's DVD company described in Problem 4. Assume that DVD production is a perfectly competitive industry. In each case, explain your answers.

a. What is Bob's break-even price? What is his shut-down price?

b. Suppose the price of a DVD is $2. What should Bob do in the short run?

c. Suppose the price of a DVD is $6. What is the profit-maximizing quantity of DVDs that Bob should produce? What will his total profit be? Will he produce or shut down in the short run? Will he stay in the industry or exit in the long run?

d. Suppose instead that the price of a DVD is $16. Now what is the profit-maximizing quantity of DVDs that Bob should produce? What will his total profit be now? Will he produce or shut down in the short run? Will he stay in the industry or exit in the long run?

6. Consider again Bob's DVD company described in Problem 4.

a. Draw Bob's marginal cost curve.

b. Over what range of prices will Bob produce no DVDs in the short run?

c. Draw Bob's individual supply curve.

7. a. A profit-maximizing firm incurs an economic loss of $10,000 per year. Its fixed cost is $15,000 per year. Should it produce or shut down in the short run? Should it stay in the industry or exit in the long run?

b. Suppose instead that this business has a fixed cost of $6,000 per year. Should it produce or shut down in the short run? Should it stay in the industry or exit in the long run?

8. Four students have each started companies selling late-night snack deliveries to dorms and student apartment complexes. Each student has estimated her or his individual supply schedule as given in the accompanying table.

Delivery charge	Quantity supplied by:			
	Aleesha	Brent	Christine	Dominic
$1	1	5	3	7
2	3	8	6	12
3	5	11	9	17
4	7	15	12	20
5	9	19	15	22

a. Graph the four individual supply curves.

b. Determine the short-run industry supply schedule. Graph the short-run industry supply curve.

9. The first sushi restaurant opens in town. Initially people are very cautious about eating tiny portions of raw fish, as this is a town where large portions of grilled meat have always been popular. Soon, however, an influential health report warns consumers against grilled meat and suggests that they increase their consumption of fish, especially raw fish. The sushi restaurant becomes very popular and its profits increase.

a. What will happen to the short-run profits of the sushi restaurant? What will happen to the number of sushi restaurants in town in the long run? Will the first sushi restaurant be able to sustain its short-run profit over the long run? Explain your answers.

b. Local steakhouses suffer from the popularity of sushi and start incurring losses. What will happen to the number of steakhouses in town in the long run? Explain your answer.

10. A perfectly competitive firm has the following short-run total cost:

Quantity	*TC*
0	$5
1	10
2	13
3	18
4	25
5	34
6	45

Market demand for the firm's product is given by the following market demand schedule:

Price	Quantity demanded
$12	300
10	500
8	800
6	1,200
4	1,800

a. Calculate this firm's marginal cost and, for all output levels except zero, the firm's average variable cost and average total cost.

b. There are 100 firms in this industry that all have identical costs to those of this firm. Draw the short-run industry supply curve. In the same diagram, draw the market demand curve.

c. What is the market price, and how much profit will each firm make?

11. A new vaccine against a deadly disease has just been discovered. Presently, 55 people die from the disease each year. The new vaccine will save lives, but it is not completely safe. Some recipients of the shots will die from adverse reactions. The projected effects of the inoculation are given in the accompanying table:

Percent of population inoculated	Total deaths due to disease	Total deaths due to inoculation	Marginal benefit of inoculation	Marginal cost of inoculation	"Profit" of inoculation
0	55	0	—	—	—
10	45	0	—	—	—
20	36	1	—	—	—
30	28	3	—	—	—
40	21	6	—	—	—
50	15	10	—	—	—
60	10	15	—	—	—
70	6	20	—	—	—
80	3	25	—	—	—
90	1	30	—	—	—
100	0	35			—

a. What are the interpretations of "marginal benefit" and "marginal cost" in this case? Calculate marginal benefit and marginal cost per each 10% increase in the rate of inoculation for each level of inoculation. Write your answers in the table.

b. What proportion of the population should optimally be inoculated?

c. What is the interpretation of "profit" in this case? Calculate the profit for all levels of inoculation.

12. Evaluate each of the following statements. If a statement is true, explain why; if it is false, identify the falsity and try to correct it.

a. A profit-maximizing firm should select the output level at which the difference between the market price and marginal cost is greatest.

b. An increase in fixed cost lowers the profit-maximizing quantity of output produced in the short run.

>web... To continue your study and review of concepts in this chapter, please visit the Krugman/Wells website for quizzes, animated graph tutorials, web links to helpful resources, and more.

www.worthpublishers.com/krugmanwellsmyatt

chapter 10

>>The Rational Consumer

A CLAM TOO FAR

TO ENTICE CUSTOMERS, RESTAURANTS sometimes offer "all-you-can-eat" specials: all-you-can-eat salad bars, all-you-can-eat breakfast buffets, and even all-you-can-eat fried-clam dinners.

But how can a restaurant owner who offers such a special be sure she won't be eaten out of business? If she charges $12.99 for an all-you-can-eat clam dinner, what prevents her average customer from wolfing down $30 worth of clams?

The answer is that even though every once in a while you see someone really take advantage of the offer—heaping a plate high with 30 or 40 fried clams—it's a rare occurrence. And even those of us who like fried clams shudder a bit at the sight. Five or even 10 fried clams can be a treat, but 30 clams is ridiculous. Anyone who pays for an all-you-can-eat meal wants to make the most of it, but a sensible person knows when one more clam would be one clam too many.

Notice what we just did in that last sentence. We said that customers in a restaurant want to "make the most" of their meal; that sounds as if they are trying to maximize something. And we also said that they will stop when consuming one more clam would be a mistake; that sounds as if they are making a marginal decision.

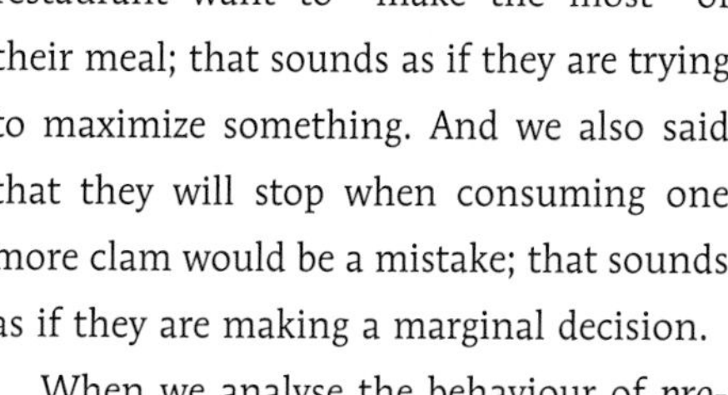

When we analyse the behaviour of *producers,* it makes sense to assume that they maximize profits. But what do consumers maximize? Isn't it all a matter of taste?

The answer is yes, it is a matter of taste—and economists can't say much about where tastes come from. But economists *can* say a lot about how a rational individual goes about satisfying his or her tastes. And that is in fact the way that economists think about consumer choice. They work with a model of a *rational consumer*—a consumer who knows what he or she wants and makes the most of the available opportunities.

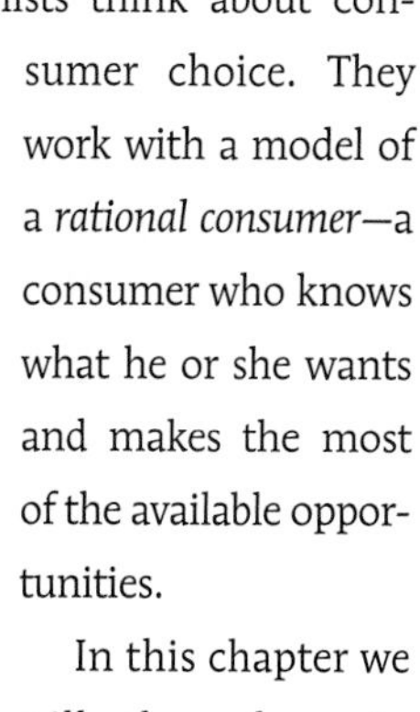

Tom Steward/Corbis

When is more of a good thing too much?

In this chapter we will show how to analyse the decisions of a rational consumer, and how this analysis can be used to derive the market demand curve.

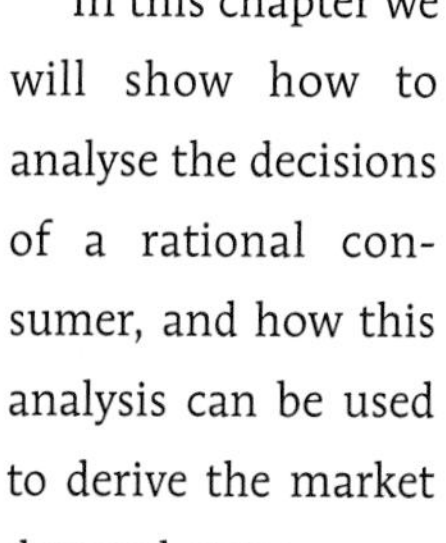

We will begin by showing how the

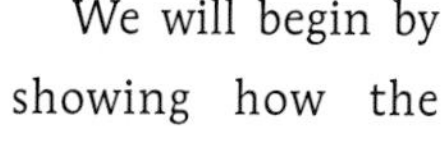

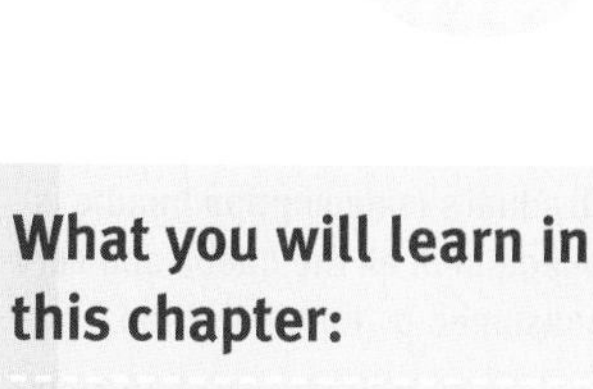

What you will learn in this chapter:

- How consumers choose to spend their income on goods and services
- Why consumers make choices by maximizing **utility,** a measure of satisfaction from consumption
- Why the principle of **diminishing marginal utility** applies to the consumption of most goods and services
- How to use marginal analysis to find the **optimal consumption bundle**
- How choices by individual consumers give rise to the market demand curve
- What **income** and **substitution effects** are

concept of *utility*—a measure of consumer satisfaction—allows us to begin thinking about rational consumer choice. We will then look at how *budget constraints* determine what a consumer can buy and how marginal analysis can be used to determine the consumption choice that maximizes utility. Finally, we will see how to use marginal analysis to derive the demand curve.

Utility: Getting Satisfaction

When analysing consumer behaviour, we're talking about people trying to get what they want—that is, about subjective feelings. Yet there is no simple way to measure subjective feelings. How much satisfaction do I get from my third fried clam? Is it less or more than yours? Does it even make sense to ask the question?

Luckily, it turns out that we don't need to make comparisons between your feelings and mine. All that is required to analyse consumer behaviour is to suppose that each individual is trying to maximize some personal measure of the satisfaction gained from consumption of goods and services. That measure is known as the consumer's **utility,** a concept we use to understand behaviour but don't expect to measure in practice. Nonetheless, we'll see that the assumption that consumers maximize utility helps us think clearly about consumer choice.

The **utility** of a consumer is a measure of the satisfaction the consumer derives from consumption of goods and services.

Utility and Consumption

An individual's utility depends on everything that individual consumes, from apples to Ziploc bags. The set of all the goods and services an individual consumes is known as the individual's **consumption bundle.** The relationship between an individual's consumption bundle and the total amount of utility it generates is known as the **utility function.** The utility function is a personal matter; two people with different tastes will have different utility functions. Someone who actually likes to consume 40 fried clams at a sitting must have a utility function that looks different from that of someone who would rather stop at 5 clams.

An individual's **consumption bundle** is the collection of all the goods and services consumed by that individual.

An individual's **utility function** gives the total utility generated by his or her consumption bundle.

This terminology closely parallels the terminology we used to describe producer decisions in Chapters 8 and 9. A producer uses inputs to produce output according to a production function; a consumer uses consumption to "produce" utility according to a utility function.

Obviously, people do not really have a little computer in their heads that calculates the utility generated by their consumption choices. Nonetheless, people must make choices, and they usually base them on at least a rough attempt to decide which choice will give them greater satisfaction. I can have either soup or salad with my dinner. Which will I enjoy more? I can go to Disney World this year or save the money towards buying a new car. Which will make me happier?

The concept of a utility function is just a way of representing the fact that people must make such choices and that they make those choices in a more or less rational way.

How do we measure utility? For the sake of simplicity, it is useful to suppose that we can measure utility in hypothetical units called—what else?—**utils.**

A **util** is a unit of utility.

Figure 10-1 illustrates a utility function. It shows the total utility that Cassie, who likes fried clams, gets from an all-you-can-eat clam dinner. We suppose that her consumption bundle consists of a side of cole slaw, which comes with the meal, plus a number of clams to be determined. The table that accompanies the figure shows how Cassie's total utility depends on the number of clams; the curve in panel (a) of the figure shows that same information graphically.

Cassie's utility function is upward sloping over most of the range shown, but it gets flatter as the number of clams consumed increases. And in this example it eventually turns downward. According to the information in the table of Figure 10-1, nine clams

Figure 10-1 **Cassie's Total Utility and Marginal Utility**

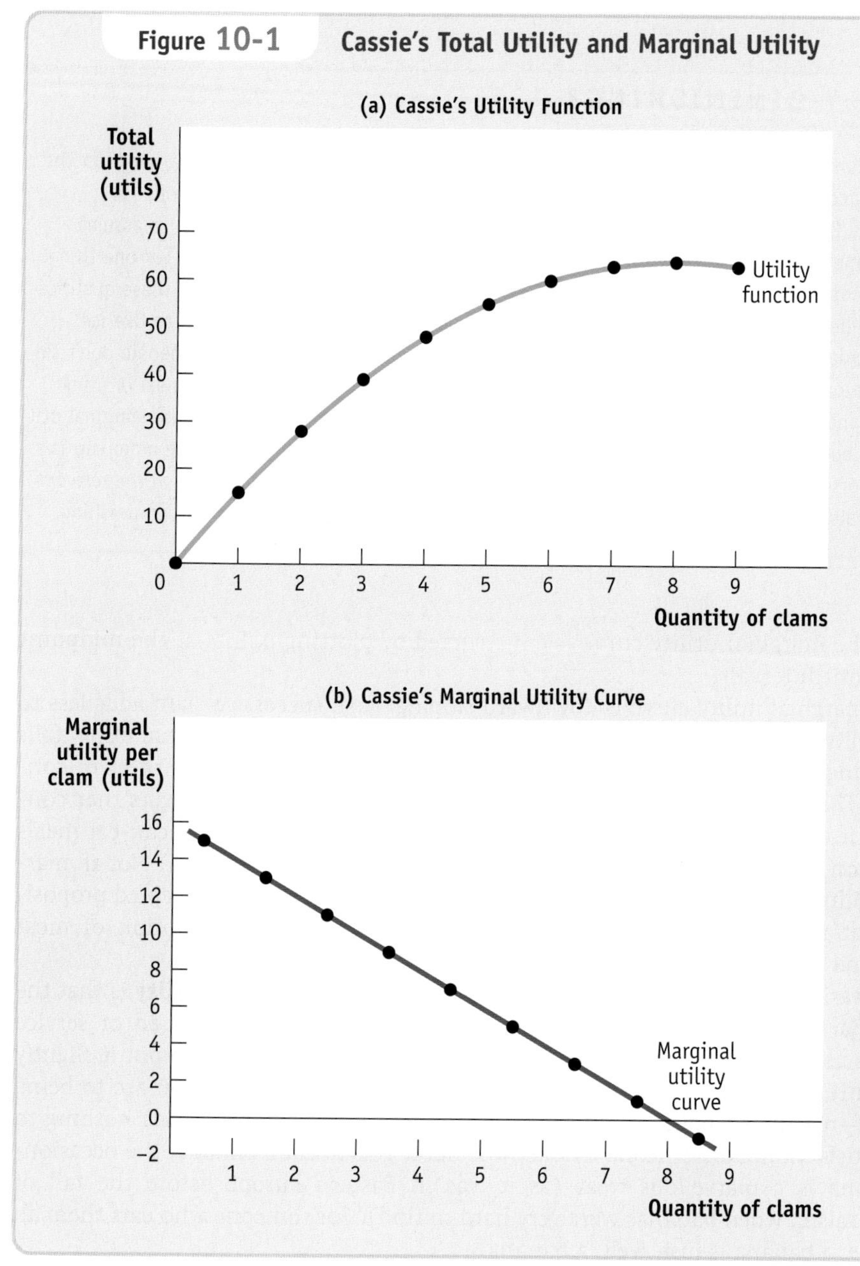

Quantity of clams	Total utility (utils)	Marginal utility per clam (utils)
0	0	
		15
1	15	
		13
2	28	
		11
3	39	
		9
4	48	
		7
5	55	
		5
6	60	
		3
7	63	
		1
8	64	
		−1
9	63	

Panel (a) shows how Cassie's total utility depends on her consumption of fried clams. It increases until it reaches its maximum utility level of 64 utils at 8 clams consumed and decreases after that. Marginal utility is calculated in the table. Panel (b) shows the marginal utility curve, which slopes downward due to diminishing marginal utility. That is, each additional clam gives Cassie less utility than the previous clam.

is one clam too many: adding that additional clam actually makes Cassie worse off. If she's rational, of course, Cassie will realize that and not consume the ninth clam.

So when Cassie chooses how many clams to consume, she will make this decision by considering the *change* in her total utility from consuming one more clam. This illustrates the general point: to maximize *total* utility, consumers must focus on *marginal* utility.

The Principle of Diminishing Marginal Utility

In addition to showing how Cassie's total utility depends on the number of clams she consumes, the table in Figure 10-1 also shows the **marginal utility** generated by consuming each additional clam—that is, the *change* in total utility from consuming an additional clam. Panel (b) shows the implied **marginal utility curve.** Following our practice in Chapters 7, 8, and 9 with the marginal cost

The **marginal utility** of a good or service is the change in total utility generated by consuming one additional unit of that good or service. The **marginal utility curve** shows how marginal utility depends on the quantity of a good or service consumed.

FOR INQUIRING MINDS

IS MARGINAL UTILITY REALLY DIMINISHING?

Are all goods really subject to diminishing marginal utility? Of course not: there are a number of goods for which, at least over some range, marginal utility is surely *increasing*.

For example, there are goods that require some experience to enjoy. The first time you do it, downhill skiing involves a lot more fear than enjoyment. It only becomes a pleasurable activity if you do it enough to become reasonably competent. And even some less strenuous forms of consumption take practice; people who are not accustomed to drinking coffee say it has a bitter taste, and can't understand its appeal.

Another example would be goods that only deliver if you buy enough; the great Victorian economist Alfred Marshall, who more or less invented the supply and demand model, gave the example of wallpaper: buying only enough to do half a room is worse than useless. If you need two rolls of wallpaper to finish a room, the marginal utility of the second roll is larger than the marginal utility of the first roll.

So why does it make sense to assume diminishing marginal utility? For one thing, most goods don't suffer from these qualifications: nobody needs to learn to like ice cream. Also, although some people don't ski or drink coffee, those who do ski or drink coffee do enough of it that the marginal utility of one more ski run or one more cup is less than that of the last. So *in the relevant range,* marginal utility is still diminishing.

curve, the marginal utility curve is constructed by plotting points at the midpoint of the unit intervals.

The marginal utility curve is downward sloping: each successive clam adds less to total utility than the previous clam. This is reflected in the table: marginal utility falls from a high of 15 utils for the first clam consumed to −1 for the ninth clam consumed. The fact that the ninth clam has negative marginal utility means that consuming it actually reduces total utility. (Restaurants that offer all-you-can-eat meals depend on the proposition that you can have too much of a good thing.) Not all marginal utility curves eventually become negative. But it is a generally accepted proposition that marginal utility curves do slope downward—that consumption of most goods and services is subject to *diminishing marginal utility.*

The **principle of diminishing marginal utility** says that each successive unit of a good or service consumed adds less to total utility than the previous unit.

The basic idea behind the **principle of diminishing marginal utility** is that the additional satisfaction a consumer gets from one more unit of a good or service declines as the amount of that good or service consumed rises. Or, to put it slightly differently, the more of a good or service you consume, the closer you are to being satiated—reaching a point at which an additional unit of the good adds nothing to your satisfaction. For someone who almost never gets to eat a banana, the occasional banana is a marvellous treat (as it was in Eastern Europe before the fall of Communism, when bananas were very hard to find). For someone who eats them all the time, a banana is just, well, a banana.

The principle of diminishing marginal utility plays the same role in the analysis of consumer behaviour that the principle of diminishing returns to an input plays in the analysis of producer behaviour. Like the principle of diminishing returns to an input, the principle of diminishing marginal utility isn't always true. But it is true in the great majority of cases, enough to serve as a foundation for our analysis of consumer behaviour.

economics in action

Lobster versus Chicken

Is a particular food a special treat, something you consume on special occasions? Or is it an ordinary, take-it-or-leave-it dish? The answer depends a lot on how much of that food people normally consume, which determines how much utility they get *at the margin* from having a bit more.

Consider chicken. Modern Canadians eat a lot of chicken, so much that they regard it as nothing special. Yet this was not always the case. Traditionally chicken was a luxury dish, because chickens were expensive to raise. Restaurant menus from two centuries ago show chicken dishes as the most expensive items listed.

What changed the status of chicken was the emergence of new, technologically advanced methods for raising and processing the birds. These methods made chicken abundant, cheap, and also—thanks to the principle of diminishing marginal utility—nothing to get excited about.

The reverse evolution took place for lobster. Most everyone who likes lobster regards it as a special treat. Lobster isn't cheap, and as a result you would be hard pressed to find an "all-you-can-eat" lobster buffet. Yet lobster was once very cheap and abundant in Atlantic Canada. In fact, just a few generations ago, it was regarded as "poverty food". When visitors came, the lobster pot would be hidden for the shame of it!

What changed? You might have guessed that the main change was a fall in the abundance of lobster. But you'd be wrong. Annual lobster landings today total about twice as much as average annual landings between 1930 and 1980. In fact, the key changes were the development, starting in the 1950s, of new technologies in freezing and canning, and improvements in our ability to store live lobsters in holding tanks.

The reason lobster was once so cheap in Atlantic Canada was that landings were highly seasonal, and at their peak, the supply greatly exceeded the ability to get the product to the lucrative export markets in Boston and New York. So, the domestic market was periodically saturated, driving prices very low.

The new technologies allowed the product to be stored, either frozen or live, and eventually sold for export. As well, increasing incomes not only expanded the size of the export market in the U.S. but also allowed diversity from a predominantly fish and crustacean diet in Atlantic Canada.

Oh, for the days when we had a surfeit of lobster! ■

>> QUICK REVIEW

- *Utility* is a measure of a person's satisfaction from consumption, expressed in units of *utils*. Consumers try to maximize their utility. A consumer's *utility function* shows the relationship between the consumption bundle and the total utility it generates.
- To maximize utility, a consumer considers the marginal utility from consuming one more unit of a good or service, illustrated by *the marginal utility curve*.
- In the consumption of most goods and services, and for most people, the *principle of diminishing marginal utility* holds: each successive unit consumed adds less to total utility than the previous unit.

>> CHECK YOUR UNDERSTANDING 10-1

1. Explain why a rational consumer who has diminishing marginal utility for a good would not consume an additional unit when it generates negative marginal utility, even when that unit is free.
2. Jennifer drinks three cups of coffee a day, for which she has diminishing marginal utility. Which of her three cups generates the greatest increase in total utility? Which generates the least?
3. In each of the following cases, does the consumer have diminishing, constant, or increasing marginal utility? Explain your answers.
   a. The more Mabel exercises, the more she enjoys each additional visit to the gym.
   b. Although Mei's classical CD collection is huge, her enjoyment from buying another CD has not changed as her collection has grown.
   c. When Dexter was a struggling student, his enjoyment from a good restaurant meal was greater than now, when he has such meals quite frequently.

Solutions appear at back of book.

Budgets and Optimal Consumption

The principle of diminishing marginal utility explains why most people eventually reach a limit, even at an all-you-can-eat buffet where the cost of another clam is measured only in future indigestion. Under ordinary circumstances, however, it costs some additional resources to consume more of a good, and consumers must take that cost into account when making choices.

What do we mean by cost? As always, the fundamental measure of cost is *opportunity cost.* Because the amount of money a consumer can spend is limited, a decision to consume more of one good is also a decision to consume less of some other good.

Budget Constraints and Budget Lines

Consider Sammy, whose appetite is exclusively for clams and potatoes (there's no accounting for tastes). He has a weekly income of $20, and since, given his appetite, more of either good is better than less, he spends all of it on clams and potatoes. We will assume that clams cost $4 per pound and potatoes cost $2 per pound. What are his possible choices?

Whatever Sammy chooses, we know that the cost of his consumption bundle cannot exceed the amount of money he has to spend. That is,

(10-1) Expenditure on clams + expenditure on potatoes $\leq$ total income

Consumers always have limited income, which constrains how much they can consume. So the requirement illustrated by Equation 10-1—that a consumer must choose a consumption bundle that costs no more than his or her total income—is known as the consumer's **budget constraint.** It's a simple way of saying that consumers can't spend more than the total amount of income available to them. In other words, consumption bundles are affordable when they obey the budget constraint. We call the set of all of Sammy's affordable consumption bundles his **consumption possibilities.** As we will see, which consumption bundles are in this set depends on the consumer's income and the prices of goods and services.

A **budget constraint** requires that the cost of a consumer's consumption bundle be no more than the consumer's total income.

A consumer's **consumption possibilities** is the set of all consumption bundles that can be consumed given the consumer's income and prevailing prices.

Figure 10-2 shows Sammy's consumption possibilities. The quantity of clams in his consumption bundle is measured on the horizontal axis and the quantity of potatoes on

Figure 10-2 **The Budget Line**

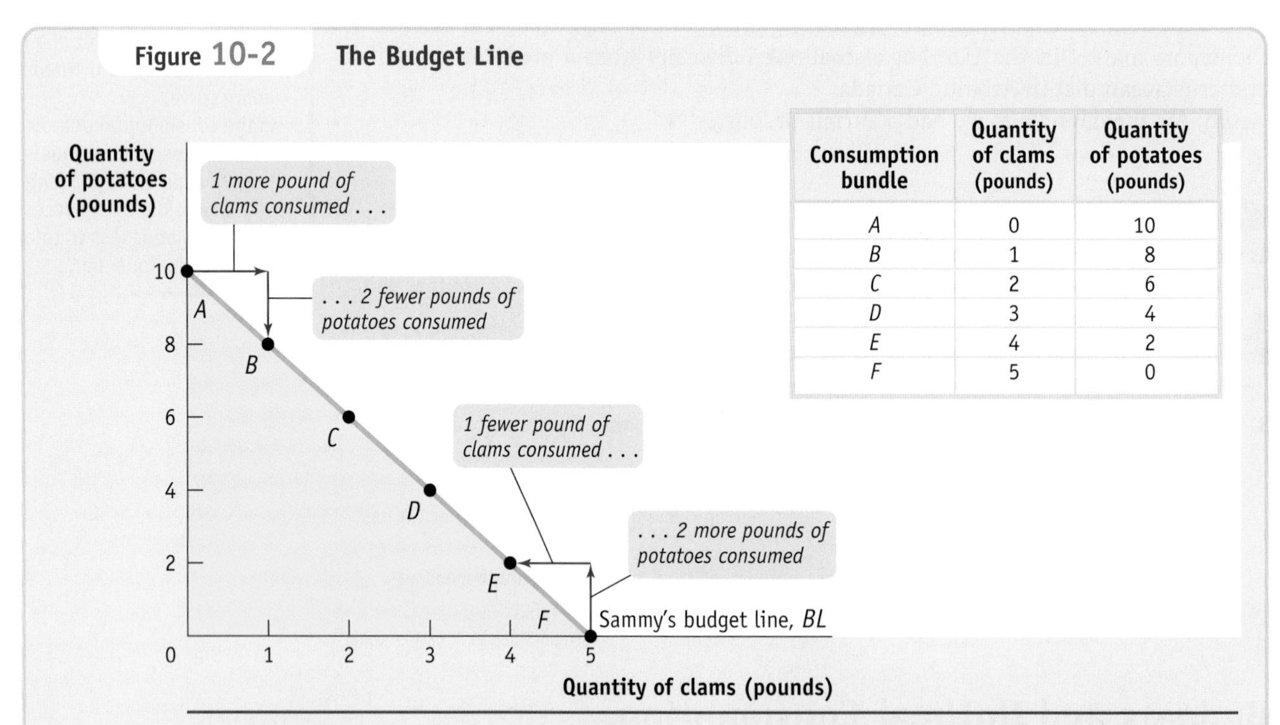

Consumption bundle	Quantity of clams (pounds)	Quantity of potatoes (pounds)
A	0	10
B	1	8
C	2	6
D	3	4
E	4	2
F	5	0

The *budget line* represents all the possible combinations of quantities of potatoes and clams that Sammy can purchase if he spends all of his income. Also, it is the boundary between the set of affordable consumption bundles (the *consumption possibilities*) and unaffordable ones. Given that clams cost $4 per pound and potatoes cost $2 per pound, if Sammy spends all of his income on clams (bundle *F*), he can purchase 5 pounds of clams; if he spends all of his income on potatoes (bundle *A*), he can purchase 10 pounds of potatoes. The slope of the budget line here is −2: 2 pounds of potatoes must be forgone for 1 more pound of clams, reflecting the opportunity cost of clams in terms of potatoes. So the location and slope of the budget line depend on the consumer's income and the prices of the goods.

the vertical axis. The downward-sloping line connecting points *A* through *F* shows which consumption bundles are affordable and which are not. Every bundle on or inside this line (the shaded area) is affordable; every bundle outside this line is unaffordable. As an example of one of the points, let's look at point *C*, representing 2 pounds of clams and 6 pounds of potatoes, and check whether it satisfies Sammy's budget constraint. The cost of bundle *C* is 6 pounds of potatoes × $2 per pound + 2 pounds of clams × $4 per pound = $12 + $8 = $20. So bundle *C* does indeed satisfy Sammy's budget constraint: it costs no more than his weekly income of $20. In fact, bundle *C* costs exactly as much as Sammy's income. By doing the arithmetic, you can check that all the other points lying on the downward-sloping line are also bundles at which Sammy spends all of his income.

The downward-sloping line has a special name, the **budget line.** It shows all the consumption bundles available to Sammy when he spends all of his income. Let's use Figure 10-2 to gain an intuitive understanding of Sammy's budget line. For brevity's sake, we will denote the quantity of clams (in pounds) by Q_C and the quantity of potatoes (in pounds) by Q_P. We will also define P_C to be the price of one pound of clams, P_P to be the price of one pound of potatoes, and N to be Sammy's income. So if we restate Sammy's budget constraint of Equation 10-1 in terms of this new notation, it becomes

A consumer's **budget line** shows the consumption bundles available to a consumer who spends all of his or her income.

(10-2) $(Q_C \times P_C) + (Q_P \times P_P) \leq N$

Whenever Sammy consumes a bundle on his *budget line,* he spends all of his income, so that his expenditure on clams and potatoes is exactly equal to his income. The equation for Sammy's budget line is therefore

(10-3) $(Q_C \times P_C) + (Q_P \times P_P) = N$

Now consider what happens when Sammy spends all $20 of his income on clams (that is, $Q_P = 0$). In that case the greatest amount of clams he can consume is

$$Q_C = N/P_C = \$20/\$4 \text{ per pound of clams} = 5 \text{ pounds of clams}$$

So the horizontal intercept of the budget line—Sammy's clam consumption when he consumes no potatoes—is at point *F*, where he consumes 5 pounds of clams.

Now consider the other extreme consumption choice given that Sammy spends all of his income: Sammy consumes all potatoes and no clams (that is, $Q_C = 0$). Then the greatest amount of potatoes he can consume would be:

$$Q_P = N/P_P = \$20/\$2 \text{ per pound of potatoes} = 10 \text{ pounds of potatoes}$$

So the vertical intercept of the budget line—Sammy's potato consumption when he consumes zero clams—is at point *A*, where he consumes 10 pounds of potatoes.

The remaining four bundles indicated on the budget line—points *B*, *C*, *D*, and *E*—can be understood by considering the trade-offs Sammy faces when spending all of his income. Starting at bundle *A*, consider what happens if Sammy wants to consume 1 pound of clams while still consuming as many pounds of potatoes as possible. Consuming 1 pound of clams, which costs $4, requires that he give up 2 pounds of potatoes, which cost $2 per pound. In order to move 1 unit to the right (an increase of 1 pound of clams), Sammy must also move 2 units down (a decrease of 2 pounds of potatoes). This places him at bundle *B* on his budget line.

Similarly, if we start at bundle *F* and allow Sammy to give up 1 pound of clams (moving 1 unit to the left), how many pounds of potatoes will he receive in return? Giving up 1 pound of clams frees up $4 of Sammy's income, which goes to purchase 2 pounds of potatoes at $2 per pound. So by moving 1 unit to the left from bundle *F*, Sammy also moves up 2 units, putting him at bundle *E* on his budget line.

This exercise shows that when Sammy spends all of his income, he trades off more clams for fewer potatoes, or vice versa, by "sliding" along his budget line. In particular, if we assume that Sammy can consume fractions of pounds of clams and potatoes as well as whole pounds, his budget line is indeed the line connecting the points *A* through *F* as shown in Figure 10-2.

Do we need to consider the other bundles in Sammy's consumption possibilities, the ones that lie *within* the shaded region in Figure 10-2 bounded by the budget line? The answer is, for all practical situations, no: as long as Sammy doesn't get satiated—that is, as long as his marginal utility from consuming either good is always positive—and he doesn't get any utility from saving income rather than spending it, then he will always choose to consume a bundle that lies on his budget line.

Because changing a consumption bundle involves sliding up or down the budget line, the *slope* of the budget line tells us the opportunity cost of each good in terms of the other. Recall from Chapter 2 that we used the slope of the production possibility frontier to illustrate the opportunity cost to the economy of an additional unit of one good in terms of how much of the other good must be forgone, a cost that arose from the economy's limited productive resources. In this case, the slope of the budget line illustrates the opportunity cost to an individual of consuming one more unit of one good in terms of how much of the other good in his or her consumption bundle must be forgone. The scarce "resource" here is money—the consumer has a limited budget.

The slope of Sammy's budget line—the rise over run—is –2; 2 pounds of potatoes must be forgone to obtain another pound of clams. Economists call the number of pounds of potatoes that must be forgone to obtain one more pound of clams the *relative price* of one pound of clams in terms of potatoes. The relative price of the good on the horizontal axis in terms of the good on the vertical axis is equal to minus the slope of the budget line.

One important point about the budget line may be obvious but nonetheless needs emphasizing: the position of a consumer's budget line—how far *out* it is from the origin—depends on that consumer's income. Suppose that Sammy's income were to rise to $32 per week. Then he could afford to buy 8 pounds of clams, or 16 pounds of potatoes, or any consumption bundle in between; as shown in Figure 10-3, his budget line would move *outward*. However, if his income were to shrink to $12 per week,

Figure 10-3

Changes in Income Shift the Budget Line

If Sammy's income increases from $20 to $32 per week, he is clearly better off: his consumption possibilities have increased, and his budget line shifts, from BL_1, outward to its new position at BL_2. If Sammy's income decreases from $20 to $12, he is clearly worse off: his consumption possibilities have decreased and his budget line shifts inward toward the origin, from BL_1 to BL_3. **>web...**

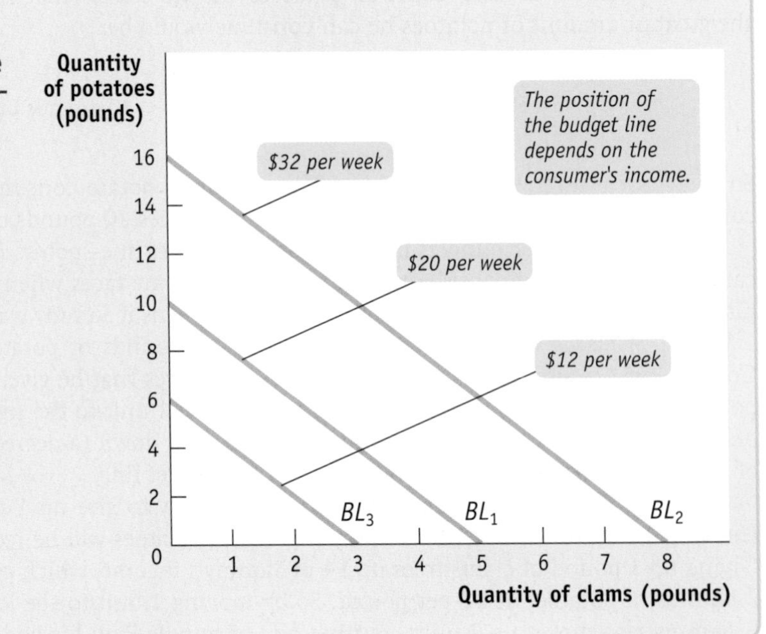

his budget line would shift *inward:* he would be able to consume at most 3 pounds of clams or 6 pounds of potatoes. In all these cases, the slope of the budget line would not change because the relative price of clams in terms of potatoes does not change: for 1 more pound of clams, Sammy still has to give up 2 pounds of potatoes.

Clearly, a larger income would increase Sammy's consumption possibilities; and utility analysis can tell us how he would take advantage of those possibilities to increase his total utility by consuming more of one or both goods. Conversely, a smaller income would reduce Sammy's consumption possibilities. He would be forced to consume less, and his utility would be lower. But for now let us continue to assume that Sammy's income is fixed at $20 per week.

Given that $20 per week budget, what point on his budget line will Sammy choose?

Optimal Consumption Choice

Because Sammy has a budget constraint, which means that he will consume a consumption bundle on the budget line, a choice to consume a given quantity of clams also determines his potato consumption, and vice versa. We want to find the consumption bundle—the point on the budget line—that maximizes Sammy's total utility. This bundle is Sammy's **optimal consumption bundle,** the consumption bundle that maximizes total utility given the budget constraint.

The **optimal consumption bundle** is the consumption bundle that maximizes a consumer's total utility given his or her budget constraint.

Table 10-1 shows how much utility Sammy gets from different levels of consumption of clams and potatoes, respectively. According to the table, Sammy has a healthy appetite; the more of either good he consumes, the higher his utility.

TABLE 10-1

Sammy's Utility from Clam and Potato Consumption

Utility from clam consumption		Utility from potato consumption	
Quantity of clams (pounds)	Utility from clams (utils)	Quantity of potatoes (pounds)	Utility from potatoes (utils)
0	0	0	0
1	15	1	11.5
2	25	2	21.4
3	31	3	29.8
4	34	4	36.8
5	36	5	42.5
		6	47.0
		7	50.5
		8	53.2
		9	55.2
		10	56.7

But because he has a limited budget, he must make a trade-off: the more pounds of clams he consumes, the fewer pounds of potatoes, and vice versa. That is, he must choose a point on his budget line.

Table 10-2 (page 252) shows how his total utility varies as he slides down his budget line. Each of six possible consumption bundles, *A* through *F* from Figure 10-2, is given in the first column. The second column shows the level of clam consumption corresponding to each choice. The third column shows the utility Sammy gets from consuming those clams. The fourth column shows the quantity of potatoes Sammy can afford *given* the level of clam consumption; this quantity goes down as his clam consumption goes up, because he is sliding down the budget line. The fifth column shows the utility he gets from consuming those potatoes. And the final column shows his *total utility.* In this example, Sammy's total utility is the sum of the utility he gets from clams and the utility he gets from potatoes.

TABLE 10-2

Sammy's Budget and Total Utility

Consumption Bundle	Quantity of clams (pounds)	Utility from clams (utils)	Quantity of potatoes (pounds)	Utility from potatoes (utils)	Total utility (utils)
A	0	0	10	56.7	56.7
B	1	15	8	53.2	68.2
C	2	25	6	47.0	72.0
D	3	31	4	36.8	67.8
E	4	34	2	21.4	55.4
F	5	36	0	0	36.0

Figure 10-4 illustrates the result graphically. Panel (a) shows Sammy's budget line, to remind us that when he decides to consume more clams he is also deciding to consume fewer potatoes. Panel (b) then shows how his total utility depends on that choice. The horizontal axis in panel (b) has two sets of labels: it shows both the quantity of clams, increasing from left to right, and the quantity of potatoes, increasing from right to left. The reason we can use the same axis to represent consumption of both goods is, of course, the budget line: the more pounds of clams Sammy consumes, the fewer pounds of potatoes he can afford, and vice versa.

Clearly, the consumption bundle that makes the best of the trade-off between clam consumption and potato consumption—the optimal consumption bundle—is the one that maximizes Sammy's total utility. That is, Sammy's optimal consumption bundle puts him at the top of the total utility curve.

As always, we can find the top of the curve by direct observation. We can see from Figure 10-4 that Sammy's total utility is maximized at point C—that his optimal consumption bundle contains 2 pounds of clams and 6 pounds of potatoes. But we know that we usually gain more insight into "how much" problems when we use marginal analysis. So in the next section we turn to representing and solving the optimal consumption choice problem with marginal analysis.

FOR INQUIRING MINDS

FOOD FOR THOUGHT ON BUDGET CONSTRAINTS

Budget constraints aren't just about money. In fact, there are many other budget constraints affecting our lives. You face a budget constraint if you have a limited amount of closet space for your clothes. All of us face a budget constraint on time: there are only so many hours in the day.

And people trying to lose weight on the Weight Watchers plan face a budget constraint on the foods they eat.

The Weight Watchers plan assigns each food a certain number of "points". A scoop of ice cream gets 4 points, a slice of pizza 7 points, a cup of grapes 1 point. You are allowed a maximum number of points each day but are free to choose which foods you eat. In other words, a dieter on the Weight Watchers plan is just like a consumer choosing a consumption bundle: points are the equivalent of prices, and the overall points limit is the equivalent of income.

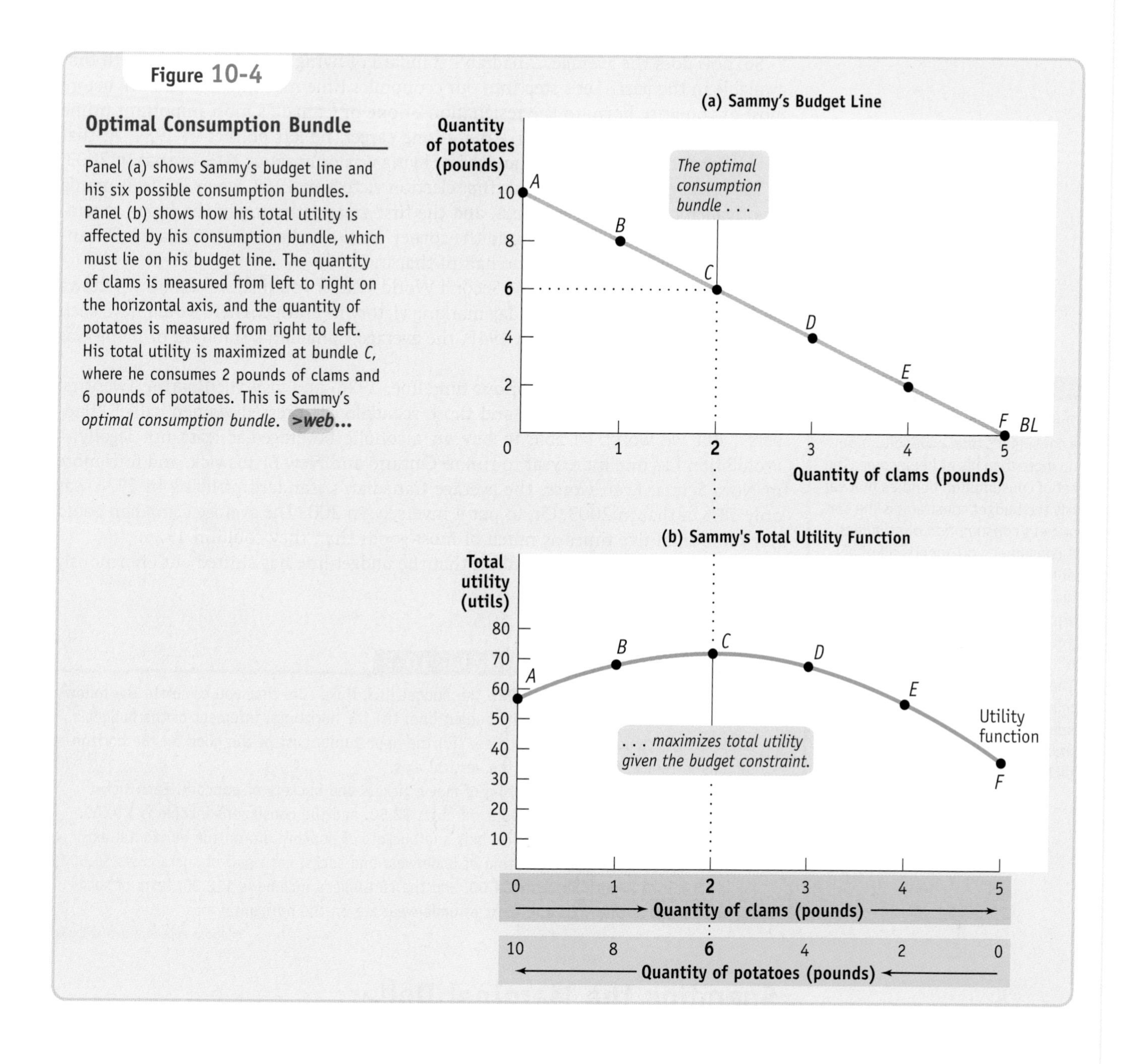

Figure 10-4

Optimal Consumption Bundle

Panel (a) shows Sammy's budget line and his six possible consumption bundles. Panel (b) shows how his total utility is affected by his consumption bundle, which must lie on his budget line. The quantity of clams is measured from left to right on the horizontal axis, and the quantity of potatoes is measured from right to left. His total utility is maximized at bundle *C*, where he consumes 2 pounds of clams and 6 pounds of potatoes. This is Sammy's *optimal consumption bundle*. >web...

economics in action

The Consumption Possibilities of Canadian Workers, 1926–2003

Over the past century, the budget line of the average Canadian has shifted radically outward as the nation has become vastly richer. One way to show this outward shift is to see how real GDP per capita has increased over time.

As most people already know, GDP is a measure of the economy's total output. But whereas nominal GDP may increase because prices increase, real GDP takes out the effect of price changes (it is adjusted for inflation). When we divide real GDP by the total population to get real GDP per capita, we get one of the most useful—though still imperfect—measures of how the average standard of living changes over time.

So, how does the average Canadian's standard of living in 2003 compare with that available in the past? Let's step into our economics time machine and go back before most of you were born, to the resignation of one of Canada's most important prime ministers, Pierre Elliot Trudeau. After a long career, he left politics in 1984. At that time, the average Canadian's standard of living was only about 70% of that in 2003.

Let's next go back to Trudeau's first election victory in 1968, when Trudeau-mania was rivalled only by Beatle-mania, and the first great gathering of the hippy generation at Woodstock was just around the corner. In 1968, the average Canadian's standard of living was just about one half of that in 2003.

Let's next go to the end of the Second World War. If you like, we can be in Ottawa on May 8, 1945, which was VE day marking victory in Europe. There would have been quite a party that night. But in 1945, the average Canadian's standard of living was only 30% of that of 2003.

Finally, let's go to the end of our time line, 1926, and visit the Roaring Twenties. We'll see those grand old cars and those scandalously dressed women called "flappers". But we won't be able to buy an alcoholic beverage—at least not legally!—Prohibition has one more year to run in Ontario and New Brunswick, and four more in Nova Scotia. Even worse, the average Canadian's standard of living in 1926 was only 18% of that in 2003. Or, to put it inversely, in 2003 the average Canadian could buy more than five times as much of most goods than they could in 1926.

By any standard, you must admit that the budget line has shifted out enormously over the years. ■

< < < < < < < < < < < < < < < < < <

>> QUICK REVIEW

- The *budget constraint* requires that a consumer's total expenditure be no more than his or her income. The set of consumption bundles that satisfy the budget constraint is the consumer's *consumption possibilities.*
- A consumer who spends all of his or her income chooses a point on his or her *budget line.* Its slope is equal to the opportunity cost of the good on the horizontal axis in terms of the good on the vertical axis.
- The consumption choice that maximizes total utility given the consumer's budget constraint is the *optimal consumption bundle.* It must lie on the consumer's budget line.

>>CHECK YOUR UNDERSTANDING 10-2

1. In the following two examples, draw the budget line. Make sure that you calculate the following: i. the vertical intercept of the budget line; (ii) the horizontal intercept of the budget line; (iii) the slope of the budget line; (iv) the opportunity cost of the good on the horizontal axis in terms of the good on the vertical axis.
   a. A consumption bundle consisting of movie tickets and buckets of popcorn. Each ticket costs $5.00, each bucket of popcorn costs $2.50, and the consumer's income is $10.00. Movie tickets are on the vertical axis and buckets of popcorn are on the horizontal axis.
   b. A consumption bundle consisting of underwear and socks. Each pair of socks costs $1.50, each pair of underwear costs $4.00, and the consumer's income is $12.00. Pairs of socks are on the vertical axis and pairs of underwear are on the horizontal axis.

Solutions appear at back of book.

Spending the Marginal Dollar

Marginal analysis is often the best way to think about "how much" decisions. In this case, Sammy is making a decision about the quantity of clams to consume, taking into account the fact that the more clams he consumes, the fewer potatoes he can afford. As we've seen, we can find his optimal consumption choice by finding the total utility he receives from each consumption bundle on his budget line and then choosing the bundle at which total utility is maximized. But is there a way to use marginal analysis instead?

The answer is yes: we can think about the problem of choosing an optimal consumption bundle in terms of the decision a consumer must make about how much to spend on each good. The marginal decision then becomes one of how to *spend the marginal dollar*—how to allocate an additional dollar between clams and potatoes. As we'll see in a moment, looking at Sammy's decision in terms of how he allocates his income gives us an important insight into the relationship between prices and consumer decisions.

The **marginal utility per dollar** spent on a good or service is the additional utility from spending one more dollar on that good or service.

Our first step is to ask how much additional utility Sammy gets from spending an additional dollar on either good—the **marginal utility per dollar** spent on either clams or potatoes.

Marginal Utility per Dollar

We've already introduced the concept of marginal utility, the additional utility a consumer gets from consuming one more unit of a good or service; now let's see how this concept can be used to derive the related measure of marginal utility per dollar.

Table 10-3 shows how to calculate the marginal utility per dollar spent on clams and potatoes, respectively.

TABLE 10-3

Marginal Utility per Dollar

(a) Clams (price of clams = $4 per pound)				(b) Potatoes (price of potatoes = $2 per pound)			
Quantity of clams (pounds)	Utility from clams (utils)	Marginal utility per pound of clams (utils)	Marginal utility per dollar (utils)	Quantity of potatoes (pounds)	Utility from potatoes (utils)	Marginal utility per pound of potatoes (utils)	Marginal utility per dollar (utils)
0	0			0	0		
		15	3.75			11.5	5.75
1	15			1	11.5		
		10	2.50			9.9	4.95
2	25			2	21.4		
		6	1.50			8.4	4.20
3	31			3	29.8		
		3	0.75			7.0	3.50
4	34			4	36.8		
		2	0.50			5.7	2.85
5	36			5	42.5		
						4.5	2.25
				6	47.0		
						3.5	1.75
				7	50.5		
						2.7	1.35
				8	53.2		
						2.0	1.00
				9	55.2		
						1.5	0.75
				10	56.7		

In panel (a) of the table, the first column shows different possible levels of clam consumption. The second column shows the utility Sammy derives from each level of clam consumption; the third column then shows the marginal utility, the increase in utility Sammy gets from consuming an additional pound of clams. Panel (b) does the same thing for potatoes. The next step is to derive marginal utility *per dollar* for each good. To do this, we must divide the marginal utility of the good by its price in dollars.

To see why we must divide by the price, compare the third and fourth columns of panel (a). Consider what happens if Sammy increases his clam consumption from 2 pounds to 3 pounds. As we can see, this increase in clam consumption raises his total utility by 6 utils. But he must spend $4 for that additional pound, so the increase in his utility per additional dollar spent on clams is 6 utils/$4 = 1.50 utils per dollar. Similarly, if he increases his clam consumption from 3 pounds to 4 pounds, his marginal utility is 3 utils per clam but his marginal utility per dollar is 3 utils/$4 = 0.75 utils per dollar. Notice that because of diminishing marginal utility per pound of clams, Sammy's marginal utility per pound of clams falls as the quantity of clams he consumes rises. As a result, his marginal utility per dollar spent on clams also falls as the quantity of clams he consumes rises.

So the last column of panel (a) shows how Sammy's marginal utility per dollar spent on clams depends on the quantity of clams he consumes. Similarly, the last column of panel (b) shows how his marginal utility per dollar spent on potatoes depends on the quantity of potatoes he consumes. Again, marginal utility per dollar spent on each good declines as the quantity of that good consumed rises, because of diminishing marginal utility.

We will use the symbols MU_C and MU_P to represent the marginal utility per pound of clams and potatoes, respectively. Then the marginal utility per dollar spent on clams is MU_C/P_C and the marginal utility per dollar spent on potatoes is MU_P/P_P. In general, the additional utility generated from an additional dollar spent on a good is equal to:

(10-4) Marginal utility per dollar spent on a good
= Marginal utility of one unit of the good / Price of one unit of the good
= MU_{good}/P_{good}

Now let's see how this concept helps us derive a consumer's optimal consumption using marginal analysis.

Optimal Consumption

The curve in panel (a) of Figure 10-5 shows Sammy's marginal utility per dollar spent on clams, MU_C/P_C, as derived in Table 10-3. The curve in panel (b) shows his marginal utility per dollar spent on potatoes, MU_P/P_P. We already know from Figure 10-4 that Sammy's optimal consumption bundle, C, consists of 2 pounds of clams and 6 pounds of potatoes. From Figure 10-5 we can read off the marginal utility per dollar

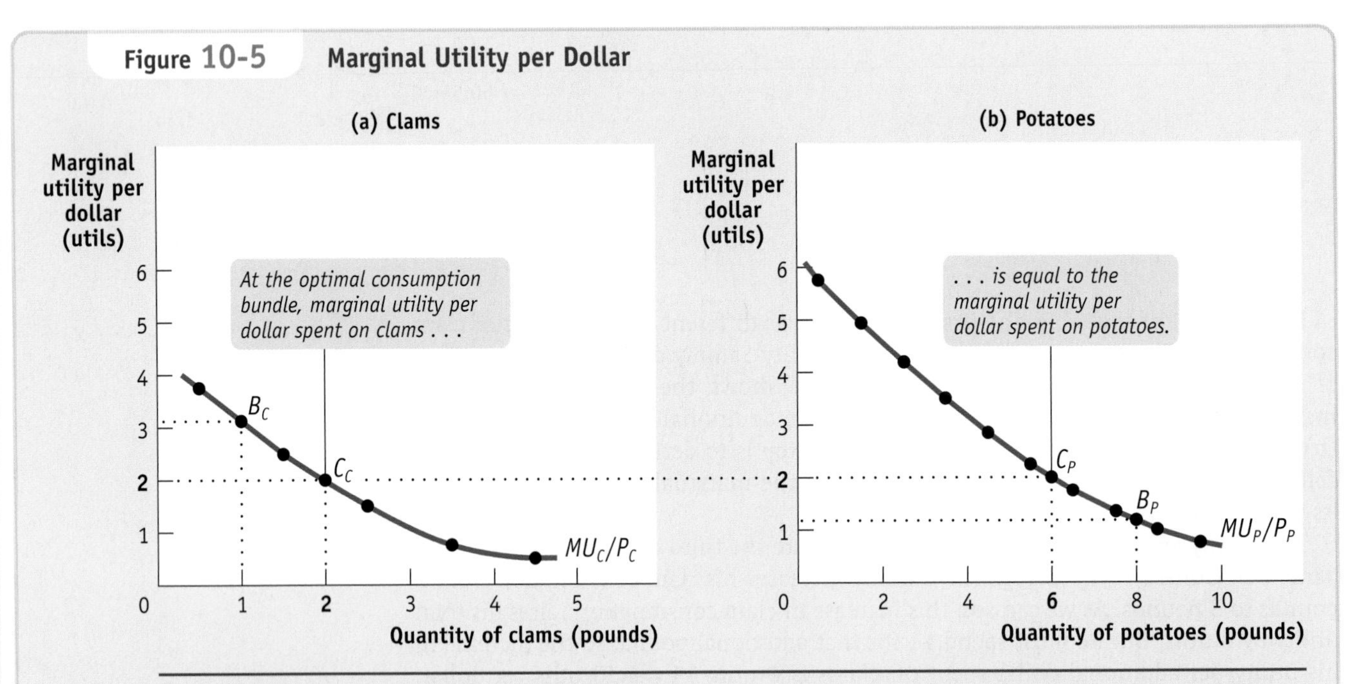

Panel (a) shows Sammy's marginal utility per dollar spent on clams; panel (b) shows his marginal utility per dollar spent on potatoes. Points C_C in panel (a) and C_P in panel (b) correspond to bundle C in Figure 10-4, Sammy's optimal consumption bundle of 2 pounds of clams and 6 pounds of potatoes. At these points his marginal utility per dollar spent on each good is 2. This illustrates the *optimal consumption rule:* at the optimal consumption bundle, the marginal utility per dollar spent on each good and service is the same. At any other consumption bundle along Sammy's budget line, such as bundle B in Figure 10-4, which is represented here by points B_C and B_P, consumption is not optimal: he can increase his utility at no additional cost by reallocating his spending.

spent on clams and potatoes, respectively, at that optimal consumption bundle, which corresponds to points C_C and C_P. And we see something interesting: when Sammy consumes 2 pounds of clams and 6 pounds of potatoes, his marginal utility per dollar spent is the same, 2, for both goods. That is, at the optimal consumption bundle $MU_C/P_C = MU_P/P_P = 2$.

FOR INQUIRING MINDS

BUT ARE CONSUMERS REALLY RATIONAL?

Would you drive across town to save $10 on a clock radio but not to save $10 on a large-screen TV? So would most people. But a $10 savings is a $10 savings, whether it is on a low-priced item or a high-priced item. So, this little piece of behaviour contradicts the conventional theory covered in this chapter.

Take another example. Is it rational for people to mow their own lawn to save $10, even though they would never agree to cut their neighbour's lawn in return for the same $10? Most of us would routinely do the same thing. But forgoing a gain of $10 to mow a neighbour's lawn has the same opportunity cost as paying somebody else to mow your own. According to theory, you either prefer the extra time or the extra money—it can't be both.

Or again, have you ever been unable to stop yourself from gorging on some tempting snack, and then felt utterly relieved when the snack was removed from your vicinity? Yet, according to accepted economic theory, a person is always better off with more rather than fewer choices.

All these examples are what are known as "anomalies"—exceptions that challenge the broader framework of the established theory of consumer choice. And they are the particular fascination of economist Richard Thaler. He has almost single-handedly spearheaded an assault on the conventional theory that models human behaviour as if we were ultra-rational *homo economicus*. Instead, Thaler proposes that people are prone to error, irrationality, and emotion. As a result, we act in ways that are not always consistent with maximizing our own financial well-being.

Thaler's view has caught on. In fact, it has come to be called "behavioural economics". He and a band of fellow dissenters are attempting to show that the anomalies fall into recognizable and predictable patterns. For example, Thaler has noticed that people are more concerned with changes in their wealth than with its absolute level. While this is a violation of standard theory, it explains many of Thaler's anomalies.

Behavioural economists hope that by illuminating these patterns new light will be shed on the economy and markets. According to Daniel McFadden, a recent Nobel laureate, behaviourism "is a fundamental re-examination of the field. It's where gravity is pulling economic science." It has important ramifications.

For example, in the United States there is a debate going on about privatizing social security and pensions. A favourite slogan for those in favour of this move is that people know what is best for themselves. The work of the behaviourists suggests that while this may be generally true, it may not be always true. Moreover, people may err in predictable ways.

Thaler has found that how choices are "framed", or positioned, affects the outcome. For example, when employees are offered the choice of a stock fund and a bond fund, they tend to invest half their savings in each. But when given a choice of three stock funds and one bond fund, they again sprinkle an equal amount in each, with the result that 75% of their savings is invested in stocks.

He has also found that people have a strong tendency to follow the path of least resistance—even over something as important as their pension! For example, the number of employees enrolling in a company's pension plan is much higher when the plan is an opt-out system (where employees are automatically enrolled unless they request otherwise) than under an opt-in system (where employees must ask to be enrolled). This tendency exists no matter how bad the employer's pension plan is. And some have been very bad indeed. In the U.S., there is nothing to stop a company from investing their employees' savings mainly in its own stock, which can be disastrous if the company gets into trouble. For example, the employees of Enron lost every cent of their pension money. Although Canadian legislation prevents an employer from investing more than 10% of a pension plan in its own stock, it is still the case that some company pension plans are much better than others.

So, framing has big implications for the debate on privatizing pensions. Neoclassicists say the more choices people have, the better off they are—therefore they should manage their own pensions. But if Thaler is right, it may not be so.

Today's behavioural economists use insights from psychology to understand behaviour that seems to be at odds with rationality. This work is having an important influence on analysis of financial markets, labour markets, and other economic concerns. But it's hard to find a behavioural economist who thinks this field should totally replace the analysis of utility maximization. The theory of the rational consumer is still the primary theory economists use to analyse consumer behaviour.

This isn't an accident. Consider another one of Sammy's possible consumption bundles, say B in Figure 10-4, at which he consumes 1 pound of clams and 8 pounds of potatoes. The marginal utility per dollar spent on each good is shown by points B_C and B_P in Figure 10-5. At that consumption bundle, Sammy's marginal utility per dollar spent on clams would be approximately 3, but his marginal utility per dollar spent on potatoes would be approximately 1. This shows that he has made a mistake: he is consuming too many potatoes and not enough clams.

How do we know this? If Sammy's marginal utility per dollar spent on clams is higher than his marginal utility per dollar spent on potatoes, he has a simple way to make himself better off while staying within his budget: spend $1 less on potatoes and $1 more on clams. By spending an additional dollar on clams, he adds about 3 utils to his total utility; meanwhile, by spending $1 less on potatoes, he subtracts only about 1 util from his total utility. Because his marginal utility per dollar spent is higher for clams than for potatoes, reallocating his spending toward clams and away from potatoes would increase his total utility. On the other hand, if his marginal utility per dollar spent on potatoes is higher, he can increase his utility by spending less on clams and more on potatoes. So if Sammy has in fact chosen his optimal consumption bundle, his marginal utility per dollar spent on clams and potatoes must be equal.

The **optimal consumption rule** says that when a consumer maximizes utility, the marginal utility per dollar spent must be the same for all goods and services in the consumption bundle.

This is a general principle, known as the **optimal consumption rule:** when a consumer maximizes utility in the face of a budget constraint, the marginal utility per dollar spent on each good or service in the consumption bundle is the same. That is, for any two goods C and P the optimal consumption rule says that at the optimal consumption bundle:

$$\text{(10-5)} \quad \frac{MU_C}{P_C} = \frac{MU_P}{P_P}$$

It's easiest to understand this rule using examples in which the consumption bundle contains only two goods, but it applies no matter how many goods or services a consumer buys: in the optimal consumption bundle, the marginal utilities per dollar spent for each and every good or service in that bundle are equal.

PITFALLS

THE RIGHT MARGINAL COMPARISON

Marginal analysis helps us understand "how much" decisions by showing us that they involve setting the marginal *benefit* of some activity equal to its marginal *cost*. But to get this right, it's important to be careful what "marginals" you compare. In the case of consumption, it's tempting but wrong to say that the marginal utility of consumption of any two goods must be the same.

The right answer is that the marginal utility *per dollar* must be the same. This takes prices into account. If a milkshake costs four times as much as an order of french fries, the optimal consumption choice isn't where you gain the same amount of utility from an extra milkshake as from an extra order of french fries; it's where the milkshake adds four times as much to utility. With the money that buys one milkshake you could have bought four orders of french fries, so the one milkshake has to add four times as much to your utility as one order of french fries. In other words, the marginal utility per dollar has to be the same for milkshakes and french fries.

economics in action

Self-Serve Gasoline

During the 1970s the price of gasoline in Canada shot up because of world oil shortages, caused mainly by Arab oil embargoes and OPEC limits on supply. At the same time, many gas stations began offering drivers a discount if they pumped their own gas.

Many people argued that the rise of self-serve gas was a response to higher gas prices, and that if gas prices ever went down again, people would once again be willing to pay the price of full service.

But economists were in general sceptical of this conclusion. Consumers, they argued, were making a calculation: the extra utility gained from spending on other goods was worth the extra effort. And gas stations offered a price break on self-serve gas because it saved them labour; so the price break would remain even if gas prices went down. Economists therefore argued that people would continue to use self-service pumps even if gasoline prices fell back to traditional levels.

In the event, gasoline prices did fall; by the late 1990s they were actually lower, adjusted for inflation, than they had been for generations. But most drivers continued to pump their own gasoline. ■

>> QUICK REVIEW

- A utility-maximizing consumer allocates spending so that the *marginal utility per dollar*—the marginal utility of a good, divided by its price—is the same for all goods. This is known as the *optimal consumption rule*. The optimal consumption bundle satisfies this rule.
- Whenever the marginal utility per dollar is higher for one good than for another good, the consumer should spend $1 more on the good with the higher marginal utility per dollar and $1 less on the other. By doing this the consumer will move closer to his or her optimal consumption bundle.

>> CHECK YOUR UNDERSTANDING 10-3

1. In Figure 10-5 you can see that marginal utility per dollar spent on clams and marginal utility per dollar spent on potatoes are approximately equal at a consumption bundle consisting of 3 pounds of clams and 8 pounds of potatoes. Explain why this is not Sammy's optimal consumption bundle. Illustrate your answer using the budget line in Figure 10-4.
2. Explain what is faulty about the following statement, using data from Table 10-3: "In order to maximize utility, Sammy should consume the bundle that gives him the maximum marginal utility per dollar for each good."

Solutions appear at back of book.

From Utility to the Demand Curve

We have now analysed the optimal consumption choice of a consumer whose income we take as given and who faces one particular set of prices—in our Sammy example, $20 income per week, $4 per pound of fried clams, and $2 per pound of fried potatoes.

But the main reason we want to understand consumer behaviour is to go behind the market demand curve—to understand how the market demand curve is explained by the utility-maximizing behaviour of individual consumers.

Individual Demand and Market Demand

Let's begin by reviewing the relationship between prices and quantity demanded, both at the individual level and at the level of the market as a whole.

The **individual demand curve** for a good shows the relationship between the quantity of a good demanded by an individual consumer and the market price of that good. For example, suppose that Bert is a consumer of fried clams, and that panel (a) of Figure 10-6 shows how many pounds of clams he will buy

The **individual demand curve** for a good shows the relationship between quantity demanded and price for an individual consumer.

Figure 10-6 Individual and Market Demand

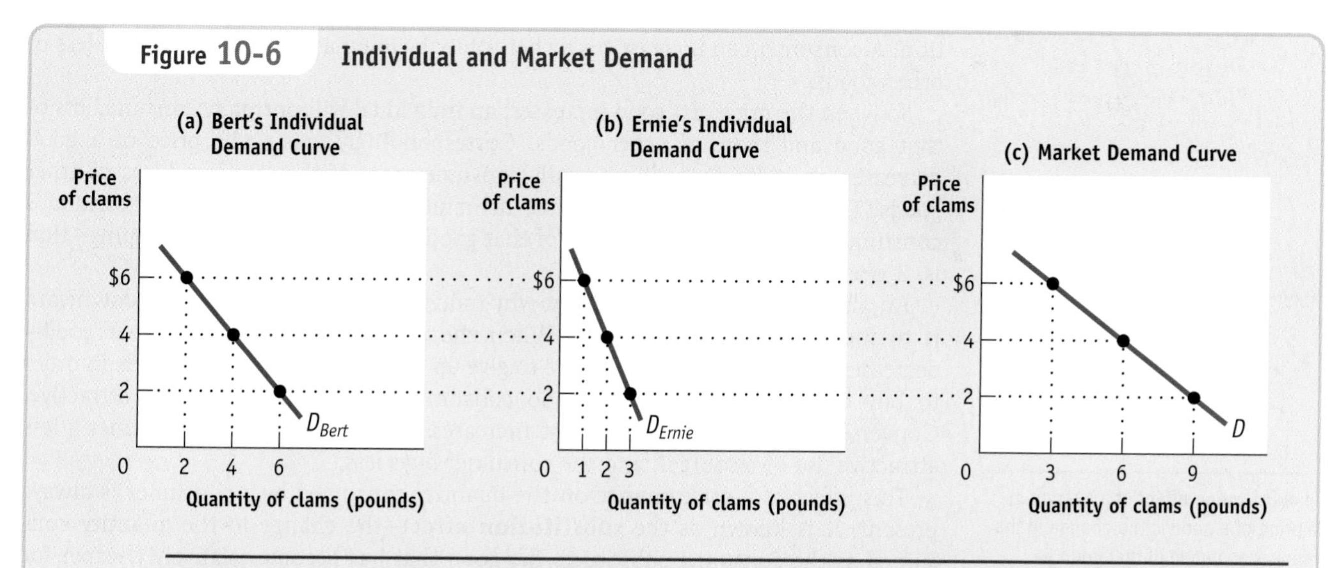

Bert and Ernie are the only two consumers of clams in the market. Panel (a) shows Bert's individual demand curve for clams and panel (b) shows Ernie's. The market demand curve, shown in panel (c), is the horizontal sum of the individual demand curves. That is, the quantity demanded by the market at any given price is the sum of the quantities demanded by Bert and by Ernie at that price. >web...

at any given market price per pound. Then D_{Bert} is Bert's individual demand curve.

The *market demand curve* shows how the quantity of a good demanded by all consumers depends on the market price of that good. The market demand curve is the *horizontal sum* of the individual demand curves of all consumers. To see what we mean by the term *horizontal sum,* assume for a moment that there are only two consumers of fried clams, Bert and Ernie. Ernie's individual demand curve is shown in panel (b). Panel (c) shows the market demand curve. At any given price, the quantity demanded by the market is the sum of the quantities demanded by Bert and Ernie. For example, at a price of $6 per pound, Bert demands 2 pounds of clams and Ernie demands 1 pound; so the quantity demanded by the market is 3 pounds. At a price of $4 per pound, Bert demands 4 pounds and Ernie demands 2 pounds; so the quantity demanded by the market is 6 pounds—and so on.

But what lies behind the individual demand curves? The *law of demand* tells us that if the price of a good increases, the quantity demanded of that good falls. But let's now use our analysis of consumer choice to get a deeper understanding of the law of demand.

Marginal Utility, the Substitution Effect, and the Law of Demand

Suppose that the price of fried clams, P_C, rises. This doesn't change the marginal utility a consumer gets from an additional pound of clams, MU_C, at any given level of clam consumption. However, it reduces the marginal utility *per dollar spent* on fried clams, MU_C/P_C. And the decrease in marginal utility per dollar spent on clams gives the consumer an incentive to consume fewer clams.

To see why, recall the optimal consumption rule: a utility-maximizing consumer chooses a consumption bundle for which the marginal utility per dollar spent on all goods is the same. If the marginal utility per dollar spent on clams falls because the price of clams rises, the consumer can increase his or her utility by purchasing fewer clams and more of other goods.

The opposite happens if the price of clams falls. In that case the marginal utility per dollar spent on clams, MU_C/P_C, increases at any given level of clam consumption. A consumer can increase his or her utility by purchasing more clams and less of other goods.

So when the price of a good increases, an individual will normally consume less of that good and more of other goods. Correspondingly, when the price of a good decreases, an individual will normally consume more of that good and less of other goods. This means that the individual demand curve, which relates an individual's consumption of a good to the price of that good, is normally downward sloping—that is, it obeys the law of demand.

An alternative way to think about why individual demand curves slope downward is to focus on opportunity costs. When the price of clams—or any other good—decreases, an individual doesn't have to give up as many units of other goods in order to buy one more unit of clams. So consuming clams becomes more attractive. Conversely, when the price of a good increases, consuming that good becomes a less attractive use of resources, and the consumer buys less.

The **substitution effect** of a change in the price of a good is the change in the quantity consumed of that good as the consumer substitutes the good that has become relatively cheaper for the good that has become relatively more expensive.

This effect of a price change on the quantity consumed by a consumer is always present. It is known as the **substitution effect**—the change in the quantity consumed as the consumer substitutes the good that has become relatively cheaper for the good that has become relatively more expensive. When a good absorbs only a small share of the consumer's spending, the substitution effect is essentially the whole story about why the individual demand curve of that consumer slopes downward. And, by implication, when a good absorbs only a small share of the typical consumer's spending, the substitution effect is essentially the sole explanation of why the market demand curve slopes downward. However, some goods such as housing absorb a large share of a typical consumer's spending. For such goods, the story behind the individual demand curve and the market demand curve becomes slightly more complicated.

The Income Effect

For the vast majority of goods, the substitution effect is pretty much the whole story behind the slopes of the individual and market demand curves. There are, however, some goods, like food or housing, that account for a substantial share of many consumers' spending. In such cases another effect, called the income effect, also comes into play.

Consider the case of a family that spends half of its income on rental housing. Now suppose that the price of housing increases. This will have a substitution effect on the family's demand: other things equal, the family will have an incentive to consume less housing—say, by moving to a smaller apartment—and more of other goods. But the family will also, in a real sense, be made poorer by that higher housing price—its income will buy less housing than before. And this reduction in its purchasing power will have an additional effect, beyond the substitution effect, on the family's consumption bundle, including its consumption of housing.

The change in the quantity consumed of a good that results from a change in the overall purchasing power of the consumer due to the change in the price of a good is known as the **income effect** of the price change. Here we find that a change in the price of a good in effect changes a consumer's income, because such a price change alters the consumer's purchasing power. This is part of the effect of prices on consumption choices.

The **income effect** of a change in the price of a good is the change in the quantity consumed of that good that results from a change in the consumer's purchasing power due to the change in the price of the good.

It's possible to give more precise definitions of the substitution effect and the income effect of a price change, and we do this in Chapter 11. For most purposes, however, there are only two things you need to know about the distinction between these two effects.

First, for the great majority of goods and services, the income effect is not important and has no significant effect on individual consumption. So most market demand curves slope downward solely because of the substitution effect—end of story.

Second, when it matters at all, the income effect usually reinforces the substitution effect. That is, when the price of a good that absorbs a substantial share of income rises, consumers of that good become a bit poorer because their purchasing power falls. And the vast majority of goods are *normal* goods, goods for which demand decreases when income falls. So this effective reduction in income leads to a reduction in the quantity demanded and reinforces the substitution effect.

However, in the case of an *inferior* good, a good for which demand increases when income falls, the income and substitution effects work in opposite directions. Although the substitution effect tends to produce a decrease in the quantity of any good demanded as its price increases, in the case of an inferior good the income effect of a price increase tends to produce an *increase* in the quantity demanded.

As a result, there are hypothetical cases involving inferior goods in which the distinction between income and substitution effects are important (see For Inquiring Minds, page 262). As a practical matter, however, it's not a subject we need to worry about when discussing the demand for most goods. Typically, income effects are important only for a very limited number of goods and when discussing *factor markets,* as we'll see in Chapter 12.

FOR INQUIRING MINDS

GIFFEN GOODS

Back when Ireland was a desperately poor country—not the prosperous "Celtic Tiger" it has lately become—it was claimed that the Irish would eat *more* potatoes when the price of potatoes went up. That is, some observers claimed that Ireland's demand curve for potatoes sloped upward, not downward. Can this happen? In theory, yes. Such goods are called "Giffen goods".

Here's the story. In nineteenth-century Ireland, potatoes absorbed a large share of consumers' budgets. People were so tired of potatoes that they would have loved to eat less of them if only they could afford it. At this time, then, potatoes were an *inferior* good for the Irish. Now a rise in the price of potatoes, *other things equal,* would cause people to substitute other foodstuffs for potatoes. But other things are not equal: given the higher price of potatoes, people are poorer. And this *increases* the demand for potatoes. If this income effect outweighs the substitution effect, a rise in the price of potatoes would increase the quantity demanded; the law of demand would not hold.

Let's take a numerical example. Suppose you have a weekly budget of $10, which you spend entirely on 5 pounds of potatoes at $1 a pound, and 1 pound of meat at $5 a pound. This provides you with a balanced diet, but a bare subsistence one—you couldn't reduce your total poundage of food intake without starving. Now suppose the price of potatoes increases to $1.67 a pound. You'd be forced to increase your consumption of potatoes to 6 pounds a week or starve. You couldn't afford to buy meat anymore, and you'd have to subsist entirely on an unbalanced diet of potatoes.

So, Giffen goods are theoretically possible. But the existence of Giffen goods in the real world has never been statistically validated, even in nineteenth-century Ireland. In a way, the point of the Irish story is how unlikely such an event is. The law of demand really has very few exceptions.

economics in action

Mortgage Rates and Consumer Demand

Most people buy houses with mortgages–loans backed by the value of the house. The interest rates on such mortgages change over time; for example, they fell quite a lot over the period from 2000 to 2003. When that happens, the cost of housing falls for millions of people–even people who have mortgages at high interest rates are often able to "refinance" them at lower rates.

It's not surprising that the demand for housing goes up when mortgage rates go down. Economists have noticed, however, that the demand for many other goods also rises when mortgage rates fall. Some of these goods are items connected with new or bigger houses, such as furniture. But people also buy new cars, eat more meals in restaurants, and take more vacations. Why?

The answer illustrates the distinction between substitution and income effects. When housing becomes cheaper, there is a *substitution effect:* people have an incentive to substitute housing for other goods in their consumption bundle. But housing also happens to be a good that absorbs a large part of consumer spending, with many families spending a quarter or more of their income on mortgage payments. So when the price of housing falls, people are in effect richer–there is a noticeable *income effect.*

The increase in the quantity of housing demanded when mortgage rates fall is the result of both effects: housing becomes a better buy compared with other consumer goods, and people also buy more and bigger houses because they feel richer. And because they feel richer, they also buy more of all other normal goods, such as cars, restaurant meals, and vacations. ■

>>QUICK REVIEW

- The market demand curve for a good is the horizontal sum of each consumer's *individual demand curve*.
- Most goods absorb only a small fraction of a consumer's spending. For such goods, the *substitution effect* of a price change is the only important effect of the price change on demand. It causes individual demand curves and the market demand curve to slope downward.
- When a good absorbs a large fraction of a consumer's spending, the *income effect* of a price change is present in addition to the substitution effect.
- For normal goods, demand rises when a consumer is richer and falls when a consumer is poorer, so that the income effect reinforces the substitution effect. For inferior goods, demand rises when a consumer is poorer and falls when a consumer is richer, so that the income and substitution effects move in the opposite direction.

>>CHECK YOUR UNDERSTANDING 10-4

In each of the following cases, state whether the income effect, the substitution effect, or both are significant. In which cases do they move in the same direction? In opposite directions? Why?

1. Orange juice represents a small share of Clare's spending. She buys more lemonade and less orange juice when the price of orange juice goes up. She does not change her purchases of other goods.

2. Apartment rents have risen dramatically this year. Since rent absorbs a major part of her income, Delia moves to a smaller apartment. Assume that rental housing is a normal good.
3. The cost of a semester-long meal ticket at the student cafeteria rises, representing a significant increase in living costs. As a result, many students have less money to spend on weekend meals at restaurants, so they eat in the cafeteria instead. Assume that cafeteria meals are an inferior good.

Solutions appear at back of book.

• A LOOK AHEAD •

At this point we have the basic tools to understand consumer behaviour; taken together with our analysis of producer behaviour (which is in Chapters 8 and 9), we have the background behind both the supply and the demand curves.

There is more to say about consumer choice; those who want to pursue the subject further should proceed to Chapter 11. Those eager to move on can, however, skip to Chapter 12 and the next subject: how the same tools that we have used to analyse the markets for *goods and services* can also be used to analyse the markets for *factors of production.*

SUMMARY

1. Consumers maximize a measure of satisfaction called **utility.** Each consumer has a **utility function** that determines the level of total utility from his or her **consumption bundle,** the goods and services that are consumed. We measure utility in hypothetical units called **utils.**
2. A good's or service's **marginal utility** is the additional utility generated by consuming one more unit of the good or service. We usually assume that the **principle of diminishing marginal utility** holds: consumption of another unit of a good or service yields less additional utility than the previous unit. As a result, the **marginal utility curve** is downward sloping.
3. A **budget constraint** limits a consumer's spending to no more than his or her income. It defines the consumer's **consumption possibilities,** the set of all affordable consumption bundles. A consumer who spends all of his or her income will choose a consumption bundle on the **budget line,** the slope of which is equal to the opportunity cost of the good on the horizontal axis in terms of the good on the vertical axis. An individual chooses the consumption bundle that maximizes total utility, the **optimal consumption bundle.**
4. We use marginal analysis to find the optimal consumption bundle by analysing how to allocate the marginal dollar. The **optimal consumption rule** says that at the optimal consumption bundle **the marginal utility per dollar** spent on each good and service—the marginal utility of a good divided by its price—is the same.
5. An **individual demand curve** for a good shows how an individual consumer's quantity demanded depends on price. Individual demand curves are summed horizontally to yield the market demand curve. Changes in the price of a good affect the quantity consumed in two possible ways: the **substitution effect** and the **income effect.** Most goods absorb only a small share of a consumer's spending; for these goods, only the substitution effect—buying less of the good that has become relatively more expensive and more of the good that has become relatively cheaper—is significant. It causes the individual and the market demand curves to slope downward. When a good absorbs a large fraction of spending, the income effect is also significant: an increase in a good's price makes a consumer poorer, but a decrease in price makes a consumer richer. This change in purchasing power makes consumers demand more or less of a good, depending on whether the good is normal or inferior. For normal goods, the substitution and income effects reinforce each other. For inferior goods, however, they work in opposite directions.

KEY TERMS

Utility, p. 244
Consumption bundle, p. 244
Utility function, p. 244
Util, p. 244
Marginal utility, p. 245
Marginal utility curve, p. 245
Principle of diminishing marginal utility, p. 246
Budget constraint, p. 248
Consumption possibilities, p. 248
Budget line, p. 249
Optimal consumption bundle, p. 251
Marginal utility per dollar, p. 254
Optimal consumption rule, p. 258
Individual demand curve, p. 259
Substitution effect, p. 260
Income effect, p. 261

PROBLEMS

1. For each of the following situations, decide whether Al has increasing, constant, or diminishing marginal utility.

   a. The more economics classes Al takes, the more he enjoys the subject. And he also finds that the more economics classes he takes, the easier each class gets, making him enjoy each additional class even more than the one before that.

   b. Al likes loud music. In fact, according to him, "the louder, the better". Each time he turns the volume up a notch, he adds 5 utils to his total utility.

   c. Al enjoys watching old episodes of the TV sitcom *Friends*. He claims that even old episodes are always funny, but he does admit that the more he sees an episode, the less funny it gets.

   d. One of Al's favourite foods is toasted marshmallows. The more he eats, however, the fuller he gets, and the less he enjoys each additional marshmallow. And there is a point at which he becomes satiated: beyond that point, more marshmallows actually make him feel worse rather than better.

2. Use the concept of marginal utility to explain the following: Newspaper vending machines are designed so that once you have paid for one paper you could take more than one paper at a time. But soda vending machines, once you have paid for one soda, dispense only one soda at a time.

3. Brenda likes to have bagels and coffee for breakfast. The accompanying table shows Brenda's total utility from various consumption bundles of bagels and coffee.

Consumption bundle		
Quantity of bagels	Quantity of coffee (cups)	Total utility (utils)
0	0	0
0	2	28
0	4	40
1	2	48
1	3	54
2	0	28
2	2	56
3	1	54
3	2	62
4	0	40
4	2	66

Suppose Brenda knows she will consume 2 cups of coffee for sure. However, she may choose to consume 0, 1, 2, 3, or 4 bagels.

   a. Calculate Brenda's marginal utility from bagels as she goes from consuming 0 bagels to 1 bagel, from 1 bagel to 2 bagels, from 2 bagels to 3 bagels, and from 3 bagels to 4 bagels.

   b. Draw Brenda's marginal utility curve of bagels. Does Brenda have increasing, diminishing, or constant marginal utility of bagels?

   c. Suppose that $1 has a constant marginal utility to Brenda, equal to 10 utils. Given your answer to part b, how much would Brenda be prepared to pay for 1 bagel, 2 bagels, and 3 bagels? Draw her demand curve for bagels.

4. Brenda from Problem 3 now has to make a decision about how many bagels and how much coffee to have for breakfast. She has $8 of income to spend on bagels and coffee. Use the information on her utility given in the table in Problem 3.

   a. Bagels cost $2 each, and coffee costs $2 per cup. Which bundles are on Brenda's budget line? For each of these bundles, what is the level of utility (in utils) that Brenda experiences? Which bundle is therefore her optimal bundle?

   b. Now the price of bagels increases to $4, while the price of coffee remains at $2 per cup. Which bundles are now on Brenda's budget line? For each of these bundles, what is the level of utility (in utils) that Brenda experiences? Which bundle is therefore her optimal bundle?

   c. Compare your answers from parts a and b. As the price of bagels increased, from $2 to $4, what happened to the quantity of bagels that Brenda chose to consume? What does this imply about the slope of Brenda's demand curve for bagels? In words, describe the substitution effect and the income effect of this increase in the price of bagels. (Bagels are a normal good.)

5. Bruno can spend his income on two different goods: Sarah McLachlan CDs and notebooks for his class notes. He is thinking about the following three bundles: bundle *A* contains 5 CDs and 5 notebooks; bundle *B* contains 10 CDs and 2 notebooks; and bundle *C* contains 3 CDs and 6 notebooks. For each of the following situations, draw the budget constraint and decide which of these bundles are possible consumption bundles; that is, which of these bundles could he consume given the information about his income and prices. Place CDs on the horizontal axis and notebooks on the vertical axis.

   a. CDs cost $10 each, and notebooks cost $2 each. Bruno has income of $60.

   b. CDs cost $10 each, and notebooks cost $5 each. Bruno has income of $110.

   c. Bruno's income and the prices for CDs and notebooks are such that he can just buy bundle *C* (that is, bundle *C* is on his budget line). The opportunity cost of one CD is one notebook.

6. The accompanying table shows Bruno's utilities from notebooks and Sarah McLachlan CDs.

Quantity of notebooks	Utility from notebooks (utils)	Quantity of CDs	Utility from CDs (utils)
0	0	0	0
2	70	1	80
4	130	2	150
6	180	3	210
8	220	4	260
10	250	5	300

The price of a notebook is $5, the price of a CD is $10, and Bruno has $50 of income to spend.

a. Which consumption bundles of notebooks and CDs can Bruno consume if he spends all his income? Draw Bruno's budget line with CDs on the horizontal axis and notebooks on the vertical axis.

b. Calculate the marginal utility of each notebook and the marginal utility of each CD. Then calculate the marginal utility per dollar spent on notebooks, and the marginal utility per dollar spent on CDs.

c. Draw a diagram like Figure 10-5 in which the marginal utility per dollar spent on notebooks is shown in one panel, and the marginal utility per dollar spent on CDs is shown in the other panel. Using this diagram and the optimal consumption rule, predict which bundle—from all the bundles on his budget line—Bruno will choose.

7. For each of the following situations, decide whether the bundle Carla is thinking about consuming is optimal or not. If it is not optimal, how could Carla improve her overall level of utility? That is, on which good should she spend more, and on which good should she spend less?

a. Carla has $200 to spend on sneakers and sweaters. Sneakers cost $50 per pair, and sweaters cost $20 each. She is thinking about buying two pairs of sneakers and five sweaters. She tells her friend that the additional utility she would get from the second pair of sneakers is the same as the additional utility she would get from the fifth sweater.

b. Carla has $5.00 to spend on pens and pencils. Each pen costs $0.50 and each pencil costs $0.10. She is thinking about buying 6 pens and 20 pencils. The last pen would add five times as much to her total utility as the last pencil.

c. Carla has $50 per season to spend on tickets to football games and tickets to soccer games. Each football ticket costs $10 and each soccer ticket costs $5. She is thinking about buying 3 football tickets and 2 soccer tickets. Her marginal utility from the third football ticket is twice as much as her marginal utility from the second soccer ticket.

8. Cal "Cool" Cooper has $200 to spend on cell phones and sunglasses. The accompanying table gives his utility of cell phones and sunglasses.

Quantity of cell phones	Utility from cell phones (utils)	Quantity of sunglasses	Utility from sunglasses (utils)
0	0	0	0
1	400	1	325
2	700	2	600
3	900	3	825
4	1,000	4	700

a. Each cell phone costs $100 and each pair of sunglasses costs $50. Which bundles lie on Cal's budget line? Draw a diagram like Figure 10-5 in which the marginal utility per dollar spent on cell phones is shown in one panel, and the marginal utility per dollar spent on sunglasses is shown in the other panel. Using this diagram and the optimal consumption rule, decide how Cal should allocate his money. That is, from all the bundles on his budget line, which bundle will Cal choose?

b. Now the price of cell phones falls to $50 each, while the price of sunglasses remains at $50 per pair. Which bundles lie on Cal's budget line? Draw a diagram like Figure 10-5 in which the marginal utility per dollar spent on cell phones is shown in one panel, and the marginal utility per dollar spent on sunglasses is shown in the other panel. Using this diagram and the optimal consumption rule, decide how Cal should allocate his money. That is, from all the bundles on his budget line, which bundle will Cal choose?

c. How has Cal's consumption of cell phones changed as the price of cell phones fell? In words, describe the income effect and the substitution effect of this fall in the price of cell phones. (Cell phones are a normal good.)

9. Damien Matthews is a busy actor. He allocates his free time to seeing movies and working out at the gym. The accompanying table shows his utility from the number of times per week he watches a movie or goes to the gym.

Quantity of gym visits per week	Utility from gym visits (utils)	Quantity of movies per week	Utility from movies (utils)
1	100	1	60
2	180	2	110
3	240	3	150
4	280	4	180
5	310	5	190
6	330	6	195

Damien has 14 hours per week to spend on watching movies and going to the gym. Each movie takes 2 hours and each gym visit takes 2 hours. (*Hint:* Damien's free time is analogous to income he can spend. The hours needed for each activity are analogous to the price of that activity.)

a. Which bundles of gym visits and movies can Damien consume per week? Draw Damien's budget line in a diagram with gym visits on the horizontal axis and movies on the vertical axis.

b. Calculate the marginal utility of each gym visit and the marginal utility of each movie. Then calculate the marginal utility per hour spent at the gym and the marginal utility per hour spent watching movies.

c. Draw a diagram like Figure 10-5 in which the marginal utility per hour spent at the gym is shown in one panel, and the marginal utility per hour spent watching movies is shown in the other panel. Using this diagram and the optimal consumption rule, decide how Damien should allocate his time.

10. Anna Jenniferson is an actress, and on the set of a new movie she meets Damien from Problem 9. She tells him that she likes watching movies much more than going to the gym. In fact, she says that if she had to give up seeing 1 movie, she would need to go to the gym twice to make up for the loss in utility from not seeing the movie. A movie takes 2 hours, and a gym visit also lasts 2 hours. Damien tells Anna that she is not watching enough movies. Is he right?

11. Paul is a low-income student who covers most of his dietary needs by eating cheap breakfast cereal, since it contains most of the important vitamins. As the price of cereal increases, he decides to buy even less of other foods and even more breakfast cereal to maintain his intake of important nutrients. This makes breakfast cereal a Giffen good for Paul. Describe in words the substitution effect from this increase in the price of cereal and the income effect from this increase in the price of cereal. In which direction does each effect move, and why? What does this imply for the slope of Paul's demand curve for cereal?

12. In each of the following situations, describe the substitution effect, and (if it is significant) the income effect. In which direction does each of these effects move? Why?

a. Ed spends a large portion of his income on his children's education. University tuition fees rise, and as a result one of his children has to withdraw from university.

b. Homer spends much of his monthly income on home mortgage payments. The interest rate on his adjustable-rate mortgage falls, lowering his mortgage payments, and Homer decides to move to a larger house.

c. Pam thinks that Spam is an inferior good. Yet as the price of Spam rises, she decides to buy less of it.

>web... To continue your study and review of concepts in this chapter, please visit the Krugman/Wells website for quizzes, animated graph tutorials, web links to helpful resources, and more.

www.worthpublishers.com/krugmanwellsmyatt

chapter 11

>>Consumer Preferences and Consumer Choice

A TALE OF TWO CITIES

DO YOU WANT TO EARN A HIGH salary? Maybe you should consider moving to Toronto. While median incomes are not as high as some other cities (like Calgary or Ottawa), some of the highest salaries are earned in Toronto. Besides being home to Canada's financial capital (on Bay Street), Toronto contains more company head offices than any other Canadian city. The size of the job market in Toronto, the opportunities for promotion, and the carrot of high salaries are the reasons why educated young people from other parts of the country routinely migrate to Ontario's capital city. For example, graduates with an MA in economics from the University of New Brunswick can usually command a starting salary in Toronto around twice as high as they could get in Fredericton, New Brunswick's provincial capital.

But before you rush to Toronto, there's something else you should know: housing is expensive there. It is the second most expensive city in Canada after Vancouver, and is about four times as expensive per square foot of living space as Fredericton. As a result, the average apartment or house in Toronto is small by Canadian standards.

So is life better or worse in Toronto than in Fredericton? It depends a lot on what you want. For young people without children, the higher wages available in Toronto might outweigh the higher price of housing. These people may be willing to accept living further from the city centre, or taking smaller accommodations, or rented accommodations, in return for the higher incomes available. This would give them the ability to consume greater quantities of other goods such as restaurant meals or clothing. On the other hand, people with big families might prefer cities like Fredericton, where the average wage is lower than it is in Toronto but where a dollar buys more

What you will learn in this chapter:

- Why economists use **indifference curves** to illustrate a person's preferences
- The importance of the **marginal rate of substitution,** the rate at which a consumer is just willing to substitute one good for another
- An alternative way of finding a consumer's optimal consumption bundle using indifference curves and the budget line
- How the shape of indifference curves helps determine whether goods are substitutes or complements
- An in-depth understanding of income and substitution effects

Ariel Skelley/Masterfile

Carol Halebein for the *New York Times*

Spacious house in the suburbs or cozy apartment in the city—how would you choose?

square feet of living space. That is, they would choose to eat fewer restaurant meals but live in more spacious housing.

For people whose preferences lie somewhere between those of young urban professionals and those of proud parents, the choice between Toronto and a city like Fredericton may not be easy. In fact, some people would be *indifferent* to living in either location. That's not to say that they would live the same way in Toronto as they would in Fredericton; rather, in Toronto they would live in small apartments and eat out a lot, but in a city like Fredericton they would be homebodies. And they would find both lifestyles equally good.

Our comparison between Toronto and Fredericton has several morals. One is that different people have different preferences. But we also see that even given an individual's preferences, there may be different consumption bundles that yield the same total utility. This insight leads to the concept of *indifference curves,* a useful way to represent individual preferences.

The example also shows that an individual's total utility depends not only on income, but also on prices—and that both income and prices affect consumer choices. We will apply this more complete analysis of consumer choice to the important distinction between *complements* and *substitutes.* Finally, we will use this insight to examine further the *income* and *substitution effects* we covered briefly in Chapter 10.

But let's begin with indifference curves.

Mapping the Utility Function

In Chapter 10 we introduced the concept of a utility function, which determines a consumer's total utility given his or her consumption bundle. In Figure 10-1 we saw how Cassie's total utility changed as we changed the quantity of fried clams consumed, holding fixed the quantities of other items in her bundle. That is, in Figure 10-1 we showed how total utility changed as consumption of only *one* good changed. But we also learned in Chapter 10, from our example of Sammy, that finding the optimal consumption bundle involves the problem of how to allocate the last dollar spent between *two* goods, clams and potatoes. In this chapter we will extend the analysis by learning how to express total utility as a function of consumption of two goods. In this way we will deepen our understanding of the trade-off involved when choosing the optimal consumption bundle and of how the optimal consumption bundle itself changes in response to changes in the prices of goods. In order to do that, we now turn to a different way of representing a consumer's utility function, based on the concept of *indifference curves.*

Indifference Curves

Ingrid is a consumer who buys only two goods: housing, measured in the number of rooms, and restaurant meals. How can we represent her utility function in a way that takes account of her consumption of both goods?

One way is to draw a three-dimensional picture. Figure 11-1 shows a three-dimensional "utility hill". The distance along the horizontal axis measures the quantity of housing Ingrid consumes in terms of numbers of rooms; the distance along the vertical axis measures the number of restaurant meals she consumes. The altitude or height of the hill at each point is indicated by a contour line, along which the height of the hill is constant. For example, point *A,* which corresponds to a consumption bundle of 3 rooms and 30 restaurant meals, lies on the contour line labelled 450. So the total utility Ingrid receives from consuming 3 rooms and 30 restaurant meals is 450 utils.

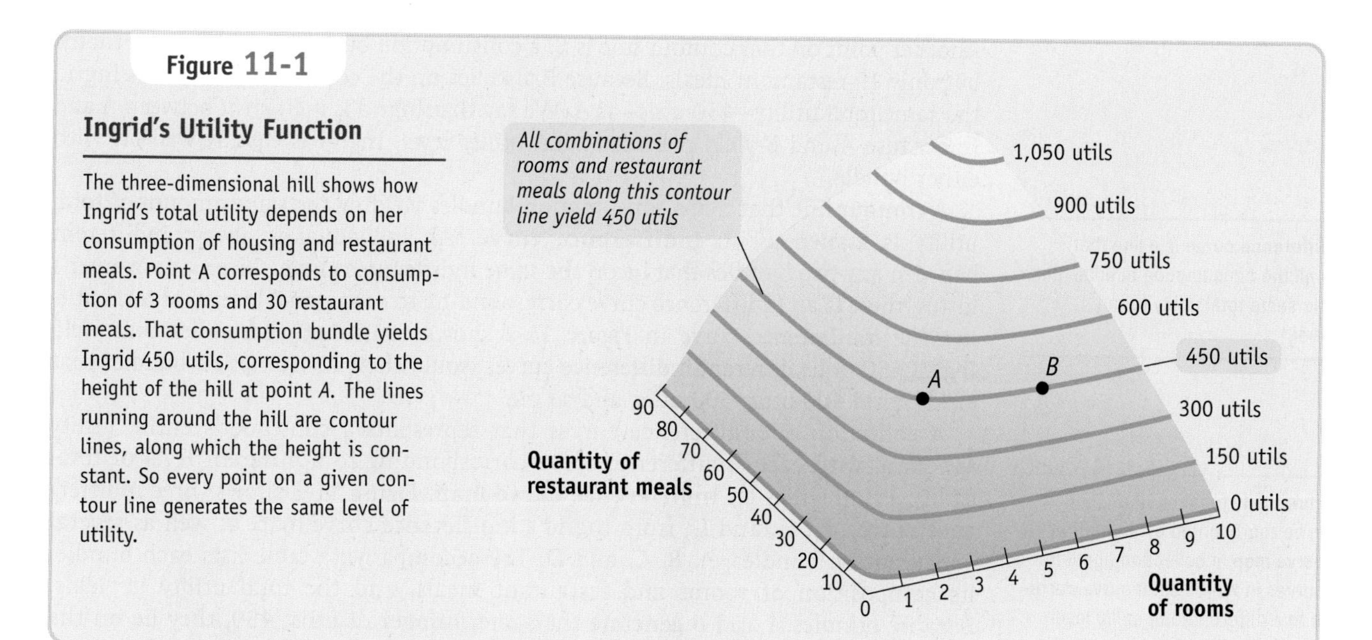

Figure 11-1

Ingrid's Utility Function

The three-dimensional hill shows how Ingrid's total utility depends on her consumption of housing and restaurant meals. Point A corresponds to consumption of 3 rooms and 30 restaurant meals. That consumption bundle yields Ingrid 450 utils, corresponding to the height of the hill at point *A*. The lines running around the hill are contour lines, along which the height is constant. So every point on a given contour line generates the same level of utility.

A three-dimensional picture like Figure 11-1 helps us think about the relationship between consumption bundles and total utility. But anyone who has ever used a topographical map to plan a hiking trip knows that it is possible to represent a three-dimensional surface in only two dimensions. A topographical map doesn't offer a three-dimensional view of the terrain; instead, it conveys information about altitude solely through the use of contour lines.

The same principle can be applied to representing the utility function. In Figure 11-2 Ingrid's consumption of rooms is measured on the horizontal axis and her consumption of restaurant meals on the vertical axis. The curve here corresponds to the contour line in Figure 11-1, drawn at a total utility of 450 utils. This curve shows all the consumption bundles that yield a total utility of 450 utils. One point on that contour line is *A*, a consumption bundle consisting of 3 rooms and 30 restaurant meals.

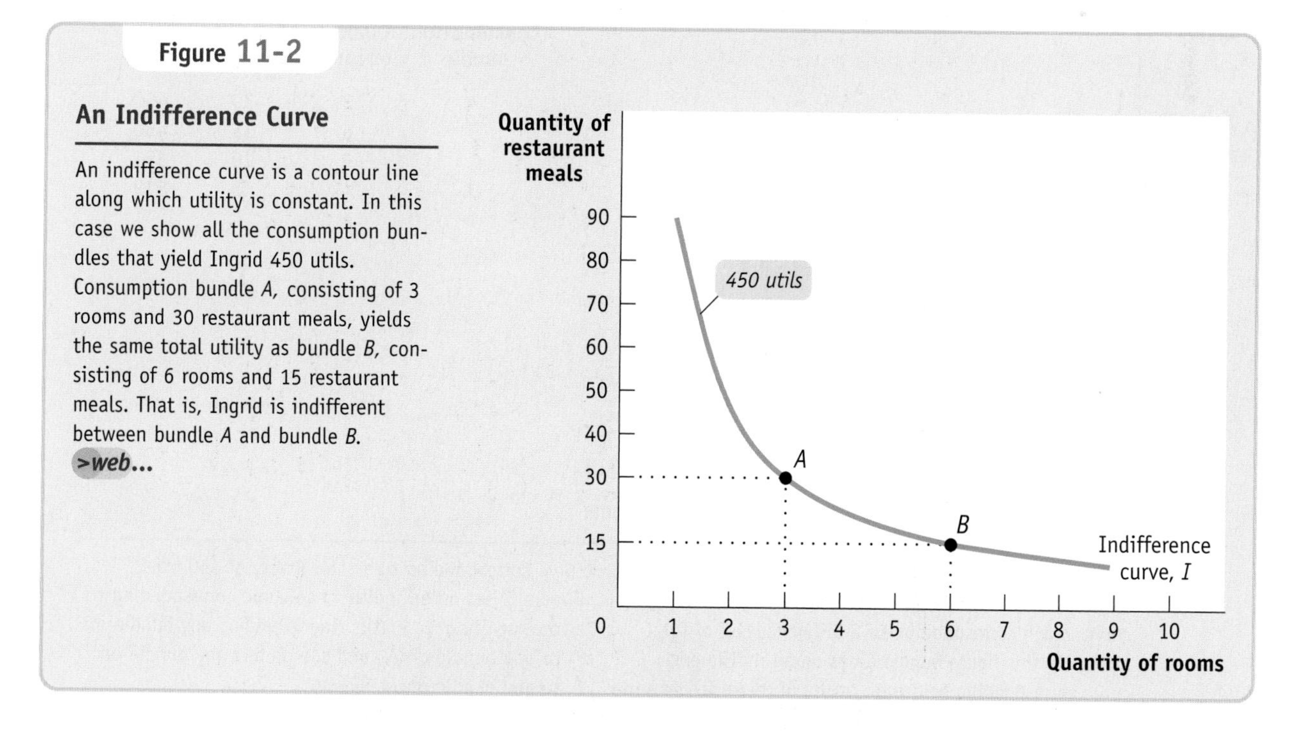

Figure 11-2

An Indifference Curve

An indifference curve is a contour line along which utility is constant. In this case we show all the consumption bundles that yield Ingrid 450 utils. Consumption bundle *A*, consisting of 3 rooms and 30 restaurant meals, yields the same total utility as bundle *B*, consisting of 6 rooms and 15 restaurant meals. That is, Ingrid is indifferent between bundle *A* and bundle *B*.

>web...

Another point on that contour line is *B*, a consumption bundle consisting of 6 rooms but only 15 restaurant meals. Because *B* also lies on the contour line, it yields Ingrid the same total utility—450 utils—as *A*. We say that Ingrid is *indifferent* between *A* and *B*: because *A* and *B* yield the same total utility level, Ingrid is equally well off with either bundle.

An **indifference curve** is a line that shows all the consumption bundles that yield the same total utility for an individual.

A contour line that maps consumption bundles yielding the same amount of total utility is known as an **indifference curve.** An individual is always indifferent between any two bundles that lie on the same indifference curve. Given a consumer's tastes, there is an indifference curve corresponding to each possible level of total utility. The indifference curve in Figure 11-2 shows consumption bundles that yield Ingrid 450 utils; different indifference curves would show consumption bundles that yield Ingrid 400 utils, 500 utils, and so on.

The entire utility function of an individual can be represented by an **indifference curve map,** a collection of indifference curves in which each curve corresponds to a different total utility level.

A collection of indifference curves that represents a consumer's entire utility function, with each indifference curve corresponding to a different level of total utility, is known as an **indifference curve map.** Figure 11-3 shows three indifference curves, I_1, I_2, and I_3, from Ingrid's indifference curve map, as well as several consumption bundles, *A*, *B*, *C*, and *D*. The accompanying table lists each bundle, its composition of rooms and restaurant meals, and the total utility it yields. Because bundles *A* and *B* generate the same number of utils, 450, they lie on the same indifference curve, I_2. Although Ingrid is indifferent between *A* and *B*, she is certainly not indifferent between *A* and *C*: as you see from the table, *C* generates only 391 utils, a lower total utility than *A* or *B*. So Ingrid prefers consumption bundles *A* and *B* to bundle *C*. This is represented by the fact that *C* is on the indifference curve I_1, and I_1 lies below I_2. Bundle *D*, though, generates 519 utils, a higher total utility level than bundles *A* or *B*. It is on I_3, an indifference curve that lies above I_2. Clearly, Ingrid prefers *D* to either *A* or *B*. And, even more strongly, she prefers *D* to *C*.

Figure 11-3 An Indifference Curve Map

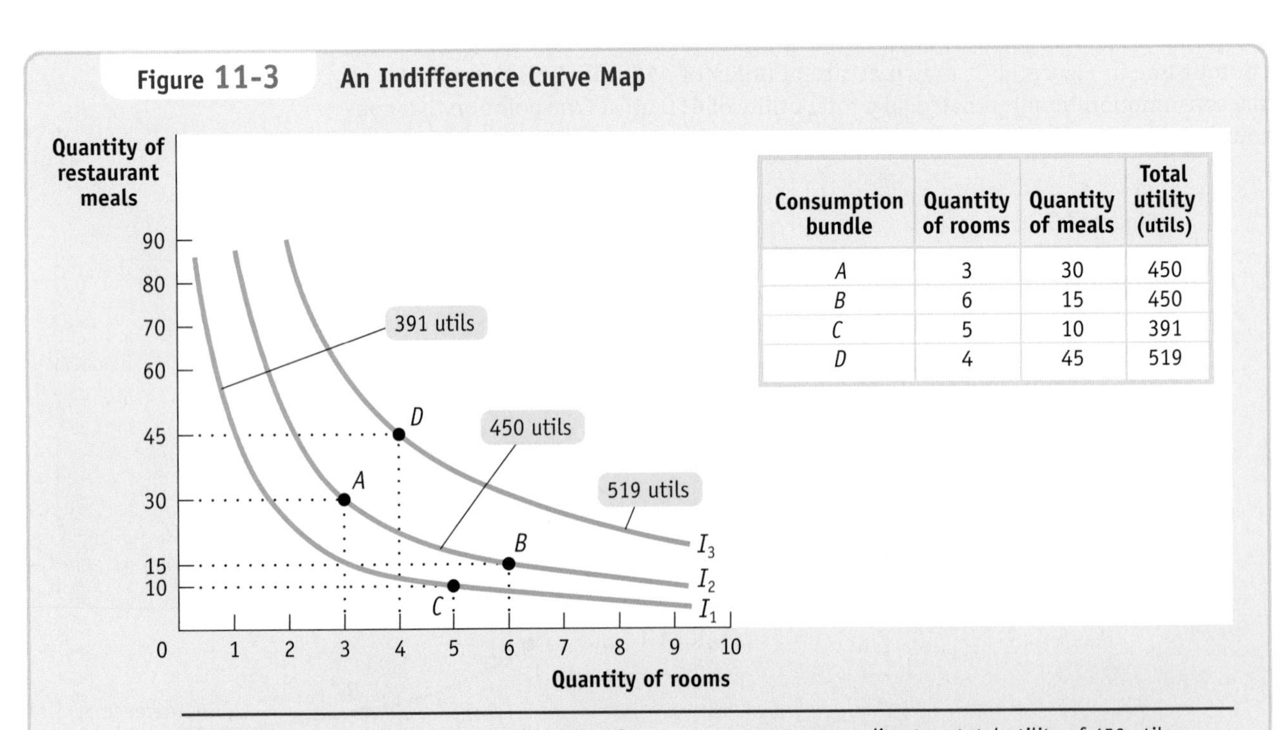

Consumption bundle	Quantity of rooms	Quantity of meals	Total utility (utils)
A	3	30	450
B	6	15	450
C	5	10	391
D	4	45	519

The utility function can be represented in as much detail as we want by showing a number of indifference curves, each corresponding to a different level of total utility. In this figure bundle *C* lies on an indifference curve corresponding to a total utility of 391 utils. As in Figure 11-2, bundles *A* and *B* lie on an indifference curve corresponding to a total utility of 450 utils. Bundle *D* lies on an indifference curve corresponding to a total utility of 519 utils. Ingrid prefers any bundle on I_2 to any bundle on I_1, and she prefers any bundle on I_3 to any bundle on I_2. **>web...**

FOR INQUIRING MINDS

ARE UTILS USEFUL?

In the table that accompanies Figure 11-3 we give the number of utils achieved at each of the indifference curves shown in the figure. But is this information actually needed?

The answer is no. As you will see shortly, the indifference curve map tells us all we need to know in order to find a consumer's optimal consumption bundle. That is, it's important that Ingrid has higher total utility along indifference curve I_2 than she does along I_1, but it doesn't matter *how much* higher her total utility is. In other words, we don't have to measure utils in order to understand how consumers make choices. Economists say that consumer theory requires an "ordinal" measure of utility—one that ranks consumption bundles in terms of desirability—so that we can say that bundle *X* is better than bundle *Y*. The theory does not, however, require "cardinal" utility, which actually assigns a specific number to the total utility yielded by each bundle.

So why introduce the concept of utils at all? The answer is that it is much easier to understand the basis of rational choice by using the concept of measurable utility.

Properties of Indifference Curves

No two individuals have the same indifference curve map because no two individuals have the same preferences. But economists believe that every indifference curve map has two general properties, illustrated in panel (a) of Figure 11-4 (page 272):

- *Indifference curves never cross.* Suppose that we tried to draw an indifference curve map like the one depicted in the left diagram in panel (a), in which two indifference curves cross at *A*. What is the total utility at *A*? Is it 100 utils or 200 utils? Indifference curves cannot cross because each consumption bundle must correspond to a unique utility level—not, as shown at *A*, two different utility levels.
- *The farther out an indifference curve lies—the farther it is from the origin—the higher the level of total utility it indicates.* The reason, illustrated in the right diagram of panel (a), is that we have assumed that more is better—over the set of consumption bundles we are considering, the consumer is not satiated. Bundle *B*, on the outer indifference curve, contains more of both goods than bundle *A* on the inner indifference curve. So *B* generates a higher total utility level (200 utils) and lies on a higher indifference curve than *A*.

Furthermore, economists believe that, for most goods, consumers' indifference curve maps also have two additional properties. They are illustrated in panel (b) of Figure 11-4:

- *Indifference curves are downward sloping.* Here, too, the reason is that more is better. The left diagram in panel (b) shows four consumption bundles on the same indifference curve: *W*, *X*, *Y*, and *Z*. By definition these consumption bundles yield the same level of total utility. But as you move along the curve to the right, the quantity of rooms consumed increases. The only way a person can consume more rooms without gaining utility is by giving up some restaurant meals. So the indifference curve must be downward sloping.
- *Indifference curves have a convex shape.* The right diagram in panel (b) shows that the slope of each indifference curve changes as you move down the curve to the right: the curve gets flatter. If you move up an indifference curve to the left, the curve gets steeper. So the indifference curve is steeper at *A* than it is at *B*. When this occurs, we say that an indifference curve has a *convex* shape—it is bowed-in towards the origin. This feature arises from diminishing marginal utility, a principle we discussed in Chapter 10. Recall that when a consumer has diminishing marginal utility, consumption of another unit of a good generates a smaller increase in total utility than the previous unit consumed. In the next section we will examine in detail how diminishing marginal utility gives rise to convex-shaped indifference curves.

Goods that satisfy all four properties of indifference curve maps are called *ordinary goods,* a term we will define more formally later in this chapter. The vast majority of goods in any consumer's utility function fall into this category. In the next section we will define ordinary goods and see the key role that diminishing marginal utility plays for them. ■

QUICK REVIEW

- An individual is indifferent between any two bundles that lie on the same *indifference curve* but prefers bundles that lie on higher indifference curves to ones that lie on lower indifference curves. A utility function can be represented by an *indifference curve map.*
- All indifference curve maps share two general properties: indifference curves never cross, and the farther out an indifference curve is, the higher the total utility it indicates.
- In addition, indifference curves for most goods, called ordinary goods, have two more properties: they are downward sloping and are convex (bowed-in towards the origin) as a result of diminishing marginal utility.

Figure 11-4 Properties of Indifference Curves

(a) Properties of All Indifference Curves

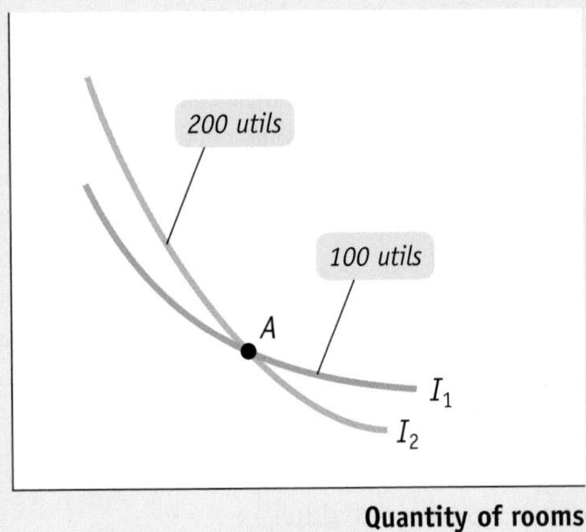

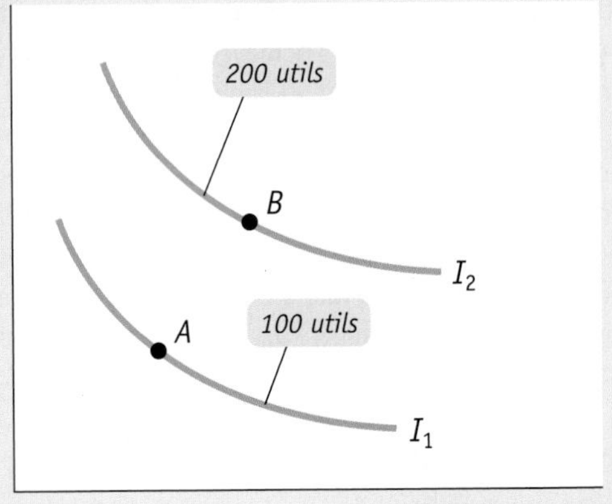

(b) Additional Properties of Indifference Curves for Ordinary Goods

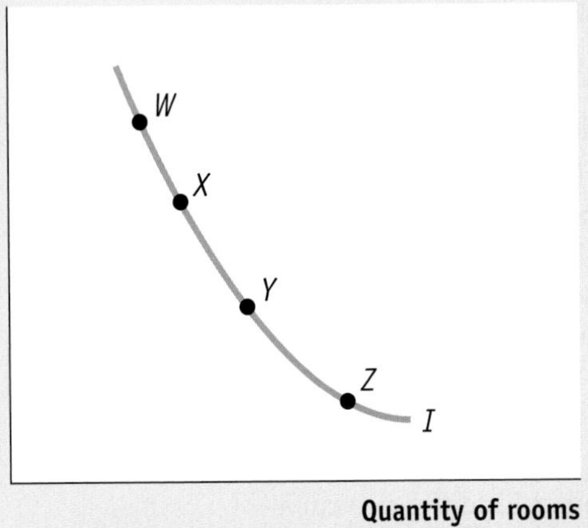

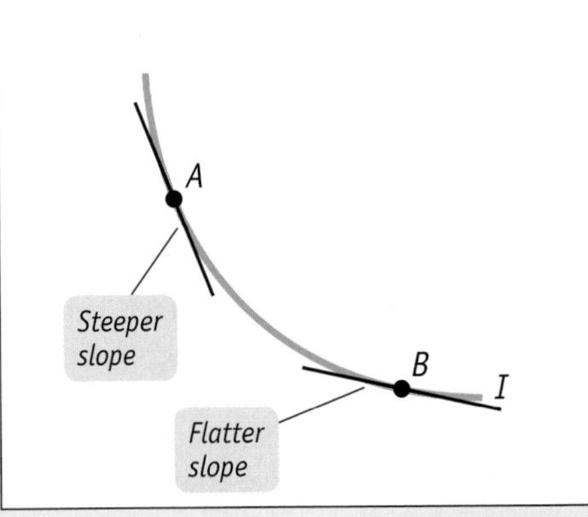

Panel (a) represents two general properties that all indifference curve maps share. The left diagram shows why indifference curves cannot cross: if they did, a consumption bundle such as *A* would yield both 100 and 200 utils, a contradiction. The right diagram of panel (a) shows that indifference curves that are further out yield higher total utility: bundle *B*, which contains more of both goods than bundle *A*, yields higher total utility. Panel (b) depicts two additional properties of indifference curves for ordinary goods. The left diagram of panel (b) shows that indifference curves slope downward. As you move down the curve from bundle *W* to bundle *Z*, consumption of rooms increases. To keep total utility constant, this must be offset by a reduction in quantity of restaurant meals. The right diagram of panel (b) shows a convex-shaped indifference curve. The slope of the indifference curve gets flatter as you move down the curve to the right, a feature arising from diminishing marginal utility.

>>CHECK YOUR UNDERSTANDING 11-1

1. The accompanying table shows Samantha's preferences for consumption bundles composed of chocolate kisses and liquorice drops.
   a. With chocolate kisses on the horizontal axis and liquorice drops on the

Consumption bundle	Quantity of chocolate kisses	Quantity of licorice drops	Total utility (utils)
A	1	3	6
B	2	3	10
C	3	1	6
D	2	1	4

vertical axis, draw hypothetical indifference curves for Samantha and locate the bundles on the curves. Assume that both items are ordinary goods.

b. Suppose you don't know the number of utils provided by each bundle. Assuming that more is better, predict Samantha's ranking of each of the four bundles to the extent possible.

2. On the left diagram in panel (a) of Figure 11-4, draw a point *B* anywhere on the 200 utils indifference curve and a point *C* anywhere on the 100 utils indifference curve (but *not* at the same location as point *A*). By comparing the utils generated by bundles *A* and *B* and those generated by bundles *A* and *C,* explain why indifference curves cannot cross.

Solutions appear at back of book.

Indifference Curves and Consumer Choice

At the beginning of the last section we used indifference curves to represent the preferences of Ingrid, whose consumption bundles consist of rooms and restaurant meals. Our next step is to show how to use Ingrid's indifference curve map to find her utility-maximizing consumption bundle given her budget constraint.

It's important to understand how our analysis here relates to what we did in Chapter 10. We are not offering a new theory of consumer behaviour in this chapter—just as in Chapter 10, consumers are assumed to maximize total utility. In particular, we know that consumers will follow the *optimal consumption rule* from Chapter 10: the optimal consumption bundle lies on the budget line, and the marginal utility per dollar is the same for every good in the bundle.

But as we'll see shortly, we can derive this optimal consumer behaviour in a somewhat different way—a way that yields deeper insights into consumer choice.

The Marginal Rate of Substitution

The first component of our approach is a new concept, the *marginal rate of substitution*. The essence of this concept is illustrated in Figure 11-5.

Recall from the last section that for most goods, consumers' indifference curves are downward sloping and convex. Figure 11-5 shows such an indifference curve. The points labelled *V, W, X, Y,* and *Z* all lie on this indifference curve—that is, they represent consumption bundles that yield Ingrid the same level of total utility. The table accompanying the figure shows the components of each of the bundles. As we move along the indifference curve from *V* to *Z,* Ingrid's consumption of housing steadily increases from 2 rooms to 6 rooms, while her total utility is kept constant. As we move down the indifference curve, then, Ingrid is trading more of one good for less of the other, with the *terms* of that trade-off—the ratio of additional rooms consumed to restaurant meals sacrificed—chosen to keep her total utility constant.

Notice that the quantity of restaurant meals that Ingrid is willing to give up in return for an additional room changes along the indifference curve. As we move from *V* to *W,* housing consumption rises from 2 to 3 rooms and restaurant meal consumption falls from 30 to 20—a trade-off of 10 restaurant meals for 1 additional room. But as we move from *Y* to *Z,* housing consumption rises from 5 to 6 rooms and restaurant meal consumption falls from 12 to 10, a trade-off of only 2 restaurant meals for an additional room.

To put it in terms of slopes: the slope of the indifference curve between *V* and *W* is −10: the change in restaurant meal consumption, −10, divided by the change in housing consumption, 1. Similarly, the slope of the indifference curve between *Y* and *Z* is −2. So the indifference curve gets flatter as we move down it to the right—that is, it has a convex shape, one of the four properties of an indifference curve for ordinary goods.

Why does the trade-off change in this way? Let's think about it intuitively, then work through it more carefully. When Ingrid moves down her indifference curve, whether from *V* to *W* or from *Y* to *Z,* she gains utility from her additional consumption of housing but loses an equal amount of utility from her reduced consumption of restaurant meals. But at each step, the initial position from which

Figure 11-5 The Changing Slope of an Indifference Curve

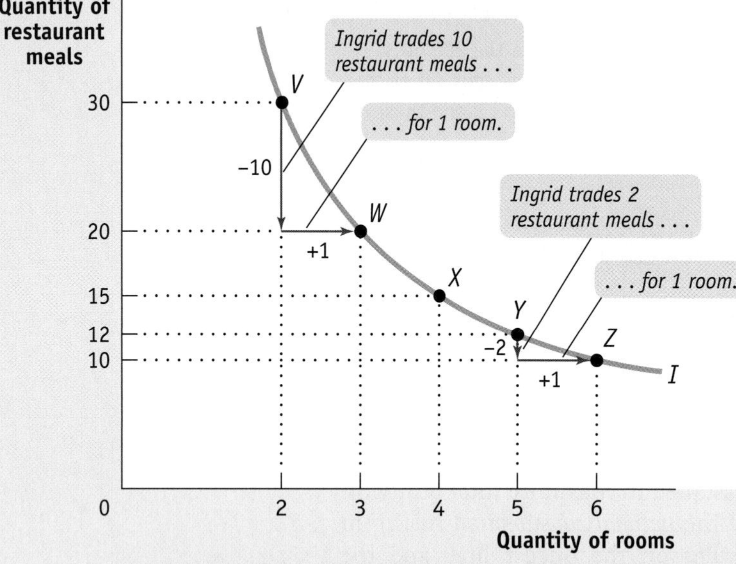

Consumption bundle	Quantity of rooms	Quantity of restaurant meals
V	2	30
W	3	20
X	4	15
Y	5	12
Z	6	10

This indifference curve is downward sloping and convex, implying that restaurant meals and rooms are ordinary goods for Ingrid. As Ingrid moves down her indifference curve from *V* to *Z,* she trades off reduced consumption of restaurant meals for increased consumption of housing. However, the terms of that trade-off change. As she moves from *V* to *W,* she is willing to give up 10 restaurant meals in return for 1 more room. As her consumption of rooms rises and her consumption of restaurant meals falls, she is willing to give up fewer restaurant meals in return for each additional room. The flattening of the slope as you move from left to right arises from diminishing marginal utility. **>*web*...**

Ingrid begins is different. At *V,* Ingrid consumes only a small quantity of rooms, so because of diminishing marginal utility her marginal utility per room at that point is high. At *V,* then, an additional room adds a lot to Ingrid's total utility. But at *V* she already consumes a large quantity of restaurant meals, so her marginal utility of restaurant meals is low at that point. This means that it takes a large reduction in her quantity of restaurant meals consumed to offset the increased utility she gets from the extra room of housing.

At *Y,* by contrast, Ingrid consumes a much larger quantity of rooms and a much smaller quantity of restaurant meals than at *V*. This means that an additional room adds fewer utils, and a restaurant meal forgone subtracts more utils, than at *V*. So Ingrid is willing to give up fewer restaurant meals in return for another room of housing at *Y* (where she gives up 2 meals for 1 room) than she is at *V* (where she gives up 10 meals for 1 room).

Now let's express the same idea—that the trade-off that Ingrid is willing to make depends on where she is starting from—by using a little math. We do this by examining how the slope of the indifference curve changes as we move down it. Moving down the indifference curve—reducing restaurant meal consumption and increasing housing consumption—will produce two opposing effects on Ingrid's total utility: lower restaurant meal consumption will reduce her total utility, but higher housing consumption will raise her total utility. And since we are moving down the indifference curve, these two effects must exactly cancel out:

Along the indifference curve:

(11-1) (Change in total utility because of lower restaurant consumption) + (Change in total utility because of higher housing consumption) = 0 or, rearranging terms,

Along the indifference curve:
(11-2) –(Change in total utility from restaurant meals) = (Change in total utility from housing)

Let's now focus on what happens as we move only a short distance down the indifference curve, trading off a small increase in housing consumption for a small decrease in restaurant meal consumption. Following our notation from Chapter 10, let's use MU_R *and* MU_M to represent the marginal utility of rooms and restaurant meals, respectively, and ΔQ_R and ΔQ_M to represent the changes in room and meal consumption, respectively. In general, the change in total utility caused by a small change in consumption of a good is equal to the change in consumption multiplied by the *marginal utility* of that good. This means that we can calculate the change in Ingrid's total utility generated by a change in her consumption bundle using the following equations:

(11-3) Change in total utility arising from a change in consumption of restaurant meals = $MU_M \times \Delta Q_M$

and

(11-4) Change in total utility arising from a change in consumption of rooms = $MU_R \times \Delta Q_R$

So we can write Equation 11-2 in symbols as

(11-5) *Along the indifference curve:* $-MU_M \times \Delta Q_M = MU_R \times \Delta Q_R$

Note that the left-hand side of Equation 11-5 has a minus sign; it represents minus the loss in total utility from decreased restaurant meal consumption. This must equal the gain in total utility from increased room consumption, represented by the right-hand side of the equation.

What we want, of course, is to know how this translates into the slope of the indifference curve. To find the slope, we divide both sides of Equation 11-5 by ΔQ_R, and again by MU_M, in order to get the ΔQ_M, ΔQ_R terms on one side and the MU_R, MU_M terms on the other. This results in:

(11-6) *Along the indifference curve:* $\frac{-\Delta Q_M}{\Delta Q_R} = \frac{MU_R}{MU_M}$

The left-hand side of Equation 11-6 is *minus* the slope of the indifference curve; it is the rate at which Ingrid is willing to trade a higher quantity of rooms (the good on the horizontal axis) in place of restaurant meals (the good on the vertical axis). The right-hand side of Equation 11-6 is the ratio of the marginal utility of rooms to the marginal utility of restaurant meals—that is, the ratio of what she gains from one more room to what she gains from one more meal.

Putting all this together, we see that Equation 11-6 shows that, along the indifference curve, the quantity of restaurant meals Ingrid is willing to give up in return for a room, $\Delta Q_M/\Delta Q_R$, is exactly equal to the ratio of the marginal utility of a room to that of a meal, MU_R/MU_M. Only when this condition is met will her total utility level remain constant as she consumes more rooms and fewer restaurant meals.

Economists have a special name for the ratio of the marginal utilities found in the right-hand side of Equation 11-6: it is called the **marginal rate of substitution,** or ***MRS,*** of rooms (the good on the horizontal axis) in place of restaurant meals (the good on the vertical axis). That's because as we slide down Ingrid's indifference curve, we are substituting more rooms for fewer restaurant meals in

The **marginal rate of substitution,** or ***MRS,*** of good *R* in place of good *M* is equal to MU_R/MU_M, the ratio of the marginal utility of *R* to the marginal utility of *M.*

her consumption bundle. As we'll see shortly, the marginal rate of substitution plays an important role in finding the optimal consumption bundle.

Recall that indifference curves get flatter as you move down them to the right. The reason, as we've just discussed, is diminishing marginal utility: as Ingrid consumes more housing and fewer restaurant meals, her marginal utility from housing falls and her marginal utility from restaurant meals rises. So her marginal rate of substitution, which is equal to minus the slope of her indifference curve, falls as she moves down the indifference curve.

The flattening of indifference curves as you slide down them to the right—which reflects the same logic as the principle of diminishing marginal utility—is known as the principle of **diminishing marginal rate of substitution.** It says that an individual who consumes only a little bit of good R and a lot of good M will be willing to trade off a lot of M in return for one more unit of R; an individual who already consumes a lot of R and not much of M will be less willing to make that trade-off.

The principle of **diminishing marginal rate of substitution** states that the more of good R a person consumes in proportion to good M, the less M he or she is willing to substitute for another unit of R.

We can illustrate this point by referring back to Figure 11-5. At point V, a bundle with a high proportion of restaurant meals to rooms, Ingrid is willing to forgo 10 restaurant meals in return for 1 room. But at point Y, a bundle with a low proportion of restaurant meals to rooms, she is willing to forgo only 2 restaurant meals in return for 1 room.

From this example we can see that, in Ingrid's utility function, rooms and restaurant meals possess the two additional properties that characterize ordinary goods. Ingrid requires additional rooms to compensate her for the loss of a meal, and vice versa; so her indifference curves for these two goods are downward sloping. And her indifference curves are convex: the slope of her indifference curve—*minus* the marginal rate of substitution—becomes flatter as we move down it. In fact, an indifference curve is convex only when it has diminishing marginal rate of substitution—these two conditions are equivalent.

With this information we can define **ordinary goods,** which account for the great majority of goods in any consumer's utility function. A pair of goods are ordinary goods in a consumer's utility function if they possess two properties: the consumer requires more of one good to compensate for less of the other, and the consumer experiences a diminishing marginal rate of substitution when substituting one good for another.

Two goods, R and M, are **ordinary goods** in a consumer's utility function when (1) the consumer requires additional units of R to compensate for less M, and vice versa; and (2) the consumer experiences a diminishing marginal rate of substitution in substituting one good for another.

Next we will see how to determine Ingrid's optimal consumption bundle using indifference curves.

The Tangency Condition

Now let's put some of Ingrid's indifference curves on the same diagram as her budget line, to get an alternative way of representing her optimal consumption choice. Figure 11-6 shows Ingrid's budget line, BL, when her income is \$2,400 per month, housing costs \$150 per room each month, and restaurant meals cost \$30 each. What is her optimal consumption bundle?

To answer this question, we show several of Ingrid's indifference curves: I_1, I_2, and I_3. Ingrid would like to achieve the total utility level represented by I_3, the highest of the three curves, but she cannot afford to because she is constrained by her income: no consumption bundle on her budget line yields that much utility. But she shouldn't settle for the level of utility generated by B, which lies on I_1: there are other bundles on her budget line, such as A, that clearly yield higher total utility than B.

In fact, A—a consumption bundle consisting of 8 rooms and 40 restaurant meals per month—is Ingrid's optimal consumption choice. The reason is that A lies on the highest indifference curve Ingrid can reach given her income.

At the optimal consumption bundle A, Ingrid's budget line just touches the relevant indifference curve—the budget line is *tangent* to the indifference curve. This **tangency condition** between the indifference curve and the budget line applies to the optimal consumption bundle when the indifference curves have the typical convex shape: *At the optimal consumption bundle, the budget line just touches the indifference curve.*

The **tangency condition** between the indifference curve and the budget line holds when the indifference curve and the budget line just touch. This condition determines the optimal consumption bundle when the indifference curves have the typical convex shape.

Figure 11-6

The Optimal Consumption Bundle

The budget line, *BL*, shows Ingrid's possible consumption bundles given an income of $2,400 per month, when rooms cost $150 per month and restaurant meals cost $30 each. I_1, I_2, and I_3 are indifference curves. Consumption bundles such as *B* and *C* are not optimal because Ingrid can get onto a higher indifference curve. The optimal consumption bundle is at *A*, where the budget line is just tangent to the highest possible indifference curve. >web...

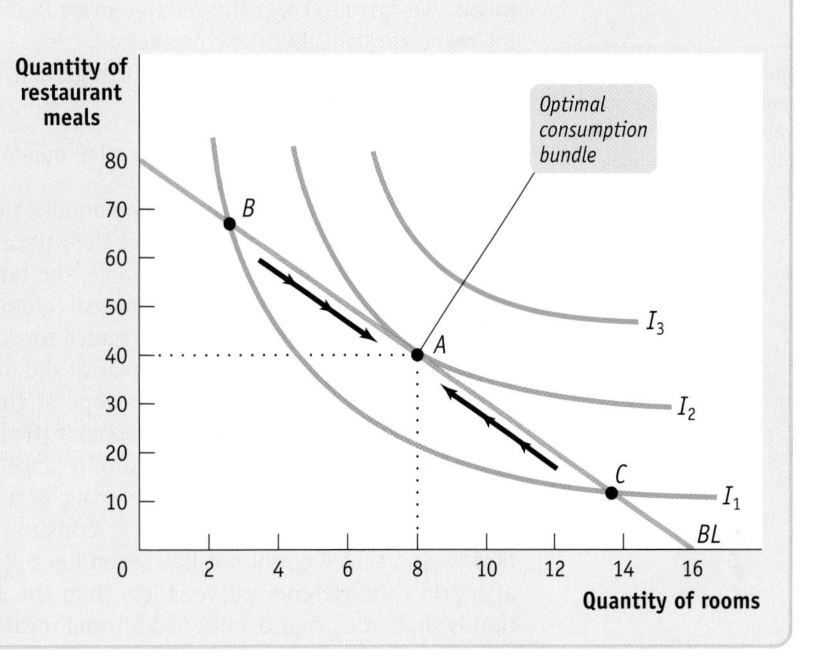

To see why, let's look more closely at how we know that a consumption bundle that *doesn't* satisfy the tangency condition can't be optimal. Re-examining Figure 11-6, we can see that the consumption bundles *B* and *C* are both affordable because they lie on the budget line. However, neither is optimal. Both of them lie on the indifference curve I_1, which cuts through the budget line at both points. But because I_1 cuts through the budget line, Ingrid can do better: she can move down the budget line from *B* or up the budget line from *C*, as indicated by the arrows. In each case this allows her to get onto a higher indifference curve, I_2, which increases her total utility.

Ingrid cannot, however, do any better than I_2: any other indifference curve either cuts through her budget line or doesn't touch it at all. And the bundle that allows her to achieve I_2 is, of course, her optimal consumption bundle, *A*.

Prices and the Marginal Rate of Substitution

Let's note one final point about the optimal consumption bundle shown in Figure 11-6. At point *A*, the slope of the indifference curve is just equal to the slope of the budget line.

From rearranging Equation 11-6 we know that the slope of the indifference curve at any point is equal to minus the marginal rate of substitution:

$$\textbf{(11-7)}\quad \text{Slope of indifference curve} = -\frac{MU_R}{MU_M}$$

But what is the slope of the budget line? As in Chapter 10, let's use the symbol N to represent Ingrid's income. As we saw in Chapter 10, the horizontal intercept of her budget line—the number of rooms she can afford if she spends all her income on rooms—is N/P_R. The vertical intercept of her budget line—the number of restaurant meals she can afford if she spends all her income on restaurant meals—is N/P_M. So the slope of her budget line when R is measured on the horizontal axis and M is measured on the vertical axis is:

$$\textbf{(11-8)}\quad \text{Slope of budget line} = -\frac{N/P_M}{N/P_R} = -\frac{P_R}{P_M}$$

The **relative price** of good R in terms of good M is equal to P_R/P_M.

The quantity P_R/P_M is known as the **relative price** of rooms in terms of restaurant meals (to distinguish it from an ordinary price in terms of dollars). Because giving up one room allows you to buy P_R/P_M quantity of restaurant meals, or 5 meals, we can interpret the relative price P_R/P_M as the rate at which a room trades for restaurant meals in the market.

The **relative price rule** says that at the optimal consumption bundle, the marginal rate of substitution between two goods is equal to their relative price.

Putting Equations 11-7 and 11-8 together, we arrive at the **relative price rule,** which says:

(11-9) *At the optimal consumption bundle:* $\frac{MU_R}{MU_M} = \frac{P_R}{P_M}$

That is, at the optimal consumption bundle, the marginal rate of substitution between any two goods is equal to the ratio of their prices. Or to put it in a more intuitive way, at Ingrid's optimal consumption bundle, the rate at which she would trade a room in exchange for having more restaurant meals along her indifference curve, MU_R/MU_M, is *equal* to the rate at which rooms are traded for restaurant meals in the market, P_R/P_M.

What would happen if this equality did not hold? We can see by examining Figure 11-7. There, at point *B*, the slope of the indifference curve, $-MU_R/MU_M$, is greater in absolute value than the slope of the budget line, $-P_R/P_M$. This means that, at *B*, Ingrid values an additional room in place of meals *more* than it costs her to buy an additional room and forgo some meals. As a result, Ingrid would be better off moving down her budget line towards *A*, consuming more rooms and fewer restaurant meals—and that *B* could not have been her optimal bundle! Likewise, at *C*, the slope of Ingrid's indifference curve is less than the slope of the budget line. The implication is that, at *C*, Ingrid values additional meals in place of a room *more* than it costs her to buy additional meals and forgo a room. Again, Ingrid would be made better off by moving along her budget line—consuming more restaurant meals and fewer rooms—until she reaches *A*, her optimal consumption bundle.

But suppose that we do the following transformation to Equation 11-9: divide both sides by P_R and multiply both by MU_M. Then the relative price rule becomes:

(11-10) *At the optimal consumption bundle:* $\frac{MU_R}{P_R} = \frac{MU_M}{P_M}$

which is the *optimal consumption rule* from Chapter 10, Equation 10-5. So using either the optimal consumption rule (from Chapter 10) or the relative price rule (from this chapter), we find the same optimal consumption bundle.

Figure 11-7

Understanding the Relative Price Rule

The *relative price* of rooms in terms of restaurant meals is equal to minus the slope of the budget line. The *marginal rate of substitution* of rooms in place of restaurant meals is equal to minus the slope of the indifference curve. The *relative price rule* says that at the optimal consumption bundle, the marginal rate of substitution must equal the relative price. This point can be demonstrated by considering what happens when the marginal rate of substitution is not equal to the relative price. At consumption bundle *B*, the marginal rate of substitution is larger than the relative price; Ingrid can increase her total utility by moving down her budget line, *BL*. At *C*, the marginal rate of substitution is smaller than the relative price, and Ingrid can increase her total utility by moving up the budget line. Only at *A*, where the relative price rule holds, is her total utility maximized, given her budget constraint.

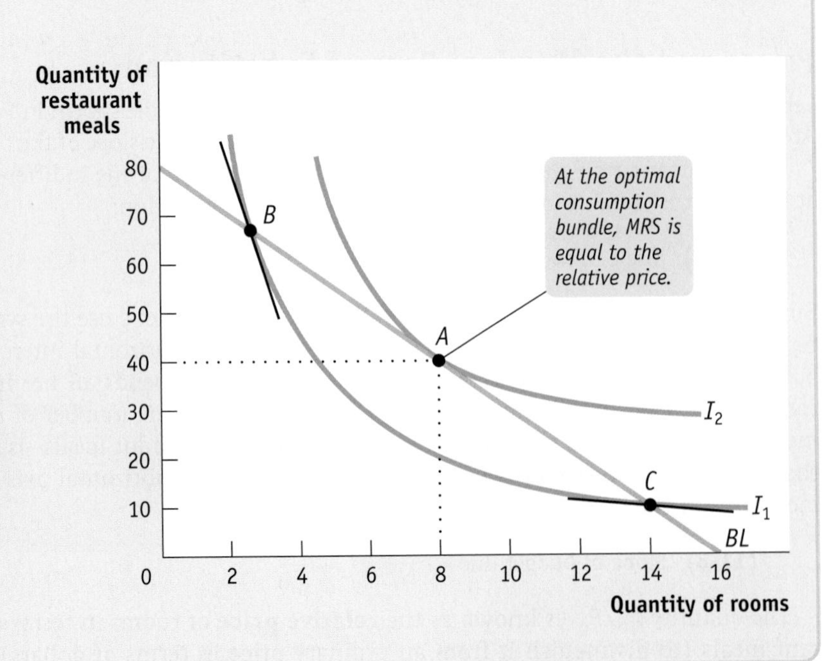

Preferences and Choices

Now that we have seen how to represent optimal consumption choice in an indifference curve diagram, we can turn briefly to the relationship between consumer preferences and consumer choices.

When we say that two consumers have different preferences, we mean that they have different utility functions. This in turn means that they will have different indifference curve maps with different shapes. And those different maps will translate into different consumption choices, even among consumers with the same income who face the same prices.

To see this, suppose that Ingrid's friend Lars also consumes only housing and restaurant meals. However, Lars has a stronger preference for restaurant meals and a weaker preference for housing. This difference in preferences is shown in Figure 11-8, which shows *two* sets of indifference curves: panel (a) shows Ingrid's preferences, and panel (b) shows Lars's preferences. Note the difference in their shapes.

Suppose, as before, that rooms cost $150 per month and restaurant meals cost $30. Let's also assume that both Ingrid and Lars have incomes of $2,400 per month, giving them identical budget lines. Nonetheless, because they have different preferences they will make different consumption choices, as shown in Figure 11-8. Ingrid will choose 8 rooms and 40 restaurant meals; Lars will choose 4 rooms and 60 restaurant meals.

Figure 11-8

Differences in Preferences

Ingrid and Lars have different preferences, reflected in the different shapes of their indifferent curve maps. So they will choose different consumption bundles even when they have the same possible choices. Both of them have an income of $2,400 per month and face prices of $30 per meal and $150 per room. Panel (a) shows Ingrid's consumption choice: 8 rooms and 40 restaurant meals. Panel (b) shows Lars's choice: even though he has the same budget line, he consumes fewer rooms and more restaurant meals.

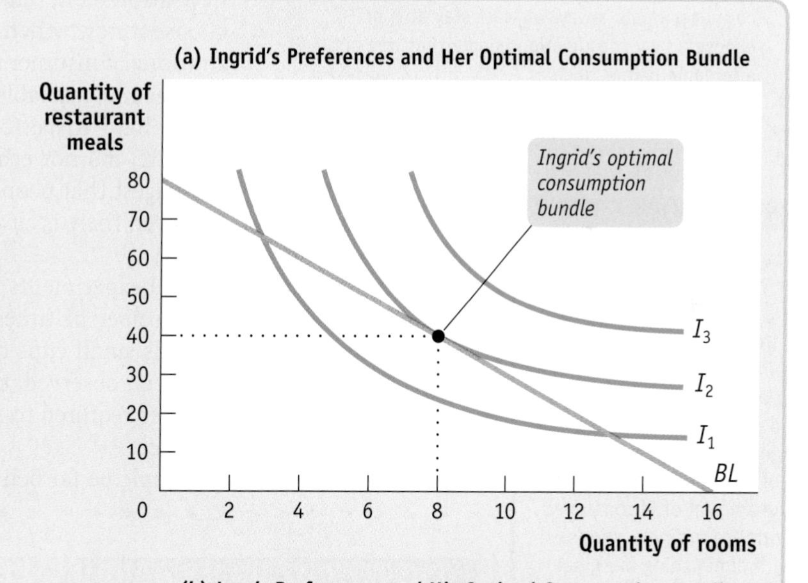

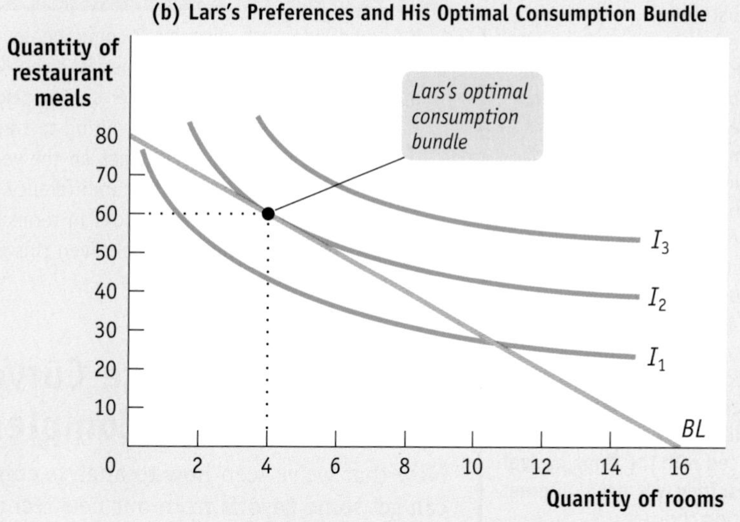

Figure 11-9 A Test for Rationality

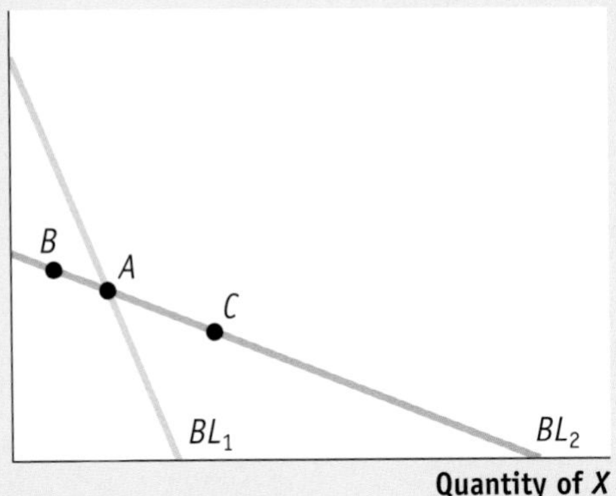

Suppose that a consumer has the budget line BL_1 and chooses the consumption bundle *A*. If that consumer is now given a new budget line such as BL_2, it would be irrational to choose a bundle such as *B;* the consumer could have afforded that bundle before but chose *A* instead. A rational consumer would always at least stay at *A* or choose a new consumption bundle that was not affordable before, such as *C*. It's difficult to test people in this way—but it works for rats!

economics in action

Rats and Rational Choice

Let's admit it: the theory of consumer choice does not bear much resemblance to the way most of us think about our consumption decisions. The purpose of the theory, however, is to help economists think systematically about how a rational consumer would behave. The practical question is whether consumers actually behave rationally.

One simple test for rationality would look like the one shown in Figure 11-9. First, give a consumer the budget line labelled BL_1, and observe what consumption bundle the consumer chooses; the result is indicated in the figure as *A*. Then change the budget constraint, so that the new budget line is BL_2. Here the consumer is still able to afford the original consumption bundle *A* but also has some new choices available.

Would a rational consumer then choose a bundle like *B*? No. The reason is that *B* lies *inside* the original budget line—that is, when the budget line was BL_1, the consumer could have afforded it, but chose *A* instead. It would be irrational to choose it now, when *A* is still available. So the new choice for a rational consumer must be either *A* or some bundle that has just become available, such as *C*.

It's hard to perform experiments like this on people—at any rate, it's not ethical (though more indirect experiments do suggest that people behave more or less rationally in their consumption choices). However, there is clear evidence that animals, such as rats, are able to make rational choices!

Economists have conducted experiments in which rats are presented with a "budget constraint"—a limited number of times per hour they can push either of two levers. One of the levers yields small cups of water; the other yields pellets of food. After the rat's choices have been observed, the budget constraint is changed by varying the number of lever pushes required to get each good. Sure enough, the rats satisfy the rule for rational choice.

If rats are rational, can people be far behind? ■

>> QUICK REVIEW

- The *marginal rate of substitution* (*MRS*) of *R* in place of *M*, MU_R/MU_M, is equal to minus the slope of the indifference curve.
- With *diminishing marginal rate of substitution,* a consumer requires more and more *R* to compensate for each forgone unit of *M* as the amount of *R* consumed grows relative to the amount of *M* consumed.
- Most goods are *ordinary goods*—goods with diminishing marginal rate of substitution.
- P_R/P_M, the *relative price* of good *R* in terms of good *M*, is equal to minus the slope of the budget line when *R* is measured on the horizontal axis and *M* is measured on the vertical axis. A utility-maximizing consumer chooses the bundle that satisfies the *tangency condition:* the indifference curve and the budget line just touch. So at the optimal consumption bundle, $MU_R/MU_M = P_R/P_M$, a condition called the *relative price rule.*
- Any two consumers will have different indifference curve maps because they have different preferences. Faced with the same budget and prices, they will make different consumption choices.

>> CHECK YOUR UNDERSTANDING 11-2

1. Brad and Kyle each consume 3 comic books and 2 video games. Brad's marginal rate of substitution of books in place of games is 2 and Kyle's is 5.
   a. For each person, find another consumption bundle that yields the same total utility as the current bundle. Who is less willing to trade games for books? In a diagram with books on the horizontal axis, and games on the vertical axis, how would this be reflected in differences in the shapes of their indifference curves?
   b. Find the relative price of books in terms of games at which Brad's current bundle is optimal. Is Kyle's bundle optimal given this relative price? If not, how should Kyle rearrange his consumption?

Solutions appear at back of book.

Using Indifference Curves: Substitutes and Complements

Now that we've seen how to analyse consumer choice using indifference curves, we can get some payoffs from our new technique. First up is a new insight into the distinction between *substitutes* and *complements*.

Way back in Chapter 3 we pointed out that the price of one good often affects the demand for another but that the direction of this effect can go either way: a rise in the price of tea increases the demand for coffee, but a rise in the price of cream reduces the demand for coffee. Tea and coffee are substitutes; cream and coffee are complements.

But what determines whether two goods are substitutes or complements? It depends on the shape of a consumer's indifference curves. This relationship can be illustrated with two extreme cases: the cases of *perfect substitutes* and *perfect complements*.

Perfect Substitutes

Consider a consumer, Champa, who likes cookies. She isn't particular: it doesn't matter to her whether she has 3 peanut butter cookies and 7 chocolate chip cookies, or vice versa. What would her indifference curves between peanut butter and chocolate chip cookies look like?

The answer is that they would be straight lines like I_1 and I_2 in Figure 11-10. For example, I_1 shows that any combination of peanut butter cookies and chocolate chip cookies that adds up to 10 cookies yields Champa the same utility.

A consumer whose indifference curves are straight lines is always willing to substitute the same amount of one good for one unit of the other, regardless of how much of either good he or she consumes. Champa, for example, is always willing to accept one fewer peanut butter cookie in exchange for one more chocolate chip cookie, making her marginal rate of substitution *constant*.

When indifference curves are straight lines, we say that goods are **perfect substitutes.** When two goods are perfect substitutes, there is only one relative price at which consumers will be willing to purchase both goods; a slightly higher or lower relative price will cause consumers to buy only one of the two goods.

Two goods are **perfect substitutes** if the marginal rate of substitution of one good in place of the other good is constant, regardless of how much of each an individual consumes.

Figure 11-11 illustrates this point. The indifference curves are the same as those in Figure 11-10, but now we include Champa's budget line, *BL*. In each panel we assume that Champa has $12 to spend. In panel (a) we assume that chocolate chip cookies cost $1.20 and peanut butter cookies cost $1.00. Champa's optimal consumption

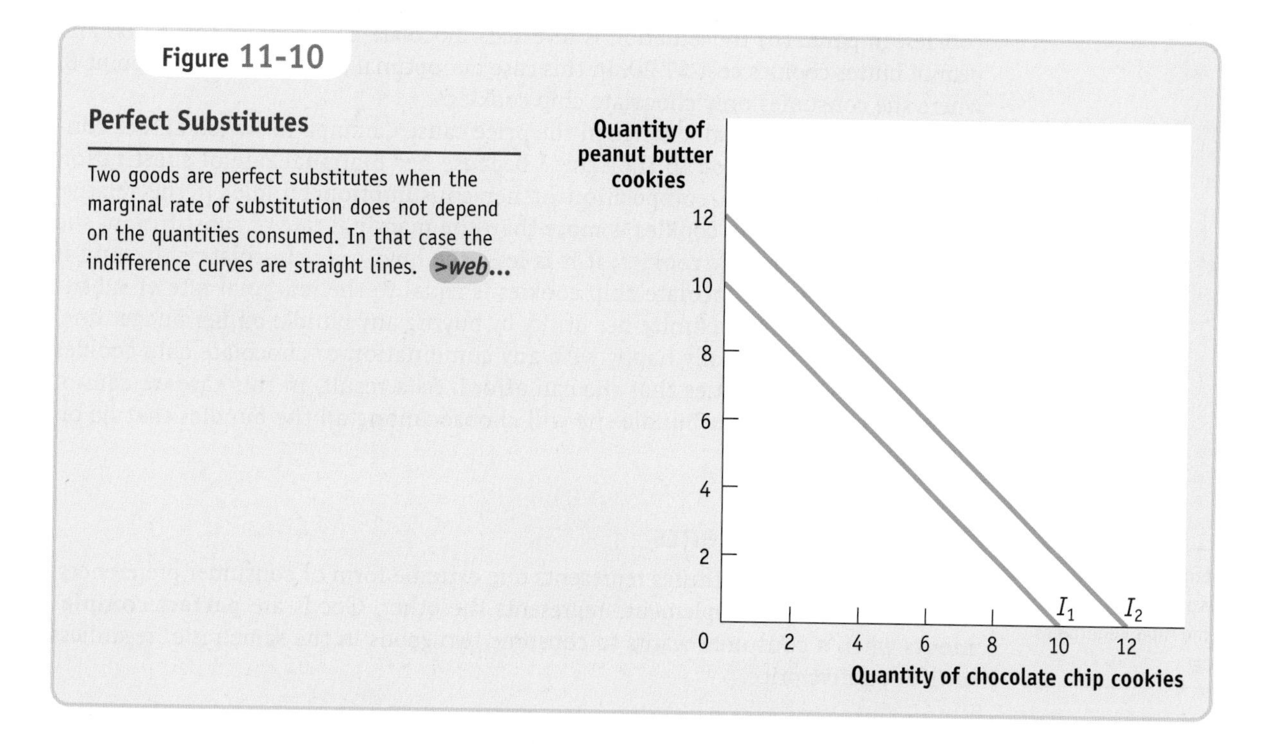

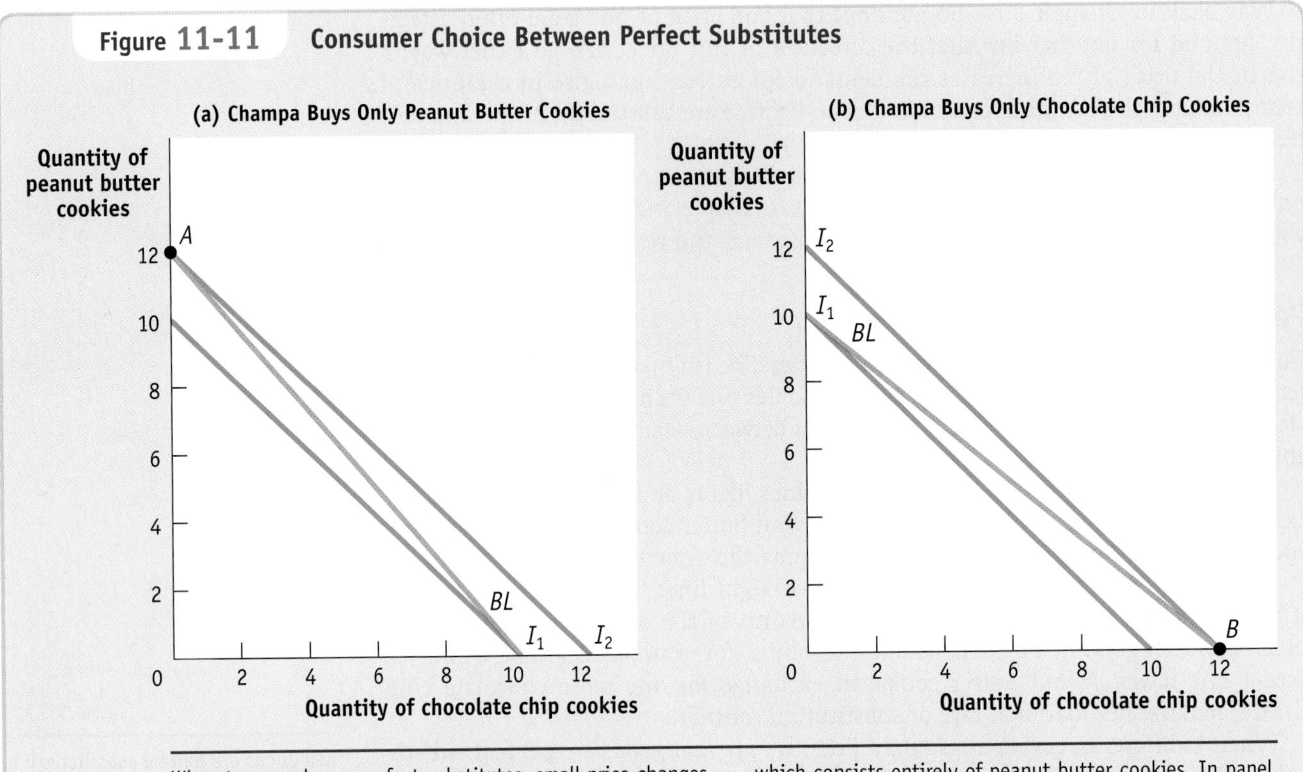

Figure 11-11 Consumer Choice Between Perfect Substitutes

When two goods are perfect substitutes, small price changes can lead to large changes in the consumption bundle. In panel (a), the relative price of chocolate chip cookies is slightly higher than the marginal rate of substitution of chocolate chip in place of peanut butter cookies; this is enough to induce Champa to choose consumption bundle *A*, which consists entirely of peanut butter cookies. In panel (b), the relative price of chocolate chip cookies is slightly lower than the marginal rate of substitution; this induces Champa to choose bundle *B*, consisting entirely of chocolate chip cookies.

bundle is then at point *A:* she buys 12 peanut butter cookies and no chocolate chip cookies. In panel (b) the situation is reversed: chocolate chip cookies cost $1.00 and peanut butter cookies cost $1.20. In this case her optimal consumption is at point *B*, where she consumes only chocolate chip cookies.

Why does such a small change in the price cause Champa to switch all her consumption from one good to the other? Because her marginal rate of substitution doesn't depend on the composition of her consumption bundle. If the relative price of chocolate chip cookies is more than the marginal rate of substitution, she buys only peanut butter cookies; if it is less, she buys only chocolate chip. And if the relative price of chocolate chip cookies is equal to the marginal rate of substitution, Champa can maximize her utility by buying any bundle on her budget line. That is, she will be equally happy with any combination of chocolate chip cookies and peanut butter cookies that she can afford. As a result, in this case we cannot predict which particular bundle she will choose among all the bundles that lie on her budget line.

Perfect Complements

Two goods are **perfect complements** when a consumer wants to consume the goods in the same ratio, regardless of their relative price.

The case of perfect substitutes represents one extreme form of consumer preferences; the case of perfect complements represents the other. Goods are **perfect complements** when a consumer wants to consume two goods in the same ratio, regardless of their relative price.

Figure 11-12

Perfect Complements

When two goods are perfect complements, a consumer wants to consume the goods in the same ratio regardless of their relative price. Indifference curves take the form of right angles. In this case, Aaron will choose to consume 4 glasses of milk and 4 cookies (bundle *B*) regardless of the slope of the budget line passing through *B*. The reason is that neither an additional glass of milk without an additional cookie (bundle *A*) nor an additional cookie without an additional glass of milk (bundle *C*) adds to his utility.
>web...

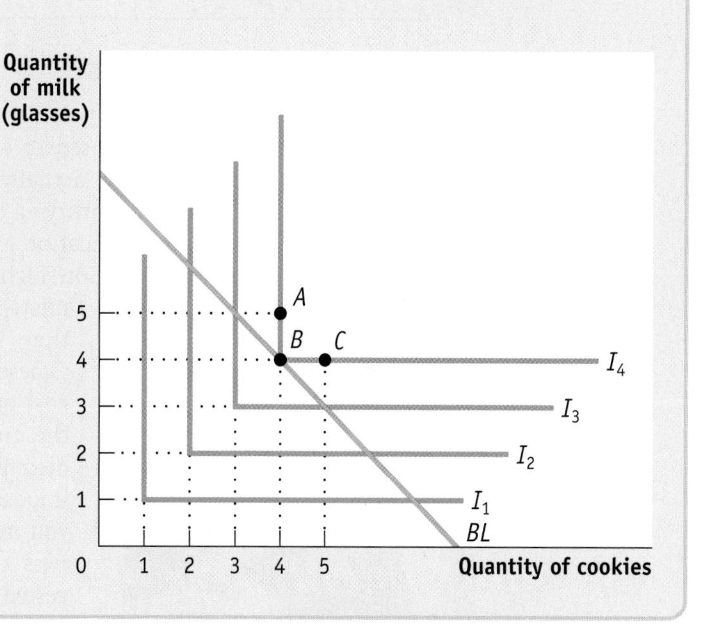

Suppose that Aaron likes cookies and milk—but only together. An extra cookie without an extra glass of milk yields no utility; neither does an extra glass of milk without another cookie. In this case, his indifference curves will form right angles, as shown in Figure 11-12.

To see why, consider the three bundles labelled *A*, *B*, and *C*. At *B*, on I_4, Aaron consumes 4 cookies and 4 glasses of milk. At *A*, directly above *B*, he consumes 4 cookies and 5 glasses of milk; but the extra glass of milk adds nothing to his utility. So *A* is on the same indifference curve as *B*, I_4. Similarly, at *C* he consumes 5 cookies and 4 glasses of milk, but this yields the same total utility as 4 cookies and 4 glasses of milk. So *C* is also on the same indifference curve, I_4.

Also shown in Figure 11-12 is a budget line that would allow Aaron to choose bundle *B*. The important point is that the slope of the budget line has no effect on his relative consumption of cookies and milk. This means that he will always consume the two goods in the same proportions regardless of prices—which makes the goods perfect complements.

You may be wondering what happened to the marginal rate of substitution in Figure 11-12. That is, exactly what is Aaron's marginal rate of substitution between cookies and milk, given that he is unwilling to make any substitutions between them? The answer is that in the case of perfect complements, the marginal rate of substitution is *undefined* because an individual's preferences don't allow *any* substitution between goods.

Less Extreme Cases

There are real-world examples of pairs of goods that are very close to perfect substitutes. For example, the list of ingredients on a package of Bisquick pancake mix says that it contains "soybean and/or cottonseed oil": the producer uses whichever is cheaper, since consumers can't tell the difference. There are other pairs of goods that are very close to perfect complements—for example, cars and tires.

In most cases, however, the possibilities for substitution lie somewhere between these extremes. In some cases, as illustrated by the following Economics in Action, it isn't easy to be sure whether goods are substitutes or complements.

Economics In Action

Who Needs Fleshmeets?

In the information technology community, "fleshmeet" is slang for a face-to-face (sorry, F2F) meeting, as opposed to an electronic interaction. Clearly the term is meant to be a bit derogatory; actually getting together with someone in the same room is so, well, twentieth century—a crude, old-fashioned way of doing business.

But are electronic communication and face-to-face meetings really substitutes? In a 1996 paper titled "Information Technology and the Future of Cities", the economists Jess Gaspar and Edward Glaeser argued that they might well be complements. Gaspar and Glaeser pointed out that over the past century the cost of telecommunications has steadily fallen and the quality of the communication has risen: long-distance phone calls, for example, went from being impossible to being cheap and routine—yet activities you might have thought were substitutes, like business travel, continued to boom. The authors suggested that although a phone call can sometimes replace a business trip, the ability to make inexpensive phone calls also generates more interaction among businesses and therefore more need for communication—both on the phone and face to face. (Think of the way that cell phones actually encourage people to get together with their friends.) In the past the net effect has actually been to increase the demand for face-to-face meetings, and the authors suggest that newer technologies will continue to be complements rather than substitutes for direct personal interaction.

Lisette LeBon/Superstock

Video conferencing might cut your commute time, but there's really no substitute for being there.

Some futurists believe that we are heading for a world in which people live wherever they please and interact via the Internet; in such a world not only business travel but also big cities, which exist mainly to facilitate face-to-face interaction, would lose much of their purpose. Gaspar and Glaeser argued, however, that this remains unlikely for the foreseeable future. ■

< < < < < < < < < < < < < < < < < <

>>QUICK REVIEW

- When two goods are *perfect substitutes*, the marginal rate of substitution is constant and the indifference curves are straight lines.
- When two goods are *perfect complements*, the indifference curves form right angles and the marginal rate of substitution is undefined.
- The relationship between most goods for most people falls somewhere between these two extremes.

>>CHECK YOUR UNDERSTANDING 11-3

In each of the following cases, determine whether the two goods are perfect substitutes, perfect complements, or ordinary goods. Explain your answer, paying particular attention to the marginal rate of substitution of one good in place of another.

1. Sanjay cares only about the number of jelly beans he receives and not about whether they are banana-flavoured or pineapple-flavoured.
2. Hillary's marginal utility of cherry pie goes up as she has more scoops of vanilla ice cream to go with each slice. But she is willing to consume some cherry pie without any vanilla ice cream.
3. Despite repeated reductions in price, customers won't buy software programs made by Omnisoft Corporation unless the company also sells the computer operating system that enables a computer to read these software programs.
4. Daniel works part-time at the campus bookstore. The manager has asked him to work additional hours this week. Daniel is willing to do additional work, but he finds that the more hours he has already worked, the less willing he is to work yet another hour. (*Hint:* Think of the goods in question as being income and leisure time.)

Solutions appear at back of book.

Prices, Income, and Demand

Let's now return to Ingrid's consumption choices. In the situation we've considered, her income was $2,400 per month, housing cost $150 per room, and restaurant meals cost $30 each. Her optimal consumption bundle, as seen in Figure 11-7 on page 278, contained 8 rooms and 40 restaurant meals.

Let's now ask how her consumption choice would change if either the rent per room or her income changed. As we'll see, we can put these pieces together to deepen our understanding of consumer demand.

The Effects of a Price Increase

Suppose that for some reason there is a sharp increase in housing prices. Ingrid must now pay $600 per room instead of $150. Meanwhile, the price of restaurant meals and her income remain unchanged. How does this change affect her consumption choices?

When the price of rooms rises, the relative price of rooms in terms of restaurant meals rises; as a result, Ingrid's budget line changes (for the worse—but we'll get to that). She responds to that change by choosing a new consumption bundle.

Figure 11-13 shows Ingrid's original (BL_1) and new (BL_2) budget lines—again, under the assumption that her income remains constant at $2,400 per month. With housing costing $150 per room and a restaurant meal costing $30, her budget line, BL_1, intersected the horizontal axis at 16 rooms, the vertical axis at 80 restaurant meals. After the price of a room rises to $600 per room, the budget line, BL_2,

PITFALLS

"OTHER THINGS EQUAL", REVISITED

One of the biggest sources of confusion and error in economics—both in the classroom and in the real world—is failure to keep in mind the principle that all economic relationships are defined "other things equal". You may recall from Chapter 3 that a demand curve shows the effect of a good's price on its quantity demanded, *other things equal*—that is, all other things that influence demand being unchanged. Among those "other things" are the prices of other goods and the incomes of consumers.

To see how important it is to be clear about what is being held constant, let's compare two experiments. First, what happens to Ingrid's budget line if we increase the price of rooms, holding the price of restaurant meals and Ingrid's income constant? Second, what happens to her budget line if we increase the price of housing and *at the same time also increase the price of restaurant meals and Ingrid's income?*

We've just seen the effects of raising the price of rooms from $150 per month to $600. But now imagine that the price of restaurant meals also quadruples from $30 to $120 and that Ingrid's income quadruples from $2,400 to $9,600 per month. How does her budget line change?

The answer (check it yourself) is that quadrupling all three numbers—the price of rooms, the price of restaurant meals, and Ingrid's income—has *no* effect on her budget line. Because the relative price is unchanged, it won't affect her consumption choice. So the law of demand, which says that increasing the price of a good reduces the quantity demanded, is only an "other things equal" proposition; a higher price results in a lower quantity demanded, holding other prices and income constant.

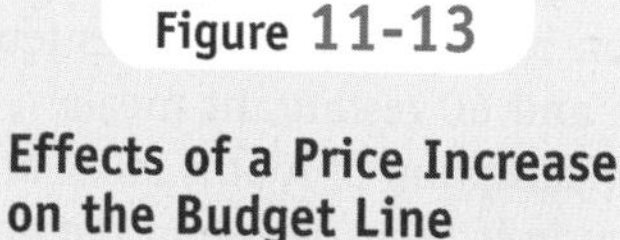

Figure 11-13

Effects of a Price Increase on the Budget Line

An increase in the price of rooms, holding the price of restaurant meals constant, increases the relative price of rooms in terms of restaurant meals. As a result, Ingrid's original budget line, BL_1, rotates inward to BL_2. Her maximum possible purchase of restaurant meals is unchanged, but her maximum possible purchase of rooms is reduced. >web...

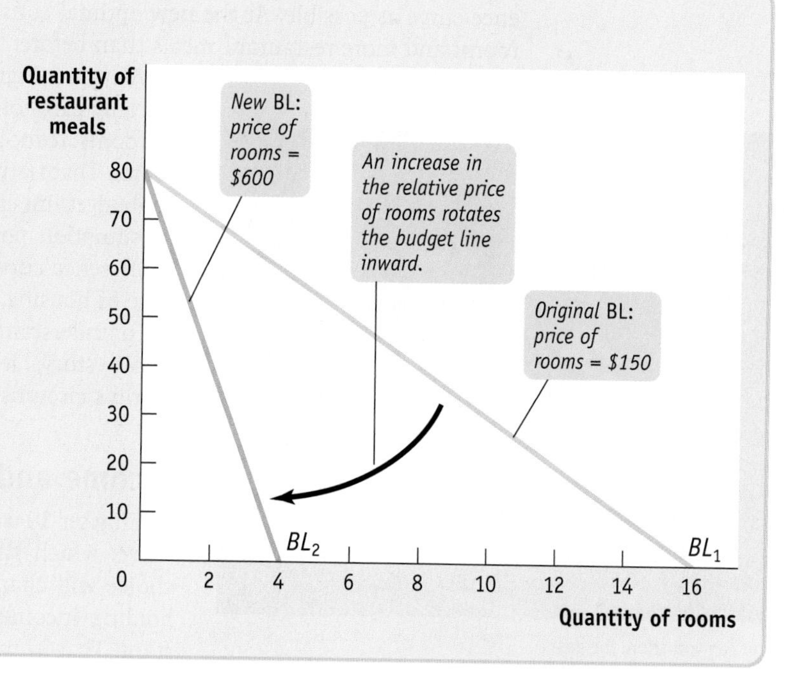

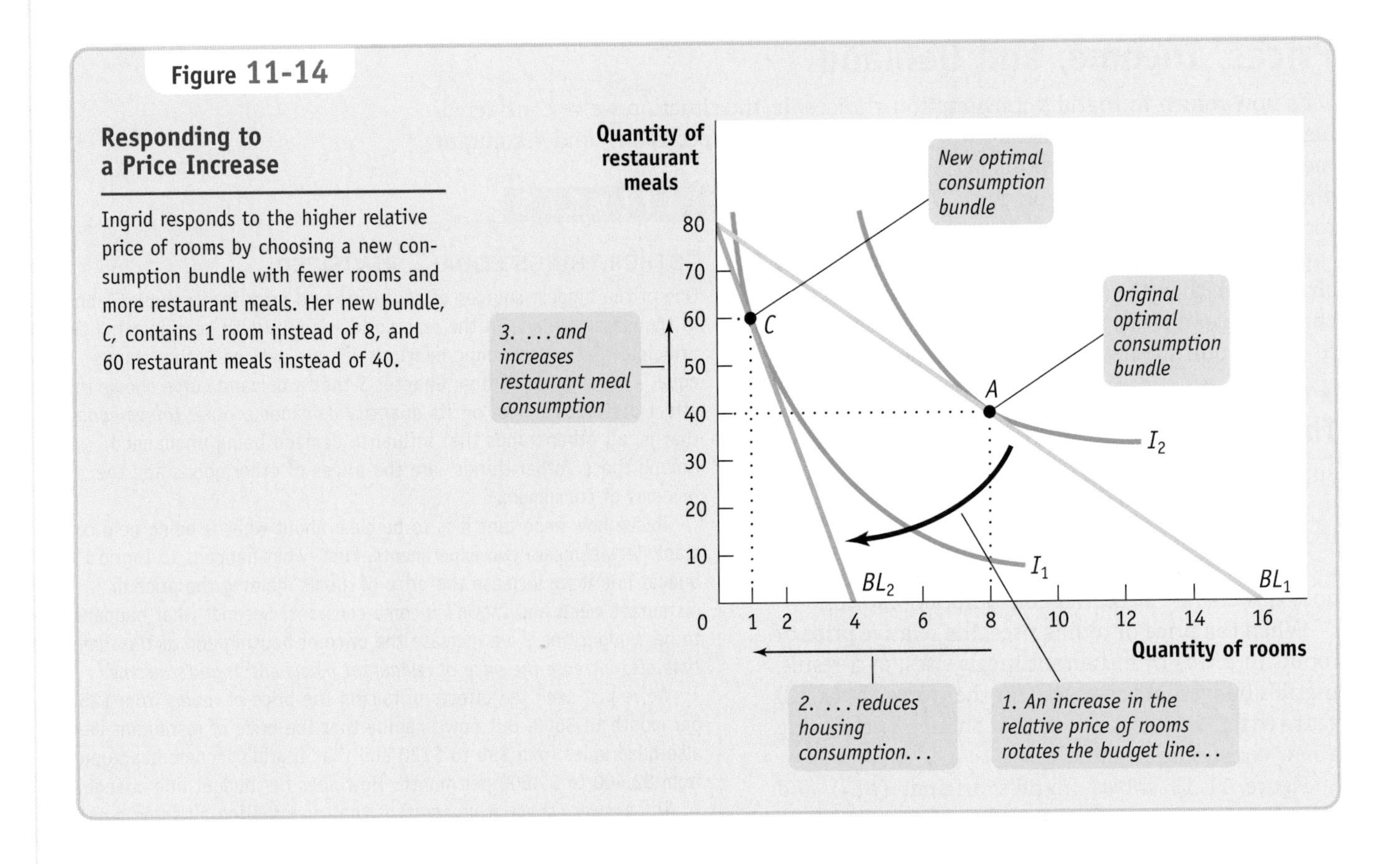

Figure 11-14

Responding to a Price Increase

Ingrid responds to the higher relative price of rooms by choosing a new consumption bundle with fewer rooms and more restaurant meals. Her new bundle, *C*, contains 1 room instead of 8, and 60 restaurant meals instead of 40.

still hits the vertical axis at 80 restaurant meals, but it hits the horizontal axis at only 4 rooms. Her budget line has rotated inward, reflecting the new, higher relative price of a room in terms of restaurant meals.

Figure 11-14 shows how Ingrid responds to her new circumstances. Her original optimal consumption bundle consists of 8 rooms and 40 meals. After her budget line rotates in response to the change in relative price, she finds her new optimal consumption bundle by choosing the point on BL_2 that brings her to as high an indifference curve as possible. At the new optimal consumption bundle, she consumes fewer rooms and more restaurant meals than before: 1 room and 60 restaurant meals.

Why does Ingrid's consumption of rooms fall? Part—but only part—of the reason is that the rise in the price of rooms reduces her purchasing power, making her poorer. That is, the higher relative price of rooms rotates her budget line inward towards the origin, reducing her consumption possibilities and putting her on a lower indifference curve. In a sense, when she faces a higher price of housing, it's as if her income declined.

To understand this effect, and to see why it isn't the whole story, let's consider a different change in Ingrid's circumstances: a change in her income.

Mark Richards/Photo Edit

Great new car, but can you afford the gas?

Income and Consumption

In Chapter 10 we learned about the individual demand curve, which shows how a consumer's consumption choice will change as the price of one good changes, holding income and the prices of other goods constant. That is, movement along the individual demand curve shows the substitution effect—how quantity consumed changes in response to changes in the *relative price* of the two goods. But we can also ask how the consumption choice will change if *income* changes, holding relative price constant.

In the previous section we considered an example in which a rise in the price of housing put Ingrid on a lower indifference curve. As we noted, it was as if her income had fallen. In this section we will consider how Ingrid responds to a direct change in income—that is, a change in her income level holding relative price constant. Figure 11-15 compares Ingrid's budget line and optimal consumption choice with an income of \$2,400 per month (BL_1) with her budget line and optimal consumption choice with an income of \$1,200 per month (BL_2), while keeping prices at \$150 per room and \$30 per restaurant meal. *A* is Ingrid's optimal consumption bundle at an income of \$2,400 and *B* is her optimal consumption bundle at an income of \$1,200. In each case, her optimal consumption bundle is given by the point at which the budget line is tangent to the indifference curve. As you can see, at the lower income her budget line shifts *inward* compared to her budget line at the higher income, but maintains the same slope because relative price has not changed. This means that she must reduce her consumption of either housing or restaurant meals, or both. As a result she is at a lower level of utility, represented by a lower indifference curve.

As it turns out, Ingrid chooses to consume less of both goods when her income falls: as her income goes from \$2,400 to \$1,200, her consumption of housing falls from 8 to 4 rooms, and her consumption of restaurant meals falls from 40 to 20. This is because in her utility function both goods are *normal goods,* as defined in Chapter 5: goods for which demand increases when income rises, and for which demand decreases when income falls.

Although most goods are normal goods, we also pointed out in Chapter 5 that some goods are *inferior goods,* goods for which demand moves in the opposite direction to the change in income: demand decreases when income rises, and demand increases when income falls. An example might be second-hand furniture. Whether a good is an inferior good depends on the consumer's indifference curve map. Figure 11-16

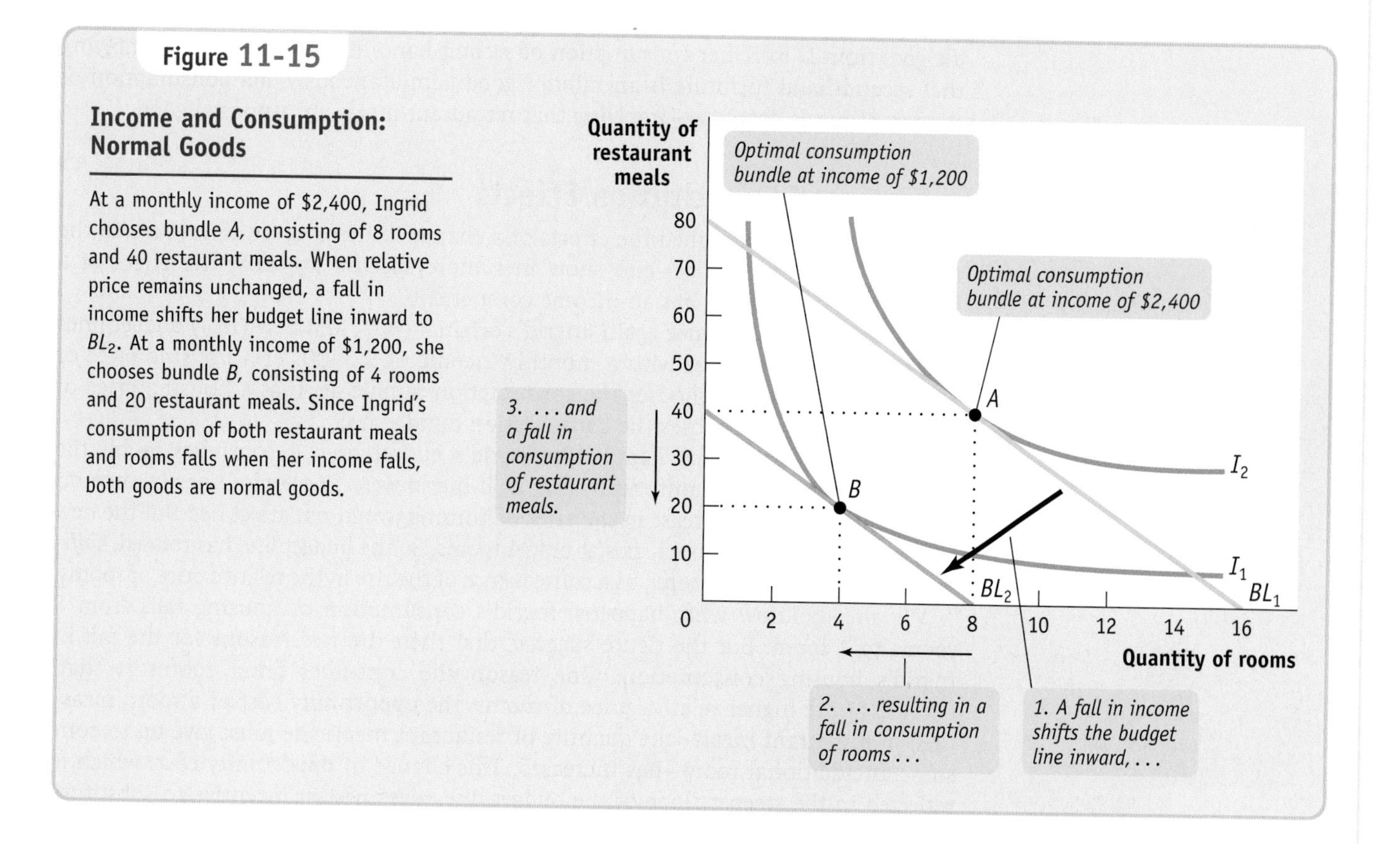

Figure 11-15

Income and Consumption: Normal Goods

At a monthly income of \$2,400, Ingrid chooses bundle *A*, consisting of 8 rooms and 40 restaurant meals. When relative price remains unchanged, a fall in income shifts her budget line inward to BL_2. At a monthly income of \$1,200, she chooses bundle *B*, consisting of 4 rooms and 20 restaurant meals. Since Ingrid's consumption of both restaurant meals and rooms falls when her income falls, both goods are normal goods.

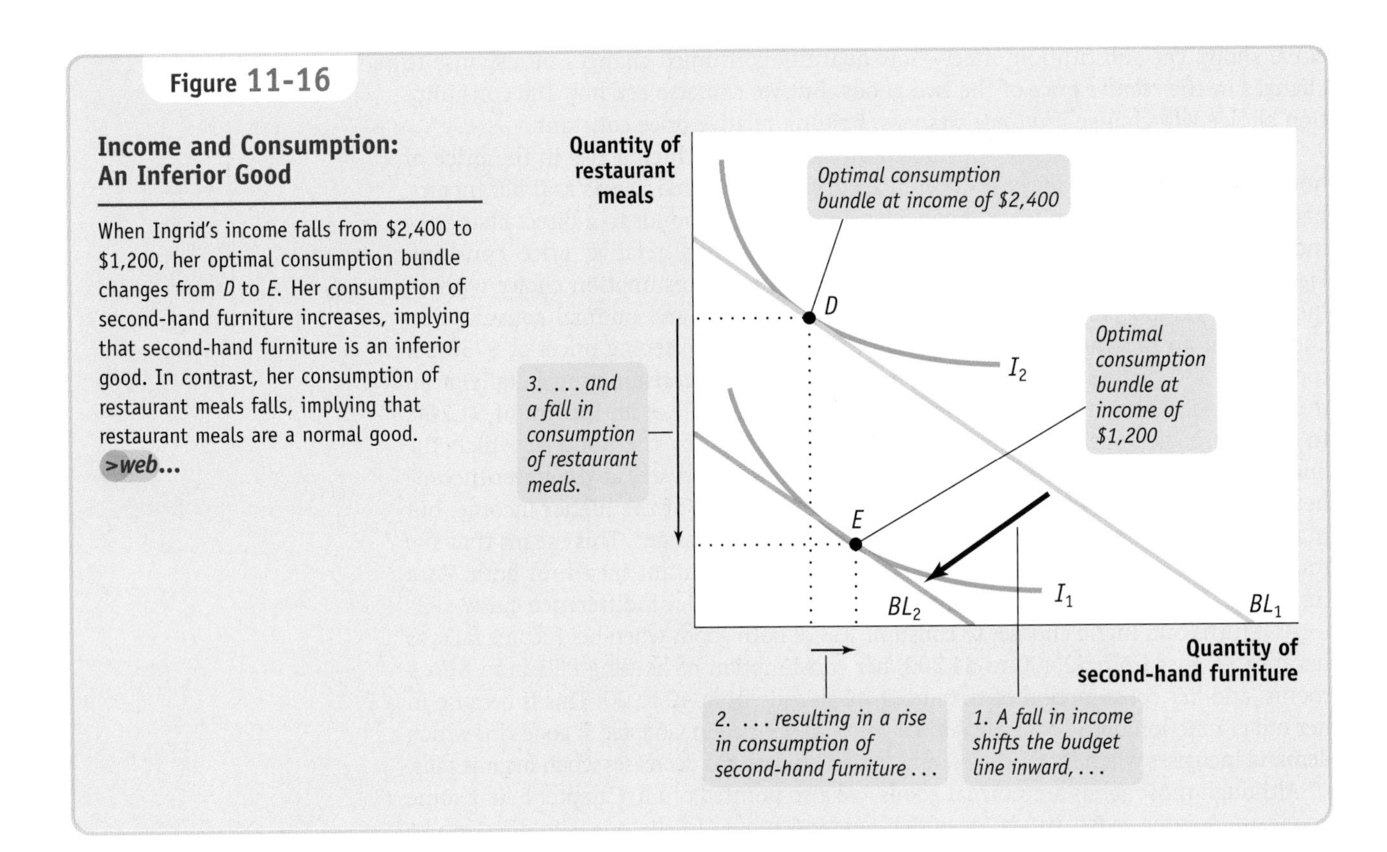

Figure 11-16

Income and Consumption: An Inferior Good

When Ingrid's income falls from $2,400 to $1,200, her optimal consumption bundle changes from *D* to *E*. Her consumption of second-hand furniture increases, implying that second-hand furniture is an inferior good. In contrast, her consumption of restaurant meals falls, implying that restaurant meals are a normal good. **>web...**

illustrates such a case, where second-hand furniture is measured on the horizontal axis and restaurant meals are measured on the vertical axis. Note that when Ingrid's income falls from $2,400 ($BL_1$) to $1,200 ($BL_2$), and her optimal consumption bundle goes from *D* to *E*, her consumption of second-hand furniture increases—implying that second-hand furniture is an inferior good. Simultaneously, her consumption of restaurant meals decreases—implying that restaurant meals are a normal good.

Income and Substitution Effects

Now that we have examined the effects of a change in income, we can return to the issue of a change in price—and show in a more specific way that the effect of a higher price on demand has an income component.

Figure 11-17 shows, once again, Ingrid's original (BL_1) and new (BL_2) budget lines and consumption choices with a monthly income of $2,400. At a housing price of $150 per room, Ingrid chooses the consumption bundle at *A;* at a housing price of $600 per room, she chooses the consumption bundle at *C*.

Let's notice again what happens to Ingrid's budget line. It continues to hit the vertical axis at 80 restaurant meals; that is, if Ingrid were to spend all her income on restaurant meals, the increase in the price of housing would not affect her. But the new budget line hits the horizontal axis at only 4 rooms. So the budget line has rotated, *shifting inward* and *becoming steeper,* as a consequence of the rise in the relative price of rooms.

We already know what happens: Ingrid's consumption of housing falls from 8 rooms to 1 room. But the figure suggests that there are *two* reasons for the fall in Ingrid's housing consumption. One reason she consumes fewer rooms is that, because of the higher relative price of rooms, the opportunity cost of a room measured in restaurant meals—the quantity of restaurant meals she must give up to consume an additional room—has increased. This change in opportunity cost, which is reflected in the steeper slope of the budget line, gives her an incentive to substitute restaurant meals for rooms in her consumption.

Figure 11-17

Income and Substitution Effects

TThe movement from Ingrid's original optimal consumption bundle when the price of rooms is $150, *A*, to her new optimal consumption bundle when the price of rooms is $600, *C*, can be decomposed into two parts. The movement from *A* to *B*—the movement along the original indifference curve, I_2, as relative price changes—is the pure substitution effect. It captures how her consumption would change if she were given a hypothetical increase in income that just compensates her for the increase in the price of rooms. The movement from *B* to *C*, the change in consumption when we remove that hypothetical income compensation, is the income effect of the price increase—how her consumption changes as a result of the fall in her purchasing power.

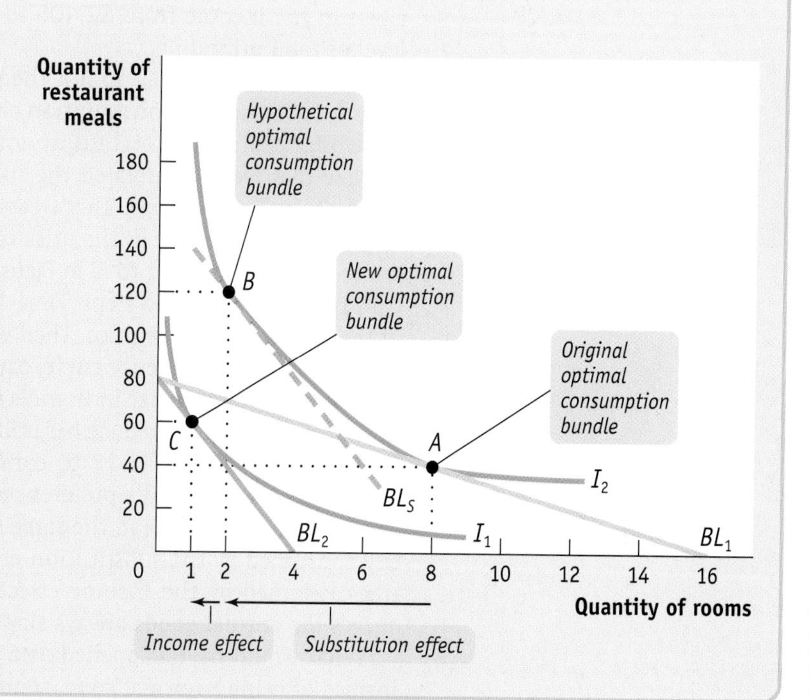

But the other reason Ingrid consumes fewer rooms after their price increases is that the rise in the price of rooms makes her *poorer*. True, her money income hasn't changed. But she must pay more for rooms, and as a result her budget line has rotated inward. So she cannot reach the same level of total utility as before. That is why she ends up on a lower indifference curve.

In the real world these effects–an increase in the price of a good raises its opportunity cost and also makes consumers poorer–usually go together. But in our imagination we can separate them. In Chapter 10 we introduced the distinction between the *substitution effect* of a price change (the change in consumption that arises from the substitution of the good that is now relatively cheaper for the good that is now relatively more expensive) and the *income effect* (the change in consumption caused by the change in purchasing power arising from a price change). Now we can show these two effects more clearly.

To isolate the substitution effect, let's temporarily change the story about why Ingrid faces an increase in rent: it's not that housing has become more expensive, it's the fact that she has moved from Fredericton to Toronto, where the rents are higher. But let's consider a hypothetical scenario–let's suppose momentarily that she earns more in Toronto, and that the higher income is just enough to *compensate* her for the higher price of housing, so that her total utility is exactly the same as before.

Figure 11-17 shows her situation before and after the move. The bundle labelled *A* represents Ingrid's original consumption choice: 8 rooms, 40 restaurant meals. When she moves to Toronto, she faces a higher price of housing, so her budget line becomes steeper. But we have just assumed that her move increases her income by just enough to compensate for the higher price of housing–that is, just enough to let her reach the original indifference curve. So her new *hypothetical* optimal consumption bundle is at *B*, where the steeper, dashed hypothetical budget line (BL_S) is just tangent to the original indifference curve (I_2). By assuming that we have compensated Ingrid for the loss in purchasing power due to the increase in the price of housing, we isolate the *pure substitution* effect of the change in relative price on her consumption.

At *B*, Ingrid's consumption bundle contains 2 rooms and 120 restaurant meals. This costs $4,800 (2 rooms at $600 each, and 120 meals at $30). So if Ingrid faces an increase in the price of housing from $150 to $600 per room, but also experiences a rise in her income from $2,400 to $4,800 per month, she ends up with the same level of total utility.

The movement from *A* to *B* is the pure substitution effect of the price change. It is the effect on Ingrid's consumption choice when we change the relative price of housing while keeping her total utility constant.

Now that we have isolated the substitution effect, we can bring back the income effect of the price change. That's easy: we just go back to the original story, in which Ingrid faces an increase in the price of housing *without* any rise in income. We already know that this leads her to C in Figure 11-17. But we can think of the move from *A* to *C* as taking place in two steps. First, Ingrid moves from *A* to *B*, the substitution effect of the change in relative price. Then we take away the extra income needed to keep her on the original indifference curve, causing her to move to C. The movement from *B* to *C* is the additional change in Ingrid's demand that results because the increase in housing prices actually does reduce her utility. So this is the income effect of the price change.

We can use Figure 11-17 to confirm that restaurant meals and rooms are both normal goods in Ingrid's preferences. For normal goods, the income effect and the substitution effect work in the same direction: a price increase induces a fall in quantity consumed by the substitution effect (the move from *A* to *B*) and a fall in quantity consumed by the income effect (the move from *B* to C). That's why demand curves for normal goods always slope downward.

What would have happened as a result of the increase in the price of housing if, instead of being a normal good, rooms had been an inferior good for Ingrid? First, the movement from *A* to *B* depicted in Figure 11-17, the substitution effect, would remain unchanged. But an income change causes quantity consumed to move in the opposite direction for an inferior good. So the movement from *B* to C shown in Figure 11-17, the income effect for a normal good, would no longer hold. Instead, the income effect for an inferior good would cause Ingrid's quantity of rooms consumed to *increase* from *B*—say, to a bundle consisting of 3 rooms and 20 restaurant meals.

In the end, the demand curves for inferior goods normally slope downward: if Ingrid consumes 3 rooms after the increase in the price of housing, it is still 5 fewer rooms than she consumed before. So although the income effect moves in the opposite direction of the substitution effect in the case of an inferior good, in this example the substitution effect is stronger than the income effect.

But what if there existed a type of inferior good in which the income effect is so strong that it dominates the substitution effect? Would a demand curve for that good then slope upward—that is, would quantity demanded increase when price increases? The answer is yes: you have encountered such a good already—it is called a *Giffen good,* and it was described in For Inquiring Minds on page 262 of Chapter 10. As we noted there, Giffen goods are rare creatures, but they cannot be ruled out.

Is the distinction between income and substitution effects important in practice? For analysing the demand for goods, the answer is that it usually isn't that important. However, in Chapter 12 we'll discuss how individuals make decisions about how much of their labour to supply to employers. In that case income and substitution effects work in opposite directions, and the distinction between them becomes crucial.

economics in action

How Much Housing and How Many Restaurants?

To illustrate the substitution effect, we offered a hypothetical example in which Ingrid moves from Fredericton to Toronto, gaining a higher income but facing a higher price of housing. We made up the numbers for that example, but the real comparison between the two cities may not be that different.

As we mentioned at the beginning of this chapter, starting salaries for economics MAs are about twice as high in Toronto as they are in Fredericton, but housing is also far more expensive. Of course, housing is just one component of the cost of living—that is, how much income a family would need to achieve a "typical" level of utility. While exhaustive estimates are hard to come by, one would not be surprised if the cost of living in Toronto exceeded that in Fredericton by just enough to offset the higher incomes available in Toronto. If this were the case, on average, families would live about as well in the two cities.

But they don't live the same way because relative prices are different. Houses are smaller in Toronto, with fewer rooms and fewer square feet; in Toronto, people are much more likely to live in townhouses or apartments. In contrast, the great majority of new homes in the Fredericton area are single-family houses on big lots. On the other hand, people in Toronto are much more likely to eat out in restaurants than people in Fredericton. ■

> > > > > > > > > > > > > > > > > >

>> QUICK REVIEW

- The change in a consumer's optimal consumption bundle caused by a change in price can be decomposed into two effects: the substitution effect, due to the change in relative price, and the income effect, due to the change in purchasing power.
- The substitution effect refers to the substitution of the good that is now relatively cheaper for the good that is now relatively more expensive, holding the utility level constant. It is represented by movement along the original indifference curve.
- When a price change alters a consumer's purchasing power, the resulting change in consumption is the income effect. It is represented by a movement to a different indifference curve, keeping the relative price unchanged.
- For normal goods, the income and substitution effects work in the same direction; so their demand curves always slope downward. Although these effects work in opposite directions for inferior goods, their demand curves usually slope downward as well because the substitution effect is typically stronger than the income effect. The exception is the case of a Giffen good.

>> CHECK YOUR UNDERSTANDING 11-4

Sammy has $60 in weekly income, the current price of clams is $5 per pound, and the current price of potatoes is $1 per pound. Both are normal goods for Sammy. For each of the following situations, construct a diagram that, like Figure 11-17, shows the substitution effect alone and also shows the substitution and income effects together. Put the quantity of clams (in pounds) on the horizontal axis and the quantity of potatoes (in pounds) on the vertical axis.

a. The price of a pound of clams falls from $5.00 to $2.50 and the price of a pound of potatoes remains at $1.00.

b. The price of a pound of clams rises from $5.00 to $10.00 and the price of a pound of potatoes remains at $1.00.

Solutions appear at back of book.

• A LOOK AHEAD •

With the end of this chapter, our analysis of consumer behaviour is complete. Chapters 8 and 9 presented a complete analysis of producer behaviour under perfect competition. Next we turn to the study of factor markets, which allocate factors of production such as physical capital and labour to various producers. In Chapter 12, we will see that producer and consumer behaviours are much like flip sides of the same coin. For example, a producer decides whether or not to hire another worker based on a comparison of the worker's cost, the wage rate, to the value of what that worker can produce. Meanwhile, an individual decides whether or not to work based on a comparison of the wage rate to the value that he or she places on leisure. The study of factor markets initiates a higher level of analysis, a first step on the path toward understanding how the market coordinates economic activity in order to, in most cases, bring about the best outcome possible.

SUMMARY

1. Preferences can be represented by an **indifference curve map,** a series of **indifference curves.** Each curve shows all the consumption bundles that yield a given level of total utility. Indifference curves have two general properties: they never cross; and greater distance from the origin indicates higher total utility levels. The indifference curves of ordinary goods have two additional properties: they are downward sloping and are *convex* in shape.
2. The **marginal rate of substitution,** or ***MRS,*** of *R* in place of *M*—the rate at which a consumer is willing to substitute more *R* for less *M*—is equal to MU_R/MU_M and is also equal to minus the slope of the indifference curve. Convex indifference curves get flatter as you move to the right along the horizontal axis and steeper as you move upward along the vertical axis because of *diminishing marginal utility:* a consumer requires more and more units of *R* to substitute for a forgone unit of *M* as the amount of *R* consumed relative to the amount of *M* consumed rises.
3. Most goods are **ordinary goods**—goods for which a consumer requires additional units of some other good as compensation for giving up some of the good, and for which there is a **diminishing marginal rate of substitution.**
4. A consumer maximizes utility by getting on the highest indifference curve his or her budget constraint allows. Using the **tangency condition,** the consumer chooses the bundle at which the indifference curve just touches the budget line. At this point, the **relative price** of *R* in terms of *M*, P_R/P_M (which is equal to minus the slope of

the budget line when R is on the horizontal axis and M is on the vertical axis), is equal to the marginal rate of substitution of R in place of M, MU_R/MU_M (which is equal to minus the slope of the indifference curve). This gives us the **relative price rule:** at the optimal consumption bundle, the relative price is equal to the marginal rate of substitution. Rearranging this equation also gives us the optimal consumption rule of Chapter 10. Two consumers faced with the same prices and income, but with different preferences and therefore different indifference curve maps, will make different consumption choices.

5. When the marginal rate of substitution is constant, two goods are **perfect substitutes** and indifference curves are straight lines: there is only one relative price at which the consumer is willing to purchase both goods. When a consumer wants to consume the two goods in the same ratio, regardless of the relative price, the goods are **perfect complements.** In this case the indifference curves form right angles and the marginal rate of substitution is undefined. The relationship between most goods for most people lies between these two extremes.
6. The effect of a change in relative price on consumer choice can be decomposed into the *substitution effect* and the *income effect.* The substitution effect is shown by the movement along the original indifference curve in response to the change in relative price, as the consumer substitutes more of the cheaper good in place of the more expensive good. The income effect is shown by a change to a new indifference curve, reflecting the fact that a change in a good's price alters the purchasing power of a given level of income.
7. The income and substitution effects work in the same direction for normal goods, ensuring that demand curves slope downward.

KEY TERMS

Indifference curve, p. 270
Indifference curve map, p. 270
Marginal rate of substitution (*MRS*), p. 275
Diminishing marginal rate of substitution, p. 276
Ordinary goods, p. 276
Tangency condition, p. 276
Relative price, p. 277
Relative price rule, p. 278
Perfect substitutes, p. 281
Perfect complements, p. 282

PROBLEMS

1. For each of the following situations, draw a diagram containing three of Isabella's indifference curves.
   a. For Isabella, cars and tires are perfect complements, but in a ratio of 1:4; that is, for each car, Isabella wants exactly four tires. Be sure to label and number the axes of your diagram. Place tires on the horizontal axis and cars on the vertical axis.
   b. Isabella gets utility only from her caffeine intake. She can consume Valley Dew or cola, and Valley Dew contains twice as much caffeine as cola. Be sure to label and number the axes of your diagram. Place cola on the horizontal axis and Valley Dew on the vertical axis.
   c. Isabella gets utility from consuming two goods: leisure time and income. Both have diminishing marginal utility. Be sure to label the axes of your diagram. Place leisure on the horizontal axis and income on the vertical axis.
   d. Isabella can consume two goods: skis and bindings. For each ski she wants exactly one binding. Be sure to label and number the axes of your diagram. Place bindings on the horizontal axis and skis on the vertical axis.
   e. Isabella gets utility from consuming soda. But she gets no utility from consuming water: any more, or any less, water leaves her utility level unchanged. Be sure to label the axes of your diagram. Place water on the horizontal axis and soda on the vertical axis.
2. Use the four properties of indifference curves for ordinary goods illustrated in Figure 11-4 to answer the following questions.
   a. Can you rank the following two bundles? If so, which property of indifference curves helps you rank them?
      Bundle *A:* 2 movie tickets and 3 cafeteria meals
      Bundle *B:* 4 movie tickets and 8 cafeteria meals
   b. Can you rank the following two bundles? If so, which property of indifference curves helps you rank them?
      Bundle *A:* 2 movie tickets and 3 cafeteria meals
      Bundle *B:* 4 movie tickets and 3 cafeteria meals
   c. Can you rank the following two bundles? If so, which property of indifference curves helps you rank them?
      Bundle *A:* 12 videos and 4 bags of chips
      Bundle *B:* 5 videos and 10 bags of chips
   d. Suppose you are indifferent between the following two bundles:
      Bundle *A:* 10 breakfasts and 4 dinners
      Bundle *B:* 4 breakfasts and 10 dinners
      Now compare bundle *A* and the following bundle:
      Bundle *C:* 7 breakfasts and 7 dinners
      Can you rank bundle *A* and bundle *C*? If so, which property of indifference curves helps you rank them? (*Hint:* It may help if you draw this, placing dinners on the horizontal axis and breakfasts on the vertical axis. And remember that breakfasts and dinners are ordinary goods.)
3. The four properties of indifference curves for ordinary goods illustrated in Figure 11-4 rule out certain indifference curves.

Determine whether those general properties allow each of the following indifference curves. If not, state which of the general principles rules out the curves.

a.

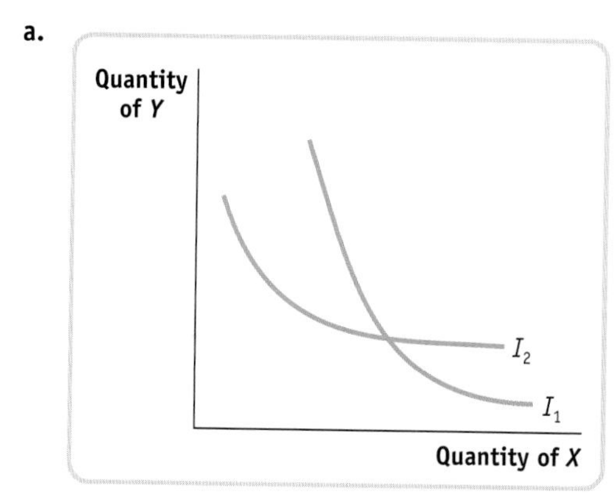

b.

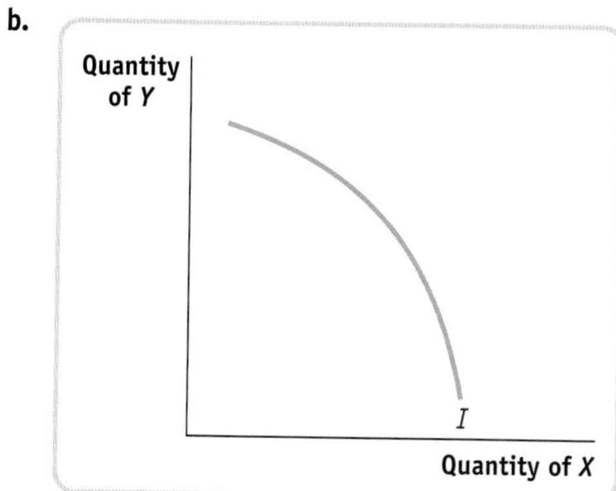

c.

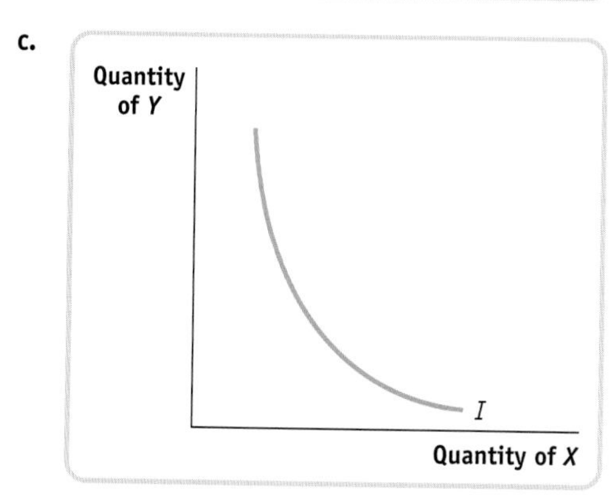

d.

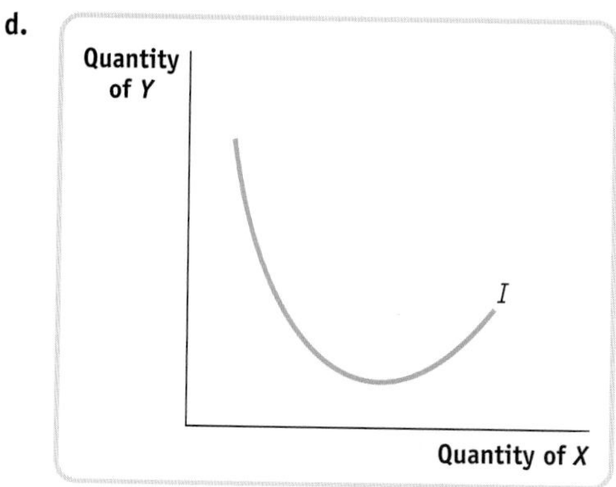

4. Kory has an income of $50, which she can spend on two goods: CDs and cups of hot chocolate. Both are normal goods for her; each CD costs $10, and each cup of hot chocolate costs $2. For each of the following situations, decide whether this is Kory's optimal consumption bundle. If not, what should Kory do to achieve her optimal consumption bundle?

a. Kory is thinking about buying 4 CDs and 5 cups of hot chocolate. At that bundle, her marginal rate of substitution of CDs in place of hot chocolate is 1; that is, she would be just willing to exchange 1 fewer cup of hot chocolate for 1 more CD.

b. Kory is thinking about buying 2 CDs and 15 cups of hot chocolate. Kory's marginal utility of the second CD is 25, and her marginal utility of the 15th cup of hot chocolate is 5.

c. Kory is thinking about buying 1 CD and 10 cups of hot chocolate. At that bundle, her marginal rate of substitution of CDs in place of hot chocolate is 5; that is, she would be just willing to exchange 5 cups of hot chocolate for 1 CD.

5. Tommy has 4 Cal Ripken and 2 Nolan Ryan baseball cards. The prices of these baseball cards are $24 for Cal and $12 for Nolan. Tommy, however, would be willing to exchange 1 Cal card for 1 Nolan card.

a. What is Tommy's marginal rate of substitution of Cal Ripken in place of Nolan Ryan baseball cards?

b. Can Tommy buy and sell baseball cards to make himself better off? How?

c. Suppose Tommy has traded baseball cards and now no longer wants to make any more trades. What is his marginal rate of substitution of Cal Ripken in place of Nolan Ryan cards now?

6. Ralph and Lauren are talking about how much they like going to the gym and how much they like eating out at their favourite restaurant. A session at the gym costs the same as a meal at the restaurant. Ralph says that, for his current consumption of gym sessions and restaurant meals, he values one more meal twice as much as he values one more session at the gym. Lauren is studying economics, and she tells him that he cannot be choosing his optimal consumption bundle.

a. Is Lauren right? Why or why not? Draw a diagram of Ralph's budget line and the indifference curve that he is on by making his current consumption choice. Place restaurant meals on the horizontal axis and gym sessions on the vertical axis.

b. How should Ralph adjust his consumption so that it is optimal? Illustrate an optimal choice in your diagram.

7. Sabine can't tell the difference between Coke and Pepsi—the two taste exactly the same to her.

a. What is Sabine's marginal rate of substitution of Coke in place of Pepsi?

b. Draw a few of Sabine's indifference curves for Coke and Pepsi. Place Coke on the horizontal axis and Pepsi on the vertical axis.

c. Sabine has $6 to spend on cola this week. Coke costs $1.50 per six-pack and Pepsi costs $1.00 per six-pack. Draw Sabine's budget line for Coke and Pepsi on the same diagram.

d. What is Sabine's optimal consumption bundle? Show this on your diagram.

e. If the price of Coke and Pepsi is the same, what combination of Coke and Pepsi will Sabine buy?

8. For Norma, both nachos and salsa are normal goods. Although she likes consuming them together, they are not perfect complements (her indifference curves are convex-shaped, not right angle–shaped). The price of nachos rises, while the price of salsa remains unchanged.
   a. Can you determine definitively whether she consumes more or fewer nachos? Explain with a diagram, placing nachos on the horizontal axis and salsa on the vertical axis.
   b. Can you determine definitively whether she consumes more or less salsa? Explain with a diagram, placing nachos on the horizontal axis and salsa on the vertical axis.

9. Tyrone is a utility maximizer. His income is $100, which he can spend on cafeteria meals and on notepads. Each meal costs $5, and each notepad costs $2. At these prices Tyrone chooses to buy 16 cafeteria meals and 10 notepads.
   a. Draw a diagram that shows Tyrone's choice using an indifference curve and his budget line, placing notepads on the vertical axis and cafeteria meals on the horizontal axis. Label the indifference curve I_1 and the budget line BL_1.
   b. The price of notepads falls to $1; the price of cafeteria meals remains the same. On the same diagram, draw Tyrone's budget line with the new prices and label it BL_H.
   c. Lastly, Tyrone's income falls to $90. On the same diagram, draw his budget line with this income and the new prices and label it BL_2. Is he worse off, better off, or equally as well off with these new prices and lower income than compared to the original prices and higher income? (*Hint:* Determine whether Tyrone can afford to buy his original consumption bundle of 16 meals and 10 notepads with the lower income and new prices.) Illustrate your answer using an indifference curve and label it I_2.
   d. Give an intuitive explanation of your answer to part c.

10. Gus spends his income on gas for his car and on food. The government raises the tax on gas, thereby raising the price of gas. But the government also lowers the income tax, thereby increasing Gus's income. And this rise in income is just enough to place Gus on the same indifference curve as the one he was on before the price of gas rose. Will Gus buy more, less, or the same amount of gas as before these changes?

11. Pam spends her money on bread and Spam, and her indifference curves obey the four properties of indifference curves for ordinary goods. Suppose that, for Pam, Spam is an inferior, but not a Giffen, good; bread is a normal good. Bread costs $2 per loaf, and Spam costs $2 per can. Pam has $20 to spend.
   a. Draw a diagram of Pam's budget line, placing Spam on the horizontal axis and bread on the vertical axis. Suppose her optimal consumption bundle is 4 cans of Spam and 6 loaves of bread. Illustrate that bundle also, and draw the indifference curve on which it lies.
   b. The price of Spam falls to $1; the price of bread remains the same. Pam now buys 7 loaves of bread and 6 cans of Spam. Illustrate her new budget line and new optimal consumption bundle in your diagram. Also draw the indifference curve on which this bundle lies.
   c. In your diagram, show the income and substitution effects from this fall in the price of Spam. Remember that Spam is an inferior good for Pam.

12. Katya commutes to work. She can use either public transport or her own car. Her indifference curves obey the four properties of indifference curves for ordinary goods.
   a. Draw Katya's budget line with car travel on the vertical axis and public transport on the horizontal axis. Suppose that Katya consumes some of both goods. Draw an indifference curve that helps you illustrate that optimal consumption bundle.
   b. Now the price of public transport falls. Draw Katya's new budget line.
   c. For Katya, public transport is an inferior, but not a Giffen, good. Draw an indifference curve that illustrates her optimal consumption bundle after the price of public transport has fallen. Is Katya consuming more or less public transport?
   d. Show the income and substitution effects from this fall in the price of public transport.

13. For Crandall, cheese cubes and crackers are perfect complements: he wants to consume exactly 1 cheese cube with each cracker. He has $2.40 to spend on cheese and crackers. One cheese cube costs $0.20, and 1 cracker costs $0.10. Draw a diagram, with crackers on the horizontal axis and cheese cubes on the vertical axis, to answer the following questions.
   a. Which bundle will Crandall consume?
   b. The price of crackers rises to $0.20. How many cheese cubes and how many crackers will Crandall consume?
   c. In your diagram, show the income and substitution effects from this price rise.

14. Carmen consumes nothing but cafeteria meals and CDs. Her indifference curves exhibit the four general properties of indifference curves. Cafeteria meals cost $5 each, and CDs cost $10. Carmen has $50 to spend.
   a. Draw Carmen's budget line and an indifference curve that illustrates her optimal consumption bundle. Place cafeteria meals on the horizontal axis and CDs on the vertical axis. You do not have enough information to know the specific tangency point, so choose one arbitrarily.
   b. Now Carmen's income rises to $100. Draw her new budget line on the same diagram, as well as an indifference curve that illustrates her optimal consumption bundle. Assume that cafeteria meals are an inferior good.
   c. Can you draw an indifference curve showing that cafeteria meals and CDs are both inferior goods?

>web... To continue your study and review of concepts in this chapter, please visit the Krugman/Wells website for quizzes, animated graph tutorials, web links to helpful resources, and more.

www.worthpublishers.com/krugmanwellsmyatt

>>Factor Markets and the Distribution of Income

chapter 12

THE VALUE OF A DEGREE

DOES HIGHER EDUCATION PAY? YES, it does: in the modern economy, employers are willing to pay a premium for workers with more education. And that premium increases as educated workers get older and gain work experience. For example, in 1995 the starting salary for university graduates with a bachelor's degree was 20% more than the earnings of those who had only graduated from high school. But for workers between 35 and 39 years of age, the premium earned with a university degree had increased to 42% more per year; and for workers between 50 and 54 years of age, it had increased to 50%. Looked at in terms of the return on your investment in university education, a bachelor's degree yields around 18% interest for every year of your working life. For a relatively risk-free investment, that is hard to beat.

But who decided that the wages of workers with university degrees would rise so much compared with those of high school grads? The answer, of course, is that nobody decided it. Wage rates are prices, the prices of different kinds of labour; and they are decided, like other prices, by supply and demand.

Still, there is a difference between the wage rate of high school grads and the price of used textbooks: the wage rate isn't the price of a *good,* it's the price of a *factor of production.* And although markets for factors of production are in many ways similar to those for goods, there are also some important differences.

In this chapter, we examine *factor markets,* the markets in which factors of production such as labour are traded. Factor markets, like goods markets, play a crucial role in the economy: they allocate productive resources to producers, and help ensure that those resources are used efficiently.

Tod Bigelow/Aurora Photos

Jon Feingersch/Corbis

If you have ever had doubts about attending university, consider this: factory workers with only high school degrees will make much less than university graduates. Currently in Canada, university grads make on average more than 18% per year more than high school grads over the course of their working lives.

This chapter begins by describing the major factors of production. Then we

What you will learn in this chapter:

- How factors of production—resources like land, labour, and both **physical capital** and **human capital**—are traded in factor markets, determining the **factor distribution of income**
- How the demand for factors leads to the **marginal productivity theory of income distribution**
- An understanding of the sources of wage disparities and the role of discrimination
- The way in which a worker's decision about **time allocation** gives rise to labour supply

consider the demand for factors of production, which leads us to a crucial insight: the *marginal productivity theory of income distribution.* We then consider some challenges to the marginal productivity theory. The final section of the chapter looks at the supply of the most important factor, labour.

The Economy's Factors of Production

You may recall that we defined a *factor of production* in Chapter 2 in the context of the circular-flow model; it is any resource that is used by firms to produce *goods* and *services*, items that are consumed by households. Factors of production are bought and sold in *factor markets*, and the prices in factor markets are known as *factor prices*.

What are these factors of production, and why do factor prices matter?

The Factors of Production

As we learned in Chapter 2, economists divide factors of production into three principal classes: labour, land, and capital. *Land* is a resource provided by nature; *labour* is the work done by human beings.

In Chapter 7 we defined *capital;* it is the assets that are used by a firm in producing its output. There are two broad types of capital. **Physical capital**—often referred to simply as "capital"—consists of manufactured resources such as buildings and machines. In the modern economy, **human capital,** the improvement in labour created by education and knowledge, and embodied in the workforce, is at least equally significant. The importance of human capital has been greatly increased by the progress of technology, which has made a high level of technical sophistication essential to many jobs—one cause of the increased premium paid for workers with advanced degrees.

Physical capital—often referred to simply as "capital"—consists of manufactured resources such as buildings and machines.

Human capital is the improvement in labour created by education and knowledge that is embodied in the workforce.

PITFALLS

WHAT IS A FACTOR, ANYWAY?

Imagine a business that produces shirts. The business will make use of workers and machines—that is, of labour and capital. But it will also use other inputs, such as electricity and cloth. Are all of these inputs factors of production? No: labour and capital are factors of production, but cloth and electricity are not.

The key distinction is that a factor of production earns income from the selling of its services over and over again but an input cannot. For example, a worker earns income over time from repeatedly selling his or her efforts; the owner of a machine earns income over time from repeatedly selling the use of that machine. So a factor of production, such as labour and capital, represents an enduring source of income. An input like electricity or cloth, however, is used up in the production process. Once exhausted, it cannot be a source of future income for its owner.

Why Factor Prices Matter: The Allocation of Resources

Factor markets and factor prices play a key role in one of the most important processes that must take place in any economy: the allocation of resources among producers.

Consider the example of Florida in 1992, in the aftermath of Hurricane Andrew, which was the costliest hurricane to hit the U.S. mainland to date, and five times stronger than the worst hurricane to ever hit Canada. Florida had an urgent need for workers in the building trades—carpenters, plumbers, and so on—to repair or replace damaged homes and businesses. What ensured that those needed workers actually came? The high demand for construction workers in Florida drove up their wages, which led large numbers of workers with the right skills to move temporarily to the state to do the work. In other words, the market for a factor of production—construction workers—allocated that factor of production to where it was needed.

In this sense factor markets are similar to goods markets, which allocate goods among consumers. But there are two features that make factor markets somewhat special. Unlike in a goods market, demand in a factor market is what we call *derived demand.* That is, demand for the factor is derived from the firm's output choice. The second feature is that factor markets are where most of us get the largest share of our income (government transfers being the next largest source of income in the economy).

Factor Incomes and the Distribution of Income

Most Canadian families get most of their income in the form of wages and salaries—that is, they get their income by selling labour. Some people, however, get most of their income from physical capital: when you own stock in a company, what you really own

FOR INQUIRING MINDS

THE FACTOR DISTRIBUTION OF INCOME AND SOCIAL CHANGE IN THE INDUSTRIAL REVOLUTION

Have you read any novels by Jane Austen? How about Charles Dickens? If you've read both, you probably noticed that they seem to be describing quite different societies. Austen's novels, set around 1800, describe a world in which the leaders of society are land-owning aristocrats. Dickens, writing about 50 years later, describes a world in which businessmen, especially factory owners, seem to be in control.

This literary shift reflects a dramatic transformation in the factor distribution of income. The Industrial Revolution, which took place between the late eighteenth century and the middle of the nineteenth century, changed England from a mainly agricultural country, in which land earned a fairly substantial share of income, to an urbanized and industrial one, in which land rents were dwarfed by capital income. Recent estimates by the economist Nancy Stokey show that between 1780 and 1850 the share of land represented in national income fell from 20 to 9%, while the share represented by capital rose from 35 to 44%. That shift changed everything—even literature.

Lewis Hines/Bettmann/Corbis

By altering how people lived and worked, the Industrial Revolution led to huge economic and social changes.

is a share of that company's physical capital. And some people get much of their income from the rents on land they own.

Obviously, then, the prices of factors of production have a major impact on how the economic "pie" is sliced among different groups. For example, a higher wage rate, other things equal, means that more of the income in the economy goes to people who derive their income from labour, as opposed to capital. Economists refer to how the economic pie is sliced as the "distribution of income".

Specifically, factor prices determine the **factor distribution of income**—how the total income of the economy is divided among labour, land, and capital.

The **factor distribution of income** is the division of total income among labour, land, and capital.

As the following Economics in Action explains, the factor distribution of income in Canada has been quite stable over the past few decades. In other times and places, however, large changes have taken place in the factor distribution. One notable example: during the Industrial Revolution, the share of total income earned by land owners fell sharply, while that earned by capital owners rose. As explained in For Inquiring Minds, this shift had a profound effect on society.

economics in action

The Factor Distribution of Income in Canada

When we talk about the factor distribution of income, what are we talking about in practice?

In Canada, as in all advanced economies, payments to labour account for most of the economy's total income. Figure 12-1 shows the factor distribution of income in Canada in 2003: in that year, 67% of total income in the economy took the form of "wages"—meaning wages, salaries, and supplementary labour income. (Supplementary labour income includes the value of employers' contributions to health and welfare schemes, pension plans, workers' compensation, Employment Insurance, Canada/Québec Pension Plans, and retirement allowances.) The share of wages in total income has been quite stable over the long run. Over the past 45 years, it has fluctuated between 66 and 75% of total income without displaying any clear trend up or down. For example, in 1961 the wage share was identical to that in 2003.

However, even though our "wage" measure includes wages, salaries, and supplementary labour income, it still doesn't capture the full income of "labour". The reason

Figure 12-1

Factor Distribution of Income in Canada in 2003

In 2003, wages (including salaries and supplementary labour income) accounted for most income earned in Canada—67% of the total. Most of the remainder—consisting of earnings paid in the form of interest, rent, and corporate profits—went to owners of physical capital. Note that "rent+", which is 9% of the total, is the sum of unincorporated business income (both farm and non-farm) and rent. This component went to individual owners of businesses, as compensation for their labour, capital, and land expended in their businesses.

Source: Statistics Canada, 2003, Table 3800001, GDP income-based.

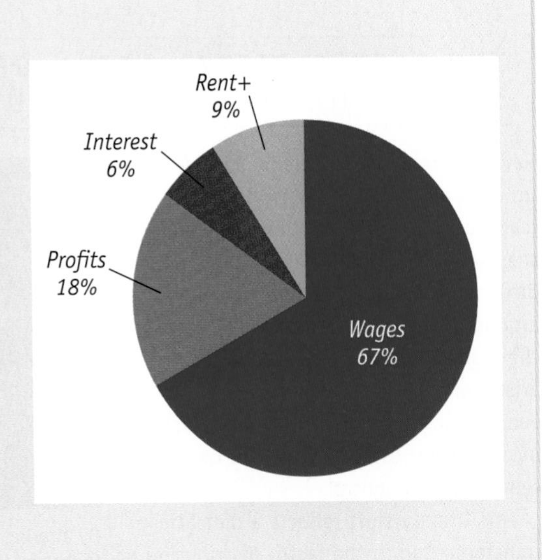

is that Statistics Canada lumps together into one aggregate number both rent and unincorporated business income—the earnings of people who own their own businesses. This could (theoretically) be decomposed into the rent these business owners "pay themselves" for the use of their own property, the interest they "pay themselves" for the use of their own financial capital, and the wages they "pay themselves" for their labour. This suggests that the true share of labour in the economy is probably several percentage points higher than the "wages" share shown in Figure 12-1.

On the other hand, much of what we call "wages" is really a return on human capital. A surgeon isn't just supplying the services of a pair of ordinary hands (at least the patient hopes not!): he or she is also supplying many years and hundreds of thousands of dollars invested in training and experience. We can't directly measure what fraction of wages is really a payment for education and training, but many economists believe that human capital has become *the* most important factor of production in modern economies. ■

>>QUICK REVIEW

- Economists usually divide the economy's factors of production into three principal categories: labour, land, and *capital*. Capital can be either *physical capital* or *human capital*.
- The demand for a factor is a derived demand. Factor prices, which are set in factor markets, determine the *factor distribution of income*.
- Labour receives the bulk—more than two thirds—of the income in the modern Canadian economy. Although the exact share is not directly measurable, much of what is called compensation of employees is a return to human capital.

>>CHECK YOUR UNDERSTANDING 12-1

1. Suppose that the government places price controls on the market for university professors, imposing a wage that is lower than the market wage. Describe the effect of this policy on the production of university degrees. What sectors of the economy do you think will be adversely affected by this policy? What sectors of the economy might benefit?

Solutions appear at back of book.

Marginal Productivity and Factor Demand

All economic decisions are about comparing costs and benefits—and usually about comparing marginal costs and marginal benefits. This goes both for a consumer, deciding whether to buy another pound of fried clams, and for a producer, deciding whether to hire an additional worker.

Although there are some important exceptions, most factors markets in the modern Canadian economy are perfectly competitive, meaning that buyers and sellers of a given factor are price-takers. And in a competitive labour market, it's clear how to define an employer's marginal cost of a worker: it is simply the worker's wage rate. But what is the marginal benefit of that worker? To answer that question, we return to a concept first introduced in Chapter 8: the *production function*, which relates inputs to output. And as in Chapter 9, we will assume throughout this chapter that all producers are price-takers—they operate in a perfectly competitive industry.

Figure 12-2 The Production Function for George and Martha's Farm

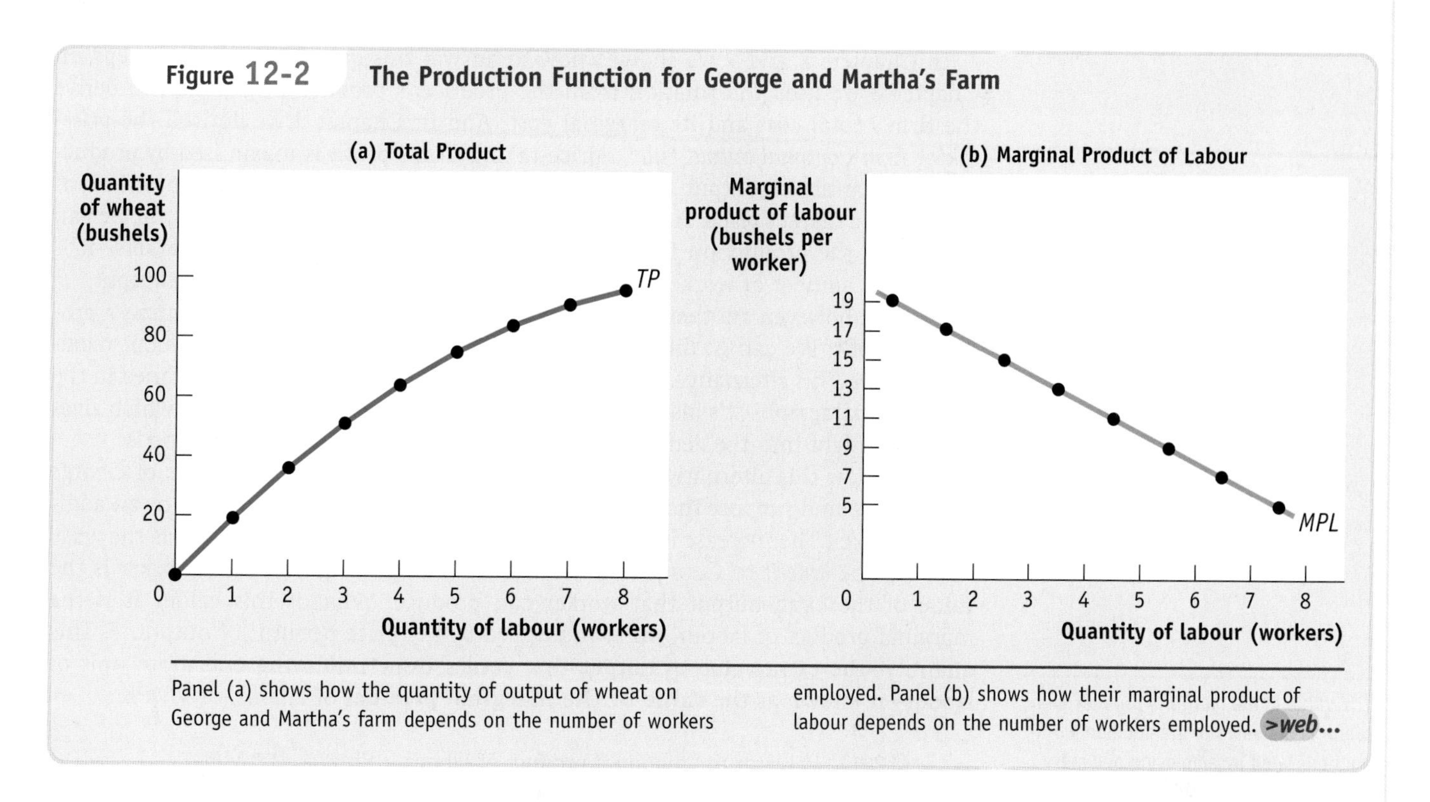

Panel (a) shows how the quantity of output of wheat on George and Martha's farm depends on the number of workers employed. Panel (b) shows how their marginal product of labour depends on the number of workers employed. >web...

Value of the Marginal Product

Figure 12-2 reproduces Figures 8-1 and 8-2, which showed the production function for wheat on George and Martha's farm. Panel (a) uses the total product curve to show how total wheat production depends on the number of workers employed on the farm; panel (b) shows how the *marginal product* of labour, the increase in output from employing one more worker, depends on the number of workers employed. Table 12-1, which reproduces the table in Figure 8-1, shows the numbers behind the figure.

Assume that George and Martha want to maximize their profit, that workers must be paid $200 each, and that wheat sells for $20 per bushel. What is their optimal number of workers? That is, how many workers should they employ to maximize profit?

TABLE 12-1

Employment and Output for George and Martha's Farm

Quantity of labour L (workers)	Quantity of wheat Q (bushels)	Marginal product of labour $MPL = \frac{\Delta Q}{\Delta L}$ (bushels per worker)
0	0	
		19
1	19	
		17
2	36	
		15
3	51	
		13
4	64	
		11
5	75	
		9
6	84	
		7
7	91	
		5
8	96	

In Chapters 8 and 9 we showed how to answer this question in several steps. In Chapter 8 we used information from the producer's production function to derive the firm's total cost and its marginal cost. And in Chapter 9 we derived the *price-taking firm's optimal output rule:* a price-taking firm's profit is maximized by producing the quantity of output at which the marginal cost of the last unit produced is equal to the market price. Having determined the optimal quantity of output, we can go back to the production function and find the optimal number of workers—it is simply the number of workers needed to produce the optimal quantity of output.

There is, however, another way to find the number of workers that maximizes a producer's profit. We can go directly to the question of what level of employment maximizes profit. This alternative approach is equivalent to the approach we outlined in the preceding paragraph—it's just a different way of looking at the same thing, which gives us more insight into the demand for factors as opposed to the supply of goods.

To see how this alternative approach works, let's return to the example of George and Martha and suppose that they are considering whether or not to employ an additional worker. The increase in *cost* from employing that additional worker is the wage rate, W. The *benefit* to George and Martha from employing that extra worker is the value of the extra output that worker can produce. What is this value? It is the marginal product of labour, MPL, multiplied by the price per unit of output, P. This quantity—the extra value of output that comes from employing one more unit of labour—is known as the **value of the marginal product** of labour, or $VMPL$:

The **value of the marginal product** of a factor is the value of the additional output generated by employing one more unit of that factor.

(12-1) Value of the marginal product of labour = $VMPL = P \times MPL$

So should George and Martha hire that extra worker? The answer is yes, if the value of the extra output is more than the cost of the worker—that is, if $VMPL > W$. Otherwise they shouldn't hire that worker.

So the decision to hire labour is a marginal decision, in which the marginal benefit to the producer from hiring an additional worker ($VMPL$) should be compared with the marginal cost to the producer (W). And as with any marginal decision, the optimal choice is where marginal benefit is just equal to marginal cost. That is, to maximize profit George and Martha will employ workers up to the point at which, for the last worker employed

(12-2) $VMPL = W$

This rule doesn't just apply to labour; it applies to any factor of production. The value of the marginal product of any factor is its marginal product times the price of the good it produces. The general rule is that *a profit-maximizing price-taking producer employs each factor of production up to the point at which the value of the marginal product of the last unit of the factor employed is equal to that factor's price.*

It's important to realize that this rule doesn't conflict with our analysis in Chapters 8 and 9. There we saw that a profit-maximizing producer of a good chooses the level of output at which the price of that good is equal to the marginal cost of production. It's just a different way of looking at the same rule. If the level of output is chosen so that price equals marginal cost, then it is also true that at that output level the value of the marginal product of labour will equal the wage rate.

Now let's look more closely at why choosing the level of employment at which the value of the marginal product of the last worker employed is equal to the wage rate works—and at how it helps us understand factor demand.

Value of the Marginal Product and Factor Demand

Table 12-2 calculates the value of the marginal product of labour on George and Martha's farm, on the assumption that the price of wheat is \$20 per bushel. In Figure 12-3 the horizontal axis shows the number of workers employed; the vertical axis

TABLE 12-2

Value of the Marginal Product of Labour for George and Martha's Farm

Quantity of labour *L* (workers)	Marginal product of labour *MPL* (bushels per worker)	Value of the marginal product of labour *VMPL* = *P* × *MPL*
0		
	19	$380
1		
	17	340
2		
	15	300
3		
	13	260
4		
	11	220
5		
	9	180
6		
	7	140
7		
	5	100
8		

measures the value of the marginal product of the last worker employed *and* the wage rate. The curve shown is the **value of the marginal product curve** of labour. This curve, like the marginal product of labour curve, is downward sloping due to diminishing returns to labour in production. That is, the value of the marginal product of each worker is less than that of the preceding worker, because the marginal product of each worker is less than that of the preceding worker.

We have just seen that to maximize profit, George and Martha must hire workers up to the point at which the wage rate is equal to the value of the marginal product of the last worker employed. Let's use the example to see that this principle really works.

The **value of the marginal product curve** of a factor shows how the value of the marginal product of that factor depends on the quantity of the factor employed.

Figure 12-3

The Value of the Marginal Product Curve

This curve shows how the value of the marginal product of labour depends on the number of workers employed. It is downward sloping due to diminishing returns to labour in production. To maximize profit, George and Martha choose the level of employment at which the value of the marginal product of labour is equal to the market wage rate. For example, at a wage rate of $200 the profit-maximizing level of employment is 5 workers, shown by point *A*. The value of the marginal product curve for a factor is the producer's individual demand curve for that factor. >web...

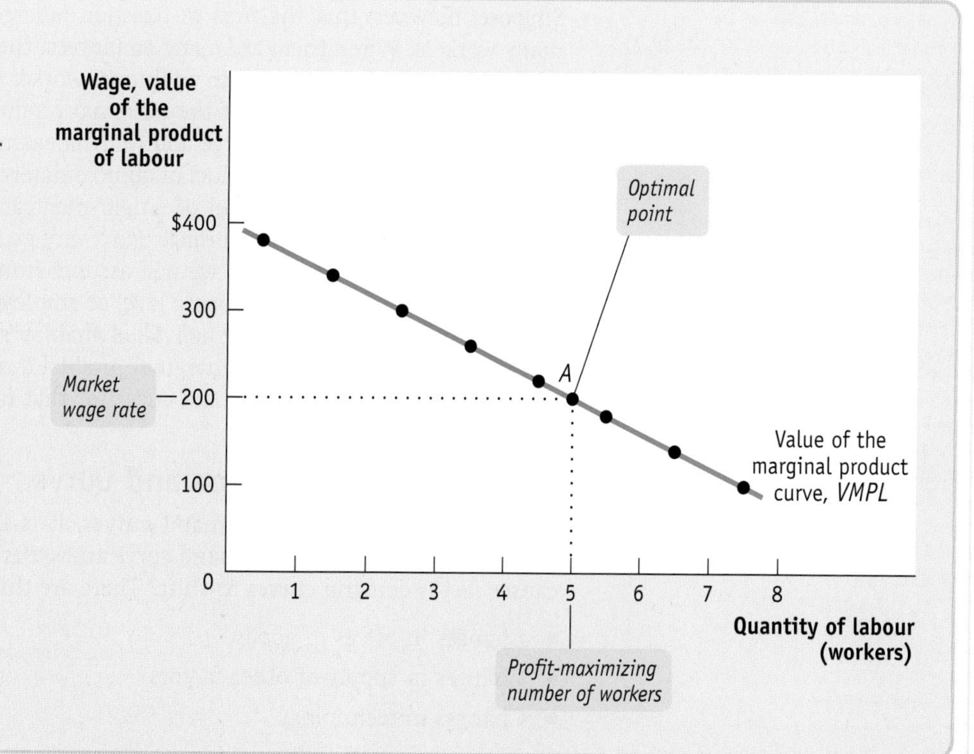

Assume that George and Martha currently employ 3 workers and that workers must be paid the market wage rate of $200. Should they employ an additional worker?

Looking at Table 12-2, we see that if George and Martha currently employ 3 workers, the value of the marginal product of an additional worker is $260. So if they employ an additional worker, they will increase the value of their production by $260 but increase their cost by only $200, yielding an increase of $60 in the farm's profit. In fact, a producer can always increase profit by employing one more unit of a factor of production as long as the value of the marginal product produced by that unit exceeds the factor price.

Alternatively, suppose that George and Martha employ 8 workers. By reducing the number of workers to 7, they can save $200 in wages. Meanwhile, the value of the marginal product of that last worker was only $100. So by reducing employment by one worker they can increase profit by $100. A producer can always increase profit by employing one less unit of a factor of production, as long as the value of the marginal product produced by that unit is less than the factor price.

Using this method, we can see from Table 12-2 that, given a wage rate of $200, the profit-maximizing employment level is 5 workers. The value of the marginal product of the 5th worker is $220, so adding that worker results in $20 of additional profit. But George and Martha should not hire any more than 5 workers: the value of the marginal product of the 6th worker is only $180, $20 less than the cost of that worker. So, to maximize profit, George and Martha should employ workers up to but not beyond the point at which the value of the marginal product of the last worker employed is equal to the wage rate.

Now look again at the value of the marginal product curve in Figure 12-3. To determine the profit-maximizing level of employment, we set the price of labour—$200 per worker—equal to the value of the marginal product of labour. This means that the profit-maximizing level of employment is at point *A*, corresponding to an employment level of 5 workers. If the price of labour were higher or lower, we would simply move up or down the curve.

In this example, George and Martha have a small farm in which the potential employment level varies from 0 to 8 workers, and they hire workers up to the point where the value of the marginal product of the last worker is no less than the wage rate. Suppose, however, that the firm in question is large and has the potential of hiring many workers. When there are many employees, the value of the marginal product of labour falls only slightly when an additional worker is employed. As a result, there will be some worker whose value of the marginal product almost exactly equals the wage rate. (In keeping with the George and Martha example, this means that some worker has a value of the marginal product of approximately $200.) In this case, the firm maximizes profit by choosing a level of employment at which the value of the marginal product of the last worker hired *equals* (to a very good approximation) the wage rate.

In the interest of simplicity, we will assume from now on that firms use this rule to determine the profit-maximizing level of employment. *This means that the value of the marginal product curve is the individual producer's labour demand curve.* And in general, a producer's value of the marginal product curve for any factor of production is that producer's individual demand curve for that factor of production.

Shifts in the Factor Demand Curve

As in the case of ordinary demand curves, it is important to distinguish between *movements along* the factor demand curve and *shifts of* the factor demand curve. What causes factor demand curves to shift? There are three main causes:

- Changes in prices of goods
- Changes in supply of other factors
- Changes in technology

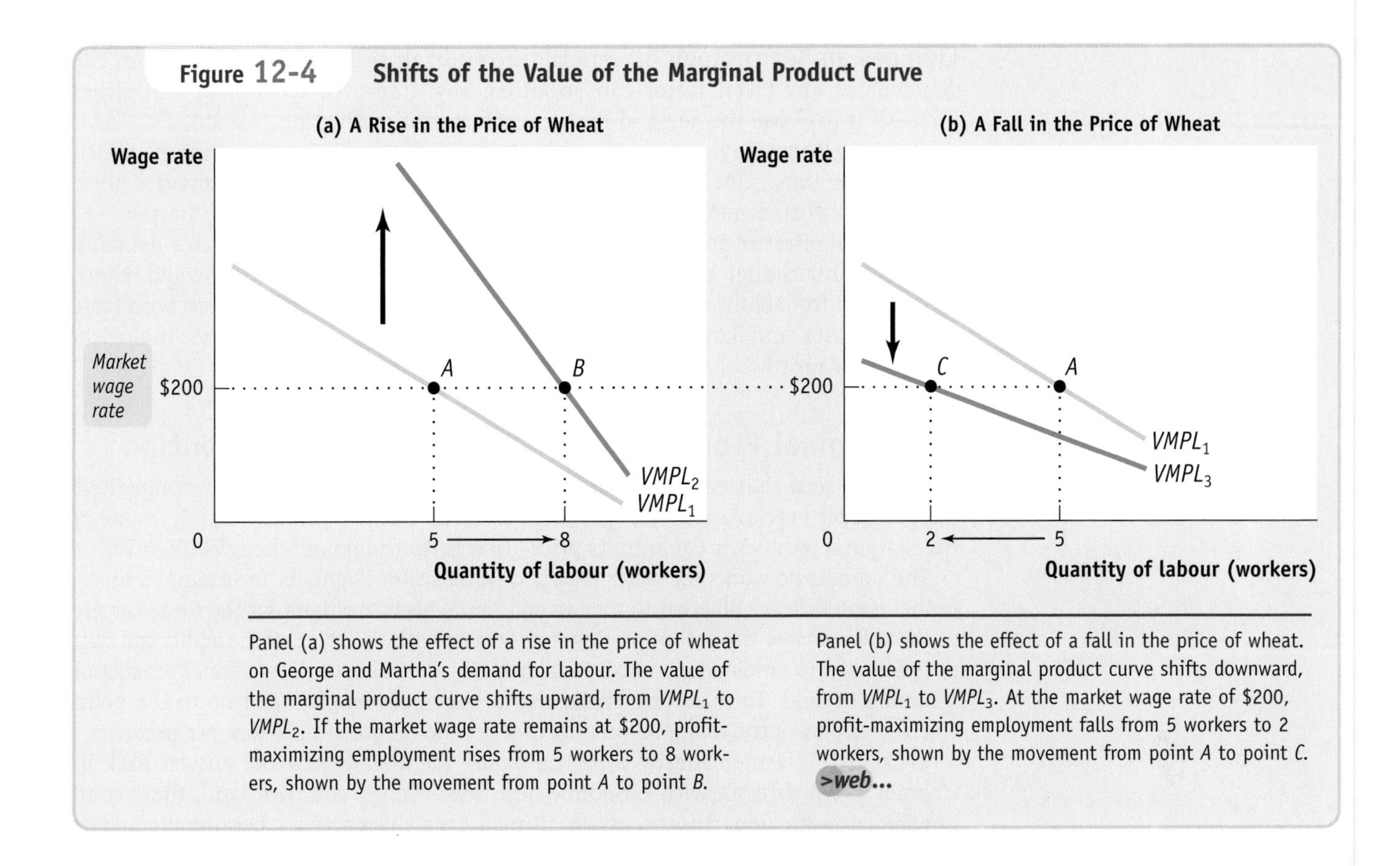

Panel (a) shows the effect of a rise in the price of wheat on George and Martha's demand for labour. The value of the marginal product curve shifts upward, from $VMPL_1$ to $VMPL_2$. If the market wage rate remains at $200, profit-maximizing employment rises from 5 workers to 8 workers, shown by the movement from point *A* to point *B*.

Panel (b) shows the effect of a fall in the price of wheat. The value of the marginal product curve shifts downward, from $VMPL_1$ to $VMPL_3$. At the market wage rate of $200, profit-maximizing employment falls from 5 workers to 2 workers, shown by the movement from point *A* to point *C*. **>web...**

Changes in Prices of Goods Remember that factor demand is derived demand: if the price of the good that is produced with a factor changes, so will the value of the marginal product of the factor. That is, if *P* changes, $VMPL = P \times MPL$ will change at any given level of employment.

Figure 12-4 illustrates the effects of changes in the price of wheat, assuming that $200 is the current wage rate. Panel (a) shows the effect of an *increase* in the price of wheat. This shifts the value of the marginal product curve upward, because *VMPL* rises at any given level of employment. If the wage rate remains unchanged at $200, the optimal point moves from *A* to *B:* the profit-maximizing level of employment rises.

Panel (b) of Figure 12-4 shows the effect of a *decrease* in the price of wheat. This shifts the value of the marginal product curve downward. If the wage rate remains unchanged at $200, the optimal point moves from *A* to *C:* the profit-maximizing level of employment falls.

Changes in Supply of Other Factors Suppose that George and Martha acquire more land to cultivate—say, by clearing a woodland on their property. Each worker could then produce more wheat because each one would have more land to work with. So the marginal product of labour on the farm would rise at any given level of employment. This would have the same effect as an increase in the price of wheat, which we have already seen in panel (a) of Figure 12-4: the value of the marginal product curve would shift upward, and at any given wage rate the profit-maximizing level of employment would increase. Similarly, if George and Martha cultivate less land, the marginal product of labour at any given employment level would fall—each worker would produce less wheat because of having less land to work with. As a result, the value of the marginal product curve would shift downward—as in panel (b) of Figure 12-4—and the profit-maximizing level of employment would decrease.

Changes in Technology In general, the effect of technological progress on the demand for any given factor can go either way: improved technology can either increase or decrease the demand for a given factor of production.

How can technological progress reduce factor demand? Consider horses, which were once an important factor of production. The development of substitutes for horse power, such as automobiles and tractors, greatly reduced the demand for horses.

The usual effect of technological progress, however, is to increase factor demand. In particular, although there have been persistent fears that machinery would reduce the demand for labour, over the long run the Canadian economy has seen both large wage increases and large increases in employment, suggesting that technological progress has greatly increased labour demand.

The Marginal Productivity Theory of Income Distribution

We've now seen that each perfectly competitive producer in a perfectly competitive factor market maximizes profit by hiring labour up to the point at which its value of the marginal product is equal to its price—that is, to the point where *VMPL* = *W*.

The same logic works for other factors of production. Suppose, for example, that a farmer is considering whether to rent an additional hectare of land for the next year. He or she will compare the cost of renting that hectare with the value of the additional output generated by employing an additional hectare—the value of the marginal product of a hectare of land. To maximize profit, the farmer must employ land up to the point where the value of the marginal product of a hectare is equal to the rent per hectare.

What if the farmer already owns the land? We already saw the answer back in Chapter 7, which dealt with economic decisions: even if you own land, there is an implicit cost—the opportunity cost—of using it for a given activity, because it could be used for something else. So a profit-maximizing producer will employ additional acres of land up to the point where the cost of the last hecatre employed, explicit or implicit, is equal to the value of the marginal product of that hectare.

The **rental rate** on either land or capital is the cost, explicit or implicit, of using a unit of that asset for a given period of time.

The same is true for capital. In general, economists say that both land and capital are employed up to the point where the **rental rate**—the cost, explicit or implicit, of using a unit of land or capital for a set period of time—is equal to that unit's value of the marginal product over that time period.

So we have learned that when the markets for goods and services and the factor markets are perfectly competitive, factors of production will be employed up to the point at which their value of the marginal product is equal to their price. What does this say about the factor distribution of income?

Suppose that the labour market is in equilibrium: at the going wage rate, the number of workers that producers want to employ is equal to the number of workers willing to work. Then all employers will pay the *same* wage rate, and *each* employer, whatever he or she is producing, will employ labour up to the point where the value of the marginal product of one more worker is equal to that wage rate.

This situation is illustrated in Figure 12-5, which shows the value of the marginal product curves of two producers—Farmer Jones, who produces wheat, and Farmer Smith, who produces corn. Despite the fact that they produce different products, they compete for the same workers, and so must pay the same wage rate, $200. So when both farmers maximize profit, both hire labour up to the point where its value of the marginal product is equal to the wage rate. In the figure, this corresponds to an employment of 5 workers by Jones and 7 by Smith.

Figure 12-6 illustrates the general situation in the labour market as a whole. The *market labour demand curve,* like the market demand curve for a good (shown in Figure 10-6), is the horizontal sum of all the individual labour demand curves—which is the same as each producer's value of the marginal product curve. For now, let's simply assume an upward-sloping supply curve for labour; we'll discuss labour supply later in this chapter. Then the equilibrium wage rate is the wage rate at which the quantity of labour supplied is equal to the quantity of labour demanded. In

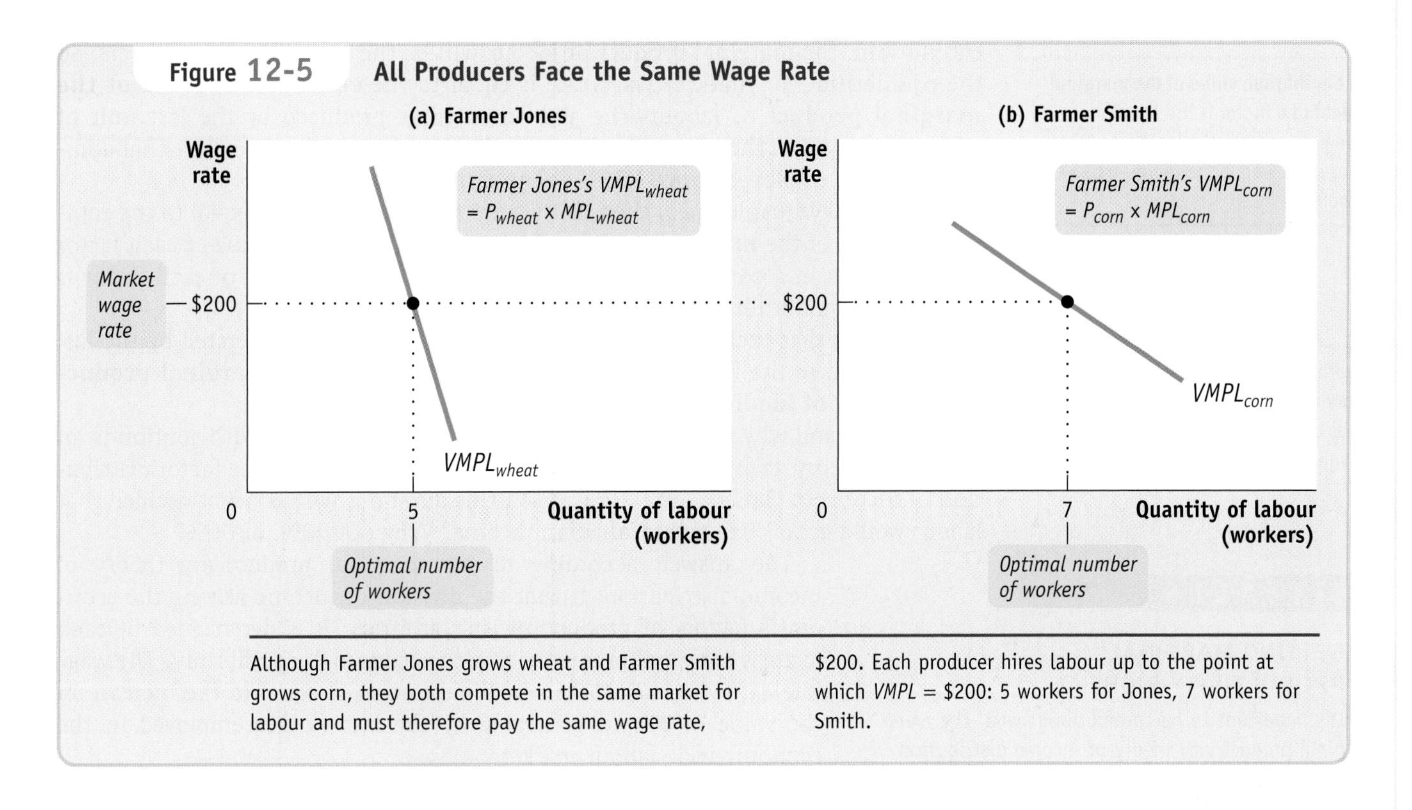

Figure 12-5 **All Producers Face the Same Wage Rate**

Although Farmer Jones grows wheat and Farmer Smith grows corn, they both compete in the same market for labour and must therefore pay the same wage rate, \$200. Each producer hires labour up to the point at which *VMPL* = \$200: 5 workers for Jones, 7 workers for Smith.

Figure 12-6, this equilibrium wage rate is W^* and the corresponding equilibrium employment level is L^*.

And as we showed in the examples of the farms of George and Martha and of Farmer Jones and Farmer Smith (where the equilibrium wage rate corresponds to \$200), each firm will hire labour up to the point at which the value of the marginal product of labour is equal to the equilibrium wage rate. This means that, in

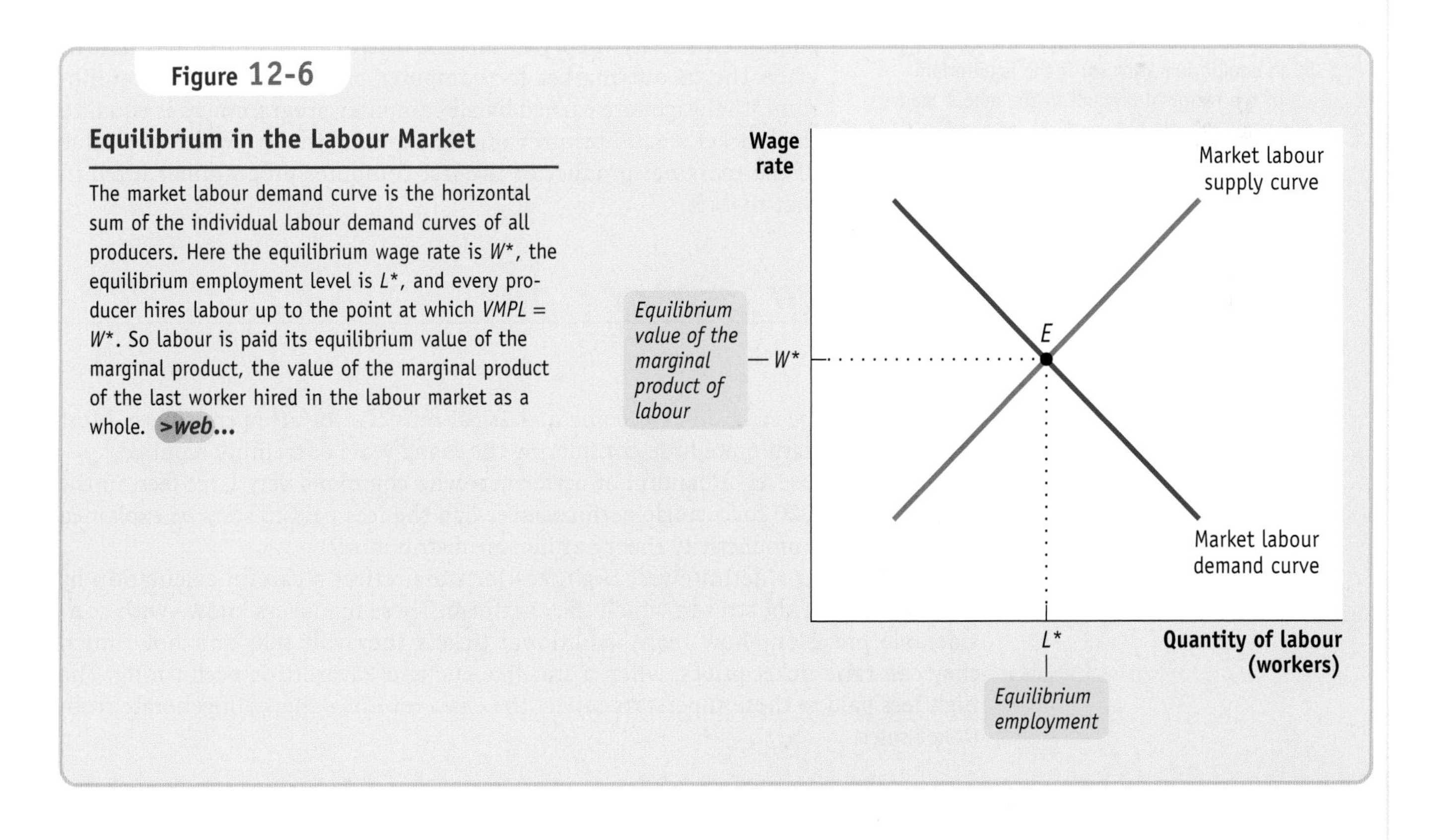

Figure 12-6

Equilibrium in the Labour Market

The market labour demand curve is the horizontal sum of the individual labour demand curves of all producers. Here the equilibrium wage rate is W^*, the equilibrium employment level is L^*, and every producer hires labour up to the point at which $VMPL = W^*$. So labour is paid its equilibrium value of the marginal product, the value of the marginal product of the last worker hired in the labour market as a whole. >web...

The **equilibrium value of the marginal product** of a factor is the additional value produced by the last unit of that factor employed in the factor market as a whole.

According to the **marginal productivity theory of income distribution,** every factor of production is paid its equilibrium value of the marginal product.

equilibrium, the marginal product of labour will be the same for all employers. So the equilibrium (or market) wage rate is equal to the **equilibrium value of the marginal product** of labour—the additional value produced by the last unit of labour employed in the labour market as a whole. It doesn't matter where that additional unit is employed, since *VMPL* is the same for all producers.

What we have just learned, then, is that the market wage rate is equal to the equilibrium value of the marginal product of labour. And the same is true of each factor of production: in a competitive market economy, the market price of each factor is equal to its equilibrium value of the marginal product.

The theory that each factor is paid the value of the output generated by the last unit employed in the factor market as a whole is known as the **marginal productivity theory of income distribution.**

To understand why the marginal productivity theory of income distribution is an important theory, take a look back at Figure 12-1, which showed the factor distribution of income in Canada, and ask yourself this question: who or what decided that labour would get 67% of total Canadian income? Why not 90%, or 50%?

The answer, according to the marginal productivity theory of income distribution, is that the division of income among the economy's factors of production isn't arbitrary: it is determined by each factor's marginal productivity at the economy's equilibrium. The wage rate earned by *all* workers in the economy is equal to the increase in the value of output generated by the last worker employed in the economy-wide labour market.

Here we have assumed that all workers are of the same ability. But in reality workers may differ considerably in ability. Rather than think of one labour market for all workers in the economy, we can instead think of different markets for different types of workers, where workers are of equivalent ability within each market. For example, the market for computer programmers is different from the market for pastry chefs. And in the market for computer programmers, all participants are assumed to have equal ability; likewise for the market for pastry chefs. In this scenario, the marginal productivity theory of income distribution still holds. That is, when the labour market for computer programmers is in equilibrium, the wage rate earned by all computer programmers is equal to the market's equilibrium value of the marginal product—the value of the marginal product of the last computer programmer hired in that market.

PITFALLS

GETTING MARGINAL PRODUCTIVITY RIGHT

It's important to be careful about what the marginal productivity theory of income distribution says: it says that *all* units of a factor get paid the factor's equilibrium value of the marginal product—the additional value produced by the *last* unit of the factor employed.

The most common source of error is to forget that the relevant value of the marginal product is the equilibrium value, not the value of the marginal products you calculate on the way to equilibrium. In looking at Table 12-2, you might be tempted to think that because the first worker has a value of the marginal product of $380 that worker is paid $380 in equilibrium. Not so: if the equilibrium value of the marginal product in the labour market is equal to $200, then *all* workers receive $200.

economics in action

Star Power

If you want to be rich, don't become a classical musician or an opera singer. Most musical artists earn quite little considering the many years of training required.

There are, however, a handful of performers who command very large fees, in the vicinity of $30,000 for a single performance. Can the fees paid to stars be explained by the marginal productivity theory of income distribution?

The answer is a definite yes. High fees for stars reflect a careful calculation by managers of the theatres in which they perform. These managers know—with considerable precision—how many additional tickets they will sell, and how much they can raise ticket prices, when a star like Luciano Pavarotti is performing. The high fees paid to these superstars reflect the extra revenues they will generate from ticket sales.

All this may seem kind of crass—aren't we talking about art and beauty here? Yes, but music—even classical music—is also a business, and the principles of economics apply to opera stars as much as they do to hamburger-flippers. ■

> > > > > > > > > > > > > > > > > >

>> QUICK REVIEW

- In a perfectly competitive market economy, the price of the good multiplied by the marginal product of labour is equal to the *value of the marginal product of labour*: $VMPL = P \times MPL$. A profit-maximizing producer hires labour up to the point at which the value of the marginal product of labour is equal to the wage rate: $VMPL = W$. The *value of the marginal product of labour curve* slopes downward due to diminishing returns to labour in production.
- The market demand curve for labour is the horizontal sum of all the individual demand curves of producers in that market. It shifts for three main reasons: changes in output price, changes in the supply of other factors, and technological progress.
- According to the *marginal productivity theory of income distribution*, in a perfectly competitive economy each factor of production is paid its *equilibrium value of the marginal product*.

>>CHECK YOUR UNDERSTANDING 12-2

1. In the following cases, state the direction of the shift of the demand curve for labour and what will happen, other things equal, to the market equilibrium wage rate and quantity of labour employed as a result.
   a. Service industries, such as home construction, retailing, and banking, experience an increase in demand. These industries use relatively more labour than non-service industries.
   b. Due to overfishing, there is a fall in the amount of fish caught per day by commercial fishers; this decrease affects their demand for workers.
2. Suppose that the price of tractors increases by 50% while the wages in the tractor-manufacturing industry remain unchanged. What is the effect on the number of workers hired?
3. Explain the following statement: "When firms in different industries all compete for the same workers, then the value of the marginal product of the last worker hired will be equal across all firms regardless of whether they are in different industries."

Solutions appear at back of book.

Is the Marginal Productivity Theory of Income Distribution Really True?

Although the marginal productivity theory of income distribution is a well-established part of economic theory, closely linked to the analysis of markets in general, it is a source of some controversy. There are two main objections to it.

First, in the real world we see large disparities in income between factors of production that, in the eyes of some observers, should receive the same payment. Perhaps the most conspicuous examples in Canada are the large differences in the average wages between women and men and among various racial and ethnic groups. Do these wage differences really reflect differences in marginal productivity, or is something else going on?

Second, many people wrongly believe that the marginal productivity theory of income distribution gives a *moral* justification for the distribution of income, implying that the existing distribution is fair and appropriate. (We'll explain in Chapter 13 why this is a misconception.) This misconception sometimes leads people who believe that the current distribution of income is unfair to reject marginal productivity theory.

To address these controversies, we'll start by looking at income disparities across gender and ethnic groups. Then, we'll ask what factors might account for these disparities, and whether these explanations are consistent with the marginal productivity theory of income distribution.

Wage Disparities in Practice

Wage rates in Canada cover a very wide range. In the year 2004, tens of thousands of workers received the legal minimum wage, a rate that varies across provinces from a high of $8.50 in Nunavut to a low of $5.90 in Alberta. At the other extreme, the chief executives of several companies were paid more than $100 million, which is $20,000 per hour even if they worked 100-hour weeks. Even leaving out these extremes, there is a huge range of wage rates. Are people really that different in their marginal productivities?

A particular source of concern is the existence of systematic wage differences across gender and ethnicity. Figure 12-7 (page 308) compares annual median earnings in 2000

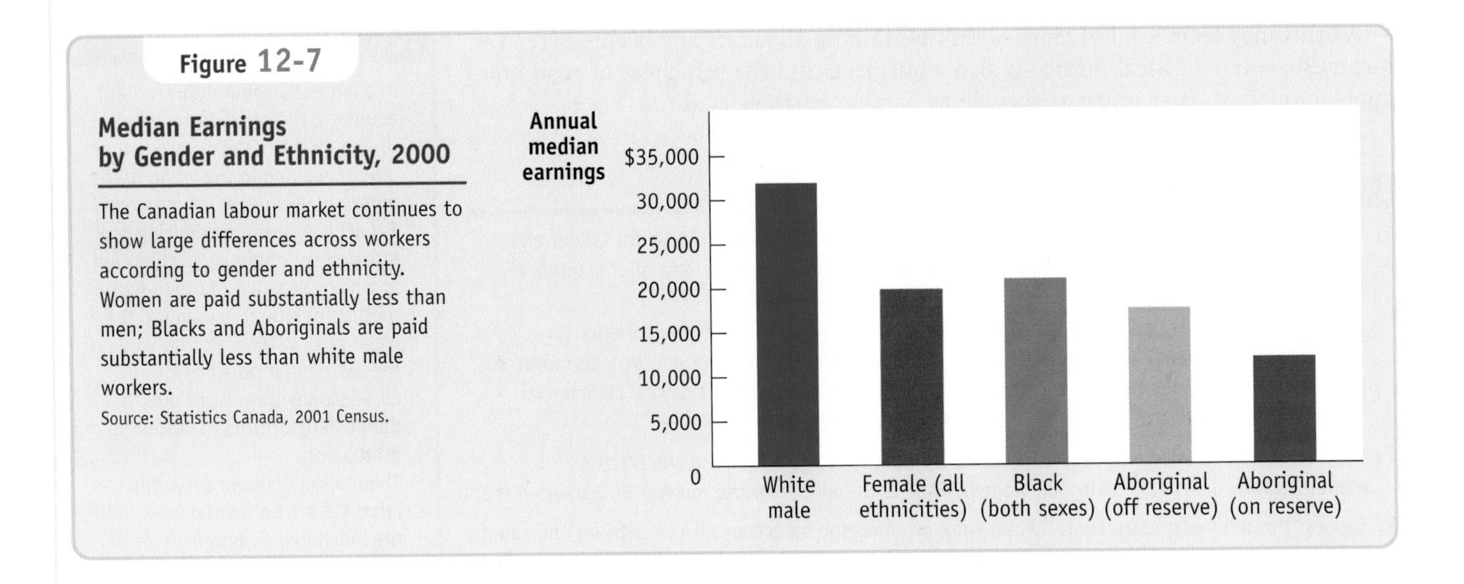

Figure 12-7

Median Earnings by Gender and Ethnicity, 2000

The Canadian labour market continues to show large differences across workers according to gender and ethnicity. Women are paid substantially less than men; Blacks and Aboriginals are paid substantially less than white male workers.

Source: Statistics Canada, 2001 Census.

of workers classified by gender and ethnicity. As a group, white males had the highest earnings. Women (averaging across all ethnicities) earned only about 62% as much; black workers (male and female combined) only 65% as much; aboriginal workers living off reserve only 55% as much; and aboriginal workers living on reserve earned only 37% as much as white males.

Every province in Canada has its own Human Rights Act. While each Act is province-specific, it generally prohibits discrimination on the grounds of sex, race, colour, religion, national origin, ancestry, age, physical disability, marital status, or sexual orientation. These Acts apply to many aspects of social life, including all aspects of employment. Moreover, they are not just paper tigers—they are backed up by provincial commissions with investigative and judicial powers.

In the face of this legal framework promoting non-discrimination, why does pay vary systematically by sex and race? Let's start with the marginal productivity explanations, then look at other influences.

Marginal Productivity and Wage Inequality

A large part of the observed inequality in wages can be explained by considerations that are consistent with the marginal productivity theory of income distribution. In particular, there are three well-understood sources of wage differences across occupations and individuals.

Compensating differentials are wage differences across jobs that reflect the fact that some jobs are less pleasant than others.

First is the existence of **compensating differentials:** across different types of jobs, wages are often higher or lower depending on how attractive or unattractive the job is. Workers with unpleasant or dangerous jobs demand a higher wage in comparison to workers with jobs that require the same skill and effort but lack the unpleasant or dangerous qualities. For example, truck-drivers who haul hazardous loads are paid more than drivers who haul normal loads. But for any *given* job, the marginal productivity theory of income distribution holds true. For example, hazardous-load truck-drivers are paid a wage equal to the equilibrium value of the marginal product of the last person employed in the market for hazardous-load drivers.

A second reason for wage inequality that is clearly consistent with marginal productivity theory is differences in talent. People differ in their abilities: a high-ability person, by producing a better product that commands a higher price compared to a lower-ability person, generates a higher value of the marginal product. And these differences in the value of the marginal product translate into differences in earning potential. We all know that this is true in sports: practice is important, but 99.9% of the population just doesn't have what it takes to hit golf balls like Tiger Woods or figure skate like Jamie Salé and David Pelletier (who won gold medals in the 2002 Winter Olympics). The same is true, though less obvious, in other fields of endeavour.

A third, very important reason for wage differences is differences in the quantity of *human capital*. Recall that human capital—education and training—is at least as important in the modern economy as physical capital in the form of buildings and machines. Different people "embody" quite different quantities of human capital, and a person with a higher quantity of human capital typically generates a higher value of the marginal product by producing a product that commands a higher price. So differences in human capital account for substantial differences in wages. People with high levels of human capital, such as skilled surgeons or engineers, generally receive high wages.

The most direct way to see the effect of human capital on wages is to look at the relationship between educational levels and earnings. As far as earnings go, the best degree is in commerce, management, or business administration, while the worst is in humanities. Figure 12-8 shows earnings differentials by gender and education. In particular, it shows earnings for the most highly rewarded degree (business administration), the least rewarded degree (humanities), and no degree, for the year 2000. While the figure brings out the fact that not all BA's have an equal impact on earnings, it remains true that, regardless of gender, higher education is associated with higher median earnings. For example, in 2000, females with a BA in the humanities had median earnings 30% higher than females without a university degree, and females with a university degree in commerce, management, or business administration had earnings 61% higher than females without a degree.

Because even now—on average in the working population—men typically have had more years of education than women, and whites have had more years of education than non-whites, differences in level of education are part of the explanation for the earnings differences shown in Figure 12-7.

It's also important to realize that formal education is not the only source of human capital; on-the-job training and experience are also very important. For example, in 2000 women with degrees in engineering and applied sciences earned on average about 40% less than men with equivalent degrees. But the influx of women into engineering is a relatively recent phenomenon. As a result, women in engineering are, on average, younger than men and have considerably less experience than their male counterparts. This difference in age and experience explains most of the earnings differential in this occupational group.

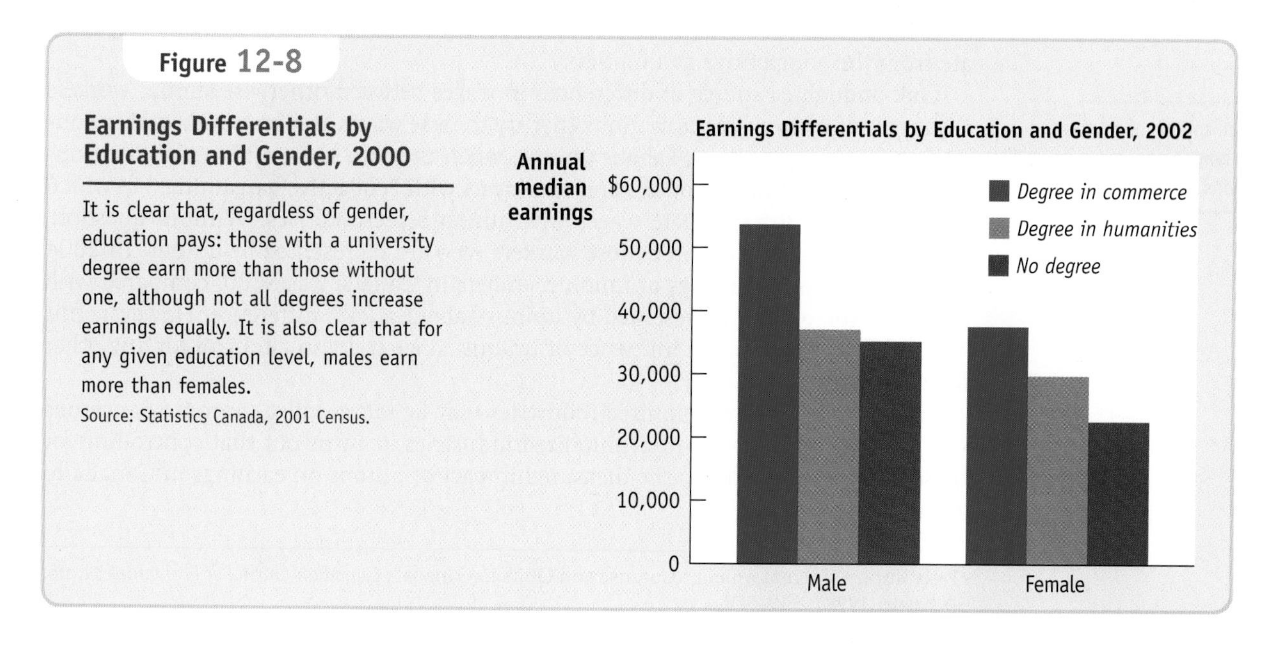

Figure 12-8

Earnings Differentials by Education and Gender, 2000

It is clear that, regardless of gender, education pays: those with a university degree earn more than those without one, although not all degrees increase earnings equally. It is also clear that for any given education level, males earn more than females.

Source: Statistics Canada, 2001 Census.

Differences in job tenure and work experience can partly explain one notable aspect of Figure 12-8: that, across all education categories, women's median earnings are less than men's median earnings for any given education level.

However, it is also important to emphasize that earnings differences that arise from differences in human capital are not necessarily "fair". For example, a society in which some children typically receive poor education because they live in poor neighbourhoods, or where only some children can afford to go to university, may have labour markets that are well described by marginal productivity theory. Yet most people would still consider the resulting distribution of income unfair.

Similarly, in the context of male-female earnings differentials, men have better job tenure and work experience than women partly because women still bear primary responsibility for child-care. Therefore, it is women (not men) who typically take time off work when a child is sick and find it necessary to interrupt their careers to have children. As a result, women are more likely than men to work part-time, to leave the workforce, and to be absent from work—all of which negatively affect their earnings. Many analysts define "systemic" discrimination as the cultural ambience that prescribes that women "should" bear primary responsibility for child care, and defines some jobs, and their associated training, as male-appropriate and some as female-appropriate.

All of this is to say that the distribution of human capital (including job experience) between different groups in society may reflect embedded and sometimes subtle (and sometimes not-so-subtle) forms of discrimination.

In sum, compensating differentials, differences in talent, and differences in human capital explain part of observed wage differentials. While these explanations are consistent with marginal productivity theory, they do not necessarily imply that the labour market is "fair" or free from discrimination. Furthermore, many observers feel that differences in marginal productivity do not explain all wage differentials. They believe that market power, *efficiency wages,* and overt discrimination also play an important role. We will examine these forces next.

Market Power

The marginal productivity theory of income distribution is based on the assumption that factor markets are perfectly competitive. In such markets we can expect workers to be paid the equilibrium value of their marginal product, regardless of who they are. But how valid is this assumption?

We haven't yet studied markets that are *not* perfectly competitive (we'll get there in Chapter 14), but let's touch briefly on the ways in which labour markets may deviate from the competitive assumption.

Unions are organizations of workers that try to raise wages and improve working conditions for their members.

One undoubted source of differences in wages between otherwise similar workers is the role of **unions**—organizations that try to raise wages and improve working conditions for their members. Labour unions, when they are successful, replace one-on-one wage deals between workers and employers with "collective bargaining," in which the employer must negotiate wages with union representatives. Without question, this leads to higher wages for those workers who are represented by unions. In 2004 the average weekly earnings of union members in Canada was \$780, compared with \$630 for workers not represented by unions—about a 24% difference. However, this statistic may overstate the influence of unions, since it doesn't control for any other factors influencing wages.

For example, jobs in unionized industries may be more skilled, or more dangerous (on average) than jobs in non-unionized industries. It turns out that controlling for these other factors reduces the measured impact of unions on earnings in Canada to around 15%.[1]

[1]Peter Kuhn, "Unemployment Insurance and Quits in Canada", *Canadian Journal of Economics* 31, no. 3 (August 1998): 549–572.

Just as workers can sometimes organize to extract higher wages than they would otherwise receive, employers may be able to pay *lower* wages than would result from competition. The clearest examples of employers having market power, and paying *lower* wages than would result from competition, occur in one-industry towns in regions of the country with relatively high unemployment rates. In these situations, worker options may be limited to either accepting the company's wage offer or uprooting their families and moving away.

Efficiency Wages

A second reason why wages may not reflect marginal productivity is the phenomenon of *efficiency wages*—a type of incentive scheme to motivate workers to work hard and reduce worker turnover. Suppose that a worker performs a job that is extremely important but in which the employer can observe only at infrequent intervals how well the job is being performed—say, serving as a caretaker for the employer's child. Then it often makes sense for the employer to pay more than the worker could earn in an alternative job—that is, more than the equilibrium wage. Why? Because earning a premium makes losing this job and having to take the alternative job quite costly for the worker. So a worker who happens to be observed performing poorly and is therefore fired is now worse off for having to accept a lower-paying job. The threat of losing a job that pays a premium motivates the worker to perform well and avoid being fired. Likewise, paying a premium also reduces worker turnover—the frequency with which an employee leaves a job voluntarily. Despite the fact that it may take no more effort and skill to be a child's caretaker than to be an office worker, efficiency wages show why it often makes economic sense for a parent to pay a caretaker more than the equilibrium wage of an office worker.

The **efficiency-wage model** explains why we may observe wages offered above their equilibrium level. Like the price floors that we studied in Chapter 4—and, in particular, much like the minimum wage—this phenomenon leads to a surplus of labour supplied in the markets for labour that are characterized by the efficiency wage model. This surplus of labour translates into unemployment—some workers are actively searching for a high-paying efficiency-wage job but are unable to get one, and other workers, more fortunate but no more deserving, are able to acquire one. As a result, two workers with exactly the same profile—the same skills and same job history—may earn unequal wages; that is, the one who is lucky enough to get an efficiency-wage job earns more than the worker who gets a standard job (or who remains unemployed while searching for a higher-paying job). Efficiency wages are a type of market failure that arises from the real-world fact that some employees don't always perform as well as they should and are able to hide that fact. As a result, employers use non-equilibrium wages in order to motivate their employees, leading to an inefficient outcome.

According to the **efficiency-wage model,** some employers pay an above-equilibrium wage as an incentive for better performance.

Discrimination

It is a real and ugly fact that throughout history there has been discrimination against workers who are considered to be the wrong race, ethnicity, or gender. How does this fit into our economic models?

The main insight economic analysis offers is that discrimination is *not* a natural consequence of market competition. On the contrary, market forces tend to work against discrimination. To see why, consider the incentives that would exist if social convention dictated that women be paid, say, 30% less than men with equivalent qualifications and experience. A company whose management was itself unbiased would then be able to reduce its costs by hiring women rather than men—and such companies would have an advantage over other companies that hired men despite their higher cost. The result would be to create an excess demand for female workers, which would tend to drive up their wages.

But if market competition works against discrimination, how is it that so much discrimination has taken place? The answer is four-fold.

First, most obviously, the above argument does not apply when workers serve the public directly (in sales, for example), and the general public prefers not to be served by the discriminated-against group.

Second, the argument does not apply when the discrimination is "justified" on statistical grounds. For example, firms know that young women have a probability of having children, and that they are still the primary caregivers for children. As a result, women are more likely than men to take parental leave and are more likely than men to be absent from work when their children are sick—both of which will adversely affect profits. Even though provincial Human Rights Codes explicitly forbid discrimination on the basis of sex or pregnancy, statistical discrimination is almost impossible to prove.

Third, the argument does not apply when labour markets don't work well. Whenever there are more job applicants than there are jobs, employers are free to discriminate among applicants without hurting their profits. This may be caused by microeconomic, macroeconomic, or regional factors. On the micro side, either market interference (such as unions or minimum-wage laws) or market failures (such as efficiency wages) can lead to wages that are above their equilibrium levels. On the macro side, deep recessions coupled with slow recoveries could lead to long periods of excessive unemployment. Finally, a particular region may suffer excessive unemployment if its dominant industries are declining faster than the population can outmigrate (or new industries replace the old).

Finally, if the discrimination is institutionalized in the form of government policy it will be easier to resist market pressure. The Economics in Action that follows this section illustrates the way government policy enforced discrimination in the world's most famous racist regime, that of South Africa.

So Does Marginal Productivity Theory Work?

The main conclusion you should draw from this discussion is that marginal productivity theory is not a perfect description of how factor incomes are determined but that it works pretty well. The deviations are important. But, by and large, in a modern economy with well-functioning labour markets, factors of production are paid the equilibrium value of the marginal product—the value of the marginal product of the last unit employed in the market as a whole.

It's important to emphasize, once again, that this does not mean that the factor distribution of income is morally justified. We'll turn to issues of fairness and equity in Chapter 13.

Joao Silva

South Africa is a democracy now, but the human legacy of apartheid persists.

economics in action

The Economics of Apartheid

The Republic of South Africa is the richest nation in Africa, but it also has a harsh political history. Until the peaceful transition to majority rule in 1994, the country was controlled by its white minority, Afrikaners, the descendants of European (mainly Dutch) immigrants. This minority imposed an economic system known as apartheid, which overwhelmingly favoured white interests over those of native Africans and other groups considered "non-white", such as Asians.

The origins of apartheid go back to the early years of the twentieth century, when large numbers of white farmers began moving into South Africa's growing cities. There they discovered, to their horror, that they did not automatically earn higher wages than other races. But they had the right to vote and non-whites did not. And so the South African government instituted "job-reservation" laws designed to ensure that only whites got jobs that paid well. The government also set about creating jobs for whites in government-owned industries. As Allister Sparks notes in *The Mind of South Africa* (1990), in its efforts to provide high-paying jobs for whites, the country "eventually acquired the largest amount of nationalized industry of any country outside the Communist bloc."

In other words, racial discrimination was possible because it was backed by the power of the government, which prevented markets from following their natural course.

A postscript: in 1994, in one of the political miracles of modern times, the white regime ceded power and South Africa became a full-fledged democracy. Apartheid was abolished. Unfortunately, large racial differences in earnings remain. The main reason is that apartheid created huge disparities in human capital, which will probably persist for many years to come. ▪

>> QUICK REVIEW

- Existing large disparities in wages both among individuals and across groups lead some to question the marginal productivity theory of income distribution.
- *Compensating differentials,* as well as differences in the values of the marginal products of workers that arise from differences in talent, job experience, and human capital, account for some wage disparities.
- Market power, in the form of *unions* or collective action by employers, as well as the *efficiency-wage model,* also explain how some wage disparities arise.
- Discrimination has historically been a major factor in wage disparities. Market competition tends to work against discrimination.

>> CHECK YOUR UNDERSTANDING 12-3

1. Assess each of the following statements. Do you think they are true, false, or ambiguous? Explain.
   a. The marginal productivity theory of income distribution is inconsistent with the presence of income disparities associated with gender, race, or ethnicity.
   b. Companies that engage in workplace discrimination but whose competitors do not are likely to have lower profits as a result of their actions.
   c. Workers who are paid less because they have less experience are not the victims of discrimination.

Solutions appear at back of book.

The Supply of Labour

Up to this point we have focused on the demand for factors, which determines the quantities demanded of labour, capital, or land by producers as a function of their factor prices. What about the supply of factors?

In this section we focus exclusively on the supply of labour. We do this for two reasons. First, in the modern Canadian economy, labour is the most important factor of production, accounting for most of factor income. Second, as we'll see, labour supply is the area in which factor markets look most different from markets for goods and services.

Work versus Leisure

In the labour market, the roles of firms and households are the reverse of what they are in markets for goods and services. On the one hand, a good such as wheat is supplied by firms and demanded by households; on the other hand, labour is demanded by firms and supplied by households. How do people decide how much labour to supply?

As a practical matter, most people have limited control over their work hours: either you take a job that involves working a set number of hours per week, or you don't get the job at all. To understand the logic of labour supply, however, it helps to put realism to one side for a bit and imagine an individual who can choose to work as many or as few hours as he or she likes.

Why wouldn't such an individual work as many hours as possible? Because workers are human beings, too, and have other uses for their time. An hour spent on the job is an hour not spent on other, presumably more pleasant, activities. So the decision about how much labour to supply involves making a decision about **time allocation**—how many hours to spend on different activities.

Decisions about labour supply result from decisions about **time allocation:** how many hours to spend on different activities.

By working, people earn income that they can use to buy goods. The more hours an individual works, the more goods he or she can afford to buy. But this increased

Leisure is time available for purposes other than earning money to buy marketed goods.

purchasing power comes at the expense of a reduction in **leisure,** the time spent not working. (Leisure doesn't necessarily mean time goofing off. It could mean time spent with one's family, pursuing hobbies, exercising, and so on.) And though purchased goods yield utility, so does leisure; indeed, we can think of leisure itself as a normal good, which most people would like to consume more of as their incomes increase.

How does a rational individual decide how much leisure to consume? By making a marginal comparison, of course. In analysing consumer choice, we asked how a utility-maximizing consumer uses a marginal *dollar.* In analysing labour supply, we ask how an individual uses a marginal *hour.*

Consider Clive, an individual who likes both leisure and the goods money can buy. And suppose that his wage rate is $10 per hour. In deciding how many hours he wants to work, he must compare the marginal utility of an additional hour of leisure with the additional utility he gets from $10 worth of goods. If $10 worth of goods adds more to his total utility than an additional hour of leisure, he can increase his total utility by giving up an hour of leisure in order to work an additional hour. If an extra hour of leisure adds more to his total utility than $10 in income, he can increase his total utility by working one fewer hour in order to gain an hour of leisure.

At Clive's optimal labour supply choice, then, his marginal utility of one hour of leisure is equal to the marginal utility he gets from the goods that his hourly wage can purchase. This is very similar to the *optimal consumption rule* we encountered in Chapter 10, except that it is a rule about time rather than money.

Our next step is to ask how Clive's decision about time allocation is affected when his wage rate changes.

Wages and Labour Supply

Suppose that Clive's wage rate doubles, from $10 per hour to $20 per hour. How will he change his time allocation?

You could argue that Clive will work longer hours, because his incentive to work has increased: by giving up an hour of leisure he can now gain twice as much money as before. But you could equally well argue that he will work less, because he doesn't need to work as many hours to generate the income to pay for the goods he wants.

As these opposing arguments suggest, the quantity of labour Clive supplies can either rise or fall when his wage rate rises. To understand why, let's recall the distinction between *substitution effects* and *income effects* that we learned in Chapters 10 and 11. We saw there that a price change affects consumer choice in two ways: by changing the opportunity cost of a good in terms of other goods (the substitution effect) and by making the consumer richer or poorer (the income effect).

Now think about how a rise in Clive's wage rate affects his demand for leisure. On the one hand, the opportunity cost of leisure—the amount of money he gives up by taking an hour off instead of working—rises. That substitution effect gives him an incentive, other things equal, to consume less leisure and work longer hours. But on the other hand, a higher wage rate makes Clive richer—and this income effect leads him, other things equal, to want to consume *more* leisure and supply less labour, because leisure is a normal good.

So in the case of labour supply, the substitution effect and the income effect work in opposite directions. If the substitution effect is so powerful that it dominates the income effect, an increase in Clive's wage rate leads him to supply more hours of labour. If the income effect is so powerful that it dominates the substitution effect, an increase in the wage rate leads him to supply *fewer* hours of labour.

The **individual labour supply curve** shows how the quantity of labour supplied by an individual depends on that individual's wage rate.

We see, then, that the **individual labour supply curve**—the relationship between the wage rate and the number of hours of labour supplied by an individual worker—is not necessarily upward sloping. If the income effect dominates, a higher wage rate will reduce the quantity of labour supplied.

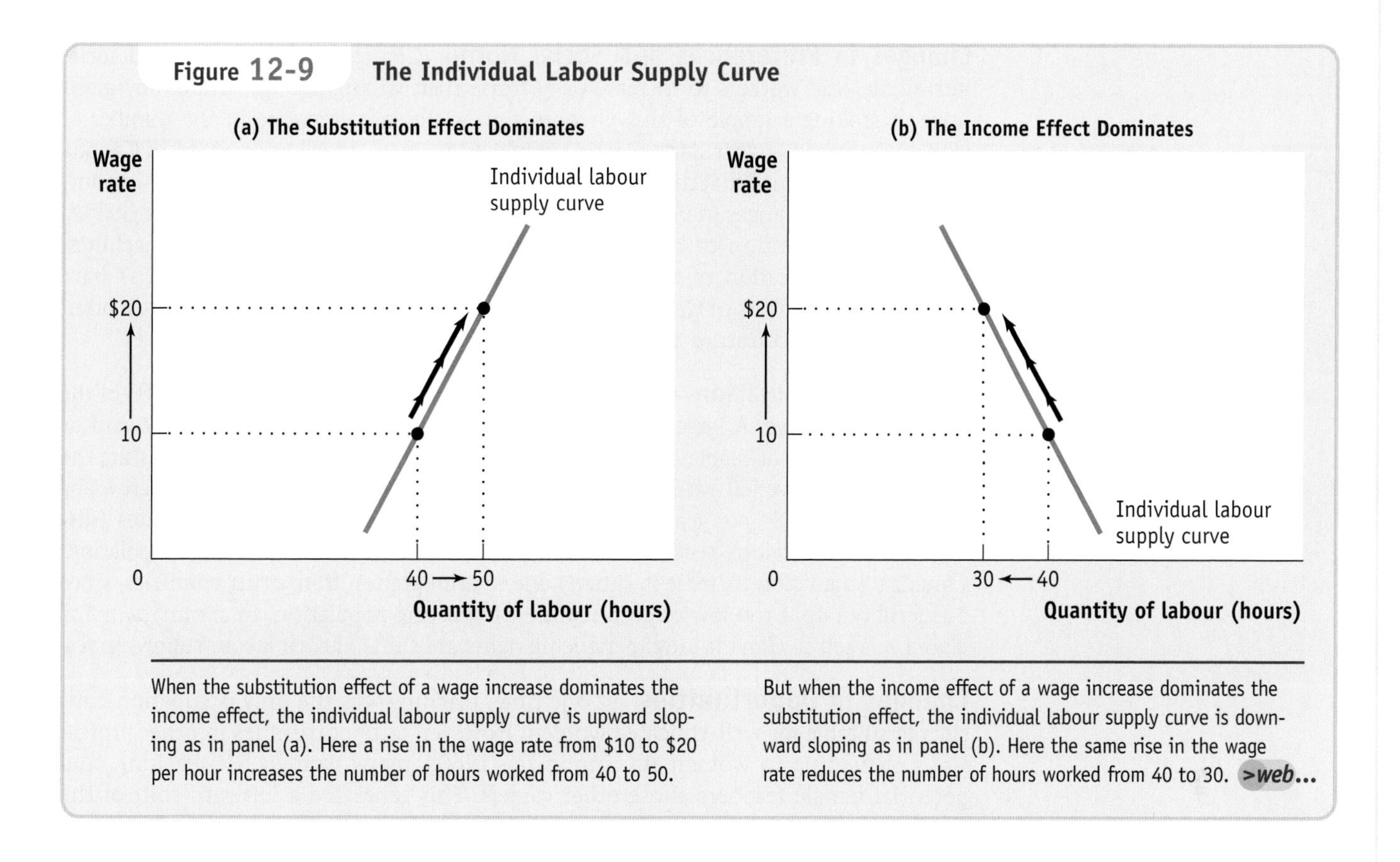

Figure 12-9 The Individual Labour Supply Curve

When the substitution effect of a wage increase dominates the income effect, the individual labour supply curve is upward sloping as in panel (a). Here a rise in the wage rate from $10 to $20 per hour increases the number of hours worked from 40 to 50. But when the income effect of a wage increase dominates the substitution effect, the individual labour supply curve is downward sloping as in panel (b). Here the same rise in the wage rate reduces the number of hours worked from 40 to 30. **>*web*...**

Figure 12-9 illustrates the two possibilities for labour supply. If the substitution effect dominates the income effect, the individual labour supply curve slopes upward; panel (a) shows an increase in the wage rate from $10 to $20 per hour leading to a rise in the number of hours worked from 40 to 50. However, if the income effect dominates, the quantity of labour supplied goes down when the wage rate increases. Panel (b) shows the same rise in the wage rate leading to a *fall* in the number of hours worked from 40 to 30. (Economists refer to an individual labour supply curve that contains both upward-sloping and downward-sloping segments as a "backward-bending labour supply curve"—a concept that we analyse in detail in this chapter's appendix.)

Is a negative response of the quantity of labour supplied to the wage rate a real possibility? Yes: many labour economists believe that income effects on the supply of labour may be somewhat stronger than substitution effects. The most compelling piece of evidence for this belief comes from Canadians' increasing consumption of leisure over the past century. At the end of the nineteenth century, wages adjusted for inflation were only about one-eighth what they are today; the typical work week was 70 hours, and very few workers retired at 65. Today the typical work week is less than 40 hours, and most people retire at 65 or earlier. So it seems that Canadians have chosen to take advantage of higher wages in part by consuming more leisure.

Shifts in the Labour Supply Curve

Now that we have examined how income and substitution effects shape the individual labour supply curve, we can turn to the market labour supply curve. In any labour market, the market supply curve is the horizontal sum of the individual labour supply curves of all workers in that market. A change in any factor *other than the wage* that alters workers' willingness to supply labour causes a shift of the labour supply curve. A variety of factors can lead to such shifts, including changes in preferences and social norms, changes in population, changes in opportunities, and changes in wealth.

Changes in Preferences and Social Norms Changes in preferences and social norms can lead workers to increase or decrease their willingness to work at any given wage. A striking example of this phenomenon is the large increase in the number of employed women—particularly married employed women—that has occurred in Canada since the 1960s. Until that time, women who could afford to largely avoided working outside the home. Changes in preferences and norms in post-World War II Canada (helped along by the invention of labour-saving home appliances such as washing machines, increasing urbanization of the population, and higher female education levels) have induced large numbers of Canadian women to join the workforce—a phenomenon often repeated in other countries that experience similar social and technological forces.

Changes in Population Changes in the population size generally lead to shifts of the labour supply curve. A larger population tends to shift the labour supply rightward as more workers are available at any given wage; a smaller population tends to shift the labour supply curve leftward. Currently the size of the Canadian labour force grows by approximately 1.7% per year—partly as a result of increasing participation rates (discussed in the previous section) but mostly as a result of an increasing population. Canada's population increase is entirely due to immigration from other countries, since our fertility rate is too low to even replace the existing population. In summary, many labour markets in Canada are experiencing rightward shifts of their labour supply curves.

Changes in Opportunities At one time, teaching was the only occupation considered suitable for well-educated women. However, as opportunities in other professions opened up to women starting in the 1960s, many women left teaching, and potential female teachers chose other careers. This generated a leftward shift of the supply curve for teachers, reflecting a fall in the willingness to work at any given wage and forcing school districts to pay more to maintain an adequate teaching staff. These events illustrate a general result: when superior alternatives arise for workers in another labour market, the supply curve in the original labour market shifts leftward as workers move to the new opportunities. Similarly, when opportunities diminish in one labour market—say, layoffs in the manufacturing industry occur because of increased foreign competition—the supply in alternative labour markets increases as workers move to these other markets.

Changes in Wealth A person whose wealth increases will buy more normal goods, including leisure. So when a class of workers experiences a general rise in wealth levels—say, due to a stock market boom—the income effect from the wealth increase will shift the labour supply curve associated with those workers leftward as workers

FOR INQUIRING MINDS

WHY YOU CAN'T FIND A CAB WHEN IT'S RAINING

Everyone says that you can't find a taxi when you really need one—say, when it's raining. That could be because everyone else is trying to get a taxi at the same time. But according to a study published in the *Quarterly Journal of Economics,* it's more than that: cab drivers actually go home early when it's raining.

The reason is that the hourly wage rate of a taxi driver depends on the weather: when it's raining, drivers get more fares, and therefore earn more per hour. And it seems that the income effect of this higher wage rate outweighs the substitution effect.

This behaviour leads the authors of the study to question drivers' rationality. They point out that if taxi drivers thought in terms of the long run, they would realize that rainy days and nice days tend to average out, and that their high earnings on a rainy day don't really affect their long-run income very much. Indeed, experienced drivers (who have probably figured this out) are less likely than inexperienced drivers to go home early on a rainy day. But leaving such issues to one side, the study does seem to show clear evidence of a labour supply curve that slopes downward instead of upward, thanks to income effects.[2]

[2]Source article: Colin Camerer et al., "Labor Supply of New York City Cabdrivers: One Day at a Time", *Quarterly Journal of Economics* 112 (May 1997): 407–441.

consume more leisure and work less. Note that *the income effect caused by a change in wealth shifts the labour supply curve,* but the *income effect from a wage increase—*as we discussed in the case of the individual labour supply curve—*is a movement along the labour supply curve.* The following Economics in Action illustrates how such a change in the wealth levels of many families during the late 1990s led to a shift in the labour supply curve associated with their employable children.

economics in action

The Decline and Rise of the Summer Job in Canada

During the boom years of the 1990s, fewer young Canadians decided to take summer jobs. According to theory, changes in family wealth could be responsible. Perhaps the economic and stock market boom in the 1990s made many more Canadian families affluent—affluent enough so that their children no longer felt under pressure to make an additional contribution by working all summer. How well does this explanation fit the facts?

Figure 12-10 shows the percentage of Canadians between the ages of 15 and 19 who were in the summer workforce. This percentage declined from 76% in 1989 to 61% in 1997, after which it gradually increased, so that by 2003 it was back to 69%.

Changes in family wealth may well play an important part in explaining these movements. But the trouble with the family wealth explanation is that the low point of teenage participation rates (1997) doesn't coincide with the high point in North American stock markets (March 2000). This suggests that other influences were at work besides changes in family wealth. What could they be?

One possibility is the increasing cost of a university degree. For example, average undergraduate fees have risen by nearly 180% between 1990 and 2003. Perhaps these rising costs began to offset increasing stock market affluence around 1997.

Another possibility is that the economic boom of the late 1990s may have made more summer jobs available, drawing teenagers into the summer workforce despite increasing levels of family wealth.

Allowing for these extra influences provides a fuller explanation, but does not negate the influence of family wealth, which seems to have its predicted effect—increases in wealth tending to shift the labour supply curve to the left. ▪

>> QUICK REVIEW

- The choice of how much labour to supply is a problem of *time allocation:* a choice between work and *leisure.*
- A rise in the wage rate causes both an income and a substitution effect on an individual's labour supply. The substitution effect of a higher wage rate induces longer work hours, other things equal. This is countered by the income effect: higher income leads to a higher demand for leisure, a normal good. If the income effect dominates, a rise in the wage rate can actually cause the *individual labour supply curve* to slope the "wrong" way: downward.
- The market labour supply curve is the horizontal sum of the individual supply curves of all workers in that market. It shifts for four main reasons: changes in preferences and social norms, changes in population, changes in opportunities, and changes in wealth.

Figure 12-10

The Percentage of Canadians Between the Ages of 15 and 19 in the Summer Workforce, 1989–1997

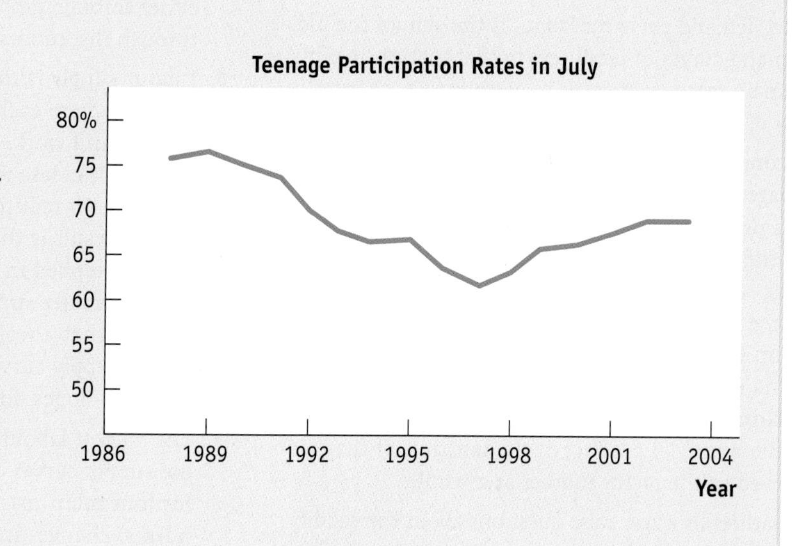

The percentage of Canadians between ages 15 and 19 in the summer workforce declined from 76% in 1989 to 61% in 1997, after which the percentage gradually increased again to 69% in 2003. One explanation is that the stock market boom made Canadian families feel more affluent, reducing the necessity for teenagers to take summer jobs. However, the timing of the rebound in participation rates (after reaching a low point in 1997) suggests the importance of other influences as well.

>>CHECK YOUR UNDERSTANDING 12-4

1. Formerly, Clive was free to choose to work as many or as few hours per week as he wanted. But a new law limits the maximum number of hours he can work per week to 35. Explain under what circumstances, if at all, he is made:
   a. Worse off
   b. Equally as well off
   c. Better off
2. Explain in terms of the income and substitution effects how a fall in Clive's wage can induce him to work more hours than before.

Solutions appear at back of book.

• A LOOK AHEAD •

We have now put together all the pieces for understanding how a perfectly competitive market economy works. We've seen how supply and demand determine market prices, how profit maximization gives rise to the supply curve for each good, and how utility maximization gives rise to the demand curve. We've also just seen how factor markets determine the prices of factors of production and therefore the factor incomes of individuals.

But the ultimate purpose of an economy is to provide people with what they want. How well does a market economy do that job? In the next chapter we finally examine the *efficiency* of a market economy and the related but different question of *equity*.

SUMMARY

1. Just as there are markets for goods and services, there are markets for factors of production, including labour, land, and both **physical capital** and **human capital.** These markets determine the **factor distribution of income.**
2. Profit-maximizing price-taking producers will employ a factor up to the point at which its price is equal to its **value of the marginal product**—the marginal product of the factor multiplied by the price of the good. The **value of the marginal product curve** is therefore the individual price-taking producer's demand curve for a factor.
3. The market demand curve for labour is the sum of the individual demand curves of producers in that market. It shifts for three main reasons: changes in output price, changes in the supply of other factors, and technological changes.
4. When a competitive labour market is in equilibrium, the market wage is equal to the **equilibrium value of the marginal product** of labour, the additional value produced by the last worker hired in the labour market as a whole. The same principle applies to other factors of production: the **rental rate** of land or capital is equal to the equilibrium value of the marginal products. This insight leads to the **marginal productivity theory of income distribution,** according to which each factor is paid the value of the marginal product of the last unit of that factor employed in the factor market as a whole.
5. Large disparities in wages raise questions about the validity of the marginal productivity theory of income distribution. Many disparities can be explained by **compensating differentials** and by differences in talent, job experience, and human capital across workers. Market interference in the forms of **unions** and collective action by employers also create wage disparities. The **efficiency-wage model,** which arises from a type of market failure, shows how wage disparities can arise from employers' attempts to increase worker performance. Free markets tend to diminish discrimination, but discrimination remains a real source of wage disparity. Discrimination is typically maintained either through problems in labour markets or (historically) through institutionalization in government policies.
6. Labour supply is the result of decisions about **time allocation,** where each worker faces a trade-off between **leisure** and work. An increase in the hourly wage rate tends to increase work hours by the substitution effect but tends to reduce work hours by the income effect. If the net result is that a worker increases the quantity of labour supplied in response to a higher wage, the **individual labour supply** curve slopes upward. If the net result is that a worker reduces work hours, the individual labour supply curve—unlike supply curves for goods and services—slopes downward.
7. The market labour supply curve is the sum of the individual supply curves of all workers in that market. It shifts for four main reasons: changes in preferences and social norms, changes in population, changes in opportunities, and changes in wealth.

KEY TERMS

Physical capital, p. 296
Human capital, p. 296
Factor distribution of income, p. 297
Value of the marginal product, p. 300
Value of the marginal product curve, p. 301
Rental rate, p. 304
Equilibrium value of the marginal product, p. 306
Marginal productivity theory of income distribution, p. 306
Compensating differentials, p. 308
Unions, p. 310
Efficiency-wage model, p. 311
Time allocation, p. 313
Leisure, p. 314
Individual labour supply curve, p. 314

PROBLEMS

1. In 2003, national income in Canada was $911 billion. In the same year, 15.7 million workers were employed, at an average wage of $38,877 per worker per year.

a. How much was paid to employees in total in Canada in 2003?

b. Analyze the factor distribution of income. What percentage of national income was received in terms of compensation of employees in 2003?

c. Suppose the demand for labour falls due to a weakening economy. What happens to the percentage of national income received in terms of compensation of employees?

d. Suppose the supply of labour increases due to an increase in the retirement age. What happens to the percentage of national income received in terms of compensation of employees?

2. Marty's Frozen Yoghurt has the production function per day shown in the accompanying table. The equilibrium wage rate for a worker is $80 per day. Each cup of frozen yoghurt sells for $2.

Quantity of labour (workers)	Quantity of frozen yoghurt (cups)
0	0
1	110
2	200
3	270
4	300
5	320
6	330

a. Calculate the marginal product of labour for each worker and the value of the marginal product per worker.

b. How many workers should Marty employ?

3. Patty's Pizza Parlour has the production function per hour shown in the accompanying table. The hourly wage rate for each worker is $10. Each pizza sells for $2.

Quantity of labour (workers)	Quantity of pizza
0	0
1	9
2	15
3	19
4	22
5	24

a. Calculate the marginal product of labour for each worker and the value of the marginal product per worker.

b. Draw the value of the marginal product curve. Use your diagram to determine how many workers Patty should employ.

c. Now the price of pizza increases to $4. Calculate the value of the marginal product per worker, and draw the new value of the marginal product curve into your diagram. Use your diagram to determine how many workers Patty should employ now.

4. The production function for Patty's Pizza Parlour is given in the table in Problem 3. The price of pizza is $2, but the hourly wage rate rises from $10 to $15. Use a diagram to determine how Patty's demand for workers responds to this wage rate increase.

5. Patty's Pizza Parlour initially had the production function given in the table in Problem 3. A worker's hourly wage rate was $10, and pizza sold for $2. Now Patty buys a new high-tech pizza oven that allows her workers to become twice as productive. That is, the first worker now produces 18 pizzas per hour instead of 9, and so on.

a. Calculate the new marginal product of labour and the new value of the marginal product of labour.

b. Use a diagram to determine how Patty's hiring decision responds to this increase in the productivity of her workforce.

6. Jameel runs a driver education school. The more driving instructors he hires, the more driving lessons he can sell. But because he only owns a limited number of training automobiles, each additional driving instructor adds less to Jameel's output of driving lessons. The accompanying table shows Jameel's production function per day. Each driving lesson can be sold at $35 per hour.

Quantity of labour (driving instructors)	Quantity of driving lessons (hours)
0	0
1	8
2	15
3	21
4	26
5	30
6	33

Determine Jameel's labour demand schedule (his demand schedule for driving instructors) for each of the following daily wage rates for driving instructors: $160, $180, $200, $220, $240, and $260.

7. Dale and Dana work at a self-service gas station and convenience store. Dale opens up every day and Dana arrives later to help stock the store. They are both paid the current market wage of $9.50 per hour. But Dale feels he should be paid much more because the revenue generated from the gas pumps he turns on every morning is much higher than the revenue generated by the items that Dana stocks. Assess this argument.

8. In the Shire, farmers can rent land for $100 per hectare per year. All the hectares are identical. Merry Brandybuck rents 30 hectares on which he grows carrots. Pippin Took rents 20 hectares on which he grows corn. They sell their produce in a perfectly competitive market. Merry boasts that his value of the marginal product of land is twice as large as Pippin's. Pippin replies that if this is true and if Merry wants to maximize his profit, Merry is renting too much land. Is Pippin right? Explain your answer.

9. For each of the following situations in which similar workers are paid different wages, find the most likely explanation for these wage differences.

a. Test pilots for new jet aircraft earn higher wages than airline pilots.

b. University graduates usually have higher earnings in their first year on the job than workers without university degrees have in their first year on the job.

c. Full professors command higher salaries than assistant professors for teaching the same class.

d. Unionized workers are generally better paid than non-unionized workers.

10. Research consistently finds that despite non-discrimination policies, female workers on average receive lower wages than male workers do. What are the possible reasons for this? Are these reasons consistent with marginal productivity theory?

11. Greta is an enthusiastic amateur gardener and spends a lot of her free time working in her yard. She also has a demanding and well-paid job as a freelance advertising consultant. The advertising business is going through a difficult time and the consulting fee Greta can charge per hour of consulting falls. Greta decides to spend more time gardening and less time consulting. Explain her decision in terms of income and substitution effects.

12. Wendy works at a fast-food restaurant. When her wage rate was $5 per hour, she worked 30 hours per week. When her wage rate rose to $6 per hour, she decided to work 40 hours. But when her wage rate rose further to $7, she decided to work only 35 hours.

a. Draw Wendy's labour supply curve.

b. Is Wendy's behaviour irrational, or can you find a rational explanation? Explain your answer.

13. You are the provincial economic policy advisor. The Premier wants to put in place policies that encourage employed people to work more hours at their job and that encourage unemployed people to find and take jobs. Assess each of the following policies in terms of reaching that goal. Explain your reasoning in terms of income and substitution effects, and indicate when the impact of the policy may be ambiguous.

a. The provincial income tax rate is lowered, which has the effect of increasing workers' after-tax wage rate.

b. The provincial income tax rate is increased, which has the effect of decreasing workers' after-tax wage rate.

c. The provincial property tax rate is increased, which reduces workers' after-tax income.

>web... To continue your study and review of concepts in this chapter, please visit the Krugman/Wells website for quizzes, animated graph tutorials, web links to helpful resources, and more.

www.worthpublishers.com/krugmanwellsmyatt

>>Chapter 12 Appendix: Indifference Curve Analysis of Labour Supply

In the body of this chapter, we explained why the labour supply curve can slope downward instead of upward: the substitution effect of a higher wage rate, which provides an incentive to work longer hours, can be outweighed by the income effect of a higher wage rate, which may lead individuals to consume more leisure. In this appendix we show how this analysis can be carried out using the *indifference curves* introduced in Chapter 11.

The Time Allocation Budget Line

Let's return to the example of Clive, who likes leisure but also likes having money to spend. We now assume that Clive has a total of 80 hours per week that he could spend either working or enjoying as leisure time. (The remaining hours in his week, we assume, are taken up with necessary activities, mainly sleeping.) Let's also assume, initially, that his hourly wage rate is $10.

His consumption possibilities are defined by the **time allocation budget line** in Figure 12A-1, a budget line that shows Clive's trade-offs between consumption of leisure and income. Hours of leisure per week are measured on the horizontal axis, and the money he earns from working is measured on the vertical axis.

A **time allocation budget line** shows an individual's trade-offs between consumption of leisure and the income that allows consumption of marketed goods.

The horizontal intercept, point *X*, is at 80 hours: if Clive didn't work at all, he would have 80 hours of leisure per week but would not earn any money. The vertical intercept, point *Y*, is at $800: if Clive worked all the time, he would earn $800 per week.

Why can we use a budget line to describe Clive's time allocation choice? The budget lines found in Chapters 10 and 11 represented the trade-offs facing consumers deciding how to allocate their income among different goods. Here, instead of asking how Clive allocates his income, we ask how he allocates his *time*. But the principles underlying the allocation of income and the allocation of time are the same: each involves allocating a fixed amount of a resource (80 hours of time in this case) with a constant

Figure 12A-1

The Time Allocation Budget Line

Clive's time allocation budget line shows his trade-off between work, which pays a wage rate of $10 per hour, and leisure. At point *X* he allocates all of his time, 80 hours, to leisure but has no income. At point *Y* he allocates all of his time to work, earning $800, but consumes no leisure. His hourly wage rate of $10, the opportunity cost of an hour of leisure, is equal to minus the slope of the time allocation budget line. We have assumed that point *A*, at 40 hours of leisure and $400 in income, is Clive's optimal time allocation. It obeys the optimal time allocation rule: the additional utility Clive gets from one more hour of leisure must equal the additional utility he gets from the goods he can purchase with one hour's wages.

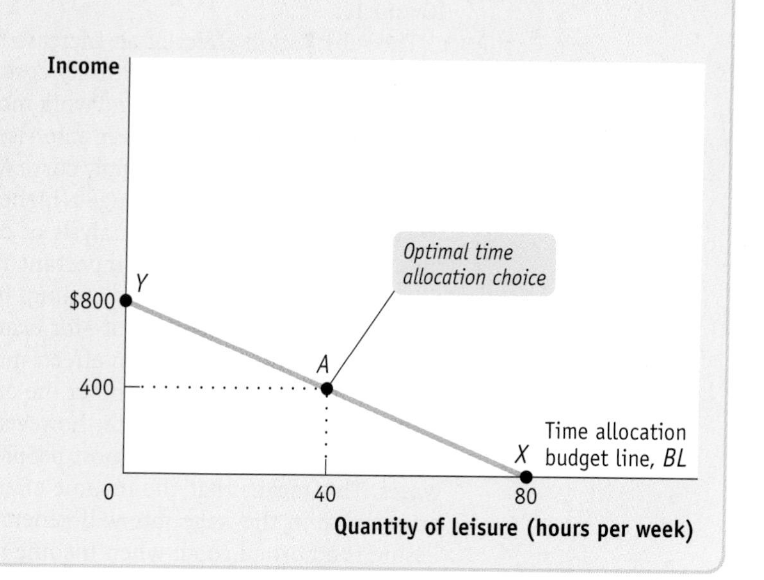

trade-off (Clive must forgo $10 for each additional hour of leisure). So using a budget line is just as appropriate for time allocation as it is for income allocation.

As in the case of ordinary budget lines, opportunity cost plays a key role. The opportunity cost of an hour of leisure is what Clive must forgo by working one less hour—$10 in income. This opportunity cost is, of course, Clive's hourly wage rate and is equal to minus the slope of his time allocation budget line. You can verify this by noting that the slope is equal to minus the vertical intercept, point *Y*, divided by the horizontal intercept, point *X*—that is, –$800/(80 hours) = –$10 per hour.

To maximize his utility, Clive must choose the optimal point on the time allocation budget line in Figure 12A-1. In Chapter 10 we saw that a consumer who allocates spending to maximize utility finds the point on the budget line that satisfies the *optimal consumption rule:* the marginal utility per dollar spent on two goods must be equal. Although Clive's choice involves allocating time rather than money, the same principles apply.

Since Clive "spends" time rather than money, the counterpart of the optimal consumption rule is the **optimal time allocation rule:** the marginal utility Clive gets from the extra money earned from an additional hour spent working must equal the marginal utility of an additional hour of leisure.

The **optimal time allocation rule** says that an individual should allocate time so that the marginal utility per hour spent working is equal to the marginal utility of an additional hour of leisure.

The Effect of a Higher Wage Rate

Depending on his tastes, Clive's utility-maximizing choice of hours of leisure and income could lie anywhere on the time allocation budget line in Figure 12A-1. Let's assume that his optimal choice is point *A*, at which he consumes 40 hours of leisure and earns $400. Now we are ready to link the analysis of time allocation to labour supply.

When Clive chooses a point like *A* on his time allocation budget line, he is also choosing the quantity of labour he supplies to the labour market. By choosing to consume 40 of his 80 available hours as leisure, he has also chosen to supply the other 40 hours as labour.

Now suppose that Clive's wage rate doubles, from $10 to $20 per hour. The effect of this increase in his wage rate is shown in Figure 12A-2. His time allocation budget line rotates outward: the vertical intercept, which represents the amount he could earn if he devoted all 80 hours to work, shifts upward from point *Y* to point *Z*. As a result of the doubling of his wage, Clive would earn $1,600 instead of $800 if he devoted all 80 hours to working.

But how will Clive's time allocation actually change? As we saw in the chapter, this depends on the *income effect* and *substitution effect* that we learned about in Chapters 10 and 11.

The substitution effect of an increase in the wage rate works as follows. When the wage rate increases, the opportunity cost of an hour of leisure increases; this induces Clive to consume less leisure and work more hours—that is, to substitute hours of work for hours of leisure as the wage rate rises. If the substitution effect were the whole story, the individual labour supply curve would look like any ordinary supply curve and would always be upward sloping—a higher wage rate leads to greater labour supply.

What we learned in our analysis of demand was that for most consumer goods, the income effect isn't very important because most goods account for only a very small share of a consumer's spending. In addition, in the few cases of goods where the income effect is significant—for example, major purchases like housing—it usually reinforces the substitution effect: most goods are normal goods, so when a price increase makes a consumer poorer, he or she buys less of that good.

In the labour/leisure choice, however, the income effect takes on a new significance, for two reasons. First, most people get the great majority of their income from wages. This means that the income effect of a change in the wage rate is *not* small: an increase in the wage rate will generate a significant increase in income. Second, leisure is a normal good: when income rises, other things equal, people tend to consume more leisure and work fewer hours.

Figure 12A-2

An Increase in the Wage Rate

The two panels show Clive's initial optimal choice, point *A*, on BL_1, the time allocation budget line corresponding to a wage rate of \$10. After his wage rate rises to \$20, his budget line rotates out to the new budget line, BL_2: if he spends all his time working, the amount of money he earns rises from \$800 to \$1,600, reflected in the movement from *Y* to *Z*. This generates two opposing effects: the substitution effect pushes him to consume less leisure and to work more hours; the income effect pushes him to consume more leisure and to work fewer hours. Panel (a) shows the change in time allocation when the substitution effect is stronger: Clive's new optimal choice is point *B*, representing a decrease in hours of leisure to 30 hours and an increase in hours of labour to 50 hours. In this case, the individual labour supply curve slopes upward. Panel (b) shows the change in time allocation when the income effect is stronger: point *C* is the new optimal choice, representing an increase in hours of leisure to 50 hours and a decrease in hours of labour to 30 hours. Now the individual labour supply curve slopes downward.

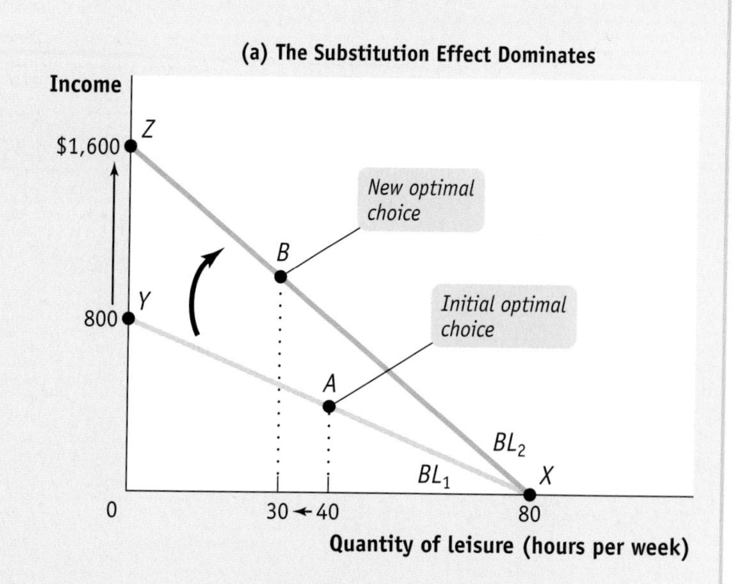

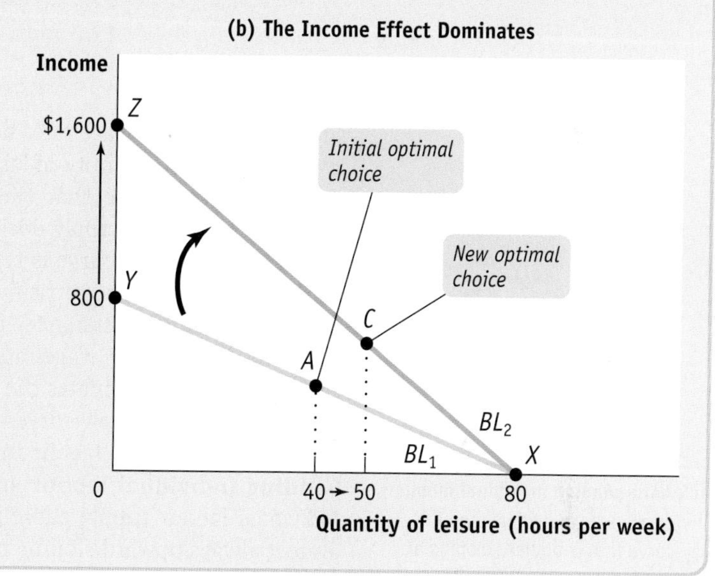

So the income effect of a higher wage rate tends to *reduce* the quantity of labour supplied, working in opposition to the substitution effect, which tends to *increase* the quantity of labour supplied. So the net effect of a higher wage rate on the quantity of labour Clive supplies could go either way—depending on his preferences, he might choose to supply more labour, or he might choose to supply less labour. The two panels of Figure 12A-2 illustrate these two outcomes. In each panel, point *A* represents Clive's initial consumption choice. Panel (a) shows the case in which Clive works more hours in response to a higher wage rate. An increase in the wage rate induces him to move from point *A* to point *B*, where he consumes less leisure than at *A* and therefore works more hours. Here the substitution effect prevails over the income effect. Panel (b) shows the case in which Clive works fewer hours in response to a higher wage rate. Here, he moves from *A* to *C*, where he consumes more leisure and works *fewer* hours than at *A*. Here the income effect prevails over the substitution effect.

When the income effect of a higher wage rate is stronger than the substitution effect, the individual labour supply curve, which shows how much labour an individual will

Figure 12A-3

A Backward-Bending Individual Labour Supply Curve

At lower wage rates, the substitution effect dominates the income effect for this individual. This is illustrated by the movement along the individual labour supply curve from point *A* to point *B*: a rise in the wage rate from W_1 to W_2 leads the quantity of labour supplied to increase from L_1 to L_2. But at higher wage rates, the income effect dominates the substitution effect, shown by the movement from point *B* to point *C*: here, a rise in the wage rate from W_2 to W_3 leads the quantity of labour supplied to decrease from L_2 to L_3.

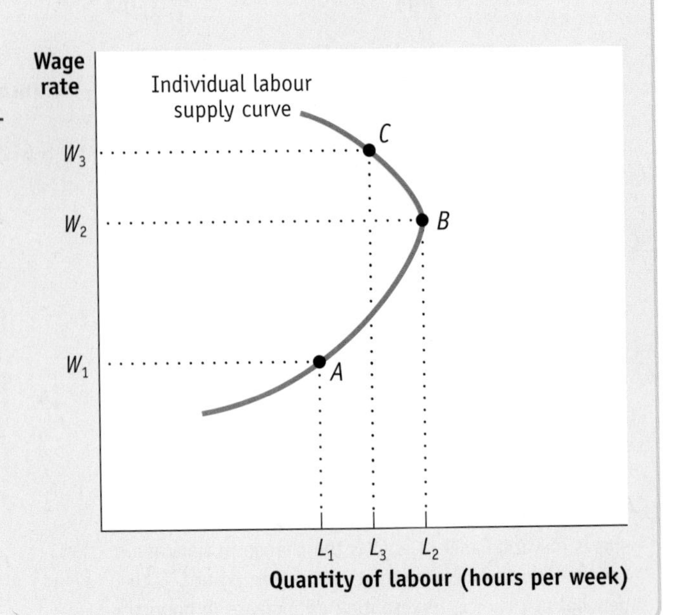

supply at any given wage rate, slopes the "wrong" way—downward: a higher wage rate leads to a smaller quantity of labour supplied.

Economists believe that the substitution effect usually dominates the income effect in the labour supply decision when an individual's wage rate is low. An individual labour supply curve is typically upward sloping for lower wage rates as people work more in response to rising wage rates. But they also believe that many individuals have stronger preferences for leisure and will choose to cut back the number of hours worked as their wage rate continues to rise. For these individuals, the income effect eventually dominates the substitution effect as the wage rate rises, leading their individual labour supply curves to change slope and to "bend backward" at high wage rates. An individual labour supply curve with this feature, called a **backward-bending individual labour supply curve,** is shown in Figure 12A-3. Although an *individual* labour supply curve may bend backward, *market* labour supply curves are almost always upward sloping over their entire range as higher wage rates draw more new workers into the labour market.

A **backward-bending individual labour supply curve** is an individual labour supply curve that is upward sloping at low to moderate wage rates and is downward sloping at higher wage rates.

Indifference Curve Analysis

In Chapter 11, we showed that consumer choice can be represented using the concept of *indifference curves,* which provide a "map" of consumer preferences. If you have covered Chapter 11, you may find it interesting to learn that indifference curves are also useful for addressing the issue of labour supply. In fact, this is one place where they are particularly helpful.

Using indifference curves, Figure 12A-4 shows how an increase in the wage rate can lead to a fall in the quantity of labour supplied. Point *A* is Clive's initial optimal choice, given an hourly wage rate of $10. It is the same as point *A* in Figure 12A-2; this time, however, we include an indifference curve to show that it is a point at which the budget line is tangent to the highest possible indifference curve.

Now consider the effect of a rise in the wage rate to $20. Imagine, for a moment, that at the same time Clive was offered a higher wage, he was told that he had to start repaying his student loan and that the good-news/bad-news combination left his

Figure 12A-4

Labour Supply Choice: The Indifference Curve Approach

Point A, on BL_1, is Clive's initial optimal choice. After a wage rate increase his income and utility level increase: his new time budget allocation line is BL_2 and his new optimal choice is point C. This change can be decomposed into the substitution effect—the fall in the hours of leisure from point A to point S, and the income effect—the increase in the number of hours of leisure from point S to point C. As shown here, the income effect dominates the substitution effect: the net result of an increase in the wage rate is an increase in the hours of leisure consumed and a decrease in the hours of labour supplied.

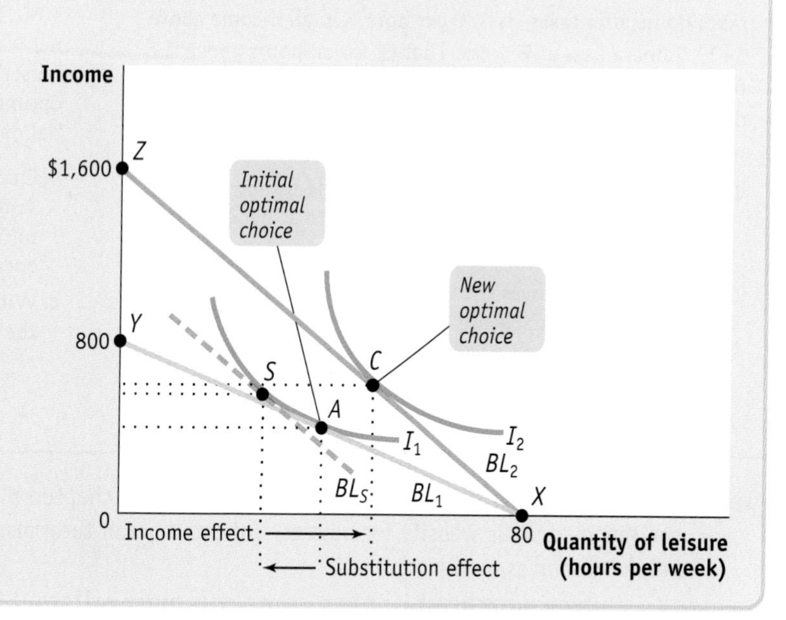

utility unchanged. Then he would find himself at point S: on the same indifference curve as at A, but tangent to a steeper budget line, the dashed line BL_S in Figure 12A-4, which is parallel to BL_2. The move from A to S is the substitution effect of his wage increase: it leads him to consume less leisure and therefore supply more labour.

But now cancel the repayment on the student loan, and Clive is able to move to a higher indifference curve. His new optimum is at C, which corresponds to C in panel (b) of Figure 12A-2. The move from S to C is the income effect of his wage increase. And we see that this income effect can outweigh the substitution effect: at C he consumes more leisure, and therefore supplies less labour, than he did at A.

PROBLEMS

1. Leandro has 16 hours per day that he can allocate to work or leisure. (The remaining 8 hours are taken up by necessary activities such as sleeping.) His job pays an hourly wage rate of $20. Leandro decides to consume 8 hours of leisure. His indifference curves have the usual shape: they are downward sloping, they do not cross, and they have the characteristic "bowed" shape.

   a. Draw Leandro's time allocation budget line for a typical day. Then illustrate the indifference curve at his optimal choice.

   Now Leandro's wage rate falls to $10 per hour.

   b. Draw Leandro's new budget line.

   c. Suppose that Leandro now works only 4 hours as a result of his reduced wage rate. Illustrate the indifference curve at his new optimal choice.

   Leandro's decision to work less as the wage rate falls is the result of a substitution effect and an income effect. In your diagram, show the income effect and the substitution effect from this reduced wage rate. Which effect is stronger?

2. Florence is a highly paid fashion consultant who earns $100 per hour. She has 16 hours per day that she can allocate to work or leisure, and she decides to work for 12 hours.

   a. Draw Florence's time allocation budget line for a typical day, and illustrate the indifference curve at her optimal choice.

   One of Florence's clients is featured on the front page of *Vague*, a fashion magazine. As a result, Florence's consulting fee now rises to $500 per hour. Florence decides to work only 10 hours per day.

   b. Draw Florence's new time allocation budget line, and illustrate the indifference curve at her optimal choice.

   c. In your diagram, show the income effect and the substitution effect from this increase in the wage. Which effect is stronger?

3. Tamara has 80 hours per week that she can allocate to work or leisure. Tamara's job pays her a wage rate of $20 per hour, but Tamara is being taxed on her income in the following way. On the first $400 that Tamara makes, she pays no tax. That

is, for the first 20 hours she works, her net wage—what she takes home after taxes—is $20 per hour. On all income above $400, Tamara pays a 75% tax. That is, for all hours above the first 20 hours, her net wage rate is only $5 per hour. Tamara decides to work 30 hours. Her indifference curves have the usual shape.

a. Draw Tamara's time allocation budget line for a typical week. Also illustrate the indifference curve at her optimal choice.

The government changes the tax scheme. Now only the first $100 of income is tax-exempt. That is, for the first 5 hours she works, Tamara's net wage rate is now $20 per hour. But the government reduces the tax rate on all other income to 50%. That is, for all hours above the first 5 hours, Tamara's net wage rate is now $10. After these changes, Tamara finds herself exactly equally as well off as before. That is, her new optimal choice is on the same indifference curve as her initial optimal choice.

b. Draw Tamara's new time allocation budget line in the same diagram. Also illustrate her optimal choice. Bear in mind that she is equally as well off (on the same indifference curve) as before the tax changes occurred.

c. Will Tamara work more or less than before the changes to the tax scheme? Why?

>web... To continue your study and review of concepts in this chapter, please visit the Krugman/Wells website for quizzes, animated graph tutorials, web links to helpful resources, and more.

www.worthpublishers.com/krugmanwellsmyatt

13

>>Efficiency and Equity

AFTER THE FALL

WHEN THE BERLIN WALL CAME down in 1989, Western observers got their first good look at the centrally planned economy of East Germany. What they found was a stunningly inefficient system. Although investment had been lavished on politically favoured industries such as energy production, producers of consumer goods and services were starved for capital. And the consumer goods that were produced were often not what consumers wanted to buy.

The revelation of East German inefficiency showed how badly such a planned economy worked compared with a market economy, like that of West Germany.

But even after the wall had come down, the government of the newly unified Federal Republic of Germany was not willing to let the free market run its course. Instead, both industry and individuals in East Germany received huge amounts of financial aid. The goal was to prevent the emergence of a politically unacceptable level of inequality between the former East Germans, many of whom lost their jobs in the aftermath of reunification, and West Germans.

Over time, many economists have come to believe that this aid actually delayed the reconstruction of the East German economy. They argue that the aid reduced incentives for workers to relocate to areas where more jobs were available or to learn new skills. But German officials insist that the price was well worth paying: sometimes a sense of fairness, they argue, is more important than efficiency.

Germany's experience reminds us that although we want our economy to be efficient, we also want it to be fair. In this chapter we will address both concerns. We begin by discussing the *efficiency* of a competitive market economy—the effectiveness of a competitive market economy at producing the goods and services that people want to consume. We then turn to the less well-defined

What you will learn in this chapter:

- ➤ How the overall concept of efficiency can be broken down into three components—**efficiency in consumption, efficiency in production,** and **efficiency in output levels**
- ➤ How a perfectly competitive market for a single good achieves efficiency in all three components
- ➤ Why an economy consisting of many perfectly competitive markets is typically, but not always, efficient
- ➤ The limits of the concept of efficiency—in particular, why efficiency is about how to achieve goals but not about which goals are chosen

Pierre Merimme/Corbis

Getty Images

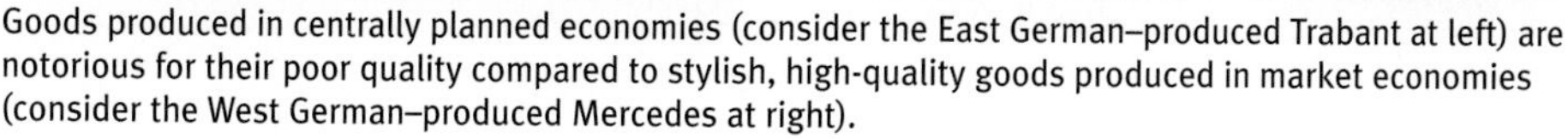

Goods produced in centrally planned economies (consider the East German–produced Trabant at left) are notorious for their poor quality compared to stylish, high-quality goods produced in market economies (consider the West German–produced Mercedes at right).

but equally important issue of *equity*—is the distribution of consumption among individuals "fair"? As we'll see, there is no generally accepted definition of *fairness;* nonetheless, societies often choose to sacrifice some efficiency in the pursuit of equity.

Supply, Demand, and the Virtues of the Market

Back in Chapter 6 we introduced the concepts of *consumer surplus* and *producer surplus.* Recall that consumer surplus is the difference between what buyers are willing to pay for a good and what they actually pay; it measures the gains to consumers from participating in the market. Similarly, producer surplus is the difference between the price that sellers of a good receive and their cost; it measures the gains to producers from participating in the market. The sum of consumer and producer surplus, *total surplus,* measures the gains from trade: the total benefits to buyers and sellers from participating in the market.

What we learned in that chapter was a remarkable fact: in equilibrium, a perfectly competitive market—a market in which both buyers and sellers are price-takers—is usually efficient. That is, in most cases such a market *maximizes total surplus.* Except in cases of market failure, there is no way to increase the gains from trade once a market has done its work.

But why is this true, and what are the conditions that make it possible?

To answer these questions, let's briefly look at this story again. It will set the stage for our discussion of efficiency in the economy as a whole.

Why a Market Maximizes Total Surplus

In Chapter 6 we showed that a market maximizes total surplus by considering the alternatives. That is, any attempt to rearrange consumption or production from the market equilibrium reduces total surplus.

How did we demonstrate this result? Figure 13-1 shows, once again, the example of a market in used textbooks. In this example the equilibrium is at *E,* where the price

Figure 13-1

Why a Market Maximizes Total Surplus

How do we know that total surplus is maximized at the equilibrium price of $30 per book and the equilibrium quantity of 1,000? First, books go to the "right" consumers: every consumer who buys a book has a willingness to pay of $30 or more, and every potential consumer who does *not* buy a book has a willingness to pay less than $30. Second, books are supplied by the "right" producers: every seller who supplies a book has a cost of $30 or less, and every potential seller who does *not* supply a book has a cost of more than $30. Finally, the "right" quantity of 1,000 books are bought and sold: any additional books would cost more than $30 to produce but would be worth less than $30 to the consumers who receive them. If any fewer books were bought and sold, some consumers would be willing to pay more than it costs producers to supply these books. >web...

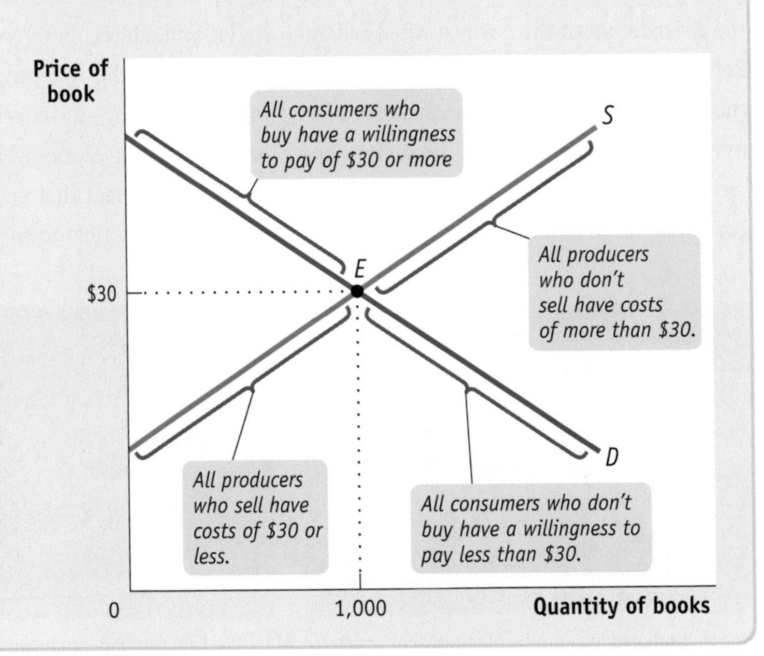

is $30, and the quantity bought and sold is 1,000 books. We then laid out the three ways in which you might try to improve on this equilibrium and showed that none of them will succeed:

- *Reallocating consumption.* You might try to increase total surplus by giving books to different consumers. But in equilibrium every consumer who gets a book is to the left of *E* on the demand curve, and every consumer who does not get a book is to the right of *E*. That is, every consumer who gets a book has a higher willingness to pay than every consumer who does not get a book. So any reallocation of consumption away from the market equilibrium would reduce the total surplus.
- *Reallocating production.* You might try to increase total surplus by getting different people to sell books. (For simplicity, let's think of sellers as "producing" the books.) But every potential seller who sells a book is to the left of *E* on the supply curve, and every potential seller who does not sell a book is to the right of *E*. That is, every potential seller who sells a book has a lower cost than every potential seller who does not. So any reallocation of production away from the market equilibrium would reduce the total surplus.
- *Changing the level of production.* You might try to increase total surplus by either increasing or decreasing the number of books sold. But at point *E*, the willingness to pay of the last buyer is just equal to the cost of the last seller. So any change in production means either producing a book that is not worth as much to the buyer as it costs to provide or *not* producing a book that is worth more to a consumer than it costs.

So we saw in Chapter 6 that when an individual competitive market is in equilibrium, the consumers who are willing to pay the most for a good are the ones who get it; the producers with the lowest cost are the ones who produce it; and the quantity produced and consumed is right, in the sense that producing either more or less would reduce total surplus.

As we'll see in the next section, a similar case for efficiency applies to the economy as a whole. But before we lay out that case, let's look at the reasons why a market manages to get so much right.

Why Markets Work So Well: Property Rights

Economists can say and have said volumes about why markets are an effective way to organize an economy. But the effectiveness of markets comes down largely to the power of two features of a well-functioning market: *property rights* and the role of prices as *economic signals.*

By **property rights** we mean a system in which valuable items in the economy—whether they are resources or goods—have specific owners who can dispose of them as they choose. Property rights are what make the mutually beneficial transactions in the used-textbook market, or any market, possible.

Property rights are the rights of owners of valuable items, whether resources or goods, to dispose of those items as they choose.

To see why property rights are crucial, imagine that students do not have full property rights in their textbooks—that they are not allowed to resell books when the semester is over.

This restriction on property rights would prevent many mutually beneficial transactions. Some students would be stuck with textbooks they do not plan to reread and would be happier receiving some cash instead. Other students would be forced to pay full price for shiny new books when they would be happier getting slightly battered copies at a lower price.

In Chapter 20, we'll see that some of the major ways in which markets go wrong have to do with a lack of clearly defined property rights in valuable goods such as fish in the sea and clean air.

Why Markets Work So Well: Prices as Economic Signals

An **economic signal** is any piece of information that helps people make better economic decisions.

Because well-defined property rights give individuals the right to engage in mutually beneficial trades, the second necessary feature of well-functioning markets—economic signals—tell individuals *which* trades are mutually beneficial. An **economic signal** is any piece of information that helps people make better economic decisions. There are thousands of signals that businesses watch in the real world. For example, business forecasters say that sales of cardboard boxes are a good early indicator of changes in industrial production: if businesses are buying lots of cardboard boxes, you can be sure that they will soon increase their production.

But prices are far and away the most important signals in a market economy, because they convey essential information about other people's costs and their willingness to pay. If the equilibrium price of used books is $30, this in effect tells everyone both that there are consumers willing to pay $30 and up and that there are producers with a cost of $30 or less.

The signal given by the market price is what ensures that total surplus is maximized, by telling people whether to buy or sell books. If the price of a book is $30, any consumer who would not be willing to pay $30 knows that there are other consumers who are willing to pay more; any producer whose cost is more than $30 knows that there are other producers with lower costs. And consumers who *are* willing to pay $30 or more, like producers with costs of $30 or less, are in effect told that it is a good idea for them to consume and produce.

Why Markets Sometimes Don't Work Well: Market Failure

We'll want to keep these two crucial features of competitive markets—property rights and prices as economic signals—in mind in later chapters when we analyse in detail how markets sometimes fail. It's worth revisiting the caution found in Chapter 6 about cases of market failure—the situation in which a market fails to maximize total surplus. First, markets can fail when one party, in an attempt to capture more resources, prevents mutually beneficial trades from occurring. Second, markets can fail when actions have side effects on others that aren't properly taken into account by the market—side effects like pollution. Finally, markets can fail because some goods, by their very nature, are unsuited for efficient management by markets. We will see in the next section how all three of these cases can be interpreted as instances in which prices give incorrect signals—that is, they fail to help people make better economic decisions. And as we will discover shortly, the failure of a particular market in an economy has implications for how well the entire economy operates.

economics in action

Smoothing Out the Bumps

The area around the departure gate is crowded, so it's obvious the plane will be full. In fact, it turns out that it's more than full. The gate agent announces that the flight is overbooked and asks for volunteers to give up their seats in return for rebooking on a later flight plus additional incentives, such as $200 toward a future ticket. If not enough volunteers come forward immediately, the incentives are increased.

This scene is familiar to any frequent flier. But it didn't always work that way. In fact, it took a couple of economists to teach the airlines how to deal efficiently with overbooking.

On busy flights, airlines have always sold tickets for more seats than actually exist. There's a good reason for this: some people with reservations always fail to show up, and an empty seat is a seat wasted. But sometimes fewer people than expected are no-shows, and a flight ends up overbooked. What happens then?

Until 1978, airlines simply "bumped" some of their passengers—informed them that their reservations had been cancelled. There were no uniform rules about who got bumped; some airlines, for example, bumped older passengers because they were less likely to complain. Needless to say, those who got bumped were not happy.

In 1968, however, the economist Julian Simon proposed a market approach, in which airlines would treat a flight reservation as if it were a property right given to the passenger, and buy that right back if the plane was overbooked. Airlines didn't think this idea was practical. But in 1978 another economist, Alfred Kahn, was appointed to head the Civil Aeronautics Board, which at the time regulated airlines in the United States. He introduced new rules requiring airlines to use an auction system to deal with overbooking, and the result was the familiar process of asking for volunteers. This system was subsequently emulated by Canadian-operated airlines and others around the world.

What's the advantage of this voluntary, market solution? Under the old system, someone who urgently needed to get on the scheduled flight was as likely to get bumped as someone who could easily take a later connection. Since 1978, those who absolutely have to make the flight don't volunteer; those who aren't that anxious to board get something that's worth more to them. The airline pays a cost to get passengers to give up their reserved seats but more than makes up for it in higher overall customer satisfaction. In short, everyone gains. By using property rights to create a market, Simon and Kahn moved that piece of the economy towards efficiency. ■

>> QUICK REVIEW

- To see why a market maximizes total surplus, we rule out various ways in which you might think total surplus could be increased. It turns out that total surplus can't be increased by reallocating consumption, and it can't be increased by rearranging production. The level of output at market equilibrium is also the right one to maximize surplus.
- A system of *property rights* and the operation of prices as *economic signals* are two key factors that enable a competitive market to maximize total surplus. But under conditions in which prices give incorrect economic signals, markets can fail.

>> CHECK YOUR UNDERSTANDING 13-1

1. Imagine that eMarkets! is a company that implements a competitive market in MP3 players. Based on information it gathers, it tells producers what the equilibrium price will be so that they can decide how much to produce. And once production has occurred, it allocates output to consumers based on the price and their willingness to pay.
   a. What information would they need to know from consumers and producers in order to find the equilibrium price and quantity of MP3 players?
   b. Suppose that eMarkets! has determined that, once production occurs and trading happens, the equilibrium price will be $199 and the equilibrium quantity will be 10,000 units. But also suppose that due to a computer glitch, it informs some producers that the price will be $299, while it informs some producers that the price will be $99. How will producer surplus be affected? Can you determine the effect on the quantity produced—will it be equal to, less than, or more than the equilibrium quantity?
   c. Also suppose that due to the computer glitch, some consumers with a willingness to pay of $299 are told that the price is $399. An equal number of consumers who have a willingness to pay of $119 are allowed to buy the good at a price of $99. How will consumer surplus be affected?

Solutions appear at back of book.

Efficiency in the Economy as a Whole

We've seen how the equilibrium outcome of an individual competitive market usually maximizes the total surplus of participants in that market. Is there an equivalent result for the economy as a whole? That is, is there a corresponding concept of equilibrium for the whole economy? And if so, does this equilibrium outcome maximize the welfare of the economy's participants?

The economy as a whole consists not of one but of many, many markets, all interrelated in two ways:

- On the consumption side, the demand for each good is affected by the prices of other goods.
- On the production side, producers of different goods compete for the same factors of production.

A **competitive market economy** is an economy in which all markets, for goods and for factors, are perfectly competitive.

An economy is in **general equilibrium** when the quantity supplied is equal to the quantity demanded in all markets.

To think about the economy as a whole, then, we have to think of many markets, for both goods and factors. A **competitive market economy** is an economy in which all of these markets are perfectly competitive, with equilibrium prices determined by supply and demand. In each market both the supply and demand curves are likely to be affected by events in other markets.

When all markets have reached equilibrium—when the quantity of each good and factor demanded is equal to the quantity of each good and factor supplied at the going market prices—we say that the economy is in **general equilibrium.** To put it another way, general equilibrium is the economy-wide counterpart of ordinary equilibrium in a single market.

Our next task is to show that, as with an individual competitive market in equilibrium, a competitive market economy in general equilibrium is usually *efficient*—that is, it is efficient except in certain well-defined cases. What do we mean by saying that the economy as a whole is efficient? Actually, we defined efficiency way back in Chapter 1. We will start by revisiting that definition to see why it is the right approach to analysing the economy as a whole. Next, we will describe the three criteria that an economy as a whole must satisfy in order to be efficient. Finally, we will learn how failures of individual markets can lead to inefficiency in the economy as a whole—failures we can view as cases in which prices fail to perform as economic signals.

Efficiency, Revisited

When economists discuss efficiency in an individual market, they usually use the concepts of consumer and producer surplus, which measure costs and benefits in monetary terms. This makes sense when you are talking about the market for just one good, because you can take the prices of other goods—and therefore the value of a dollar—as

FOR INQUIRING MINDS
DEFINING ECONOMIC EFFICIENCY

The economist's definition of *efficiency*—that an economy is efficient if nobody can be made better off without making others worse off—may seem to be oddly indirect. Why can't we define efficiency in terms of a positive achievement rather than the absence of something?

Many other definitions of efficiency have been proposed, but none of them have survived careful scrutiny—all of them turn out either to be incomplete or to involve unacceptable implications. A good example is the fate of the principle known as utilitarianism, proposed by the nineteenth-century English philosopher Jeremy Bentham.

Bentham offered a simple principle: "the greatest good for the greatest number". In effect, he argued that society should try to maximize the total utility of its members. This sounded persuasive but eventually ran into two problems. First, how do we add up the utility of different people? We may loosely say that Ms. Martineau is happier than Mr. Ricardo, but is she twice as happy or three times as happy? You may argue that it makes no sense even to ask that question—but in that case Bentham's principle becomes meaningless because we have no way to add up the total utility of all members of society.

Ray Laskowitz/Lonely Planet

Whose util counts more? Efficiency has been difficult to define because we can't compare utility across people.

Second, even if we imagine that it is somehow possible to add up the utility of different people, critics of Bentham point out that his doctrine has the disturbing implication that we should cater to the tastes of "utility monsters"—people who derive especially high pleasure from excessive consumption. Bentham's criterion implies that if Martineau really likes owning luxury automobiles and going to fancy restaurants but Ricardo is a modest sort who can make do with a bicycle and macaroni-and-cheese dinners, we should take money from Ricardo and give it to Martineau—even if Ricardo is a hard worker and Martineau notably lazy. This doesn't seem right.

Because of these difficulties, Bentham's principle has pretty much vanished from economic thought. The same is true of other ideas, such as the Marxist slogan "from each according to his ability, to each according to his needs". The only definition of efficiency that has managed to survive practical and logical criticism is the negative one: an economy is inefficient if there is a way to make at least one person better off without making others worse off, and it is efficient if it is not inefficient.

given. When we are analysing the economy as a whole, however, measuring costs and benefits in dollar terms no longer makes sense, because all prices are "to be determined".

Instead, economists focus on the basic definition of efficiency. Recall from Chapter 1: An economy is efficient if it does not pass up any opportunities to make some people better off without making other people worse off.

To achieve efficiency, an economy must meet three criteria, which closely parallel the three features ensuring that total surplus is maximized in an individual market. The economy must be *efficient in consumption, efficient in production,* and *efficient in output levels.* Let's look at these criteria and see how a competitive market economy satisfies them.

Efficiency in Consumption

An economy is **efficient in consumption** if there is no way to redistribute goods among consumers that makes some consumers better off without making others worse off.

An economy is **efficient in consumption** if there is no way to redistribute goods among consumers that makes some consumers better off without making others worse off.

To see what efficiency in consumption involves, it helps to imagine scenarios for inefficiency. Imagine, for example, an economy that produces both cornflakes and shredded wheat but that provides those who prefer shredded wheat with cornflakes, and vice versa. Then it would be possible to make at least one person better off without making anyone else worse off by redistributing the goods, giving people the breakfast cereal they prefer.

The first piece of good news is that as long as prices perform properly as economic signals, this kind of inefficiency won't occur in a competitive market economy. We've seen this already in the case of market equilibrium in one individual market: the consumers who actually receive a good at the market equilibrium are those with the greatest willingness to pay—thanks to the role prices play in helping people make the right economic decisions. Consumers who prefer an additional box of cornflakes will be willing to pay more for that box than consumers who would rather have an additional box of shredded wheat. So if the markets for cornflakes and shredded wheat are both in equilibrium, there won't be any way to make at least one consumer better off without making others worse off by redistributing the available quantities of breakfast cereals.

In other words, prices in goods markets ensure that you can't increase total surplus in a single market by taking a good away from one person and giving it to another. Similarly, prices also ensure that when all markets in an economy are in perfectly competitive general equilibrium, there is no way to redistribute goods that makes some consumers better off without making others worse off.

It's important, however, to realize the limitations of that statement: even though an economy is efficient, you can always make *some* consumers better off if you are willing to make others worse off. We'll come back to that point shortly.

Efficiency in Production

Economists say that an economy is **efficient in production** if it is not possible to produce more of some goods without producing less of others.

An economy is **efficient in production** if there is no way to produce more of some goods without producing less of other goods.

We can use the *production possibility frontier* model from Chapter 2 to understand this. This model uses a diagram like Figure 13-2 to illustrate the economy's trade-offs: the more wheat it produces, the less corn it can produce, and vice versa. If the economy produces the quantities at either point *A* or point *B* on the production possibility frontier, it is efficient in production: it is possible to produce more corn than the economy produces at *A,* but only by producing less wheat; it is possible to produce more wheat than the economy produces at *B,* but only by producing less corn. The economy is not efficient in production, however, if it produces at point *C:* it is possible to produce more wheat *and* more corn than the economy does at that point.

An economy will be efficient in production if it has an **efficient allocation of resources**—if there is no way to reallocate factors of production among producers to produce more of some goods without producing less of others. This is an important result: *An economy that is efficient in allocation of resources is efficient in production, and vice versa.*

An economy has an **efficient allocation of resources** if there is no way to reallocate factors of production among producers to produce more of some goods without producing less of others.

Here is another way to think about Figure 13-2: at point *A* the economy can produce more corn only by taking resources away from wheat production. Similarly, at

Figure 13-2

The Production Possibility Frontier and Efficiency in Production

An economy is efficient in production if it cannot produce more of one good without producing less of other goods. Equivalently, an economy is efficient in production if it is on its production possibility frontier. Here *A* and *B* are efficient production points—at each point the economy can produce more of one good only by producing less of the other. *C* is not an efficient production point because more corn *and* more wheat can be produced. **>*web*...**

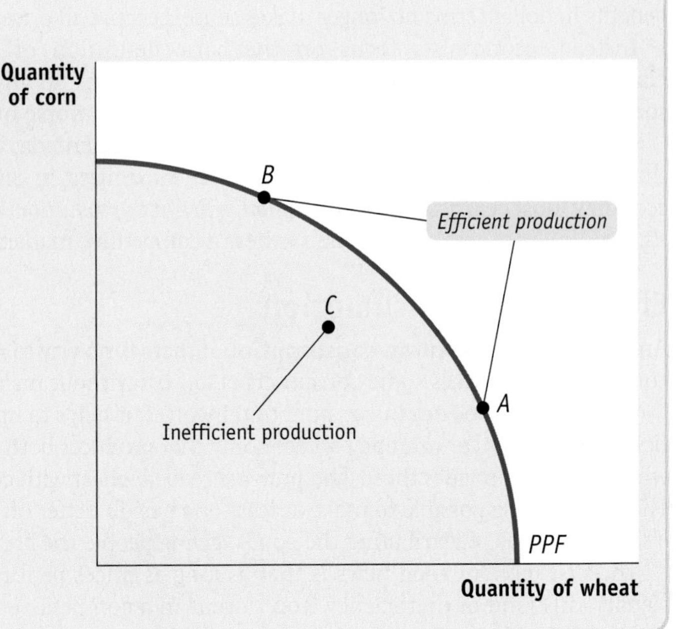

point *B* the economy can produce more wheat only by taking resources away from corn production.

Just as in the case of efficiency in consumption, it helps to imagine scenarios for inefficiency. In Canada, the Prairies are ideally suited for growing wheat, while land in Ontario is (generally speaking) better suited for growing corn, and most land in Newfoundland isn't well suited for growing anything. It would clearly be inefficient if good land in the Prairies were left idle while farmers struggled with the stony soil of Newfoundland; it would also be inefficient if all of Canada's wheat were grown in Ontario and all its corn were grown on the Prairies.

The second piece of good news is that, just as in the case of consumption, the role of prices as economic signals ensures that an economy in general equilibrium achieves efficiency in production. The logic is similar, but this time it applies to prices in factor markets rather than prices in goods markets. Corn farmers are willing to pay more for Ontario land than wheat farmers; wheat farmers are willing to pay more for land on the Prairies. And no one has farmed much in Newfoundland, because traditionally labour and capital in that province could be more productively employed in fishing. In short, when factor markets are competitive, resources are allocated to the producers that can make the best use of them, and the economy is indeed efficient in production.

Notice, however, that this does not say *what* the economy produces. Both *A* and *B* in Figure 13-2 represent efficient production. We still need to ask whether the economy produces at the "right" place on the production possibility frontier—or rather, *a* right place, because there may be many efficient outcomes. But let's hold off on that for a moment, and finish our description of efficiency in the economy as a whole.

Efficiency in Output Levels

Suppose that a competitive market economy is efficient in production—it cannot produce more of some goods without producing less of others. Suppose also that it is efficient in consumption—there is no way to redistribute the goods produced that will make some consumers better off without making others worse off. There is still the question of whether the competitive market economy is producing the *right mix* of goods to start with. For example, suppose that point *A* in Figure 13-3 corresponds to producing enough wheat to let everyone have shredded wheat five times a week and cornflakes two times a

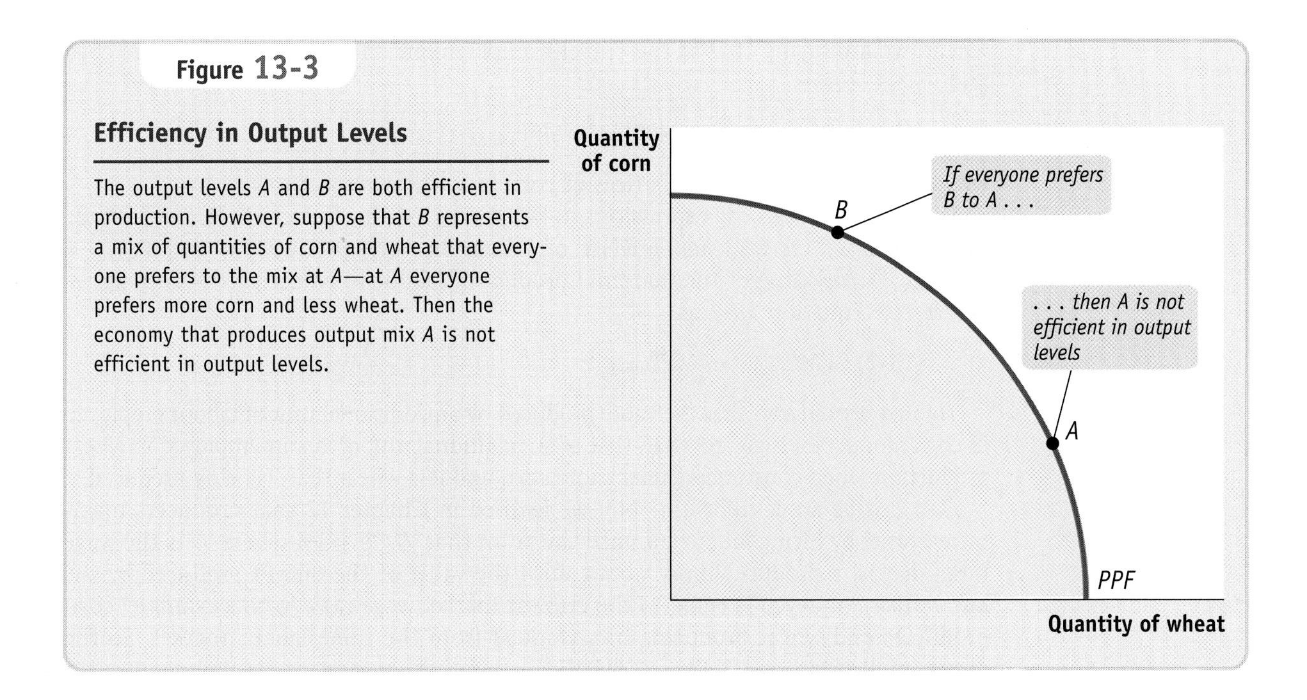

Figure 13-3

Efficiency in Output Levels

The output levels *A* and *B* are both efficient in production. However, suppose that *B* represents a mix of quantities of corn and wheat that everyone prefers to the mix at *A*—at *A* everyone prefers more corn and less wheat. Then the economy that produces output mix *A* is not efficient in output levels.

week. This will still be inefficient if everyone prefers to have shredded wheat only three times a week but cornflakes four times a week—*and* if point *B* would allow them to do so. In that case, moving from *A* to *B*—that is, shifting resources into corn production—would make everyone better off. Our third criterion for efficiency, then, is that the economy be **efficient in output levels:** there must not be a different mix of output that would make some people better off without making others worse off.

An economy is **efficient in output levels** if there isn't a different mix of output that would make some people better off without making others worse off.

The third and final piece of good news about the equilibrium of a competitive market economy is that it will be efficient in output levels when prices perform properly as economic signals.

How do we know this? We already saw that in an individual competitive market producers produce the quantity of output that maximizes total surplus. The reason is that consumers and producers face the same price—the market price is an economic signal telling producers what one more unit of output is worth to consumers. This signal induces producers to produce that extra unit of output if the cost of the resources they need to produce it is less than the market price.

In the economy as a whole, producers learn how much consumers are willing to pay for a bit more of one good versus a bit more of another when market prices operate as economic signals. This process ensures that a competitive market economy in general equilibrium produces the right mix of goods.

To see how this happens, imagine an economy in which the only resource that can be shifted between industries is labour, and all producers are hiring from the same labour market. (We'll also assume there are no complications like compensating differentials that make wages differ.) Imagine that right now consumers would prefer more corn and less wheat than the economy is currently producing. The economy can provide what consumers want by transferring labour from wheat production to corn production—by forgoing some wheat output in order to produce more corn. But will this adjustment take place?

Yes, it will, because consumers are willing to pay more for the additional corn that one more worker employed in corn production can produce than they are willing to pay for the wheat forgone by employing one fewer worker in wheat production. We can express this algebraically. The extra corn that a unit of labour can produce is MPL_{corn}, the marginal product of labour in corn. The wheat that unit of labour would have produced is MPL_{wheat}, the marginal product of labour in wheat. When we say that consumers are willing to pay more for the extra corn than for the wheat, we are saying that at the current employment and output levels in the corn and wheat sectors

(13-1) $P_{corn} \times MPL_{corn} > P_{wheat} \times MPL_{wheat}$

where P_{corn} and P_{wheat} are the prices of corn and wheat respectively.

We've already seen the expressions in Equation 13-1 in Chapter 12. $P_{corn} \times MPL_{corn}$ is the *value of the marginal product* of labour in corn production, and $P_{wheat} \times MPL_{wheat}$ is the value of the marginal product of labour in wheat production. So we can restate Equation 13-1 as

(13-2) $VMPL_{corn} > VMPL_{wheat}$

This expression says that the value produced by an additional unit of labour employed in corn production is greater than that of an additional unit of labour employed in wheat production when consumers prefer more corn and less wheat than is being produced.

Can this be an equilibrium? No; we learned in Chapter 12 that producers maximize profits by hiring labour up until the point that $VMPL = W$, where W is the wage rate. That is, a producer hires labour until the value of the output produced by the last worker employed is equal to the current market wage rate. In this example, corn producers and wheat producers hire workers from the same labour market. So the direct implication of $VMPL_{corn} > VMPL_{wheat}$ is that, at current employment levels, corn producers are willing to pay a higher wage rate than wheat producers. Corn producers will hire workers away from wheat producers.

When will this process stop? When the wage rate that corn producers are willing to pay is equal to the wage rate that wheat producers are willing to pay; that is, when $VMPL_{corn} = VMPL_{wheat}$. The evolution of this process is illustrated in Figure 13-4. In

Figure 13-4 How an Economy Achieves Efficiency in Output Levels

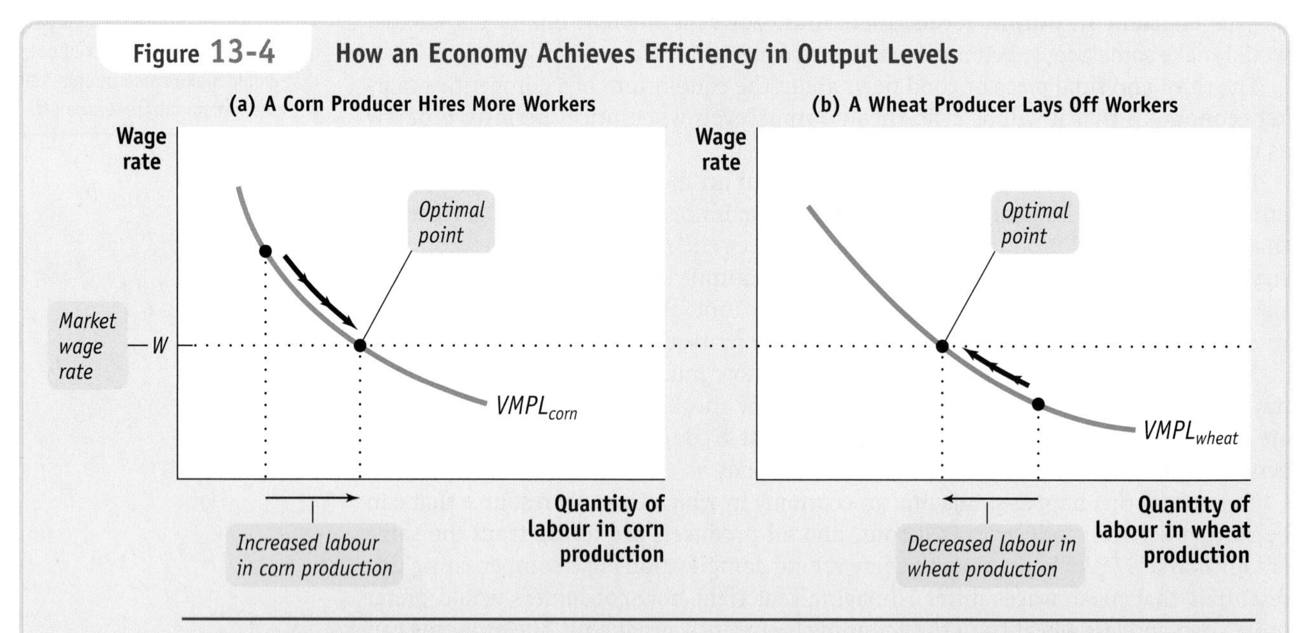

If at current employment levels $VMPL_{corn} > VMPL_{wheat}$, then corn producers will increase their profits by hiring workers away from wheat producers, who will, in turn, increase their profits by laying off workers. This process is illustrated for a corn producer in panel (a). As a corn producer hires workers, she increases her corn production and moves down her *VMPL* curve until she reaches her optimal employment level, the number of workers at which $VMPL_{corn} = W$, the market wage rate. Panel (b) shows the corresponding changes for a wheat producer: he decreases his wheat production and moves up his *VMPL* curve as he lays off workers. He also reaches his optimal employment level at $VMPL_{wheat} = W$. Workers cease moving between sectors once $VMPL_{corn} = VMPL_{wheat}$. It is an equilibrium because at that point the value of the additional output produced by a worker in the corn sector no longer exceeds the value of the additional output produced by a worker in the wheat sector and corn producers are no longer willing to pay a higher wage than wheat producers. >web...

panel (a), a corn producer starts at a $VMPL_{corn}$ greater than the current market wage rate. She increases her profits by hiring more workers and moves down her *VMPL* curve until she reaches her optimal employment level, at which $VMPL_{corn} = W$.

Where are these new workers in the corn sector coming from? They are coming from the wheat sector. This is illustrated in panel (b), where a wheat producer is losing workers and in the process is moving up his *VMPL* curve. He increases his profits by laying off workers, letting them go until he reaches his optimal employment level, at which $VMPL_{wheat} = W$.

So as labour in the economy is reallocated from wheat production to corn production, the output of corn rises and the output of wheat falls. Eventually, workers cease moving from the wheat sector to the corn sector when $VMPL_{corn} = VMPL_{wheat}$. At this point the value of the additional output produced by a worker in the corn sector no longer exceeds the value of the additional output produced by a worker in the wheat sector. That is, we have finally reached an equilibrium.

This example helps us understand that, in a market economy, markets for goods and services are linked via the factor markets. Or to put it a slightly different way, any change in the amount of one good or service produced will ultimately affect the amounts of other goods and services as factors of production shift from one sector to another. Figure 13-5 helps us make sense of the interconnectedness of markets for goods and services and

Figure 13-5 Efficiency in Output Levels in a Circular-Flow Framework

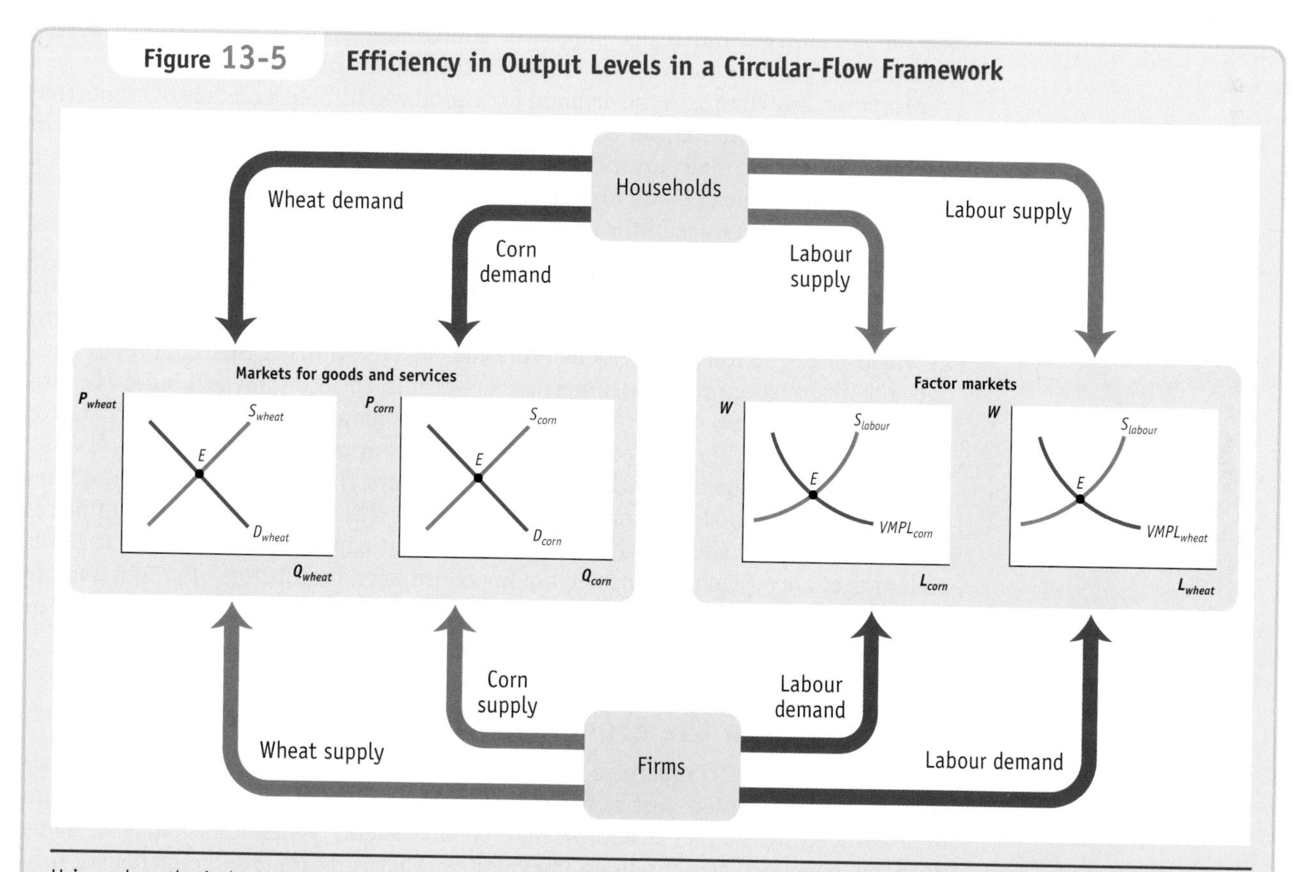

Using a hypothetical economy in which corn and wheat are the only goods and labour is the only factor of production, we can see how the markets for goods and services are linked via the factor markets. The factor markets bring the supply of labour from households and the demand for labour by firms into equilibrium, and the markets for goods and services bring the supply of goods and services from firms and the demand for goods and services by households into equilibrium. But supply and demand in all these markets are interrelated: households' earnings in the labour market determine their demand for goods and services, and vice versa; firms' profits from hiring labour in the labour market and producing output determine their supply of goods and services, and vice versa. Any change in one market will ultimately generate corresponding changes in all the other markets. When every market for goods and services and every factor market in the economy is in equilibrium, the economy as a whole is in general equilibrium.

factor markets in a market economy. To appreciate its significance, it may help to recall the circular-flow diagram of Chapter 2. There we saw how firms and households are linked via the factor markets and the markets for goods and services through flows of money. That is, in the factor markets, firms pay households for factors of production; in the markets for goods and services, households pay firms for goods and services.

Figure 13-5 presents an alternative and richer version of the same phenomenon, this time expressed in terms of the forces of supply and demand for resources that underlie the money flows of the circular-flow diagram. Here, we imagine that the only goods in the economy are corn and wheat and that labour is the only factor of production. The right portion of the figure represents how the supply of labour from households and the demand for labour from firms meet and are brought into equilibrium in the factor markets. But supply and demand in the labour market are themselves affected by supply and demand in the markets for goods and services: firms' demand for labour is derived from the demand for their goods and services, and households' supply of labour is determined by the earnings required for purchases in the markets for goods and services.

Similarly, the left portion of Figure 13-5 represents how the supply of goods and services from firms and the demand for goods and services from households meet and are brought into equilibrium in the markets for goods and services. Again, there is an interrelationship between the market for goods and services and factor markets: households' demand for goods and services is determined by the wages they earn in the labour market, and firms' supply of goods and services is determined by the returns they generate from hiring labour in the labour market.

Moreover, any change in the demand for a good will initiate a cascade of events that will ripple through the entire economy as resources shift among various sectors in response. So, for example, an increase in demand for corn relative to wheat causes a rightward shift in the demand for corn and a leftward shift in the demand for wheat. This results in an increase in the equilibrium quantity of corn supplied and a decrease in the equilibrium quantity of wheat supplied, which in turn causes an increase in the equilibrium employment level in the corn sector and a decrease in the equilibrium employment in the wheat sector. So the incentives in a competitive market economy in which prices perform properly as economic signals will lead the economy to produce the mix of goods that consumers prefer—that is, the economy will indeed be efficient in output levels. When each market for goods and services and each factor market is in equilibrium, the economy as a whole is in general equilibrium.

How does a competitive market economy achieve this amazing result? It comes down to the point we have emphasized throughout this discussion: the role of prices as *economic signals*. The fact that everyone faces the same prices ensures that goods and services are efficiently allocated among consumers, that factors of production are efficiently allocated among producers, and that the mix of goods and services produced reflects what people want.

Inefficiency in the Economy: When Prices Go Astray

The efficiency of a competitive market economy, however, is not something we should take for granted. Just as individual markets can fail, the general equilibrium of a competitive market economy may be inefficient. When this happens, some mutually beneficial trades will go unexploited. That is, there is some reallocation of consumption or production, or some change in output levels, that would make someone better off without making others worse off.

Why is a competitive market economy sometimes inefficient? For the same three reasons that individual markets sometimes fail. And when markets fail, prices fail to provide accurate economic signals.

First, recall that a market fails when attempts by one party to capture more resources prevents mutually beneficial transactions from occurring. We can illustrate this phenomenon by returning to our Chapter 4 example of agricultural quotas.

Recall that the current quota on Canadian poultry production results in a shortage of poultry compared to the unrestricted competitive market equilibrium. As a result, existing owners of poultry quota licenses gain (earning higher returns than they would have otherwise), but mutually beneficial transactions in poultry go unexploited. If the quota didn't exist, the fact that the market price of poultry exceeds the unrestricted competitive market price would draw new producers into the market. So supply would increase until the willingness to pay of the last buyer in the market equalled the cost of the last seller in the market, and the market would achieve efficiency. Or, to put it slightly differently, the quota prevents the market price from operating as an economic signal that would draw new producers into the market to eliminate the shortage. As a result, the larger economy (of which the poultry market is a part) is inefficient. It is not efficient in production because some producers with higher costs have poultry quota licenses but some with lower costs do not, implying that output could be increased without using more resources by reallocating production to those producers with the lowest cost. And it is not efficient in output levels because there are too few poultry producers relative to other goods. We will study a similar kind of inefficiency in detail in Chapter 14, where we investigate monopoly, an industry that has only a single seller.

The second source of market failure is the side effects of actions that aren't properly accounted for in the existing markets. For example, consider the pollution caused by a large pig farm whose wastes foul nearby streams and reduce the welfare of nearby residents. The cost savings that the farm gains by dumping its waste rather than having it properly disposed of are smaller in value than the discomfort experienced by its neighbours—that is, what the neighbours would be willing to pay to get rid of the pollution. But a mutually beneficial trade between the farm and the neighbours is going unexploited. Efficiency could be achieved if there were a "market for pollution"—if either the farm could purchase from the residents the right to dump so many barrels of waste or the residents could purchase from the farm the right to water of a certain purity. Either way, efficiency would be achieved: consumers would buy and the seller would sell until the willingness to pay for the last unit bought and sold equals the seller's cost of producing it. The problem here arises because the relevant market doesn't exist—there is no market for either pollution rights or water-purity rights. As a result, there is no relevant market price that can function as an economic signal to direct individuals to buy and sell. This economy is inefficient: the total welfare of individuals in the economy would be higher if less pollution and, correspondingly, fewer pigs were produced. We will analyze these side effects, called *externalities,* in detail in Chapter 19. There we will see how governments can intervene in ways that ensure that market prices do indeed provide the proper economic signals.

The third and final reason that markets fail is that some goods, by their nature, are unsuited for efficient management by markets. Consider a song that can be downloaded from the Internet. Once the song is recorded, the marginal cost to the record company of allowing someone to download it is virtually zero. So efficiency implies that people should be allowed to download the song until the last downloader's willingness to pay is equal to zero. That is, efficiency is achieved only if there is free and unrestricted downloading of music. But an inconvenient fact arises at this point: if the record company can't charge for downloads, then it won't have revenues to pay its artists. And if it can't pay its artists, then artists won't record in the first place. And that, too, is inefficient. The problem here lies in the nature of the good itself, called an *information good,* which is the subject of Chapter 22. For information goods, efficiency in consumption means that the price to consumers must be zero, but efficiency in output levels means that the price received by producers must be greater than zero. For these goods, inefficiency is simply unavoidable. A similar inefficiency arises for what are called *public goods* and *common resources*—goods for which, by their nature, the producer cannot charge consumers. We will study public goods and common resources in Chapter 20.

In most cases, however, market failures can be corrected. Indeed, although it is important to understand how they occur, this analysis isn't a reason to reject markets. Instead, the analysis of market failures tells policy-makers how to correct them and take advantage of the remarkable ability of a competitive market economy to allocate resources efficiently.

>>QUICK REVIEW

- To achieve efficiency, an economy must be *efficient in consumption, efficient in production,* and *efficient in output levels.*
- When prices perform properly as economic signals, a *competitive market economy* in *general equilibrium* is efficient. It is efficient in consumption because goods and services are allocated to consumers according to their prices, which are signals of consumers' willingness to pay. Second, it is efficient in production because factors of production are allocated to producers according to their prices, signals of producer's valuation of those factors. Finally, it is efficient in output levels: because everyone faces the same prices, the mix of goods and services will be the mix that people prefer.
- The same factors that lead to market failure lead to inefficiency of the economy as a whole, with prices failing to perform properly as economic signals and mutually beneficial transactions going unexploited.

economics in action

A Great Leap—Backward

We began this chapter with the observation that the planned economy of East Germany did not, as its founders had hoped, surpass the market economies of the West. But possibly the most compelling example of inefficiency in a planned economy comes from China.

In the late 1950s, China's leader Mao Zedong put into effect an ambitious plan, the so-called Great Leap Forward, to speed up the nation's industrialization. Key to this plan was a shift from urban to rural manufacturing: farming villages were supposed to start producing such heavy industrial goods as steel.

Unfortunately, this plan backfired. Diverting farmers from their usual work led to a sharp fall in food production. Meanwhile, because raw materials like coal and iron ore were sent to ill-equipped and inexperienced rural producers rather than to urban factories, industrial output declined as well. The plan, in short, led to a fall in the production of everything.

Because China was a very poor nation to start with, the results were catastrophic. The famine that followed is estimated to have reduced China's population by as much as 30 million. ■

>>CHECK YOUR UNDERSTANDING 13-2

1. In the small country of Bountiful, labour is the only factor of production, all workers are paid the same wage, all food is produced domestically, and all markets are perfectly competitive. Imagine that, due to health concerns, each Bountifullian experiences a greater demand for breakfast cereals and a lower demand for sausage.
   a. Explain how the change in preferences will lead to a reallocation of labour between the sausage and breakfast cereal industries. Use the concepts of $VMPL_S$, $VMPL_C$, and wage rate in your answer (the subscript S refers to sausage and C to cereal).
   b. How will you know that the Bountiful economy has fully adjusted to the change in preferences? Use the three conditions of efficiency in your answer.

Solutions appear at back of book.

Efficiency and Equity

We have now shown why a perfectly competitive market economy is typically efficient: there is no way to make some people better off without making others worse off.

This conclusion refutes the claims of would-be economic planners, who insist that markets are disorganized free-for-alls and that centralized decision making would be more efficient. But we need to be careful: it is easy to get carried away with the idea that markets get it right and to then draw inappropriate conclusions about economic policy.

It's important to remember that efficiency is about *how to achieve goals;* it does not say anything about what your goals should be. Saying that the market outcome is efficient doesn't mean that that outcome is necessarily desirable. In fact, in some circumstances a well-thought-out economic policy may deliberately choose an outcome that is *not* efficient.

When can an outcome be efficient without being desirable? When it's not fair.

What's Fair?

Imagine an economy in which a dictator controls everything, keeping almost everything the economy produces for himself and allowing his subjects only the bare minimum they need to survive. Could such an economy be efficient?

Yes, it could. If there is no way to make one of the suffering citizens better off without making the dictator worse off, then the economy is efficient. But that doesn't mean we have to approve of it. The situation is clearly unjust; the contrast between the dictator's wealth and his subjects' poverty isn't fair.

This extreme example shows that we want something more than efficiency from an economy. We also want **equity:** we want the distribution of utility among individuals to be reasonably fair.

Equity means that the distribution of utility among individuals is fair.

But what exactly is "fair"? That turns out to be a very hard question to answer. To see why it's such a tricky question, let's consider how plausible ideas about fairness become problematic when you start to think about them carefully.

First, you sometimes hear that people should be given an equal chance at the starting line—that is, at birth, or maybe at the age of 18, everyone should have the same opportunities to be successful in life. That sounds fair—but what about the natural desire of parents to do well by their children? Shouldn't parents who own their own businesses have the right to appoint their children to executive positions in those businesses? Shouldn't parents who can afford to do so have the right to send their children to expensive private schools? It seems unfair that children of successful parents should have an advantage over children whose parents don't have the same resources. Yet it would also seem unfair to prevent successful parents from helping their children. How do you resolve this contradiction?

"FAIR IS FAIR... IF IT'S TURN-OFF-YOUR-TV WEEK FOR ME, THEN IT'S UNPLUG-YOUR-E-MAIL WEEK FOR YOU."

Another familiar concept is that people should be rewarded for the work they do. And that too seems reasonable: if you are a skilled worker, with twice my marginal product, it seems only fair that you should receive twice my wage. But what about someone who suffers an injury and cannot work? To say that that person should go without any income seems unfair.

The attempt to define fairness has led to some fascinating debates among philosophers; we describe the views of one influential thinker, John Rawls, in For Inquiring Minds below. However, those debates have not led to any generally accepted definition.

FOR INQUIRING MINDS
THEORIES OF JUSTICE

In 1971 the philosopher John Rawls published *A Theory of Justice,* which represents the most famous attempt to date to develop a theory of economic fairness. He asked readers to imagine deciding economic and social policies behind a "veil of ignorance" about your identity. That is, suppose that you knew you would be a human being, but you did not know whether you would be rich or poor, healthy or sick, and so on. What kind of policies would you want?

Rawls answered that you would probably want to choose policies that placed a high weight on the utility of the worst-off members of society: after all, you might end up being one of them. And because of diminishing marginal utility, having a few more dollars will do you a lot of good if you find yourself poor, while having a few dollars less won't do you much harm if you find yourself well-off.

Do we need a definition of *fairness?* Not necessarily—virtually everyone agrees that some outcomes, like our hypothetical dictator-dominated economy, are unfair, and in other cases we can agree to differ. But sometimes the lack of agreement on fairness means that economic analysis alone cannot be used to decide between alternative policies. To see why, let's introduce a new concept, the *utility possibility frontier.*

The Utility Possibility Frontier

Let's think of an economy that contains only two kinds of people, Easterners and Westerners. In Figure 13-6, the horizontal axis measures the total utility of the typical Westerner and the vertical axis measures the total utility of the typical Easterner.

An efficient outcome in this economy would be one in which there was no way to make either Easterners or Westerners better off without making members of the other group worse off. But there may be many such possible outcomes. In the figure we show what the possibilities might look like by drawing a **utility possibility frontier,** which shows how well-off each group *could* be given the economy's resources and the total utility of the other. Any point on the utility possibility frontier is efficient—that is, once you are on the frontier, the only way to make some people better off is to make others worse off. Any point inside the frontier is inefficient.

A **utility possibility frontier** shows how well-off one individual or group could be for each given total utility level of another individual or group.

So suppose that you were asked to choose between two sets of economic policies—one that would bring the economy to point *A* and one that would bring it to point *B.* For example, suppose there is a question of who should receive ownership of some disputed land. As long as the property rights are clearly defined, the economy will be efficient, but Westerners would prefer that they get the rights, and Easterners would prefer the reverse. So which outcome is better?

The answer is that it's a matter of taste. Westerners would, of course, prefer *A;* Easterners would prefer *B.* For government officials trying to decide how to assign the property rights, the answer would depend on what relative weight they give to the welfare of the two groups. The question of whether *A* or *B* is better is, in other words, a question of values that economics cannot answer.

Notice, by the way, that *A* and *B* don't differ just in how goods and services are distributed to individuals; they might well involve producing a different mix of goods and services. If Westerners like cornflakes but Easterners prefer shredded wheat, the

Figure 13-6

The Utility Possibility Frontier

The utility possibility frontier reminds us that there may be many efficient outcomes for an economy. The utility possibility frontier shows the maximum level of total utility of a typical Easterner, given the level of total utility of a typical Westerner. Any point on the curve is efficient because at such a point there is no way to make a typical Easterner better off without making a typical Westerner worse off, and vice versa. But this means that we cannot decide on economic grounds alone whether point *A* or *B* is better. **>web...**

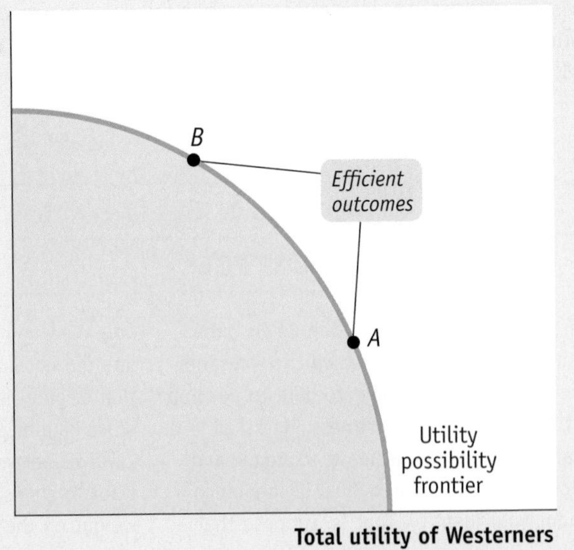

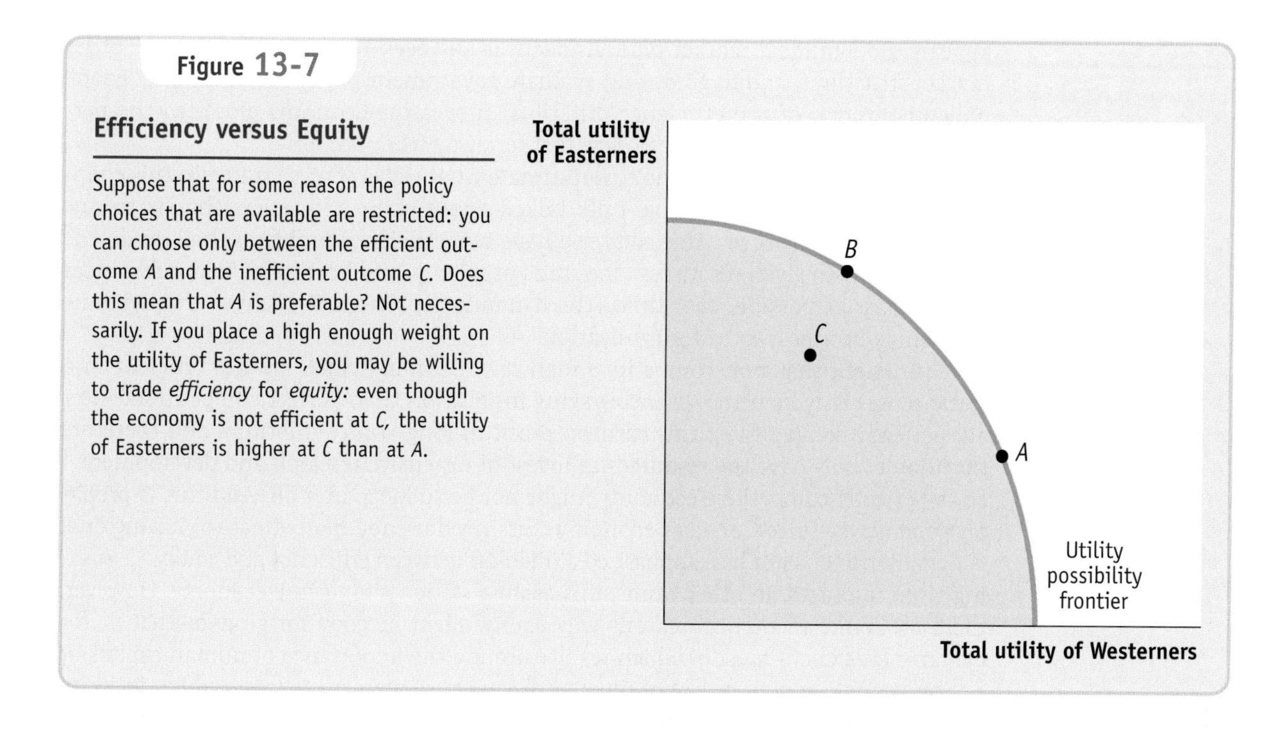

Figure 13-7

Efficiency versus Equity

Suppose that for some reason the policy choices that are available are restricted: you can choose only between the efficient outcome *A* and the inefficient outcome *C*. Does this mean that *A* is preferable? Not necessarily. If you place a high enough weight on the utility of Easterners, you may be willing to trade *efficiency* for *equity:* even though the economy is not efficient at *C*, the utility of Easterners is higher at *C* than at *A*.

economy probably produces more corn and less wheat at *B* than at *A*. Is it more efficient to produce corn or wheat? There is no answer to this question, because both can be efficient, depending on our goals.

The point that efficiency is a means to achieve goals, not a goal in itself, can be further illustrated by considering what is wrong with *inefficient* policies. Figure 13-7 shows the same utility possibility frontier as Figure 13-6 but now also shows point *C*—an inefficient outcome, one that lies inside the frontier. You might think of *C* as the result of a policy that favours Easterners in an inefficient way. In fact, many economists believe that the actual policies the newly reunited Germany followed to help the former East Germans were poorly designed, providing them with few incentives to take new jobs or acquire new skills. That is, many economists believe that Germany as a whole ended up at a point like *C*.

Is there any reason why you might want to choose an inefficient point such as *C*? Not if better choices are genuinely available: there are points on the utility possibility frontier that are better than *C*, whatever relative weight you give to the welfare of the two groups. For example, *B* is better than *C* by any standard.

But what if the real choices are limited to *A* or *C*? Should you as a voter prefer the efficient policies proposed by the Western party?

Not necessarily. *A* is efficient, and *C* is not; but it is still true that Easterners are better off at *C* than they are at *A*. So if the utility of Easterners matters enough to you, you might well prefer *C* to *A* even though you would prefer *B* to either. As economists say, it is often—but by no means always—worth trading less efficiency for more equity.

So it's important to remember what efficiency is *not*. Efficiency is not a goal in itself, to be pursued at the expense of other goals. It is only a way to achieve our goals more effectively—whatever those goals may be.

economics in action

When Theory Meets Policy

It's important not to underestimate what we've demonstrated in this chapter: that an economy where all markets are perfectly competitive will be efficient in consumption, production, and output levels. Since this avoids all waste, perfect competition may appear to be an ideal market type. As such, it has been used both to evaluate other market structures, and to guide and evaluate government policy intervention: "good" policy (in terms of the efficiency criterion) moves the economy closer to the perfectly competitive ideal; "bad" policy, further away from it.

But it is equally important not overestimate what we've demonstrated in this chapter. One problem is that we've only talked about static efficiency; that is to say, assuming *given* resources. In reality, we have two efficiency problems: how to do the best we can with given resources (the static problem), and how to make our resources grow as fast as possible over time (the dynamic problem). The key to the dynamic problem is how best to foster innovation.

It turns out that non-competitive market structures (which are not efficient in a static sense) may be better at encouraging innovation than perfect competition. After all, perfectly competitive firms earn no profit in long-run equilibrium, and therefore they don't really have the resources to invest in expensive research and development.[1] So, a perfectly competitive economy might not be so ideal after all. And this is probably good news—since Canada's economy certainly does not approximate to having one.

Finally, this chapter has emphasized a trade-off between efficiency and equity—assuming given resources. In other words, it is again a static vision of the economy. However, there are sound theoretical reasons why equity might be good for growth—that is, for dynamic efficiency—most of which revolve around the importance of human capital.

For example, a high degree of inequality can cause high crime rates, which increase the social costs associated with law enforcement and the judicial process—meaning more police, more courts, more lawyers, more prisoners, and more prisons; and fewer universities, fewer engineers, fewer scientists, and less innovation. Second, inequality and poverty tend to be associated with a lack of educational opportunities for the poor; and it is well known that a better-educated workforce is more productive than a less-educated one.

In Canada, eligibility for a student loan depends on family income. Despite this, those from high-income families are almost twice as likely to receive post-secondary education than those from low-income families. And a recent Statistics Canada study found that 36% of students who drop out of college or university cited financial barriers as the major reason. Thus, despite the structures we have put in place to increase educational opportunities for the poor, inequality in family incomes still provides an obstacle to education.

These linkages between inequality and growth are not just theoretical. They have been validated by a large amount of empirical work.[2] And this may not be such good news for Canada—since we have a good deal of inequality here, which may be hindering investment in human capital. ■

>> QUICK REVIEW

- We want an economy to be fair—to deliver *equity*—as well as efficient. There is, however, no agreed-upon definition of *fairness*.
- A useful concept for illustrating the limitations of efficiency as a goal is the *utility possibility frontier*. It shows that there are usually many efficient outcomes for an economy and that economics alone cannot tell us which one is better.
- It's not necessarily true that everyone prefers a given efficient outcome to a given inefficient one. There are many efficient policies, but you might prefer a given inefficient policy to some efficient policies.

>> CHECK YOUR UNDERSTANDING 13-3

1. Explain why it is easier to determine whether an economy is efficient than to determine whether it is fair.
2. Explain why the following statements are problematic to use in determining whether or not a society is fair.
   a. In a fair society, each person contributes to society according to his or her means, and each person receives benefits according to his or her needs.
   b. In a fair society, a person is rewarded in proportion to how hard he or she works.

Solutions appear at back of book.

[1]William J. Baumol, *The Free Market Innovation Machine* (Princeton, NJ: Princeton University Press, 2002).

[2]For example, see Xavier Sala-i-Martin, "Cross-Sectional Regressions and the Empirics of Economic Growth", *European Economic Review* 38 (1995): 739–747.

• A LOOK AHEAD •

We have now answered the first of the big questions we raised in the Introduction: *Why does a competitive market economy generally work so well?* Part of the answer involved defining what it means to work "well": an economy works badly if it misses opportunities to make at least one person better off without making others worse off, and it works well if it does not miss those opportunities.

What we've now seen is that in a well-functioning competitive market economy in equilibrium, consumers can buy as much or as little as they choose at the same price, and producers can sell as much or as little as they choose, also at the same price. And this means that all the opportunities to make at least one person better off without making others worse off—whether by redistributing goods among consumers, rearranging output among producers, or changing what the economy produces—will *already have been taken.*

One question down, another to go. Why do things sometimes go wrong? Why do market economies sometimes work badly? The short answer, as we saw in Chapter 6, is "market failure". The long answer will require a few more chapters!

SUMMARY

1. Except in cases of market failure, an individual competitive market in equilibrium maximizes total surplus, the sum of consumer and producer surplus. Rearranging consumption, rearranging production, or changing the level of output will all reduce total surplus.
2. **Property rights** and prices as **economic signals** are two features of competitive markets that are crucial to their ability to work well. The three causes of market failure—mutually beneficial transactions that are unexploited due to attempts to capture surplus, side effects that are not accounted for in the market, and goods whose nature prevents their efficient management by markets—can all be linked to the failure of prices to perform properly as economic signals.
3. When we turn to the performance of the economy as a whole, we use the economic definition of efficiency: the **general equilibrium** of a **competitive market economy** is efficient if there is no way to make some people better off without making others worse off.
4. Economic efficiency requires **efficiency in consumption**—there is no way to redistribute goods and services that makes some consumers better off without making others worse off. It requires **efficiency in production,** which arises from an **efficient allocation of resources**—there is no way to reallocate resources that allows the economy to produce more of some goods and services without producing less of others. And it requires **efficiency in output levels**—there is no other choice of output mix that makes some people better off without making others worse off. In the same way in which a competitive market maximizes total surplus, the general equilibrium of a competitive market economy as a whole is efficient—in consumption, in production, and in output levels—when prices perform properly as market signals. In cases of market failure, however, prices fail to lead people to exploit all mutually beneficial transactions; as a result, when markets fail, the economy as a whole is inefficient.
5. It is not enough for an economy to be efficient. We also want it to deliver an outcome that is "fair" in terms of the distribution of utility among individuals. Economic fairness is known as **equity.**
6. Unfortunately, there is no generally accepted definition of *fairness*. The ambiguity this sometimes creates for evaluating economic policy can be illustrated with the **utility possibility frontier,** which shows the trade-offs between the utility achieved by one individual or group and that achieved by other individuals or groups.

KEY TERMS

Property rights, p. 329
Economic signal, p. 330
Competitive market economy, p. 332
General equilibrium, p. 332
Efficient in consumption, p. 333
Efficient in production, p. 333
Efficient allocation of resources, p. 333
Efficient in output levels, p. 335
Equity, p. 341
Utility possibility frontier, p. 342

PROBLEMS

1. The Medici family in Florence produces all the wool in Italy. The five Medici children each have a factory in which they can produce one pound of wool per day. Their costs of producing each pound of wool are given on the left side of the accompanying table. Wool is demanded by the Visconti family in Milan. Each of the five Visconti children can demand one pound of wool per day. Their willingness to pay is given on the right side of the table.

Medici family		Visconti family	
Name	Cost (per pound)	Name	Willingness to pay (per pound)
Lucrezia	$8	Ennio	$14
Bianca	10	Lucchino	13
Luisa	12	Matteo	12
Contessina	14	Giovanni	11
Maddalena	16	Filippo	10

   a. The market in wool is perfectly competitive. What will the equilibrium price be?

   b. Does the equilibrium price lead to efficiency in this market?

   c. The Visconti family argues that the price of wool should be fixed at a maximum of $10 so that all their operations can buy wool. Is this efficient? Why or why not?

2. Lakshmi and Sam have a cake that they want to divide in an efficient way, and the cake is the only good in their little economy. Both Lakshmi and Sam like cake and would always prefer to have more of it. Using the standard of efficiency in consumption, determine whether the following ways of dividing the cake are efficient.

   a. Lakshmi and Sam each get half of the cake.

   b. Lakshmi and Sam each get one-third of the cake and one-third is thrown away.

   c. Lakshmi gets the whole cake and Sam gets nothing.

3. A city block with 25 residents has a garden in the center. Some of the residents are very busy, but others have lots of leisure time. And their preferences also differ: some enjoy yard work, others don't. The garden requires a total of 1,000 hours of work per year—planting, mowing grass, and so on. One resident suggests that each resident should contribute 40 hours per year to maintain the garden. Another resident, an economist, objects that this will be inefficient.

   a. Explain why the economist thinks that the proposal will be inefficient.

   b. Describe how a market in which residents can trade hours of yard work leads to an efficient allocation of yard work among residents.

4. In the town of Blind River, only two goods are produced: left shoes and right shoes. And this economy produces on the production possibility frontier. That is, there is no way of producing more left shoes without producing fewer right shoes, and vice versa. What else would you need to know, if anything, to determine whether the economy of Blind River as a whole is efficient? That is, does it satisfy efficiency in production, efficiency in consumption, and efficiency in output levels? Explain your answer.

5. The economy of Dunk, Alberta, produces only two goods, bagels and doughnuts, using labour as the only factor of production. There are 8 workers in Dunk and all are paid the same wage. The accompanying table shows the amount of output that can be produced with a certain number of workers.

Quantity of labor in doughnut production (workers)	Quantity of doughnuts	Quantity of labor in bagel production (workers)	Quantity of bagels
0	0	0	0
1	34	1	50
2	40	2	86
3	46	3	92
4	49	4	98
5	52	5	104
6	53	6	106

   a. Suppose that the price of a doughnut is $0.50 and the price of a bagel is also $0.50. There are 2 workers producing doughnuts and 3 workers producing bagels. The other 3 workers are unemployed. Given what you know about the relationship between the value of the marginal products and efficiency, determine whether this economy is efficient in the production of doughnuts versus the production of bagels—that is, is the economy efficient in output levels? Also determine whether the economy is efficient in production—that is, is it producing on the production possibility frontier?

   b. Suppose that the price of doughnuts is $0.20, and the price of bagels is $0.10. There are 4 workers producing doughnuts and 4 workers producing bagels, and nobody is unemployed. Is this economy efficient in production? Is it efficient in output levels?

   c. Initially, the price of doughnuts is $0.20, the price of bagels is $0.10, and there are 4 workers producing doughnuts and 4 workers producing bagels, just as in part b. Now consumers' tastes change: due to health concerns, consumers are now willing to pay $0.75 per bagel but only $0.10 per doughnut. These new prices act as signals of consumers' preferences. In response to this change, will the allocation of workers to bagel or doughnut production change?

6. Land in the Shire can be used for growing carrots or potatoes, and the only variable input into production is labour (land is fixed). All workers are paid the same wage. There are two farmers: Sam grows carrots, and the marginal product of

labour on his farm is 30 pounds of carrots per month. Merry grows potatoes, and the marginal product of labour on his farm is 44 pounds of potatoes per month. Each experiences diminishing returns to labour. The price of carrots is $3 per pound, and the price of potatoes is $2 per pound.

a. Calculate the value of the marginal product of labour in carrots and in potatoes to assess whether the economy of the Shire is efficient in output levels. Is the economy in general equilibrium?

b. Do the prices of carrots and potatoes signal that farmers should produce more or less of their crops? In which direction will employment levels adjust in response to the market prices for the two crops? Describe how the economy reaches general equilibrium.

7. The economy of Leisureville, BC, produces only two goods: skis and bikes. Labour is the only variable input into production, there are diminishing returns to labour, and all workers are paid the same wage. All markets are competitive, and initially the economy is in general equilibrium. Now, due to a change in tastes, consumers' preferences change away from skis and toward bikes.

a. What will happen to consumers' willingness to pay for bikes and for skis? What will therefore happen to the market prices for bikes and skis?

b. As the prices adjust, what will happen to the value of the marginal product of labour in bikes and in skis? What will happen to bike producers' and ski producers' willingness to pay for workers?

c. As adjustments are made in employment, what happens to the output of bikes and of skis? How does the marginal product of labour in bikes and in skis respond? What therefore happens to the value of the marginal product of labour in bikes and in skis?

d. At what point does this process stop?

8. Gulliver travels to a country in which there are two types of creatures, the Houyhnhnms and the Yahoos, and there are equally as many Houyhnhnms as there are Yahoos. The accompanying table lists the possible combinations of utility levels. That is, the points in the table lie on this economy's utility possibility frontier.

Point	Total utility of Houyhnhnms (utils)	Total utility of Yahoos (utils)
A	200	0
B	180	30
C	140	60
D	80	90
E	0	120

a. Draw the utility possibility frontier. When Gulliver arrives, he notices that the Houyhnhnms have a utility of 120 and the Yahoos have a utility of 50. Is this an efficient outcome?

b. Gulliver remembers that Jeremy Bentham argued that the best outcome is the one that maximizes the sum of everyone's utility. Which of the points *A* through *E* on the utility frontier would Bentham have chosen as the best outcome?

c. Gulliver then recalls that John Rawls argued that the best outcome is the one that gives the most utility to whoever happens to be the worst-off member in society. Which of the points *A* through *E* would Rawls have chosen?

9. Consider the utility possibility frontier in the accompanying diagram.

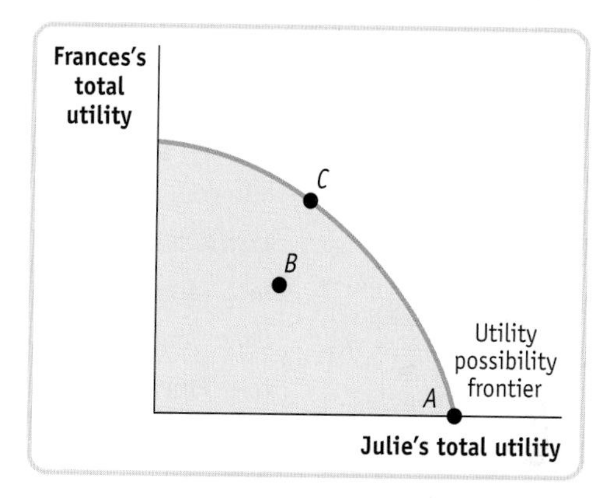

a. Is point *A* efficient? Would you describe point *A* as fair? Why or why not?

b. Is point *B* efficient?

c. Is point *C* better than point *B*? Why or why not?

d. Is point *A* better than point *B*? Why or why not?

>web... To continue your study and review of concepts in this chapter, please visit the Krugman/Wells website for quizzes, animated graph tutorials, web links to helpful resources, and more.

www.worthpublishers.com/krugmanwellsmyatt

chapter 14

>>Monopoly

EVERYBODY MUST GET STONES

A FEW YEARS AGO DE BEERS, THE world's main supplier of diamonds, ran an ad urging men to buy their wives diamond jewellery. "She married you for richer, for poorer", read the ad. "Let her know how it's going."

Crass? Yes. Effective? No question. For generations diamonds have been a symbol of luxury, valued not only for their appearance but also for their rarity.

But geologists will tell you that diamonds aren't all that rare. In fact, according to the *Dow Jones-Irwin Guide to Fine Gems and Jewelry,* diamonds are "more common than any other gem-quality coloured stone. They only seem rarer . . ."

Corbis

Got stones?

Why do diamonds seem rarer than other gems? Part of the answer is a brilliant marketing campaign (we'll talk more about marketing and product differentiation in Chapter 16). But mainly diamonds seem rare because De Beers *makes* them rare: the company controls most of the world's diamond mines, and limits the quantity of diamonds supplied to the market.

Up to now we have concentrated exclusively on perfectly competitive markets—markets in which the producers are perfect competitors. But De Beers isn't like the producers we've studied so far: it is a *monopolist,* the sole (or almost sole) producer of a good. Monopolists behave differently from producers in perfectly competitive industries: where perfect competitors take the price at which they can sell their output as given, monopolists like De Beers know that their actions affect market prices, and take that effect into account when deciding how much to produce. Before we begin our analysis of monopoly, let's step back and look at monopoly and perfect competition as parts of a broader system for classifying markets.

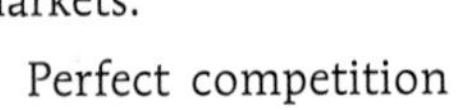

Perfect competition and *monopoly* are particular types of *market structure.* They are particular categories in a system economists use to classify markets and industries according to two main dimensions. This chapter begins with a brief overview of types of market

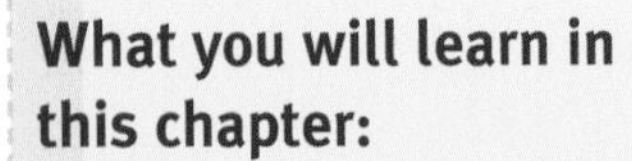

What you will learn in this chapter:

- The significance of **monopoly,** where a single **monopolist** is the only producer of a good
- How a monopolist determines its profit-maximizing output and price
- The difference between monopoly and perfect competition, and the effects of that difference on society's welfare
- How policy makers address the problems posed by monopoly
- What **price discrimination** is, and why it is so prevalent when producers have **market power**

structure. It will help us in this chapter and in subsequent chapters to understand on a deeper level why markets differ and why producers in those markets behave quite differently.

Types of Market Structure

In the real world, there is a mind-boggling array of different markets. We observe widely different patterns of behaviour by producers across markets: in some markets producers are extremely competitive; in others, they seem to somehow coordinate their actions to avoid competing with one another; and, as we have just described, some markets are monopolies in which there is no competition at all. In order to develop principles and make predictions about markets and how producers will behave in those markets, economists have developed four principal market structure models: *perfect competition, monopoly, oligopoly,* and *monopolistic competition.* This system of market structures is based on two dimensions:

- The number of producers in the market (one, few, or many)
- Whether the goods offered are identical or *differentiated*

Differentiated goods are goods that are different but considered somewhat substitutable by consumers (think Coke versus Pepsi).

Figure 14-1 provides a simple visual summary of the types of market structure classified according to the two dimensions. Let's briefly look at each type. In *monopoly,* a single producer sells a single, undifferentiated product. In *oligopoly,* a few producers—more than one but not a large number—sell products that may be either identical or differentiated. In *monopolistic competition,* many producers each sell a differentiated product (think of producers of economics textbooks). And finally, as we know, in *perfect competition* many producers each sell an identical product.

You might wonder what determines the number of firms in a market: whether there is one (monopoly), few (oligopoly), or many (perfect competition and monopolistic competition). We won't answer that question here, because it will be covered in detail later in this chapter and in Chapters 15 and 16, which analyse oligopoly and monopolistic competition. We will just briefly note that in the long run it depends

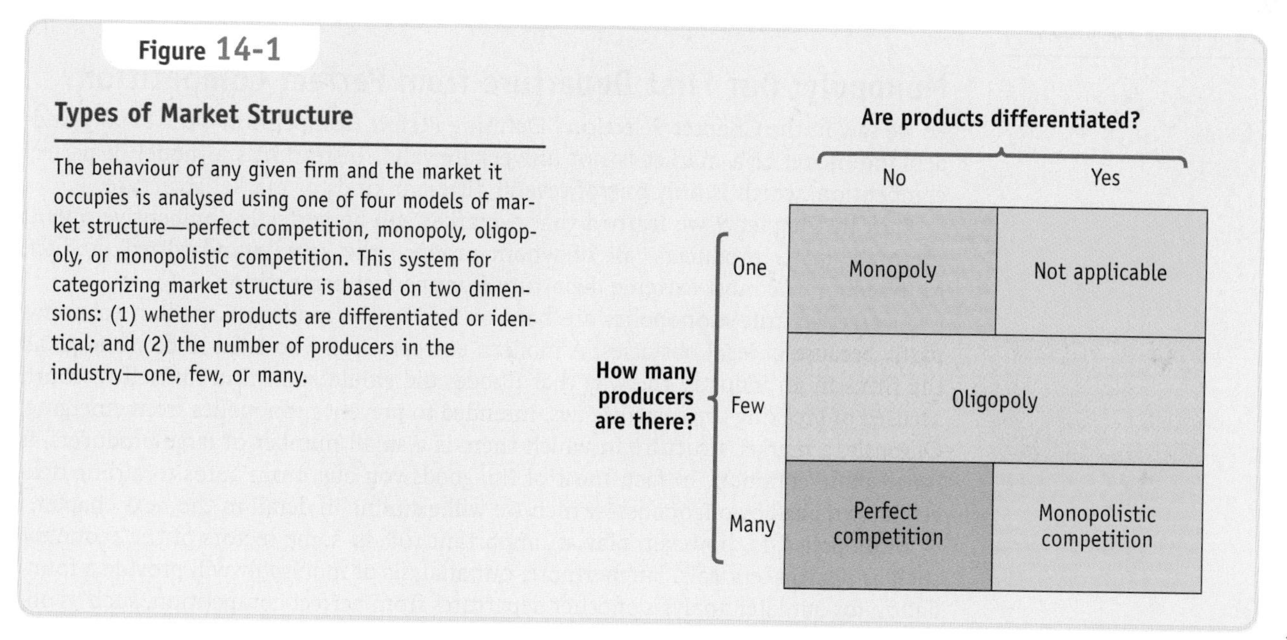

Figure 14-1

Types of Market Structure

The behaviour of any given firm and the market it occupies is analysed using one of four models of market structure—perfect competition, monopoly, oligopoly, or monopolistic competition. This system for categorizing market structure is based on two dimensions: (1) whether products are differentiated or identical; and (2) the number of producers in the industry—one, few, or many.

on whether there are conditions that make it difficult for new firms to enter the market—conditions such as government regulations that discourage entry, economies of scale in production, technological superiority, or control of necessary resources or inputs. When these conditions are present, industries tend to be monopolies or oligopolies; when they are not present, industries tend to be perfectly competitive or monopolistically competitive.

You might also wonder why some markets have differentiated products but others have identical ones. The answer is that it depends on the nature of the good and consumers' preferences. Some goods—soft drinks, economics textbooks, breakfast cereals—can readily be made into different varieties in the eyes and tastes of consumers. Other goods—hammers, for example—are much less easy to differentiate.

Although this chapter is devoted to the topic of monopoly, important aspects of monopoly carry over to other market structures—to oligopoly and monopolistic competition. In the next section we will define monopoly and review the conditions that make it possible. These same conditions, in less extreme form, also give rise to oligopoly. We then show how a monopolist can increase profit by limiting the quantity supplied to a market—behaviour that also occurs in oligopoly and monopolistic competition. As we'll see, this kind of behaviour is good for the producer but bad for consumers; it also causes inefficiency. An important topic of study will be the ways in which public policy tries to limit the damage. Finally, we turn to one of the surprising effects of monopoly—one that is very often present in oligopoly and monopolistic competition as well: the fact that different consumers often pay different prices for the same good.

The Meaning of Monopoly

The De Beers monopoly was created in the 1880s by Cecil Rhodes, a British businessman. By 1880 mines in South Africa already dominated the world's supply of diamonds. There were, however, many mining companies, all competing with each other. During the 1880s Rhodes bought up the great majority of those mines, and consolidated them into a single company, De Beers. By 1889 De Beers controlled almost all of the world's diamond production.

A **monopolist** is a firm that is the only producer of a good that has no close substitutes. An industry controlled by a monopolist is known as a **monopoly.**

De Beers, in other words, became a **monopolist.** A producer is a monopolist if it is the sole supplier of a good that has no close substitutes. When a firm is a monopolist, we say that the industry is a **monopoly.**

Monopoly: Our First Departure from Perfect Competition

As we saw in the Chapter 9 section "Defining Perfect Competition", the supply-and-demand model of a market is not universally valid. Instead, it's a model of perfect competition, which is only one of several different kinds of market structure.

Back in Chapter 9 we learned that a market will be perfectly competitive only if there are many producers, all of whom produce the same standardized product. Monopoly is the most extreme departure from perfect competition.

In practice, true monopolies are hard to find in the modern Canadian economy, partly because of legal obstacles. A modern entrepreneur who tried to consolidate all the firms in an industry the way that Rhodes did would soon find himself in court, accused of breaking the *combine laws,* intended to prevent monopolies from emerging. *Oligopoly,* a market structure in which there is a small number of large producers, is much more common. In fact, most of the goods you buy, from autos to airline tickets, are supplied by oligopolies—which we will examine in detail in the next chapter.

Monopolies do, however, play an important role in some sectors of the economy, such as pharmaceuticals. Furthermore, our analysis of monopoly will provide a foundation for our later analysis of other departures from perfect competition, such as oligopoly and monopolistic competition.

What Monopolists Do

Why did Rhodes want to consolidate South African diamond producers into a single company? What difference did it make to the world diamond market?

Figure 14-2 offers a preliminary view of the effects of monopoly. The figure shows an industry in which the supply curve under perfect competition intersects the demand curve at *C*, leading to the price P_C and the output Q_C.

Suppose that this industry is consolidated into a monopoly. The monopolist *moves up the demand curve* by reducing quantity supplied to a point like *M*, at which the price, P_M, paid by consumers is higher than under perfect competition, while the quantity produced, Q_M, is lower.

The ability of a monopolist to raise its price above the competitive level is known as the monopolist's **market power.** And market power is what monopoly is all about. A wheat farmer who is one of 100,000 wheat farmers has no market power: he or she must sell wheat for the going market price. Your local cable TV company, on the other hand, does have market power: it can raise prices and still keep many (though not all) of its customers, because they have nowhere else to go. In short, it's a monopolist.

Market power is the ability of a producer to raise prices.

The reason a monopolist raises its price above the competitive level and reduces output is to increase profit. Cecil Rhodes consolidated the diamond producers into De Beers because he realized that the whole would be worth more than the sum of its parts—the monopoly would generate more profit than the sum of the profits of the individual competitive firms. In fact, we saw in Chapter 9 that under perfect competition economic profits normally vanish in the long run. Under monopoly the profits don't go away—a monopolist is able to continue earning profits in the long run.

In fact, monopolists are not the only types of firms that possess market power. In the next chapter we will study *oligopolists*, firms that can have market power as well. Under certain conditions, oligopolists can earn positive economic profits in the long run by restricting output like monopolists do.

But why don't monopoly profits get competed away? What allows monopolists to be monopolists?

Figure 14-2

What a Monopolist Does

Under perfect competition, the price and quantity are determined by supply and demand. Here, the equilibrium is at *C*, where the price is P_C and the quantity is Q_C. A monopolist reduces the quantity supplied, to Q_M, and moves up the demand curve from *C* to *M*, raising the price to P_M. >web...

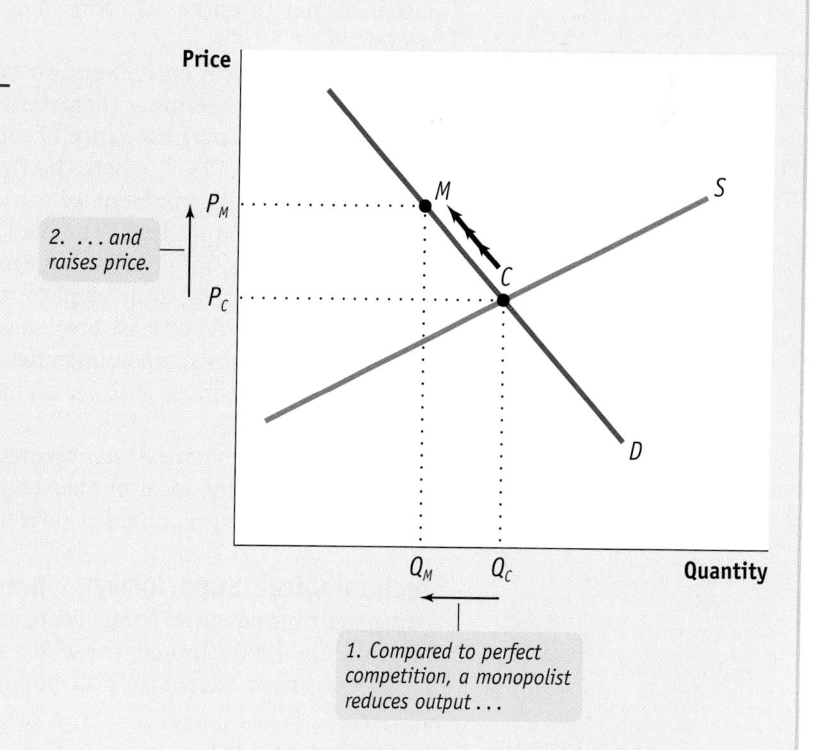

Why Do Monopolies Exist?

A monopolist making monopoly profits will not go unnoticed by others. But won't other firms crash the party, grab a piece of the action, and drive down prices and profits in the long run? For a profitable monopoly to persist, something must keep others from going into the same business; that "something" is known as a **barrier to entry.** There are four principal types of barriers to entry: control of scarce resources or inputs, economies of scale, technological superiority, and government-created barriers.

To earn profits, a monopolist must be protected by a **barrier to entry**—something that prevents other firms from entering the industry.

Control of a Scarce Resource or Input A monopolist that controls a resource crucial to an industry can prevent other firms from entering its market. Cecil Rhodes created the De Beers monopoly by establishing control over the mines that produced the great bulk of the world's diamonds.

Economies of Scale Many Canadians have natural gas piped into their homes for cooking and heating. Invariably, the local gas company is a monopolist. But why don't rival companies compete to provide gas?

When we look at the history of the gas industry around the world, we find that it often begins with several companies competing for local customers. But invariably this competition doesn't last long; soon local gas supply becomes a monopoly no matter where we look. This happens because of the large fixed costs involved in providing a town with gas lines. Since the cost of laying gas lines doesn't depend on how much gas a company sells, firms with a larger volume of sales have an advantage: because they are able to spread the fixed costs over a larger volume, they have lower average total costs than smaller firms.

Local gas supply is an industry in which average total costs always fall as output increases. As we learned in Chapter 8, this phenomenon is called *economies of scale*. There we learned that when average total cost falls as output increases, firms tend to grow larger. In an industry characterized by economies of scale, bigger companies are more profitable and drive out smaller companies. For the same reason, established companies have a cost advantage over any potential entrant—a potent barrier to entry. So economies of scale can both give rise to and sustain monopoly.

A monopoly that is created and sustained by economies of scale is called a **natural monopoly.** The defining characteristic of a natural monopoly is that it possesses economies of scale over the range of output that is relevant for the industry. This is illustrated in Figure 14-3, where the firm's average total cost curve and the market demand curve are drawn. Here we can see that the natural monopolist's *ATC* curve declines over the output levels at which price is greater than or equal to average total cost. So, the natural monopolist has economies of scale over the entire range of output for which any firm would want to remain in the industry—the range of output at which the firm would at least break even in the long run. The source of this condition is large fixed costs: when large fixed costs are required to operate, a given quantity of output is produced at lower average total cost by one large firm than by two or more smaller firms.

A **natural monopoly** exists when economies of scale provide a large cost advantage to having all of an industry's output produced by a single firm.

The most visible natural monopolies in the modern economy are local utilities—water, gas, electricity, local phone service, and cable television. As we'll see later in this chapter, natural monopolies pose a special challenge to public policy.

Technological Superiority A firm that maintains a consistent technological advantage over potential competitors can establish itself as a monopolist. For example, from the 1970s through the 1990s the chip manufacturer Intel was able to maintain a consistent advantage over potential competitors in both the design and the

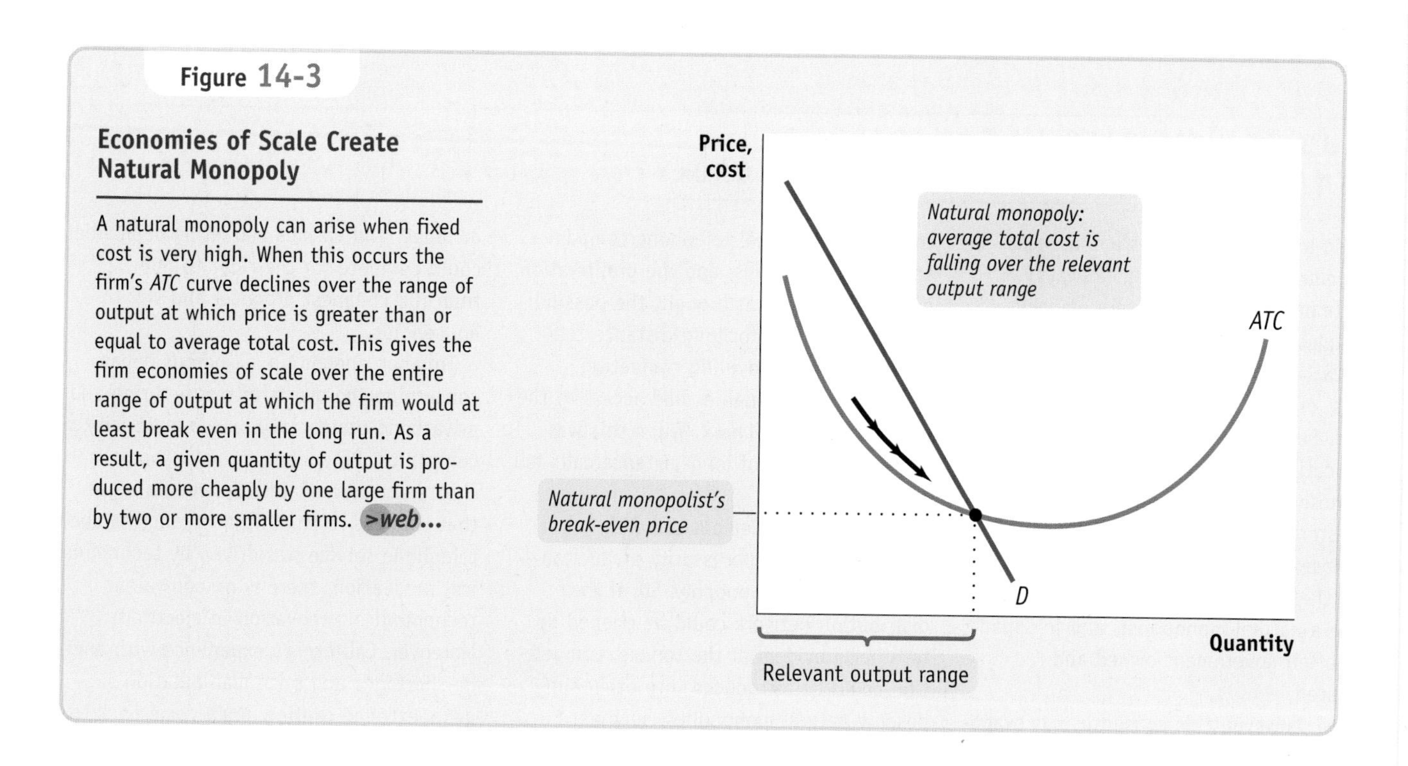

Figure 14-3

Economies of Scale Create Natural Monopoly

A natural monopoly can arise when fixed cost is very high. When this occurs the firm's *ATC* curve declines over the range of output at which price is greater than or equal to average total cost. This gives the firm economies of scale over the entire range of output at which the firm would at least break even in the long run. As a result, a given quantity of output is produced more cheaply by one large firm than by two or more smaller firms. **>web...**

production of microprocessors, the chips that run computers. But technological superiority is typically a short-run, not a long-run, barrier to entry: over time competitors will invest in upgrading their technology to match the technology leader. In fact, in the last few years Intel has found its technological superiority eroded by a competitor, Advanced Micro Devices (also known as AMD), which now produces chips that are approximately as fast and powerful as Intel chips.

We should note, however, that in certain high technology industries, technological superiority is not a guarantee of success against competitors. Some high technology industries are characterized by *network externalities,* a condition that arises when the value to the consumer of a good rises as the number of people who also use the good rises. In these industries, the firm possessing the largest network—that is, the largest number of consumers currently using its product—has an advantage over its competitors in attracting new customers, an advantage that may allow it to become a monopolist. For example, Microsoft is often cited as an example of a company with a technologically inferior product—its computer operating system—that grew into a monopolist through the phenomenon of network externalities. (You can read more about network externalities in Chapter 22.)

Government-Created Barriers The most important legally created monopolies in today's world arise from *patents* and *copyrights.* Patents, which currently last for 20 years, are given to inventors of new products, such as drugs. Copyrights are given to the authors of literature or music; they usually last for the creator's lifetime or for 50 years, whichever is longer.

Why does the government create these legal monopolies? To encourage innovation through the promise of profits. Pharmaceutical companies are willing to invest large sums in developing new drugs precisely because they expect to profit from having a 20-year monopoly in producing that drug. In Chapter 22, we'll go into the reasons why governments use this method of encouraging innovation. For now, the important point is that in some cases the government creates monopolies.

FOR INQUIRING MINDS

PUBLIC UTILITIES IN CANADA: WHAT CONSTITUTES A NATURAL MONOPOLY?

Not so long ago there was a consensus that electricity, gas, water, railways, and telecommunications were obvious examples of natural monopolies. All were "tentacle industries" requiring wires, pipes, or roadbeds linking suppliers to users. Such networks are expensive, and duplicating them is inefficient. Moreover, all these industries provide important, non-storable services, for which there were no close substitutes. Therefore, in each case the producer-distributor was thought to be a natural monopolist, and in Canada, was often government owned and operated.

Now, however, this consensus has evaporated, driven largely by technological changes that have created new possibilities for competition. For example, cell phones and home satellite dishes brought competition to local telephone companies and cable companies; and the proliferation of orbiting satellites brought the possibility of competition for long-distance telephone service—providing competing long-distance companies had access to the local telephone network. When this was allowed, the cost of long-distance calls fell dramatically.

These changes demonstrated that distribution—not necessarily production—causes a natural monopoly. So, if the distribution network could be opened up to other providers of the service, competition could be introduced into other supposedly natural monopolies, such as electricity or gas.

For example, producers could compete to supply electricity (or gas) along publicly owned or publicly regulated wires or pipes, and various marketing companies could compete for the right to buy from the cheapest producer and sell to households.

This has opened up a vigorous debate concerning the merits of restructuring and privatizing provincially owned electricity companies. Proponents promise more choice and lower rates. Opponents argue that whereas restructuring in long-distance telephone service was driven by technological innovation, there is no equivalent technological innovation in electricity. Moreover, California's experience with energy shortages and price manipulation suggests extreme caution. We'll come back to the topic of restructuring and privatizing electricity in the Economics in Action on page 361.

economics in action

Are Diamond Monopolies Forever?

When Cecil Rhodes created the De Beers monopoly, it was a particularly opportune moment. The new diamond mines in South Africa dwarfed all previous sources, so almost all of the world's diamond production was concentrated in a few square miles.

Since that time, however, diamond deposits similar to those in South Africa have been found in a number of places—other African countries, Russia, and Australia, which is now the largest producer. So how does De Beers remain a monopolist?

Until quite recently De Beers was able to extend its control of resources even as new mines were opened—De Beers either bought up new producers or entered into agreements with local governments that controlled some of the new mines, effectively making them part of the De Beers monopoly. The most remarkable of these was an agreement with the former Soviet Union, which ensured that Russian diamonds were marketed through De Beers, preserving its ability to control world supplies.

In recent years, however, the spread of diamond production—together with competition from synthetic diamonds, which are becoming better substitutes for natural stones—has led to some erosion of De Beers' control, and prices have even dropped somewhat. De Beers is arguably the most successful monopolist in history—but even diamond monopolies may not be forever. ■

< < < < < < < < < < < < < < < < < <

>> QUICK REVIEW

- A *monopolist* has *market power* and as a result will charge higher prices and produce less output than a competitive industry. This generates profit for the monopolist in both the short run and long run.
- Profits will not persist in the long run unless there is a *barrier to entry*. This can take the form of control of natural resources or inputs, economies of scale, technological superiority on the part of the monopolist, or legal restrictions imposed by governments, including patents and copyrights.
- A *natural monopoly* arises when average total cost is declining over the output range relevant for the industry. This creates a barrier to entry because an established monopolist has lower average total cost than any smaller firm.

>>CHECK YOUR UNDERSTANDING 14-1

1. Currently, Lightning Oil Co. is the only local supplier of home heating oil in Frigid, Manitoba. This winter residents were shocked to find that the cost of a litre of heating oil had doubled and believed that they were the victims of market power. Which of the following pieces of evidence support that conclusion? Which do not? Explain.
   a. There is a national shortage of heating oil, and Lightning could procure only a limited amount.
   b. Last year, Lightning and several other competing local oil-supply firms merged into a single firm.
   c. The cost of heating oil from the refineries has gone up significantly.
   d. Recently, some non-local firms have begun offering heating oil to Lightning's regular customers at a price much lower than Lightning's.
   e. Lightning has acquired the exclusive license to draw oil from the only heating oil pipeline in the province.

Solutions appear at back of book.

How a Monopolist Maximizes Profit

As we've suggested, once Cecil Rhodes consolidated the diamond producers of South Africa into a single company, the industry's behaviour changed: the quantity supplied fell and the market price rose. In this section we will learn how a monopolist increases its profits by reducing output below the amount that would be supplied by a perfectly competitive industry. And we will see the crucial role that market demand plays in leading a monopolist to behave differently from a perfectly competitive industry.

The Monopolist's Demand Curve and Marginal Revenue

In Chapter 9 we derived the producers's optimal output rule: a profit-maximizing producer produces the quantity of output at which the marginal cost of producing the last unit of output equals marginal revenue—the change in total revenue generated by that last unit of output. That is, $MR = MC$ at the profit-maximizing output level. Although the optimal output rule holds for *all* producers, we will see shortly that its application leads to different optimal output levels for a monopolist compared to a perfectly competitive producer—that is, a price-taking producer. The source of that difference lies in the comparison of the demand curve faced by a monopolist to the demand curve faced by an individual, perfectly competitive producer.

In addition to the optimal output rule, we also learned in Chapter 9 that even though the *market* demand curve is always downward sloping, each of the producers that make up a perfectly competitive industry faces a horizontal, *perfectly elastic* demand curve, like D_C in panel (a) of Figure 14-4 (page 356). Any attempt by an individual producer in a perfectly competitive industry to charge more than the going market price will cause it to lose all its sales. It can, however, sell as much as it likes at the going market price. As we saw in Chapter 9, the marginal revenue of a perfectly competitive producer is simply the market price. As a result, the price-taking firm's optimal output rule is to produce the output level at which the marginal cost of the last unit produced is equal to the market price.

A monopolist, in contrast, is the sole supplier of its good. So its demand curve is simply the market demand curve, which is downward sloping, like D_M in panel (b) of Figure 14-4. This downward slope creates a "wedge" between the price of the good and the marginal revenue of the good—the change in revenue generated by producing one more unit.

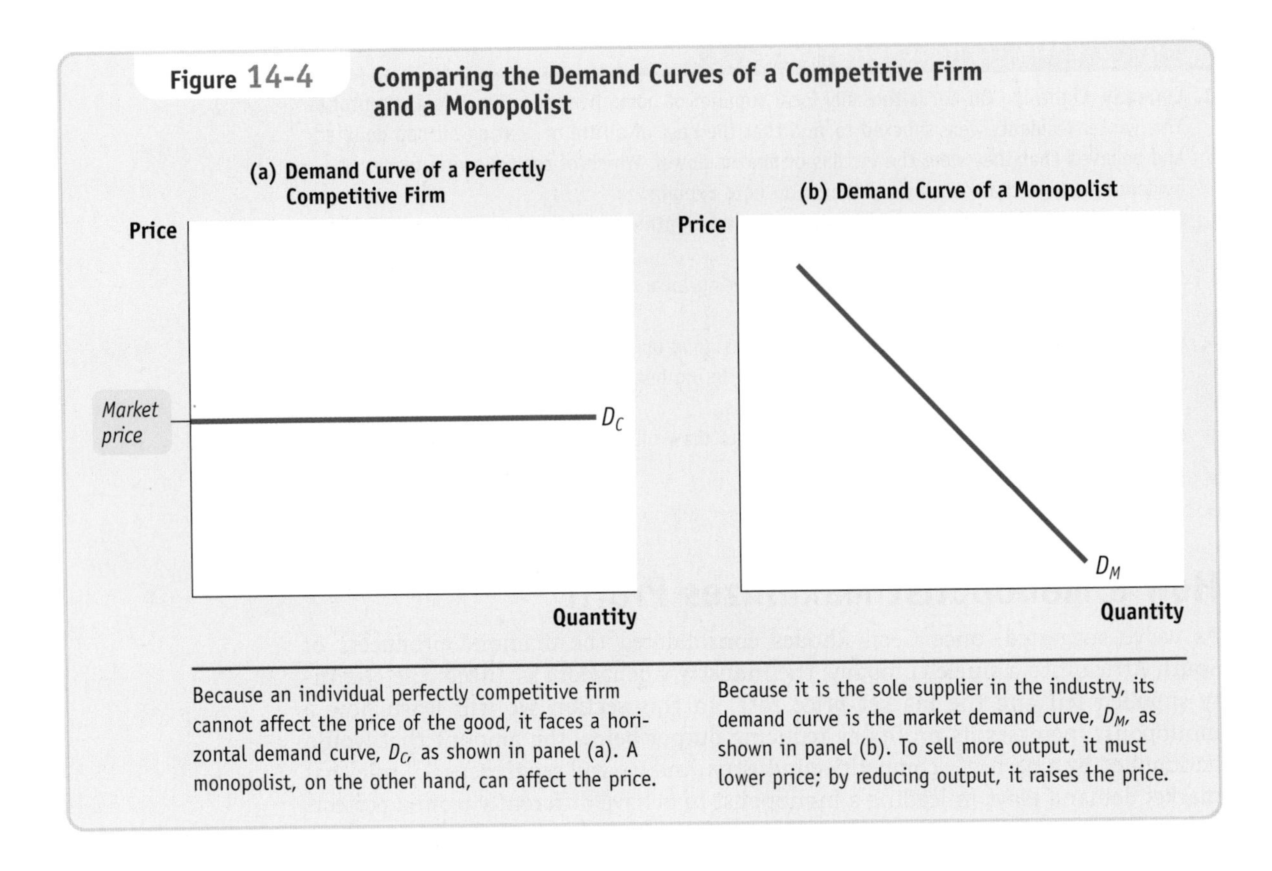

Figure 14-4 Comparing the Demand Curves of a Competitive Firm and a Monopolist

Because an individual perfectly competitive firm cannot affect the price of the good, it faces a horizontal demand curve, D_C, as shown in panel (a). A monopolist, on the other hand, can affect the price. Because it is the sole supplier in the industry, its demand curve is the market demand curve, D_M, as shown in panel (b). To sell more output, it must lower price; by reducing output, it raises the price.

Table 14-1 shows this wedge between price and marginal revenue for a monopolist, by calculating the monopolist's total revenue and marginal revenue schedules from its demand schedule.

The first two columns of Table 14-1 show a hypothetical demand schedule for De Beers diamonds. For the sake of simplicity, we assume that all diamonds are exactly alike. To make the arithmetic easy, we suppose that the number of diamonds sold is far smaller than is actually the case. For instance, at a price of $500 per diamond, we assume that only 10 diamonds are sold. The demand curve implied by this schedule is shown in panel (a) of Figure 14-5.

The third column of Table 14-1 shows De Beers's total revenue from selling each quantity of diamonds—the price per diamond multiplied by the number of diamonds sold. The last column of Table 14-1 calculates marginal revenue, the change in revenue from producing and selling one more diamond.

Clearly, after the 1st diamond, the marginal revenue a monopolist receives from selling one more unit is less than the price at which that unit is sold. For example, if De Beers sells 10 diamonds, the price at which the 10th diamond is sold is $500. But the marginal revenue—the change in total revenue in going from 9 to 10 diamonds—is only $50.

Why is the marginal revenue from that 10th diamond less than the price? An increase in production by a monopolist has two opposing effects on revenue:

- A *quantity effect:* one more unit is sold, increasing total revenue by the price at which the unit is sold (in this case $500).
- A *price effect:* in order to sell that last unit, the monopolist must cut the market price on *all* units sold. This decreases total revenue (in this case by $9 \times \$50 = \$450$ decrease in total revenue).

The quantity effect and the price effect are illustrated by the two shaded areas in panel (a) of Figure 14-5 (page 358). Increasing diamond sales from 9 to 10 means moving down the demand curve from *A* to *B*, reducing the price per diamond from $550 to $500. The green-shaded area represents the quantity effect: De Beers sells the 10th diamond at a price of $500. This is offset, however, by the price effect, represented by the orange-shaded area. In order to sell that 10th diamond, De Beers must reduce the price on all its diamonds from $550 to $500. So it loses 9 × $50 = $450 in revenue, the orange-shaded area. So, as point *C* indicates, the total effect on revenue of selling one more diamond—the marginal revenue—from an increase in diamond sales from 9 to 10 is only $50.

Point *C* lies on the monopolist's marginal revenue curve, labelled *MR* in panel (a) of Figure 14-5 and taken from the last column of Table 14-1. The crucial point about the monopolist's marginal revenue curve is that it is always *below* the demand curve. That's because of the price effect, which means that a monopolist's marginal revenue from producing an additional unit is always less than the price the monopolist receives for that unit. It is the price effect that creates the wedge between the monopolist's marginal revenue curve and the demand curve: in order to sell an additional diamond, De Beers must cut the market price on all units sold.

TABLE 14-1

Demand, Total Revenue, and Marginal Revenue for the De Beers Monopoly

Price of diamond P	Quantity of diamonds Q	Total revenue $TR = P \times Q$	Marginal revenue $MR = \Delta TR/\Delta Q$
$1,000	0	$0	
			$950
950	1	950	
			850
900	2	1,800	
			750
850	3	2,550	
			650
800	4	3,200	
			550
750	5	3,750	
			450
700	6	4,200	
			350
650	7	4,550	
			250
600	8	4,800	
			150
550	9	4,950	
			50
500	10	5,000	
			−50
450	11	4,950	
			−150
400	12	4,800	
			−250
350	13	4,550	
			−350
300	14	4,200	
			−450
250	15	3,750	
			−550
200	16	3,200	
			−650
150	17	2,550	
			−750
100	18	1,800	
			−850
50	19	950	
			−950
0	20	0	

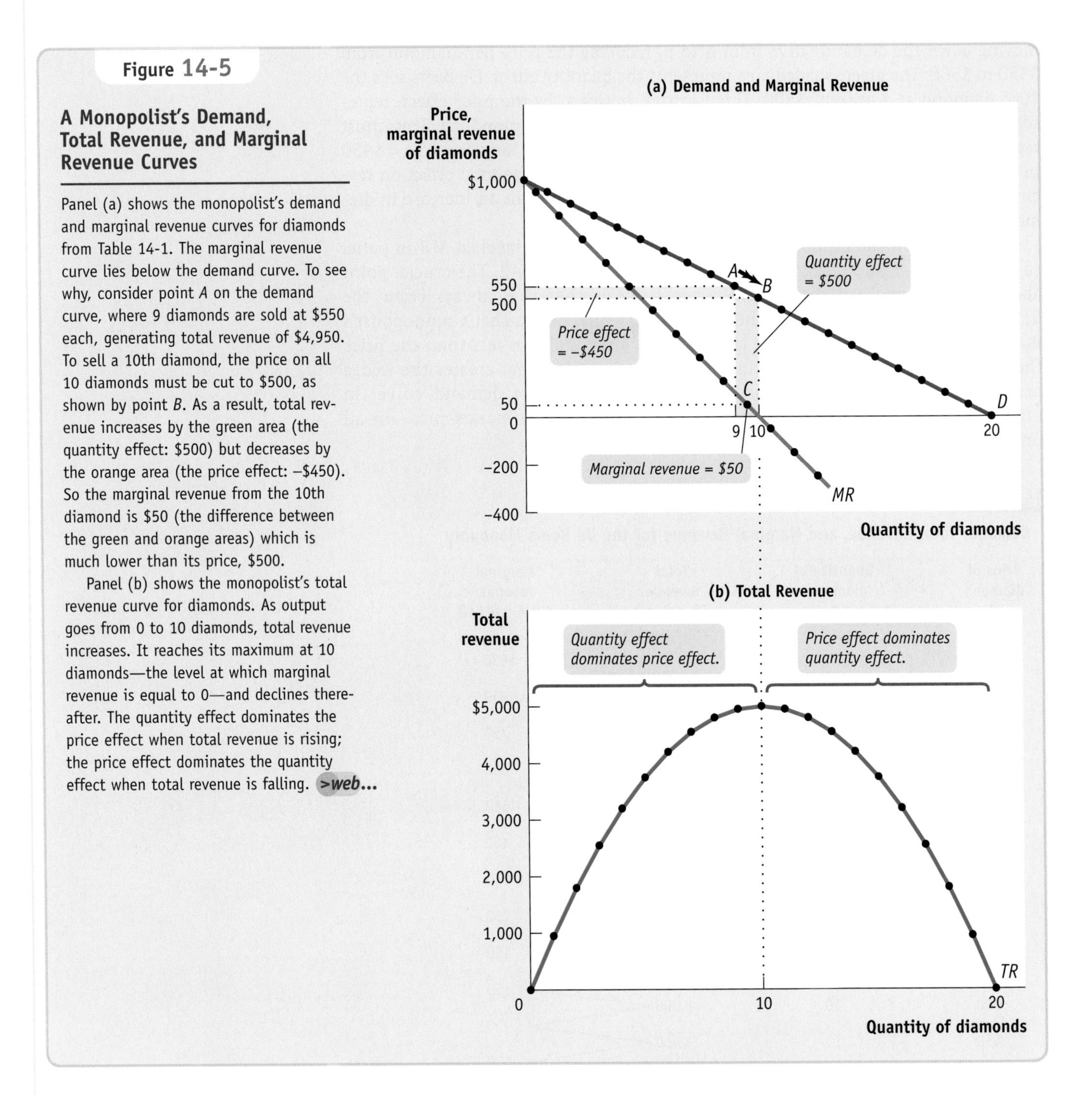

Figure 14-5

A Monopolist's Demand, Total Revenue, and Marginal Revenue Curves

Panel (a) shows the monopolist's demand and marginal revenue curves for diamonds from Table 14-1. The marginal revenue curve lies below the demand curve. To see why, consider point *A* on the demand curve, where 9 diamonds are sold at $550 each, generating total revenue of $4,950. To sell a 10th diamond, the price on all 10 diamonds must be cut to $500, as shown by point *B*. As a result, total revenue increases by the green area (the quantity effect: $500) but decreases by the orange area (the price effect: −$450). So the marginal revenue from the 10th diamond is $50 (the difference between the green and orange areas) which is much lower than its price, $500.

Panel (b) shows the monopolist's total revenue curve for diamonds. As output goes from 0 to 10 diamonds, total revenue increases. It reaches its maximum at 10 diamonds—the level at which marginal revenue is equal to 0—and declines thereafter. The quantity effect dominates the price effect when total revenue is rising; the price effect dominates the quantity effect when total revenue is falling. **>web...**

In fact, this wedge is present for any firm that possesses market power, such as oligopolists. Having market power means that the monopolist faces a downward-sloping demand curve; as a result, there will always be a price effect from an increase in its output. So for a firm with market power, the marginal revenue curve always lies below its demand curve.

Take a moment to compare the monopolist's marginal revenue curve with the marginal revenue curve for a perfectly competitive producer, one without market power. For such a producer there is no price effect from an increase in output: its marginal revenue curve is simply its horizontal demand curve. So for a perfectly competitive producer, market price and marginal revenue are always equal.

To emphasize how the quantity and price effects offset one another for a producer with market power, De Beers's total revenue curve is drawn in the lower panel of Figure 14-5. Notice that it is hill-shaped: as output rises from 0 to 10 diamonds, total revenue increases. This reflects the fact that *at low levels of output, the quantity effect is stronger than the price effect.* This is because as the monopolist sells more, it has to lower the price on only very few units, so the price effect is small. As output rises beyond 10 diamonds, total revenue actually falls; this reflects the fact that *at high levels of output, the price effect is stronger than the quantity effect.* This is because as the monopolist sells more, it now has to lower the price on many units of output, making the price effect very large. Correspondingly, the marginal revenue curve lies below zero at output levels above 10 diamonds. For example, an increase in diamond production from 11 to 12 yields only $400 for the 12th diamond, while reducing the revenue from diamonds 1 through 11 by $550. As a result, the marginal revenue of the 12th diamond is –$150.

The Monopolist's Profit-Maximizing Output and Price

To complete the story of how a monopolist maximizes profit, we now bring in the monopolist's marginal cost. Let's assume that there is no fixed cost of production; and we'll also assume that the marginal cost of producing an additional diamond is constant at $200, no matter how many diamonds De Beers produces. Then marginal cost will always equal average total cost and the marginal cost curve (and the average total cost curve) is a horizontal line at $200, as shown in Figure 14-6.

To maximize profit, the monopolist compares marginal cost with marginal revenue. If marginal revenue exceeds marginal cost, De Beers increases profit by producing more; if marginal revenue is less than marginal cost, De Beers increases profit by producing less. So the monopolist maximizes its profit by using the optimal output rule:

(14-1) *$MR = MC$ at the monopolist's profit-maximizing output level*

Figure 14-6

The Monopolist's Profit-Maximizing Output and Price

This figure shows the demand, marginal revenue, and marginal cost curves. Marginal cost per diamond is $200, so the marginal cost curve is horizontal at $200. According to the optimal output rule, the profit-maximizing level of output for the monopolist is at $MR = MC$, shown by point *A*, where the marginal cost and marginal revenue curves cross at an output of 8 diamonds. The price De Beers can charge per diamond is found by going to the point on the demand curve directly above point *A*, which is point *B* here—a price of $600 per diamond. It makes a profit of $400 × 8 = $3,200. A competitive industry produces the output level at which $P = MC$, given by point *C*, where the demand curve and marginal cost curves cross. So a perfectively competitive industry produces 16 diamonds, sells at a price of $200, and makes zero profit.

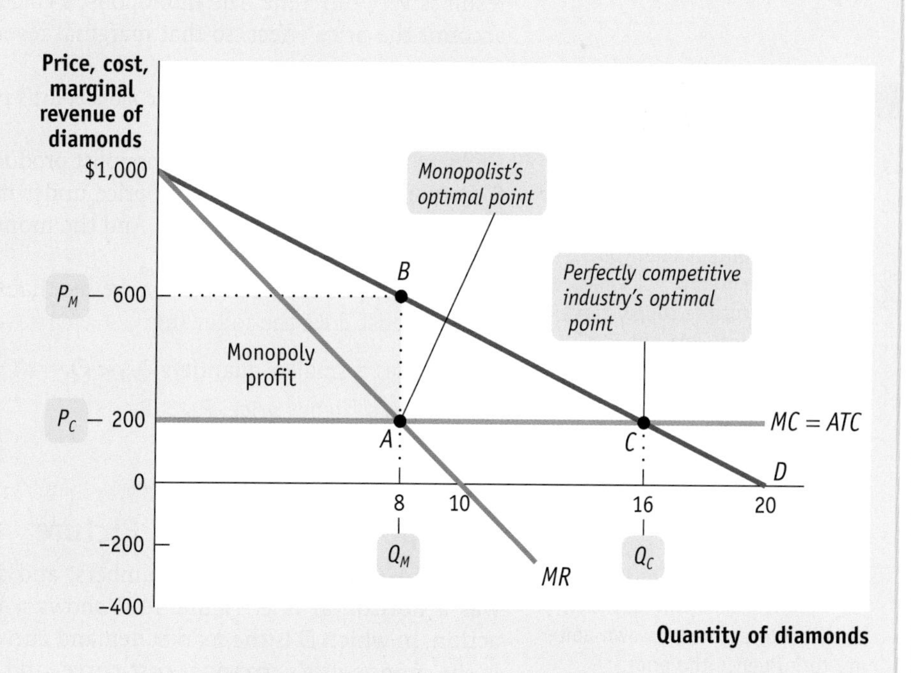

PITFALLS

FINDING THE MONOPOLY PRICE

In order to find the *profit-maximizing quantity of output* for a monopolist, you look for the point where the marginal revenue curve crosses the marginal cost curve. Point *A* in Figure 14-6 is an example.

However, it's important not to fall into a common error: imagining that point *A* also shows the *price* at which the monopolist sells its output. It doesn't: it shows the *marginal revenue* received by the monopolist, which we know is less than the price.

To find the monopoly price, you have to go up vertically from *A* to the demand curve. There you find the price at which consumers demand the profit-maximizing quantity. So the profit-maximizing price–quantity combination is always a point on the demand curve, like *B* in Figure 14-6.

The monopolist's optimal point is shown in Figure 14-6. At *A*, the marginal cost curve, *MC*, crosses the marginal revenue curve, *MR*. The corresponding output level, 8 diamonds, is the monopolist's profit-maximizing quantity of output, Q_M. The price at which consumers demand 8 diamonds is \$600, so the monopolist's price, P_M, is \$600—corresponding to point *B*. The cost of producing each diamond is \$200, so the monopolist earns \$600 − \$200 = \$400 per diamond, and total profit is 8 × \$400 = \$3,200, as indicated by the shaded area.

Monopoly versus Perfect Competition

When Cecil Rhodes consolidated many independent diamond producers into De Beers, he converted a perfectly competitive industry into a monopoly. We can now use our analysis to see the effects of such a consolidation.

Let's look again at Figure 14-6 and ask how this same market would work if, instead of being a monopoly, the industry were perfectly competitive. We will continue to assume that there is no fixed cost and that marginal cost is constant, so average total cost and marginal cost are equal.

If the diamond industry consists of many perfectly competitive firms, each of those producers takes the market price as given. That is, each producer acts as if its marginal revenue is equal to the market price. So each firm within the industry uses the price-taking firm's optimal output rule:

(14-2) $P = MC$ *at the perfectly competitive firm's profit-maximizing output*

In Figure 14-6, this would correspond to producing at *C*, where the price per diamond, P_C, is \$200, equal to the marginal cost of production. Profit-maximizing industry output under perfect competition, Q_C, is therefore 16 diamonds.

But does the perfectly competitive industry earn any profits at *C*? No: the price of \$200 is equal to the production cost per diamond. So there are no economic profits for this industry when it produces at the perfectly competitive output level.

We've already seen that once the industry is consolidated into a monopoly, the result is very different. The monopolist's calculation of marginal revenue takes into account the price effect, so that marginal revenue is less than the price. That is,

(14-3) $P > MR = MC$ *at the monopolist's profit-maximizing output level*

As we've already seen, the monopolist produces less than the competitive industry—8 diamonds rather than 16. The price under monopoly is \$600, compared with only \$200 under perfect competition. And the monopolist earns positive profits, while the competitive industry does not.

So, just as we suggested earlier, we see that compared with a competitive industry, a monopolist does the following:

- Produces a smaller quantity: $Q_M < Q_C$
- Charges a higher price: $P_M > P_C$
- Earns profits

PITFALLS

IS THERE A MONOPOLY SUPPLY CURVE?

Given how a monopolist applies the optimal output rule, you might be tempted to ask what this implies for the supply curve of a monopolist. But this is a meaningless question: *monopolists don't have supply curves.*

Remember that a supply curve shows the quantity that producers are willing to supply for any given market price. A monopolist, however, does not take the price as given; it chooses a profit-maximizing quantity, taking into account its own ability to influence the price.

Monopoly: The General Picture

Figure 14-6 involved specific numbers, and assumed that the marginal cost curve was a horizontal line. Figure 14-7 shows a more general picture of monopoly in action, in which *D* is the market demand curve, *MR* the marginal revenue curve, *MC* is the monopolist's marginal cost curve, and *ATC* its average total cost curve. Here we return to the usual assumption that both marginal and average cost curves are U-shaped.

Figure 14-7

The Monopolist's Profit

In this case, the marginal cost is upward sloping and the average total cost curve is U-shaped. The monopolist maximizes profit by producing the level of output at which $MR = MC$, given by point A, generating quantity Q_M. It finds its monopoly price, P_M, from the point on the demand curve directly above point A, point B here. The average total cost at Q_M is shown by point C. Profit is given by the area of the shaded rectangle. >web...

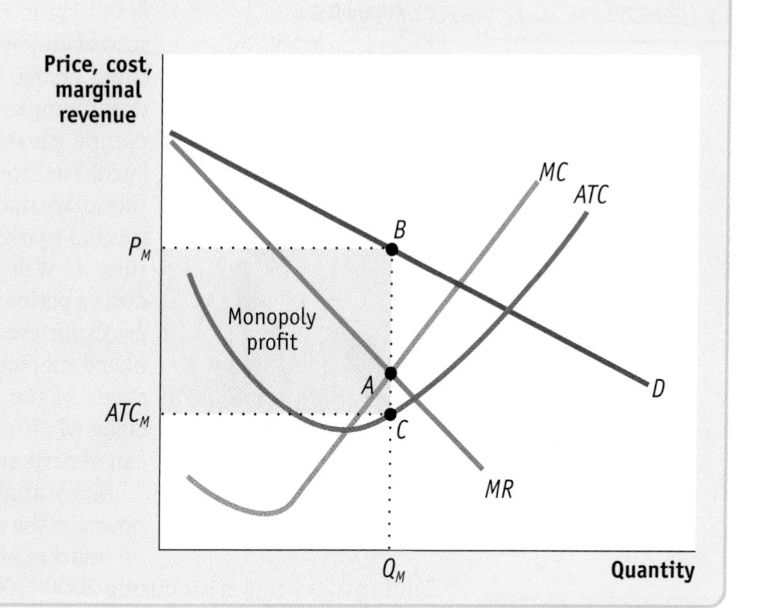

Applying the optimal output rule, the profit-maximizing level of output is the output at which marginal revenue equals marginal cost, indicated by point A. The profit-maximizing quantity of output is Q_M; the price charged by the monopolist is P_M. At the profit-maximizing level of output, the monopolist's average total cost is ATC_M, shown by point C.

Recalling how we calculated profit in Equation 9-5 on page 227, profit is equal to the difference between total revenue and total cost. Total revenue is equal to price times output; total cost is equal to average total cost times output. So we have:

(14-4) $$\begin{aligned} \textit{Monopoly profit} &= \textit{total revenue } (TR) - \textit{total cost } (TC) \\ &= (P_M \times Q_M) - (ATC_M \times Q_M) \\ &= (P_M - ATC_M) \times Q_M \end{aligned}$$

Profit is equal to the area of the shaded rectangle in Figure 14-7, with a height of $P_M - ATC_M$ and a width of Q_M.

In Chapter 9 we learned that a perfectly competitive industry can have profits *in the short run but not in the long run.* In the short run price can exceed average total cost, allowing a perfectly competitive firm to make a profit. But we also know that this cannot persist. In the long run, any profit in a perfectly competitive industry will be competed away as new firms enter the market. In contrast, a monopolist will make profits in both the short run and the long run.

economics in action

Privatizing Power: Lessons from California

The winter of 2000–2001 was a grim time for the state of California, as power shortages gripped the state. One factor involved was the soaring price of natural gas. Yet, strangely, natural gas prices in California were much higher than the cost of buying natural gas in Texas and pumping it through interstate pipelines. So why wasn't more gas supplied?

The answer is that pipelines are a natural monopoly. As a result, there was only one set of pipelines—operated by the El Paso Corporation, which appears to have

deliberately restricted supplies to drive up market prices. It didn't stand to gain anything directly by this, since it was subject to government regulation that limited the prices it could charge for transporting natural gas. But since there was "competition" between companies that marketed the natural gas in California, the marketing sector was unregulated. The trouble was that El Paso also had an unregulated subsidiary marketing natural gas in California that had substantial market share. So, by running pipelines at low pressure, as well as by scheduling non-essential maintenance during periods of peak demand, El Paso was able to drive up prices for everyone and reap the benefit through its unregulated marketing subsidiary. The moral of the story is to be aware of the structure of ownership in an industry—especially when one part of a company has market power that can benefit an unregulated subsidiary downstream.

Many analysts believe that El Paso's exercise of market power in the natural gas market was part of a broad pattern of market manipulation that played a key role in California's energy crisis during 2000–2001. For example, Enron bought up supplies of electricity from power-generating companies and appears to have deliberately withheld this electricity from the California market in order to drive up prices. The point is that if competition isn't perfect, producers or traders will still have market power and be able to influence prices. So, deregulating electricity isn't easy, and it may be a good idea to have a public body responsible for monitoring for possible price manipulation. In the Enron case, the need for *effective* government regulators was particularly apparent. ■

>> QUICK REVIEW

- The crucial difference between a producer with market power, such as a monopolist, and a producer in a perfectly competitive industry is that perfectly competitive producers are price-takers that face horizontal demand curves, but a producer with market power faces a downward-sloping demand curve.
- Due to the price effect of an increase in output, the marginal revenue curve of a producer with market power always lies below its demand curve. So a profit-maximizing monopolist chooses the output level at which marginal cost is equal to marginal revenue—*not* to price.
- As a result, the monopolist produces less, and sells its output at a higher price, than a perfectly competitive industry would. It earns a profit in the short run and the long run.

>> CHECK YOUR UNDERSTANDING 14-2

1. Use the accompanying total revenue schedule of Emerald, Inc., a monopoly producer of 10-carat emeralds, to calculate the answers to parts a–d. Then answer part e.
   a. The demand schedule
   b. The marginal revenue schedule
   c. The quantity effect component of marginal revenue for each output level
   d. The price effect component of marginal revenue for each output level
   e. What additional information is needed to determine Emerald, Inc.'s profit-maximizing output?

Quantity of emeralds demanded	Total revenue
1	$100
2	186
3	252
4	280
5	250

2. Use Figure 14-6 to show what happens to the following when the marginal cost of diamond production rises from $200 to $400. Assume, as before, that fixed cost is zero.
   a. Marginal cost curve
   b. Profit-maximizing quantity
   c. Profits of the monopolist
   d. Perfectly competitive industry profits

Solutions appear at back of book.

Monopoly and Public Policy

It's good to be a monopolist; but it's not so good to be a monopolist's customer. A monopolist, by raising prices, benefits at the expense of consumers. But buyers and sellers always have conflicting interests. Is the conflict of interest under monopoly any different than it is under perfect competition?

The answer is yes, because monopoly is a source of inefficiency: the losses to consumers from monopoly behaviour are larger than the gains to the monopolist. Because monopoly leads to net losses for the economy, governments often try either to prevent the emergence of monopolies or to limit their effects. In this section we will see why monopoly leads to inefficiency and examine the policies governments adopt in an attempt to prevent this inefficiency.

Welfare Effects of Monopoly

By restricting output below the level at which marginal cost is equal to the market price, a monopolist increases its profit but hurts consumers. To assess whether this is a net benefit or loss to society, we must compare the monopolist's gain in profit to the consumer loss. And what we learn is that the consumer loss is larger than the monopolist's gain. Monopoly causes a net loss for the economy.

To see why, let's return to the case where the marginal cost curve is horizontal, as shown in the two panels of Figure 14-8. Here the marginal cost curve is *MC*, the demand curve is *D*, and, in panel (b), the marginal revenue curve is *MR*.

Panel (a) shows what happens if this industry is perfectly competitive. Equilibrium output is Q_C; the price of the good, P_C, is equal to marginal cost, and marginal cost is also equal to average total cost because there is no fixed cost and marginal cost is constant. Each firm is earning exactly its cost per unit of output, so there is no producer surplus in this equilibrium. The consumer surplus generated by the market is equal to the area of the blue-shaded triangle CS_C shown in panel (a). Since there is no producer surplus, CS_C also represents the total surplus.

Panel (b) shows the results for the same market, but this time we assume that the industry is a monopoly. The monopolist produces the level of output, Q_M, at which marginal cost is equal to marginal revenue. It charges the price P_M. The industry now earns profit—which is also the producer surplus—equal to the area of the green

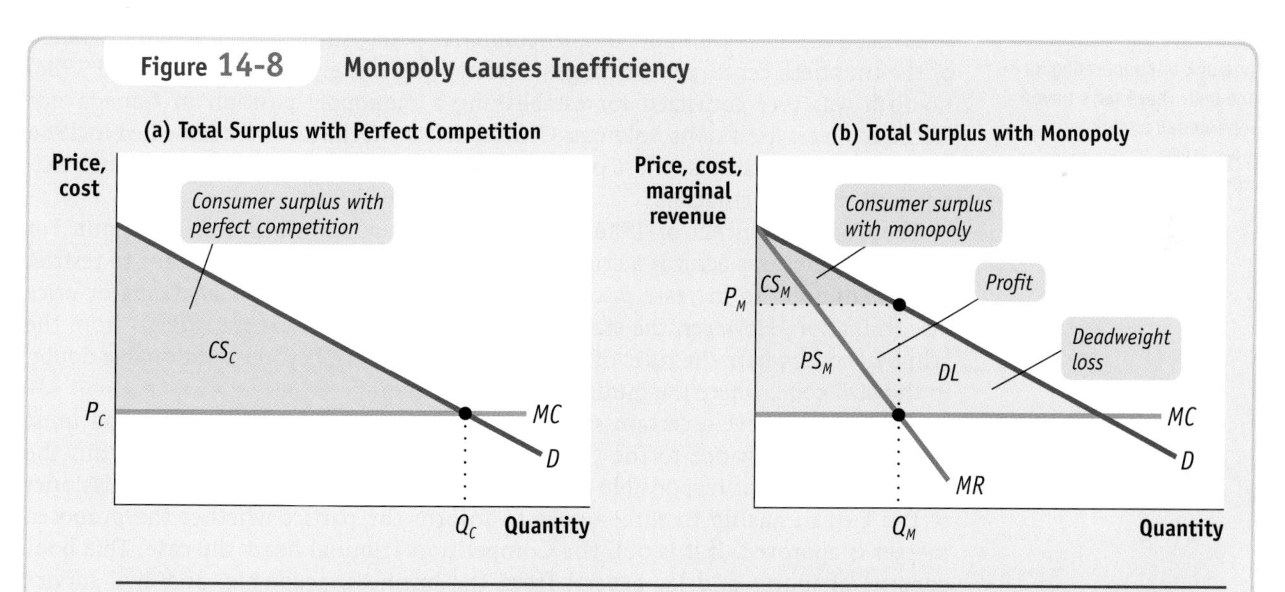

Panel (a) depicts a perfectly competitive industry: output is Q_C and market price, P_C, is equal is to *MC*. Since price is exactly equal to each producer's cost of production per unit, there is no producer surplus. Total surplus is therefore equal to consumer surplus, the entire shaded area. Panel (b) depicts the industry under monopoly: the monopolist decreases output to Q_M and charges P_M. Consumer surplus (blue area) has shrunk because a portion of it is has been captured as monopoly profits (green area). Total surplus falls: the deadweight loss (orange area) represents the value of mutually beneficial transactions that do not occur because of monopoly behaviour. >web...

rectangle, PS_M. Note that this profit is surplus that has been captured from consumers, as consumer surplus shrinks to the area of the blue triangle, CS_M.

By comparing panels (a) and (b), we see that in addition to the redistribution of surplus from consumers to the monopolist, another important change has occurred: the sum of monopoly profits and consumer surplus—total surplus—is *smaller* under monopoly than it is under perfect competition. That is, the sum of CS_M and PS_M is less than the area CS_C in panel (a). In Chapter 6, we introduced the concept of *deadweight loss*, the net loss caused by government policies such as taxes. Here we show that monopoly creates a deadweight loss to society equal to the area of the orange triangle, *DL*. So monopoly produces a net loss for the economy.

This net loss exists because some mutually beneficial transactions do not occur. There are people for whom an additional unit of the good is worth more than the marginal cost of producing it, but who don't consume it because they are not willing to pay P_M.

Those who recall our discussion of the deadweight loss from taxes in Chapter 6 will notice that the deadweight loss from monopoly looks quite similar. Indeed, by driving a wedge between price and marginal cost, monopoly acts much like a tax on consumers and produces the same kind of inefficiency.

So monopoly hurts the welfare of society as a whole and is a source of market failure. Is there anything government policy can do about it?

Preventing Monopoly

Policy toward monopoly depends crucially on whether the industry in question is a natural monopoly—one in which economies of scale ensure that bigger producers have lower average total cost. If the industry is *not* a natural monopoly, the best policy is to prevent monopoly from arising or break it up if it already exists. Government policies used to prevent or eliminate monopolies are referred to as *anti-trust policy* in the U.S., and as **combine laws** or *competition policy* in Canada.

Combine laws were first adopted in the 1880s to prevent firms from either combining into one unit or cooperating as if they were one unit. These laws have now been superceded by the Competition Act (1986).

Canada has had some sort of anti-combines policy since 1889, though for much of the twentieth century it was largely ineffective. Tellingly, between 1889 and 1986, no firm was ever convicted for establishing a monopoly position in Canada nor forced to divest itself of its holdings. Crucial defects in the law were remedied in 1986 when two new statutes, the Competition Act and the Competition Tribunal Act, replaced the old legislation.

The Competition Act of 1986 regulates many aspects of business behaviour. For example, under this act it is a criminal offence to collude with other firms to restrict output (in order to increase prices), or to engage in misleading advertising or price discrimination. However, the statute dealing with mergers was transferred from the criminal code, where the rules of evidence required proof beyond a reasonable doubt, to the civil code, where the burden of proof is easier.

All mergers above a certain size are now subject to automatic review and must be reported in advance to the Competition Bureau, which is the unit within the federal government responsible for enforcing competition law. The Commissioner of the bureau has up to three weeks to inform the parties whether the proposed merger is approved. If it is not, the Competition Tribunal hears the case. This body consists of judges and lay experts from the business, academic, and civil service communities. If it concludes that the merger is likely to "prevent or lessen competition substantially", the Tribunal can block a merger or require that the merged entity divest itself of some of its assets. For example, in 1990 the Tribunal ruled that the merger of two of Canada's largest integrated petroleum companies, Imperial Oil and Texaco Canada, would have substantial anticompetitive effects. Although the merger was allowed to proceed, the Tribunal ordered that many of the merged entity's assets be given up. This divestiture involved 414 service stations, 13 terminals, and 1 refinery.

The new Act is a definite improvement on the old one. In the first three years of its existence alone, some 369 mergers were investigated; of these, the Commissioner objected to 19. As a result, several were abandoned, eight were restructured to satisfy the Commissioner, and four cases went to the Tribunal. Of course, what is impossible to know is the number of mergers that have not been attempted because a more effective law is in place.

Dealing with Natural Monopoly

Breaking up a monopoly that isn't natural is clearly a good idea: the gains to consumers outweigh the loss to the producer. But it's not so clear whether a natural monopoly, one in which large producers have lower average total costs than small producers, should be broken up, because this would raise average total costs. For example, a town government that tried to prevent a single company from dominating local gas supply—which, as we've seen, is almost surely a natural monopoly—would raise the costs of providing gas to its residents.

Yet even in the case of a natural monopoly, a profit-maximizing monopolist acts in a way that causes inefficiency—it charges consumers a price that is higher than marginal cost, and therefore prevents some potentially beneficial transactions. Also, it can seem unfair that a firm that has managed to establish a monopoly position earns large profits at the expense of consumers.

What can public policy do about this? There are two common answers.

Public Ownership In many countries, the preferred answer to the problem of natural monopoly has been **public ownership.** Instead of allowing a private monopolist to control an industry, a government establishes a public agency to provide the good and protect consumers' interests.

In **public ownership** of a monopoly, the good is supplied by the government or by a firm owned by the government.

This is a common solution in many European countries. It is also relatively common in Canada, although somewhat less so in recent years. In Canada, the government has often assumed control of a monopoly industry, or nationalized it. Publicly owned companies in Canada are referred to as Crown corporations, and they may be owned federally or provincially. Federally owned firms with monopoly positions include Canada Post and Atomic Energy of Canada Limited. In the past decade, the federal government has privatized many of its Crown corporations, including the Canadian National Railway, Air Canada, and Petro-Canada. Most electric utilities are provincially owned monopolies, as well as several telephone companies (B.C. Tel, SaskTel).

Not all Crown corporations were established because a natural monopoly existed. For example, Petro-Canada was established as the federal government's response to the energy crisis of the 1970s and competed in the marketplace with other private energy companies.

The advantage of public ownership, in principle, is that a publicly owned natural monopoly can set prices based on the criterion of efficiency rather than profit maximization. In the case of a perfectly competitive industry, profit-maximizing behaviour *is* efficient, because producers set prices equal to marginal cost. That is why there is no economic argument for public ownership of, say, wheat farms.

Experience suggests that public ownership, as a solution to the problem of natural monopoly, may not always work well in practice. One reason is that publicly owned firms are often less eager than private companies to keep costs down or offer high-quality products (consider the mountain of debt built up by Ontario Hydro). Another reason is that publicly owned companies all too often end up serving political interests—providing contracts or jobs to people with the right connections. On the other hand, France has a superb publicly owned railway network, and the TGV (the network of high-speed trains) is the envy of the world. Closer to home, SaskTel is recognized as one of the 50 best employers in Canada, regularly donates millions to the provincial coffers, and is sufficiently competitive internationally to have been awarded the contract to establish all the telecommunications and control systems in the Channel Tunnel linking England and France.

Price regulation limits the price that a monopolist is allowed to charge.

Regulation An alternative to operating a natural monopoly as a Crown corporation is to leave the industry in the private sector and regulate the prices it charges. This has typically been the approach in the United States. In Canada, both public ownership and **price regulation** have occurred, depending on the industry. Indeed, sometimes the industry has been both publicly owned and price regulated. For example, in some provinces, Crown corporations provide telephone services and the federal government regulates their prices; in others, electricity companies are privately owned and their prices regulated provincially.

We saw in Chapter 4 that imposing a *price ceiling* on a competitive industry is a recipe for shortages, black markets, and other nasty side effects. Doesn't imposing a limit on the price that, say, a local gas company can charge have the same effects?

Not necessarily: a price ceiling on a monopolist need not create a shortage—in the absence of a price ceiling, a monopolist would charge a price that is higher than its marginal cost of production. So, even if forced to charge a lower price—as long as that price is above *MC* and the monopolist at least breaks even on total output—the monopolist still has an incentive to produce the quantity demanded at that price.

Figure 14-9 shows an example of price regulation of a natural monopoly—a highly simplified version of a local gas company. The company faces a demand curve *D*, with an associated marginal revenue curve *MR*. For simplicity, we assume that the firm's total costs consist of two parts: a fixed cost and variable costs that are incurred at a constant proportion to output. So the marginal cost curve, which in this case is also the average variable cost curve, is a horizontal line at *MC*. The average total cost curve is the downward-sloping curve *ATC*; it is downward sloping because the higher

Figure 14-9 Regulated and Unregulated Natural Monopoly

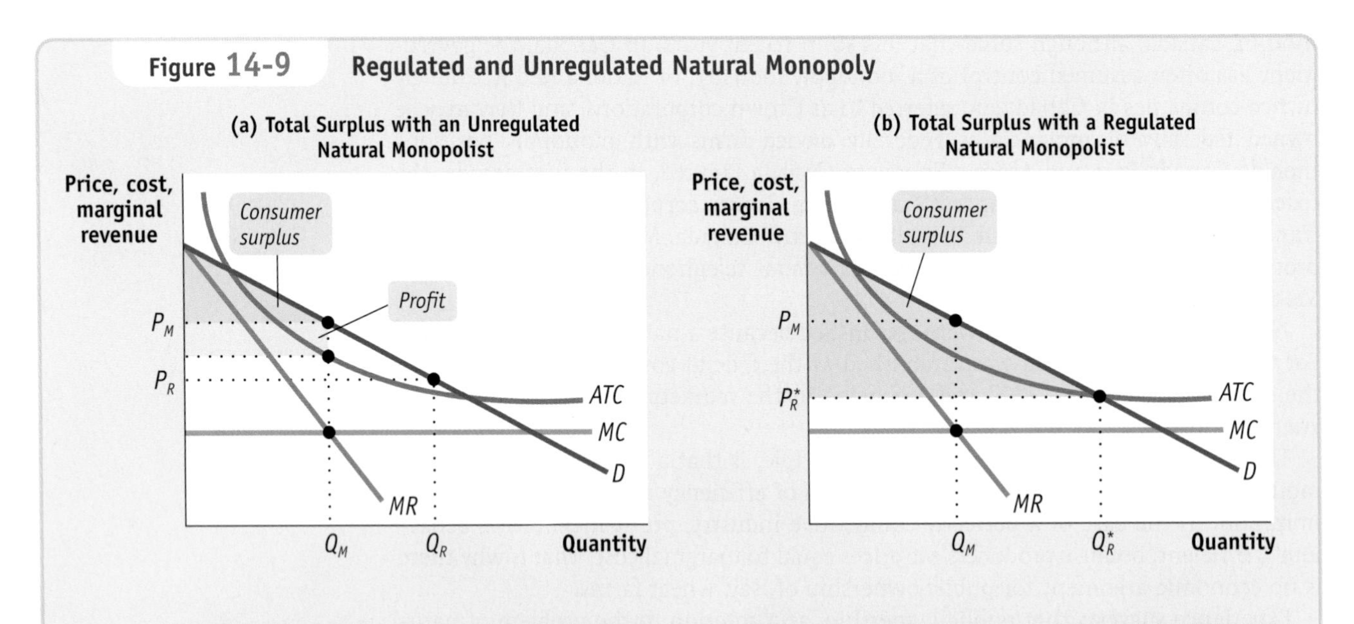

This figure shows the case of a natural monopolist. In panel (a), if the monopolist is allowed to charge P_M, it makes a profit given by the green area and consumer surplus is given by the blue area. If it is regulated and must charge the lower price P_R, output increases from Q_M to Q_R, and consumer surplus increases.

Panel (b) shows what happens when the monopolist must charge a price equal to average total cost, the price P_R^*. Output expands to Q_R^*, and consumer surplus is now the entire blue area. The monopolist makes zero profit. This is the greatest consumer surplus possible when the monopolist is allowed to at least break even, making P_R^* the best regulated price.

the output, the lower the average fixed cost (the fixed cost per unit of output). Because average total cost is downward sloping over the range of output relevant for market demand, this is a natural monopoly.

Panel (a) of Figure 14-9 illustrates a case of natural monopoly without regulation. The unregulated natural monopolist chooses the monopoly output Q_M and charges the price P_M. Since the monopolist receives a price greater than its average total cost, it earns a profit. This profit is exactly equal to the producer surplus in this market, represented by the green-shaded rectangle.

Now suppose that regulators impose a price ceiling on local gas deliveries—one that falls below the monopoly price P_M but above *ATC*, say, at P_R as shown in panel (a). At that price the quantity demanded is Q_R.

Does the company have an incentive to produce that quantity? Yes. If the price at which the monopolist can sell its product is fixed by regulators, the firm's output no longer affects the market price—so it ignores the *MR* curve and is willing to expand output as long as the price it receives for the next unit is greater than marginal cost and the monopolist at least breaks even on total output. So with price regulation, the monopolist produces more, at a lower price.

Of course, the monopolist will not be willing to produce at all if the imposed price means producing at a loss. That is, the price ceiling has to be set high enough to allow the firm to cover its average total cost. Panel (b) of Figure 14-9 shows a situation in which regulators have pushed the price down as far as possible, at the level where the average total cost curve crosses the demand curve. At any lower price the firm loses money. The price here, P_R^*, is the best regulated price: the monopolist is just willing to operate and produces Q_R^*, the quantity demanded at that price. Consumers and society gain as a result.

The welfare effects of this regulation can be seen by comparing the shaded areas in the two panels of Figure 14-9. Consumer surplus is increased by the regulation, with the gains coming from two sources. First, profits are eliminated and added instead to consumer surplus. Second, the larger output and lower price leads to an overall welfare gain—an increase in total surplus.

This all looks terrific: consumers are better off, profits are eliminated, overall welfare increases. Unfortunately, things are rarely that easy in practice. The main problem is that regulators don't have the information required to set the price exactly at the level at which the demand curve crosses the average total cost curve. Sometimes they set it too low, creating shortages; at other times they set it too high. Also, regulated monopolies tend to exaggerate their costs to regulators and to provide inferior quality to consumers.

Must Monopoly Be Controlled? Sometimes the cure is worse than the disease. Some economists have argued that the best solution to the problem of monopoly may be to live with it. The case for doing nothing is that attempts to control monopoly will, one way or another, do more harm than good.

For example, some argue that blocking mergers (through the review process and the Competition Tribunal) may prevent companies from realizing important synergies. Moreover, since the Canadian market is relatively small, it is argued that Canadian firms must be large relative to the domestic market in order to realize economies of scale and to compete internationally.

With regard to natural monopolies, neither public regulation nor public ownership is a perfect solution. The aim of regulation is to allow a firm to earn a "fair" return on its capital. So, when a firm succeeds in reducing costs, the regulated price is reduced too. But this eliminates the incentive to innovate and keep costs down. Even worse, regulators may lose track of the public interest—they may become "captured" by those they attempt to regulate. This could happen through bribery and corruption, or, more innocently, through cross-hiring. Regulators tend to hire personnel who have previously worked in the industry being regulated because of their expertise and knowledge.

And after leaving government service, regulators who have shown "understanding" are often rewarded with good jobs back in the same industry.

Public ownership of the industry involves the same pitfalls as regulation—no incentive to minimize costs, and management by personnel who could lose track of the public interest. For example, politicians may give lucrative management positions of Crown corporations to those who are most loyal, rather than to those who have the most expertise. George Stigler, who won the Nobel Prize for his work in industrial organisation, often remarked that in his opinion the costs of "market failure" are much smaller than the costs of "political failure" found in real political systems.

Finally, doing nothing may involve a relatively small cost if monopoly power is relatively fleeting and the monopolies themselves relatively dynamic. All firms want monopoly profits. It creates the carrot that drives the search for technological superiority. Joseph Schumpeter believed that dominant firms are constantly subjected to competition as new innovations supplant the old. For example, at one time (throughout the 1960s, 1970s, and 1980s) IBM had a near-monopoly in the production of computers. This was swept aside by the development of the personal computer and successive waves of technological innovations. Either the dominant firm maintains its monopoly position by reinvesting its profits to develop technological innovation, or it is swept away.

Moreover, it is argued that since competitive firms earn zero profits (in long-run equilibrium), they do not have the necessary resources to invest in technological innovation. Most research and development spending is done by larger firms with market power. In Schumpeter's view, the disadvantage of imperfect markets—the reduction of output—is more than offset by the advantages of greater research funded by the extra profits.

economics in action

Are Canada's Merger Guidelines Too Strict?

While the "Big Five" banks may be large in terms of the domestic market, they are small fry compared to their international competitors. In an attempt to realize so-called "synergies", four of them sought permission to merge in 1998: the Royal Bank with the Bank of Montreal, and CIBC with the Toronto Dominion Bank—but both merger deals were rejected by the federal government. Does Canada's merger review process stop companies from growing to the size necessary to allow them to compete internationally? Those bankers thought so.

The Competition Bureau will routinely investigate any merger that leads to a firm having more than 35% of market share (or the top four firms having more than 65% of market share). But on the other hand, the Competition Act explicitly instructs the Competition Tribunal not to rule against a merger *solely* on the basis of large market share. Rather, the Tribunal is explicitly instructed to consider other factors such as the extent of foreign competition and whether the merger is likely to bring about efficiency gains.

Nevertheless, in 1998 the federal government refused permission for the bank mergers. The reason was that at that time banking industry regulations excluded potential competitors from entering the market. That changed in 2001. Changes to federal regulations opened up new opportunities for foreign banks to operate in Canada, encouraged the start-up of new banks with new ownership rules, and gave certain non-bank financial institutions direct access to the payments system. This led to several large retail firms moving into the banking sector. For example, Canadian Tire, Sears Canada, and Loblaw Companies (President's Choice Bank) have all established banking subsidiaries. Given these changes, many observers feel the government would not block another merger attempt by the big banks some time in the future.

But not everyone contends that Canada's merger guidelines are too strict. Many feel they are too lenient. They note that many of Canada's leading exporters are relatively small companies, which leads them to question the importance of economies of scale. They argue that enhancing competition through strict anti-combines policies not only makes consumers better off through lower prices but also sharpens the edge of businesses, making the more successful firms better able to compete internationally.

Moreover, Canada is already more lenient than either the U.S. or Europe when it comes to tolerating domestically owned companies that have significant market power. For example, it is noteworthy that towards the end of 2004 the huge Canadian aluminium producer, Alcan, announced that it was voluntarily spinning off its rolled products manufacturing into a separate company called Novelis, Inc. Alcan took this action to address antitrust concerns—not in Canada, but in the U.S. and Europe.

The bottom line is that how and when anti-combines legislation should be enforced remains a controversial issue in Canada. ■

>> QUICK REVIEW

- By reducing output and raising price above marginal cost, a monopolist captures some of the consumer surplus as profit and causes deadweight loss. To avoid deadweight loss, government policy attempts to prevent monopoly behaviour.
- When monopolies are "created" rather than natural, governments should act to prevent monopolies from forming and break up existing ones.
- Natural monopoly poses a more difficult policy problem. One answer is *public ownership*, but publicly owned companies are sometimes poorly run.
- Another response is *price regulation*. A price ceiling imposed on a monopolist does not create shortages as long as it is not set too low.
- There always remains the option of doing nothing; monopoly is a bad thing, but the cure may be worse than the disease.

>> CHECK YOUR UNDERSTANDING 14-3

1. What policy should the government adopt in the following cases? Explain.
   a. Internet service in Anytown, Manitoba, is provided by cable. Customers feel that they are being gouged for service, but the cable company claims it must charge prices that let it recover the costs of laying cable in the town.
   b. The only two airlines that fly to Kamloops, BC, wish to merge but must get government approval. As a condition of its consent, the government can give away some of the airport landing slots in Kamloops to other airlines.
2. True or false? Explain your answer.
   a. Society's welfare is lower under a monopoly because some consumer surplus is transformed into profit for the monopolist.
   b. A monopolist causes inefficiency because there are consumers who are willing to pay a price greater than or equal to marginal cost but less than the monopoly price.
3. Suppose a monopolist mistakenly believes that its marginal revenue is always equal to the market price, though it correctly perceives that it faces a downward sloping demand function. Assuming constant marginal cost, draw a diagram comparing the level of profit, consumer surplus, total surplus, and deadweight loss for this misguided monopolist compared to a smart monopolist.

Solutions appear at back of book.

Price Discrimination

Up to this point we have considered only the case of a **single-price monopolist,** one who charges all consumers the same price. As the term suggests, not all monopolists do this. In fact, many if not most monopolists find that they can increase their profits by charging different customers different prices for the same good: they engage in **price discrimination.**

A **single-price monopolist** offers its product to all consumers at the same price.

Sellers engage in **price discrimination** when they charge different prices to different consumers for the same good.

The most striking example of price discrimination most of us encounter regularly involves airline tickets. Canada currently has one dominant national airline, Air Canada, and several smaller competitors such as WestJet and CanJet. As a result, most routes are serviced by only one or two carriers. These carriers have market power and can set prices. So any regular airline passenger quickly becomes aware that the question "How much will it cost me to fly there?" rarely has a simple answer. If you are willing to buy a non-refundable ticket to Anytown, Manitoba, a month in advance and stay over a Saturday night, your round trip may cost only $150—or less if you are a senior citizen or a student. On the other hand, if your boss has just told you that you have to go to Anytown tomorrow, which happens to be Tuesday, and come back on Wednesday, the round trip might cost $550. Yet the business traveller and the visiting grandparent will receive the same product—the same cramped seat, the same awful food.

You might object that airlines are not usually monopolists—that the airline industry is an oligopoly. In fact, price discrimination takes place under oligopoly and monopolistic competition as well as monopoly. But it doesn't happen under perfect competition. And once we've seen why monopolists sometimes price-discriminate, we'll be in a good position to understand why it happens in other cases, too.

The Logic of Price Discrimination

To get a preliminary view of why price discrimination might be more profitable than charging all consumers the same price, imagine that Air Sunshine offers the only non-stop flights between Edmonton, Alberta, and Ottawa, Ontario. Assume that there are no capacity problems—the airline can fly as many planes as the number of passengers warrants. For simplicity, also assume that there is no fixed cost. The marginal cost to the airline of providing a seat is $125, however many passengers the airline carries.

Further assume that the airline knows that there are two kinds of potential passengers. First, there are business travellers, 2,000 of whom want to travel between the destinations each week. Second, there are students, 2,000 of whom also want to travel each week.

Will potential passengers take the flight? It depends on the price. The business travellers, it turns out, really want to fly; they will take the plane as long as the price is no more than $550. The students, on the other hand, have less money and more time; if the price goes above $150, they will take the bus.

So what should the airline do? If it has to charge everyone the same price, its options are limited. It could charge $550; that way it would get as much as possible out of the business travellers but lose the student market. Or it could charge only $150; that way it would get both types of travellers, but would not make as much money on the business travellers as it might have.

We can quickly calculate the profits from each of these alternatives. If the airline charged $550, it would sell 2,000 tickets to the business travellers, getting total revenues of 550 × 2,000 = $1.1 million and incurring costs of 125 × 2,000 = $250,000; so its total profit would be $850,000. If the airline were to charge only $150, it would sell 4,000 tickets, receiving revenue of 4,000 × 150 = $600,000; its costs would be 4,000 × 125 = $500,000, so its profit would be $100,000. If the airline must charge everyone the same price, charging the higher price is clearly more profitable.

But what the airline would really like to do is charge the business travellers the full $550 and at the same time offer $150 tickets to the students. That's a lot less than the price paid by business travellers, but it's still above marginal cost; so if the airline could sell those extra 2,000 tickets to the students, it would make an additional $50,000 in profit.

In this example we assume that cutting the price below $550 will not lead to *any* additional business travel and that at a price above $150 *no* students will fly. The implied demand curve is shown in Figure 14-10.

It would be more realistic to suppose that there is some "give" in the demand of each group. But this, it turns out, does not do away with the argument for price discrimination. The important thing about the example is that the two groups of consumers differ in their *sensitivity to price*—that a high price has a larger effect in discouraging purchases by students than by business travellers. As long as differ-

Figure 14-10

Two Types of Airline Customers

Air Sunshine has two types of customers, business travellers who are willing to pay $550 per ticket and students willing to pay $150 per ticket. There are 2,000 of each kind of customer. Air Sunshine has a constant marginal cost of $125 per seat. If Air Sunshine could charge these two types of customers different prices, it would maximize its profits by charging business travellers $550 and students $150 per ticket. It would capture all of the consumer surplus as profit. **>web...**

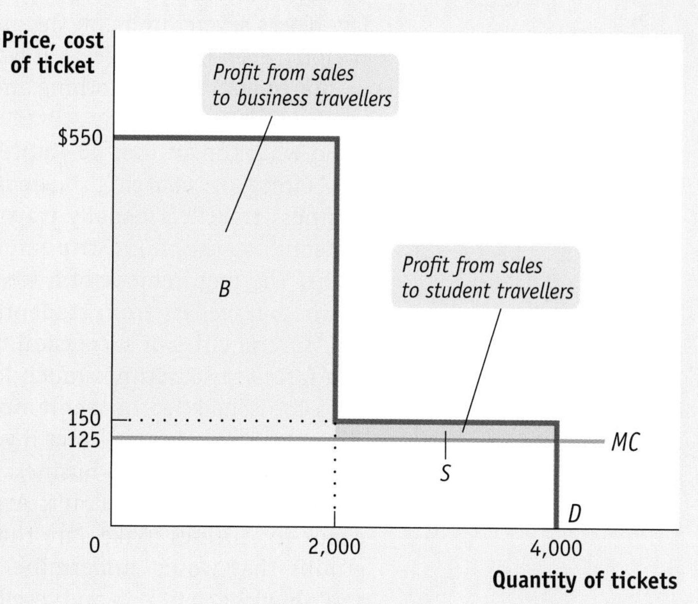

ent groups of customers respond differently to the price, a monopolist will find that it can capture more consumer surplus and increase its profit by charging them different prices.

Price Discrimination and Elasticity

A more realistic description of the demand that airlines face would not specify particular prices at which different types of travellers would choose to fly. Instead, it would distinguish between the groups on the basis of their *sensitivity* to the price—their price elasticity of demand.

Suppose that a company sells its product to two easily identifiable groups of people—call them business travellers and students. It just so happens that business travellers are very insensitive to the price: there is a certain amount of the product that they just have to have whatever the price, but they cannot be persuaded to buy much more than that no matter how cheap it is. Students, on the other hand, are more flexible: offer a good enough price and they will buy quite a lot, but raise the price too high and they will switch to something else. What should the company do?

The answer is the one already suggested by our simplified example: the company should charge business travellers, with their low price elasticity of demand, a higher price than it charges students, with their high price elasticity of demand.

The actual situation of the airlines is very much like this hypothetical example. Business travellers typically place a high priority on being at the right place at the right time and are not too sensitive to the price. But non-business travellers faced with a high price might take the bus, drive to another airport to get a lower fare, or skip the trip altogether.

On many airline routes, the fare you pay depends on the type of traveller you are.

So why doesn't an airline simply announce different prices for business and non-business customers? One reason is that this would probably be illegal (in Canada the law places severe limits on the ability of companies to practice open price discrimination). Even if it were legal, it would be hard to enforce: business travellers might be willing to wear casual clothing and claim they were visiting family in Ottawa in order to save $400.

So what the airlines do—quite successfully—is impose rules that indirectly have the effect of charging business and non-business travellers different fares. Business travellers usually travel during the week and want to be home on the weekend; so the round-trip fare is much higher if you don't stay over a Saturday night. The requirement of a weekend stay for a cheap ticket effectively separates business travellers from students and tourists. Similarly, business travellers often visit several cities in succession rather than making a simple round trip; so round-trip fares are sometimes much lower than twice the one-way fare. Many business trips are scheduled on short notice; so fares are much lower if you book far in advance. Fares are also lower if you travel standby, taking your chances on whether you actually get a seat—business travellers have to make it to that meeting, people visiting their relatives don't. And by requiring customers to show their ID upon check-in, airlines make sure that there are no resales of tickets between the two groups that would undermine their ability to price-discriminate—i.e., students can't buy cheap tickets and resell them to business travellers. Look at the rules that govern ticket pricing, and you will see an ingenious implementation of profit-maximizing price discrimination.

Perfect Price Discrimination

Let's return to the example of business travellers and students travelling between Edmonton and Ottawa, illustrated in Figure 14-10, and ask what would happen if the airline could distinguish between the two groups of customers in order to charge each a different price.

Clearly, then, the airline would charge each group its willingness to pay—that is, as we learned in Chapter 6, the maximum that each group is willing to pay. In the case of business travellers, the willingness to pay is $550, and it is $150 for students. We have assumed that the marginal cost is $125 and does not depend on output, so that the marginal cost curve is a horizontal line. We can easily read off the airline's profit: it is the sum of the areas of the rectangle *B* and the rectangle *S*.

In this case, the consumers do not get any consumer surplus! The entire surplus is captured by the monopolist in the form of profit. When a monopolist is able to capture the entire surplus in this way, we say that it achieves **perfect price discrimination.**

Perfect price discrimination takes place when a monopolist charges each consumer his or her willingness to pay—the maximum that consumer is willing to pay.

In general, the greater the number of different prices a monopolist manages to charge, the closer it can get to perfect price discrimination. Figure 14-11 shows a monopolist facing a downward-sloping demand curve; we suppose that this monopolist is able to charge different prices to different groups of consumers, with the consumers who are willing to pay the most being charged the most. In panel (a) the monopolist charges two different prices; in panel (b) the monopolist charges three different prices. Two things are apparent:

- The greater the number of prices the monopolist charges, the lower the lowest price—that is, some consumers will pay prices that approach marginal cost.
- The greater the number of prices the monopolist charges, the more money it extracts from consumers.

With a very large number of different prices, the picture would look like panel (c), a case of perfect price discrimination. Here, consumers least willing to buy the good pay marginal cost, and the entire consumer surplus is extracted as profit.

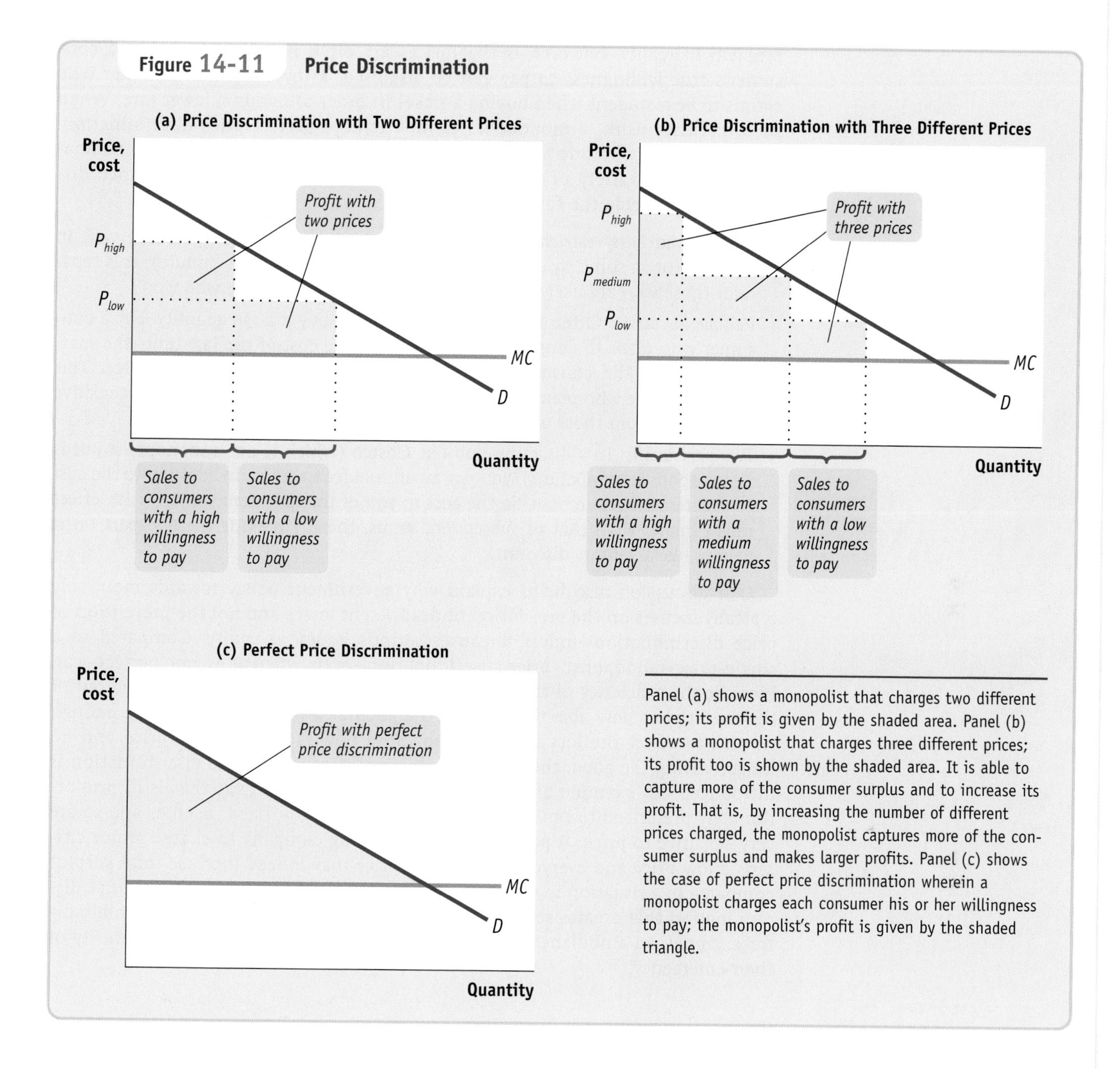

Panel (a) shows a monopolist that charges two different prices; its profit is given by the shaded area. Panel (b) shows a monopolist that charges three different prices; its profit too is shown by the shaded area. It is able to capture more of the consumer surplus and to increase its profit. That is, by increasing the number of different prices charged, the monopolist captures more of the consumer surplus and makes larger profits. Panel (c) shows the case of perfect price discrimination wherein a monopolist charges each consumer his or her willingness to pay; the monopolist's profit is given by the shaded triangle.

Both our airline example and the example in Figure 14-11 can be used to make another point: a monopolist that can engage in perfect price discrimination doesn't cause any inefficiency! The reason is that the source of inefficiency is eliminated: there are no potential consumers who would be willing to purchase the good at a price equal to or above marginal cost but do not get the chance to do so. Instead, the monopolist manages to "scoop up" these consumers by offering them lower prices than it charges others.

Perfect price discrimination is probably never possible in practice. At a fundamental level, the inability to achieve perfect price discrimination is a problem of prices as economic signals, a phenomenon we noted in Chapter 13. When prices work as economic signals, they convey the information needed to ensure that all mutually beneficial transactions will indeed occur: the market price signals the seller's cost, and a consumer signals willingness to pay by purchasing the good whenever that willingness to pay is at least as high as the market price. The problem in reality, however, is that prices are often not perfect signals: a consumer's true willingness to pay can be disguised, as by a business traveller who claims to be a student when buying a ticket in order to obtain a lower fare. When such disguises work, a monopolist cannot achieve perfect price discrimination. However, monopolists do try to move in the direction of perfect price discrimination through a variety of pricing strategies. Common techniques for price discrimination include the following:

- *Advance purchase restrictions.* Prices are lower for those who purchase well in advance (or in some cases for those who purchase at the last minute); this separates those who are likely to shop for better prices from those who won't.
- *Volume discounts.* Often the price is lower if you buy a large quantity. For a consumer who plans to consume a lot of a good, the cost of the last unit—the marginal cost to the consumer—is considerably less than the average price. This separates those who plan to buy a lot and are therefore likely to be more sensitive to the price from those who don't.
- *Two-part tariffs.* In a discount club like Costco (which is not a monopolist but is a monopolistic competitor), you pay an annual fee to get in, in addition to the cost of the items you purchase. So the cost to you of the first item you buy is in effect much higher than that of subsequent items, thereby making the two-part tariff behave like a volume discount.

Our discussion also helps explain why government policy towards monopoly typically focuses on the prevention of deadweight losses and not the prevention of price discrimination—unless it causes serious issues of equity. Compared to a single-price monopolist, price discrimination—even when it is not perfect—can increase the efficiency of the market. If sales to consumers formerly priced out of the market but now able to purchase the good at a lower price generate enough surplus to offset the loss in surplus to those now facing a higher price and no longer buying the good, then total surplus increases when price discrimination is introduced. An example of this phenomenon might be a drug that is disproportionately prescribed to senior citizens, who are often on fixed incomes and so are very sensitive to price. A policy that allows a drug company to charge senior citizens a low price and everyone else a high price may indeed increase total surplus compared to a situation in which everyone is charged the same price. But price discrimination that creates serious concerns about equity is likely to be prohibited—for example, an ambulance service that charges patients based on the severity of their emergency.

economics in action

But Isn't Price Discrimination Illegal in Canada?

It is a criminal offence in Canada to collude with other firms to fix prices, to engage in misleading advertising, or to practice price discrimination. The outlawing of these three practices predates the 1986 Competition Act. For example, price discrimination has been illegal in Canada since 1935. But if price discrimination is illegal, why then do cinemas, public transit authorities, theme parks, and restaurants offer age-related discounts to senior citizens and children? Why do airlines discriminate against those who cannot stay over a Saturday night or who are unable to book early? Why do utility companies routinely charge less per kilowatt of electricity to those who use the most? The reason is that the law against price discrimination is rarely enforced. There have been only three convictions since 1935, and all cases involved sales to retailers, not customers. Why so few?

The most compelling reason for allowing such pricing practices is that they might improve the efficiency of the market over the single-price solution. For example, as long as the movie house is not full to capacity, who is made worse off by offering discounts to children? The children are better off, the theatre owners are better off (since otherwise the children couldn't afford the admission price), and the adults are no worse off (unless they suffer from a bout of envy). Price discrimination that induces greater use of a facility that has excess capacity is "efficiency enhancing", and society would be worse off by banning the practice.

Why, then, does the law make price discrimination illegal? The answer is that the law seems to be concerned with situations where the monopolist discriminates among buyers to expand its market power and keep out potential competitors. And in these situations, complaints involving price discrimination are dealt with under other parts of the Competition Act, such as abuse of dominant position.

But if the law against price discrimination among consumers is rarely enforced, the same is not true about the laws banning price fixing or misleading advertising. Engage in these practices and you can expect to have the book thrown at you—like the four Toronto businessmen who had the bright idea to set up a company called "Yellow Business Pages.com" and who sent out solicitations for business that looked just like bills for regular advertising in the yellow pages of the telephone directory. Businesses thought they were paying their yellow pages invoices, and the Toronto businessmen made a lot of money. But in October 2004, they received jail time and a fine of nearly a million dollars for misleading advertising. ■

>>QUICK REVIEW

- Not every monopolist is a *single-price monopolist*. Many monopolists, as well as oligopolists and monopolistic competitors, engage in *price discrimination*.
- Price discrimination is profitable when consumers differ in their sensitivity to the price. A monopolist would like to charge high prices to those consumers willing to pay them, without driving away other consumers who are willing to pay less.
- It is profit maximizing to charge higher prices to consumers with a low elasticity of demand and lower prices to those with a high elasticity of demand.
- A monopolist able to charge each consumer his or her willingness to pay for the good achieves *perfect price discrimination* and does not cause any inefficiency because all mutually beneficial transactions are exploited.

>>CHECK YOUR UNDERSTANDING 14-4

1. True or false? Explain your answer.
   a. A single-price monopolist sells to some customers that a price-discriminating monopolist refuses to.
   b. A price-discriminating monopolist creates more inefficiency than a single-price monopolist because it captures more of the consumer surplus.
   c. Under price discrimination, a customer with highly elastic demand will pay a lower price than a customer with inelastic demand.

2. Which of the following are cases of price discrimination and which are not? In the cases of price discrimination, identify the consumers with high and those with low price elasticity of demand.
   a. Damaged merchandise is marked down.
   b. Restaurants have senior citizen discounts.
   c. Food manufacturers place discount coupons for their merchandise in newspapers.
   d. Airline tickets cost more during the summer peak flying season.

Solutions appear at back of book.

• A LOOK AHEAD •

We've now taken one large step away from the world of perfect competition. As we have seen, a monopolistic industry behaves quite differently from a perfectly competitive industry.

But pure monopoly is actually quite rare in the modern economy. More typical are industries in which there is some competition, but not perfect competition—that is, where there is *imperfect competition*. In the next two chapters we examine two types of imperfect competition: oligopoly and monopolistic competition.

You might expect an oligopoly to act something like a cross between a monopoly and a perfectly competitive industry, but it turns out that oligopoly raises issues that arise neither in perfect competition nor in monopoly, issues of *strategic interaction* and *collusion* between firms. Likewise, monopolistic competition creates yet another set of issues, such as tastes, product differentiation, and advertising.

SUMMARY

1. There are four main types of market structure based on number of firms in the industry and product differentiation: perfect competition, monopoly, oligopoly, and monopolistic competition.
2. A **monopolist** is a producer who is the sole supplier of a good without close substitutes. An industry controlled by a monopolist is a **monopoly.**
3. The key difference between a monopoly and a perfectly competitive industry is that an individual perfectly competitive firm faces a horizontal demand curve, but a monopolist faces a downward-sloping demand curve. This gives the monopolist **market power,** the ability to raise the market price by reducing output.
4. To persist, a monopoly must be protected by a **barrier to entry.** This can take the form of control of natural resources or inputs, economies of scale that give rise to **natural monopoly,** technological advantage, or government rules that prevent entry by other firms.
5. The marginal revenue of a monopolist is composed of a quantity effect (the price received from the additional unit) and a price effect (the reduction in the price at which all units are sold). Because of the price effect, a monopolist's marginal revenue is always less than the market price, and the marginal revenue curve lies below the demand curve.
6. At the monopolist's profit-maximizing output level, marginal cost equals marginal revenue, which is less than market price. At the perfectly competitive firm's profit-maximizing output level, marginal cost equals the market price. So in comparison to competitive industries, monopolies produce less, charge higher prices, and earn higher profits in both the short run and the long run.
7. A monopoly creates deadweight (efficiency) losses by charging a price above marginal cost: the loss in consumer surplus exceeds the monopolist's profit. Thus monopolies are a source of market failure and should be prevented or broken up, except in the case of natural monopolies.
8. Natural monopolies still cause deadweight losses. To limit these losses, governments sometimes impose **public ownership** and at other times impose **price regulation.** A price ceiling on a monopolist, as opposed to a perfectly competitive industry, need not cause shortages and can increase total surplus.
9. Not all monopolists are **single-price monopolists.** Monopolists, as well as oligopolists and monopolistic competitors, often engage in **price discrimination** to make higher profits, using various techniques to differentiate consumers based on their sensitivity to price, and charging those with less elastic demand higher prices. A monopolist that achieves **perfect price discrimination** charges each consumer a price equal to his or her willingness to pay and captures the total surplus in the market. Although perfect price discrimination creates no inefficiency, it is practically impossible to implement.

KEY TERMS

Monopolist, p. 350
Monopoly, p. 350
Market power, p. 351
Barrier to entry, p. 352
Natural monopoly, p. 352
Combine laws, p. 364
Public ownership, p. 365
Price regulation, p. 366
Single-price monopolist, p. 369
Price discrimination, p. 369
Perfect price discrimination, p. 372

PROBLEMS

1. Each of the following firms possesses market power. Explain its source.
   a. Merck, the producer of the patented cholesterol-lowering drug Zetia
   b. Aliant, a provider of local telephone service
   c. Chiquita, a supplier of bananas and owner of most banana plantations
2. Skyscraper City has a subway system, for which a one-way fare is $1.50. There is pressure on the mayor to reduce the fare by one third, to $1.00. The mayor is dismayed, thinking this means that Skyscraper City will lose one-third of its revenue from subway ticket sales. The mayor's economic adviser reminds her that she is only focusing on the price effect and ignoring the quantity effect. Explain why the mayor's estimate of a one-third loss of revenue is likely to be an overestimate. Illustrate with a diagram.
3. Consider an industry with the demand curve and marginal cost (*MC*) curve shown in the accompanying diagram. There is no fixed cost. If the industry is a single-price monopoly, the monopolist's marginal revenue curve would be *MR*. Answer the following questions by naming the appropriate points or areas.

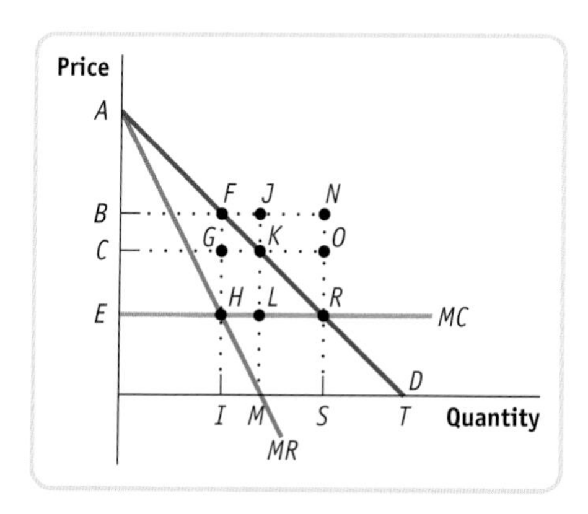

a. If the industry is perfectly competitive, what will be the total quantity produced? At what price?

b. Which area reflects consumer surplus under perfect competition?

c. If the industry is a single-price monopoly, what quantity will the monopolist produce? Which price will it charge?

d. Which area reflects the single-price monopolist's profit?

e. Which area reflects consumer surplus under single-price monopoly?

f. Which area reflects the deadweight loss to society from single-price monopoly?

g. If the monopolist can price-discriminate perfectly, what quantity will the perfectly price-discriminating monopolist produce?

4. Bob, Bill, Ben, and Brad Baxter have just made a documentary movie about their hockey team. They are thinking about making the movie available for download on the Internet, and they can act as a single-price monopolist if they choose. Each time the movie is downloaded, their Internet service provider charges them a fee of $4. The Baxter brothers argue about which price to charge customers per download. The accompanying table shows the demand schedule for their film.

Price of download	Quantity of downloads demanded
$10	0
8	1
6	3
4	6
2	10
0	15

a. Calculate the total revenue and the marginal revenue per download.

b. Bob is proud of the film and wants as many people as possible to download it. Which price would he choose? How many downloads would be sold?

c. Bill wants as much total revenue as possible. Which price would he choose? How many downloads would be sold?

d. Ben wants to maximize profit. Which price would he choose? How many downloads would be sold?

e. Brad wants to charge the efficient price. Which price would he choose? How many downloads would be sold?

5. Jimmy has a room that overlooks, from some distance, a major league baseball stadium. He decides to rent a telescope for $50.00 a week and charge his friends and classmates to use it to "peep" at the game for 30 seconds. He can act as a single-price monopolist for renting out "peeps". For each person who takes a 30-second peep, it costs Jimmy $0.20 to clean the eyepiece. The accompanying table shows the information Jimmy has gathered about the demand for the service.

Price of peep	Quantity of peeps demanded
$1.20	0
1.00	100
0.90	150
0.80	200
0.70	250
0.60	300
0.50	350
0.40	400
0.30	450
0.20	500
0.10	550

a. For each price in the table above, calculate the total revenue from selling peeps and the marginal revenue per peep.

b. At what quantity will Jimmy's profit be maximized? What price will he charge? What will be his total profit?

c. Jimmy's landlady complains about all the visitors coming into the building and tells Jimmy to stop selling peeps. Jimmy discovers, however, that if he gives the landlady $0.20 for every peep he sells, she will stop complaining. What effect does the $0.20-per-peep bribe have on Jimmy's marginal cost per peep? What is the new profit-maximizing quantity of peeps? What effect does the $0.20-per-peep bribe have on Jimmy's total profit?

6. Suppose that De Beers is a single-price monopolist in the market for diamonds. De Beers has five potential customers: Greta, Jackie, Joan, Mia, and Sophia. Each of these customers will buy at most one diamond, and only if the price is just equal to, or lower than, her willingness to pay. Greta's willingness to pay is $400; Jackie's, $300; Joan's, $200; Mia's, $100; and Sophia's, $0. De Beers's marginal cost per diamond is $100. This leads to the demand schedule for diamonds shown in the accompanying table.

Price of diamond	Quantity of diamonds demanded
$500	0
400	1
300	2
200	3
100	4
0	5

a. Calculate De Beers's total revenue and its marginal revenue. From your calculation, draw the demand curve and the marginal revenue curve.

b. Explain why De Beers faces a downward-sloping demand curve.

c. Explain why the marginal revenue from an additional diamond sale is less than the price of the diamond.

d. Suppose De Beers currently charges $200 for its diamonds. If it lowered the price to $100, how large is the price effect? How large is the quantity effect?

e. Draw the marginal cost curve into your diagram and determine which quantity maximizes De Beers's profit and which price De Beers will charge.

7. Use the demand schedule for diamonds given in Problem 6. The marginal cost of producing diamonds is constant at $100. There is no fixed cost.

a. If De Beers charges the monopoly price, how large is the consumer surplus that each buyer experiences? How large, therefore, is total consumer surplus? How large is producer surplus?

Suppose that upstart Russian and Asian producers enter the market and the market becomes perfectly competitive.

b. What is the perfectly competitive price? What quantity will be sold in this perfectly competitive market?

c. At the competitive price and quantity, how large is the consumer surplus that each buyer experiences? How large is total consumer surplus? How large is producer surplus?

d. Compare your answer to part c of this question with your answer to part a. How large is the deadweight loss associated with monopoly in this case?

8. Use the demand schedule for diamonds given in Problem 6. De Beers is the monopolist, but it can now price-discriminate perfectly amongst all five of its potential customers. De Beers's marginal cost is constant at $100. There is no fixed cost.

a. If De Beers can price-discriminate perfectly, to which customers will it sell diamonds and at what prices?

b. How large is each consumer's consumer surplus? How large is total consumer surplus? Calculate producer surplus by summing the producer surplus generated by each sale.

9. Download Records decides to release an album by the group Mary and the Little Lamb. It produces the album with no fixed cost, but the total cost of downloading an album to a CD and paying Mary her royalty is $6 per album. Download Records can act as a single-price monopolist. Its marketing division finds that the demand schedule for the album is as shown in the accompanying table.

Price of album	Quantity of albums demanded
$22	0
20	1,000
18	2,000
16	3,000
14	4,000
12	5,000
10	6,000
8	7,000

a. Calculate the total revenue and marginal revenue per album.

b. The marginal cost of producing each album is constant at $6. To maximize profit, what level of output should Download Records choose, and what price should it therefore charge?

c. Mary renegotiates her contract and now needs to be paid a royalty of $14 per album. The marginal cost therefore rises to be constant at $14. To maximize profit, what level of output should Download Records now choose, and which price should it charge for each album?

10. The accompanying diagram illustrates your local electricity company's natural monopoly. The diagram shows the demand (*D*) curve for kilowatt-hours (kWh) of electricity, the company's marginal revenue (*MR*) curve, the marginal cost (*MC*) curve, and its average total cost (*ATC*) curve. The government wants to regulate the monopolist by imposing a price ceiling.

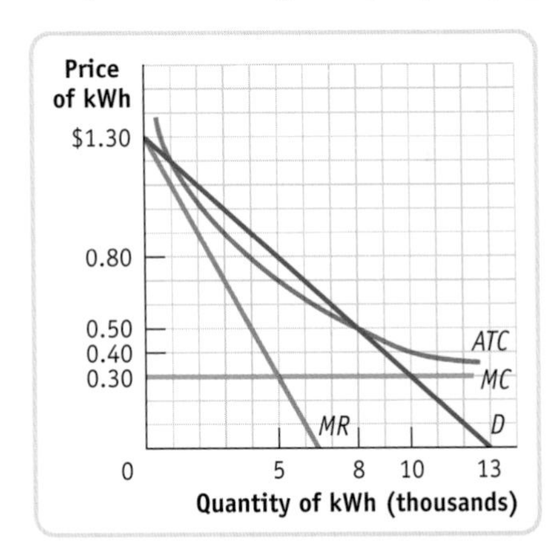

a. If the government does not regulate this monopolist, which price will it charge? Illustrate the inefficiency this creates by shading the deadweight loss from monopoly.

b. If the government imposes a price ceiling equal to the marginal cost, $0.30, will the monopolist make profits or lose money? Shade the area of profit (or losses) for the monopolist. If the government imposes this price ceiling, do you think the firm will continue to produce in the long run?

c. If the government imposes a price ceiling of $0.50, will the monopolist make a profit or lose money?

11. The movie theatre in Collegetown serves two kinds of customers: students and professors. There are 900 students and 100 professors in Collegetown. Each student's willingness to pay for a movie ticket is $5. Each professor's willingness to pay for a movie ticket is $10. Each will buy at most one ticket. The movie theatre's marginal cost per ticket is constant at $3, and there is no fixed cost.

a. Suppose the movie theatre cannot price-discriminate and needs to charge both students and professors the same price per ticket. If the movie theatre charges $5, who will buy movie tickets, and what will the movie theatre's profit be? How large is consumer surplus?

b. If the movie theatre charges a price of $10, who will buy movie tickets, and what will the movie theatre's profit be? How large is consumer surplus?

c. Now suppose that, if it chooses to, the movie theatre can price-discriminate between students and professors by requiring students to show their student ID. If the movie theatre charges students $5 and professors $10, how much profit will the movie theatre make? How large is consumer surplus?

>web... To continue your study and review of concepts in this chapter, please visit the Krugman/Wells website for quizzes, animated graph tutorials, web links to helpful resources, and more.

www.worthpublishers.com/krugmanwellsmyatt

15 >>Oligopoly

CAUGHT IN THE ACT

IT IS A CRIMINAL OFFENCE IN CANADA for firms to conspire to restrict output and increase prices. But given the increasing importance of international trade, more and more conspiracies are international in nature. To counter this, Canada's Competition Bureau actively cooperates with other international law enforcement agencies, especially those in the United States. Some of the biggest fines in the history of the Competition Act have been imposed on multinational corporations engaged in global conspiracies that have adversely affected Canadians. Archer Daniels Midland (also known as ADM) has the dubious distinction of having received the largest fine ever imposed on a single company in Canada—some $17.5 million in 1998.

ADM is a multinational "agribusiness" corporation based in the U.S. Its name will be familiar to Canadian farmers who buy ADM's livestock and chicken feed, as well as to Canadians who tune into American public television—of which ADM is a generous sponsor. But on October 25, 1993, ADM itself was on camera.

On that day executives from ADM and its Japanese competitor Ajinomoto met at the Marriott Hotel in Irvine, California, to discuss the market for lysine, an additive used in animal feed. (How is lysine produced? It's excreted by genetically engineered bacteria.) In this and subsequent meetings, the two companies joined with several other competitors to set targets for the market price of lysine. Each company also agreed to limit its production in order to achieve those targets. Agreeing on specific limits would be their biggest challenge—or so they thought.

What the participants in the meeting didn't know was that they had a bigger problem: the FBI had bugged the room and was filming them with a camera hidden in a lamp.

What the companies were doing was illegal. To understand why it was illegal and why the companies were doing it anyway, we need to examine the issues posed by industries that are neither perfectly competitive nor pure monopolies. In this chapter we focus on the case of *oligopoly,* an industry in which

AP/Wide World Photos

The law catches up with a colluding oligopolist.

What you will learn in this chapter:

- The meaning of **oligopoly,** and why it occurs
- Why **oligopolists** have an incentive to act in ways that reduce their combined profit, and why they can benefit from **collusion**
- How our understanding of oligopoly can be enhanced by using **game theory,** especially the concept of the **prisoners' dilemma**
- How repeated interactions among oligopolists can help them achieve **tacit collusion**
- How oligopoly works in practice, under the legal constraints of the Competition Act.

there are only a few producers. As we'll see, oligopoly is a very important reality—much more important, in fact, than monopoly, and arguably more typical of modern economies than perfect competition.

Although much that we have learned about both perfect competition and monopoly is relevant to oligopoly, oligopoly also raises some entirely new issues. Among other things, firms in an oligopoly are often tempted to engage in the kind of behaviour that got ADM, Ajinomoto, and other lysine producers into trouble with the law.

We will begin by examining what oligopoly is and why it is so important. Then we'll turn to the behaviour of oligopolistic industries. Finally, we'll look again at those aspects of Canada's competition law that are primarily concerned with trying to keep oligopolies "well behaved".

The Prevalence Of Oligopoly

At the time of that elaborately bugged meeting, no one company controlled the world lysine industry, but there were only a few major producers. An industry with only a few sellers is known as an **oligopoly;** a firm in such an industry is known as an **oligopolist.**

An **oligopoly** is an industry with only a small number of producers. A producer in such an industry is known as an **oligopolist.**

Oligopolists obviously compete with each other for sales. But ADM and Ajinomoto weren't like firms in a perfectly competitive industry, which take the price at which they can sell their product as given. Each of these firms knew that its decision about how much to produce would affect the market price. That is, like monopolists, each of the firms had some *market power*. So the competition in this industry wasn't "perfect".

Economists refer to a situation in which firms compete but also possess market power—which enables them to affect market prices—as **imperfect competition.** As we saw in Chapter 14, there are actually two important forms of imperfect competition: oligopoly and *monopolistic competition*. Of these, oligopoly is probably the more important in practice.

When no one firm has a monopoly, but producers nonetheless realize that they can affect market prices, an industry is characterized by **imperfect competition.**

Although lysine is a multibillion-dollar business, it is not exactly a product familiar to most consumers. However, many familiar goods and services are supplied by only a few competing sellers, which means the industries in question are oligopolies. For example, if you want to buy hockey skates you must choose either CCM or Bauer. Most air routes are served by only two or three airlines. Most cola beverages are sold by Coca-Cola and Pepsi. Most breakfast cereals are produced by Kellogg, General Mills, General Foods (Post cereals), and Quaker. This list could go on for many pages.

It's important to realize that an oligopoly isn't necessarily made up of large firms. What matters isn't size per se; the question is how many competitors there are. When a small town has only two grocery stores, grocery service there is just as much an oligopoly as air shuttle service between Montreal and Toronto.

Why are oligopolies so prevalent? Essentially, oligopoly is the result of the same factors that sometimes produce monopoly, but in somewhat weaker form. Probably the most important source of oligopoly is the existence of *economies of scale,* which give bigger producers a cost advantage over smaller ones. When these economies of scale are very strong, they lead to monopoly, but when they are not that strong they lead to competition among a small number of firms. For example, larger grocery stores typically have lower costs than smaller stores. But the advantages of

Rhonda Sidney/The Image Works

Froot Loops or Wheaties? Four firms control nearly 83 percent of the breakfast cereal market.

large scale taper off once grocery stores are reasonably large, which is why two or three stores often survive in small towns.

If oligopoly is so common, why has most of this book focused on competition in industries where the number of sellers is very large? And why did we study monopoly, which is relatively uncommon, first? The answer has two parts. First, much of what we learn from the study of perfectly competitive markets—about costs, entry and exit, and efficiency—remains valid despite the fact that many industries are not perfectly competitive. Second, the analysis of oligopoly turns out to present some puzzles for which there is no easy solution. It is almost always a good idea—in exams and in life—to first deal with the questions you can answer, then puzzle over the harder ones. We have simply followed the same strategy, developing the relatively clear-cut theories of perfect competition and monopoly first, and only then turning to the puzzles presented by oligopoly.

economics in action

Some Oligopolistic Industries

In practice, it is not always easy to determine an industry's market structure just by looking at the number of sellers. Many oligopolistic industries contain a number of small "niche" producers, which don't really compete with the major players. For example, the Canadian airline industry includes a number of regional airlines like Pacific Coastal, which is based in Vancouver and flies propeller-driven planes to places like Campbell River and Port Hardy. If you count these airlines along with foreign carriers operating out of Canada's bigger cities, the Canadian airline industry may contain dozens of sellers, which doesn't sound like competition among a small group. But there is currently only one dominant national carrier—Air Canada—with WestJet (based in Calgary) providing an increasingly national service, and CanJet (based in Halifax) providing competition mainly in the East. Most routes are serviced by only one or two carriers.

To get a better picture of market structure, economists often make use of the "four-firm concentration ratio", which asks what share of industry sales is accounted for by the top four firms. (Why four? Statistics Canada normally doesn't release data on share of industry sales by individual firms within the top four, lest it be accused of giving away corporate secrets.)

Table 15-1 shows some industries with high four-firm concentration ratios, along with the names of the biggest firms in each industry. These names are familiar—not just because these are big companies, but also because they advertise a lot. And that is not an

TABLE 15-1

Four-Firm Concentration Ratios

Industry	Concentration ratio	Largest firms
1. Steel smelting	100	Stelco, Dofasco
2. Cigarettes	99.8	Imperial Tobacco, Rothmans (Benson and Hedges), JTI-Macdonald
3. Automobiles	86.2	General Motors, Ford, DaimlerChrysler
4. Batteries	82.9	Duracell, Energizer, Rayovac
5. Breakfast cereals	77.5	Kellogg, General Mills, Post, Quaker Oats
6. Refined petroleum products	72.6	Imperial (Esso), Petro-Canada, Irving, Ultramar
7. Book publishing	57	McClelland and Stewart, Random House (Canada), Harper-Collins (Canada)

Source: From data tabulated by the Manufacturing, Construction and Energy Division, Statistics Canada, 2002.

accident. As we will see shortly, oligopolistic firms often choose *not* to compete much on price, trying instead to win customers in other ways—such as through ad campaigns. ■

>> QUICK REVIEW

- In addition to perfect competition and monopoly, *oligopoly* and monopolistic competition are also important types of market structure. They are forms of *imperfect competition.*
- Oligopoly is a common market structure. It arises from the same forces that lead to monopoly, except in weaker form.

>> CHECK YOUR UNDERSTANDING 15-1

1. What factors caused each of the following industries to be structured as an oligopoly, rather than a perfectly competitive industry?
   a. The world oil industry, in which a few countries near the Persian Gulf control much of the world's oil reserves
   b. The microprocessor industry, where two firms, Intel and its bitter rival AMD, dominate the technology
   c. The wide-bodied passenger jet industry, in which all planes are manufactured by either Boeing or Airbus, and production is characterized by extremely high fixed cost

Solutions appear at back of book.

Understanding Oligopoly

How much will a firm produce? Up to this point we have always answered: the quantity that maximizes its profit. The assumption that firms maximize profit is enough to determine their output when they are perfect competitors or when the industry is a monopoly.

When it comes to oligopoly, however, we run into some difficulties. Indeed, economists often describe the behaviour of oligopolistic firms as a "puzzle".

A Duopoly Example

Let's begin looking at the puzzle of oligopoly with the simplest version, an industry in which there are only two producing firms—a **duopoly**—and each firm is known as a **duopolist.**

An oligopoly consisting of only two firms is a **duopoly.** Each firm is known as a **duopolist.**

Going back to our chapter-opening story, imagine that ADM and Ajinomoto are the only two producers of lysine. To make things even simpler, let's suppose that once a company has incurred the fixed cost needed to produce lysine, the marginal cost of producing another pound is zero. So the companies are only concerned with the revenue they receive from sales.

Table 15-2 shows a hypothetical demand schedule for lysine and the total revenue of the industry at each price-quantity combination.

TABLE 15-2

Demand Schedule for Lysine

Price of lysine (per pound)	Quantity of lysine demanded (millions of pounds)	Total revenue (millions)
$12	0	$0
11	10	110
10	20	200
9	30	270
8	40	320
7	50	350
6	60	360
5	70	350
4	80	320
3	90	270
2	100	200
1	110	110
0	120	0

If this were a perfectly competitive industry, each firm would have an incentive to produce more as long as the market price was above marginal cost. Since the marginal cost is assumed to be zero, this would mean that at equilibrium lysine would be provided free. Firms would produce until price equals zero, yielding a total output of 120 million pounds and zero revenue for all firms.

However, surely the firms would not be that stupid. With only two firms in the industry, each would realize that by producing more it would drive down the market price. So each firm would, like a monopolist, realize that profits would be higher if it limited its production.

So how much will the two firms produce?

Sellers engage in **collusion** when they cooperate to raise each other's profits. A **cartel** is an agreement by several producers that increases their combined profits by telling each one how much to produce.

One possibility is that the two companies will engage in **collusion**—they will cooperate to raise each other's profits. The strongest form of collusion is a **cartel,** an arrangement that determines how much each firm produces. The world's most famous cartel is the Organization of Petroleum Exporting Countries, described in Economics in Action on page 395. As its name indicates, it's actually an agreement among governments rather than firms. There's a reason this most famous of cartels is an agreement among governments: cartels among firms are illegal in Canada and most other jurisdictions. But let's ignore the law for a moment (which is, of course, what ADM and Ajinomoto did in real life—to their own detriment).

So suppose that ADM and Ajinomoto were to form a cartel and that this cartel decided to act as if it were a monopolist, maximizing total industry profits. It's obvious from Table 15-2 that in order to maximize the combined profits of the firms, this cartel should set total industry output at 60 million pounds of lysine, which would sell at a price of $6 per pound, leading to revenue of $360 million, the maximum possible. Then the only question would be how much of that 60 million pounds each firm gets to produce. A "fair" solution might be for each firm to produce 30 million pounds.

But even if the two firms agreed on such a deal, they might have a problem: each of the firms would have an incentive to break its word and produce more than the agreed-upon quantity.

Collusion and Competition

Suppose that the presidents of ADM and Ajinomoto were to agree that each would produce 30 million pounds of lysine over the next year. Both would understand that this plan maximizes their combined profits. And both would have an incentive to cheat.

To see why, consider what would happen if Ajinomoto honoured its agreement, producing only 30 million pounds, but ADM ignored its promise and produced 40 million pounds. This increase in total output would drive the price down from $6 to $5 per pound, the price at which 70 million pounds are demanded. The industry's total revenue would fall from $360 million ($\$6 \times 60$ million pounds) to $350 million ($\$5 \times 70$ million pounds). However, ADM's revenue would *rise,* from $180 million to $200 million. Since we are assuming a marginal cost of zero, this would mean a $20 million increase in ADM's profits.

But Ajinomoto's president might make exactly the same calculation. And if *both* firms were to produce 40 million pounds of lysine, the price would drop to $4 per pound. So each firm's profits would fall, from $180 million to $160 million.

Why do individual firms have an incentive to produce more than the quantity that maximizes their joint profits? Because neither firm has as strong an incentive to limit its output as a true monopolist would.

Let's go back for a minute to the theory of monopoly. We know that a profit-maximizing monopolist sets marginal cost (which in this case is zero) equal to marginal revenue. But what is marginal revenue? Producing an additional unit of a good has two effects:

1. A positive *quantity* effect: one more unit is sold, increasing total revenue by the price at which that unit is sold.
2. A negative *price* effect: in order to sell one more unit, the monopolist must cut the market price on *all* units sold.

The negative price effect is the reason marginal revenue for a monopolist is less than the market price. But when considering the effect of increasing production, a firm is concerned only with the price effect on its own units of output, not those of its fellow oligopolists. Both ADM and Ajinomoto suffer a negative price effect if ADM decides to produce extra lysine and so drives down the price. But ADM cares only about the negative price effect on the units it produces, not about the loss to Ajinomoto.

This tells us that an individual firm in an oligopolistic industry faces a smaller price effect from an additional unit of output than a monopolist; therefore, the marginal revenue that such a firm calculates is higher. So it will seem to be profitable for any one company in an oligopoly to increase production, even if that increase reduces the profits of the industry as a whole. But if everyone thinks that way, the result is that everyone earns a lower profit!

Until now, we have been able to analyse producer behaviour by asking what a producer should do to maximize profits. But even if ADM and Ajinomoto are both trying to maximize profits, what does this predict about their behaviour? Will they engage in collusion, reaching and holding to an agreement that maximizes their combined profits? Or will they engage in **non-cooperative behaviour,** with each firm acting in its own self-interest, even though this has the effect of driving down everyone's profits? Both strategies sound like profit maximization. Which will actually describe their behaviour?

When firms ignore the effects of their actions on each other's profits, they engage in **non-cooperative behaviour**.

Now you see why oligopoly presents a puzzle: there are only a small number of players, making collusion a real possibility. If there were dozens or hundreds of firms, it would be safe to assume they would behave non-cooperatively. When there are only a handful of firms in an industry, however, it's hard to determine whether collusion will actually materialize.

Since collusion is ultimately more profitable than non-cooperative behaviour, firms have an incentive to collude if they can. One way to do so is to formalize it—sign an agreement (maybe even make a legal contract) or establish some financial incentives for the companies to set their prices high. But in Canada and many other nations, you can't do that—at least not legally. Companies cannot make a legal contract to keep prices high: not only is the contract unenforceable, but writing it is a one-way ticket to jail. Neither can they sign a gentlemen's agreement, which lacks the force of law but perhaps exerts moral force—that's illegal, too. In fact, executives from rival companies rarely meet without lawyers present, who make sure that the conversation does not stray into inappropriate territory. Even hinting at how nice it would be if prices were higher can bring you an unwelcome interview with the investigative branch of the Competition Bureau that enforces the laws against oligopolistic collusion.

Sometimes, as we've seen, oligopolistic firms just ignore the rules. But more often they find ways to achieve collusion without a formal agreement. As we'll see in the next section, one important factor in determining how hard it is to achieve collusion without a formal agreement is how easy it is for a firm to increase its output quickly in order to capture sales from its rival.

Competing in Prices versus Competing in Quantities

In our duopoly example, we've assumed that firms choose a quantity of output and sell that output at whatever the market price turns out to be. That's actually a pretty good description of the way the lysine market works. But in other industries, such as automobiles, firms don't choose a level of output; they choose a *price* and sell as much as they can at that price. Does this make any difference?

Yes, it does, at least when we analyse non-cooperative behaviour. In choosing what to do, an oligopolist must always be concerned about whether a non-cooperative rival firm will respond by *undercutting* her. The oligopolist must be concerned that a rival firm will take some action that allows it to steal some of her sales and capture a larger share of the market. And, it turns out, the answer to whether a rival is willing to engage in undercutting behaviour depends on how difficult it is for him to increase output to satisfy the additional customers he gains by his undercutting.

Let's consider a hypothetical example using Airbus and Boeing, duopolists in the large passenger aircraft industry, to gain some intuition. For these firms, deciding their production capacity—how much output they can produce over, say, the next two or three years—is their most important decision. Why? Passenger aircraft are very large and are built in batches, a few planes at a time, in huge hangars. The determining factor in how many planes can be built at any given time is the size of the company's existing production facilities, which can take years to build.

So this means that when Airbus, for example, sets its maximum production capacity at 50 planes per year, Boeing can feel comfortably assured that Airbus won't easily be able to increase this number anytime soon. This, in turn, has important implications for Boeing's actions. If Boeing also sets its production capacity at 50 planes per year, it can safely assume that Airbus's production capacity is *given* and that, as a result, the market will be split 50–50 between the two manufacturers. Airbus won't be able to quickly increase its output and steal some of Boeing's customers by offering them a lower price. The end result is that the total output of the industry is less than the output under perfect competition, and each firm earns a profit. Economists refer to this kind of behaviour as *quantity competition* or *Cournot behaviour,* after the nineteenth-century French economist who devised the model. The basic insight of the Cournot model is that when firms are restricted in how much they can produce, it is easier for them to avoid excessive competition and to "divvy up" the market, thereby pricing above marginal cost and earning profits. It is easier for them to achieve an outcome that looks like collusion without a formal agreement.

But how does the behaviour of oligopolists change when they are not constrained by limited production capacity? Let's assume that Air Canada and British Airways are duopolists and that they have exclusive rights to fly the Toronto–London route. When the economy is strong and lots of people want to fly between Toronto and London, Air Canada and British Airways are likely to find the number of passengers they can carry constrained by their production capacity—for example, the number of landing slots available. So in this environment they are likely to behave according to the Cournot model and price above marginal cost—say, charging \$800 per round trip. But when the business climate is poor, the two airlines are likely to find that they have lots of empty seats at a fare of \$800 and that capacity constraints are no longer an issue. What will they do?

Recent history tells us they will engage in a price war by slashing ticket prices. They are no longer able to maintain Cournot behaviour because at the ticket price of \$800, each has excess capacity. If Air Canada were to try to maintain a price of \$800, it would soon find itself undercut by British Airways, which would charge \$750 and steal all its customers. In turn, Air Canada would undercut British Airways by charging \$700, and so on. As long as each firm finds that it can make additional sales by cutting price, each will continue cutting until price is equal to marginal cost. (Going any lower would cause them to incur an avoidable loss.) This type of behaviour is known as *price competition* or *Bertrand behaviour,* after another nineteenth-century French economist. The logic behind the Bertrand model is that when firms produce perfect substitutes and have sufficient capacity to satisfy demand when price is equal to marginal cost, then each firm will be compelled to engage in competition by undercutting its rival's price until the price reaches marginal cost—that is, perfect competition.

Oligopolists would, understandably, prefer to avoid Bertrand behaviour because it earns them zero profits. Lacking an environment that imposes constraints on their output capacity, firms try other means to avoid direct price competition—such as producing products that are not perfect substitutes but are instead differentiated. We'll examine this strategy in more detail later in this chapter, just noting here that producing differentiated products allows oligopolists to cultivate a loyal set of customers and to charge prices higher than marginal cost.

Even in the absence of limitations on production capacity, firms are often able to maintain collusive behaviour (although it may be somewhat harder to do). In the next section, we'll see why such informal collusion often works but sometimes fails.

economics in action

The Great Vitamin Conspiracy

It was a bitter pill to swallow. In late 1999 some of the world's largest drug companies (mainly European and Japanese) agreed to pay billions of dollars in damages to customers after being convicted of a huge conspiracy to rig the world vitamin market.

The conspiracy began in 1989 when the Swiss company Roche and the German company BASF began secret talks about raising prices for vitamins. Soon a French company, Rhone-Poulenc, joined in, followed by several Japanese companies and other companies around the world. The members of the group, which referred to itself as "Vitamins Inc.", met regularly—sometimes at hotels, sometimes at the private homes of executives—to set prices and divide up markets for "bulk" vitamins (like vitamin A, vitamin C, and so on). These bulk vitamins are sold mainly to other companies, such as animal feed makers, food producers, and so on, which include them in their products. Indeed, it was the animal feed companies that grew suspicious about the prices they were being charged, which led to a series of investigations and eventually to huge fines in both Canada and the U.S. The ten companies involved in the Canadian link of this international conspiracy were fined a staggering $91 million in 1999 by the Canadian courts.

This was a huge conspiracy—it makes the lysine case look like, well, chicken feed. How could it have happened?

The main answer probably lies in different national traditions about how to treat oligopolists. Both Canada and the United States have a long tradition of taking tough legal action against price-fixing, as we have just described. European governments, however, have historically been much less stringent. Indeed, in the past some European governments have actually encouraged major companies to form cartels. Modern European law on competition is not that different from that in North America, but the European cultural tradition of viewing conspiracies to raise prices as normal business practice has not entirely died out. ■

>>QUICK REVIEW

- Some of the key issues in oligopoly can be understood by looking at the simplest case, a *duopoly*.
- By acting as if they were a single monopolist, oligopolists can maximize their combined profits. So there is an incentive to form a *cartel*.
- However, each firm has an incentive to cheat—to produce more than it is supposed to under the cartel agreement. So there are two principal outcomes: successful *collusion* or behaving *non-cooperatively* by cheating.
- It is likely to be easier to achieve informal collusion when firms in an industry face capacity constraints.

>>CHECK YOUR UNDERSTANDING 15-2

1. Which of the following factors increase the likelihood that an oligopolist will collude with other firms in the industry? Which factors increase the likelihood that an oligopolist will act non-cooperatively and raise output to capture sales from its rivals? Explain your answer.
   a. The firm's initial market share is small.
   b. The firm has a cost advantage over its rivals.
   c. The firm's customers face additional costs when they switch from the use of one firm's product to another firm's product.
   d. The firm and its rivals are currently operating at maximum production capacity, which cannot be altered in the short run.

Solutions appear at back of book.

Games Oligopolists Play

In our duopoly example and in real life, each oligopolist realizes both that its profit depends on what its competitor does and that its competitor's profit depends on what it does. That is, the two firms are in a situation of **interdependence.**

When the decisions of two or more firms significantly affect each other's profits, they are in a situation of **interdependence.**

The study of behaviour in situations of interdependence is known as **game theory.**

In effect, the two firms are playing a "game" in which the profit of each player depends not only on its own actions but also on those of the other player. The area of study of such games, known as **game theory,** has many applications, not just to economics but also to military strategy, politics, and other social sciences.

Let's see how game theory helps us understand oligopoly.

The Prisoners' Dilemma

The reward received by a player in a game, such as the profits earned by an oligopolist, is that player's **payoff.**

A **payoff matrix** shows how the payoff to each of the participants in a two-player game depends on the actions of both. Such a matrix helps us analyse interdependence.

Game theory deals with any situation in which the reward to any one player—the **payoff**—depends not only on his or her own actions but also on those of other players in the game. In the case of oligopolistic firms, the payoff is simply the firm's profit.

When there are only two players, as in a duopoly, the interdependence between the players can be represented with a **payoff matrix** like that shown in Figure 15-1. Each row corresponds to an action by one player (in this case, ADM); each column corresponds to an action by the other (in this case, Ajinomoto). For simplicity, let's assume that ADM can pick only one of two alternatives: produce 30 million pounds of lysine or produce 40 million pounds. Ajinomoto has the same pair of choices.

The matrix contains four boxes, each divided by a diagonal line. Each box shows the payoff to the two firms that results from a pair of choices; the number below the diagonal shows ADM's profits, the number above the diagonal shows Ajinomoto's profits.

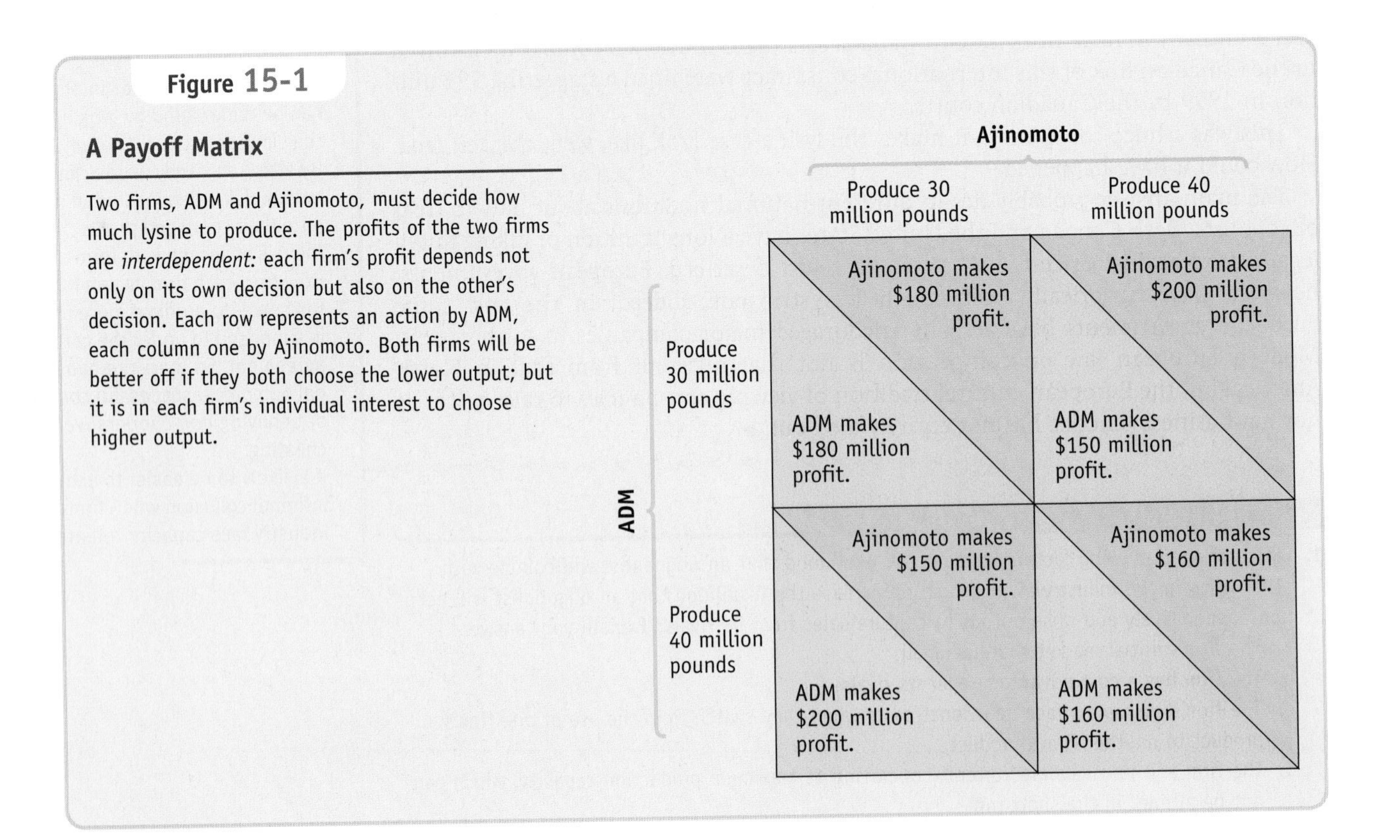

Figure 15-1

A Payoff Matrix

Two firms, ADM and Ajinomoto, must decide how much lysine to produce. The profits of the two firms are *interdependent:* each firm's profit depends not only on its own decision but also on the other's decision. Each row represents an action by ADM, each column one by Ajinomoto. Both firms will be better off if they both choose the lower output; but it is in each firm's individual interest to choose higher output.

These payoffs show what we concluded from our earlier analysis: the combined profit of the two firms is maximized if they each produce 30 million pounds. Either firm can, however, increase its own profits by producing 40 million pounds while the other produces only 30 million pounds. But if both produce the larger quantity, both will have lower profits than if they had both held their output down.

The particular situation shown here is a version of a famous—and seemingly paradoxical—case of interdependence that appears in many contexts. Known as the **prisoners' dilemma,** it is a type of game in which the payoff matrix implies the following:

- Each player has an incentive, regardless of what the other player does, to "cheat"—that is, to take an action that benefits him or her at the other's expense.
- When both players cheat, both are worse off than they would have been if neither had cheated.

Prisoners' dilemma is a game based on two premises: (1) Each player has an incentive to choose an action that benefits him or herself at the other player's expense. (2) When both players act in this way, both are worse off than if they had chosen different actions.

The original illustration of the prisoners' dilemma occurred in a fictional story about two accomplices in crime—let's call them Thelma and Louise—who have been caught by the police. The police have enough evidence to put them behind bars for 5 years. They also know that the pair have committed a more serious crime, one that carries a 20-year sentence; unfortunately, they don't have enough evidence to convict the women on that charge. To do so, they would need each of the prisoners to implicate the other in the second crime.

So the police put the miscreants in separate cells and say the following to each: "Here's the deal: If neither of you confesses, you know that we'll send you to jail for 5 years. If you confess and implicate your partner, and she doesn't do the same, we'll reduce your sentence from 5 years to 2. But if your partner confesses and you don't, you'll get the maximum 20 years. And if both of you confess, we'll give you both 15 years."

Figure 15-2 shows the payoffs that face the prisoners, depending on the decision of each to remain silent or to confess. (Usually the payoff matrix reflects the

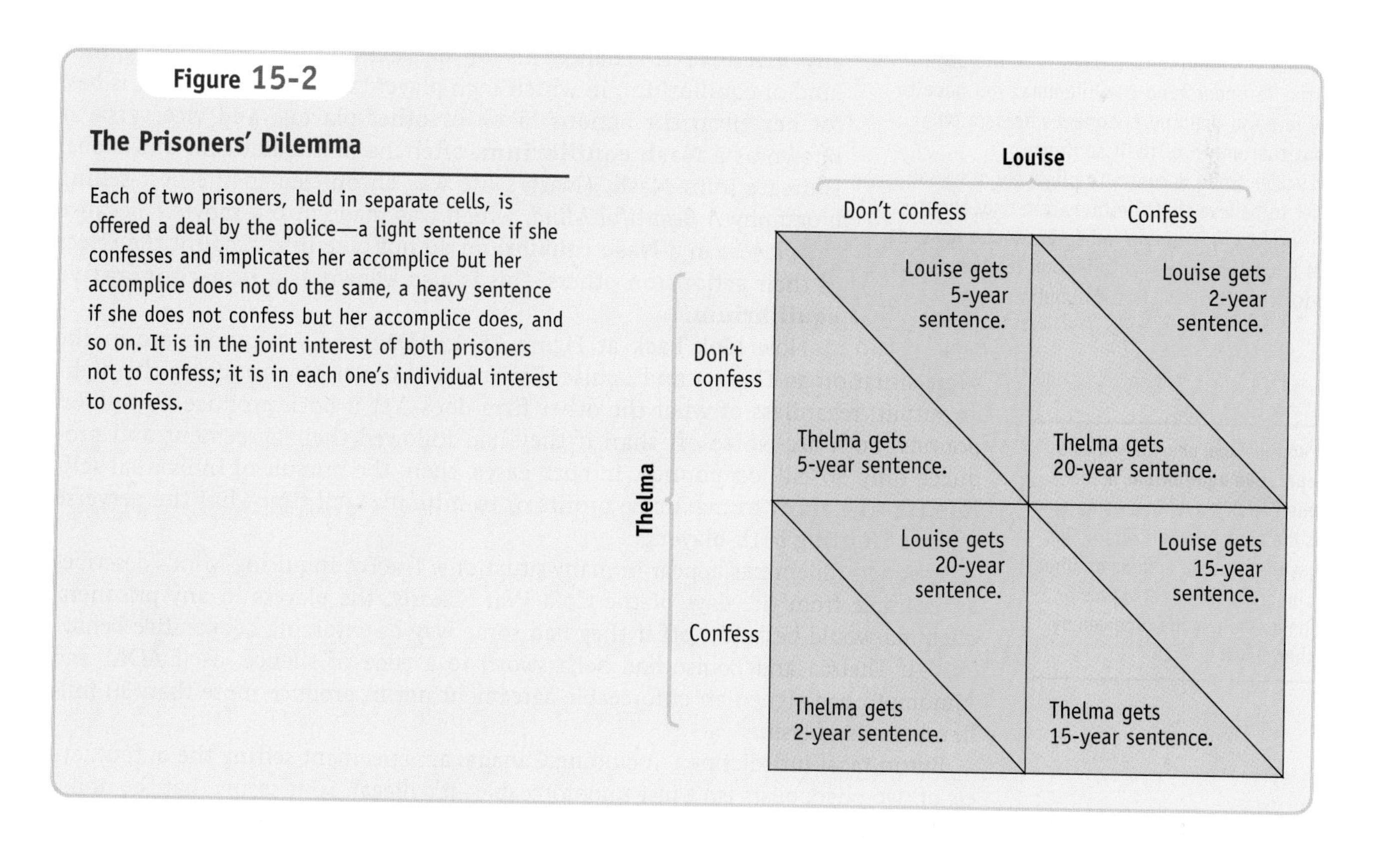

Figure 15-2

The Prisoners' Dilemma

Each of two prisoners, held in separate cells, is offered a deal by the police—a light sentence if she confesses and implicates her accomplice but her accomplice does not do the same, a heavy sentence if she does not confess but her accomplice does, and so on. It is in the joint interest of both prisoners not to confess; it is in each one's individual interest to confess.

players' payoffs, and higher payoffs are better than lower payoffs. This case is an exception: a higher number of years in prison is bad, not good!) Let's assume that the prisoners have no way to communicate and that they have not sworn an oath not to harm each other or anything of that sort. So each acts in her own self-interest. What will they do?

The answer is clear: both will confess. Look at it first from Thelma's point of view: she is better off confessing, regardless of what Louise does. If Louise doesn't confess, Thelma's confession reduces her own sentence from 5 years to 2. If Louise *does* confess, Thelma's confession reduces her sentence from 20 to 15 years. Either way, it's clearly in Thelma's interest to confess. And because she faces the same incentives, it's clearly in Louise's interest to confess, too. To confess in this situation is a type of action that economists call a *dominant strategy*. An action is a **dominant strategy** when it is the player's best action regardless of what action the other player takes. It's important to note that not all games have a dominant strategy—it depends on the structure of payoffs in the game. But in the case of Thelma and Louise, it is clearly in the interest of the police to structure the payoffs so that confessing is a dominant strategy for each person. So as long as the two prisoners have no way to make an enforceable agreement that neither will confess (something they can't do if they can't communicate, which the police certainly won't allow them to do because the police want to compel each one to confess), Thelma and Louise will each act in a way that hurts the other.

An action is a **dominant strategy** when it is a player's best action regardless of the action taken by the other player.

So if each prisoner acts rationally in her own interest, both will confess. Yet if neither of them had confessed, both would have received a much lighter sentence! In a prisoners' dilemma, each player has a clear incentive to act in a way that hurts the other player—but when both make that choice, it leaves both of them worse off.

When Thelma and Louise both confess, they reach an *equilibrium* of the game. We have used the concept of equilibrium many times in this book; it is an outcome in which no individual or firm has any incentive to change his or her action. In game theory, this kind of equilibrium, in which each player takes the action that is best for her given the actions taken by other players, and vice versa, is known as a **Nash equilibrium,** after the mathematician and Nobel Laureate John Nash. (Nash's life was chronicled in the best-selling biography *A Beautiful Mind*, which was made into a movie.) Because the players in a Nash equilibrium do not take into account the effect of their actions on others, this is also known as a **non-cooperative equilibrium.**

PITFALLS

PLAYING FAIR ON THE PRISONERS' DILEMMA

One common reaction to the prisoners' dilemma is to assert that it isn't really rational for either prisoner to confess—that Thelma wouldn't dare confess, because she'd be afraid that Louise would beat her up, or Thelma would feel guilty because Louise wouldn't do that to her.

But this kind of answer is, well, cheating—it amounts to changing the payoffs in the payoff matrix. To understand the dilemma, you have to play fair and imagine prisoners who care *only* about the length of their sentence.

Luckily, when it comes to oligopoly, it's a lot easier to believe that the firms care only about their profits. There is no indication that anyone at ADM felt either fear of or affection for Ajinomoto, or vice versa; it was strictly about business.

Now look back at Figure 15-1; ADM and Ajinomoto are in the same situation as Thelma and Louise. Each firm is better off producing the higher output, regardless of what the other firm does. Yet if both produce 40 million pounds, both are worse off than if they had followed their agreement and produced only 30 million pounds. In both cases, then, the pursuit of individual self-interest—the effort to maximize profits or to minimize jail time—has the perverse effect of hurting both players.

A **Nash equilibrium,** also known as a **non-cooperative equilibrium,** is the result when each player in a game chooses the action that maximizes his or her payoff given the actions of other players, ignoring the effects of his or her action on the payoffs received by those other players.

Prisoners' dilemmas appear in many situations. The For Inquiring Minds describes an example from the days of the Cold War. Clearly, the players in any prisoners' dilemma would be better off if they had some way of enforcing cooperative behaviour—if Thelma and Louise had both sworn to a code of silence, or if ADM and Ajinomoto had signed an enforceable agreement not to produce more than 30 million pounds of lysine.

But in most jurisdictions, including Canada, an agreement setting the output levels of two oligopolists isn't just unenforceable—it's illegal. So it seems that the undesirable non-cooperative equilibrium is the only possible outcome. Or is it?

FOR INQUIRING MINDS

PRISONERS OF THE ARMS RACE

Political history between World War II and the late 1980s was dominated by the Cold War—a seemingly endless struggle between the United States (and its allies) and the Soviet Union. During the Cold War, both countries spent huge sums on arms, sums that were a significant drain on the U.S. economy and eventually proved a crippling burden for the Soviet Union, whose underlying economic base was much weaker. Yet neither country was ever able to achieve a decisive military advantage.

As many people pointed out, both nations would have been better off if they had both spent less on arms. Yet the arms race continued for 40 years.

Why? As political scientists were quick to notice, one way to explain the arms race was to suppose that the two countries were locked in a classic prisoners' dilemma. Each government would have liked to achieve decisive military superiority, and feared military inferiority; but both would have preferred a stalemate with low military spending to one with high spending. However, each government rationally chose to engage in high spending: if its rival did not spend heavily, this would lead to military superiority, while *not* spending heavily would lead to inferiority if the other government continued its arms buildup. So the countries were trapped.

The answer to this trap could have been an agreement not to spend as much; indeed, the two sides tried repeatedly to negotiate limits on some kinds of weapons. But these agreements weren't very effective. In the end the issue was resolved by the collapse of the Soviet Union in 1991.

TASS/Soufoto

Caught in the prisoners' dilemma: heavy military spending hastened the collapse of the Soviet Union.

Overcoming the Prisoners' Dilemma: Repeated Interaction and Tacit Collusion

Thelma and Louise in their cells are playing what is known as a *one-shot* game—that is, they play the game with each other only once. They get to choose once and for all whether to confess or hang tough, and that's it. However, most of the games that oligopolists play aren't one-shot; instead, they expect to play the game repeatedly with the same competitors. An oligopolist usually expects to be in business for many years, and it knows that its decision today about whether to cheat is likely to affect the way other firms treat it in the future. So a smart oligopolist doesn't just decide what to do based on the effect on profit in the short run. Instead, he or she engages in **strategic behaviour,** taking account of the effects of the action he or she chooses today on the future actions of other players in the game. And under some conditions, oligopolists that behave strategically can manage to behave as if they had a formal agreement to collude.

A firm engages in **strategic behaviour** when it attempts to influence the future behaviour of other firms.

Suppose that ADM and Ajinomoto expect to be in the lysine business for many years and therefore expect to play the game of cheat versus collude shown in Figure 15-1 many times. Would they really betray each other time and again?

Probably not. Suppose that ADM considers two strategies. In one strategy it always cheats, producing 40 million pounds of lysine each year, regardless of what Ajinomoto does. In the other strategy, it starts off with good behaviour, producing only 30 million pounds in the first year, and watches to see what its rival does. If Ajinomoto also keeps its production down, ADM will stay cooperative, producing 30 million pounds again for the next year. But if Ajinomoto produces 40 million pounds, ADM will take the gloves off and also produce 40 million pounds next year. This latter strategy—start off behaving cooperatively, but thereafter do whatever the other player did in the previous period—is generally known as **tit for tat.**

A strategy of **tit for tat** involves playing cooperatively at first, then doing whatever the other player did the previous period.

"Tit for tat" is a form of strategic behaviour, which we have just defined as behaviour intended to influence the future actions of other players. "Tit for tat" offers a reward to the other player for cooperative behaviour—if you behave cooperatively, so will I. It also provides a punishment for cheating—if you cheat, don't expect me to be nice in the future.

The payoff to ADM of each of these strategies would depend on which strategy Ajinomoto chooses. Consider the four possibilities, shown in Figure 15-3:

1. If ADM plays "tit for tat" and so does Ajinomoto, both firms will make a profit of $180 million each year.
2. If ADM plays "always cheat" but Ajinomoto plays "tit for tat", ADM makes a profit of $200 million the first year but only $160 million per year thereafter.
3. If ADM plays "tit for tat" but Ajinomoto plays "always cheat", ADM makes a profit of only $150 million in the first year but $160 million per year thereafter.
4. If ADM plays "always cheat" and Ajinomoto does the same, both firms will make a profit of $160 million each year.

Which strategy is better? In the first year, ADM does better playing "always cheat", whatever its rival's strategy: it assures itself that it will get either $200 million or $160 million (which of the two payoffs it actually receives depends upon whether Ajinomoto plays "always cheat" or "tit for tat"). This is better than it would get in the first year if it played "tit for tat": either $180 million or $150 million. But by the second year, a strategy of "always cheat" gains ADM only $160 million per year for the second and all subsequent years, regardless of Ajinomoto's actions. This amount is inferior to the amount ADM would gain by playing "tit for tat": for the second and all subsequent years, it would never get any less than $160 million and would get as

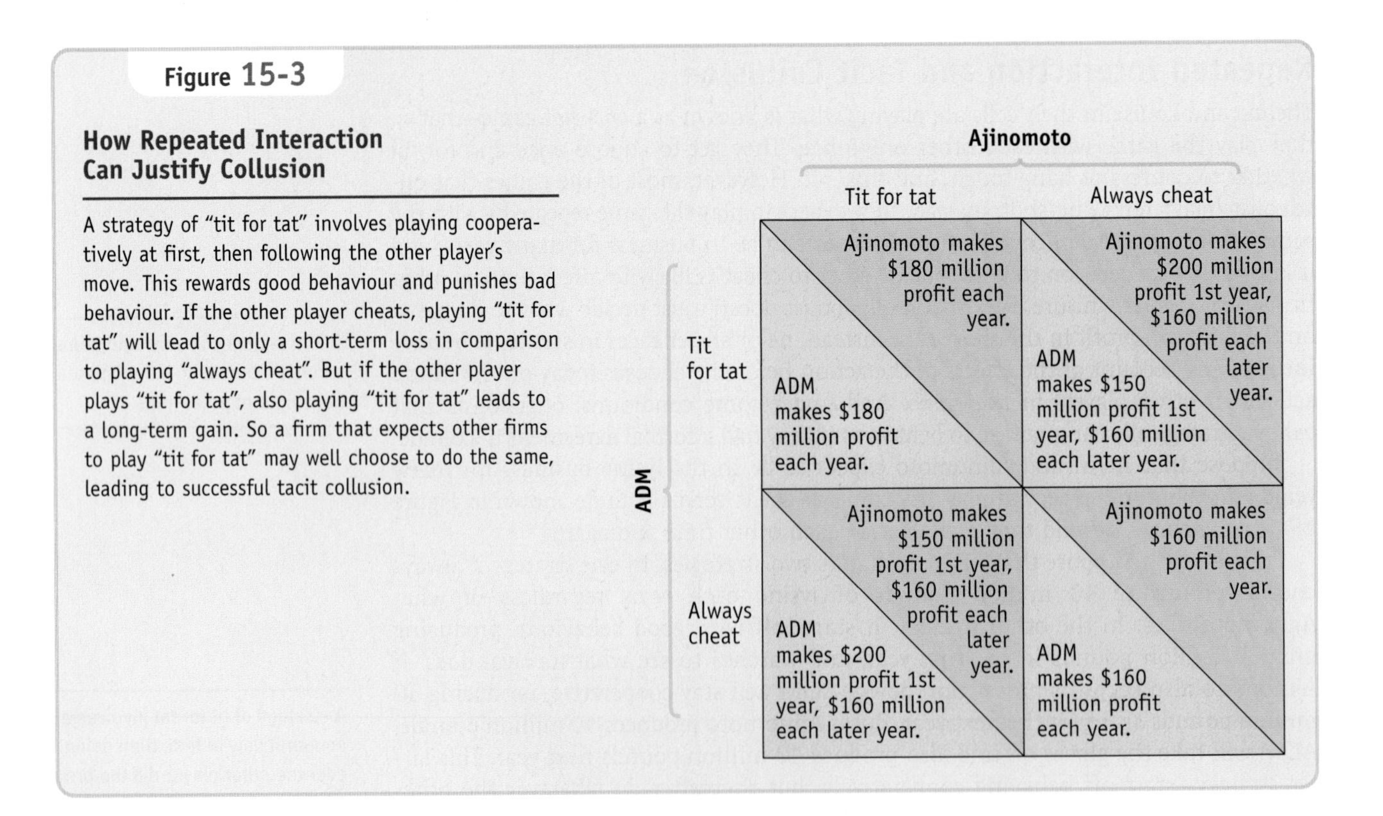

Figure 15-3

How Repeated Interaction Can Justify Collusion

A strategy of "tit for tat" involves playing cooperatively at first, then following the other player's move. This rewards good behaviour and punishes bad behaviour. If the other player cheats, playing "tit for tat" will lead to only a short-term loss in comparison to playing "always cheat". But if the other player plays "tit for tat", also playing "tit for tat" leads to a long-term gain. So a firm that expects other firms to play "tit for tat" may well choose to do the same, leading to successful tacit collusion.

much as $180 million if Ajinomoto played "tit for tat" as well. So which strategy is more profitable depends on two things: how many years ADM expects to play the game and what strategy its rival follows.

If ADM expects the lysine business to end in the near future, it is in effect playing a one-shot game. So it might as well grab what it can. Even if ADM expects to remain in the lysine business for many years (therefore to find itself repeatedly playing this game with Ajinomoto) and expects, for some reason, Ajinomoto always to cheat, it should also always cheat. That is, ADM should follow the old rule "Do unto others before they do unto you".

But if ADM expects to be in the business for a long time and thinks Ajinomoto is likely to play "tit for tat", it will make more profits over the long run by playing "tit for tat", too. It could have made some extra short-term profits by cheating at the beginning, but this would provoke Ajinomoto into cheating too, and would in the end mean lower profits.

The lesson of this story is that when oligopolists expect to compete with each other over an extended period of time, each individual firm will often conclude that it is in its own best interest to be helpful to the other firms in the industry. So it will restrict its output in a way that raises the profits of the other firms, expecting them to return the favour. Even though the firms have no way of making an enforceable agreement to limit output and raise prices, they manage to act "as if" they had such an agreement. When this happens, we say that firms engage in **tacit collusion.**

When firms limit production and raise prices in a way that raises each other's profits, even though they have not made any formal agreement, they are engaged in **tacit collusion.**

But one problem remains: how do firms commit to the tit-for-tat policy? One possibility is that they simply demonstrate their commitment through their actions. Actions speak louder than words, after all. However, there is another very interesting possibility—that a firm announces its "tit-for-tat" commitment to its customers! It advertises that "we will not knowingly be undersold" or "we'll match any price our competitors offer". So, "lowest price guarantees" may not be in the consumer's best interest. In fact, they may turn the consumer into a zero-cost means of enforcing tacit collusion!

The Kinked Demand Curve

Once an oligopoly has achieved tacit collusion, individual producers have an incentive to behave carefully—they don't want to do anything to disrupt the collusion. They must behave carefully because under tacit collusion there is no safe communication channel between producers. When a producer changes her output, there is a danger that tacit collusion will collapse as rivals interpret her action as a non-cooperative move. In consequence, the output of an oligopolist may not respond to changes in marginal cost. If she increases her output, her rivals may interpret this as cheating, leading them to retaliate and cut prices. But if she reduces her output, she has no assurance that rivals will follow her actions by cutting output and raising their prices. In fact, they may respond by leaving their prices unchanged and stealing some of her sales.

Figure 15-4 illustrates this behaviour. At the original tacit collusion outcome, the oligopolist produces the quantity Q^* and receives the price P^*, located on her demand curve, D. This demand curve shows how the price she receives for her good varies as she changes her output. As you can see, this demand curve has a special shape—it is *kinked* at the price and quantity combination associated with the tacit collusion outcome, P^* and Q^*.

On one side, the demand curve slopes steeply downward at output levels greater than Q^*. The reason is that the oligopolist believes that if she produces more than Q^*, she will gain very few sales because her rivals will retaliate by also producing more and cutting their prices.

Figure 15-4

The Kinked Demand Curve

This oligopolist believes that her demand curve is kinked at the tacit collusion price and quantity levels, P^* and Q^*. That is, she believes that if she increases her output and lowers her price her rivals will retaliate, increasing their output and lowering their prices as well, leading to only a small gain in sales. So her demand curve is very steep to the right of Q^*. But the oligopolist believes that if she lowers her output and raises her price her rivals will refuse to reciprocate and will steal a substantial number of her customers, leading to a large fall in sales. So her demand curve is very flat to the left of Q^*. The kink in the demand curve leads to the break XY in the marginal revenue curve. As shown by the marginal cost curves, MC_1 and MC_2, any marginal cost curve that lies within the break leads the oligopolist to produce the same output level, Q^*. So starting at the tacit collusion outcome, changes in marginal cost within a certain range will leave the firm's output unchanged. But large changes in marginal cost—changes that cause the marginal cost curve to cut the marginal revenue curve in the segment WX or the segment YZ—will lead to changes in output. **>web...**

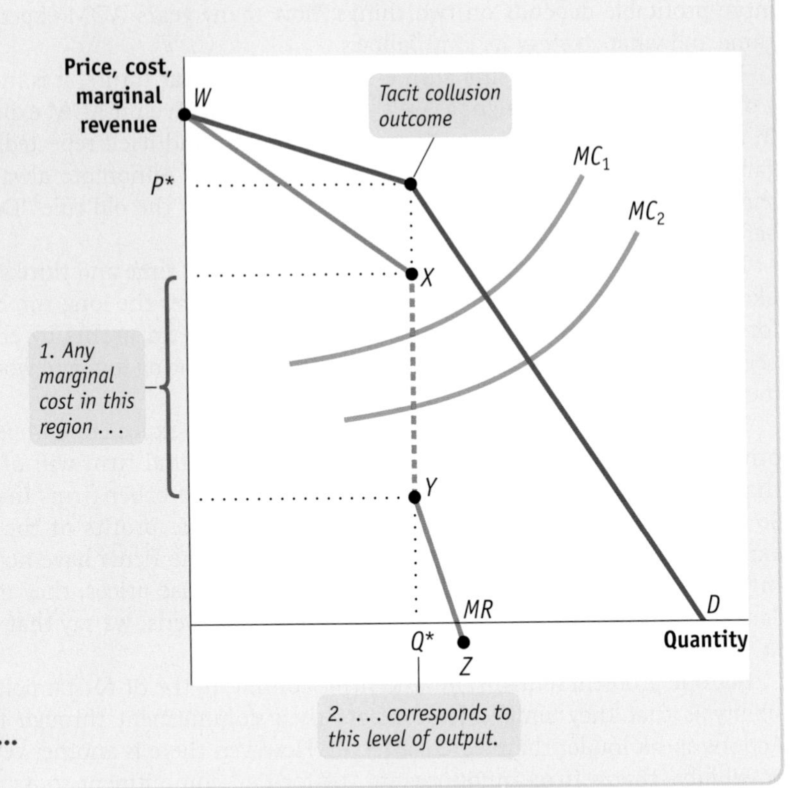

On the other side, the demand curve is very flat. If the oligopolist reduces her output below Q*, she does not expect rivals to reduce their output as well. Consequently, she will lose a relatively large number of sales if she lowers her output and raises her price as her rivals capture a substantial share of her customers. You might ask why the industry can't reestablish tacit collusion at a higher price and lower output after our oligopolist cuts her output and raises her price. It is possible, but by no means assured, that the industry can reestablish tacit collusion. So it is reasonable for an oligopolist to fear that tacit collusion will not be reestablished and to behave as if her demand curve is kinked as in Figure 15-4.

An oligopolist who believes that she will lose a substantial number of sales if she increases her price but will gain only few additional sales if she lowers her price, away from the tacit collusion outcome, faces a **kinked demand curve.**

Now that we have explained the source of the oligopolist's **kinked demand curve,** let's examine how this affects her response to a change in marginal cost. The kink in the demand curve *D* generates a break in the oligopolist's marginal revenue curve, *MR*, shown by the gap between the points X and Y. Two marginal cost curves pass through that break in the marginal revenue curve: MC_1 corresponds to a situation of higher marginal cost, and MC_2 corresponds to a situation of lower marginal cost.

Recall that according to the optimal output rule, a firm will maximize profits by producing the output quantity at which marginal revenue is equal to marginal cost. But given the break between X and Y in the oligopolist's marginal revenue curve, any marginal cost curves that lie within that break–like MC_1 and MC_2–will generate the same output level, Q*. To put it in a slightly different way, starting from the tacit collusive output level Q*, the oligopolist's output level is unresponsive to changes in marginal cost within a certain range. If marginal cost falls substantially, the oligopolist is more likely to risk a breakdown in collusion and increase her output; in this case, the marginal cost curve cuts the marginal revenue curve in the segment *YZ*. And if marginal cost rises substantially, shifting the marginal cost curve up so that it cuts the marginal revenue curve in the segment *WX*, then the oligopolist is likely to reduce output and raise her price despite the risk of losing significant sales to rivals. But if marginal cost changes within a limited range—the range defined by XY—the producer will leave her output level unchanged rather than risk a breakdown in tacit collusion.

The behaviour described by the kinked demand curve appears justified when a producer believes that she alone is facing a change in marginal cost—that is, when the change is unique to her. But when the change in marginal cost is clearly shared throughout the industry, this behaviour is much less plausible. In that case, each producer knows that a change in a rival's output level and price is just a response to a change in the general level of marginal cost, not a hostile act of non-cooperation. Consequently, all the producers in the industry are likely to respond to a change in marginal cost by adjusting their output and prices, and thereby maintain collusion.

economics in action

The Rise and Fall and Rise of OPEC

Call it the cartel that does not need to meet in secret. The Organization of Petroleum Exporting Countries, usually referred to as OPEC, includes 11 national governments (Algeria, Indonesia, Iran, Iraq, Kuwait, Libya, Nigeria, Qatar, Saudi Arabia, United Arab Emirates, and Venezuela). Two other oil-exporting countries, Norway and Mexico, are not formally part of the cartel but act as if they were. (Russia, also an important oil exporter, has not yet become part of the club.) Unlike corporations, which are often legally prohibited by governments from reaching agreements about production and prices, national governments can talk about whatever they feel like. OPEC members routinely meet to try to set targets for production.

These nations are not particularly friendly with one another. Indeed, OPEC members Iraq and Iran fought a spectacularly bloody war with each other in the 1980s. And, in 1990, Iraq invaded another member, Kuwait. (A mainly American force based in yet another OPEC member, Saudi Arabia, drove the Iraqis out of Kuwait.)

Yet the members of OPEC, whether they like one another or not, are effectively players in a game with repeated interactions. In any given year it is in their combined interest to keep output low and prices high. But it is also in the interest of any one producer to cheat and produce more than the agreed-upon quota—unless that producer believes that this action will bring future retaliation.

So how successful is the cartel? Well, it's had its ups and downs.

Figure 15-5 shows the price of oil in constant dollars (that is, the value of a barrel of oil in terms of other goods) since 1947. OPEC first demonstrated its muscle in 1974: in the aftermath of a war in the Middle East, several OPEC producers limited their output—and they liked the results so much that they decided to continue the practice. Following a second wave of turmoil in the aftermath of Iran's 1979 revolution, prices shot still higher.

By the mid-1980s, however, there was a growing glut of oil on world markets, and cheating by cash-short OPEC members became widespread. The result, in 1985, was that producers who had tried to play by the rules—especially Saudi Arabia, the largest producer—got fed up, and collusion collapsed.

Figure 15-5 The Ups and Downs of the Oil Cartel

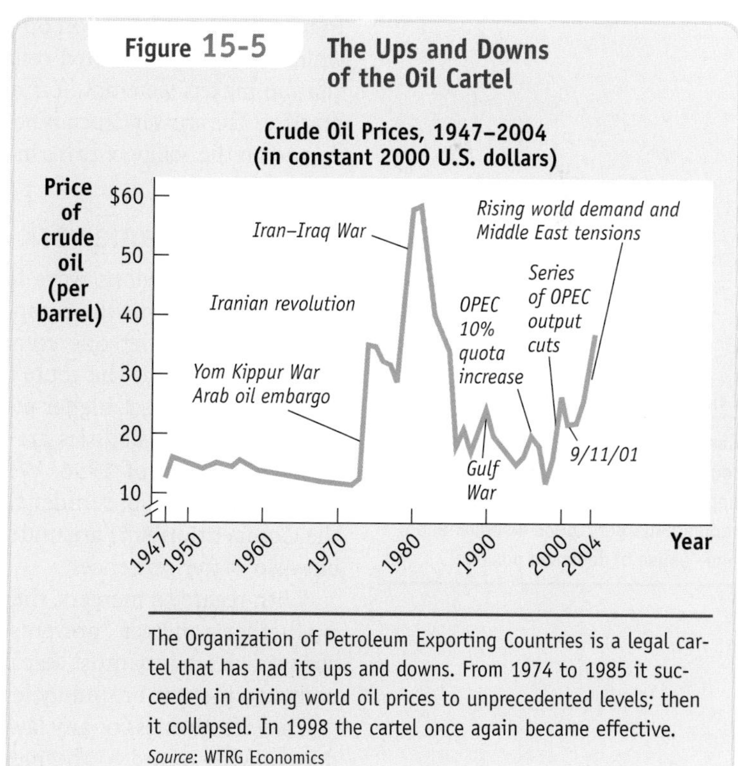

The Organization of Petroleum Exporting Countries is a legal cartel that has had its ups and downs. From 1974 to 1985 it succeeded in driving world oil prices to unprecedented levels; then it collapsed. In 1998 the cartel once again became effective.
Source: WTRG Economics

The cartel began to act effectively again at the end of the 1990s, thanks largely to the efforts of Mexico's oil minister to orchestrate output reductions. To assure greater adherence to production targets, OPEC meets very frequently—seven times in 2003 alone—seeking to keep the price of a barrel of oil in the range of US$22 to $28. And this discipline appears to be paying off; a decrease of 900,000 barrels per day in late 2003 coupled with rising demand from China and production difficulties in Iraq resulted in oil prices above US$55 a barrel in 2004. ■

>> QUICK REVIEW

- Economists use *game theory* to study firms' behaviour when there is *interdependence* between their *payoffs*. The game can be represented with a *payoff matrix*. Depending on the payoffs, a player may or may not have a *dominant strategy*.
- When each firm has an incentive to cheat, but both are worse off if both cheat, the situation is known as a *prisoners' dilemma*.
- Players who don't take their interdependence into account arrive at a *Nash*, or *non-cooperative, equilibrium*. But if a game is played repeatedly, players may engage in *strategic behaviour*, sacrificing short-run profit to influence future behaviour.
- In repeated prisoners' dilemma games, *tit for tat* is often a good strategy, leading to successful *tacit collusion*.
- The *kinked demand curve* illustrates how tacit collusion can make an oligopolist unresponsive to changes in marginal cost within a certain range when those changes are unique to her.

>> CHECK YOUR UNDERSTANDING 15-3

1. Find the Nash (non-cooperative) equilibrium actions of the accompanying payoff matrix. Each *column* corresponds to a choice by Nikita, and each *row* corresponds to a choice by Margaret. Which actions maximize the total payoff of the two players? Why is it unlikely that the players will choose those actions without some additional communication?

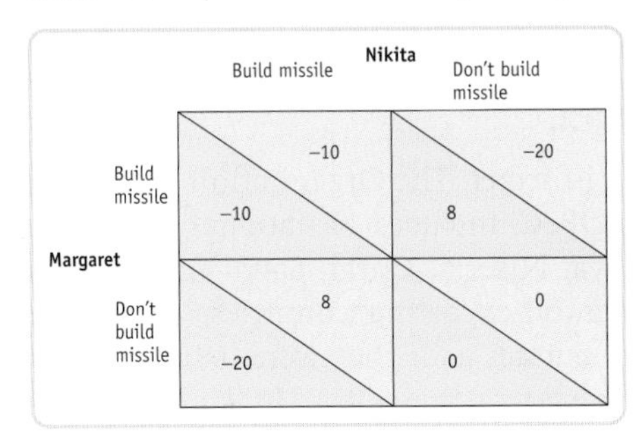

2. Which factors make it more likely that oligopolists will play non-cooperatively? Which make it more likely that they will engage in tacit collusion? Explain.
   a. Each oligopolist expects several new firms to enter the market in the future.
   b. It is very difficult for a firm to detect if another firm has raised output.
   c. The firms have coexisted while maintaining high prices for a long time.

Solutions appear at back of book.

Oligopoly in Practice

In the Economics in Action on p. 387 we described the cartel known as "Vitamins Inc.", which effectively promoted collusion for many years. The conspiratorial dealings of the vitamin makers were not, fortunately, the norm. But how do oligopolies usually work in practice? The answer depends both on the legal framework that limits what companies can do and on the ability of firms in a given industry to cooperate without formal agreements.

The Legal Framework

There are two obvious ways for companies to avoid getting trapped in a prisoners' dilemma. One is for the companies to eliminate conflict by combining the two companies into one—let one company buy the other, or let them exchange stock and merge. The other is the route that ADM tried—to meet with each other and agree to produce less and get higher prices.

Competition policy is a set of laws that regulate the business environment. Important parts of the Competition Act regulate mergers, price discrimination, and "abuse of dominant position".

Both these possibilities are regulated by **competition policy** as embodied in the Competition Act of 1986. Whereas the merger provisions (sections 91–107 of the Competition Act) are under the civil code, the conspiracy provisions (section 45 of the Competition Act) are under the criminal code—implying a harder burden of proof but also stiffer sentences.

With regard to mergers, the key point for the Competition Tribunal to decide upon is whether a merger "prevents or lessens competition substantially". With regard to conspiracies, a jury must determine whether there have been "agreements or arrangements to prevent or unduly lessen competition".

The effectiveness of any law is determined by how well such wording can be nailed down. With regard to the merger provisions, what does *substantially* mean in practice? Is it possible for one individual to own every newspaper in a province without *substantially* lessening competition? Obviously, competition will be eliminated in the newspaper business, but is that the relevant market? Corporate lawyers may argue that the relevant market is not the newspaper business but the "information dissemination" business and that it should be defined to include radio, television, magazines, and the Internet along with newspapers. The definition of "the market" is crucial. (By the way, the lawyers of K. C. Irving successfully made that argument back in 1968. Ever since, the Irving family has owned all the English-language newspapers in New Brunswick, several radio stations, and for many years a TV station besides.)

With regard to conspiracies, what does it mean to *unduly* lessen competition? Considerable case law has been developed that provides guidance on this issue. Unfortunately for the crown, since conspiracies are a criminal matter, the crown must also show *intent*. For example, in February 1993, the Pharmacy Association of Nova Scotia was acquitted of price-fixing prescription drugs in Nova Scotia. The Court found that the accused had entered into an agreement that had lessened competition *unduly,* but was not satisfied that the accused had *intended* the agreement to have that effect.

The details of competition policy can be exceedingly complex, especially because corporations (and associations) can and do fight costly legal battles against decisions they dislike. But the legislation is not without teeth. On the contrary, Canada has taken a particularly aggressive approach to conspiracies in recent years to ensure that the activities of criminal cartels are stopped and stringent penalties are levied as a deterrent. Between 1980 and 2000 there were 51 conspiracy cases prosecuted, two-thirds of which were won by the crown, resulting in fines of about $158 million.

So, if colluding is out, and if the Competition Tribunal refuses to allow a merger, what's an oligopolist to do?

Tacit Collusion and Price Wars

If a real industry were as simple as our hypothetical lysine example, it probably wouldn't be necessary for the company presidents to meet or do anything that could land them in jail. Both firms would realize that it was in their mutual interest to restrict output to 30 million pounds each and that any short-term gains to either firm from producing more would be much less than the later losses as the other firm retaliated. So even without any explicit agreement, the firms would probably achieve the tacit collusion needed to maximize their combined profits.

Real industries are nowhere near that simple; nonetheless, in most oligopolistic industries, most of the time, the sellers do appear to succeed in keeping prices above their non-cooperative level. Tacit collusion, in other words, is the normal state of oligopoly.

Although tacit collusion is common, it rarely allows an industry to push prices all the way up to their monopoly level; collusion is usually far from perfect. A variety of factors make it hard for an industry to coordinate on high prices.

Large Numbers Suppose that there were three instead of two firms in the lysine industry and that each was currently producing only 20 million pounds. You can confirm for yourself that in that case any one firm that decided to produce an extra 10 million pounds would gain more in short-term profits—and lose less once another firm responded in kind—than in our original example. The general point is that the more firms there are in an oligopoly, the less the incentive of any one firm to behave cooperatively, taking into account the impact of its actions on the profits of the other firms. Large numbers of firms in an industry typically are an indication that there are low barriers to entry.

Complex Products and Pricing Schemes In our structuring of the lysine example, the two firms produce only one product. In reality, however, oligopolists often sell thousands or even tens of thousands of different products. Under these circumstances, keeping track of what other firms are producing and what prices they are charging is difficult. This makes it hard to determine whether a firm is cheating on the tacit agreement.

Differences in Interests In the simplified lysine example, a tacit agreement for the firms to split the market equally is a natural outcome, probably acceptable to both firms. In real industries, however, firms often differ both in their perceptions about what is fair and in their real interests.

For example, suppose that Ajinomoto was a long-established lysine producer and ADM a more recent entrant to the industry. Ajinomoto might feel that it deserved to continue producing more than ADM, but ADM might feel that it was entitled to 50% of the business. (A disagreement along these lines was one of the contentious issues in those meetings the FBI was filming.)

Alternatively, suppose that ADM's marginal costs were lower than Ajinomoto's. Even if they could agree on market shares, they would then disagree about the profit-maximizing level of output.

Bargaining Power of Buyers Often oligopolists sell not to individual consumers but to large buyers—other industrial enterprises, nationwide chains of stores, and so on. These large buyers are in a position to bargain for lower prices from the oligopolists: they can ask for a discount from an oligopolist, and warn that they will go to a competitor if they don't get it. An important reason why large retailers like Wal-Mart are able to offer lower prices to customers than small retailers is precisely their ability to use their size to extract lower prices from their suppliers.

These difficulties in enforcing tacit collusion have sometimes led companies to defy the law and create illegal cartels. We've already examined the cases of the lysine industry and the bulk vitamin industry. A classic example that occurred in the U.S. was the electrical equipment conspiracy of the 1950s, which led to the indictment of and jail sentences for some executives. The industry was one in which tacit collusion was especially difficult because of all the reasons just mentioned. There were many firms—40 companies were indicted. They produced a very complex array of products, often more or less custom-built for particular clients. They differed greatly in size, from giants like General Electric to family firms with only a few dozen employees. And the customers in many cases were large buyers like electrical utilities, which would normally try to force suppliers to compete for their business. Tacit collusion just didn't seem practical—so executives met secretly and illegally to decide who would bid what price for which contract.

The For Inquiring Minds describes yet another price-fixing conspiracy: the one between the very posh auction houses Sotheby's and Christie's.

Because tacit collusion is often hard to achieve, most oligopolies charge prices that are well below what the same industry would charge if it were controlled by a single

FOR INQUIRING MINDS

THE ART OF CONSPIRACY

If you want to sell a valuable work of art, there are really only two places to go: Christie's, the London-based auction house, or Sotheby's, its New York counterpart and competitor. Both are classy operations—literally: many of the employees of Christie's come from Britain's aristocracy, and many of Sotheby's come from blue-blooded American families that might as well have titles. They're not the sort of people you would expect to be seeking plea bargains from prosecutors.

But on October 6, 2000, Diana D. Brooks, the very upper-class former president of Sotheby's, pleaded guilty to a conspiracy. Together with her counterpart at Christie's she had engaged in the illegal practice of price-fixing—in this case, agreeing on the fees they would charge people who sold artwork through either house. As part of her guilty plea, and in an effort to avoid going to jail, she agreed to help in the investigation of her boss, the former chairman of the company.

Why would such upper-crust types engage in illegal practices? For the same reasons that respectable electrical industry executives did the same thing. By definition, no two works of art are alike; it wasn't easy for the two houses to collude tacitly, because it was too hard to determine what commissions they were charging on any given transaction. To increase profits, then, the companies felt that they needed to reach a detailed agreement. They did, and they got caught.

firm—or what they would charge if they were able to collude explicitly. In addition, sometimes collusion breaks down and there is a **price war.** A price war sometimes involves simply a collapse of prices to their non-cooperative level. Sometimes they even go *below* that level, as sellers try to put each other out of business or at least punish what they regard as cheating.

A **price war** occurs when tacit collusion breaks down, and prices collapse.

Product Differentiation and Price Leadership

Lysine is lysine: there was no question in anyone's mind that ADM and Ajinomoto were producing the same good and that consumers would make their decision about which company's lysine to buy based on the price.

In many oligopolies, however, firms produce products that consumers regard as similar but not identical. A $10 difference in the price won't make many customers switch from a Ford to a Chrysler, or vice versa. Sometimes the differences between products are real, like differences between Froot Loops and Wheaties; sometimes, like differences between brands of vodka (which is *supposed* to be tasteless), they exist mainly in the minds of consumers. Either way, the effect of perceived product differences is to reduce the intensity of the competition among the firms: consumers will not all rush to buy whichever product is cheapest.

As you might imagine, oligopolists welcome the extra market power that comes when consumers think that their product is different from that of competitors. So in many oligopolistic industries, firms make considerable efforts to create the perception that their product is different—that is, they engage in **product differentiation.**

Firms engage in **product differentiation** when they try to convince buyers that their product is different from the products of other firms in the industry.

A firm that tries to differentiate its product may do so by altering what it actually produces, adding "extras", or choosing a different design. It may also use advertising and marketing campaigns to create a differentiation in the minds of consumers, even though its product is more or less identical to the products of rivals.

A classic case of how products may be perceived as different even when they are really pretty much the same is over-the-counter medication. For many years there were only three widely sold pain relievers—aspirin, ibuprofen, and acetaminophen. Yet these generic pain relievers were marketed under a number of brand names, each brand using a marketing campaign implying some special superiority (one classic slogan was "contains the pain reliever doctors recommend most"—that is, aspirin).

Whatever the nature of product differentiation, oligopolists producing differentiated products often reach a tacit understanding not to compete on price. For example, during the years when the great majority of cars sold in North America were produced by the Big Three auto companies, there was a sort of unwritten rule that none of the three companies would try to gain market share by making its cars noticeably cheaper than those of the other two.

But then who would decide on the overall price of cars? The answer was normally that General Motors, the biggest of the three, would announce its prices for the year first; then the other companies would match it. This pattern of behaviour, in which some company tacitly sets prices for the industry as a whole, is known as **price leadership.**

In **price leadership,** one firm sets its price first, and other firms then follow.

Interestingly, firms that have a tacit agreement not to compete on price often engage in vigorous **non-price competition**—adding new features to their products, spending large sums on ads that proclaim the inferiority of their rivals' offerings, and so on.

Firms that have a tacit understanding not to compete on price often engage in intense **non-price competition,** using advertising and other means to try to increase their sales.

Perhaps the best way to understand the mix of cooperation and competition in such industries is with a political analogy. During the long Cold War between the United States and the Soviet Union, the two countries engaged in intense rivalry for global influence. They not only provided financial and military aid to their allies; they sometimes supported forces trying to overthrow governments allied with their rival (as the Soviet Union did in Vietnam in the 1960s and early 1970s, and as the United States did in Afghanistan from 1979 until the collapse of the Soviet Union in 1991). They even sent their own soldiers to support allied governments against rebels (as the United States did in Vietnam and the Soviet Union did in Afghanistan). But they did *not* get into direct military confrontations with each other; open warfare between the two superpowers was regarded by both as too dangerous—and tacitly avoided.

Price wars aren't as serious as shooting wars, but the principle is the same.

economics in action

Air Wars in Canada

Not so very long ago, the Canadian airline industry was regulated, which limited competition between airlines in terms of the routes they could fly and the prices they could offer. This system subsidized flights to less densely populated areas at the cost of higher prices elsewhere. Opponents of this system argued that it impeded competition and efficiency, and led to higher overall prices. Proponents argued that it facilitated a national network of air travel, and worried that Canada's population was spread too thin over too large a distance. Deregulation, they thought, would lead to the dominance of a small number of large firms with market power and much-reduced service to the smaller markets.

The opponents of regulation won out. In 1987, the National Transportation Act deregulated the Canadian airline industry (along with the trucking and railway industries). As far as air travel goes, the effects have been mixed.

Price competition led to price wars and lower prices on some routes, but also to a series of mergers and takeovers that led to two national carriers—Air Canada and Canadian Airlines—dominating the market for a decade. But many routes in Canada are natural monopolies, and price competition put both airlines in a precarious financial position. Since Canadian Airlines was on the brink of bankruptcy, the Competition Bureau approved their merger with Air Canada in December 1999. Now we are seeing the emergence of two new airlines—WestJet and CanJet—each striving to compete in the national market, again resulting in price wars on certain routes.

Why are airlines so prone to price wars? There are at least three reasons, all bearing on the problems of tacit collusion we have just discussed. First, although each airline tries to differentiate its product, creating a perception among consumers that it offers better service, most fliers choose airlines on the basis of schedule and price—period. So competition is intense. Second, airline pricing is complex: as discussed in Chapter 14, airlines engage in complex price-discrimination schemes that make it hard to figure out when tacit collusion is being broken. Third, airlines often differ in their interests: many of the most severe price wars have been set off by attempts of a new competitor to break into established markets. And this indicates yet another source of airline price wars: low barriers to entry. ■

>>QUICK REVIEW

- Oligopolies operate under legal restrictions in the form of *competition policy.* Nonetheless, many succeed in achieving tacit collusion.
- Tacit collusion is limited by a number of factors, including large numbers of firms, complex pricing, and conflicts of interest among firms. When collusion breaks down, there is a *price war.*
- To limit competition, oligopolists often try to achieve *product differentiation*. When products are differentiated, it is sometimes possible for an industry to achieve tacit collusion through *price leadership*.
- Oligopolists often avoid competing directly on price, engaging in *nonprice competition* through advertising and other means instead.

>>CHECK YOUR UNDERSTANDING 15-4

1. Which of the following factors are likely to support the conclusion that there is tacit collusion in this industry? Which are not? Explain.
   a. For many years the price in the industry has changed infrequently, and all the firms in the industry charge the same price. The largest firm publishes a catalogue containing a "suggested" retail price. Changes in price coincide with changes in the catalogue.
   b. There has been considerable variation in the market shares of the firms in the industry over time.
   c. Firms in the industry build into their products unnecessary features that make it hard for consumers to switch from one company's products to another's.
   d. Firms meet yearly to discuss their yearly sales forecasts.
   e. Firms tend to adjust their prices upward at the same times.

Solutions appear at back of book.

How Important Is Oligopoly?

We have seen that, across industries, oligopoly is far more common than either perfect competition or monopoly. When we try to analyse oligopoly, the economist's usual way of thinking—asking how self-interested individuals would behave, then analysing their interaction—does not work as well as we might hope, because we do not know whether rival firms will engage in non-cooperative behaviour or manage to engage in some kind of collusion. Given the prevalence of oligopoly, then, is the analysis we developed in earlier chapters, which was based on perfect competition, still useful?

The conclusion of the great majority of economists is yes. For one thing, important parts of the economy—forest and fish products, agriculture, and many raw materials such as iron ore, tin, and copper—are fairly well described by perfect competition. And even though many industries are oligopolistic, in many cases the limits to collusion keep prices relatively close to marginal costs—in other words, the industry behaves "almost" as if it were perfectly competitive.

It is also true that predictions from supply and demand analysis are often valid for oligopolies. For example, in Chapter 4 we saw that price controls will produce shortages. Strictly speaking, this conclusion is certain only for perfectly competitive industries. But in the 1970s, when the U.S. government imposed price controls on the definitely oligopolistic oil industry, the result was indeed to produce shortages and lines at the gas pumps.

So how important is it to take account of oligopoly? Most economists adopt a pragmatic approach. As we have seen in this chapter, the analysis of oligopoly is far more difficult and messy than that of perfect competition; so in situations where they do not expect the complications associated with oligopoly to be crucial, economists prefer to adopt the working assumption of perfectly competitive markets. They always keep in mind the possibility that oligopoly might be important; they recognize that there are important issues, from competition policies to price wars, where trying to understand oligopolistic behaviour is crucial.

We will follow the same approach in the chapters that follow.

• A LOOK AHEAD •

We're not yet done with our investigation of market structures other than perfect competition. There are quite a few industries that don't seem to fit either the definition of oligopoly or our definition of perfect competition. Consider, for example, the restaurant business. There are many restaurants, so it's not an oligopoly. But restaurants aren't price-takers, like wheat farmers, so it's not perfectly competitive. What is it?

The answer lies in our next chapter, which turns to the concept of *monopolistic competition*.

SUMMARY

1. Many industries are **oligopolies:** there are only a few sellers. In particular, a **duopoly** has only two sellers. Oligopolies exist for more or less the same reasons that monopolies exist, but in weaker form. They are characterized by **imperfect competition:** firms compete but possess market power.
2. Predicting the behaviour of **oligopolists** poses something of a puzzle. The firms in an oligopoly could maximize their combined profits by acting as a **cartel,** setting output levels for each firm as if they were a single monopolist; to the extent that firms manage to do this, they engage in **collusion.** But each individual firm has an incentive to produce more than it would in such an arrangement—to engage in **non-cooperative behaviour.** Informal collusion is likely to be easier to achieve in industries in which firms face capacity constraints.
3. The situation of **interdependence,** in which each firm's profit depends noticeably on what other firms do, is the

subject of **game theory.** In the case of a game with two players, the **payoff** of each player depends both on its own actions and on the actions of the other; this interdependence can be represented as a **payoff matrix.** Depending upon the structure of payoffs in the payoff matrix, a player may have a **dominant strategy**—an action that is always the best regardless of the other player's actions.

4. **Duopolists** face a particular type of game known as a **prisoners' dilemma;** if each acts independently in its own interest, the resulting **Nash equilibrium** or **non-cooperative equilibrium** will be bad for both. However, firms that expect to play a game repeatedly tend to engage in **strategic behaviour,** trying to influence each other's future actions. A particular strategy that seems to work well in such situations is **tit for tat,** which often leads to **tacit collusion.**
5. The **kinked demand curve** illustrates how an oligopolist who faces unique changes in her marginal cost within a certain range may choose not to adjust her output and price in order to avoid a breakdown in tacit collusion.
6. In order to limit the ability of oligopolists to collude and act like monopolists, most governments pursue **competition policy,** which regulates business practice. In Canada and most other jurisdictions, conspiracies to collude are illegal. In practice, however, tacit collusion is widespread.
7. A variety of factors make tacit collusion difficult: large numbers of firms, complex products and pricing, differences in interests, and bargaining power of buyers. When tacit collusion breaks down, there is a **price war.** Oligopolists try to avoid price wars in various ways, such as through **product differentiation** and through **price leadership,** in which one firm sets prices for the industry. Another is through **non-price competition,** like advertising.

KEY TERMS

Oligopoly, p. 381
Oligopolist, p. 381
Imperfect competition, p. 381
Duopoly, p. 383
Duopolist, p. 383
Collusion, p. 384
Cartel, p. 384
Non-cooperative behaviour, p. 385
Interdependence, p. 388
Game theory, p. 388
Payoff, p. 388
Payoff matrix, p. 388
Prisoners' dilemma, p. 389
Dominant strategy, p. 390
Nash equilibrium, p. 390
Non-cooperative equilibrium, p. 390
Strategic behaviour, p. 391
Tit for tat, p. 391
Tacit collusion, p. 393
Kinked demand curve, p. 394
Price war, p. 399
Product differentiation, p. 399
Price leadership, p. 399
Non-price competition, p. 399

PROBLEMS

1. The accompanying table shows the demand schedule for vitamin D. Suppose that the marginal cost of producing vitamin D is zero.

Price of vitamin D (per ton)	Quantity of vitamin D demanded (tons)
$8	0
7	10
6	20
5	30
4	40
3	50
2	60
1	70

   a. Suppose that BASF is the only producer of vitamin D and acts as a monopolist. Suppose BASF currently produces 40 tons of vitamin D at $4 per ton. If BASF were to produce 10 tons more, what would be the price effect for BASF? What would be the quantity effect? Would BASF therefore have an incentive to produce those 10 additional tons?

   b. Now suppose that Roche enters the market by also producing vitamin D, and the market is now a duopoly. BASF and Roche agree to produce 40 tons of vitamin D in total, 20 tons each. BASF cannot be punished for deviating from the agreement with Roche. If BASF, on its own, were to deviate from that agreement and produce 10 tons more, what would be the price effect for BASF? What would be the quantity effect for BASF? Would BASF have an incentive to produce those 10 additional tons?

2. The market for olive oil in Montreal is controlled by two families, the Sopranos and the Contraltos. Both families will ruthlessly eliminate any other family that attempts to enter the Montreal olive oil market. The marginal cost of producing olive oil is constant and equal to $40 per gallon. There is no

fixed cost. The accompanying table gives the market demand schedule for olive oil.

Price of olive oil (per gallon)	Quantity of olive oil demanded (gallons)
$100	1,000
90	1,500
80	2,000
70	2,500
60	3,000
50	3,500
40	4,000
30	4,500
20	5,000
10	5,500

a. Suppose the Sopranos and the Contraltos form a cartel. For each of the quantities given in the table, calculate the total revenue for their cartel and the marginal revenue for each additional gallon. How many gallons of olive oil would the cartel sell in total and at what price? The two families share the market equally (each produces half of the total output of the cartel). How much profit does each family make?

b. Uncle Junior, the head of the Soprano family, decides to break the agreement and sells 500 more gallons of olive oil than under the cartel agreement. Assuming the Contraltos maintain the agreement, how does this affect the price for olive oil and the profits earned by each family?

c. Anthony Contralto, the head of the Contralto family, decides to punish Uncle Junior by increasing his sales by 500 gallons as well. How much profit does each family earn now?

3. In France, the market for bottled water is controlled by two large firms, Perrier and Evian. Each firm has a fixed cost of € 1 and marginal cost of € 2 per litre of bottled water (€ = 1 euro). The accompanying table gives the market demand schedule for bottled water in France.

Price of bottled water (per litre)	Quantity of bottled water demanded (litres)
€10	0
9	1
8	2
7	3
6	4
5	5
4	6
3	7
2	8
1	9

a. Suppose the two firms form a cartel and act as a monopolist. Calculate marginal revenue for the cartel. What will the monopoly price and output be? Assuming the firms divided the output evenly, how much will each produce and what will each firm's profits be?

b. Now suppose Perrier decides to increase production by 1 litre. Evian doesn't change its production. What will the new market price and output be? What is Perrier's profit? What is Evian's profit?

c. What if Perrier increases production by 3 litres? Evian doesn't change its production. What would its output and profits be relative to those in part b?

d. What do your results tell you about the likelihood of cheating on such agreements?

4. To preserve the North Atlantic fish stocks, it is decided that only two fishing fleets, one from Canada and the other from the European Union, can fish in those waters. The accompanying table shows the market demand schedule per week for fish from these waters. The only costs are fixed costs, so fishing fleets maximize profit by maximizing revenue.

Price of fish (per pound)	Quantity of fish demanded (pounds)
$17	1,800
16	2,000
15	2,100
14	2,200
12	2,300

a. If both fishing fleets collude, what is the revenue-maximizing output for the North Atlantic fishery? What price will a pound of fish sell for?

b. If both fishing fleets collude and share the output equally, what is the revenue to the EU fleet? To the Canadian fleet?

c. Suppose the EU fleet cheats by expanding its own catch by 100 pounds per week. The Canadian fleet doesn't change its catch. What is the revenue to the Canadian fleet? To the EU fleet?

d. In retaliation for the cheating by the EU fleet, the Canadian fleet also expands its catch by 100 pounds per week. What is the revenue to the Canadian fleet? To the EU fleet?

5. Suppose that the fisheries agreement in Problem 4 breaks down, so that the fleets behave non-cooperatively. Assume the two sides can send out 1 or 2 fleets each; and the more fleets in the area, the more fish they catch in total but the lower the catch of each fleet. The matrix below shows the profit (in dollars) per week earned by the two sides.

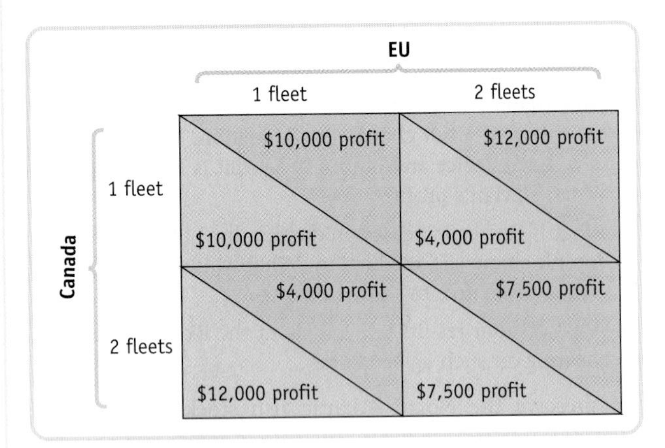

a. What is the non-cooperative Nash equilibrium? Will each side choose to send out 1 or 2 fleets?

b. Suppose the fish stocks are being depleted. Each side considers the future and comes to a tit-for-tat agreement whereby each side will send out only 1 fleet as long as the other does the same. If either breaks the agreement and sends out a 2nd fleet, the other country will also send out 2 and will continue to do so until the other country sends out only 1 fleet. If both countries play this "tit-for-tat" strategy, how much profit will each country make every week?

6. Two airlines, Untied and Air 'R' Us, are the only two airlines operating flights between Collegeville and Bigtown. That is, they operate in a duopoly. Each airline can charge either a high price or a low price for a ticket. The accompanying matrix shows their payoffs, in profits per seat (in dollars), for any choice that the two airlines can make.

		Air 'R' Us: Low price	Air 'R' Us: High price
Untied	Low price	Air 'R' Us: $20 profit; Untied: $20 profit	Air 'R' Us: $0 profit; Untied: $50 profit
Untied	High price	Air 'R' Us: $50 profit; Untied: $0 profit	Air 'R' Us: $40 profit; Untied: $40 profit

a. Suppose the two airlines play a one-shot game; that is, they interact only once and never again. What will be the non-cooperative Nash equilibrium in this one-shot game?

b. Now suppose the two airlines play this game twice. And suppose each airline can play one of two strategies: it can play either "always charge the low price" or "tit-for-tat"—that is, it starts off charging the high price in the first period, and then in the second period it does whatever the other airline did in the previous period. Write down the payoffs to Untied from the following four possibilities:

i. Untied plays "always charge the low price" when Air 'R' Us also plays "always charge the low price".

ii. Untied plays "always charge the low price" when Air 'R' Us plays "tit-for-tat".

iii. Untied plays "tit-for-tat" when Air 'R' Us plays "always charge the low price".

iv. Untied plays "tit-for-tat" when Air 'R' Us also plays "tit-for-tat".

7. Suppose that Coke and Pepsi are the only two producers of cola drinks, so they are duopolists. Both companies have zero marginal cost and a fixed cost of $100,000.

a. Assume first that consumers regard Coke and Pepsi as perfect substitutes. Currently both are sold for a price of $0.20 per can, and at that price each company sells 4 million cans per day.

i. How large is Pepsi's profit?

ii. If Pepsi were to raise its price to $0.30 per can, what would happen to its profit?

b. Now suppose that each company advertises to differentiate its product from the other company's. As a result of advertising, Pepsi realizes that if it raises or lowers its price, it will sell less or more of its product, as shown by the demand schedule in the accompanying table.

Price of Pepsi (per can)	Quantity of Pepsi demanded (millions of cans)
$0.10	5
0.20	4
0.30	3
0.40	2
0.50	1

If Pepsi now were to raise its price to $0.30 per can, what would happen to its profit?

c. Comparing your answer to part a (i) and to part b, how much at most do you think Pepsi would be willing to spend on advertising?

8. Imperial and Rothmans spend huge sums of money each year to advertise their tobacco products in an attempt to steal consumers from each other. Suppose each year Imperial and Rothmans have to decide whether or not they want to spend money on advertising. If neither firm advertises, each will earn a profit of $2 million. If both advertise, each will earn a profit of $1.5 million. If one firm advertises and the other does not, the firm that advertises will earn a profit of $2.8 million while the other firm will earn $1 million.

a. Use a payoff matrix to depict this problem.

b. Suppose Imperial and Rothmans can write a binding contract about what they will do. What is the cooperative solution to this game?

c. What is the Nash equilibrium? Explain why in the absence of any binding agreement this is the likely outcome.

9. Over the last 30 years the Organization of Petroleum Exporting Countries (OPEC) has had varied success in forming and maintaining its cartel agreements. Explain how the following factors may contribute to the difficulty of forming and/or maintaining its price and output agreements.

a. New oil fields are discovered and drilling is increased in the Gulf of Mexico and the North Atlantic by non-OPEC members.

b. Crude oil is a product that is differentiated by sulphur content: it costs less to refine low-sulphur crude oil into gasoline. Different OPEC countries possess oil reserves of different sulphur content.

c. Cars powered by hydrogen are developed.

10. Suppose you are an economist working for the Competition Bureau. You are given the task of determining whether three firms in a particular industry are guilty of forming a collusive agreement. However, there is no direct evidence that these firms formed any explicit agreements. You are provided with the following facts. Assess each of these facts and explain whether or not each supports the allegation of collusive behaviour.

a. The three major firms in the industry have market shares of 45%, 20%, and 15%. There are many other firms in the industry, but none of the other firms has more than a 2% share of the market.

b. Last year when the largest firm announced a price increase of 16%, the other two major firms increased their prices to the same level within a day.

c. Each firm sells a differentiated product.

d. Each of the three firms advertises that it will match the lowest price of any other firm in the industry.

11. The industry for small single-engine airplanes is oligopolistic, and it has achieved tacit collusion. Each firm currently sells 10 airplanes at a price of $200,000 each. Each firm believes that it will sell one less airplane if it raises the price by $5,000. And each firm also believes that it can sell one more airplane if it lowers the price by $10,000. That is, each firm has a kinked demand curve.

a. How much additional revenue will a firm generate if it produces one more (the 11th) airplane?

b. How much revenue will a firm lose if it produces one less airplane?

c. If the marginal cost of producing an airplane is $120,000, how many airplanes will each firm produce, and at what price?

d. If the marginal cost of producing an airplane is $140,000, how many airplanes will each firm produce, and at what price?

>web... To continue your study and review of concepts in this chapter, please visit the Krugman/Wells website for quizzes, animated graph tutorials, web links to helpful resources, and more.

www.worthpublishers.com/krugmanwellsmyatt

chapter 16

>> Monopolistic Competition and Product Differentiation

FAST-FOOD DIFFERENTIATION

A RECENT BEST-SELLING BOOK titled *Fast Food Nation* offered a fascinating if rather negative report on the burgers, pizza, tacos, and fried chicken that make up so much of the modern North American diet. According to the book, all fast-food chains produce and deliver their food in pretty much the same way. In particular, a lot of the taste of your fast food—whatever kind of fast food it is—comes from food additives manufactured in New Jersey.

But each fast-food provider goes to great lengths to convince you that it has something special to offer. Everyone recognizes Ronald McDonald the clown, a symbol of McDonald's carefully cultivated image as the place kids love. Rival Wendy's took a bite out of McDonald's market share with a little old lady yelling "Where's the beef?", an advertising campaign that emphasized Wendy's somewhat bigger burgers.

So how would you describe the fast-food industry? On the one hand, it clearly isn't a monopoly. When you go to a fast-food court, you have a choice among vendors, and there is real competition between the different burger outlets and between the burgers and the fried chicken. On the other hand, in a way each vendor *does* possess some aspects of a monopoly: at one point McDonald's had the slogan "Nobody does it like McDonald's." That was literally true—though McDonald's competitors would say that they did it *better*. In any case, the point is that each fast-food provider offers a product that is *differentiated* from its rivals' products.

Jeff Greenberg/PhotoEdit

Competing for your tastebuds.

What you will learn in this chapter:

- The meaning of **monopolistic competition**
- Why oligopolists and monopolistically competitive firms differentiate their products
- How prices and profits are determined in monopolistic competition in the short run and the long run
- Why monopolistic competition poses a trade-off between lower prices and greater product diversity
- The economic significance of advertising and brand names

In the fast-food industry, many firms compete to satisfy more or less the same demand—the desire of consumers for something tasty but quick. But each firm offers to satisfy that demand with a distinctive, differentiated product—products that consumers typically view as close but not perfect substitutes. When there are many firms offering competing, differentiated products, as there are in the fast-food industry, economists say that the industry is characterized by *monopolistic competition*. This is the fourth and final market structure that we will discuss, after perfect competition, monopoly, and oligopoly.

First we'll define monopolistic competition more carefully and explain its characteristic features. Then we'll explore how firms differentiate their products; this will allow us to analyse how monopolistic competition works. The chapter concludes with a discussion of some controversies about product differentiation—in particular, the question of why advertising is effective.

The Meaning of Monopolistic Competition

Joe manages the Wonderful Wok stand in the food court of a big shopping mall. He offers the only Chinese food there, but there are more than a dozen alternatives, from Bodacious Burgers to Pizza Paradise. When deciding what to charge for a meal, Joe knows that he must take those alternatives into account: even people who normally prefer stir-fry won't order a $15 lunch from Joe when they can get a burger, fries, and drink for $4.

But Joe also knows that he won't lose all his business even if his lunches cost a bit more than the alternatives. Chinese food isn't the same thing as burgers or pizza. Some people will really be in the mood for Chinese that day, and they will buy from Joe even if they could have dined more cheaply on burgers. Of course, the reverse is also true: even if Chinese is a bit cheaper, some people will choose burgers instead. In other words, Joe does have some market power: he has *some* ability to set his own price.

So how would you describe Joe's situation? He definitely isn't a price-taker, so he isn't in a situation of perfect competition. But you wouldn't exactly call him a monopolist, either. Although he's the only seller of Chinese food in that food court, he does face competition from other food vendors.

Yet it would also be wrong to call him an oligopolist. Oligopoly, remember, involves competition among a small number of firms in an industry protected by some—albeit limited—barriers to entry and whose profits are highly interdependent. This interdependence provides an incentive for oligopolists to try to find a way to collude, if only tacitly. But in Joe's case there are *lots* of vendors in the shopping mall, too many to make tacit collusion feasible.

Economists describe Joe's situation as one of **monopolistic competition.** Monopolistic competition is particularly common in service industries like restaurants and gas stations, but it also exists in some manufacturing industries. It involves three conditions: large numbers of competing producers, differentiated products, and free entry into and exit from the industry in the long run. In a monopolistically competitive industry, each producer has some ability to set the price of her differentiated good. But exactly how high she can set it is limited by the competition she faces from other existing and potential producers that produce close, but not identical, products.

Monopolistic competition is a market structure in which there are many competing producers in an industry, each producer sells a differentiated product, and there is free entry into and exit from the industry in the long run.

Large Numbers

In a monopolistically competitive industry there are many producers. Such an industry does not look like either a monopoly, where the firm faces no competition, or an oligopoly, where each firm has only a few rivals. Instead, each seller has many competitors. There are many vendors in a big food court, many gas stations along a major highway, and many hotels in a popular beach resort town.

Differentiated Products

In a monopolistically competitive industry, each producer has a product that consumers view as somewhat distinct from the products of competing firms but at the same time are considered close substitutes. If Joe's food court contained 15 vendors selling exactly the same kind and quality of food, there would be perfect competition: any seller who tried to charge a higher price would have no customers. But suppose that Wonderful Wok is the only Chinese food vendor, Bodacious Burgers is the only hamburger stand, and so on. The result of this differentiation is that each seller has some ability to set his own price: each producer has some—albeit limited—market power.

Free Entry and Exit in the Long Run

In monopolistically competitive industries, new producers, with their own distinct products, can enter the industry freely in the long run. For example, other food vendors would open outlets in the shopping mall if they thought it would be profitable to do so. In addition, firms will exit the industry if they find they are not covering their costs in the long run.

Monopolistic competition, then, differs from the three market structures we have examined so far. It's not the same as perfect competition: firms have some power to set prices. It's not pure monopoly: firms face some competition. And it's not the same as oligopoly: because there are many firms and free entry, the potential for collusion, so important in oligopoly, no longer exists.

We'll see in a moment how prices, output, and the number of products available are determined in monopolistically competitive industries. But first, let's look a little more closely at what it means to have differentiated products.

Product Differentiation

We pointed out in Chapter 15 that product differentiation often plays an important role in oligopolistic industries. In such industries, product differentiation reduces the intensity of competition between firms when tacit collusion cannot be achieved. Product differentiation plays an even more crucial role in monopolistically competitive industries. Because tacit collusion is virtually impossible when there are many producers, product differentiation is the only way monopolistically competitive firms can acquire some market power.

How do firms in the same industry—such as fast-food vendors, gas stations, or chocolate companies—differentiate their products? Sometimes the difference is mainly in the minds of consumers rather than in the products themselves. We'll discuss the role of advertising and the importance of brand names in achieving this kind of product differentiation later in the chapter. But, in general, firms differentiate their products by—surprise!—actually making them different.

The key to product differentiation is that consumers have different preferences and that each producer can carve out a market niche by producing something that caters to the particular preferences of some group of consumers better than the products of other firms. There are three important forms of product differentiation: differentiation by style or type, differentiation by location, and differentiation by quality.

Differentiation by Style or Type

The sellers in Joe's food court offer different types of fast food: hamburgers, pizza, Chinese food, Mexican food, and so on. Each consumer arrives at the food court with some preference for one or another of these offerings. This preference may depend on the consumer's mood, her diet, or what she has already eaten that day. These preferences will not make consumers indifferent to price: If Wonderful Wok were to charge $15 for an egg roll, everybody would go to Bodacious Burgers or Pizza Paradise instead. But some people will choose a more expensive meal if that type of food is closer to their preference. So the products of the different vendors are substitutes, but they aren't *perfect* substitutes—they are *imperfect substitutes.*

FOR INQUIRING MINDS
ANYONE FOR A SECOND CUP?

The coffee shop industry has always been monopolistically competitive, with each local shop selling a somewhat differentiated product. Until the mid-1980s, however, products were mainly differentiated by location: customers chose a coffee shop because it was near their workplace or on the way to work. There was also a bit of differentiation by quality—some places made better coffee than others—but that was it. After all, coffee was coffee.

That is, coffee was coffee until it started becoming cappuccino, latte, frappuccino, and other more or less Italian-style beverages. In Canada, this trend toward specialty coffee was led by the Second Cup (the Toronto-based chain grew from one store in 1975 to more than 400 nationwide by 2004)—though Starbucks leads the worldwide market.

Is this a true expansion of the choices available to consumers? Are the coffee varieties now available really different? Yes, they are. The authors are old enough to remember what typical coffee-shop coffee tasted like in the dark ages: things really have improved. Is the improvement worth the price of a Starbucks latte? Well, people are willing to pay those prices, and the customer is always right.

AP/Wide World Photos

Mocha lattes served here—the Starbucks revolution comes to Beijing.

Vendors in a food court aren't the only sellers who differentiate their offerings by type. Clothing stores concentrate on women's or men's clothes, on business attire or sportswear, on trendy or classic styles, and so on. Auto manufacturers offer sedans, minivans, sport-utility vehicles, and sports cars, each type aimed at drivers with different needs and tastes.

Books offer yet another example of differentiation by type and style. Mysteries are differentiated from romances; among mysteries, we can differentiate among hard-boiled detective stories, whodunits, and police procedurals. And no two writers of hard-boiled detective stories are exactly alike: Raymond Chandler and Howard Engel each have their devoted fans.

In fact, product differentiation is characteristic of most consumer goods. As long as people differ in their tastes, producers find it possible and profitable to produce a range of varieties.

Differentiation by Location

Gas stations along a road offer differentiated products. True, the gas may be exactly the same. But the location of the stations is different, and location matters to consumers: it's more convenient to stop for gas near your home, near your workplace, or near wherever you are when the gas gauge gets low.

In fact, many monopolistically competitive industries supply goods differentiated by location. This is especially true in service industries, from dry cleaners to hairdressers, where customers often choose the seller who is closest rather than the one who is cheapest.

Differentiation by Quality

Do you have a craving for chocolate? How much are you willing to spend on it? You see, there's chocolate and then there's chocolate: although ordinary chocolate may not be very expensive, gourmet chocolate can cost dollars for every bite.

With chocolate, as with many goods, there is a range of possible qualities. You can get a usable bicycle for less than $100; you can get a much fancier bicycle for 10 times as much. It all depends on how much the additional quality matters to you and how much you will miss the other things you could have purchased with that money.

Because consumers vary in what they are willing to pay for higher quality, producers can differentiate their products by quality—some offering lower-quality, inexpensive products and others offering higher-quality products at a higher price.

Product differentiation, then, can take several forms. Whatever form it takes, however, there are two important features of industries with differentiated products: *competition among sellers* and *value in diversity*.

Competition among sellers means that even though sellers of differentiated products are not offering identical goods, they are to some extent competing for a limited market. If more businesses enter the market, each will find that it sells less quantity at any given price. For example, if a new gas station opens along a road, each of the existing gas stations will sell a bit less.

Value in diversity refers to the gain to consumers from the proliferation of differentiated products. A food court with eight vendors makes consumers happier than one with only six vendors, even if the prices are the same, because some customers will get a meal that is closer to what they had in mind. A road on which there is a gas station every two miles is more convenient for motorists than a road where gas stations are five miles apart. When a product is available in many different qualities, fewer people are forced to pay for more quality than they need or to settle for lower quality than they want. There are, in other words, benefits to consumers from a greater diversity of available products.

As we'll see next, competition among the sellers of differentiated products is the key to understanding how monopolistic competition works.

economics in action

Any Colour, So Long as It's Black

The early history of the auto industry offers a classic illustration of the power of product differentiation.

The modern automobile industry was created by Henry Ford, who first introduced assembly-line production. This technique made it possible for him to offer the famous Model T at a far lower price than anyone else was charging for a car; by 1920, Ford dominated the automobile business.

Ford's strategy was to offer just one style of car, which maximized his economies of scale but made no concessions to differences in taste. He supposedly declared that customers could get the Model T in "any colour, so long as it's black."

This strategy was challenged by Alfred P. Sloan, who had merged a number of smaller automobile companies into General Motors. Sloan's strategy was to offer a range of car types, differentiated by quality and price. Chevrolets were basic cars that directly challenged the Model T, Buicks were bigger and more expensive, and so on up to Cadillacs. And you could get each model in several different colours.

By the 1930s the verdict was clear: customers preferred a range of styles, and General Motors, not Ford, became the dominant North American auto manufacturer for the rest of the twentieth century. ■

>> QUICK REVIEW

- In *monopolistic competition* there are many competing producers, each with a differentiated product, and free entry and exit in the long run.
- Product differentiation can occur in oligopolies that fail to achieve tacit collusion as well as in monopolistic competition. It takes three main forms: by style or type, by location, or by quality. The products of competing sellers are considered imperfect substitutes.
- Producers compete for the same market, so entry by more producers reduces the quantity each existing producer sells at any given price. In addition, consumers gain from the increased diversity of products.

>>CHECK YOUR UNDERSTANDING 16-1

1. Each of the following goods and services are differentiated products. Which are differentiated as a result of monopolistic competition and which are not? Explain.
   a. Ladders
   b. Soft drinks
   c. Department stores
   d. Steel
2. You must determine which of two types of market structure best describes an industry, but you are allowed to ask only one question about the industry. What question should you ask to determine if an industry is:
   a. Perfectly competitive or monopolistically competitive?
   b. A monopoly or monopolistically competitive?

Solutions appear at back of book.

Understanding Monopolistic Competition

Suppose an industry is monopolistically competitive: it consists of many producers, all competing for the same consumers but offering differentiated products. How does such an industry behave?

As the term *monopolistic competition* suggests, this market structure combines some features typical of monopoly with others typical of perfect competition. Because each firm is offering a distinct product, it is in a way like a monopolist: it faces a downward-sloping demand curve and has some market power—the ability within limits to determine the price of its product. However, unlike a pure monopolist, a monopolistically competitive firm does face competition: the amount it can sell of its product depends on the prices and products offered by other firms in the industry.

The same, of course, is true of an oligopoly. In a monopolistically competitive industry, however, there are *many* producers, as opposed to the small number that defines an oligopoly. This means that the "puzzle" of oligopoly—will firms collude or will they behave non-cooperatively?—does not arise in the case of monopolistically competitive industries. True, if all the gas stations or all the restaurants in a town could agree—explicitly or tacitly—to raise prices, it would be in their mutual interest to do so. But such collusion is virtually impossible when the number of firms is large and, by implication, there are no barriers to entry. So in situations of monopolistic competition, we can safely assume that firms behave non-cooperatively and ignore the potential for collusion.

Monopolistic Competition in the Short Run

We introduced the distinction between short-run and long-run equilibrium back in Chapter 9. The short-run equilibrium of an industry takes the number of firms as given. The long-run equilibrium, by contrast, is reached only after enough time has elapsed for firms to enter or exit the industry. To analyse monopolistic competition, we focus first on the short run and then on how an industry moves from the short run to the long run.

Panels (a) and (b) of Figure 16-1 (page 412) show two possible situations that a typical firm in a monopolistically competitive industry might face in the short run. In each case the firm looks like any monopolist: it faces a downward-sloping demand curve, which implies a downward-sloping marginal revenue curve.

We assume that every firm has an upward-sloping marginal cost curve but that it also faces some fixed costs, so that its average total cost curve is U-shaped. This assumption doesn't matter in the short run, but, as we'll see shortly, it is crucial to understanding the long-run equilibrium.

In each case the firm, in order to maximize profit, sets marginal revenue equal to marginal cost. So how do these two figures differ? In panel (a) the firm is profitable; in panel (b) it is unprofitable.

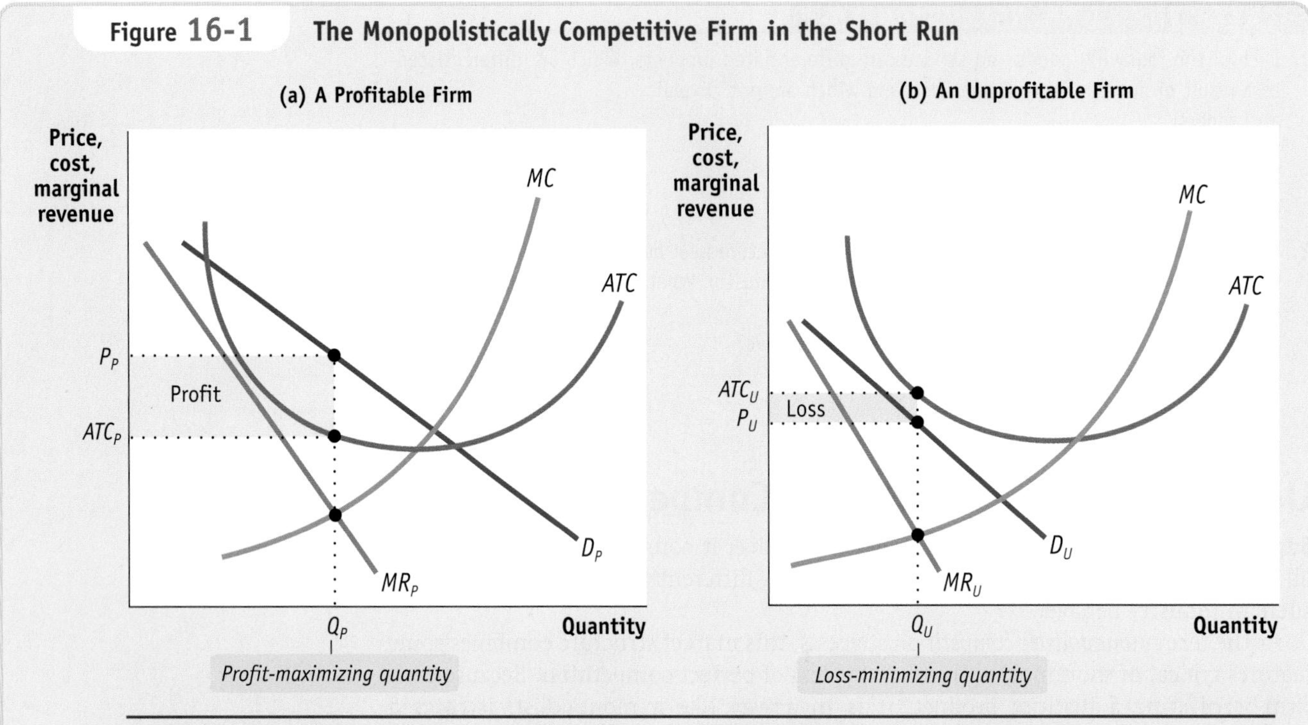

The firm in panel (a) can be profitable for some output quantity: the quantity at which its average total cost curve, *ATC*, lies below its demand curve, D_P. The profit-maximizing output quantity is Q_P, the output at which marginal revenue, MR_P, is equal to marginal cost, *MC*. The firm charges price P_P and earns a profit, represented by the area of the shaded rectangle. The firm in panel (b), however, can never be profitable because its average total cost curve lies above its demand curve, D_U, for every output quantity. The best that it can do if it produces at all is to produce quantity Q_U and charge price P_U. This generates a loss, indicated by the area of the shaded rectangle. Any other output quantity results in a greater loss. **>web...**

In panel (a) the firm faces the demand curve D_P and the marginal revenue curve MR_P. It produces the profit-maximizing output Q_P, the quantity at which marginal revenue is equal to marginal cost, and sells it at the price P_P. This price is above the average total cost at this output, ATC_P. The firm's profit is indicated by the area of the shaded rectangle.

In panel (b) the firm faces the demand curve D_U and the marginal revenue curve MR_U. It chooses the quantity Q_U at which marginal revenue is equal to marginal cost. However, in this case the price P_U is *below* the average total cost ATC_U; so at this quantity the firm loses money. Its loss is equal to the area of the shaded rectangle. Since Q_U is the profit-maximizing quantity—which means, in this case, the loss-minimizing quantity—there is no way for a firm in this situation to make a profit. We can confirm this by noting that at *any* quantity of output, the average total cost curve in panel (b) lies above the demand curve D_U. Because $ATC > P$ at all quantities of output, this firm always suffers a loss.

As this comparison suggests, the key to whether a firm with market power is profitable or unprofitable in the short run lies in the relationship between its demand curve and its average total cost curve. In panel (a) the demand curve D_P crosses the average total cost curve, meaning that some of the demand curve lies above the average total cost curve. So there are some price-quantity combinations available at which price is higher than average total cost, indicating that the firm can choose a quantity at which it makes positive profit.

In panel (b), by contrast, the demand curve D_U does not cross the average total cost curve—it always lies below it. So the price corresponding to each quantity demanded is always less than the average total cost of producing that quantity. There is no quantity at which the firm can avoid losing money.

These figures, showing firms facing downward-sloping demand curves and their associated marginal revenue curves, look just like ordinary monopoly analysis. The "competition" aspect of monopolistic competition comes into play, however, when we move from the short run to the long run.

Monopolistic Competition in the Long Run

Obviously, an industry in which existing firms are losing money, like the one in panel (b) of Figure 16-1, is not in long-run equilibrium. When existing firms are losing money, some firms will *exit* the industry. The industry will not be in long-run equilibrium until the persistent losses have been eliminated by the exit of some firms.

It may be less obvious that an industry in which existing firms are earning profits, like the one in panel (a) of Figure 16-1, is also not in long-run equilibrium. Given that there is *free entry* into the industry, persistent profits by the firms already existing will lead to the entry of additional producers. The industry will not be in long-run equilibrium until the persistent profits have been eliminated by the entry of new producers.

How will entry or exit by other firms affect the profits of a typical existing firm? Because the differentiated products offered by firms in a monopolistically competitive industry compete for the same set of customers, entry or exit by other firms will affect the demand curve facing every existing producer. If new gas stations open along a highway, each of the existing gas stations will sell less gas at any given price. So, as illustrated in panel (a) of Figure 16-2, entry of additional producers into a monopolistically competitive industry will lead to a *leftward* shift of the demand curve and the marginal revenue curve facing a typical existing producer.

Figure 16-2 Entry and Exit Shift Each Firm's Demand Curve and Marginal Revenue Curve

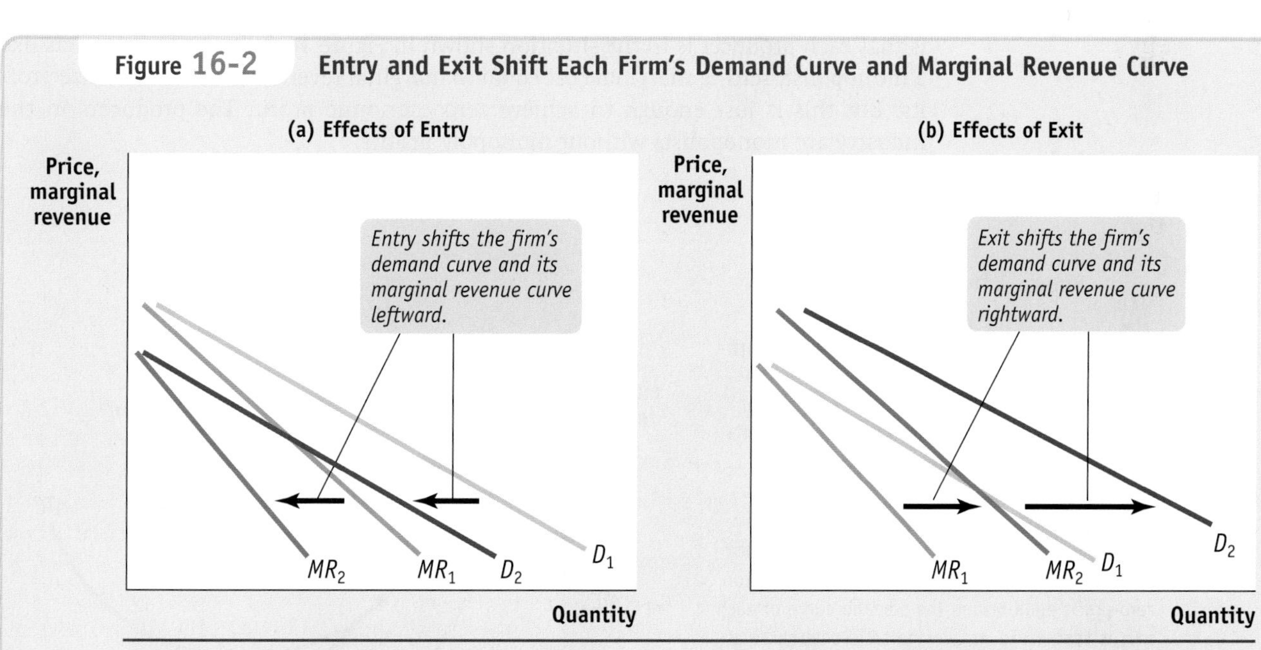

Entry will occur in the long run when existing firms are profitable. In panel (a), entry causes each existing firm's demand curve and marginal revenue curve to shift to the left. The firm receives a lower price for every unit it sells, and its profit falls. Entry will cease when firms make zero profit. Exit will occur in the long run when existing firms are unprofitable. In panel (b), exit from the industry shifts each remaining firm's demand curve and marginal revenue curve to the right. The firm receives a higher price for every unit it sells, and profit rises. Exit will cease when the remaining firms make zero profit.

Conversely, suppose that some of the gas stations along the highway close. Then each of the remaining stations will sell more gasoline at any given price. So as illustrated in panel (b), exit of firms from an industry leads to a *rightward* shift of the demand curve and marginal revenue curve facing a typical remaining producer.

The industry will be in long-run equilibrium when there is neither entry nor exit. This will occur only when every firm earns zero profit. So in the long run, a monopolistically competitive industry will end up in **zero-profit equilibrium,** in which firms just manage to cover their costs at their profit-maximizing output quantities.

In the long run, a monopolistically competitive industry ends up in **zero-profit equilibrium:** each firm makes zero profit at its profit-maximizing quantity.

We have seen that a firm facing a downward-sloping demand curve will earn positive profits if any part of that demand curve lies above its average total cost curve; it will incur a loss if its demand curve lies anywhere below its average total cost curve. So in zero-profit equilibrium, the firm must be in a borderline position between these two cases; its demand curve must just touch its average total cost curve. That is, it must be just *tangent* to it at the firm's profit-maximizing output quantity—the output quantity at which marginal revenue equals marginal cost.

If this is not the case, the firm operating at its profit-maximizing quantity will find itself making either a profit or loss, as illustrated in the panels of Figure 16-1. But we also know that free entry and exit means that this cannot be a long-run equilibrium. Why? In the case of a profit, new firms will enter the industry, shifting the demand curve of every existing firm leftward until all profits are extinguished. In the case of a loss, some existing firms will exit the industry and so shift the demand curve of every remaining firm to the right until all losses are extinguished. All entry and exit ceases only when every existing firm makes zero profit at its profit-maximizing quantity of output.

Figure 16-3 shows a typical monopolistically competitive firm in such a zero-profit equilibrium. The firm produces Q_{MC}, the output at which $MR = MC$, and charges price P_{MC}. At this price and quantity, represented by point Z, the demand curve is just tangent to its average total cost curve. The firm earns zero profit because price, P_{MC}, is equal to average total cost, ATC_{MC}.

The normal long-run condition of a monopolistically competitive industry, then, is that each producer is in the situation shown in Figure 16-3. Each producer acts like a monopolist, setting marginal cost equal to marginal revenue so as to maximize profits. But this is just enough to achieve zero economic profit. The producers in the industry are monopolists without monopoly profits.

Figure 16-3

The Long-Run Zero-Profit Equilibrium

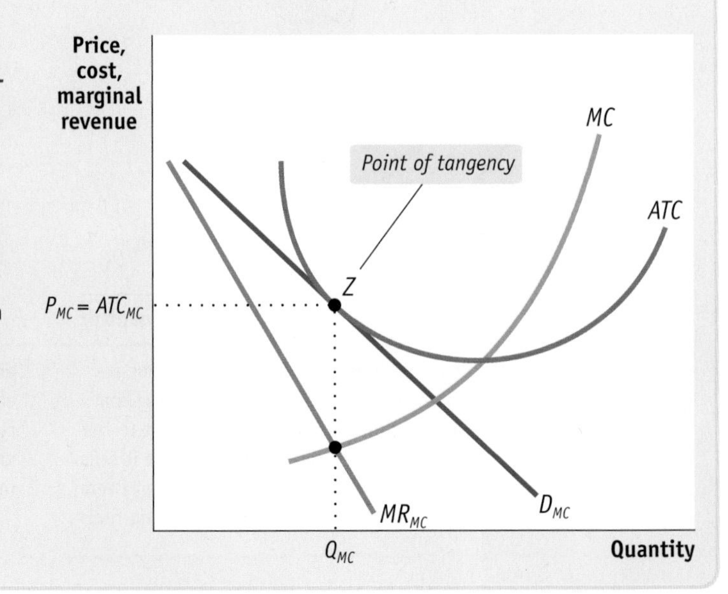

If existing firms are profitable, entry will occur and shift each existing firm's demand curve leftward. If existing firms are unprofitable, each existing firm's demand curve shifts rightward as some firms exit the industry. Entry and exit will cease when every existing firm makes zero profit at its profit-maximizing quantity. So, in long-run zero-profit equilibrium, the demand curve of each firm is tangent to its average total cost curve at its profit-maximizing quantity: at the profit-maximizing quantity, Q_{MC}, price, P_{MC}, equals average total cost, ATC_{MC}. A monopolistically competitive firm is like a monopolist without monopoly profits. >web...

FOR INQUIRING MINDS

HITS AND FLOPS

On the face of it, the movie business seems to meet the criteria for monopolistic competition. Movies compete for the same consumers; each movie is different from the others; new companies can and do enter the business. But where's the zero-profit equilibrium? After all, some movies are enormously profitable.

The key is to realize that for every successful blockbuster, there are several flops—and that the movie studios don't know in advance which will be which. (One observer of Hollywood summed up his conclusions as follows: "Nobody knows anything.") And by the time it becomes clear that a movie will be a flop, it's too late to cancel it.

The difference between moviemaking and the type of monopolistic competition we model in this chapter is that the fixed costs of making a movie are also *sunk costs*—once they've been incurred, they can't be recovered.

Yet there is still, in a way, a zero-profit equilibrium. If movies on average were highly profitable, more studios would enter the industry and more movies would be made. If movies on average lost money, fewer movies would be made. In fact, as you might expect, the movie industry on average earns just about enough to cover the cost of production—that is, it earns roughly zero economic profit.

This kind of situation—in which firms earn zero profit on average but have a mixture of highly profitable hits and money-losing flops—can be found in other industries, characterized by high, upfront sunk costs. A notable example is the pharmaceutical industry, where many research projects lead nowhere, but a few lead to highly profitable drugs.

economics in action

Bagels from Boom to Bust

Bagels have always been big in Montreal, but in the mid-1990s they suddenly became popular across the entire country. Nobody was quite sure why. One factor may have been health consciousness (bagels are low in fat and cholesterol—until you smother them in cream cheese). In any case, bagel consumption surged. Those who already owned bagel shops suddenly found their businesses highly profitable.

The fresh-bagel sector fits the definition of monopolistic competition quite well: there are many shops, all competing with one another, but the shops are differentiated by location as well as by style (some shops offer traditional bagels; others offer new items like bagels with blueberries or jalapenos). Each has some market power—it will not lose all its business if it charges slightly higher prices than other shops. And the industry is also characterized by free entry. Sure enough, once bagel shops became highly profitable, many new competitors entered the business. This, in turn, reduced the profitability of every bagel shop. By the end of the 1990s bagels were no longer a highly profitable business. Indeed, quite a few companies dropped out of the business or went bankrupt.

Meanwhile, a similar story seems to be emerging among specialty coffee shops: Second Cup is the most visible Canadian company but by no means the only one. When Canadians developed a taste for high-end coffee, the business became highly profitable, and many firms entered the industry. Second Cup is being challenged by Starbucks and Coffee & Company, as well as a host of independent operators. Demand for specialty coffee is still going up, but thanks to the rapid growth in the number of coffee shops, experts no longer think that the business offers easy opportunities for high profits. ■

>> QUICK REVIEW

- Like a monopolist, each firm in a monopolistically competitive industry faces a downward-sloping demand curve and marginal revenue curve. In the short run, it may earn a profit or incur a loss at its profit-maximizing quantity.
- If the typical firm earns positive profit, new firms will enter the industry in the long run, shifting each existing firm's demand curve to the left. If the typical firm incurs a loss, some existing firms will exit the industry in the long run, shifting the demand curve of each remaining firm to the right.
- In the long-run equilibrium of a monopolistically competitive industry, the *zero-profit equilibrium*, firms just break even. The typical firm's demand curve is tangent to its average total cost curve at its profit-maximizing quantity.

>>CHECK YOUR UNDERSTANDING 16-2

1. A monopolistically competitive industry, composed of firms with U-shaped average total cost curves, is currently in long-run equilibrium. Describe how the industry adjusts, in both the short and long run, in each of the following situations.
   a. A technological change that increases fixed cost for every firm in the industry
   b. A technological change that decreases marginal cost for every firm in the industry
2. Why, in the long run, is it impossible for firms in a monopolistically competitive industry to create a monopoly by joining together to form a single firm?

Solutions appear at back of book.

Monopolistic Competition Versus Perfect Competition

In a way, long-run equilibrium in a monopolistically competitive industry looks a lot like long-run equilibrium in a perfectly competitive industry. In both cases, there are many firms; in both cases, profits have been competed away; in both cases, the price received by every firm is equal to the average total cost of production.

However, the two versions of long-run equilibrium are different—in ways that are economically significant.

Price, Marginal Cost, and Average Total Cost

Figure 16-4 compares the long-run equilibrium of a typical firm in a perfectly competitive industry with that of a typical firm in a monopolistically competitive industry. Panel (a) shows a perfectly competitive firm facing a market price equal to its minimum average total cost; panel (b) reproduces Figure 16-3. Comparing the panels, we see two important differences.

First, in the case of the perfectly competitive firm shown in panel (a), the price, P_C, received by the firm at the profit-maximizing quantity, Q_C, is equal to the firm's marginal cost of production, MC_C, at that quantity of output. By contrast, at the profit-maximizing quantity chosen by the monopolistically competitive firm in panel (b), Q_{MC}, the price, P_{MC}, *is higher* than the marginal cost of production, MC_{MC}.

This difference translates into a difference in the attitude of firms towards consumers. A wheat farmer, who can sell as much wheat as he likes at the going market price, would not get particularly excited if you offered to buy some wheat at the market price. Since he has no desire to produce more at that price and can sell the wheat to someone else, you are not doing him a favour.

But if you decide to fill up your tank at Jamil's gas station rather than at Katy's, you are doing Jamil a favour. He is not willing to cut his price to get more customers—he's already made the best of that trade-off. But if he gets a few more customers than he expected at the *posted* price, that's good news: an additional sale at the posted price increases his revenue more than it increases his costs because the posted price exceeds marginal cost.

The fact that monopolistic competitors, unlike perfect competitors, want to sell more at the going price is crucial to understanding why they engage in activities like advertising that help increase sales.

The other difference between monopolistic competition and perfect competition that is visible in Figure 16-4 involves the position of each firm on its average total cost curve. In panel (a), the perfectly competitive firm produces at point Q_C, at the bottom of the U-shaped average total cost curve. That is, each firm produces the quantity at which average total cost is minimized—the *minimum-cost output*. As a consequence, the total cost of industry output is also minimized.

Under monopolistic competition, in panel (b), the firm produces at Q_{MC}, on the *downward-sloping* part of the U-shaped *ATC* curve: it produces less than the quantity that would minimize average total cost. This failure to produce enough to minimize average total cost is sometimes described as the **excess capacity** issue. The typical vendor in a food court or gas station along a road is not big enough to take maximum

Firms in a monopolistically competitive industry have **excess capacity:** they produce less than the output at which average total cost is minimized.

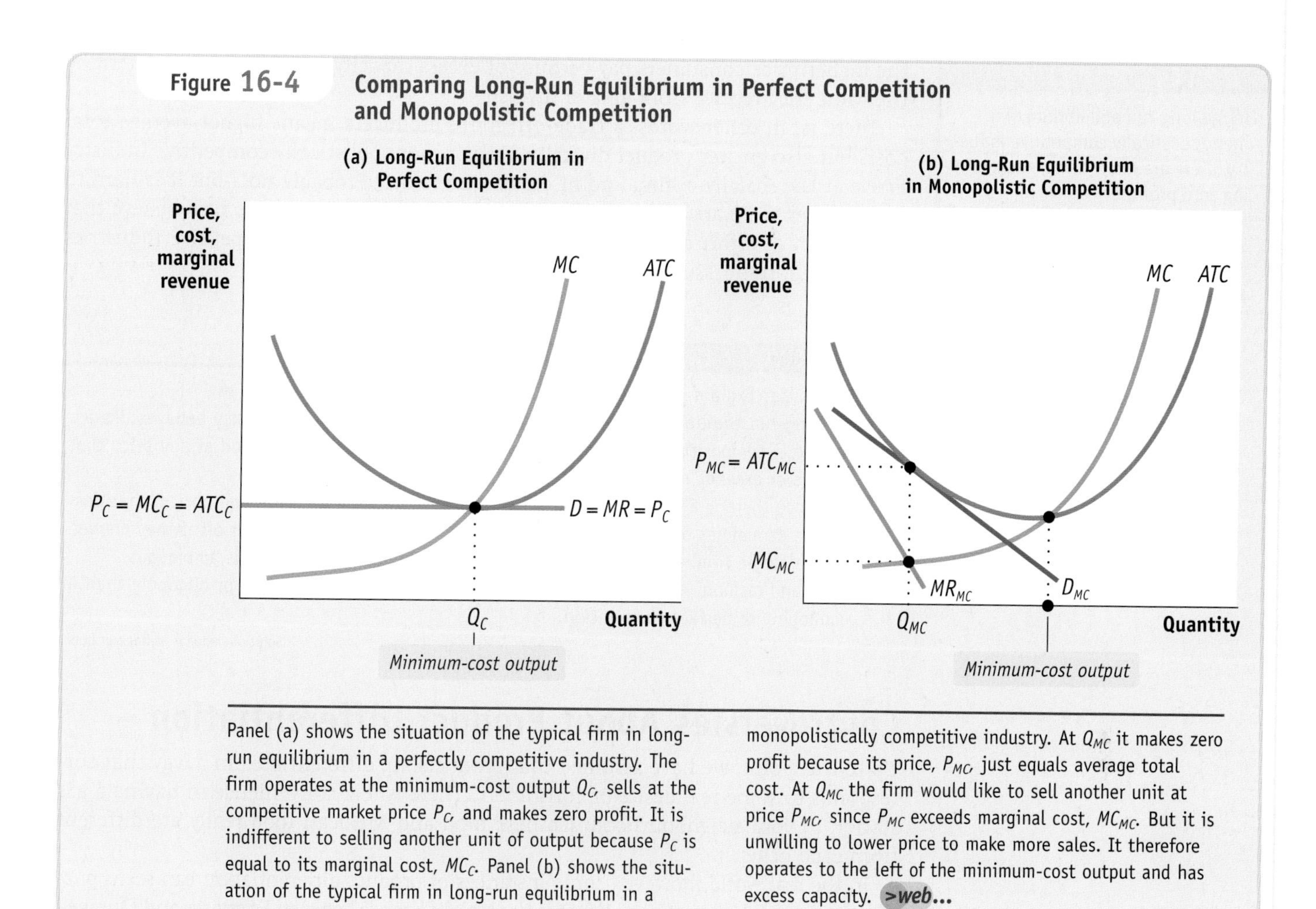

Figure 16-4 Comparing Long-Run Equilibrium in Perfect Competition and Monopolistic Competition

Panel (a) shows the situation of the typical firm in long-run equilibrium in a perfectly competitive industry. The firm operates at the minimum-cost output Q_C, sells at the competitive market price P_C, and makes zero profit. It is indifferent to selling another unit of output because P_C is equal to its marginal cost, MC_C. Panel (b) shows the situation of the typical firm in long-run equilibrium in a monopolistically competitive industry. At Q_{MC} it makes zero profit because its price, P_{MC}, just equals average total cost. At Q_{MC} the firm would like to sell another unit at price P_{MC}, since P_{MC} exceeds marginal cost, MC_{MC}. But it is unwilling to lower price to make more sales. It therefore operates to the left of the minimum-cost output and has excess capacity. >web...

advantage of available cost savings. So, the total cost of industry output is not minimized in the case of a monopolistically competitive market.

Some people have argued that, because every monopolistic competitor has excess capacity, monopolistically competitive industries are inefficient. But the issue of efficiency under monopolistic competition turns out to be a subtle one that does not have a clear answer.

Is Monopolistic Competition Inefficient?

A monopolistic competitor, like a monopolist, charges a price that is above marginal cost. As a result, some people who are willing to pay at least as much for an egg roll at Wonderful Wok as it costs to produce it are deterred from doing so. In monopolistic competition, some mutually beneficial transactions go unexploited.

Furthermore, it is often argued that monopolistic competition is subject to a further kind of inefficiency: that the excess capacity of every monopolistic competitor implies *wasteful duplication:* monopolistically competitive industries offer too many varieties. According to this argument, it would be better if there were only two or three vendors in the food court, not six or seven. If there were fewer vendors, each would have lower average total costs and so could offer food more cheaply.

Is this argument against monopolistic competition right—that it lowers total surplus by causing inefficiency? Not necessarily. It's true that if there were fewer gas stations along a highway, each gas station would sell more gasoline and so would have lower costs per gallon. But there is a drawback: motorists would be inconvenienced because gas stations would be farther apart. The point is that the diversity of products offered in a monopolistically competitive industry is itself beneficial to consumers. So the higher price consumers pay because of excess capacity is offset to some extent by the value they receive from greater diversity.

There is, in other words, a trade-off: more producers means higher average total costs but also greater product diversity. Does a monopolistically competitive industry arrive at the socially optimal point on this trade-off? Probably not—but it is hard to say whether there are too many firms or too few! Most economists now believe that duplication of effort and excess capacity in monopolistically competitive industries are not important issues in practice. ■

< < < < < < < < < < < < < < < < < < <

>> QUICK REVIEW

- In the long-run equilibrium of a monopolistically competitive industry, there are many firms, each earning zero profit.
- Price exceeds marginal cost, so some mutually beneficial trades are unexploited.
- Monopolistically competitive firms have *excess capacity* because they do not minimize average total cost. But it is not clear that this is actually a source of inefficiency since consumers gain from product diversity.

>> CHECK YOUR UNDERSTANDING 16-3

1. True or false? Explain your answer.
   a. In long-run equilibrium, a firm in a monopolistically competitive industry behaves like a perfectly competitive firm in one respect: both are willing to sell a good at any price that equals or exceeds marginal cost.
   b. Suppose there is a monopolistically competitive industry in long-run equilibrium that possesses economies of scale. All the firms in the industry would be better off if they merged into a single firm, but whether consumers are made better off by this is ambiguous.
   c. Fads and fashions are more likely to arise in monopolistic competition or oligopoly than in monopoly or perfect competition.

Solutions appear at back of book.

Controversies About Product Differentiation

Up to this point, we have assumed that products are differentiated in a way that corresponds to some real desire of consumers. There is real convenience in having a gas station in your neighbourhood; Chinese food and Mexican food really are different from each other.

In the real world, however, some instances of product differentiation can seem puzzling if you think about them. What is the real difference between Energizer and Duracell batteries? Between the beer brewed by Molson or that by Labatt? Or a Delta and a Ramada hotel room? Most people would be hard pressed to answer any of these questions. Yet the producers of these goods make considerable efforts to convince consumers that their products are different from and better than those of their competitors.

No discussion of product differentiation is complete without spending at least a bit of time on the two related issues—and puzzles—of *advertising* and *brand names*.

The Role of Advertising

Wheat farmers don't advertise their wares on TV; car dealers do. That's not because farmers are shy and car dealers are outgoing; it's because advertising is worthwhile only in industries in which firms have at least some market power. The purpose of advertisements is to get people to buy more of a seller's product at the going price. A perfectly competitive firm, which can sell as much as it likes at the going market price, would have no incentive to spend money convincing consumers to buy more. Only a firm that has some market power, and therefore charges a price that is above marginal cost, can gain from advertising. (Industries that are more or less perfectly competitive, like the milk industry, do advertise—but these ads are sponsored by an association on behalf of the industry as a whole, not on behalf of the milk that comes from the cows on a particular farm.)

Given that advertising "works", it's not hard to see why firms with market power would spend money on it. But the big question about advertising is *why* it works. A related question is whether advertising is, from society's point of view, a waste of resources.

Not all advertising poses a puzzle. Much of it is straightforward: it's a way for sellers to inform potential buyers about what they have to offer (or, occasionally, for buyers to inform potential sellers about what they want). Nor is there much controversy about the economic usefulness of ads that provide information: the real estate ad that declares "sunny, charming, 2 br, 1 ba, a/c" tells you things you need to know (even if a few euphemisms are involved—"charming", of course, means "small").

But what information is being conveyed when a TV actress proclaims the virtues of one or another long-distance telephone service or a sports hero declares that some company's batteries are better than those inside that pink mechanical rabbit? Surely nobody believes that the sports star is an expert on batteries—or that he chose the company that he personally believes makes the best batteries, as opposed to the company that offered to pay him the most. Yet companies believe, with good reason, that money spent on such promotions increases their sales—and that they would be in big trouble if they stopped advertising but their competitors continued to do so.

© Reprinted with special permission of King Features Syndicate.

Why are consumers influenced by ads that do not really provide any information about the product? One answer is that consumers are not as rational as economists typically assume. Perhaps consumers' judgments, or even their tastes, can be influenced by things that economists think ought to be irrelevant, such as which company has hired the most charismatic celebrity to endorse its product. And there is surely some truth to this. Consumer rationality is a useful working assumption; it is not an absolute truth.

However, another answer is that consumer response to advertising is not entirely irrational, because ads can serve as indirect "signals" in a world where consumers don't have good information about products. Suppose, to take a common example, that you need to avail yourself of some local service that you don't use regularly—bodywork on your car, say, or furniture moving. You turn to the Yellow Pages, where you see a number of small listings and several large display ads. You know that those display ads are large because the firms paid extra for them; still, it may be quite rational to call one of the firms with a big display ad. After all, the big ad probably means that it's a relatively large, successful company—otherwise, the company wouldn't have found it worth spending the money for the larger ad.

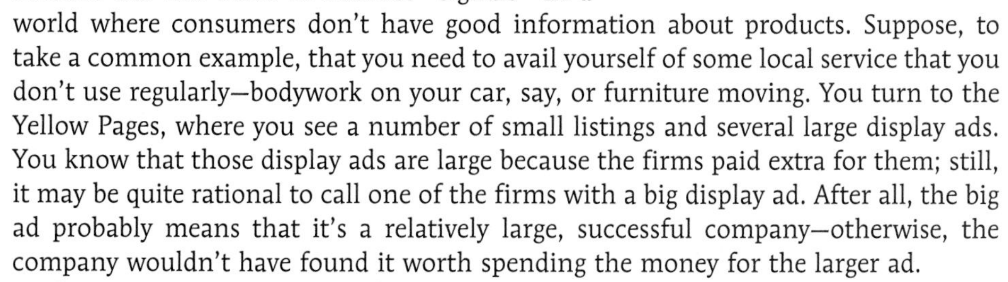

The same principle may partly explain why ads feature celebrities. You don't really believe that the supermodel prefers that watch; but the fact that the watch manufacturer is willing and able to pay her fee tells you that it is a major company that is likely to stand behind its product. According to this reasoning, an expensive advertisement serves to establish the quality of a firm's products in the eyes of consumers.

The possibility that it is rational for consumers to respond to advertising also has some bearing on the question of whether advertising is a waste of resources. If ads only work by manipulating the weak-minded, the $5 billion businesses spent on advertising in Canada in 2002 would have been an economic waste—except to the extent that ads sometimes provide entertainment. To the extent that advertising conveys important information, however, it is an economically productive activity after all.

Brand Names

You've been driving all day, and you decide that it's time to find a place to sleep. On your right, you see a sign for the Bates Motel; on your left, you see a sign for a Holiday Inn, or a Best Western, or some other national chain. Which one do you choose?

Unless they were familiar with the area, most people would head for the chain. While independent motels still exist in Canada, most motels are members of major chains; the same is true of most fast-food restaurants and many, if not most, stores in shopping malls.

A **brand name** is a name owned by a particular firm that distinguishes its products from those of other firms.

Motel chains and fast-food restaurants are only two examples illustrating a broader phenomenon: the role of **brand names,** names owned by particular companies that differentiate their products in the minds of consumers. In many cases, a company's brand name is the most important asset it has: clearly, McDonald's is worth far more than the sum of the deep-fat fryers and hamburger grills the company owns.

In fact, companies often go to considerable lengths to defend their brand names, suing anyone else who uses them without permission. You may talk about blowing your nose on a kleenex or xeroxing a term paper, but unless the product in question comes from Kleenex or Xerox, the seller must describe it as a facial tissue or a photocopier.

As with advertising, with which they are closely linked, the social usefulness of brand names is a source of dispute. Does the preference of consumers for known brands reflect consumer irrationality? Or do brand names convey real information? That is, do brand names create unnecessary market power, or do they serve a real purpose?

As in the case of advertising, the answer is probably some of both. On the one hand, brand names often do create unjustified market power. Consumers often pay more for brand-name goods in the supermarket even though consumer experts assure us that the cheaper store brands are equally good. Similarly, many common medicines, like aspirin, are cheaper—with no loss of quality—in their generic form.

On the other hand, for many products the brand name does convey information. A traveller arriving in a strange town can be sure of what awaits at a Holiday Inn or a McDonald's; a tired and hungry traveler may find this preferable to trying an independent hotel or restaurant that might be better—but might be worse.

In addition, brand names offer some assurance that the seller is engaged in repeated interaction with its customers and so has a reputation to protect. If a traveller eats a bad meal at a restaurant in a tourist trap and vows never to eat there again, the restaurant owner may not care, since the chance is small that the traveller will be in the same area again in the future. But if that traveller eats a bad meal at McDonald's and vows never to eat at a McDonald's again, that matters to the company. This gives McDonald's an incentive to provide consistent quality and so gives travellers some assurance that quality controls are in place.

economics in action

Absolut Irrationality

Advertising often serves a useful function. Among other things, it can make consumers aware of a wider range of alternatives, which leads to increased competition and lower prices. Indeed, in some cases the courts have viewed industry agreements *not* to advertise as violations of antitrust law. For example, in 2003 the Re/Max franchise (of real estate agents) was found to be in violation of the Competition Act by prohibiting its agents from advertising commission rates. Re/Max settled the case with the Competition Bureau, and agreed to allow its sales associates to set their commission rates independently and to advertise such rates.

Conversely, advertising sometimes creates product differentiation and market power where there is no real difference in the product. Consider, for example, the spectacularly successful advertising campaign of Absolut vodka.

In *Twenty Ads That Shook the World,* James B. Twitchell puts it this way: "The pull of Absolut's magnetic advertising is curious because the product itself is so bland. Vodka is aquavit, and aquavit is the most unsophisticated of alcohols. . . . No taste, no smell. . . . In fact, the Swedes, who make the stuff, rarely drink Absolut. They prefer cheaper brands such as Explorer, Brannvin, or Skåne. That's because Absolut can't advertise in Sweden, where alcohol advertising is against the law."

But here's a metaphysical question: if Absolut doesn't really taste any different from other brands, but advertising convinces consumers that they are getting a distinctive product, who are we to say that they aren't? Isn't distinctiveness in the mind of the beholder? ■

>> QUICK REVIEW

- In industries with product differentiation, firms advertise in order to increase the demand for their products.
- Advertising is not a waste of resources when it gives consumers useful information about products.
- Advertising that simply touts a product is harder to explain. Either consumers are irrational, or expensive advertising communicates that the firm's products are of high quality.
- Some firms create *brand names*. As with advertising, the economic value of brand names can be ambiguous. They convey real information when they assure consumers of the quality of a product.

< < < < < < < < < < < < < < < < < < < <

>>CHECK YOUR UNDERSTANDING 16-4

1. In which of the following cases is advertisement likely to be economically useful? Economically wasteful? Explain.
   a. Advertisements on the benefits of aspirin
   b. Advertisements for Bayer aspirin
   c. Advertisements on the benefits of drinking orange juice
   d. Advertisements for Tropicana orange juice
   e. Advertisements that state how long a plumber or an electrician has been in business
2. Some industry analysts have stated that a successful brand name is like a barrier to entry. Explain.

Solutions appear at back of book.

• A LOOK AHEAD •

Over the last three chapters we have taken the basic analysis of a perfectly competitive market and extended it in one important direction: to include other kinds of *market structures*. Next we turn to a different kind of extension: to different kinds of *markets*. We begin by asking how economic analysis changes when a national economy can exchange goods and services with other national economies. Next stop: international trade.

SUMMARY

1. **Monopolistic competition** is a market structure in which there are many competing producers, each producing a differentiated product, and there is free entry and exit in the long run. Product differentiation takes three main forms: by style or type, by location, or by quality. Products of competing sellers are considered imperfect substitutes, and each firm has its own downward-sloping demand curve and marginal revenue curve.
2. Short-run profits will attract entry of new firms. This reduces the quantity each existing producer sells at any given price and shifts its demand curve to the left. Short-run losses will induce exit by some firms. This shifts the demand curve of each remaining firm to the right.
3. In the long run, a monopolistically competitive industry is in **zero-profit equilibrium:** at its profit-maximizing quantity, the demand curve for each existing firm is tangent to its average total cost curve. There are zero profits in the industry and no entry or exit.
4. In long-run equilibrium, firms in a monopolistically competitive industry sell at a price greater than marginal cost. They also have **excess capacity** because they produce less than the minimum-cost output; as a result, they have higher costs than firms in a competitive industry. Whether or not monopolistic competition is inefficient is ambiguous because consumers value the diversity of products that it creates.
5. A monopolistically competitive firm will always prefer to make an additional sale at the going price, so it will engage in advertising to increase demand for its product and enhance its market power. Advertising and **brand names** that provide useful information to consumers are economically valuable. But they are economically wasteful when their only purpose is to create market power. In reality, advertising and brand names are likely to be some of both: economically valuable and economically wasteful.

KEY TERMS

Monopolistic competition, p. 407
Zero-profit equilibrium, p. 414
Excess capacity, p. 416
Brand name, p. 420

PROBLEMS

1. Use the three conditions for monopolistic competition discussed in the chapter to decide which of the following firms are likely to be operating as monopolistic competitors. If they are not monopolistically competitive firms, are they monopolists, oligopolists, or perfectly competitive firms?
   a. A local band that plays for weddings, parties, and so on
   b. Minute Maid, a producer of individual-serving juice boxes
   c. Your local dry cleaner
   d. A farmer who produces soybeans

2. You are thinking of setting up a coffee shop. The market structure for coffee shops is monopolistic competition. There are two Second Cup shops in your town already. In order for you to have some degree of market power, you may want to differentiate your coffee shop. Thinking about the three different ways in which products can be differentiated, explain how you would decide whether you should copy Second Cup or whether you should sell coffee in a completely different way.

3. The restaurant business in town is a monopolistically competitive industry in long-run equilibrium. One restaurant owner asks for your advice. She tells you that, each night, not all tables in her restaurant are full. She also tells you that if she lowered the prices on her menu, she would attract more customers and that doing so would lower her average total cost. Should she lower her prices? Draw a diagram showing the demand curve, marginal revenue curve, marginal cost curve, and average total cost curve for this restaurant to explain your advice. Show in your diagram what would happen to the restaurant owner's profit if she were to lower the price so that she sells the minimum-cost output.

4. The structure of the local gas station industry is monopolistic competition. Suppose that currently each gas station incurs a loss. Draw a diagram for a typical gas station to show this short-run situation. Then, in a separate diagram, show what will happen to the typical gas station in the long run. Explain your reasoning.

5. The local hairdresser industry has the structure of monopolistic competition. Your hairdresser boasts that he is making a profit and that if he continues to do so, he will be able to retire in five years. Use a diagram to illustrate your hairdresser's current situation. Do you expect this to last? In a separate diagram, draw what you expect to happen in the long run. Explain your reasoning.

6. Magnificent Blooms is a florist in a monopolistically competitive industry. It is a successful operation, producing the quantity that minimizes its average total cost and making a profit. The owner also boasts that at its current level of output, its marginal cost is above marginal revenue. Illustrate the current situation of Magnificent Blooms in a diagram. Answer the following questions by illustrating with a diagram.
   a. In the short run, could Magnificent Blooms increase its profit?
   b. In the long run, could Magnificent Blooms increase its profit?

7. "In the long run, there is no difference between monopolistic competition and perfect competition." True, false, or ambiguous? Discuss this statement with respect to the following:
   a. The price charged to consumers
   b. The average total cost of production
   c. The efficiency of the market outcome
   d. The typical firm's profit in the long run

8. "In both the short run and in the long run, the typical firm in monopolistic competition and a monopolist each make a profit." Do you agree with this statement? Explain your reasoning.

9. The market for clothes has the structure of monopolistic competition. What impact will fewer firms in this industry have on you as a consumer? Address the following issues:
   a. Variety of clothes
   b. Differences in quality of service
   c. Price

10. For each of the following situations, decide whether advertising is directly informative about the product or simply an indirect signal of its quality. Explain your reasoning.
   a. Hockey legend Wayne Gretzky drives a Buick in a TV commercial and claims that he prefers it to any other car.
   b. A newspaper ad states "For sale: 1989 Honda Civic, 160,000 miles, new transmission."
   c. McDonald's spends millions of dollars on an advertising campaign that proclaims: "I'm lovin' it."
   d. Subway advertises one of its sandwiches, claiming that it contains 6 grams of fat and fewer than 300 calories.

11. In each of the following cases, explain how the advertisement functions as a signal to a potential buyer. Explain what information the buyer lacks that is being supplied by the advertisement and how the information supplied by the advertisement is likely to affect the buyer's willingness to buy the good.
   a. "Looking for work. Excellent references from previous employers available."
   b. "Electronic equipment for sale. All merchandise carries a 1-year, no-questions-asked warranty."
   c. "Car for sale by original owner. All repair and maintenance records available."

12. McDonald's spends millions of dollars each year on legal protection of its brand name, thereby preventing any unauthorized use of it. Explain what information this conveys to you as a consumer about the quality of McDonald's products.

>web... To continue your study and review of concepts in this chapter, please visit the Krugman/Wells/Myatt website for quizzes, animated graph tutorials, web links to helpful resources, and more.

www.worthpublishers.com/krugmanwellsmyatt

>>International Trade

chapter 17

A ROSE BY ANY OTHER NATION

Giving your beloved roses on Valentine's Day is a well-established tradition in Canada. But in the past it was a very expensive gesture: in the northern hemisphere, Valentine's Day falls not in summer, when roses are in bloom, but in the depths of winter. Until recently, that meant that the roses in the florist's shop were grown at great cost in heated greenhouses. Nowadays, however, most of the Valentine's Day roses sold in this country are flown in from South America, mainly from Ecuador and Colombia, where growing a rose in February is no trouble at all.

Is it a good thing that we now buy our winter roses from abroad? The vast majority of economists say yes: international trade, in which countries specialize in producing different goods and trade those goods with each other, is a source of mutual benefit to the countries involved. In Chapter 2 we laid out the basic principle that there are *gains from trade;* it's a principle that applies to countries as well as individuals.

But some politicians and sections of the public are not convinced. For example, in 1988 there was a great debate in Canada about whether free trade, and the particular Free Trade Agreement (FTA) negotiated by the Progressive Conservative government with the United States, was a good idea. The federal election that year became the battleground for the debate, and in a memorable moment John Turner, the Liberal leader, accused then–Prime Minister Brian Mulroney of having "sold out" the country. The Conservatives won that election, and the FTA was ratified.

Rolf/Bruderer/Masterfile

Pablo Corral V/Corbis

What do these sweethearts and this rose farmer have in common? They are enjoying the mutual benefits of international trade.

What you will learn in this chapter:

- How comparative advantage leads to mutually beneficial international trade
- The sources of international comparative advantage
- Who gains and who loses from international trade, and why the gains exceed the losses
- How **tariffs** and **import quotas** cause inefficiency and reduce total surplus
- Why governments might rationally choose **trade protection** for some industries
- The relationship between free trade and **international trade agreements** and the role of the **World Trade Organization**

Since then, trade issues have hardly left world headlines. There have been mass demonstrations and protests against the meetings of the World Trade Organization (WTO) in Seattle (1999) and Cancún (2003). Yet most economists insist that there is nothing sinister about the WTO. It exists, they say, solely to enforce the rules of international trade and to occasionally provide a forum for further rounds of trade liberalization. For an informed opinion on these issues, we must study international trade and the impact of trade agreements on the national economy. These are the goals of this chapter.

We start from the beginning, with the model of comparative advantage, which, as we saw in Chapter 2, explains why there are gains from international trade. We go on to show how some individuals can be hurt by international trade and the effects of trade policies that countries use to limit imports or promote exports.

Comparative Advantage and International Trade

Goods and services purchased from other countries are **imports;** goods and services sold to other countries are **exports.**

Canada buys roses—and many other goods and services—from other countries. At the same time, it sells many goods and services to other countries. Goods and services purchased from abroad are **imports;** goods and services sold abroad are **exports.**

Trade is increasingly important for the Canadian economy. Over the last 40 years, both imports and exports have grown faster than the Canadian economy. Panel (a) of Figure 17-1 shows how the values of imports and exports have grown from about 15% of gross domestic product in 1961 to more than 40% in 2004. As panel (b) demonstrates, foreign trade is more important for Canada than it is for many other countries. In fact, Canada is among the ten largest trading countries in the world, with most of our trade being with the United States. The United States currently

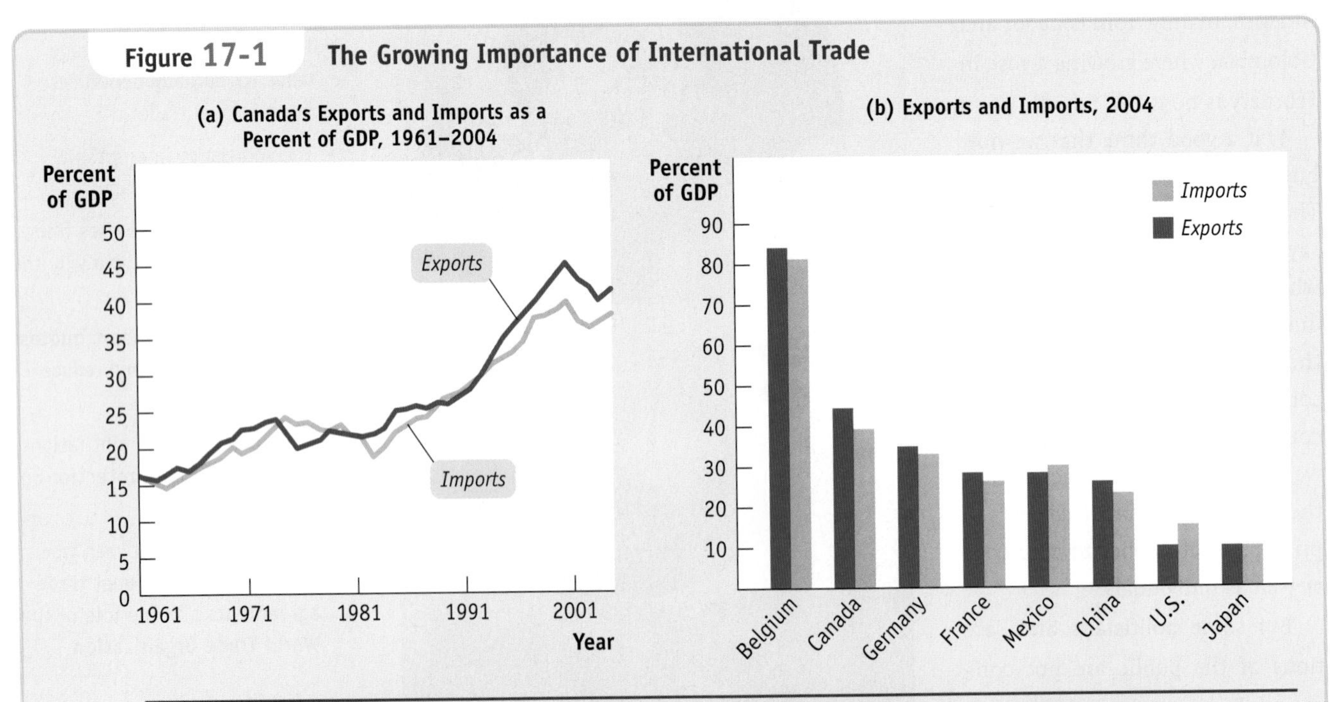

Figure 17-1 The Growing Importance of International Trade

Panel (a) illustrates the fact that over the past 40 years, Canada has exported a steadily growing share of its output (that is, its gross domestic product) to other countries and imported a growing share of what it consumes from abroad.

Panel (b) demonstrates that international trade is even more important to many other countries than it is to Canada.

Source: Statistics Canada, Cansim II, table 3800002 [for panel (a)] and United Nations Human Development Report 2004 [for panel (b)].

absorbs more than 80% of our exports. Indeed, the United States is now a larger market for Canadian manufactured goods than Canada itself.

To understand why international trade occurs and why economists believe it is beneficial to the economy, we will first review the concept of comparative advantage.

Production Possibilities and Comparative Advantage, Revisited

To grow Valentine's Day roses, any country must use resources—labour, energy, capital, and so on—that could have been used to produce other things. The potential production of other goods a country must forgo to produce a rose is the opportunity cost of that rose.

It's a lot easier to grow Valentine's Day roses in Colombia, where the weather in January and February is nearly ideal, than it is in Canada. Conversely, other goods are not produced as easily in Colombia as in Canada. Not only is Canada resource-rich, it also possesses a skilled labour force and excellent infrastructure that make it good at producing industrial and agricultural machinery, small aircraft, motor vehicles, and information technology equipment and services. Colombia doesn't have this base of skilled workers and technological know-how. So the opportunity cost of a Valentine's Day rose, in terms of other goods—say, a chainsaw winch (one of the best is made by Lewis, Inc., based in British Columbia)—is much less in Colombia than it is in Canada. (The Lewis winch fits any chainsaw, converting it into a motorized pulley to load trucks or free equipment stuck in mud.)

And so we say that Colombia has a comparative advantage in producing roses. Let's repeat the definition of comparative advantage from Chapter 2: *A country has a comparative advantage in producing a good if the opportunity cost of producing the good is lower for that country than for other countries.*

Figure 17-2 provides a hypothetical numerical example of comparative advantage in international trade. We assume that only two goods are produced and

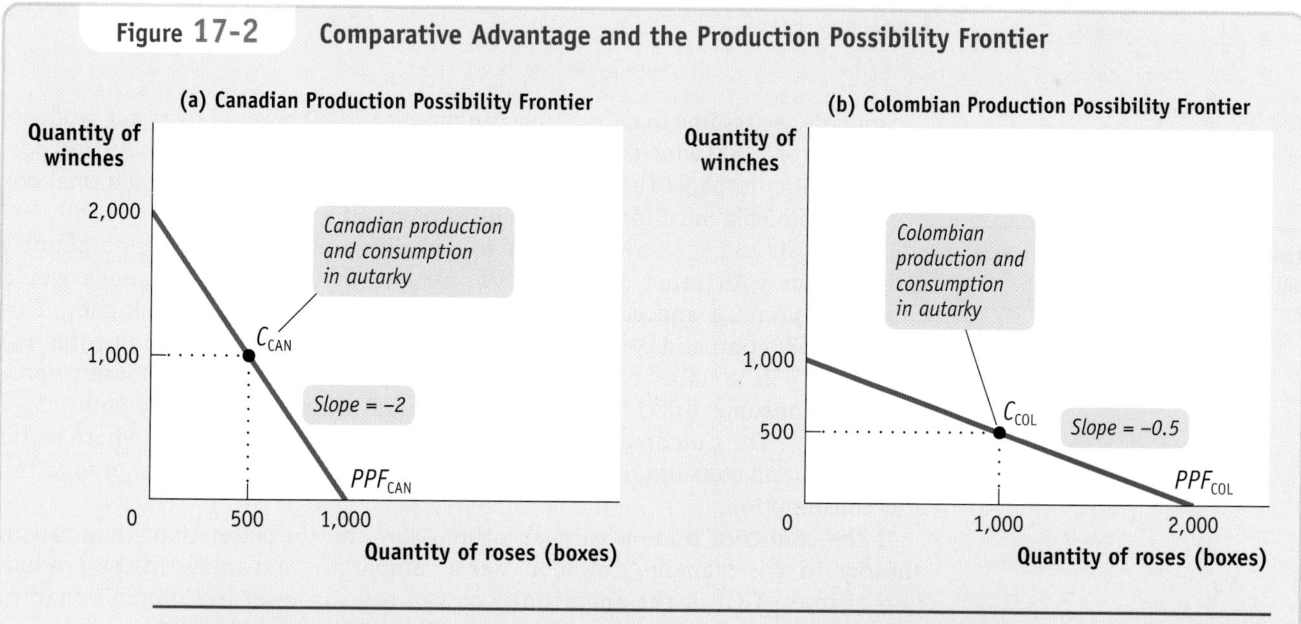

The Canadian opportunity cost of a box of roses in terms of a winch is 2: 2 winches must be forgone for every additional box of roses produced. The Colombian opportunity cost of a box of roses in terms of a winch is 0.5: only 0.5 winch must be forgone for every additional box of roses produced. Therefore, Colombia has a comparative advantage in roses and Canada has a comparative advantage in winches. In autarky, C_{CAN} is the Canadian production and consumption bundle and C_{COL} is the Colombian production and consumption bundle. **>web...**

consumed, roses and winches, and there are only two countries in the world, Canada and Colombia. We also assume that roses are shipped in standard refrigerated boxes, each containing 100 roses. The figure shows hypothetical production possibility frontiers for Canada and Colombia. As in Chapter 2, we simplify the model by assuming that the production possibility frontiers are straight lines, rather than the more realistic bowed-out shape shown in Figure 2-1. The straight-line shape implies that the opportunity cost of a box of roses in terms of winches in each country is constant—it does not depend on how many units of each good the country produces. The analysis of international trade under the assumption that opportunity costs are constant and therefore production possibility frontiers are straight lines is known as the **Ricardian model of international trade,** named after the English economist David Ricardo, who introduced this analysis in the early nineteenth century.

The **Ricardian model of international trade** analyses international trade under the assumption that opportunity costs are constant.

Table 17-1 presents the same information that is shown in Figure 17-2. We assume that Canada can produce 1,000 boxes of roses if it produces no winches or 2,000 winches if it produces no roses. The slope of the production possibility frontier in panel (a) is –2,000/1,000, or –2: to produce an additional box of roses, Canada must forgo the production of 2 winches.

TABLE 17-1

Production Possibilities

(a) Canada	Production	
	One possibility	Another possibility
Quantity of roses (boxes)	1,000	0
Quantity of winches	0	2,000
(b) Colombia	**Production**	
	One possibility	**Another possibility**
Quantity of roses (boxes)	2,000	0
Quantity of winches	0	1,000

Similarly, we assume that Colombia can produce 2,000 boxes of roses if it produces no winches or 1,000 winches if it produces no roses. The slope of the production possibility frontier in panel (b) is –1,000/2,000, or –0.5: to produce an additional box of roses, Colombia must forgo the production of half a winch.

Autarky is a situation in which a country cannot trade with other countries.

Economists use the term **autarky** to describe a situation in which a country cannot trade with other countries. We assume that in autarky Canada would choose to produce and consume 500 boxes of roses and 1,000 winches. This autarky production and consumption bundle is shown by point C_{CAN} in panel (a) of Figure 17-2. We also assume that in autarky Colombia would choose to produce and consume 1,000 boxes of roses and 500 winches, shown by point C_{COL} in panel (b). The outcome in autarky is summarized in Table 17-2, where world production and consumption is the sum of Canadian and Colombian production and consumption.

If the countries trade with each other, they can do better than they can in autarky. In this example, Colombia has a comparative advantage in the production of roses. That is, the opportunity cost of roses is lower in Colombia than in Canada: 0.5 winches per box of roses in Colombia versus 2 winches per box of roses in Canada. Conversely, Canada has a comparative advantage in the production of winches: to produce an additional winch, Canada must forgo the production of 0.5 boxes of roses, but producing an additional winch in Colombia requires forgoing the production of 2 boxes of roses. International trade allows

TABLE 17-2

Production and Consumption Under Autarky

(a) Canada	Production	Consumption
Quantity of roses (boxes)	500	500
Quantity of winches	1,000	1,000
(b) Colombia	**Production**	**Consumption**
Quantity of roses (boxes)	1,000	1,000
Quantity of winches	500	500
(c) World (Canada and Colombia)	**Production**	**Consumption**
Quantity of roses (boxes)	1,500	1,500
Quantity of winches	1,500	1,500

each country to specialize in producing the good in which it has a comparative advantage: winches in Canada, roses in Colombia. And that leads to gains for both when they trade.

The Gains from International Trade

Figure 17-3 illustrates how both countries gain from specialization and trade. Again, panel (a) represents Canada and panel (b) represents Colombia. As a result of international trade, Canada produces at point Q_{CAN}: 2,000 winches but no

Figure 17-3 The Gains from International Trade

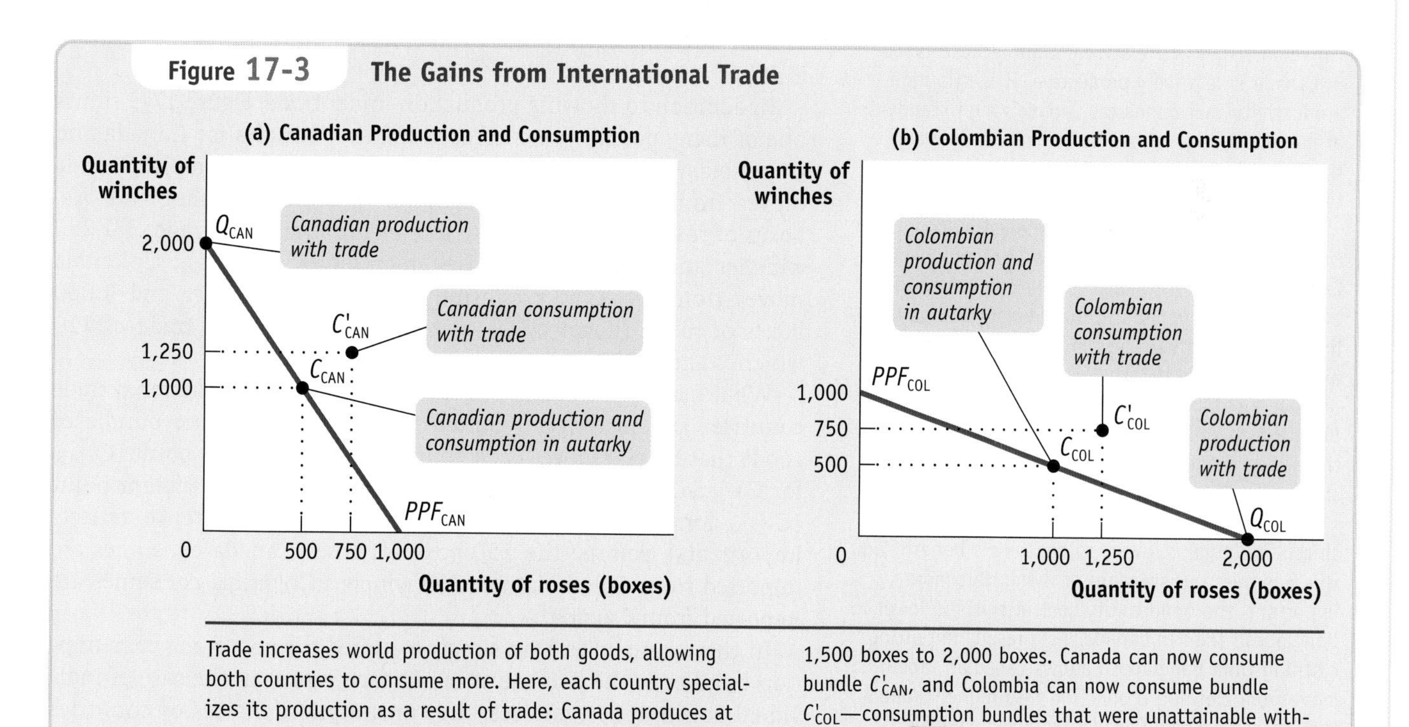

Trade increases world production of both goods, allowing both countries to consume more. Here, each country specializes its production as a result of trade: Canada produces at Q_{CAN} and Colombia produces at Q_{COL}. Total world production of winches has risen from 1,500 to 2,000 and of roses from 1,500 boxes to 2,000 boxes. Canada can now consume bundle C'_{CAN}, and Colombia can now consume bundle C'_{COL}—consumption bundles that were unattainable without trade. >web...

TABLE 17-3

Production and Consumption After International Trade

(a) Canada	**Production**	**Consumption**
Quantity of roses (boxes)	500	750
Quantity of winches	2,000	1,250
(b) Colombia	**Production**	**Consumption**
Quantity of roses (boxes)	2,000	1,250
Quantity of winches	500	750
(c) World (Canada and Columbia)	**Production**	**Consumption**
Quantity of roses (boxes)	2,000	2,000
Quantity of winches	2,000	2,000

roses. Colombia produces at Q_{COL}: 2,000 boxes of roses but no winches. The new production choices are given in the second column of Table 17-3.

By comparing Table 17-3 with Table 17-2, you can see that specialization increases total world production of *both* goods. In the absence of specialization, total world production consists of 1,500 winches and 1,500 boxes of roses. After specialization, total world production rises to 2,000 winches and 2,000 boxes of roses. These goods can now be traded, with Canada consuming roses produced in Colombia and Colombia consuming winches produced in Canada. The result is that each country can consume more of *both* goods than it did in autarky.

In addition to showing production under trade, Figure 17-3 shows one of many possible pairs of consumption bundles for Canada and Colombia, which is also given in Table 17-3. In this example, Canada moves from its autarky consumption of 1,000 winches and 500 boxes of roses, shown by C_{CAN}, to consumption after trade of 1,250 winches and 750 boxes of roses, represented by C'_{CAN}. Colombia moves from its autarky consumption of 500 winches and 1,000 boxes of roses, shown by C_{COL}, to consumption after trade of 750 winches and 1,250 boxes of roses, shown by C'_{COL}.

What makes this possible is the fact that with international trade countries are no longer required to consume the same bundle of goods that they produce. Each country produces at one point (Q_{CAN} for Canada, Q_{COL} for Colombia) but consumes at a different point (C'_{CAN} for Canada, C'_{COL} for Colombia). The difference reflects imports and exports: the 750 boxes of roses Canada consumes are imported from Colombia; the 750 winches Colombia consumes are imported from Canada.

In this example we have simply assumed the post-trade consumption bundles of the two countries. In fact, just as in the case of individual consumption choices, the consumption choices of countries reflect both the preferences of its residents and the *relative prices* in international markets—the prices of one good in terms of another. Although we have not explicitly given the price of winches in terms

PITFALLS

THE PAUPER LABOUR FALLACY

One common argument about international trade goes as follows: wages are so low in many developing countries ("pauper labour") that they can produce almost everything more cheaply than we can. Free trade with these countries would drive most Canadian products off the market. Canadians would lose their jobs, and the Canadian standard of living would fall.

Why is this a misconception? First of all, Canadian wages are relatively high because labour in Canada is relatively productive. It is this high productivity that generates Canada's high standard of living. So, high wages don't necessarily mean that Canadian products are uncompetitive relative to products made in low-wage countries.

Second, trade flows are determined by *comparative advantage,* not by *absolute advantage.* Even if Canada were more efficient in the production of every good, we would still improve our standard of living by trading with less productive nations. For example, suppose it takes *fewer* hours of labour to produce a shirt in Canada than in Bangladesh, but Bangladeshi shirts are cheaper solely because of their lower wages. Should we prohibit imports of shirts from Bangladesh?

No. We benefit from importing Bangladeshi shirts. The price *is* lower; so consumers benefit, and this improves our standard of living. But more important, the opportunity cost of shirts is lower in Bangladesh than in Canada. As a result, importing clothing from Bangladesh allows Canadian labour to move from clothing production into higher productivity sectors where Canada has a comparative advantage. This raises the average productivity of workers in Canada and further improves the Canadian standard of living.

of roses, that price is implicit in our example: Colombia exports 750 boxes of roses and receives 750 winches in return, so that each box of roses is traded for 1 winch. This tells us that the price of a winch on world markets must be equal to the price of a box of roses in our example. What determines the actual relative prices in international trade? The answer is supply and demand—and we'll turn to supply and demand in international trade in the next section.

We have also assumed that each country ends up completely specializing in the production of its export good. In part, this is because we assumed a straight-line production possibility frontier, which implies constant opportunity costs. We saw in Chapter 2 that a bowed-out production possibility frontier implies that the opportunity costs of producing a good increase as more of that good is produced. This usually prevents complete specialization, since as the export industry expands its opportunity costs increase, and as the import-competing industry contracts its opportunity costs decrease.

In our supply and demand analysis in the next section, we'll consider incomplete specialization by a country to be the norm. We should also emphasize that although countries often specialize incompletely, this fact does not change in any way the conclusion that there are gains from trade. However, first let's look behind the production possibility frontiers and ask what determines a country's comparative advantage.

Sources of Comparative Advantage

International trade is driven by comparative advantage, but where does comparative advantage come from? Economists who study international trade have found three main sources of comparative advantage: international differences in *climate*, international differences in *factor endowments*, and international differences in *technology*.

Differences in Climate A key reason the opportunity cost of producing a Valentine's Day rose in Colombia is less than in Canada is that nurseries in Colombia can grow roses outdoors all year round but nurseries in Canada can't. In general, differences in climate are a significant source of international trade. Tropical countries export tropical products like coffee, sugar, and bananas. Countries in the temperate

FOR INQUIRING MINDS

DOES TRADE HURT POOR COUNTRIES?

It's a good bet that the clothes you are wearing right now were produced in a labour-abundant country such as Bangladesh, Sri Lanka, or China. If so, the workers who produced those clothes were paid very low wages by Western standards: in 2002 (the most recent data available) workers in Sri Lankan factories were paid an average of $0.33 an hour. Doesn't this mean that Sri Lankan workers are getting a bad deal?

The answer of most economists is that it doesn't. The wages paid to export workers in poor countries should be compared not to what workers get in rich countries but to what they would get if those export jobs weren't available. The reason Sri Lankans are willing to work for so little is that in an underdeveloped economy, with lots of labour but very little of other factors of production like capital, the opportunities available to workers are very limited. It's almost certain that international trade makes Sri Lanka and other low-wage countries *less* poor than they would be otherwise and raises workers' wages relative to what they would be without international trade.

Nonetheless, many people in advanced countries—students in particular—are disturbed by the thought that their consumer goods are produced by such poorly paid workers and want to see those workers receive higher pay and better working conditions.

The dilemma is whether it is possible to insist on higher wages and better working conditions without eliminating the job altogether, thereby choking off the benefits of international trade and making poor workers even poorer. Some argue that we should trust market forces to work things out in the long run. But some problems do need to be addressed through international agreements. For example, countries are now allowed to ban the import of goods produced by prison labour. Should similar agreements be negotiated to ban the products of child labour?

zones export crops like wheat and corn. Some trade is even driven by the difference in seasons between the northern and southern hemispheres: winter deliveries of Chilean grapes and New Zealand apples have become commonplace in North American and European supermarkets.

Differences in Factor Endowments Canada is a major exporter of forest products—lumber and products derived from lumber, like pulp and paper—to the United States. These exports don't reflect the special skill of Canadian lumberjacks. Instead, Canada has a comparative advantage in forest products because its forested area is much greater compared to the size of its labour force than the ratio of forestland to the labour force in the United States.

Forestland, like labour and capital, is a factor of production. Due to history and geography, the mix of available factors of production differs among countries, providing an important source of comparative advantage. And while geography is relatively immutable, history can be shaped. Capital can be accumulated through saving. Human capital can be acquired by devoting resources to education. In this way, the availability of factors of production can be influenced by policy, and comparative advantage can be shaped through time by acquiring capital and know-how.

The relationship between factor availability and comparative advantage is found in an influential model of international trade, the *Heckscher-Ohlin model,* developed by two Swedish economists in the first half of the twentieth century. A key concept in the model is *factor intensity*. Producers use different ratios of factors of production in the production of different goods. For example, at any given wage rate and rental rate of capital, oil refineries will use much more capital per worker than clothing factories. Economists use the term **factor intensity** to describe this difference among goods: oil refining is capital-intensive, because it tends to use a high ratio of capital to labour, but clothing manufacture is generally labour-intensive, because it tends to use a high ratio of labour to capital.

The **factor intensity** of production of a good is a measure of which factor is used in relatively greater quantities than other factors in production.

According to the **Heckscher–Ohlin model,** a country has a comparative advantage in a good whose production is intensive in the factors that are abundantly available in that country.

According to the **Heckscher–Ohlin model,** a country will have a comparative advantage in a good whose production is intensive in the factors that are abundantly available in that country. So a country that has an abundance of capital will have a comparative advantage in capital-intensive industries such as pharmaceuticals, but a country that has an abundance of labour will have a comparative advantage in labour-intensive industries such as clothing production. The basic

FOR INQUIRING MINDS

INCREASING RETURNS AND INTERNATIONAL TRADE

Most analysis of international trade focuses on how differences between countries—differences in climate, factor endowments, and technology—create national comparative advantage. However, economists have also pointed out another reason for international trade: the role of *increasing returns.*

Production of a good is characterized by increasing returns if the productivity of labour and other resources rises with the quantity of output. For example, in an industry characterized by increasing returns, increasing output by 10% might require only 8% more labour and 9% more raw materials. Increasing returns (sometimes also called economies of scale) can give rise to monopoly, because they give large firms an advantage over small firms.

But increasing returns can also give rise to international trade. The logic runs as follows: if production of a good is characterized by increasing returns, it makes sense to concentrate production in only a few locations, so as to achieve a high level of production in each location. But that also means that the good is produced in only a few countries, which export that good to other countries. A commonly cited example is the North American auto industry: although both Canada and the United States produce automobiles and their components, each particular model or component tends to be produced in only one of the two countries and exported to the other. Increasing returns probably play a large role in the trade in manufactured goods between economically advanced countries, which is about 25% of the total value of world trade.

intuition behind this result is simple and based on opportunity cost. The opportunity cost of a given factor—the value that the factor would generate in alternative uses—is low for a country when it possesses an abundance of that factor. (For example, in Canada, the opportunity cost of water for residences is low because there is a plentiful supply for other uses, such as agriculture.) So the opportunity cost of producing goods that are intensive in the use of an abundantly available factor is also low.

The most dramatic example of the validity of the Heckscher–Ohlin model is world trade in clothing. Clothing production is generally a labour-intensive activity: it doesn't need much physical capital, nor does it require a lot of human capital in the form of highly educated workers. So you would expect labour-abundant countries such as China and Bangladesh to have a comparative advantage in clothing production. And they do.

Differences in Technology In the 1970s and 1980s, Japan became by far the world's largest exporter of automobiles, selling large numbers to North America and the rest of the world. Japan's comparative advantage in automobiles wasn't the result of climate. Nor can it easily be attributed to differences in factor endowments: aside from a scarcity of land, Japan's mix of available factors is quite similar to that in other economically advanced countries. Instead, Japan's comparative advantage in automobiles was based on the superior production techniques developed by that country's manufacturers, which allowed them to produce more cars with a given amount of labour and capital than their North American or European counterparts.

Japan's comparative advantage in automobiles was a case of comparative advantage caused by differences in technology—the techniques used in production.

The causes of differences in technology are somewhat mysterious. Sometimes they seem to be based on knowledge accumulated through experience—for example, Switzerland's comparative advantage in watches reflects a long tradition of watchmaking. Sometimes they are the result of a set of innovations that for some reason occur in one country but not in others. Sometimes a technological advantage can be acquired or supported by government funds for research. For instance, government support for the nuclear and aerospace industries has helped Canada occupy a niche in the world markets for those products. In another example, the semiconductor industry in the United States was the recipient of large amounts of government research funds that helped U.S. semiconductor manufacturers to dominate the world market in that industry.

Technological advantage is also often transitory. North American auto manufacturers have now closed much of the gap in productivity with their Japanese competitors; Europe's aircraft industry has closed a similar gap with the U.S aircraft industry. At any given point in time, however, differences in technology are a major source of comparative advantage.

economics in action

The Comparative Advantage of Canada

Canada is a country of superlatives: a country not only richly endowed with resources such as lumber, metals, oil, and hydroelectricity, but also possessing a skilled labour force, technological know-how, and excellent infrastructure. So with all these absolute advantages, where does Canada's *comparative* advantage lie? It lies in two types of goods.

First, Canada's comparative advantage lies in resource-intensive products: in pulp and paper, lumber, wheat, fish and fish products, ores and concentrates, precious metals, aluminium, oil, coal, and electricity. Second, Canada's comparative advantage lies in goods utilizing Canada's technological know-how and excellent infrastructure: motor vehicles and parts (General Motors Canada, Chrysler Canada, and Ford Canada); small aircraft, engines, and locomotives (Pratt and Whitney, Bombardier); telephone equipment (Nortel); personal communication devices (Research in Motion, manufacturer of the BlackBerry device); and computer software and support (IBM Canada). Most of these industries produce differentiated products with high volumes of imports as well as exports. For example, Canada's automobile industry specializes in certain lines that it exports throughout North America, and it imports other lines from the United States and Mexico.

The sorts of industries where Canada definitely does *not* have a comparative advantage are those that are not favoured by our climate—such as citrus fruit, vegetables, and cotton—and those that intensively use less-skilled labour, such as most of the garment and textile industry and consumer goods assembly.

In brief, Canada's exports tend to be either resource-intensive or capital-intensive—especially human-capital-intensive—whereas Canada's imports tend to be unskilled-labour-intensive. ■

>>QUICK REVIEW

- *Imports* and *exports* account for a growing share of the Canadian economy and of the economies of many other countries.
- International trade is driven by comparative advantage. The *Ricardian model of international trade* shows that trade between two countries makes both countries better off than they would be in *autarky*—that is, there are gains from trade.
- The main sources of comparative advantage are international differences in climate, factor endowments, and technology.
- The *Heckscher–Ohlin model* shows how comparative advantage can arise from differences in factor endowments: goods differ in their *factor intensity*, and countries tend to export goods that are intensive in the factors they have in abundance.
- Trade in manufactured goods amongst developed countries is best explained by increasing returns in production.

>>CHECK YOUR UNDERSTANDING 17-1

1. In Canada, the opportunity cost of 1 ton of corn is 50 bicycles. In China, the opportunity cost of 1 bicycle is 0.01 ton of corn.
   a. Determine the pattern of comparative advantage.
   b. In autarky, Canada can produce 200,000 bicycles if no corn is produced, and China can produce 3,000 tons of corn if no bicycles are produced. Draw each country's production possibility frontier assuming constant opportunity cost, with tons of corn on the vertical axis and bicycles on the horizontal axis.
   c. With trade, each country specializes its production. Canada consumes 1,000 tons of corn and 200,000 bicycles; China consumes 3,000 tons of corn and 100,000 bicycles. Indicate the production and consumption points on your diagrams, and use them to explain the gains from trade.
2. Explain the following patterns of trade using the Heckscher–Ohlin model:
   a. France exports wine to Canada, and Canada exports paper to France.
   b. Brazil exports shoes to Canada, and Canada exports shoe-making machinery to Brazil.

Solutions appear at back of book.

Supply, Demand, and International Trade

Simple models of comparative advantage are helpful for understanding the fundamental causes of international trade. However, to analyse the effects of international trade at a more detailed level and to understand trade policy, it helps to return to the supply and demand model. We'll start by looking at the effects of imports on domestic producers and consumers, then turn to the effect of exports.

The Effects of Imports

Figure 17-4 shows the Canadian market for roses, ignoring international trade for a moment. It introduces a few new concepts: the *domestic demand curve*, the *domestic supply curve*, and the domestic or autarky price.

The **domestic demand curve** shows how the quantity of a good demanded by domestic consumers depends on the price of that good.

The **domestic demand curve** shows how the quantity of a good demanded by residents of a country depends on the price of that good. Why "domestic"? Because people living in other countries may demand the good, too. Once we introduce international trade, we need to distinguish between purchases of a good by domestic

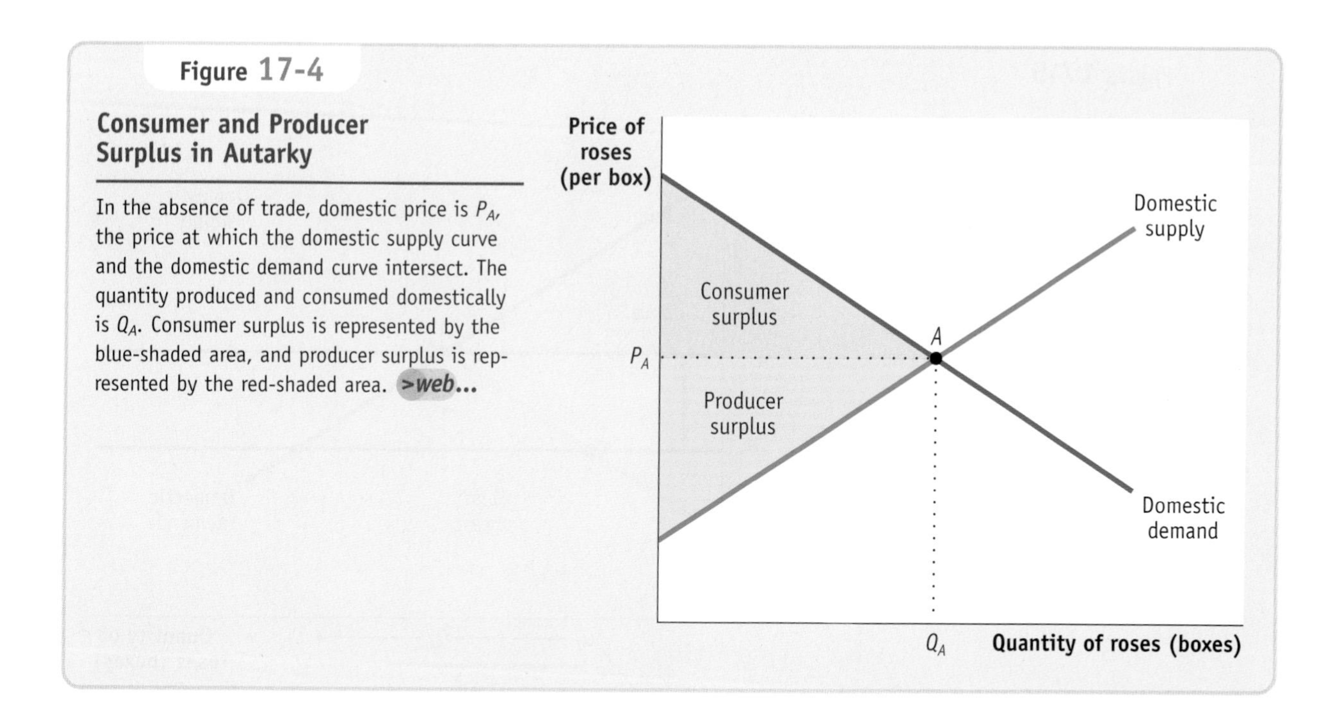

Figure 17-4

Consumer and Producer Surplus in Autarky

In the absence of trade, domestic price is P_A, the price at which the domestic supply curve and the domestic demand curve intersect. The quantity produced and consumed domestically is Q_A. Consumer surplus is represented by the blue-shaded area, and producer surplus is represented by the red-shaded area. >web...

consumers and purchases by foreign consumers. So the domestic demand curve reflects only the demand of residents of our own country. Similarly, the **domestic supply curve** shows how the quantity of a good supplied by producers inside a country depends on the price of that good. Once we introduce international trade, we need to distinguish between the supply of domestic producers and foreign supply—supply brought in from abroad.

The **domestic supply curve** shows how the quantity of a good supplied by domestic producers depends on the price of that good.

In autarky, with no international trade in roses, the equilibrium in this market would be determined by the intersection of the domestic demand and domestic supply curves, point *A*. The equilibrium price of roses would be P_A, and the equilibrium quantity of roses produced and consumed would be Q_A. As always, both consumers and producers would gain from the existence of the domestic market. Consumer surplus would be equal to the area of the upper shaded triangle in Figure 17-4. Producer surplus would be equal to the area of the lower shaded triangle. And total surplus would be equal to the sum of these two shaded triangles.

Now let's imagine opening up this market to imports. To do this, we must make some assumption about the supply of imports. The simplest assumption, which we will adopt here, is that unlimited quantities of roses can be purchased from abroad at a fixed price, known as the **world price** of roses. Figure 17-5 shows a situation in which the world price of roses, P_W, is lower than the price of roses that would prevail in the domestic market in autarky, P_A.

The **world price** of a good is the price at which that good can be bought or sold abroad.

Given that the world price of roses is below the domestic price of roses, it is profitable for importers to buy roses abroad and resell them domestically. The imported roses increase the supply of roses to the domestic market, driving down the domestic market price. Roses will continue to be imported until the domestic price falls to a level equal to the world price.

The result is shown in Figure 17-5. Because of imports, the domestic price of roses falls from P_A to P_W. The quantity of roses demanded by domestic consumers rises from Q_A to C_T, and the quantity supplied by domestic producers falls from Q_A to Q_T. The difference between the domestic quantity demanded and the domestic quantity supplied, $C_T - Q_T$, is filled by imports.

Now let's turn to the effects of imports on consumer surplus and producer surplus. Because imports of roses lead to a fall in their domestic price, consumer surplus

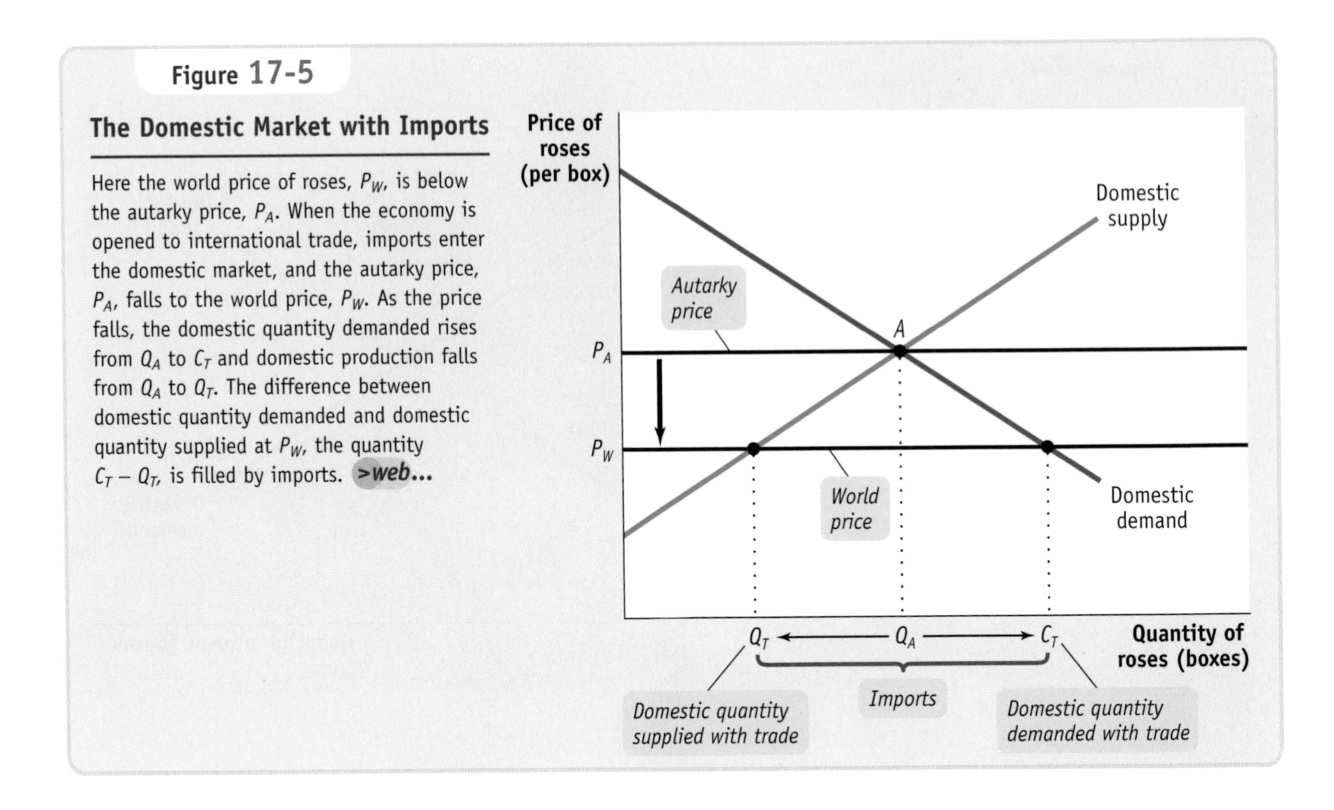

Figure 17-5

The Domestic Market with Imports

Here the world price of roses, P_W, is below the autarky price, P_A. When the economy is opened to international trade, imports enter the domestic market, and the autarky price, P_A, falls to the world price, P_W. As the price falls, the domestic quantity demanded rises from Q_A to C_T and domestic production falls from Q_A to Q_T. The difference between domestic quantity demanded and domestic quantity supplied at P_W, the quantity $C_T - Q_T$, is filled by imports. >web...

rises and producer surplus falls. Figure 17-6 shows how this works. We label four areas: *W*, *X*, *Y*, and *Z*. The autarky consumer surplus we identified in Figure 17-4 corresponds to *W*, and the autarky producer surplus corresponds to the sum of *X* and *Y*. The fall in the domestic price to the world price leads to an increase in consumer

Figure 17-6 **The Effects of Imports on Surplus**

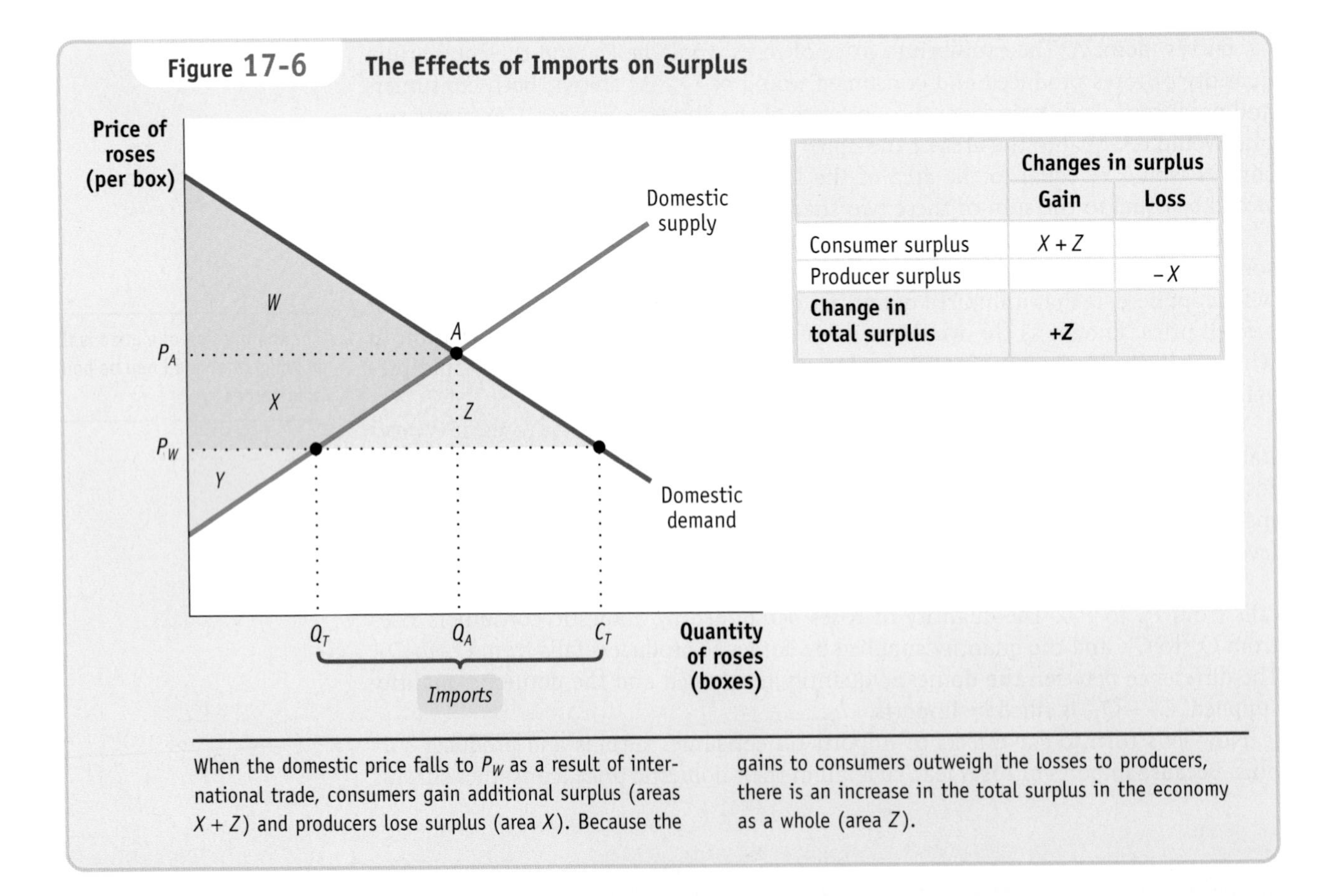

	Changes in surplus	
	Gain	**Loss**
Consumer surplus	$X + Z$	
Producer surplus		$-X$
Change in total surplus	**$+Z$**	

When the domestic price falls to P_W as a result of international trade, consumers gain additional surplus (areas $X + Z$) and producers lose surplus (area X). Because the gains to consumers outweigh the losses to producers, there is an increase in the total surplus in the economy as a whole (area Z).

surplus; it increases by the areas X and Z, so that it now equals the sum of W, X, and Z. At the same time, producers lose the area X in surplus, so that producer surplus now equals only Y.

The table in Figure 17-6 summarizes the changes in consumer and producer surplus when the rose market is opened to imports. Consumers gain surplus equal to the area $X + Z$. Producers lose surplus equal to the area X. So the sum of producer and consumer surplus—the total surplus generated in the rose market—increases by the area Z. As a result of trade, consumers gain and producers lose, but the gain to consumers exceeds the loss to producers.

This is an important result. We have just shown that opening up a market to imports leads to a net gain in total surplus, which is what we should have expected given the proposition that there are gains from international trade. However, we have also learned that although the country as a whole gains, some groups—in this case, domestic producers of roses—lose as a result of international trade. As we'll see shortly, the fact that international trade typically creates losers as well as winners is crucial for understanding the politics of trade policy.

We turn next to the case in which a country exports a good.

The Effects of Exports

Figure 17-7 shows the effects on a country when it exports a good, in this case a universal chainsaw winch. For this example, we assume that unlimited quantities of winches can be sold abroad at a given world price, P_W, which is higher than the price that would prevail in the domestic market in autarky, P_A.

The higher world price makes it profitable for exporters to buy winches domestically and sell them overseas. The purchases of domestic winches drives the domestic price up until the domestic price is equal to the world price. As a result, the quantity demanded by domestic consumers falls from Q_A to C_T, and the quantity supplied by domestic producers rises from Q_A to Q_T. This difference between domestic production and domestic consumption, $Q_T - C_T$, is exported.

Figure 17-7

The Domestic Market with Exports

Here the world price, P_W, is greater than the autarky price, P_A. When the economy is opened to international trade, some of the domestic supply is now exported. The domestic price, P_A, rises to the world price, P_W. As the price rises, the domestic quantity demanded falls from Q_A to C_T and domestic production rises from Q_A to Q_T. The remainder of the domestic quantity supplied, $Q_T - C_T$, is exported. >web...

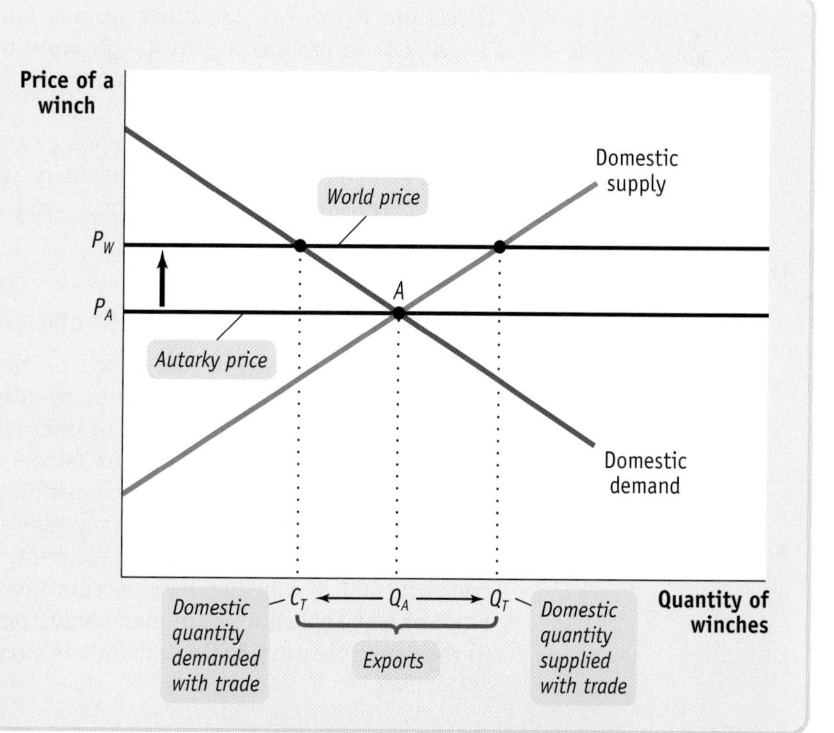

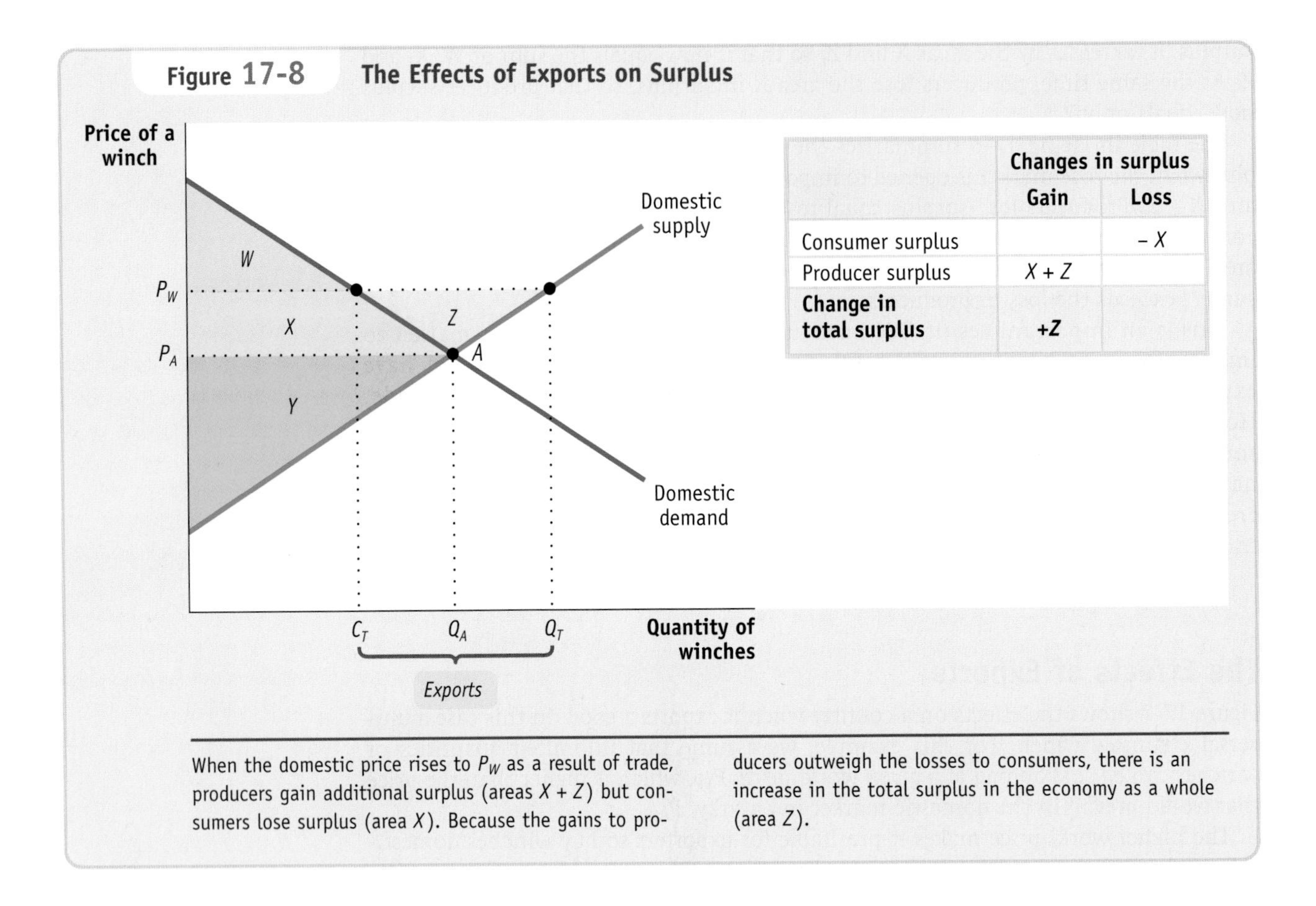

Figure 17-8 The Effects of Exports on Surplus

	Changes in surplus	
	Gain	Loss
Consumer surplus		$-X$
Producer surplus	$X + Z$	
Change in total surplus	**$+Z$**	

When the domestic price rises to P_W as a result of trade, producers gain additional surplus (areas $X + Z$) but consumers lose surplus (area X). Because the gains to producers outweigh the losses to consumers, there is an increase in the total surplus in the economy as a whole (area Z).

Like imports, exports lead to an overall gain in total surplus for the exporting country, but also create losers as well as winners. Figure 17-8 shows the effects of winch exports on producer and consumer surplus. In the absence of trade, the price of winches would be P_A. Consumer surplus in the absence of trade is the sum of the areas W and X, and producer surplus would be the area Y. As a result of trade, price rises from P_A to P_W, consumer surplus falls to W, and producer surplus rises to $Y + X + Z$. So producers gain $X + Z$, consumers lose X, and, as shown in the table accompanying the figure, the economy as a whole gains total surplus in the amount of Z.

We have learned, then, that imports of a particular good hurt domestic producers of that good but help domestic consumers, whereas exports of a particular good hurt domestic consumers but help domestic producers of that good. In each case, the gains are larger than the losses.

International Trade and Factor Markets

So far we have focused on the effects of international trade on producers and consumers in a particular industry. For many purposes this is a very helpful approach. But to understand the long-run effects of international trade on income distribution, this approach can be inadequate, because factors of production move between industries.

To see the problem, consider the position of Maria, a trained accountant who currently works for a Canadian company that grows flowers. If the economy is opened up to imports of roses from South America, the domestic rose-growing industry will contract, and it will hire fewer accountants. But accounting is a profession with employment opportunities in many industries, and Maria might well find a better job in the winch industry, which expands as a result of international trade. So it may not be appropriate to think of her as a producer of flowers who is hurt by competition from imported roses. Rather, what matters to her is the effect of international trade on the salaries of accountants, wherever they are employed. In other words, sometimes it is important to analyse the effect of trade on *factor prices*.

Earlier in this chapter we described the Heckscher-Ohlin model of trade, which states that comparative advantage is determined by a country's factor endowment. This model also suggests how international trade affects factor prices in a country: compared to autarky, international trade tends to raise the prices of factors that are abundantly available and reduce the prices of factors that are scarce.

We won't work this out in detail, but the idea is intuitively simple. Think of a country's industries as consisting of two kinds: **exporting industries,** which produce goods and services that are sold abroad, and **import-competing industries,** which produce goods and services that are also imported. Compared with autarky, international trade leads to higher production in exporting industries and lower production in import-competing industries. This indirectly increases the demand for the factors used by exporting industries and decreases the demand for factors used by import-competing industries. In addition, the Heckscher-Ohlin model says that a country tends to export goods that are intensive in its abundant factors and to import goods that are intensive in its scarce factors. *So international trade tends to increase the demand for factors that are abundant in our country compared with other countries, and to decrease the demand for factors that are scarce in our country compared with other countries. As a result, the prices of abundant factors tend to rise, and the prices of scarce factors tend to fall.*

Exporting industries produce goods and services that are sold abroad.

Import-competing industries produce goods and services that are also imported.

The Economics in Action on page 431 pointed out that Canadian exports tend to be either resource-intensive or human-capital-intensive, and Canadian imports tend to be unskilled-labour-intensive. This suggests that the effect of international trade on Canadian factor markets is to raise the price of resources and the wage rate of highly skilled workers, and to reduce the wage rate of unskilled workers.

This effect has been a source of some concern in recent years. Earnings inequality—the gap between the earnings of high-paid and low-paid workers—has increased over the last 25 years. Some economists believe that growing international trade is an important factor in that trend. If international trade has the effects predicted by the Heckscher-Ohlin model, it raises the earnings of highly skilled workers, who already have relatively high earnings, and lowers the earnings of less skilled workers, who already have relatively low earnings.

How important are these effects? In some historical episodes, the impacts of international trade on factor prices have been very large. As we explain in the Economics in Action that follows, the opening of transatlantic trade in the late nineteenth century had a large negative impact on land rents in Europe, hurting landowners but helping workers and owners of capital.

But interpreting the recent shifts is more difficult. First, the effects in Canada have been much smaller than those in the United States. Second, the large increase in inequality in the United States has set off a heated debate as to the cause. Increased international trade is one possible cause. However, technological change—such as the introduction of computers—that makes skilled workers even more productive is another. Meanwhile, dissenters point out that increases in inequality between observationally equivalent workers—that is, workers who have identical skills, education, and work experience—accounts for much of the increase in total inequality.[1] These economists think that declining relative minimum wages, deregulation, the decline of unions, and higher unemployment rates are also important in explaining recent increases in inequality in the United States.

[1]Daron Acemoglu, "Technical Change, Inequality, and the Labor Market", *Journal of Economic Literature* 40, no. 1 (2002): 7–72.

economics in action

Trade, Wages, and Land Prices in the Nineteenth Century

Beginning around 1870, there was an explosive growth of world trade in agricultural products, based largely on the steam engine. Steam-powered ships could cross the ocean much more quickly and reliably than sailing ships. Until about 1860, steamships had higher costs than sailing ships, but after that rates dropped sharply. At the same time, steam-powered rail transport made it possible to bring grain and other bulk goods cheaply from the interior to ports. The result was that land-abundant countries—Canada, the United States, Argentina, Australia—began shipping large quantities of agricultural goods to the densely populated, land-scarce countries of Europe.

This opening up of international trade led to higher prices of agricultural products, such as wheat, in exporting countries and a decline in their prices in importing countries. Notably, the difference between wheat prices in North America and England plunged.

The change in agricultural prices created both winners and losers on both sides of the Atlantic as factor prices adjusted. In England, land prices fell by half compared with average wages; landowners found their purchasing power sharply reduced, but workers benefited from cheaper food. In the United States, the reverse happened: land prices doubled compared with wages. Landowners did very well, but workers found the purchasing power of their wages dented by rising food prices.

Did the grain trade cause land prices to rise in Canada too? No. In Canada land prices were held in check by the availability of free homesteads (right up until 1914, and then off-and-on till 1939) to anyone wanting to claim one, and farm it; whereas, the free land had run out in the United States by 1890. This combination of free land in Canada and rising land prices in the United States led to one of the few periods in history where there was large-scale immigration into Canada from the United States. ■

< < < < < < < < < < < < < < < < < < < <

>> QUICK REVIEW

- The intersection of the *domestic demand curve* and the *domestic supply curve* determines the autarky price of a good. When a market is opened to international trade, the domestic price is driven to equal the *world price.*
- If the world price is lower than the autarky price, trade leads to imports, and the domestic price falls to the world price. There are overall gains from trade because the gain in consumer surplus exceeds the loss in producer surplus.
- If the world price is higher than the autarky price, trade leads to exports, and the domestic price rises to the world price. There are overall gains from trade because the gain in producer surplus exceeds the loss in consumer surplus.
- Trade leads to an expansion of *exporting industries,* which increases demand for a country's abundant factors, and a contraction of *import-competing industries,* which decreases demand for its scarce factors.

>>CHECK YOUR UNDERSTANDING 17-2

1. Due to a strike by truckers, trade in food between Canada and Mexico is halted. In autarky, the price of Mexican grapes is lower than that of Canadian grapes. Using a diagram of the Canadian domestic demand curve and the Canadian domestic supply curve for Canadian grapes, explain the effect of these events on the following:
   a. Canadian grape consumers' surplus
   b. Canadian grape producers' surplus
   c. Canadian total surplus
2. What effect do you think these events have on Mexican grape producers? Mexican grape pickers? Mexican grape consumers? Canadian grape pickers?

Solutions appear at back of book.

The Effects of Trade Protection

An economy has **free trade** when the government does not attempt either to reduce or to increase the levels of exports and imports that occur naturally as a result of supply and demand.

Ever since David Ricardo laid out the principle of comparative advantage in the early nineteenth century, most economists have advocated **free trade.** That is, they have argued that government policy should not attempt either to reduce or to increase the levels of exports and imports that occur naturally as a result of supply and demand. Despite the free-trade arguments of economists, however, many governments use taxes and other restrictions to limit imports. Much less frequently, governments offer subsidies to encourage exports. Policies that limit imports, usually with the goal of protecting domestic producers in import-competing industries from foreign competition, are known as **trade protection** or simply as **protection.**

Policies that limit imports are known as **trade protection** or simply as **protection.**

Let's look at the two most common protectionist policies, tariffs and import quotas, then turn to the reasons governments pursue these policies.

The Effects of a Tariff

A **tariff** is a form of excise tax, one that is levied only on sales of imported goods. For example, the Canadian government could declare that anyone bringing in roses from Colombia must pay a tariff of \$2 per rose, or \$200 per box of 100 roses. In the distant past, tariffs were an important source of government revenue because they were relatively easy to collect. But in the modern world, tariffs are usually intended to discourage imports and protect import-competing domestic producers rather than as a source of government revenue.

A **tariff** is a tax levied on imports.

The effect of a tariff is to raise both the price received by domestic producers and the price paid by domestic consumers. Suppose, for example, that our country imports roses, and a box of 100 roses is available on the world market at \$400. As we saw earlier, under free trade the domestic price would also be \$400. But if a tariff of \$200 per box is imposed, the domestic price will rise to \$600, and it won't be profitable to import roses unless the price in the domestic market is high enough to compensate importers for the cost of paying the tariff.

Figure 17-9 illustrates the effects of a tariff on rose imports. As before, we assume that P_W is the world price of roses. Before the tariff is imposed, imports have driven the domestic price down to P_W, so that pre-tariff domestic production is Q_1, pre-tariff domestic consumption is C_1, and pre-tariff imports are $C_1 - Q_1$.

Now suppose that the government imposes a tariff on each box of roses imported. As a consequence, it is no longer profitable to import roses unless the domestic price received by the importer is greater than or equal to the world price plus the tariff. So the domestic price rises to P_T, which is equal to the world price, P_W, plus the tariff.

Figure 17-9

The Effect of a Tariff

A tariff raises the domestic price of the good from P_W to P_T. Domestic demand shrinks from C_1 to C_2 and domestic supply increases from Q_1 to Q_2. As a result, imports—which had been $C_1 - Q_1$ before the tariff was imposed—shrink to $C_2 - Q_2$ after the tariff is imposed. >web...

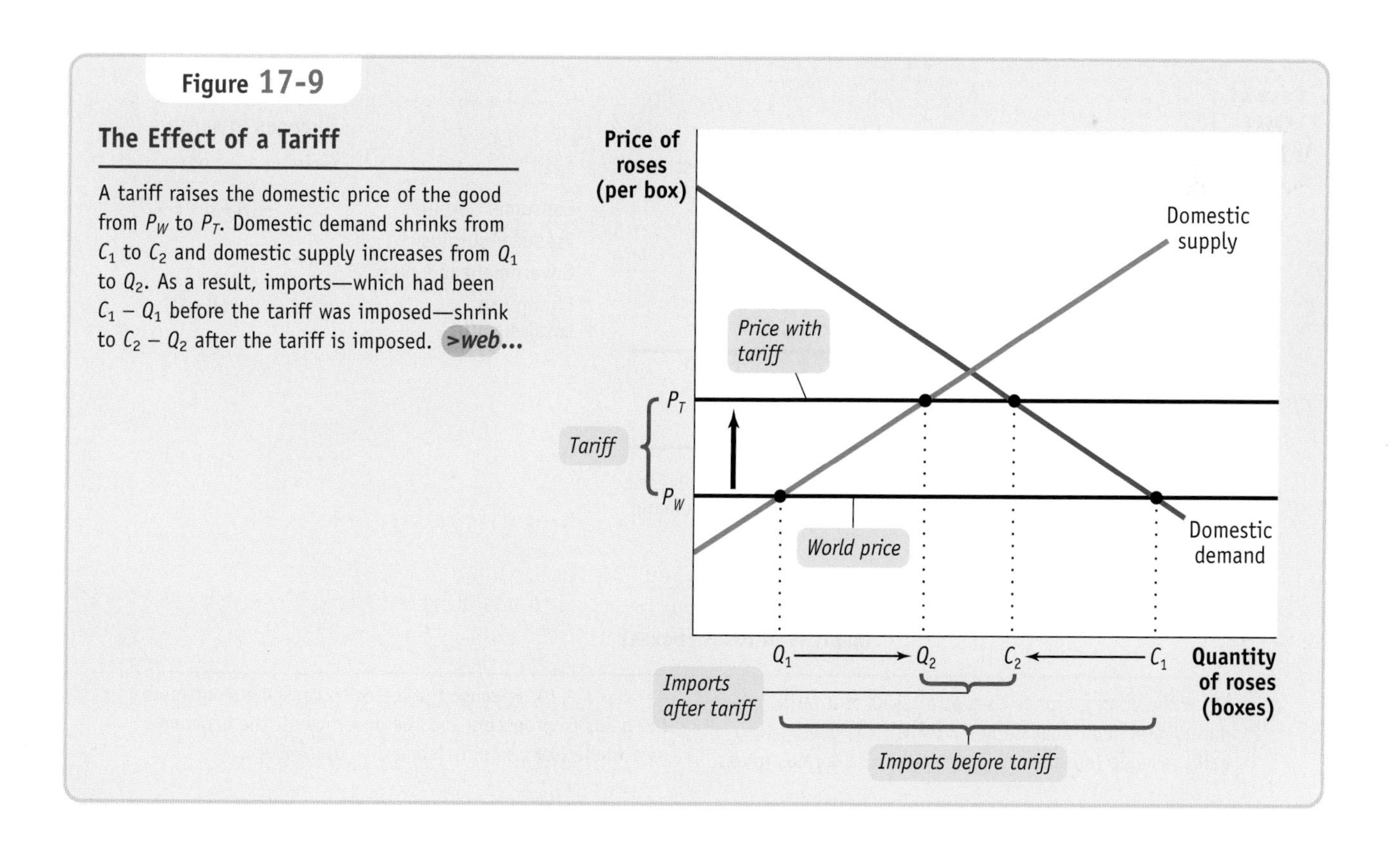

Domestic production rises to Q_2, domestic consumption falls to C_2, and imports fall to $C_2 - Q_2$.

A tariff, then, raises domestic prices, and leads to increased domestic production and reduced domestic consumption compared to the situation under free trade. Figure 17-10 shows the effects on producer and consumer surplus. There are three effects. First, the higher domestic price increases producer surplus, a gain equal to area *A*. Second, the higher domestic price reduces consumer surplus, a reduction equal to the sum of areas *A*, *B*, *C*, and *D*. Finally, the tariff yields revenue to the government. How much revenue? The government collects the tariff—which, remember, is equal to the difference between P_T and P_W on each of the $(C_2 - Q_2)$ roses imported. So total revenue is $(P_T - P_W) \times (C_2 - Q_2)$. This is equal to area *C*.

The welfare effects of a tariff are summarized in the table in Figure 17-10. Producers gain, consumers lose, the government gains. But consumer losses are greater than the sum of producer and government gains, leading to a net reduction in total surplus equal to areas $B + D$.

Recall that in Chapter 4 we analysed the effect of an excise tax—a tax on buyers or sellers of a good. We saw that an excise tax creates inefficiency, or deadweight loss, because it prevents mutually beneficial trades from occurring. The same is true of a tariff, where its deadweight loss on society is equal to the loss in total surplus represented by areas $B + D$. Tariffs generate deadweight losses because they create inefficiencies in two ways. First, some mutually beneficial trades go unexploited: some consumers who are willing to pay more than the world price, P_W, do not purchase the good, even though P_W is the true cost of a unit of the good to the economy. The cost of this inefficiency is represented in Figure 17-10 by area *D*. Second, the economy's resources are wasted on inefficient production: some producers whose cost exceeds P_W produce the good, even though an additional unit of the good can be purchased abroad for P_W. The cost of this inefficiency is represented in Figure 17-10 by area *B*.

Figure 17-10 A Tariff Reduces Total Surplus

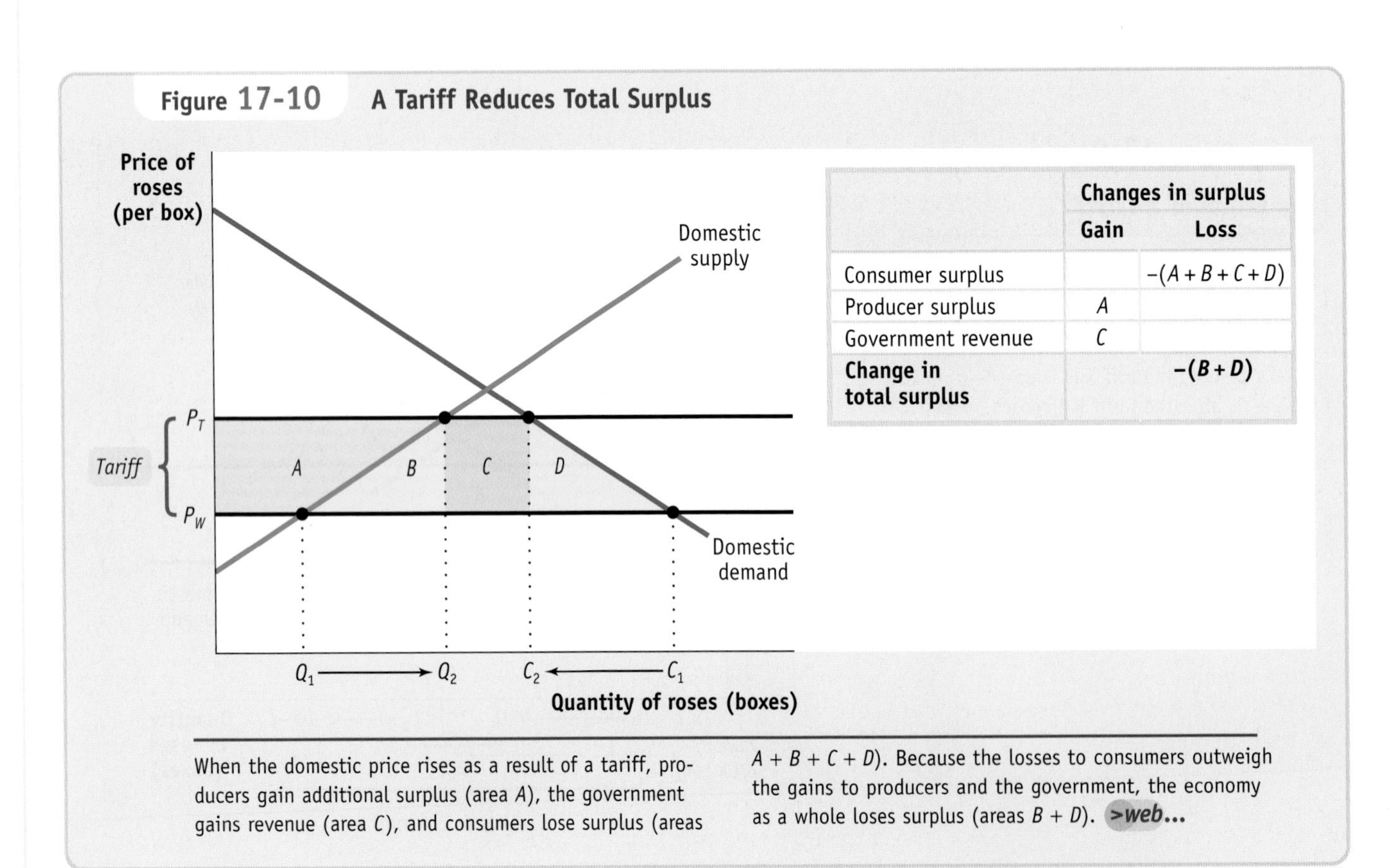

	Changes in surplus	
	Gain	Loss
Consumer surplus		$-(A + B + C + D)$
Producer surplus	*A*	
Government revenue	*C*	
Change in total surplus		$-(B + D)$

When the domestic price rises as a result of a tariff, producers gain additional surplus (area *A*), the government gains revenue (area *C*), and consumers lose surplus (areas $A + B + C + D$). Because the losses to consumers outweigh the gains to producers and the government, the economy as a whole loses surplus (areas $B + D$). **>web...**

The Effects of an Import Quota

An **import quota,** another form of trade protection, is a legal limit on the quantity of a good that can be imported. For example, a Canadian import quota on Colombian roses might limit the number imported each year to 50 million. Import quotas are usually administered through licenses: a number of licenses are issued, each giving the license-holder the right to import a limited quantity of the good each year.

An **import quota** is a legal limit on the quantity of a good that can be imported.

We discussed quotas in Chapter 4, where we saw that a quota on sales has the same effect as an excise tax, with one difference: the money that would otherwise have accrued to the government as tax revenue under an excise tax becomes quota rents to license-holders under a quota. Similarly, an import quota has the same effect as a tariff, with one difference: the money that would otherwise have been government revenue becomes quota rents to license-holders. Look again at Figure 17-10. An import quota that limits imports to $C_2 - Q_2$ will raise the domestic price of roses by the same amount as the tariff we considered previously. That is, it will raise the domestic price from P_W to P_T. However, area C will now represent quota rents rather than government revenue.

Who receives import licenses and so collects the quota rents? In the case of Canadian import protection, the answer may surprise you: the most important import licenses—mainly for clothing, to a lesser extent for sugar—are granted to foreign governments. Because the quota rents for most Canadian import quotas go to foreigners, the cost to the nation of such quotas is larger than that of a comparable tariff (a tariff that leads to the same level of imports). In Figure 17-10 the net loss to Canada from such an import quota would be equal to $B + C + D$, the difference between consumer losses and producer gains.

economics in action

Trade Protection in Canada

Canada was created as a nation by the British North America Act of 1867. At that time, Canada's western provinces were barely settled, most of the country's trading links were north-south, there was no transcontinental railway, and Canada's fledgling manufacturing faced stiff competition from the United States and Britain.

In an attempt to forge Canada's small, diverse, and far-flung people into a nation, the government of Sir John A. Macdonald implemented a "National Policy" in 1879. This policy had several pillars. It involved encouraging western settlement with homestead grants of free land. It involved building a transcontinental railway to transport manufactured goods from the East, and to route food from the West. And, most significant, it involved a system of high tariffs designed to protect and promote Canadian manufacturing. The aim of the National Policy was to replace existing north-south trading relationships with newly created east-west ones, to create a national market, and achieve a truly east-west transcontinental union. The tariffs were part of this nation-building enterprise.

Courtesy of the National Archives of Canada

Prime Minister John A. Macdonald, architect of the "National Policy" in 1879.

Since then, Canada and her infant industries have grown up. In 1947, Canada and 22 other countries signed the General Agreement on Tariffs and Trade (GATT) with the aim of reducing trade barriers. Successive waves of negotiations resulted in additional rounds of GATT, the most notable being the Uruguay Round, completed in 1994. This round had success on four broad fronts. First, it succeeded in reducing world tariffs by about 40%. Second, while Canada and the European Union prevented an agreement on liberalizing trade in agricultural goods, both were forced to replace agricultural quotas with "tariff equivalents". Those countries pushing for free trade in agricultural goods hoped that pressure would build for reduction of the high tariffs over subsequent decades. Third, quotas restricting trade in textiles and garments had to be phased out over a 10-year period ending January 1, 2005. Fourth, and perhaps most significant, the Uruguay Round eliminated the GATT structure and replaced it with the World Trade Organization, which has a formal dispute settlement mechanism whose rulings are binding on member governments.

Besides these multilateral agreements towards trade liberalization, Canada has also negotiated separately with the United States. In 1989 Canada and the United States signed a Free Trade Agreement (FTA), and in 1994 the North American Free Trade Agreement (NAFTA) extended it to include Mexico. Currently, there are negotiations to extend NAFTA from 3 members to 30 as it becomes a hemispheric Free Trade Area of the Americas (FTAA).

Canada today generally follows a policy of free trade, at least in comparison with other countries and in comparison with its own past. Most manufactured goods are subject to either no tariff or a low tariff. However, Canada does still limit imports on many agricultural goods, and protects its "cultural industries". Canada has always tried to protect its magazines, book publishers, film distributors, and other cultural industries from U.S. competition, and has succeeded in exempting them from both the FTA and NAFTA. ■

>> QUICK REVIEW

- Most economists advocate *free trade,* although many governments engage in *trade protection* of import-competing industries. The two most common protectionist policies are tariffs and import quotas. In rare instances, governments subsidize export industries.
- A *tariff* is a tax on imports. It raises the domestic price above the world price, leading to a fall in trade and total consumption and a rise in domestic production. Domestic producers and the government gain, but consumer losses more than offset this gain, leading to deadweight loss in total surplus.
- An *import quota* is a legal quantity limit on imports. Its effect is like that of a tariff, except that revenues—the quota rents—accrue to the license-holder, not to the government.

>> CHECK YOUR UNDERSTANDING 17-3

1. Suppose that the world price of butter is $0.50 per pound and the domestic price in autarky is $1.00 per pound. Use a diagram similar to Figure 17-9 to show the following:
   a. If there is free trade, domestic butter producers want the government to impose a tariff of no less than $0.50 per pound.
   b. What happens if a tariff of $0.25 per pound is imposed?
   c. What happens if a tariff greater than $0.50 per pound is imposed?
2. Suppose the government imposes an import quota rather than a tariff on butter. What quota limit would generate the same quantity of imports as a tariff of $0.50 per pound?

Solutions appear at back of book.

The Political Economy of Trade Protection

Up to this point we have focused on understanding the arguments in favour of free trade. We have presented arguments that international trade produces mutual benefits to the countries that engage in it. We have also argued that tariffs and import quotas, although they produce winners as well as losers, reduce total surplus. Yet many countries continue to impose tariffs and import quotas, and to enact other protectionist measures.

To understand why trade protection takes place, we will first look at some common justifications for protection. Then we will look at the politics of both trade protection and trade agreements, many of which are policed by international organizations such as the WTO.

Arguments for Trade Protection

Advocates of tariffs and import quotas offer a variety of arguments. We will deal with a number of them here.

Protect Domestic Jobs It is often suggested that we need to protect our industries from low-wage and low-cost foreign competitors. We have already touched on this when we discussed the pauper labour fallacy in the Pitfalls on page 428. But because the argument is so prevalent, it is worth considering Frederic Bastiat's satire of it.

Frederic Bastiat, a French economist and wit, published *Economic Sophisms* in 1845. In it he imagines a petition from all the producers of artificial light—manufacturers of candles, lanterns, street lamps, waxes, oils, and resins—to their elected representatives. They complain of unfair and ruinous foreign competition that produces at zero cost. From the moment it appears, all consumption of their products ceases. This foreign rival is none other than . . . the sun. So they request the passing of a law forbidding windows, chinks, or fissures in all buildings. Surely, they argue, producers of artificial light would gain from such a law. Then how could France lose?

Obviously, France would lose by denying a gratuitous gift of nature. But the petitioners argue that other goods have been excluded *because* and *in proportion as* they approximate gratuitous gifts. In particular, when coal, iron, wheat, and textiles come from abroad, and can be acquired for less labour than if they were produced domestically, the difference is no less a gratuitous gift. Yet, their importation is banned. Therefore, let's ban the sun!

Bastiat's point was, if we are going to trade, we gain the most by trading with the lowest-cost supplier. And why should everyone be denied the benefit of the sun to protect the narrow interests of a few producers?

Keep the Money at Home A corollary of the argument that we should protect domestic jobs is that we should spend on domestically produced goods (buy Canadian) in order to keep the money (and the jobs) at home. Besides ignoring the benefits of comparative advantage, this argument ignores the fact that foreign countries pay for Canadian goods using Canadian dollars. They get these dollars from us when we buy imports from them. So, our imports from other countries facilitate their purchase of our exports. In a global sense, if all countries restrict imports, they will all find it difficult to export. Globally, without imports there can be no exports.

Let's next turn our attention to arguments for trade protection that have some merit.

Adjustment Costs May Be Too High In demonstrating the mutual benefits of free trade, we assumed full employment as each country moved resources out of the import-competing industry and into the export industry. We acknowledged that jobs will be lost in the import-competing sector, but argued that jobs will be created in the export sector. On page 436 we mentioned that Maria, who is an accountant in the Canadian rose-growing industry, may lose her current job but may well find a better one in the winch-manufacturing industry. But what about Ted, who is a 50-year-old, unskilled worker in the rose-growing industry? What will happen to him?

The expansion of the export sector and the contraction of the import-competing sector may involve a redistribution of benefits not only among people but also among regions of a country. Workers may need to relocate and retrain. Older workers with low skills may suffer long-term unemployment and severe costs. How do we know that the long-term gains more than offset the short-term pain? Certainly, this is Frederic Bastiat's assumption in his satire about banning sunshine. But how do we know?

In reality, we don't know. We believe that the gains are permanent and the pain is temporary, which certainly lends a strong *presumption* that the benefits outweigh the costs. But in a positive science like economics, we need more than presumption and belief. We need to look at the evidence. Fortunately the tenth anniversary of the Canada–U.S. Free Trade Agreement (FTA), which occurred in 1999, produced many first-rate studies into its effects. One of the most thorough was by Daniel Trefler, published in the *American Economic Review.*

Trefler found that in Canada's import-competing industries where tariff cuts were the deepest, employment fell by 12% and productivity rose by 15% as low-productivity plants contracted. In the export industries that received the largest U.S. tariff cuts, plant-level productivity soared 14%, but there were no employment gains. On balance, the FTA was associated with "substantial employment losses". Nevertheless, he concludes that the FTA likely raised welfare as a whole through lower import prices and increased productivity. His results highlight the conflict between those who bear the short-run adjustment costs—displaced workers and struggling plants—and those who garner the long-run gains, that is, consumers and efficient plants.[2]

Most economists would argue that unemployed workers are not an argument against free trade as such, but rather highlight the need for assistance to those harmed by free trade, in the form of retraining and/or relocation.

The Infant Industry Argument Historically, the United Kingdom was the first country to industrialize. By the mid-nineteenth century, it had become the "workshop of the world"—meaning that it could produce almost every manufactured good, from textiles to machinery, more cheaply than any other country. Current manufacturing powers (including the United States, Germany, and Japan) protected themselves from British competition, and nurtured their fledgling manufacturing industries behind high tariff walls, until they were able to compete.

Whenever an industry has large economies of scale, costs will fall as the industry grows. In such industries, the first country in the field has a tremendous advantage. Theoretically, a temporary trade restriction can help an infant industry withstand foreign competition. The hope is that it will mature into a strong industry with an acquired, but real, comparative advantage. If such an industry were undercut and driven out of business at the beginning of its life, that comparative advantage might never develop.

The trouble is that some infant industries never grow up, but instead continue to rely on tariff protection for their existence. Even worse, it is very hard to tell which industries will be successful and which will not.

For example, the Japanese auto industry received extensive tariff protection in its early years, and grew up to be a strong competitor on the world stage. But recently Japanese subsidies to a number of high-tech industries such as semiconductors have been less successful. In Canada, federal government subsidies to Atomic Energy of Canada led to the development of the CANDU nuclear reactor. But sales of CANDU reactors have been at extremely subsidized rates, and the program has not come close to being a financial success. In Latin America in the 1950s, many countries imposed tariffs and import quotas on manufactured goods in an effort to nurture domestic industries. Most of the resulting industries remained inefficient, high-cost producers dependent on subsidies and tariff protection.

So, while the infant industry argument is theoretically valid, in practice, picking winners is very difficult.

Unfair Trade Practices It is accepted under international trade law (GATT) that a country can protect its domestic industry against unfair foreign competition. Suppose, for example, a foreign firm *dumps* its product—meaning that it sells below costs of production—in an effort to drive domestic producers out of business, so as to achieve and later exploit a monopoly position. In this case, the domestic government can impose *antidumping* duties on the offending firm. Alternatively, suppose foreign competitors are unfairly helped by subsidies from their governments. In this case *countervailing* duties may be levied on foreign imports. Antidumping and countervailing duties are often referred to as *trade-remedy laws*. However, all too often such laws are misused to protect inefficient domestic industries.

Indeed, several features of the antidumping system that is now in place in many countries make it highly protectionist. For example, antidumping law in the United States presumes guilt once a charge is made, and gives foreign producers only a short time to prove their innocence. Once implemented, U.S. antidumping duties often persist long after foreign firms alter the prices that gave rise to them.

---

[2]Daniel Trefler, "The Long and Short of the Canada-U.S. Free Trade Agreement", *American Economic Review* (September 2004): 870–895.

More fundamentally, the definition of dumping as "selling below costs of production" is not sophisticated enough. For example, if the industry were in a recession, the profit-maximizing price might be below average costs of production. Worse still, many countries consider it "dumping" for a firm to charge a lower price in the foreign market than in its domestic market. This precludes setting a profit-maximizing price in each market based on the varying elasticity of demand.

In the case of countervailing duties, it is easy to blame hidden subsidies for the inability of inefficient domestic producers to compete with foreign competition. For example, in the context of NAFTA, U.S. lumber producers allege that their Canadian counterparts receive a hidden subsidy from the government in terms of low stumpage fees. (These are the fees the government charges lumber companies for cutting trees on crown land.) In the United States stumpage fees are set by open auction, which results in higher fees. Canadian producers claim that higher U.S. stumpage fees reflect better services provided by the government by way of infrastructure. In the early 1990s two dispute-settlement panels found in favour of Canada, but mostly on narrow technical grounds. In response, the U.S. changed its law to get around those technical difficulties. In April 2004, another NAFTA dispute-settlement panel again ruled in favour of Canadian softwood lumber producers. Initially the U.S. International Trade Commission threatened to defy this ruling, but by September 2004 had decided to accept it.

Many worry that when one starts taking a microscope to every government tax and every government subsidy, no matter how indirect, there is no end to it. It leads them to worry about pressure for harmonization not just of taxes and subsidies but also of social programs, employment standards, and environmental legislation. The fact that numerous dispute-settlement panels have sided with Canada on the softwood lumber dispute should serve to allay these concerns.

Objectives Other Than Maximizing National Income The argument for free trade is that it maximizes national income. But this may not be a country's only goal. Economists cannot say that it is irrational for a society to sacrifice some income to achieve other goals.

For example, national security may be compromised by free trade if overseas sources of goods are vulnerable to disruption in times of international conflict; therefore a country might protect domestic suppliers of crucial goods with the aim of self-sufficiency in those goods. However, European nations took precisely the opposite approach. They reasoned that their security lay in integrating their economies so closely that another war between them would be impossible.

Just as imports may be vulnerable to disruption in times of international conflict, so might exports. Since September 11, 2001, Canadian exporters have had more difficulty moving their goods across the Canada/U.S. border. This matters because of Canada's increasing dependence on U.S. markets. With over 80% of Canada's exports going to the U.S., we are also vulnerable to U.S. decisions to ban Canadian products out of safety concerns. For example, the U.S. decision to ban Canadian beef because of a single case of BSE (or mad cow disease) severely damaged Alberta's beef industry. And some argue that this dependence may make Canada vulnerable to political pressure from the U.S. on other issues.

The goal of protecting cultural identity has led Canada to protect its magazines, books, and film distributors. It has also led to strict national content guidelines in broadcasting, in both TV and radio.

So, national security and cultural objectives may mitigate the adoption of free trade policies.

Environmental Concerns Pollution could be worsened by free trade if production is relocated from a country where environmental standards are high to one where they are low. Many fear that such relocations could produce political pressures leading to a general erosion of environmental standards in a "race to the bottom". Free traders counter by arguing that poor countries can't afford to be as concerned about the environment, and claim that trade leads to higher incomes, which in turn allows better environmental standards. Militant free traders even go so far as to argue that less developed countries have a comparative advantage in "dirty" industries, allowing environmental standards to be raised in developed countries.

The problem of different environmental standards doesn't arise within the European Union, because that is more than a free-trade area—Europe is moving towards a full economic (and perhaps political) union where all economic policies are harmonized. And in working to unify social and environmental policy, the European Union's goal is to raise standards to meet the highest levels achieved by member nations. Although particular interests may sometimes prevent this goal being met, at least we can say that standards are not being lowered.

Things are different in free-trade areas. A fundamental principle of the General Agreement on Tariffs and Trade (GATT) is that trade rules may not be used to force one country's domestic laws on another nation. This means that environmental goals must be met through the negotiation of multilateral agreements.

In the context of NAFTA, a parallel environmental agreement established the Commission for Environmental Cooperation (CEC) to address regional environmental concerns, help prevent environmental conflicts, and promote the enforcement of environmental law. One interesting feature is that it allows citizens to submit complaints to the CEC when a NAFTA member is failing to effectively enforce its own environmental law. The CEC is currently investigating a citizen complaint that the province of Québec has failed to apply its own law limiting carbon monoxide emissions from automobiles.

One of the CEC's important achievements is the development of an analytical framework for assessing the environmental effects of NAFTA. We eagerly await its findings.

In evaluating environmental concerns, it has been necessary to discuss specific international free-trade agreements, rather than free trade as an abstraction. This distinction needs drawing out.

The Difference Between Free Trade and Free Trade Agreements

Although free trade might in general be beneficial, any particular free-trade agreement may contain clauses that are detrimental to the interests of a particular country, or potentially shift the balance of power between citizens of all countries and corporations.

For example, many Canadians opposed the Canada–U.S. free-trade agreement on the grounds that it failed to specifically exclude water resources or publicly-provided Medicare. As a result, some commentators worry about Canada's potential loss of sovereignty over its water resources and the pressure towards privatization of Medicare. Both issues hinge on the principle that no country is allowed to give "preferential treatment" to its domestic industry. Thus, should the Province of Ontario, for example, allow a Canadian firm to export water from the Great Lakes, it may not be able to deny a U.S. firm the right to do the same thing. Similarly, should some component of the Canadian medical system be contracted out to a private Canadian firm, American firms could claim that any public provision of that aspect of Medicare violated the FTA (and now NAFTA). While such consequences are entirely speculative, Canadian governments have to be careful in deciding what they allow Canadian firms to do in these sensitive areas.

Increasingly, trade agreements are not primarily about the trade of goods and services but about the rights of multinational corporations and the protection of intellectual property. These issues are quite distinct from the benefits of trade that were our focus when studying comparative advantage. It is possible to be in favour of free trade in goods and services but oppose the strengthening of corporate or intellectual property rights.

International Trade Agreements and the World Trade Organization

Some trade agreements are between two or more countries; others are global, extending to most of the countries in the world. **International trade agreements** are treaties in which a country promises to engage in less trade protection against the exports of another country in return for a promise by the other country to do the same for its exports. Most world trade is now governed by such agreements.

International trade agreements are treaties in which a country promises to engage in less trade protection against the exports of other countries in return for a promise by other countries to do the same for its own exports.

The Canada–U.S. Free Trade Agreement The original Canadian objective behind the free-trade initiative with the United States was to have guaranteed access to the U.S. market. Canadian policy-makers worried about the strong protectionist tendencies that sometimes arise in the United States, partly because of the nature of the U.S. political system, and partly because producers are generally a more cohesive group than consumers and therefore have better lobbying success. Consequently, the interests of consumers often end up being sacrificed.

Canada's aim was to eliminate all the trade-remedy laws—which permit antidumping and countervailing duties—in both countries, and replace them with a system of rules that would be enforced through binding dispute settlement.

That aim was not achieved. There is a binding dispute-settlement mechanism consisting of binational panels. But each country is free to establish any laws it wishes, as long as those laws do not discriminate on the basis of nationality. This is known as the principle of *national treatment,* and it is a fundamental principle guiding the FTA and now NAFTA. Canada can have tough environmental laws and Mexico weak ones, but each country must enforce its rules equally on all firms in its jurisdiction regardless of nationality.

Ironically—given Canada's concerns about loss of sovereignty—this retention of sovereignty over trade-remedy laws has led to unfortunate consequences for the Canadian softwood lumber industry. The U.S. has consistently alleged that unfair government subsidies are given to this industry, and slapped countervailing duties on Canadian exports. As noted earlier, twice in the 1990s the binational panel found in favour of Canada, saying that the duties were not justified under U.S. law. However, the United States responded by modifying its trade-remedy law and reinstating its protectionist measures, necessitating another lengthy appeal process to the dispute-settlement mechanism. Despite such irritants as these, the dispute-settlement mechanism seems to have worked reasonably well on the whole. Numerous disputes have arisen and been referred to binational panels. Panel members have usually reacted as professionals rather than partisan nationals, and most cases have been decided on their merit.

The World Trade Organization Besides being a member of NAFTA, Canada has also taken part in global trade agreements, first through GATT and now through the **World Trade Organization** (or WTO). The WTO provides the framework for the massively complex negotiations involved in major international trade agreements (the full text of the last major agreement, approved in 1994, was 24,000 pages long). The WTO also has its own trade-dispute-settlement mechanism.

The **World Trade Organization** oversees international trade agreements and rules on disputes between countries over those arguments.

The WTO is sometimes, with great exaggeration, described as a world government. In fact, it has no army, no police, and no direct enforcement power. The grain of truth in that description is that when a country joins the WTO, it agrees to accept the organization's judgments—and these judgments apply not only to tariffs and import quotas but also to domestic policies that, according to the organization, are, in effect, trade protection under another name. So in joining the WTO, a country does give up a bit of its sovereignty.

The third ministerial conference of the WTO, held in Seattle in 1999, became an unexpected focus for citizens' protests. Four main concerns were expressed: first, that WTO rulings were systematically biased against the environment; second, that trade

FOR INQUIRING MINDS

THE MULTILATERAL AGREEMENT ON INVESTMENT

In the 1990s, Canada joined other members of the Organisation for Economic Co-operation and Development (OECD) in negotiations towards a Multilateral Agreement on Investment (MAI). The aim of the agreement was to reduce uncertainty about how foreign-located assets would be treated by foreign governments. The key idea was that all participating governments undertook to treat foreign-owned firms no differently from domestically owned firms, and it included a mechanism for settlements of disputes.

Essentially, the MAI was like a "Charter of Rights" for corporations. For example, the MAI would have given multinational corporations the right to compete against (or buy) domestic companies in *all* economic sectors, including strategic industries such as communications and defence; freedom from "performance requirements" placed on foreign investment; the right to convert currency and move money across borders without constraints; and the right to sue governments for cash damages (paid from public funds) for restitution if an investor claimed its rights had been violated under the agreement.

Many citizens groups around the world worried that the MAI would shift the balance of power in favour of corporations and against citizens and their elected governments. They worried that the MAI said nothing about corporate responsibilities, but instead seemed to eliminate them; and they worried that developing countries would be particularly at risk since foreign investments could easily overwhelm their infant industries. As a result, there was a clamour of public protest.

In addition, some countries (including Canada and France) pushed for some industries to be exempt. They wanted to be able to discriminate against foreign-owned firms in politically sensitive "cultural" industries such as publishing and broadcasting.

By 1998 negotiations had stalled and were subsequently abandoned. But the issue may well resurface, perhaps next time under the auspices of the WTO. After success in liberalizing trade in goods and services, attention seems to be swinging back towards accomplishing the same thing for foreign direct investment.

took precedence over human rights; third, that the WTO pushed a globalization agenda; and fourth and finally, that all this was achieved through secret meetings that bypassed the democratic process.

Trade officials argue that reaching a trade agreement is difficult enough without bringing other issues or non-governmental organizations to the negotiating table. They argue that human rights and workers' rights have to be taken to the International Labour Organization and dealt with there. Finally, they argue that the WTO is not intended as an environmental protection agency, although there is no necessary conflict between environmental protection and trade liberalization.

We'll investigate claims that the WTO undermines environmental protection laws in the next Economics in Action. First, let's clarify what is meant by the term "globalization".

The Globalization Controversy

"Globalization" differs from "free trade" in at least three important respects. First, globalization suggests the emergence of a single world economy and world culture. Free trade has never implied such close cultural, political, and economic ties as are now emerging.

Second, free trade is concerned with the free movement of goods and services, whereas globalization also implies the free movement of capital. This movement of capital reduces the sovereignty of all but the largest economies. For example, it limits a country's ability to redistribute income from capital to labour—if capital is taxed too heavily, it can move to a more accommodating location.

Third, with globalization we recognize that many multinational companies are huge. Many have worldwide sales that exceed the GDPs of many countries. America's largest multinational, General Motors, has annual sales about the size of the economy of Indonesia, which means it is bigger than Denmark, South Africa, or Norway.

Certainly, the sheer size of multinational corporations gives them enormous scope for achieving production efficiencies. It also gives them enormous economic and political influence. Some worry that their tremendous lobbying powers can subvert even our own democratic processes.

For example, in the late 1990s scientists working for Health Canada decided that a new growth hormone for dairy cattle was unsafe. (The hormone is called recombinant bovine somatotrophin, or rBST.) A lot of profit was at stake, and the scientists were pressured to change their report. After a Senate inquiry, a Labour Board hearing, and a federal court case, the scientists were vindicated. But the point is that the corporation in question had so much profit at stake, and the pressure it exerted was so great, that government officials caved in, although the scientists did not.

Less developed countries often court multinational corporations. They want the jobs, the training, and the transfer of technology that such investment seems to promise. Critics claim that ultimately many end up with foreign managers parachuted in, very little training of indigenous workers, very little technology transfer, and a stifling of indigenous/domestic industry. Domestic resources are exhausted, and most of the money flows out of the country.

Champions of globalization point to countries that have successfully industrialized by embracing the global economy—countries such as Taiwan, Singapore, South Korea, Indonesia, Malaysia, and even the Philippines. Certainly, globalization is bringing with it the relative decline of the economic power of the Western hemisphere. For example, in 1928, 84% of world's manufactured output came from the West; today this has fallen to less than 50%.

economics in action

Are WTO Rulings Biased Against the Environment?

WTO trading rules do not prohibit international environmental agreements—even when they interfere with trade. There are many examples of environmental agreements that allow for a ban on trade on certain products, or allow countries to restrict trade in certain circumstances. Two examples are the Montreal Protocol for Protection of the Ozone Layer, and the CITES Convention on International Trade on Endangered Species.

However, several decisions of the WTO's dispute-settlement mechanism have reinforced the public perception that it is biased against the environment. For example, in 1991 it overturned a U.S. ban on imported Mexican tuna that had been caught with nets that endangered the safety of dolphins (the Tuna/Dolphin Case). In 1996 it ruled that the U.S. Clean Air Act did not allow the United States to ban imports of gasoline from Venezuela and Brazil that contained an impurity (olephin) that caused pollution (the Reformulated Gasoline Case). In 1998, it ruled against the European Economic Community's ban on the importation of meat and meat products that had been treated with growth hormones (the Beef Hormone Case). And finally, in 1998 it ruled against a U.S. ban on imported shrimp and shrimp products from Southeast Asia (India, Malaysia, Pakistan, and Thailand), even though their fishing methods led to the drowning of species of turtles protected under the CITES convention (the Shrimp/Turtle Case).

Superficially, all these cases seem to confirm the view that the WTO is anti-environment. But looking deeper, we find there is a flip side containing some good news for the environment. Let's first compare the Tuna/Dolphin Case with the Shrimp/Turtle Case.

In the Tuna/Dolphin Case (1991) the affected species, dolphin, was not on an endangered species list. Therefore, following the principle that *no country can use trading rules to impose its domestic policies on another country,* the WTO overturned the U.S. ban on Mexican tuna. It ruled that labelling U.S. tuna as "dolphin-safe" was sufficient to give consumers the choice as to which tuna to buy.

On the other hand, in the Shrimp/Turtle Case (1998) the adversely affected species (turtles) was covered by the CITES convention on endangered species. This did give the United States the right to ban imports of products that put turtles at danger. However, the U.S. ban discriminated among WTO members. It banned the products of Southeast Asia but gave extra funding and extra time to countries in the Caribbean to adjust to using turtle-excluding devices (TEDs). Discrimination is not permitted under WTO rules, and so the U.S. ban was overturned.

With regard to the Reformulated Gasoline Case (1998), the WTO ruling insisted that the United States *did have the right to set standards for clean air* within its borders. But it overturned the U.S. ban on imported "dirty" gasoline because the United States applied stricter rules on the chemical characteristics of imported gasoline than it did on those of domestically refined gasoline, and was therefore discriminatory.

Finally, in the Beef Hormone Case (1998), the WTO ruling insisted that *member states do have the right to establish higher levels of health protection than the prevailing international standards*—as long as there is established scientific evidence linking the product to health problems. It overturned the European ban on hormone-treated beef for lack of evidence. This raises the question as to whether the WTO's standard of scientific proof is unrealistically high. However, in 2001 it upheld a European ban on asbestos products for health safety reasons, against the wishes of Canada, indicating that its standards of proof can at least sometimes be met.

The good news is that evolving jurisprudence of the WTO panels indicates that it is acceptable under WTO rules to employ trade measures for health or environmental reasons providing these measure are, first, necessary to achieve their objective (and this must be backed up with scientifically sound evidence); and, second, not discriminatory or a disguised restriction on trade. ■

>>QUICK REVIEW

- The major justifications for trade protection are preservation of domestic jobs, fear of high adjustment costs to free trade, protection of infant industries, protection against unfair foreign competition, and pursuance of non-economic goals like domestic security.
- Despite the deadweight losses, import protections are often imposed because groups representing import-competing industries are smaller and more cohesive, and therefore more influential, than groups of consumers.
- To further trade liberalization, countries engage in *international trade agreements.* Some agreements are for only a small number of countries, such as the North American Free Trade Agreement. The *World Trade Organization* (WTO) is a multinational organization that seeks to negotiate global trade agreements as well as adjudicate trade disputes between members.

>>CHECK YOUR UNDERSTANDING 17-4

1. In 2002 Canadian steel producers were adversely affected when the United States imposed tariffs on steel imports. These imports are an input in a large number and variety of U.S. industries. Explain why political lobbying to eliminate these tariffs is more likely to be effective than political lobbying to eliminate tariffs on consumer goods such as sugar or clothing.
2. Over the years, the WTO has increasingly found itself adjudicating trade disputes that involve not just tariffs or quota restrictions but also restrictions based on quality, health, and environmental considerations. Why do you think this has occurred? What method would you, as a WTO official, use to decide whether a quality, health, or environmental restriction is in violation of a free-trade agreement?

Solutions appear at back of book.

• A LOOK AHEAD •

As we move ahead to new topics, it is important that we carry with us the insights learned here about the logic of comparative advantage and the gains from international trade. They will provide us with a deeper understanding of what drives the world economy and of the reasons countries differ economically. In addition, the study of international trade teaches us how economic policies can create both winners and losers despite the fact that society as a whole gains, an important consideration in any study of how policies are actually made.

SUMMARY

1. International trade is of growing importance to Canada and of even greater importance to most other countries. International trade, like trade among individuals, arises from comparative advantage: the opportunity cost of producing an additional unit of a good is lower in some countries than in others. Goods and services purchased abroad are **imports;** those sold abroad are **exports.**
2. The **Ricardian model of international trade** assumes that opportunity costs are constant. It shows that there are gains from trade: two countries are better off with trade than in **autarky.**
3. In practice, comparative advantage reflects differences between countries in climate, factor endowments, and technology. The **Heckscher–Ohlin model** shows how differences in factor endowments determine comparative advantage: goods differ in **factor intensity,** and countries tend to export goods that are intensive in the factors they have in abundance.
4. The **domestic demand curve** and the **domestic supply curve** determine the price of a good in autarky. When international trade occurs, the domestic price is driven to equality with the **world price,** the price at which the good may be bought or sold abroad.
5. If the world price is below the autarky price, a good is imported. This leads to an increase in consumer surplus, a fall in producer surplus, and a gain in total surplus. If the world price is above the autarky price, a good is exported. This leads to an increase in producer surplus, a fall in consumer surplus, and a gain in total surplus.
6. International trade leads to expansion in **exporting industries** and contraction in **import-competing industries.** This raises the domestic demand for abundant factors of production, reduces the demand for scarce factors, and so affects factor prices.
7. Most economists advocate **free trade,** but in practice many governments engage in **trade protection.** The two most common forms of **protection** are tariffs and quotas; in rare instances, export industries are subsidized.
8. A **tariff** is a tax levied on imports. It raises the domestic price above the world price, hurting consumers, benefiting domestic producers, and generating government revenue. As a result, total surplus falls. An **import quota** is a legal limit on the quantity of a good that can be imported. It has the same effects as a tariff, except that the revenue goes not to the government but to those who receive import licenses.
9. Although several popular arguments have been made in favour of trade protection, in practice the main reason for protection is probably political: import-competing industries are well organized and well informed about how they gain from trade protection, while consumers are unaware of the costs they pay. Still, Canadian trade is fairly free, mainly because of the role of **international trade agreements,** in which countries agree to reduce trade protection against each other's exports. Trade negotiations are overseen, and the resulting agreements are enforced, by the **World Trade Organization.**

KEY TERMS

Imports, p. 424
Exports, p. 424
Ricardian model of international trade, p. 426
Autarky, p. 426
Factor intensity, p. 430
Heckscher–Ohlin model, p. 430
Domestic demand curve, p. 432
Domestic supply curve, p. 433
World price, p. 433
Exporting industries, p. 437
Import-competing industries, p. 437
Free trade, p. 438
Trade protection, p. 439
Protection, p. 439
Tariff, p. 439
Import quota, p. 441
International trade agreements, p. 447
World Trade Organization, p. 447

PROBLEMS

1. Assume Saudi Arabia and Canada face the production possibilities for oil and cars shown in the accompanying table.

Saudi Arabia		Canada	
Quantity of oil (millions of barrels)	Quantity of cars (millions)	Quantity of oil (millions of barrels)	Quantity of cars (millions)
0	4	0	10.0
200	3	100	7.5
400	2	200	5.0
600	1	300	2.5
800	0	400	0

   a. What is the opportunity cost of producing a car in Saudi Arabia? In Canada? What is the opportunity cost of producing a barrel of oil in Saudi Arabia? In Canada?

   b. Which country has the comparative advantage in producing oil? In producing cars?

   c. Suppose that in autarky, Saudi Arabia produces 200 million barrels of oil and 3 million cars; and that Canada produces 300 million barrels of oil and 2.5 million cars. Without trade, can Saudi Arabia produce more oil and more cars? Without trade, can Canada produce more oil *and* more cars?

2. The production possibilities for Canada and Saudi Arabia are given in Problem 1. Suppose now that each country specializes in the good in which it has the comparative advantage, and the two countries trade. Also assume that for each country the value of imports must equal the value of exports.

   a. What is the total quantity of oil produced? What is the total quantity of cars produced?

   b. Is it possible for Saudi Arabia to consume 400 million barrels of oil and 5 million cars, and for Canada to consume 400 million barrels of oil and 5 million cars?

   c. Suppose that, in fact, Saudi Arabia consumes 300 million barrels of oil and 4 million cars and Canada consumes 500 million barrels of oil and 6 million cars. How many barrels of oil does Canada import? How many cars does Canada export? Suppose a car costs $10,000 on the world market. How much, then, does a barrel of oil cost on the world market?

3. Both Canada and the United States produce lumber and music CDs with constant opportunity costs. The U.S. can produce either 10 tons of lumber and no CDs, or 1,000 CDs and no lumber, or any combination in between. Canada can produce either 8 tons of lumber and no CDs, or 400 CDs and no lumber, or any combination in between.

   a. Draw the U.S. and Canadian production possibility frontiers in two separate diagrams, with CDs on the horizontal axis and lumber on the vertical axis.

   b. In autarky, if the U.S. wants to consume 500 CDs, how much lumber can it consume at most? Label this point *A* in your diagram. Similarly, if Canada wants to consume 1 ton of lumber, how many CDs can it consume in autarky? Label this point C in your diagram.

   c. Which country has the absolute advantage in lumber production?

   d. Which country has the comparative advantage in lumber production?

   Suppose each country specializes in the good in which it has the comparative advantage, and there is trade.

   e. How many CDs does the U.S. produce? How much lumber does Canada produce?

   f. Is it possible for the U.S. to consume 500 CDs and 7 tons of lumber? Label this point *B* in your diagram. Is it possible for Canada at the same time to consume 500 CDs and 1 ton of lumber? Label this point *D* in your diagram.

4. For each of the following trade relationships, explain the likely source of the comparative advantage of each of the exporting countries.

   a. Canada exports software to Ecuador, and Ecuador exports roses to Canada.

   b. Canada exports executive airplanes to China, and China exports clothing to Canada.

   c. Canada exports wheat to Colombia, and Colombia exports coffee to Canada.

5. Shoes are labour-intensive and satellites are capital-intensive to produce. Canada has abundant capital. China has abundant labour. According to the Heckscher–Ohlin model, which good will China export? Which good will Canada export? In Canada, what will happen to the price of labour (the wage) and to the price of capital?

6. Before the North American Free Trade Agreement (NAFTA) gradually eliminated import tariffs on goods, the autarky price of tomatoes in Mexico was below the world price and in Canada was above the world price. Similarly, the autarky price of beef in Mexico was above the world price and in Canada was below the world price. Draw diagrams with domestic supply and demand curves for each country and each of the two goods. As a result of NAFTA, Canada now imports tomatoes from Mexico and Canada now exports beef to Mexico. How would you expect the following groups to be affected?

   a. Mexican and Canadian consumers of tomatoes. Illustrate the effect on consumer surplus in your diagram.

   b. Mexican and Canadian producers of tomatoes. Illustrate the effect on producer surplus in your diagram.

   c. Mexican and Canadian tomato workers.

   d. Mexican and Canadian consumers of beef. Illustrate the effect on consumer surplus in your diagram.

   e. Mexican and Canadian producers of beef. Illustrate the effect on producer surplus in your diagram.

   f. Mexican and Canadian beef workers.

7. The accompanying table indicates the Canadian domestic demand schedule and domestic supply schedule for executive jet airplanes. Suppose that the world price of an executive jet airplane is $10 million.

Price of jet (millions)	Quantity of jets demanded	Quantity of jets supplied
$12	100	1,000
11	150	900
10	200	800
9	250	700
8	300	600
7	350	500
6	400	400
5	450	300
4	500	200

a. In autarky, how many executive jet airplanes does Canada produce, and at what price are they bought and sold?

b. With trade, what will the price for executive jet airplanes be? Will Canada import or export airplanes? How many?

8. The accompanying table shows the Canadian domestic demand schedule and domestic supply schedule for apples. Suppose that the world price of apple is $0.30 per apple.

Price of apple	Quantity of apples demanded (thousands)	Quantity of apples supplied (thousands)
$1.00	2	11
0.90	4	10
0.80	6	9
0.70	8	8
0.60	10	7
0.50	12	6
0.40	14	5
0.30	16	4
0.20	18	3

a. Draw the Canadian domestic supply curve and domestic demand curve.

b. With free trade, how many apples will Canada import or export?

Suppose that the Canadian government imposes a tariff on apples of $0.20 per apple:

c. How many apples will Canada import or export after introduction of the tariff?

d. In your diagram, shade the gain or loss to the economy as a whole from the introduction of this tariff.

9. The Canadian domestic demand schedule and domestic supply schedule for apples was given in Problem 8. Suppose that the world price of apples is $0.30. Canada introduces an import quota of 3,000 apples. Draw the domestic demand and supply curves and answer the following questions.

a. What will the domestic price of apples be after introduction of the quota?

b. What is the value of the quota rents that importers of apples receive?

10. The accompanying diagram illustrates the Canadian domestic demand curve and domestic supply curve for textiles.

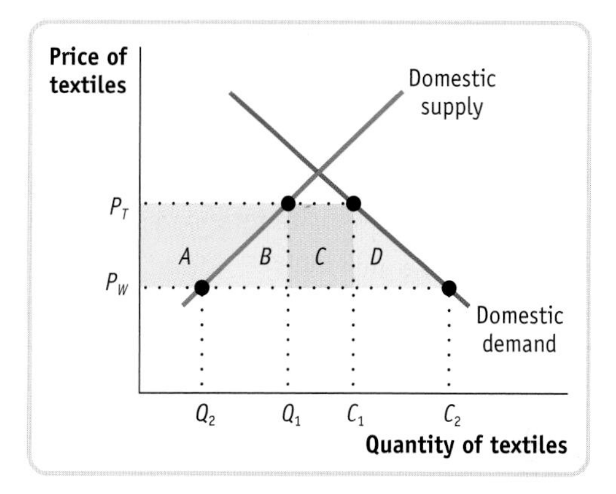

The world price of textiles is P_W. Canada currently imposes an import tariff on textiles, so the price of textiles is P_T. The Canadian government decides to eliminate the tariff. In terms of the areas marked in the diagram, answer the following questions.

a. What is the gain/loss in consumer surplus?

b. What is the gain/loss in producer surplus?

c. What is the gain/loss to the government?

d. What is the gain/loss to the economy as a whole?

11. As Canada has opened up to trade, it has lost many of its low-skill manufacturing jobs, but it has gained jobs in high-skill industries, such as the software industry. Explain whether Canada as a whole has been made better off by trade.

12. Canada is extremely protective of its agricultural industry, imposing very high tariffs on imports of milk products and poultry. This chapter presented several arguments for trade protection, amongst which were: to protect domestic jobs, to protect an infant industry, and to protect national security. For each of these arguments, discuss whether it is a valid justification for trade protection of Canadian agricultural products.

13. Producers in import-competing industries often make the following argument: "Other countries have an advantage in production of certain goods purely because workers abroad are paid lower wages. In fact, Canadian workers are much more productive than foreign workers. So import-competing industries need to be protected." Is this a valid argument? Explain your answer.

14. In World Trade Organization (WTO) negotiations, if a country agrees to reduce trade barriers (tariffs or quotas), it usually refers to this as a *concession* to other countries. Do you think that this terminology is appropriate?

15. The WTO's dispute-settlement mechanism overturned a European ban on imported beef from the United States (the Beef Hormone Case, 1998). However, the European Union ignored the ruling and has continued to refuse U.S. beef. Therefore, the WTO granted the United States the right to impose retaliatory tariffs of equivalent worth. (The estimated value of the lost U.S. beef exports is $117 million annually.) Therefore, the United States imposed 100% duties on a variety of European products, including European pork, French mustard, truffles, Roquefort cheese, and fruit juices.

Now suppose the WTO had overturned the European ban on asbestos products (produced mainly in Canada), but the European Union had continued to refuse these products. If Canada were given the right to impose retaliatory tariffs, would this hurt the European Union? Could it hurt Canada? Does this imply that the WTO should be strengthened, rather than weakened as some of its critics suggest?

>web... To continue your study and review of concepts in this chapter, please visit the Krugman/Wells website for quizzes, animated graph tutorials, web links to helpful resources, and more.

www.worthpublishers.com/krugmanwellsmyatt

chapter 18

>>Uncertainty, Risk, and Private Information

AFTER THE FLOOD

THE RED RIVER SYSTEM IS ONE OF the few river systems in Canada that flows north—first into Lake Winnipeg, and ultimately into the Hudson Bay. Because it flows north, the southern waters thaw while the northern reaches are still frozen. It should come as no surprise, then, that Winnipeg, built on the Red River's banks, has repeatedly suffered disastrous flooding—in 1950, 1966, 1979, and again, dramatically, in 1997.

In contrast, the floods that occurred in the Saguenay–Lac-Saint-Jean region of Québec in 1996 were completely unexpected. Torrential rains caused floodwaters so powerful they swept away a whole shopping complex, ripped apart homes, and buried cars under mud. It was the worst flood in the province's history. Scientists said it was a natural disaster likely to happen only once in 10,000 years. The government called it "an act of God".

Jacques Boissinot/AP Photo

The Saguenay flood: The risk of flooding is just one of the many uncertainties present in the real world.

Uncertainty is an important feature of real-world economies. Up to this point, we have assumed that people make decisions with knowledge of exactly how those decisions will affect their welfare. In reality, people often make economic decisions—such as whether to build a house near a river—without full knowledge of their future consequences. As the residents of Saguenay learned, making decisions when the future is uncertain carries with it the *risk* of loss.

Yet it is often possible for individuals to use markets to reduce the risk they face. Through insurance and other devices, the modern economy offers many ways for individuals to reduce their exposure to risk.

Does this mean that a market economy can solve all the problems created by uncertainty? Alas, no. Markets do very well at coping with situations in which nobody knows what will happen. But they run into trouble when some people know things that others do not—a situation known as *private information*. We'll see that private information can cause inefficiency by preventing mutually beneficial transactions.

In this chapter we'll examine the economics of risk and private information.

What you will learn in this chapter:

- That **risk** is an important feature of the economy, and that most people are **risk-averse**—they would like to avoid risk
- Why diminishing marginal utility makes people risk-averse and determines the **premium** they are willing to pay to reduce risk
- How risk can be traded, with risk-averse people paying others to assume part of their risk
- How exposure to risk can be reduced through **diversification** and **pooling**
- The special problems posed by **private information**—situations in which some people know things that other people do not

We'll start by looking at why people dislike risk. Then we'll explore how a market economy allows people to reduce risk, at a price. Finally, we'll turn to the special problems created when some people have information that others don't.

The Economics of Risk Aversion

In general, people don't like risk and are willing to pay a price to avoid it. Just think of all the money paid out for insurance premiums every year. But what exactly is risk? And why don't people like it? To answer these questions, we need to look briefly at the concept of *expected value* and the meaning of uncertainty. Then we can turn to why people dislike *risk.*

Expectations and Uncertainty

The Lee family doesn't know how big its dental bills will be next year. If all goes well, it won't have any dental expenses at all. Let's assume that there's a 50% chance of that happening. But if a family member requires a root canal and the children need braces, they will face dental expenses of $10,000. Let's assume that there's also a 50% chance that these high dental expenses will materialize.

A **random variable** is a variable with an uncertain future value.

The **expected value** of a random variable is the weighted average of all possible values, where the weights on each possible value correspond to the probability of that value occurring.

In this example—which is designed to illustrate a point, rather than to be realistic—the Lees' dental expenses for the coming year are a **random variable,** a variable that has an uncertain future value. No one can predict which of its possible values, or outcomes, a random variable will take. But that doesn't mean we can say nothing about the Lees' future dental expenses. On the contrary, an actuary (a person trained in evaluating uncertain future events) could calculate the **expected value** of expenses next year—the weighted average of all possible values, where the weights on each possible value correspond to the probability of that value occurring. In this example, the expected value of the Lees' dental expenses is $(0.5 \times \$0) + (0.5 \times \$10{,}000) = \$5{,}000$.

A **state of the world** is a possible future event.

To derive the general formula for the expected value of a random variable, we imagine that there are a number of different **states of the world,** possible future events. Each state is associated with a different realized value—the value that actually occurs—of the random variable. You don't know which state of the world will actually occur, but you can assign probabilities, one for each state of the world. Let's assume that P_1 is the probability of state 1, P_2 the probability of state 2, and so on. And you know the realized value of the random value in each state of the world: S_1 in state 1, S_2 in state 2, and so on. Let's also assume that there are N possible states. Then the expected value of the random variable is:

(18-1) *Expected value of a random variable*

$$EV = (P_1 \times S_1) + (P_2 \times S_2) + \ldots + (P_N \times S_N)$$

In the case of the Lee family, there are only two possible states of the world, each with a probability of 0.5.

Notice, however, that the Lee family doesn't actually expect to pay $5,000 in dental bills next year, regardless of what occurs. That's because in this example there is no state of the world in which the family pays exactly $5,000. Either the family pays nothing, or it pays $10,000. So the Lees face considerable uncertainty about their future dental expenses.

But what if the Lee family can buy insurance that will cover its dental expenses, whatever they turn out to be? Suppose, in particular, that the family can pay $5,000 up front in return for full coverage of whatever dental expenses actually arise during the coming year. Then the Lees' future dental expenses are no longer uncertain *for them:* in return for $5,000—an amount equal to the expected value of the dental expenses—the insurance company assumes all responsibility for paying those dental expenses. Would this be a good deal from the Lees' point of view?

Yes, it would—or at least most families would think so. Most people prefer, other things equal, to reduce **risk**—uncertainty about future outcomes. (We'll focus here on **financial risk,** in which the uncertainty is about monetary outcomes, as opposed to uncertainty about outcomes that can't be assigned a monetary value.) In fact, most people are willing to pay a substantial price to reduce their risk; that's why we have an insurance industry. But before we study the market for insurance, we need to understand why people feel that risk is a bad thing, an attitude that economists call *risk aversion.* The answer, as we'll now see, is a concept we first encountered in our analysis of consumer demand, back in Chapter 10: *diminishing marginal utility.*

Risk is uncertainty about future outcomes. When the uncertainty is about monetary outcomes, it becomes **financial risk.**

The Logic of Risk Aversion

To understand how diminishing marginal utility gives rise to risk aversion, we need to look not only at the Lees' dental costs but also at how those costs affect the income the family has left after dental expenses. Let's assume that the family knows that it will have an income of $30,000 next year. If the family has no dental expenses, it will be left with all of that income. If its dental expenses are $10,000, its income after dental expenses will be only $20,000. Since we have assumed that there is an equal chance of these two outcomes, the expected value of the Lees' income after dental expenses is (0.5 × $30,000) + (0.5 × $20,000) = $25,000. At times we will simply refer to this as expected income.

But as we'll now see, if the family's utility function has the shape typical of most families', its **expected utility**—the expected value of its total utility given uncertainty about future outcomes—is less than it would be if the family didn't face any risk and knew with certainty that its income after dental expenses would be $25,000.

Expected utility is the expected value of an individual's total utility given uncertainty about future outcomes.

To see why, we need to look at how total utility depends on income. Panel (a) of Figure 18-1 (page 458) shows a hypothetical utility function for the Lee family, where total utility depends on income—the amount of money the Lees have available for consumption of goods and services (after they have paid any dental bills). The table within the figure shows how the family's total utility varies over the income range of $20,000 to $30,000. As usual, the utility function is upward sloping, because more income leads to higher total utility. Notice as well that the curve gets flatter as we move up and to the right, which reflects diminishing marginal utility.

In Chapter 10 we applied the principle of diminishing marginal utility to individual goods and services: each successive unit of a good or service that a consumer purchases adds less to his or her total utility. The same principle applies to income used for consumption: each successive dollar of income adds less to total utility than the previous dollar. Panel (b) shows how marginal utility varies with income, confirming that marginal utility of income falls as income rises. As we'll see in a moment, diminishing marginal utility is the key to understanding the desire of individuals to reduce risk.

To analyse how a person's utility is affected by risk, economists start from the assumption that individuals facing uncertainty maximize their *expected* utility. We can use the data in Figure 18-1 to calculate the Lee family's expected utility. We'll first do the calculation assuming that the Lees have no insurance, and then we'll recalculate it assuming that they have purchased insurance.

Without insurance, if the Lees are lucky and don't incur any dental expenses, they will have an income of $30,000, generating total utility of 1,080 utils. But if they have no insurance and are unlucky, incurring $10,000 in dental expenses, they will have just $20,000 of their income to spend on consumption, and total utility of only 920 utils. So *without insurance,* the family's expected utility is (0.5 × 1,080) + (0.5 × 920) = 1,000 utils.

Now let's suppose that an insurance company offers to pay whatever dental expenses the family incurs during the next year in return for a **premium**—a payment to

A **premium** is a payment to an insurance company in return for the insurance company's promise to pay a claim in certain states of the world.

Figure 18-1 The Utility Function and Marginal Utility Curve of a Risk-Averse Family

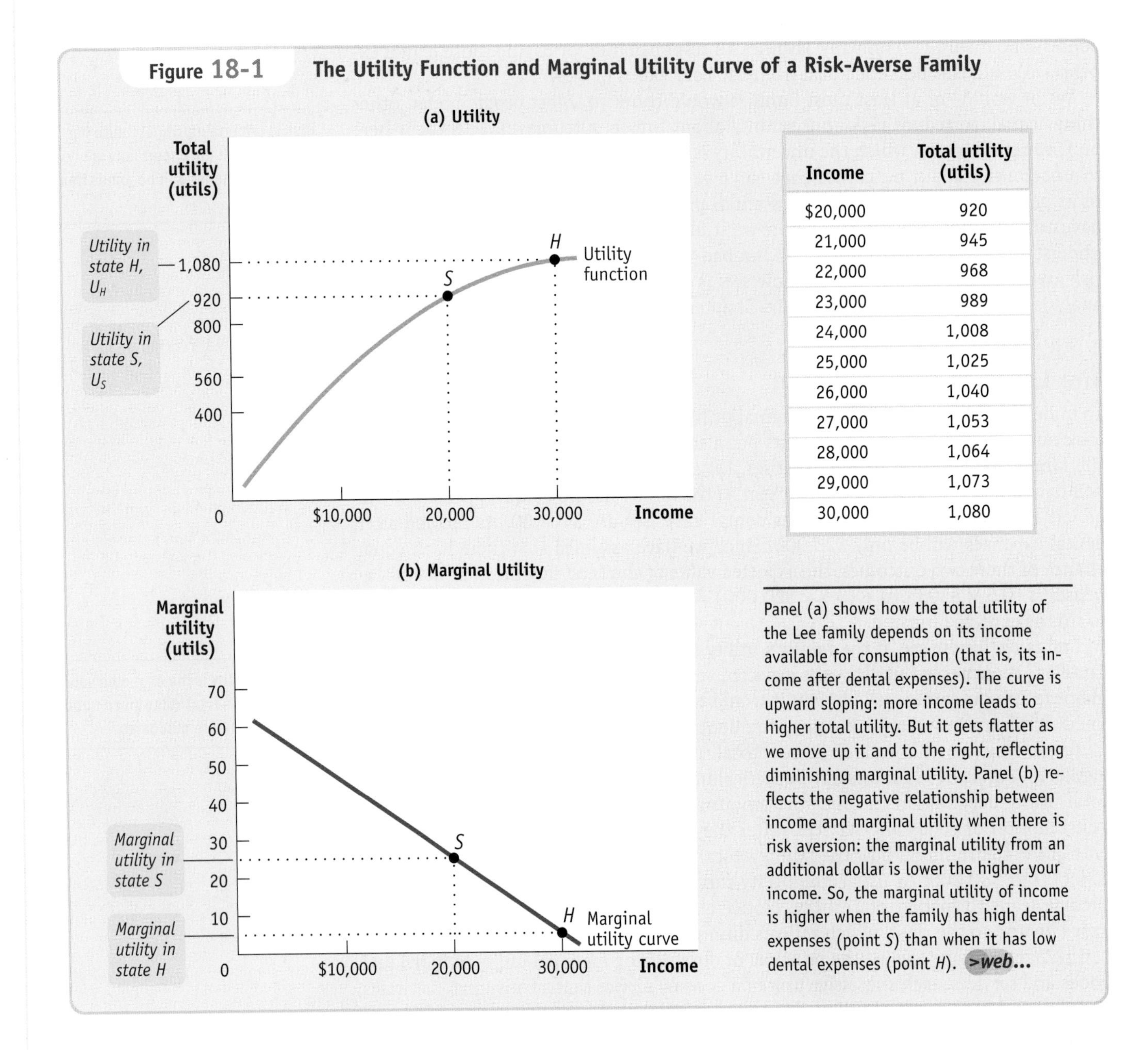

Income	Total utility (utils)
$20,000	920
21,000	945
22,000	968
23,000	989
24,000	1,008
25,000	1,025
26,000	1,040
27,000	1,053
28,000	1,064
29,000	1,073
30,000	1,080

Panel (a) shows how the total utility of the Lee family depends on its income available for consumption (that is, its income after dental expenses). The curve is upward sloping: more income leads to higher total utility. But it gets flatter as we move up it and to the right, reflecting diminishing marginal utility. Panel (b) reflects the negative relationship between income and marginal utility when there is risk aversion: the marginal utility from an additional dollar is lower the higher your income. So, the marginal utility of income is higher when the family has high dental expenses (point *S*) than when it has low dental expenses (point *H*). >web...

the insurance company—of $5,000. Note that the amount of the premium in this case is equal to the expected value of the Lees' dental expenses—the expected value of their future claim against the policy. An insurance policy with this feature, for which the premium is equal to the expected value of the claim, has a special name—a **fair insurance policy.**

A **fair insurance policy** is an insurance policy for which the premium is equal to the expected value of the claim.

If the family purchases this fair insurance policy, the expected value of its income available for consumption is the *same* as it would be without insurance: $25,000—that is, $30,000 minus the $5,000 premium. But the family's risk has been eliminated: the family has an income available for consumption of $25,000 *for sure,* which means that it receives the utility level associated with an income of $25,000. Reading from the table in Figure 18-1, we see that this utility level is 1,025 utils. Or to put it a slightly different way, their expected utility with insurance is $1 \times 1{,}025 = 1{,}025$ utils, because with insurance they will receive a utility of 1,025 utils with a probability of 1. And this is higher than the level of expected utility without insurance—only 1,000 utils. So by eliminating risk through the purchase of a fair insurance policy, the family increases its expected utility even though its expected income hasn't changed.

TABLE 18-1

The Effect of Fair Insurance on the Lee Family's Expected Income and Expected Utility

	Income in different states of the world			
	$0 in dental expenses (0.5 probability)	$10,000 in dental expenses (0.5 probability)	Expected income	Expected utility
Without insurance	$30,000	$20,000	(0.5 × $30,000) + (0.5 × $20,000) = $25,000	(0.5 × 1,080 utils) + (0.5 × 920 utils) = 1,000 utils
With fair insurance	$25,000	$25,000	(0.5 × $25,000) + (0.5 × $25,000) = $25,000	(0.5 × 1,025 utils) + (0.5 × 1,025 utils) = 1,025 utils

The calculations for this example are summarized in Table 18-1. This example shows that the Lees, like most people in real life, are **risk-averse:** they will choose to reduce the risk they face when the cost of that reduction leaves the expected value of their income or wealth unchanged. So the Lees, like most people, will be willing to buy fair insurance.

Risk-averse individuals will choose to reduce the risk they face when that reduction leaves the expected value of their income or wealth unchanged.

You might think that this result depends on the specific numbers we have chosen. In fact, however, the proposition that purchase of a fair insurance policy increases expected utility depends on only one assumption: diminishing marginal utility. The reason is that *with diminishing marginal utility, a dollar gained when income is low adds more to utility than a dollar lost when income is high.* That is, having an additional dollar matters more when you are facing hard times than when you are facing good times. And as we will shortly see, a fair insurance policy is desirable because it transfers a dollar from high-income states (where it is valued less) to low-income states (where it is valued more).

But first, let's see how diminishing marginal utility leads to risk aversion by examining expected utility more closely. In the case of the Lee family, there are two states of the world; let's call them *H* and *S*, for healthy and sick. In state *H* the family has no dental expenses; in state *S* it has $10,000 in dental expenses. Let's use the symbols U_H and U_S to represent the Lee family's utility in each state. Then the family's expected utility is

(18-2) $$\text{Expected utility} = (\text{Probability of healthy state} \times \text{Total utility in healthy state}) + (\text{Probability of sick state} \times \text{Total utility in sick state}) = (0.5 \times U_H) + (0.5 \times U_S)$$

The fair insurance policy *reduces* the family's income available for consumption in state *H* by $5,000, but it *increases* it in state *S* by the same amount. As we've just seen, we can use the utility function to directly calculate the effects of these changes on expected utility. But as we have also seen in many other contexts, we gain more insight into individual choice by focusing on *marginal* utility.

To use marginal utility to analyse the effects of fair insurance, let's imagine introducing the insurance a bit at a time, say in 5,000 small steps. At each of these steps, we reduce income in state *H* by $1 and simultaneously increase income in state *S* by $1. At each of these steps, utility in state *H* falls by the marginal utility of income in that state but utility in state S rises by the marginal utility of income in that state.

Now look again at panel (b) of Figure 18-1, which shows how marginal utility varies with income. Point *S* shows marginal utility when the Lee family's income is $20,000; point *H* shows marginal utility when income is $30,000. Clearly, marginal utility is higher when income after dental expenses is low. Because of diminishing marginal utility, an additional dollar of income adds more to utility when the family has low income (point *S*) than when it has high income (point *H*).

This tells us that the gain in expected utility from increasing income in state *S* is larger than the loss in expected utility from reducing income in state *H*. So at each step of the process of reducing risk, by transferring $1 of income from state *H* to state *S*, expected utility increases. This is the same as saying that the family is risk-averse; that is, risk aversion is a result of diminishing marginal utility.

Almost everyone is risk-averse, because almost everyone has diminishing marginal utility. But the degree of risk aversion varies among individuals—some people are more risk-averse than others. To illustrate this point, Figure 18-2 compares two individuals, Danny and Mel. We suppose that each of them earns the same income now but is confronted with the possibility of earning either $1,000 more or $1,000 less. Panel (a) shows how each individual's total utility would be affected by the change in income. Danny would gain very few utils from a rise in income, which moves him from *N* to H_D, but would lose a large number of utils from a fall in income, which moves him

Figure 18-2

Differences in Risk Aversion

Danny and Mel have different utility functions. Danny is highly risk-averse: a gain of $1,000 in income, which moves him from *N* to H_D, adds only a few utils to his total utility, but a $1,000 fall in income, which moves him from *N* to L_D, reduces his total utility by a large number of utils. By contrast, Mel gains almost as many utils from a $1,000 rise in income (the movement from *N* to H_M) as he loses from a $1,000 fall in income (the movement from *N* to L_M). This difference—reflected in the differing slopes of the two men's marginal utility curves—means that Danny would be willing to pay much more than Mel for insurance. >web...

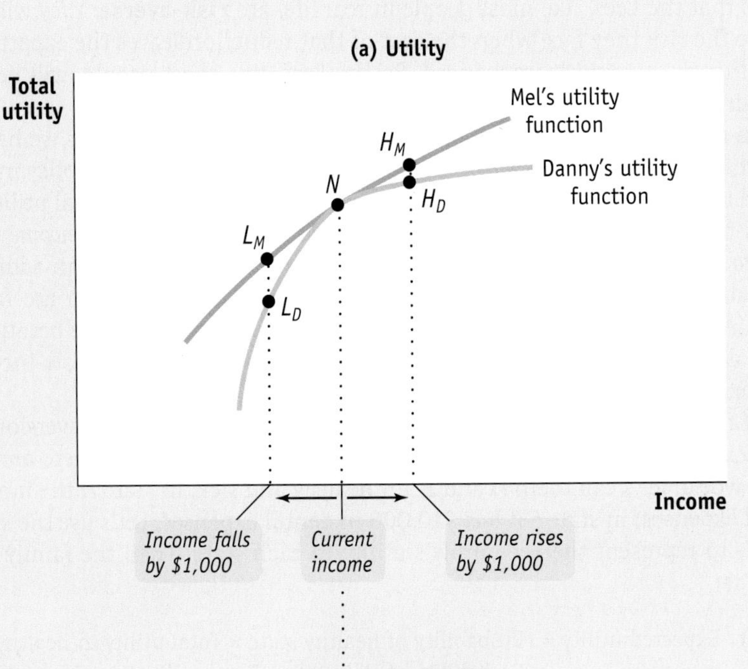

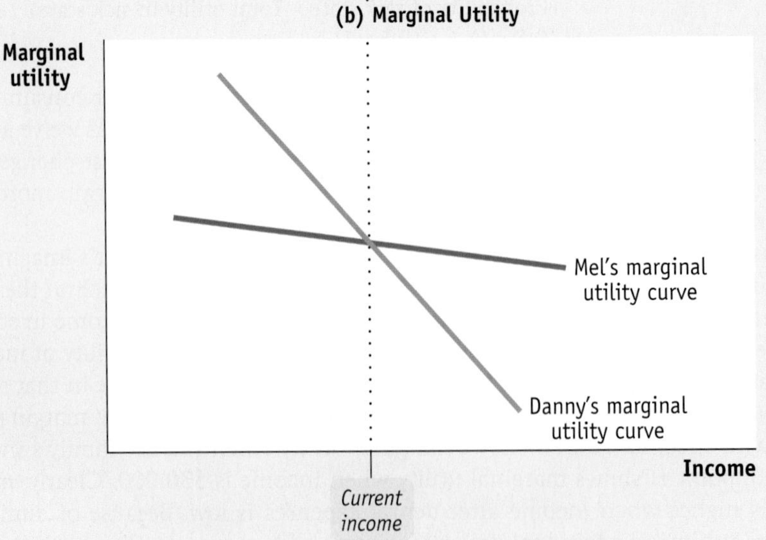

FOR INQUIRING MINDS

THE PARADOX OF GAMBLING

If most people are risk-averse and risk-averse individuals won't take a fair gamble, how come casinos do so much business? After all, a casino doesn't even offer gamblers a fair gamble: all the games in any gambling facility are designed so that, on average, the casino makes money. So why would anyone play their games?

You might argue that the gambling industry caters to the minority of people who are actually the opposite of risk-averse: risk-loving. But a glance at the customers of most casinos quickly refutes that hypothesis: most of them aren't daredevils who also skydive and hang-glide. Instead, most of them are ordinary people who have dental plans and life insurance and who wear seat belts. In other words, they are risk-averse like the rest of us.

So why do people gamble? Presumably because they enjoy the experience.

Also, gambling may be one of those areas where the assumption of rational behavior goes awry. Psychologists have concluded that gambling can be addictive in ways that are not that different from the addictive effects of smoking or hard recreational drugs. Taking dangerous drugs is irrational; so is excessive gambling. Alas, both happen all the same.

James Marshall/Corbis

Gambling: Enjoyment or addiction?

from N to L_D. That is, he is highly risk-averse. This is reflected in the lower part of the figure by his steeply declining marginal utility curve. Mel, though, would gain almost as many utils from higher income, which moves him from N to H_M, as he would lose from lower income, which moves him from N to L_M. He is barely risk-averse at all. This is reflected in his marginal utility curve, which is almost horizontal. So other things equal, Danny will gain a lot more utility from insurance than Mel will.

Individuals differ in risk aversion for two main reasons: differences in preferences and differences in initial income or wealth.

- *Differences in preferences.* Other things equal, people simply differ in how much their marginal utility is affected by their level of income. Someone whose marginal utility does not depend very much on income won't be highly risk-averse.
- *Differences in initial income or wealth.* The possible loss of $1,000 makes a big difference to a family living below the poverty line; it makes very little difference to someone who earns $1 million a year. In general, people with high incomes or high wealth will be less risk-averse.

Differences in risk aversion have an important consequence: they affect how much an individual is willing to pay to avoid risk.

Paying to Avoid Risk

The risk-averse Lee family is clearly better off taking out a fair insurance policy—a policy that leaves their expected income unchanged but eliminates their risk. Unfortunately, real insurance policies are rarely fair: because insurance companies have to cover other costs,

PITFALLS

BEFORE THE FACT VERSUS AFTER THE FACT

Why is an insurance policy different from a doughnut?

No, it's not a riddle. Although the supply and demand for insurance behave like the supply and demand for any good or service, the payoff is very different. When you buy a doughnut, you know what you're going to get; when you buy insurance, by definition you *don't* know what you're going to get. If you bought fully comprehensive car insurance and then didn't have an accident where you were at fault, you got nothing from the policy except peace of mind, and you might wish you hadn't bothered. But if you did have an accident where you were at fault, you probably wished that you had bought the most expensive policy with the smallest deductibles.

This means we have to be careful in assessing the rationality of insurance purchases (or, for that matter, any decision made in the face of uncertainty). *After the fact*—after the uncertainty has been resolved—such decisions are almost always subject to second-guessing. But that doesn't mean that the decision was wrong *before the fact,* given the information available at the time.

One highly successful stock market investor told us that he never looks back—that as long as he believes he made the right decision given what he knew when he made it, he never reproaches himself if things turn out badly. That's the right attitude, and it almost surely contributes to his success.

such as salaries for salespeople and actuaries, they charge more than they expect to pay in claims. Will the Lee family still want to purchase an "unfair" insurance policy—one for which the premium is larger than the expected claim?

It depends on the size of the premium. Look again at Table 18-1. We know that without insurance expected utility is 1,000 utils and that insurance costing $5,000 raises expected utility to 1,025 utils. If the premium were $6,000, the Lees would be left with an income of $24,000, which, as you can see from Figure 18-1, would give them a total utility of 1,008 utils—which is still higher than their expected utility if they had no insurance at all. So the Lees would be willing to buy insurance with a $6,000 premium. But they wouldn't be willing to pay $7,000, which would reduce their income to $23,000 and their total utility to 989 utils.

This example shows that risk-averse individuals are willing to make deals that reduce their expected income but also reduce their risk: they are willing to pay a premium that exceeds their expected claim. The more risk-averse they are, the higher the premium they are willing to pay. That willingness to pay is what makes the insurance industry possible.

economics in action

Warranties

Many expensive consumer goods—stereos, major appliances, cars—come with some form of *warranty*. Typically, the manufacturer guarantees to repair or replace the item if something goes wrong with it during some specified period after purchase—usually six months or one year.

Why do manufacturers offer warranties? Part of the answer is that warranties *signal* to consumers that the goods are of high quality (see the discussion of private information later in this chapter). But mainly warranties are a form of consumer insurance. For many people, the cost of repairing or replacing an expensive item like a refrigerator—or, worse yet, a car—would be a serious burden. If they were obliged to come up with the cash, their consumption of other goods would be restricted; as a result, their marginal utility of income would be higher than if they didn't have to pay for repairs.

So a warranty that covers the cost of repair or replacement increases the consumer's expected utility, even if the cost of the warranty is greater than the expected future claim paid by the manufacturer. ■

< < < < < < < < < < < < < < < < < < <

>> QUICK REVIEW

- Uncertainty about future outcomes entails *risk*. When faced with uncertainty, a consumer chooses the option that yields the highest level of *expected utility*.
- Most people are *risk-averse:* they would be willing to purchase a *fair insurance* policy—a policy in which the premium is equal to the expected value of the claim.
- Risk aversion arises from diminishing marginal utility. Differences in preferences and in income or wealth lead to differences in risk aversion.
- Depending on the size of the *premium*, a risk-averse person may be willing to purchase an "unfair" insurance policy—a policy with a premium larger than the expected claim. The greater your risk aversion, the greater the premium you are willing to pay.

>>CHECK YOUR UNDERSTANDING 18-1

1. In which of the following circumstances would you be more likely to buy fully comprehensive car insurance (that covers your loss even when you're to blame)?
   a. You must work to pay your living expenses, and you need a car to get to work.
   b. Your parents are wealthy and can easily buy you another car if you need it.
2. Karma's income next year is uncertain: there is a 60% probability she will make $22,000 and a 40% probability she will make $35,000. The accompanying table shows some income and utility levels for Karma:

Income	Total utility (utils)
$22,000	850
25,000	1,014
26,000	1,056
35,000	1,260

   a. What is Karma's expected income? her expected utility?
   b. What certain income level leaves her as well off as her uncertain income? What does this imply about Karma's attitudes toward risk? Explain.
   c. Would Karma be willing to pay some amount of money greater than zero for an insurance policy that guarantees her an income of $26,000? Explain.

Solutions appear at back of book.

Buying, Selling, and Reducing Risk

Lloyd's of London is the oldest existing commercial insurance company, and it is an institution with an illustrious past. Originally formed in the eighteenth century as a commercial venture to help merchants cope with the risks of commerce, it grew in the heyday of the British Empire into a mainstay of imperial trade.

The basic idea of Lloyd's was simple. In the eighteenth century, shipping goods via sailing vessels was risky: the chance that a ship would sink in a storm or be captured by pirates was fairly high. The merchant who owned the ship and its cargo could easily be ruined financially by such an event. Lloyd's matched shipowners seeking insurance with wealthy investors who promised to compensate a merchant if his ship was lost. In return, the merchant paid the investor a fee in advance; if his ship *didn't* sink, the investor still kept the fee. In effect, the merchant paid a price to relieve himself of risk. By matching people who wanted to purchase insurance with people who wanted to provide it, Lloyd's performed the functions of a market. The fact that British merchants could use Lloyd's to reduce their risk made many more people in Britain willing to undertake merchant trade.

Insurance companies have changed quite a lot from the early days of Lloyd's. They no longer consist of wealthy individuals deciding on insurance deals over port and boiled mutton. But asking why Lloyd's worked to the mutual benefit of merchants and investors is a good way to understand how the market economy as a whole "trades" and thereby transforms risk.

The insurance industry rests on two principles. The first is that trade in risk, like trade in any good or service, can produce mutual gains. In this case, the gains come when people who are less willing to bear risk transfer it to people who are more willing to bear it. The second is that some risk can be made to disappear through *diversification.* Let's consider each principle in turn.

Trading Risk

It may seem a bit strange to talk about "trading" risk. After all, risk is a bad thing—and aren't we supposed to be trading goods and services?

But people often trade away things they don't like to other people who dislike them less. Suppose you have just bought a house for $100,000, the average price for a house in your community. But you have now learned, to your horror, that the building next door is being turned into an all-night disco. You want to sell the house immediately and are willing to accept $95,000 for it. But who will now be willing to buy it? The answer: a person who doesn't really mind late-night noise. Such a person might be willing to pay up to $100,000. So there is an opportunity here for a mutually beneficial deal—you are willing to sell for as little as $95,000, and the other person is willing to pay as much as $100,000, so any price in between will benefit both of you.

The key point is that the two parties have different sensitivities to noise, which enables those who most dislike noise, in effect, to pay other people to make their lives quieter. Trading risk works exactly the same way: people who want to reduce the risk they face can pay other people who are less sensitive to risk to take some of their risk away.

As we saw in the previous section, individual preferences account for some of the variations in people's attitudes towards risk, but differences in income and wealth are probably the principal reason behind different risk sensitivities. Lloyd's made money by matching wealthy investors who were more risk-tolerant with less wealthy and therefore more risk-averse shipowners.

Suppose, staying with our Lloyd's of London story, that a merchant whose ship went down would lose £1,000, and that there was a 10% chance of such a disaster. The expected loss in this case, then, would be $0.10 \times$ £1,000 = £100. But the merchant, whose whole livelihood was at stake, might have been willing to pay £150 to be compensated in the amount of £1,000 if the ship sank. Meanwhile, a wealthy investor for whom the loss of £1,000 was no big deal would have been willing to take this risk for a return only slightly better than the expected loss—say, £110. Clearly, there is room for a mutually beneficial deal here: the merchant pays something less than £150 and more than £110—say, £130—in return for compensation if the ship goes down. In effect, he has paid a less risk-averse individual to bear the burden of his risk. Everyone has been made better off by this transaction.

The funds that an insurer places at risk when providing insurance is called his or her **capital at risk**.

The funds that an insurer places at risk when providing insurance are called his or her **capital at risk.** In our example, the wealthy Lloyd's investor places capital of £1,000 at risk in return for a premium of £130. In general, the amount of capital that potential insurers are willing to place at risk depends, other things equal, on the premium offered. If every ship is worth £1,000 and has a 10% chance of going down, nobody would offer insurance for less than a £100 premium, equal to the expected claim. In fact, only an investor who isn't risk-averse at all would be willing to offer a policy at that price, because accepting a £100 premium would leave the insurer's expected income unchanged while increasing his or her risk. Suppose there is one investor who isn't risk-averse; but the next most willing investor is slightly risk-averse and insists on a £105 premium. The next investor, being somewhat more risk-averse, demands a premium of £110, and so on. By varying the premium and asking how many insurers would be willing to provide insurance at that premium, we can trace out a supply curve for insurance, as shown in Figure 18-3. As the premium increases as we move up the supply curve, more risk-averse investors are induced to provide coverage.

Meanwhile, potential buyers will consider their willingness to pay a given premium, defining the demand curve for insurance. In Figure 18-4, the highest premium that any shipowner is willing to pay is £200. Who's willing to pay this? The most risk-averse shipowner, of course. A slightly less risk-averse shipowner might be willing to pay £190, an even slightly less risk-averse shipowner is willing to pay £180, and so on.

Now imagine a market in which there are thousands of shipowners and potential insurers, so that the supply and demand curves for insurance are smooth lines. In this market, as in markets for ordinary goods and services, there will be an equilibrium price and quantity. Figure 18-5 illustrates such a market equilibrium at a premium of £130, with a total quantity of 5,000 policies bought and sold, representing a total capital at risk of £5,000,000.

Figure 18-3

The Supply of Insurance

This is the supply of insurance policies to provide £1,000 in coverage to a merchant ship that has a 10% chance of being lost. Each investor has £1,000 of capital at risk. The lowest possible premium at which a policy is offered is £100, equal to the expected claim, and only a non-risk-averse investor is willing to supply this policy. As the premium increases, investors who are more risk-averse are induced to supply policies to the market, increasing the quantity of policies supplied.

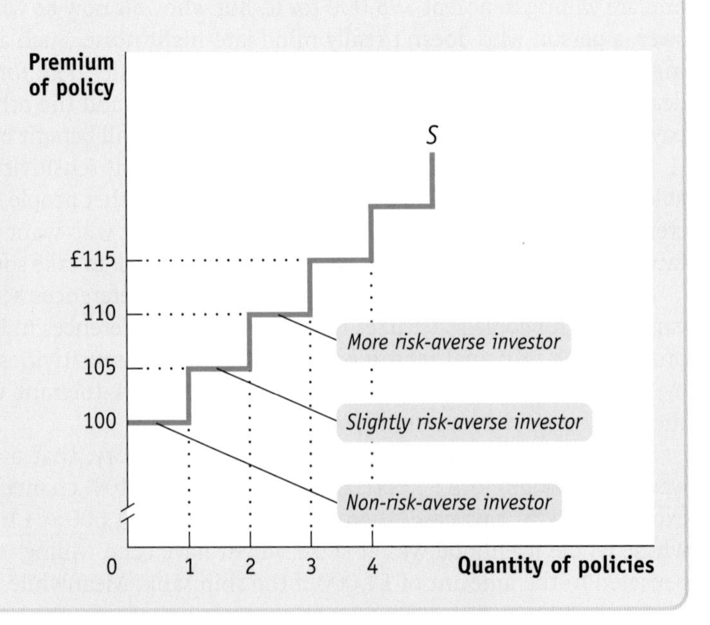

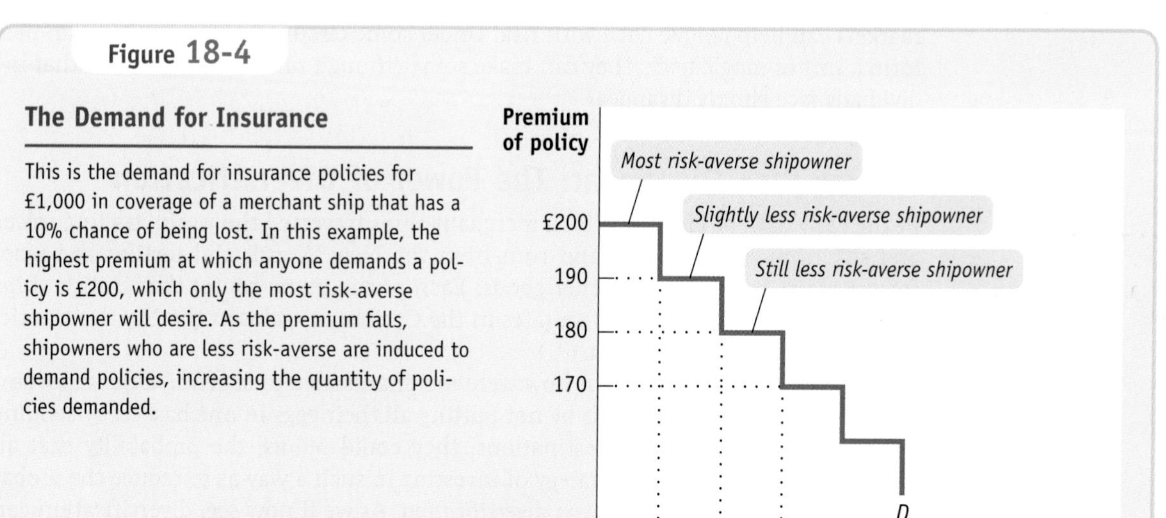

Figure 18-4

The Demand for Insurance

This is the demand for insurance policies for £1,000 in coverage of a merchant ship that has a 10% chance of being lost. In this example, the highest premium at which anyone demands a policy is £200, which only the most risk-averse shipowner will desire. As the premium falls, shipowners who are less risk-averse are induced to demand policies, increasing the quantity of policies demanded.

Notice that in this market, risk is transferred from the people who most want to get rid of it (the most risk-averse shipowners) to the people least bothered by risk (the least risk-averse investors). So just as markets for goods and services typically produce an efficient allocation of resources, markets for risk also typically lead to an **efficient allocation of risk**—an allocation of risk in which those who are most willing to bear risk are those who end up bearing it. But as in the case of the markets for goods and services, there is an important qualification to this result: there are well-defined cases in which the market for risk fails to achieve efficiency. These arise from the presence of private information, an important topic that we will cover in the next section.

An **efficient allocation of risk** is an allocation of risk in which those who are most willing to bear risk are those who end up bearing it.

The trading of risk between individuals who differ in their degree of risk aversion plays an extremely important role in the economy, but it is not the only way that

Figure 18-5

The Insurance Market

Here we represent the hypothetical market for insuring a merchant ship, where each ship requires £1,000 in coverage. The demand curve is made up of shipowners who wish to buy insurance, and the supply curve is made up of wealthy investors who wish to supply insurance. In this example, at a premium of £200, only the most risk-averse shipowners will purchase insurance; at a premium of £100, only non-risk-averse investors are willing to supply insurance. The equilibrium is at a premium of £130 with 5,000 policies bought and sold. In the absence of private information, the insurance market leads to an efficient allocation of risk. >web...

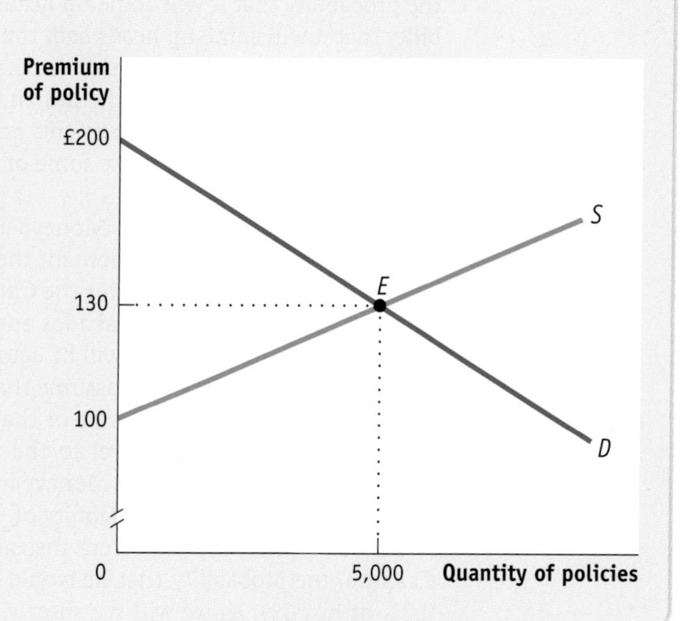

markets can help people cope with risk. Under some circumstances, markets can perform a sort of magic trick: they can make some (though rarely all) of the risk that individuals face simply disappear.

Making Risk Disappear: The Power of Diversification

In the early days of Lloyd's, British merchant ships traversed the world, trading spices and silk from Asia, tobacco and rum from the New World, and textiles and wool from Britain, among many other goods. Each of the many routes that British ships took had its own unique risks—pirates in the Caribbean, gales in the North Atlantic, typhoons in the Indian Ocean.

In the face of all these risks, how were merchants able to survive? One important way was by reducing their risks by not putting all their eggs in one basket: by sending different ships to different destinations, they could reduce the probability that all their ships would be lost. A strategy of investing in such a way as to reduce the probability of severe losses is known as *diversification.* As we'll now see, diversification can often make some of the economy's risk disappear.

Let's stay with our shipping example. It was all too likely that a pirate might seize a merchant ship in the Caribbean or that a typhoon might sink another ship in the Indian Ocean. But the key point here is that the various threats to shipping didn't have much to do with each other. So it was considerably less likely that a merchant who had one ship in the Caribbean and another ship in the Indian Ocean in a given year would lose them both, one to a pirate and the other to a typhoon. After all, there was no connection: the actions of cutthroats in the Carribean had no influence on weather in the Indian Ocean, or vice versa.

Two possible events are **independent events** if each of them is neither more nor less likely to happen if the other one happens.

Statisticians refer to such events—events that have no connection, so that one is no more likely to happen if the other does than if it does not—as **independent events.** Many unpredictable events are independent of each other. If you toss a coin twice, the probability that it will come up heads on the second toss is the same whether it came up heads or tails on the first toss. If your house burns down today, it does not affect the probability that my house will burn down the same day (unless we live next door to each other or share the services of the same incompetent electrician).

There is a simple rule for calculating the probability that two independent events will both happen: multiply the probability that one event would happen on its own by the probability that the other event would happen on its own. If you toss a coin once, the probability that it will come up heads is 0.5; if you toss the coin twice, the probability that it will come up heads *both* times is $0.5 \times 0.5 = 0.25$.

But what did it matter to shipowners or Lloyd's investors that ship losses in the Caribbean and ship losses in the Indian Ocean were independent events? The answer is that by spreading their investments across different parts of the world, shipowners or Lloyd's investors could make some of the riskiness of the shipping business simply disappear.

Let's suppose that Joseph Moneypenny, Esq., is wealthy enough to outfit two ships—and let's ignore for a moment the possibility of insuring his ships. Should Mr. Moneypenny equip two ships for the Caribbean trade and send them off together? Or should he send one ship to Barbados and one to Calcutta?

Assume that both voyages will be equally profitable if successful, yielding £1,000 if the voyage is completed. Also assume that there is a 10% chance both that a ship sent to Barbados will run into a pirate or that a ship sent to Calcutta will be sunk by a typhoon. And if two ships travel to the same destination, we will assume that they share the same fate. So if Mr. Moneypenny were to send both his ships to either destination, he would face a probability of 10% of losing all his investment.

But if Mr. Moneypenny were instead to send one ship to Barbados and one to Calcutta, the probability that he would lose both of them would be only $0.1 \times 0.1 = 0.01$, or just 1%. As we will see shortly, his expected payoff would be the same—but

TABLE 18-2

How Diversification Reduces Risk

(a) If both ships sent to the same destination

State	Probability	Payoff	Expected payoff
Both ships arrive	0.9 = 90%	£2,000	(0.9 × £2,000) + (0.1 × £0) = £1,800
Both ships lost	0.1 = 10%	0	

(b) If one ship sent east, one west

State	Probability	Payoff	Expected payoff
Both ships arrive	0.9 × 0.9 = 81%	£2,000	(0.81 × £2,000) + (0.01 × £0) + (0.18 × £1,000) = £1,800
Both ships lost	0.1 × 0.1 = 1%	0	
One ship arrives	(0.1 × 0.9) + (0.1 × 0.9) = 18%	1,000	

the chance of losing it all would be much less. So by engaging in **diversification**—investing in several different things, where the possible losses are independent events—he could make some of his risk disappear.

An individual can engage in **diversification** by investing in several different things, so that the possible losses are independent events.

Table 18-2 summarizes Mr. Moneypenny's options and their possible consequences. If he sends both ships to the same destination, he runs a 10% chance of losing them both. If he sends them to different destinations, there are three possible outcomes. Both ships could arrive safely: because there is a 0.9 probability of either one making it, the probability that both will make it is 0.9 × 0.9 = 81%. Both could be lost—but the probability of that happening is only 0.1 × 0.1 = 1%. Finally, there are two ways that only one ship can arrive. The probability that the first ship arrives and the second ship is lost is 0.9 × 0.1 = 9%. The probability that the first ship is lost but the second ship arrives is 0.1 × 0.9 = 9%. So the probability that only one ship makes it is 9% + 9% = 18%.

You might think that diversification is a strategy available only to those with a lot of money to begin with. How could Mr. Moneypenny have diversified if he were able to finance only one ship? But there are ways for even small investors to diversify. Even if Mr. Moneypenny were only wealthy enough to equip one ship, he could enter a partnership with another merchant. They could jointly outfit two ships, agreeing to share the profits equally, and then send those ships to different destinations. That way each would face less risk than if he equipped one ship on his own.

A **share** in a company is a partial ownership of that company.

In the modern economy, diversification is made much easier for investors by the fact that they can easily buy shares in many companies by using the *stock market*. The owner of a **share** in a company is the owner of part of that company—typically a very small part, one-millionth or less. An individual who put all of his or her wealth in shares of a single company would lose all of that wealth if the company went bankrupt. But most investors hold shares in many companies, which makes the chance of losing all their investment very small.

In fact, Lloyd's of London wasn't just a way to trade risks; it was also a way for investors to diversify. To see how this worked, let's introduce Lady Penelope Smedley-Smythe, a wealthy aristocrat, who decides to increase her income by placing £1,000 of her capital at risk via Lloyd's. She could use that capital to insure just one ship. But more typically she would enter a "syndicate", a group of investors, who would jointly insure a

"Your mother called to remind you to diversify."

number of ships going to different destinations, agreeing to share the cost if any one of those ships went down. Because it would be much less likely for all the ships insured by the syndicate to sink than for any one of them to go down, Lady Smedley-Smythe would be at much less risk of losing her entire capital.

Pooling is a strong form of diversification in which an individual takes a small share in many independent events. This produces a payoff with very little risk.

In some cases, an individual can make risk almost entirely disappear by taking a small share in many independent events. This strategy is known as **pooling.** Consider the case of a supplementary health and dental insurance company, which has millions of policyholders, with thousands of them requiring expensive dental treatment each year. The insurance company can't know whether any given individual will require expensive dental work. But dental problems for two different individuals are pretty much independent events. And when there are many possible independent events, it is possible, using statistical analysis, to predict with great accuracy *how many* events of a given type will happen. For example, if you toss a coin 1,000 times, it will come up heads about 500 times—and it is very unlikely to be more than 1 or 2% off that figure. So a company offering fire insurance can predict very accurately how many of its clients' homes will burn down in a given year; a company offering supplementary health and dental insurance can predict very accurately how many of its clients will need root canals in a given year; a life insurance company can predict how many of its clients will . . . Well, you get the idea.

When an insurance company is able to take advantage of the predictability that comes from looking at large numbers of independent events, it is said to engage in *pooling of risks*. And this pooling often means that even though insurance companies protect people from risk, the owners of the insurance companies may not themselves face much risk.

Lloyd's of London wasn't just a way for wealthy individuals to get paid for taking on some of the risks of less wealthy merchants. It was also a vehicle for pooling some of those risks. The effect of that pooling was to shift the supply curve in Figure 18-5 rightward: to make people willing to accept more risk, at a lower price, than would otherwise have been possible.

The Limits of Diversification

Diversification can reduce risk. In some cases it can eliminate it. But these cases are not typical, because there are important limits to diversification. We can see the most important reason for these limits by returning to Lloyd's one more time.

During the period when Lloyd's was creating its legend, there was one important hazard facing British shipping other than pirates or storms: war. Between 1690 and 1815, Britain fought a series of wars, mainly with France (which, among other things, went to war with Britain in support of the American Revolution). Each time, France would sponsor "privateers"—basically pirates with official backing—to raid British shipping and thus indirectly damage Britain's war effort.

Whenever war broke out between Britain and France, losses of British merchant ships would suddenly increase. Unfortunately, merchants could not protect themselves against this eventuality by sending ships to different ports: the privateers would prey on British ships anywhere in the world. So the loss of a ship to French privateers in the Caribbean and the loss of another ship to French privateers in the Indian Ocean would *not* be independent events. It would be quite likely that they would happen in the same year.

Two events are **positively correlated** if each event is more likely to occur if the other event also occurs.

When an event is more likely to occur if some other event occurs, these two events are said to be **positively correlated.** And like the risk of having a ship seized by French privateers, many financial risks are, alas, positively correlated.

Here are some of the positively correlated financial risks that investors in the modern world face:

- *Severe weather.* Within any given province of Canada, losses due to weather are definitely not independent events. The ice storm of 1998 caused severe damage to homes across eastern Ontario and southern Québec. To some extent, insurance companies can diversify away this risk by insuring homes in many provinces.

- *Political events.* Modern governments do not, thankfully, license privateers—although submarines served much the same function during World War II. Even today, however, some kinds of political events—say, a war in the Middle East, or revolution in a key raw-material-producing area—can damage business around the globe.
- *Business cycles.* The causes of *business cycles,* fluctuations in the output of the economy as a whole, are a subject for macroeconomics. What we can say here is that if one company suffers a decline in business because of a nationwide economic slump, many other companies will also suffer such declines. So these events will be positively correlated.

When events are positively correlated, the risks they pose cannot be diversified away. An investor can protect herself from the risk that any one company will do badly by investing in many companies; she cannot use the same technique to protect against an economic slump in which *all* companies do badly. An insurance company can protect itself against the risk of losses from local flooding by insuring houses in many different places; but a global weather pattern that produces floods in many places will defeat this strategy.

So institutions like insurance companies and stock markets cannot make risk go away completely. There is always an irreducible core of risk that cannot be diversified. Markets for risk, however, do accomplish two things: First, they enable the economy to eliminate the risk that can be diversified. Second, they allocate the risk that remains to the people most willing to bear it.

economics in action

When Lloyd's Almost Llost It

At the end of the 1980s, the venerable institution of Lloyd's found itself in severe trouble. Investors who had placed their capital at risk, believing that the risks were small and the return on their investments more or less assured, found themselves required to make large payments to satisfy enormous claims. A number of investors, including members of some very old aristocratic families, found themselves pushed into bankruptcy.

What happened? Part of the answer is that ambitious managers at Lloyd's had persuaded investors to take on risks that were much larger than the investors realized. (Or to put it a different way, the premiums the investors accepted were too small for the true level of risk contained in the policies.)

But the biggest single problem was that many of the events against which Lloyd's had become a major insurer were *not* independent. In the 1970s and 1980s, Lloyd's had become a major provider of corporate liability insurance in the United States: it protected American corporations against the possibility that they might be sued for selling defective or harmful products. Everyone expected such suits to be more or less independent events. Why should one company's legal problems have much to do with another's?

The answer turned out to lie in one word: asbestos. For decades, this fireproofing material had been used in many products, which meant that many companies were responsible for its use. Then it turned out that asbestos can cause severe damage to the lungs, especially in children. The result was a torrent of lawsuits by people who believed they were injured by asbestos and billions of dollars in damage awards—many of them ultimately paid by Lloyd's investors. ■

>> QUICK REVIEW

- Insurance markets exist because there are gains from trade in risk. Except in the case of private information, they lead to an *efficient allocation of risk*: those who are most willing to bear risk place their *capital at risk* to cover the financial losses of those least willing to bear risk.
- When *independent events* are involved, a strategy of *diversification* can substantially reduce risk. Diversification is made easier by the existence of institutions like the stock market, in which people trade *shares* of companies. A form of diversification, relevant especially to insurance companies, is *pooling*.
- When events are *positively correlated*, there is a core of risk that will not go away no matter how much individuals diversify.

>> CHECK YOUR UNDERSTANDING 18-2

1. Explain how each of the following events would change the equilibrium premium and quantity of insurance in the market, indicating any shifts in the supply and demand curves.
   a. An increase in the number of ships travelling the same trade routes and so facing the same kinds of risks

b. An increase in the number of trading routes, with the same number of ships travelling a greater variety of routes and so facing different kinds of risk
c. An increase in the degree of risk aversion among the shipowners in the market
d. An increase in the degree of risk aversion among the investors in the market
e. An increase in the risk affecting the economy as a whole
f. A fall in the wealth levels of investors in the market

Solutions appear at back of book.

Private Information: What You Don't Know Can Hurt You

Private information is information that some people have that others do not.

Markets do very well at dealing with risk due to uncertainty: situations in which nobody knows what is going to happen, whose roof will be blown off by high winds, or who will need dental care. However, markets have much more trouble with situations in which *some people know things that other people don't know*—situations of **private information.** As we will see, private information can distort economic decisions and sometimes prevent mutually beneficial economic transactions from taking place. (Sometimes economists use the term *asymmetric information* rather than private information, but they are equivalent.)

Why is some information private? The most important reason is that people generally know more about themselves than other people do. You know whether or not you are a careful driver; but unless you have already been in several accidents, your insurance company does not. You also probably know more about objects you deal with regularly than anyone else. So if you are selling me your used car, you are more likely to be aware of any problems with it than I am.

But why should such differences in who knows what be a problem? It turns out that there are two distinct sources of trouble: *adverse selection,* which arises from having private information about the way things are, and *moral hazard,* which arises from having private information about what people do.

Adverse Selection: The Economics of Lemons

Suppose that someone offers to sell you an almost brand-new car—purchased just three months ago, with only 2,000 miles on the odometer and no dents or scratches. Will you be willing to pay almost the same for it as for a car direct from the dealer?

Probably not, for one main reason: you cannot help but wonder why this car is being sold. Is it because the owner has discovered that something is wrong with it—that it is a "lemon"? Having driven the car for a while, the owner knows more about it than you do—and people are more likely to sell cars that give them trouble.

You might think that the fact that sellers of used cars know more about them than the buyers do represents an advantage to the sellers. But potential buyers know that potential sellers are likely to offer them lemons—they just don't know exactly which car is a lemon. Because potential buyers of a used car know that potential sellers are more likely to sell lemons than good cars, buyers will offer a lower price than they would if they had a guarantee of the car's quality. Worse yet, this poor opinion of used cars tends to be self-reinforcing, precisely because it depresses the prices that buyers offer. Used cars sell at a discount because buyers expect a disproportionate share of those cars to be lemons. Even a used car that is not a lemon would sell only at a large discount, because buyers don't know whether it's a lemon or not. But potential sellers who have good cars are unwilling to sell them at a deep discount, except under exceptional circumstances. So good used cars are rarely offered for sale; and used cars that are offered for sale have a strong tendency to be lemons. (This is why people who have a compelling reason to sell a car, such as moving overseas, make a point of revealing that information to potential buyers—as if to say "This car is not a lemon!")

The end result, then, is not only that used cars sell for low prices and that there are a large number of used cars with hidden problems. Equally important, many potentially beneficial transactions—sales of good cars by people who would like to get rid of them to people who would like to buy them—end up being frustrated by the inability of potential sellers to convince potential buyers that their cars are actually worth the higher price demanded. So some mutually beneficial trades between those who want to sell used cars and those who want to buy them go unexploited.

Although economists sometimes refer to situations like this as the "lemons problem" (the issue was introduced in a famous 1970 paper by economist and Nobel Laureate George Akerlof entitled "The Market for Lemons"), the more formal name of the problem is **adverse selection.** The reason for the name is obvious: because the potential sellers know more about the quality of what they are selling than the potential buyers, they have an incentive to select the worst things to sell.

Adverse selection occurs when an individual knows more about the way things are than other people do. Private information leads buyers to expect hidden problems in items offered for sale, leading to low prices and the best items being kept off the market.

Adverse selection does not apply only to used cars. It is a problem for many parts of the economy—most notably for insurance companies. Suppose that an insurance company were to offer a standard policy for repairing cars after accidents, with the same premium for all drivers. This premium would reflect the *average* risk of accidents across all drivers. But that would make the policy look very expensive to drivers who know they are particularly careful or skillful and so less likely than the average driver to have an accident. So safe drivers would be less likely than less-safe drivers to buy this policy, leaving the insurance company with exactly the customers it doesn't want: people who have a higher-than-average risk of having accidents. Mutually beneficial transactions between safe drivers and insurance companies go unexploited because when drivers possess private information about their risk characteristics, the insurance company cannot set premiums according to the true riskiness of the driver. Safe drivers would get "priced out" of the market.

In practice, people or firms faced with the problem of adverse selection follow one of several well-established strategies for dealing with it. One strategy is **screening:** using observable information to make inferences about private information. Auto insurance provides a very good example. An insurance company may not know whether you are a careful driver, but it has statistical data on the accident rates of people who resemble your profile—and it uses those data in setting premiums. A 19-year-old male who drives a sports car and has already had a fender-bender is likely to pay a very high premium. A 40-year-old female who drives a minivan and has never had an accident is likely to pay much less. In some cases, this may be quite unfair: some adolescent males are very careful drivers, and some mature women drive their minivans as if they were Formula One racing cars. But nobody can deny that the insurance companies are right on average.

Adverse selection can be reduced through **screening:** using observable information about people to make inferences about their private information.

Another strategy is for people who are good prospects to do something that **signals** their private information—taking some action that wouldn't be worth taking unless they were indeed good prospects. Reputable used-car dealers often offer warranties—promises to repair any problems with the cars they sell that arise within a given amount of time. This isn't just a way of insuring their customers against possible expenses; it's a way of credibly showing that they are not selling lemons. As a result, more sales occur and dealers can command higher prices for their used cars.

Adverse selection can be diminished by people **signalling** their private information through actions that credibly reveal what they know.

Finally, in the face of adverse selection, it can be very valuable to establish a good **reputation:** a used-car dealer will often advertise how long it has been in business to show that it has continued to satisfy its customers. New customers, therefore, will be willing to purchase cars and to pay more for that dealer's cars.

A long-term **reputation** allows an individual to reassure others that he or she isn't concealing adverse private information.

Moral Hazard

In the late 1970s, New York and other major cities experienced an epidemic of "suspicious" fires—fires that appeared to be deliberately set. Some of the fires were probably started by teenagers on a lark, others by gang members struggling over turf. But investigators eventually became aware of patterns in a number of the fires. Particular landlords who owned several buildings seemed to have an unusually large number of their buildings burn down. Although it was difficult to prove, police had few doubts that most of these "fire-prone" landlords were hiring professional arsonists to torch their own properties.

Why burn your own building? These buildings were typically in declining neighborhoods, where rising crime and middle-class flight had led to a decline in property values. But the insurance policies on the buildings were written to compensate owners based on historical property values, and so would actually pay the owner of a destroyed building more than the building was worth in the current market. For an unscrupulous landlord who knew the right people, this presented a profitable opportunity.

The arson epidemic became less severe during the 1980s, partly because insurance companies began making it difficult to overinsure properties, and partly because a boom in real estate values made many previously arson-threatened buildings worth more unburned.

The episode makes it clear that it is a bad idea for insurance companies to let customers insure buildings for more than their value—it gives the customers some destructive incentives. You might think, however, that the incentive problem goes away as long as the insurance is no more than 100% of the value of what is being insured.

But, unfortunately, anything close to 100% insurance still distorts incentives—it induces policyholders to behave differently than they would in the absence of insurance. The reason is that preventing fires requires effort and cost on the part of a building's owner. Fire alarms and sprinkler systems have to be kept in good repair, fire safety rules have to be strictly enforced, and so on. All of this takes time and money—time and money that the owner may not find worth spending if the insurance policy will provide close to full compensation for any losses.

Of course, the insurance company could specify in the policy that it won't pay if basic safety precautions have not been taken. But it isn't always easy to tell how careful a building's owner has been—the owner knows, but the insurance company does not.

The point is that the building's owner has private information about his or her own actions, about whether he or she has really taken all appropriate precautions. As a result, the insurance company is likely to face greater claims than if it were able to determine exactly how much effort a building owner exerts to prevent a loss. The problem of distorted incentives arises when an individual has private information about his own actions but someone else bears the costs of a lack of care or effort. This is known as **moral hazard.**

Moral hazard occurs when an individual knows more about his or her own actions than other people do. This leads to a distortion of incentives to take care or to exert effort when someone else bears the costs of the lack of care or effort.

To deal with moral hazard, it is necessary to give individuals with private information some personal stake in what happens, a stake that gives them a reason to exert effort even if others cannot verify that they have done so. Moral hazard is the reason salespeople in many stores receive a commission on sales: it's hard for managers to be sure how hard the salespeople are really working, and if they were paid only straight salary, they would not have an incentive to exert effort to make those sales. As described in the following Economics in Action, similar logic explains why many stores and restaurants, even if they are part of national chains, are actually franchises—licensed outlets owned by the people who run them.

Insurance companies deal with moral hazard by requiring a **deductible:** they compensate for losses only above a certain amount, so that coverage is always less than 100%. The insurance on your car, for example, may pay for repairs only after the first $500 in loss. This means that a careless driver who gets into a fender-bender will end up paying $500 for repairs even if he is insured, which provides at least some incentive to be careful and reduce moral hazard.

A **deductible** in an insurance policy is a sum that the insured individual must pay before being compensated for a claim.

In addition to reducing moral hazard, deductibles provide a partial solution to the problem of adverse selection. Your insurance premium often drops substantially if you are willing to accept a large deductible. This is an attractive option to people who know they are low-risk customers; it is less attractive to people who know they are high-risk—and so are likely to have an accident and end up paying the deductible. By offering a menu of policies with different premiums and deductibles, insurance companies can screen their customers, inducing them to sort themselves out on the basis of their private information.

As the example of deductibles suggests, moral hazard limits the ability of the economy to allocate risks efficiently. You generally can't get full (100%) insurance on your home or car, even though you would like to buy it, and you bear the risk of large deductibles even though you would prefer not to. The following Economics in Action illustrates how in some cases moral hazard limits the ability of investors to diversify their investments.

economics in action

Franchise Owners Try Harder

When Canadians go out for a quick meal, they often end up at one of the fast-food chains—McDonald's, Wendy's, and so on. Because these are large corporations, most customers probably imagine that the people who serve them are themselves employees of large corporations. But usually they aren't. Most fast-food restaurants—for example, 85% of McDonald's outlets—are franchises. That is, some individual has paid the parent company for the right to operate a restaurant selling its product; he or she may look like an arm of a giant company but is in fact a small-business owner.

Becoming a franchisee is not a guarantee of success. You must put up a large amount of money, both to buy the license and to set up the restaurant itself (to open a Taco Bell, for example, cost over $1 million in 1997). And although McDonald's takes care that its franchises are not too close to each other, they often face stiff competition from rival chains and even from a few truly independent restaurants. Becoming a franchise owner, in other words, involves taking on quite a lot of risk.

But why should people be willing to take these risks? Didn't we just learn that it is better to diversify, to spread your wealth among many investments? The logic of diversification would seem to say that it's better for someone with $1 million to invest in a wide range of stocks rather than put it all into one Taco Bell. This implies that Taco Bell would find it hard to attract franchisees: nobody would be willing to be a franchisee unless they expected to earn considerably more than if they invested their wealth in a diversified portfolio of stocks and found a paying job as a manager. But in that case, wouldn't it be more profitable for McDonald's or Taco Bell simply to hire managers to run their restaurants?

It turns out that it isn't, because the success of a restaurant depends a lot on how hard the manager works, on the effort he or she puts into choosing the right employees, on keeping the place clean and attractive to customers, and so on. Could McDonald's get the right level of effort from a salaried manager? Probably not. The problem is moral hazard: the manager knows whether he or she is really putting 100% into the job; but company headquarters, which bears the costs of a poorly run restaurant, does not. So a salaried manager, who gets a salary even without doing everything possible to make the restaurant a success, does not have the incentive to do that extra bit—an incentive the owner does have because he or she has a substantial personal stake in the success of the restaurant.

In other words, there is a moral hazard problem when a salaried manager runs a McDonald's, where the private information is how hard the manager works. Franchising resolves this problem. A franchisee, whose wealth is tied up in the business and who stands to profit personally from its success, has every incentive to work extremely hard.

The result is that fast-food chains rely mainly on franchisees to operate their restaurants, even though the contracts with these owner-managers allow the franchisees on average to make much more than it would have cost the companies to employ store managers. The higher earnings of franchisees compensate them for the risk they accept, and the companies are compensated by higher sales that lead to higher license fees. In addition, franchisees are forbidden by the licensing agreement with the company from reducing their risk by taking actions such as selling shares of the franchise to outside investors and using the proceeds to diversify. It's an illustration of the fact that moral hazard prevents the elimination of risk through diversification. ■

< < < < < < < < < < < < < < < < < <

>>QUICK REVIEW

- *Private information* can distort incentives and prevent mutually beneficial transactions from occurring. One source is *adverse selection:* sellers have private information about their goods and buyers offer low prices, leading the sellers of quality goods to drop out and leaving the market dominated by "lemons".
- Adverse selection can be reduced by revealing private information through *screening* or *signalling,* or by cultivating a long-term *reputation.*
- Another source of problems is *moral hazard.* In the case of insurance, it leads individuals to exert too little effort to prevent losses. This gives rise to features like *deductibles,* which limit the efficient allocation of risk.

>>CHECK YOUR UNDERSTANDING 18-3

1. Your car insurance premiums are lower if you have had no moving violations for several years. Explain how this feature tends to decrease the potential inefficiency caused by adverse selection.
2. A common feature of home construction contracts is that when it costs more to construct a building than was originally estimated, the contractor must absorb the additional cost. Explain how this feature reduces the problem of moral hazard but also forces the contractor to bear more risk than she would like.
3. True or false? Explain your answer, stating what concept analysed in this chapter accounts for the feature.

   People with higher deductibles on their auto insurance:

   a. Generally drive more carefully
   b. Pay lower premiums
   c. Generally are wealthier

Solutions at back of book.

• A LOOK AHEAD •

We began this chapter with a discussion of yet another thing markets can do right: they allow individuals to trade risk, to their mutual benefit. But our discussion of private information shows that markets have difficulty handling some problems.

In the next two chapters, we will begin discussing in earnest the problem of *market failure*—situations in which markets, left to themselves, can lead to inefficient outcomes. As we'll see, one of the key roles of government is to correct market failure.

SUMMARY

1. The **expected value** of a **random variable** is the weighted average of all possible values, where the weight corresponds to the probability of a given value occurring.
2. **Risk** is uncertainty about future events or **states of the world.** It is **financial risk** when the uncertainty is about monetary outcomes.
3. Under uncertainty, people maximize **expected utility.** A **risk-averse** person will choose to reduce risk when that reduction leaves the expected value of his or her income or wealth unchanged. A **fair insurance policy** has that feature: the **premium** is equal to the expected value of the claim.
4. Risk aversion arises from diminishing marginal utility: an additional dollar of income generates higher marginal utility in low-income states than in high-income states. A fair insurance policy increases a risk-averse person's utility because it transfers a dollar from a high-income state (a state when no loss occurs) to a low-income state (a state when a loss occurs).
5. Differences in preferences and income or wealth lead to differences in risk aversion. Depending on the size of the premium, a risk-averse person is willing to purchase unfair insurance, a policy for which the premium exceeds the expected value of the claim. The greater your risk aversion, the higher the premium you are willing to pay.
6. There are gains from trade in risk, leading to an **efficient allocation of risk:** those who are most willing to bear risk put their **capital at risk** to cover the losses of those least willing to bear risk.
7. Risk can also be reduced through **diversification,** investing in several different things that correspond to **independent events.** The stock market, where **shares** in companies are traded, offers one way to diversify. Insurance companies can engage in **pooling,** insuring

many independent events so as to eliminate almost all risk. But when the underlying events are **positively correlated,** all risk cannot be diversified away.

8. **Private information** can cause inefficiency in the allocation of risk. One problem is **adverse selection,** private information about the way things are. It creates the "lemons problem" in used car markets where sellers of high-quality cars drop out of the market. Adverse selection can be limited in several ways—through **screening** of individuals, through **signalling** that people use to reveal their private information, and through the building of a **reputation.**

9. A related problem is **moral hazard:** individuals have private information about their actions, which distorts their incentives to exert effort or care when someone else bears the costs of that lack of effort or care. It limits the ability of markets to allocate risk efficiently. Insurance companies try to limit moral hazard by imposing **deductibles,** placing more risk on the insured.

KEY TERMS

Random variable, p. 456
Expected value, p. 456
State of the world, p. 456
Risk, p. 457
Financial risk, p. 457
Expected utility, p. 457
Premium, p. 457
Fair insurance policy, p. 458
Risk-averse, p. 459
Capital at risk, p. 464
Efficient allocation of risk, p. 465
Independent events, p. 466
Diversification, p. 467
Share, p. 467
Pooling, p. 468
Positively correlated, p. 468
Private information, p. 470
Adverse selection, p. 471
Screening, p. 471
Signalling, p. 471
Reputation, p. 471
Moral hazard, p. 472
Deductible, p. 472

PROBLEMS

1. For each of the following situations, calculate the expected value.

   a. Tanisha owns one share of IBM stock, which is currently trading at $80. There is a 50% chance that the share price will rise to $100 and a 50% chance that the share price will fall to $70. What is the expected value of the future share price?

   b. Sharon buys a ticket in a small lottery. There is a probability of 0.7 that she will win nothing, a probability of 0.2 that she will win $10, and a probability of 0.1 that she will win $50. What is the expected value of Sharon's winnings?

   c. Tom is a farmer whose rice crop depends on the weather. If the weather is favourable, he will make a profit of $100. If the weather is unfavourable, he will make a profit of –$20 (that is, he will lose money). The weather forecast reports that the probability of weather being favourable is 0.9, and the probability of weather being unfavourable is 0.1. What is the expected value of Tom's profit?

2. Vicky N. Vestor is considering investing some of her money in a startup company. She currently has income of $4,000, and she is considering investing $2,000 of that income into the company. There is a 0.5 probability that the company will succeed and will pay out $8,000 to Vicky (her original investment of $2,000 plus $6,000 of the company's profits). And there is a 0.5 probability the company will fail and Vicky will get nothing (and lose her investment). The accompanying table illustrates Vicky's utility function.

Income	Total utility (utils)
$0	0
1,000	50
2,000	85
3,000	115
4,000	140
5,000	163
6,000	183
7,000	200
8,000	215
9,000	229
10,000	241

   a. Calculate Vicky's marginal utility of income, for each income level. Is Vicky risk-averse?

   b. Calculate the expected value of Vicky's income from this investment.

   c. Calculate Vicky's expected utility from making the investment.

   d. What is Vicky's utility from not making the investment? Will Vicky therefore invest in the company?

3. Vicky N. Vestor's utility function was given in Problem 2. As in Problem 2, Vicky currently has $4,000 income. Vicky is considering investing in a startup company, but the investment now costs $4,000. If the company fails, Vicky will get

nothing from the company. But if the company succeeds, Vicky will get $10,000 from the company (her original investment of $4,000 plus $6,000 of the company's profits). Will Vicky invest in the company?

4. You have $1,000 that you can invest. If you buy Ford stock, you face the following returns and probabilities from holding the stock for one year: with a probability of 0.2 you will get $1,500; with a probability of 0.4 you will get $1,100; and with a probability of 0.4 you will get $900. If you put the money into the bank, in one year's time you will get $1,100 for certain.

   a. What is the expected value of your earnings from investing in Ford stock?

   b. Suppose you are risk-averse. Can we say for sure whether you will invest in Ford stocks or put your money into the bank?

5. You have $1,000 that you can invest. If you buy General Motors stock, then, in one year's time: with a probability of 0.4 you will get $1,600; with a probability of 0.4 you will get $1,100; and with a probability of 0.2 you will get $800. If you put the money into the bank, in one year's time you will get $1,100 for certain.

   a. What is the expected value of your earnings from investing in General Motors stock?

   b. Suppose you prefer putting your money into the bank, over investing it in General Motors stocks. What does that tell us about your attitude to risk?

6. Wilbur is an airline pilot who currently has income of $60,000. If he gets sick and loses his flight medical certificate, he loses his job and only has $10,000 income. His probability of staying healthy is 0.6, and his probability of getting sick is 0.4. His utility function is given in the accompanying table.

Income	Total utility (utils)
$0	0
10,000	60
20,000	110
30,000	150
40,000	180
50,000	200
60,000	210

   a. What is the expected value of Wilbur's income?

   b. What is Wilbur's expected utility?

   Wilbur thinks about buying "loss-of-license" insurance that will compensate him if he loses his flight medical certificate.

   c. One insurance company offers Wilbur full compensation for his income loss (that is, the insurance company pays Wilbur $50,000 if he loses his flight medical certificate), and it charges a premium of $40,000. That is, regardless of whether or not he loses his flight medical certificate, Wilbur's income after insurance will be $20,000. What is Wilbur's utility? Will he buy the insurance?

   d. What is the highest premium Wilbur would just be willing to pay for full insurance (insurance that completely compensates him for the income loss)?

7. Hugh's income is currently $5,000. His utility function is shown in the accompanying table.

Income	Total utility (utils)
$0	0
1,000	100
2,000	140
3,000	166
4,000	185
5,000	200
6,000	212
7,000	222
8,000	230
9,000	236
10,000	240

   a. Calculate Hugh's marginal utility of income. What is his attitude to risk?

   b. Hugh is thinking about gambling in a casino. With a probability of 0.5 he loses $4,000, and with a probability of 0.5 he wins $4,000. What is the expected value of Hugh's income? What is Hugh's expected utility? Will he decide to gamble? (Suppose that he gets no extra utility from going to the casino.)

   c. Suppose that the "spread" (how much he can win versus how much he can lose) of the gamble narrows, so that with a probability of 0.5 he loses $2,000, and with a probability of 0.5 he wins $2,000. What is the expected value of Hugh's income? What is Hugh's expected utility? Is this gamble better for him than the gamble in part b? Will he decide to gamble?

8. Eva is risk-averse. Currently she has $50,000 to invest. She faces the following choice. She can invest in the stock of a dot-com company, or she can invest in IBM stock. If she invests in the dot-com company, then with a probability of 0.5 she will lose $30,000, but with a probability of 0.5 she will gain $50,000. If she invests in IBM stock, then with a probability of 0.5 she will lose only $10,000, but with a probability of 0.5 she will gain only $30,000. Can you tell which investment she will prefer to make?

9. Suppose you have $1,000 that you can invest in Ted and Larry's Ice Cream Parlour and Ethel's House of Cocoa. The price of a share of stock in either company is $100. The fortunes of each company are closely linked to the weather. When it is warm, the stock price of Ted and Larry's increases to $150, while the value of Ethel's stock falls to $60. When it is cold, the value of Ethel's stock increases to $150, while Ted and Larry's stock falls to $60. There is an equal chance of the weather being warm or cold.

a. If you invest all of your money in Ted and Larry's, what is your expected payoff? What if you invested all of your money in Ethel's?

b. Suppose you diversify and invest half of your $1,000 in each company. How much money will you have if the weather is warm? What if it is cold?

c. Suppose you are risk-averse. Would you prefer to put all your money in Ted and Larry's, as in part a? Or would you prefer to diversify, as in part b? Explain your reasoning.

10. You are considering buying a second-hand Volkswagen. From reading car magazines you know that half of all Volkswagens have problems of some kind (they are "lemons") and the other half run just fine (they are "plums"). If you knew that you were getting a plum, you would be willing to pay $10,000 for it: this is how much a plum is worth to you. You would also be willing to buy a lemon, but only if its price were no more than $4,000: this is how much a lemon is worth to you. And someone who owns a plum would be willing to sell it at any price above $8,000. Someone who owns a lemon would be willing to sell it for any price above $2,000.

a. For now, suppose that you can immediately tell whether the car that you are being offered is a lemon or a plum. Suppose someone offers you a plum. Will there be trade?

Now suppose that the seller has private information about the car she is selling: the seller knows whether she has a lemon or a plum to sell. But when a seller offers you a Volkswagen to buy, you do not know whether it is a lemon or a plum. This is therefore a situation of adverse selection.

b. Since you do not know whether you are offered a plum or a lemon, you base your decision on the expected value to you of a Volkswagen, assuming that you are just as likely to end up with a lemon as a plum. Calculate this expected value.

c. Suppose, from driving the car, the seller knows she has a plum. However, you don't know whether this particular car is a lemon or a plum, so the most you are willing to pay for this car is your expected value. Will there be trade?

11. You own a company that produces chairs, and you are thinking about hiring one more employee. Each chair that is produced gives you revenue of $10. There are two potential employees, Fred Ast and Sylvia Low. Fred is a fast worker who produces 10 chairs per day, creating revenue for you of $100. Fred knows that he is fast and so will work for you only if you pay him more than $80 per day. Sylvia is a slow worker who produces only 5 chairs per day, creating revenue for you of $50. Sylvia knows that she is slow and she will therefore work for you if you pay her more than $40 per day. While Sylvia knows she is slow, and Fred knows he is fast, you do not know who is fast and who is slow. So this is a situation of adverse selection.

a. Since you do not know which type of worker you get, you think about what the expected value of your revenue will be if you hire one of the two. What is that expected value?

b. Suppose you offered to pay a daily wage equal to the expected revenue you calculated in part a. Who would you be able to hire: Fred or Sylvia, or either?

12. For each of the following situations, do the following: First describe whether it is a situation of moral hazard or a situation of adverse selection. Then explain what inefficiency can arise from this situation and explain how the proposed solution reduces the inefficiency.

a. When you buy a second-hand car, you do not know whether it is a lemon (low quality) or a plum (high quality), but the seller knows. The proposed solution: sellers should offer a warranty with the car that pays for repair costs.

b. When airlines sell tickets, they do not know whether a buyer is a business traveller (who is willing to pay a lot for an airline seat), or a leisure traveller (who has a low willingness to pay). A solution for a profit-maximizing airline is to offer an expensive ticket that is very flexible (it allows date and route changes) and a cheap ticket that is very inflexible (it has to be booked in advance and cannot be changed).

c. Shareholders in a company do not know whether the CEO in fact maximizes the firm's profit. The proposed solution: shareholders should pay part of the CEO's salary in stock options, which are worth a lot if the company's profits are high and worth very little if the company's profits are low.

d. A company does not know whether workers on an assembly line work hard or whether they shirk. The proposed solution: the company should pay the workers "piece rates"—that is, pay them according to how much they have produced each day. All workers are risk-averse, and the company is not risk-averse.

e. When making a decision about hiring you, prospective employers do not know whether you are a productive or unproductive worker. A solution is for productive workers to provide potential employers with references from previous employers.

>web... To continue your study and review of concepts in this chapter, please visit the Krugman/Wells website for quizzes, animated graph tutorials, web links to helpful resources, and more.

www.worthpublishers.com/krugmanwellsmyatt

chapter 19

>>Externalities

WHO'LL STOP THE RAIN?

In the summertime, many Canadians can think of no better way to relax than freshwater fishing. But in the 1960s avid fishermen—especially in central and eastern Canada—noticed something alarming: lakes that had formerly teemed with fish were now almost empty. What had happened?

The answer turned out to be acid rain, caused mainly by coal-burning power plants and ore-smelting operations in the midwestern United States and central Canada. When coal is burned, it releases sulphur dioxide and nitric oxide into the atmosphere; these gases react with water, producing sulphuric acid and nitric acid. The result is a dilute acid that stays in the air for 2 to 5 days, travelling sometimes thousands of kilometres on the prevailing northeasterly winds before eventually falling as rain (or snow) that can be as acidic as lemon juice. Acid rain didn't just kill fish; it also damaged trees and crops and, over time, even began to dissolve limestone buildings.

You'll be glad to hear that the acid rain problem today is much less serious than it was in the 1960s. Power plants and ore smelters have reduced their emissions by switching to low-sulphur coal and by installing scrubbers in their smokestacks. But they didn't do this out of the goodness of their hearts; they did it in response to government policy. Without such intervention, power companies would have had no incentive to take the environmental effects of their actions into account.

When individuals impose costs on or provide benefits for others, but don't have an economic incentive to take those costs or benefits into account, economists say that the situation includes *externalities*. You may recall that we briefly noted this phenomenon

AP/Wide World Photos

For many polluters, acid rain is someone else's problem.

What you will learn in this chapter:

- What **externalities** are and why they can lead to inefficiency in a market economy and support for government intervention
- The difference between **negative** and **positive externalities**
- The importance of the **Coase theorem,** which explains how private individuals can sometimes solve externalities
- Why some government policies to deal with externalities, such as **emissions taxes, tradable permits,** or **Pigouvian subsidies,** are efficient, although others, like **environmental standards,** are inefficient
- How positive externalities give rise to arguments for **industrial policy**

in Chapters 1, 6, and 13. There we stated that one of the principal sources of market failure are actions that create *side effects* that are not properly taken into account—that is, externalities. In this chapter, we'll examine the economics of externalities, seeing how they can get in the way of economic efficiency and lead to market failure, why they provide a reason for government intervention in markets, and how economic analysis can be used to guide government policy.

Because externalities arise from the side effects of actions, we need to study them from two slightly different vantage points. First, we consider the situation in which the side effect—that is, pollution—can be directly observed and quantified. Whenever an activity can be directly observed and quantified, it can be regulated: by imposing direct controls on it, by taxing it, or by subsidizing it. As we will see, government intervention in this case should be aimed directly at moving the market to the right quantity of the side effect.

But in many situations, only the original activity, not its side effect, can be observed. For example, we can't observe the congestion caused by a single car, so the government is unable to implement policies that control the side effect directly. What it can do is employ policies that affect the *original* activity—driving. So in the second part of our analysis we will consider how governments can indirectly achieve the right quantity of the side effect through influencing the activity that generates it. In a fundamental way, however, the two approaches are equivalent: each one involves, at the margin, setting the benefit of doing a little bit more of something equal to the cost of doing that little bit more.

The Economics Of Pollution

Pollution is a bad thing. Yet most pollution is a side effect of activities that provide us with good things: our air is polluted by power plants generating the electricity that lights our cities, and our rivers are damaged by fertilizer runoff from farms that grow our food. Why don't we accept a certain amount of pollution as the cost of a good life?

Actually, we do. Even highly committed environmentalists don't think that we can or should completely eliminate pollution—even an environmentally conscious society would accept *some* pollution as the cost of producing useful goods and services. What environmentalists argue is that unless there is a strong and effective environmental policy, our society will generate *too much* pollution—too much of a bad thing. And the great majority of economists agree.

To see why, we need a framework that lets us think about how much pollution a society *should* have. We'll then be able to see why a market economy, left to itself, will produce more pollution than it should. We'll start by adopting the simplest framework to study the problem—assuming that the amount of pollution emitted by a polluter is directly observable and controllable.

Costs and Benefits of Pollution

How much pollution should society allow? We learned in Chapter 7 that "how much" decisions always involve comparing the marginal benefit from an additional unit of something with the marginal cost of that additional unit. The same is true of pollution.

PITFALLS

SO HOW DO YOU MEASURE THE MARGINAL SOCIAL COST OF POLLUTION?

It might be confusing to think of marginal *social* cost—after all, we have up to this point always defined marginal cost as being incurred by an individual or a firm, not society as a whole. But it is easily understandable once we link it to the familiar concept of willingness to pay: the marginal social cost of a unit of pollution is equal to the *highest willingness to pay among all members of society* to avoid that unit of pollution. But calculating the true cost to society of pollution—marginal or average—is a difficult matter, requiring a great deal of scientific knowledge, as the Economics in Action on page 484 illustrates. As a result, society often underestimates the true marginal social cost of pollution.

The **marginal social cost of pollution** is the additional cost imposed on society as a whole by an additional unit of pollution.

The **marginal social benefit of pollution** is the additional gain to society as a whole from an additional unit of pollution.

The **socially optimal quantity of pollution** is the quantity of pollution that society would choose if all the costs and benefits of pollution were fully accounted for.

The **marginal social cost of pollution** is the additional cost imposed on society as a whole by an additional unit of pollution. For example, acid rain damages fisheries, crops, and forests; and each additional ton of sulphur dioxide released into the atmosphere increases the damage.

The **marginal social benefit of pollution**—the additional gain to society from an additional unit of pollution—may seem like a confusing concept. What's good about pollution? However, avoiding pollution requires using scarce resources that could have been used to produce other goods and services. For example, to reduce the quantity of sulphur dioxide they emit, power companies must either buy expensive low-sulphur coal or install special scrubbers to remove sulphur from their emissions. The more sulphur dioxide they are allowed to emit, the lower these extra costs. Suppose that we can calculate how much money the power industry would save if it were allowed to emit an additional ton of sulphur dioxide. That saving is the marginal benefit to society of emitting an extra ton of sulphur dioxide.

Using hypothetical numbers, Figure 19-1 shows how we can determine the **socially optimal quantity of pollution**—the quantity of pollution society would choose if all its costs and benefits were fully accounted for. The upward-sloping marginal social cost curve, *MSC*, shows how the marginal cost to society of an additional ton of pollution emissions varies with the quantity of emissions. (An upward slope is likely because nature can often safely handle low levels of pollution but is increasingly harmed as pollution reaches high levels.) The marginal social benefit curve, *MSB*, is downward sloping because it is progressively harder, and therefore more expensive, to achieve a further reduction in pollution as the total amount of pollution falls—increasingly expensive technology must be used. As a result, as pollution falls, the cost savings to a polluter of being allowed to emit one more ton rises.

PITFALLS

SO HOW DO YOU MEASURE THE MARGINAL SOCIAL BENEFIT OF POLLUTION?

Similar to the problem of measuring the marginal social cost of pollution, the concept of willingness to pay helps us understand the marginal social benefit of pollution in contrast to the marginal benefit to an individual or firm. The marginal social benefit of a unit of pollution is simply equal to the highest willingness to pay for the right to emit that unit across all polluters. But unlike the marginal social cost of pollution, the value of the marginal social benefit of pollution is a number likely to be known—to polluters, that is.

Figure 19-1

The Socially Optimal Quantity of Pollution

Pollution yields both costs and benefits. Here the curve *MSC* shows how the marginal cost to society as a whole from emitting one more ton of pollution emissions depends on the quantity of emissions. The curve *MSB* shows how the marginal benefit to society as a whole of emitting an additional ton of pollution emissions depends on the quantity of pollution emissions. The socially optimal quantity of pollution is Q_{OPT}; at that quantity, the marginal social benefit of pollution is equal to the marginal social cost, corresponding to $200.

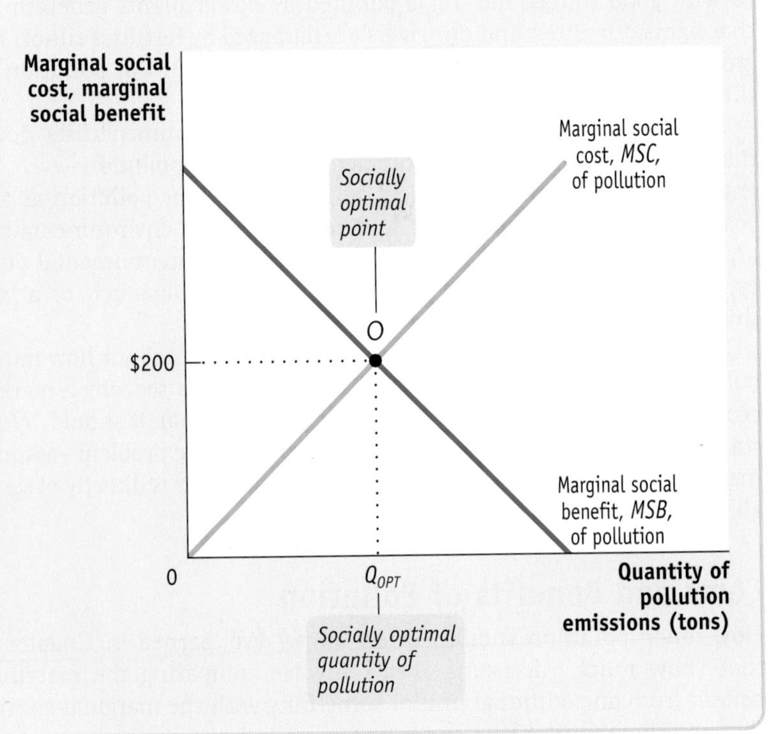

The socially optimal quantity of pollution in this example isn't zero. It's Q_{OPT}, the quantity corresponding to point O, where *MSB* crosses *MSC*. At Q_{OPT}, the marginal social benefit from an additional ton of emissions and its marginal social cost are equalized at $200.

But will a market economy, left to itself, arrive at the socially optimal quantity of pollution? No, it won't.

Pollution: An External Cost

Pollution yields both benefits and costs to society. But in a market economy without government intervention, those who benefit from pollution—like the owners of power companies—decide how much pollution occurs. They have no incentive to take into account the costs of pollution that they impose on others.

To see why, remember the nature of the benefits and costs from pollution. For polluters, the benefits take the form of monetary savings: by emitting an extra ton of sulphur dioxide, any given polluter saves the cost of buying expensive, low-sulphur coal or installing pollution-control equipment. So the benefits of pollution accrue directly to the polluters.

The costs of pollution, though, fall on people who have no say in the decision about how much pollution takes place: people who fish in freshwater lakes do not control the decisions of power plants or smelting operations.

Figure 19-2 shows the result of this asymmetry between who reaps the benefits and who pays the costs. In a market economy without government intervention to protect the environment, only the benefits of pollution are taken into account in choosing the quantity of pollution. So the quantity of emissions won't be at the socially optimal quantity Q_{OPT}; it will be Q_{MKT}, the quantity at which the marginal social benefit of an additional ton of pollution is zero, but the marginal social cost of that additional ton is much larger—$400. The quantity of pollution in a market economy without government intervention will be higher than its

Figure 19-2

Why a Market Economy Produces Too Much Pollution

In the absence of government intervention, the quantity of pollution will be Q_{MKT}, the level at which the marginal social benefit of pollution to polluters is zero. This is an inefficiently high quantity of pollution: the marginal social cost, $400, greatly exceeds the marginal social benefit, $0. The marginal social cost of pollution equals the marginal social benefit of pollution at a value of $200. Therefore, a tax of $200 would be an optimal Pigouvian tax. It would move the market to the socially optimal quantity of pollution, Q_{OPT}. >web...

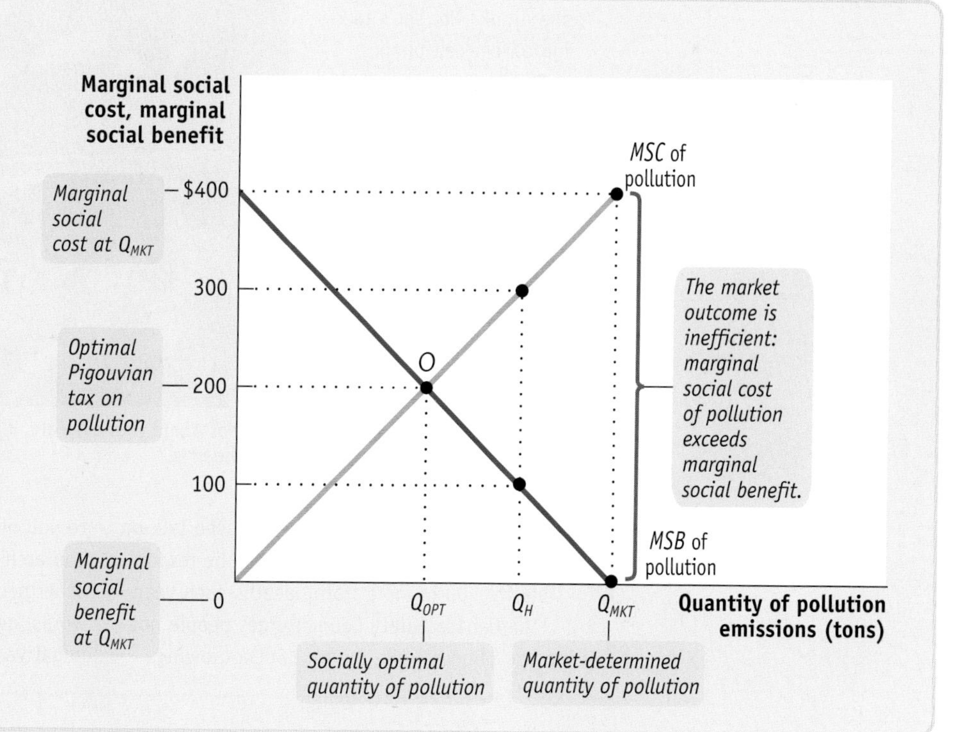

socially optimal quantity. (The Pigouvian tax noted in Figure 19-2 will be explained shortly.)

The reason is that in the absence of government intervention, those who derive the benefits from pollution—in this case, the owners of power plants and ore-smelting operations—don't have to compensate those who bear the costs. So, the marginal cost of pollution to any given polluter is zero: polluters have no incentive to limit the amount of emissions. For example, before the U.S. and Canada passed their Clean Air Acts in the early 1970s, power plants and ore smelters used the cheapest type of coal available, regardless of how much pollution it caused, and did nothing to scrub their emissions.

An **external cost** is an uncompensated cost that an individual or firm imposes on others.

The environmental costs of pollution are the best-known and most important example of an **external cost**—an uncompensated cost that an individual or firm imposes on others. There are many other examples of external costs besides pollution. Another important, and certainly very familiar, external cost is traffic congestion—an individual who chooses to drive during rush hour increases congestion and so increases the travel time of other drivers.

An **external benefit** is a benefit that an individual or firm confers on others without receiving compensation.

External costs and benefits are known as **externalities;** external costs are **negative externalities,** and external benefits are **positive externalities.**

We'll see later in this chapter that there are also important examples of **external benefits,** benefits that individuals or firms confer on others without receiving compensation. External costs and benefits are jointly known as **externalities,** with external costs called **negative externalities** and external benefits called **positive externalities.**

As we've already suggested, externalities can lead to individual decisions that are not optimal for society as a whole. Let's take a closer look at why, focusing on the case of pollution.

FOR INQUIRING MINDS

TALKING AND DRIVING

Why is that woman in the car in front of us driving so erratically? Is she drunk? No, she's talking on her cell phone.

Traffic safety experts take the risks posed by driving while talking very seriously. Using hands-free, voice-activated phones doesn't seem to help much because the main danger is distraction. As one traffic safety consultant put it, "It's not where your eyes are; it's where your head is." And we're not talking about a trivial problem. One estimate suggests that people who talk on their cell phones while driving may be responsible for 600 or more traffic deaths each year.

Bob Daemmrich/The Image Works

"It's not where your eyes are, it's where your head is."

The Canada Safety Council urges people not to use phones while driving. But a growing number of people say that voluntary standards aren't enough; they want the use of cell phones while driving made illegal, as it already is in Japan, Israel, and several other countries.

Why not leave the decision up to the driver? Because the risk posed by driving while talking isn't just a risk to the driver; it's also a safety risk to others—especially people in other cars. Even if you decide that the benefit to you of taking that call is worth the cost, you aren't taking into account the cost to other people. Driving while talking, in other words, generates a serious—sometimes fatal—negative externality.

The Inefficiency of Excess Pollution

We have just shown that in the absence of government action, the quantity of pollution will be *inefficient:* polluters will pollute up to the point at which the marginal social benefit of pollution is zero, as shown by the pollution quantity Q_{MKT} in Figure 19-2. Recall that an outcome is inefficient if some people could be made better off without making others worse off. In Chapter 6 we showed why the market equilibrium quantity in a perfectly competitive market is the efficient quantity of the good, the quantity that maximizes total surplus. Here, we can use a variation of that analysis to show how the presence of a negative externality upsets that result.

Because the marginal social benefit of pollution is zero at Q_{MKT}, reducing the quantity of pollution by one ton would subtract very little from the total social benefit from pollution. In other words, the benefit to polluters of that last unit of pollution is very low—virtually zero. Meanwhile, the marginal social cost imposed on the rest of society of that last ton of pollution at Q_{MKT} is quite high—$400. This means that by reducing the quantity of pollution at Q_{MKT} by one ton, the total social cost of pollution falls by $400, while total social benefits fall by virtually zero. So total surplus rises by approximately $400 if the quantity of pollution at Q_{MKT} is reduced by one ton.

If the quantity of pollution is reduced further, there will be more gains in total surplus, though they will be smaller. For example, if the quantity of pollution is Q_H in Figure 19-2, the marginal social benefit of a ton of pollution is $100, but the marginal social cost is still $300. This means that reducing the quantity of pollution by one ton leads to a net gain in total surplus of approximately $300 – $100 = $200. This tells us that Q_H is still an inefficiently high quantity of pollution. Only if the quantity of pollution is reduced to Q_{OPT}, where the marginal social cost and the marginal social benefit of an additional ton of pollution are both $200, is the outcome efficient.

Private Solutions to Externalities

Can the private sector solve the problem of externalities without government intervention? Bear in mind that when an outcome is inefficient, there is potentially a deal that makes people better off. Why don't individuals find a way to make that deal?

In an influential 1960 article, the economist and Nobel laureate Ronald Coase pointed out that in an ideal world the private sector could indeed deal with all externalities. According to the **Coase theorem,** even in the presence of externalities an economy can always reach an efficient solution provided that the costs of making a deal are sufficiently low. The costs of making a deal are known as **transaction costs.**

According to the **Coase theorem,** even in the presence of externalities an economy can always reach an efficient solution as long as **transaction costs**—the costs to individuals of making a deal—are sufficiently low.

To get a sense of Coase's argument, imagine two neighbours, Mick and Britney, who both like to barbecue in their backyards on summer afternoons. Mick likes to play golden oldies on his boom box while barbecuing; but this annoys Britney, who can't stand that kind of music.

Who prevails? You might think that it depends on the legal rights involved in the case: if the law says that Mick has the right to play whatever music he wants, Britney just has to suffer; if the law says that Mick needs Britney's consent to play music in his backyard, Mick has to live without his favourite music while barbecuing.

But as Coase pointed out, the outcome need not be determined by legal rights, because Britney and Mick can make a private deal. Even if Mick has the right to play his music, Britney could pay him not to. Even if Mick can't play the music without an OK from Britney, he can offer to pay her to give that OK. These payments allow them to reach an efficient solution, regardless of who has the legal upper hand. If the benefit of the music to Mick exceeds its cost to Britney, the music will go on; if the benefit to Mick is less than the cost to Britney, there will be silence.

The implication of Coase's analysis is that externalities need not lead to inefficiency because individuals have an incentive to make mutually beneficial deals—deals that lead them to take externalities into account when making decisions. When individuals *do* take externalities into account when making decisions, economists say that they **internalize the externality.** If externalities are fully internalized, the outcome is efficient even without government intervention.

When individuals take external costs or benefits into account, they **internalize the externality.**

Why can't individuals always internalize externalities? Our barbecue example implicitly assumes the transaction costs are low enough for Mick and Britney to be able to make a deal. In many situations involving externalities, however, transaction costs prevent individuals from making efficient deals. Examples of transaction costs include the following:

- The costs of communication among the interested parties—costs that may be very high if many people are involved or if they are separated by international frontiers
- The costs of making legally binding agreements—costs that may be high if the employment of expensive lawyers is required
- Costly delays involved in bargaining—even if there is a potentially beneficial deal, both sides may hold out in an effort to extract more favourable terms, leading to increased effort and forgone utility

In some cases, people do find ways to reduce transaction costs, allowing them to internalize externalities. For example, many people live in private communities that set rules for home maintenance and behaviour, making bargaining between neighbours unnecessary. But in many other cases, transaction costs are too high to make it possible to deal with externalities through private action. For example, tens of millions of people are adversely affected by acid rain. It would be prohibitively expensive to try to make a deal among all those people and all those power companies.

When transaction costs prevent the private sector from dealing with externalities, it is time to look for government solutions. We turn to public policy in the next section.

economics in action

Thank You for Not Smoking

In the depths of winter, when most other animals are in hibernation, it is relatively easy to spot the common "huff-and-puff". This strange beast likes to congregate outside office buildings, flapping its arms and stamping its feet, blowing smoke into the frozen air.

The phenomenon of the "huff-and-puff" has been caused by increasingly strict rules against smoking in spaces shared by others. This is partly a matter of personal dislike—non-smokers really don't like to smell other people's cigarette smoke—but it also reflects concerns over the health risks of second-hand smoke. As Health Canada's warning on many packs says, "Smoking causes lung cancer, heart disease, and emphysema, and may complicate pregnancy." And there's no question that being in the same room as someone who smokes exposes you to at least some health risk.

Second-hand smoke, then, is clearly an example of a negative externality. But how important is it? Putting a dollars-and-cents value on it—that is, measuring the marginal social cost of cigarette smoke—requires not only estimating the health effects but putting a value on these effects. Despite the difficulty, economists have tried. A paper published in 1993 in the *Journal of Economic Perspectives* surveyed the research on the external costs of both cigarette smoking and alcohol consumption.

According to this paper, valuing the health costs of cigarettes depends on whether you count the costs imposed on members of smokers' families, including unborn children, in addition to costs borne by smokers. If you don't, the external costs of second-hand smoke have been estimated at about only $0.25 per pack smoked. (Using this method of calculation, $0.25 corresponds to the *average* social cost of smoking per pack at the current level of smoking in society.) If you include effects on smokers' families, the number rises considerably—family members who live with smokers are exposed to a lot more smoke. (They are also exposed to the risk of fires, which alone is estimated at $0.12 per pack.) If you include the effects of smoking by pregnant women on their unborn children's future health, the cost is immense—$5.90 per pack, which is more than twice the wholesale price charged by cigarette manufacturers.[1] (The amounts in this example are cited in 1993 U.S. dollars.)■

> > > > > > > > > > > > > > > > > >

>> QUICK REVIEW

- There are costs as well as benefits to reducing pollution, so the optimal quantity of pollution isn't zero. Instead, the *socially optimal quantity of pollution* is the quantity at which the *marginal social cost of pollution* is equal to the *marginal social benefit of pollution*.
- Left to itself, a market economy will typically generate too much pollution because polluters have no incentive to take into account the costs they impose on others.
- Pollution is an example of an *external cost*, or *negative externality;* in contrast, some activities can give rise to *external benefits*, or *positive externalities*. External costs and benefits are known as *externalities*.
- According to the *Coase theorem*, the private sector can sometimes resolve externalities on its own: if *transaction costs* aren't too high, individuals can reach a deal to *internalize the externality*.

>> CHECK YOUR UNDERSTANDING 19-1

1. Waste-water runoff from large poultry farms adversely affects their neighbours. Explain the following:
   a. The nature of the external cost imposed
   b. The outcome in the absence of government intervention or a private deal
   c. The socially optimal outcome
2. According to Yasmin, any student who borrows a book from the university library and fails to return it on time imposes a negative externality on other students. He claims that rather than charging a modest fine for late returns, the library should charge a huge fine, so that borrowers will never return a book late. Is Yasmin's economic reasoning correct?

Solutions appear at back of book.

Policies Towards Pollution

At one time, there were no rules governing the emissions of sulphur dioxide in either Canada or the United States—which is why acid rain got to be such a problem. But in the early 1970s, both countries passed Clean Air Acts that set objectives (in the case of Canada) or rules (in the case of the United States) about sulphur dioxide emissions—and the acidity of rainfall declined significantly. Economists argued, however, that a more flexible system of rules that exploited the effectiveness of markets could achieve lower pollution at less cost. In 1990, the United States put this theory into effect when it modified its Clean Air Act. And guess what? The economists were right!

In this section we'll look at the policies governments use to deal with pollution and at how economic analysis has been used to improve those policies.

Environmental Standards

The most serious external costs in the modern world are surely those associated with actions that damage the environment—air pollution, water pollution, habitat destruction, and so on. Protection of the environment has become a major role of government in all economically advanced nations.

In Canada, environmental legislation is shared among all levels of government. While the federal government has the power to sign international treaties to protect air resources on a global scale, it cannot implement these treaties without legal permission from the provinces. For example, in 1971 the federal government's Clean Air Act established national air-quality objectives, but the provinces were free to choose their own regulations in deciding how (and to what degree) to conform with those objectives.

How does a country protect its environment? At present the main policy tools worldwide are **environmental standards,** rules that protect the environment by specifying actions by producers and consumers. A familiar example is the law that requires all new automobiles to have catalytic converters, which reduce the emission of chemicals that can cause smog and lead to health problems. Other rules require

Environmental standards are rules that protect the environment by specifying actions by producers and consumers.

[1] M. Gross, J. L. Sindelar, J. Mullahy, and R. Anderson, "Policy Watch: Alcohol and Cigarette Taxes", *Journal of Economic Perspectives* 7 (1993): 211–222.

communities to treat their sewage, factories to avoid or limit certain kinds of pollution, and so on.

Environmental standards came into widespread use in the 1960s and 1970s, and they have had considerable success in reducing pollution. For example, through the use of standards the governments of the seven eastern provinces were able to cut their sulphur dioxide emissions significantly. By 1994, sulphur dioxide emissions in eastern Canada were 54% lower than 1980 levels, even though the provinces had larger economies and larger populations in 1994.

Despite some success with standards, economists believe that while regulators can control a polluter's emissions directly, there are more efficient ways than environmental standards to deal with pollution. By using methods grounded in economic analysis, society can achieve a cleaner environment at lower cost. Environmental standards are an inflexible tool and don't allow reductions in pollution to be achieved at minimum cost. For example, Plant A and Plant B might be ordered to reduce pollution by the same percentage, even if their costs of achieving that objective are very different.

How does economic theory suggest that pollution should be directly controlled? There are actually two approaches: taxes and tradable permits. As we'll see, either approach can achieve the efficient outcome at the minimum feasible cost.

Emissions Taxes

An **emissions tax** is a tax that depends on the amount of pollution a firm produces.

One way to deal with pollution directly is to charge polluters an **emissions tax.** Emissions taxes are taxes that depend on the amount of pollution a firm produces. For example, power plants might be charged $200 for every ton of sulphur dioxide they emit.

Look again at Figure 19-2, which shows that the socially optimal quantity of pollution is Q_{OPT}. At that quantity of pollution, the marginal social benefit and marginal social cost of an additional ton of emissions are equal at $200. But in the absence of government intervention, power companies have no incentive to limit pollution to the socially optimal quantity Q_{OPT}; instead, they will push pollution up to the quantity Q_{MKT}, at which marginal social benefit is zero.

It's now easy to see how an emissions tax can solve the problem. If power companies are required to pay a tax of $200 per ton of emissions, they now face a marginal cost of $200 per ton and have an incentive to reduce emissions to Q_{OPT}, the socially optimal quantity. This illustrates a general result: an emissions tax equal to the marginal social cost at the socially optimal quantity of pollution induces polluters to internalize the externality—to take into account the true costs to society of their actions.

Why is an emissions tax an efficient way (that is, a cost-minimizing way) to reduce pollution but environmental standards generally are not? Because an emissions tax ensures that the marginal benefit of pollution is equal for all sources of pollution but an environmental standard does not. Figure 19-3 shows a hypothetical industry consisting of only two plants, Plant A and Plant B. We'll assume that Plant A uses newer technology than Plant B and so has a lower cost of reducing pollution. Reflecting this difference in costs, Plant A's marginal benefit of pollution curve, MB_A, lies below Plant B's marginal benefit of pollution curve, MB_B. Because it is more costly for Plant B to reduce its pollution at any output quantity, an additional ton of pollution is worth more to Plant B than to Plant A.

In the absence of government action, we know that polluters will pollute until the marginal social benefit of an additional unit of emissions is equal to zero. Recall that the marginal social benefit of pollution is the cost savings, at the margin, to polluters of an additional unit of pollution. This means that without government intervention each plant will pollute until its own marginal benefit of pollution is equal to zero. This corresponds to an emissions quantity of 600 tons each for Plants A and B—the quantity of pollution at which MB_A and MB_B are each equal to zero. So although Plant A and Plant B value a ton of emissions differently, without government action they will each choose to emit the same amount of pollution.

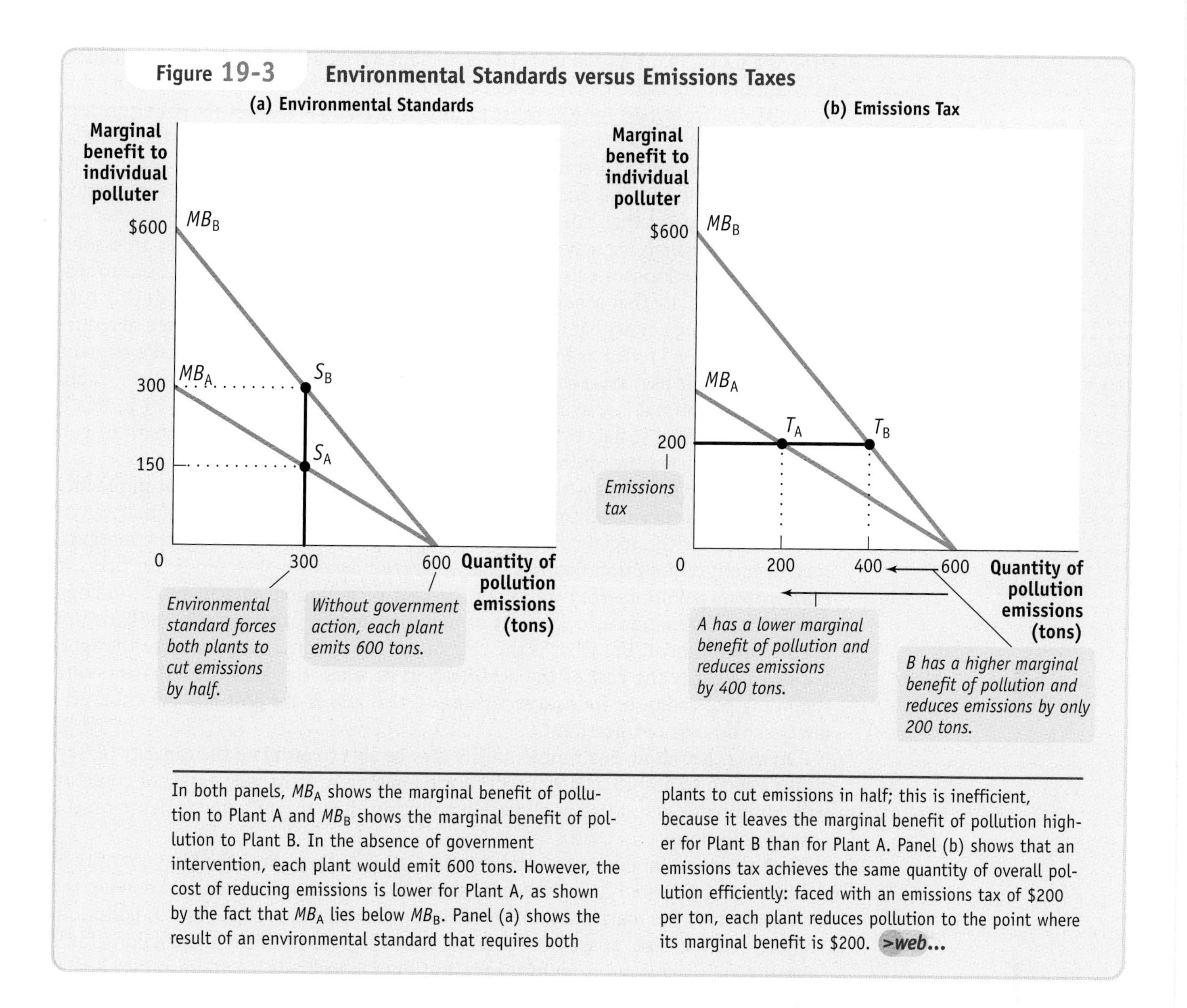

Figure 19-3 Environmental Standards versus Emissions Taxes

In both panels, MB_A shows the marginal benefit of pollution to Plant A and MB_B shows the marginal benefit of pollution to Plant B. In the absence of government intervention, each plant would emit 600 tons. However, the cost of reducing emissions is lower for Plant A, as shown by the fact that MB_A lies below MB_B. Panel (a) shows the result of an environmental standard that requires both plants to cut emissions in half; this is inefficient, because it leaves the marginal benefit of pollution higher for Plant B than for Plant A. Panel (b) shows that an emissions tax achieves the same quantity of overall pollution efficiently: faced with an emissions tax of $200 per ton, each plant reduces pollution to the point where its marginal benefit is $200. >web...

Now suppose that the government decides that overall pollution from this industry should be cut in half, from 1,200 tons to 600 tons. Panel (a) of Figure 19-3 shows how this might be achieved with an environmental standard that requires each plant to cut its emissions in half, from 600 to 300 tons. The standard has the desired effect of reducing overall emissions from 1,200 to 600 tons but accomplishes it in an inefficient way. As you can see from panel (a), the environmental standard leads Plant A to produce at point S_A, where its marginal benefit of pollution is $150, but Plant B produces at point S_B, where its marginal benefit of pollution is twice as high, $300.

This difference in marginal benefits between the two plants tells us that the same quantity of pollution can be achieved at lower total cost by allowing Plant B to pollute more than 300 tons but inducing Plant A to pollute less. In fact, the efficient way to reduce pollution is to ensure that at the industry-wide outcome, the marginal benefit of pollution is the same for all plants. When each plant values a unit of pollution equally, there is no way to re-arrange pollution reduction among the various plants that achieves the optimal quantity of pollution at a lower total cost.

We can see from panel (b) how an emissions tax achieves exactly that result. Suppose both Plant A and Plant B pay an emissions tax of $200 per ton, so that the marginal cost of an additional ton of emissions to each plant is now $200 rather than zero. As a result, Plant A produces at T_A and Plant B produces at T_B. So Plant A reduces its pollution more than it would under an inflexible environmental standard, cutting its emissions from 600 to 200 tons; meanwhile, Plant B reduces its pollution less, going from 600 to 400 tons. In the end, total pollution—600 tons—is the same as under the environmental standard, but total surplus is higher. That's because the reduction in pollution has been achieved efficiently, allocating most of the reduction to Plant A, the plant that can reduce emissions at lower cost.

The term *emissions tax* may convey the misleading impression that taxes are a solution to only one kind of external cost, pollution. In fact, taxes can be used to discourage any activity that generates negative externalities, such as driving during rush hour or operating a noisy bar in a residential area. In general, taxes designed to reduce external costs are known as **Pigouvian taxes,** after the economist A. C. Pigou, who emphasized their usefulness in a classic 1920 book, *The Economics of Welfare*. In our example, the optimal Pigouvian tax is $200; as you can see from Figure 19-2, this is where the marginal social cost of pollution equals the marginal social benefit of pollution, and achieves the optimal output quantity, Q_{OPT}.

Taxes designed to reduce external costs are known as **Pigouvian taxes.**

Are there any problems with emissions taxes? The main concern is that in practice government officials usually aren't sure how high the tax should be set. It may not be easy to calculate the social costs and benefits of pollution. Calculating the marginal social benefit of pollution requires that we know how costly it would be for firms to refrain from pollution—that we know the cost of pollution abatement technology. Calculating the marginal social costs of pollution requires that we put a dollar value on the environment. But what is the cost of the extinction of a species like the spotted owl? What is the cost of the acidification of lakes that kills the fish—and with them any possibility of freshwater fishing? Calculations are possible, but there will always be a range of uncertainty.

On the other hand, environmentalists may be able to estimate the capacity of, say, a lake system to absorb acid rain without damaging it. It may be easier to come up with sustainable quantities of allowable pollution than to put a dollar figure on the cost of pollution.

One advantage of environmental standards is that they allow the total quantity of pollution to be limited in a given geographical area without regulators knowing the details of either the marginal social benefits or the marginal social costs of pollution. The big disadvantage, as we have seen, is that they are inefficient. Emissions taxes solve the inefficiency problem in theory. But in practice their big disadvantage is that we don't know how high to set the tax to achieve a given reduction in pollution. Is there no way of combining the advantages of environmental standards and emissions taxes, while avoiding their disadvantages? Happily, there is such a solution: tradable emissions permits.

Tradable Emissions Permits

Tradable emissions permits are licenses to emit limited quantities of pollutants that can be bought and sold by polluters. These permits work very much like taxes on emissions, only instead of paying a tax for every unit of pollution, the firm buys a permit for every unit of pollution—the cost of the permit operates just like the tax. However, by controlling the total quantity of permits issued, the government more easily controls the total amount of pollution that occurs. The fact that the permits are tradable ensures that pollution is reduced in the most efficient way.

Tradable emissions permits are licenses to emit limited quantities of pollutants that can be bought and sold by polluters.

In some schemes, the government will sell the initial allocation of permits at an auction. But this isn't necessary. Tradable emissions permits work equally well even when the government initially gives them away—as long as permits are scarce and *tradable,* they will command a price that reflects their scarcity value.

For example, each power plant might be issued permits equal to 50% of its emissions before the system went into effect. Firms with differing costs of reducing pollution can now engage in mutually beneficial transactions: those that find it easier to reduce pollution will sell some of their permits to those that find it more difficult. In other words, firms will use transactions in permits to reallocate pollution reduction among themselves, so that in the end those with the lowest cost will reduce their pollution the most, while those with the highest cost will reduce their pollution the least. Using our original example, this means that Plant A will find it profitable to sell 100 of its 300 government-issued licenses to Plant B. The effect of a tradable permit system is to create a market in rights to pollute.

Just like emissions taxes, tradable permits provide polluters with an incentive to take into account the marginal social cost of pollution. To see why, suppose that the market price of a permit to emit one ton of sulphur dioxide is $200. Then every plant has an incentive to limit its emissions of sulphur dioxide to the point where the marginal benefit of emissions is $200. This is obvious for plants that buy rights to pollute: if a plant must pay $200 for the right to emit an additional ton of sulphur dioxide, it faces the same incentives as a plant facing an emissions tax of $200 per ton. But it's equally true for plants that have more permits than they plan to use: by *not* emitting a ton of sulphur dioxide, a plant frees up a permit that it can sell for $200, so the opportunity cost of a ton of emissions to the plant's owner is $200.

In short, tradable emissions permits have the same cost-minimizing advantage as emissions taxes over environmental standards: either system ensures that those who can reduce pollution most cheaply are the ones who do so. The socially optimal quantity of pollution shown in Figure 19-2 could be efficiently achieved either way: by imposing an emissions tax of $200 per ton of pollution or by issuing tradable permits to emit Q_{OPT} tons of pollution. If regulators choose to issue Q_{OPT} permits, where one permit allows the release of one ton of emissions, then the equilibrium market price of a permit among polluters will indeed be $200. Why? You can see from Figure 19-2 that at Q_{OPT}, only polluters with a marginal benefit of pollution of $200 or more will buy a permit. And the last polluter who buys—who has a marginal benefit of exactly $200—sets the market price.

It's important to realize that emissions taxes and tradable permits do more than induce polluting industries to reduce their output. They also provide incentives to create and use less-polluting technology. In the United States, where tradable permit schemes have been used to reduce sulphur dioxide emissions, the main effect has been to change *how* electricity is produced rather than to reduce electricity output. For example, power companies have shifted to the use of alternative fuels such as low-sulphur coal and natural gas; they have also installed scrubbers that take much of the sulphur dioxide out of a power plant's emissions.

We have emphasized that tradable emissions permits combine the best features of emissions standards and emissions taxes: they can achieve a given reduction in emissions (like emissions standards) in the most efficient way (like emissions taxes). They also have two other attractive features. First, there is nothing to stop environmental groups from buying up some permits themselves and taking them off the market, if they feel the government has issued too many. Second, the price fetched by permits is a very good signal of how difficult it is for firms to reduce their pollution emissions. A very high price indicates that abatement is difficult and still costly. But over time, we would expect firms to invest in new, cost-effective methods of pollution abatement. As this occurs, the price firms are willing to pay for emission permits will drop. This indicates that it may be time to tighten environmental controls and issue fewer permits.

Canadian regulators have yet to experiment with tradable emissions permits to enforce pollution standards. However, the United States has had several successful experiences using them. They were used to control lead in gasoline by issuing refineries an ever-smaller number of tradable permits, until lead in gasoline was eliminated completely. The United States is currently using tradable emissions permits to reduce sulphur dioxide emissions from coal-burning electric power plants, the major source of acid rain. In 2004, the price of a permit to release one ton of sulphur dioxide into the atmosphere was US$260. This is well below the price most analysts expected, and some environmentalists have taken the low price as a sign that the government should seek further reductions in pollution levels.

economics in action

Environmental Regulation in Canada

In Canada, environmental legislation is shared among all levels of government. The federal government has legislative control over the oceans (and ocean fisheries), shipping (including spills), and international pollution problems. The provinces and municipalities are concerned with environmental matters within their own territorial jurisdictions, such as water and drainage systems, garbage disposal, and sewage treatment. However, there is also considerable overlap in jurisdiction between the federal and provincial governments, partly because in some areas (such as agriculture and the inland fisheries) responsibility is explicitly shared, and partly because the responsibility for environmental control is not completely spelled out in the Constitution. Thus, the provinces each have their own environmental legislation that attempts to control the discharge of contaminants into the air, water, and soil, alongside similar controls placed by federal legislation. On several occasions the court system has been called upon to determine which government, provincial or federal, has the power to enact environmental legislation when laws conflict.

This division of powers complicates environmental legislation in Canada. Currently, the provinces and the federal government are working through the Canadian Council of Ministers of the Environment (CCME) to try to harmonize regulations across jurisdictions. This painfully slow process absorbs valuable energy and personnel.

Canadian environmental legislation has also been hampered by an almost total reliance on emissions standards—the "command and control" approach. This involves outright prohibitions, pollution approvals and licenses, and the establishment of minimum standards. This system is inefficient for several reasons. First, there is no efficient distribution of pollution reduction among firms. Second, once firms comply with the standards there is no ongoing incentive to adopt the most efficient pollution-reduction technology. Not only is this system inefficient, it also susceptible to political blackmail—companies might threaten to shut down rather than comply with regulations; and given the importance of jobs, governments are tempted to issue waivers or give generous subsidies to facilitate compliance. Once firms realize that exemptions are a possibility, all companies with enough influence begin to play the same game.

It is interesting that since the federal government has signed the Kyoto Accord, tradable permits will be used in Canada to control carbon dioxide emissions (the principal greenhouse gas). However, not all provinces have agreed to cooperate with the federal government to implement Canada's commitment under this accord—which is to reduce our greenhouse gas emissions to 6% below 1990 levels by 2012. Again, we see how the division of powers between the federal and provincial governments complicates environmental legislation in Canada. ■

< < < < < < < < < < < < < < < < < <

>>QUICK REVIEW

- Governments often limit pollution with *environmental standards.* Generally such standards are an inefficient way to reduce pollution because they are inflexible.
- When the quantity of pollution emitted can be directly observed and controlled, environmental goals can be achieved efficiently in two ways: *emissions taxes* and *tradable emissions permits*. These methods are efficient because they are flexible, allocating more pollution reduction to those who can do it more cheaply.
- An emissions tax is a form of *Pigouvian tax*. The optimal Pigouvian tax is equal to the marginal social cost of pollution at the socially optimal quantity of pollution.

>>CHECK YOUR UNDERSTANDING 19-2

1. Some opponents of tradable emissions permits object to them on the ground that polluters that sell their permits benefit monetarily from their contribution to polluting the environment. Assess this argument.
2. Explain the following:
   a. Why an emissions tax smaller than or greater than the marginal social cost at Q_{OPT} reduces total surplus
   b. Why a system of tradable emissions permits that sets the total quantity of allowable pollution higher or lower than Q_{OPT} reduces total surplus

Solutions appear at back of book.

Production, Consumption, and Externalities

Nobody imposes external costs like pollution out of malice. Pollution, traffic congestion, and other harmful externalities are side effects of activities, like electricity generation or driving, that are otherwise desirable. We've just learned how government regulators can move the market to the socially optimal quantity when the side effect can be directly controlled. But as we cautioned earlier, in some cases it's not possible to directly control the side effect; only the original activity can be influenced. As we'll see shortly, government policies in these situations must instead be geared to changing the quantity of the original activity, which in turn changes the quantity of the side effect produced.

This approach, although slightly more complicated, has several advantages. First, it gives us a clear understanding of how the quantity of the original, desirable activity is altered by policies designed to manage its side effects (such alteration will, in fact, typically occur both when the side effect can be directly controlled and when it can't). Second, it lets us evaluate arguments against environmental policy—arguments that arise from the fact that desirable activities are unavoidably impeded by policies intended to control their negative side effects. Finally, it helps us think about a phenomenon that is different but related to the problem of external costs: what should be done when an activity generates external *benefits*.

National Trust Photographic Library/Joe Cornish/ The Image Works

Muck and methane gas: the costly side effects of producing a side of bacon.

Private versus Social Costs

Given current technology, there is no affordable way to breed and raise livestock on a commercial scale without hurting the environment. Whatever it is—cows, pigs, chicken, sheep, or salmon—livestock farming produces prodigious amounts of what is euphemistically known as "muck". But that's not all: scientists estimate that the amount of methane gas produced by livestock currently rivals the pollution caused by the burning of fossil fuels in the creation of greenhouses gases. From the point of view of society as a whole, then, the cost of livestock farming includes both direct production costs to the farmer (payments for factors of production and inputs such as animal feed) and the external environmental costs imposed as a by-product. In the absence of government intervention, however, livestock farmers have no incentive to take into account the environmental costs of their production decisions. As a result, in the absence of government intervention, livestock farmers will produce too much output.

Panel (a) of Figure 19-4 (page 492) illustrates this point. The market demand curve for livestock by consumers is represented by the curve D; the market, or industry, supply curve is given by the curve S. In the absence of government intervention, market equilibrium will be at point E_{MKT}, yielding the amount produced and consumed Q_{MKT} and the market price P_{MKT}. At that point, the marginal benefit to society of another unit of livestock (measured by the market price) is equal to the marginal cost *incurred by the industry* for producing that unit.

Let's look a little more closely at the supply curve. Assuming that the livestock industry is competitive, we know from Chapter 9 that the industry supply curve corresponds to the horizontal sum of all the individual supply curves of producers in the industry. In addition, we know that each individual producer's supply curve corresponds to its marginal cost curve. These two facts taken together imply that the industry supply curve is the horizontal sum of the individual producers' marginal cost curves: a given point on S corresponds to the total industry-wide marginal cost at the corresponding output level. But we also know from our earlier discussion that this estimation of marginal cost does not include the external cost that production imposes on others. In other words, when external costs are present, the industry supply curve does not reflect the true cost to society of production of the good.

The **marginal social cost of a good or activity** is equal to the marginal cost of production plus its marginal external cost.

In order to account for the true cost to society of an additional unit of the good, we must define the **marginal social cost of a good or activity,** which is equal to

Figure 19-4 Negative Externalities and Production

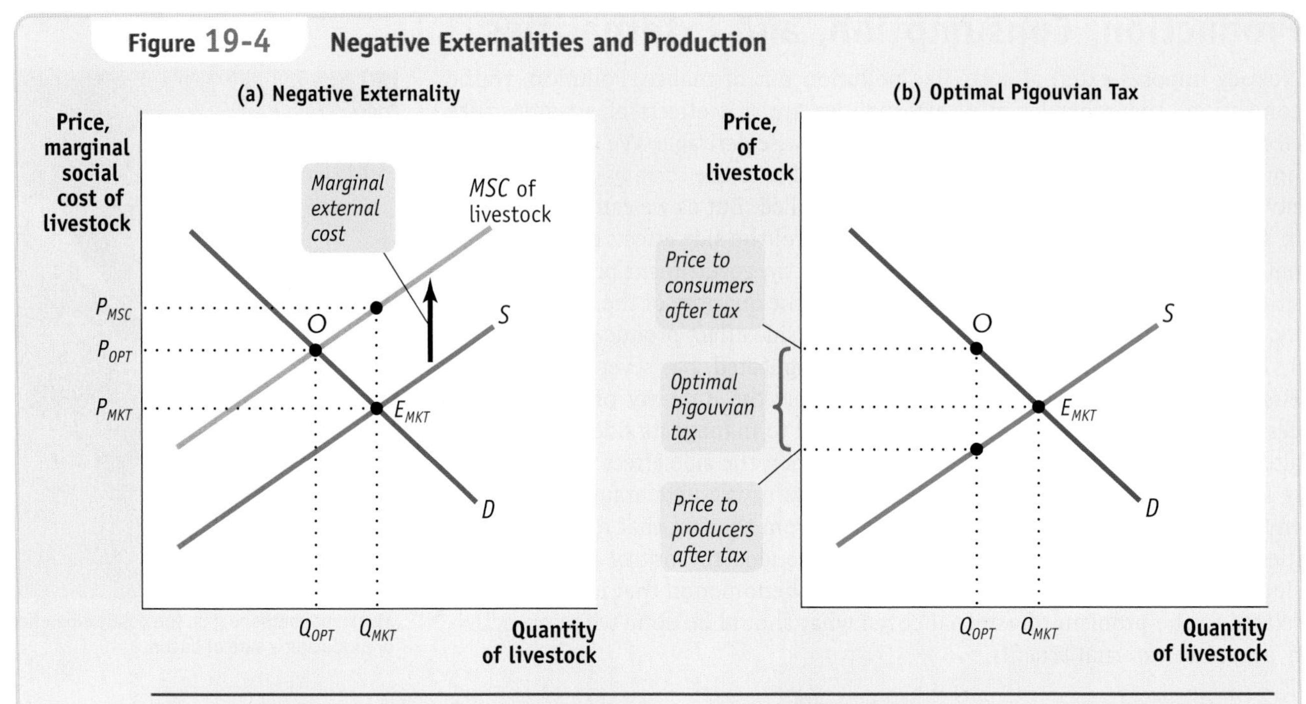

Livestock production generates external costs, so the marginal social cost curve of livestock, *MSC*, corresponds to the supply curve, *S*, shifted upward by the marginal external cost. Panel (a) shows that without government action, the market produces the amount Q_{MKT}. It is greater than the socially optimal quantity of livestock production, Q_{OPT}, the quantity at which *MSC* crosses the demand curve, *D*. At Q_{MKT}, the market price, P_{MKT}, is less than P_{MSC}, the true marginal cost to society of livestock production. Panel (b) shows how an optimal Pigouvian tax on livestock production, equal to its marginal external cost, moves the production to Q_{OPT}, resulting in lower output and a higher price to consumers. **>web...**

the marginal cost of production plus the marginal external cost generated by an additional unit of the good or activity. It captures the increase in production cost to the industry *and* the increase in external cost to the rest of society caused by producing one more unit. Panel (a) of Figure 19-4 shows the marginal social cost of livestock curve, *MSC*; it corresponds to the industry supply curve *shifted upward* by the amount of the marginal external cost. With the marginal social cost curve and the demand curve, we can find the socially optimal quantity of a good or activity that creates external costs: it is the quantity Q_{OPT}, the quantity corresponding to *O*, the point at which *MSC* and *D* cross. Reflecting the proper accounting for external cost, Q_{OPT} is less than Q_{MKT}. So, left to its own, a market will result in too much of a good that carries external costs being produced and consumed. Correspondingly, without government action, the price to consumers of such a good is too low: at the output level Q_{MKT}, the unregulated market price P_{MKT} is lower than P_{MSC}, the true marginal cost to society of a unit of livestock.

Environmental Policy, Revisited

We have already seen two efficient methods for controlling pollution when government regulators can control it directly: an emissions tax and a system of tradable emissions permits. Are there similar methods that lead to an efficient quantity of pollution when regulators can target only the original activity or good, such as livestock production? Yes, there are—although they will take the form of a tax on livestock sales or a license to produce a unit of livestock rather than on the pollution created. These methods will move the market to the efficient quantity by compelling producers to internalize the externality caused by livestock production in their decisions.

Consider first the case of a Pigouvian tax on livestock transactions. Once such a tax is in effect, the cost to a livestock farmer of producing an additional unit of livestock includes both the marginal cost of production and the tax. If the tax is set at the right amount, it is exactly equal to the marginal external cost. As shown in panel (b) of Figure 19-4, the optimal Pigouvian tax will move the market outcome to the optimal point O.

A system of tradable production permits that restricts the industry-wide quantity of livestock produced to the optimal level has the same effect. Suppose that in order to produce an additional unit of livestock, a farmer must purchase a permit. The cost of this permit behaves like a Pigouvian tax, and once again external costs are completely internalized in the private decisions of producers. Even if the farmer already possesses the permit, its opportunity cost—the price it could command in the market for permits—acts like a Pigouvian tax.

So Q_{OPT}, the efficient quantity of livestock produced and consumed, corresponds to the efficient quantity of pollution generated by livestock production. You might ask yourself at this point how this analysis, in terms of the optimal amount of a good or activity that gives rise to an external cost, relates to our earlier analysis of the optimal amount of pollution. Except for the effect that emissions taxes and tradable emissions permits have on the creation and adoption of less-polluting production methods, the two approaches are equivalent: the difference between the two comes down to a matter of units. The first analysis was carried out in units of pollution and the second in units of a good or activity that yields pollution. But regardless of the framework we use, the underlying method is the same: to find the level at which society's marginal benefit from another unit equals society's marginal cost.

But our second analysis does create additional insights: we see how consumption choices are affected by policies designed to counteract external costs. Note that in panel (b) of Figure 19-4, consumers consume less livestock (in the form of meat purchased at supermarkets and restaurants) and pay a higher market price at the socially optimal quantity. (We know from Chapter 5 that exactly how the burden of the tax is allocated between producers and consumers depends on the price elasticities of demand and supply.) Moreover, this shows us that criticisms of environmental policies made exclusively on the basis that they "hurt consumers" are misguided.

Finally, you might ask which method a regulator would choose if a choice existed between policies that target pollution directly and policies that target production of the original good or activity. Generally, whenever feasible it is a good idea to target the pollution directly. The main reason, as we mentioned earlier, is that it gives incentives for the creation and adoption of less-polluting production methods. This, in turn, lessens the disincentive to produce the good—which is something, after all, that people want.

An example of this phenomenon was recently reported. A Florida-based company, Agcert, has developed technology whereby methane from pig-waste tanks can be drawn off and either burned or used as "biofuel" to generate electricity. The company claims that this technology can achieve an average emissions reduction of one ton of methane gas per pig per year, a sizable savings in an industry where farms can have as many as 10,000 animals. Farmers could then be granted "credits" for their emissions reductions, which they could sell to producers in other industries who want to purchase a license to pollute. Such credits could be a lucrative source of income for farmers, given that the current market price in the United States for a one-ton credit for emissions is about US$7 to US$8. Agcert is currently valued at around $128 million. As some have commented, this invention has given new life to an old saying among plumbers and sewer workers: "Where there's muck, there's gold."

Private versus Social Benefits

Not all externalities are negative. In some important cases, an economic activity creates external benefits—that is, individual actions provide benefits to other people for which the producers are not compensated.

The most important source of external benefits in the modern economy probably involves creation of knowledge. In high-tech industries like semiconductors, innovations by one firm are quickly emulated and improved upon both by rival firms in the same industry and by firms in other industries. Such spreading of knowledge among individuals and firms is known as a **technology spillover.**

A **technology spillover** is an external benefit that results when knowledge spreads among individuals and firms.

In Chapter 22 we'll discuss the economics of goods whose value lies principally in the knowledge or information they embody. For now, let's just look at the implications of external benefits in general for economic efficiency and economic policy. Suppose that the production of some good—say, semiconductor chips—yields positive externalities. How does this affect our analysis of the chip market, and does it create a justification for government intervention?

Just as external costs cause the marginal social *cost* of producing a good to exceed the industry's marginal cost, when there are external benefits from a good, the marginal social *benefit* exceeds consumers' marginal benefit. This is illustrated in panel (a) of Figure 19-5, which shows the market for semiconductor chips. Since there are no external costs in this case, the industry supply curve, *S*, represents the true marginal social cost to society of production. The demand curve, *D*, represents the marginal benefit that accrues to *consumers of the good:* each point on the demand curve corresponds to the willingness to pay of the last consumer to purchase the good at the corresponding price. But it does not incorporate the benefits to society as a whole

Figure 19-5 Positive Externalities and Production

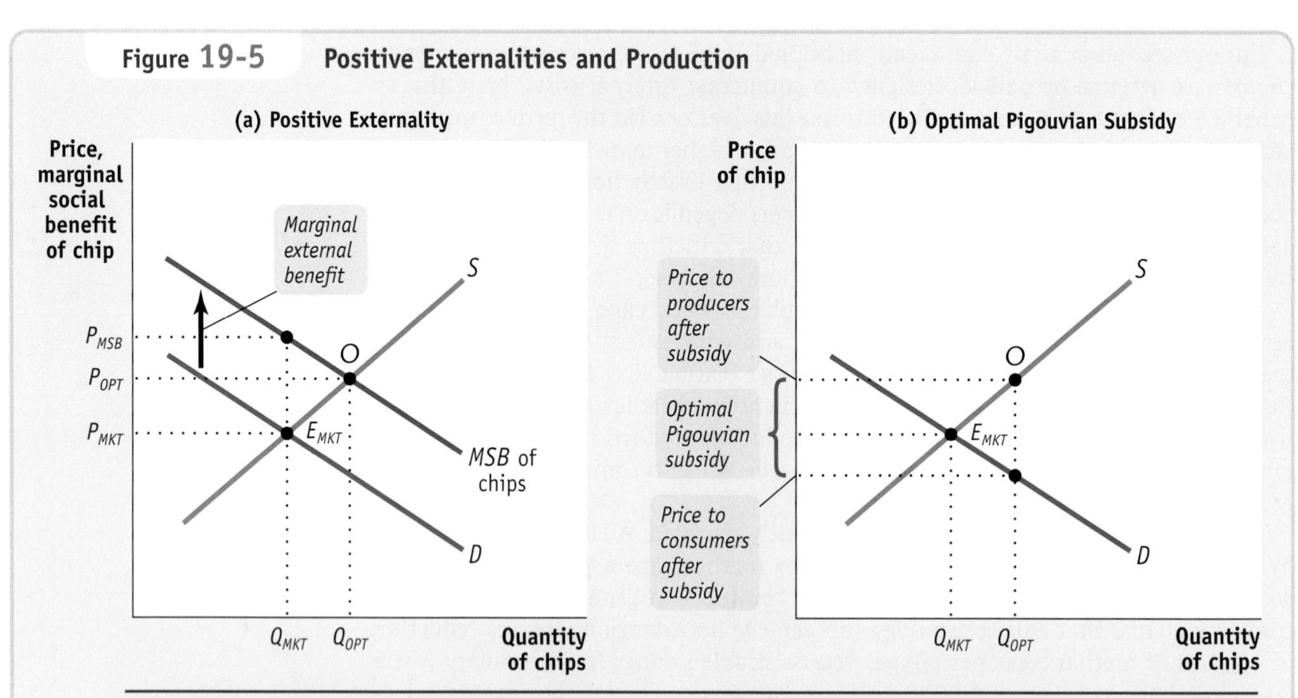

Semiconductor chip production generates external benefits, so the marginal social benefit curve of chips, *MSB*, corresponds to the demand curve, *D*, shifted upward by the marginal external benefit. Panel (a) shows that without government action, the market produces Q_{MKT}. It is lower than the socially optimal quantity of production, Q_{OPT}, the quantity at which *MSB* crosses the supply curve, *S*. At Q_{MKT}, the market price, P_{MKT}, is less than P_{MSB}, the true marginal benefit to society of semiconductor chip production. Panel (b) shows how an optimal Pigouvian subsidy to chip producers, equal to its marginal external benefit, moves the production to Q_{OPT}, resulting in higher output and a higher price to producers. **>web...**

from production of the good—the technological spillover an additional unit provides to the economy as a whole.

To explore this phenomenon we need a new concept, the **marginal social benefit of a good or activity**—the marginal benefit that accrues to consumers from an additional unit of the good or activity, plus the marginal external benefit to society from an additional unit. As you can see from panel (a) of Figure 19-5, the marginal social benefit curve, *MSB*, corresponds to the demand curve *D shifted upward* by the amount of the marginal external benefit.

The **marginal social benefit of a good or activity** is equal to the marginal benefit that accrues to consumers plus its marginal external benefit.

The analysis in this case is very similar to that of external costs. Left to itself, the market will reach an equilibrium at E_{MKT}, the point at which the demand curve *D* crosses the supply curve *S* at a market price P_{MKT}. But the quantity of output at this equilibrium, Q_{MKT}, is inefficiently low: at that output level, the marginal social benefit of an additional unit, P_{MSB}, exceeds the industry's marginal cost of producing that unit, P_{MKT}. The optimal quantity of production and consumption is Q_{OPT}, the quantity at which marginal cost is equal to marginal social benefit.

How can the economy be induced to produce Q_{OPT} chips? The answer is a **Pigouvian subsidy:** a payment designed to encourage activities that yield external benefits. The optimal Pigouvian subsidy, shown in panel (b) of Figure 19-5, is equal to the marginal external benefit of producing an additional unit. Producers receive the price paid by consumers plus the per-unit subsidy, inducing them to produce more output. Such a subsidy is an example of an **industrial policy,** a general term for a policy of supporting industries believed to yield positive externalities.

A **Pigouvian subsidy** is a payment designed to encourage activities that yield external benefits.

An **industrial policy** is a policy that supports industries believed to yield positive externalities.

Although the strict economic logic supporting such efforts is impeccable, economists are generally less enthusiastic about industrial policies to promote positive externalities than they are about fees and permit schemes to discourage negative externalities. This lack of enthusiasm reflects a mixture of practical and political judgments. First, positive externalities—which most often involve the creation of knowledge and new technologies—are typically much harder to identify and measure than negative externalities. (A simple sensor can keep track of how many tons of sulphur dioxide come out of a smokestack. But how do you tell whether and when a new product embodies a technology that will benefit other producers and consumers?) In addition, producers gain monetarily from subsidies: they receive a higher price than they otherwise would. So, many economists also fear, with some historical justification, that a program intended to promote industries that yield positive externalities will degenerate into a program that promotes industries with political pull.

However, there is one activity that is widely believed to generate positive externalities and is provided with considerable subsidies: education!

economics in action

Is Education Subsidized Too Little in Canada? Or Too Much?

It is well established that the private returns to education are large, and seem to be increasing. Nevertheless, high private returns to education do not necessarily translate into high social returns. There are two competing theories in this regard: human capital theory, and the "ability-sorting" theory.

Human capital theory supposes that students learn useful stuff at university, which has value when they get a job afterwards. This is why firms pay higher wages to people with a university degree—because they are more productive. Moreover, if one person's education makes others more productive, then the social returns to education will be even greater than the private returns. Such positive externalities justify governments giving subsidies to education on efficiency grounds.

However, the "ability-sorting" theory is more pessimistic. It supposes that students learn nothing of any use at university! Firms prefer to hire university graduates simply because they tend to have more innate ability. The education process sorts people according to their innate ability, which otherwise would be unobservable. This theory suggests that there are negative externalities to education—the more education everyone has, the less having an education indicates innate ability—and suggests that governments should not subsidize education but should tax it!

Happily, two types of empirical evidence support the human capital theory. First, cross-country empirical studies on the determinants of economic growth have definitively shown that "countries with a better-educated work force tend to grow faster".[2] Second, detailed empirical studies have shown the existence of substantial positive externalities associated with education. According to Davies (2003), these education externalities may be equivalent to a rate of return of 6 to 8 percentage points.[3]

Interestingly, this implies that current education subsidies in Canada are about right. Ideally, they should make the private rate of return to education equal to the social return. Estimates by Vaillancourt and Bourdeau-Primeau (2002) suggest that subsidies to education raise the private return to education by about 8% (from about 10% to about 18%).[4] This difference of 8% is approximately the size of the estimated positive externality (between 6 and 8%). ■

>> QUICK REVIEW

- When there are external costs, the *marginal social cost of a good or activity* exceeds the industry's marginal cost of producing the good. In the absence of government intervention, the industry typically produces too much of the good.
- The socially optimal quantity can be achieved by an optimal Pigouvian tax, equal to the marginal external cost, or by a system of tradable production permits.
- The most common examples of external benefits are *technology spillovers*. When these occur, the *marginal social benefit of a good or activity* exceeds the marginal benefit to consumers, and too little of the good is produced in the absence of government intervention. The socially optimal quantity can be achieved by an optimal *Pigouvian subsidy*—a type of *industrial policy*—equal to the marginal external benefit.

>> CHECK YOUR UNDERSTANDING 19-3

1. Explain how the London congestion charge described in Chapter 3 (page 65), in which cars entering central London during business hours must pay a fee of £5, can be an optimal policy to manage inner-city pollution and congestion.
2. In each of the following cases, determine whether an external cost or an external benefit is imposed and what an appropriate policy response would be.
   a. Trees planted in urban areas improve air quality and lower summer temperatures.
   b. Water-saving toilets reduce the need to pump water from rivers and aquifers. The cost of a litre of water to homeowners is virtually zero.
   c. Old computer monitors contain toxic materials that pollute the environment when improperly disposed of.

Solutions appear at back of book.

• A LOOK AHEAD •

Externalities are an important justification for government intervention in the economy. As we've seen, government programs such as emissions taxes or tradable permit systems may be necessary to bring individual incentives in line with social costs or benefits.

In the next chapter, we'll turn to some related justifications for government intervention: the problems of *public goods* like lighthouses, which won't be provided in the absence of government action, and *common resources* like fish in the sea, which will be overused in the absence of government action.

[2]Xavier Sala-i-Martin, "Cross-Sectional Regressions and the Empirics of Economic Growth", *European Economic Review* 38 (1994): 739–747.
[3]Jim Davies, "Empirical Evidence on Human Capital Externalities", Department of Finance, Working Paper 11 (2003).
[4]Francois Vaillancourt and Sandrine Bourdeau-Primeau, "The Returns to University Education in Canada, 1990 and 1995", in *Renovating the Ivory Tower: Canadian Universities and the Knowledge Economy*, ed. David Laidler, 215–240 (Toronto: C. D. Howe Institute, 2002).

SUMMARY

1. When pollution can be directly observed and controlled, government policies should be geared directly to producing the **socially optimal quantity of pollution,** the quantity at which the **marginal social cost of pollution** is equal to the **marginal social benefit of pollution.** In the absence of government intervention, a market produces too much pollution because polluters take only their benefit from polluting into account, not the costs imposed on others.
2. The costs to society of pollution are an example of an **external cost;** in some cases, however, economic activities yield **external benefits.** External costs and benefits are jointly known as **externalities,** with external costs called **negative externalities** and external benefits called **positive externalities.**
3. According to the **Coase theorem,** individuals can find a way to **internalize the externality,** making government intervention unnecessary, as long as **transaction costs**—the costs of making a deal—are sufficiently low. However, in many cases transaction costs are too high to permit such deals.
4. Governments often deal with pollution by imposing **environmental standards,** a method, economists argue, that is usually an inefficient way to reduce pollution. Two efficient (cost-minimizing) methods for reducing pollution are **emissions taxes,** a form of **Pigouvian tax,** and **tradable emissions permits.** The optimal Pigouvian tax on pollution is equal to its marginal social cost at the socially optimal quantity of pollution. These methods also provide incentives for the creation and adoption of less-polluting production technologies.
5. When only the original good or activity can be controlled, government policies are geared to influencing how much of it is produced. When there are external costs from production, the **marginal social cost of a good or activity** exceeds its marginal cost to producers, the difference being the marginal external cost. Without government action, the market produces too much of the good or activity. The optimal Pigouvian tax on production of the good or activity is equal to its marginal external cost, yielding lower output and a higher price to consumers. A system of tradable production permits for the right to produce the good or activity can also achieve efficiency at minimum cost.
6. When a good or activity yields external benefits, such as **technology spillovers,** the **marginal social benefit of the good or activity** is equal to the marginal benefit accruing to consumers plus its marginal external benefit. Without government intervention, the market produces too little of the good or activity. An optimal **Pigouvian subsidy** to producers, equal to the marginal external benefit, moves the market to the socially optimal quantity of production. This yields higher output and a higher price to producers. It is a form of **industrial policy,** a policy to support industries that are believed to generate positive externalities. Economists are often skeptical of industrial policies because external benefits are hard to measure and they motivate producers to lobby for lucrative benefits.

KEY TERMS

Marginal social cost of pollution, p. 480
Marginal social benefit of pollution, p. 480
Socially optimal quantity of pollution, p. 480
External cost, p. 482
External benefit, p. 482
Externalities, p. 482
Negative externalities, p. 482
Positive externalities, p. 482
Coase theorem, p. 483
Transaction costs, p. 483
Internalize the externality, p. 484
Environmental standards, p. 485
Emissions tax, p. 486
Pigouvian taxes, p. 488
Tradable emissions permits, p. 488
Marginal social cost of a good or activity, p. 491
Technology spillover, p. 494
Marginal social benefit of a good or activity, p. 495
Pigouvian subsidy, p. 495
Industrial policy, p. 495

PROBLEMS

1. What type of externality (positive or negative) is described in each of the following examples? Is the marginal social benefit of the activity greater than or equal to the marginal benefit to the individual? Is the marginal social cost of the activity greater than or equal to the marginal cost to the individual? Consequently, without intervention, will there be too little or too much (relative to what would be socially optimal) of this activity?

   a. Mrs. Chau plants lots of colorful flowers in her front yard.

   b. Anna Crombie and Fritz, a popular clothing store, opens in a mall, attracting more shoppers who also visit other stores.

   c. Your neighbour plays loud music, keeping you from studying.

d. Maija, who lives next to an apple orchard, decides to keep bees to produce honey.

e. Justine buys a large SUV that consumes a lot of gasoline.

2. The Poets Club meets in the neighbouring residence, and regularly plays German opera at extreme decibel levels. The loud music is a negative externality that can be directly quantified. The accompanying table shows the marginal social benefit and the marginal social cost per decibel (dB, a measure of volume) of music.

Volume of music (dB)	Marginal social benefit of dB	Marginal social cost of dB
90		
	$36	$0
91		
	30	2
92		
	24	4
93		
	18	6
94		
	12	8
95		
	6	10
96		
	0	12
97		

a. Draw the marginal social benefit curve and the marginal social cost curve. Use your diagram to determine the socially optimal volume of music.

b. Only the members of the Poets Club benefit from the music and they bear none of the cost. Which volume of music will they choose?

c. The university imposes a Pigouvian tax of $3 per decibel of music played. From your diagram, determine the volume of music the Poets Club will now choose.

3. Many dairy farmers in Quebec are adopting a new technology that allows them to produce their own electricity from methane gas captured from animal wastes. (One cow can produce up to 2 kilowatts a day.) This practice reduces the amount of methane gas released into the atmosphere. In addition to reducing their own utility bills, the farmers are allowed to sell any electricity they produce at favourable rates.

a. Explain how the ability to earn money from capturing and transforming methane gas behaves like a Pigouvian tax on methane gas pollution and can lead dairy farmers to emit the efficient amount of methane gas pollution.

b. Suppose some dairy farmers have lower costs of transforming methane into electricity than others. Explain how this system leads to an efficient allocation of emissions reduction among farmers.

4. The accompanying table shows the total social benefit from steel production and the total cost to steel producers of producing steel. Producing a ton of steel imposes a marginal external cost of $60 per ton.

Quantity of steel (tons)	Total social benefit	Total cost to producers
1	$115	$10
2	210	30
3	285	60
4	340	100
5	375	150

a. Calculate the marginal social benefit per ton of steel and the marginal cost per ton of steel to steel producers. Then calculate the marginal social cost per ton of steel.

b. What is the market equilibrium quantity of steel production?

c. What is the socially optimal quantity of steel production?

d. If you wanted to impose a Pigouvian tax to remedy the problem created by the negative externality, how high would the Pigouvian tax have to be per ton of steel?

5. Education is an example of a positive externality: acquiring more education benefits the individual student, and having a more highly educated work force is good for the economy as a whole. The accompanying table illustrates the marginal benefit to Sian per year of education and the marginal cost per year of education. Each year of education has a marginal external benefit to society equal to $8,000. Assume that the marginal social cost is the same as the marginal cost paid by an individual student.

Quantity of education (years)	Sian's marginal benefit per year	Sian's marginal cost per year
9		
	$20,000	$15,000
10		
	19,000	16,000
11		
	18,000	17,000
12		
	17,000	18,000
13		
	16,000	19,000
14		
	15,000	20,000
15		
	14,000	21,000
16		
	13,000	22,000
17		

a. Find Sian's market equilibrium number of years of education.

b. Calculate the marginal social benefit schedule. What is the socially optimal number of years of education?

c. You are in charge of education funding. Would you use a Pigouvian tax or a Pigouvian subsidy to induce Sian to choose the socially optimal amount of education? How high would you set this tax or subsidy per year of education?

6. Getting a flu shot reduces not only your chance of getting the flu but also the chance that you will pass it on to someone else.

a. Draw a diagram showing the supply and demand curves of inoculating different proportions of the population. Assume that the marginal cost of each flu shot is constant and is equal to the marginal social cost, and that the demand curve is downward sloping.

b. Will the marginal social benefit curve be higher, lower, or the same as the demand curve? Why? Draw the marginal social benefit curve into your diagram.

c. In your diagram, show the market equilibrium quantity and the socially optimal quantity of flu shots. Is the market equilibrium quantity of flu shots socially efficient? Why or why not?

d. Many university health centres offer free flu shots to students and employees. Does this solution necessarily achieve efficiency? Explain, using your diagram.

7. Draw a diagram of the supply and demand curves for telephone service. The marginal cost of connecting another household to the telephone network is increasing, as it is more costly to connect another household as the size of the network grows larger. Assume that the demand curve is downward sloping.

a. Label the market equilibrium in your diagram E_{MKT}.

Telephone service is a positive externality (sometimes called a "network externality"). There is a marginal external benefit to connecting one more household to the telephone network, the benefit to everybody else of being able to call the newly connected household.

b. Draw the marginal social benefit curve into your diagram, find the socially optimal point, and label it O.

c. Explain why the market equilibrium E_{MKT} is inefficient.

d. Governments subsidize phone service for rural households. Describe how such a Pigouvian subsidy eliminates the inefficiency.

8. According to a report from the Statistics Canada's Census, "the average [lifetime] earnings of a full-time, year-round worker with a high school education are about $1.2 million compared with $2.1 million for a university graduate". This indicates that there is a considerable benefit to a graduate from investing in his or her own education. Tuition at most universities covers at most about one-third of the cost—the rest is covered by the provinces, effectively applying a Pigouvian subsidy to university education.

If a Pigouvian subsidy is appropriate, is the externality created by a university education a positive or a negative externality? What does this imply about the differences between the costs and benefits to students compared to social costs and benefits? What are some reasons for the differences?

9. Fishing for sablefish off the coast of Florida has been so intensive that sablefish were threatened with extinction. After several years of banning such fishing, the U.S. government is now proposing to introduce tradable vouchers, each of which entitles its holder to a catch of a certain size. Explain how fishing is a negative externality and how the voucher scheme may overcome the inefficiency created by this externality.

10. The two dry-cleaning companies in Collegetown, College Cleaners and Big Green Cleaners, are a major source of air pollution. Together they currently produce 350 units of air pollution, which the town wants to reduce to 200 units. The accompanying table shows the current pollution level produced by each company and each company's marginal cost of reducing its pollution. The marginal cost is constant.

Companies	Initial pollution level (units)	Marginal cost of reducing pollution (per unit)
College Cleaners	230	$5
Big Green Cleaners	120	$2

a. Suppose that Collegetown were to pass an environmental standards law that limits each company to 100 units of pollution. What would be the total cost to the two companies of each reducing its pollution emissions to 100 units?

Suppose instead that Collegetown issues 100 pollution vouchers to each company, each entitling the company to one unit of pollution, and that these vouchers can be traded.

b. How much is each pollution voucher worth to College Cleaners? To Big Green Cleaners? (That is, how much would each company, at most, be willing to pay for one more voucher?)

c. Who will sell vouchers and who will buy them? How many vouchers will be traded?

d. What is the total cost to the two companies of the pollution controls under this voucher system?

11. Ronald owns a cattle farm at the source of a long river. His cattle's waste flows into the river, and down many miles to where Carla lives. Carla gets her drinking water from the river. By allowing his cattle's waste to flow into the river, Ronald imposes a negative externality on Carla. In each of the two following cases, do you think that through negotiation Ronald and Carla can find an efficient solution? What might this solution look like?

a. There are no telephones, and for Carla to talk to Ronald, she has to travel for two days on a rocky road.

b. Carla and Ronald both have e-mail access, making it costless for them to communicate.

>web... To continue your study and review of concepts in this chapter, please visit the Krugman/Wells website for quizzes, animated graph tutorials, web links to helpful resources, and more.

www.worthpublishers.com/krugmanwellsmyatt

chapter

20 >>Public Goods and Common Resources

THE GREAT STINK

BY THE MIDDLE OF THE NINETEENTH century, London had become the world's largest city, with close to 2.5 million inhabitants. Unfortunately, all those people produced a lot of waste—and there was no place for the stuff to go except the Thames, the river flowing through the city. Nobody with a working nose could ignore the results. And the river didn't just smell bad—it carried waterborne diseases like cholera and typhoid. London neighbourhoods close to the Thames had death rates from cholera more than six times greater than the neighbourhoods farthest away. And the great majority of Londoners drew their drinking water from the Thames.

What the city needed, said reformers, was a sewage system that would carry waste away from the river. Yet no private individual was willing to build such a system, and influential people were opposed to the idea that the government should take responsibility for the problem. For example, the magazine *The Economist* weighed in against proposals for a government-built sewage system, declaring that "suffering and evil are nature's admonitions—they cannot be got rid of."

But the hot summer of 1858 brought what came to be known as the Great Stink, which was so bad that one health journal reported "men struck down with the stench." Even the privileged and powerful suffered: Parliament met in a building next to the river. After unsuccessful efforts to stop the smell by covering the windows with chemical-soaked curtains, Parliament

What you will learn in this chapter:

- A way to classify goods that predicts whether a good can be efficiently provided by markets
- What **public goods** are, and why markets fail to supply them
- What **common resources** are, and why they are overused
- What **artificially scarce goods** are, and why they are underconsumed
- How government intervention in the production and consumption of these types of goods can make society better off
- Why finding the right level of government intervention is difficult

UPPA/Topham/The Image Works

London's River Thames then . . .

Corbis

. . . and the same river now, thanks to government intervention.

finally approved a plan for an immense system of sewers and pumping stations to direct sewage away from the city. The system, opened in 1865, brought dramatic improvement in the city's quality of life; cholera and typhoid epidemics, which had been regular occurrences, completely disappeared. The Thames was turned from the filthiest to the cleanest metropolitan river in the world, and the sewage system's principal engineer, Sir Joseph Bazalgette, was lauded as having "saved more lives than any single Victorian public official." It was estimated at the time that Bazalgette's sewer system added 20 years to the life span of the average Londoner.

The story of the Great Stink and the policy response that followed illustrate two important reasons for government intervention in the economy. London's new sewage system was a clear example of a *public good*—a good that benefits many people, whether or not they have paid for it, and whose benefits to any one individual do not depend on how many others also benefit. As we will see shortly, public goods differ in important ways from the *private goods* we have studied so far—and these differences mean that public goods cannot be efficiently supplied by the market.

In addition, clean water in the Thames is an example of a *common resource,* a good that many people can consume whether or not they have paid for it but whose consumption by each person reduces the amount available to others. Such goods tend to be overused by individuals in a market system unless the government takes action.

In earlier chapters, we saw that markets sometimes fail to deliver efficient levels of production and consumption of a good or activity. We saw how inefficiency can arise from market power, which leads producers to charge prices that are higher than marginal cost, thereby preventing mutually beneficial transactions from occurring. We also saw how inefficiency can arise from externalities, which cause a divergence between the costs and benefits of an individual's or industry's actions and the costs and benefits of those actions borne by society as a whole, and from private information, which distorts incentives and leads to market failure.

In this chapter, we will take a somewhat different approach to the question of why markets sometimes fail. Here we focus on how the characteristics of goods often determine whether markets can deliver them efficiently. When goods have the "wrong" characteristics, the resulting market failures resemble those associated with externalities or market power. This alternative way of looking at sources of inefficiency deepens our understanding of why markets sometimes don't work well, and how government can serve a useful purpose.

Private Goods—and Others

What's the difference between installing a new bathroom in a house and building a municipal sewage system? What's the difference between growing wheat and fishing in the open ocean?

These aren't trick questions. In each case there is a basic difference in the characteristics of the goods involved. Bathroom appliances and wheat have the characteristics needed to allow markets to work efficiently. Sewage systems and fish in the sea do not.

Let's look at these crucial characteristics and why they matter.

Characteristics of Goods

Goods like bathroom fixtures or wheat have two characteristics that, as we'll soon see, are essential if a good is to be efficiently provided by a market economy.

A good is **excludable** if the supplier of that good can prevent people who do not pay from consuming it.

A good is **rival in consumption** if the same unit of the good cannot be consumed by more than one person at the same time.

A good that is both excludable and rival in consumption is a **private good.**

When a good is **non-excludable,** the supplier cannot prevent consumption by people who do not pay for it.

- They are **excludable:** suppliers of the good can prevent people who don't pay from consuming it.
- They are **rival in consumption:** the same unit of the good cannot be consumed by more than one person at the same time.

When a good is both excludable and rival in consumption, it is called a **private good.** Wheat is an example of a private good. It is *excludable:* the farmer can sell a bushel to one consumer without having to provide wheat to everyone in the county. And it is *rival in consumption:* if I eat bread baked with a farmer's wheat, that bread can no longer be eaten by someone else.

But not all goods have these two characteristics. Some goods are **non-excludable**—the supplier cannot prevent consumption of the good by people who do not pay for it. Fire protection is one example: a fire department that puts out fires before they spread protects the whole city, not just people who have made contributions to the Firemen's Benevolent Association. An improved environment is another: the city of London couldn't have ended the Great Stink for some residents while leaving the River Thames foul for others.

A good is **non-rival in consumption** if more than one person can consume the same unit of the good at the same time.

Nor are all goods rival in consumption. Goods are **non-rival in consumption** if more than one person can consume the same unit of the good at the same time. TV programs are non-rival in consumption: your decision to watch a show does not prevent other people from watching the same show.

Because goods can be either excludable or non-excludable, rival or non-rival in consumption, there are four types of goods, illustrated by the matrix in Figure 20-1:

- *Private goods,* which are excludable and rival in consumption, like wheat
- *Public goods,* which are non-excludable and non-rival in consumption, like a public sewer system
- *Common resources,* which are non-excludable but rival in consumption, like clean water in a river or fish in the ocean
- *Artificially scarce goods,* which are excludable but non-rival in consumption, like pay-per-view movies on cable TV

There are, of course, many other characteristics that distinguish between types of goods—necessities versus luxuries, normal versus inferior, and so on. Why focus on whether goods are excludable and rival in consumption?

Figure 20-1

Four Types of Goods

There are four types of goods. The type of a good depends on (1) whether or not it is excludable—whether a producer can prevent someone from consuming it; and (2) whether or not it is rival in consumption—whether it is impossible for the same unit of a good to be consumed by more than one person at the same time.

	Rival in consumption	Non-rival in consumption
Excludable	**Private goods** • Wheat • Bathroom fixtures	**Artificially scarce goods** • Pay-per-view movies • Computer software
Non-excludable	**Common resources** • Clean water • Biodiversity	**Public goods** • Public sanitation • National defense

Why Markets Can Supply Only Private Goods Efficiently

A market economy, as we learned in earlier chapters, is an amazing system for delivering goods and services. But it cannot supply goods and services efficiently unless they are private goods—excludable and rival in consumption.

To see why excludability is crucial, suppose that a farmer had only two choices: either produce no wheat or provide a bushel of wheat to every resident of the county who wants it, whether or not that resident pays for it. It seems unlikely that anyone would grow wheat under those conditions.

Yet the operator of a municipal sewage system faces pretty much the same problem as our hypothetical farmer. A sewage system makes the whole city cleaner and healthier—but that benefit accrues to all the city's residents, whether or not they pay the system operator. That's why no private entrepreneur came forward with a plan to end London's Great Stink.

The general point is that if a good is non-excludable, rational consumers won't be willing to pay for it—they will take a "free ride" on anyone who *does* pay. So there is a **free-rider problem.** Examples of the free-rider problem are familiar from daily life. One example you may have encountered happens when students are required to do a group project. There is often a tendency of some members of the group to shirk, relying on others in the group to get the work done. The shirkers *free-ride* on someone else's effort.

Goods that are non-excludable suffer from the **free-rider problem:** individuals have no incentive to pay for their own consumption and instead will take a "free ride" on anyone who does pay.

Because of the free-rider problem, the forces of self-interest alone do not lead to an efficient level of production for a non-excludable good. Even though consumers would benefit from increased production of the good, no one individual is willing to pay for more, and so no producer is willing to supply it. The result is that non-excludable goods suffer from *inefficiently low production* in a market economy. In fact, in the face of the free-rider problem, self-interest may not ensure that any amount of the good—let alone the efficient quantity—is produced.

Goods that are excludable and non-rival in consumption, like pay-per-view movies, suffer from a different kind of inefficiency. As long as a good is excludable, it is possible to earn a profit by making the good available only to those who pay. But the marginal cost of letting an additional viewer watch a pay-per-view movie is zero because it is non-rival in consumption. So the efficient price to the consumer is also zero—or, to put it another way, individuals should watch TV movies up to the point where their marginal benefit is zero. But if the cable company actually charges viewers $4, viewers will consume the good only up to the point where their marginal benefit is $4. When consumers must pay a price greater than zero for a good that is nonrival in consumption, the price they pay is higher than the marginal cost of allowing them to consume that good, which is zero. So in a market economy goods that are non-rival in consumption suffer from *inefficiently low consumption.*

Now we can see why private goods are the only goods that can be efficiently produced and consumed in a competitive market. (That is, a private good will be efficiently produced and consumed in a market free of market power, externalities, or private information.) Because private goods are excludable, producers can charge for them and so have an incentive to produce them. And because they are also rival in consumption, it is efficient for consumers to pay a positive price—a price equal to the marginal cost of production. If one or both of these characteristics are lacking, a market economy will not lead to efficient production and consumption of the good.

Fortunately for the market system, most goods are private goods. Food, clothing, shelter, and most other desirable things in life are excludable and rival in consumption, so markets can provide us with most things. Yet there are crucial goods that don't meet these criteria—and in most cases, that means that government must step in.

PITFALLS

MARGINAL COST OF WHAT EXACTLY?

In the case of a good that is non-rival in consumption, it's easy to confuse the marginal cost of *producing* a unit of the good with the marginal cost of *allowing* a unit of the good *to be consumed.* For example, your local cable company incurs a marginal cost in making a movie available to its subscribers that is equal to the cost of the resources it uses to produce and broadcast that movie. However, *once that movie is being broadcast,* no marginal cost is incurred by letting an additional family watch it. In other words, no costly resources are "used up" when one more family consumes a movie that has already been produced and is being broadcast.

This complication does not arise, however, when a good is rival in consumption. In that case, the resources used to produce a unit of the good are "used up" by a person's consumption of it—they are no longer available to satisfy someone else's consumption. So when a good is rival in consumption, the marginal cost to society of allowing an individual to consume a unit is equal to the resource cost of producing that unit—that is, equal to the marginal cost of producing it.

economics in action

What Kind of Good Is Health Care?

Canada's universal public health care system helps define our identity as Canadians, and maintaining its viability has been one of the most important political issues of recent times. But on the face of it, health care seems to meet the definition of a private good. It is excludable—a doctor could turn away patients who were unwilling or unable to pay the fee. And it is rival in consumption—each patient requires time, care, and medicine that are therefore not available to other patients.

But if health care is a private good, and private goods can be efficiently supplied by markets, why don't we leave health care up to the market? Why do so many developed countries treat health care as a government responsibility?

There are several reasons. First, when it comes to controlling infectious diseases, health care is more like a public good than a private one. Disease makes our health interdependent. It makes your health not purely a matter of your concern but also a social concern. The benefits of stamping out infectious diseases are neither excludable nor rival in consumption. I can't enjoy the benefits of living in a disease-free society while excluding you from also enjoying those same benefits. And my gain from living in a disease-free society does not come at your expense.

More generally, though, private markets don't function well when there is a problem of information asymmetry between buyers and sellers. In a market system, patients buy health care and doctors sell it. But patients rely on doctors for diagnosis—to tell them what they need—and also for treatment. This is like having the salesperson dictate what the customer should buy. Sure, patients could get a second opinion, but getting this information would be costly in a private market. Moreover, in the face of uncertainty there is a rational tendency for the prospective patient to use price as an indicator of quality. All of these factors interfere with the ability of markets to efficiently allocate resources.

There are two other factors suggesting that private provision of health care is problematic. First, private health insurance companies would naturally prefer not to insure unhealthy people. Second, drug companies selling patented drugs have market power. Public provision of health care offsets the power of monopolistic sellers by confronting them with a monopolistic buyer. In Canada, the Patented Medicine Prices Review Board (an independent quasi-judicial tribunal) limits the prices set by manufacturers for all patented medicines sold in Canada, whether under prescription or over the counter, to ensure they are not excessive.

It is said that "the proof of the pudding is in the eating". Not only does Canada have universal publicly provided health care, it also spends less on health care as a proportion of GDP than the United States, where health care is (mostly) privately funded and coverage is not universal. In the U.S., health care absorbs about 14% of GDP; whereas, including private spending, Canada spends about 9% of GDP. It is also said, "if it ain't broke . . .". ■

< < < < < < < < < < < < < < < < < <

>> QUICK REVIEW

- Goods can be classified according to two attributes: whether they are *excludable* and whether they are *rival in consumption.*
- Goods that are both excludable and rival in consumption are *private goods.* Private goods can be efficiently produced and consumed in a competitive market.
- When goods are *non-excludable,* there is a *free-rider problem:* consumers will not pay producers, leading to inefficiently low production.
- When goods are *non-rival in consumption,* the efficient price for consumption is zero. But if a positive price is charged to compensate producers for the cost of production, the result is inefficiently low consumption.

>> CHECK YOUR UNDERSTANDING 20-1

1. Classify each of the following goods according to whether they are excludable and whether they are rival in consumption. What kind of good is each?
   a. Use of a river for recreational purposes, such as swimming, water skiing, or jet skiing
   b. A cheese burrito
   c. Information from a website that is password-protected
   d. Publicly announced information on the path of an incoming hurricane
2. Which of the goods in Question 1 will be provided by a competitive market? Which will not? Explain.

Solutions appear at back of book.

Public Goods

A **public good** is the exact opposite of a private good: it is a good that is both non-excludable and non-rival in consumption. A sewage system is an example of a public good: you can't keep a river clean without making it clean for everyone who lives near its banks, and my protection from great stinks does not come at my neighbour's expense.

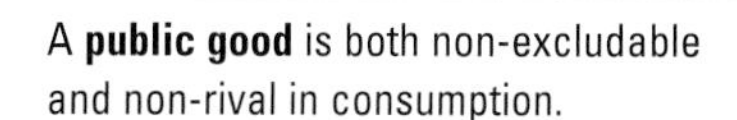
A **public good** is both non-excludable and non-rival in consumption.

Here are some other examples of public goods:

- *Disease prevention.* When doctors act to stamp out the beginnings of an epidemic before it can spread, they protect people around the world.
- *National defence.* A strong military protects all citizens.
- *Scientific research.* More knowledge benefits everyone.

Because these goods are non-excludable, they suffer from the free-rider problem, so no private firm would be willing to produce them. And because they are non-rival in consumption, it would be inefficient to charge people for consuming them. As a result, society must find non-market methods for providing these goods.

Providing Public Goods

Public goods are provided through a variety of means. The government doesn't always get involved—in many cases a non-governmental solution has been found for the free-rider problem. But these solutions are usually imperfect in some way.

Some public goods are supplied through voluntary contributions. For example, private donations support a considerable amount of scientific research. But private donations are insufficient to finance huge, socially important projects like basic medical research.

Some public goods are supplied by self-interested individuals or firms because those who produce them are able to make money in an indirect way. The classic example is broadcast television, which in the United States is supported entirely by advertising. The downside of such indirect funding is that it skews the nature and quantity of the public goods that are supplied, as well as imposing additional costs on consumers. TV stations show the programs that yield the most advertising revenue (that is, programs best suited for selling antacids, hair-loss remedies, antihistamines, and the like to the segment of the population that buys them), which are not necessarily the programs people most want to see. And viewers must also endure many commercials.

Some potentially public goods are deliberately made excludable and therefore subject to charge, like pay-per-view movies. In the U.K., where most television programming is paid for by a yearly license fee assessed on every television owner, television viewing is made artificially excludable by the use of "television detection vans": vans that roam neighbourhoods in an attempt to detect televisions in non-licensed households and fine them. However, as noted earlier, when suppliers charge a price greater than zero for a non-rival good, consumers will consume an inefficiently low quantity of that good.

In small communities, a high level of social encouragement or pressure can be brought to bear on people to contribute money or time to provide the efficient level of a public good. Volunteer fire departments, which depend both on the volunteered services of the firefighters themselves and on contributions from local residents, are a good example. But as communities grow larger and more anonymous, social pressure is increasingly difficult to apply, so that larger towns and cities must depend on salaried firefighters.

Touhig Sion/Corbis Sygma

On the prowl: a British TV detection van at work.

As this last example suggests, when these other solutions fail, it is up to the government to provide public goods. Indeed, the most important public goods—national defence, the legal system, disease control, fire protection in large cities, and so on—are provided by government and paid for by taxes. Economic theory tells us that the provision of public goods is one of the crucial roles of government.

How Much of a Public Good Should Be Provided?

In some cases, provision of a public good is an "either-or" decision: London would either have a sewage system—or not. But in most cases, governments must decide not only whether to provide a public good but also *how much* of that public good to provide. For example, street cleaning is a public good—but how often should the streets be cleaned? Once a month? Twice a month? Every other day?

Imagine a city in which there are only two residents, Ted and Alice. Assume that the public good in question is street cleaning and that Ted and Alice truthfully tell the government how much they value a unit of the public good, where a unit is equal to one street cleaning per month. Specifically, each of them tells the government *his or her willingness to pay for another unit of the public good supplied*—an amount that corresponds to that *individual's marginal benefit* of another unit of the public good.

Using this information plus information on the cost of providing the good, the government can use marginal analysis to find the efficient level of providing the public good: the level at which the *marginal social benefit* of the public good is equal to the marginal cost of producing it. Recall from Chapter 19 that the marginal social benefit of a good is the benefit that accrues to society as a whole from the consumption of one additional unit of the good.

But what is the marginal social benefit of another unit of a public good—a unit that generates utility for *all* consumers, not just one consumer, because it is non-excludable and non-rival in consumption? This question leads us to an important principle: *in the special case of a public good, the marginal social benefit of a unit of the good is equal to the sum of the individual marginal benefits that are enjoyed by all consumers of that unit.* Or to consider it from a slightly different angle, if a consumer could be compelled to pay for a unit before consuming it (the good is made excludable), then the marginal social benefit of a unit is equal to the *sum* of each consumer's willingness to pay for that unit. Using this principle, the marginal social benefit of an additional street cleaning per month is equal to Ted's individual marginal benefit from that additional cleaning *plus* Alice's individual marginal benefit.

AP/Wide World Photos

We all benefit when someone does the cleaning up.

Why? Because a public good is non-rival in consumption—Ted's benefit from a cleaner street does not diminish Alice's benefit from that same clean street, and vice versa. Because people can all simultaneously consume the same unit of a public good, the marginal social benefit of an additional unit of that good is the *sum* of the individual marginal benefits of all who enjoy the public good. And the efficient quantity of a public good is the quantity at which the marginal social benefit is equal to the marginal cost of providing it.

Figure 20-2 illustrates the efficient provision of a public good, showing three marginal benefit curves. Panel (a) shows Ted's individual marginal benefit curve from street cleaning, MB_T: he would be willing to pay \$25 for the city to clean its streets once per month, an additional \$18 to have it done a second time, and so on. Panel (b) shows Alice's individual marginal benefit curve from street cleaning, MB_A. Panel (c) shows the marginal social benefit curve from street cleaning, *MSB:* it is the vertical sum of Ted's and Alice's individual marginal benefit curves, MB_T and MB_A.

To maximize society's welfare, the government should clean the street up to the level at which the marginal social benefit of an additional cleaning is no longer greater than the marginal cost. Suppose that the marginal cost of street cleaning is \$6 per cleaning. Then the city should clean its streets 5 times per month, because the

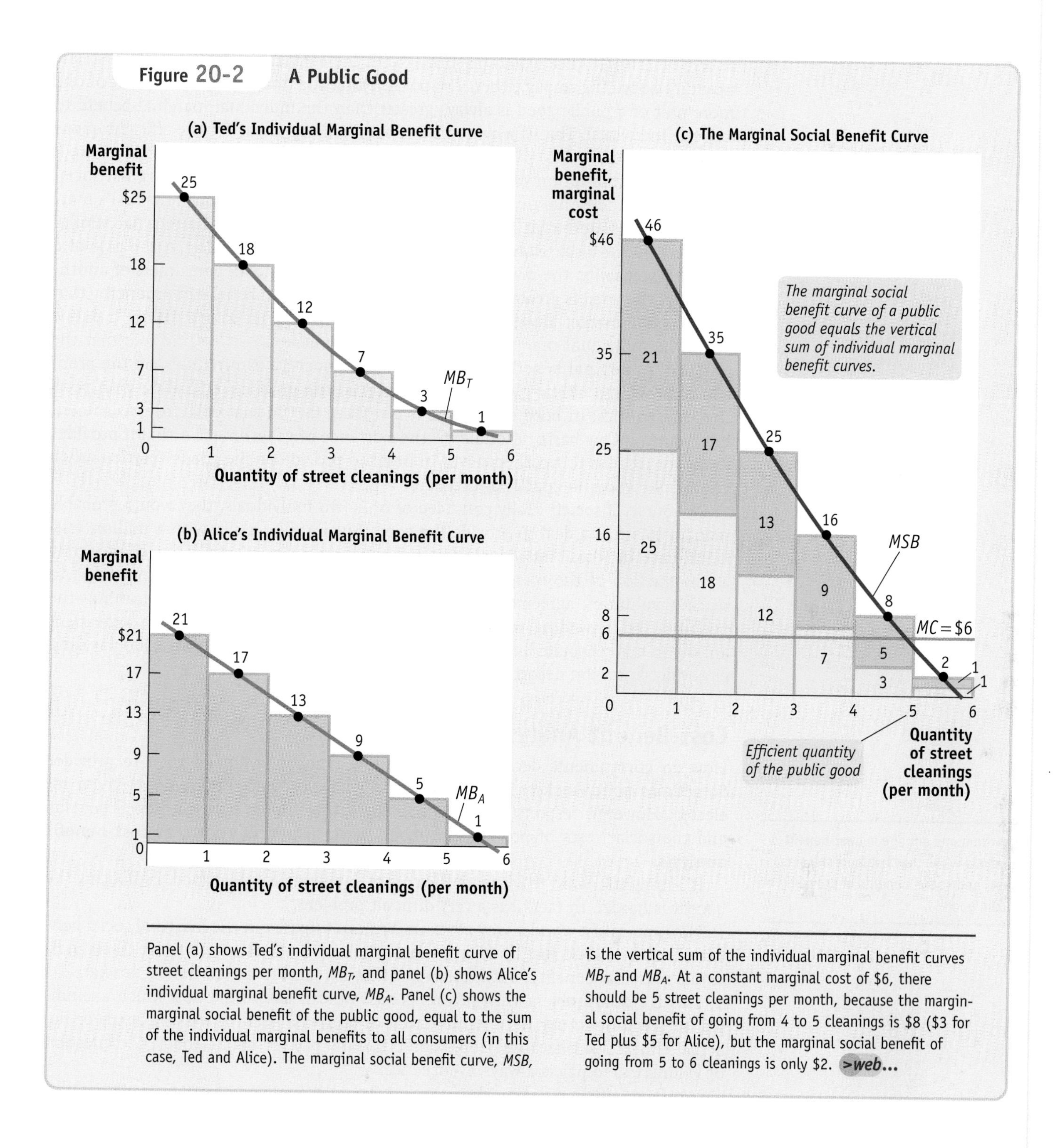

Panel (a) shows Ted's individual marginal benefit curve of street cleanings per month, MB_T, and panel (b) shows Alice's individual marginal benefit curve, MB_A. Panel (c) shows the marginal social benefit of the public good, equal to the sum of the individual marginal benefits to all consumers (in this case, Ted and Alice). The marginal social benefit curve, *MSB*, is the vertical sum of the individual marginal benefit curves MB_T and MB_A. At a constant marginal cost of $6, there should be 5 street cleanings per month, because the marginal social benefit of going from 4 to 5 cleanings is $8 ($3 for Ted plus $5 for Alice), but the marginal social benefit of going from 5 to 6 cleanings is only $2. **>web...**

marginal social benefit of going from 4 to 5 cleanings is $8, but going from 5 to 6 cleanings would yield a marginal social benefit of only $2.

Figure 20-2 can help reinforce our understanding of why we cannot rely on individual self-interest to yield provision of an efficient quantity of public goods. Suppose that the city did one fewer street cleaning than the efficient quantity and that either Ted or Alice was asked to pay for the last cleaning. Neither one would be willing to pay for it! Ted would personally gain only the equivalent of $3 in utility from adding one more street cleaning—so he wouldn't be willing to pay the $6 marginal cost of another cleaning. Alice would personally gain the equivalent of $5 in utility—so she wouldn't be willing to pay either. The point is that the marginal social benefit of one more unit of a public good is always greater than the individual marginal benefit to any one individual. That is why no individual is willing to pay for the efficient quantity of the good.

Does this description of the public good problem, in which the marginal social benefit of an additional unit of the public good is greater than any individual's marginal benefit, sound a bit familiar? It should: we encountered a somewhat similar situation in our discussion of *positive externalities.* Remember that in the case of a positive externality, the marginal social benefit accruing to all consumers of another unit of the good is greater than the producer's marginal benefit of producing that unit and the market alone produces too little of the good. In the case of a public good, the individual marginal benefit of a consumer plays the same role that the producer's marginal benefit plays in the case of positive externalities. So the problem of providing public goods is very similar to the problem of dealing with positive externalities; in both cases there is a market failure that calls for government intervention. One basic rationale for the existence of government is that it provides a way for citizens to tax themselves in order to provide public goods—particularly a vital public good like national defence.

Of course, if society really consisted of only two individuals, they would probably manage to strike a deal to provide the good. But imagine a city with a million residents, each of whose individual marginal benefit from provision of the good is only a tiny fraction of the marginal social benefit. It would be impossible for people to reach a voluntary agreement to pay for the efficient level of street cleaning—the potential for free-riding makes it too difficult to make and enforce an agreement among so many people. But they could and would vote to tax themselves to pay for a city-wide sanitation department.

Cost-Benefit Analysis

How do governments decide in practice how much of a public good to provide? Sometimes policy-makers just guess—or do whatever they think will get them re-elected. However, responsible governments try to estimate both the social benefits and the social costs of providing a public good, a process known as **cost-benefit analysis.**

Governments engage in **cost-benefit analysis** when they estimate the social costs and social benefits of providing a public good.

It's straightforward to estimate the cost of supplying a public good. Estimating the benefit is harder. In fact, it is a very difficult problem.

Now you might wonder why governments can't figure out the marginal social benefit of a public good just by asking people their willingness to pay for it (their individual marginal benefit). But it turns out that it's hard to get an honest answer.

This is not a problem with private goods: we can determine how much an individual is willing to pay for one more unit of a private good by looking at his or her actual choices. But because people don't actually pay for public goods, the question of willingness to pay is always hypothetical.

Worse yet, it's a question that people have an incentive not to answer truthfully. People naturally want more rather than less. Because they cannot be made to pay for whatever quantity of the public good they use, when asked how much they desire a public good people are apt to overstate their true feelings. For example, if street cleaning were scheduled according to the stated wishes of homeowners alone, the streets would be cleaned every day—an inefficient level of provision. So governments must be aware that they cannot simply rely on the public's statements when deciding how much of a public good to provide—if they do, they are likely to provide too much. In contrast, as the For Inquiring Minds explains, relying on the public to indicate how much of the public good they want through voting has problems as well—and is likely to lead to too little of the public good being provided.

FOR INQUIRING MINDS

VOTING AS A PUBLIC GOOD

It would be an oversimplification to think that governments build lighthouses because lighthouses are inherently public goods. Or to think that that we have socialized medicine because it too has elements of being a public good. Or to think that we have free primary and secondary education because governments recognize the beneficial externalities associated with them. It is probably more accurate to say that the reason we have socialized medicine is because people have demanded it, organized in favour of it, and refused to allow it to be taken away. Socially financed education and medicine exist not primarily because the government saw the logic of when it should intervene and when it should not, but more because people fought for them and demanded them politically.

So it is an unfortunate fact of life that political involvement is itself a public good—one that is subject to severe free-rider problems—that explains why people in general devote too little effort to defending their own interests.

For example, imagine that you are one of a million people who would stand to gain the equivalent of $100 each if a particular political party wins in a provincial election—say, this party plans to improve public schools. And suppose that the opportunity cost of the time it would take you to vote is $10. Will you be sure to go to the polls and vote? If you are rational, the answer is no! The reason is that it is very unlikely that your vote will decide the issue, either way. If the party wins, you benefit even if you don't bother to vote—the benefits are non-excludable. If the party loses, your vote would not have changed the outcome. Either way, by not voting—by free-riding on those who do vote—you save $10.

Of course, many people do vote out of a sense of civic duty. But because political action is a public good, when a large group of people share a common political interest, they are likely to exert too little effort promoting their cause and so will be ignored. Conversely, small, well-organized interest groups that act on issues narrowly targeted in their favour tend to have disproportionate power.

Is this a reason to distrust democracy? George Bernard Shaw said that democracy is where the ignorant masses periodically replace the corrupt few. On the other hand, perhaps Winston Churchill said it best when he quipped: "Democracy is the worst form of government, with the exception of every other system that has ever been tried."

economics in action

Publicly Funded But Privately Provided Education?

If a good is non-exclusive, the private sector cannot commercially produce it. If it is non-rival, it is inefficient for the private sector to produce it. But essentially these arguments are about the funding of a good, not about who produces it. Public funding does not stop the government from contracting out to the lowest bidder. This way government "interference" is kept to a minimum and the market is allowed fuller scope. In practice, more and more public services are being handled this way—especially municipal services like garbage collection.

Some have suggested, controversially, that this practice be applied to education. Instead of the government hiring teachers and providing schools, the government could give parents "education vouchers", each one worth the equivalent of the total education budget per student (we divide the total amount of money the government spends on education by the total number of students–this becomes the value of an education voucher). Schools then become private firms that compete for students and their education vouchers. Such competition is deemed good for education standards, and allows more scope for consumer choice.

However, the effect of the plan depends on whether the government imposes a price ceiling on education–meaning that school fees could be legally fixed at the value of one voucher. The alternative would be to adopt a more market-driven approach, and allow schools to charge whatever amount they want.

Consider first the option of the price ceiling–prohibiting schools from charging more than one government voucher per student. This proposal could facilitate competition among schools for students, and may allow parents more choice. Because schools would have to compete for students, they may become more open to parents' concerns. It would also introduce more competition among schools to hire the very best teachers. And it would create an incentive for teachers to try to show they were the very best.

However, having taken these steps towards a market system, it may be difficult to impose a price ceiling on school fees—especially in societies where private schools already exist. If all schools were suddenly allowed to charge whatever amount they wanted, the proposal mainly benefits those who already send their children to private schools: under the new system, part of their cost of doing so would be funded by a government voucher. So, the rich clearly benefit, and middle-income families might be willing and able to pay additional amounts above the voucher. The poor, however, could not. Better-funded schools would offer higher wages for teachers and so attract the best teachers. The poor, then, might be left with a choice between schools that could only afford mediocre teachers. On balance, the effect would be the abandonment of the liberal idea of *equality of opportunity*, and barriers to upward income mobility would become entrenched. ■

>> QUICK REVIEW

- A *public good* is both non-excludable and non-rival in consumption.
- Because most forms of public good provision by the private sector have serious defects, they are typically provided by the government and paid for with taxes.
- The marginal social benefit of an additional unit of a public good is equal to the sum of each consumer's individual marginal benefit from that unit. At the efficient quantity, the marginal social benefit equals the marginal cost.
- No individual has an incentive to pay for providing the efficient quantity of a public good because each individual's marginal benefit is less than the marginal social benefit. This is a primary justification for the existence of government.
- Although governments should rely on *cost-benefit analysis* to determine how much of a public good to supply, doing so is problematic because individuals tend to overstate the good's value to them.

>> CHECK YOUR UNDERSTANDING 20-2

1. The town of Centreville, population 16, has two types of residents, Homebodies and Revellers. Using the accompanying table, the town must decide how much to spend on its New Year's Eve party. No individual resident expects to directly bear the cost of the party.
   a. Suppose there are 10 Homebodies and 6 Revellers. Determine the marginal social benefit schedule of money spent on the party. What is the efficient level of spending?
   b. Suppose there are 6 Homebodies and 10 Revellers. How do your answers to part a change? Explain.
   c. Suppose that the individual marginal benefit schedules are known but no one knows the true numbers of Homebodies and Revellers. Individuals are asked their preferences. What is the likely outcome? Why is it likely to result in an inefficiently high level of spending? Explain.

Money spent on party	Individual marginal benefit of additional $1 spent on party	
	Homebody	Reveller
$0		
	$0.05	$0.13
1		
	0.04	0.11
2		
	0.03	0.09
3		
	0.02	0.07
4		

Solutions appear at back of book.

Common Resources

A **common resource** is non-excludable and rival in consumption: you can't stop me from consuming the good, and more consumption by me means less of the good available for you.

A **common resource** is a good that is non-excludable but is rival in consumption. An example is the stock of fish in a limited fishing area, like the fisheries off the coast of Newfoundland and Nova Scotia. Traditionally, anyone who had a boat could go out to sea and catch fish—fish in the sea were a non-excludable good. Yet, because the total number of fish is limited, the fish that one person catches are no longer available to be caught by someone else. So fish in the sea are rival in consumption.

Other examples of common resources are clean air and water as well as the diversity of animal and plant species on the planet (biodiversity). In each of these cases the fact that the good, though rival in consumption, is non-excludable poses a serious problem.

The Problem of Overuse

Because common resources are non-excludable, individuals cannot be charged for their use. Yet, because they are rival in consumption, an individual who uses a unit depletes the resource by making that unit unavailable to others. As a result, a common resource is subject to **overuse:** an individual will continue to use it until his or her marginal benefit of its use is equal to zero, ignoring the cost that this action inflicts on society as a whole. As we will see shortly, the problem of overuse of a common resource is similar to a problem we studied in Chapter 19: the problem of a good that generates a negative externality, such as pollution-creating electricity generation or livestock farming.

Common resources left to the market suffer from **overuse:** individuals ignore the fact that their use depletes the amount of the resource remaining for others.

Fishing is a classic example of a common resource. In heavily fished waters, my fishing imposes a cost on others by reducing the fish population and making it harder for others to catch fish. But I have no personal incentive to take this cost into account, since I cannot be charged for fishing. As a result, from society's point of view, I catch too many fish. Traffic congestion is another example of overuse of a common resource. A major highway during rush hour can accommodate only a certain number of vehicles per hour. If I decide to drive alone to work rather than carpool or work at home, I make the commute of many other people a bit longer; but I have no incentive to take these consequences into account.

In the case of a common resource, the *marginal social cost* of my use of that resource is higher than my *individual marginal cost,* the cost to me of using an additional unit of the good.

Figure 20-3 illustrates the point. It shows the demand curve for fish, which measures the marginal benefit of fish—the benefit to consumers when an additional unit of fish is caught and consumed. It also shows the supply curve for fish, which measures the marginal cost of production of the fishing industry. We know from Chapter 9 that the industry supply curve is the horizontal sum of each individual fisherman's supply curve—equivalent to his or her individual marginal cost curve. The fishing industry supplies the quantity where its marginal cost is equal to the price, the quantity Q_{MKT}. But the efficient outcome is to catch the quantity Q_{OPT}, the quantity of output that equates the marginal benefit to the marginal social cost, not to the fishing industry's marginal cost of production. The market outcome results in overuse of the common resource.

As we noted, there is a close parallel between the problem of managing a common resource and the problem posed by negative externalities. In the case of an activity that generates a negative externality, the marginal social cost of production is greater than the industry's marginal cost of production, the difference being the

Figure 20-3

A Common Resource

The supply curve *S,* which shows the marginal cost of production of the entire fishing industry, is composed of the individual supply curves of the individual fishermen. But each fisherman's individual marginal cost does not include the cost that his or her actions impose on others: the depletion of the common resource. As a result, the marginal social cost curve, *MSC,* lies above the supply curve; in an unregulated market, the quantity of the common resource used, Q_{MKT}, exceeds the efficient quantity of use, Q_{OPT}.

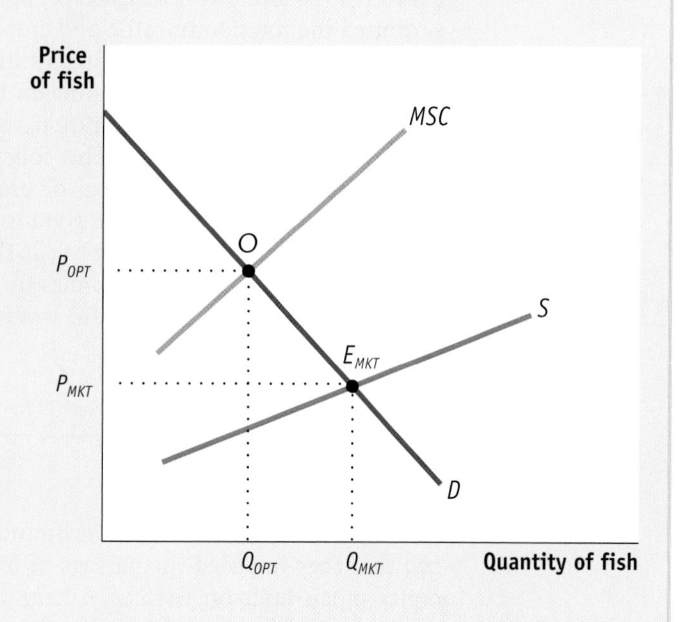

marginal external cost imposed on society. Here, the loss to society arising from a fisherman's depletion of the common resource plays the same role as the external cost plays when there is a negative externality. In fact, many negative externalities (such as pollution) can be thought of as involving common resources (such as clean air).

The Efficient Use and Maintenance of a Common Resource

Because common resources pose problems similar to those created by negative externalities, the solutions are also similar. To ensure efficient use of a common resource, society must find a way of getting individual users of the resource to take into account the costs they impose on other users. This is basically the same principle as that of getting individuals to internalize a negative externality that arises from their actions.

There are three fundamental ways to induce people who use common resources to internalize the costs they impose on others.

- Tax or otherwise regulate the use of the common resource
- Make the common resource excludable and assign property rights to some individuals
- Create a system of tradable licenses for the right to use the common resource

Like activities that generate negative externalities, use of a common resource can be reduced to the efficient quantity by imposing a Pigouvian tax. For example, some countries have imposed "congestion charges" on those who drive during rush hour, in effect charging them for use of the common resource of highway space. Likewise, visitors to national parks must pay a fee, and the number of visitors to any one park is restricted.

But when it comes to common resources, often the most natural solution is simply to assign property rights. At a fundamental level, common resources are subject to overuse because *nobody owns them.* The essence of ownership of a good—the *property right* over the good—is that you can limit who can and cannot use the good, and how much of it can be used. So one way to correct the problem of overuse is to make the good excludable and assign property rights over it to someone. The good now has an owner who has an incentive to protect the value of the good—to use it efficiently rather than overuse it. For example, common pasture land in England was overused and underfertilized because nobody owned it. The "enclosure movement" (that reached its peak between 1750 and 1815) assigned property rights over these fields to individuals. This permitted the rotation of cattle and crops, which improved the fertility of the soil. In this way the enclosure movement permitted vast increases in agricultural productivity.

A third way to correct the problem of overuse is to create a system of tradable licenses for the use of the common resource, much like the systems designed to address negative externalities. The policy-maker issues the number of licenses that corresponds to the efficient level of use of the good. Making the licenses tradable assures that the right to use the good is allocated efficiently—that is, those who end up using the good (those willing to pay the most for a license) are those who gain the most from its use. As the Economics in Action that follows shows, a system of tradable licenses has been a successful strategy in some fisheries.

economics in action

A Tale of Two Fisheries

When John Cabot discovered Newfoundland in 1497 the seas were so teeming with cod that they impeded the passage of his ship. The economy of Newfoundland was pretty much built on the cod fishery, and for five hundred years the cod off the

Grand Banks attracted fishing fleets from all over the world. But all this came to an end in 1992. By that stage, there was hardly any fishery left. So it was finally shut down in the hope that the cessation of fishing would allow stocks to recover. We're still waiting.

Fortunately for the East Coast, however, there remains a profitable and vibrant lobster fishery that provides direct employment for about 32,000 people and has a substantial impact on the Atlantic community. In an effort to protect this fishery, a tradable license system was established in 1967. To set a lobster trap, you must have a license, and only a limited number of licenses have been issued. A license for Grand Manan Island in the Bay of Fundy will change hands for around $250,000. At first Atlantic lobstermen were sceptical of a system that limited their fishing. But they now support the system enthusiastically, because it sustains the value of their licenses—and also sustains their livelihood. Without this system in place, the Atlantic lobster fishery would have gone the way of the cod fishery—or indeed, the way of the lobster fishery in parts of New England. The United States has not limited the catch of lobster fishers, who have discovered anew the "tragedy of the commons". ■

> > > > > > > > > > > > > > > > > >

>> QUICK REVIEW

- A *common resource* is rival in consumption but non-excludable.
- The problem with common resources is *overuse:* a user depletes the amount of the common resource available to others but does not take this cost into account when deciding how much to use the common resource.
- Like negative externalities, a common resource can be efficiently managed by Pigouvian taxes, by the creation of a system of tradable licenses for its use, or by making it excludable and assigning property rights.

>>CHECK YOUR UNDERSTANDING 20-3

1. Rocky Mountain Forest is a government-owned forest in which private citizens were allowed in the past to harvest as much timber as they wanted free of charge. State in economic terms why this is problematic from society's point of view.
2. You are the new Forest Service Commissioner and have been instructed to come up with ways to preserve the forest for the general public. Name three different methods you could use to maintain the efficient level of tree harvesting and explain how each would work. For each method, what information would you need to know in order to achieve an efficient outcome?

Solutions appear at back of book.

Artificially Scarce Goods

An **artificially scarce good** is a good that is excludable but non-rival in consumption. As we've already seen, pay-per-view movies are a familiar example. The marginal cost to society of allowing an individual to watch the movie is zero, because one person's viewing doesn't interfere with other people's viewing. Yet cable companies prevent an individual from seeing a movie if he or she hasn't paid. Many *information goods* like computer software are also artificially scarce; we will discuss the economics of information goods at greater length in Chapter 22.

An **artificially scarce good** is excludable but non-rival in consumption.

As we've already seen, markets will supply artificially scarce goods: because they are excludable, the producers can charge people for consuming them.

But artificially scarce goods are non-rival in consumption, which means that the marginal cost of an individual's consumption is zero. So the price that the supplier of an artificially scarce good charges exceeds marginal cost. Because the efficient price is equal to the marginal cost of zero, the good is "artificially scarce," and consumption of the good is inefficiently low. However, unless the producer can somehow earn revenue for producing and selling the good, he or she will be unwilling to produce at all—an outcome that leaves society even worse off than it would otherwise be with positive but inefficiently low consumption.

Figure 20-4 (page 514) illustrates the loss in total surplus caused by artificial scarcity. The demand curve shows the quantity of pay-per-view movies watched at any given price. The marginal cost of allowing an additional person to watch the movie is zero; so the efficient quantity of movies viewed is Q_{OPT}. The cable company charges a positive price, in this case $4, to unscramble the signal, and as a result only Q_{MKT}

Figure 20-4

An Artificially Scarce Good

An artificially scarce good is excludable and non-rival in consumption. It is made artificially scarce because producers charge a positive price but the marginal cost of allowing one more person to consume the good is zero. In this example the market price of a pay-per-view movie is $4 and the quantity demanded at that price is Q_{MKT}. But the efficient level of consumption is Q_{OPT}, the quantity demanded when the price is zero. The efficient quantity, Q_{OPT}, exceeds the quantity demanded in an unregulated market, Q_{MKT}. The shaded area represents the loss in total surplus from charging a price of $4. >web...

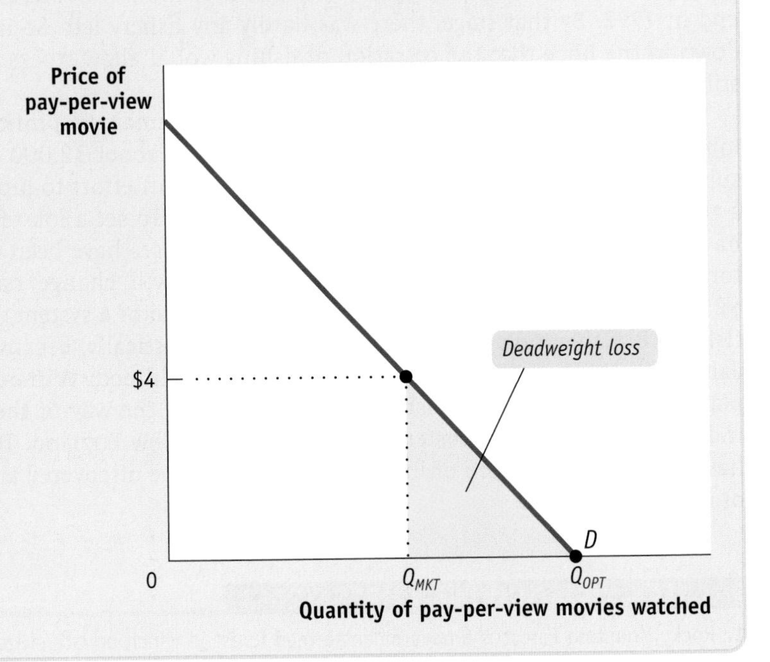

pay-per-view movies will be watched. This leads to a deadweight loss equal to the area of the shaded triangle.

Does this look familiar? Like the problems that arise with public goods and common resources, the problem created by artificially scarce goods is similar to something we have already seen: in this case, it is the problem of *natural monopoly.* A natural monopoly, you will recall, is an industry in which average total cost is above marginal cost for the relevant output range. In order to be willing to produce output, the producer must charge a price at least as high as average total cost—that is, a price above marginal cost. But a price above marginal cost leads to inefficiently low consumption.

economics in action

Blacked-Out Games

It's the night of the big game for your local CFL team—a game that is being nationally televised by one of the major networks. So you flip to the local channel that is an affiliate of that network—but the game isn't on. Instead, you get some other show with a message scrolling across the bottom of the screen that this game has been blacked out in your area. What the message probably doesn't say, though you understand quite well, is that this blackout is at the insistence of the team's owners, who don't want potential ticket buyers to have the option of staying home and watching the game for free on TV. So the good in question—watching the game on TV—has been made artificially scarce. Because the game is being broadcast anyway, no scarce resources would be used to make it available in its immediate locality as well. But it isn't available—which means a loss in welfare to those who would have watched the game on TV but are not willing to pay the price, in time and money, to go to the stadium. By the way, it seems that NHL hockey games don't need to create artificial scarcity with local TV blackouts—the hockey arenas fill up anyway. ■

>> QUICK REVIEW

- An *artificially scarce good* is excludable but non-rival in consumption.
- Because the good is non-rival in consumption, the efficient price to consumers is zero. However, because it is excludable, sellers charge a positive price, which leads to inefficiently low consumption.
- The problems of artificially scarce goods are similar to those posed by a natural monopoly.

>>CHECK YOUR UNDERSTANDING 20-4

1. Xena is a software program produced by Xenoid. Each year Xenoid produces an upgrade that costs $300,000 to produce. It costs nothing to allow customers to download it from the company's website. The demand schedule for the upgrade is shown in the accompanying table.
   a. What is the efficient price to a consumer of this upgrade? Explain.
   b. What is the lowest price at which Xenoid is willing to produce and sell the upgrade? Draw the demand curve and show the loss of total surplus that occurs when Xenoid charges this price compared to the efficient price.

Price of upgrade	Quantity of upgrades demanded
$180	1,700
150	2,000
120	2,300
90	2,600
0	3,500

Solutions appear at back of book.

• A LOOK AHEAD •

In 2001 the various levels of Canadian government—federal, provincial, and local—spent about $439 billion. Where did the money go?

The answer, in large part, is that it went to provide public goods. National defence and police took only a small chunk—around 8%; education and health, which are widely regarded as public goods, took up nearly 30%. Then there was spending on highways, fire prevention, and so on.

Not all government spending is on items that can easily be described as public goods. As we'll see in Chapter 21, much spending at the federal level goes for *social insurance,* programs intended to help individuals and families in trouble. But providing public goods is still a central feature of government budgets.

And that brings us to the next question: where does the money that pays for public goods come from? The answer, of course, is that it comes from tax revenue. But taxes, in turn, have economic effects, because they change incentives.

In the next chapter we'll take a deeper look at how taxes affect a market economy. We'll also look at the related effects of social insurance.

SUMMARY

1. Goods may be classified according to whether or not they are **excludable** and whether or not they are **rival in consumption.**
2. Free markets can deliver efficient levels of production and consumption for **private goods,** which are both excludable and rival in consumption. When goods are non-excludable, non-rival in consumption, or both, free markets cannot achieve efficient outcomes.
3. When goods are **non-excludable,** there is a **free-rider problem:** consumers will not pay for the good, leading to inefficiently low production. When goods are **non-rival in consumption,** they should be free, and any positive price leads to inefficiently low consumption.
4. A **public good** is non-excludable and non-rival in consumption. In most cases a public good must be supplied by the government. The marginal social benefit of a public good is equal to the sum of the individual marginal benefits to each consumer. The efficient quantity of a public good is the quantity at which marginal social benefit equals marginal cost. Like a positive externality, marginal social benefit is greater than any one individual's marginal benefit, so no individual is willing to provide the efficient quantity.
5. One rationale for the presence of government is that it allows citizens to tax themselves in order to provide public goods. Governments use **cost-benefit analysis** to determine the efficient provision of a public good. Such analysis is difficult, however, because individuals have an incentive to overstate the good's value to them.
6. A **common resource** is rival in consumption but non-excludable. It is subject to **overuse,** because an individual does not take into account the fact that his or her use depletes the amount available for others. This is similar to the problem of a negative externality: the marginal social cost of use of an individual's common resource is always higher than his or her individual marginal cost. Pigouvian taxes, the creation of a system of tradable licenses, or the assignment of property rights are possible solutions.

7. **Artificially scarce goods** are excludable but non-rival in consumption. Because no marginal cost arises from allowing another individual to consume the good, the efficient price is zero. A positive price compensates the producer for the cost of production but leads to inefficiently low consumption. The problem of an artificially scarce good is similar to that of a natural monopoly.

KEY TERMS

PROBLEMS

1. The government is involved in providing many goods and services. For each of the goods or services listed, determine whether it is rival or non-rival in consumption and whether it is excludable or non-excludable. What type of good is it? Without government involvement, would the quantity provided be efficient, inefficiently low, or inefficiently high?
   a. Street signs
   b. Via Rail service
   c. Regulations limiting pollution
   d. A highway without tolls
   e. A lighthouse on the coast

2. An economist gives the following advice to a museum director: "You should introduce 'peak pricing': at times when the museum has few visitors, you should admit visitors for free. And at times when the museum has many visitors, you should charge a higher admission fee."
   a. When the museum is quiet, is it rival or non-rival in consumption? Is it excludable or non-excludable? What type of good is the museum at those times? What would be the efficient price to charge visitors during that time, and why?
   b. When the museum is busy, is it rival or non-rival in consumption? Is it excludable or non-excludable? What type of good is the museum at those times? What would be the efficient price to charge visitors during that time, and why?

3. In many planned communities, various aspects of community living are subject to regulation by a homeowners' association. These rules can regulate house architecture, require snow removal from sidewalks, exclude outdoor equipment such as backyard swimming pools, require appropriate conduct in shared spaces such as the community clubhouse, and so on. There has been some conflict, as some homeowners feel that some of the regulations are overly intrusive. You have been called in to mediate. Using economics, how would you decide what types of regulations are warranted and what types are not?

4. A residential community's 100 residents are concerned about security. The accompanying table gives the total cost of hiring a 24-hour security service, as well as each individual resident's total benefit.

Quantity of security guards	Total cost	Total individual benefit to each resident
0	$0	$0
1	150	10
2	300	16
3	450	18
4	600	19

   a. Explain why the security service is a public good for the residents of the community.
   b. Calculate the marginal cost, the individual marginal benefit for each resident, and the marginal social benefit.
   c. If an individual resident were to decide about hiring and paying for security guards on his or her own, how many guards would that resident hire?
   d. If the residents act together, how many security guards will they hire?

5. The accompanying table shows Tanisha's and Ari's individual marginal benefit of different amounts of street cleanings per month. Suppose that the marginal cost of street cleanings is constant at $9 each.

Quantity of street cleanings per month	Tanisha's individual marginal benefit	Ari's individual marginal benefit
0		
	$10	$8
1		
	6	4
2		
	2	1
3		

a. If Tanisha had to pay for street cleaning on her own, how many street cleanings would there be?

b. Calculate the marginal social benefit of street cleaning. What is the optimal number of street cleanings?

c. Consider the optimal number of street cleanings. The last street cleaning of that number costs $9. Is Tanisha willing to pay for that last cleaning on her own? Is Ari willing to pay for that last cleaning on his own?

6. Anyone with a radio receiver can listen to public radio, which is funded largely by donations.

a. Is public radio excludable or non-excludable? Is it rival in consumption or non-rival? What type of good is it?

b. Should the government support public radio? Explain your reasoning.

c. In order to finance itself, public radio decides to transmit only to satellite radios, for which users have to pay a fee. What type of good is public radio then? Will the quantity of radio listening be efficient? Why or why not?

7. The village of Upper Bigglesworth has a village "commons", a piece of land on which each villager, by law, is free to graze his or her cows. Use of the commons is measured in units of the number of cows grazing on it. Assume that each resident has a constant marginal cost of sending cows to graze (that is, the marginal cost is the same, whether 1 or 10 cows are grazing). But each additional cow grazed means less grass available for others, and the damage done by overgrazing of the commons increases as the number of cows grazing increases. Finally, assume that the benefit to the villagers of each additional cow grazing on the commons declines as more cows graze, since each additional cow has less grass to eat than the previous one.

a. Is the commons excludable or non-excludable? Is it rival in consumption or non-rival? What kind of good is the commons?

b. Draw a diagram, with the quantity of cows that graze on the commons on the horizontal axis. How does the quantity of cows grazing in the absence of government intervention compare to the efficient quantity? Show both in your diagram.

c. The villagers hire you to tell them how to achieve an efficient use of the commons. You tell them that there are three possibilities: a Pigouvian tax, the assignment of property rights over the commons, and a system of tradable licenses for the right to graze a cow. Explain how each one of these options would lead to an efficient use of the commons. Draw a diagram that shows the Pigouvian tax.

8. The accompanying table shows six consumers' willingness to pay (his or her individual marginal benefit) for one MP3 file copy of a Dr. Dre album. The marginal cost of making the file accessible to one additional consumer is constant, at zero.

Consumer	Individual marginal benefit
Adriana	$2
Bhagesh	15
Chizuko	1
Denzel	10
Emma	5
Frank	4

a. What would be the efficient price to charge for a download of the file?

b. All six consumers are able to download the file for free from a file-sharing service, Pantster. Which consumers will download the file? What will be the total consumer surplus to those consumers?

c. Pantster is shut down for copyright law infringement. In order to download the file, consumers now have to pay $4.99 at a commercial music site. Which consumers will download the file? What will be the total consumer surplus to those consumers? How much producer surplus accrues to the commercial music site? What is the total surplus? What is the deadweight loss from the new pricing policy?

9. Butchart Gardens is a very large garden in Victoria, British Columbia, renowned for its beautiful plants. It is so large that it could hold many times more visitors than currently visit it. The garden charges an admission fee of $10. At this price, 1,000 visitors visit the garden each day. If admission were free, 2,000 visitors would visit the garden each day.

a. Are visits to Butchart Gardens excludable or non-excludable? Are they rival in consumption or non-rival? What type of good is it?

b. In a diagram, illustrate the demand curve for visits to Butchart Gardens. Indicate the situation when Butchart Gardens charges an admission fee of $10. Also indicate the situation when Butchart Gardens charges no admission fee.

c. Illustrate the deadweight loss from charging a $10 admission fee. Explain why charging a $10 admission fee is inefficient.

10. In developing a vaccine for a new virus called SARS, a pharmaceutical company incurs a very high fixed cost. The marginal cost of delivering the vaccine to patients, however, is negligible (consider it to be equal to zero). The pharmaceutical company holds the exclusive patent to the vaccine. You are a regulator who must decide what price the pharmaceutical company is allowed to charge.

a. Draw a diagram that shows the price for the vaccine that would arise if the company is unregulated, and label it P_M. What is the efficient price for the vaccine? Show the deadweight loss that arises from the price P_M.

b. On another diagram, show the lowest price that the regulator can enforce that would still induce the pharmaceutical company to develop the vaccine. Label it P^*. Show the deadweight loss that arises from this price. How does it compare to the deadweight loss that arises from the price P_M?

c. Suppose you have accurate information about the pharmaceutical company's fixed cost. How could you use price regulation of the pharmaceutical company, combined with a subsidy to the company, to have the efficient quantity of the vaccine provided at the lowest cost to the government?

To continue your study and review of concepts in this chapter, please visit the Krugman/Wells website for quizzes, animated graph tutorials, web links to helpful resources, and more.

www.worthpublishers.com/krugmanwellsmyatt

chapter 21

>>Taxes, Social Insurance, and Income Distribution

A TAX RIOT

On March 31, 1990, hundreds of thousands of British citizens marched across London, protesting a new tax that had been introduced by Prime Minister Margaret Thatcher. As some protestors clashed with police, the initially peaceful demonstration turned into a riot, with hundreds injured. The violence came as a surprise, but maybe it shouldn't have: the tax had aroused angry opposition throughout Britain. Later that year Mrs. Thatcher was forced to resign, and many observers believed that the tax controversy was the prime cause of her fall.

The tax at issue was officially known as the "Community Charge" but was popularly known as the "poll tax". Until 1989 local public services like street cleaning and trash collection had been financed with "the rates", a tax that depended on the value of peoples' homes. Most local services in Canada are financed with similar property-based taxes. Mrs. Thatcher, however, replaced these property taxes with a payment from each individual over the age of 18. While the tax varied from town to town, every adult in a particular town owed the same amount, regardless of his or her income or how much his or her property was worth.

Supporters of the poll tax argued that it was better for efficiency than the tax it replaced. Because the old tax depended on the value of property, it discouraged people both from buying more expensive homes and from improving the homes they had. Supporters also argued that the poll tax was fair, because the cost of providing public services depended mainly on how many people lived in a town, not on how rich those people were.

But opponents argued that the poll tax was extremely unfair because it did not take into account differences in people's ability to

What you will learn in this chapter:

- Why designing a tax system involves **a trade-off between equity and efficiency**
- Two concepts of fairness (or equity) in taxation: the **benefits principle** and the **ability-to-pay principle**
- The difference between horizontal equity and vertical equity
- The different kinds of taxes and their effects on people at different levels of income
- The major types of government spending and how they are justified
- What income inequality is and why there is a policy debate about it

HIP-Archive/Topham/The Image Works

AP/Wide World Photos

Margaret Thatcher and these protesters differed sharply over the fairness of the poll tax.

pay—a single mother who worked as a waitress and a millionaire stockbroker owed the same amount if they lived in the same town.

One moral of the story is that making tax policy isn't easy—in fact, if you are a politician it can be dangerous to your professional health. But the deeper moral is that making tax policy always involves striking a balance between the pursuit of efficiency and the pursuit of perceived fairness (or equity). Or as economists say, there is a *trade-off between equity and efficiency*. In this chapter we will show why this trade-off exists and how attempts to make the best of the trade-off influence the design of actual tax systems.

Principles of Tax Policy

A tax system achieves **tax efficiency** when it minimizes the direct and indirect costs to the economy of tax collection.

A tax system achieves **tax fairness,** or **tax equity,** when the "right" people actually bear the burden of taxes.

Tax policy always has two goals. On the one hand, governments strive to achieve **tax efficiency:** they try to minimize the direct and indirect costs to the economy of the government's tax collection. On the other hand, governments seek **tax fairness,** or **tax equity:** they try to ensure that the "right" people actually bear the burden of taxes. The central dilemma in tax policy—the dilemma that led to London's poll tax riot—is that an efficient tax may not seem fair, and a fair tax may not be efficient.

The Burden of Taxes: A Quick Review

We analysed some of the basic economics of taxation in Chapters 4 and 6. Here we revisit briefly the results of that analysis. Figure 21-1 shows the effects of an *excise tax*—a tax on sales or purchases—imposed on some good, in this case automobiles. Excise taxes are only part of the Canadian tax system, but the principles suggested by this analysis apply to all taxes.

In the absence of a tax, the equilibrium price of autos would be P_E, and the quantity bought and sold would be Q_E. If a tax is imposed on the purchase or sale of an automobile, it *drives a wedge* between the price paid by buyers and that received by sellers. In this case, a tax of $\$T$ per unit is imposed. In the new equilibrium the price paid by buyers rises to P_C, while the price received by sellers falls to P_P. The difference,

Figure 21-1

The Deadweight Loss of a Tax

Here an excise tax of the amount $T = P_C - P_P$ is imposed per auto sold. The quantity transacted falls from Q_E to Q_T, and there is a deadweight loss equal to the shaded area. The tax creates a wedge between the price paid by consumers, P_C, and the price received by producers, P_P. As a result, incentives are distorted and inefficiency arises: consumers consume less than is efficient and producers produce less than is efficient.

>web...

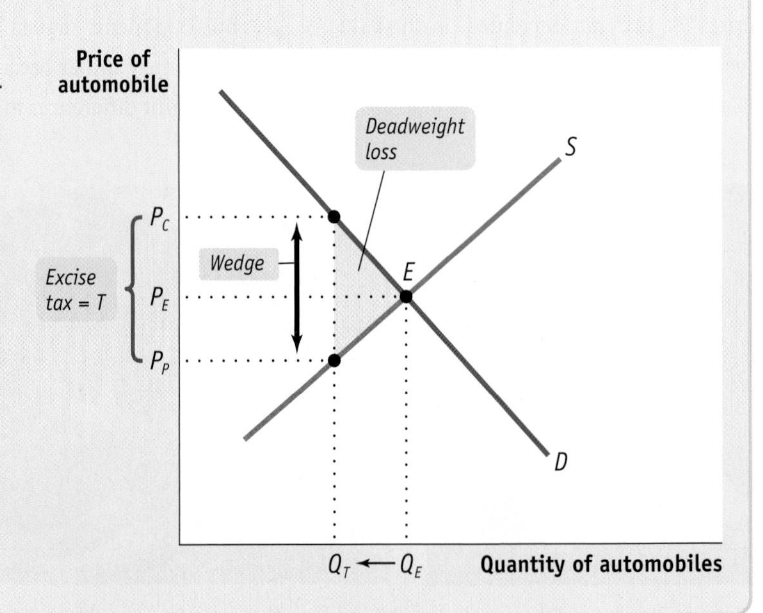

$P_C - P_P$, is equal to the tax. As a result of the tax, the quantity bought and sold falls from Q_E to Q_T. So the tax changes people's behaviour: producers produce less of the taxed good, and consumers consume less.

Our analysis in Chapters 4 and 6 revealed three key results:

1. Buyers are hurt by the tax to the extent that the price they pay rises; sellers are hurt to the extent that the price they receive falls. But how much P_C rises and how much P_P falls does not depend on who pays the tax—in fact, in Figure 21-1 we have not even specified whether this is a tax on producers or on consumers. So the *incidence* of a tax—who actually bears the burden—cannot be determined simply by looking at who pays the money to the government.
2. What does determine the incidence of the tax is the price elasticity of supply and demand. The higher the price elasticity of supply, the more the price paid by consumers rises as a result of the tax, and therefore the greater the tax burden on consumers. The higher the elasticity of demand, the more the price received by producers falls and the greater the tax burden on producers.
3. The tax causes a loss in efficiency—a deadweight loss—by creating a wedge between the price paid by consumers and the price paid by producers. At Q_T in Figure 21-1, the marginal value of an additional unit of consumption is greater than the marginal cost of producing that additional unit. This means that the economy misses the potential gain from producing and consuming more of the good. The total deadweight loss from the tax can be measured by the area of the shaded triangle. This deadweight loss represents the *excess burden* of the tax, that is, the cost to society over and above the tax revenue the government collects.

A tax system causes deadweight losses because taxes *distort incentives:* the incentives at the margin for producers to produce and consumers to consume are different from what they would have been without the tax, and so people change their behaviour. This means that the most efficient tax will be one that distorts incentives the least.

In considering the efficiency of a tax, we must also take into account something not shown in Figure 21-1: the resources actually used both to collect the tax and to pay it. These are called the **administrative costs** of the tax. The most familiar administrative cost is the time that individuals spend filling out their personal income tax forms, or the money that they spend on accountants who do their taxes for them. The administrative costs to businesses of complying with the government's tax regulations (remitting sales taxes, paying corporate income taxes, and making tax and payroll deductions from employee wages) have been estimated to be between $2.3 and $4.5 billion a year (for the year 1996)—greater than the cost of running the whole of Revenue Canada ($1.7 billion).[1]

The **administrative costs** of a tax are the resources used both to collect the tax and to pay it.

If maximizing efficiency were the only goal, a tax system should be designed to minimize the sum of its excess burden and its administrative costs. But tax policy is not driven by efficiency alone, because the voters who must approve a tax system also care about fairness, or *equity*. As we will see, fairness in a tax system usually (but not always!) comes at the expense of efficiency.

Tax Fairness

We have just seen how economic analysis can be used to determine who bears the burden of a tax. But who *should* bear the burden? Governments have wide discretion in choosing what to tax and how to tax it. How should they exercise this discretion?

One answer is that the tax system should be fair. But what exactly does fairness mean? Fairness, like beauty, is often in the eyes of the beholder. Nevertheless, most people would probably agree that similar or identical people should face similar or

[1] David Zussman and Robert Plamondon, "Cutting the Costs of Tax Collection Down to Size" (Public Policy Forum, 1998), http://www.ppforum.com/bbg/bbg_p_01_1998.PDF.

Horizontal equity is the principle that identical or similar individuals should face identical or similar tax burdens.

identical taxes. This principle is known as **horizontal equity,** and it plays an important role in the Canadian tax system: "Similar or identical" individuals may live in different provinces, some of which are relatively wealthy (like Alberta), and some of which are relatively poor (like New Brunswick). An architect living in Alberta may make about the same money as an architect living in New Brunswick. But because Alberta is a richer province with enormous oil revenues and low unemployment, while New Brunswick has generally lower incomes and high unemployment, Alberta has a lot more tax revenue than New Brunswick. So, to ensure that these two architects pay "similar or identical" taxes *and* have the same access to public services, the federal government redistributes (or transfers) tax revenue from the provinces that are better off to those that are worse off. These **transfers** are known as **equalization payments.**

Transfer payments are government payments to individuals, firms, or other levels of government that are not made in exchange for goods or services.

Equalization payments are transfers paid by the federal government to the provinces whose tax capacities are below average, designed to equalize their ability to provide public service to their residents.

Vertical equity refers to fair tax treatment for people in different economic circumstances.

According to the **benefits principle** of tax fairness, those who benefit from public spending should bear the burden of the tax that pays for that spending.

Vertical equity refers to fair tax treatment for people in different economic circumstances—with different incomes or different levels of consumption of public goods. Now we are comparing, for example, the tax treatment of architects (who tend to make a lot of money) with that of poor labourers (who struggle to make ends meet). As far as vertical equity is concerned, there are two conflicting principles: the benefits principle and the ability-to-pay principle.

According to the **benefits principle** of tax fairness, those who benefit from public spending should bear the burden of the tax that pays for that spending. For example, those who benefit from a road should pay for the road's upkeep, and those who fly on airplanes should pay for air traffic control. Approaching this from another direction, we can ask why someone who never flies should pay for air traffic control. Those who benefit can be made to pay either through user fees or through taxes that target users. For example, motorists could pay for roads through road tolls (a user fee) or through fuel taxes. While road tolls *are* used in Canada, tolls are costly to collect and are unpopular with electorates. Instead, most provinces have fuel taxes that fund road maintenance and improvement. In this way motorists, who benefit from the highway system, also pay for it.

User fees are perhaps the clearest application of the benefits principle in action. University tuition fees can be regarded as a provincial government user fee—though one that does not fully pay for the service provided, because university tuition amounts to only about 20% of university revenues (in 2001). Similarly, marriage license fees can be justified on the "benefits principle"—those who benefit from receiving a marriage license are contributing to the government's cost of issuing it.

The benefits principle is attractive from an economic point of view because it matches well with one of the major justifications for public spending, the theory of public goods. If government's role is to provide people with goods that could not otherwise be made available, it seems natural to charge people in proportion to the benefits they get from those goods.

Practical considerations, however, make it impossible to base the whole tax system on the benefits principle. It would be too cumbersome to have a specific tax for each of the many distinct programs that the government offers. Also, attempts to base taxes on the benefits principle often conflict with the other major principle of tax fairness: the **ability-to-pay principle,** according to which those with greater ability to pay a tax should pay more.

According to the **ability-to-pay principle** of tax fairness, those with greater ability to pay a tax should pay more tax.

The ability-to-pay principle is usually interpreted to mean that high-income individuals should pay more in taxes than low-income individuals. Often the ability-to-pay principle is used to argue not just that high-income individuals should pay more taxes but that they should pay a higher *percentage* of their income in taxes. We'll consider the issue of how taxes vary as a percentage of income later.

The London protest we described at the beginning of this chapter was basically a protest against the failure of the poll tax to take the ability-to-pay principle into account. In some parts of Britain, the poll tax was as high as $900 per year. For a highly paid executive or professional, $900 is not a lot of money. But for a struggling British family, a tax of $900 per adult was a crushing burden. It's not surprising that many people were upset that the new tax completely disregarded the ability-to-pay principle.

Equity versus Efficiency

Margaret Thatcher's poll tax was an example of a **lump-sum tax,** a tax that is the same for everyone regardless of any actions that people take. It was widely perceived as much less fair than the tax it replaced, under which taxes were proportional to property values. Under the old system, the biggest tax bills were paid by the people with the most expensive houses; since these people tended to be wealthy, they were also the people best able to bear the burden.

But the old system definitely distorted incentives. People considering home improvements knew that such improvements, by making their property more valuable, would also increase their tax bills. The result, surely, was that the tax discouraged homeowners from making some home improvements that they would have made had the tax not been there.

In contrast, a lump-sum tax like the poll tax does not distort incentives, because people have to pay the tax regardless of their actions. So lump-sum taxes, although unfair, are usually more efficient than other taxes.

The example of the poll tax debate illustrates a general point. Unless a tax system is badly designed, it can only be made fairer by sacrificing efficiency; conversely, it can only be made more efficient by making it less fair. So there is normally a **trade-off between equity and efficiency.**

Economic analysis cannot say how much weight a tax system should give to equity and how much to efficiency. That choice is a value judgement, one we make through the political process.

A **lump-sum tax** is the same for everyone, regardless of any actions people take.

In a well-designed tax system there is a **trade-off between equity and efficiency:** the system can be made more efficient only by making it less fair, and vice versa.

FOR INQUIRING MINDS

MUST TAXES ALWAYS CAUSE EFFICIENCY LOSSES?

We have said that the most efficient taxes are those that distort incentives the least. A poll tax is an efficient tax because it cannot be avoided (except by emigration or death!) and it has no effect on incentives. Other lump-sum taxes may not be quite as efficient as the poll tax, since in some cases individuals may completely avoid the activity that is taxed. For example, a lump-sum tax on a firm's payroll could cause the firm to close down. However, if one does still undertake the taxed activity, a lump-sum tax will have no effect on any decisions at the margin. Thus, in general, lump-sum taxes distort incentives the least.

But what if we want to distort incentives? Or, to be more precise, what if we want to correct incentives for a distortion that already exists? For example, we saw in Chapter 19 that a tax on pollution emissions can improve economic efficiency. In this case, the government corrects market incentives for the fact that a scarce good (clean air or water) is free. Taxes on pollution emissions give society a double dividend: not only is the tax itself beneficial but society also gains from the additional public goods financed by the tax.

Because negative externalities are so prevalent, numerous taxes could be introduced that that might have beneficial effects on resource allocation. Indeed, some environmentalists suggest that the entire tax system should be revamped and geared to reducing emissions that damage air quality and produce greenhouse gases.

economics in action

Employment Insurance in Canada

Let's look at employment insurance (EI) in Canada and see if we can identify the tax equity principle behind it.

Regular EI benefits can be paid if you lose your job through no fault of your own—for example, through seasonal layoffs or corporate downsizing—and you are available

TABLE 21-1

Employment Insurance Benefits Relative to Contributions, by Province, 1986–1990

Province	Benefits relative to contributions
Newfoundland	4.3
PEI	3.4
New Brunswick	2.4
Nova Scotia	1.6
Québec	1.3
British Columbia	1.2
Saskatchewan	0.9
Manitoba	0.8
Alberta	0.8
Ontario	0.6
CANADA	1

Source: Myles Corak and Wendy Pyper, "Firms, Industries, and Cross-Subsidies: Patterns in the Distribution of UI Benefits and Taxes", Unemployment Insurance Evaluation Series, Human Resources Development Canada (Ottawa: Ministry of Supply and Services, 1995), Table 3, p. 14.

for work. To be eligible for EI benefits, you must have worked the required number of hours, which varies according to where you live and the unemployment rate in your economic region.

EI benefits are funded by a payroll tax on both workers and employers. In 2005, workers paid 1.95% of their earnings, with a ceiling on insurable earnings of $39,000. Employer contributions are 1.4 times worker contributions.

If the EI system were self-financing (meaning that total contributions just equalled total benefits) and if every contributor had the same probability of receiving benefits, EI contributions would unambiguously be based on the benefits principle. This follows since both contributions and benefits are proportionately related to earnings up to a maximum insurable limit.

Although as of 2005 the system is running a surplus, it is designed to be approximately self-financing over the long run. However, it is not the case that all contributors are equally likely to receive benefits. In fact, the statistical likelihood of becoming unemployed depends on workers' location and income class, and the industry in which they work. Thus, the EI system not only insures against unemployment but also redistributes income among industries, regions, and income classes.

In terms of income classes, the lower middle class benefits the most from the EI system. This is because the poorest individuals typically have difficulty qualifying for EI benefits, while the richest rarely need to claim them. On the other hand, Table 21-1 shows us that the poorest regions benefit most—they have the highest EI benefits relative to contributions. Though this conforms with the "ability-to-pay" principle of vertical equity, it creates considerable horizontal inequity between individuals. For example, two individuals who earn the same wage and make the same contributions to EI but who live in different regions will receive different benefits. This is because both qualification requirements and benefit periods depend on the regional unemployment rate.

So the payroll taxes that fund the EI system cannot be easily categorized. They are based primarily on the benefits principle, but since the lower middle class and the poorest regions are favoured, they are also influenced by the ability-to-pay principle. Add to the mix some horizontal inequity among individuals and a pinch of arbitrariness, and that about sums up the EI system.

The moral of the story is that it is often difficult to discover what principle lies behind a tax. As with the EI system in Canada, several principles may work in combination. ■

< < < < < < < < < < < < < < < < < <

>> QUICK REVIEW

- The *incidence* of a tax—who actually bears the burden of the tax—does not necessarily depend on who pays the money to the government.
- Taxes usually cause a deadweight loss, an *excess burden* over and above the money collected by the government. They also typically incur *administrative costs.*
- Other things equal, governments try to achieve *tax efficiency*. But they also try to achieve *tax fairness* or *equity.*
- There are two ways of gauging tax fairness: by *horizontal equity* or by *vertical equity*.
- There are two important principles of vertical equity: the *benefits principle* and the *ability-to-pay principle.*
- A *lump-sum tax on individuals* is efficient because it does not distort incentives, but it is also unfair. In a well-designed tax system, there is a *trade-off between equity and efficiency.*

>> CHECK YOUR UNDERSTANDING 21-1

1. Assess each of the following taxes in terms of the benefit principle versus the ability-to-pay principle. What actions, if any, are distorted by the tax? Assume for simplicity that in each case the purchaser of the good bears 100% of the tax burden.
   a. A federal tax of $500 for each new car purchased that finances highway safety programs
   b. A local tax of 20% on hotel rooms that finances local government expenditures
   c. A local tax of 1% of the assessed value of homes that finances local schools
   d. A 1% sales tax on food that pays for government food safety regulation and inspection programs

Solutions appear at back of book.

Understanding the Tax System

An excise tax is the easiest tax to analyse, making it a good vehicle for understanding the general principles of tax analysis. However, excise taxes are only one of many taxes used in Canada today. In this section, we develop a framework for understanding more general forms of taxation, and look at some of the major taxes used in Canada.

Tax Bases and Tax Rate Structure

Every tax consists of two pieces: a *base* and a *structure*. The **tax base** is the measure or value that determines how much an individual pays. It is usually a monetary measure, like income or property value. The **tax structure** specifies how the tax depends on the tax base. It is usually expressed in percentage terms; for example, homeowners in some area might pay taxes equal to 2% of the value of their homes.

Some important taxes and their tax bases are:

- **Income tax:** a tax that depends on the income of an individual or family
- **Payroll tax:** a tax that depends on the earnings an employer pays to an employee
- **Sales tax or excise tax:** a tax that depends on the value of goods sold
- **Profits tax:** a tax that depends on a firm's profits
- **Property tax:** a tax that depends on the value of property, such as the value of a home
- **Wealth tax:** a tax that depends on an individual's or family's wealth

Once the tax base has been defined, the next question is how the tax depends on the base. The simplest tax structure is a **proportional tax,** also sometimes called a *flat tax,* which is the same percentage of the base regardless of the taxpayer's income or wealth. For example, a property tax that is set at 2% of the value of the property, whether the property is worth $10,000 or $10,000,000, is a proportional tax. Many taxes, however, are not proportional. Instead, different people pay different percentages, usually because the tax law tries to take account of either the benefits principle or the ability-to-pay principle.

Because taxes are ultimately paid out of income, economists classify taxes according to how they vary with the income of individuals. A tax that rises *more* than in proportion to income, so that high-income taxpayers pay a larger percentage of their income than low-income taxpayers, is a **progressive tax.** A tax that rises *less* than in proportion to income, so that higher-income taxpayers pay a smaller percentage of their income than low-income taxpayers, is a **regressive tax.** A proportional tax on income would be neither progressive nor regressive.

Figure 21-2 illustrates the relationship between tax payment and income for proportional, progressive, and regressive taxes with three curves, one corresponding to each type of tax. In the case of a proportional tax, plotting the tax due against income

The **tax base** is the measure or value, such as income or property value, that determines how much tax an individual pays.

The **tax structure** specifies how the tax depends on the tax base.

An **income tax** is a tax on an individual's or family's income.

A **payroll tax** is a tax on the earnings an employer pays to an employee.

A **sales tax,** or **excise tax,** is a tax on the value of goods sold.

A **profits tax** is a tax on a firm's profits.

A **property tax** is a tax on the value of property, such as the value of a home.

A **wealth tax** is a tax on an individual's wealth.

A **proportional tax** is the same percentage of the tax base regardless of the taxpayer's income or wealth.

A **progressive tax** takes a larger share of the income of high-income taxpayers than of low-income taxpayers.

A **regressive tax** takes a smaller share of the income of high-income taxpayers than of low-income taxpayers.

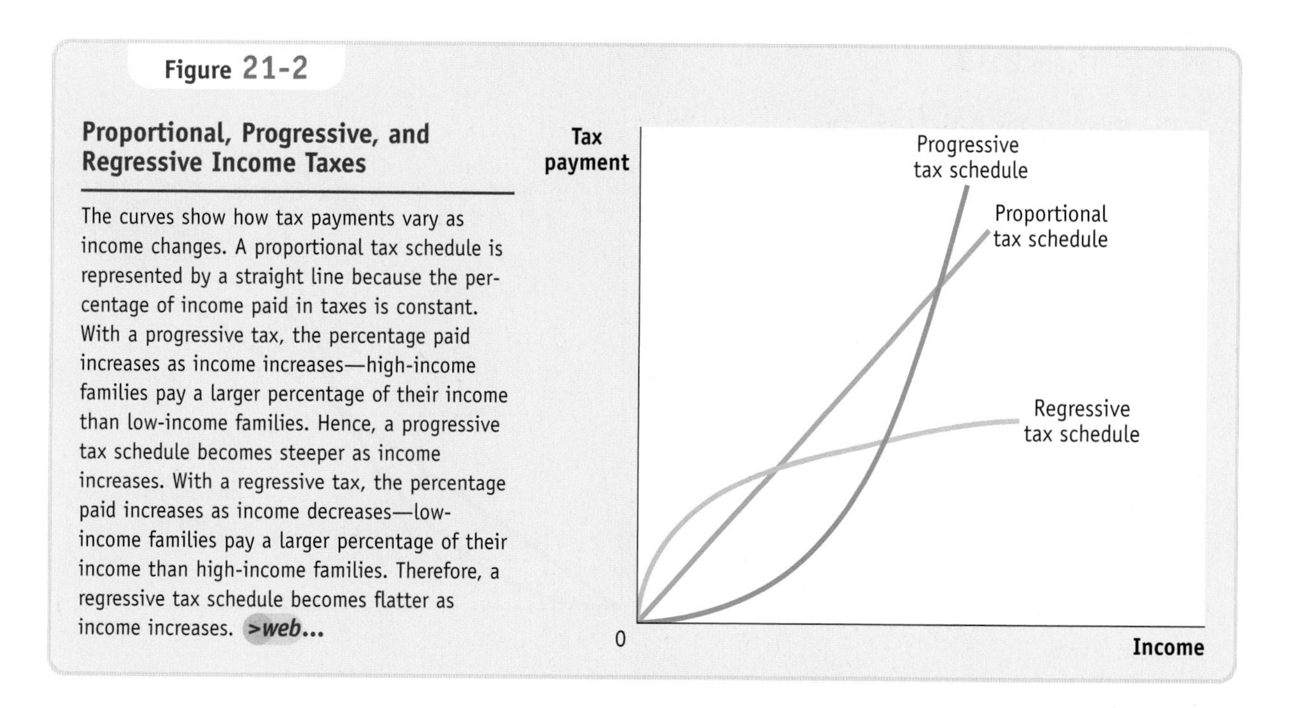

Figure 21-2

Proportional, Progressive, and Regressive Income Taxes

The curves show how tax payments vary as income changes. A proportional tax schedule is represented by a straight line because the percentage of income paid in taxes is constant. With a progressive tax, the percentage paid increases as income increases—high-income families pay a larger percentage of their income than low-income families. Hence, a progressive tax schedule becomes steeper as income increases. With a regressive tax, the percentage paid increases as income decreases—low-income families pay a larger percentage of their income than high-income families. Therefore, a regressive tax schedule becomes flatter as income increases. >web...

yields a tax schedule that is a straight line from the origin. For a progressive tax, the curve gets steeper as income increases; for a regressive tax, the curve gets flatter as income increases.

The Canadian tax system contains a mixture of progressive and regressive taxes, though as we'll see it is somewhat progressive overall.

Equity, Efficiency, and Progressive Taxation

Most people—though not all—view a progressive tax system as fairer than a regressive system. The reason is the ability-to-pay principle: a high-income family that pays 35% of its income in taxes is still left with a lot more money than a low-income family that pays only 15% in taxes. But attempts to make taxes strongly progressive run up against the trade-off between equity and efficiency.

Figure 21-3 shows once again a progressive tax schedule on income. Consider a particular individual whose income is N; given that income, he will find himself at point A on the tax schedule and will pay taxes equal to T. His **average tax rate on income** is the ratio of tax payment to income, equal to T/N. As shown in Figure 21-3, it is equal to the slope of a line from the origin to point A.

The **average tax rate on income** is the ratio of income taxes paid by an individual to his or her income.

The **marginal tax rate on income** is the additional tax an individual pays if his or her income goes up by $1.

But what effect does the tax have on his incentive to earn income—say, by working longer hours, or by investing? The answer depends on his **marginal tax rate on income,** the additional tax he pays if his income goes up by $1. It is the marginal tax rate, not the average tax rate, that affects an individual's incentive to earn another $1.

In Figure 21-3, the marginal tax rate of an individual with income N is the slope of a line tangent to the tax schedule at point A. Clearly, in this example the marginal tax rate is higher than the average tax rate. This is always true in the case of a progressive tax: *when a tax is progressive, the marginal tax rate is higher than the average tax rate at every income level.*

To deepen our understanding of this point, let's consider a simplified tax system. Imagine that income taxes work as follows: families pay no tax on the first $40,000 of income but pay a 50% tax rate on any income over $40,000. This system would be strongly progressive: families with less than $40,000 in income will pay no taxes, but families with high incomes will pay up to 50% of their income in taxes.

Figure 21-3

The Marginal Tax Rate versus the Average Tax Rate for a Progressive Tax

Under the progressive tax schedule shown here, a taxpayer with income *N* finds himself at point *A* on the tax schedule and pays taxes of *T*. His average tax rate at income *N* is the total tax paid divided by the total income, *T/N*, which is equal to the slope of the line connecting the origin to *A*. His marginal tax rate at income *N* is the tax rate paid on an additional $1 of income at point *A*. This is equal to the slope of the line tangent to the tax schedule at *A*. As shown, for a progressive tax the marginal tax rate is greater than the average tax rate. As a result, compared to a proportional or regressive tax, progressive taxes result in reduced incentives for higher-income people to work and invest. >web...

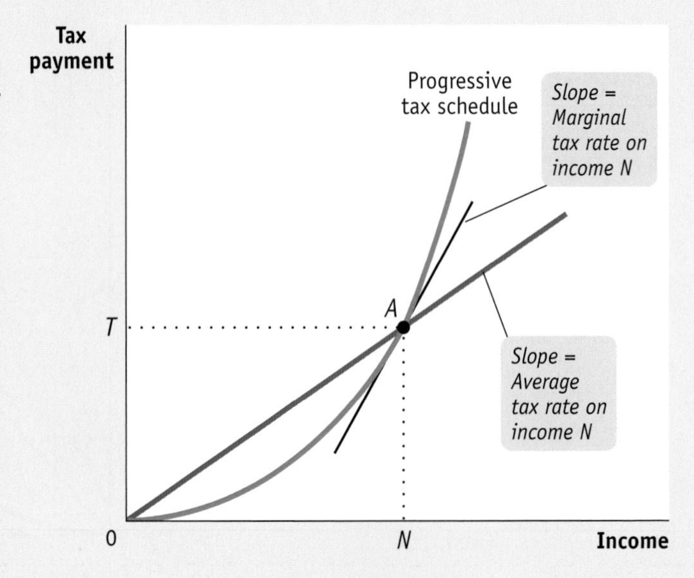

At the same time, this system will lead to a high marginal tax rate for many families, even if their *average* tax rates aren't very high. Consider a family with an income of $50,000. It will pay taxes only on the last $10,000 of that income, so its average tax rate will be $5,000/$50,000, or 10 percent. However, the family will pay $0.50 in taxes for each additional $1 it earns; its marginal tax rate is 50%.

In fact, the federal income tax works a lot like that. Family income below a certain amount (the amount depends on the size of the family and other criteria) isn't taxed. Income above that amount is taxed at a rate of 16%, up to another threshold at which the tax rate rises to 22%, and so on. In 1998 the combined federal–provincial *average* income tax rate was about 19%, but taxpayers in the highest tax bracket (with incomes over $100,000) faced *marginal* rates as high as 49%. These are actually moderate by historical standards. In the past, marginal rates in Canada have been as high as 80%. Even today, marginal rates are as high as 70% in some European countries.

The excess burden of a tax comes from its effect on marginal incentives. Suppose that a highly progressive tax system implied a marginal tax rate of 70% on successful businesspeople. An entrepreneur might look at that rate and decide that the risk and effort of expanding her business just wasn't worth it. So high marginal tax rates distort incentives, reducing the incentive to earn more income by working more or investing money rather than spending it. In short, the ability-to-pay principle pushes governments toward a highly progressive tax system, but efficiency considerations push them the other way.

Taxes in Canada

In this section we are going to provide a brief description of the major taxes in Canada, and examine whether they are progressive or regressive. This is an important question because there seems to be something unfair about a regressive tax system. So let's see how Canada's taxes measure up.

Table 21-2 shows the revenue raised by the major taxes in Canada in fiscal year 2001. It's noticeable that there is a major tax corresponding to five of the six tax bases we previously identified. There are taxes on incomes, payrolls, profits (or corporate income), sales, and property. Indeed, for most categories there are two layers of taxes—one paid to the federal government and one to the provincial or local governments. The only exception is property, which is not taxed by the federal government.

What about wealth taxes? For many years they took the form of estate and inheritance taxes, but these were abolished in the 1970s. Canada is now one

TABLE 21-2

Major Taxes in Canada, Fiscal Year 2001 (billions of dollars)

	Federal	Provincial and local	Percent of total taxes
Income tax	$88	$53	32.0%
Sales tax	39	47	19.7
Profits tax	28	14	9.6
Property tax	0	41	9.4
Payroll tax	23	10	7.5
Other	16	78	21.5

Source: Karin Treff and David Perry, *Finances of the Nation 2001* (Toronto: Canadian Tax Foundation, 2001).

of the few industrialized countries that do not tax transfers of wealth between individuals.

Of all the taxes in Canada, income taxes are easily the most important. Of the $437 billion paid in taxes in 2001, 32% was raised through personal income taxes alone. Sales taxes are the next in importance, constituting 20% of total tax revenue. Corporate income taxes and property taxes each raise nearly 10% of total tax revenue. Payroll taxes are fifth, at 7.5% of total tax revenue.

Having delineated the major taxes in Canada, let's now examine whether they can be categorized as progressive or regressive so we can discover the general trend of the tax system.

Intuitively, we would expect different answers for different taxes. We would expect the personal income tax to be strongly progressive because low incomes are exempt, and higher incomes are taxed at increasing marginal tax rates. We would expect sales taxes to be regressive since the rich spend a smaller proportion of their income and are more able to spend part of it in tax-free jurisdictions. We would expect corporate income taxes to be progressive since ultimately these taxes fall on the shareholders of corporations who are likely to have higher incomes. Intuitively, we would expect property taxes to be progressive (since the poor don't own much property), and payroll taxes—which are paid only on earnings up to a maximum level—to be proportional up to that maximum, but regressive thereafter.

So much for intuition—what about the reality? Answering this question is complicated by two factors.

First, as we have already emphasized, the *incidence* of a tax—who actually bears the burden—cannot be determined simply by looking at who pays the money to the government. The incidence of a tax is determined by the elasticity of demand and supply—and must be *estimated*. For example, in practice the incidence of payroll taxes paid by employers falls mostly onto workers in the form of lower wages.

Second, to determine an effective tax *rate*, we need to divide the *estimated* tax liability of each income class by their total income. This should include their market income, plus government transfers received in cash, plus the value of government transfers received in kind. If we did not include both kinds of government transfers, "effective" tax rates would be incomplete. In particular, they would be arbitrarily affected by how the government allocates its expenditure between direct spending and transfers.

Suppose, for example, that the federal government decides to help students. It could give them a non-taxable grant, which increases their incomes and reduces their tax rate. Or, the government could give students the same amount of financial help by transferring more money to the provinces to be used to reduce university tuition fees. If government transfers received in kind were excluded, there would be no effect on the effective tax rate of students. Yet, they are clearly benefiting from the lower tuition fees.

Once we accept that both kinds of government transfers (in cash and in kind) must be included, we realize that the whole question of the incidence of taxes, and whether they are progressive or regressive, depends on who gets the benefits that result from government spending.

Studies have been done that take these points into account. Recently, Ruggeri, Van Wart, and Howard used a highly detailed micro-database for the year 1986.[2] If the

[2] G. C. Ruggeri, D. Van Wart, and R. Howard, "The Redistributional Impact of Taxation in Canada", *Canadian Tax Journal* 42, No. 2 (1994): 417–451.

study were repeated using today's income tax system, the results would be very similar. Let's see how our intuition compares to the results of Ruggeri.

It turns out that our intuition was right about the personal income tax—it is unambiguously progressive. But we were slightly wrong about payroll taxes, since they are initially progressive (rather than proportional) at income levels below $35,000. The main reason is that payroll taxes are assessed against earned income, and low-income households have a lower ratio of earned to total income. As incomes rise above $35,000, however, payroll taxes become strongly regressive.

Finally, the annual incidence of sales taxes is similar to that of payroll taxes. The surprise here is that sales taxes are progressive for income levels below $25,000! There are two reasons for this. First, low-income families receive a GHT tax credit that partially insulates them from the effects of sales taxes. Second, sales taxes are generally shifted onto consumers, resulting in higher prices. But low-income households are more likely to be receiving transfers (such as Canada Pension Plan, EI benefits, or the Canada Child Tax Benefit), which are indexed to the consumer price index.

Summing up, our intuition didn't do too badly. But although intuition is useful, the incidence of taxation is too complicated to be left to intuition alone. We also need the results of detailed studies.

Figure 21-4 shows us that overall, taking into account all levels of government and all taxes, Canada has a progressive system of taxation. Overall, progressive taxes at the federal and provincial levels more than offset taxes at the local level that are essentially regressive.

Figure 21-4 The Overall Tax Rate by Income Class—All Taxes and All Levels of Government

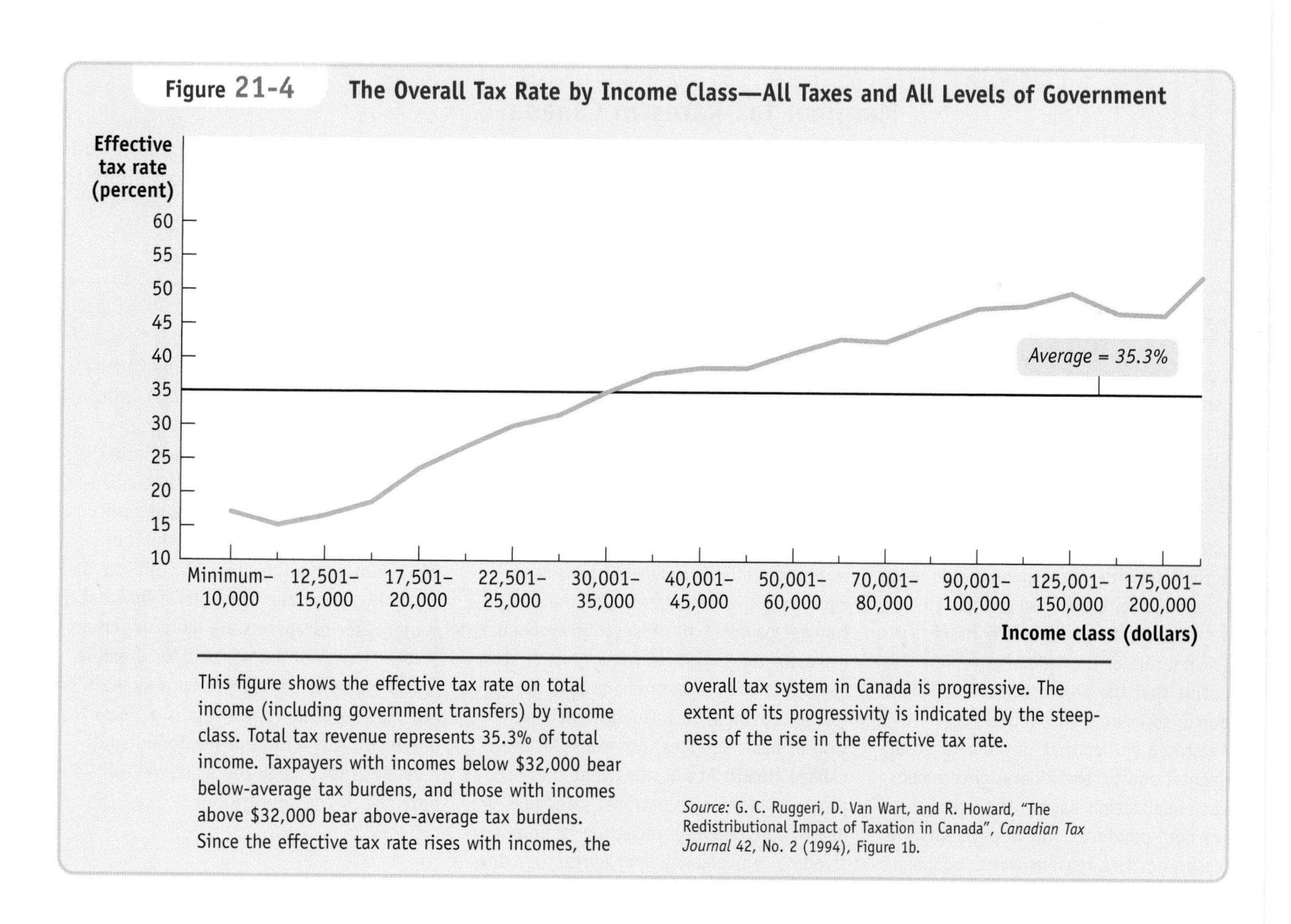

This figure shows the effective tax rate on total income (including government transfers) by income class. Total tax revenue represents 35.3% of total income. Taxpayers with incomes below $32,000 bear below-average tax burdens, and those with incomes above $32,000 bear above-average tax burdens. Since the effective tax rate rises with incomes, the overall tax system in Canada is progressive. The extent of its progressivity is indicated by the steepness of the rise in the effective tax rate.

Source: G. C. Ruggeri, D. Van Wart, and R. Howard, "The Redistributional Impact of Taxation in Canada", *Canadian Tax Journal* 42, No. 2 (1994), Figure 1b.

Different Taxes, Different Principles

Why are some taxes progressive but others regressive? Can't the government make up its mind?

There are two main reasons for the mixture of regressive and progressive taxes in the Canadian system: the difference between lower and upper levels of government, and the fact that different taxes are based on different principles.

Provincial and especially local governments are limited in the extent to which they can apply the ability-to-pay principle. This is largely because they are subject to *tax competition:* a local or provincial government that tried to impose high taxes on people with high incomes might find those people moving to other locations where taxes are lower. This is less of a concern at the national level, although some very rich people have opted to live outside Canada to reduce their tax burden. A famous example in Atlantic Canada is that of the New Brunswick industrialist K. C. Irving, who lived 6 months plus a day each year in Bermuda.

While the federal government is therefore in the best position to apply principles of fairness, it applies different principles to different taxes, as we have just seen. The most important tax, the income tax, is strongly progressive, reflecting the ability-to-pay principle. But while the second most important tax, the sales tax, is also based on the ability-to-pay principle, it is regressive at high income levels. Finally, the regressive nature of payroll taxes (above moderate income levels) stems from the vagaries of specific programs—Canada Pension Plan and Employment Insurance—and in part reflects the benefits principle.

economics in action

Marginal Tax Rates in Canada

Every year, usually around February, the federal government brings down a new budget. Usually the changes are minor. However, there have been several attempts to

FOR INQUIRING MINDS

CANADIAN FISCAL FEDERALISM

In Canada, powers and responsibilities are shared between the central authority—the federal government—and the ten provinces and three territories. The fiscal interaction of these bodies is known as "fiscal federalism"—the essence of which is the necessity for the various fiscal authorities to coordinate their activities to respond to the needs and desires of citizens, who are free to move from one area to another. In particular, a vital role of the federal government is to ensure that the provinces have sufficient resources to meet their obligations.

We stated earlier that in order to ensure horizontal equity, the federal government makes equalization payments to the "have-not" provinces. These payments are necessary for two reasons. First, economic resources are not distributed evenly across the country. Second, the constitution establishes that the provinces have jurisdiction over health, education, and welfare. This precludes the federal government from simply providing equal access to these services itself. Instead, it must work indirectly, through the provinces. Equalization payments are not the only transfer payment the federal government makes to the provinces. As a general strategy, the federal government uses grants to the provinces to influence their provision of basic services. For example, the Canada Health Act ensures that the provinces adhere to national principles of health care delivery, including comprehensiveness, universality, and portability. In return, the provinces receive the Canada Health and Social Transfer (CHST), which assists the financing of health care, social assistance, education, and other things. Together, the CHST and equalization payments amount to 90% of total federal-provincial transfers—which in 2003–2004 amounted to $53.5 billion. Naturally, given the principle of horizontal equity, these transfers are more important to the "have-not" provinces. For example, federal transfers amounted to only 9.2% of Alberta's revenue (since this is a "'have" province); but 41.4% of Newfoundland's revenue (historically the least well-off province in the country).

overhaul the whole income tax system—most notably in 1972 and 1987—the general aims being simplification, elimination of loopholes, broadening of the tax base, and reduction of marginal tax rates.

The 1972 reforms cut the highest combined federal/provincial marginal tax rates from 84% to 60%. They fell further to 48% in 1982, rose in the mid-1980s to over 53% because of deficit problems, and fell back to around current levels of 44% by the early 1990s. This trend towards lower marginal tax rates is largely justified by economic arguments: many politicians have picked up on the idea that high marginal tax rates discourage productive activity.

The Canadian tax system still imposes a substantial wedge between the pre-tax earnings of families and their after-tax income. But the wedge is considerably smaller than it was a generation ago. ■

> > > > > > > > > > > > > > > > > > >

>> QUICK REVIEW

- Every tax consists of a *tax base* and a *tax structure*.
- Among the types of taxes classified by tax base are *income taxes, payroll taxes, sales taxes, profits taxes, property taxes,* and *wealth taxes.*
- A *proportional tax* is the same percentage of the tax base for everyone. If higher-income people pay a higher percentage, a tax is *progressive;* if they pay a lower percentage, it is *regressive.*
- Progressive taxes are often justified by the ability-to-pay principle. However, they distort incentives to work, save, and invest because the *marginal tax rate on income* is higher than the *average tax rate on income.*
- Canada has a mixture of progressive and regressive taxes, both because we have different levels of government and because different principles of fairness are applied to different taxes. However, the overall structure of taxes is progressive.

>> CHECK YOUR UNDERSTANDING 21-2

1. A wealth tax taxes 1% of the first $10,000 of wealth and 2% on all wealth above $10,000. Show that the average rate is lower than the marginal rate for someone with wealth of $20,000.
2. When comparing households at different income levels, economists find that consumption spending grows more slowly than income. Assume that when income grows by 50%, from $10,000 to $15,000, consumption grows by 25%, from $8,000 to $10,000. Under a 1% tax on consumption purchases, compare the percentage of income paid in taxes by a family with $15,000 in income to that paid by a family with $10,000 in income. Is this tax proportional, progressive, or regressive?
3. True or false? Explain your answers.
   a. Payroll taxes do not affect a person's incentive to take a job because they are paid by employers.
   b. A lump-sum tax is a proportional tax because it is the same amount for each person.

Solutions appear at back of book.

Understanding Government Spending

One way or another, governments in Canada collect about 40% of total income in taxes. That's about average by international standards: the United States collects less (about 30%), while some European countries collect more (about 50%). Where does all the money go?

It's easy to make fun of government spending—everyone has his or her favourite story of wasted money. But most government spending is done for reasons that seem sensible to a large fraction of the electorate. Let's take a look at the major types of spending in Canada.

Types of Spending

Broadly speaking, governments spend money for three reasons: to provide *public goods,* to provide *social insurance,* and to engage in *redistribution.*

We defined public goods in Chapter 20: they are goods that are non-excludable, so that people cannot be forced to pay for consuming them, and non-rival, so that people *should* not have to pay. The government therefore provides many public goods. One public good in particular—national defence—used to account for over 20% of spending by the federal government in the 1950s. However, defence spending has since been gradually declining; by 2001, it amounted to little more than 5% of federal spending.

Much modern government spending is not for public goods but for **social insurance:** programs intended to protect people against some of the financial risks in life. Canada provides universal health care for the sick, employment insurance for those who are temporarily unemployed, workers' compensation for those who are injured

Social insurance is government spending intended to protect people against financial risks.

on the job, and disability pensions for those who are forced to retire early because of injury. Social insurance programs are sometimes referred to as the social safety net.

Governments engage in **redistribution of income** when they tax the well-off and use the money to support those less well-off.

Finally, most governments also engage in **redistribution of income:** taking money via taxes from the relatively well-off and using that money either to support the incomes of the poor or to provide the poor with benefits like public housing. The case for redistribution can be made in at least four different ways—and all of them are worth making.

1. First, one could think of it as an extension of the ability-to-pay principle: the poor, one could argue, are not only less able to pay taxes than the affluent—they could actually use some help.
2. Second, one can think of poverty reduction as a sort of public good. Most of us prefer to live in a society where everyone has enough to eat, decent housing, and so on—this is why we give to charity. But each of us is tempted to free-ride on the positive effects of charitable giving by others. So, just as most people agree that they should be taxed to provide for national defence, many agree that they should be taxed to provide aid to the poor.
3. Third, one can think of poverty reduction as an extension of the government's commitment to maintain equality of opportunity—in particular, to ensure that children who live in poverty are not deprived of the chance for a good education. This deprivation can take many forms, from lack of shoes to lack of money for school field trips.
4. Fourth and finally, if redistributing income to the poor helps them to receive a better education (an optimal rather than sub-optimal level of education), this redistribution can be justified on efficiency grounds.

You might wonder how one draws the line between social insurance and redistribution. Both typically involve transfer payments, and both typically help the poor. Moreover, since any of us might end up poor one day, poverty reduction programs are, in a sense, part of the social safety net. These points serve to emphasize that the line between social insurance and redistribution is a fuzzy one. However, in practice everyone benefits from social insurance programs—not just the poor. Moreover, transfers directed to those in need are always **means-tested**. A means-tested program is available only to someone who can show that he or she has a sufficiently low income to qualify. Roughly speaking, then, programs that provide support to people—but are *not* means-tested—are social insurance; whereas programs that are means-tested clearly redistribute income.

Means-tested government programs are available only to those with sufficiently low income.

Spending in Canada

Table 21-3 shows some of the major components of spending by all levels of Canadian government in the year 2001, the most recent year for which this breakdown was available. These components fit, more or less, into the categories of spending we have just described.

Protection of persons and property includes national defence, police, and judiciary. This is clearly a public good: the government can't protect some people without protecting others, and my protection doesn't come at your expense.

Education could also be defined as a quasi-public good. It is not a pure public good since it is excludable—children can be prevented from attending school. But there are so many important positive externalities with regard to having an educated populace that most governments provide education as a public good.

Social services are the largest single government expenditure item, absorbing nearly 30% of total expenditures. This item is a mixture of transfers and social insurance. It includes Employment Insurance and the Canada Pension Plan (neither of which is means-tested), along with several important means-tested transfers: old-age pensions, guaranteed income supplements, social welfare, and the child tax benefit.

TABLE 21-3

Major Components of Total Government Spending, 2001 (billions of dollars)

	Billions of dollars	Percentage of total spending
Social services	$133	30%
Health	70	16
Education	62	14
Debt charges	60	14
Protection of persons and property	33	8
Other	81	8
TOTAL	$439	

Source: Karin Treff and David Perry, *Finances of the Nation 2001* (Toronto: Canadian Tax Foundation, 2001), table A.4.

Next comes health care expenditure—the most popular item in Canada's social insurance scheme. This absorbed nearly 16% of total government spending in 2001.

Perhaps most surprising is that debt service charges were as high as $60 billion in 2001, since the federal government declared victory over its deficit problem around that time. However, the high debt charges reflect not only past federal deficits but also the debts incurred by provincial and local governments. Some would argue that the federal government solved its deficit problem on the backs of the provincial and local governments.

What's in the "other" component that absorbs around 20% of government spending? This includes a host of things involved in administering the affairs of a nation, such as expenditures on transportation and communications, resource conservation and industrial development, foreign affairs and international assistance, and the grab bag category "general services".

Comparisons Across Time and Space

Economic analysis cannot tell us whether the government spends too much or too little. But it is useful to have some sense of both how the level of government spending in Canada compares with its level in the past, and how spending here compares with spending in other major nations.

Figure 21-5 (page 534) shows the share of all government spending in Canada (for all levels of government) in *gross domestic product* (or GDP) over the past three decades. GDP is a measure of all the income generated in the economy—that is, it is the sum of wages, profits, and so on.

As can be seen from Figure 21-5, the overall size of the government has been on quite a roller-coaster ride. Throughout the 1970s and early 1980s, the relative size of combined government spending was on an upward trend. We can identify three causes.

First, in 1971 the federal government overhauled the unemployment insurance system (as it was then called), making it many times more generous than previously. The effect of this didn't really kick in until the major recession of 1981.

Second, in 1973, all federal transfers and income tax brackets were indexed for inflation. Since the average rate of inflation for the 1970s was over 7%, this had a double whammy effect: government spending automatically increased as prices increased; simultaneously, however, the government deprived itself of automatic increases in tax revenue. The effect was ballooning federal deficits, which in turn increased the need for government spending on debt service charges. In the background of all of this was an inflation rate that seemed to be accelerating.

Third, the attempt to beat inflation out of the economic system in the early 1980s led to higher interest rates—as high as 22% in 1981. This dramatically increased government

Figure 21-5

Consolidated Government Spending at All Levels, as a Percent of GDP

This graph show the percent of GDP devoted to government spending at all levels—federal, provincial, and municipal. The sharp increase between 1990 and 1992 was due to the 1990 recession that adversely affected growth of GDP. Since 1992 there has been a sharp downward trend in total government spending as a proportion of GDP as a result of government cutbacks that aimed to eliminate government deficits and bring down the level of government debt.

Source: Table A.4, *Finances of the Nation* (various years).

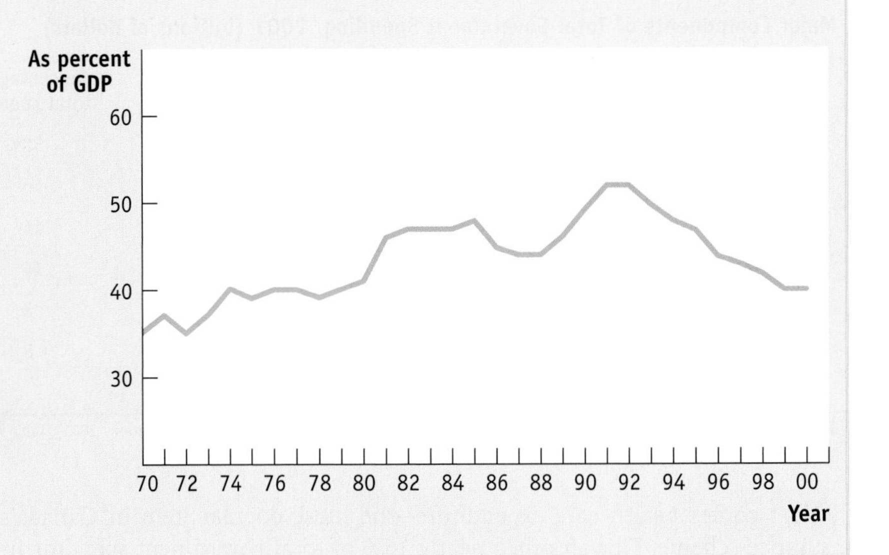

spending on debt service charges. It also dramatically increased unemployment rates, which further increased government spending on social insurance payments.

Getting Canada's economic house in order has taken the better part of 20 years. After beating inflation in the early 1980s, a process of "belt tightening" began in the mid-1980s. Tax brackets and some transfers were partially de-indexed, and the federal government systematically cut back on its transfers to the provinces—money the provinces needed for health care, education, and social welfare spending.

This roller coaster that we see in Figure 21-5 has dominated the political landscape and discussion for the last 20 years. However, government spending as a percent of GDP has now been brought back down to its lowest level in over 20 years. Moreover, at 40% of GDP, the size of the government sector in Canada is about average by international standards. Figure 21-6 compares government spending as a percent of GDP for the seven largest economies in 2002. Canada is right in the middle of the pack.

Figure 21-6

Government Spending as a Percent of GDP in 2002

In 2002, France devoted the largest share of its GDP (53.4%) to government spending among the major industrial countries. The United States devoted the smallest share among these countries, at 35.3%. Canada's government spending was close to the average at 40.6%.

Source: OECD Economic Outlook.

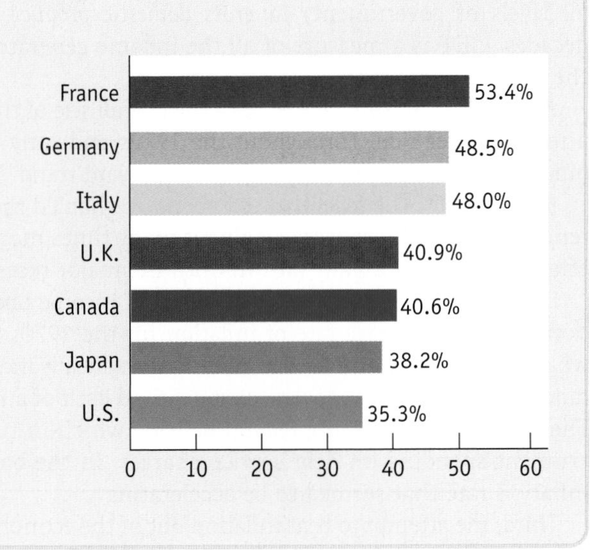

economics in action

Health Care in Crisis?

Social insurance and transfers account for over 50% of total government spending in Canada, of which health care is the single most expensive item. One hears that Canada's health care system is inefficient and that we can no longer afford it because the costs are spiralling out of control. Is it true?

According to the Romanow Commission, publicly funded health care is both feasible and efficient.[3] The much-publicized problems of Canada's health care system stem from the fact that it is chronically underfunded.

Figure 21-7 provides some context for the discussion. The orange line plots total health care spending as a ratio of total government spending. This shows that health care spending has been gradually absorbing an increasing share of total government spending. That share increased from 12% in 1985 to 16% in 2001. Looking just at this line, one may get the impression of health care expenditures that are out of control. We need to remember what we learned from Figure 21-5—that government spending has been rapidly declining as a proportion of GDP since 1992.

The green line in Figure 21-7 plots health care spending as a proportion of GDP, and this line gives a very different impression. There is a bulge around 1991–1993 caused by the recession of 1991, which slowed growth in GDP. But overall it appears that health care spending has been quite stable as a percentage of GDP.

Does this mean there is no cause for concern? Not necessarily. Health care will become more expensive in the future for two reasons. First, the most intensive users of health care are the elderly, and the percentage of Canadians aged 65 and over will dramatically increase after 2011, with the aging of the baby-boom generation. Second, medical care is becoming more expensive. Experts in health economics say

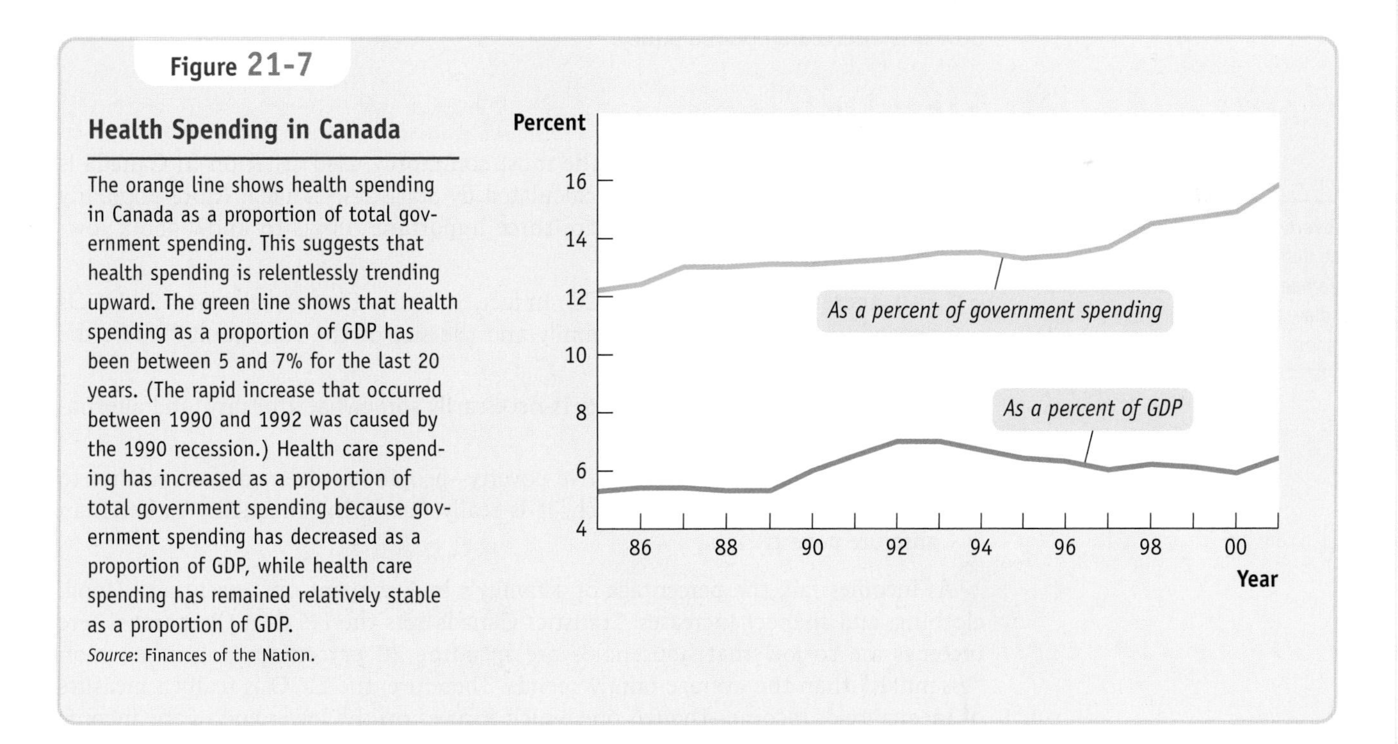

Figure 21-7

Health Spending in Canada

The orange line shows health spending in Canada as a proportion of total government spending. This suggests that health spending is relentlessly trending upward. The green line shows that health spending as a proportion of GDP has been between 5 and 7% for the last 20 years. (The rapid increase that occurred between 1990 and 1992 was caused by the 1990 recession.) Health care spending has increased as a proportion of total government spending because government spending has decreased as a proportion of GDP, while health care spending has remained relatively stable as a proportion of GDP.

Source: Finances of the Nation.

[3] Roy Romanow, "The Commission on the Future of Health Care in Canada", Government of Canada Royal Commission (2002, November).

this is primarily because progress in medicine has made it possible to do more. Many treatments now commonly used, such as heart bypass surgery, were experimental, rare, or not yet developed 30 years ago.

Despite the advantages of a publicly funded system, we cannot expect it to perform well if it is underfunded. We will have to spend more on health care not only to solve its current problems but also to meet increased future needs. ▪

< < < < < < < < < < < < < < < < < <

>> QUICK REVIEW

- There are three main types of government spending: spending on public goods, *social insurance,* and *redistribution of income.*
- Although the line between social insurance and redistribution is somewhat blurry, a program that is *means-tested* is usually considered redistribution and one that is not means-tested is considered social insurance.
- The Canadian government spends substantial sums on all three types of programs. Public goods account for about 40% of total government spending; social insurance and transfers for about 56%. Health care is the largest single item.
- While health expenditure as a percent of GDP has not risen much in the past, there are good reasons to think that it will need to be increased in the future.

>>CHECK YOUR UNDERSTANDING 21-3

1. Suppose there are only two provinces in Canada, Lotusland and Eastario, each with the same number of workers. Further suppose that each province has its own employment insurance program that is financed by taxes on employed workers, who collect benefits if they become unemployed. Finally, suppose that during even-numbered years, workers in Lotusland are unemployed and workers in Eastario are employed, but that the opposite is true during odd-numbered years. Explain why workers in these two provinces can benefit from an employment insurance program that covers both provinces.
2. Classify the following programs according to whether they redistribute income or provide social insurance.
   a. Natural disaster emergency relief
   b. Heating cost assistance for low-income families
   c. Employment insurance payments
   d. Aid grants to low-income students

Solutions appear at back of book.

Poverty and Public Aid

Governments in Canada provide help to the poor through many different types of programs. This section explores the programs used and their relative effectiveness. Let's begin by looking at how poverty is defined, how it has changed over time, and how it is affected by public policy.

Defining Poverty

What does it mean to be "poor"? The most commonly used criterion in Canada is the "low-income cut-off" (LICO) calculated by Statistics Canada. More popularly known as **"poverty lines",** there are three important things to know about low-income cut-offs.

The **poverty line** is a minimum annual income defined as adequate for a family's needs. Families whose income falls below the poverty line are considered poor.

1. First, there is more than one LICO. In fact, Statistics Canada calculates 35 LICOs depending on the size of the family and the size of the community where the family lives.
2. Second, any definition of poverty is necessarily somewhat arbitrary, and alternative definitions exist.
3. Third, the LICO measures *relative* poverty—people are deemed poor *relative* to how well-off others are. As such, it is really measuring inequality rather than absolute poverty.

As incomes fall, the percentage of a family's budget spent on "essentials" (food, clothing, and shelter) increases. Statistics Canada sets the LICO at the point where incomes are so low that households are spending 20 percentage points more on "essentials" than the average family spends. Therefore, the LICO is really a measure of inequality of income—though one which focuses on the lower end of the income distribution. Growth in average incomes alone will not affect the proportion of people living below the poverty line. To reduce that proportion, a more equal distribution of income is required.

Using Statistics Canada's measure of poverty, the Canadian **poverty rate**—the percentage of the population living below the low-income cut-off—has been relatively stable since 1980. Currently, about 17% of all people in Canada live below the poverty line. Who are they?

The **poverty rate** is the percentage of the population living below the poverty line.

A Portrait of the Poor

Because certain groups of the population have a high incidence of poverty, it is relatively easy to paint a portrait of the poor. In broad brushstrokes, they are the least educated; those only partly employed; Aboriginals, members of visible minorities or recent immigrants; or those living in a single-parent household. Let's consider these points in turn.

The more education an individual has, the less likely they are to live in poverty. On average, the poverty rate among people with a post-secondary degree is around 16%; in contrast, the rate among people without a high school certificate is almost double, at 30%.

Poverty rates decrease with increased employment. Among individuals with no employment, 46% were poor. Among those with full-time, year-round employment, only 7.5% were poor. Nevertheless, the working poor make up a large proportion of those living below the poverty line. It may be surprising to learn that 55% of the poor work either full-time for part of the year, or part-time throughout the year.

City-dwelling Aboriginals have one of the highest poverty rates. Whereas the average poverty rate among all city residents is around 24%, the rate for Aboriginal people is 54%. The next highest poverty rate is for recent immigrants, though this is mainly a transition problem since the longer they reside in Canada, the lower the rate becomes. Visible minorities also have a high poverty rate. They account for about 21.6% of city populations, but for 33% of the poor populations.

Single-parent families have a very high incidence of poverty—on average, nearly 60% are poor. Of course, the children in these families also live below the poverty line. This partly explains why children are over-represented among the poor population. They account for 32% of the total population, but for 40% of the poor population.

The incidence of poverty on children is particularly painful. Childhood poverty is associated with higher chances of poor health, low educational attainment, riskier environments, and riskier behaviours. Children raised in poverty have a greater likelihood of living in poverty as adults, and a greater risk of mental health problems and behavioural disorders. These are all negative outcomes both for the long-term development of individuals and for the nation as a whole.

Anti-Poverty Programs

Strictly speaking, **"welfare"** is the generic term used for all monetary aid given to poor families. It includes all cash benefits, income supplements, sales tax rebates, and income assistance. However, in Canada the term "welfare" has come to mean "social assistance"—a specific program administered by the province or municipality. This is the primary anti-poverty program in Canada. Note that social assistance is sometimes called income support, income assistance, and a few other program names, depending on the jurisdiction.

Welfare is monetary aid to poor families.

Social assistance payments are available only to Canadians who have no other source of income and have spent down their assets, though each province has its own definition of assets. In Ontario, for example, a single employable person in 1999 could not have more than $520 in liquid assets; in Manitoba, it was $0. Support levels are determined by the provinces, and depend on family size.

But regardless of where one lives, support levels are well below the poverty line. They are least generous for single employable persons: in 2001, support levels ranged from a low of 21% of the poverty line in New Brunswick to a high of 36% in Ontario. A single parent with one child does slightly better: in 2001, support levels ranged from a low of 49% of the poverty line in Alberta to a high of 64% in New Brunswick.

In-kind transfers provide poor families with specific goods and services.

In addition to cash transfers, **in-kind transfers** can provide those who qualify with specific goods and services. In Canada, the most important transfer of this kind is public housing, or equivalent programs such as cooperative housing, shelter allowances, or rent supplements. However, there are also important programs that provide prescription drug coverage, vision care, and dental care to welfare recipients.

Trends in Poverty

How effective have these programs been in fighting poverty? Figure 21-8 shows the Canadian poverty rate between 1980 and 1997. The poverty rate for all persons has been relatively stable—though it is apparent that it responds to the overall level of economic activity. For example, when the economy boomed in 1989 the overall poverty rate reached a 20-year low.

But while the overall poverty rate has been relatively stable, there have been substantial changes in its composition. Traditionally, poverty has been most common in two groups: the elderly (who often cannot work) and single-parent households.

Figure 21-8 shows us that while the incidence of poverty among children and the elderly is greater than average, these two components have had very different trends over the last 20 years. The poverty rate of the elderly has been declining steadily and is now nearly the same as that of "all persons". On the other hand, the poverty rate for children rose during the 1990s, implying higher absolute numbers of children living in poverty than ever before. The incidence of poverty among children is now greater than it is among the elderly. Why this divergence?

Figure 21-8 **Poverty Rates in Canada**

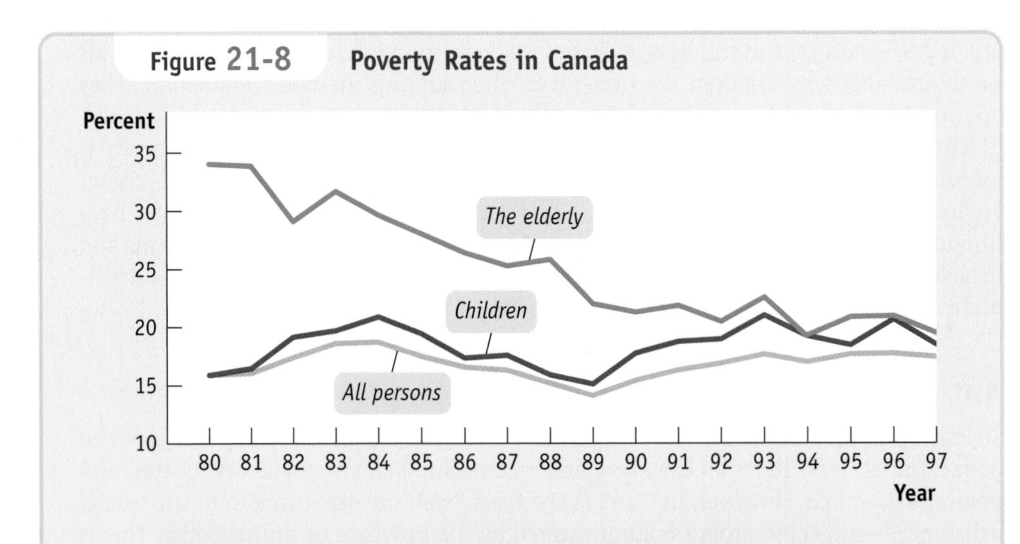

The overall poverty rate has hovered around 15% over the last 20 years. The figure shows that while the incidence of poverty among children and the elderly is greater than average, these two components have had very different trends over the last 20 years. Programs targeting the elderly have been successful in reducing their poverty rate significantly, so that it is now nearly the same as that of "all persons". On the other hand, the poverty rate for children rose during the 1990s, implying more absolute numbers of children living in poverty than ever before. The incidence of poverty on children is now greater than it is on the elderly.

Source: Harvey Rosen, Beverly Dahlby, Roger Smith, and Paul Boothe, *Public Finance in Canada* (McGrawHill, 2003), Figure 6.3.

economics in action

Old Poor, Young Poor

The divergence in the poverty rates of children and the elderly has been essentially policy-driven. In effect, anti-poverty programs have targeted the elderly while neglecting the poorest children. But why has child poverty been neglected?

A key fact is that 70% of children living beneath the poverty line are living in families that depend on government welfare, paid for by provincial governments. These governments are afraid that assisting children in these families will reduce incentives for the parents to find work.

No such worry exists when helping the elderly. As a result, a number of programs have been designed to help the elderly—old-age security, guaranteed income supplements, and spousal allowances—the success of which is evident from Figure 21-8.

Similarly, there are programs designed to help children. The Canada Child Tax Benefit provides monthly payments to families with children. Although means-tested, it is not particularly targeted to the poor. It also helps middle-class families. However, the National Child Benefit program (NCB) is a supplement, introduced in 1997 by the federal government, targeted to low-income families with children. The combination of these programs *has* succeeded in raising family incomes for the children of the working poor. But National Child Benefits for families receiving welfare were clawed back by the provinces. In effect, a family's welfare check was reduced by $1 for every dollar received under the National Child Benefit scheme. The federal government allowed them to do this, providing the provinces "reinvested" this money in programs for the working poor.

Only one province refused to **claw back** NCB payments—and that province was New Brunswick. This explains why, in 2001, the support levels for a single parent with one child were higher in New Brunswick than in any other province in Canada. Happily, several provinces are now following New Brunswick's example. By 2003, five provinces had stopped clawing back NCB payments.■

A **clawback** occurs when government takes away with one hand what was given with the other. Usually, this results when benefits that appear universal are in fact means-tested. Sometimes one level of government can take away what was given by another level of government.

>> QUICK REVIEW

- Families are considered poor if their income falls below the *poverty line*, an income considered necessary to maintain an adequate standard of living. Statistics Canada's "low-income cut-off" (LICO) is a measure of relative poverty.
- The *poverty rate* is the percentage of the population with incomes below the poverty line. The overall poverty rate in Canada has remained fairly stable over the last 20 years.
- However, there have been important changes in the composition of the officially poor. The incidence of the elderly living in poverty has fallen dramatically. However, the incidence of children living in poverty has increased.
- All low-income families receive various cash transfers that are means-tested. These include GST rebates, and for families with children, the Canada Child Tax Benefit. Families without employment and without savings are eligible to receive social assistance or welfare payments.
- In addition to cash payments, low-income families may also receive *in-kind transfers* to pay for specific goods, such as housing.

>> CHECK YOUR UNDERSTANDING 21-4

1. Explain why the poverty rate for Canadians over 65 has fallen over time, while the poverty rate for Canadian children has risen over time.
2. Explain why Statistics Canada's "low-income cut-off" is a measure of relative poverty, not absolute poverty.
3. Is it possible to eradicate poverty using Statistics Canada's low-income cut-off (LICO) as a measure of poverty?

Solutions appear at back of book.

The Big Debate: Taxes, Transfers, and Income Distribution

The great majority of Canadians agree that the ability-to-pay principle should be given some weight in tax and spending policy—that high-income individuals should pay more in taxes than low-income individuals, and that at least some public aid should be offered to the poor. But how *much* weight should ability to pay be given?

That is not a question of economic analysis; it is a political question, perhaps *the* political question. Roughly speaking, fiscal conservatives believe that at present Canada gives too much weight to the ability-to-pay principle, that taxes are excessively progressive, that too much aid is given to those with low incomes, and that all this causes serious disincentive effects. Fiscal liberals believe the opposite.

Although we can't resolve this debate, we can shed some light on it by clarifying the issues involved.

The Distribution of Income

A starting point for the big debate is to have a sense of the extent to which families differ in their ability to pay, that is, of the distribution of income among families.

Table 21-4 summarizes the distribution of income among Canadian families in 1997. Families are grouped by quintile from the poorest 20% to the richest 20%. Column 1 shows the distribution of "market" income, which includes both labour income and investment income. Column 1 is the result of market outcomes, before government transfers and taxes. The numbers show a considerable amount of inequality: the poorest 20% of families received just over 2% of total market income in Canada, while the richest 20% received just over 44%. Column 2 adds government transfers to market income. This is called "total income". As we can see, government transfers benefit the poor relative to the rich. The share of the poorest quintile increases to 6.1% (up from 2.1%), while the share of the richest quintile falls to 40.2%(down from 44.3%). These transfers are financed by taxation, and, to the degree that taxes are progressive, that tax burden should further reduce inequality. Column 3 confirms that it does. This column shows us after-tax income: total income minus taxation. Again, this has the effect of favouring the least well-off. The poorest 20% receives just over 7% of after-tax income (up from 6.1%), while the richest 20% receives 37.5% (down from 40.2%).

The most commonly used summary measure of inequality is called the Gini coefficient—the value of which is shown just below each column of Table 21-4. The value of the Gini coefficient can range from 0 to 1. A coefficient of 0 means uniform income for all groups (perfect income equality); a coefficient of 1 means that the highest income group receives all the income (extreme inequality). Used with caution, Gini coefficients are a useful way of comparing inequality between countries, and movements in inequality over time. For example, Gini coefficients in many Eastern European countries before the fall of the Berlin Wall were in the neighbourhood of 0.25 (indicating very little inequality), while many Latin American countries today (such as Brazil, Colombia, and Guatemala) have values around 0.6 (indicating a good deal of inequality).

From Table 21-4 we can see that in 1997, the Gini coefficient in Canada for market income was 0.425. But inequality was reduced by .082 as a result of transfers, and further reduced by .041 as a result of taxes. So transfers had twice the impact of taxes in reducing income inequality. The Gini coefficient for total income (after taxes and after transfers) was only 0.302.

What about the trend in inequality in Canada? In recent years, inequality has increased by a small but significant amount. Between 1989 and 2000, inequality in total income, after taxes and after transfers, increased by about 7%. This was driven by increased inequality in market incomes at a time when transfers were being cut back to reduce deficits.

TABLE 21-4

Income Shares in Canada, Families, 1997

Quintile	Market income	Total income: Market income plus transfers	After-tax income: Total income minus taxes
Poorest 20%	2.1%	6.1	7.4
Second 20%	10.1	11.9	13.2
Middle 20%	17.7	17.6	18.1
Fourth 20%	25.8	24.1	23.9
Richest 20%	44.3	40.2	37.5
Total	100	100	100
Gini coefficient	*0.425*	*0.343*	*0.302*

Source: David N. Hyman and John C. Strick, *Public Finance in Canada* (Toronto: Harper, 2001), Table 7.1.

This increased inequality in market incomes is not just a phenomenon restricted to Canada. Increases in inequality have been even more pronounced in the United States. Most economists favour two explanations: it is either the result of rapid technological change or the effect of increased international trade. Both of these may have increased the demand for highly skilled workers more rapidly than the demand for less-skilled workers. However, dissenters point out that increases in inequality between observationally equivalent workers account for much of the increase in total inequality, especially in the United States.[4] These economists think that institutional factors, such as declining minimum wages, deregulation, weaker unions, and higher unemployment rates are important in explaining the increase in inequality.

The fact that some people in Canada are very well off, indeed better off than ever before, while others remain quite poor, leads advocates of redistribution to argue for higher taxes on those with high incomes, and greater aid to those with low incomes. Let's look briefly at their argument, and then at the arguments that others make against redistribution.

The Case for Redistribution

Those who advocate more progressive taxation and redistribution of income to people in the lower part of the income distribution base their position on an extended version of the ability-to-pay principle. High-income families should pay high taxes, they argue, because they will still have after-tax income that is higher than average. Low-income families not only should not pay taxes, they should receive aid from the government, because even with that aid they will have incomes lower than average. So the redistribution is justified because the money transferred adds more to the welfare of the recipients than it subtracts from the welfare of the taxpayers.

Others argue that equity might even be good for efficiency—*at least up to a point.* For example, a high degree of inequality can cause high crime rates, which increase the social costs associated with law enforcement and the judicial process—more police, more courts, more lawyers, more prisoners, and more prisons—fewer universities, fewer engineers, and fewer scientists. Moreover, inequality and poverty tend to be associated with a lack of educational opportunities for the poor; and it is well known that a better-educated workforce is more productive than a less-educated one.

Furthermore, recent work emphasizes that equity promotes "social cohesion" and trust, which have economic payoffs for efficiency and growth. Trust between workers and management facilitates the adoption of new and more productive techniques, whereas polarized groups engage in wasteful conflict that brings production to a standstill. Where there is trust, parties can reach handshake agreements; without trust, elaborate contracts are required.

Wouldn't the logical conclusion of this argument be that the government should tax away any income above the average and top up the income of anyone who makes less than the average? No, because even the most ardent advocates of progressive taxes and redistribution recognize that *eventually* more equity must push against the barrier of less efficiency. This is the trade-off between equity and efficiency again—that the tax and spending policies of the government must take care not to do too much damage to incentives. That brings us to the case, or rather cases, against income redistribution.

Arguments Against Redistribution

There are two different kinds of arguments against income redistribution. One is based on philosophical concerns about the proper role of government. Some political theorists believe that redistributing income is not a legitimate role of government—

[4] Daron Acemoglu, "Technical Change, Inequality, and the Labor Market", *Journal of Economic Literature* 40, No. 1 (2002): 7–72.

that government's role should be limited to maintaining the rule of law, providing public goods, and controlling externalities. We cannot go into this debate at length, but because it is an influential point of view, you should be aware that it exists.

The more conventional argument against taxing the rich and making transfers to the poor involves the trade-off between efficiency and equity. We've already seen part of this argument: a tax system that tries to put all of the burden on the very well off will have to be highly progressive. A highly progressive system implies high marginal tax rates, and high marginal tax rates reduce the incentive to work hard or otherwise increase a family's income. As a result, a highly progressive tax system makes society as a whole poorer, and may hurt even those who pay little or no tax. That's why even economists who strongly favour progressive taxation don't support a return to the extremely progressive system that prevailed in the 1950s, when the top marginal rate was more than 80%.

A similar trade-off between equity and efficiency occurs as a result of programs that aid people with low incomes. Consider the following example: suppose there is some means-tested benefit, worth $1,000 per year, that is available only to individuals with earnings of less than $10,000 per year. Now suppose that an individual is currently earning $9,800 per year and is deciding whether to take a new job that will raise his income to $10,200. He will actually make himself worse off by taking the job because he will lose the $1,000 government benefit.

This situation, in which earning more actually leaves an individual worse off, is known as a *notch*. It is a well-known problem with programs that aid the poor, and behaves much like a high marginal rate on income. Most programs are designed to avoid creating a notch. This is typically done by setting a sliding scale for benefits, so that they fall off gradually as the recipient's income rises rather than coming to an abrupt end. Even so, as the following Economics in Action illustrates, means-tested programs have indeed led to high effective marginal tax rates for low-income workers.

economics in action

Effective Marginal Tax Rates on the Poor

Because means-tested programs are available only to families with sufficiently low incomes, families that manage to increase their earnings find that they lose benefits. So in effect they face a high marginal tax rate on their earnings, although the stated marginal tax rate is quite low.

For example, consider the taxes of a married couple with two dependent children in 2001. GST rebates and Child Tax Benefits are offered to all Canadians, but both benefits are lost (or "clawed back") at moderate income levels. Combining these lost benefits with regular taxes, the marginal tax rate for less well-off families can exceed that for the better off. For example, if the family were in Alberta and their income was around $32,000, they would have faced a marginal tax rate over 42%. In comparison, those earning over $80,000 had a marginal tax rate of 36%.

The highest marginal tax rates aren't at the top of the income distribution; they're toward the lower end, where families find that higher income leads to reductions in means-tested benefits. ■

< < < < < < < < < < < < < < < < < < <

>> QUICK REVIEW

- The amount of weight that should be placed on the ability-to-pay principle is a political question, not an economic one.
- Market incomes in Canada are unequally distributed. Both government taxes and transfers help to moderate the amount of inequality, but inequality has increased in recent years due to increased inequality in market incomes and reductions in transfers.
- Those who oppose redistributing income argue that it would be bad for efficiency.
- Those who favour redistributing income base their case mainly on the ability-to-pay principle. Some also argue that a certain amount redistribution can be good for efficiency.
- Programs designed to aid people with low incomes often weaken incentives to work because of notches created in the tax system. As earnings increase, the loss of benefits may create high effective marginal tax rates.

>> CHECK YOUR UNDERSTANDING 21-5

1. Suppose that the government offered free prescription drugs, vision care, and dental care to families with income of less than $15,000 per year, but not to families with income of $15,000 per year or more.
   a. What problem would this program create for incentives? Explain this problem in terms of a marginal tax rate.
   b. How would you restructure the program to make the problem less severe? Again, explain in terms of a marginal tax rate.

2. Describe the trade-off between equity and efficiency in the following programs:
   a. A program that supplements the income of farmers during poor crop years
   b. A program that pays rental expenses for low-income families

Solutions appear at back of book.

Economists and the Tax System

As our opening story of Britain's poll tax suggested, tempers often run high when it comes to tax policy. The same is true when it comes to government spending for social insurance or redistribution. What makes these disputes especially hard to resolve is that there is *no right answer:* there is always a trade-off between equity and efficiency, and two people who agree about that trade-off can disagree about what weight to give to each goal.

What role can economics play in this eternal debate? First, the economist can try to keep the debate honest. Politics being politics, those who advocate policy changes that will increase equity are always tempted to deny that their proposals will come at the expense of efficiency, and vice versa. It is the job of economists to point out when a proposed change in taxes or spending is being offered under false pretences.

The other job of economists is to point out opportunities for clear improvement. An ideal tax system would offer no way to improve efficiency without reducing equity. Real tax systems probably can be made better, allowing progress on both goals, and economic analysis should try to show the way.

• A LOOK AHEAD •

We have now almost completed our study of microeconomics. We've learned a lot about how the economy works, and about the role of government policy.

But do the models we have studied—models that reflect a couple of centuries of economic analysis and observation—still apply? In recent years there have been dramatic changes on the economic scene, as information technology has transformed the way we live and work. Some people talk of a "new economy" whose rules differ drastically from those of the past. In the next chapter, we'll look at how technology changes microeconomics—and how it doesn't.

SUMMARY

1. **Tax efficiency** is achieved when the costs of a tax—the sum of the deadweight loss or excess burden due to distorted incentives and the **administrative costs** of the tax—are minimized. However, **tax fairness,** or **tax equity,** ensuring that the right people pay taxes, is also a goal of tax policy.
2. There are two major principles of tax fairness or equity: the **benefits principle** and the **ability-to-pay principle.** The most efficient tax, a **lump-sum tax,** does not distort incentives but performs badly in terms of fairness. The fairest taxes in terms of the ability-to-pay principle, however, distort incentives the most and perform badly on efficiency grounds. So in a well-designed tax system, there is a **trade-off between equity and efficiency.**
3. Every tax consists of a **tax base,** which defines what is taxed, and a **tax structure.** Different tax bases give rise to different taxes—the **income tax, payroll tax, sales** or **excise tax, profits tax, property tax,** and **wealth tax.** A **proportional tax** is the same percentage of the tax base for all taxpayers.
4. A tax is **progressive** if higher-income people pay a higher percentage of their income in taxes than lower income people, and **regressive** if they pay a lower percentage. Progressive taxes are often justified by the ability-to-pay principle. However, a progressive tax on income can distort incentives to work, save, and invest because the **marginal tax rate on income** is higher than the **average tax rate on income.**
5. Money raised in taxes is spent in three main ways: for **social insurance** and for **redistribution of income** (which are implemented through **transfer payments** to individuals) and for public goods. Public goods (including education, protection of persons and property, and other expenditures) account for about 40% of total government spending; social insurance and transfers for about 56%. Health care is the largest single item.
6. The **poverty line** is an estimate of the minimum annual income needed to achieve an acceptable standard of living.

The **poverty rate** is the fraction of the population with incomes below the poverty line.

7. The overall poverty rate in Canada has remained fairly stable over the last 20 years. However, there have been important changes in its composition. The incidence of poverty among the elderly has fallen dramatically, while the incidence among children rose during the 1990s. The effects of poverty are often severe, particularly for children.
8. Aid to the poor takes two main forms: **welfare** (or social assistance), which is all forms of cash payments to the poor; and **in-kind transfers** such as public housing or rent supplements.
9. Income redistribution is often justified by the inequality of income distribution. But a highly progressive tax system makes society as a whole poorer, a fact that limits the level of progressivity that supporters advocate. Like progressive taxation, redistribution forces a trade-off between equity and efficiency. An example of this is a **means-tested** program, which places high effective marginal tax rates on low-income families.

KEY TERMS

Tax efficiency, p. 520
Tax fairness, p. 520
Tax equity, p. 520
Administrative costs, p. 521
Horizontal equity, p. 522
Transfer payments, p. 522
Equalization payments, p. 522
Vertical equity, p. 522
Benefits principle, p. 522
Ability-to-pay principle, p. 522
Lump-sum tax, p. 523
Trade-off between equity and efficiency, p. 523
Tax base, p. 525
Tax structure, p. 525
Income tax, p. 525
Payroll tax, p. 525
Sales tax, p. 525
Excise tax, p. 525
Profits tax, p. 525
Property tax, p. 525
Wealth tax, p. 525
Proportional tax, p. 525
Progressive tax, p. 525
Regressive tax, p. 525
Average tax rate on income, p. 526
Marginal tax rate on income, p. 526
Social insurance, p. 531
Redistribution of income, p. 532
Means-tested, p. 532
Poverty line, p. 536
Poverty rate, p. 537
Welfare, p. 537
In-kind transfers, p. 538
Clawback, p. 539

PROBLEMS

1. Assume that the demand for gasoline is inelastic. The government imposes an excise tax on gasoline.
   a. Who bears more of the excess burden of this tax: consumers or producers? Show in a diagram who bears how much of the excess burden.
   b. Suppose the tax revenue is used to fund research into clean fuel alternatives to gasoline, which will improve the air we breathe. Is this tax based on the benefits principle or on the ability-to-pay principle? Explain.
2. Assess the following three taxes in terms of the benefits principle versus the ability-to-pay principle.
   a. A tax on gasoline that finances maintenance of provincial roads
   b. A property tax, assessed on the value of a person's house, that finances local schools
   c. Airline-flight landing fees that pay for air-traffic control
3. Consider the following deductions, which reduce the amount of income tax an individual must pay. Can they be justified on the basis of the ability-to-pay principle?
   a. Charitable contributions
   b. Number of dependent children
4. You are advising the government on how to pay for national defence. There are two proposals for a tax system to fund national defence. Under both proposals, the tax base is an individual's income. Under proposal A, all citizens pay exactly the same lump-sum tax, regardless of income. Under proposal B, individuals with higher income pay a greater proportion of their income in taxes.
   a. Is the tax in proposal A progressive, proportional, or regressive? What about the tax in proposal B?
   b. Is the tax in proposal A based on the ability-to-pay principle or on the benefits principle? What about the tax in proposal B?
   c. In terms of efficiency, which tax is better? Explain.
5. Each of the following tax proposals have income as the tax base. In a diagram with the tax base—income, ranging from $0 to $50,000—on the horizontal axis and the taxes paid on the vertical axis, draw the income tax for each of the following tax proposals. For an individual who earns $25,000, what is the marginal tax rate under each proposal? What is the average tax rate for that individual? Is the marginal tax rate higher, lower, or equal to the average tax rate? Accordingly, classify the tax as being proportional, progressive, or regressive.
   a. All income is taxed at 20%.
   b. All income up to $10,000 is tax-free. All income above $10,000 is taxed at a constant rate of 20%.

c. All income between $0 and $10,000 is taxed at 10%. All income between $10,000 and $20,000 is taxed at 20%. All income higher than $20,000 is taxed at 30%.

d. Each individual who earns more than $10,000 pays a lump-sum tax of $10,000. If the individual's income is less than $10,000, that individual pays in tax exactly what his or her income is.

6. In Sylvania the basic income tax system is fairly simple. The first 40,000 sylvers (the official currency of Sylvania) earned each year are free of income tax. Any additional income is taxed at a rate of 25%. In addition, every individual pays a social security tax, which is calculated as follows: all income up to 80,000 sylvers is taxed at an additional 20%, but there is no additional social security tax on income above 80,000 sylvers.

a. Calculate the average and the marginal tax rates for Sylvanians with the following levels of income: 20,000 sylvers, 40,000 sylvers, 80,000 sylvers, and 120,000 sylvers.

b. For each of the income levels in part a of this question, is the tax system progressive, regressive, or proportional?

7. You work for the federal government in the Department of Finance, providing economic advice. The government wants to overhaul the income tax system and you are assigned the job of making recommendations. Suppose that the current income tax system consists of a proportional tax of 10% on all income and that there is one person in the country who earns $110 million; everyone else earns less than $100 million. The president proposes a tax cut targeted at the very rich so that the new tax system would consist of a proportional tax of 10% on all income up to $100 million and a marginal tax rate of 0% (no tax) on income above $100 million. You are asked to evaluate this tax proposal.

a. Is this tax system progressive, regressive, or proportional? Explain.

b. Would this tax system create more or less tax revenue, everything else remaining equal? Is this tax system more or less efficient than the current tax system? Explain.

8. In the city of Metropolis, there are 100 residents, each of whom lives until age 75. Residents of Metropolis have the following incomes over their lifetime: through age 14, they earn nothing. From age 15 until age 29, they earn 200 metros (the currency of Metropolis) per year. From age 30 to age 49, they earn 400 metros. From age 50 to age 64, they earn 300 metros. And finally at age 65 they retire and are paid a pension of 100 metros per year until they die at age 75. Everyone consumes each year whatever their income is that year (that is, there is no saving and no borrowing). Currently, 20 residents are 10 years old, 20 residents are 20 years old, 20 residents are 40 years old, 20 residents are 60 years old, and 20 residents are 70 years old.

a. Study the income distribution amongst all citizens of Metropolis. Split the population into quintiles according to their income. How much income does a resident in the lowest quintile have? In the second, third, fourth, and top quintiles? Which share of total income of all residents goes to the residents in each quintile? Construct a table with the share of total income that goes to each quintile. Does this income distribution show inequality?

b. Now look only at the 20 residents of Metropolis who are currently 40 years old, and study the income distribution amongst only those residents. Split those 20 residents into quintiles according to their income. How much income does a resident in the first quintile have? In the second, third, fourth, and fifth, quintiles? Which share of total income of all 40-year-olds goes to the residents in each quintile? Does this income distribution show inequality?

c. What is the relevance of these examples for assessing data on the distribution of income in any country?

9. The country of Marxland has the following income tax and social insurance system. Each citizen's income is taxed at an average tax rate of 100%. A social insurance system then provides transfers to each citizen such that each citizen's after-tax income is exactly equal. That is, each citizen gets (through a government transfer payment) an equal share of the income tax revenue. What is the incentive for one individual citizen to work and earn income? What will the total tax revenue in Marxland therefore be? What will be the after-tax income (including the transfer payment) for each citizen? Do you think such a tax system that creates perfect equality will work?

10. In the city of Notchingham, each worker is paid a wage rate of $10 per hour. Notchingham administers its own unemployment benefit, which is structured as follows: If you are unemployed (that is, if you do not work at all), you get unemployment benefits (a transfer from the government) of $50 per day. As soon as you work for only 1 hour, you are no longer eligible for unemployment benefits. That is, there is a "notch" in the benefit system.

a. How much income does an unemployed person have per day? How much daily income does an individual have who works 4 hours per day? How many hours do you need to work to earn just the same as if you were unemployed?

b. Will anyone ever accept a part-time job that requires working 4 hours per day, rather than being unemployed?

c. Suppose that Notchingham now changes the eligibility rules: working no longer makes you ineligible for unemployment benefits. Instead, for each additional dollar that an individual earns, $0.50 of the unemployment benefit is withdrawn. How much daily income does an individual now have who works 4 hours per day? Is there an incentive now to work 4 hours rather than being unemployed?

>web... To continue your study and review of concepts in this chapter, please visit the Krugman/Wells website for quizzes, animated graph tutorials, web links to helpful resources, and more.

www.worthpublishers.com/krugmanwellsmyatt

chapter

22 >>Technology, Information Goods, and Network Externalities

What you will learn in this chapter:

- The growing importance of goods embodying new technology and the unique economic problems they pose
- How the economics of **information goods** differs from that of other goods
- The importance of **network externalities** and why they lead a consumer to prefer the good used by most other consumers
- Why information goods can lead to **critical mass** effects, in which a market suddenly explodes in size, or to **tipping,** in which the market swings to favour one good over another
- The special dilemmas information goods pose for antitrust policy

SUING CHILDREN

IN SEPTEMBER 2003, THE RECORDING Industry Association of America—a group representing big record labels—sued Brianna Lahara, a 12-year-old schoolgirl, for copyright infringement. Her mother settled the case for $2,000.

Was Brianna in the music piracy business? Not exactly. All she did was participate in Kazaa, a file-swapping network whose members use the Internet to download digitized music, among other things, from each other's computers. But recordings of musical performances are copyrighted—and by swapping files of these recordings with other Kazaa members, Brianna was indeed breaking the law. By the way, the reason the recording industry went after individuals like Brianna was that the company behind Kazaa—chastened by the legal action brought against Napster, the company that made file-swapping famous—insisted that it bore no responsibility for what other people did with its software.

But what about the economics of the case? Are people who swap music files truly engaged in theft? File-swappers and the companies whose software facilitates their activities say no—they're not making off with physical goods, and they aren't doing anyone any harm. If I listen to a bootleg recording of my favourite band, I don't make the band's music any less available to you. Or do I?

The fight over file-swapping flared up just two years after another high-tech legal drama. In 2001 a judge in a federal court in the United States ordered the breakup of

Photographer's Choice

Daily News Pix

New technology has changed the way we access music, but it has also created new economic challenges. Brianna Lahara (shown at right) learned this the hard way.

Microsoft, the producer of the Windows software that runs most personal computers, only to have his ruling thrown out on appeal. Both cases vividly illustrate the extent to which changing technology—and in particular the growing importance of digital products—is changing the economic landscape and presenting new problems for economic policy.

Why does technology change the landscape? Because products like software and music files, unlike most of the goods and services traded in an economy, are *information goods:* their value comes not from their physical attributes but from the information they embody. They are also goods whose value to a consumer depends in large part on how many other consumers use the same good. As we'll see, the growing importance of information goods takes some issues we have discussed in earlier chapters—monopoly, positive externalities, and the dilemmas of antitrust policy—to a new and higher level.

The Economics of Information Goods

Even now most workers in the Canadian economy are employed in the production of conventional goods and services: cars, houses, haircuts, and so on. But considerable resources are now also devoted to producing **information goods**—products whose value comes not from their physical characteristics but from the information they embody.

An **information good** is a good whose value comes from the information it contains.

There is no sharp line dividing information goods from other goods. A computer file is clearly an information good, but conventional goods also contain information. For example, the value of a piece of furniture is partly the result of the knowledge of the furniture-maker, embodied in its form. But although almost all recordings sold these days are in digital form and can be sent over the Internet, many consumers still prefer a physical CD to a downloadable file. By any definition, however, the importance of information goods in the economy has clearly been increasing. As we'll see next, this creates some new challenges for a market economy.

Producing and Selling Information Goods

The fight over file-swapping is widely seen as a landmark dispute, with significance that goes well beyond the music industry. Why? Because the dispute poses, in a very clear way, the question of how society should deal with the production, sale, and distribution of information goods.

To understand why this is an issue, let's start by examining the production costs for an information good. It seems clear that the marginal cost of producing an additional unit of an information good is very low. For example, once the master of a recording has been created, the cost of making an additional digital copy—or burning a copy onto a compact disc—is very small. Similarly, it costs Microsoft very little to produce and ship another copy of Windows. Indeed, many information goods have nearly zero marginal cost.

But that doesn't mean that an information good is costless to produce. A master recording requires many hours of work by songwriters, musicians, audio technicians, producers, and so on, many of them working with expensive equipment. Producing a large software program may require tens of thousands of hours of work by highly skilled and highly paid programmers. These costs are, however, *fixed*—they are the same regardless of how many copies of the product are sold. Whether a recording goes multiple platinum or is never released, the costs of making it are the same. So the characteristic cost structure of information goods involves *high fixed cost* and *very low marginal cost*. This means that information goods have the kind of cost structure we discussed in our analysis of natural monopolies in Chapter 14.

Figure 22-1 illustrates the typical cost structure of an information good and its consequences. Here we imagine that Def Ear Ventures, a record company, is considering producing a new recording by a group that has a large but not huge potential audience. If the recording is made, Def Ear will have a monopoly on its sales, since it owns the copyright. But the company must decide whether the recording is worth producing.

Def Ear's management believes that the demand curve for the new recording is shown by the demand schedule in Figure 22-1: at a price of $10, sales are zero, but if the recording were free, 1 million people would take it. The graph in Figure 22-1 shows the demand curve *D*, along with its associated marginal revenue curve *MR*. (Remember from Chapter 14 that a monopolist's marginal revenue curve is always below the demand curve.)

Figure 22-1

The Profit-Maximizing Quantity of an Information Good

An information good such as a musical recording has high fixed cost and low marginal cost, a situation similar to natural monopoly. Here, Def Ear's fixed cost is $1.5 million, and the marginal cost of manufacturing a single recording is zero. As a result, the average total cost curve, *ATC*, is downward sloping. Given the demand curve, *D*, with its associated marginal revenue curve, *MR*, the profit-maximizing quantity of output is 500,000 recordings, the quantity at which marginal revenue equals marginal cost, as indicated by the optimal point *M*. The profit-maximizing price, P_M, is $5; and the average total cost, ATC_M, is $3, resulting in a per-unit profit of $2. >web...

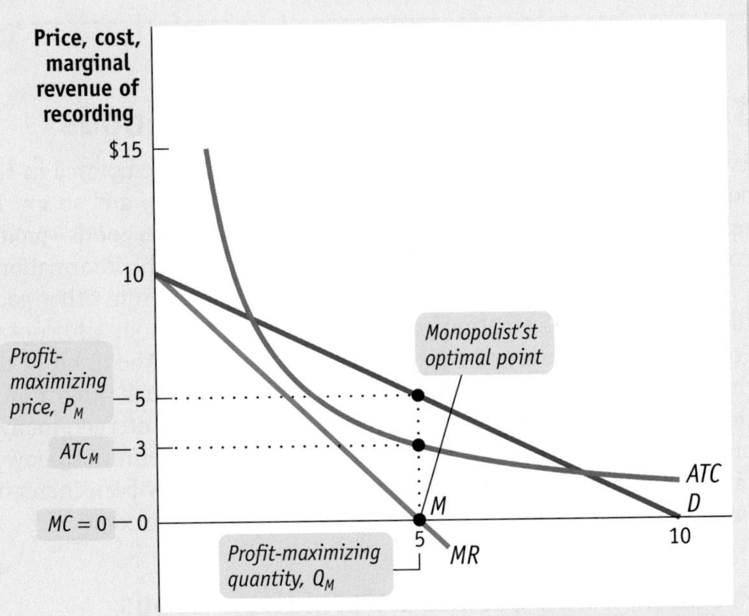

Demand for Recording		Production Cost of Recording		
Price of recording	Quantity of recordings demanded (hundreds of thousands)	Quantity of recordings produced (hundreds of thousands)	Fixed cost (millions)	Average total cost
$10	0	0	$1.5	—
9	1	1	1.5	$15.00
8	2	2	1.5	7.50
7	3	3	1.5	5.00
6	4	4	1.5	3.75
5	5	5	1.5	3.00
4	6	6	1.5	2.50
3	7	7	1.5	2.14
2	8	8	1.5	1.88
1	9	9	1.5	1.67
0	10	10	1.5	1.50

The company also believes that it will cost \$1.5 million to produce the master recording, but that no additional costs will arise from distributing it. This cost structure is also shown in Figure 22-1. Average total cost is equal to \$1.5 million divided by the number of recordings sold; so average total cost falls as the number of recordings sold increases, leading to the downward-sloping average total cost curve *ATC*. When only 100,000 recordings are sold, the average total cost per recording is \$15, but the average total cost is \$1.50 when 1,000,000 recordings are sold. Marginal cost, though, is always zero.

We can apply the *optimal output rule* from Chapters 9 and 14 to find Def Ear's profit-maximizing quantity. The company should produce the quantity at which marginal revenue equals marginal cost, as indicated by the optimal point *M*. Because marginal cost is zero, the profit-maximizing quantity, Q_M, is 500,000 recordings, the quantity at which marginal revenue is equal to zero.

The price at this profit-maximizing quantity, P_M, is \$5 per recording and the average total cost, ATC_M, is \$3 per recording. So the recording is profitable: Def Ear earns \$2 per recording sold, generating a profit of \$1 million on sales of 500,000 recordings.

Pricing Problems for Information Goods

The economic analysis we just applied to Def Ear's recording is standard monopoly theory. So what makes an information good different from any other good?

The answer is illustrated by the problem of file-swapping. Suppose that a music-copying technology, such as the one exploited by file-swappers, allows some potential buyers to download copies of Def Ear's new recording for free. Is this good or bad from an economic perspective?

It depends on whether the recording would still be produced. If Def Ear, knowing that some customers will make free copies, still produces the recording, free downloading increases total surplus. Remember, the marginal cost to the company of producing one more copy is zero. So inefficiency arises whenever anyone decides not to buy the recording because the price is greater than zero. If a person who wouldn't have bought the recording downloads a free copy, the music company doesn't lose anything, the listener gains something, and total surplus increases.

Figure 22-2 (page 550) shows the gains to total surplus from free copying, compared with the original monopoly outcome: they are equal to the area of the triangle labelled *E*, the gain in consumer surplus from letting those who would not otherwise have bought the recording listen to the music for free. Q_O, 1 million copies, is the socially optimal quantity of output because at Q_O, the marginal benefit to the consumer of the last copy (the millionth copy) is equal to marginal cost—that is, zero. Those who defend file-swapping are in effect basing their argument on these potential gains to total surplus represented by the area *E*.

This analysis may look familiar: it is basically the same as the analysis of *artificially scarce goods* in Chapter 20. These are goods that are non-rival in consumption, so the marginal cost of allowing an additional individual to consume the good is zero. For such goods, efficiency is achieved when the price to consumers is zero.

But you may already have seen the problem: consumers can't download music that hasn't been produced. If Def Ear expects many listeners to download its recording for free—not just those who would not otherwise have bought the recording, but some or all of those who *would* have bought one—producing the master recording won't be profitable in the first place.

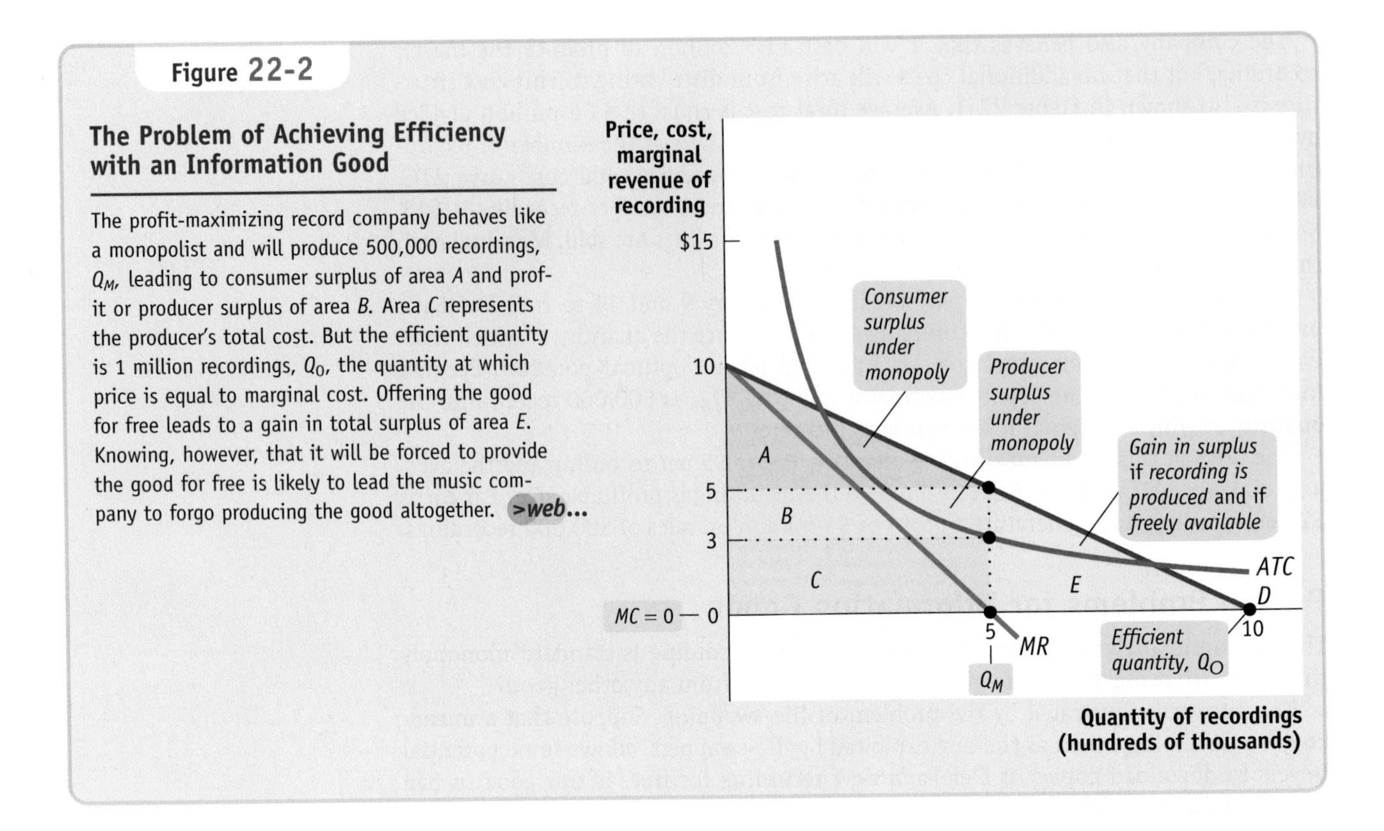

Figure 22-2

The Problem of Achieving Efficiency with an Information Good

The profit-maximizing record company behaves like a monopolist and will produce 500,000 recordings, Q_M, leading to consumer surplus of area *A* and profit or producer surplus of area *B*. Area *C* represents the producer's total cost. But the efficient quantity is 1 million recordings, Q_O, the quantity at which price is equal to marginal cost. Offering the good for free leads to a gain in total surplus of area *E*. Knowing, however, that it will be forced to provide the good for free is likely to lead the music company to forgo producing the good altogether. **>web...**

And if the recording isn't produced, both Def Ear and its potential consumers are worse off than if the recording were produced, even if it is priced above marginal cost. In Figure 22-2, if Def Ear is able to charge the profit-maximizing monopoly price of $5, it earns enough to cover its total cost, measured by the area of the rectangle *C*, and earn profits equal to the area of the rectangle *B*. The profits represented by the area *B* are the producer surplus compared to a situation in which the good is not produced at all. In addition, consumers receive the consumer surplus measured by the area of the triangle *A*. So if the company is deterred from producing the recording, both producer and consumer surplus (the sum of areas *A* and *B*) are sacrificed.

Clearly, then, information goods create a special tension. Monopoly is a bad thing, other things equal: it is inefficient to charge a price that is above marginal cost. But the expectation of monopoly profits is necessary to induce the company to produce the good at all. Indeed, economists generally agree that when it comes to information goods, a *temporary* monopoly may be the necessary price of progress.

Why temporary? As we will now see, both law and natural forces tend to limit the duration of the monopolies associated with information goods.

Property Rights in Information

The conundrum we have just seen is not new; indeed, it has plagued inventors for centuries. Some, like Samuel Morse, who invented the telegraph in 1837, were criticized for allowing their inventions to become the source of monopoly power. Others, like Eli Whitney, who invented the cotton gin in 1793, couldn't make money from their inventions. (Whitney's design was easy to copy, and he was never able to enforce his patent.) But the growing importance of information goods has made the dilemma more critical today than ever before. How has it been dealt with?

To make it worthwhile for people to incur the cost of producing information goods, they must be given some kind of property rights to the information the goods embody that, in turn, allows them to earn revenue. Traditionally this has been done through two closely related legal instruments: **patents** and **copyrights.** Both instruments give creators of knowledge property rights to the knowledge. Patents give inventors the sole right to make, use, or sell their invention for a period that in most countries lasts between 16 and 20 years. Copyrights give the creators of literary or artistic works a similar monopoly for a longer period. One of the strange aspects of the digital revolution, by the way, is the blurring of the distinction between items subject to patent law and those subject to copyright law. Is a piece of software, which takes the form of thousands of lines of program code, an invention or a literary work? Because copyrights last much longer than patents, millions or even billions of dollars depend on how that question is answered.

A **patent** gives an inventor a temporary monopoly in the use or sale of an invention; a **copyright** similarly gives the creator of a literary or artistic work sole rights to profit from that work.

The justification for patent and copyright law is clear from our earlier discussion. If inventors were not protected by patents, they would gain little reward from their efforts: as soon as a valuable invention was made public, other people would copy it and sell products based on it. And if inventors could not expect to profit from their inventions, they would not incur the costs of invention in the first place. So the law gives a temporary monopoly through the creation of temporary property rights to encourage invention. In effect, the law tries to ensure that the gains measured by the areas *A* and *B* in Figure 22-2 take place.

But why are patents temporary? Again, Figure 22-2 illustrates the logic that underlies the law. As long as production of an information good is assured, it is efficient to set its price at marginal cost. But granting a permanent monopoly means creating a permanent gap between price and marginal cost. As a result, the gains from making the invention freely available, measured by the area *E*, would be permanently forgone.

Patent and copyright laws try to strike a compromise. Inventors are granted a temporary monopoly, which, it is hoped, will compensate them for the cost of invention. Because the monopoly eventually ends, the gap between marginal cost and marginal benefit is ultimately eliminated.

Because the length of the temporary monopoly cannot be tailored to specific cases, this system is imperfect and leads to some missed opportunities. Although some potential inventions are not created because the property rights don't last long enough, some monopolies go on longer than necessary. So the length of patents involves a trade-off. Furthermore, it's not clear whether the actual duration of patents makes the best of this trade-off.

In any case, the effectiveness of patents and copyrights varies, depending on the characteristics of the product and industry. In some industries, patents are a highly effective protection for innovators and are the principal incentive for invention. The following Economics in Action describes one such industry, pharmaceuticals. In other industries, however, innovations are less easy to patent. For example, the innovation may not be a discrete, patentable invention as much as a combination of existing ideas. A case in point is Wal-Mart, which was able to achieve rapid growth by, among other things, building large stores away from traditional downtowns and using information technology to manage inventories efficiently. Nothing in that system could be patented, yet the combination gave Wal-Mart a huge cost advantage over competitors. Or it may be possible for competitors to engage in what is known as "reverse engineering": taking a patented product apart, figuring out how it works and how it was made, then developing something similar that avoids violating the letter (but perhaps not the spirit) of the patent.

Even in cases where innovations cannot be patented, however, innovators often have "first-mover" advantages over potential rivals that allow them to establish temporary monopoly positions. The innovating firm's head start in production can give it a technological advantage. If reputation is important to consumers, the first firm into a market can establish brand-name recognition. And in an industry characterized by *network externalities,* which we describe later in this chapter, the first firm in an industry can have a powerful advantage. All of these first-mover advantages arise because reverse engineering and other forms of copying take time.

A good, relatively recent example of first-mover advantage is Amazon, the first large-scale online book retailer. Its leadership is based not on patents—other online booksellers offer similar services—but on the advantages of size and name recognition among book buyers.

Such monopoly positions created by first movers, unlike those created by patents, are real even though they have no legal standing. Despite the fact that companies don't have legal property rights to their innovation, they are able to use their head start to gain a privileged market position. Even so, the monopoly positions established by innovators tend to erode over time, much as if patents were expiring. There are two reasons for this. One is that eventually competitors manage to duplicate the innovation. The other is that newer innovators come up with products that make the original innovation obsolete. For example, in the late 1990s AOL dominated the residential market for Internet access, which at that time relied almost completely on dial-up connections. But its position has rapidly eroded in recent years as broadband access via DSL and cable has become widely available at home.

So temporary monopoly tends to be the norm for many kinds of innovation, including those that cannot be effectively protected by patents.

economics in action

Canada's Drug-Patent Legislation

The trade-off between the good aspects of a monopoly (it encourages innovation) and the bad aspects (it discourages consumption) is vividly illustrated by the pharmaceutical industry.

It may not be apparent that prescription drugs are information goods. But once they have been developed, most drugs are relatively inexpensive to manufacture. It's the initial research and development and the clinical tests that cost hundreds of millions of dollars. In other words, the drug embodies the information created by researchers, which gives it a high fixed cost but a low marginal cost.

Drugs are protected by patents, which give the producer a temporary monopoly. In 1991, Canada increased drug patent protection from 17 years to 20 years—mostly to comply with the World Trade Organization's TRIPS agreement (the agreement on trade-related intellectual property rights). But if 20 years seems like a long time, the impression may be misleading. Drug patents are filed *after* laboratory testing suggests that a drug might be medically useful, but *before* clinical tests on human subjects show that the drug is safe and effective. Since these tests often take more than a decade, the actual period during which a drug company can make use of its monopoly is more like 10 years than 20 years. After that, it faces competition from generic versions of the drug. So some observers have wondered whether pharmaceutical drug companies should be given longer periods of patent protection to stimulate research and development.

The length of drug patents is not just a matter of academic interest. In Chapter 21 we noted that health care spending in Canada has been gradually absorbing an increasing share of total government spending. The main reason for this is the rapid increase in the cost of pharmaceutical drugs. This cost is increasing more rapidly than any other component of health care costs, and is increasing in Canada at a faster rate than anywhere else in the world. Generic drugs help keep these costs down. For example, in 2002 generic drugs filled more than 40% of all prescriptions in Canada, but accounted for only 13.8% of Canada's $13 billion annual prescription drug expenditure.

The brand-name drug companies argue that a longer period of patent protection is necessary to cover fixed costs of development. These fixed costs, they claim, are as high as US$800 million per drug, on average. The generic companies point out that this figure comes from the Tufts Center for the Study of Drug Development, which receives 65% of its funding from drug companies. They argue that the Tufts figure includes the costs of advertising, marketing, and sales—which are substantial. Removing these components brings the figure down to around US$200 million per new drug. Moreover, *Fortune* magazine in 2003 ranked the pharmaceutical industry first overall in terms of profitability. It would seem that the pharmaceutical industry does not need more profit incentives at this time.

If anything, it is Canada's generic drug companies that need patent law reformed in their favour. Currently, under *Notice of Compliance regulations,* Canada allows brand-name drug companies to put additional patents on drugs whose original patents are about to expire. Called "evergreening", the additional patents can involve new features as minor as a new coating on a pill, changing from a capsule to a tablet, or listing the inactive chemicals used as "filler" in the pills. Each new patent allows the brand-name company to allege patent infringement and litigate against generic producers, resulting in an automatic 24-month stay as the legal complexities are sorted out. The United States repealed its Notice of Compliance regulations in August 2003, leaving Canada as the only country in the world to allow this process of "evergreening" of patents by brand-name drug companies. Such legislation unnecessarily prolongs patent protection and introduces needless uncertainty as to when generic products can be produced. ■

>> QUICK REVIEW

- *Information goods* are of growing importance in the economy.
- Efficiency requires that goods sell at their marginal cost, and information goods have low marginal cost. However, because they have high fixed costs, they won't be created unless the producer can expect to cover the cost of production by charging a price well above marginal cost. But like natural monopoly, this leads to an inefficiently low quantity of output.
- By creating temporary monopolies, *patents* and *copyrights* facilitate the production of some information goods. When this legal protection is not available, producers of information goods often manage to establish temporary monopolies by exploiting first-mover advantages.

>> CHECK YOUR UNDERSTANDING 22-1

1. Which of the following are information goods? Which are not? Explain your answers.
   a. A premium cable show delivered to cable viewers
   b. A winter coat made from a newly developed high-tech fabric
   c. A newspaper
   d. A car that contains a new, highly fuel-efficient motor
2. It is often said that "bigger is better" in industries in which the good has the characteristics of an information good. Explain this statement.

Solutions appear at back of book.

Network Externalities

Suppose you owned the only fax machine in the world. What would it be worth to you?

The answer, of course, is nothing. A fax machine derives its value only from the fact that other people also possess fax machines so that you and they can exchange faxes. And in general, the more people who have fax machines, the more valuable a fax machine is to you.

This phenomenon, in which a good's value to an individual is greater when many other people own or use the same good, is common in technology-driven sectors of the economy. This is called a **network externality** because the most obvious versions of the "fax machine effect" occur when the goods involved form some kind of communications or transportation network. But the phenomenon is considerably more widespread than that.

A good is subject to a **network externality** when the value of the good to an individual is greater when a large number of other people also use that good.

Network externalities play a key role both in the modern economy and in a number of policy controversies. Let's look at where and how network externalities occur and then at some of the issues they raise.

Types of Network Externality

The most obvious examples of network externalities involve communications. At different points in history the prime examples have been telegraphs, telephones, fax machines, and e-mail accounts. In each case the value of the good is derived entirely from its ability to link many people possessing the same good. As a result, the marginal benefit of the good to any one individual depends on the number of other individuals who use it.

However, network externalities can also arise in less dramatic ways. For example, network externalities can exist when other users are not strictly necessary for the use of a good, as long as they enhance its usefulness. In the early days of railroad development, a railroad from Winnipeg to Montreal would have had considerable value all by itself, as would a railroad from Halifax to Montreal. However, each line was worth more given the existence of the other, because once both were in place, goods could be shipped via Montreal between Halifax and Winnipeg. In the modern world, a scheduled flight between two airports becomes more valuable if one or both of those airports is a hub with connections to other places.

Even this kind of direct link need not be necessary to create important network externalities. Any way in which other people's consumption of a good increases your own marginal benefit from consumption of that good can give rise to network effects.

Perhaps the classic case of indirect network externalities is that of computer operating systems. The operating system of a computer is the underlying software that runs the machine's basic operations, underpinning and coordinating the various programs—word processors, spreadsheets, e-mail programs, and so on—that the user runs. Most personal computers around the world run on Windows, the system sold by Microsoft—although a significant minority of users own computers produced by Apple, which has its own operating system. And a growing number of computers run on Linux, a system designed by programmers who believe that operating systems should not be corporate property.

Why is Windows so dominant? Is a personal computer running Windows like a fax machine, which is useful only to the extent that other people possess the same good? Not in a direct sense: a computer can be used to type a term paper, do calculations on a spreadsheet, and even to send and receive e-mail regardless of how many other people have computers running the same operating system. So there isn't a literal network issue making Windows the preferred system.

Nonetheless, the dominance of Windows turns out to be self-reinforcing, for at least two indirect reasons. First, it is easier for a Windows user to get help and advice from other computer users than for someone using a less popular system. So it's a good idea, if possible, to use the same system that your colleague in the next office uses. Second, because Windows is used so widely, it attracts more attention from software developers. As a result, there are more programs that run on Windows than on any other operating system.

Network externalities in this broad sense occur for many goods. Even your choice of a car is influenced by a form of network externalities. Most people would be reluctant to switch to a car that does not run on ordinary gasoline—for example, a vehicle that runs on natural gas—if only because fuelling the car would be difficult: very few gas stations offer alternative fuels. But the reason they do not offer alternative fuels is, of course, that few people drive anything other than gasoline-powered cars. Or to take a less drastic example, people who live in small towns are reluctant to drive an unusual imported vehicle: Where would they find a mechanic who knows how to fix it? So the circularity that makes one person choose Windows because everyone else uses Windows also applies to non-high-tech goods like cars.

Nonetheless, experience suggests that network externalities are more important for information goods than for other goods. And network externalities lead to two characteristic features of markets for information goods: *positive feedback* and *tipping.*

Positive Feedback

Goods subject to network externalities experience **positive feedback:** success breeds success, failure breeds failure.

When a good is subject to a network externality, it is likely to be subject to **positive feedback.** If large numbers of people buy the good, other people become more likely to buy it. If people *don't* buy the good, others become less likely to buy it. So both success and failure tend to be self-reinforcing.

Because of positive feedback, certain "story lines" recur in the history of information good industries. One of these is the story of a small network that suddenly takes off when it reaches *critical mass*. Another is that of competition between two alternative technologies, neither obviously better than the other, that is resolved decisively through market *tipping*. Let's look at each story line in turn.

Critical Mass and Industry Takeoffs Fax machines have existed for a remarkably long time. The basic technology was developed by the Scottish inventor Alexander Bain in 1843, and AT&T introduced a wire photo service using fax technology in 1925. Really widespread use of fax machines, however, began only in the 1980s. And the rise was sudden indeed. Sharp introduced the first low-priced fax machine in 1984 and sold 80,000 that first year. In 1987 a million fax machines were sold, and by 1989 they were everywhere.

E-mail and the Internet present a similar picture. The first e-mail message was sent in 1969, but at the beginning of the 1990s only a relative handful of people were online; by about 1996, e-mail had become essential to business, and tens of millions of people had access to the Internet.

What accounts for these sudden explosions? In each case the technology improved: low-priced high-quality fax machines like the one Sharp introduced in 1984 were made possible by the rapid progress of microelectronics. But the explosive growth of fax machine use wasn't just because the technology improved; it also resulted from the network externality in fax use.

To see why, let's consider a simplified description of the decision to acquire a fax machine. We assume that there are two types of potential buyers. First, there are "unconditional" fax users—people who will want a fax machine regardless of how many other people have them. (An example might be corporations, which use faxes to send documents between their own branches.) Second, there are "conditional" users, who will want a fax machine only if the network of fax machines is large enough—that is, if enough other people already have them. In addition, both the number of unconditional users and the level of fax machine ownership that would persuade the conditional users to buy machines depend on how much the machines cost and how well they work.

Suppose that there are 1 million potential fax machine users, the total number of conditional and unconditional users. Suppose also that given the current technology and price of fax machines, 100,000 of them are unconditional users. But the other 900,000 potential users will find it worthwhile to buy a machine only if the number of machines already out there exceeds a **threshold network size** of 300,000. That is, they will buy machines only if 300,000 other people (the unconditional users) have machines because they won't have enough occasions to send or receive faxes otherwise.

In a market subject to network externalities, the **threshold network size** for a given individual is the smallest number of current members of the network that leads the individual to join the network.

The initial situation of the demand for fax machines is shown in panel (a) of Figure 22-3 (page 556). Here we assume for simplicity that all fax machines are produced with the same technology so that all consumers face the same price and quality. On the horizontal axis is the quantity of fax machines currently in use at the given price and quality. On the vertical axis is the quantity of fax machines demanded—the number of people who *want* fax machines. The two blue lines show what we have assumed about the demand for fax machines. The blue line on the left shows that there is an unconditional demand for 100,000 fax machines—100,000 people will acquire fax machines regardless of how many other people have them. The blue line on the right shows that if the number of fax machines in use reaches 300,000, the number of users suddenly increases to 1 million. (In this case we have assumed that all conditional users have the *same* threshold network size, but the story would stay the same as long as they have sufficiently similar thresholds.)

How many people will acquire fax machines in this situation? There are two possible equilibria, represented by points L_1 and H. The point labelled L_1, at which

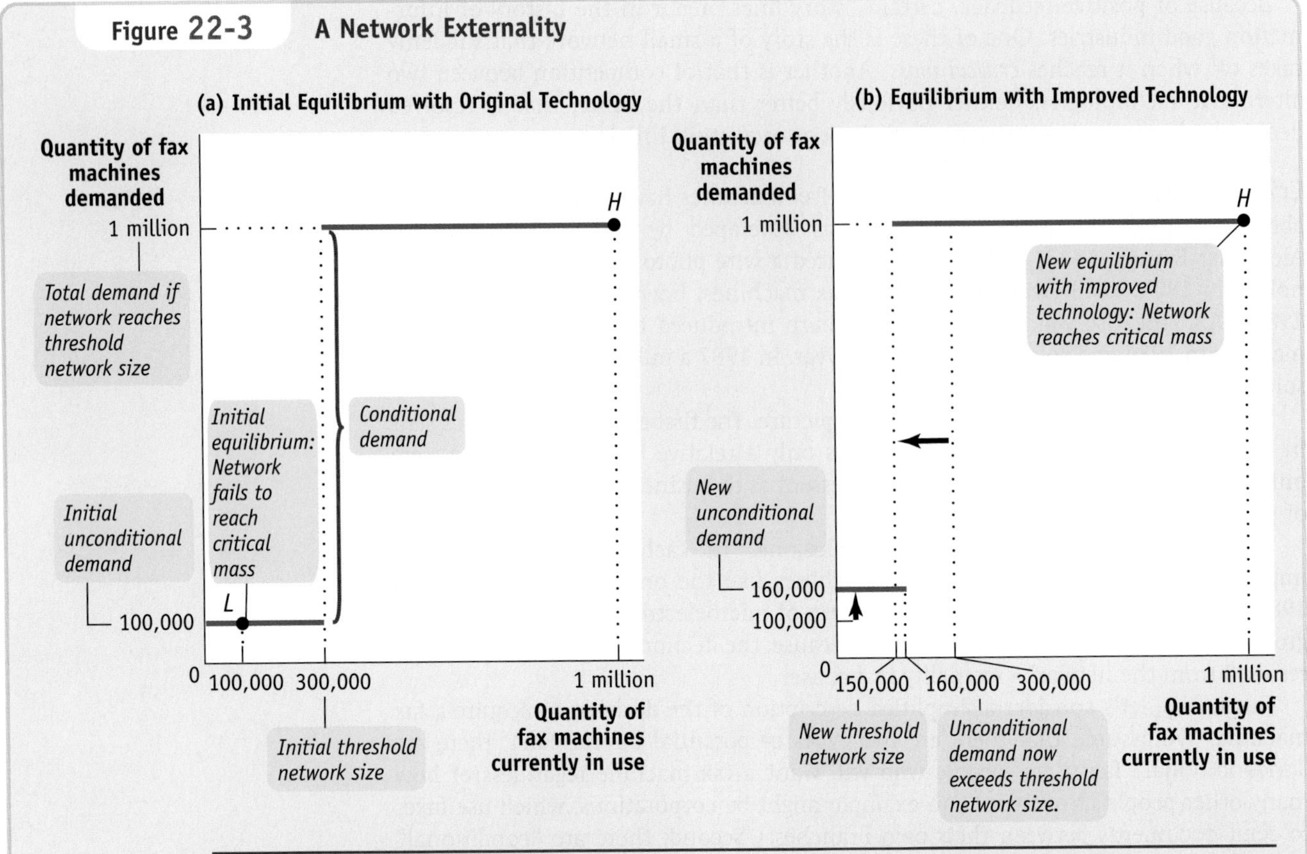

Figure 22-3 A Network Externality

With a network externality, small changes in the cost or quality of a good can lead the market to suddenly explode. Here, conditional users will not participate in the network unless the number of users (the unconditional demand) equals or exceeds the threshold network size. Panel (a) illustrates the network under the original technology, where the initial threshold network size is 300,000. The initial equilibrium is L_1. The network fails to reach critical mass because the unconditional demand, 100,000, is less than the threshold network size under the original technology, 300,000, and conditional users refuse to participate. Panel (b) illustrates the network when the technology has improved. Due to the better technology the threshold network size falls to 150,000, the unconditional demand rises to 160,000, and the new equilibrium is *H*. The network has now reached critical mass: conditional users participate in the network because unconditional demand exceeds the threshold network size.

100,000 people acquire fax machines, is a possible equilibrium—each individual is making his or her best choice given what everyone else is doing. The point labelled *H*, with 1 million fax machines in use, is also a possible equilibrium. But if, as is typically the case, machines built with the original technology are relatively expensive given the quality, you would expect the number of unconditional users to be relatively small. So we can safely assume that L_1 is indeed the initial equilibrium in this market, and not *H*.

Now suppose that improved technology makes faxes cheaper and better. This will both increase the number of unconditional users and reduce the threshold network size for conditional users. If the improvement in technology is substantial enough, the new number of unconditional users will equal or exceed the threshold network size and the fax machine industry will take off.

Panel (b) of Figure 22-3 shows how this might happen. Due to the cheaper and better machines, the number of unconditional users rises from 100,000 to 160,000, and the threshold network size drops from 300,000 to 150,000. The number of cur-

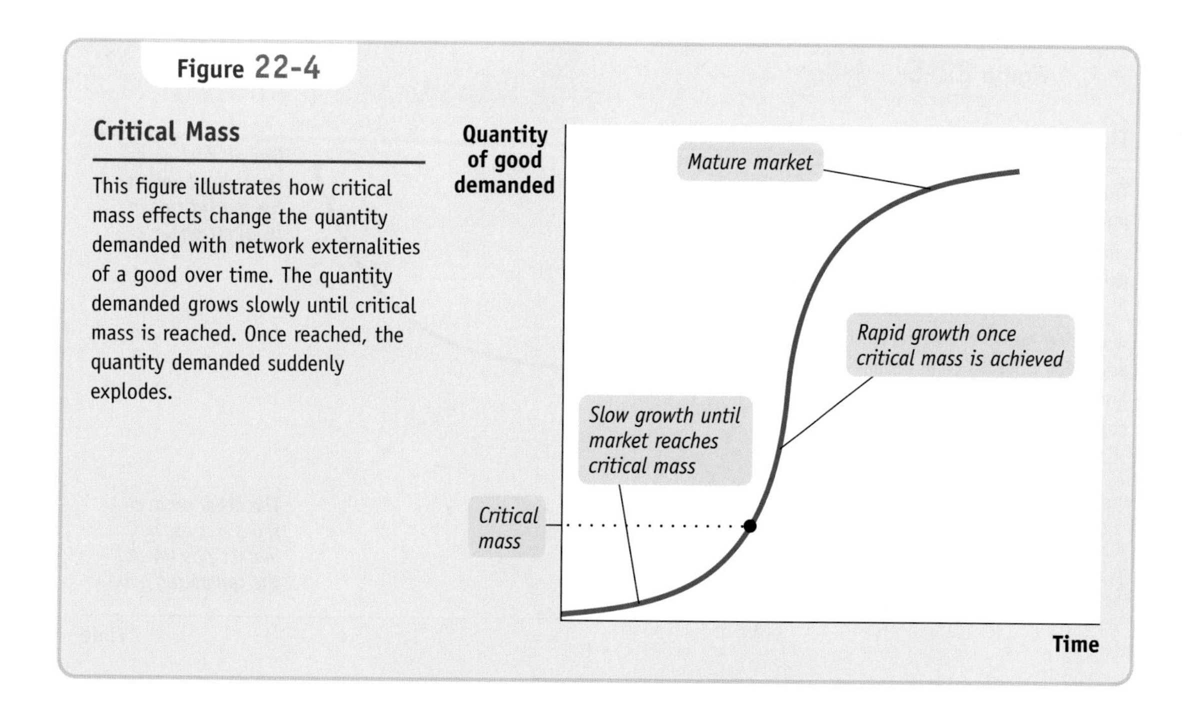

Figure 22-4

Critical Mass

This figure illustrates how critical mass effects change the quantity demanded with network externalities of a good over time. The quantity demanded grows slowly until critical mass is reached. Once reached, the quantity demanded suddenly explodes.

rent users now exceeds the threshold network size, leading the 840,000 conditional users to jump in and buy fax machines. The network quickly expands and a new equilibrium is reached at *H*.

The moral of this story is that improvements in the technology of goods subject to network externalities may at first lead to only gradual increases in the size of the network. But when the network reaches a certain size—a **critical mass**—it suddenly explodes.

The **critical mass** of a network is the size at which it suddenly begins to grow rapidly.

Because of the critical mass effect, industries subject to network externalities often exhibit the pattern of growth shown in Figure 22-4: a long period of slow growth, followed by a sudden, rapid expansion, with growth levelling off again once the conditional buyers have been brought in.

Tipping During the 1980s, when the fax machine was becoming a standard feature of American life, Americans also began to buy large numbers of video cassette recorders. VCRs allow people to watch rented movies at home and also (with some difficulty) to tape TV shows for later viewing. But in the early 1980s there were two different kinds of VCRs. To this day there is debate about whether VHS (produced by several companies) or Betamax (produced only by Sony) was the better system. However, after a period in which both were in use, consumers swung decisively to VHS and Betamax eventually disappeared.

What made consumers choose VHS over Betamax? The key point was that VHS enjoyed an initial advantage. Most of the videos available for rental were VHS—and that was because most of the customers to whom rental stores catered had VHS players. So ultimately consumers chose VHS because other consumers had chosen VHS—a case of positive feedback at work.

The situation in which a small initial advantage for one of two competing goods or technologies proves self-reinforcing, eventually driving the other competitor out of the market, is known as **tipping.** Tipping is similar in its logic to the critical mass effect on sales of a single good. And it leads to somewhat similar patterns of change over time. Figure 22-5 (page 558) shows the characteristic path of a market subject to tipping. On the horizontal axis is time; on the vertical axis is the quantity of a good demanded. A good that has a substantial but not dominant share of the market may stay in

Tipping occurs when positive feedback due to network externalities causes consumers to swing to one of two competing goods or technologies.

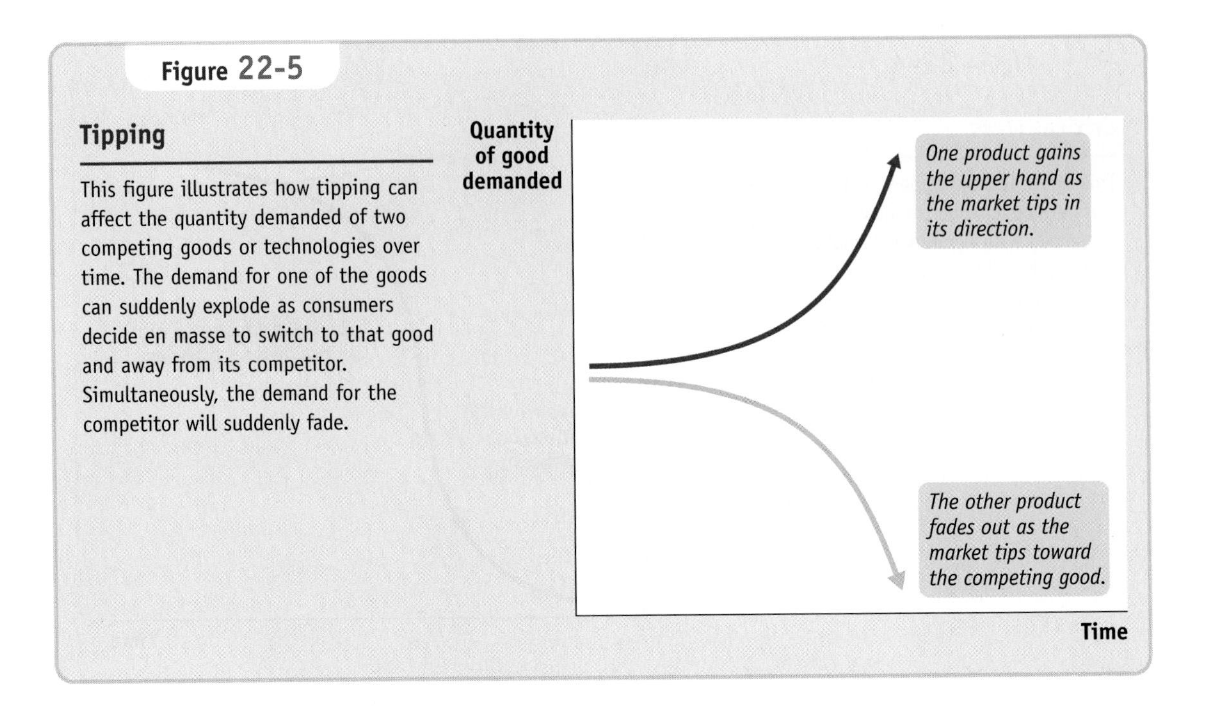

Figure 22-5

Tipping

This figure illustrates how tipping can affect the quantity demanded of two competing goods or technologies over time. The demand for one of the goods can suddenly explode as consumers decide en masse to switch to that good and away from its competitor. Simultaneously, the demand for the competitor will suddenly fade.

that range for an extended period. Then, quite suddenly, and often for no obvious reason, the market tips either for or against it, and the good either becomes dominant or fades away.

Competition in the Face of Network Externalities

Companies that produce information goods are aware of the importance of network externalities. But how do these effects change the behaviour of firms? The general answer is that when companies believe their products are subject to strong network externalities, they typically place a strong emphasis on building their sales network, even at the expense of short-term profits. This strategy is reflected by the saying that in information industries sometimes you need to lose money to make money.

To see why, consider the case of a good subject to a critical mass effect—say, camera phones that also allow speakers to see each other. If only a few companies are supplying those phones, it is clearly in their interest to get the industry to critical mass—to get the explosion of sales that will occur when many people feel that they should have camera phones because so many other people have them. But how can these companies get the industry to critical mass? One way is to sell the product cheaply—perhaps at a loss—in order to increase the size of the network. So we often see companies introducing new high-technology products at a price well below production cost.

The same kind of logic applies in markets subject to tipping. Because a company wants to do all it can to induce the market to tip towards its product, it has an incentive to offer the product cheaply until the market has swung decisively in its favour. Of course, firms offering rival products have the same incentive, so the early stages of competition in information goods often involve rival firms offering their products for very little—in some cases nothing. The most famous case may be the "browser wars" of the 1990s. A browser is software used to access the Internet; the two main competitors—Netscape Navigator and Microsoft Internet Explorer—were both available for free.

In the real world, of course, nobody can be quite sure if a new product will ever achieve critical mass or if it is possible to tip the market towards a product by offering it cheaply. The result is that there are many cases of attempts to launch products that seem foolish in retrospect: goods sold cheaply, with lots of money lost, that never took off.

FOR INQUIRING MINDS

WHOSE NETWORK IS IT, ANYWAY?

Suppose that Sharp, when it introduced the first cheap fax machine, had engineered it so that it could send and receive faxes only from other Sharp machines. That would not have been good for the fax network—but it might have been very good for Sharp.

Sound implausible? Consider the case of America Online and instant messaging.

AOL is a sort of Internet within the Internet—subscribers can access all the usual web pages and also have special access to services only AOL offers. And at the end of the 1990s, AOL introduced a new service: instant messaging, e-mail that pops up immediately on the recipient's screen. This was supposed to be available only between AOL subscribers: the company viewed it as an additional selling point that would increase the number of subscribers. But AOL subscribers wanted to be able to send instant messages to non-AOL subscribers, and vice versa. So a sort of arms race developed, as programmers wrote software that allowed non-AOL users to send instant messages and to receive them from AOL users, to which AOL responded by introducing countermeasures, to which the programmers responded with new software, and so on.

Who was serving the public interest? As in the case of file-sharing, the answer is ambiguous. Instant messaging is more useful if it's available to everyone; but companies like AOL won't make innovations unless they believe that they can profit from them. So although AOL eventually opened up their instant messaging service to non-AOL users after it became the subject of antitrust scrutiny, the original belief that sales would be increased by the threat of excluding non-AOL users made the innovation possible.

economics in action

Apple's Big Mistake

In 1984 Apple Computer introduced the Macintosh, a personal computer that co-founder Steve Jobs described as "insanely great". Many observers agreed. Before the Mac, personal computers were operated by typing in cumbersome commands or possibly by choosing a command from a menu. The Mac introduced the much more powerful graphical user interface, also known as point-and-click: you use a mouse to move an arrow to an image on the screen, then click a button. Graphical user interfaces have now become standard for all personal computers.

But sales of the Mac were never as good as Apple expected. And even though Apple's computers were clearly technologically superior to the alternatives well into the 1990s (devotees say they still are), they have remained a small part of the market.

What happened? At the time the Mac was introduced, most computer users had PCs that ran on DOS, an operating system created by Microsoft. Apple knew that its product was better and so charged a premium price. This kept Apple's customer base relatively small. Apple failed to recognize the strength of the network externality that caused many users to stick with an inferior product that was widely used, especially given the fact that the superior alternative was considerably more expensive.

Over time, Microsoft developed its own version of a graphical user interface, Windows. Windows, especially in its early versions, was still technologically inferior to Apple's system: it took a long time to boot, and it was notoriously vulnerable to crashes. (The joke went around that if Microsoft made cars, they would take five minutes to start and would occasionally stop suddenly for no apparent reason.) But again, the network externalities already achieved by DOS induced many people to stay with the technologically inferior Microsoft system.

In retrospect, it seems likely that if Apple had understood the force of network externalities and priced the Macintosh lower, it would have come to dominate the industry. ■

< < < < < < < < < < < < < < < < < <

>> QUICK REVIEW

- Many information goods are subject to *network externalities*. Industries producing goods subject to network externalities exhibit *positive feedback*.
- Under a network externality, a large proportion of consumers may not be willing to purchase a good unless the number of existing users exceeds a *threshold network size*. This leads to the *critical mass* effect, a sudden rapid increase in the network size. Network externalities also lead to *tipping*, in which a small initial advantage for one of two competing goods becomes self-reinforcing.

>> CHECK YOUR UNDERSTANDING 22-2

1. For each of the following goods explain the nature of the network externality present.
   a. Appliances using a particular voltage, such as 110 volt versus 220 volt
   b. $8\frac{1}{2}$-by-11-inch paper versus 8-by-$12\frac{1}{2}$-inch paper
2. Suppose there are two competing companies in an industry that has critical mass effects. Explain why the market is likely to tip to the company that can sustain the largest initial losses.

Solutions appear at back of book.

Policy Towards Information Goods

Does the growing importance of information goods require new kinds of economic policy? Most economists would answer with a qualified no. The principles of economics remain the same as ever, and the issues raised by information goods are not new. Still, the emphasis shifts: issues that may have seemed unimportant in the past become very important in this new world.

Let's look at two types of policy concerns raised by the growing importance of information goods: competition policy and standards.

Competition Policy

We saw in Chapters 14 and 15 that market power creates problems for economic efficiency. As a result, governments worldwide attempt both to limit the growth of monopolies and to keep oligopolies from behaving like monopolies. But how should competition policy be conducted in information goods industries?

As we saw earlier in this chapter, monopoly is a natural outcome in industries with high fixed costs but low marginal costs, which is the case for information goods. Furthermore, it is the hope of achieving a monopoly that leads potential producers to incur those high fixed costs in the first place.

However, Canada's competition laws do not, strictly speaking, forbid monopoly. Rather, they only constrain "monopolization"—efforts to create a monopoly. If you just happen to end up ruling an industry, that's okay providing you don't "abuse your dominant position". If you do abuse it—if you take actions designed to drive out potential competition, or competition in other markets—that's not okay. So we could argue that monopolies in information goods, because they occur naturally, should not pose legal problems.

Unfortunately, it isn't that simple. Firms investing in new technologies are clearly trying to establish monopoly positions. Furthermore, in the face of positive feedback, firms have an incentive to engage in aggressive strategies to push their goods to critical mass, or to tip the market in their direction. So what is the dividing line between legal and illegal actions?

At this point the issue really hasn't arisen in Canada, so it's difficult to predict how Canadian case history will evolve when dealing with information goods. But it's a different matter in the United States. Microsoft has a near-monopoly on the operating system of personal computers, and in 2000 the U.S. Justice Department decided to take on Microsoft in perhaps the most celebrated antitrust case of modern times. This case is interesting not only in its own right but also because competition law in Canada is not that dissimilar from antitrust law in the United States. In the Economics in Action on page 562, we will see that reasonable economists and legal experts disagreed sharply about both whether the company had broken U.S. law by pursuing a monopoly position, and whether the company should be broken up to diminish its ability to tip new markets in its favour.

Setting Standards

Canada has always had a pretty decent phone service—tribute perhaps to the legacy of a great Canadian, Alexander Graham Bell. But when it comes to cell phones, we lag noticeably behind Europe. Why?

The answer has to do with the European decision, at the end of the 1980s, to adopt a common **standard** for digital cellular phones—a set of rules for operation that induced competing cell phone companies to form a common network—so that every cellular phone would work everywhere on the continent. A GSM (General Standard for Mobiles) phone works equally well even in the most remote areas in Europe; because of the common standard, supporting antennas are plentiful and there is good coverage almost everywhere. In Canada, by contrast, there is no common standard among competing cell phone companies: some use the GSM, but others use alternative standards. Even if there is a transmission tower near you, it may not carry a signal your phone can use. Currently, the severity of this problem is being mitigated by the appearance of new cell phones that can receive several different types of signals. Even so, the signals themselves resemble a patchwork, with some areas where signals overlap and others where there is no signal at all.

A **standard** is a set of rules for operation that induces competing goods to operate as a single network.

Standards are by no means a new issue. In the nineteenth century the most important choice of standard was the gauge of railroads—how far apart the rails of a track were. The problems created when two railroads with different gauges met were obvious. In the United Kingdom, narrow-gauge rail eventually came to dominate despite the superior safety of the wide gauge. In the United States in 1860, there were no fewer than seven different railroad gauges in use. In both countries, a common gauge was eventually established at the cost of a massive effort in ripping up miles of rail that had already been laid.

Both the old railroad example and the modern cell phone example suggest that the need for common standards creates a justification for government intervention in the economy. Left to itself, the market may fail to converge on a common standard. And as in the case of early railroads or contemporary Canadian cell phones, an industry may suffer from avoidable inefficiency because of failure to converge. So the government can play a useful role by prodding the private sector into that convergence, as it did in the case of European cell phones.

An important point about standards is that getting *some* standard is often more important than *which* standard is chosen. For example, it was less important whether the early railway companies used wide-gauge or narrow-gauge rail than that they all coordinate on a single choice. And it isn't always necessary for the government to enforce a standard; sometimes industries do it voluntarily. A number of companies agreed on the standard for digital video discs (DVDs), which are rapidly replacing video cassettes. In other cases a standard simply evolves as firms try to match each other.

But do unplanned standards—standards that arise as a natural market outcome—get it right? In some cases, different standards will lead to different results: one standard may lead to lower costs or higher quality than another, and there is no guarantee that the market will choose the better standard. So could an industry get "stuck" with one standard when some other standard is clearly better?

Economists have long debated this issue, which has come to be known as the **QWERTY problem**. The name comes from the top row on a standard keyboard, which reads QWERTYUIOP. Why are keyboards laid out that way? Basically because they started out with that layout, which was chosen partly because it helped prevent keys on a mechanical typewriter from jamming—not a concern on a computer—and partly because it allowed salesmen to quickly pick out the letters "TYPEWRITER", which are all in the top row of the QWERTY keyboard. So that is what typists learn, and that is what typewriter manufacturers, and more recently computer keyboard manufacturers, provide—it's a self-reinforcing loop.

An industry that gets stuck using an inferior standard suffers from the **QWERTY problem.**

The question is whether QWERTY is the best keyboard layout. Might there be a better layout, one that would allow faster typing, that nobody uses because network externalities have locked us into the standard layout?

The evidence on keyboards is mixed. Other layouts seem to be somewhat better. But a computer can be easily reprogrammed to use a different keyboard layout, so if the gains from a switch were really large we would expect a widespread move away from the QWERTY layout; this hasn't happened. Nonetheless, in principle government intervention might be useful in moving an industry to a superior standard.

economics in action

The Microsoft Case

In 2000 the U.S. Justice Department took on Microsoft in one of the most watched antitrust cases in history. By that time, Microsoft had become the world's most valuable corporation, and its founder, Bill Gates, was the world's richest man. What the government sought was nothing less than the breakup of the company.

The case involved almost all of the issues raised by information goods. Microsoft was, by any reasonable definition, a monopoly: leaving aside the niches of Apple customers and Linux users, just about all personal computers ran the Windows operating system. The key fact sustaining the Windows system was the force of a network externality: people used Windows because other people used Windows.

Reuters

The Microsoft case involved almost all of the issues raised by information goods.

The U.S. government did not challenge the Windows monopoly itself, however (although some economists urged it to). Basically, everyone agreed that monopoly per se is a natural thing in such industries and should not be prevented. Instead, what the U.S. government claimed was that Microsoft had "abused its monopoly position"—that it had used its market power to give its products an advantage over competitors in other markets. For example, by including Internet Explorer as part of the Windows system, it was alleged, Microsoft was giving itself an unfair advantage over its rival Netscape in the browser software market.

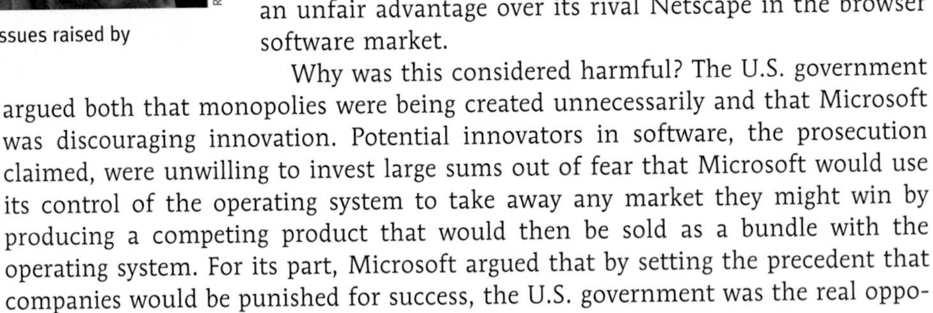

Why was this considered harmful? The U.S. government argued both that monopolies were being created unnecessarily and that Microsoft was discouraging innovation. Potential innovators in software, the prosecution claimed, were unwilling to invest large sums out of fear that Microsoft would use its control of the operating system to take away any market they might win by producing a competing product that would then be sold as a bundle with the operating system. For its part, Microsoft argued that by setting the precedent that companies would be punished for success, the U.S. government was the real opponent of innovation.

At first the case went against Microsoft when a judge ordered the company split in two—into an operating-system company and a company selling the firm's other products. But this judgment was overturned on appeal. In November 2001, the U.S. government reached a settlement with Microsoft in which the company agreed to provide other companies with the technology to develop products that interacted seamlessly with Microsoft's software, thus removing the company's special advantage acquired through bundling its products.

Competitors complained bitterly that this settlement had far too many loopholes, and that Microsoft's ability to exploit its monopoly position would remain. And by early 2004, the U.S. government agreed: antitrust lawyers from the Justice Department reported to the judge who negotiated the original settlement that they were increasingly uneasy about the plan's ability to spur competition. A particular concern was a rumoured Microsoft move to take over the market in publishing software, in which Adobe Acrobat was the current leader. ▪

>>CHECK YOUR UNDERSTANDING 22-3

1. As described in the For Inquiring Minds on page 559, America Online (AOL), the biggest Internet service provider in North America, was at one time the subject of U.S. antitrust scrutiny of its instant messaging service. In the original form of the program, when an AOL customer sent a message to another AOL customer, the message instantly popped up on the receiver's screen. But AOL did not allow non-AOL senders to access the service when they sent messages to an AOL customer. Did this action represent an "abuse of dominant position"? Was AOL trying to suppress competition and create a monopoly? Give arguments pro and con.

>>QUICK REVIEW

- Information goods pose difficult problems for antitrust policy.
- Information goods also create a possible role for the government in setting *standards*. Left to themselves, industries may fail to arrive at a common standard or suffer from the *QWERTY problem*, getting stuck with an inferior standard.

SUMMARY

1. **Information goods**—goods whose value derives mainly from the information they embody—are increasingly important in the economy.
2. Information goods typically have high fixed costs but low or zero marginal costs. This means that once an information good has been created, efficiency requires that it be free or almost free to consumers. But innovators must have some way to earn back their fixed costs if the good is to be produced at all.
3. To enhance efficiency, governments have created **patents** and **copyrights,** which give innovators a temporary monopoly. But these temporary monopolies often arise naturally due to first-mover advantages from innovation.
4. Many information goods are also characterized by **network externalities:** the value of the good to an individual is greater when a large number of people also use the good. Network externalities cause **positive feedback,** in which either initial success or initial failure is self-reinforcing.
5. Because consumers may have a **threshold network size** at which they are willing to purchase a good, information goods may have a **critical mass,** a market size at which growth explodes. Or they may experience **tipping,** in which a small advantage to one of two competing goods leads it to become dominant. These features often lead firms to price their goods or technologies very low in the hope of greatly increasing sales.
6. Information goods pose difficulties for antitrust policy because firms investing in new technologies may engage in aggressive tactics to establish monopolies, tactics that may or may not be legal.
7. To facilitate network externalities, industries must coordinate on **standards** that let competing goods work together. Government can play a useful role both in helping an industry establish a standard and in helping it avoid getting trapped in an inferior standard, known as the **QWERTY problem.**

KEY TERMS

PROBLEMS

1. Information goods are characterized by high fixed cost and very low or zero marginal cost. Suppose the government grants the producer of an information good a patent so that the producer is the only seller of that good.

   a. If the government forces the producer to charge a price equal to marginal cost, would the firm's profit be greater than, equal to, or less than zero?

b. If the government forces the producer to charge a price equal to average total cost, would the firm's profit be greater than, equal to, or less than zero?

2. Werck, a pharmaceutical company, is developing a new AIDS drug. The demand schedule for the drug, once it has been developed, is shown in Table 2a. If Werck can act as a monopolist, its marginal revenue from selling the drug will be as given in Table 2b.

Table 2a

Price of dose	Quantity of doses demanded (thousands)
$100	0
90	20
80	40
70	60
60	80
50	100
40	120
30	140
20	160
10	180
0	200

Table 2b

Quantity of doses (thousands)	Marginal revenue (per dose)
0	
	$90
20	
	70
40	
	50
60	
	30
80	
	10
100	
	−10
120	

Werck's fixed cost in developing the drug is $4 million. The marginal cost of producing the drug is zero.

a. If Werck develops the drug and can act as a monopolist, which quantity of output will it choose to produce? What will its profit be? Does Werck therefore have an incentive to engage in the costly development of the drug?

b. Suppose now that the government announces that in order to make AIDS drugs more widely available, it will force the producer to sell the drug at marginal cost. If Werck develops the drug, what will the price be and how much of the drug will be sold? What will its profit be? Does Werck have an incentive to engage in the costly development of the drug?

3. British Biotech is developing a new cancer drug. The demand schedule for the drug, once the drug has been developed, is shown in Table 3a. If British Biotech can act as a monopolist, its marginal revenue from selling the drug will be as shown in Table 3b.

Table 3a

Price of dose	Quantity of doses demanded (millions)
$50	0
45	1
40	2
35	3
30	4
25	5
20	6
15	7
10	8
5	9
0	10

Table 3b

Quantity of doses (millions)	Marginal revenue (per dose)
0	
	$45
1	
	35
2	
	25
3	
	15
4	
	5
5	
	−5
6	

British Biotech's fixed cost of developing the drug is $750 million. Its marginal cost is zero.

a. If British Biotech is granted a monopoly for one year, what will its revenue be that year?

b. If British Biotech does not have a monopoly, other drug makers will copy its product without incurring any development cost, and the price will fall to marginal cost. What will British Biotech's yearly revenue be in that case?

c. If the government sets the length of British Biotech's patent at 4 years so that British Biotech is a monopolist for 4 years and then other firms can imitate the product (and therefore after 4 years the price falls to marginal cost), what will British Biotech's revenue be over those 4 years? Is this enough to cover British Biotech's fixed cost of developing the drug? (Ignore the issue of discounting over time.)

d. How long would the patent have to be for British Biotech to cover its fixed cost and so want to invest in development of the drug?

4. Explain the following situations.

a. In Europe, many cell phone service providers give away for free what would otherwise be very expensive cell phones when a service contract is purchased. Why might a company want to do that?

b. In the United Kingdom, the country's antitrust authority banned one cell phone service provider (Vodaphone) from offering a plan that gave customers free calls to other customers of Vodaphone. Why might Vodaphone have wanted to offer these calls for free? Why might a government want to step in and ban this practice? Why might it not be a good idea for the government to interfere in this way?

>web... To continue your study and review of concepts in this chapter, please visit the Krugman/Wells website for quizzes, animated graph tutorials, web links to helpful resources, and more.

www.worthpublishers.com/krugmanwellsmyatt

>> Solutions to "Check Your Understanding" Questions

This section offers suggested answers to the "Check Your Understanding" questions found within chapters.

Chapter One

Check Your Understanding 1-1

1. **a.** This illustrates the concept of opportunity cost. Given that one can only eat so much, having an additional slice of coconut cream pie requires that you forgo eating something else, such as a slice of the chocolate cake.
   b. This illustrates the concept of scarce resources. Even if there were more resources in the world, the total amount of those resources is limited. As a result, scarcity would still arise. For there to be no scarcity, there would have to be unlimited amounts of everything (including unlimited time in a human life)—which is clearly impossible.
   c. This illustrates the concept that people usually exploit opportunities to make themselves better off. Students will seek to make themselves better off by signing up for the tutorials of teaching assistants with good reputations, while avoiding the tutorials of teaching assistants with poor reputations.
   d. This illustrates the concept of marginal analysis. Your decision about allocating your time is a "how much" decision: how much time spent exercising versus how much time spent studying. You make your decision by comparing the benefit of doing an additional hour of exercising to its cost, which is the effect on your grades of one less hour spent studying.
2. **a.** Yes. The increased time, but not the total time, spent commuting is a cost you will incur if you accept the new job. That additional time spent commuting, or equivalently, the use you would get from spending that time doing something else, is an opportunity cost of the new job.
   b. Yes. One of the benefits of the new job is that you will be making $50,000. But if you take the new job, you will have to give up your current job; that is, you have to give up your current salary of $45,000. So, $45,000 is one of the opportunity costs of taking the new job.
   c. No. A more spacious office at your new job is an additional benefit to your new job, and does not involve forgoing something else.

Check Your Understanding 1-2

1. **a.** This illustrates the concept that markets usually lead to efficiency. Any seller who wants to sell a book for at least $X does indeed sell to someone who is willing to buy a book for $X. As a result, there is no way to change how used textbooks are distributed among buyers and sellers that would make one person better off without making someone else worse off.
   b. This illustrates the concept that there are gains from trade. Students here trade tutoring services based upon their different abilities in academic subjects.
   c. This illustrates the concept that when markets don't achieve efficiency, government intervention can improve society's welfare. In this case the market, left alone, will permit bars and nightclubs to impose costs on their neighbours in the form of loud music, costs that the bars and nightclubs have no incentive to take into account. This is an inefficient outcome because society as a whole can be made better off if bars and nightclubs are induced to reduce their noise.
   d. This illustrates the concept that resources should be used as efficiently as possible to achieve society's goals. By closing neighbourhood clinics and shifting funds to the main hospital, better health care can be provided, and at a lower cost.
   e. This illustrates the concept that markets move towards equilibrium. Here, because books of the same level of wear and tear sell for about the same price, no buyer and no seller can be made better off by engaging in a trade different than he or she undertook. This means that the market for used textbooks has moved to an equilibrium.
2. **a.** No. Many students should want to change their behaviour and switch to eating at the restaurants. Therefore the situation described is not an equilibrium. An equilibrium will be established when students are equally as well off eating at the restaurant as eating at the dining hall—which would happen if, say, prices at the restaurants are higher than at the dining hall.
   b. Yes. By changing your behaviour and riding the bus you will not be made better off. Therefore, you have no incentive to change your behaviour.

Chapter Two

Check Your Understanding 2-1

1. a. False. An increase in the resources available to Tom for use in producing coconuts and fish changes his production possibility frontier by shifting it outwards. This is because he can now produce more fish and coconuts than before. In the figure below, the green line represents Tom's old production possibility frontier, while the red line represents the new production possibility frontier that results from an increase in resources.

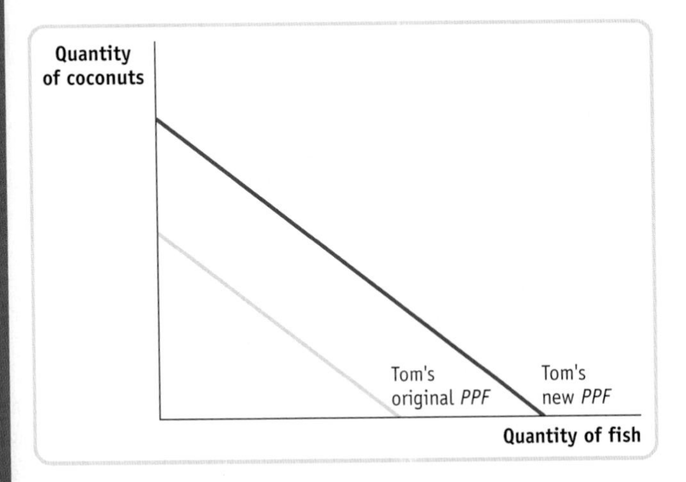

b. True. A technological change that allows Tom to catch more fish for any amount of coconuts gathered results in a change in his production possibility frontier. This is illustrated in the figure below: the new production possibility frontier is represented by the red line, while the old production possibility frontier is represented by the green line. Since the maximum amount of coconuts that Tom can gather is the same as before, the new production possibility frontier intersects the vertical axis at the same point as the old frontier. But since the maximum possible number of fish is now greater then before, the new frontier intersects the horizontal axis to the right of the old frontier.

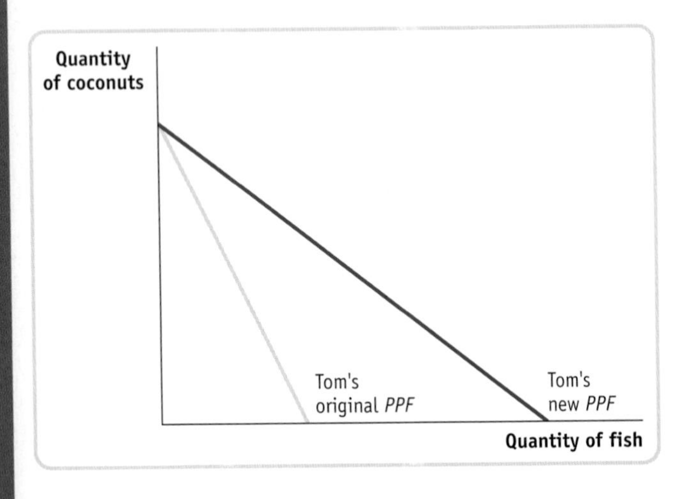

c. False. The production possibility frontier illustrates how much an economy must give up of one good in order to get more of another good only when resources are used efficiently. If an economy is producing inefficiently—that is, inside the frontier—then it does not have to give up a unit of one good in order to get another unit of the other good. Instead, by becoming more efficient, this economy can have more of both goods.

2. a. Canada has an absolute advantage in automobile production because it takes fewer Canadian workers (6) to produce a car in one day than Italian workers (8). Likewise, Canada also has an absolute advantage in washing machine production: it takes fewer Canadians (2) to produce a washing machine in one day than Italians (3).

b. In Italy the opportunity cost of a washing machine in terms of an automobile is $3/8$: $3/8$ of a car can be produced with the same number of workers and in the same time it takes to produce 1 washing machine. In Canada the opportunity cost of a washing machine in terms of an automobile is $2/6 = 1/3$ $1/3$: $1/3$ of a car can be produced with the same number of workers, and in the same time it takes to produce 1 washing machine. Since $1/3 < 3/8$, Canada has a comparative advantage in the production of washing machines: to produce a washing machine, only $1/3$ of a car must be given up in Canada, while $3/8$ of a car must be given up in Italy. This means that Italy has a comparative advantage in automobiles. This can be checked as follows. The opportunity cost of an automobile in terms of a washing machine in Italy is $8/3$, equal to $2\frac{2}{3}$: $2\frac{2}{3}$ washing machines can be produced in the time it takes to produce 1 car in Italy. And the opportunity cost of an automobile in terms of a washing machine in Canada is $6/2$, equal to 3: 3 washing machines can be produced in the time it takes to produce 1 car in Canada.

c. The greatest gains are realized when each country specializes in producing the good for which it has a comparative advantage. Hence Canada should specialize in producing washing machines, while Italy should specialize in producing automobiles.

3. An increase in the amount of money spent by households results in an increase in the flow of goods to households. This, in turn, generates an increase in demand for factors of production by firms. Therefore there is an increase in the number of jobs in the economy.

Check Your Understanding 2-2

1. a. This is a normative statement because it stipulates what should be done. In addition, it may have no "right" answer. That is, should people be prevented from all dangerous personal behaviour if they enjoy that behaviour—like skydiving? Your answer may depend upon your point of view.

b. This is a positive statement because it provides a description of fact.

2. a. True. Economists often have different value judgments about the desirability of a particular social goal. But despite those differences in value judgments, they will tend to agree that once society has decided to pursue a given social goal, society should adopt the most efficient policy to achieve that goal. Hence economists are likely to agree on adopting policy choice B.

b. False. Disagreements between economists are more likely to arise because they base their conclusions on different models or because they have different value judgments about the desirability of the policy.

c. False. Deciding which goals a society should try to achieve is a matter of value judgments, not a question of economic analysis.

Chapter Three

Check Your Understanding 3-1

1. **a.** The demand for umbrellas is higher at any given price. This is a rightward *shift of* the demand curve, since at any given price the quantity demanded increases. But this implies that any specific quantity can now be sold at a higher price.

   b. The quantity of weekend calls demanded increases in response to a reduction in price. This is a *movement along* the demand curve for weekend calls.

   c. The demand for roses increases the week of Valentine's Day although prices are higher. This is a rightward *shift of* the demand curve.

   d. The quantity of gasoline demanded falls in response to an increase in price. This is a *movement along* the demand curve.

Check Your Understanding 3-2

1. **a.** The quantity of houses supplied rises as a result of an increase in prices. This is a *movement along* the supply curve.

   b. The supply of strawberries is higher even at lower prices. This is a rightward *shift of* the supply curve.

   c. The supply of labor is lower at any given wage. This is a leftward *shift of* the supply curve, so in order to attract workers, firms have to offer higher wages (that is, a movement along the new supply curve).

   d. The quantity of labor supplied increases in response to an increase in wages. This is a *movement along* the supply curve.

   e. The supply of berths is higher at lower prices. This is a rightward *shift of* the supply curve.

Check Your Understanding 3-3

1. **a.** At the original price, the quantity of wheat supplied exceeds the quantity of wheat demanded at current prices. This is a case of surplus. The price of wheat will fall.

   b. At the original price, the quantity of hotel rooms supplied exceeds the quantity demanded. This is a case of surplus. The rates for hotel rooms will fall.

   c. At the original price, the quantity of second-hand snowblowers demanded exceeds the quantity supplied. This is a case of shortage. The price of second-hand snowblowers will rise.

Check Your Understanding 3-4

1. **a.** The market for large cars: This is a rightward shift in demand induced by a decrease in the price of a complement, gasoline. As a result of the shift, the price of large cars will rise and the number of large cars sold will increase.

   b. The market for fresh paper made from recycled paper: This is a rightward shift in supply due to a technological innovation. As a result of this shift, the price of fresh paper made from recycled paper will fall, while the quantity supplied will increase.

   c. The market for movies at a cinema: This is a leftward shift in demand induced by a decrease in the price of a substitute, pay-per-view movies. As a result of this shift, movie tickets will get cheaper and the number of people who go to cinemas will decrease.

2. Upon the announcement of the next generation chip, the demand curve for computers using earlier chips shifts leftward, as demand decreases, while the supply curve for these computers shifts rightward, as supply increases. If demand decreases relatively more than supply increases, then the equilibrium quantity decreases, as shown here:

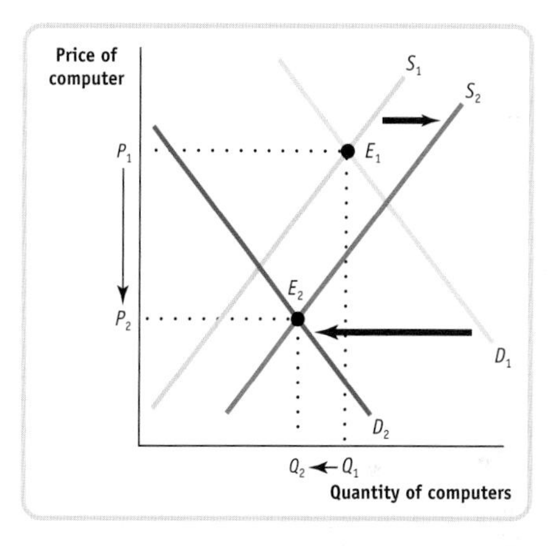

And if supply increases relatively more than demand decreases, then the equilibrium quantity increases, as shown here:

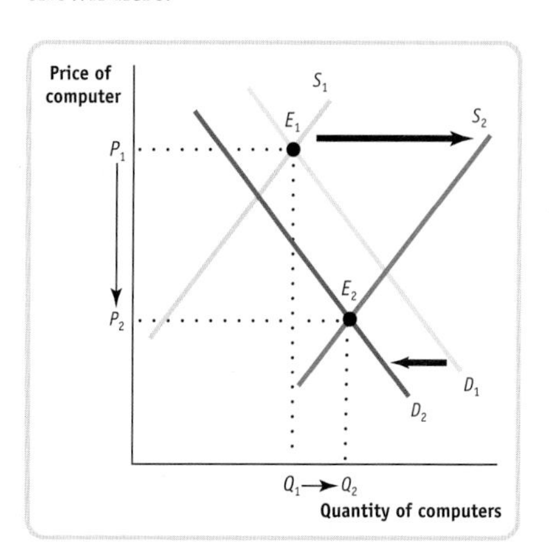

Note that in both cases, the equilibrium price falls.

Chapter Four

Check Your Understanding 4-1

1. **a.** Fewer homeowners are willing to rent out their driveways because the price ceiling has caused a decrease in the price they receive. This reflects the concept that the quantity supplied falls as the price falls. It is shown in the diagram by the movement from point *E* to point *A* along the supply curve.

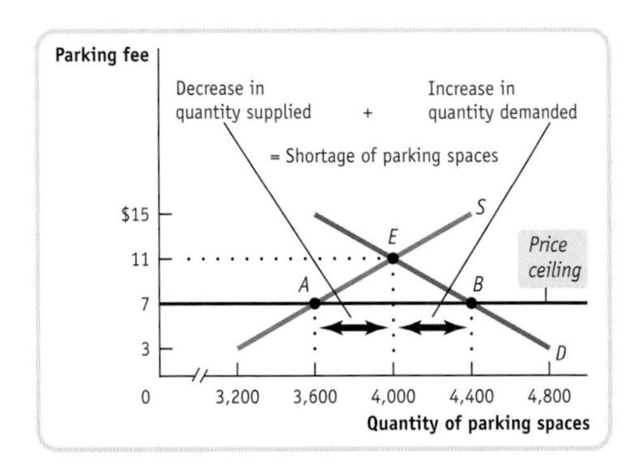

b. The quantity demanded increases by 400 spaces as the price falls. Thus, at a lower price more football fans are willing to drive and rent a parking space. It is shown in the diagram by the movement from point *E* to point *C* along the demand curve.

c. Under a price ceiling, the quantity demanded exceeds the quantity supplied; as a result, shortages arise. In this case, there will be a shortage of 800 parking spaces. The shortage is shown by the horizontal distance between points *A* and *B*.

d. Price ceilings result in wasted resources. The additional time spent by football fans in order to guarantee a parking space is wasted time.

e. Price ceilings lead to inefficient allocation of a good—here, the parking spaces—to consumers.

f. Price ceilings lead to black markets.

2. **a.** False. By lowering the price that producers receive, price ceilings lead to a decrease in the quantity supplied.

b. True. Price ceilings lead to a lower quantity supplied than is supplied in a free market. As a result, some consumers who would have been willing to pay the market price, and therefore would have gotten the good in a free market, are unable to obtain it when a price ceiling is imposed.

c. True. Those producers who still sell the product now receive less for it, and are therefore worse off. In addition, because the price falls, some producers who previously sold the product will no longer find it worthwhile to offer the product at all and will therefore also be made worse off.

Check Your Understanding 4-2

1. **a.** Some gas station owners will benefit from getting a higher price. Point *A* indicates the sales (0.8 million litres) made by these station owners. But some will lose; there are those who made sales at the market price of $1.10 but do not make sales at the regulated price of $1.30. These missed sales are indicated on the graph by the fall in the quantity demanded along the demand curve, from point *E* to point *A*. Overall, the effect on station owners is ambiguous.

b. Those who buy gas at the higher price of $1.30 probably will receive better service; this is an example of *inefficiently high quality* caused by a price floor as gas station owners compete on quality rather than price. But opponents are correct to claim that consumers are generally worse off—those who buy at $1.30 would have been happy to buy at $1.10, and many who were willing to buy at a price between $1.30 and $1.10 are now unwilling to buy. This is indicated on the graph by the fall in the quantity demanded along the demand curve, from point *E* to point *A*.

c. Proponents are wrong because consumers and some gas station owners are hurt by the price floor, which creates missed opportunities—desirable transactions between consumers and station owners that never take place. Moreover, the inefficiency of wasted resources arises as consumers spend time and money driving to other provinces or to the United States. The price floor tempts people to engage in black market activity. With the price floor of $1.30, only 0.8 million litres are sold. But at prices between $1.30 and $1.10 per litre, there are drivers who cumulatively want to buy more than 0.8 million litres and owners who are willing to sell to them, a situation likely to lead to illegal activity.

Check Your Understanding 4-3

1. **a.** The price of a litre is $1.60 since the quantity demanded at this price is 10 million: $1.60 is the *demand price* of 10 million litres. This is represented by point A in the accompanying figure.

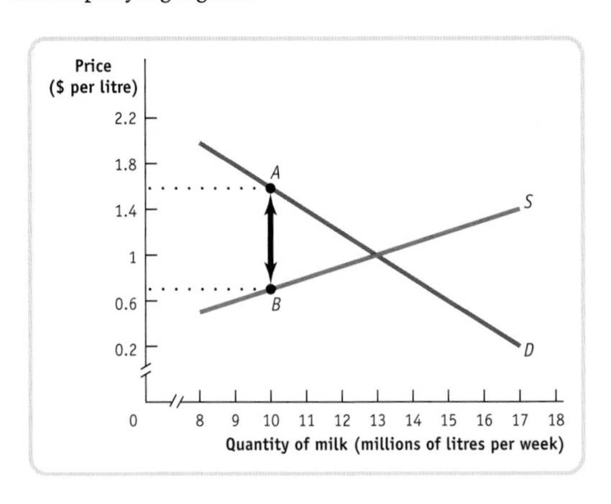

b. At 10 million litres, the supply price is $0.70, represented by point *B* in the figure. The wedge between the demand price of $1.60 and the supply price of $0.70 is the quota rent per litre, $0.90. This is represented in the figure by the vertical distance between points *A* and *B*.

2. a. At 12 million litres, the demand price is $1.20, indicated by point *A* on the accompanying figure, and the supply price is $0.90, indicated by point *B*. The quota rent is the difference between the demand price and the supply price, in this case, $0.30 per litre.

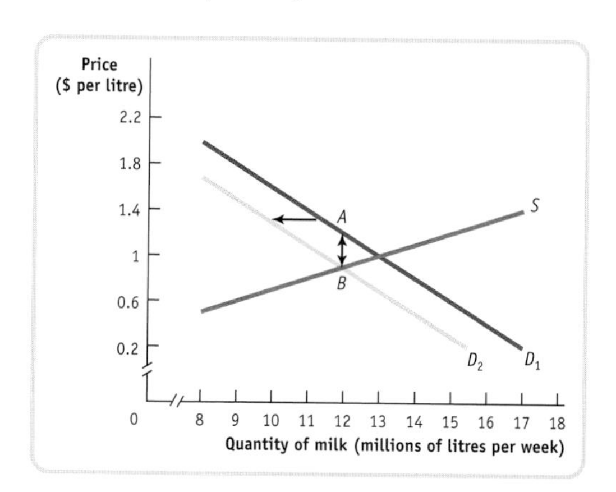

b. The figure shows how a fall in demand, represented by a leftward shift of the demand curve from D_1 to D_2, eliminates the effect of a quota limit of 12 million litres. The new market equilibrium occurs at point *B*, and the equilibrium quantity is equal to the quota limit; as a result, the quota has no effect on the market.

Check Your Understanding 4-4

1. a. Under the quota, only 9 million pint boxes of blueberries are transacted. We can limit the amount of blueberries that growers want to sell to 9 million pint boxes by setting the supply price to $3.50, as indicated by point *D* in the accompanying figure, which is derived from the same data as Figure 4-4. Similarly, we can limit the amount of blueberries consumers want to buy by setting the demand price to $5, as indicated by point *C* in the figure. The difference between these two prices, $1.50, is therefore equal to the tax that reduces sales to only 9 million pint boxes of blueberries, indicated by the vertical distance between points *C* and *D*. Thus a tax of $1.50 per pint box generates the same inefficiency as a quota of 9 million pint boxes.

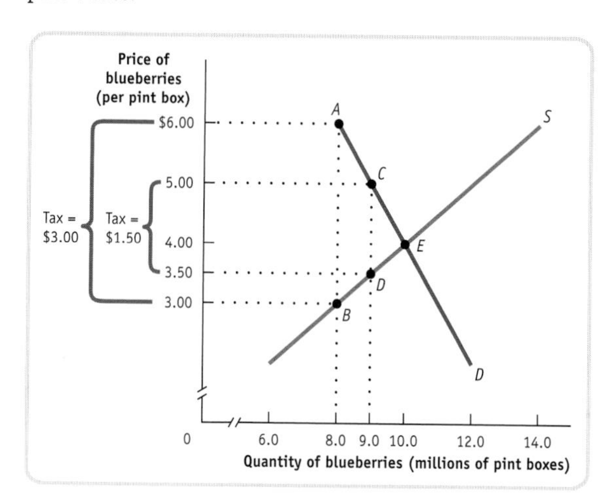

b. To answer this question, one must find a supply price and a demand price that generate the same quantity of blueberries but differ by $3. Examination of the supply and demand schedules shows that the supply price of $3 (indicated by point *B*) and the demand price of $6 (indicated by point *A*) satisfy these conditions: they give rise to the same quantity transacted, 8 million pint boxes, and they differ by $3. Therefore, a quota of 8 million pint boxes will generate the same level of inefficiency as a tax of $3.

c. For part a: The unrestricted equilibrium price is $4 per pound. So consumers bear $1($5 – $4 = $1) of the $1.50 tax, while producers bear $0.50($4 – $3.50 = $0.50). For part b: Here consumers bear $2($6 – $4 = $2) of the total tax of $3, while producers bear $1($4 – $3 = $1).

Chapter Five

Check Your Understanding 5-1

1. By the midpoint method, the percent change in the price of strawberries is

$$\frac{\$1.50 - \$1.00}{(\$1.50 + \$1.00)/2} \times 100 = \frac{\$0.50}{\$1.25} \times 100 = 40\%$$

Similarly, the percent change in the quantity of strawberries demanded is

$$\frac{200{,}000 - 100{,}000}{(100{,}000 + 200{,}000)/2} \times 100 = \frac{100{,}000}{150{,}000} \times 100 = 67\%$$

Therefore the price elasticity of demand using the midpoint method is (67%/40%) = 1.7.

2. By the midpoint method, the percent change in the quantity of movie tickets in going from 4,000 tickets to 5,000 tickets is

$$\frac{5{,}000 - 4{,}000}{(4{,}000 + 5{,}000)/2} \times 100 = \frac{1{,}000}{4{,}500} \times 100 = 22\%$$

Since the price elasticity of demand is 1 at the current consumption level, it will take a 22% drop in the price of movie tickets to generate a 22% increase in quantity demanded.

3. Since price rises, we know that quantity demanded must fall. Given the current price of $0.50, a $0.05 increase in price represents a 10% change, using the method in Equation 5-2. This implies that

$$\frac{\%\text{ change in quantity demanded}}{10\%} = 1.2$$

so that (% change in quantity demanded) is 12%. A 12% decrease in quantity demanded represents 100,000 × 0.12 sandwiches, or 12,000.

Check Your Understanding 5-2

1. a. Elastic demand. Consumers are highly responsive to changes in price. For an increase in price, the quantity effect, which tends to lower revenue, outweighs the price effect, which tends to raise revenue. Overall, this leads to a fall in total revenue.

b. Unit-elastic demand. Here the revenue lost to the price decline is exactly equal to the revenue gained from higher sales. The quantity effect exactly offsets the price effect.

c. Inelastic demand. Consumers are relatively unresponsive to price. For consumers to purchase a given percent increase in output, the price must fall by an even greater percent. The price effect of a fall in price, which tends to lower revenue, outweighs the quantity effect, which tends to raise revenue. As a result, total revenue decreases.

d. Inelastic demand. Consumers are relatively unresponsive to price, so a given percent fall in output is accompanied by an even greater percent rise in price. The price effect of a rise in price, which tends to raise revenue, outweighs the quantity effect, which tends to lower revenue. As a result, total revenue increases.

2. a. Once someone has been bitten by a venomous snake, his or her demand for an antidote is very likely to be perfectly inelastic because there is no substitute and it is necessary for survival. The demand curve will be vertical, at a quantity equal to the needed dose.

b. Students' demand for green erasers is likely to be perfectly elastic because there are easily available substitutes: non-green erasers. The demand curve will be horizontal, at a price equal to the available price of non-green erasers.

Check Your Understanding 5-3

1. By the midpoint method, the percent increase in Kathy's income is:

$$\frac{\$18{,}000 - \$12{,}000}{(\$12{,}000 + \$18{,}000)/2} \times 100 = \frac{\$6{,}000}{\$15{,}000} \times 100 = 40\%$$

Similarly, the percent increase in her consumption of CDs is

$$\frac{40 - 10}{(10 + 40)/2} \times 100 = \frac{30}{25} \times 100 = 120\%$$

Kathy's income elasticity of demand for CDs is therefore 120%/40% = 3.

2. Sanjay's consumption of expensive restaurant meals will fall more than 10% because a given percent change in income (10% here) induces a larger percent change in consumption of a superior good.

3. The cross-price elasticity of demand is 5%/20% = 0.25. Since the cross-price elasticity of demand is positive, the two goods are substitutes.

Check Your Understanding 5-4

1. By the midpoint method, the percent change in the number of hours of web-design services contracted is:

$$\frac{500{,}000 - 300{,}000}{(300{,}000 + 500{,}000)/2} \times 100 = \frac{200{,}000}{400{,}000} \times 100 = 50\%$$

Similarly, the percent change in the price of web-design services is:

$$\frac{\$150 - \$100}{(\$100 + \$150)/2} \times 100 = \frac{\$50}{\$125} \times 100 = 40\%$$

The elasticity of supply is 50%/40% = 1.25; hence supply is elastic.

2. True. An increase in demand raises price. If the price elasticity of supply of milk is low, then relatively little additional supply will be forthcoming as the price rises. As a result, the price of milk will rise substantially to satisfy the higher demand for milk. If the price elasticity of supply is high, then a relatively large amount of additional supply will be produced as price rises. In this case, the price of milk will rise only by a little to satisfy the higher demand for milk.

3. False. It is true that long-run price elasticities of supply are generally higher than short-run elasticities of supply. But this means that the short-run supply curves are generally steeper, not flatter, than the long-run supply curves.

4. True. When supply is perfectly elastic, the supply curve is a horizontal line at the supply price. A change in demand therefore has no effect on price; it only affects the quantity bought and sold.

Check Your Understanding 5-5

1. The fact that demand is very inelastic means that consumers will reduce their demand for textbooks very little in response to an increase in the price caused by the tax. The fact that supply is somewhat elastic means that suppliers will respond to the fall in the price by reducing supply. As a result, the incidence of the tax will fall heavily on consumers of economics textbooks and very little on publishers, as shown in the accompanying figure.

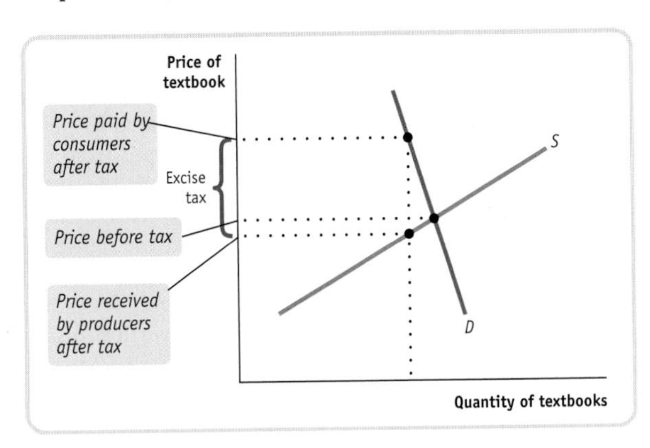

2. True. When a substitute is readily available, demand is elastic. That implies that producers cannot easily pass on the cost of the tax to consumers, because consumers will respond to an increased price by switching to the substitute. Furthermore, when producers have difficulty adjusting the amount of the good produced, supply is inelastic. That is, producers cannot easily reduce output in response to a lower price net of the tax. So the tax burden will fall more heavily on producers than consumers.

3. The fact that supply is very inelastic means that producers will reduce their supply of bottled water very little in response to the fall in price caused by the tax. Demand, on the other hand, will fall in response to an increase in price because demand is somewhat elastic. As a result, the incidence of the tax will fall heavily on producers of bottled spring water and very little on consumers, as shown in the accompanying figure.

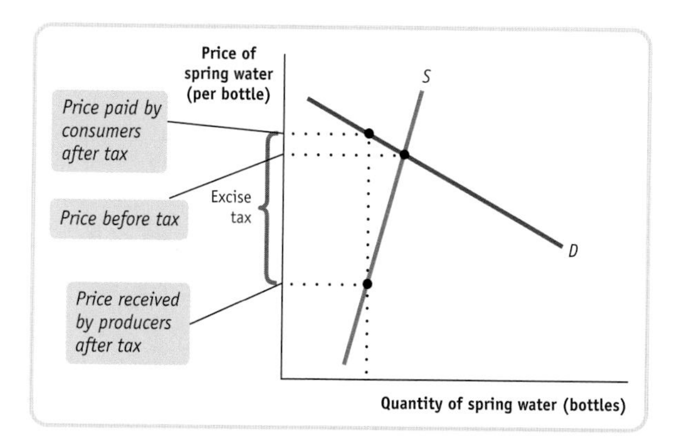

4. True. The lower the elasticity of supply, the more the burden of a tax will fall on producers rather than consumers, other things equal.

Chapter Six

Check Your Understanding 6-1

1. A consumer buys each pepper if the price of a pepper is less than (or just equal to) the consumer's willingness to pay for that pepper. The demand schedule is constructed by asking how many peppers will be demanded at any price. The accompanying table illustrates the demand schedule.

Price of pepper	Quantity of peppers demanded	Quantity of peppers demanded by Casey	Quantity of peppers demanded by Josie
$0.90	1	1	0
0.80	2	1	1
0.70	3	2	1
0.60	4	2	2
0.50	5	3	2
0.40	6	3	3
0.30	8	4	4
0.20	8	4	4
0.10	8	4	4
0.00	8	4	4

When the price is $0.40, Casey's consumer surplus from the first pepper is $0.50, from his second pepper $0.30, from his third pepper $0.10, and he does not buy any more peppers. Casey's individual consumer surplus therefore is $0.90. Josie's consumer surplus from her first pepper is $0.40, from her second pepper $0.20, from her third pepper $0.00 (she is just indifferent between buying it and not buying it, so let's assume she does buy it), and she does not buy any more peppers. Josie's individual consumer surplus therefore is $0.60. Total consumer surplus at a price of $0.40 is therefore $0.90 + $0.60 = $1.50.

Check Your Understanding 6-2

1. A producer supplies each pepper if the price of a pepper is greater than (or just equal to) the producer's cost of producing that pepper. The supply schedule is constructed by asking how many peppers will be supplied at any price. The accompanying table illustrates the supply schedule.

Price of pepper	Quantity of peppers supplied	Quantity of peppers supplied by Cara	Quantity of peppers supplied by Jamie
$0.90	8	4	4
0.80	7	4	3
0.70	7	4	3
0.60	6	4	2
0.50	5	3	2
0.40	4	3	1
0.30	3	2	1
0.20	2	2	0
0.10	2	2	0
0.00	0	0	0

When the price is $0.70, Cara's producer surplus from the first pepper is $0.60, from her second pepper $0.60, from her third pepper $0.30, from her fourth pepper $0.10, and she does not supply any more peppers. Cara's individual producer surplus therefore is $1.60. Jamie's producer surplus from his first pepper is $0.40, from his second pepper $0.20, from his third pepper $0.00 (he is just indifferent between supplying it and not supplying it, so let's assume he does supply it), and he does not supply any more peppers. Jamie's individual producer surplus therefore is $0.60. Total producer surplus at a price of $0.70 is therefore $1.60 + $0.60 = $2.20.

Check Your Understanding 6-3

1. The quantity demanded equals the quantity supplied at a price of $0.50, the equilibrium price. At that price, a total quantity of five peppers will be bought and sold. Casey will buy three peppers and receive consumer surplus of $0.40 on his first, $0.20 on his second, and $0.00 on his third pepper. Josie will buy two peppers and receive consumer surplus of $0.30 on her first and $0.10 on her second pepper. Total consumer surplus is therefore $1.00. Cara will supply three peppers and receive producer surplus of $0.40 on her first, $0.40 on her second, and $0.10 on her third pepper. Jamie will supply two peppers and receive producer surplus of $0.20 on his first and $0.00 on his second pepper. Total producer surplus is therefore $1.10. Total surplus in this market is therefore $1.00 + $1.10 = $2.10.

2. **a.** If Josie consumes one less pepper, she loses $0.60 (her willingness to pay for her second pepper), and if Casey consumes one more pepper, he gains $0.30 (his willingness to pay for his fourth pepper). This results in an overall loss of consumer surplus of $0.60 − $0.30 = $0.30.

b. Cara's cost of the last pepper she supplied (the third pepper) is $0.40, and Jamie's cost of producing one more (his third pepper) is $0.70. Total cost therefore increases by $0.70 – $0.40 = $0.30.

c. Josie's willingness to pay for her second pepper is $0.60; this is what she would lose if she were to consume one less pepper. And Cara's cost of producing her third pepper is $0.40; this is what she would save if she were to produce one less pepper. If we therefore reduced quantity by one pepper, we would lose $0.60 – $0.40 = $0.20 of surplus.

Check Your Understanding 6-4

1. a. At a price paid by consumers of $0.70, Casey's consumer surplus is $0.20 from his first pepper (he loses $0.20 compared to the market equilibrium), $0.00 from his second pepper (he loses $0.20), and he no longer buys the third pepper. Josie's consumer surplus is $0.10 from her first pepper (she loses $0.20), and she no longer buys the second pepper (she loses $0.10 of surplus that she previously got from that second pepper). So the loss in consumer surplus is $0.70.

b. At a price received by producers of $0.30, Cara's producer surplus is $0.20 from her first pepper (she loses $0.20), $0.20 from her second pepper (she loses $0.20), and she no longer produces the third pepper (she loses $0.10 that she previously got from that third pepper). Jamie's producer surplus is $0.00 from his first pepper (he loses $0.20), and he no longer produces his second pepper. So the loss in producer surplus is $0.70.

c. Since now three peppers are sold, and the tax on each is $0.40, the government tax revenue is 3 × $0.40 = $1.20.

d. Introduction of the tax resulted in a loss of total surplus of $1.40. Of that amount, $1.20 went to the government in the form of tax revenue. But $0.20 is lost: that is the amount of deadweight loss from this tax.

2. a. The demand for gasoline is inelastic because there is no close substitute for gasoline itself, and it is difficult for drivers to arrange substitutes for driving such as taking public transportation. As a result, the deadweight loss from a tax on gasoline would be relatively small.

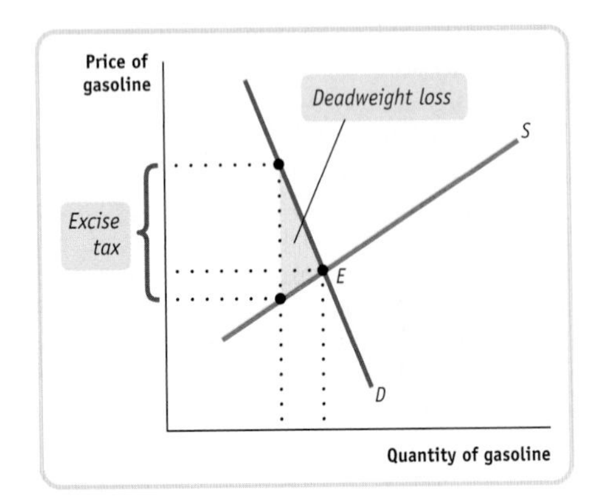

b. The demand for milk chocolate bars is elastic because there are close substitutes: dark chocolate bars, milk chocolate kisses, etc. As a result, the deadweight loss from a tax on milk chocolate bars would be relatively large.

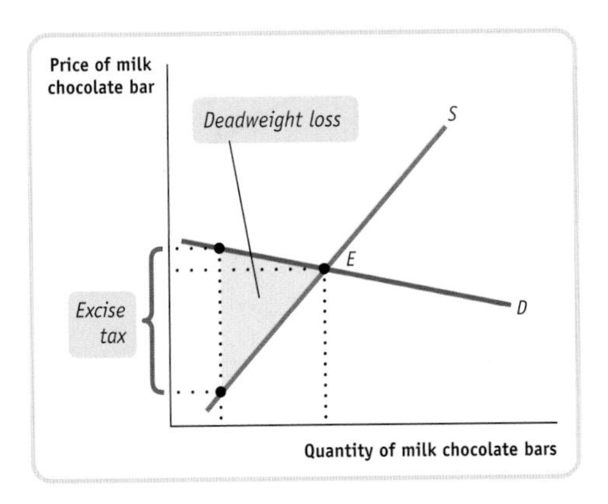

Chapter Seven

Check Your Understanding Question 7-1

1. a. Supplies are an explicit cost since they require an outlay of money.

b. If the basement can be used in some other way that generates money, such as renting it to a student, then the implicit cost is the money forgone. Otherwise, the implicit cost is zero.

c. Wages are an explicit cost.

d. By using the van for their business, Karma and Don forgo the money they could have gained by selling it. So the use of the van is an implicit cost.

e. Karma's forgone wages from her job are an implicit cost.

Check Your Understanding 7-2

1. a. The marginal cost of doing your laundry is the opportunity cost of your time spent doing laundry today—that is, the value you would place on spending time today on your next best alternative activity, like seeing a movie. The marginal benefit is having more clean clothes today to choose from.

b. The marginal cost of changing your oil is the opportunity cost of time spent changing your oil now, as well as the explicit cost of the oil change. The marginal benefit is the improvement in the car's performance.

c. The marginal benefit of another jalapeno on your nachos is the pleasant taste that you receive from it. The marginal cost is the unpleasant feeling of a burning mouth that you receive from it, plus any explicit cost of the jalapeno.

d. The marginal benefit of hiring another worker in your company is the value of the output that worker produces. The marginal cost is the wage you must pay that worker.

e. The marginal benefit of another dose of the drug is the value of the reduction in the patient's disease. The marginal cost is value of the increased side effects from this additional dose.

f. The marginal benefit of assigning one more soldier to your invasion force is the increased probability of a successful invasion generated by that extra soldier. The marginal cost is the decreased probability of success in the alternative project for which you could use that soldier, such as defending your borders.

2. a. As can be seen from Table 7-6, the optimal quantity of lawns is 6 lawns when marginal cost is constant at $18.50. At the 6th lawn, Felix's marginal benefit is $19.00, exceeding marginal cost by $0.50. At the 7th lawn, however, marginal benefit is $18.00, implying a loss of $0.50 on the 7th lawn if he mows it. His total net gain is equal to ($35 – $18.50) + ($30 – $18.50) + ($26 – $18.50) + ($23 – $18.50) + ($21 – $18.50) + ($19 – $18.50) = $43.

b. The lawn that generates the highest marginal benefit is the 1st lawn; it generates $35 in marginal benefit. So the optimal quantity is 0 when marginal cost is always greater than $35. In that case, it would never benefit Felix to do even the 1st lawn. In going from the 3rd to 4th lawn, marginal benefit goes from $26 to $23. So any marginal cost lower than $26 but higher than $23 implies an optimal quantity of 3.

Check Your Understanding 7-3

1. a. Your sunk cost is $8,000 because none of the $8,000 you spent on the truck is recoverable.

b. Your sunk cost is $4,000 because 50% of the $8,000 spent on the truck is recoverable.

2. a. This is an invalid argument because the time and money already spent are a sunk cost.

b. This is also an invalid argument because what you should have done two years ago is irrelevant to what you should do now.

c. This is a valid argument because it recognizes that sunk costs are irrelevant to what you should do now.

d. This is a valid argument given that you are concerned about disappointing your parents. But your parents' views are irrational because they do not recognize that the time already spent is a sunk cost.

Check Your Understanding 7-4

1. a. The net present value of Project A is unaffected by the interest rate since it is money received today; its present value is still $100. The net present value of Project B is now (–$10 + $115/1.02) = $102.75. The net present value of Project C is now ($119 – $20/1.02) = $99.39. Project B is now preferred.

b. When the interest rate is lower, the cost of waiting for money that arrives in the future is lower. For example, at a 10% interest rate, a dollar arriving 1 year from today is worth only 1/1.10 = $0.91. But when the interest rate is 2%, a dollar arriving 1 year from today is worth 1/1.02 = $0.98, a sizeable increase. As a result, Project B, which has a benefit 1 year from today, becomes more attractive. And Project C, which has a cost 1 year from today, becomes less attractive.

Chapter Eight

Check Your Understanding 8-1

1. a. The fixed input is the 10-ton machine, and the variable input is electricity.

b. As one can see from the declining numbers in the third column of the accompanying table, electricity does indeed exhibit diminishing returns: the marginal product of each additional kilowatt of electricity is less than that of the previous kilowatt.

Quantity of electricity (kilowatts)	Quantity of ice (kilograms)	Marginal product of electricity (kilograms per kilowatt)
0	0	
		1,000
1	1,000	
		800
2	1,800	
		600
3	2,400	
		400
4	2,800	

c. A 50% increase in the size of the fixed input means that Bernie now has a 15-ton machine. So the fixed input is now the 15-ton machine. Since it generates a 100% increase in output for any given amount of electricity, the quantity of output and marginal product are now as shown in the accompanying table:

Quantity of electricity (kilowatts)	Quantity of ice (kilograms)	Marginal product of electricity (kilograms per kilowatt)
0	0	
		2,000
1	2,000	
		1,600
2	3,600	
		1,200
3	4,800	
		800
4	5,600	

Check Your Understanding 8-2

1. a. As shown in the accompanying table, the marginal cost for each pie is found by multiplying the marginal cost of the previous pie by 1.5. Variable cost for each output level is found by summing the marginal cost for all the pies produced to reach that output level. So, for example, the variable cost of 3 pies is $1.00 + $1.50 + $2.25 = $4.75. Average fixed cost for Q pies is calculated as $9.00/Q since fixed cost is $9.00. Average variable cost for Q pies is equal to variable cost for the Q pies divided by Q; for example, the average variable cost of five pies is $13.19/5, or approximately $2.64. Finally, average total cost can be calculated two equivalent ways: as *TC*/*Q*, or as *AVC* + *AFC*.

Quantity of pies	Marginal cost of pie	Variable cost	Average fixed cost of pie	Average variable cost of pie	Average total cost of pie
0		$0.00	—	—	—
	$1.00				
1		1.00	$9.00	$1.00	$10.00
	1.50				
2		2.50	4.50	1.25	5.75
	2.25				
3		4.75	3.00	1.58	4.58
	3.38				
4		8.13	2.25	2.03	4.28
	5.06				
5		13.19	1.80	2.64	4.44
	7.59				
6		20.78	1.50	3.46	4.96

b. The spreading effect dominates the diminishing returns effect when average total cost is falling: the fall in *AFC* dominates the rise in *AVC* for pies 1 to 4. The diminishing returns effect dominates when average total cost is rising: the rise in *AVC* dominates the fall in *AFC* for pies 5 and 6.

c. Alicia's minimum-cost output is 4 pies; this generates the lowest average total cost, $4.28. When output is less than 4, the marginal cost of a pie is less than the average total cost of the pies already produced. So making an additional pie lowers average total cost. For example, the marginal cost of pie 3 is $2.25, while the average total cost of pies 1 and 2 is $5.75. So making pie 3 lowers Alicia's average total cost to $4.58, equal to (2 × $5.75 + $2.25)/3. When output is more than 4, the marginal cost of a pie is greater than the average total cost of the pies already produced. Consequently, making an additional pie raises average total cost. So, although the marginal cost of pie 6 is $7.59, the average total cost of pies 1 through 5 is $4.44. Making pie 6 raises average total cost to $4.96, equal to (5 × $4.44 + $7.59)/6.

Check Your Understanding 8-3

1. a. The accompanying table shows the average total cost of producing 12,000, 22,000, and 30,000 units for each of the three choices of fixed cost. For example, if the firm makes choice 1, the total cost of producing 12,000 units of output is $8,000 + 12,000 × $1.00 = $20,000. The average total cost of producing 12,000 units of output is therefore $20,000/12,000 = $1.67. The other average total costs are calculated similarly.

	12,000 units	22,000 units	30,000 units
Average total cost from choice 1	$1.67	$1.36	$1.27
Average total cost from choice 2	1.75	1.30	1.15
Average total cost from choice 3	2.25	1.34	1.05

Therefore, if the firm wanted to produce 12,000 units, it would make choice 1 because this gives it the lowest average total cost. If it wanted to produce 22,000 units, it would make choice 2. If it wanted to produce 30,000 units, it would make choice 3.

b. Having historically produced 12,000 units, the firm would have adopted choice 1. When producing 12,000 units, the firm would have had an average total cost of $1.67. When output jumps to 22,000, the firm cannot alter its choice of fixed cost in the short run, so its average total cost in the short run will be $1.36. In the long run, however, it will adopt choice 2, making its average total cost fall to $1.30.

c. If the firm believes that the increase in demand is temporary, it should not alter its fixed cost from choice 1 because choice 2 generates higher average total cost as soon as output falls back to its original quantity of 12,000 units: $1.75 versus $1.67.

2. a. This firm is likely to experience constant returns to scale. To increase output, the firm must hire more workers, purchase more computers, and pay additional telephone charges. Because these inputs are easily available, their long-run costs are unlikely to change as output increases.

b. This firm is likely to experience diseconomies of scale. As the firm takes on more projects, the costs of communication and coordination required to implement the expertise of the firm's owner are likely to increase.

c. This firm is likely to experience economies of scale. Because diamond mining requires a large initial set-up cost for excavation equipment, long-run average total cost will fall as output increases.

Chapter Nine

Check Your Understanding 9-1

1. a. With only two producers in the world, each producer will represent a sizable share of the market. Therefore the industry will not be perfectly competitive.

b. Because each producer of gas from the North Sea has only a small market share of total world supply of natural gas, and since natural gas is a standardized product, the market for natural gas will be perfectly competitive.

c. Because each designer has a distinctive style, high-fashion clothes are not a standardized product. Therefore the market will not be perfectly competitive.

d. The market described here is the market in each city for tickets to hockey games. Since there are only one or two teams in each major city, each team will represent a sizable share of the market. Therefore, the market will not be perfectly competitive.

Check Your Understanding 9-2

1. a. The firm should shut down immediately when price is less than minimum average variable cost, the shut-down price. In the accompanying diagram, this is optimal for prices in the range 0 to P_1.

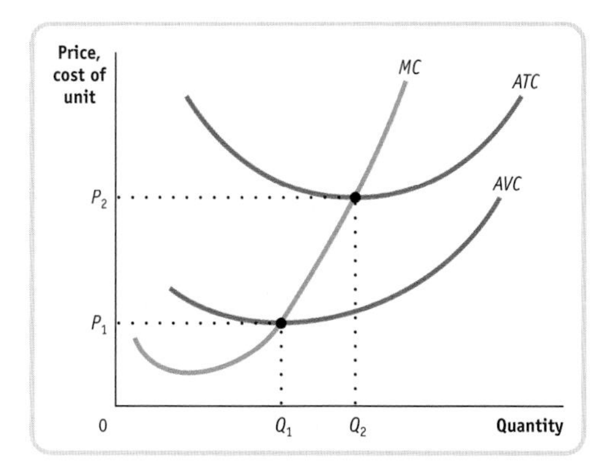

b. When price is greater than minimum average variable cost (the shut-down price) but less than minimum average total cost (the break-even price),the firm should continue to operate in the short-run even though it is incurring a loss. This is optimal for prices in the range P_1 to P_2 and quantities Q_1 to Q_2.

c. When price exceeds minimum average total cost (the break-even price) the firm makes a profit. This happens for prices in excess of P_2 and results in quantities greater than Q_2.

2. This is an example of a temporary shut-down by a firm when the market price lies below the shut-down price, the minimum average variable cost. In this case, the market price is the price of a lobster meal, and variable cost is the variable cost of serving such a meal, such as the cost of the lobster, employee wages, and so on. In this example, both the average variable cost curve and the market price of a lobster meal shift over time, due to seasonal changes. On the cost side, New Brunswick lobster shacks find that they have relatively low average variable cost during the summer, when cheap New Brunswick lobsters are available; during the rest of the year, their average variable cost is relatively high due to the high cost of imported lobsters, and the extra cost of heating the lobster shack. On the demand side, the dearth of tourist traffic implies less demand for lobster meals, and hence a lower market price. As a result of both sets of factors, minimum average variable cost lies below price during the summer months when the lobster shacks are open for business; but they close during the rest of the year, when price lies below their minimum average variable cost.

Check Your Understanding 9-3

1. a. A fall in the fixed cost of production generates a fall in the average total cost of production, and, in the short run, an increase in each firm's profit at the current output level. So in the long run new firms will enter the industry. The increase in supply drives down price and profits. Once profits are driven back to zero, entry will cease.

b. An increase in wages generates an increase in the average total cost of production at every output level. In the short run, firms incur losses at the current output level, and therefore in the long run some firms will exit the industry. As firms exit, supply decreases, price rises, and losses are reduced. Exit will cease once losses return to zero.

c. Price will rise as a result of the increased demand, leading to a short-run increase in profits at the current output level. In the long run, firms will enter the industry, generating an increase in supply, a fall in price, and a fall in profits. Once profits are driven back to zero, entry will cease.

d. The shortage of a key input causes that input's price to rise, resulting in an increase in average total costs for producers. Firms incur losses in the short run, and some firms will exit the industry in the long run. The fall in supply generates an increase in price and a decrease in losses. Exit will cease when losses have returned to zero.

2. In the accompanying diagram, point X_{MKT} in panel (b), the intersection of S_1 and D_1, represents the long-run industry equilibrium before the change in consumer tastes. When tastes change, demand decreases, and the industry moves in the short run to point Y_{MKT} in panel (b), at the intersection of the new demand curve D_2 and S_1, the short-run supply curve representing the same number of beef producers as in the original equilibrium at point X_{MKT}. As the market price falls, an individual firm reacts by producing less, as shown in panel (a), as long as the market price remains above the minimum average variable cost. If market price falls below average variable cost, the firm would shut down immediately. At point Y_{MKT} the price of beef is below minimum average total cost, creating losses for producers. This leads some firms to exit, which shifts the short-run industry supply curve leftward to S_2. A new long-run equilibrium is established at point Z_{MKT}. As this occurs, the market price rises again, and, as shown in panel (c), each remaining producer reacts by increasing output (here, from point Y to point Z). All remaining producers again make zero profits. The reduction in the quantity of beef supplied in the industry comes entirely from the exit of some producers out of the industry. The long-run industry supply curve is the curve labelled *LRS* in panel (b).

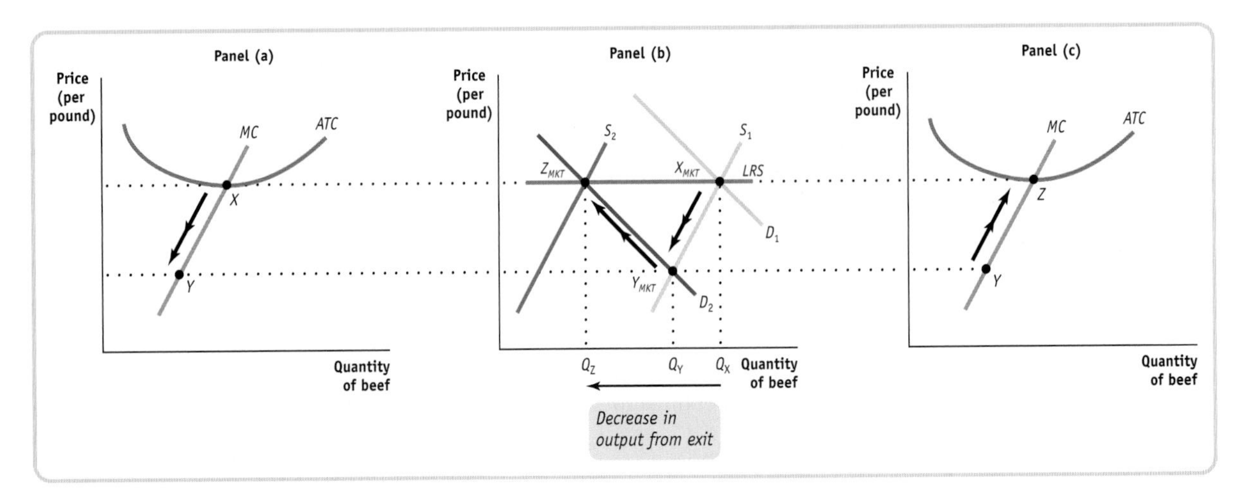

Chapter Ten

Check Your Understanding 10-1

1. Consuming a unit that generates negative marginal utility leaves the consumer with lower total utility than not consuming that unit at all. A rational consumer, a consumer who maximizes utility, would not do that. For example, from Figure 10-1 you can see that Cassie receives 64 utils if she consumes 8 clams; but if she consumes the 9th clam, she loses 1 util, netting her a total utility of only 63 utils. So whenever consuming a unit generates negative marginal utility, the consumer is made better off by not consuming that unit.

2. Since Jennifer has diminishing marginal utility of coffee, her first cup of coffee of the day generates the greatest increase in total utility for her. Her third and last cup of the day generates the least.

3. **a.** Mabel has increasing marginal utility since each additional unit consumed brings more additional enjoyment than the previous unit.

   b. Mei has constant marginal utility because each additional unit generates the same additional satisfaction as the previous unit.

   c. Dexter has diminishing marginal utility since the additional utility generated by a good restaurant meal is less when he consumes lots of them than when he consumed few of them.

Check Your Understanding 10-2

1. **a.** At a price of $5.00 for a movie ticket and income of $10.00, the maximum quantity of tickets that can be purchased is $10.00/$5.00 = 2, as shown in the accompanying diagram. This corresponds to the vertical intercept. At a price of $2.50 for a bucket of popcorn, the horizontal intercept—the maximum quantity of popcorn that can be purchased given the budget—is $10.00/$2.50 = 4. The slope of the budget line is equal to the rise over run: $-2/4 = -1/2$ (there is a negative sign because the line is downward sloping). The opportunity cost of a bucket of popcorn in terms of movie tickets is equal to minus the slope of the budget line, in this case equal to ½: 1 bucket of popcorn can be obtained if ½ movie ticket is forgone.

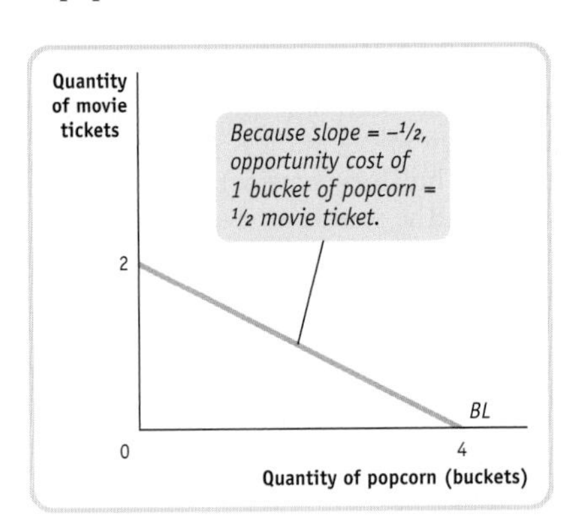

   b. At a price of $1.50 for a pair of socks and income of $12.00, the vertical intercept—the maximum quantity of pairs of socks that can be purchased—is $12.00/$1.50 = 8, as shown in the accompanying diagram. The horizontal intercept—the maximum quantity of pairs of underwear that can be purchased—is $12.00/$4.00 = 3. The slope of the budget line is equal to $-8/3 = -2\frac{2}{3}$. The opportunity cost of underwear in terms of socks is equal to minus the slope of the budget line, in this case equal to 2⅔: 1 pair of underwear can be obtained if 2⅔ pairs of socks are forgone.

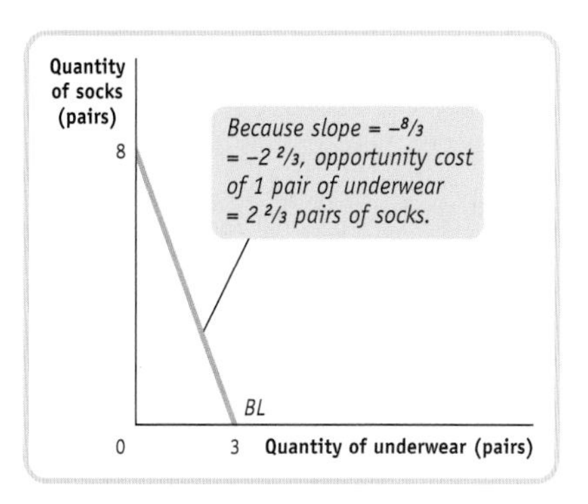

Check Your Understanding 10-3

1. From Figure 10-5 you can see that the marginal utility per dollar at 3 pounds of clams and the marginal utility per dollar at 8 pounds of potatoes is approximately the same, at a value of about 1. But it is not Sammy's optimal consumption bundle because it is not affordable given his income of \$20; 3 pounds of clams and 8 pounds of potatoes costs $\$4 \times 3 + \$2 \times 8 = \$28$, \$8 more than Sammy's income. This can be illustrated with Sammy's budget line from Figure 10-4. A bundle of 3 pounds of clams and 8 pounds of potatoes is represented by point *X* in the accompanying diagram, a point that lies outside Sammy's budget line.

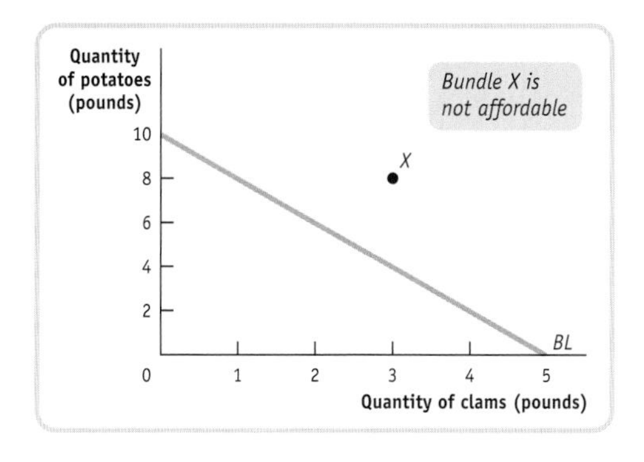

2. If Sammy chose the bundle that maximized his marginal utility per dollar for each good, he would choose to consume 1 pound of potatoes, where $MU_P/P_P = 5.75$, and 1 pound of clams, where $MU_C/P_C = 3.75$. But this bundle generates 26.5 utils for him. Instead, Sammy should choose the consumption bundle that satisfies his budget constraint and for which the marginal utility per dollar for both goods is equal.

Check Your Understanding 10-4

1. Since spending on orange juice is a small share of Clare's spending, the income effect from a rise in the price of orange juice is insignificant. Only the substitution effect, represented by the substitution of lemonade for orange juice, is significant.

2. Since rent is a large share of Delia's expenditures, the increase in rent generates an income effect, making Delia feel poorer. Since housing is a normal good for Delia, the income and substitution effects move in the same direction, leading her to reduce her consumption of housing by moving to a smaller apartment.

3. Since a meal ticket is a significant share of the students' living costs, an increase in the price will generate an income effect. Students respond to the increase in price by eating more often at the cafeteria. So in this case the substitution effect (which would induce them to eat at the cafeteria less often) and the income effect (which would induce them to eat at the cafeteria more often than at restaurants because they are poorer) move in opposite directions. This happens because cafeteria meals are an inferior good for the students. In fact, since the income effect outweighs the substitution effect (students eat at the cafeteria more as the price of meal tickets increases), cafeteria meals are a Giffen good.

Chapter Eleven

Check Your Understanding 11-1

1. **a.** As you can see from the accompanying diagram, the four bundles are associated with three indifference curves: *B* on the 10-util indifference curve, *A* and *C* on the 6-util indifference curve, and *D* on the 4-util indifference curve.

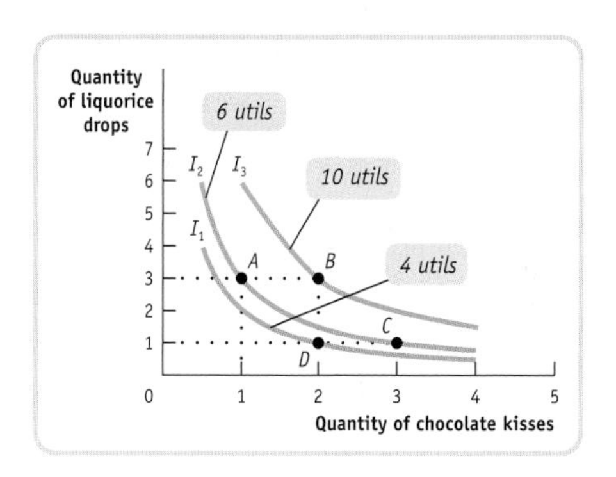

b. By comparing the quantity of chocolate kisses and liquorice drops, you can predict that Samantha will prefer *B* to *A* because *B* gives her one more chocolate kiss and the same amount of liquorice drops as *A*. Next, you can predict that she will prefer *C* to *D* because *C* gives her one more chocolate kiss and the same amount of liquorice drops as *D*. You can also predict that she prefers *B* to *D* because *B* gives her two more liquorice drops and the same amount of chocolate kisses as *D*. But without data about utils, you cannot predict how Samantha would rank *A* versus *C* or *D* because each of those have more chocolate kisses but fewer liquorice drops than *A*. Neither can you rank *B* versus *C*, for the same reason.

2. Bundles *A* and *B* each generate 200 utils since they both lie on the 200-util indifference curve. Likewise, bundles *A* and *C* each generate 100 utils since they both lie on the 100-util indifference curve. But this implies that *A*

generates 100 utils and also that *A* generates 200 utils. This is a contradiction, and so cannot be true. It shows that indifference curves cannot cross.

Check Your Understanding 11-2

1. **a.** The marginal rate of substitution between books and games, MU_B/MU_G, is 2 for Brad and 5 for Kyle. This implies that Brad is willing to trade 1 book for 2 games, and Kyle is willing to trade 1 book for 5 games. So starting from a bundle of 3 books and 2 games, Brad would be equally content with a bundle of 2 books and 4 games, while Kyle would be equally content with a bundle of 2 books and 7 games. Kyle finds it more difficult to trade games for books: he demands 5 games as compensation for the loss of a book, while Brad demands only 2. If books are measured on the horizontal axis and games on the vertical axis, Kyle's indifference curve will be steeper than Brad's at the current consumption bundle.

   b. Brad's current consumption bundle is optimal if P_B/P_G, the relative price of books in terms of games, is 2. Kyle's current consumption bundle is not optimal at this relative price; his bundle would be optimal only if the relative price of books in terms of games is 5. Since, for Kyle, $MU_B/MU_G = 5$ but $P_B/P_G = 2$, Kyle should consume fewer games and more books, thereby lowering his MU_B/MU_G until it is equal to 2.

Check Your Understanding 11-3

1. Since Sanjay cares only about the number of jelly beans, and not whether they are banana-flavoured or pineapple-flavoured, he is always willing to exchange one for the other at the same rate. This implies that his marginal rate of substitution between them is constant. So they are perfect substitutes.

2. Cherry pie and vanilla ice cream are complements for Hillary since her marginal utility of cherry pie goes up as she has another scoop of vanilla ice cream. But they are ordinary goods, not perfect complements, because she gains some utility from having cherry pie without any vanilla ice cream.

3. Omnisoft's software programs and its operating system are perfect complements for its customers: they gain no utility from the software programs without the operating system. So their marginal rate of substitution between the two goods is undefined, and their indifference curves have a right-angle shape.

4. Income and leisure are ordinary goods for Daniel: the more income he has made by working more hours, the less willing he is to earn yet more by giving up additional leisure time.

Check Your Understanding 11-4

1. **a.** Sammy's original budget line is illustrated in the accompanying diagram by BL_1. His original consumption is at point *A*. When the price of clams falls, his budget line rotates outward to BL_2, allowing him to achieve a higher level of utility. The pure substitution effect would involve the same change in the slope of his budget line, but without any increase in utility. So the pure substitution effect is illustrated by the movement from *A* to *B*. In fact, his utility does rise, so his consumption moves from *A* to *C*. The movement from *B* to *C* is the income effect.

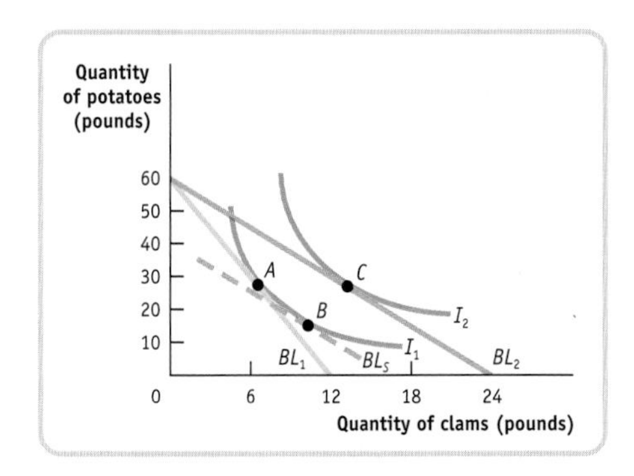

   b. Again, Sammy's original budget line is BL_1, and his original consumption is at point *A*. The increase in the price of clams causes his budget line to rotate inward to BL_2. This reduces his utility. The pure substitution effect is what would happen if the slope of the budget line changed but his total utility did not; it is shown as the movement from *A* to *B*. The full effect of the price change is the movement from *A* to *C*. The movement from *B* to *C* is the income effect.

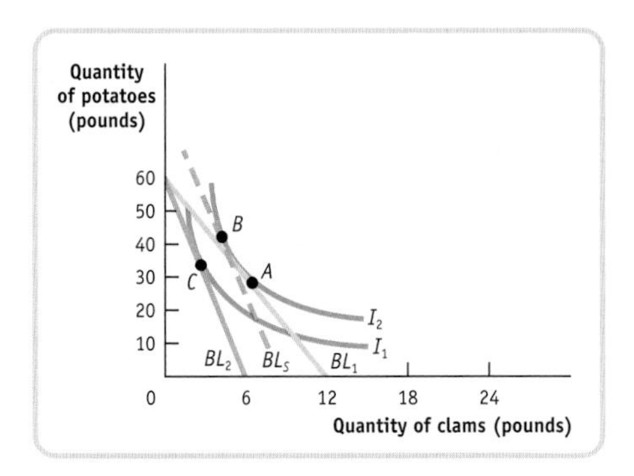

Chapter Twelve

Check Your Understanding 12-1

1. Many university professors will depart for other lines of work if the government imposes a wage that is lower than the market wage. Fewer professors will result in fewer courses taught and fewer university degrees produced. It will adversely affect parts of the economy that depend directly on universities, such as the local shopkeepers who sell goods and services to the universities and their faculty, university textbook publishers, and so on. But it will also adversely affect firms that use the "output" produced by universities: new university graduates. Firms that need to hire new employees with university degrees will be hurt as a smaller supply results in a higher market wage for university graduates. Ultimately, the reduced supply of university-educated workers will result in a lower level of the human capital in the entire economy relative to what it would have been without the

policy. And this will hurt all sectors of the economy that depend on human capital. The parts of the economy that might benefit are firms that compete with universities in the hiring of would-be university professors. For example, accounting firms will find it easier to hire people who would otherwise have been professors of accounting, and publishers will find it easier to hire people who would otherwise have been professors of English (easier in the sense that the firms can recruit would-be professors with a lower wage than before). In addition, workers who already have university degrees will benefit; they command higher wages as the supply of university-educated workers falls.

Check Your Understanding 12-2

1. a. As the price of the output produced by the industries increases, this shifts the *VMPL* curve up; that is, the demand for labour rises. This results in an increase in the equilibrium wage rate and an increase in the quantity of labour employed.
   b. The fall in the catch per day means that the marginal product of labour in the industry declines. The VMPL curve shifts downwards, generating a fall in the equilibrium wage rate and the equilibrium quantity of labour employed.
2. By the marginal productivity theory of income distribution, $P \times MPL = W$ at the market equilibrium for labour. Suppose the labour market in the tractor industry is initially in equilibrium; then the price of tractors, P, goes up by 50% but the wage, W, remains unchanged. As a result of these events, $P \times MPL > W$, and the market for workers in this industry is no longer in equilibrium. Tractor manufacturers will respond by hiring more workers. This will generate a fall in the marginal product of labour, MPL. Hiring will continue until MPL falls to the level at which $P \times MPL = W$ again, at which point equilibrium is re-established.
3. When firms from different industries compete for the same workers, then each worker in the various industries will be paid the same equilibrium wage, W. And since, by the marginal productivity theory of income distribution, $VMPL = P \times MPL = W$ for the last worker hired in equilibrium, the last worker hired in each of these different industries will have the same value of the marginal product of labour.

Check Your Understanding 12-3

1. a. False. Income disparities associated with gender, race, or ethnicity can be explained by the marginal productivity theory of income distribution provided that differences in marginal productivity across people are correlated with gender, race, or ethnicity. One possible source for such correlation is past discrimination. Such discrimination can lower a person's marginal productivity by, for example, preventing them from acquiring human capital that would raise their productivity. Another possible source of the correlation is differences in work experience that are associated with gender, race, or ethnicity. For example, in jobs where work experience or length of tenure are important, women may earn lower wages because on average more women than men take child-care-related absences from work.
   b. True. Companies that discriminate when their competitors do not are likely to hire less able workers because they discriminate against more able workers who are considered of the wrong gender, race, or ethnicity. And with less able workers, such companies are likely to earn lower profits than their competitors who don't discriminate.
   c. Ambiguous. In general, workers who are paid less because they have less experience may or may not be the victims of discrimination. The answer depends on the reason for the lack of experience. If workers have less experience because they are young or have chosen to do something else rather than gain experience, then they are not the victims of discrimination if they are paid less. On the other hand, if a person lacks experience because previous job discrimination prevented them from gaining experience, then they are indeed victims of discrimination when they are paid less as a result.

Check Your Understanding 12-4

1. a. Clive is made worse off if, before the new law, he had preferred to work more than 35 hours per week. As a result of the law, he can no longer choose his preferred time allocation; he now consumes fewer goods and more leisure than he would like.
   b. Clive's utility is unaffected by the law if, before the law, he had preferred to work 35 or fewer hours per week. The law has not changed his preferred time allocation.
   c. Clive can never be made better off by a law that restricts the number of hours he can work unless he is working more hours than he wants to. This could occur at a wage-hours combination to the right of his labour supply curve. If employers have the right to set working hours, some employees could find themselves in this position.
2. The substitution effect would induce Clive to work fewer hours and consume more leisure after his wage falls—the fall in wage means the price of an hour of leisure falls, leading Clive to consume more leisure. But a fall in his wage also generates a fall in Clive's income. The income effect of this is to induce Clive to consume less leisure and therefore work more hours, since he is now poorer and leisure is a normal good. If the income effect outweighs the substitution effect, Clive will in the end work more hours than before.

Chapter Thirteen

Check Your Understanding 13-1

1. a. eMarkets! will have to know the willingness to pay of every potential consumer—that is, the demand schedule. It will also have to know the seller's cost for each unit of output of every potential producer—that is, the supply schedule. (Equivalently, it must know the marginal cost curve of every potential producer.)
   b. Some producers who have a seller's cost greater than $199 will produce because they were mistakenly told that the

price would be $299; some who have a seller's cost equal to or less than $199 will not produce because they were mistakenly told that the price would be $99. So producer surplus is lower because the market price cannot allocate production efficiently among producers. You cannot tell whether the output will be equal to, less than, or greater than the equilibrium output. Overproduction may occur if a relatively high number of producers think the price will be $299, and underproduction may occur if a relatively high number of producers think the price will be $99.

c. Consumers with a willingness to pay of $299, who are told that the price is $399, will not purchase the good. For each of these consumers, consumer surplus of $299 – $199 = $100 is lost. Consumers with a willingness to pay of $119, who are allowed to buy the good at a price of $99 each, gain $119 – $99 = $20 surplus. So this transfer of units from high-willingness-to-pay consumers to low-willingness-to-pay consumers results in a net loss of consumer surplus of $100 – $20 = $80 per unit.

Check Your Understanding 13-2

1. a. Before the change in preferences, the Bountifullian labour market is in equilibrium, defined by the condition $VMPL_C$ = wage rate = $VMPL_S$. After preferences change, a greater demand for breakfast cereal will induce an increase in the price of cereal, P_C. $VMPL_C = P_C \times MPL_C$ will therefore rise, with the result that $VMPL_C >$ wage rate. A lower demand for sausage will induce a fall in the price of sausage, P_S. $VMPL_S = P_S \times MPL_S$ will fall, with the result that $VMPL_S <$ wage rate. Sausage producers will let some of their workers go, and these workers will move to cereal producers, who are hiring additional workers. As labour moves from the sausage industry to the cereal industry, MPL_C and $VMPL_C$ fall, while MPL_S and $VMPL_S$ rise.

b. One knows that the economy has fully adjusted when the labour market has reattained equilibrium; that is, when $VMPL_C$ = wage rate = $VMPL_S$ again. Because all consumers face the same price for cereal, P_C, and the same price for sausage, P_S, there will be *efficiency in consumption:* every consumer who consumes a good has a higher willingness to pay for it than someone who does not. Next, because cereal producers and sausage producers compete for workers in a perfectly competitive labour market, there is no surplus of labour and all labour is fully employed. So there will be *efficiency in production:* there is no way to produce more of one good without producing less of the other. Finally, there will be *efficiency in the levels of output:* any other mix of cereal and sausage reduces welfare. Because $VMPL_C$ = wage rate = $VMPL_S$ in equilibrium, the allocation of labour to the two industries, and therefore the mix of outputs of the two goods, fully reflects consumers' valuations of the two goods.

Check Your Understanding 13-3

1. There is an objective way to determine whether an economy is efficient: determine whether it is possible to rearrange production and/or consumption in a way that makes someone better off without making anyone else worse off. If the economy is inefficient, then people should be able to agree to adopt policies which make it efficient: those who are made better off would gladly accept them, and those who are no worse off would be willing to go along. But because there is no objective measure of what is fair, it is much harder to determine whether an economy is fair. What a person deems is fair typically depends upon his or her viewpoint.

2. a. The problem with this statement is that what one "should contribute" or "should receive" is subject to interpretation. Suppose a person has worked extremely hard to become wealthy, while another person is born wealthy and has never worked. Should each person be required to contribute the same to society? Some would say yes (those who think the amount of money a person has is the only criterion), while others would say no (those who think that people should be rewarded for working hard relative to those who don't)—it depends upon one's viewpoint. Similarly, suppose one person needs a surgical operation to be able to see, another person needs an operation to be able to walk, and society doesn't have the resources to perform both operations. Whose need is more important? Again, the answer is unclear because society has no way of measuring whether one person's needs are more compelling than another's.

b. This statement is also subject to very different interpretations. First, how does one define "work hard"? Do people who spend years working on something they enjoy, such as writing a classical sonata, "work harder" than someone who does less intense but very unappealing work? Also, this statement implies that people who cannot work very hard for reasons outside their control—say, due to illness—should be rewarded less. Whether this is fair or not is again subject to a person's viewpoint.

Chapter Fourteen

Check Your Understanding 14-1

1. a. This does not support the conclusion. Lightning has a limited amount of oil, and the price has risen in order to equalize supply and demand.

b. This supports the conclusion because the market for home heating oil has become monopolized, and a monopolist will reduce the quantity supplied and raise price to generate monopoly profit.

c. This does not support the conclusion. Lightning has raised its price to consumers because the price of its input, home heating oil, has increased.

d. This supports the conclusion. The fact that other firms have begun to supply heating oil at a lower price implies that Lightning must have earned monopoly profits—profits that attracted the other firms to Frigid, and that allowed those other firms to sell oil at a lower price.

e. This supports the conclusion. It indicates that Lightning enjoys a barrier to entry because it controls access to the only heating oil pipeline.

Check Your Understanding 14-2

1. a. The price at each output level is found by dividing the total revenue by the number of emeralds produced; for example, the price when 3 emeralds are produced is

$252/3 = $84. The price at the various output levels is then used to construct the demand schedule in the accompanying table.

b. The marginal revenue schedule is found by calculating the change in total revenue for each one-unit increase in output quantity. For example, the marginal revenue generated by increasing output from 2 to 3 emeralds is ($252 – $186) = $66.

c. The quantity effect component of marginal revenue is the additional revenue generated by selling one more unit of the good at the market price. For example, as shown in the accompanying table, at 3 emeralds, the market price is $84; so, when going from 2 to 3 emeralds, the quantity effect is equal to $84.

d. The price effect component of marginal revenue is the decline in revenue caused by the fall in price when one more unit is sold. For example, when only 2 emeralds are sold, each emerald sells at a price of $186 / 2 = $93. However, when Emerald, Inc. sells an additional emerald, the price must fall by $9 to $84. So the price effect component in going from 2 to 3 emeralds is (–$9) x 2 = –$18. That's because 2 emeralds can only be sold at a price of $84 when 3 emeralds in total are sold, whereas they could have been sold at a price of $93 when only 2 in total were sold.

Quantity of emerald demanded	Price of emerald	Marginal revenue	Quantity effect component	Price effect component
1	$100			
		$86	$93	–$7
2	93			
		66	84	–18
3	84			
		28	70	–42
4	70			
		–30	50	–80
5	50			

e. In order to determine Emerald, Inc.'s profit-maximizing output level, one must know its marginal cost at each output level. Its profit-maximizing output level is the one at which marginal revenue is equal to marginal cost.

2. As the accompanying diagram shows, the marginal cost curve shifts upward to $400. The profit-maximizing quantity falls, and so does profit, from $3,200 to $300 x 6 = $1,800. Competitive industry profits, though, are unchanged at zero.

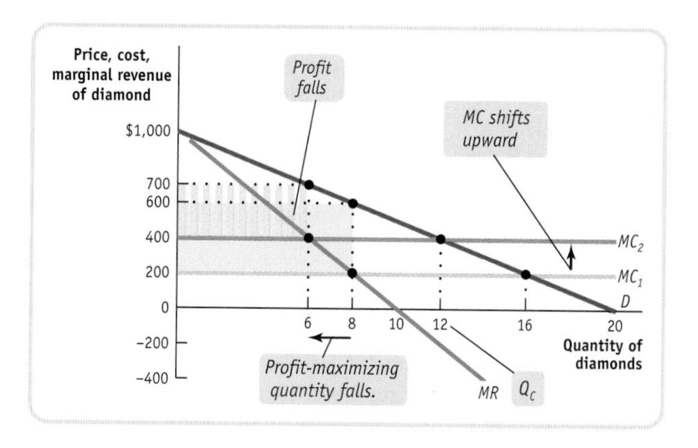

Check Your Understanding 14-3

1. a. Cable Internet service is a natural monopoly. So the government should intervene only if it believes that price exceeds average total cost, where average total cost is based on the cost of laying the cable. In this case it should impose a price ceiling equal to average total cost. Otherwise, it should do nothing.

b. The government should approve the merger only if it fosters competition by transferring some of the company's landing slots to another, competing airline.

2. a. False. As can be see from Figure 14-8, panel b., the inefficiency arises from the fact that some of the consumer surplus is transformed into deadweight loss (the orange area), not that it is transformed into profit for the monopolist (the green area).

b. True. If a monopolist sold to all customers who have a valuation greater than or equal to marginal cost, all mutually beneficial transactions would occur and there would be no deadweight loss.

3. As shown in the accompanying diagram, a monopolist produces Q_M, *the output level at which* MR = *MC*. A monopolist who mistakenly believes that *P* = *MR* produces the output level at which *P* = *MC* (when, in fact, *P* > *MR*, and at the true profit-maximizing level of output, P > MR = *MC*). This misguided monopolist will produce the output level Q_C, the output level at which the demand curve crosses the marginal cost curve—the same output level produced if the industry were perfectly competitive. It will charge a price P_C, which is equal to marginal cost, and make zero profit. The entire shaded area is equal to the consumer surplus, which is also equal to total surplus in this case (since the monopolist receives zero producer surplus). There is no deadweight loss, since every consumer who has a willingness to pay equal to or greater than marginal cost gets the good. A smart monopolist, on the other hand, will produce output level Q_M, the output level at which the marginal revenue curve crosses the marginal cost curve, and charge the price P_M. Profit equals the green area, consumer surplus corresponds to the blue area, and total surplus is equal to the sum of the green and blue areas. The orange area is the deadweight loss generated by the monopolist.

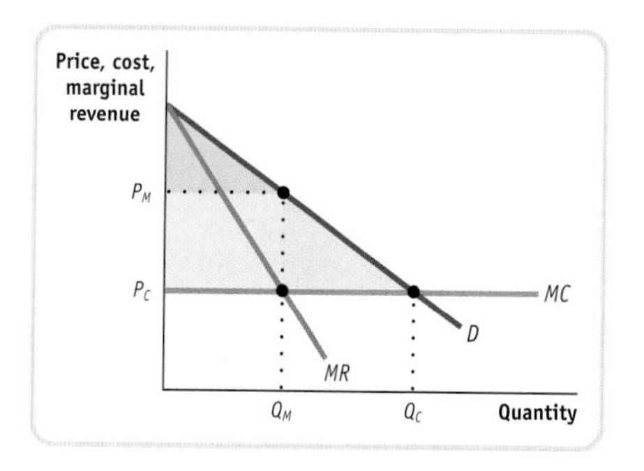

Check Your Understanding 14-4

1. a. False. A price-discriminating monopolist will sell to some customers that a single-price monopolist will refuse to; namely, customers with a high price elasticity of demand who are willing to pay only a relatively low price for the good.
   b. False. Although a price-discriminating monopolist does indeed capture more of the consumer surplus, inefficiency is lower: mutually beneficial transactions occur because the monopolist makes more sales to customers with a low willingness to pay for the good.
   c. True. Under price discrimination, consumers are charged prices that depend on their price elasticity of demand. A consumer with highly elastic demand will pay a lower price than a consumer with inelastic demand.
2. a. This is not a case of price discrimination because all consumers, regardless of their price elasticities of demand, value the damaged merchandise less than undamaged merchandise. So price must be lowered in order to sell the merchandise.
   b. This is a case of price discrimination. Senior citizens have a higher price elasticity of demand for restaurant meals (their demand for restaurant meals is more responsive to price changes) than other patrons. Restaurants lower the price to high-elasticity consumers (senior citizens). The consumers with low price elasticity of demand will pay the full price.
   c. This is a case of price discrimination. Consumers with a high price elasticity of demand will pay a lower price by collecting and using discount coupons. Consumers with a low price elasticity of demand will not use coupons.
   d. This is not a case of price discrimination; it is simply a case of supply and demand.

Chapter Fifteen

Check Your Understanding 15-1

1. a. The world oil industry is an oligopoly because a few countries control a necessary resource for production, oil reserves.
   b. The microprocessor industry is an oligopoly because two firms possess superior technology and so dominate industry production.
   c. The wide-bodied passenger jet industry is an oligopoly because there are economies of scale in production.

Check Your Understanding 15-2

1. a. The firm is likely to act non-cooperatively and raise output, which will generate a negative price effect. But because the firm's current market share is small, the negative price effect will fall much more heavily on its rivals' revenues than on its own. At the same time, the firm benefits from a positive quantity effect.
   b. The firm is likely to act non-cooperatively and raise output, which will generate a fall in price. Because its rivals have higher costs, they will lose money at the lower price while the firm continues to make profits. So the firm may be able to drive its rivals out of business by increasing its output.
   c. The firm is likely to collude. Because it is costly for consumers to switch products, the firm would have to lower its price quite substantially (by increasing quantity a lot) to induce consumers to switch to its product. So increasing output is likely to be unprofitable given the large negative price effect.
   d. The firm is likely to collude. It cannot increase sales because it is currently at maximum production capacity.

Check Your Understanding 15-3

1. When Margaret builds a missile, Nikita's payoff from building a missile as well is –10; it is –20 if he does not. The same set of payoffs holds for Margaret when Nikita builds a missile: her payoff is –10 if she builds one as well, –20 if she does not. So it is a Nash (or non-cooperative) equilibrium for both Margaret and Nikita to build missiles, and their total payoff is (–10) + (–10) = –20 in this case. But their total payoff is greatest when neither builds a missile: in that case, their total payoff is 0 + 0 = 0. But this outcome—the cooperative outcome—is unlikely. If Margaret builds a missile but Nikita does not, Margaret gets a payoff of +8, rather than the 0 she gets if she doesn't build a missile. So Margaret is better off if she builds a missile but Nikita doesn't. Similarly, Nikita is better of if he builds a missile but Margaret does not: he gets a payoff of +8, rather than the 0 he gets if he doesn't build a missile. So both players have an incentive to build a missile. Both will build a missile, and each gets a payoff of –10. Thus, unless Nikita and Margaret are able to communicate in some way to enforce cooperation, they will act in their own individual interests, and each will build a missile.
2. a. Future entry by several new firms will increase competition and drive down industry profits. As a result, there is less future profit to protect by behaving cooperatively today. So each oligopolist is more likely to behave non-cooperatively today.
   b. When it is very difficult for a firm to detect if another firm has raised output, then it is very difficult to enforce cooperation by playing "tit-for-tat". So it is more likely that a firm will behave non-cooperatively.
   c. When firms have co-existed while maintaining high prices for a long time, each expects cooperation to continue. So the value of behaving cooperatively today is high and it is likely that firms will engage in tacit collusion.

Check Your Understanding 15-4

1. a. This is likely to be interpreted as evidence of tacit collusion. Firms in the industry are able to tacitly collude by setting their prices according to the published "suggested" price of the largest firm in the industry. This is a form of price leadership.
   b. This is not likely to be interpreted as evidence of tacit collusion. Considerable variation in market share indicates that firms have been competing to capture each other's business.
   c. This is not likely to be interpreted as evidence of tacit collusion. These features make it more unlikely that consumers will switch products in response to lower prices. So this is a way for firms to avoid any temptation to gain market share by lowering price. This is a form of product differentiation used to avert direct competition.

d. This is likely to be interpreted as evidence of tacit collusion. In the guise of discussing sales targets, firms can create a cartel by designating quantities to be produced by each firm.

e. This is likely to be interpreted as evidence of collusion. By raising prices together, each firm in the industry is refusing to undercut its rivals by leaving its price unchanged or lowering it. Because it could gain market share by doing so, refusing to do it is evidence of collusion.

Chapter Sixteen

Check Your Understanding 16-1

1. a. Ladders are not differentiated as a result of monopolistic competition. A ladder producer makes different ladders (i.e., tall ladders versus short ladders) in order to satisfy different consumer needs, not in order to avert competition with rivals. As a result, two tall ladders made by two different producers will be indistinguishable by consumers.

b. Soft drinks are an example of product differentiation resulting from monopolistic competition. For example, several producers make a cola-flavoured drink; each one is differentiated in terms of taste, which fast-food restaurant chains sell it, and so on.

c. Department stores are an example of product differentiation resulting from monopolistic competition. They serve different clienteles, who have different sensitivities to price and different tastes. They also offer different levels of customer service, and are sited in different locations.

d. Steel is not differentiated as a result of monopolistic competition. Different types of steel (i.e., beams versus sheets) are made for different purposes, not to distinguish one steel manufacturer's products from another's.

2. a. Perfectly competitive industries and monopolistically competitive industries both have many sellers; therefore, it may be hard to distinguish them in terms of number of firms alone. And, in both market structures, there is free entry into and exit from the industry in the long run. But firms in monopolistically competitive industries have some market power in the short run, while firms in perfectly competitive industries do not. So you should ask whether or not firms have market power in order to distinguish between the two market structures. Equivalently, you could ask whether products are differentiated in the industry.

b. In a monopolized industry there is only one firm, while a monopolistically competitive industry contains many firms. So, you should ask whether there is only a single firm in the industry.

Check Your Understanding 16-2

1. a. An increase in fixed costs raises average total cost and shifts the average total cost curve upward. Firms incur losses, and some are compelled to exit the industry. This results in a rightward shift of the demand curves for those firms that remain in the industry, as each one now serves a larger share of the market. Long-run equilibrium is re-established when the demand curve for each remaining firm has shifted rightward to the point that it is tangent to the firm's new, higher average total cost curve. At this point each firm's price just equals its marginal cost, and each firm makes zero profit.

b. A decrease in marginal cost lowers average total cost and shifts the average total cost curve downward. Firms make profits, and this attracts new entrants into the industry. This results in a leftward shift of each firm's demand curve, as each firm now has a smaller share of the market. Long-run equilibrium is re-established when each firm's demand curve has shifted leftward to the point that it is tangent to the new, lower average total cost curve. At this point each firm's price just equals marginal cost, and each firm makes zero profit.

2. If all the existing firms in the industry were to join together to create a monopoly, they would achieve monopoly profits. But this would induce new firms to enter the industry with new, differentiated products and capture some of the monopoly profits. So in the long run it would be impossible to maintain a monopoly. The problem arises because new firms can create new products, so there is no barrier to entry that can maintain a monopoly.

Check Your Understanding 16-3

1. a. False. As can be seen from panel (b) of Figure 16-4, a monopolistically competitive firm produces at a point where average total cost exceeds marginal cost—unlike a perfectly competitive firm, which produces where average total cost equals marginal cost (at the point of minimum average total cost). A monopolistically competitive firm will refuse to sell at marginal cost. This would be below average total cost and the firm would incur a loss.

b. True. In the short run firms in a monopolistically competitive industry could achieve higher profits (monopoly profits) if they all joined together. The effect on consumers, however, is ambiguous. They would experience less choice; but if consolidation substantially reduces industry-wide average total cost and therefore substantially increases industry-wide output, in the short run consumers may experience lower prices under monopoly.

c. True. Fads and fashions are created and promulgated by advertising, which is found frequently in oligopolies or monopolistically competitive industries but less often in monopolies or perfectly competitive industries.

Check Your Understanding 16-4

1. a. Such advertisements are likely to focus on the medical benefits of aspirin and are therefore likely to be economically useful.

b. Such advertisements are likely to focus on promoting Bayer aspirin versus a rival's aspirin product, although the two products are medically indistinguishable. Therefore, the advertisement is likely to be economically wasteful.

c. Such advertisements are likely to focus on the health and enjoyment benefits of orange juice, and are therefore economically useful.

d. Such advertisements are likely to be economically wasteful, as they are likely to focus on promoting Tropicana orange juice versus a rival's product, although the two are likely to be indistinguishable by consumers.

e. Such advertisements are likely to be economically useful because the longevity of a business gives a potential customer information about its quality.

2. A successful brand name indicates a desirable attribute, such as quality, to a potential customer. So, other things equal—such as price—a firm with a successful brand name will achieve higher sales than will a rival with a comparable product but without a successful brand name. This is likely to act as a barrier to entry by deterring new firms from entering an industry in which an existing firm has a successful brand name.

Chapter Seventeen

Check Your Understanding 17-1

1. a. To determine comparative advantage, we must compare the two countries' opportunity costs for a given good. Take the opportunity cost of 1 ton of corn in terms of bicycles. In China, the opportunity cost of 1 bicycle is .01 ton of corn; so the opportunity cost of 1 ton of corn is 1/0.01 bicycles = 100 bicycles. Canada has the comparative advantage in corn since its opportunity cost in terms of bicycles is 50, a smaller number. Similarly, the opportunity cost in Canada of 1 bicycle in terms of corn is 1/50 tons of corn = 0.02 ton of corn. This is greater than 0.01, the Chinese opportunity cost of 1 bicycle in terms of corn, implying that China has a comparative advantage in bicycles.

b. Given that Canada can produce 200,000 bicycles if no corn is produced, it can produce 200,000 bicycles × (0.02 ton of corn/bicycle) = 4,000 tons of corn when no bicycles are produced. Likewise, if China can produce 3,000 tons of corn when no bicycles are produced, it can produce 3,000 tons of corn × 100 bicycles/ton of corn = 300,000 bicycles when no corn is produced. These points determine the vertical and horizontal intercepts of the Canadian and Chinese production possibility frontiers as shown in the accompanying diagram.

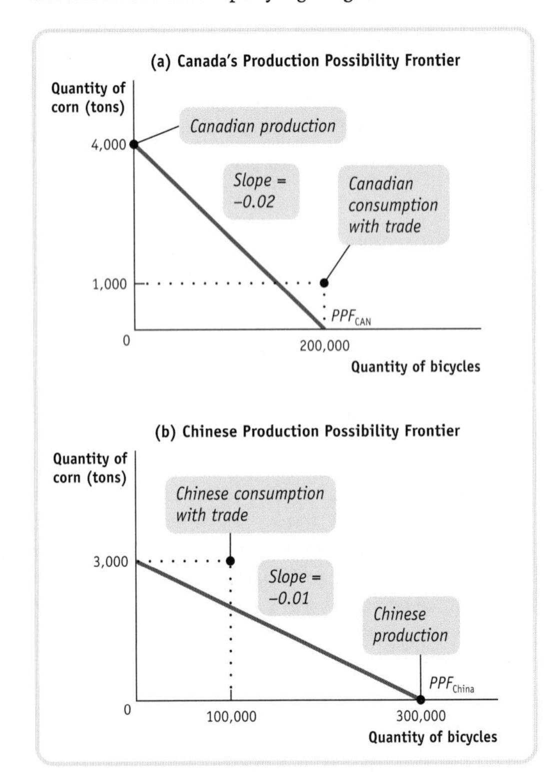

c. The accompanying figure shows the production and consumption points of the two countries. Each country is clearly better off under international trade because each now consumes a bundle of the two goods that lies outside its own production possibility frontier, indicating that these bundles were unattainable when each country was in autarky.

2. a. According to the Heckscher–Ohlin model, this pattern occurs because Canada has a relatively larger endowment of factors of production such as forest resources, capital, and labour skills that are suited to the production of paper, whereas France has a relatively larger endowment of factors of production suited to wine-making, such as vineyards and the human capital of vintners.

b. According to the Heckscher–Ohlin model, this pattern occurs because Canada has a relatively larger endowment of factors of production such as human and physical capital suited to making machinery, whereas Brazil has a relatively larger endowment of factors of production suited to shoe-making, such as labour and leather.

Check Your Understanding 17-2

1. In the accompanying diagram, P_A is the Canadian price of grapes in autarky and P_W is the world price of grapes under international trade. With trade, Canadian consumers pay a price of P_W for grapes and consume quantity C_T, Canadian grape producers produce quantity Q_T, and the difference, $C_T - Q_T$, represents imports of Mexican grapes. As a consequence of the strike, imports are halted, the price paid by Canadian consumers rises to the autarky price, P_A, and Canadian consumption falls to the autarky quantity Q_A.

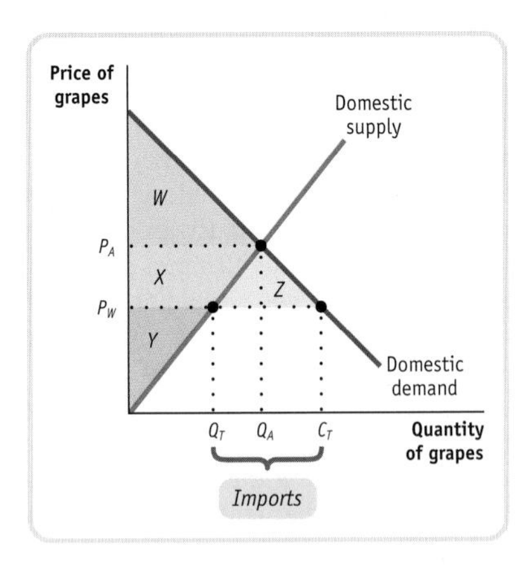

a. Before the strike, Canadian consumers enjoy consumer surplus equal to the areas $W + X + Z$. After the strike, their consumer surplus shrinks to the area W. So consumers are worse off, losing consumer surplus represented by the areas $X + Z$.

b. Before the strike, Canadian producers have producer surplus equal to the area Y. After the strike, their producer surplus increases to the area $Y + X$. So Canadian producers are better off, gaining producer surplus represented by the area X.

c. Canadian total surplus falls as a result of the strike by an amount represented by the area Z, the loss in consumer surplus that does not accrue to producers.

2. Mexican grape producers are worse off because they lose sales in the amount of $C_T - Q_T$, and Mexican grape pickers are worse off because they lose the wages that were associated with the lost sales. The lower demand for Mexican grapes caused by the strike implies that the price that Mexican consumers pay for grapes falls, making them better off. And Canadian grape pickers are better off because their wages increase as the result of the increase of $Q_A - Q_T$ in Canadian sales to Mexico.

Check Your Understanding 17-3

1. a. If the tariff is $0.50, the price paid by domestic consumers for a pound of imported butter is $0.50 + $0.50 = $1.00, the same price as a pound of domestic butter. Imported butter will no longer have a price advantage over domestic butter, imports will cease, and domestic producers will capture all the feasible sales to domestic consumers, selling the amount Q_A in the accompanying figure.

b. If the tariff is only $0.25, the price paid by domestic consumers for a pound of imported butter is $0.25 + $0.50 = $0.75, $0.25 cheaper than domestic butter. Canadian butter producers will gain sales in the amount of $Q_T - Q_F$ as a result of the $0.25 tariff. But this is smaller than the amount they would have gained under the $0.50 tariff, the amount $Q_A - Q_F$.

c. As long as the tariff is at least $0.50, increasing it more has no effect. At a tariff of $0.50, all imports are effectively blocked.

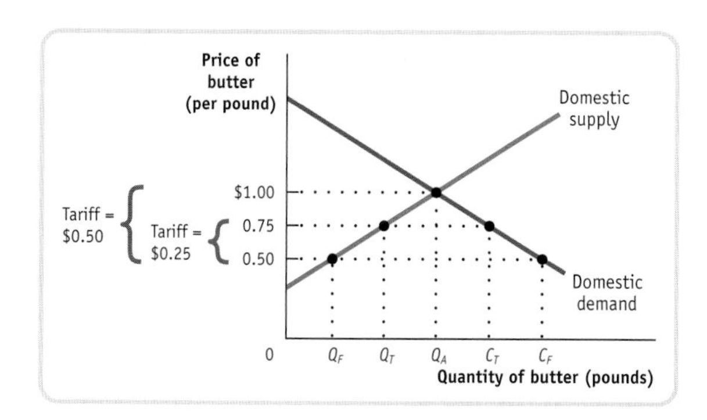

2. All imports are effectively blocked at a tariff of $0.50. Such a tariff therefore corresponds to an import quota of zero.

Check Your Understanding 17-4

1. There are many fewer businesses that use steel as an input than there are consumers who buy sugar or clothing. So it will be easier for such businesses to communicate and coordinate among themselves to lobby against tariffs than it will be for consumers. In addition, each business will perceive that the cost of a steel tariff is quite costly to their profits, but an individual consumer is either unaware or perceives little loss from tariffs on sugar or clothing.

2. Countries are often tempted to protect domestic industries by claiming that an import poses a quality, health, or environmental danger to domestic consumers. A WTO official should examine whether domestic producers are subject to the same stringency in the application of quality, health, or environmental regulations as foreign producers. If they are, then it is more likely that the regulations are for legitimate, non-trade protection purposes; if they are not, then it is more likely that the regulations are intended as trade protection measures.

Chapter Eighteen

Check Your Understanding 18-1

1. a. This will make it more likely that you will buy fully comprehensive auto insurance. Suppose you have only accident insurance. If you are at fault, this insurance does not cover your own damages. If the bad state of the world occurs (an accident that is your fault) and your car is damaged, you can no longer get to work. That is, in the bad state of the world, not only is your income reduced because you have to pay for repairs to your car, but your income is reduced further because you no longer have income from work. This increases the risk to your income you experience from damage to your car. If you are risk-averse, you are therefore more likely to buy fully comprehensive insurance.

b. This will make it less likely that you will buy fully comprehensive auto insurance. Suppose you have only accident insurance. If the bad state of the world occurs (an accident that is your fault) and your car is damaged, your parents can easily buy you another car. In other words, when the bad state of the world occurs, your income is not reduced by as much as if you did not have wealthy parents. The risk to your income from damage to your car is therefore lower, and as a result you are less likely to buy fully comprehensive insurance.

2. a. Karma's expected income is the weighted average of all possible values of her income, weighted by the probabilities with which she earns each possible value of her income. Since she makes $22,000 with a probability of 0.6 and $35,000 with a probability of 0.4, her expected income is 0.6 × $22,000 + 0.4 × $35,000 = $13,200 + $14,000 = $27,200. Her expected total utility is just the expected value of the utilities she will experience. Since with a probability of 0.6 she will experience a utility of 850 utils (the utility to her from making $22,000), and with a probability of 0.4 she will experience a utility of 1,260 utils (the utility to her from making $35,000), her expected total utility is (0.6 × 850 utils) + (0.4 × 1,260 utils) = 510 utils + 504 utils = 1,014 utils.

b. If Karma makes $25,000 for certain, she experiences a utility level of 1,014 utils. From the answer to part a, we know that this leaves her equally as well off as when she has a risky expected income of $27,200. Since Karma is indifferent between a risky expected income of $27,200 and a certain income of $25,000, you can conclude that she would prefer a certain income of $27,200 to a risky expected income of $27,200. That is, she would definitely be willing to reduce the risk she faces when this reduction in risk leaves her expected income unchanged. In other words, Karma is risk-averse.

c. Yes. Karma experiences a utility level of 1,056 utils when she has a certain income of $26,000. This is higher than the expected utility level of 1,014 utils generated by a risky expected income of $27,200. So Karma is willing to pay a premium to guarantee her a certain income of $26,000.

Check Your Understanding 18-2

1. a. An increase in the number of ships implies an increase in the quantity of insurance demanded at any given premium. This is a rightward shift of the demand curve, resulting in a rise in both the equilibrium premium and the equilibrium quantity of insurance bought and sold.

b. An increase in the number of trading routes means that investors can diversify more. In other words, they can reduce risk further. At any given premium, there are now more investors willing to supply insurance. This is a rightward shift of the supply curve for insurance, leading to a fall in the equilibrium premium and a rise in the equilibrium quantity of insurance bought and sold.

c. If shipowners in the market become even more risk-averse, they will be willing to pay higher premiums for insurance. That is, at any given premium there are now more people willing to buy insurance. This is a rightward shift of the demand curve for insurance, leading to a rise in both the equilibrium premium and the equilibrium quantity of insurance bought and sold.

d. If investors in the market become more risk-averse, they will be less willing to accept risk at any given premium. This is a leftward shift of the supply curve for insurance, leading to a rise in the equilibrium premium and a fall in the equilibrium quantity of insurance bought and sold.

e. As the overall level of risk increases, those willing to buy insurance will be more willing to buy insurance at any given premium; that is, the demand curve for insurance shifts to the right. But since overall risk cannot be diversified away, those willing to take on risk will be less willing to do so, leading to a leftward shift in the supply curve for insurance. As a result, the equilibrium premium will rise; the effect on the equilibrium quantity of insurance is uncertain.

f. If the wealth levels of investors fall, these people will become more risk-averse and therefore less willing to supply insurance at any given premium. This is a leftward shift of the supply curve for insurance, leading to a rise in the equilibrium premium and a fall in the equilibrium quantity of insurance bought and sold.

Check Your Understanding 18-3

1. The inefficiency caused by adverse selection is that an insurance policy with a premium based on the average risk of all drivers will attract only an adverse selection of bad drivers. Good (that is, safe) drivers will find this insurance premium too expensive and so will remain uninsured. This is inefficient. However, safe drivers are also those drivers who have had fewer moving violations for several years. Lowering premiums for those drivers allows the insurance company to screen its customers, and sell insurance to safe drivers, too. This means that at least some of the good drivers now are also insured, which decreases the inefficiency that arises from adverse selection. In a way, having no moving violations for several years is building a reputation for being a safe driver.

2. The moral hazard problem in home construction arises from private information about what the contractor does: whether she takes care to reduce the cost of home construction or allows costs to increase. The homeowner cannot, or can only imperfectly, observe the cost-reduction effort of the contractor. If the contractor were fully reimbursed for all costs she incurs during construction, she would have no incentive to reduce costs. Making the contractor responsible for paying any additional costs above the original estimate means that she now has an incentive to keep costs low. However, this imposes risk on the contractor. For instance, if the weather is bad, home construction will take longer, and will be more costly, than if the weather had been good. Since the contractor pays for any additional costs (such as weather-induced delays) above the original estimate, she now faces risk that she cannot control.

3. a. True. Drivers with higher deductibles have more incentive to take care in their driving, to avoid paying the deductible. This is a moral hazard phenomenon.

b. True. Suppose you know that you are a safe driver. You have a choice of a policy with a high premium and a low deductible or one with a lower premium but a higher deductible. In this case, you would be more likely to choose the cheap policy with the high deductible because you know that you will be unlikely to have to pay the deductible. When there is adverse selection, insurance companies use screening devices such as this to make inferences about people's private information about how skilful they are as drivers.

c. True. The wealthier you are, the less risk-averse you are. If you are less risk-averse, you are more willing to bear risk yourself. Having an insurance policy with a high deductible means that you are exposed to more risk: you have to pay more of any insurance claim yourself. This is an implication of how risk aversion changes with a person's income or wealth.

Chapter Nineteen

Check Your Understanding 19-1

1. a. The external cost is the pollution caused by the waste-water runoff, an uncompensated cost imposed by the poultry farms on their neighbours.

b. Since poultry farmers do not take the external cost of their actions into account when making decisions about how much waste water to generate, they will create more runoff than is socially optimal in the absence of government intervention or a private deal. They will produce runoff up to the point at which the marginal social benefit of an additional unit of runoff is zero; however, their neighbours experience a high, positive level of marginal social cost of runoff from this output level. So the quantity of waste-water runoff is inefficient: reducing runoff by one unit would reduce total social benefit by less than it would reduce total social cost.

c. At the socially optimal quantity of waste-water runoff, the marginal social benefit is equal to the marginal social cost. This quantity is lower than the quantity of waste-water runoff that would be created in the absence of government intervention or a private deal.

2. Yasmin's reasoning is not correct: allowing some late returns of books is likely to be socially optimal. Although you impose a marginal social cost on others every day that you are late in returning a book, there is some positive marginal social benefit to you of returning a book late—for example, you get a longer period to use it in working on a term paper.

The socially optimal number of days that a book is returned late is the number at which the marginal social benefit equals the marginal social cost. A fine so stiff that it prevents any late returns is likely to result in a situation in which people return books although the marginal social benefit of keeping them another day is greater than the marginal social cost—an inefficient outcome. In that case, allowing an overdue patron another day would increase total social benefit more than it would increase total social cost. So charging a moderate fine that reduces the number of days that books are returned late to the socially optimal number of days is appropriate.

Check Your Understanding 19-2

1. This is a misguided argument. Allowing polluters to sell emissions permits makes polluters face a cost of polluting: the opportunity cost of the permit. If a polluter chooses not to reduce its emissions, it cannot sell its emissions permits. As a result, it forgoes the opportunity of making money from the sale of the permits. So despite the fact that the polluter receives a monetary benefit from selling the permits, the scheme has the desired effect: to make polluters internalize the externality of their actions.

2. a. If the emissions tax is smaller than the marginal social cost at Q_{OPT}, a polluter will face a marginal cost of polluting (equal to the amount of the tax) that is less than the marginal social cost at the socially optimal quantity of pollution. Since a polluter will produce emissions up to the point where the marginal social benefit is equal to its marginal cost, the resulting amount of pollution will be larger than the socially optimal quantity. As a result, there is inefficiency: if the amount of pollution is larger than the socially optimal quantity, the marginal social cost exceeds the marginal social benefit, and society could gain from a reduction in emissions levels.

If the emissions tax is greater than the marginal social cost at Q_{OPT}, a polluter will face a marginal cost of polluting (equal to the amount of the tax) that is greater than the marginal social cost at the socially optimal quantity of pollution. This will lead the polluter to reduce emissions below the socially optimal quantity. This also is inefficient: whenever the marginal social benefit is greater than the marginal social cost, society could benefit from an increase in emissions levels.

b. If the total amount of allowable pollution is set too high, the supply of emissions permits will be high and so the equilibrium price at which permits trade will be low. That is, polluters will face a marginal cost of polluting (the price of a permit) that is "too low"—lower than the marginal social cost at the socially optimal quantity of pollution. As a result, pollution will be greater than the socially optimal quantity. This is inefficient.

If the total level of allowable pollution is set too low, the supply of emissions permits will be low and so the equilibrium price at which permits trade will be high. That is, polluters will face a marginal cost of polluting (the price of a permit) that is "too high"—higher than the marginal social cost at the socially optimal quantity of pollution. As a result, pollution will be lower than the socially optimal quantity. This also is inefficient.

Check Your Understanding 19-3

1. The London congestion charge acts like a Pigouvian tax on driving in central London. If the marginal external cost in terms of pollution and congestion of an additional car driven in central London is indeed £5, then the scheme is an optimal policy.

2. a. Planting trees imposes an external benefit: the marginal social benefit of planting trees is higher than the marginal benefit to individual tree planters, since many people (not just those who plant the trees) can benefit from the increased air quality and lower summer temperatures. The difference between the marginal social benefit and the marginal benefit to individual tree planters is the marginal external benefit. A Pigouvian subsidy could be placed on each tree planted in urban areas in order to increase the marginal benefit to individual tree planters to the same level as the marginal social benefit.

b. Water-saving toilets impose an external benefit: the marginal benefit to individual homeowners from replacing a traditional toilet with a water-saving toilet is zero, since water is virtually costless. But the marginal social benefit is large, since fewer rivers and aquifers need to be pumped. The difference between the marginal social benefit and the marginal benefit to individual homeowners is the marginal external benefit. A Pigouvian subsidy on installing water-saving toilets could bring the marginal benefit to individual homeowners in line with the marginal social benefit.

c. Disposing of old computer monitors imposes an external cost: the marginal cost to those disposing of old computer monitors is lower than the marginal social cost, since environmental pollution is borne by people other than the person disposing of the monitor. The difference between the marginal social cost and the marginal cost to those disposing of old computer monitors is the marginal external cost. A Pigouvian tax on disposing of computer monitors, or a system of tradable permits for their disposal, could raise the marginal cost to those disposing of old computer monitors sufficiently to make it equal to the marginal social cost.

Chapter Twenty

Check Your Understanding 20-1

1. a. Use of a river is non-excludable, but it may or may not be rival in consumption depending on the circumstances. For example, if both you and I use the river for swimming, then your use will not prevent my use—use of the river is non-rival in consumption. In this case, the river is a public good. But use of the river is rival in consumption when if there are many people trying to use it at the same time, or when your use of your jet ski prevents me from swimming. In this case, the river is a common resource.
   b. A cheese burrito is both excludable and rival in consumption. Therefore it is a private good.
   c. Information from a password-protected website is excludable but non-rival in consumption. Therefore it is an artificially scarce good.
   d. Publicly announced information on the path of an incoming hurricane is non-excludable and non-rival in consumption. So it is a public good.
2. A private producer will only supply a good that is excludable; otherwise, the producer won't be able to charge a price for it that covers the costs of production. So a private producer would be willing to supply a cheese burrito and information from a password-protected website, but unwilling to clean up a river or supply publicly announced information about an incoming hurricane.

Check Your Understanding 20-2

1. a. With 10 Homebodies and 6 Revellers, the marginal social benefit schedule of money spent on the party is as shown in the accompanying table:

Money spent on party	Marginal social benefit
\$0	
	(10 × \$0.05) + (6 × \$0.13) = \$1.28
1	
	(10 × \$0.04) + (6 × \$0.11) = \$1.06
2	
	(10 × \$0.03) + (6 × \$0.09) = \$0.84
3	
	(10 × \$0.02) + (6 × \$0.07) = \$0.62
4	

Therefore the efficient spending level is \$2, the highest level for which the marginal social benefit is greater than the marginal cost (\$1).

   b. With 6 Homebodies and 10 Revellers, the marginal social benefit schedule of money spent on the party is shown in the accompanying table:

Money spent on party	Marginal social benefit
\$0	
	(6 × \$0.05) + (10 × \$0.13) = \$1.60
1	
	(6 × \$0.04) + (10 × \$0.11) = \$1.34
2	
	(6 × \$0.03) + (10 × \$0.09) = \$1.08
3	
	(6 × \$0.02) + (10 × \$0.07) = \$0.82
4	

The efficient spending level is now \$3, the highest level for which the marginal social benefit is greater than the marginal cost (\$1). The efficient level of spending has increased from that in part a because with relatively more Revellers than Homebodies, an additional dollar spent on the party generates a higher level of social benefit compared to when there are relatively more Homebodies than Revellers.

   c. When the numbers of Homebodies and Revellers are unknown and residents are asked their preferences, then Homebodies will pretend to be Revellers to induce a higher level of spending on the public party. That's because a Homebody still receives a positive individual marginal benefit from an additional \$1 spent, despite the fact that his or her individual marginal benefit is lower than that of a Reveller for every additional \$1. In this case the "reported" marginal social benefit schedule of money spent on the party will be as shown in the accompanying table:

Money spent on party	Marginal social benefit
\$0	
	16 × \$0.13 = \$2.08
1	
	16 × \$0.11 = \$1.76
2	
	16 × \$0.09 = \$1.44
3	
	16 × \$0.07 = \$1.12
4	

As a result, \$4 will be spent on the party, the highest level for which the "reported" marginal social benefit is greater than the marginal cost (\$1). Regardless of whether there are 10 Homebodies and 6 Revellers (case a), or 6 Homebodies and 10 Revellers (case b), spending \$4 in total on the party is clearly inefficient because marginal cost exceeds marginal social benefit at this spending level.

As a further exercise, consider how much Homebodies gain by this misrepresentation. In part a, the efficient level of spending is \$2. So by misrepresenting their preferences, the 10

Homebodies gain, in total, 10 × ($0.03 + $0.02) = $0.50—that is, they gain the marginal individual benefit in going from a spending level of $2 to a spending level of $4. Note that the 6 Revellers also gain from the misrepresentations of the Homebodies; they gain 6 × ($0.09 + $0.07) = $0.96 in total. This outcome is clearly inefficient—when $4 in total is spent, the marginal cost is $1, while the marginal social benefit is only $0.56, indicating that too much money is being spent on the party.

In part b, the efficient level of spending is actually $3. The misrepresentation by the 6 Homebodies gains them, in total, 6 × $0.02 = $0.12, but the 10 Revellers gain 10 × $0.07 = $0.70 in total. This outcome is also clearly inefficient—when $4 is spent, marginal social benefit is only $0.12 + $0.70 = $0.82, while marginal cost is $1.

Check Your Understanding 20-3

1. When individuals are allowed to harvest freely, the government-owned forest becomes a common resource, and individuals will overuse it—they will harvest an inefficiently excessive number of trees. In economic terms, the marginal social cost of harvesting a tree is greater than a private logger's marginal individual cost.

2. The three methods consistent with economic theory are: (a) Pigouvian taxes, (b) a system of tradable licenses, and (c) allocating property rights.
   - **a.** *Pigouvian taxes.* You would enforce a tax on tree loggers that equals the difference between marginal social cost and the individual marginal cost of logging a tree at the socially efficient harvest amount. In order to do this, you must know the marginal social cost schedule and the marginal individual cost schedule.
   - **b.** *System of tradable licenses.* You would issue tradable licenses, setting the total number of trees harvested equal to the socially efficient harvest number. The market that arises in these licenses will allocate the right to log efficiently when loggers differ in their costs of logging: licenses will be purchased by those who have a relatively lower cost of logging. The market price of a license will be equal to the difference between the marginal social cost and the individual marginal cost of logging a tree at the socially efficient harvest amount. In order to implement this level, you need to know the socially efficient harvest amount.
   - **c.** *Allocating property rights.* Here you would sell or give the forest to a private party. This party will have the right to exclude others from harvesting trees. Harvesting is now a private good—it is excludable and rival in consumption. As a result, there is no longer any divergence between social and private costs, and the private party will harvest the efficient level of trees. You need no additional information to use this method.

Check Your Understanding 20-4

1. **a.** The efficient price to a consumer is $0, since the marginal cost of allowing a consumer to download it is $0.
   b. Xenoid will not produce the software unless it can charge a price that allows it at least to make back the $300,000 cost of producing it. So the lowest price at which Xenoid is willing to produce is $150. At this price, it makes total revenue of $150 × 2,000 = $300,000; at any lower price Xenoid will not cover its cost.

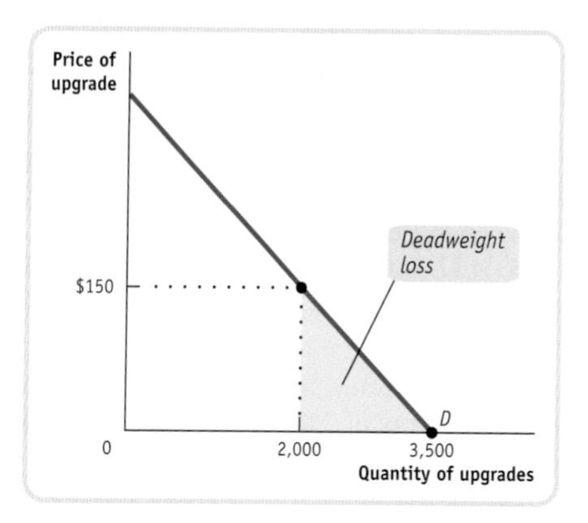

The shaded area shown in the accompanying diagram shows the deadweight loss when Xenoid charges a price of $150.

Chapter Twenty-one

Check Your Understanding 21-1

1. **a.** Since drivers are the beneficiaries of highway safety programs, this tax performs well according to the benefits principle. But since the level of the tax does not depend on ability to pay, it does not perform well according to the ability-to-pay principle. Since higher-income car purchasers are likely to spend more on a new car, a tax assessed as a percentage of the purchase price of the car would have performed better on the ability-to-pay principle. This tax will distort the action of car buying: people will purchase fewer cars, less expensive cars, or second-hand cars as a result of the tax.
   b. This tax does not perform well according to the benefits principle because the payers are non-residents of the local area, while the beneficiaries are residents of the local area who enjoy greater government services. But to the extent that people who stay in more expensive hotels have higher incomes compared to those who don't, the tax performs well according to the ability-to-pay principle. It will distort the action of staying in an expensive hotel room in this area, resulting in fewer nights of expensive hotel room stays.
   c. This tax performs well according to the benefits principle because local homeowners are the users of local schools. It also performs well according to the ability-to-pay principle because it is assessed as a percentage of home value: higher-income residents, who own more expensive homes, will pay higher taxes. It will distort the action of buying a house in this area versus another area with a lower property tax rate, as well as the action of making changes to a house that increase its assessed value.
   d. This tax performs well according to the benefits principle because food consumers are the beneficiaries of government food-safety programs. It does not perform well according to the ability-to-pay principle because food is a

necessity, and lower-income people will pay approximately as much as higher-income people. This tax will distort the action of buying food, leading people to purchase cheaper varieties of food.

Check Your Understanding 21-2

1. A taxpayer who has $20,000 of wealth will pay a tax of (1% × $10,000) + (2% × $10,000) = $100 + $200 = $300. This is equivalent to an average tax rate of 1.5%; that is, 1.5% × $20,000 = $300. But the marginal tax rate—the rate paid on an additional dollar of wealth accrued—is higher, at 2%.

2. A 1% tax on consumption means that a family that earns $15,000 will pay a tax of 1% × $10,000 = $100, equivalent to 0.67% of their income: ($100/$15,000) × 100 = 0.67%. On the other hand, a family that earns $10,000 will pay a tax of 1% × $8,000 = $80, equivalent to 0.80% of their income: ($80/$10,000) × 100 = 0.8%. So the tax is regressive, since the lower-income family pays a higher percentage of their income in tax than the higher-income family.

3. **a.** False. Recall from Chapter 5 that a seller always bears some burden of a tax as long as his or her supply of the good is not perfectly inelastic—that is, as long as quantity supplied is not completely insensitive to the price offered. Since the supply of labour a worker offers is not perfectly inelastic (he or she will always respond to some degree to a change in the wage offered), the worker will bear some burden of a payroll tax, and therefore the tax will affect the person's incentive to take a job.

   b. False. Under a proportional tax, the percentage of the tax base is the same for everyone. Under a lump-sum tax, the total tax paid is the same for everyone, regardless of their income. A lump-sum tax is regressive.

Check Your Understanding 21-3

1. With an insurance program that covers both provinces, workers in one province who are employed in a given year can contribute tax payments that are then used to pay unemployment benefits to workers in the other province who are unemployed during that year. So in even-numbered years employed workers in Lotusland will help unemployed workers in Eastario, and in odd-numbered years employed workers in Eastario will help unemployed workers in Lotusland. Workers in the two provinces are better off with this program because they are assured of having benefits when unemployed.

2. **a.** National disaster emergency relief is not means-tested; therefore, it is social insurance.

   b. Heating cost assistance for low-income families is means-tested; therefore, it redistributes income.

   c. Employment insurance is not means tested. Therefore, it is social insurance.

   d. Aid grants to low income students are means-tested; therefore, they redistribute income.

Check Your Understanding 21-4

1. Government spending programs that benefit Canadians over 65 have increased in generosity over time. Programs such as old-age security, guaranteed income supplements, and spousal allowances have successfully reduced poverty among the elderly. Meanwhile, aid payments that benefit families with children have not kept up with inflation, making them less generous over time. Although the Federal government's National Child Benefit program specifically targets poor families, many provinces have reacted by reducing welfare payments dollar for dollar. As a consequence, the poverty rate for Canadians under 18 has risen, while the poverty rate for Canadians over 65 has fallen.

2. When families spend 20% more of their incomes on essentials than the average family, they are deemed poor. This is a relative measure. As incomes rise, the average family can be expected to spend less and less of its income on essentials. Accordingly, essentials would absorb an ever smaller percent of the budget of "poor" families.

3. The relative measure of poverty is really measuring inequality. It would be possible to eradicate poverty, but only by eradicating inequality of family incomes.

Check Your Understanding 21-5

1. **a.** A family will experience a very high marginal tax rate on the dollar it earns in going from an income of $14,999 to $15,000, because earning this additional dollar will cause it to lose all its benefits (free prescription drugs, vision care, and dental care). As a result, the marginal tax rate on that dollar may be several hundred or several thousand percent (depending on the family's supplementary health costs). This will severely discourage a family from earning any more than $14,999 per year.

   b. A decrease in benefits as an additional dollar is earned is experienced by the family as a marginal tax rate on that dollar. As a result, a large decrease in benefits as an additional dollar is earned translates into a large disincentive to the family to earn that dollar. This means that one should restructure the program so that benefits are reduced gradually as income increases in an effort to reduce the disincentive effects on work.

2. **a.** This program improves equity by aiding farmers in years when their income is low. However, it can generate inefficiency in farmers' incentives—for example, taking insufficient precautions against crop failures, farming in overly risky ways (such as on flood-prone land), and so on.

   b. This program improves equity because rent is often a sizable expense for low-income families. It can generate inefficiency in their incentives, however, such as reducing the incentive to earn more income.

Chapter Twenty-two

Check Your Understanding 22-1

1. a. This is an information good because the value to a consumer, the viewer, is the information conveyed in the program. And it also satisfies the cost conditions of an information good: there are high fixed costs associated with creating the show and installing cables to homes; there is low marginal cost associated with delivering the show over cable lines to homes.
   b. This is not an information good. Although the coat embodies a lot of information through its high-tech fabric, the value to the consumer comes from its use as a garment.
   c. This is an information good because the value to the consumer is in the information conveyed in the newspaper. It also satisfies the cost conditions of an information good: it has high fixed cost (the cost of gathering and reporting the news) and low marginal cost (the cost of printing and distributing the paper).
   d. This is not an information good. Despite the fact that the car engine embodies a lot of information in its engineering, the value to a consumer comes from its use as a vehicle.

2. The fact that fixed cost is high but marginal cost is low explains the statement that "bigger is better". A bigger market for the good means more sales over which to defray the fixed cost of production, while low marginal cost means that the cost of making an additional sale is low. So the larger the market, the better off the firm, because its average total cost falls as it produces more output.

Check Your Understanding 22-2

1. a. The voltage of an appliance must be consistent with the voltage of the electrical outlet it is plugged into. So consumers will wish to have 110-volt appliances when houses are wired for 110-volt outlets, and builders will want to install 110-volt outlets when most prospective homeowners use 110-volt appliances. Therefore a network externality arises because a consumer will want to use appliances that operate with the same voltage as the appliances used by most other consumers.
   b. Printers, copy machines, fax machines, and so on are designed for specific paper sizes. Consumers will want to purchase paper of a size that can be used in these machines, and machine manufacturers will want to manufacture their machines for the size of paper that most consumers use. So a network externality arises because a consumer will want to use the size of paper used by most other consumers—namely, 8½-by-11-inch paper rather than 8-by-12½-inch paper.

2. Of the two competing companies, the company that can achieve the higher number of sales is likely to see the market tip in its favour, as more new consumers want to use its standard because more existing consumers have already adopted it. So it is important for a company to make a high number of sales early on. It can do this by pricing its good cheaply—by taking a loss on each unit sold. So the company that can best afford to subsidize a large number of sales early on is likely to be the winner of this competition.

Check Your Understanding 22-3

1. **Pro:** It can be argued that AOL is attempting to create a monopoly by creating artificial barriers to other Internet service providers. As the biggest Internet service provider, a potential customer will be more likely to use AOL than a rival company if AOL restricts its pop-up message service to its own customers. If you wanted to reach the largest number of people possible with pop-up messages, and most people were AOL users, and AOL restricted its pop-up messaging to its own customers, then you would have had to become an AOL user. So by pursuing this policy AOL believed it could eventually achieve a monopoly position in the Internet service provider industry.
   Con: It can be argued that AOL was simply offering a superior product to its customers and that it had no obligation to offer this product without charge to customers of competing firms. To put it another way, if AOL had been required to provide to customers of other companies with the superior products it developed and provided to its own customers, then it could never charge its own customers a price high enough to recoup its investment in developing the product. So it had to restrict this product to its own customers in order to make it worthwhile to offer it. Using a term from Chapter 20, AOL must make the good "excludable" in order to earn revenue from it.

Glossary

Italicized terms within definitions are key terms that are defined elsewhere in this glossary.

ability-to-pay principle: the principle of *tax fairness* by which those with greater ability to pay a tax should pay more tax.

absolute advantage: the advantage conferred by the ability to produce a good more efficiently—at lower cost of *resources*—than other producers.

absolute value: the value of a number without regard to a plus or minus sign.

accounting profit: revenue minus *explicit costs* and depreciation.

administrative costs (of a tax): the *resources* used (which is a cost) both to collect the tax and to pay it.

adverse selection: occurs when an individual knows more about the way things are than other people do. Adverse selection problems can lead to market problems: private information leads buyers to expect hidden problems in items offered for sale, which leads to low prices, which leads to the best items being kept off the market.

artificially scarce good: a good that is *excludable* but *non-rival in consumption.*

autarky: a situation in which a country cannot trade with other countries.

average cost: an alternative term for *average total cost;* the *total cost* divided by the total quantity of output.

average fixed cost: the *fixed cost* per unit of output.

average tax rate on income: the ratio of income taxes paid to income.

average total cost: *total cost* divided by the total quantity of output.

average variable cost: the *variable cost* per unit of output.

backward-bending individual labour supply curve: an *individual labour supply curve* that is upward sloping when the *substitution effect* predominates (usually at low to moderate wage rates) and downward sloping when the *income effect* predominates (at very high wage rates).

bar graph: a graph that uses bars of varying height or length to show the comparative sizes of different observations of a variable.

barrier to entry: something that prevents other firms from entering an industry. Crucial in protecting the profits of a *monopolist.* There are four types of barriers to entry: control over scarce resources or inputs, *economies of scale,* technological superiority, and government-created barriers such as *licenses.*

barter: the direct exchange of goods or services without the use of money.

benefits principle: the principle of *tax fairness* by which those who benefit from public spending should bear the burden of the tax that pays for that spending.

binding price constraint: describes a *price ceiling* that is set below the *equilibrium price* or a *price floor* that is set above it.

black market: a market in which goods or services are bought and sold illegally, either because it is illegal to sell them at all or because the prices charged are legally prohibited by a *price ceiling.*

brand name: a name owned by a particular firm that distinguishes its products from those of other firms.

break-even price: the market price at which a firm earns zero profits.

budget constraint: the cost of a consumer's *consumption bundle* cannot exceed the consumer's total income.

budget line: all the *consumption bundles* available to a consumer, assuming all income is spent.

capital: the combined value of assets; includes equipment, buildings, tools, inventory, and financial assets.

capital at risk: funds that an insurer places at risk when agreeing to provide insurance.

cartel: an agreement among several producers setting production quotas for each, thereby leading to oligopoly profits.

causal relationship: the relationship between two variables in which the value taken by one variable directly influences or determines the value taken by the other variable.

circular-flow diagram: a model that represents the transactions in an *economy* by two kinds of flows around a circle: a flow of physical things such as goods or labour and the flow of money to pay for these physical things.

clawback: a taking away by government of a conferred benefit, as results when benefits that appear universal are in fact *means-tested;* can occur between levels of government.

Coase theorem: the proposition that even in the presence of *externalities* an *economy* can always reach an *efficient* solution as long as *transaction costs* are sufficiently low.

collusion: cooperation among producers to limit production and raise prices so as to raise one another's profits.

combine laws: laws that prevent firms from either combining into one unit or behaving as if they were one unit.

commodity: output of different producers regarded by consumers as all the same good; also referred to as a *standardized product.*

common resource: a *resource* that is *non-excludable* and *rival in consumption.*

comparative advantage: the advantage conferred on an individual or nation if it can produce a good at a lower *opportunity cost* than another producer.

compensating differentials: wage differences across jobs that reflect the fact that some jobs are less pleasant or more dangerous than others.

competition policy: a set of laws embodied in the Competition Act (1986) designed to prevent the erosion of competition by regulating mergers, and prevent the exercise of monopoly power by "abuse of dominant position".

competitive market: a market in which all market participants are price-takers.

competitive market economy: an *economy* in which all markets, for goods and for factors, are perfectly competitive. All market participants are price-takers.

complements: pairs of goods for which a fall in the price of one good results in greater demand for the other.

constant returns to scale: a range of production in which *long-run average total cost* is constant as output increases.

consumer surplus: a term often used to refer both to *individual consumer surplus* and to *total consumer surplus.*

consumption bundle (of an individual)**:** the collection of all the goods and services consumed by a given individual.

consumption possibilities: the set of all *consumption bundles* available to a consumer, given that consumer's income and prevailing prices.

copyright: the exclusive legal right of the creator of a literary or artistic work to profit from that work; like a *patent,* it is a temporary monopoly.

cost (of potential seller)**:** the lowest price at which a seller is willing to sell a good.

cost-benefit analysis: an estimate of the costs and benefits of providing a good. When governments use cost-benefit analysis, they estimate the social costs and social benefits of providing a public good.

critical mass: the size at which a network suddenly begins to grow rapidly.

cross-price elasticity of demand: the ratio of the percent change in the *quantity demanded* of one good to the percent change in the price of another good; a measure of the effect of the change in the price of one good on the quantity demanded of the other.

curve: a line on a graph, which may be curved or straight, that depicts a relationship between two variables.

deadweight loss (from a tax)**:** the extra cost in the form of inefficiency that results because a tax discourages mutually beneficial transactions; also referred to as *excess burden.*

decreasing marginal benefit: *marginal benefit* that decreases with each additional unit of the activity.

deductible: a sum specified in an insurance policy that the insured must pay before being compensated for a loss; deductibles reduce *moral hazard.*

demand curve: a graphical representation of the *demand schedule,* showing how much of a good or service consumers would buy at a given price.

demand price: the price of a given quantity at which consumers will demand that quantity.

demand schedule: a list or table showing the relationship between price and the quantity of a good consumers would buy.

dependent variable: the determined variable in a causal relationship.

diminishing marginal rate of substitution: the principle that the more of one good that is consumed in proportion to another, the less of the second good the consumer is willing to substitute for another unit of the first good.

diminishing marginal utility: the principle that each successive unit of a good or service consumed adds less to total utility than the previous unit.

diminishing returns to an input: the effect observed when an increase in the quantity of an *input,* while holding the levels of all other inputs fixed, leads to a decline in the *marginal product* of that input.

diseconomies of scale: a range of production in which *long-run average total cost* increases as output increases.

diversification: reducing risk by investing in several different enterprises, so that the possible losses are *independent events.*

domestic demand curve: a *demand curve* for domestic consumers.

domestic supply curve: a *supply curve* for domestic producers.

dominant strategy: in *game theory,* an action that is a player's best action regardless of the action taken by the other player.

duopolist: one of the two firms in a *duopoly.*

duopoly: an *oligopoly* consisting of only two firms.

economic growth: a *long-run* trend toward the production of more goods and services.

economic profit: revenue minus the *opportunity cost of resources;* often less than *accounting profit.*

economic signal: any piece of information that helps people make better economic decisions.

economics: the study of *economies,* at the level of individuals and of society as a whole.

economies of scale: a range of production in which *long-run average total cost* declines as output increases.

economy: a system for coordinating a society's productive activities.

efficiency-wage model: a model in which some employers pay an above-equilibrium wage as an *incentive* to better performance.

efficient: description of a market or *economy* that uses its resources in such a way as to exploit all opportunities to make some individuals better off without making others worse off.

efficient allocation of resources: the case in which there is no way for an economy to reallocate *factors of production* among producers to produce more of some goods without producing less of others.

efficient allocation of risk: the case in which those most willing to bear *risk* are those who bear it.

efficient in consumption: description of an *economy* in which there is no way to redistribute goods that makes some consumers better off without making others worse off.

efficient in output levels: description of an *economy* in which no different mix of output would make some consumers better off without making others worse off.

efficient in production: description of an *economy* in which there is no way to produce more of some goods without producing less of others.

elastic demand: when the *price elasticity of demand* is greater than 1. A percentage increase in price will cause a correspondingly greater percentage decrease in quantity demanded, and vice versa.

emissions tax: a tax that depends on the amount of pollution a firm produces.

environmental standards: rules established by a government to protect the environment by specifying actions to be taken by producers and consumers.

equalization payments: transfers paid by the federal government to the provinces whose tax capacities are below average.

equilibrium: an economic balance in which no individual would be better off doing something different; an equality of supply and demand.

equilibrium price: the price at which the market is in *equilibrium,* that is, the quantity of a good demanded equals the quantity supplied; also referred to as the *market-clearing price.*

equilibrium quantity: the quantity of a good bought and sold at the *equilibrium* (or *market-clearing*) *price.*

equilibrium value of the marginal product: the additional value produced by the last unit of a factor employed in the *factor market* as a whole.

equity: fairness; because individuals can disagree about what is "fair", equity is not as well defined a concept as efficiency.

excess burden (from a tax)**:** the extra cost in the form of inefficiency that results because a tax discourages mutually beneficial transactions; also referred to as *deadweight loss.*

excess capacity: when firms produce less than the output at which *average total cost* is minimized; characteristic of *monopolistically competitive* firms.

excise tax: a tax on the sale of a particular good or service.

excludable: referring to a good, describes the case in which the supplier can prevent those who do not pay from consuming the good.

expected utility: the expected value of total *utility,* given uncertainty about outcomes.

expected value: in reference to a *random variable,* the weighted average of all possible variables; the weights on each possible value correspond to the probability of that value.

explicit cost: a cost that requires an outlay of money.

exporting industries: industries that produce goods or services for sale abroad.

exports: goods and services sold to other countries.

external benefit: an uncompensated benefit that an individual or firm confers on others; also known as *positive externalities.*

external cost: an uncompensated cost that an individual or firm imposes on others; also known as *negative externalities.*

externalities: *external benefits* and *external costs.*

factor distribution of income: the division of total income among labour, land, and *capital.*

factor intensity: the difference in the ratio of *factors* used to produce a good in various industries. For example, oil refining is capital-intensive compared to clothing manufacture because oil refiners use a higher ratio of capital to labour than do clothing producers.

factor markets: markets in which *firms* buy *factors of production.*

factors of production: the *resources* needed to produce goods or services. Labour and capital are examples of factors.

fair insurance policy: an insurance policy for which the *premium* is equal to the expected value of the claims.

financial risk: uncertainty about monetary outcomes.

firm: an organization that produces goods or services for sale.

fixed cost: a cost that does not depend on the quantity of output produced; the cost of a *fixed input.*

fixed input: an *input* whose quantity is fixed and cannot be varied (for example, land).

forecast: a simple prediction of the future under current assumptions.

free entry and exit: describes an industry that potential producers can easily enter or current producers can leave.

free trade: *trade* that is unregulated by government *tariffs* or other artificial barriers; the levels of *exports* and *imports* occur naturally, as a result of supply and demand.

free-rider problem: when individuals have no *incentive* to pay for their own consumption of a good, they will take a "free ride" on anyone who does pay; a problem with goods that are *non-excludable.*

gains from trade: the benefit that each party receives from a trade, which, because of *specialization,* is greater than if each attempted to be self-sufficient.

game theory: the study of behaviour in situations of *interdependence.* Used to explain the behaviour of an *oligopoly.*

general equilibrium: an economic balance in which the *quantity supplied* is equal to the *quantity demanded* in all markets in an economy.

Heckscher–Ohlin model: a *model* of international trade that shows how a country's *comparative advantage* can be determined by its supply of *factors of production.*

horizontal axis: the horizontal number line of a graph along which values of the *x*-variable are measured; also referred to as the *x-axis.*

horizontal intercept: the point at which a curve intersects the horizontal axis, showing the value of the *x*-variable when the value of the *y*-variable is zero.

horizontal equity: the principle that identical or similar individuals should face identical or similar tax burdens.

household: a group of people that share a dwelling and their income (a household may also consist of one person).

human capital: the improvement in labour created by education and knowledge.

imperfect competition: a market structure in which no firm is a *monopolist,* but producers nonetheless have *market power* they can use to affect market prices.

implicit cost: a cost that does not require the outlay of money; it is measured by the value, in dollar terms, of forgone benefits.

implicit cost of capital: the *opportunity cost* of the capital used; that is, the income that could have been realized had the capital been used in the next best alternative way.

import quota: a legal limit on the quantity of a good that can be imported.

import-competing industries: industries that produce goods or services that are also imported.

imports: goods and services purchased from other countries.

in-kind transfers: specific goods and services (such as food stamps) provided to poor families by government.

incentive: a reward offered to people who change their behaviour.

incidence (of a tax)**:** a measure of who actually bears the burden of a tax.

income effect: the change in the quantity of a good consumed that results from the change in a consumer's purchasing power due to the change in the price of the good.

income elasticity of demand: the ratio of the percentage change in *quantity demanded* of a good or service to the percentage change in a consumer's income.

income tax: a tax on the income of an individual or family.

income-elastic demand: when the *income elasticity of demand* is greater than 1. Occurs when the demand for certain goods (such as luxury goods) rises faster than the increase in income.

income-inelastic demand: when the *income elasticity of demand* is positive but less than 1. Occurs when the demand for certain goods (such as food and clothing) rises but more slowly than the increase in income.

increasing marginal cost: *marginal cost* that becomes greater with each additional unit of the activity.

independent events: events for which the occurrence of one does not affect the likelihood of occurrence of any of the others.

independent variable: the determining variable in a causal relationship.

indifference curve: a contour line showing all *consumption bundles* that yield the same amount of total *utility* for an individual.

indifference curve map: a collection of *indifference curves* for a given individual that represents the individual's total *utility function*; each curve corresponds to a different total utility level.

individual choice: the decision by an individual of what to do, which necessarily involves a decision of what not to do.

individual consumer surplus: the net gain to an individual buyer from the purchase of a good; equal to the difference between the buyer's *willingness to pay* and the price paid.

individual demand curve: a graphical representation of the relationship between *quantity demanded* and price for an individual consumer.

individual labour supply curve: a graphical representation of the relationship between the wage rate and the number of hours supplied by an individual worker.

individual producer surplus: the net gain to an individual seller from selling a good; equal to the difference between the price received and the seller's *cost.*

industrial policy: a policy that supports industries believed to yield *positive externalities.*

industry supply curve: a graphical representation that shows the relationship between the price of a good and the total output of the industry for that good.

inefficient: describes a market or *economy* in which there are missed opportunities for making some individuals better off without making others worse off.

inefficient allocation to consumers: a form of inefficiency in which consumers who are willing to pay a high price for a good do not get it, and those willing to pay only a low price do; often a result of a *price ceiling.*

inefficient allocation of sales among sellers: a form of inefficiency in which sellers who are willing to sell a good at a lower price are not always those who actually manage to sell it; often the result of a *price floor*.

inefficiently high quality: a form of inefficiency in which sellers offer high-quality goods at a high price even though buyers would prefer a lower quality at a lower price; often the result of a *price floor.*

inefficiently low quality: a form of inefficiency in which sellers offer low-quality goods at a low price even though buyers would prefer a higher quality at a higher price; often a result of a *price ceiling.*

inelastic demand: when the *price elasticity of demand* is less than 1. A percentage increase in price will cause a correspondingly lesser percentage decrease in quantity demanded, and vice versa.

inferior good: a good for which a rise in income decreases the demand for the good.

information good: a good whose value derives from the information it contains.

input: a good used to produce another good.

interaction (of choices)**:** the mutual influence of the choices of various parties (the results are often quite different from what was intended).

interdependence: the relationship among firms when their decisions significantly affect one another's profits; characteristic of oligopolies.

interest rate: the price, calculated as a percentage of the amount borrowed, charged by the lender.

internalize the externality: take into account *external costs* and *external benefits.*

international trade agreements: treaties by which countries agree to lower *trade protections* against one another.

invisible hand: a phrase used by Adam Smith to describe the way in which an individual's pursuit of self-interest can lead, without the individual intending it, to good results for society as a whole.

kinked demand curve: a model used to explain the stability of oligopoly pricing; a *demand curve* that kinks (bends) because the *oligopolist* will lose sales if price is increased but gain only momentarily if price is lowered (because the lower price will be matched at once by other oligopolists).

law of demand: a higher price charged for a good, other things equal, leads to a smaller quantity of the good demanded.

leisure: the time available for purposes other than earning money to buy marketed goods.

license: the right, conferred by the government or an owner, to supply some good or perform some activity, often in exchange for a fee.

linear relationship: the relationship between two variables in which the *slope* is constant and therefore is depicted on a graph by a *curve* that is a straight line.

long run: the time period in which all *inputs* can be varied.

long-run average total cost curve: a graphical representation showing the relationship between output and *average total cost* when *fixed cost* has been chosen to minimize *total cost* for each level of output.

long-run industry supply curve: a graphical representation that shows how *quantity supplied* responds to price once producers have had time to enter or exit the industry.

long-run market equilibrium: an economic balance in which, given sufficient time for producers to enter or exit an industry, the *quantity supplied* equals the *quantity demanded.*

lump-sum tax: a tax that is the same for everyone, regardless of any actions individuals take.

macroeconomics: the branch of *economics* concerned with the overall ups and downs in the *economy.*

marginal analysis: the study of *marginal decisions,* those resulting from small changes in an activity.

marginal benefit: the additional benefit derived by performing one more unit of an activity.

marginal benefit curve: a graphical representation showing how the benefit from undertaking one more unit of an activity depends on the quantity of that activity that has already been done.

marginal cost: the additional cost incurred by performing one more unit of an activity.

marginal cost curve: a graphical representation showing how the cost of undertaking one more unit of an activity depends on the quantity of that activity that has already been done.

marginal decision: a decision made at the "margin" of an activity to do a little more or a little less.

marginal product: the additional quantity of output produced by using one more unit of a given *input.*

marginal productivity theory of income distribution: the proposition that every *factor of production* is paid its *equilibrium value of the marginal product.*

marginal rate of substitution (MRS): the ratio of the *marginal utility* of one good to the marginal utility of another.

marginal revenue: the change in *total revenue* generated by an additional unit of output.

marginal revenue curve: a graphical representation showing how *marginal revenue* varies as output varies.

marginal social benefit of a good or activity: the *marginal benefit* that accrues to consumers plus the marginal *external benefit.*

marginal social benefit of pollution: the additional gain to society from an additional unit of pollution.

marginal social cost of a good or activity: the *marginal cost* of production plus the marginal *external cost* to society of that production.

marginal social cost of pollution: the additional cost imposed on society by an additional unit of pollution.

marginal tax rate on income: the additional income tax paid if income increases by $1.

marginal utility: the change in total *utility* generated by consuming one additional unit of a good or service.

marginal utility curve: a graphical representation showing how *marginal utility* depends on the quantity of the good or service consumed.

marginal utility per dollar: the additional *utility* gained from spending an additional dollar on a good or service.

market-clearing price: the price at which the market is in *equilibrium,* that is, the quantity of a good demanded equals the quantity supplied; also referred to as the *equilibrium price.*

market economy: an *economy* in which decisions about production and consumption are made by individual producers and consumers.

market failure: occurs when a market fails to be efficient.

market power: the ability of a firm to raise prices.

market share: the fraction of the total industry output represented by a given producer's output.

markets for goods and services: markets in which households buy goods and services from *firms.*

maximum: the highest point on a *nonlinear curve,* where the *slope* changes from positive to negative.

means-tested: having an income qualification, as certain government social programs.

microeconomics: the branch of *economics* that studies how individuals make decisions and how those decisions interact.

midpoint method: a technique for calculating the percent change in which changes in a variable are compared with the average, or midpoint, of the starting and final values.

minimum-cost output: the quantity of output at which the *average total cost* is lowest—the bottom of the *U-shaped average total cost curve.*

minimum: the lowest point on a *nonlinear curve,* where the *slope* changes from negative to positive.

minimum wage: a legal floor on the wage rate. The wage rate is the market price of labour.

model: a simplified representation of a real-life situation that uses data and assumptions to make predictions about that situation and understand it better.

monopolist: a firm that is the only producer of a good that has no close substitutes.

monopolistic competition: a market structure in which there are many competing producers in an industry, each producer sells a differentiated product, and there is *free entry and exit* into and from the industry in the *long run.*

monopoly: an industry controlled by a *monopolist.*

moral hazard: the situation that can exist when an individual knows more about his or her own actions than other people do. This leads to a distortion of incentives to take care or to expend effort, especially when someone else bears the costs of the lack of care or effort.

movement along the demand curve: a change in the *quantity demanded* of a good that results from a change in the price of that good.

movement along the supply curve: a change in the *quantity supplied* of a good that results from a change in the price of that good.

Nash equilibrium: in *game theory,* the *equilibrium* that results when all

players choose their optimal action given the actions of other players, ignoring the effect of that action on the *payoffs* of other players; also known as *non-cooperative equilibrium.*

natural monopoly: a *monopoly* that arises because *economies of scale* over the range of output of an industry provide a large cost advantage to having all output produced by a single firm.

negative externalities: *external costs.*

negative relationship: a relationship between two variables in which an increase in the value of one variable is associated with a decrease in the value of the other variable. It is described by a *curve* that slopes downward from left to right.

net present value: the *present value* of current and future benefits minus the present value of current and future costs.

network externality: the increase in the value of a good to an individual is greater when a large number of others own or use the same good.

non-cooperative behaviour: actions by firms that ignore the effects of those actions on the profits of other firms.

non-cooperative equilibrium: in *game theory,* the *equilibrium* that results when all players choose their optimal action given the actions of other players, ignoring the effect of that action on the *payoffs* of other players; also known as *Nash equilibrium.*

non-excludable: referring to a good, describes the case in which the supplier cannot prevent those who do not pay from consuming the good.

nonlinear curve: a curve whose *slope* is not constant.

nonlinear relationship: the relationship between two variables in which the *slope* is not constant and therefore is depicted on a graph by a *curve* that is not a straight line.

non-price competition: competition in areas other than price to increase sales, such as new product features and advertising; especially engaged in by firms that have a tacit understanding not to compete on price.

non-rival in consumption: referring to a good, describes the case in which the same unit can be consumed by more than one person at the same time.

normal good: a good for which a rise in income increases the demand for that good—the "normal" case.

normative economics: the branch of economic analysis that makes prescriptive statements about how the *economy* should work.

oligopolist: a firm in an industry with only a small number of producers.

oligopoly: an industry with only a small number of producers.

omitted variable: an unobserved *variable* that, through its influence on other variables, creates the erroneous appearance of a direct *causal relationship* among those variables.

opportunity cost: the real cost of an item, including what must be given up to obtain it.

optimal consumption bundle: the *consumption bundle* that maximizes a consumer's total *utility,* given that consumer's *budget constraint.*

optimal consumption rule: when a consumer maximizes *utility,* the *marginal utility per dollar* spent is the same for all goods and services in the *consumption bundle.*

optimal output rule: profit is maximized by producing the quantity of output at which the *marginal cost* of the last unit produced is equal to its *marginal revenue.*

optimal quantity: the level of activity that generates the maximum possible total net gain.

optimal time allocation rule: an individual should allocate time in such a way that the *marginal utility* of an hour spent working is equal to the marginal utility of an additional hour of *leisure.*

ordinary goods: in a consumer's *utility function,* those for which additional units of one good are required to compensate for fewer units of another, and for which the consumer experiences a *diminishing marginal rate of substitution* in substituting one good for another.

origin: the point where the axes of a two-variable graph meet.

other things equal assumption: in the development of a model, the assumption that all relevant factors except the one under study remain unchanged.

overuse: the depletion of a *common resource* that occurs when individuals ignore the effect their use has on the amount of the resource remaining for others.

patent: a temporary monopoly given by the government to an inventor for the use or sale of an invention.

payoff: in *game theory,* the reward received by a player (for example, the profit earned by an *oligopolist*).

payoff matrix: in *game theory,* a diagram that shows how the *payoffs* to each of the participants in a two-player game depend on the actions of both; a tool in analyzing *interdependence.*

payroll tax: a tax on the amount an employer pays to an employee.

perfect complements: goods a consumer wants to consume in a given ratio, regardless of their *relative price.*

perfect price discrimination: charging each consumer the maximum that consumer is willing to pay.

perfect substitutes: goods for which the *indifference curves* are straight lines; the *marginal rate of substitution* is constant, no matter how much of each is consumed.

perfectly competitive industry: an industry in which all producers are price-takers.

perfectly competitive market: a market in which all participants are price-takers.

perfectly elastic supply: the case in which even small changes in price lead to large changes in the *quantity supplied,* so the *price elasticity of supply* is infinite; the *supply curve* is a horizontal line.

perfectly elastic demand: the case in which any price increase causes the *quantity demanded* to fall to zero; the *demand curve* is a horizontal line.

perfectly inelastic supply: the case in which the *price elasticity of supply* is zero, so changes in price have no effect on the *quantity supplied;* the *supply curve* is a vertical line.

perfectly inelastic demand: the case in which the *quantity demanded* does

not respond to price; the *demand curve* is a vertical line.

physical capital: manufactured resources, such as buildings and machines; often referred to simply as "capital".

pie chart: a circular graph that shows how some total is divided among its components; the proportions are indicated by the sizes of the "wedges".

Pigouvian subsidy: a payment designed to encourage activities that yield *external benefits.*

Pigouvian taxes: taxes designed to reduce *external costs.*

pooling: a strong form of *diversification;* the individual investor takes a small share in many *independent events,* so the *payoff* has very little uncertainty.

positive economics: the branch of economic analysis that describes the way the *economy* actually works.

positive externalities: *external benefits.*

positive feedback: put simply, success breeds success, failure breeds failure; the effect is seen with goods that are subject to *network externalities.*

positive relationship: a relationship between two variables in which an increase in the value of one variable is associated with an increase in the value of the other variable. It is described by a *curve* that slopes upward from left to right.

positively correlated: a relationship between events such that each event is more likely to occur if the other also occurs.

poverty line: a minimum income defined by the government as adequate; families whose income falls below the poverty line are considered poor.

poverty rate: the percentage of the population living below the *poverty line.*

premium: a payment to an insurance company in return for the promise to pay in certain circumstances.

present value: the amount of money needed at the present time to produce, at the prevailing *interest rate,* a given amount of money at a specified future time.

price ceiling: a government-set maximum price that sellers are allowed to charge for a good; a form of *price control.*

price controls: legal restrictions on how high or low a market price may go.

price discrimination: charging different prices to different consumers for the same good.

price elasticity of demand: the ratio of the percent change in the *quantity demanded* to the percent change in price at a given point on the *demand curve.*

price elasticity of supply: the ratio of the percent change in the *quantity supplied* to the percent change in price at a given point on the *supply curve.*

price floor: a government-set minimum price that buyers are required to pay for a good; a form of price control.

price leadership: a pattern of behaviour in which one firm sets its price and other firms in the industry follow.

price regulation: a limitation by the government on the price a *monopolist* is allowed to charge.

price war: a collapse of prices when *tacit collusion* breaks down.

price-taking consumer: a consumer whose actions have no effect on the market price of the good bought.

price-taking firm's optimal output rule: the profit of a price-taking firm is maximized by producing the quantity of output at which the *marginal cost* of the last unit produced is equal to the market price.

price-taking producer: a producer whose actions have no effect on the market price of the good sold.

principle of diminishing marginal utility: the proposition that each successive unit of a good or service consumed adds less to total *utility* than did the previous unit.

principle of marginal analysis: the proposition that the *optimal quantity* of an activity is that at which *marginal benefit* is equal to *marginal cost.*

prisoners' dilemma: a game for two players in which the pursuit of self-interest rather than cooperation, if followed by both players, makes both worse off.

private good: a good that is both *excludable* and *rival in consumption.*

private information: information affecting all parties to a transaction or decision that only some parties have.

producer surplus: a term often used to refer both to *individual producer surplus* and to *total producer surplus.*

product differentiation: the effort by firms to convince buyers that their products are different from those of other firms in the industry. If firms can so convince buyers, they can charge a higher price.

production function: the relationship between the quantity of *inputs* used and the quantity of output produced.

production possibility frontier: illustrates the trade-offs facing an economy that produces only two goods. It shows the maximum quantity of one good that can be produced for any given production of the other.

profits tax: a tax on the profits of a firm.

progressive tax: a tax that takes a larger share of the income of high-income taxpayers than of low-income taxpayers.

property rights: the rights of owners of *resources* or goods to dispose of them as they choose.

property tax: a tax on the value of property, such as a home.

proportional tax: a tax that is the same percentage of the *tax base* regardless of the taxpayer's income or wealth.

protection: an alternative term for *trade protection;* policies that limit *imports.*

public good: a good that is both *non-excludable* and *non-rival in consumption.*

public ownership: control of an industry by a public agency of the government to provide a good and protect the interests of the consumer; a response to *natural monopoly.*

quantity control: an upper limit, set by the government, on the quantity of some good that can be bought or sold; also referred to as a *quota.*

quantity demanded: the actual amount of a good or service consumers are willing to buy at some specific price.

quantity supplied: the actual amount of a good or service sellers are willing to sell at some specific price.

quota: an upper limit, set by the government, on the quantity of some good that can be bought or sold; also referred to as a *quantity control.*

quota-license: the right to supply a certain quantity of a good.

quota limit: the total amount of a good under a *quota* or *quantity control* that can be legally transacted.

quota rent: the difference between the *demand price* and the *supply price* at the *quota limit;* this difference, the earnings that accrue to the license-holder, is equal to the market price of the *license* when the license is traded.

QWERTY problem: an inferior industry standard that has prevailed, possibly because of historical accident. Refers to the first six letters of a typewriter keyboard.

random variable: a *variable* with an uncertain future value.

recession: a downturn in the *economy.*

redistribution of income: a movement of income, such as revenue from taxes on the well-off, that is used to support those less well off.

regressive tax: a tax that takes a smaller share of the income of high-income taxpayers than of low-income taxpayers.

relative price: the ratio of the price of one good to the price of another.

relative price rule: at the *optimal consumption bundle,* the *marginal rate of substitution* between two goods is equal to their *relative price.*

rental rate: the cost, implicit or explicit, of using a unit of land or capital for a given period of time.

reputation: a long-term standing in the public regard that serves to reassure others that *private information* is not being concealed; a valuable asset in the face of *adverse selection.*

resource: anything, such as land, labour, and capital, that can be used to produce something else; includes natural resources (from the physical environment) and human resources (labour, skill, intelligence).

reverse causality: the error committed when the true direction between *variables* is reversed, and the *independent variable* and the *dependent variable* are incorrectly identified.

Ricardian model of international trade: a model that analyzes international *trade* under the assumption that *production possibility frontiers* are straight lines.

risk: uncertainty about outcomes.

risk-averse: describes individuals who choose to reduce *risk* when that reduction leaves the expected value of income or wealth unchanged.

rival in consumption: referring to a good, describes the case in which one unit cannot be consumed by more than one person at the same time.

sales tax: a tax on the value of goods sold.

scarce: in short supply; a *resource* is scarce when the quantity available is insufficient to satisfy all productive uses.

scatter diagram: a graph that displays points that correspond to actual observations of the *x*- and *y*-variables; a curve is usually fitted to the scatter of points to indicate the trend in the data.

screening: using observable information to make inferences about *private information;* a way to reduce *adverse selection.*

share: a partial ownership of a company.

shift of the demand curve: a change in the *quantity demanded* at any given price, represented graphically by the movement of the original *demand curve* to a new position.

shift of the supply curve: a change in the *quantity supplied* at any given price, represented graphically by the movement of the original *supply curve* to a new position.

short run: the time period in which at least one *input* is fixed.

short-run individual supply curve: a graphical representation showing how an individual producer's optimal output quantity depends on the market price, taking *fixed cost* as given.

short-run industry supply curve: a graphical representation that shows how the quantity supplied by an industry depends on the market price, given a fixed number of producers.

short-run market equilibrium: an economic balance that results when the *quantity supplied* equals the *quantity demanded,* taking the number of producers as given.

shortage: the insufficiency of a good when the quantity supplied is less than the quantity demanded; shortages occur when the price is below the *equilibrium price.*

shut-down price: the price at which a firm ceases production in the short run because the market price has fallen below the minimum *average variable cost.*

signalling: taking some action to establish credibility despite possessing *private information;* a way to reduce *adverse selection.*

single-price monopolist: a *monopolist* that charges all consumers the same price.

slope: the ratio of the "rise" (the change between two points on the *y*-axis) to the "run" (the difference between the same two points on the *x*-axis); a measure of the steepness of a curve.

social insurance: government programs intended to protect individuals against financial risk.

socially optimal quantity of pollution: the quantity of pollution that society would choose if all the costs and benefits of pollution were fully accounted for.

specialization: occurs when each person concentrates on the task that he or she is good at performing; generally leads to improved quality or to increase in output.

standardized product: output of different producers regarded by consumers as all the same good; also referred to as a *commodity.*

standard: a set of rules for operation that allows competing goods to operate as a single network.

state of the world: a possible future event.

strategic behaviour: actions taken by a firm that attempt to influence the behaviour of other firms.

substitutes: pairs of goods for which a fall in the price of one results in less demand for the other.

substitution effect: the change in the quantity consumed when a consumer substitutes a good that has become relatively cheaper for one that has become relatively more expensive.

sunk cost: a cost that has already been incurred and is not recoverable.

supply and demand model: a model that describes how a *competitive market* works.

supply curve: a graphical representation of the *supply schedule,* showing how much of a good or service would be supplied at a given price.

supply price: the price of a given quantity at which producers will supply that quantity.

supply schedule: a list or table showing the relationship between price and the quantity of a good or service that would be supplied to consumers.

surplus: the excess of a good that occurs when the quantity supplied is greater than the quantity demanded; surpluses occur when the price is above the *equilibrium price.*

tacit collusion: cooperation among producers, without a formal agreement, to limit production and raise prices so as to raise one another's profits.

tangency condition: on a graph of a consumer's *budget line* and available *indifference curves* of available *consumption bundles,* the point at which an indifference curve and the budget line touch. When the indifference curves have the typical convex shape, this point determines the *optimal consumption bundle.*

tangent line: a straight line that touches a *nonlinear curve* at a given point; the *slope* of the tangent line equals the slope of the nonlinear curve at that point.

tariff: a tax levied on *imports.*

tax base: the measure or value, such as income or property value, that determines how much tax an individual pays.

tax efficiency: the degree to which a tax system minimizes the cost to the *economy* of tax collection.

tax fairness (also known as **tax equity**): the degree to which the "right" people bear the burden of taxes.

tax structure: specifies how a tax depends on the *tax base;* usually expressed in percentage terms.

technology spillover: an *external benefit* that is conferred when knowledge spreads among individuals and firms.

threshold network size: in a market subject to *network externalities,* the smallest number of current members of the network that leads a given individual to join.

time allocation: the decision about how many hours to expend on different activities, which leads to a decision about how much labour to supply.

time allocation budget line: an individual's possible trade-offs between consumption of *leisure* and the income that allows consumption of marketed goods.

time-series graph: a two-variable graph in which the values on the *horizontal axis* are dates and those on the *vertical axis* are values of a variable that occurred on those dates.

tipping: a sudden rapid increase in the network size that occurs when *positive feedback* due to *network externalities* causes consumers to swing to one of two competing goods or technologies.

tit for tat: in *game theory,* a strategy in which players begin cooperatively, then each repeats the other player's action in the previous round.

total consumer surplus: the sum of the *individual consumer surpluses* of all the buyers of a good.

total cost: the sum of the *fixed cost* and the *variable cost* of producing a given quantity of output.

total cost curve: a graphical representation of the *total cost,* showing how total cost depends on the quantity of output.

total producer surplus: the sum of the *individual producer surpluses* of all the sellers of a good.

total product curve: a graphical representation of the *production function,* showing how the quantity of output depends on the quantity of the *variable input* for a given amount of *fixed input.*

total revenue: the total value of sales of a good (the price of the good multiplied by the quantity sold).

total surplus: the total net gain to consumers and producers from trading in a market; the sum of the *consumer surplus* and the *producer surplus.*

tradable emissions permits: *licenses* to emit limited quantities of pollutants that can be bought and sold by polluters.

trade: the exchange of goods or services for other goods or services.

trade protection: policies that limit *imports.*

trade-off: a comparison of costs and benefits; the amount of a good that must be sacrificed to obtain another good.

trade-off between equity and efficiency: the dynamic whereby a well-designed tax system can be made more efficient only by making it less fair, and vice versa.

transaction costs: the costs of making a deal.

transfer payment: money received by an individual from the government for which no good or service is returned to the government.

truncated: cut; in a truncated axis, some of the range of values are omitted, usually to save space.

U-shaped average total cost curve: a distinctive graphical representation of the relationship between output and *average total cost;* the average total cost curve at first falls when output is low and then rises as output increases.

unions: organizations of workers that engage in collective bargaining to raise wages and improve working conditions for their members.

unit-elastic demand: the case in which the *price elasticity of demand* is 1. A specific percentage increase in price leads to an equal percentage decrease in quantity demanded, and vice versa.

util: a unit of *utility.*

utility (of a consumer): a measure of the satisfaction derived from consumption of goods and services.

utility function (of an individual): the relationship between an individual's *consumption bundle* and the total amount of *utility* it generates.

utility possibility frontier: on a graph plotting the total *utility* of two

individuals or groups, the curve that shows how well off one individual or group could be for each given total utility level of the other.

value of the marginal product: the value of the additional output generated by employing one more unit of a given factor, such as labour.

value of the marginal product curve: a graphical representation showing how the *value of the marginal product* of a factor depends on the quantity of the factor employed.

variable: a quantity that can take on more than one value.

variable cost: a cost that depends on the quantity of output produced; the cost of a *variable input.*

variable input: an *input* whose quantity can be varied (for example, labour).

vertical axis: the vertical number line of a graph along which values of the *y*-variable are measured; also referred to as the *y-axis.*

vertical equity: the principle of fair tax treatment for people in different economic circumstances.

vertical intercept: the point at which a curve intersects the vertical axis, showing the value of the *y*-variable when the value of the *x*-variable is zero.

wasted resources: a form of inefficiency; consumers waste resources when they must spend money and expend effort to deal with shortages caused by a *price ceiling.*

wealth tax: a tax on the wealth of an individual.

wedge: the difference between the *demand price* of the quantity transacted and the *supply price* of the quantity transacted for a good when the supply of the good is legally restricted. Often created by a quota or a tax.

welfare: government monetary aid to poor families.

willingness to pay: the maximum price a consumer is prepared to pay for a good.

world price: the price at which a good can be bought or sold abroad.

World Trade Organization: an international organization of member countries that oversees *international trade agreements* and rules on *trade* disputes.

***x*-axis:** the horizontal number line of a graph along which values of the *x*-variable are measured; also referred to as the *horizontal axis.*

***x*-coordinate:** the value that the *x*-variable takes on for a given point.

***y*-axis:** the vertical number line of a graph along which values of the *y*-variable are measured; also referred to as the *vertical axis.*

***y*-coordinate:** the value that the *y*-variable takes on for a given point.

zero-profit equilibrium: an economic balance in which each firm makes zero profit at its profit-maximizing output level.

Index

Key terms and the pages on which they are defined appear in **boldface** in this index.

LUXE
R-B-Q

F

LUXE
R-B-Q

J

K

L

M

LUXE
R-B-Q

N

O

P

LUXE
R-B-Q

USED CARS

LUXE
R-B-Q

USED CARS

Visit the Krugman/Wells/Myatt website

econ X change

www.worthpublishers.com/krugmanwellsmyatt

The companion Web site for Krugman/Wells/Myatt *Microeconomics* offers valuable tools, including online simulations designed to help students master economic concepts. This completely customized Web site provides your students with a virtual study guide, twenty-four hours a day, seven days a week. The site provides your students with a pedagogically sound means of testing their understanding of text material. One of the features of ECon X-Change is the **Graphing Center.** Selected graphs from the textbook have been animated in a Flash format, allowing students to manipulate curves and plot data points when appropriate. Every interactive graph has accompanying questions that quiz students on key concepts from the textbook and provide feedback on student progress. Student responses and interactions are tracked and stored in an online database that can be accessed by the instructor. The following list indicates the graphs in *Microeconomics* that are available at the Graphing Center.

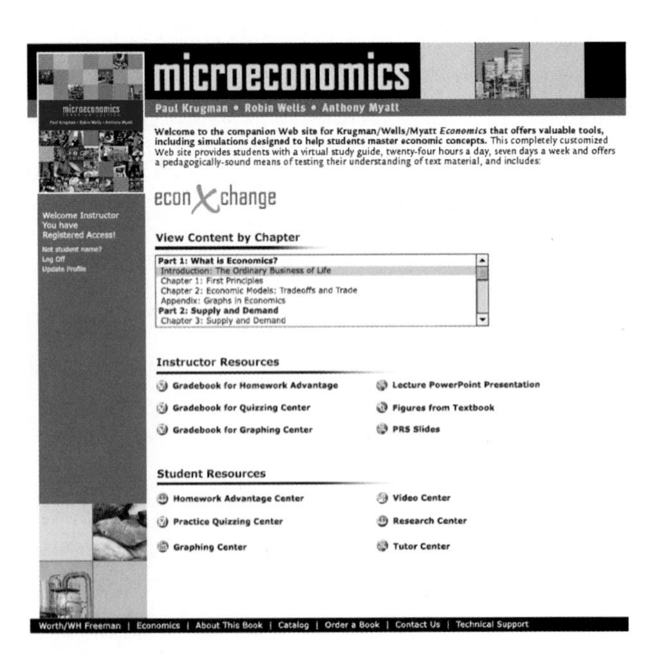

LIST OF ANIMATED FIGURES